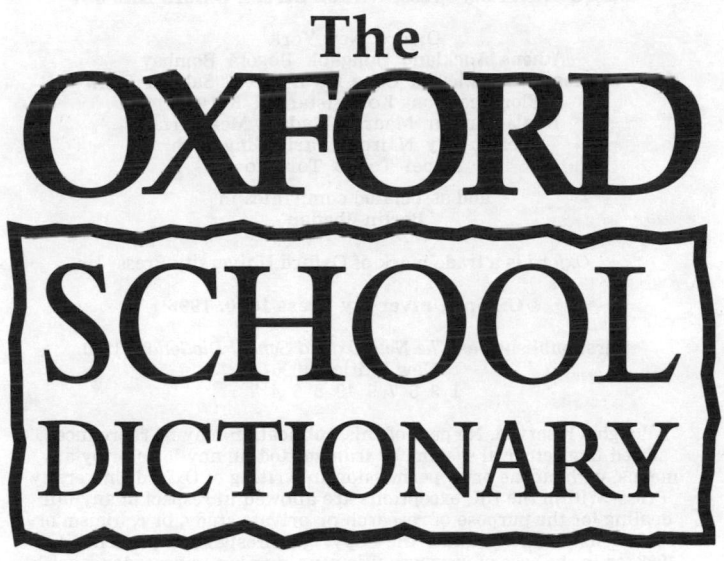

The OXFORD SCHOOL DICTIONARY

Compiled by
Joyce M. Hawkins
Revised by
Andrew Delahunty and Fred McDonald

OXFORD UNIVERSITY PRESS

Oxford University Press, Walton Street, Oxford OX2 6DP

Oxford New York
Athens Auckland Bangkok Bogotá Bombay
Buenos Aires Calcutta Cape Town Dar es Salaam Delhi
Florence Hong Kong Istanbul Karachi
Kuala Lumpur Madras Madrid Melbourne
Mexico City Nairobi Paris Singapore
Taipei Tokyo Toronto

and associated companies in
Berlin Ibadan

Oxford is a trade mark of Oxford University Press

© Oxford University Press 1990, 1996

First published as *The New Oxford School Dictionary* 1990
New Edition 1996
1 3 5 7 9 10 8 6 4 2

ISBN 019 910377 1 (Trade Edition)
ISBN 019 910378 X (Educational Edition)

A CIP catalogue record for this book is available from the British Library

Typeset by Pentacor PLC, High Wycombe

Printed in Great Britain by The Bath Press, Bath

OWLS
OXFORD ENGLISH
DICTIONARY
WORD AND
LANGUAGE
SERVICE

Do you have a query about words, their origin, meaning, use, spelling,
pronunciation, or any other aspect of the English language? Then write to
OWLS at Oxford University Press, Walton Street, Oxford, OX2 6DP.

All queries will be answered using the full resources of the
Oxford Dictionary Department

Contents

Preface

This dictionary has been specially written for secondary school students aged 11–16 years. It should serve as a working tool in the classroom and accustom its users to the style in which most adult dictionaries are written, but at the same time be easy to use because it avoids abbreviations and similar conventions.

For this edition we have kept and expanded the features of the first edition. Inflections of all verbs and plurals of nouns are spelt out in full, and comparatives and superlatives of many adjectives and adverbs are also given. Pronunciation of difficult words is given in a simple look-and-say system without special symbols. Definitions are clearly expressed, with careful explanations of difficult concepts (e.g. *hindsight, hypothesis, irony*), and many examples of words in use are provided. There are a number of notes on correct usage, grammatical points, and words that are easily confused (e.g. *alternate/alternative*). Direct opposites or parallel terms are sometimes indicated (e.g. *maximum/minimum, optimist/pessimist, libel/slander*). Prefixes and suffixes are entered at the appropriate place in the alphabetical sequence; lists of them are contained in Appendix 1. Etymologies are given for all words, with the exception of obvious derivatives and compounds. While it is not always possible to show the details of a word's derivation, the most significant language of origin and important changes of meaning are given. The etymologies are intended to introduce the idea that words have a history as well as a meaning, to demonstrate the connection between related words and help with recognition of word elements, and to show the variety of languages that have contributed to English. It is hoped that the etymologies will also arouse the curiosity of users so that they will be encouraged to look in a larger dictionary for more detailed information.

Acknowledgements

The publisher and editors are indebted to all the people who helped in the production of this dictionary, and to those who were involved in the planning and preparation of the previous edition, particularly the late Joyce Hawkins. We are grateful to the teachers who advised us in the initial stages, to John Butterworth and Clive Johnson for their helpful comments on this revision, to the keyboarders and to the proof-readers Richard Jeffery, Janet Foot, and Steve Siddle.

The English Language

English is the chief language of Britain, the USA, Australia, and a number of other countries. More than 300 million people speak it as their first or their only language, and millions more in all parts of the world learn it as a foreign language for use in communicating with people of other nations. It is the official language used between airline pilots and their air traffic controllers in all countries, and in shipping, and the main language of international business, science, medicine, and computing.

All languages have a history: they are constantly changing and evolving. It is probable that nearly all the languages of Europe, and some of those in the Middle East and India, came from one ancient community, who lived in Eastern Europe about 5,000 years ago. Scholars call the language of this community Indo-European. As people moved away to the east and west they lost contact with each other and developed new and different lifestyles. Naturally their language needs changed too. They invented new words and forgot old ones, and the grammar of the language also changed. Many varied languages grew from the original parent tongue, until the time came when people with the same ancestors would no longer have understood each other.

Invasions and conquests complicated the process. The English language shows this very well, for invaders brought their own languages to Britain, and British travellers took theirs to lands overseas. The earliest known inhabitants of Britain spoke a form of **Celtic**, related to modern Welsh and Gaelic. Very little of this Celtic survived the waves of invasion that drove its speakers into western and highland parts of the country, but the names of some cities, rivers, and hills date back to Celtic times (e.g. *Carlisle, Avon, Pendle*).

Old English

Old English, which is also called Anglo-Saxon, does not look very much like modern English (for example *Faeder ure, þu þe eart in heofonum* = Our Father, who is in heaven) but many words, especially the most frequently used ones, can be traced back to it. *Eat, drink, sleep, speak, work, play,* and *sing* are all from Old English; so are *house, door, meat, bread, milk, fish*; and *head, nose, eye, man, woman, husband, wife*. The prepositions and conjunctions that we use to join words together in sentences, such as *and, but, to, from*, come from Old English, and so do many common adverbs, for example *up, down, here, there, over, under*.

Old English did not originate in Britain. It was the language of the Angles, Saxons, and Jutes, Germanic tribes who came to Britain from the Continent in about AD 450. By about AD 700 the Anglo-Saxons had occupied most of the country and their language was the dominant one. Even the name of the country itself became 'England', which means 'land of the Angles', and from it came 'Englisc', the Old English spelling of 'English'.

The next great influence on Old English came from the Vikings, who arrived from Norway and Denmark in the 9th and 10th centuries and occupied much of northern and eastern England. They also settled in parts of Scotland, Wales, and Ireland. Their language was Old Norse, and from it we get many common words, such as *call, cast*, and *take*, and a number of words beginning with 'sc' or 'sk', including *scare, scrap, skirt*, and *sky*.

Middle English

In 1066 the Normans, led by William the Conqueror, invaded England. English life was greatly changed in the years that followed and the language changed too, so much so that, with a little practice, we can now read and understand the language of that time. These lines, for example, were written in about 1390: *This carpenter hadde wedded newe a wyf, Which that he lovede moore than his lyf.* We call this language 'Middle English' to distinguish it from Old English or Anglo-Saxon.

For much of this period the language used by the ruling classes was the French of the victorious Norman invaders, though most of the ordinary people still spoke English. Many words connected with government and law came into the language at this time through their French use, e.g. *advise, command, court, govern, people, reign, royalty, rule*.

Throughout all these centuries, although scholars in different countries spoke different languages, they all understood Latin, which had been the language of the ancient Roman Empire, and used it for writing about every subject that they studied. Some Latin words (e.g. *mint, pound, sack*, and *street*) had already been adopted by the Anglo-

Saxons before they came to Britain, because they had lived on the fringe of the Roman Empire; others (e.g. *font*, *pope*, and *school*) arrived with the spread of Christianity. Then in the 14–16th centuries (the *Renaissance*) people throughout Europe became especially interested in Greek and Roman literature, philosophy, art, and buildings, and many more words from Greek and Latin were introduced into English (e.g. *architecture*, *column*, *comedy*, *educate*, *history*, *physics*, *tributary*). The Christian Church in all western countries had always used Latin, and continued to use this (not English or other local languages) in all its services.

Modern English

From about 1500 onwards the English language continued to change, and developed enormously. It adopted words from other languages with which people came into contact through trade or travel, and it was exported to other lands when English-speaking people travelled abroad. In the early 17th century colonies began to be established, first in North America and in India, then in the West Indies, and later in Australia, New Zealand, Hong Kong, and Africa. To each country the settlers took the English language of their own time, and in each country it changed, little by little, until it differed in various ways not only from the English of other settlements but from its parent form in Britain—where, of course, the language was changing too. Some words, such as names for birds and animals found only in one country, were adopted into the form of English used there and are not known elsewhere; others (e.g. *banana*, *potato*, and *tornado*) have made their way into international English and are known everywhere.

In the 20th century, people who came from the Caribbean and Asia to settle in England brought with them their own cultures and vocabulary, and many words from these have been adopted into standard English (e.g. *chapatti*, *reggae*).

Nowadays travel is not the only way in which people acquire words from other countries. Films made in one country are shown in many others, and television programmes from all over the world are received in people's homes. The result is that while American, Australian, and other vocabulary becomes familiar in Britain, British English continues to be exported.

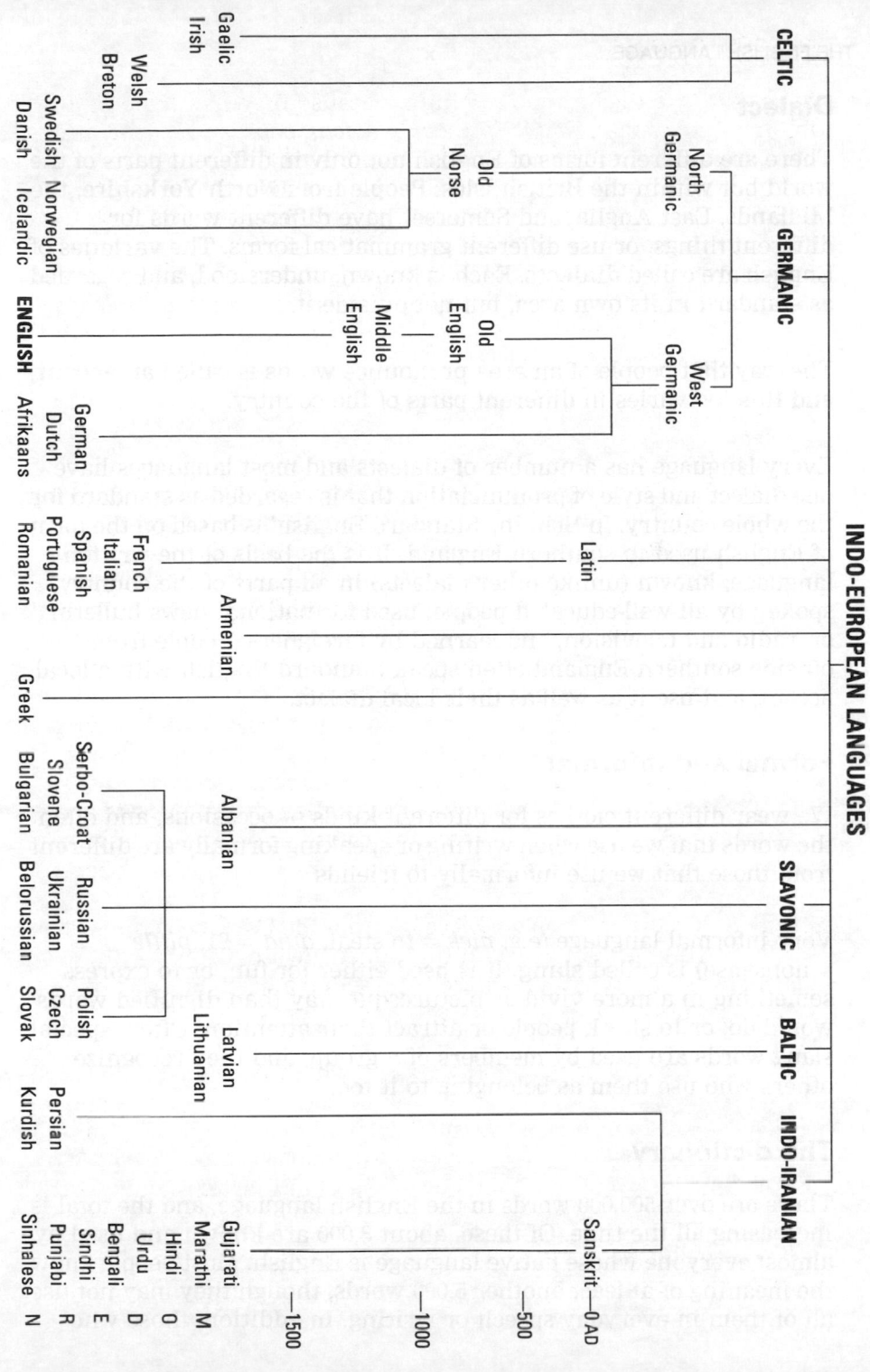

INDO-EUROPEAN LANGUAGES

CELTIC

Gaelic
Irish

Welsh
Breton

GERMANIC

North Germanic

Old Norse

Swedish
Danish

Norwegian
Icelandic

West Germanic

Old English

Middle English

ENGLISH

German
Dutch

Afrikaans

Latin

French
Italian
Spanish
Portuguese
Romanian

Armenian

Greek

SLAVONIC

Albanian

Serbo-Croat
Slovene
Bulgarian

Russian
Ukrainian
Belorussian

Polish
Czech
Slovak

BALTIC

Latvian
Lithuanian

INDO-IRANIAN

Persian
Kurdish

Sanskrit — 0 AD

Gujarati
Marathi
Hindi
Urdu
Bengali
Sindhi
Punjabi
Sinhalese

M
O
D
E
R
N

—500

—1000

—1500

Dialect

There are different forms of English not only in different parts of the world but within the British Isles. People from North Yorkshire, the Midlands, East Anglia, and Somerset have different words for different things, or use different grammatical forms. The varieties of English are called **dialects**. Each is known, understood, and regarded as standard in its own area, but not outside it.

The way that people of an area pronounce words is called an **accent**, and this too varies in different parts of the country.

Every language has a number of dialects and most languages have one dialect and style of pronunciation that is regarded as standard for the whole country. In Britain, 'Standard English' is based on the form of English used in southern England. It is the basis of the written language, known (unlike other dialects) in all parts of the country, spoken by all well-educated people, used for national news bulletins on radio and television, and learned by foreigners. People from outside southern England often speak Standard English with a local accent, and use it as well as their local dialect.

Formal and informal

We wear different clothes for different kinds of occasions, and often the words that we use when writing or speaking formally are different from those that we use informally to friends.

Very informal language (e.g. *nick* = to steal, *quid* = £1, *piffle* = nonsense) is called **slang**. It is used either for fun, or to express something in a more vivid or picturesque way than dignified words would do, or to shock people or attract their attention. Often, special slang words are used by members of a group, and they recognize others who use them as belonging to it too.

The dictionary

There are over 500,000 words in the English language, and the total is increasing all the time. Of these, about 3,000 are known and used by almost everyone whose native language is English. Most people know the meaning of at least another 5,000 words, though they may not use all of them in everyday speech or writing. In addition, those who specialize in a particular subject (e.g. music, chemistry, medicine, computers) have a wide vocabulary of words that are used by people working in that subject but are not generally known to others.

The biggest dictionary in the world is the *Oxford English Dictionary*, which fills twenty very large volumes, and it contains most of these words. Small dictionaries can find room for only a fraction of the whole language; they include most of the words that are in common use, but (in order to make the book a convenient size and not too expensive) they have to miss out a considerable number of words, and a larger dictionary must be consulted for information about these.

Notes on the use of the dictionary

Dictionary entries

Words defined are arranged in alphabetical order. The words derived
from each word (*derivatives*) are often included in the same entry
without definitions if their meaning can easily be worked out from
the meaning of the main word.

Words with the same spelling but with a different meaning or origin
(*homographs*) are given separate entries with a space between them,
and numbered with a raised figure, e.g.

peer[1] *verb* (peers, peering, peered)
look at something closely or with
difficulty. [from *appear*]

peer[2] *noun* (*plural* peers)
1 a noble. 2 someone who is equal to
another in rank, merit, or age etc.,
She had no peer. **peeress** *noun*
[from Latin *par* = equal]

Pronunciation

Help is given with this when the word is difficult, or when two words
with the same spelling are pronounced differently. The pronunciation
is given in brackets with *say* or *rhymes with*, e.g.

toll (rhymes with *hole*) *noun*
chaos (*say* kay-oss) *noun*

Words are broken up into small units (usually of one syllable), and the
syllable that is spoken with most stress is shown in thick black letters.
In the pronunciation guide, note the following distinctions:

oo shows the sound as in *soon*
uu " " " " " *book*
th " " " " " *thin*
th " " " " " *this*
zh " " " " " *vision*

Parts of speech

These are printed in italic or sloping print (e.g. *noun, adjective, verb*) after the word and before its definition. Some words can be used as more than one part of speech. When these are defined, no space is left between the entries, e.g.

barricade *noun* (*plural* **barricades**)
a barrier, especially one put up hastily across a street or door.
barricade *verb* (**barricades, barricading, barricaded**)
block a street or door with a barricade.

Inflections and plurals

Derived forms of verbs, plurals of nouns, and some comparative and superlative forms of adjectives and adverbs are given after the part of speech. The first verb form given (ending in *-s*) is used for the present tense. The second form given (ending in *-ing*) is the present participle. When three verb forms are given, e.g.

admit *verb* (**admits, admitting, admitted**)

the third form is both the past tense (as in 'he *admitted* it') and the past participle ('it was *admitted*'). When four forms are given, e.g.

come *verb* (**comes, coming, came, come**)
freeze *verb* (**freezes, freezing, froze, frozen**)

the third is the past tense (as in 'he *came*'; 'it *froze*'), and the fourth is the past participle ('he had *come*'; 'it was *frozen*').

Meanings

Many words have more than one meaning. Each meaning is numbered separately.

Labels

Words that are not standard English are labelled as *informal* or *slang* etc.

Examples

Examples of words in use are given in italic or sloping print *like this* to help make a definition clearer, e.g.

beware *verb*
be careful, *Beware of pickpockets*.

Phrases

These are listed and defined under the part of speech to which they belong, e.g.

jump *verb* **(jumps, jumping, jumped)**
move up suddenly from the ground into the air.
jump at (*informal*) accept something eagerly.
jump the gun start before you should.
jump the queue not wait your turn.
jump *noun* (*plural* **jumps**)
a jumping movement.

Usage notes

The dictionary includes over 200 notes on correct usage, grammatical points, and words that are easily confused, e.g.

less *adjective* & *adverb*

USAGE: Do not use *less* when you mean *fewer*. You should use *fewer* when you are talking about a number of individual things, and *less* when you are talking about a quantity or mass of something: *The less batter you make, the fewer pancakes you'll get.*

Origins of words

The derivation (or *etymology*) of a word is given in square brackets at the end of the entry, e.g.

alligator *noun* (*plural* **alligators**)
a large reptile of the crocodile family. [from Spanish *el lagarto* = the lizard]

These derivations often shed light on the word's meaning or how its meaning has changed, or show the connection between words that have the same set of letters in them (e.g. *attract*, *contract*, *extract*, and *tractor*) and also help to indicate the number of languages from which words have been taken into English. For instance, *alligator* comes from Spanish, *algebra* from Arabic, *mammoth* from Russian, *bungalow* from Hindi, *shawl* from Persian or Urdu, and *skunk* from a Native American language.

Other examples:

bread [from Old English, from Germanic]
butter [from Old English, taken via Latin from Greek]
cake [from a Scandinavian language]
cereal [from *Ceres*, the Roman goddess of farming]
cheese [from Old English, taken from Latin]
chocolate [via French or Spanish from Nahuatl (a Central American language spoken by the Aztecs)]
coffee [from Arabic *kahwa*]
cream [from old French]
liquorice [from Greek *glykys* = sweet + *rhiza* = root]
tea [via Dutch from Chinese]

No origin is given if the word is obviously related to another word nearby, for which there is an etymology (e.g. the origin of *determine* is given, but not those of *determination*, *determined*, or *determiner*). Etymology is not always given for words made up of two other words in the dictionary (e.g. *seafood*, *racecourse*), or of a word and a prefix or suffix (e.g. *regenerate*, *radiography*, *sleepless*, *unfortunate*). Some words have very complicated origins, and it is not always possible to show all the details; users who are interested in discovering more about word origins should look in a larger dictionary.

Aa

a *adjective* (called the *indefinite article* and changing to **an** before most vowel sounds) **1** one (but not any special one), *Can you lend me a book?* **2** each; per, *We see it once a day* or *once an hour*.
[from Old English *an* = one]

a-¹ *prefix*
1 on; to; towards (as in *afoot, ashore, aside*). **2** in the process of (as in *a-hunting*).
[from the preposition *on*]

a-² *prefix* (**an-** is used before a vowel sound)
not; without (as in *asymmetrical, anarchy*).
[from Greek *a-* = not]

ab- *prefix* (changing to **abs-** before *c* and *t*)
away; from (as in *abduct, abnormal, abstract*). [from Latin *ab* = away]

aback *adverb*
taken aback surprised.
[from Old English *on baec* = backwards]

abacus (*say* ab-a-kus) *noun* (*plural* abacuses)
a frame used for counting with beads sliding on wires. [from Greek]

abandon *verb* (abandons, abandoning, abandoned)
1 give up, *We never abandoned hope*. **2** leave something without intending to return, *Abandon ship!* **abandonment** *noun*
abandon *noun*
a careless and uncontrolled manner, *dancing with great abandon*.
[from old French]

abase *verb* (abases, abasing, abased)
make a person feel humble or humiliated.
[from old French]

abashed *adjective*
embarrassed.
[from old French *esbair* = astound]

abate *verb* (abates, abating, abated)
make or become less; die down, *The storm had abated*. **abatement** *noun*
[from Latin *battuere* = to beat]

abattoir (*say* ab-at-wahr) *noun* (*plural* abattoirs)
a place where animals are killed for food; a slaughterhouse. [French, from *abattre* = knock down, destroy]

abbey *noun* (*plural* abbeys)
1 a monastery or convent. **2** a church that was once part of a monastery, *Westminster Abbey*. [same origin as *abbot*]

abbot *noun* (*plural* abbots)
the head of an abbey. [via Latin and Greek from Aramaic (a language once spoken in the Middle East), *abba* = father]

abbreviate *verb* (abbreviates, abbreviating, abbreviated)
shorten something.
[from Latin *brevis* = short, brief]

abbreviation *noun* (*plural* abbreviations)
1 a shortened form of a word or words, especially one using the initial letters, such as GCSE, St., USA. **2** abbreviating something.

abdicate *verb* (abdicates, abdicating, abdicated)
1 resign from a throne. **2** give up an important responsibility. **abdication** *noun*
[from Latin]

abdomen (*say* ab-dom-en) *noun* (*plural* abdomens)
1 the lower front part of a person's or animal's body, containing the stomach, intestines, and other digestive organs. **2** the rear section of an insect's body. **abdominal** (*say* ab-dom-in-al) *adjective*
[Latin]

abduct *verb* (abducts, abducting, abducted)
take a person away illegally; kidnap. **abduction** *noun*, **abductor** *noun*
[from *ab-* + Latin *ductum* = led]

abet *verb* (abets, abetting, abetted)
help or encourage someone to commit a crime. [from old French *abeter* – urge]

abeyance (*say* ab-ay-ans) *noun*
in abeyance not being used at the moment; suspended, *More serious punishments are being held in abeyance*.
[from old French]

abhor *verb* (abhors, abhorring, abhorred)
(*formal*) hate something very much.
abhorrent *adjective*, **abhorrence** *noun*
[from Latin *abhorrere* = shrink away in
horror]

abide *verb* (abides, abiding, abided)
1 (*old use*; *past tense* **abode**) remain or
dwell somewhere. 2 bear or tolerate, *I can't
abide wasps*.
abide by keep a promise etc.
[from Old English]

abiding *adjective*
lasting or permanent.

ability *noun* (*plural* **abilities**)
1 being able to do something. 2 cleverness
or talent.

abject (*say* ab-jekt) *adjective*
1 wretched or miserable, *living in abject
poverty*. 2 humble, *an abject apology*.
[from *ab-* + Latin *-jectum* = thrown]

ablaze *adjective*
blazing; on fire.

able *adjective*
1 having the power or skill or opportunity
to do something. 2 skilful or clever. **ably**
adverb [from old French]

-able *suffix* (*also* **-ble**, **-ible**, and **-uble**)
forms adjectives (e.g. *readable*, *legible*). The
nouns formed from these end in **-bility** (e.g.
readability, *legibility*). [from Latin]

able-bodied *adjective*
fit and healthy; not disabled.

abnormal *adjective*
not normal; unusual. **abnormally** *adverb*,
abnormality *noun* [from *ab-* + *normal*]

aboard *adverb* & *preposition*
on or into a ship or aircraft or train.
[from *a-¹* + *board*]

abode *noun* (*plural* **abodes**) (*old use*)
the place where someone lives.
[from *abide*]

abolish *verb* (abolishes, abolishing,
abolished)
put an end to a law or custom etc.
abolition (*say* ab-ol-ish-on) *noun*
[from Latin *abolere* = destroy]

abominable *adjective*
very bad or unpleasant. **abominably** *adverb*

abominate *verb* (abominates, abominating,
abominated)
hate something very much. **abomination**
noun [from Latin *abominari* = regard as a
bad omen]

aborigine (*say* ab-er-ij-in-ee) *noun* (*plural*
aborigines)
one of the original inhabitants of a
country. **aboriginal** *adjective* & *noun*
Aborigine one of the original inhabitants of
Australia. [from Latin *ab origine* = from
the beginning]

abort *verb* (aborts, aborting, aborted)
put an end to something before it has been
completed, *They aborted the space flight
because of problems*.
[from Latin *aboriri* = miscarry]

abortion *noun* (*plural* **abortions**)
removal of a baby from the womb before it
has developed enough to survive.

abortive *adjective*
unsuccessful, *an abortive attempt*.

abound *verb* (abounds, abounding,
abounded)
1 be plentiful or abundant, *Fish abound in
the river*. 2 have something in great
quantities, *The river abounds in fish*.
[from Latin *abundare* = overflow]

about *preposition*
1 near in amount or size or time etc., *It
costs about £5. Come about two o'clock*. 2 on
the subject of; in connection with, *Tell me
about your holiday*. 3 all round; in various
parts of, *They ran about the playground*.
about *adverb*
1 in various directions, *They were running
about*. 2 not far away, *He is somewhere
about*.
be about to be going to do something.
[from *a-¹* + Old English *butan* = outside]

above *preposition*
1 higher than. 2 more than.
above *adverb*
at or to a higher place. [from Old English]

above board *adjective* & *adverb*
honest; without deception.
[from card-players cheating by changing
their cards under the table]

abrade *verb* (abrades, abrading, abraded)
scrape or wear something away by rubbing
it. **abrasion** *noun*
[from *ab-* + Latin *radere* = to scrape]

abrasive *adjective*
1 that abrades things, *an abrasive wheel*.
2 harsh, *an abrasive manner*.
abrasive *noun* (*plural* abrasives)
a rough substance used for rubbing or
polishing things.

abreast *adverb*
1 side by side. 2 keeping up with
something. [from *a*¹ + *breast*]

abridge *verb* (abridges, abridging, abridged)
shorten a book etc. by using fewer words,
an abridged edition. **abridgement** *noun*
[same origin as *abbreviate*]

abroad *adverb*
in or to another country.
[from *a-*¹ + *broad*]

abrupt *adjective*
1 sudden or hasty, *his abrupt departure*.
2 rather rude and unfriendly; curt, *She has
quite an abrupt manner*. **abruptly** *adverb*,
abruptness *noun*
[from *ab-* + Latin *ruptum* = broken]

abs- *prefix*
away; from. see **ab-**.

abscess (*say* ab-sis) *noun* (*plural* abscesses)
an inflamed place where pus has formed in
the body. [from Latin]

abscond *verb* (absconds, absconding,
absconded)
go away secretly, *The cashier had
absconded with the money*. [from Latin]

abseil *verb* (abseils, abseiling, abseiled)
lower yourself down a steep cliff or rock by
sliding down a rope.
[from German *ab* = down + *Seil* = rope]

absent *adjective*
not here; not present, *absent from school*.
absence *noun*

absent (*say* ab-sent) *verb* (absents,
absenting, absented)
absent yourself stay away.
[from *abs-* + Latin *esse* = to be]

absentee *noun* (*plural* absentees)
a person who is absent. **absenteeism** *noun*

absent-minded *adjective*
having your mind on other things;
forgetful.

absolute *adjective*
complete; not restricted.
[same origin as *absolve*]

absolutely *adverb*
1 completely. 2 (*informal*) yes, I agree.

absolute zero *noun*
the lowest possible temperature, calculated
as −273.15°C.

absolution *noun*
a priest's formal statement that someone's
sins are forgiven.

absolve *verb* (absolves, absolving, absolved)
1 clear a person of blame or guilt. 2 release
a person from a promise or obligation.
[from *ab-* + Latin *solvere* = set free]

absorb *verb* (absorbs, absorbing, absorbed)
1 soak up a liquid or gas. 2 receive
something and reduce its effects, *The
buffers absorbed most of the shock*. 3 take
up a person's attention or time.
[from *ab-* + Latin *sorbere* = suck in]

absorbent *adjective*
able to soak up liquids easily, *absorbent
paper*.

abstain *verb* (abstains, abstaining,
abstained)
1 keep yourself from doing something;
refrain. 2 choose not to use your vote.
abstainer *noun*, **abstention** *noun*
[from *abs-* + Latin *tenere* = hold]

abstemious (*say* ab-steem-ee-us) *adjective*
eating or drinking only small amounts;
not greedy. **abstemiously** *adverb*,
abstemiousness *noun* [from *abs-* + Latin
temetum = alcoholic drink]

abstinence *noun*
abstaining, especially from alcohol.
abstinent *adjective* [same origin as *abstain*]

abstract (*say* ab-strakt) *adjective*
1 concerned with ideas, not solid objects,
Truth, hope, danger are all abstract. 2 (of a
painting or sculpture) showing the artist's
ideas or feelings, not showing a
recognizable person or thing.
abstract (*say* ab-strakt) *verb* (abstracts,
abstracting, abstracted)
take out; remove, *He abstracted some cards
from the pack.* **abstraction** *noun*
abstract (*say* ab-strakt) *noun* (*plural*
abstracts)
a summary.
[from *abs-* + Latin *trahere* = pull]

abstracted *adjective*
with your mind on other things; not paying
attention.

abstruse (*say* ab-strooss) *adjective*
hard to understand; obscure.
[from Latin *abstrusus* = hidden]

absurd *adjective*
ridiculous or foolish.
absurdly *adverb*, **absurdity** *noun*
[from Latin *absurdus* = out of tune]

abundance *noun*
plenty. [same origin as *abound*]

abundant *adjective*
plentiful. **abundantly** *adverb*

abuse (*say* ab-yooz) *verb* (abuses, abusing,
abused)
1 use something badly or wrongly; misuse.
2 ill-treat a person. 3 say unpleasant things
about a person or thing.
abuse (*say* ab-yooss) *noun* (*plural* abuses)
1 a misuse, *the abuse of power.* 2 ill-
treatment. 3 words abusing a person or
thing; insults. [from *ab-* + *use*]

abusive *adjective*
rude and insulting, *abusive remarks.*

abut *verb* (abuts, abutting, abutted)
end against something, *Their shed abuts
against ours.* **abutment** *noun*
[from old French]

abysmal (*say* ab-iz-mal) *adjective*
extremely bad, *abysmal ignorance.*
[from *abyss*]

abyss (*say* ab-iss) *noun* (*plural* abysses)
an extremely deep pit.
[from Greek *abyssos* = bottomless]

ac- *prefix*
to; towards. see **ad-**.

academic *adjective*
1 to do with education or studying,
especially at a school or college or
university. 2 theoretical; having no
practical use, *an academic point.*
academic *noun* (*plural* academics)
a university or college teacher.

academy *noun* (*plural* academies)
1 a school or college, especially one for
specialized training. 2 a society of scholars
or artists, *The Royal Academy.*
[from *Akademeia*, the name of the garden
where the Greek philosopher Plato taught
his pupils]

accede (*say* ak-seed) *verb* (accedes,
acceding, acceded)
1 agree to what is asked or suggested,
accede to a request. 2 take office; become
king or queen, *She acceded to the throne.*
[from *ac-* + Latin *cedere* = go]

accelerate *verb* (accelerates, accelerating,
accelerated)
make or become quicker; increase speed.
[from *ac-* + Latin *celer* = swift]

acceleration *noun* (*plural* accelerations)
1 the rate at which the speed of something
increases. 2 the rate of change of velocity.

accelerator *noun* (*plural* accelerators)
1 the pedal that a driver presses to make a
motor vehicle go faster. 2 a thing used to
increase the speed of something.

accent (*say* ak-sent) *noun* (*plural* accents)
1 the way a person pronounces words, *She
has a French accent.* 2 emphasis or stress,
In 'fairy', the accent is on 'fair-'. 3 a mark
placed over a letter to show how it is
pronounced, e.g. on *café*.

accent (*say* ak-sent) *verb* (accents, accenting, accented)
pronounce part of a word more strongly than the other parts; emphasize.
[from *ac-* + Latin *cantus* = song]

accentuate (*say* ak-sent-yoo-ayt) *verb* (accentuates, accentuating, accentuated)
make something more obvious; emphasize.
accentuation *noun*

accept *verb* (accepts, accepting, accepted)
1 take a thing that is offered or presented.
2 say yes to an invitation, offer, etc.
acceptance *noun*
[from *ac-* + Latin *capere* = take]

USAGE: Do not confuse with *except*.

acceptable *adjective*
good enough to accept; pleasing.
acceptably *adverb*, **acceptability** *noun*

access (*say* ak-sess) *noun*
1 a way to enter or reach something. **2** the right to use or look at something.
access *verb* (accesses, accessing, accessed)
find information that has been stored in a computer. [same origin as *accede*]

accessible *adjective*
able to be reached.
accessibly *adverb*, **accessibility** *noun*

accession *noun* (*plural* accessions)
1 reaching a rank or position; becoming king or queen. **2** an addition, *recent accessions to our library*.
[from Latin *accessio* = coming to, something come to or added]

accessory (*say* ak-sess-er-ee) *noun* (*plural* accessories)
1 an extra thing that goes with something. **2** a person who helps another with a crime.
[from Latin *accessorius* = added]

accident *noun* (*plural* accidents)
an unexpected happening, especially one causing injury or damage.
by accident by chance; without its being arranged in advance.
[from Latin *accidere* = happen]

accidental *adjective*
happening or done by accident.
accidentally *adverb*

acclaim *verb* (acclaims, acclaiming, acclaimed)
welcome or applaud.
acclaim *noun*, **acclamation** *noun*
[from *ac-* + Latin *clamare* = to shout]

acclimatize *verb* (acclimatizes, acclimatizing, acclimatized)
make or become used to a new climate or new surroundings. **acclimatization** *noun*
[from *ac-* + French *climat* = climate + *-ize*]

accolade (*say* ak-ol-**ayd**) *noun* (*plural* accolades)
praise or a prize given to someone for something they have done.
[from *ac-* + Latin *collum* = neck (because in olden days, when a man was knighted, the king embraced him round the neck)]

accommodate *verb* (accommodates, accommodating, accommodated)
1 provide somebody with a place to live, work, or sleep overnight. **2** help by providing something, *We can accommodate you with skis.*
[from Latin *accommodare* = make suitable for]

accommodating *adjective*
willing to help or cooperate.

accommodation *noun*
somewhere to live, work, or sleep overnight.

accompanist *noun* (*plural* accompanists)
a pianist etc. who accompanies a singer or another musician.

accompany *verb* (accompanies, accompanying, accompanied)
1 go somewhere with somebody. **2** be present with something, *Thunder accompanied the storm.* **3** play music, especially on a piano, that supports a singer or another player etc.
accompaniment *noun*
[from old French]

accomplice (*say* a-**kum**-pliss) *noun* (*plural* accomplices)
a person who helps another in a crime etc.
[from old French]

accomplish *verb* (accomplishes, accomplishing, accomplished)
do something successfully.
accomplishment *noun*
[from *ac-* + Latin *complere* = to complete]

accomplished *adjective*
skilled.

accord *noun*
agreement; consent.
of your own accord voluntarily; without being asked or compelled.
accord *verb* (accords, according, accorded)
1 be consistent with something. **2** (*formal*) give, *He was accorded this privilege.*
[from old French]

accordance *noun*
in accordance with in agreement with, *This is done in accordance with the rules.*

according *adverb*
according to 1 as stated by, *According to him, we are stupid.* **2** in relation to, *Price the apples according to their size.*

accordingly *adverb*
1 in the way that is required, *I've given you your instructions and I expect you to act accordingly.* **2** therefore.

accordion *noun* (*plural* accordions)
a portable musical instrument like a large concertina. [via German from Italian *accordare* = to tune an instrument]

accost *verb* (accosts, accosting, accosted)
approach and speak to a person.
[via French from Italian]

account *noun* (*plural* accounts)
1 a statement of money owed, spent, or received; a bill. **2** an arrangement to keep money in a bank etc. **3** a description or report.
on account of because of.
on no account under no circumstances; certainly not.
take something into account consider or include it when making a decision or calculation.
account *verb* (accounts, accounting, accounted)
account for make it clear why something happens.
[from *ac-* + old French *counte* = story, sum]

accountable *adjective*
responsible; having to explain why you have done something.
accountability *noun*

accountant *noun* (*plural* accountants)
a person whose job is keeping or inspecting financial accounts.
accountancy *noun*

accounting *noun*
keeping financial accounts.

accoutrements (*say* a-koo-trim-ents)
plural noun
equipment. [French]

accredited *adjective*
officially recognized, *our accredited agent.*
[from French *accréditer* = vouch for]

accretion (*say* a-kree-shon) *noun* (*plural* accretions)
a growth or increase in which things are added gradually. [same origin as *accrue*]

accrue (*say* a-kroo) *verb* (accrues, accruing, accrued)
1 gradually increase over a period of time. **2** accumulate. **accrual** *noun*
[from *ac-* + Latin *crescere* = grow]

accumulate *verb* (accumulates, accumulating, accumulated)
collect; pile up. **accumulation** *noun*
[from *ac-* + Latin *cumulus* = heap]

accumulator *noun* (*plural* accumulators)
a storage battery.

accurate *adjective*
correct or exact. **accurately** *adverb*, **accuracy** *noun* [from *ac-* + Latin *cura* = care]

accusation *noun* (*plural* accusations)
accusing someone; a statement accusing a person of a fault or crime etc.

accuse *verb* (accuses, accusing, accused)
say that a person has committed a crime etc.; blame. **accuser** *noun*
[from *ac-* + Latin *causa* = cause]

accustom *verb* (accustoms, accustoming, accustomed)
make a person become used to something.
[from *ac-* + *custom*]

ace *noun* (*plural* aces)
1 a playing card with one spot. **2** a very skilful person or thing. **3** (in tennis) a serve that is too good for the other player to reach. [from Latin *as* = unit]

acetylene (*say* a-set-il-een) *noun*
a gas that burns with a bright flame, used in cutting and welding metal. [from Latin]

ache *noun* (*plural* aches)
a dull continuous pain.
ache *verb* (aches, aching, ached)
have an ache. [from Old English]

achieve *verb* (achieves, achieving, achieved)
succeed in doing or producing something.
achievable *adjective*, **achievement** *noun*
[from old French *a chief* = to a head]

acid *noun* (*plural* acids)
a chemical substance that contains hydrogen and neutralizes alkalis. **acidic** *adjective*, **acidity** *noun*
acid *adjective*
1 sharp-tasting; sour. **2** looking or sounding bitter, *an acid reply*. **acidly** *adverb*
[from Latin *acere* = to be sour]

acid rain *noun*
rain made acid by mixing with waste gases from factories etc.

acknowledge *verb* (acknowledges, acknowledging, acknowledged)
1 admit that something is true. **2** state that you have received or noticed something, *Acknowledge this letter*. **3** express thanks or appreciation for something.
acknowledgement *noun* [from Old English *acknow* = confess, + *knowledge*]

acme (*say* ak-mee) *noun*
the highest degree of something, *the acme of perfection*.
[from Greek *akme* = highest point]

acne (*say* ak-nee) *noun*
inflamed red pimples on the face and neck.
[same origin as *acme*]

aconite *noun* (*plural* aconites)
a plant of the buttercup family.
[from Greek]

acorn *noun* (*plural* acorns)
the seed of the oak tree. [from Old English]

acoustic (*say* a-koo-stik) *adjective*
1 to do with sound or hearing. **2** (of a musical instrument) not electronic, *an acoustic guitar*. **acoustically** *adverb*
[from Greek *akouein* = hear]

acoustics (*say* a-koo-stiks) *plural noun*
1 the qualities of a hall etc. that make it good or bad for carrying sound. **2** the properties of sound.

acquaint *verb* (acquaints, acquainting, acquainted)
tell somebody about something, *Acquaint him with the facts*.
be acquainted with know slightly.
[from old French]

acquaintance *noun* (*plural* acquaintances)
1 a person you know slightly. **2** being acquainted.

acquiesce (*say* ak-wee-ess) *verb* (acquiesces, acquiescing, acquiesced)
agree to something. **acquiescent** *adjective*, **acquiescence** *noun*
[from *ac-* + Latin *quiescere* = to rest]

acquire *verb* (acquires, acquiring, acquired)
obtain. **acquirement** *noun*, **acquisition** *noun*
[from *ac-* + Latin *quaerere* = seek]

acquisitive (*say* a-kwiz-it-iv) *adjective*
eager to acquire things.

acquit *verb* (acquits, acquitting, acquitted)
decide that somebody is not guilty, *The jury acquitted her*. **acquittal** *noun*
acquit yourself well perform or do something well.
[from *ac-* + Latin *quietus* = at rest]

acre (*say* ay-ker) *noun* (*plural* acres)
an area of land measuring 4,840 square yards or 0.405 hectares. **acreage** *noun*
[from Old English *aecer* = field]

acrid *adjective*
bitter, *an acrid smell*.
[from Latin *acer* = sharp, pungent, bitter]

acrimonious (*say* ak-rim-oh-nee-us) *adjective*
(of a person's manner or words) sharp and bad-tempered or bitter.
acrimony (*say* ak-rim-on-ee) *noun*
[same origin as *acrid*]

acrobat *noun* (*plural* **acrobats**)
a person who performs spectacular
gymnastic stunts for entertainment.
acrobatic *adjective*, **acrobatics** *plural noun*
[from Greek *akrobatos* = walking on tiptoe]

acronym (*say* ak-ron-im) *noun* (*plural*
acronyms)
a word or name that is formed from the
initial letters of other words, *Nato is an
acronym of North Atlantic Treaty
Organization.*
[from Greek *akros* = top + *onyma* = name]

across *preposition* & *adverb*
1 from one side to the other, *Swim across
the river. Are you across yet?* 2 on the
opposite side, *the house across the street.*
[from French *à croix* = crosswise]

acrostic *noun* (*plural* **acrostics**)
a word-puzzle or poem in which the first or
last letters of each line form a word or
words. [from Greek *akros* = top + *stikhos*
= a line of verse]

acrylic (*say* a-kril-ik) *noun*
a kind of fibre, plastic, or resin made from
an organic acid. [from *acrolein*, the
substance from which acrylic is made]

acrylics *plural noun*
a type of paint used by artists.

act *noun* (*plural* **acts**)
1 an action. 2 a law passed by a
parliament. 3 one of the main divisions of
a play or opera. 4 a short performance in a
programme of entertainment, *a juggling
act.* 5 a pretence, *She is only putting on an
act.*

act *verb* (**acts, acting, acted**)
1 do something; perform actions.
2 perform a part in a play or film etc.
3 function; have an effect.
[from Latin *actus* = doing, performing]

action *noun* (*plural* **actions**)
1 doing something. 2 something done.
3 a battle; fighting, *He was killed in action.*
4 a lawsuit.
out of action not working or functioning.
take action do something.

action replay *noun* (*plural* **action replays**)
playing back a piece of sports action on
television, especially in slow motion.

activate *verb* (**activates, activating,
activated**)
start something working.
activation *noun*, **activator** *noun*

active *adjective*
1 lively or energetic. 2 functioning or
working; in operation, *an active volcano.*
3 radioactive. 4 (of a form of a verb) used
when the subject of the verb is performing
the action. In 'The shop *sells* sweets' the
verb is active; in 'Sweets *are sold* by the
shop' the verb is passive.
actively *adverb*, **activeness** *noun*

activist *noun* (*plural* **activists**)
a person who believes in vigorous action,
especially in politics.

activity *noun* (*plural* **activities**)
1 an action or occupation, *outdoor
activities.* 2 being active or lively.

actor *noun* (*plural* **actors**)
a person who acts a part in a play or film
etc.

actress *noun* (*plural* **actresses**)
a woman who acts a part in a play or film
etc.

actual *adjective*
real. **actually** *adverb*, **actuality** *noun*
[from Latin *actualis* = active, practical]

actuate *verb* (**actuates, actuating, actuated**)
start something working; activate.
actuation *noun*

acumen (*say* ak-yoo-men) *noun*
sharpness of mind. [Latin, = a point]

acupuncture (*say* ak-yoo-punk-cher) *noun*
pricking parts of the body with needles to
relieve pain or cure disease. **acupuncturist**
noun [from Latin *acu* = with a needle,
+ *puncture*]

acute *adjective*
1 sharp or strong, *acute pain.* 2 having a
sharp mind. **acutely** *adverb*, **acuteness** *noun*
[from Latin *acus* = needle]

acute accent *noun* (*plural* **acute accents**)
a mark over a vowel, as over *é* in *café.*

acute angle *noun* (*plural* **acute angles**)
an angle of less than 90°.

AD *abbreviation*
Anno Domini (Latin = in the year of Our Lord), used in dates counted from the birth of Jesus Christ.

ad- *prefix* (changing to **ac-, af-, ag-, al-, an-, ap-, ar-, as-, at-** before certain consonants) to; towards (as in *adapt, admit*). [from Latin *ad* = to]

adamant (*say* ad-am-ant) *adjective*
firm and not giving way to requests. [from Greek]

Adam's apple *noun* (*plural* **Adam's apples**)
the lump at the front of a man's neck. [from the story that when Adam (the first man, according to the Bible) ate an apple, which God had forbidden him to, a piece of it stuck in his throat]

adapt *verb* (**adapts, adapting, adapted**)
change something so that it is suitable for a new purpose or situation.
adaptable *adjective*, **adaptation** *noun*
[from *ad-* + Latin *aptus* = suitable, apt]

adaptor *noun* (*plural* **adaptors**)
a device to connect pieces of electrical or other equipment.

add *verb* (**adds, adding, added**)
1 put one thing with another. 2 make another remark.
add up 1 make or find a total. 2 (*informal*) make sense; seem reasonable.
[from Latin]

addenda *plural noun*
things added at the end of a book.
[Latin, = things to be added]

adder *noun* (*plural* **adders**)
a small poisonous snake.
[from Old English; originally called *a nadder*, which became *an adder*]

addict *noun* (*plural* **addicts**)
a person who does or uses something that he or she cannot give up. **addicted** *adjective*, **addiction** *noun* [from Latin]

addictive *adjective*
causing people to become addicts, *an addictive drug*.

addition *noun* (*plural* **additions**)
1 the process of adding. 2 something added.
In addition also; as an extra thing.
additional *adjective*, **additionally** *adverb*

additive *noun* (*plural* **additives**)
a substance added to another in small amounts for a special purpose, e.g. as a flavouring.

addled *adjective*
(of eggs) rotted and producing no chick after being brooded. [from Old English]

address *noun* (*plural* **addresses**)
1 the details of the place where someone lives or of where letters etc. should be delivered to a person or firm. 2 a speech to an audience.
address *verb* (**addresses, addressing, addressed**)
1 write an address on a parcel etc. 2 make a speech or remark etc. to somebody. [from old French]

addressee *noun* (*plural* **addressees**)
the person to whom a letter etc. is addressed.

adenoids *plural noun*
thick spongy flesh at the back of the nose and throat, which may hinder breathing. [from Greek *aden* = gland]

adept (*say* a-dept) *adjective*
very skilful. [from Latin]

adequate *adjective*
enough or good enough. **adequately** *adverb*, **adequacy** *noun* [from Latin]

adhere *verb* (**adheres, adhering, adhered**)
stick to something. **adhesion** *noun*
[from *ad-* + Latin *haerere* = to stick]

adherent (*say* ad-heer-ent) *noun* (*plural* **adherents**)
a person who supports a certain group or theory etc. **adherence** *noun*

adhesive *adjective*
sticky; causing things to stick together.
adhesive *noun* (*plural* **adhesives**)
a substance used to stick things together; glue. [same origin as *adhere*]

ad hoc (*adjective* & *adverb*)
done or arranged only when necessary and
not planned in advance, *We had to make a
number of ad hoc decisions.*
[Latin, = for this]

adieu (*say* a-**dew**) *interjection*
goodbye.
[from French *à* = to + *Dieu* = God]

ad infinitum (*say* in-fin-I-tum) *adverb*
without limit; for ever.
[Latin, = to infinity]

adjacent *adjective*
near or next to, *I waited in an adjacent
room.* [from *ad-* + Latin *jacens* = lying]

adjective *noun* (*plural* **adjectives**)
a word that describes a noun or adds to its
meaning, e.g. *big, honest, strange, our.*
adjectival *adjective*, **adjectivally** *adverb*

adjoin *verb* (**adjoins, adjoining, adjoined**)
be next or nearest to something.
[same origin as *adjunct*]

adjourn (*say* a-**jern**) *verb* (**adjourns,
adjourning, adjourned**)
1 break off a meeting etc. until a later time.
2 break off and go somewhere else, *They
adjourned to the library.* **adjournment** *noun*
[from Latin, = to another day]

adjudge *verb* (**adjudges, adjudging,
adjudged**)
judge; give a decision, *He was adjudged to
be guilty.* [same origin as *adjudicate*]

adjudicate (*say* a-**joo**-dik-ayt) *verb*
(**adjudicates, adjudicating, adjudicated**)
act as judge in a competition etc.
adjudication *noun*, **adjudicator** *noun*
[from *ad-* + Latin *judex* = a judge]

adjunct (*say* aj-unkt) *noun* (*plural* **adjuncts**)
something added that is useful but not
essential.
[from *ad-* + Latin *junctum* = joined]

adjust *verb* (**adjusts, adjusting, adjusted**)
1 put a thing into its proper position or
order. 2 alter something so that it fits or
is suitable.
adjustable *adjective*, **adjustment** *noun*
[from *ad-* + Latin *juxta* = close to]

ad lib *adverb*
as you like; freely.

ad lib *verb* (**ad libs, ad libbing, ad libbed**)
say or do something without any rehearsal
or preparation. [from Latin *ad libitum*
= according to pleasure]

administer *verb* (**administers,
administering, administered**)
1 give or provide something, *He
administered medicine.* 2 manage business
affairs; administrate.
[from *ad-* + Latin *ministrare* = serve]

administrate *verb* (**administrates,
administrating, administrated**)
manage public or business affairs.
administrator *noun*, **administrative** *adjective*
[same origin as *administer*]

administration *noun* (*plural*
administrations)
1 administering. 2 the management of
public or business affairs. 3 the people who
manage an organization etc.; the
government.

admirable *adjective*
worth admiring; excellent.
admirably *adverb*

admiral *noun* (*plural* **admirals**)
a naval officer of high rank.
[from Arabic *amir* = commander]

admire *verb* (**admires, admiring, admired**)
1 look at something and enjoy it. 2 think
that someone or something is very good.
admiration *noun*, **admirer** *noun*
[from *ad-* + Latin *mirari* = wonder at]

admissible *adjective*
able to be admitted or allowed, *admissible
evidence.*

admission *noun* (*plural* **admissions**)
1 admitting. 2 the charge for being allowed
to go in. 3 a statement admitting
something; a confession.

admit *verb* (**admits, admitting, admitted**)
1 allow someone or something to come in.
2 state reluctantly that something is true;
confess, *We admit that the task is difficult.
He admitted his crime.*
[from *ad-* + Latin *mittere* = send]

admittance *noun*
being allowed to go in, especially to a private place.

admittedly *adverb*
as an agreed fact; without denying it.

admonish *verb* (**admonishes, admonishing, admonished**)
advise or warn someone firmly but mildly. **admonition** *noun*
[from *ad-* + Latin *monere* = advise]

ad nauseam (*say* naw-see-am) *adverb*
until people are sick of it.
[Latin, = to sickness]

ado *noun*
without more or **further ado** without wasting any more time.
[originally in *much ado* = much to do]

adolescence (*say* ad-ol-ess-ens) *noun*
the time between being a child and being an adult.
[from *ad-* + Latin *alescere* = grow up]

adolescent *noun* (*plural* **adolescents**)
a young person at the age between being a child and being an adult.
adolescent *adjective*

adopt *verb* (**adopts, adopting, adopted**)
1 take someone into your family as your own child. **2** accept something; take something and use it, *They adopted new methods of working.* **adoption** *noun*
[from *ad-* + Latin *optare* = choose]

adore *verb* (**adores, adoring, adored**)
love a person or thing very much.
adorable *adjective*, **adoration** *noun*
[from *ad-* + Latin *orare* = pray]

adorn *verb* (**adorns, adorning, adorned**)
decorate. **adornment** *noun* [from *ad-* + Latin *ornare* = furnish, decorate]

adrenalin (*say* a-dren-al-in) *noun*
a hormone that stimulates the nervous system. [from *ad-* + *renal* (because adrenalin is made by the adrenal glands, above the kidneys)]

adrift *adjective* & *adverb*
drifting. [from *a-*[1] + *drift*]

adroit (*say* a-droit) *adjective*
skilful.
[from French *à droit* = according to right]

adulation *noun*
very great flattery. [from old French]

adult (*say* ad-ult) *noun* (*plural* **adults**)
a fully grown or mature person.
[from Latin *adultus* = grown up]

adulterate *verb* (**adulterates, adulterating, adulterated**)
make a thing impure or less good by adding something to it. **adulteration** *noun*
[from Latin]

adultery *noun*
being unfaithful to your wife or husband by having sexual intercourse with someone else. **adulterer** *noun*, **adulterous** *adjective* [from Latin]

advance *noun* (*plural* **advances**)
1 a forward movement; progress. **2** an increase. **3** a loan; payment made before it is due.
in advance beforehand; ahead.
advance *verb* (**advances, advancing, advanced**)
1 move forward; make progress. **2** lend or pay money ahead of the proper time, *Advance her a month's salary.* **advancement** *noun* [from old French]

advantage *noun* (*plural* **advantages**)
1 something useful or helpful. **2** the next point won after deuce in tennis.
take advantage of use a person or thing profitably or unfairly.
to advantage making a good effect, *The painting can be seen to its best advantage here.*
to your advantage profitable or helpful to you.
[from French *avant* = before]

advantageous (*say* ad-van-tay-jus) *adjective*
giving an advantage; beneficial.

Advent *noun*
the period just before Christmas, when Christians celebrate the coming of Christ.

advent *noun*
the arrival of a new person or thing, *the advent of computers.*
[from *ad-* + Latin *ventum* = arrived]

adventure *noun* (*plural* **adventures**)
1 an exciting or dangerous experience.
2 willingness to take risks. **adventurer** *noun* [same origin as *advent*]

adventurous *adjective*
willing to take risks and do new things.

adverb *noun* (*plural* **adverbs**)
a word that adds to the meaning of a verb or adjective or another adverb and tells how, when, or where something happens, e.g. *gently*, *soon*, and *upstairs*.
adverbial *adjective*, **adverbially** *adverb*
[from *ad-* + Latin *verbum* = word]

adversary (*say* ad-ver-ser-ee) *noun* (*plural* **adversaries**)
an opponent or enemy.

adverse *adjective*
unfavourable or harmful, *adverse effects.*
adversely *adverb*, **adversity** *noun*
[from Latin *adversus* = opposite, from *ad-* + *versus* = turned]

USAGE: Do not confuse with *averse.*

advert *noun* (*plural* **adverts**)
(*informal*) an advertisement.

advertise *verb* (**advertises, advertising, advertised**)
1 make something publicly known, *advertise a meeting.* **2** praise goods etc. in order to encourage people to buy or use them. **3** ask or offer by a public notice, *advertise for a secretary.* **advertiser** *noun*
[from old French]

advertisement *noun* (*plural* **advertisements**)
a public notice or announcement, especially one advertising goods or services in newspapers, on posters, or in broadcasts.

advice *noun*
1 telling a person what you think he or she should do. **2** a piece of information, *We*

received advice that the goods had been dispatched. [originally = opinion, point of view: from *ad-* + Latin *videre* = see]

USAGE: Do not confuse with the verb *advise.*

advisable *adjective*
that is the wise thing to do.
advisability *noun*

advise *verb* (**advises, advising, advised**)
1 give somebody advice; recommend.
2 inform. **adviser** *noun*, **advisory** *adjective*
[same origin as *advice*]

advocate (*say* ad-vok-ayt) *verb* (**advocates, advocating, advocated**)
speak in favour of something; recommend, *We advocate changing the law.*

advocate (*say* ad-vok-at) *noun* (*plural* **advocates**)
1 a person who advocates a policy etc., *She is an advocate of women's rights.* **2** a lawyer presenting someone's case in a lawcourt.
[from *ad-* + Latin *vocare* = call, speak]

aegis (*say* ee-jiss) *noun*
under the aegis of, under the protection or with the support of, *The scheme is under the aegis of the Scout Association.*
[from Greek *aigis* = magical shield of the god Zeus]

aerate (*say* air-ayt) *verb* (**aerates, aerating, aerated**)
1 add air to something. **2** add carbon dioxide to a liquid, *aerated water.*
[same origin as *aero-*]

aerial *adjective*
1 in or from the air. **2** to do with aircraft.

aerial *noun* (*plural* **aerials**)
a wire or rod etc. for receiving or transmitting radio or television signals.
[same origin as *aero-*]

aero- *prefix*
to do with air or aircraft (as in *aeronautics*). [from Greek *aer* = air]

aerobatics *plural noun*
spectacular performances by flying aircraft. **aerobatic** *adjective*
[from *aero-* + *acrobatics*]

aerobics *plural noun*
exercises to stimulate breathing and strengthen the heart and lungs. **aerobic** *adjective* [from *aero-* + Greek *bios* = life]

aerodrome *noun* (*plural* **aerodromes**)
an airfield. [from *aero-* + Greek *dromos* = running-track]

aerodynamic *adjective*
designed to move through the air quickly and easily.

aeronautics *noun*
the study of aircraft and flying.
aeronautic *adjective*, **aeronautical** *adjective* [from *aero-* + *nautical*]

aeroplane *noun* (*plural* **aeroplanes**)
a flying machine with wings.
[from *aero-* + *plane*[1]]

aerosol *noun* (*plural* **aerosols**)
a container that holds a liquid under pressure and can let it out in a fine spray. [from *aero-* + *solution*]

aerospace *noun*
the earth's atmosphere and space beyond it. [from *aero-* + *space*]

aesthetic (*say* iss-**thet**-ik) *adjective*
to do with the appreciation of beautiful things. [from Greek *aisthesthai* = perceive]

af- *prefix*
to; towards. see **ad-**.

afar *adverb*
far away, *The din was heard from afar.*
[from *a-*[1] + *far*]

affable *adjective*
polite and friendly. **affably** *adverb*, **affability** *noun* [from *af-* + Latin *fari* = speak]

affair *noun* (*plural* **affairs**)
1 an event or matter, *The party was a grand affair.* **2** a temporary sexual relationship between two people who are not married to each other.
[from French *à faire* = to do]

affairs *plural noun*
the business and activities that are part of private or public life, *Keep out of my affairs*; *current affairs.*

affect *verb* (**affects, affecting, affected**)
1 have an effect on; influence. **2** pretend, *She affected ignorance*
[from *af-* + Latin *facere* = do]

USAGE: The word *affect* is a verb. Do not confuse it with the noun *effect.*

---

affectation *noun* (*plural* **affectations**)
a pretence; behaviour that is put on for show and not natural.

affected *adjective*
pretended and unnatural.

affection *noun* (*plural* **affections**)
a strong liking for a person.

affectionate *adjective*
showing affection; loving. **affectionately** *adverb* [from Latin *affectionatus* = devoted]

affidavit (*say* af-id-**ay**-vit) *noun* (*plural* **affidavits**)
a statement written down and sworn to be true, for use as legal evidence. [Latin, = he or she has stated on oath]

affiliated *adjective*
officially connected with a larger organization. [from Latin *affiliatum* = adopted, from *af-* + *filius* = son]

affinity *noun* (*plural* **affinities**)
attraction, relationship, or similarity to each other, *There are many affinities between the two languages.* [from French]

affirm *verb* (**affirms, affirming, affirmed**)
state something definitely or firmly.
affirmation *noun*
[from *af-* + Latin *firmus* = firm]

affirmative *adjective*
that says 'yes', *an affirmative reply.*
(Compare *negative.*)

affix (*say* a-**fiks**) *verb* (**affixes, affixing, affixed**)
attach; add in writing, *affix a stamp*; *affix your signature.*

affix (*say* **aff**-iks) *noun* (*plural* **affixes**)
a prefix or suffix.
[from *af-* + Latin *fixare* = fix]

afflict *verb* (**afflicts, afflicting, afflicted**)
cause somebody to suffer, *He is afflicted with arthritis.* **affliction** *noun*
[from *af-* + Latin *flictum* = struck]

affluent (*say* af-loo-ent) *adjective*
rich. **affluence** *noun* [from Latin *affluens* = overflowing, from *af-* + *fluens* = flowing]

afford *verb* (**affords, affording, afforded**)
1 have enough money to pay for something. **2** have enough time or resources etc. to do something.
[from Old English]

afforestation *noun*
the planting of trees to form a forest.
[from *af-* + Latin *foresta* = forest]

affray *noun* (*plural* **affrays**)
fighting or rioting in public.
[from old French]

affront *verb* (**affronts, affronting, affronted**)
insult or offend someone.
affront *noun* (*plural* **affronts**)
an insult.
[from Latin *ad frontem* = to the face]

afield *adverb*
at or to a distance; away from home,
travelling far afield. [from *a-*[1] + *field*]

aflame *adjective* & *adverb*
in flames; glowing. [from *a-*[1] + *flame*]

afloat *adjective* & *adverb*
floating; on the sea. [from *a-*[1] + *float*]

afoot *adjective*
happening, *Great changes are afoot.*
[originally = on foot, moving: from *a-*[1] + *foot*]

aforesaid *adjective*
mentioned previously.
[from *afore* = before, + *said*]

afraid *adjective*
frightened or alarmed.
I'm afraid I regret, *I'm afraid I'm late.*
[past participle of an old word *affray* = attack, frighten]

afresh *adverb*
again; in a new way, *We must start afresh.*
[from *a-*[1] + *fresh*]

African *adjective*
to do with Africa or its people.
African *noun* (*plural* **Africans**)
an African person.

Afrikaans (*say* af-rik-ahns) *noun*
a language developed from Dutch, used in South Africa. [Dutch, = African]

Afrikaner (*say* af-rik-ah-ner) *noun* (*plural* **Afrikaners**)
a White person in South Africa whose language is Afrikaans.

Afro- *prefix*
African.

Afro-Caribbean *adjective*
to do with Caribbean (especially West Indian) people whose ancestors came from Africa.

aft *adverb*
at or towards the back of a ship or aircraft.
[from Old English, related to *after*]

after *preposition*
1 later than, *Come after tea.* **2** behind in place or order, *Which letter comes after H?* **3** trying to catch; pursuing, *Run after him.* **4** in spite of, *We can come after all.* **5** in imitation or honour of, *She is named after her aunt.* **6** about or concerning, *He asked after you.*
after *adverb*
1 behind, *Jill came tumbling after.* **2** later, *It came a week after.*
after *adjective*
coming or done afterwards, *in after years*; *the after-effects.* [from Old English]

afterbirth *noun*
the placenta and other membranes that come out of the mother's womb after she has given birth.

aftermath *noun*
the conditions after a disaster, war, etc., *the aftermath of the earthquake.*
[from *after* + *math* = mowing (i.e. new grass that grows after a mowing)]

afternoon *noun* (*plural* **afternoons**)
the time from noon or lunchtime to evening.

aftershave *noun*
a pleasant-smelling lotion that men put on their skin after shaving.

afterthought *noun* (*plural* afterthoughts)
something thought of or added later.

afterwards *adverb*
at a later time. [from *after* + *-wards*]

ag- *prefix*
to; towards. see **ad-**.

again *adverb*
1 another time; once more, *try again*. 2 as before, *You will soon be well again.*
3 besides; moreover.
[from Old English *ongean* = in the opposite direction, back to the beginning]

against *preposition*
1 touching or hitting, *He leant against the wall.* 2 in opposition to; not in favour of, *They voted against the proposal.* 3 in preparation for, *Protect them against the cold.* [from *again*]

age *noun* (*plural* ages)
1 the length of time a person has lived or a thing has existed. 2 a special period of history or geology, *the ice age.*
ages *plural noun* (*informal*) a very long time, *We've been waiting for ages.*
come of age reach the age at which you have an adult's legal rights and obligations (now at 18 years; formerly 21).
age *verb* (ages, ageing, aged)
make or become old. [from old French]

aged *adjective*
1 (*say* ayjd) having the age of, *a girl aged 9.*
2 (*say* **ay**-jid) very old, *an aged man.*

age group *noun* (*plural* age groups)
people who are all of the same age.

agency *noun* (*plural* agencies)
1 the office or business of an agent, *a travel agency.* 2 the means by which something is done, *Flowers are pollinated by the agency of bees.* [same origin as *agent*]

agenda (*say* a-jen-da) *noun* (*plural* agendas)
a list of things to be done or discussed, *The agenda is rather long.*
[Latin, = things to be done]

agent *noun* (*plural* agents)
1 a person who organizes things for other people. 2 a spy, *a secret agent.*
[from Latin *agens* – doing things]

agglomeration *noun* (*plural* agglomerations)
a mass of things collected together.
[from *ag-* + Latin *glomus* = mass]

aggravate *verb* (aggravates, aggravating, aggravated)
1 make a thing worse or more serious.
2 annoy. **aggravation** *noun*
[from *ag-* + Latin *gravare* = load heavily]

aggregate (*say* **ag**-rig-at) *adjective*
combined or total, *the aggregate amount.*
aggregate *noun* (*plural* aggregates)
a total amount or score.
[from *ag-* + Latin *gregatum* = herded together]

aggression *noun*
starting an attack or war etc.; aggressive behaviour. [from Latin *aggredi* = attack, from *ag-* = against + *gradi* = step, move]

aggressive *adjective*
likely to attack people; forceful.
aggressively *adverb*, **aggressiveness** *noun*

aggressor *noun* (*plural* aggressors)
the person or nation that started an attack or war etc.

aggrieved (*say* a-greevd) *adjective*
resentful because of being treated unfairly.
[same origin as *aggravate*]

aghast *adjective*
horrified. [from Old English]

agile *adjective*
moving quickly or easily. **agilely** *adverb*, **agility** *noun* [from Latin *agere* = do]

agitate *verb* (agitates, agitating, agitated)
1 make someone feel upset or anxious.
2 stir up public interest or concern; campaign, *They agitated for a new bypass.*
3 shake something about. **agitation** *noun*, **agitator** *noun* [from Latin *agitare* = shake]

aglow *adjective*
glowing. [from *a-*[1] + *glow*]

agnostic (*say* ag-**nost**-ik) *noun* (*plural* **agnostics**)
a person who believes that it is impossible to know whether God exists. **agnosticism** *noun*
[from a-² + Greek *gnostikos* = knowing]

ago *adverb*
in the past, *long ago.*
[from Middle English *agone* = gone by]

agog *adjective*
eager and excited. [from French *en gogues* = in a happy mood, ready for fun]

agony *noun* (*plural* **agonies**)
extremely great pain or suffering.
agonizing *adjective*
[from Greek *agon* = a struggle]

agoraphobia (*say* ag-er-a-**foh**-bee-a) *noun*
abnormal fear of being in open spaces.
[from Greek *agora* = market place, + *phobia*]

agrarian (*say* a-**grair**-ee-an) *adjective*
to do with farm land or its cultivation.
[from Latin *ager* = field]

agree *verb* (**agrees, agreeing, agreed**)
1 think or say the same as another person etc. **2** consent, *She agreed to come.* **3** suit a person's health or digestion, *Curry doesn't agree with me.* **4** correspond in grammatical number, gender, or person. In 'They were good teachers', *they* agrees with *teachers* (both are plural forms) and *were* agrees with *they*; *was* would be incorrect because it is singular. [from old French]

agreeable *adjective*
1 willing, *We shall go if you are agreeable.* **2** pleasant, *an agreeable place.*
agreeably *adverb*

agreement *noun* (*plural* **agreements**)
1 agreeing. **2** an arrangement that people have agreed on.

agriculture *noun*
cultivating land on a large scale and rearing livestock; farming. **agricultural** *adjective* [from Latin *agri* = of a field, + *culture*]

aground *adverb* & *adjective*
stranded on the bottom in shallow water.
[from a-¹ + *ground*]

ah *interjection*
an exclamation of surprise, pity, admiration, etc.

ahead *adverb*
1 further forward; in front. **2** forwards, *Full steam ahead!* [from a-¹ + *head*]

ahoy *interjection*
an exclamation used by seamen to call attention.

aid *noun* (*plural* **aids**)
1 help. **2** something that helps, *a hearing aid.* **3** money, food, etc. sent to another country to help it, *overseas aid.*
in aid of for the purpose of; to help something.
aid *verb* (**aids, aiding, aided**)
help. [from old French]

aide *noun* (*plural* **aides**)
an assistant. [French]

aide-de-camp (*say* ay-der-**kahm**) *noun* (*plural* **aides-de-camp**)
a military officer who is the assistant to a senior officer. [French, = camp-helper]

Aids *noun*
a disease that greatly weakens a person's ability to resist infections.
[from the initial letters of 'acquired immune deficiency syndrome']

ail *verb* (**ails, ailing, ailed**) (*old use*)
be ill; make a person ill, *What ails you?*
[from Old English]

ailing *adjective*
1 ill; in poor health. **2** in difficulties; not successful, *the ailing ship industry.*

ailment *noun* (*plural* **ailments**)
a slight illness.

aim *verb* (**aims, aiming, aimed**)
1 point a gun etc. **2** throw or kick in a particular direction. **3** try or intend to do something.
aim *noun* (*plural* **aims**)
1 aiming a gun etc. **2** a purpose or intention. [via old French *amer* from Latin *aestimare* = estimate]

aimless *adjective*
without a purpose. **aimlessly** *adverb*

air *noun* (*plural* **airs**)
1 the mixture of gases that surrounds the earth and which everyone breathes. **2** the open space above the earth. **3** a tune or melody. **4** an appearance or impression of something, *an air of mystery*. **5** an impressive or haughty manner, *He puts on airs*.
by air in or by aircraft.
on the air on radio or television.

air *verb* (**airs, airing, aired**)
1 put clothes etc. in a warm place to finish drying. **2** ventilate a room. **3** express, *He aired his opinions*. [from old French]

airborne *adjective*
1 (of an aircraft) in flight. **2** carried by the air or by aircraft.

air-conditioning *noun*
a system for controlling the temperature, purity, etc. of the air in a room or building. **air-conditioned** *adjective*

aircraft *noun* (*plural* **aircraft**)
an aeroplane, glider, or helicopter etc.

aircraft carrier *noun* (*plural* **aircraft carriers**)
a large ship with a long deck where aircraft can take off and land.

airfield *noun* (*plural* **airfields**)
an area equipped with runways etc. where aircraft can take off and land.

air force (*plural* **air forces**)
the part of a country's armed forces that is equipped with aircraft.

airgun *noun* (*plural* **airguns**)
a gun in which compressed air shoots a pellet or dart.

airline *noun* (*plural* **airlines**)
a company that provides a regular service of transport by aircraft.

airliner *noun* (*plural* **airliners**)
a large aircraft for carrying passengers.

airlock *noun* (*plural* **airlocks**)
1 a compartment with an airtight door at each end, through which people can go in and out of a pressurized chamber. **2** a bubble of air that stops liquid flowing through a pipe.

airmail *noun*
mail carried by air.

airman *noun* (*plural* **airmen**)
a man who is a member of an air force or of the crew of an aircraft.

airport *noun* (*plural* **airports**)
an airfield for aircraft carrying passengers and goods.

air raid (*plural* **air raids**)
an attack by aircraft.

airship *noun* (*plural* **airships**)
a large balloon with engines, designed to carry passengers or goods.

airstrip *noun* (*plural* **airstrips**)
a strip of ground prepared for aircraft to land and take off.

airtight *adjective*
not letting air in or out.

airworthy *adjective*
(of an aircraft) fit to fly. **airworthiness** *noun*

airy *adjective*
1 with plenty of fresh air. **2** light as air. **3** light-hearted and insincere, *airy promises*. **airily** *adverb*

aisle (*say* I'll) *noun* (*plural* **aisles**)
1 a passage between or beside rows of seats or pews. **2** a side part of a church. [from old French]

ajar *adverb* & *adjective*
slightly open, *Leave the door ajar*. [literally = turned: from a-^{1} + Old English *cerr* = a turn]

akimbo *adverb*
arms akimbo with hands on hips and elbows out. [from Old Norse]

akin *adjective*
related or similar to, *a feeling akin to regret*. [from Old English a = of, + *kin*]

al- *prefix*
to; towards. see **ad-**.

alabaster (*say* al-a-bast-er) *noun*
a kind of hard stone, usually white. [from Greek]

à la carte *adjective* & *adverb*
ordered and paid for as separate items
from a menu. (Compare *table d'hôte*.)
[French, = from the menu]

alacrity *noun*
speed and willingness, *She accepted with
alacrity.* [from Latin]

alarm *noun* (*plural* **alarms**)
1 a warning sound or signal; a piece of
equipment for giving this. **2** a feeling of
fear or worry. **3** an alarm clock.
alarm *verb* (**alarms, alarming, alarmed**)
make someone frightened or anxious.
alarming *adjective* [from Italian *all' arme!*
= to arms!: compare this with *alert*]

alarm clock *noun* (*plural* **alarm clocks**)
a clock that can be set to make a sound at a
fixed time to wake a sleeping person.

alarmist *noun* (*plural* **alarmists**)
a person who raises unnecessary alarm.

alas *interjection*
an exclamation of sorrow.
[from Latin *lassus* = weary]

albatross *noun* (*plural* **albatrosses**)
a large seabird with very long wings.
[from Arabic]

albino (*say* al-**been**-oh) *noun* (*plural*
albinos)
a person or animal with no colour in the
skin and hair (which are white).
[from Latin *albus* = white]

album *noun* (*plural* **albums**)
1 a book with blank pages in which to keep
a collection of photographs, stamps,
autographs, etc. **2** a collection of songs on a
CD, record, or tape. [Latin, = white piece of
stone etc. on which to write things]

albumen (*say* al-**bew**-min) *noun*
white of egg. [from Latin *albus* = white]

alchemy (*say* al-kim-ee) *noun*
an early form of chemistry, the chief aim of
which was to turn ordinary metals into
gold. **alchemist** *noun* [from Arabic *al-kimiya*
= the art of changing metals]

alcohol *noun*
1 a colourless liquid made by fermenting
sugar or starch. **2** drinks containing this
liquid (e.g. wine, beer, whisky), that can
make people drunk. [from Arabic]

alcoholic *adjective*
containing alcohol.
alcoholic *noun* (*plural* **alcoholics**)
a person who is seriously addicted to
alcohol. **alcoholism** *noun*

alcove *noun* (*plural* **alcoves**)
a section of a room etc. that is set back
from the main part; a recess.
[from Arabic *al-kubba* = the arch]

alder *noun* (*plural* **alders**)
a kind of tree, often growing in marshy
places. [from Old English]

alderman (*say* **awl**-der-man) *noun* (*plural*
aldermen)
a senior member of an English county or
borough council. [from Old English *aldor*
= elder, chief, + *man*]

ale *noun* (*plural* **ales**)
beer. [from Old English]

alert *adjective*
watching for something; ready to act.
alertly *adverb*, **alertness** *noun*
alert *noun* (*plural* **alerts**)
a warning or alarm.
on the alert on the lookout; watchful.
alert *verb* (**alerts, alerting, alerted**)
warn someone of danger etc.; make
someone aware of something.
[from Italian *all' erta!* = to the watchtower!:
compare this with *alarm*]

A level *noun* (*plural* **A levels**)
advanced level in GCSE.

alfresco *adjective* & *adverb*
in the open air, *an alfresco meal.*
[from Italian *al fresco* = in the fresh air]

algae (*say* al-jee) *plural noun*
plants that grow in water, with no true
stems or leaves. [Latin, = seaweed]

algebra (*say* al-jib-ra) *noun*
mathematics in which letters and symbols
are used to represent quantities. **algebraic**
(*say* al-jib-**ray**-ik) *adjective* [from Arabic *al-
jabr* = putting together broken parts]

alias (*say* ay-lee-as) *noun* (*plural* **aliases**)
a false or different name.
alias *adverb*
also named, *Clark Kent, alias Superman.*
[Latin, = at another time, otherwise]

alibi (*say* al-ib-I) *noun* (*plural* **alibis**)
evidence that a person accused of a crime
was somewhere else when it was
committed. [Latin, = at another place]

USAGE: This word is sometimes used as if
it simply means 'an excuse'. Some people
dislike this use, so it is probably best to
avoid it.

alien (*say* ay-lee-en) *noun* (*plural* **aliens**)
1 a person who is not a citizen of the
country where he or she is living; a
foreigner. **2** a being from another world.
alien *adjective*
1 foreign. **2** unnatural, *Cruelty is alien to
her nature.* [from Latin *alius* = other]

alienate (*say* ay-lee-en-ayt) *verb* (**alienates,
alienating, alienated**)
make a person become unfriendly or
hostile. **alienation** *noun*

alight¹ *adjective*
1 on fire. **2** lit up. [from *a-¹* + *light¹*]

alight² *verb* (**alights, alighting, alighted**)
1 get out of a vehicle or down from a horse
etc. **2** fly down and settle, *The bird alighted
on a branch.* [from *a-¹* + *light²*]

align (*say* al-I'n) *verb* (**aligns, aligning,
aligned**)
1 arrange things in a line. **2** join as an ally,
They aligned themselves with the Germans.
alignment *noun*
[from French *à ligne* = into line]

alike *adjective* & *adverb*
like one another; in the same way, *The
twins are very alike. Treat them alike.*
[from Old English]

alimentary canal *noun* (*plural* **alimentary
canals**)
the tube along which food passes from the
mouth to the anus while it is being digested
and absorbed by the body.
[from Latin *alimentum* = food]

alimony *noun*
money paid by someone to his or her wife
or husband after they are separated or
divorced; maintenance.
[from Latin *alimonia* = nourishment]

alive *adjective*
1 living. **2** alert, *Be alive to the possible
dangers.* [from Old English *on life* = in life]

alkali (*say* alk-al-I) *noun* (*plural* **alkalis**)
a substance that neutralizes acids.
alkaline *adjective*
[from Arabic *al-kali* = the ashes (because
alkali was first obtained from the ashes of
seaweed)]

all *adjective*
the whole number or amount of, *All my
books are here; all day.*
all *noun*
1 everything, *That is all I know.*
2 everybody, *All are agreed.*
all *adverb*
1 completely, *She was dressed all in white.*
2 to each team or competitor, *The score is
fifteen all.*
all in (*informal*) exhausted, *I'm all in.*
all-in *adjective* including or allowing
everything, *an all-in price.*
all there (*informal*) having an alert mind.
all the same in spite of this; making no
difference, *I like him, all the same.*
[from Old English]

Allah *noun*
the Muslim name of God.

allay (*say* a-lay) *verb* (**allays, allaying, allayed**)
calm or relieve, *to allay their fears.*
[from Old English *alecgan* = lay down]

all-clear *noun*
a signal that a danger has passed.

allegation (*say* al-ig-ay-shon) *noun* (*plural*
allegations)
a statement made without proof.

allege (*say* a-lej) *verb* (**alleges, alleging,
alleged**)
say something without being able to prove
it, *He alleged that I had cheated.* **allegedly**
(*say* a-lej-id-lee) *adverb* [from old French]

allegiance (*say* a-lee-jans) *noun* (*plural*
allegiances)
loyalty. [from old French; related to *liege*]

allegory (*say* al-ig-er-ee) *noun* (*plural* **allegories**)
a story in which the characters and events represent or symbolize a deeper meaning, e.g. to teach a moral lesson. **allegorical** (*say* al-ig-o-rik-al) *adjective* [from Greek *allos* = other + -*agoria* = speaking]

alleluia *interjection*
praise to God. [from Hebrew]

allergic *adjective*
very sensitive to something that may make you ill, *He is allergic to pollen, which gives him hay fever.* **allergy** (*say* al-er-jee) *noun* [via German from Greek *allos* = other, different]

alleviate (*say* a-lee-vee-ayt) *verb* (**alleviates, alleviating, alleviated**)
make a thing less severe, *to alleviate pain.* **alleviation** *noun* [from Latin *alleviare* = lighten the weight of]

alley *noun* (*plural* **alleys**)
1 a narrow street or passage. 2 a place where you can play bowls or skittles. [from French *aller* = go]

alliance (*say* a-leye-ans) *noun* (*plural* **alliances**)
an association formed by countries or groups who wish to support each other. [same origin as *ally*]

allied *adjective*
1 joined as allies; on the same side. 2 of the same kind.

alligator *noun* (*plural* **alligators**)
a large reptile of the crocodile family. [from Spanish *el lagarto* = the lizard]

alliteration *noun*
having the same letter or sound at the beginning of several words, e.g. in *Sit in solemn silence.*
[from *al-* + Latin *littera* = letter]

allocate *verb* (**allocates, allocating, allocated**)
allot; set something aside for a particular purpose. **allocation** *noun*
[from *al-* + Latin *locus* = a place]

allot *verb* (**allots, allotting, allotted**)
give portions, jobs, etc. to different people. [from old French *aloter* = distribute by lot (sense 2)]

allotment *noun* (*plural* **allotments**)
1 a small rented piece of public land used for growing vegetables, fruit, or flowers. 2 allotting; the amount allotted.

allow *verb* (**allows, allowing, allowed**)
1 permit, *Smoking is not allowed.* 2 permit someone to have something; provide with, *She was allowed £10 for books.* 3 agree, *I allow that you have been patient.* **allowable** *adjective* [from old French]

allowance *noun* (*plural* **allowances**)
an amount of money that is given regularly for a particular purpose.
make allowances be considerate; excuse, *Make allowances for his age.*

alloy *noun* (*plural* **alloys**)
a metal formed by mixing two or more metals etc.
[from old French; related to *ally*]

all right *adjective* & *adverb*
1 satisfactory. 2 in good condition. 3 as desired. 4 yes, I consent.

all-round *adjective*
general; not specialist, *an all-round athlete.* **all-rounder** *noun*

allude *verb* (**alludes, alluding, alluded**)
mention something briefly or indirectly, *He alluded to his wealth.* **allusion** *noun* [from Latin]

USAGE: Do not confuse with *elude.*

allure *verb* (**allures, alluring, allured**)
attract or fascinate someone.
allure *noun*, **alluring** *adjective*
[from old French; related to *lure*]

alluvium (*say* a-loo-vee-um) *noun*
sand and soil etc. deposited by a river or flood. **alluvial** *adjective*
[from *al-* + Latin *luere* = to wash]

ally (*say* al-eye) *noun* (*plural* **allies**)
1 a country in alliance with another.
2 a person who cooperates with another.

ally *verb* (allies, allying, allied)
form an alliance.
[from *al-* + Latin *ligare* = bind]

almanac *noun* (*plural* almanacs)
an annual publication containing a
calendar and other information.
[from Greek]

almighty *adjective*
1 having complete power. 2 (*informal*)
very great, *an almighty din*.

almond (*say* ah-mond) *noun* (*plural*
almonds)
an oval edible nut. [from Greek]

almost *adverb*
near to being something but not quite,
almost ready. [from Old English]

alms (*say* ahmz) *plural noun* (*old use*)
money and gifts given to the poor.
[from Old English]

almshouse *noun* (*plural* almshouses)
a house founded by charity for poor people.

aloft *adverb*
high up; up in the air. [from Old Norse]

alone *adjective*
without any other people or things;
without help. [from *all one*]

along *preposition*
following the length of something, *Walk
along the path*.
along *adverb*
1 on or onwards, *Push it along*.
2 accompanying somebody, *I've brought
my brother along*. [from Old English]

alongside *preposition* & *adverb*
next to something; beside.

aloof *adverb*
apart; not taking part, *We stayed aloof from
their quarrels*.
aloof *adjective*
distant and not friendly in manner, *She
seemed aloof*. [from old French]

aloud *adverb*
in a voice that can be heard.
[from *a-*[1] + *loud*]

alpha *noun*
the first letter of the Greek alphabet, = a.

alphabet *noun* (*plural* alphabets)
the letters used in a language, usually
arranged in a set order. **alphabetical**
adjective, **alphabetically** *adverb*
[from *alpha, beta*, the first two letters of the
Greek alphabet]

alpine *adjective*
to do with high mountains, *alpine plants*.
[from the Alps, mountains in Switzerland]

already *adverb*
by now; before now. [from *all* + *ready*]

Alsatian (*say* al-say-shan) *noun* (*plural*
Alsatians)
a German shepherd dog.
[from *Alsace*, in north-eastern France: the
name was adopted during the First World
War, when British people disliked
anything that was German]

also *adverb*
in addition; besides.
[from Old English]

altar *noun* (*plural* altars)
a table or similar structure used in
religious ceremonies.
[via Old English from Latin *altus* = high]

USAGE: Do not confuse with the verb *alter*.

alter *verb* (alters, altering, altered)
make or become different; change.
alteration *noun*
[from Latin *alter* = other]

USAGE: Do not confuse with the noun
altar.

altercation (*say* ol-ter-kay-shon) *noun*
(*plural* altercations)
a noisy argument or quarrel. [from Latin]

alter ego *noun* (*plural* alter egos)
another, very different, side of someone's
personality, *Superman's alter ego, Clark
Kent*. [Latin, = other self]

alternate (*say* ol-tern-at) *adjective*
1 happening or coming one after the other,
alternate layers of sponge and cream.

2 one in every two, *We meet up on alternate Fridays.*
alternately *adverb*

USAGE: See the note at *alternative*.

alternate (*say* ol-tern-ayt) *verb* (**alternates, alternating, alternated**)
use or come alternately. **alternation** *noun*, **alternator** *noun* [from Latin *alternus* = every other one, from *alter* = other]

alternating current *noun* (*plural* **alternating currents**)
electric current that keeps reversing its direction at regular intervals.

alternative *adjective*
available instead of something else.
alternatively *adverb*

USAGE: Do not confuse *alternative* with *alternate*. If there are *alternative colours* it means that there is a choice of two or more colours, but *alternate colours* means that there is first one colour and then the other.

alternative *noun* (*plural* **alternatives**)
one of two or more possibilities.
no alternative no choice.

alternative medicine *noun*
types of medical treatment that are not based on ordinary medicine. Acupuncture, homeopathy, and osteopathy are all forms of alternative medicine.

although *conjunction*
though. [from *all* + *though*]

altimeter *noun* (*plural* **altimeters**)
an instrument used in aircraft etc. for showing the height above sea level. [from Latin *altus* = high, + *meter*]

altitude *noun* (*plural* **altitudes**)
the height of something, especially above sea level. [from Latin *altus* = high]

alto *noun* (*plural* **altos**)
1 an adult male singer with a very high voice. **2** a contralto. [Italian, = high]

altogether *adverb*
1 with all included; in total, *The outfit costs £20 altogether.* **2** completely, *The stream*

dries up altogether in summer. **3** on the whole, *Altogether, it was a good concert.* [from *all* + *together*]

USAGE: Do not confuse *altogether* and *all together*.

altruistic (*say* al-troo-ist-ik) *adjective*
unselfish; thinking of other people's welfare. **altruist** *noun*, **altruism** *noun* [from Italian *altrui* = somebody else]

aluminium *noun*
a lightweight silver-coloured metal. [from Latin]

always *adverb*
1 at all times. **2** often, *You are always crying.* **3** whatever happens, *You can always sleep on the floor.* [from Old English]

Alzheimer's disease *noun*
a serious disease of the brain which affects some old people and makes them confused and forgetful. [named after a German scientist, A. Alzheimer]

a.m. *abbreviation*
ante meridiem [Latin, = before noon]

amalgam *noun* (*plural* **amalgams**)
1 an alloy of mercury. **2** a mixture or combination. [from Latin]

amalgamate *verb* (**amalgamates, amalgamating, amalgamated**)
mix or combine. **amalgamation** *noun* [originally = make an amalgam]

amass *verb* (**amasses, amassing, amassed**)
heap up; collect. [from *ad-* + *mass*[1]]

amateur (*say* am-at-er) *noun* (*plural* **amateurs**)
a person who does something as a hobby, not as a professional. **amateurish** *adjective* [from Latin *amator* = lover]

amaze *verb* (**amazes, amazing, amazed**)
surprise somebody greatly; fill with wonder. **amazement** *noun* [from Old English]

amazing *adjective*
very surprising or remarkable.

ambassador *noun* (*plural* **ambassadors**)
a person sent to a foreign country to represent his or her own government. [from old French; related to *embassy*]

amber *noun*
1 a hard clear yellowish substance used for making ornaments. 2 a yellow traffic light shown as a signal for caution, placed between red (= stop) and green (= go). [from Arabic]

ambi- *prefix*
both; on both sides (as in *ambidextrous*). [from Latin *ambo* = both]

ambidextrous *adjective*
able to use either your left hand or your right hand equally well. [from *ambi-* + *dextrous* = skilful (related to *dexterity*)]

ambiguous *adjective*
having more than one possible meaning; unclear. **ambiguously** *adverb*, **ambiguity** *noun* [from Latin *ambiguus* = doubtful, shifting, from *ambi-* + *agere* = drive, go]

ambition *noun* (*plural* **ambitions**)
1 a strong desire to achieve something. 2 the thing desired. [from Latin *ambire* = go around, especially to persuade people to vote for you]

ambitious *adjective*
full of ambition.

ambivalent (*say* am-**biv**-al-ent) *adjective*
having mixed feelings about something (e.g. liking and disliking it). **ambivalence** *noun* [from *ambi-* + Latin *valens* = strong]

amble *verb* (**ambles, ambling, ambled**)
walk at a slow easy pace. [from Latin *ambulare* = walk]

ambrosia (*say* am-**broh**-zee-a) *noun*
something delicious. [in Greek mythology, ambrosia was the food of the gods]

ambulance *noun* (*plural* **ambulances**)
a vehicle equipped to carry sick or injured people. [from French *hôpital ambulant*, a mobile military hospital; from Latin *ambulare* = walk]

ambush *noun* (*plural* **ambushes**)
a surprise attack from troops etc. who have concealed themselves.

ambush *verb* (**ambushes, ambushing, ambushed**)
attack someone after lying in wait for them. [from old French]

ameliorate (*say* a-**mee**-lee-er-ayt) *verb* (**ameliorates, ameliorating, ameliorated**)
make or become better; improve. **amelioration** *noun* [from *ad-* + Latin *melior* = better]

amen *interjection*
a word used at the end of a prayer or hymn, meaning 'may it be so'. [Hebrew, = certainly]

amenable (*say* a-**meen**-a-bul) *adjective*
willing to be guided or controlled by something, *He is not amenable to discipline.* [from French *amener* = to lead]

amend *verb* (**amends, amending, amended**)
alter something in order to improve it. **make amends** make up for having done something wrong; atone. **amendment** *noun* [same origin as *emend*]

amenity (*say* a-**men**-it-ee or a-**meen**-it-ee) *noun* (*plural* **amenities**)
a pleasant or useful feature of a place, *The town has many amenities, such as a sports centre and a multiplex cinema.* [from Latin *amoenus* = pleasant]

American *adjective*
1 to do with the continent of America. 2 to do with the United States of America. **American** *noun*

amethyst *noun* (*plural* **amethysts**)
a purple precious stone. [from Greek *lithos amethystos* = stone against drunkenness (because people believed that they would not get drunk if there was an amethyst in their drink)]

amiable *adjective*
friendly and good-tempered. **amiably** *adverb* [same origin as *amicable*]

amicable *adjective*
friendly. **amicably** *adverb* [from Latin *amicus* = friend]

amid or **amidst** *preposition*
in the middle of; among. [from *a-1* + *mid*]

amino acid (*say* a-**meen**-oh) *noun* (*plural* amino acids)
an acid found in proteins. [from *ammonia*, because the amino acids contain the same group of atoms as ammonia]

amir (*say* a-**meer**) *noun* (*plural* amirs)
a different spelling of *emir*.

amiss *adjective*
wrong or faulty, *She knew something was amiss.*
amiss *adverb*
wrongly or faultily.
take amiss be offended by, *Don't take what I'm about to say amiss.*
[from Old Norse]

ammonia *noun*
a colourless gas or liquid with a strong smell. [from Latin]

ammunition *noun*
a supply of bullets, shells, grenades, etc. for use in fighting. [from French *la munition*, wrongly taken as *l'ammunition*]

amnesia (*say* am-**nee**-zee-a) *noun*
loss of memory. [from Greek *a-* = without, + *-mnesis* = memory]

amnesty *noun* (*plural* amnesties)
a general pardon for people who have committed a crime.
[from Greek *amnestia* = forgetfulness (because the crimes are legally 'forgotten')]

amoeba (*say* a-**mee**-ba) *noun* (*plural* amoebas)
a microscopic creature consisting of a single cell which constantly changes shape. [from Greek *amoibe* = change]

amok *adverb*
run amok rush about wildly in a violent rage.
[from Malay (a language spoken in Malaysia), = fighting mad]

among or **amongst** *preposition*
1 surrounded by; in, *There were weeds among the flowers.* 2 between, *Divide the sweets among the children.*
[from Old English *ongemang* = in a crowd]

amoral (*say* ay-**moral**) *adjective*
not based on moral standards; neither moral nor immoral. [from a-^{2} + *moral*]

amorous *adjective*
showing or feeling sexual love, *amorous glances.* [from Latin *amor* = love]

amorphous (*say* a-**mor**-fus) *adjective*
shapeless, *an amorphous mass.*
[from a-^{2} + Greek *morphe* = form]

amount *noun* (*plural* amounts)
1 a quantity. 2 a total.
amount *verb* (amounts, amounting, amounted)
amount to 1 add up to. 2 be equivalent to, *Their reply amounts to a refusal.*
[from Latin *ad montem* = to the mountain, upwards]

amp *noun* (*plural* amps)
1 an ampere. 2 (*informal*) an amplifier.

ampere (*say* am-**pair**) *noun* (*plural* amperes)
a unit for measuring electric current.
[named after the French scientist A. M. Ampère]

ampersand *noun* (*plural* ampersands)
the symbol & (= and). [from the phrase *and per se and* = '& by itself means and' (Latin *per se* = by itself). The symbol '&' was added to the end of the alphabet in children's school books, and when they came to it, pupils reciting the alphabet would say the phrase; they thought it was the name of the symbol]

amphetamine *noun* (*plural* amphetamines)
a drug used as a stimulant. [from the names of chemicals from which it is made]

amphi- *prefix*
both; on both sides; in both places (as in *amphibian*). [from Greek *amphi* = around]

amphibian *noun* (*plural* amphibians)
1 an amphibious animal; an animal (e.g. a frog) that at first (as a tadpole) has gills and lives in water but later develops lungs and breathes air. 2 an amphibious aircraft or tank etc. [from *amphi-* + Greek *bios* = life]

amphibious *adjective*
able to live or move both on land and in water.

amphitheatre *noun* (*plural* **amphitheatres**)
an oval or circular unroofed building with tiers of seats round a central arena. [from Greek *amphi* = all round, + *theatre*]

USAGE: This word does not mean 'an ancient theatre'. Greek and Roman theatres were semicircular.

ample *adjective*
1 quite enough, *ample provisions*. 2 large. **amply** *adverb*
[from Latin *amplus* = large, plentiful]

amplifier *noun* (*plural* **amplifiers**)
a piece of equipment for making a sound or electrical signal louder or stronger.

amplify *verb* (**amplifies, amplifying, amplified**)
1 make a sound or electrical signal louder or stronger. 2 give more details about something, *Could you amplify that point?* [from Latin *amplificare* = make larger]

amplitude *noun*
1 the strength of a sound wave or electronic signal. 2 largeness or abundance.
[same origin as *ample*]

amputate *verb* (**amputates, amputating, amputated**)
cut off an arm or leg by a surgical operation. **amputation** *noun* [from Latin *amb-* = around + *putare* cut off, prune]

amuse *verb* (**amuses, amusing, amused**)
1 make a person laugh or smile. 2 make time pass pleasantly for someone. **amusing** *adjective* [from French *amuser* = distract; related to *muse*]

amusement *noun* (*plural* **amusements**)
1 being amused. 2 a way of passing time pleasantly.

amusement arcade *noun* (*plural* **amusement arcades**)
an indoor area where people can play on automatic game machines.

amusement park *noun* (*plural* **amusement parks**)
a large outdoor area with fairground rides and other amusements.

an *adjective* see **a**.

an-[1] *prefix*
not; without. see **a-**[2].

an-[2] *prefix*
to; towards. see **ad-**.

ana- *prefix*
up; back (as in *analysis*).
[Greek, = up]

anachronism (*say* an-ak-ron-izm) *noun* (*plural* **anachronisms**)
something wrongly placed in a particular historical period, or regarded as out of date, *Bows and arrows would be an anachronism in modern warfare.*
[from *ana-* + Greek *chronos* = time]

anaemia (*say* a-nee-mee-a) *noun*
a poor condition of the blood that makes a person pale. **anaemic** *adjective*
[from *an-*[1] + Greek *haima* = blood]

anaesthetic (*say* an-iss-thet-ik) *noun* (*plural* **anaesthetics**)
a substance or gas that makes you unable to feel pain. **anaesthesia** *noun*
[from *an-*[1] + Greek *aisthesis* = sensation]

anaesthetist (*say* an-ees-thet-ist) *noun* (*plural* **anaesthetists**)
a person trained to give anaesthetics. **anaesthetize** *verb*

anagram *noun* (*plural* **anagrams**)
a word or phrase made by rearranging the letters of another, *'Trap' is an anagram of 'part'.*
[from *ana-* + Greek *gramma* = letter]

anal (*say* ay-nal) *adjective*
to do with the anus.

analgesic (*say* an-al-jee-sik) *noun* (*plural* **analgesics**)
a substance that relieves pain.
[from *an-*[1] + Greek *algesis* = pain]

analogy (*say* a-nal-oj-ee) *noun* (*plural* **analogies**)
comparing two things that are alike in some ways, *the analogy between the human heart and a pump*. **analogous** *adjective*
[from Greek]

analyse verb (analyses, analysing, analysed)
1 separate something into its parts.
2 examine and interpret something,
analyse the causes.

analysis noun (plural analyses)
1 a separation of something into its parts.
2 a detailed examination of something.
analytic adjective, **analytical** adjective
[from Greek, = dissolving, loosening]

analyst noun (plural analysts)
a person who analyses things.

anarchist (say an-er-kist) noun (plural
anarchists)
a person who believes that all forms of
government are bad and should be
abolished.

anarchy (say an-er-kee) noun
1 lack of government or control, resulting
in lawlessness. 2 complete disorder.
[from an-¹ + -archy]

anathema noun
something you detest, Bigotry of any kind is
anathema to me. [from Greek]

anatomy (say an-at-om-ee) noun
the study of the structure of the bodies of
humans or animals. **anatomical** adjective,
anatomist noun
[from ana- + Greek tome = cutting]

ancestor noun (plural ancestors)
anyone from whom a person is descended.
ancestral adjective, **ancestry** noun [from
Latin, literally = one who goes before]

anchor noun (plural anchors)
a heavy object joined to a ship by a chain
or rope and dropped to the bottom of the
sea to stop the ship from moving.
anchor verb (anchors, anchoring, anchored)
1 fix or be fixed by an anchor. 2 fix
something firmly. [from Latin]

anchorage noun (plural anchorages)
a place where a ship can be anchored.

anchovy noun (plural anchovies)
a small fish with a strong flavour. [from
Spanish or Portuguese]

ancient adjective
1 very old. 2 belonging to the distant past,
ancient history. [from old French]

ancillary (say an-sil-er-ee) adjective
helping or supporting the people who do
the main work, ancillary staff.
[from Latin ancilla = servant]

and conjunction
1 together with; in addition to, We had
cakes and buns. 2 so that; with this result,
Work hard and you will pass. 3 to, Go and
buy a pen. [from Old English]

anecdote noun (plural anecdotes)
a short amusing or interesting story about
a real person or thing.
[from Greek anekdota = things that have
not been published]

anemone (say a-nem-on-ee) noun (plural
anemones)
a plant with cup-shaped red, purple, or
white flowers.
[from Greek, = windflower (from the belief
that the flower opens when it is windy)]

anew adverb
again; in a new or different way, begin
anew. [from Old English of = from, + new]

angel noun (plural angels)
1 an attendant or messenger of God. 2 a
very kind or beautiful person. **angelic** (say
an-jel-ik) adjective
[from Greek angelos = messenger]

angelica noun
a sweet-smelling plant whose crystallized
stalks are used in cookery as a decoration.
[from Latin herba angelica = angelic plant
(because it was believed to cure plague)]

anger noun
a strong feeling that makes you want to
quarrel or fight.
anger verb (angers, angering, angered)
make a person angry. [from Old Norse]

angle noun (plural angles)
1 the space between two lines or surfaces
that meet; the amount by which a line or
surface must be turned to make it lie along
another. 2 a point of view.
angle verb (angles, angling, angled)
1 put something in a slanting position.
2 present news etc. from one point of view.
[from Latin angulus = corner]

angler *noun* (*plural* **anglers**)
a person who fishes with a fishing rod and line. **angling** *noun*
[from Old English *angul* = fishing-hook]

Anglican *adjective*
to do with the Church of England.
Anglican *noun*

Anglo- *prefix*
English or British, *an Anglo-French agreement.*
[from the *Angles*, a Germanic tribe who came to England in the 5th century and eventually gave their name to it]

Anglo-Saxon *noun* (*plural* **Anglo-Saxons**)
1 an English person, especially of the time before the Norman conquest in 1066. **2** 'Old English'. [from Old English *Angulseaxe* = an English Saxon (contrasted with the Old Saxons on the Continent)]

angry *adjective* (**angrier, angriest**)
feeling anger. **angrily** *adverb*

anguish *noun*
severe suffering or misery. **anguished** *adjective* [same origin as *anxious*]

angular *adjective*
1 having angles or sharp corners. **2** (of a person) bony, not plump.

animal *noun* (*plural* **animals**)
1 a living thing that can feel and usually move about, *Horses, birds, fish, bees, and people are all animals.* **2** a brutish person; someone not worthy of being called human.
[from Latin *animalis* = having breath]

animate *verb* (**animates, animating, animated**)
1 make a thing lively. **2** produce something as an animated cartoon.
animation *noun*, **animator** *noun*

animated cartoon *noun* (*plural* **animated cartoons**)
a film made by photographing a series of drawings.

animosity (*say* an-im-oss-it-ee) *noun*
(*plural* **animosities**)
a feeling of hostility. [originally = courage: from Latin *animus* = spirit]

aniseed *noun*
a sweet-smelling seed used for flavouring things. [from Greek *anison* + *seed*]

ankle *noun* (*plural* **ankles**)
the part of the leg where it joins the foot.
[from Old English; distantly related to *angle*]

annals *plural noun*
a history of events, especially when written year by year.
[from Latin *annales* = yearly books]

annex *verb* (**annexes, annexing, annexed**)
1 take possession of something and add it to what you have already. **2** add or join a thing to something else.
[from *an-²* + Latin *nexum* = tied]

annexe *noun* (*plural* **annexes**)
a building added to a larger or more important building. [same origin as *annex*]

annihilate (*say* an-I-il-ayt) *verb* (**annihilates, annihilating, annihilated**)
destroy something completely. **annihilation** *noun* [from *an-²* + Latin *nihil* = nothing]

anniversary *noun* (*plural* **anniversaries**)
a day when you remember something special that happened on the same day in a previous year. [from Latin *annus* = year + *versum* = turned]

annotate (*say* an-oh-tayt) *verb* (**annotates, annotating, annotated**)
add notes of explanation to something written or printed. **annotation** *noun*
[from *an-²* + Latin *notare* = to note]

announce *verb* (**announces, announcing, announced**)
make something known, especially by saying it publicly or to an audience.
announcement *noun*
[from *an-²* + Latin *nuntius* = messenger]

announcer *noun* (*plural* **announcers**)
a person who announces items in a broadcast.

annoy *verb* (**annoys, annoying, annoyed**)
1 make a person slightly angry. **2** be troublesome to someone. **annoyance** *noun*
[from Latin *in odio* = hateful]

annual *adjective*
1 happening or done once a year, *her annual visit*. **2** calculated over one year, *our annual income*. **3** living for one year or one season, *an annual plant*.
annually *adverb*

annual *noun* (*plural* **annuals**)
1 a book that comes out once a year. **2** an annual plant. [from Latin *annus* = year]

annuity (*say* a-**new**-it-ee) *noun* (*plural* **annuities**)
a fixed annual allowance of money, especially from a kind of investment. [same origin as *annual*]

annul *verb* (**annuls, annulling, annulled**)
cancel a law or contract; end something legally, *Their marriage was annulled*.
annulment *noun*
[from *an-*² + Latin *nullus* = none]

anode *noun* (*plural* **anodes**)
the electrode by which electric current enters a device. (Compare *cathode*.)
[from *ana-* = up + Greek *hodos* = way]

anoint *verb* (**anoints, anointing, anointed**)
put oil or ointment on something, especially in a religious ceremony. [from Latin]

anomaly (*say* an-**om**-al-ee) *noun* (*plural* **anomalies**)
something that does not follow the general rule or that is unlike the usual or normal kind.
[from *an-*¹ = not + Greek *homalos* = even]

anon *adverb* (*old use*)
soon, *I will say more about this anon*.
[from Old English *on ane* = in one, at once]

anon. *abbreviation*
anonymous.

anonymous (*say* an-**on**-im-us) *adjective*
without the name of the person responsible being known or made public, *an anonymous donor*. **anonymously** *adverb*, **anonymity** (*say* an-on-**im**-it-ee) *noun*
[from *an-*¹ + Greek *onyma* = name]

anorak *noun* (*plural* **anoraks**)
a thick warm jacket with a hood. [from an Eskimo word]

anorexia (*say* an-er-**eks**-ee-a) *noun*
an illness that makes a person so anxious to lose weight that he or she refuses to eat.
anorexic *adjective*
[from *an-*¹ + Greek *orexis* = appetite]

another *adjective* & *pronoun*
a different or extra person or thing, *another day*; *choose another*.

answer *noun* (*plural* **answers**)
1 a reply. **2** the solution to a problem.

answer *verb* (**answers, answering, answered**)
1 give or find an answer to; reply.
2 respond to a signal, *Answer the telephone*.
answer back reply cheekily.
answer for be responsible for.
answer to correspond to, *This answers to the description of the stolen bag*.
[from Old English]

answerable *adjective*
1 able to be answered. **2** having to be responsible for something.

answering machine *noun* (*plural* **answering machines**)
a machine that records messages from people who telephone while you are out.

answerphone *noun* (*plural* **answerphones**)
a telephone answering machine.

ant *noun* (*plural* **ants**)
a very small insect that lives as one of an organized group. [from Old English]

ant- *prefix*
against; preventing. see **anti-**.

antagonism (*say* an-**tag**-on-izm) *noun*
an unfriendly feeling; hostility. **antagonist** *noun*, **antagonistic** *adjective*
[from *ant-* + Greek *agon* = struggle]

antagonize *verb* (**antagonizes, antagonizing, antagonized**)
make a person feel hostile or angry.

ante- *prefix*
before (as in *ante-room*). [from Latin]

anteater *noun* (*plural* **anteaters**)
an animal that feeds on ants and termites.

antediluvian (*say* an-tee-dil-**oo**-vee-an)
adjective
1 belonging to the time before Noah's Flood in the Old Testament. **2** (*informal*) very old or out of date.
[from *ante-* + Latin *diluvium* = deluge]

antelope *noun* (*plural* **antelope** or **antelopes**)
an animal like a deer. [from Greek]

antenatal (*say* an-tee-**nay**-tal) *adjective*
before birth; during pregnancy.

antenna *noun*
1 (*plural* **antennae**) a feeler on the head of an insect or crustacean. **2** (*plural* **antennas**) an aerial. [Latin]

anterior *adjective*
1 at or near the front. (The opposite is *posterior*.) **2** earlier.
[Latin, = further forward]

ante-room *noun* (*plural* **ante-rooms**)
a room leading to a more important room.

anthem *noun* (*plural* **anthems**)
a religious or patriotic song, usually sung by a choir or group of people. [from Latin]

anther *noun* (*plural* **anthers**)
the part of a flower's stamen that contains pollen. [from Greek *anthos* = flower]

anthill *noun* (*plural* **anthills**)
a mound over an ants' nest.

anthology *noun* (*plural* **anthologies**)
a collection of poems, stories, songs, etc. in one book. [from Greek *anthos* = flower + *-logia* = collection]

anthracite *noun*
a kind of hard coal.
[from Greek *anthrax* = coal, carbuncle]

anthrax *noun*
a disease of sheep and cattle that can also infect people.
[same origin as *anthracite* (because of the carbuncles that the disease causes)]

anthropoid *adjective*
like a human being, *Gorillas are anthropoid apes.*
[from Greek *anthropos* = human being]

anthropology *noun*
the study of human beings and their customs. **anthropological** *adjective*, **anthropologist** *noun* [from Greek *anthropos* = human being, + *-logy*]

anti- *prefix* (changing to **ant-** before a vowel)
against; preventing (as in *antifreeze*).
[from Greek *anti* = against]

anti-aircraft *adjective*
used against enemy aircraft.

antibiotic *noun* (*plural* **antibiotics**)
a substance (e.g. penicillin) that destroys bacteria or prevents them from growing.
[from *anti-* + Greek *bios* = life]

antibody *noun* (*plural* **antibodies**)
a protein that forms in the blood as a defence against certain substances which it then attacks and destroys.
[from *anti-* + *body* (sense 5)]

anticipate *verb* (**anticipates, anticipating, anticipated**)
1 do something before the proper time or before someone else, *Others may have anticipated Columbus in discovering America.* **2** foresee, *They had anticipated our needs.* **3** expect, *We anticipate that it will rain.* **anticipation** *noun*, **anticipatory** *adjective* [from *ante-* + Latin *capere* = take]

USAGE: Many people regard use **3** as incorrect; it is better to avoid it and use 'expect'.

anticlimax *noun* (*plural* **anticlimaxes**)
a disappointing ending or result where something exciting had been expected.

anticlockwise *adverb* & *adjective*
moving in the direction opposite to clockwise.

antics *plural noun*
funny or foolish actions.
[from *antic* = strange, grotesque, from Italian *antico* = ancient, antique]

anticyclone *noun* (*plural* **anticyclones**)
an area where air pressure is high, usually producing fine settled weather.
[from *anti-* + *cyclone*, because the pressure at the centre of a cyclone is low]

antidote *noun* (*plural* **antidotes**)
something that acts against the effects of a
poison or disease.
[from *anti-* + Greek *dotos* = given]

antifreeze *noun*
a liquid added to water to make it less
likely to freeze.

antihistamine *noun* (*plural*
antihistamines)
a drug that protects people against
unpleasant effects when they are allergic to
something. [from *anti-* + *histamine*, a
substance in the body which is released
when someone meets whatever they are
allergic to, and which causes the
unpleasant effects]

antimony *noun*
a brittle silvery metal. [from Latin]

antipathy (*say* an-**tip**-ath-ee) *noun*
a strong dislike.
[from *anti-* + Greek *pathos* = feeling]

antipodes (*say* an-**tip**-od-eez) *plural noun*
places on opposite sides of the earth.
the Antipodes Australia, New Zealand, and
the areas near them, which are almost
exactly opposite Europe. **antipodean**
adjective [from Greek, = having the feet
opposite (*podes* = feet)]

antiquarian (*say* anti-**kwair**-ee-an) *adjective*
to do with the study of antiques.

antiquated *adjective*
old-fashioned.

antique (*say* an-**teek**) *adjective*
very old; belonging to the distant past.
antique *noun* (*plural* **antiques**)
something that is valuable because it is
very old. [from Latin *antiquus* = ancient,
from *ante* = before]

antiquities *plural noun*
objects that were made in ancient times.

antiquity (*say* an-**tik**-wit-ee) *noun*
ancient times.

anti-Semitic (*say* anti-sim-**it**-ik) *adjective*
unfriendly or hostile towards Jews.
anti-Semitism (*say* anti-**sem**-it-izm) *noun*

antiseptic *adjective*
1 able to destroy bacteria, especially those
that cause things to become septic or to
decay. **2** thoroughly clean and free from
germs.
antiseptic *noun* (*plural* **antiseptics**)
a substance with an antiseptic effect.

antisocial *adjective*
unfriendly or inconsiderate towards other
people.

antistatic *adjective*
counteracting the effects of static
electricity.

antithesis (*say* an-**tith**-iss-iss) *noun* (*plural*
antitheses)
1 the exact opposite of something, *Slavery
is the antithesis of freedom.* **2** a contrast of
ideas. [from *anti-* + Greek *thesis* = placing]

antitoxin *noun* (*plural* **antitoxins**)
a substance that neutralizes a toxin and
prevents it from having a harmful effect.
antitoxic *adjective*

antivivisectionist *noun* (*plural*
antivivisectionists)
a person who is opposed to making
experiments on live animals.

antler *noun* (*plural* **antlers**)
the branching horn of a deer.
[from old French]

antonym (*say* **ant**-on-im) *noun* (*plural*
antonyms)
a word that is opposite in meaning to
another, *'Soft' is an antonym of 'hard'.*
[from *ant-* + Greek *onyma* = name]

anus (*say* **ay**-nus) *noun* (*plural* **anuses**)
the opening at the lower end of the
alimentary canal, through which solid
waste matter is passed out of the body.
[Latin]

anvil *noun* (*plural* **anvils**)
a large block of iron on which a blacksmith
hammers metal into shape.
[from Old English *an* = on + *filt-* = beat]

anxious *adjective*
1 worried. **2** eager, *She is anxious to please
us.* **anxiously** *adverb*, **anxiety** *noun* [from
Latin *angere* = choke, squeeze, oppress]

any *adjective & pronoun*
1 one or some, *Have you any wool? There isn't any.* 2 no matter which, *Come any day you like.* 3 every, *Any fool knows that!*
any *adverb*
at all; in some degree, *Is that any better?* [from Old English]

anybody *noun & pronoun*
any person.

anyhow *adverb*
1 anyway. 2 (*informal*) carelessly, *He does his work anyhow.*

anyone *noun & pronoun*
anybody.

anything *noun & pronoun*
any thing.

anyway *adverb*
whatever happens; whatever the situation may be.

anywhere *adverb*
in or to any place.
anywhere *pronoun*
any place, *Anywhere will do.*

aorta (*say* ay-or-ta) *noun* (*plural* aortas)
the main artery that carries blood away from the left side of the heart. [from Greek]

ap-¹ *prefix*
to; towards. see **ad-**.

ap-² *prefix*
from; out or away. see **apo-**.

apace *adverb*
quickly. [from French *à pas* = step by step]

apart *adverb*
1 away from each other; separately, *Keep your desks apart.* 2 into pieces, *It fell apart.* 3 excluded, *Joking apart, what do you think of it?* [from French *à* = to + *part* = side]

apartheid (*say* a-part-hayt) *noun*
the political policy that used to be practised in South Africa, of keeping people of different races apart.
[Afrikaans, = being apart]

apartment *noun* (*plural* apartments)
1 a set of rooms. 2 (*American*) a flat.
[from Italian *appartare* = to separate]

apathy (*say* ap-ath-ee) *noun*
lack of interest or concern. **apathetic** (*say* ap-a-thet-ik) *adjective*
[from *a-²* + Greek *pathos* = feeling]

ape *noun* (*plural* apes)
any of the four kinds of monkey (gorillas, chimpanzees, orang-utans, gibbons) that do not have a tail.
ape *verb* (apes, aping, aped)
imitate or mimic. [from Old English]

aperient (*say* a-peer-ee-ent) *noun*
a laxative. [from Latin *aperiens* = opening]

aperitif (*say* a-perri-teef) *noun* (*plural* aperitifs)
an alcoholic drink taken before a meal to stimulate the appetite. [French]

aperture *noun* (*plural* apertures)
an opening. [from Latin *aperire* = to open]

apex (*say* ay-peks) *noun* (*plural* apexes)
the tip or highest point. [Latin]

aphid (*say* ay-fid) *noun* (*plural* aphids)
a tiny insect (e.g. a greenfly) that sucks the juices from plants. [from *aphis*]

aphis (*say* ay-fiss) *noun* (*plural* aphides (*say* ay-fid-eez))
an aphid. [Latin]

aphorism (*say* af-er-izm) *noun* (*plural* aphorisms)
a short witty saying.
[from Greek *aphorizein* = define, limit]

apiary (*say* ay-pee-er-ee) *noun* (*plural* apiaries)
a place with a number of hives where bees are kept. **apiarist** *noun*
[from Latin *apis* = bee]

apiece *adverb*
to, for, or by each, *They cost five pence apiece.* [from *a piece*]

aplomb (*say* a-plom) *noun*
dignity and confidence, *She handled the press conference with aplomb.*
[from French = straight as a plumb line]

apo- *prefix* (changing to **ap-** before a vowel or h)
from; out or away (as in *Apostle*).
[from Greek *apo* = away from]

apocryphal (*say* a-**pok**-rif-al) *adjective*
not likely to be true; invented, *This account of his travels is apocryphal.*
[from the *Apocrypha*, books of the Old Testament that were not accepted by the Jews as part of the Hebrew Scriptures]

apologetic *adjective*
making an apology. **apologetically** *adverb*

apologize *verb* (apologizes, apologizing, apologized)
make an apology.

apology *noun* (*plural* apologies)
1 a statement saying that you are sorry for having done something wrong or badly. 2 something very poor, *this feeble apology for a meal.* [from Greek *apologia* = a speech in your own defence]

apoplexy (*say* ap-op-lek-see) *noun*
1 sudden loss of the ability to feel and move, caused by the blocking or breaking of a blood vessel in the brain. 2 (*informal*) rage or anger. **apoplectic** *adjective*
[from Greek, = a stroke]

Apostle *noun* (*plural* Apostles)
any of the twelve men sent out by Christ to preach the Gospel.
[from Greek *apostellein* = send out]

apostrophe (*say* a-**poss**-trof-ee) *noun*
(*plural* apostrophes)
the punctuation mark ' used to show that letters have been missed out (as in *I can't* = I cannot) or to show possession (as in *the boy's book*; *the boys' books*).
[from *apo-* + Greek *strophe* = turning]

apothecary (*say* a-**poth**-ik-er-ee) *noun*
(*plural* apothecaries) (*old use*)
a chemist who prepares medicines.
[from Latin *apothecarius* = storekeeper]

appal *verb* (appals, appalling, appalled)
fill a person with horror; shock somebody very much.
[from Old French *apalir* = become pale]

appalling *adjective*
shocking; very unpleasant.

apparatus *noun*
the equipment for a particular experiment or job etc.
[from Latin *apparare* = prepare, get ready]

apparel *noun*
(*formal*) clothing. [from old French]

apparent *adjective*
1 clear or obvious, *His embarrassment was apparent to everyone.* 2 seeming; appearing to be true but not really so, *I could not understand her apparent indifference.*
apparently *adverb* [same origin as *appear*]

apparition *noun* (*plural* apparitions)
1 a ghost. 2 something strange or surprising that appears.
[same origin as *appear*]

appeal *verb* (appeals, appealing, appealed)
1 ask for something earnestly or formally, *They appealed for funds.* 2 ask for a decision to be changed, *He appealed against the prison sentence.* 3 seem attractive or interesting, *Cricket doesn't appeal to me.*

appeal *noun* (*plural* appeals)
1 the action of appealing for something or about a decision; an earnest or formal request. 2 attraction or interest.
[from old French]

appear *verb* (appears, appearing, appeared)
1 come into sight. 2 seem. 3 take part in a play, film, or show etc.
[from *ap-*[1] + Latin *parere* = come into]

appearance *noun* (*plural* appearances)
1 appearing. 2 what somebody looks like; what something appears to be.

appease *verb* (appeases, appeasing, appeased)
calm or pacify someone, especially by giving in to demands. **appeasement** *noun*
[from French *à* = to + *paix* = peace]

appellation *noun* (*plural* appellations)
a name or title. [from old French]

append *verb* (appends, appending, appended)
add at the end; attach.
[from *ap-*[1] + Latin *pendere* = hang]

appendage *noun* (*plural* appendages)
something added or attached; a thing that forms a natural part of something larger.

appendicitis *noun*
inflammation of the appendix.

appendix *noun*
1 (*plural* appendixes) a small tube leading off from the intestine. 2 (*plural* appendices) a section added at the end of a book. [same origin as *append*]

appetite *noun* (*plural* appetites)
1 desire for food. 2 an enthusiasm for something, *an appetite for violent films.* [from *ap-*¹ + Latin *petere* = seek]

appetizer *noun* (*plural* appetizers)
a small amount of food eaten before the main meal.

appetizing *adjective*
(of food) looking and smelling good to eat.

applaud *verb* (applauds, applauding, applauded)
show that you like something, especially by clapping your hands. [from *ap-*¹ + Latin *plaudere* = clap hands]

applause *noun*
clapping.

apple *noun* (*plural* apples)
a round fruit with a red, yellow, or green skin.
the apple of your eye a person or thing that you love and are proud of. [from Old English]

appliance *noun* (*plural* appliances)
a device or piece of equipment, *electrical appliances.* [from *apply*]

applicable (*say* ap-lik-a-bul) *adjective*
able to be applied; suitable or relevant.

applicant *noun* (*plural* applicants)
a person who applies for a job or position.

application *noun* (*plural* applications)
1 the action of applying. 2 a formal request. 3 the ability to apply yourself.

applied *adjective*
put to practical use, *applied maths.*

appliqué (*say* a-plee-kay) *noun*
needlework in which cut-out pieces of material are sewn or fixed decoratively on another piece. [French, = put on]

apply *verb* (applies, applying, applied)
1 put one thing on another. 2 start using something. 3 concern; be relevant, *This rule does not apply to you.* 4 make a formal request, *apply for a job.*
apply yourself give all your attention to a job; work diligently.
[from *ap-*¹ + Latin *plicare* = to fold]

appoint *verb* (appoints, appointing, appointed)
1 choose a person for a job. 2 arrange something officially, *They appointed a time for the meeting.* [from old French]

appointment *noun* (*plural* appointments)
1 an arrangement to meet or visit somebody at a particular time. 2 choosing somebody for a job. 3 a job or position.

apportion *verb* (apportions, apportioning, apportioned)
divide something into shares; allot. [from old French]

apposite (*say* ap-o-zit) *adjective*
(of a remark) suitable or relevant. [from Latin *appositus* = applied]

apposition *noun*
placing things together, especially nouns and phrases in a grammatical relationship. In *the reign of Elizabeth, our Queen,* 'our Queen' is in apposition to 'Elizabeth'. [from Latin]

appraise *verb* (appraises, appraising, appraised)
estimate the value or quality of a person or thing. **appraisal** *noun*
[from old French; related to *price*]

appreciable *adjective*
enough to be noticed or felt; perceptible. **appreciably** *adverb*

appreciate *verb* (appreciates, appreciating, appreciated)
1 enjoy or value something. 2 understand. 3 increase in value. **appreciation** *noun,* **appreciative** *adjective*
[from *ap-*¹ + Latin *pretium* = price]

apprehend *verb* (apprehends, apprehending, apprehended)
1 seize or arrest someone. 2 understand. 3 expect something with fear or worry. [from *ap-*¹ + Latin *prehendere* = to grasp]

apprehension *noun*
1 fear or worry. 2 understanding. 3 the arrest of a person.

apprehensive *adjective*
anxious or worried.

apprentice *noun* (*plural* **apprentices**)
a person who is learning a trade or craft by a legal agreement with an employer.
apprenticeship *noun*
apprentice *verb* (**apprentices, apprenticing, apprenticed**)
place a person as an apprentice.
[from French *apprendre* = learn]

approach *verb* (**approaches, approaching, approached**)
1 come near. 2 go to someone with a request or offer, *They approached me for help.* 3 set about doing something or tackling a problem.
approach *noun* (*plural* **approaches**)
1 approaching. 2 a way or road.
[from old French]

approachable *adjective*
friendly and easy to talk to.

approbation *noun*
approval. [same origin as *approve*]

appropriate (*say* a-proh-pree-at) *adjective*
suitable. **appropriately** *adverb*
appropriate (*say* a-proh-pree-ayt) *verb*
(**appropriates, appropriating, appropriated**)
take something and use it as your own.
appropriation *noun*
[from Latin]

approval *noun*
approving somebody or something.
on approval received by a customer to examine before deciding to buy.

approve *verb* (**approves, approving, approved**)
say or think that a person or thing is good or suitable.
[from *ap-*[1] + Latin *probus* = good]

approximate (*say* a-proks-im-at) *adjective*
almost exact or correct but not completely so. **approximately** *adverb*

approximate (*say* a-proks-im-ayt) *verb*
(**approximates, approximating, approximated**)
make or be almost the same as something.
[from *ap-*[1] + Latin *proximus* = very near]

apricot *noun* (*plural* **apricots**)
a juicy orange-coloured fruit with a stone in it. [from Spanish or Portuguese]

apron *noun* (*plural* **aprons**)
1 a piece of clothing worn over the front of the body, especially to protect other clothes. 2 a hard-surfaced area on an airfield where aircraft are loaded and unloaded. [originally *a naperon*, from French *nappe* = tablecloth]

apron stage *noun* (*plural* **apron stages**)
a part of a theatre stage in front of the curtain.

apropos (*say* ap-rop-oh) *adverb*
concerning, *Apropos of money, where's that £10 you owe me?*
[from French *à propos* = to the purpose]

apse *noun* (*plural* **apses**)
a domed semicircular part at the east end of a church.
[from Greek *apsis* = arch, vault, wheel]

apt *adjective*
1 likely, *He is apt to be careless.* 2 suitable, *an apt quotation.* **aptly** *adverb*, **aptness** *noun*
[from Latin *aptus* = fitted]

aptitude *noun*
a talent or skill, *an aptitude for languages.*

aqualung *noun* (*plural* **aqualungs**)
a diver's portable breathing-apparatus, with cylinders of compressed air connected to a face mask.
[from Latin *aqua* = water, + *lung*]

aquamarine *noun* (*plural* **aquamarines**)
a bluish-green precious stone.
[from Latin *aqua marina* = sea water]

aquarium *noun* (*plural* **aquariums**)
a tank or building in which live fish and other water animals are displayed.
[from Latin *aquarius* = of water]

aquatic *adjective*
to do with water, *aquatic sports.*
[from Latin *aqua* = water]

aquatint *noun* (*plural* aquatints)
an etching made on copper by using nitric acid. [from Italian]

aqueduct *noun* (*plural* aqueducts)
a bridge carrying a water-channel across low ground or a valley. [from Latin *aqua* = water + *ducere* = to lead]

aquiline (*say* ak-wil-I'n) *adjective*
hooked like an eagle's beak, *an aquiline nose*. [from Latin *aquila* = eagle]

ar- *prefix*
to; towards. see **ad-**.

Arab *noun* (*plural* Arabs)
a member of a people living in Arabia and other parts of the Middle East and North Africa. **Arabian** *adjective*

arabesque (*say* a-rab-esk) *noun* (*plural* arabesques)
1 (in dancing) a position with one leg stretched backwards in the air. **2** an ornamental design of leaves and branches. [French, = Arabian (because the leaf and branch designs were first used in Arabic art)]

Arabic *adjective*
to do with the Arabs or their language.
Arabic *noun*
the language of the Arabs.

arabic numerals *plural noun*
the symbols 1, 2, 3, 4, etc. (Compare *Roman numerals*.)

arable *adjective*
suitable for ploughing or growing crops on, *arable land*. [from Latin *arare* = to plough]

arachnid (*say* a-rak-nid) *noun* (*plural* arachnids)
a member of the group of animals that includes spiders and scorpions. [from Greek *arachne* = spider]

arbiter *noun* (*plural* arbiters)
a person who has the power to decide what shall be done or used etc. [Latin, = judge, supreme ruler]

arbitrary (*say* ar-bit-rer-ee) *adjective*
chosen or done on an impulse, not according to a rule or law, *an arbitrary decision*. **arbitrarily** *adverb* [originally = according to an arbiter's decision, not according to rules]

arbitration *noun*
settling a dispute by calling in someone from outside to make a decision. **arbitrate** *verb*, **arbitrator** *noun*
[from Latin *arbitrari* = to judge]

arboreal (*say* ar-bor-ee-al) *adjective*
to do with trees; living in trees.
[from Latin *arbor* = tree]

arboretum (*say* ar-ber-ee-tum) *noun* (*plural* arboretums or arboreta)
a place where trees are grown for study and display. [from Latin *arbor* = tree]

arbour (*say* ar-ber) *noun* (*plural* arbours)
a shady place among trees.
[from Latin *arbor* = tree]

arc *noun* (*plural* arcs)
1 a curve; part of the circumference of a circle. **2** a luminous electric current passing between two electrodes.
[from Latin *arcus* = a bow or curve]

arcade *noun* (*plural* arcades)
a covered passage or area, especially for shopping. [French or Italian, from Latin *arcus* = curve (because early arcades had curved roofs)]

arcane *adjective*
secret or mysterious. [from Latin *arcere* = to shut up, from *arca* = box]

arch[1] *noun* (*plural* arches)
1 a curved structure that helps to support a bridge or other building etc. **2** something shaped like this.
arch *verb* (arches, arching, arched)
form something into an arch; curve, *The cat arched its back and hissed.*
[same origin as *arc*]

arch[2] *adjective*
pretending to be playful; mischievous, *an arch smile*. **archly** *adverb*
[from Greek *archos* = a chief]

arch- *prefix*
chief or principal (as in *arch-enemy*).

-arch and **-archy** *suffixes*
form nouns meaning 'ruler' or 'rule,
ruling' (e.g. *monarch, monarchy*).
[from Greek *archein* = to rule]

archaeology (*say* ar-kee-ol-oj-ee) *noun*
the study of the remains of ancient
civilizations. **archaeological** *adjective*,
archaeologist *noun*
[from Greek *archaios* = old, + *-logy*]

archaic (*say* ar-**kay**-ik) *adjective*
belonging to former or ancient times.
[from Greek *arche* = beginning]

archangel *noun* (*plural* **archangels**)
an angel of the highest rank.

archbishop *noun* (*plural* **archbishops**)
the chief bishop of a province of the
Church.

archdeacon *noun* (*plural* **archdeacons**)
a senior priest ranking next below a
bishop.

arch-enemy *noun* (*plural* **arch-enemies**)
the chief enemy.

archer *noun* (*plural* **archers**)
a person who shoots with a bow and
arrows.
[from Latin *arcus* = a bow or curve]

archery *noun*
the sport of shooting at a target with a
bow and arrows.

archetype (*say* **ark**-i-typ) *noun* (*plural*
archetypes)
the original form or model from which
others are copied. [from *arch-* + *type*]

archipelago (*say* ark-i-**pel**-ag-oh) *noun*
(*plural* **archipelagos**)
a large group of islands, or the sea
containing these.
[from *arch-* + Greek *pelagos* = sea]

architect (*say* **ark**-i-tekt) *noun* (*plural*
architects)
a person who designs buildings.
[from *arch-* + Greek *tekton* = builder]

architecture *noun*
1 the process of designing buildings. **2** a
particular style of building, *Elizabethan
architecture*. **architectural** *adjective*

archives (*say* ark-**I**'vz) *plural noun*
the historical documents etc. of an
organization or community.
[from Greek *archeia* = public records]

archivist (*say* **ar**-kiv-ist) *noun* (*plural*
archivists)
a person trained to deal with archives.

archway *noun* (*plural* **archways**)
an arched passage or entrance.

-archy *suffix* see **-arch**.

arc lamp or **arc light** *noun* (*plural* **arc
lamps, arc lights**)
a light using an electric arc.

arctic *adjective*
very cold, *The weather was arctic*. [from the
Arctic, the area round the North Pole]

ardent *adjective*
enthusiastic or passionate. **ardently** *adverb*
[from Latin *ardens* = burning]

ardour (*say* **ar**-der) *noun*
enthusiasm or passion.
[from old French; related to *ardent*]

arduous *adjective*
needing much effort; laborious. **arduously**
adverb [from Latin *arduus* = steep]

area *noun* (*plural* **areas**)
1 the extent or measurement of a surface.
2 a particular region or piece of land.
3 a subject or activity.
[Latin, = piece of ground]

arena (*say* a-**reen**-a) *noun* (*plural* **arenas**)
the level area in the centre of an
amphitheatre or sports stadium.
[Latin, = sand (because the floors of
Roman arenas were covered with sand)]

aren't (*mainly spoken*)
are not.
aren't I? (*informal*) am I not?

argosy *noun* (*plural* **argosies**) (*poetic*)
a large merchant ship.
[from Italian *Ragusea* = ship from Ragusa
(now called Dubrovnik)]

arguable *adjective*
1 able to be asserted; likely to be correct.
2 able to be doubted; not certain.
arguably *adverb*

argue *verb* (**argues, arguing, argued**)
1 say that you disagree; exchange angry
comments. 2 state that something is true
and give reasons. [from Latin]

argument *noun* (*plural* **arguments**)
1 a disagreement or quarrel. 2 a reason or
series of reasons put forward.

argumentative *adjective*
fond of arguing.

aria (*say* ar-ee-a) *noun* (*plural* **arias**)
a solo in an opera or oratorio.
[Italian; related to *air*]

-arian *suffix*
forms nouns and adjectives (e.g.
vegetarian) showing members of a group.
[from Latin]

arid *adjective*
dry and barren. [from Latin]

arise *verb* (**arises, arising, arose, arisen**)
1 come into existence; come to people's
notice, *Problems arose.* 2 (*old use*) rise;
stand up, *Arise, Sir Francis.*
[from Old English]

aristocracy (*say* a-ris-tok-ra-see) *noun*
people of the highest social rank; members
of the nobility.
[from Greek *aristos* = best, + *-cracy*]

aristocrat (*say* a-ris-tok-rat) *noun* (*plural*
aristocrats)
a member of the aristocracy.
aristocratic *adjective*

arithmetic *noun*
the science or study of numbers;
calculating with numbers. **arithmetical**
adjective [from Greek *arithmos* = number]

ark *noun* (*plural* **arks**)
1 (in the Bible) the ship in which Noah and
his family escaped the Flood. 2 a wooden
box in which the writings of the Jewish
Law were kept. [from Latin *arca* = box]

arm¹ *noun* (*plural* **arms**)
1 either of the two upper limbs of the body,
between the shoulder and the hand. 2 a
sleeve. 3 something shaped like an arm or
jutting out from a main part. 4 the raised
side part of a chair. **armful** *noun*
[Old English]

arm² *verb* (**arms, arming, armed**)
1 supply someone with weapons. 2 prepare
for war. [from Latin *arma* = weapons]

armada (*say* ar-mah-da) *noun* (*plural*
armadas)
a fleet of warships.
the Armada or **Spanish Armada** the
warships sent by Spain to invade England
in 1588.
[Spanish, = navy, from Latin *armata*
= armed]

armadillo *noun* (*plural* **armadillos**)
a small burrowing South American animal
whose body is covered with a shell of bony
plates. [Spanish, = little armed man]

armaments *plural noun*
the weapons of an army etc.
[from Latin *arma* = weapons]

armature *noun* (*plural* **armatures**)
the current-carrying part of a dynamo or
electric motor. [from Latin]

armchair *noun* (*plural* **armchairs**)
a chair with arms.

armed forces or **armed services** *plural
noun*
a country's military forces; the army,
navy, and air force.

armistice *noun* (*plural* **armistices**)
an agreement to stop fighting in a war or
battle. [from Latin *arma* = weapons
+ *sistere* = stop]

armour *noun*
1 a protective covering for the body,
formerly worn in fighting. 2 a metal
covering on a warship, tank, or car to
protect it from missiles. **armoured** *adjective*
[same origin as *arm*²]

armoury *noun* (*plural* **armouries**)
a place where weapons and ammunition
are stored.

armpit *noun* (*plural* **armpits**)
the hollow underneath the top of the arm, below the shoulder.

arms *plural noun*
1 weapons. 2 a coat of arms.
up in arms protesting vigorously.
[same origin as *arm²*]

arms race *noun*
competition between nations in building up supplies of weapons, especially nuclear weapons.

army *noun* (*plural* **armies**)
1 a large number of people trained to fight on land. 2 a large group. [via old French *armée* from Latin *armata* = armed]

aroma (*say* a-**roh**-ma) *noun* (*plural* **aromas**)
a smell, especially a pleasant one. **aromatic** (*say* a-ro-**mat**-ik) *adjective*
[from Greek *aroma* = spice]

around *adverb* & *preposition*
all round; about. [from *a-¹* + *round*]

arouse *verb* (**arouses, arousing, aroused**)
1 stir up a feeling in someone, *You've aroused my curiosity*. 2 wake someone up.
[from *a-¹* + *rouse*]

arpeggio (*say* ar-**pej**-ee-oh) *noun* (*plural* **arpeggios**)
the notes of a musical chord played one after the other instead of together.
[from Italian *arpa* = harp]

arrange *verb* (**arranges, arranging, arranged**)
1 put things into a certain order; adjust.
2 form plans for something, *We arranged to be there*. 3 prepare music for a particular purpose. **arrangement** *noun*
[from old French; related to *range*]

arrant *adjective*
thorough and obvious, *Arrant nonsense!*
[a different spelling of *errant*]

array *noun* (*plural* **arrays**)
1 a display. 2 an orderly arrangement.

array *verb* (**arrays, arraying, arrayed**)
1 arrange in order. 2 dress or adorn.
[from *ar-* + old form of *ready*]

arrears *plural noun*
1 money that is owing and ought to have been paid earlier. 2 a backlog of work etc.
in arrears behind with payments.
[from *ar-* + Latin *retro* = backwards, behind]

arrest *verb* (**arrests, arresting, arrested**)
1 seize a person by authority of the law.
2 stop a process or movement.
arrest *noun* (*plural* **arrests**)
1 arresting somebody, *The police made several arrests*. 2 stopping something.
[from old French]

arrive *verb* (**arrives, arriving, arrived**)
1 reach the end of a journey or a point on it. 2 come, *The great day arrived*. **arrival** *noun* [from *ar-* + Latin *ripa* = shore]

arrogant *adjective*
behaving in an unpleasantly proud way because you think you are superior to other people. **arrogantly** *adverb*, **arrogance** *noun*
[from Latin *arrogare* = claim, demand]

arrow *noun* (*plural* **arrows**)
1 a pointed stick to be shot from a bow. 2 a sign with an outward-pointing V at the end, used to show direction or position.
arrowhead *noun* [from Old Norse]

arsenal *noun* (*plural* **arsenals**)
a place where weapons and ammunition are stored or manufactured.
[from Arabic *dar-sinaa* = workshop]

arsenic *noun*
a very poisonous metallic substance.
[originally the name of arsenic sulphide, which is yellow; from Persian *zar* = gold]

arson *noun*
the crime of deliberately setting fire to a house or building. **arsonist** *noun*
[from Latin *ardere* = burn]

art *noun* (*plural* **arts**)
1 producing something beautiful, especially by painting or drawing; things produced in this way. 2 a skill, *the art of sailing*. [from Latin]

artefact *noun* (*plural* **artefacts**)
a man-made object.
[from Latin *arte* = by art + *factum* = made]

artery *noun* (*plural* **arteries**)
1 one of the tubes that carry blood away from the heart to all parts of the body. (Compare *vein*.) 2 an important road or route. **arterial** (*say* ar-**teer**-ee-al) *adjective* [from Latin]

artesian well *noun* (*plural* **artesian wells**)
a well that is bored straight down into a place where water will rise easily to the surface. [French *artésien* = of Artois, a region of France where wells of this type were first made]

artful *adjective*
crafty. **artfully** *adverb*

arthritis (*say* arth-**ry**-tiss) *noun*
a disease that makes joints in the body stiff and painful. **arthritic** (*say* arth-**rit**-ik) *adjective* [from Greek *arthron* = joint]

arthropod *noun* (*plural* **arthropods**)
an animal of the group that includes insects, spiders, crabs, and centipedes. [from Greek *arthron* = joint + *podes* = feet (because arthropods have jointed limbs)]

artichoke *noun* (*plural* **artichokes**)
a kind of plant with a flower head used as a vegetable. [from Arabic]

article *noun* (*plural* **articles**)
1 a piece of writing published in a newspaper or magazine. 2 an object.
definite article the word 'the'.
indefinite article the word 'a' or 'an'.
[same origin as *articulate*]

articulate *adjective*
able to express things clearly and fluently.
articulate *verb* (**articulates, articulating, articulated**)
1 say or speak clearly. 2 connect by a joint. **articulation** *noun* [from Latin *artus* = joint]

articulated *adjective*
(of a vehicle) in two sections that are connected by a flexible joint, *an articulated lorry.*

artifice *noun* (*plural* **artifices**)
a piece of trickery; a clever device. [same origin as *artificial*]

artificial *adjective*
not natural; made by human beings in imitation of a natural thing. **artificially** *adverb*, **artificiality** *noun*
[from Latin *ars* = art + *facere* = make]

artificial intelligence *noun*
the use of computers to perform tasks normally requiring human intelligence, e.g. decision-making.

artificial respiration *noun*
helping somebody to start breathing again after their breathing has stopped.

artillery *noun*
1 large guns. 2 the part of the army that uses large guns. [from old French]

artisan (*say* art-iz-**an**) *noun* (*plural* **artisans**)
a skilled worker.
[from Italian; related to *art*]

artist *noun* (*plural* **artists**)
1 a person who produces works of art, especially a painter. 2 an entertainer. **artistry** *noun*

artistic *adjective*
1 to do with art or artists. 2 having a talent for art. **artistically** *adverb*

artless *adjective*
simple and natural; not artful. **artlessly** *adverb*

arts *plural noun*
subjects (e.g. languages, literature, history) in which opinion and understanding are very important, as opposed to sciences where measurements and calculations are used.
the arts painting, music, and writing etc., considered together.

-ary *suffix*
to do with; of that kind: forms adjectives (e.g. *contrary, primary*) or nouns (e.g. *dictionary, January*). [from Latin]

as *adverb*
equally or similarly, *This is just as easy.*
as *preposition*
in the function or role of, *Use it as a handle.*
as *conjunction*
1 when or while, *She slipped as she got off the bus.* 2 because, *As he was late, we*

missed the train. **3** in a way that, *Leave it as it is.*
as for with regard to, *As for you, I despise you.*
as it were in a way, *She became, as it were, her own enemy.*
as well also.
[from Old English]

as- *prefix*
to; towards. see **ad-**.

A/S *abbreviation*
advanced supplementary level in GCSE.

asbestos *noun*
a soft fireproof material.
[from Greek, = unquenchable]

ascend *verb* (**ascends, ascending, ascended**)
go up.
ascend the throne become king or queen.
[from Latin *ascendere* = climb up]

ascendancy *noun*
being in control, *They gained ascendancy over others.*

ascendant *adjective*
rising.
in the ascendant rising, especially in power or influence.

ascension *noun*
ascending.

ascent *noun* (*plural* **ascents**)
1 ascending. **2** a way up; an upward path or slope.

ascertain (*say* as-er-tayn) *verb* (**ascertains, ascertaining, ascertained**)
find something out by asking. **ascertainable** *adjective* [from old French]

ascetic (*say* a-set-ik) *adjective*
not allowing yourself pleasure and luxuries. **asceticism** *noun*
ascetic *noun* (*plural* **ascetics**)
a person who leads an ascetic life, often for religious reasons.
[from Greek *asketes* = hermit]

ascribe *verb* (**ascribes, ascribing, ascribed**)
regard something as belonging to or caused by; attribute, *She ascribes her success to good luck.*
[from *as-* + Latin *scribere* = write]

aseptic (*say* ay-sep-tik) *adjective*
clean and free from bacteria that cause things to become septic.
[from a^{-2} = not + *septic*]

asexual *adjective*
(in biology, to do with reproduction) by other than sexual methods.
[from a^{-2} = not + *sexual*]

ash[1] *noun* (*plural* **ashes**)
the powder that is left after something has been burned. **ashy** *adjective*
[from Old English *aesce*]

ash[2] *noun* (*plural* **ashes**)
a tree with silver-grey bark.
[from Old English *aesc*]

ashamed *adjective*
feeling shame.

ashen *adjective*
grey or pale, *his ashen face.*

ashore *adverb*
to or on the shore.

ashtray *noun* (*plural* **ashtrays**)
a small bowl for tobacco ash.

Ash Wednesday *noun*
the first day of Lent.

Asian *adjective*
to do with Asia or its people.
Asian *noun* (*plural* **Asians**)
an Asian person.

Asiatic *adjective*
to do with Asia.

aside *adverb*
1 to or at one side, *pull it aside.* **2** away; in reserve.
aside *noun* (*plural* **asides**)
words spoken so that only certain people will hear.

asinine (*say* ass-in-I'n) *adjective*
silly or stupid. [same origin as *ass*]

ask *verb* (**asks, asking, asked**)
1 speak so as to find out or get something.
2 invite, *Ask her to the party.*
[from Old English]

askance (*say* a-skanss) *adverb*
look askance at regard a person or situation with distrust or disapproval.
[origin unknown]

askew *adverb* & *adjective*
crooked; not straight or level.
[from *a-¹* + *skew*]

asleep *adverb* & *adjective*
sleeping.

asp *noun* (*plural* **asps**)
a small poisonous snake. [from Greek]

asparagus *noun*
a plant whose young shoots are eaten as a vegetable. [from Greek]

aspect *noun* (*plural* **aspects**)
1 one part of a problem or situation, *Violence was the worst aspect of the crime.* **2** a person's or thing's appearance, *The forest had a sinister aspect.* **3** the direction a house etc. faces, *This room has a southern aspect.* [from *as-* + Latin *specere* = to look]

aspen *noun* (*plural* **aspens**)
a tree with leaves that move in the slightest wind. [from Old English]

asperity *noun*
harshness or severity.
[from Latin *asper* = rough]

aspersions *plural noun*
cast aspersions on somebody attack his or her reputation or integrity.
[from *asperse* = spatter (with water or mud), from *as-* + Latin *spergere* = sprinkle]

asphalt (*say* ass-falt) *noun*
a sticky black substance like tar, often mixed with gravel to surface roads, etc.
[from French]

asphyxia (*say* ass-fiks-ee-a) *noun*
suffocation.
[Greek, = stopping of the pulse]

asphyxiate (*say* ass-fiks-ee-ayt) *verb*
(**asphyxiates, asphyxiating, asphyxiated**)
suffocate. **asphyxiation** *noun*
[from *asphyxia*]

aspic *noun*
a savoury jelly used for coating meats, eggs, etc. [French]

aspidistra *noun* (*plural* **aspidistras**)
a house-plant with broad leaves.
[from Greek *aspis* = a shield]

aspirant (*say* asp-er-ant) *noun* (*plural* **aspirants**)
a person who aspires to something.

aspirate (*say* asp-er-at) *noun* (*plural* **aspirates**)
the sound of 'h'. [same origin as *aspire*]

aspiration *noun* (*plural* **aspirations**)
ambition; strong desire.

aspire *verb* (**aspires, aspiring, aspired**)
have an ambition to achieve something, *He aspired to be world champion.*
[from *ad-* = to + Latin *spirare* = breathe]

aspirin *noun* (*plural* **aspirins**)
a medicinal drug used to relieve pain or reduce fever. [German]

ass *noun* (*plural* **asses**)
1 a donkey. **2** (*informal*) a stupid person.
[from Latin *asinus* = donkey]

assail *verb* (**assails, assailing, assailed**)
attack. **assailant** *noun*
[from Latin *assilire* = leap upon]

assassin *noun* (*plural* **assassins**)
a person who assassinates somebody.
[from Arabic *hashishi* = hashish-takers, used as a name for a group of Muslims at the time of the Crusades, who were believed to take hashish before going out to kill Christian leaders]

assassinate *verb* (**assassinates, assassinating, assassinated**)
kill an important person deliberately and violently, especially for political reasons.
assassination *noun*

assault *noun* (*plural* **assaults**)
a violent or illegal attack.
assault *verb* (**assaults, assaulting, assaulted**)
make an assault on someone.
[same origin as *assail*]

assay (*say* a-say) *noun* (*plural* **assays**)
a test made on metal or ore to discover its quality. [from French *essai* = trial]

assegai (*say* ass-ig-I) *noun* (*plural* assegais)
an iron-tipped spear used by South African peoples. [from Arabic]

assemble *verb* (assembles, assembling, assembled)
1 bring or come together. 2 fit or put together the parts of something. **assemblage** *noun*
[from *as-* + Latin *simul* = together]

assembly *noun* (*plural* assemblies)
1 assembling. 2 a regular meeting, such as when everybody in a school meets together. 3 people who regularly meet for a special purpose; a parliament.

assembly line *noun* (*plural* assembly lines)
a series of workers and machines along which a product passes to be assembled part by part.

assent *verb* (assents, assenting, assented)
consent; say you agree.
assent *noun*
consent or approval.
[from *as-* + Latin *sentire* = feel, think]

assert *verb* (asserts, asserting, asserted)
state something firmly. **assertion** *noun*
assert yourself use firmness or forcefulness.
[from Latin]

assertive *adjective*
asserting yourself; firm and forceful.

assess *verb* (assesses, assessing, assessed)
decide or estimate the value or quality of a person or thing. **assessment** *noun*, **assessor** *noun*
[from Latin *assessor* = an assistant judge]

asset *noun* (*plural* assets)
something useful. [from old French]

assets *plural noun*
a person's or firm's property, reckoned as having value.

assiduous (*say* a-sid-yoo-us) *adjective*
working hard; persevering. **assiduously** *adverb*, **assiduity** *noun* [from Latin]

assign *verb* (assigns, assigning, assigned)
1 give or allot. 2 appoint a person to perform a task.
[from *as-* + Latin *signare* = mark out]

assignation (*say* ass-ig-nay-shon) *noun* (*plural* assignations)
1 an arrangement to meet someone.
2 assigning something.

assignment *noun* (*plural* assignments)
1 assigning. 2 something assigned; a task given to someone.

assimilate *verb* (assimilates, assimilating, assimilated)
take in and absorb something, e.g. nourishment into the body or knowledge into the mind. **assimilation** *noun*
[from *as-* + Latin *similis* = similar]

assist *verb* (assists, assisting, assisted)
help. **assistance** *noun*
[from Latin *assistere* = stand by]

assistant *noun* (*plural* assistants)
1 a person who assists another; a helper.
2 a person who serves customers in a shop.
assistant *adjective*
helping a person and ranking next below him or her, *the assistant manager*.

associate *verb* (associates, associating, associated)
1 connect things in your mind, *I don't associate Ryan with fitness and healthy living*. 2 spend time or have dealings with a group of people.
associate *noun* (*plural* associates)
a colleague or companion; a partner.
associate *adjective*
[from *as-* + Latin *socius* = an ally]

association *noun* (*plural* associations)
1 an organization of people; a society.
2 associating. 3 a connection or link in your mind.

Association football *noun*
a form of football using a round ball that may not be handled during play except by the goalkeeper.

assonance (*say* ass-on-ans) *noun*
similarity of vowel sounds, e.g. in *vermin* and *furnish*.
[from *as-* + Latin *sonus* = sound]

assorted *adjective*
of various sorts put together; mixed, *assorted sweets*.

assortment *noun* (*plural* assortments)
a mixed collection of things.

assuage (*say* a-**sway**]) *verb* (assuages,
assuaging, assuaged)
soothe; make something less severe, *We
drank to assuage our thirst.*
[from *as-* + Latin *suavis* = pleasant]

assume *verb* (assumes, assuming, assumed)
1 accept (without proof or question) that
something is true or sure to happen. **2** take
on; undertake, *She assumed the extra
responsibility.* **3** put on, *He assumed an
innocent expression.*
assumed name a false name. **assumption**
noun [from *as-* + Latin *sumere* = take]

assurance *noun* (*plural* assurances)
1 a promise or guarantee that something is
true or will happen. **2** life insurance. **3** self-
confidence.

assure *verb* (assures, assuring, assured)
1 tell somebody confidently; promise.
2 make certain.
[from *as-* + Latin *securus* = secure]

aster *noun* (*plural* asters)
a garden plant with daisy-like flowers in
various colours. [from Greek *aster* = star]

asterisk *noun* (*plural* asterisks)
a star-shaped sign * used to draw attention
to something.
[from Greek *asteriskos* = little star]

astern *adverb*
1 at the back of a ship or aircraft.
2 backwards, *Full speed astern!*

asteroid *noun* (*plural* asteroids)
one of the small planets found mainly
between the orbits of Mars and Jupiter.
[same origin as *aster*]

asthma (*say* ass-ma) *noun*
a disease that makes breathing difficult.
asthmatic *adjective* & *noun* [Greek]

astigmatism (*say* a-**stig**-mat-izm) *noun*
a defect that prevents an eye or lens from
focusing properly. **astigmatic** *adjective*
[from *a-²* = not + Greek *stigma* = a point]

astir *adverb* & *adjective*
in motion; moving. [from *a-¹* + *stir*]

astonish *verb* (astonishes, astonishing,
astonished)
surprise somebody greatly. **astonishment**
noun [same origin as *astound*]

astound *verb* (astounds, astounding,
astounded)
astonish; shock somebody greatly.
[from old French; related to *stun*]

astral *adjective*
to do with the stars.
[from Greek *astron* = star]

astray *adverb* & *adjective*
away from the right path or place or course
of action.

astride *adverb* & *preposition*
with one leg on each side of something.

astringent *adjective*
1 causing skin or body tissue to contract.
2 harsh or severe, *astringent criticism.*
[from *as-* + Latin *stringere* − bind tightly]

astrology *noun*
the study of how the stars and planets may
influence people's lives. **astrologer** *noun*,
astrological *adjective*
[from Greek *astron* = star, + *-logy*]

astronaut *noun* (*plural* astronauts)
a person who travels in a spacecraft.
astronautics *noun*
[from Greek *astron* = star + *nautes* = sailor]

astronomical *adjective*
1 to do with astronomy. **2** extremely large,
The restaurant's prices are astronomical.

astronomy *noun*
the study of the stars and planets and their
movements. **astronomer** *noun* [from Greek
astron = star + *-nomia* = arrangement]

astute *adjective*
clever and good at understanding
situations quickly; shrewd.
astutely *adverb*, **astuteness** *noun*
[from Latin *astus* = cleverness, cunning]

asunder *adverb*
apart; into pieces. [from Old English]

asylum *noun* (*plural* **asylums**)
1 refuge and safety; a place of refuge, *The defeated rebels sought political asylum in another country.* 2 (*old use*) a mental hospital. [from Greek *asylon* = refuge]

asymmetrical (*say* ay-sim-et-rik-al) *adjective*
not symmetrical. **asymmetrically** *adverb*

at *preposition*
This word is used to show 1 position (*at the top*), 2 time (*at midnight*), 3 condition (*Stand at ease*), 4 direction towards something (*Aim at the target*), 5 level or price etc. (*Sell them at £1 each*), 6 cause (*We were annoyed at his failure*).
at all in any way.
at it doing or working at something.
at once 1 immediately. **2** at the same time, *It all came out at once.*
[from Old English]

at- *prefix*
to; towards. see **ad-**.

-ate *suffix*
forms 1 adjectives (e.g. *passionate*), 2 nouns showing status or function (e.g. *magistrate*) or (in scientific use) nouns meaning salts of certain acids (e.g. *nitrate*; compare **-ite**), 3 verbs (e.g. *create*, *fascinate*). [from Latin]

atheist (*say* ayth-ee-ist) *noun* (*plural* **atheists**)
a person who believes that there is no God. **atheism** *noun* [from *a-*[2] + Greek *theos* = god]

athlete *noun* (*plural* **athletes**)
a person who is good at sport, especially athletics. [from Greek *athlein* = compete for a prize]

athletic *adjective*
1 physically strong and active. 2 to do with athletes. **athletically** *adverb*

athletics *plural noun*
physical exercises and sports, e.g. running, jumping, and throwing.

-ation *suffix*
forms nouns, often from verbs (e.g. *creation*, *organization*, *starvation*). [from Latin]

atlas *noun* (*plural* **atlases**)
a book of maps. [named after Atlas, a giant in Greek mythology, who was made to support the universe on his shoulders]

atmosphere *noun* (*plural* **atmospheres**)
1 the air round the earth. 2 a feeling or mood given by surroundings, *the happy atmosphere of the fairground.* **atmospheric** *adjective*
[from Greek *atmos* = vapour, + *sphere*]

atoll *noun* (*plural* **atolls**)
a ring-shaped coral reef. [from Maldivian (the language spoken in the Maldives)]

atom *noun* (*plural* **atoms**)
the smallest particle of a substance. [from Greek *atomos* = indivisible]

atom bomb *noun* (*plural* **atom bombs**)
a bomb using atomic energy.

atomic *adjective*
1 to do with an atom or atoms. 2 to do with atomic energy or atom bombs.

atomic bomb *noun* (*plural* **atomic bombs**)
a bomb using atomic energy.

atomic energy *noun*
energy created by splitting the nuclei of certain atoms.

atomic number *noun* (*plural* **atomic numbers**)
the number of protons in the nucleus of the atom of a chemical element.

atomizer *noun* (*plural* **atomizers**)
a device for making a liquid into a fine spray.

atone *verb* (**atones, atoning, atoned**)
make amends; make up for having done something wrong. **atonement** *noun*
[from *at one*]

atrocious (*say* a-troh-shus) *adjective*
extremely bad or wicked, *atrocious weather.* **atrociously** *adverb*
[from Latin *atrox* = cruel]

atrocity (*say* a-tross-it-ee) *noun* (*plural* **atrocities**)
something extremely bad or wicked; wickedness.

attach *verb* (attaches, attaching, attached)
1 fix or join to something else. 2 regard as belonging to something, *We attach great importance to fitness.* **attachment** *noun*
attached to fond of.
[via old French from Germanic]

attaché (*say* a-tash-ay) *noun* (*plural* attachés)
a special assistant to an ambassador, *our military attaché.* [French, = attached]

attaché case *noun* (*plural* attaché cases)
a small case in which documents etc. may be carried.

attack *noun* (*plural* attacks)
1 a violent attempt to hurt or overcome somebody. 2 a piece of strong criticism. 3 sudden illness or pain.
attack *verb* (attacks, attacking, attacked)
make an attack. **attacker** *noun*
[from French; related to *attach*]

attain *verb* (attains, attaining, attained)
accomplish; succeed in doing or getting something. **attainable** *adjective*, **attainment** *noun* [from *at-* + Latin *tangere* = touch]

attempt *verb* (attempts, attempting, attempted)
make an effort to do something; try.
attempt *noun* (*plural* attempts)
an effort to do something; a try.
[from *at-* + Latin *temptare* = try]

attend *verb* (attends, attending, attended)
1 give care and thought to something; look and listen, *Why don't you attend to your teacher?* 2 be present somewhere; go regularly to a meeting etc. 3 look after someone; be an attendant. **attendance** *noun* [from old French]

attendant *noun* (*plural* attendants)
a person who helps or accompanies someone.

attention *noun*
1 giving concentration and careful thought, *Pay attention to what I'm saying.* 2 a position in which a soldier etc. stands with feet together and arms straight downwards.

attentive *adjective*
giving attention to something.
attentively *adverb*, **attentiveness** *noun*

attenuate *verb* (attenuates, attenuating, attenuated)
make a thing thinner or weaker.
attenuation *noun*
[from *at-* + Latin *tenuis* = thin]

attest *verb* (attests, attesting, attested)
declare or prove that something is true or genuine. **attestation** *noun*
[from *at-* + Latin *testari* = be a witness]

attic *noun* (*plural* attics)
a room in the roof of a house.
[via French from Greek]

attire *noun* (*formal*)
clothes.
attire *verb* (attires, attiring, attired) (*formal*)
dress. [from old French *atirer* = equip]

attitude *noun* (*plural* attitudes)
1 the position of the body or its parts; posture. 2 a way of thinking or behaving.
[French]

attorney *noun* (*plural* attorneys)
1 a person who is appointed to act on behalf of another in business matters.
2 (*American*) a lawyer. [from old French]

attract *verb* (attracts, attracting, attracted)
1 get someone's attention or interest; seem pleasant to someone. 2 pull something by an invisible force, *Magnets attract metal pins.* **attraction** *noun*
[from *at-* + Latin *tractum* = pulled]

attractive *adjective*
1 pleasant or good-looking. 2 interesting or appealing, *an attractive plan.*
attractively *adverb*, **attractiveness** *noun*

attribute (*say* a-trib-yoot) *verb* (attributes, attributing, attributed)
regard something as belonging to or created by, *We attribute his success to hard work.* **attribution** *noun*
attribute (*say* at-rib-yoot) *noun* (*plural* attributes)
a quality or characteristic, *Kindness is one of his attributes.*
[from *at-* + Latin *tribuere* = allot]

attributive (*say* a-trib-yoo-tiv) *adjective*
expressing an attribute and placed before the word it describes, e.g. *old* in *the old dog.*
(Compare *predicative.*) **attributively** *adverb*

attrition (*say* a-**trish**-on) *noun*
gradually wearing down an enemy by
repeatedly attacking them. [from Latin]

attuned *adjective*
adjusted to something, *My eyes were now
attuned to the darkness.* [from *at-* + *tune*]

aubergine (*say* oh-ber-*zheen*) *noun* (*plural*
aubergines)
the deep-purple fruit of the eggplant.
[via French and Arabic from Sanskrit]

auburn *adjective*
(of hair) reddish-brown. [from old French]

auction *noun* (*plural* **auctions**)
a public sale where things are sold to the
person who offers the most money for
them.
auction *verb* (**auctions, auctioning,
auctioned**)
sell something by auction. **auctioneer** *noun*
[from Latin *auctum* = increased]

audacious (*say* aw-**day**-shus) *adjective*
bold or daring. **audaciously** *adverb*, **audacity**
noun [from Latin *audax* = bold]

audible *adjective*
loud enough to be heard. **audibly** *adverb*,
audibility *noun* [from Latin *audire* = hear]

audience *noun* (*plural* **audiences**)
1 people who have gathered to hear or
watch something. **2** a formal interview
with an important person.
[from Latin *audire* = hear]

audio *noun*
reproduced sounds.

audio typist *noun* (*plural* **audio typists**)
a person who types from dictation that has
been recorded.

audio-visual *adjective*
using both sound and pictures to give
information.

audit *noun* (*plural* **audits**)
an official examination of financial
accounts to see that they are correct.
audit *verb* (**audits, auditing, audited**)
make an audit of accounts. **auditor** *noun*
[from Latin *audire* = hear (because
originally the accounts were read out)]

audition *noun* (*plural* **auditions**)
a test to see if an actor or musician
is suitable for a job.
audition *verb*
[same origin as *audience*]

auditorium *noun* (*plural* **auditoriums**)
the part of a building where the audience
sits. [Latin, = place for hearing]

au fait (*say* oh **fay**) *adjective*
knowing a subject or procedure etc. well.
[French, = to the point]

augment *verb* (**augments, augmenting,
augmented**)
increase or add to something.
augmentation *noun*
[from Latin *augere* = increase]

au gratin (*say* oh **grat**-an) *adjective*
cooked with a crisp topping of
breadcrumbs or grated cheese. [French]

augur (*say* **awg**-er) *verb* (**augurs, auguring,
augured**)
be a sign of what is to come, *These exam
results augur well.*
[from Latin *augur* = prophet]

august (*say* aw-**gust**) *adjective*
majestic or imposing.
[from Latin *augustus* = majestic]

auk *noun* (*plural* **auks**)
a kind of seabird. [from Old Norse]

aunt *noun* (*plural* **aunts**)
the sister of your father or mother; your
uncle's wife. [from Latin]

auntie or **aunty** *noun* (*plural* **aunties**)
(*informal*) aunt.

au pair (*say* oh **pair**) *noun* (*plural* **au pairs**)
a young person from overseas who works
for a time in someone's home.
[French]

aura (*say* **or**-a) *noun* (*plural* **auras**)
a general feeling surrounding a person or
thing, *an aura of happiness.*
[Greek, = breeze]

aural (*say* or-al) *adjective*
to do with the ear or hearing. **aurally** *adverb*
[from Latin *auris* = ear]

USAGE: Do not confuse with *oral*.

au revoir (*say* oh rev-**wahr**) *interjection*
goodbye for the moment.
[French, literally = to be seeing again]

aurora (*say* aw-**raw**-ra) *noun* (*plural*
auroras)
bands of coloured light appearing in the
sky at night, the **aurora borealis** (*say* bor-ee-
ay-liss) in the northern hemisphere and the
aurora australis (*say* aw-**stray**-liss) in the
southern hemisphere.
[Latin: *aurora* = dawn; *borealis* = of the
north; *australis* = of the south]

auspices (*say* aw-spiss-eez) *plural noun*
protection or support, *under the auspices of
the Red Cross.*
[originally = omens; later = influence,
protection; same origin as *auspicious*]

auspicious (*say* aw-**spish**-us) *adjective*
fortunate or favourable, *an auspicious
start.* [from Latin *auspicium* = telling the
future from the behaviour of birds, from
avis = bird]

austere (*say* aw-**steer**) *adjective*
very simple and plain; without luxuries.
austerely *adverb*, **austerity** *noun*
[from Greek *austeros* = severe]

aut- *prefix*
self-; of or by yourself or itself. see **auto-**.

authentic *adjective*
genuine, *an authentic signature.*
authentically *adverb*, **authenticity** *noun*
[from Greek]

authenticate *verb* (**authenticates,
authenticating, authenticated**)
confirm something as being authentic.
authentication *noun*

author *noun* (*plural* **authors**)
the writer of a book, play, poem, etc.
authorship *noun*
[from Latin *auctor* = originator]

authoritarian *adjective*
believing that people should be completely
obedient to those in authority.

authoritative *adjective*
having proper authority or expert
knowledge; official.

authority *noun* (*plural* **authorities**)
1 the right or power to give orders to other
people. 2 a person or organization with the
right to give orders. 3 an expert; a book etc.
that gives reliable information, *an
authority on spiders.*
[same origin as *author*]

authorize *verb* (**authorizes, authorizing,
authorized**)
give official permission for something.
authorization *noun*

autistic (*say* aw-**tist**-ik) *adjective*
unable to communicate with other people
or respond to surroundings. **autism** *noun*
[from *auto-*]

auto- *prefix* (changing to **aut-** before a
vowel)
self-; of or by yourself or itself (as in
autograph, automatic).
[from Greek *autos* – self]

autobiography *noun* (*plural*
autobiographies)
the story of a person's life written by
himself or herself.
autobiographical *adjective*

autocracy (*say* aw-**tok**-ra-see) *noun* (*plural*
autocracies)
rule by a person with unlimited power;
despotism. [from *auto-* + *-cracy*]

autocrat *noun* (*plural* **autocrats**)
a ruler with unlimited power.
autocratic *adjective*, **autocratically** *adverb*

autocue *noun* (*plural* **autocues**) (*trade
mark*)
a device that displays the script for a
television presenter or newsreader to read.

autograph *noun* (*plural* **autographs**)
a person's signature.
autograph *verb* (**autographs,
autographing, autographed**)
sign your name on or in a book etc.
[from *auto-* + *-graph*]

automate *verb* (**automates, automating,
automated**)
work something by automation.

automatic *adjective*
1 working on its own without continuous attention or control by people. 2 done without thinking. **automatically** *adverb*
[from Greek *automatos* = self-operating]

automation *noun*
making processes automatic; using machines instead of people to do jobs.

automaton (*say* aw-**tom**-at-on) *noun* (*plural* **automatons**)
1 a robot. 2 a person who seems to act mechanically without thinking.
[same origin as *automatic*]

automobile *noun* (*plural* **automobiles**)
(*American*) a car. [from *auto-* + *mobile*]

autonomy (*say* aw-**ton**-om-ee) *noun*
1 self-government. 2 the right to act independently without being told what to do. **autonomous** *adjective*
[from *auto-* + Greek *-nomia* = arrangement]

autopsy (*say* **aw**-top-see) *noun* (*plural* **autopsies**)
a post-mortem. [from Greek *autopsia* = seeing with your own eyes]

autumn *noun* (*plural* **autumns**)
the season between summer and winter. **autumnal** *adjective* [from old French]

auxiliary *adjective*
giving help and support, *auxiliary services*.
auxiliary *noun* (*plural* **auxiliaries**)
a helper. [from Latin *auxilium* = help]

auxiliary verb *noun* (*plural* **auxiliary verbs**)
a verb used in forming tenses etc. of other verbs, e.g. *have* in *I have finished*.

avail *noun*
to or **of no avail** of no use; without success, *Their pleas for mercy were all to no avail*.
avail *verb* (**avails, availing, availed**)
be useful or helpful, *Nothing availed against the storm*.
avail yourself of make use of something, *Could I avail myself of your bicycle?*
[from Latin *valere* = be strong]

available *adjective*
ready or able to be used; obtainable. **availability** *noun*

avalanche *noun* (*plural* **avalanches**)
a mass of snow or rock falling down the side of a mountain.
[French, from *avaler* = descend]

avant-garde (*say* av-ahn-**gard**) *noun*
people who use a very modern style in art or literature etc. [French, = vanguard]

avarice (*say* **av**-er-iss) *noun*
greed for money or possessions. **avaricious** *adjective* [from Latin *avarus* = greedy]

avenge *verb* (**avenges, avenging, avenged**)
take vengeance for something done to harm you. **avenger** *noun*
[from old French; related to *vindicate*]

avenue *noun* (*plural* **avenues**)
1 a wide street. 2 a road with trees along both sides.
[from French *avenir* = approach]

average *noun* (*plural* **averages**)
1 the value obtained by adding several quantities together and dividing by the number of quantities. 2 the usual or ordinary standard.
average *adjective*
1 worked out as an average, *Their average age is ten*. 2 of the usual or ordinary standard.
average *verb* (**averages, averaging, averaged**)
work out, produce, or amount to as an average. [from Arabic]

averse *adjective*
unwilling; feeling opposed to something, *I'm not averse to a bit of hard work*.
[same origin as *avert*]

USAGE: Do not confuse with *adverse*.

aversion *noun*
a strong dislike.

avert *verb* (**averts, averting, averted**)
1 turn something away, *People averted their eyes from the accident*. 2 prevent, *We averted a disaster*.
[from *ab-* = away + Latin *vertere* = turn]

aviary *noun* (*plural* **aviaries**)
a large cage or building for keeping birds.
[from Latin *avis* = bird]

aviation *noun*
the flying of aircraft. **aviator** *noun*
[from Latin *avis* = bird]

avid (*say* av-id) *adjective*
eager, *an avid reader*. **avidly** *adverb*, **avidity**
noun [from Latin *avere* = long for]

avocado (*say* av-ok-**ah**-doh) *noun* (*plural*
avocados)
a pear-shaped tropical fruit.
[via Spanish from Nahuatl (a Central
American language)]

avoid *verb* (avoids, avoiding, avoided)
1 keep yourself away from someone or
something. **2** keep yourself from doing
something; refrain from, *Avoid rash
promises*. **avoidable** *adjective*, **avoidance**
noun [from old French]

avoirdupois (*say* av-er-dew-**poiz**) *noun*
a system of weights using the unit of 16
ounces = 1 pound. [French, = goods of
weight (goods sold by weight)]

avuncular *adjective*
like a kindly uncle. [from Latin]

await *verb* (awaits, awaiting, awaited)
wait for. [from old French]

awake *verb* (awakes, awaking, awoke,
awoken)
wake up.
awake *adjective*
not asleep. [from Old English]

awaken *verb* (awakens, awakening,
awakened)
wake up. **awakening** *noun*
[from Old English]

award *verb* (awards, awarding, awarded)
give something officially as a prize,
payment, or penalty.
award *noun* (*plural* awards)
something awarded, such as a prize or a
sum of money. [from old French]

aware *adjective*
knowing or realizing something, *Were you
aware of the danger?* **awareness** *noun*
[from Old English]

awash *adjective*
with waves or water flooding over it.
[from *a-*¹ + *wash*]

away *adverb*
1 to or at a distance; not at the usual place.
2 out of existence, *The water had boiled
away*. **3** continuously or persistently, *We
worked away at it*.
away *adjective*
played on an opponent's ground, *an away
match*. [from Old English]

awe *noun*
fearful or deeply respectful wonder, *The
mountains always fill me with awe*. **awed**
adjective, **awestricken** *adjective*, **awestruck**
adjective [from Old English]

aweigh *adverb*
hanging just clear of the sea-bottom, *The
anchor is aweigh*. [from *a-*¹ + *weigh*]

awesome *adjective*
causing awe. [from *awe* + *-some*]

awful *adjective*
1 very bad, *an awful accident*. **2** (*informal*)
very great, *That's an awful lot of money*.
awfully *adverb* [from *awe* + *-ful*]

awhile *adverb*
for a short time. [from *a* + *while*]

awkward *adjective*
1 difficult to use or deal with; not
convenient. **2** clumsy; not skilful.
awkwardly *adverb*, **awkwardness** *noun* [from
Old Norse *ofugr* = turned the wrong way]

awl *noun* (*plural* awls)
a small pointed tool for making holes in
leather, wood, etc. [from Old English]

awning *noun* (*plural* awnings)
a roof-like shelter made of canvas etc.
[origin unknown]

awry *adverb* & *adjective*
1 twisted to one side; crooked. **2** wrong; not
according to plan, *plans went awry*.
[from *a-*¹ + *wry*]

axe *noun* (*plural* axes)
1 a tool for chopping things. **2** (*informal*)
being axed.
have an axe to grind have a personal
interest in something and want to take
care of it.

axe *verb* (axes, axing, axed)
1 cancel or abolish something. **2** reduce
something greatly. [from Old English]

axiom *noun* (*plural* axioms)
an established general truth or principle.
axiomatic *adjective* [from Greek]

axis *noun* (*plural* axes)
1 a line through the centre of a spinning
object. **2** a line dividing a thing in half.
[Latin, = axle]

axle *noun* (*plural* axles)
the rod through the centre of a wheel, on
which the wheel turns. [from Old Norse]

ayatollah (*say* I-a-**tol**-a) *noun* (*plural*
ayatollahs)
a Muslim religious leader in Iran.
[from Arabic *ayatu-llah* = sign from God]

aye (*say* I) *adverb*
yes. [origin unknown]

azalea (*say* a-**zay**-lee-a) *noun* (*plural*
azaleas)
a kind of flowering shrub.
[from Greek, = dry (because the plant
grows well in dry soil)]

azure *adjective*
sky-blue. [via old French from Persian]

Bb

baa *noun* (*plural* baas)
the cry of a sheep or lamb.

babble *verb* (babbles, babbling, babbled)
1 talk very quickly without making sense.
2 make a murmuring sound. **babble** *noun*,
babbler *noun* [imitating the sound]

babe *noun* (*plural* babes)
a baby. [same as *baby*]

baboon *noun* (*plural* baboons)
a kind of large monkey from Africa and
Asia. Baboons have long muzzles and short
tails. [from French]

baby *noun* (*plural* babies)
a very young child or animal. **babyish**
adjective [probably from the sounds a baby
makes when it first tries to speak]

babysitter *noun* (*plural* babysitters)
someone who looks after a child while its
parents are out.

bachelor *noun* (*plural* bachelors)
a man who has not married.
Bachelor of Arts or **Science** a person who
has taken a first degree in arts or science.
[from French]

bacillus (*say* ba-**sil**-us) *noun* (*plural* bacilli)
a rod-shaped bacterium.
[Latin, = little stick]

back *noun* (*plural* backs)
1 the part that is furthest from the front.
2 the back part of the body from the
shoulders to the buttocks. **3** the part of a
chair etc. that your back rests against.
4 a defending player near the goal in
football, hockey, etc.
back *adjective*
1 placed at or near the back. **2** to do with
the back, *back pain*.
back *adverb*
1 to or towards the back. **2** to the place you
have come from, *Go back home*. **3** to an
earlier time or position, *Put the clocks back
one hour*.
back *verb* (backs, backing, backed)
1 move backwards. **2** give someone
support or help. **3** bet on something.
4 cover the back of something, *Back the
rug with canvas*. **backer** *noun*
back out refuse to do what you agreed to do.
back up give support or help to a person or
thing. **back-up** *noun*
[from Old English]

backbencher *noun* (*plural* backbenchers)
a Member of Parliament who does not hold
an important position.

backbiting *noun*
saying unkind or nasty things about
someone who is not there.

backbone *noun* (*plural* backbones)
the column of small bones down the centre
of the back; the spine.

backdrop *noun* (*plural* backdrops)
a large, painted cloth that is hung across
the back of a stage.

backfire *verb* (**backfires, backfiring, backfired**)
1 if a car backfires, it makes a loud noise, caused by an explosion in the exhaust pipe.
2 if a plan backfires, it goes wrong.

backgammon *noun*
a game played on a board with draughts and dice. [from *back* (because sometimes pieces must go back to the start) + Old English *gamen* = game]

background *noun*
1 the back part of a scene or view etc.
2 the conditions influencing something.
3 a person's family, upbringing, and education.

backhand *noun* (*plural* **backhands**)
a stroke made in tennis etc. with the back of the hand turned outwards.
backhanded *adjective*

backing *noun*
1 support. 2 material that is used to line the back of something. 3 musical accompaniment.

backlash *noun* (*plural* **backlashes**)
a violent reaction to an event.

backlog *noun* (*plural* **backlogs**)
an amount of work that should have been finished but is still waiting to be done.

backpack *noun* (*plural* **backpacks**)
a rucksack. **backpacker** *noun*

backside *noun* (*plural* **backsides**)
(*informal*)
the buttocks.

backstroke *noun*
a way of swimming lying on your back.

backward *adjective*
1 going backwards. 2 slow at learning or developing. **backwardness** *noun*
backward *adverb*
backwards.

USAGE: The adverb *backward* is mainly used in American English.

backwards *adverb*
1 to or towards the back. 2 with the back end going first. 3 in reverse order, *Count backwards.*
backwards and forwards in each direction alternately; to and fro.

backwater *noun* (*plural* **backwaters**)
1 a branch of a river that comes to a dead end with stagnant water. 2 a quiet place that is not affected by progress or new ideas.

bacon *noun*
smoked or salted meat from the back or sides of a pig. [via French from Germanic; related to *back*]

bacterium *noun* (*plural* **bacteria**)
a microscopic organism. **bacterial** *adjective* [from Greek *bakterion* = little cane]

USAGE: Note that it is a mistake to use the plural form *bacteria* as if it were the singular. It is incorrect to say 'a bacteria' or 'this bacteria'; correct usage is *this bacterium* or *these bacteria*.

bad *adjective* (**worse, worst**)
1 not having the right qualities; not good.
2 wicked or evil. 3 serious or severe, *a bad accident*. 4 ill or unhealthy. 5 harmful, *Sweets are bad for your teeth*. 6 decayed or rotten, *This meat has gone bad*. **badness** *noun*
not bad quite good.
[*bad* is probably from Old English; *worse* and *worst* are from Old English *wyrsa*, related to *war*]

bade *old past tense* of **bid²**.

badge *noun* (*plural* **badges**)
a button or sign that you wear to show people who you are or what school or club etc. you belong to. [origin unknown]

badger *noun* (*plural* **badgers**)
a grey burrowing animal with a black and white head.
badger *verb* (**badgers, badgering, badgered**)
keep asking someone to do something; pester. [perhaps from *badge* (because of the markings on a badger's head)]

badly *adverb* (**worse, worst**)
1 in a bad way; not well. 2 severely; causing much injury, *He was badly wounded*. 3 very much, *She badly wanted to win*.

badminton *noun*
a game in which players use rackets to hit a light object called a shuttlecock across a high net. [the name of a stately home in SW England where the game was first played]

baffle *verb* (baffles, baffling, baffled)
puzzle or confuse somebody. **bafflement** *noun* [origin unknown]

bag *noun* (*plural* bags)
a container made of a soft material, for holding or carrying things.
bags (*informal*) plenty, *bags of room.*
bag *verb* (bags, bagging, bagged)
1 (*informal*) catch or claim something. 2 put something into bags.
[from Old Norse]

bagatelle *noun*
a game played on a board in which small balls are struck into holes. [from Italian]

baggage *noun*
luggage. [from old French]

baggy *adjective*
(of clothes) large and loose.

bagpipes *plural noun*
a musical instrument in which air is squeezed out of a bag into pipes. Bagpipes are played especially in Scotland.

bail¹ *noun*
money that is paid or promised as a guarantee that a person who is accused of a crime will return for trial if he or she is released in the meantime.
bail *verb* (bails, bailing, bailed)
provide bail for a person.
[from old French *bail* = custody, jurisdiction; related to *bail²*]

bail² *noun* (*plural* bails)
one of the two small pieces of wood placed on top of the stumps in cricket.
[from old French *bail* = palisade]

bail³ *verb* (bails, bailing, bailed)
scoop out water that has got into a boat.
[from French *baille* = bucket]

bailey *noun* (*plural* baileys)
the courtyard of a castle; the wall round this courtyard. [same origin as *bail²*]

bailiff *noun* (*plural* bailiffs)
1 a law officer who helps a sheriff by serving writs and performing arrests. 2 an official who takes people's property when they owe money.
[from old French; related to *bail¹*]

Bairam (*say* by-**rahm**) *noun*
either of two Muslim festivals, one in the tenth month and one in the twelfth month of the Islamic year. [from Turkish]

bairn *noun* (*plural* bairns) (*Scottish*)
a child. [from Old English]

Baisakhi *noun*
a Sikh festival held in April.

bait *noun*
1 food that is put on a hook or in a trap to catch fish or animals. 2 something that is meant to tempt someone.
bait *verb* (baits, baiting, baited)
1 put bait on a hook or in a trap. 2 try to make someone angry by teasing them.
[from Old Norse; related to *bite*]

baize *noun*
the thick green cloth that is used for covering snooker tables.
[same origin as *bay⁵* (because the cloth was originally reddish-brown)]

bake *verb* (bakes, baking, baked)
1 cook in an oven. 2 make or become very hot. 3 make a thing hard by heating it.
[from Old English]

baked beans *plural noun*
cooked white beans, usually tinned with tomato sauce.

baker *noun* (*plural* bakers)
a person who bakes and sells bread or cakes. **bakery** *noun*

baking soda *noun*
sodium bicarbonate.

balaclava or **balaclava helmet** *noun*
(*plural* balaclavas, balaclava helmets)
a hood covering the head and neck and part of the face. [named after *Balaclava*, a village in the Crimea (because the helmets were worn by soldiers fighting near there during the Crimean War)]

balance *noun* (*plural* **balances**)
1 a steady position, with the weight or amount evenly distributed. **2** a machine for weighing things, with two containers hanging from a bar. **3** the difference between money paid into an account and money taken out of it. **4** the money left after something has been paid for.
balance *verb* (**balances, balancing, balanced**)
make or be steady or equal. [from Latin]

balcony *noun* (*plural* **balconies**)
1 a platform that sticks out from an outside wall of a building. **2** the upstairs part of a theatre or cinema. [from Italian]

bald *adjective*
1 without hair on the top of the head. **2** with no details; blunt, *a bald statement*.
baldly *adverb*, **baldness** *noun*
[origin unknown]

bale[1] *noun* (*plural* **bales**)
a large bundle of hay, straw, cotton, etc., usually tied up tightly.
[probably from Dutch; related to *ball*[1]]

bale[2] *verb* (**bales, baling, baled**)
bale out jump out of an aircraft with a parachute.
[a different spelling of *bail*[3]]

baleful *adjective*
menacing or harmful, *a baleful frown*.
balefully *adverb*
[from Old English *balu* = evil]

ball[1] *noun* (*plural* **balls**)
1 a round object used in many games. **2** anything that has a round shape, *a ball of string*. [from Old Norse]

ball[2] *noun* (*plural* **balls**)
a formal party where people dance.
[same origin as *ballet*]

ballad *noun* (*plural* **ballads**)
a simple song or poem that tells a story.
[from old French]

ballast (*say* bal-ast) *noun*
heavy material that is carried in a ship to keep it steady.
[probably from a Scandinavian language]

ball-bearings *plural noun*
small steel balls rolling in a groove on which machine parts can move easily.

ballcock *noun* (*plural* **ballcocks**)
a floating ball that controls the water level in a cistern. [from *ball*[1] + *cock* = tap]

ballerina (*say* bal-er-een-a) *noun* (*plural* **ballerinas**)
a female ballet dancer.
[Italian, = female dancing teacher]

ballet (*say* bal-ay) *noun* (*plural* **ballets**)
a stage entertainment that tells a story with dancing, mime, and music.
[via French from Italian]

ballistic (*say* bal-ist-ik) *adjective*
to do with objects that are fired through the air, especially bullets and missiles.
[from Greek *ballein* = to throw]

ballistic missile *noun* (*plural* **ballistic missiles**)
a missile that is initially powered and guided and then falls under gravity on its target.

balloon *noun* (*plural* **balloons**)
1 a bag made of thin rubber that can be inflated and used as a toy or decoration. **2** a large round bag inflated with hot air or light gases to make it rise in the air. **3** an outline round spoken words in a strip cartoon.
[from French or Italian; related to *ball*[1]]

ballot *noun* (*plural* **ballots**)
1 a secret method of voting, usually by making a mark on a piece of paper. **2** a piece of paper on which a vote is made.
ballot *verb* (**ballots, balloting, balloted**)
invite people to vote for something by a ballot.
[from Italian *ballotta* = small ball (because one way of voting is by placing a ball in a box; the colour of the ball shows whether you are voting for something or against it)]

ballpoint pen *noun* (*plural* **ballpoint pens**)
a pen with a tiny ball round which the ink flows.

ballroom *noun* (*plural* **ballrooms**)
a large room where dances are held.

balm *noun*
1 a sweet-scented ointment. 2 something that soothes you. [same origin as *balsam*]

balmy *adjective*
1 sweet-scented like balm. 2 soft and warm, *a balmy breeze.*

balsa *noun*
a kind of very lightweight wood. [Spanish, = raft (because balsa was used for building rafts and small boats)]

balsam *noun* (*plural* **balsams**)
1 a kind of sweet-smelling gum produced by certain trees. 2 a tree producing balsam. [from Latin *balsamum*]

balti *noun* (*plural* **baltis**)
a type of Pakistani curry, cooked in a bowl-shaped pan. [perhaps from *Baltistan*, a region in the Himalayas]

balustrade *noun* (*plural* **balustrades**)
a row of short posts or pillars that supports a rail or strip of stonework round a balcony or staircase. [from Italian *balustra* = pomegranate flower (because the pillars of a balustrade were the same shape as the flower)]

bamboo *noun* (*plural* **bamboos**)
1 a tall plant with hard hollow stems. 2 a stem of the bamboo plant. [via Dutch from Malay (a language spoken in Malaysia)]

bamboozle *verb* (**bamboozles, bamboozling, bamboozled**) (*informal*)
puzzle or trick someone. [origin unknown]

ban *verb* (**bans, banning, banned**)
forbid something officially.

ban *noun* (*plural* **bans**)
an order that bans something. [from Old English]

banal (*say* ban-**ahl**) *adjective*
ordinary and uninteresting. **banality** *noun* [from French]

banana *noun* (*plural* **bananas**)
a long curved fruit with a yellow or green skin. [via Spanish and Portuguese from Mande (a group of languages spoken in west Africa)]

band[1] *noun* (*plural* **bands**)
1 a strip or loop of something. 2 a range of values, wavelengths, etc. [via French from Germanic; related to *bind*]

band[2] *noun* (*plural* **bands**)
1 an organized group of people doing something together, *a band of robbers.*
2 a group of people playing music together.

band *verb* (**bands, banding, banded**)
form an organized group. [from French]

bandage *noun* (*plural* **bandages**)
a strip of material for binding up a wound.

bandage *verb* [French; related to *band*[1]]

bandit *noun* (*plural* **bandits**)
a member of a gang of robbers who attack travellers. [from Latin *bannire* = banish]

bandstand *noun* (*plural* **bandstands**)
a platform for a band playing music outdoors, usually in a park.

bandwagon *noun*
jump or **climb on the bandwagon** join other people in something that is successful.

bandy[1] *adjective*
having legs that curve outwards at the knees. [from *bandy* = a kind of hockey stick]

bandy[2] *verb* (**bandies, bandying, bandied**)
if a word or story is bandied about, it is mentioned or told by a lot of different people. [probably from French]

bane *noun*
a cause of trouble or worry etc., *Exams are the bane of our lives!* [from Old English]

bang *noun* (*plural* **bangs**)
1 a sudden loud noise like that of an explosion. 2 a sharp blow or knock.

bang *verb* (**bangs, banging, banged**)
1 hit or shut something noisily. 2 make a sudden loud noise.

bang *adverb*
1 with a bang; suddenly. 2 (*informal*) exactly, *bang in the middle.* [imitating the sound]

banger *noun* (*plural* **bangers**)
1 a firework that explodes noisily. 2 (*slang*) a sausage. 3 (*slang*) a noisy old car.

bangle *noun* (*plural* bangles)
a stiff bracelet. [from Hindi]

banish *verb* (banishes, banishing, banished)
1 punish a person by ordering them to leave a place. **2** if you banish doubts or fears, you drive them away.
banishment *noun*
[via French from Germanic; related to *ban*]

banisters *plural noun*
a handrail with upright supports beside a staircase. [a different spelling of *baluster*, related to *balustrade*]

banjo *noun* (*plural* banjos)
an instrument like a guitar with a round body. [a Black American word]

bank¹ *noun* (*plural* banks)
1 a slope. **2** a long piled-up mass of sand, snow, cloud, etc. **3** a row of lights or switches etc.
bank *verb* (banks, banking, banked)
1 build or form a bank. **2** tilt sideways while changing direction, *The plane banked as it prepared to land.*
[from Old Norse]

bank² *noun* (*plural* banks)
1 a business that looks after people's money. **2** a reserve supply, *a blood bank.*
bank *verb* (banks, banking, banked)
put money in a bank.
bank on rely on.
[from Italian]

banker *noun* (*plural* bankers)
a person who runs a bank.

bank holiday *noun* (*plural* bank holidays)
a public holiday, when banks are officially closed.

banknote *noun* (*plural* banknotes)
a piece of paper money issued by a bank.

bankrupt *adjective*
a person or business that is bankrupt is unable to pay debts. **bankruptcy** *noun*
[from *bank²* + Latin *ruptum* = broken]

banner *noun* (*plural* banners)
1 a flag. **2** a strip of cloth with a design or slogan on it, carried on a pole or two poles in a procession or demonstration.
[from Latin]

banns *plural noun*
an announcement in a church that the two people named are going to marry each other. [plural of *ban* = proclamation]

banquet *noun* (*plural* banquets)
a formal public meal. **banqueting** *noun*
[French, = little bench]

bantam *noun* (*plural* bantams)
a kind of small hen. [from *Bantam*, the name of a district of Java]

banter *noun*
playful teasing or joking. **banter** *verb*
[origin unknown]

Bantu *noun* (*plural* Bantu or Bantus)
1 a member of a group of central and southern African peoples. **2** the group of languages spoken by these peoples.
[the Bantu word for *people*]

bap *noun* (*plural* baps)
a soft flat bread roll. [origin unknown]

baptism *noun* (*plural* baptisms)
baptizing.

Baptist *noun* (*plural* Baptists)
a member of a group of Christians who believe that a person should not be baptized until he or she is old enough to understand what baptism means.

baptize *verb* (baptizes, baptizing, baptized)
receive a person into the Christian Church in a ceremony in which he or she is sprinkled with or dipped in water, and usually given a name or names.
[from Greek *baptizein* = to dip]

bar *noun* (*plural* bars)
1 a long piece of something hard, *a gold bar.* **2** a counter or room where refreshments, especially alcoholic drinks, are served. **3** a barrier or obstruction. **4** one of the small equal sections into which music is divided, *three beats to the bar.*
the Bar barristers.
bar *verb* (bars, barring, barred)
1 fasten something with a bar or bars. **2** block or obstruct, *A man with a dog barred the way.* **3** forbid or ban.
[from French]

barb *noun* (*plural* barbs)
the backward-pointing spike of a spear, arrow, or fish-hook, which makes the point stay in. [from Latin *barba* = beard]

barbarian *noun* (*plural* barbarians)
an uncivilized or brutal person. **barbaric** *adjective*, **barbarous** *adjective*, **barbarity** *noun*, **barbarism** *noun* [from Greek *barbaros* = babbling, not speaking Greek]

barbecue *noun* (*plural* barbecues)
1 a metal frame for grilling food over an open fire outdoors. 2 a party where food is cooked in this way.
barbecue *verb* (barbecues, barbecuing, barbecued)
cook food on a barbecue.
[via Spanish from Arawak (a South American language)]

barbed *adjective*
1 having a barb or barbs. 2 a barbed comment or remark is deliberately hurtful.

barbed wire *noun*
wire with small spikes in it, used to make fences.

barber *noun* (*plural* barbers)
a men's hairdresser.
[from Latin *barba* = beard]

bar chart *noun* (*plural* bar charts)
a diagram that shows amounts as bars of equal width but varying height.

bar code *noun* (*plural* bar codes)
a set of black lines that are printed on goods, library books, etc., and can be read by a computer to give information about the goods, books, etc.

bard *noun* (*plural* bards) (*formal*)
a poet or minstrel. [a Celtic word]

bare *adjective*
1 without clothing or covering. 2 empty, *The cupboard was bare.* 3 plain; without details, *the bare facts.* 4 only just enough, *the bare necessities of life.*
barely *adverb*, **bareness** *noun*
bare *verb* (bares, baring, bared)
uncover or reveal, *The dog bared its teeth in a snarl.* [from Old English]

bareback *adjective* & *adverb*
riding on a horse without a saddle.

barefaced *adjective*
shameless; bold and unconcealed, *He told a barefaced lie.*

bargain *noun* (*plural* bargains)
1 an agreement about buying or selling or exchanging something. 2 something that you buy cheaply.
bargain *verb* (bargains, bargaining, bargained)
argue over the price to be paid or what you will do in return for something.
bargain for be prepared for or expect, *He got more than he bargained for.*
[from French]

barge *noun* (*plural* barges)
a long flat-bottomed boat used on canals.
barge *verb* (barges, barging, barged)
push or knock against roughly.
barge in rush into a room rudely.
[from Latin *barca* = boat]

baritone *noun* (*plural* baritones)
a male singer with a voice between a tenor and a bass.
[from Greek *barys* = heavy, + *tone*]

barium (*say* bair-ee-um) *noun*
a soft silvery-white metal. [from Greek]

bark[1] *noun* (*plural* barks)
the short harsh sound made by a dog or fox. **bark** *verb* [from Old English *beorc*, imitating the sound]

bark[2] *noun*
the outer covering of a tree's branches or trunk. [from Old Norse]

barley *noun*
a cereal plant from which malt is made. [from Old English]

barley sugar *noun* (*plural* barley sugars)
a sweet made from boiled sugar.

bar mitzvah *noun* (*plural* bar mitzvahs)
a religious ceremony for Jewish boys aged 13. [Hebrew, = son of the commandment]

barmy *adjective* (*slang*)
crazy. [literally full of *barm* = yeast, froth]

barn *noun* (*plural* barns)
a farm building for storing hay or grain etc. **barnyard** *noun* [from Old English]

barnacle *noun* (*plural* **barnacles**)
a shellfish that attaches itself to rocks and the bottoms of ships. [from Latin]

barn dance *noun* (*plural* **barn dances**)
a kind of country dance; an informal gathering for dancing.

barometer (*say* ba-**rom**-it-er) *noun* (*plural* **barometers**)
an instrument that measures air pressure, used in forecasting the weather.
[from Greek *baros* = weight, + *meter*]

baron *noun* (*plural* **barons**)
1 a member of the lowest rank of noblemen. 2 a powerful owner of an industry or business, *a newspaper baron*.
barony *noun*, **baronial** (*say* ba-**roh**-nee-al) *adjective* [from Latin *baro* = man, warrior]

baroness *noun* (*plural* **baronesses**)
a female baron or a baron's wife.

baronet *noun* (*plural* **baronets**)
a nobleman ranking below a baron but above a knight. **baronetcy** *noun*
[same origin as *baron*]

baroque (*say* ba-**rok**) *noun*
an elaborately decorated style of architecture used in the 17th and 18th centuries. [from French]

barracks *noun*
a large building or group of buildings for soldiers to live in.
[via French from Spanish or Italian]

barrage (*say* ba-**rah**zh) *noun* (*plural* **barrages**)
1 a dam built across a river. 2 heavy gunfire. 3 a large amount of something, *a barrage of questions*.
[from French; related to *bar*]

barrel *noun* (*plural* **barrels**)
1 a large rounded container with flat ends. 2 the metal tube of a gun, through which the shot is fired.
[from Latin *barriculus* = a small cask]

barrel organ *noun* (*plural* **barrel organs**)
a musical instrument which you play by turning a handle.

barren *adjective*
1 a barren woman is not able to have children. 2 barren land is not fertile.
barrenness *noun* [from old French]

barricade *noun* (*plural* **barricades**)
a barrier, especially one put up hastily across a street or door.
barricade *verb* (**barricades, barricading, barricaded**)
block a street or door with a barricade.
[French, from Spanish *barrica* = barrel (because barrels were sometimes used to build barricades)]

barrier *noun* (*plural* **barriers**)
something that prevents people or things from getting past; an obstacle.
[from old French; related to *bar*]

barrister *noun* (*plural* **barristers**)
a lawyer who represents people in the higher lawcourts.
[originally one who was allowed to pass the *bar*, a partition separating qualified lawyers from students]

barrow[1] *noun* (*plural* **barrows**)
1 a wheelbarrow. 2 a small cart that is pushed or pulled by hand.
[from Old English; related to *bear*[2]]

barrow[2] *noun* (*plural* **barrows**)
a mound of earth over a prehistoric grave.
[from Old English; related to *burrow*]

barter *verb* (**barters, bartering, bartered**)
trade by exchanging goods for other goods, not for money.

USAGE: This word does not mean 'to bargain'.

barter *noun* (*plural* **barters**)
the system of bartering.
[probably from old French]

basalt (*say* **bas**-awlt) *noun*
a kind of dark volcanic rock. [from Greek]

base[1] *noun* (*plural* **bases**)
1 the lowest part of something; the part on which a thing stands. 2 a starting point or foundation; a basis. 3 a headquarters.
4 each of the four corners that must be reached by a runner in baseball. 5 a substance that can combine with an acid to form a salt. 6 the number in terms of which

other numbers can be expressed in a number system. 10 is the base of the decimal system and 2 is the base of the binary system.

base *verb* (bases, basing, based)
use something as a starting point or foundation, *The story is based on facts.* [same origin as *basis*]

base² *adjective*
1 dishonourable, *base motives.* 2 not of great value, *base metals.* **basely** *adverb*, **baseness** *noun* [from French *bas* = low]

baseball *noun* (*plural* baseballs)
1 an American ball game rather like rounders. 2 the ball used in this game.

basement *noun* (*plural* basements)
a room or rooms below ground level. [probably via Dutch from Italian; related to *base¹*]

bash *verb* (bashes, bashing, bashed)
hit hard.
bash *noun* (*plural* bashes)
1 a hard hit. 2 (*informal*) a try, *Have a bash at it.* [imitating the sound]

bashful *adjective*
shy and self-conscious. **bashfully** *adverb* [from *abash*]

Basic *noun*
a computer language that is designed to be easy to learn.
[from the initials of *Beginners' all-purpose symbolic instruction code*]

basic *adjective*
forming a basis or starting point; very important, *Bread is a basic food.* [from *base¹*]

basically *adverb*
at the simplest or most fundamental level.

basilica (*say* ba-**zil**-ik-a) *noun* (*plural* basilicas)
a large oblong church with two rows of columns and an apse at one end. [Latin, = royal palace]

basilisk (*say* **baz**-il-isk) *noun* (*plural* basilisks)
a mythical reptile that was said to be able to kill people just by looking at them. [from Greek *basilikos* = a kind of snake]

basin *noun* (*plural* basins)
1 a deep bowl. 2 a washbasin. 3 a sheltered area of water for mooring boats. 4 the area from which water drains into a river, *the Amazon basin.* [from old French]

basis *noun* (*plural* bases)
something to start from or add to; the main principle or ingredient.
[Greek, = step, stepping]

bask *verb* (basks, basking, basked)
sit or lie comfortably warming yourself in the sun. [origin unknown]

basket *noun* (*plural* baskets)
a container for holding or carrying things, made of strips of flexible material or wire woven together. [probably from Latin]

basketball *noun* (*plural* basketballs)
1 a game in which goals are scored by putting a ball through high nets. 2 the ball used in this game.

bass¹ (*say* bayss) *adjective*
deep-sounding; the bass part of a piece of music is the lowest part.
bass *noun* (*plural* basses)
1 a male singer with a very deep voice. 2 a bass instrument or part. [from *base²* = low]

bass² (*say* bas) *noun* (*plural* bass)
a fish of the perch family.
[from Old English]

basset *noun* (*plural* bassets)
a short-legged dog used for hunting hares. [same origin as *base²*]

bassoon *noun* (*plural* bassoons)
a bass woodwind instrument.
[from Italian *basso* = low]

bastard *noun* (*plural* bastards)
1 (*old use*) an illegitimate child. 2 (*slang*) an unpleasant or difficult person or thing. **bastardy** *noun* [from old French]

baste *verb* (bastes, basting, basted)
moisten meat with fat while it is cooking. [origin unknown]

bastion *noun* (*plural* bastions)
1 a projecting part of a fortified building. 2 something that protects a belief or way of life. [from Italian *bastire* = to build]

bat¹ *noun* (*plural* bats)
1 a shaped piece of wood used to hit the ball in cricket, baseball, etc. 2 a batsman, *their opening bat.*
off your own bat without help from other people.
bat *verb* (bats, batting, batted)
use a bat in cricket etc. [from Old English]

bat² *noun* (*plural* bats)
a flying animal that looks like a mouse with wings.
[from a Scandinavian language]

batch *noun* (*plural* batches)
a set of things or people dealt with together.
[from Old English; related to *bake*]

bated *adjective*
with bated breath anxiously; hardly daring to speak.
[from *abate*]

bath *noun* (*plural* baths)
1 washing your whole body while sitting in water. 2 a large container for water in which to wash your whole body; this water, *Your bath is getting cold.* 3 a liquid in which something is placed, *an acid bath.*
bath *verb* (baths, bathing, bathed)
wash in a bath.
[from Old English; related to *bathe*]

bathe *verb* (bathes, bathing, bathed)
1 go swimming. 2 wash something gently.
bathe *noun*, **bather** *noun*, **bathing suit** *noun*
[from Old English; related to *bath*]

bathos *noun*
a sudden change from a serious subject or tone to a ridiculous or trivial one.
[Greek, = depth]

bathroom *noun* (*plural* bathrooms)
a room containing a bath.

baths *plural noun*
1 a building with rooms where people can bath. 2 a public swimming pool.

baton *noun* (*plural* batons)
a short stick, e.g. one used to conduct an orchestra or in a relay race. [from French]

batsman *noun* (*plural* batsmen)
a player who uses a bat in cricket etc.

battalion *noun* (*plural* battalions)
an army unit containing two or more companies. [from Italian *battaglia* = battle]

batten *noun* (*plural* battens)
a strip of wood or metal that holds something in place.
batten *verb* (battens, battening, battened)
fasten something down firmly.
[from old French]

batter *verb* (batters, battering, battered)
hit hard and often.
batter *noun* (*plural* batters)
1 a beaten mixture of flour, eggs, and milk, used for making pancakes etc. 2 a batsman in baseball. [from Latin *battuere* = to beat]

battering ram *noun* (*plural* battering rams)
a heavy pole that is used to break down walls or gates.

battery *noun* (*plural* batteries)
1 a device for storing and supplying electricity. 2 a set of similar pieces of equipment; a group of large guns. 3 a series of cages in which poultry or animals are kept close together, *battery farming.*
[same origin as *batter*]

battle *noun* (*plural* battles)
1 a fight between two armies. 2 a struggle.
battlefield *noun*, **battleground** *noun*
battle *verb* (battles, battling, battled)
fight or struggle. [same origin as *batter*]

battlements *plural noun*
the top of a castle wall, often with gaps from which the defenders could fire at the enemy.

battleship *noun* (*plural* battleships)
a heavily armed warship.

batty *adjective* (*slang*)
crazy.
[from the phrase *bats in the belfry* = crazy]

bauble *noun* (*plural* baubles)
a bright, showy, but valueless ornament.
[from old French *baubel* = toy]

baulk *verb* (baulks, baulking, baulked)
1 stop and refuse to go on, *The horse baulked at the fence.* 2 frustrate; prevent from doing or getting something.
[from Old Norse]

bauxite *noun*
the clay-like substance from which aluminium is obtained. [from *Les Baux*, a place in France, where it was first found]

bawdy *adjective* (**bawdier**, **bawdiest**)
referring to sex in a humorous way.
bawdiness *noun*
[from *bawd* = a brothel-keeper]

bawl *verb* (**bawls**, **bawling**, **bawled**)
1 shout. 2 cry noisily.
[imitating the sound]

bay¹ *noun* (*plural* **bays**)
a place where the shore curves inwards.
[from Spanish]

bay² *noun* (*plural* **bays**)
an alcove. [from Latin *batare* = gape]

bay³ *noun* (*plural* **bays**)
a kind of laurel tree. Bay leaves are used as a flavouring in cooking. [originally = laurel berry, from Latin *bacca* = berry]

bay⁴ *noun* (*plural* **bays**)
the long deep cry of a hunting hound or other large dog.
at bay cornered but defiantly facing attackers, *a stag at bay*.
keep at bay prevent something from coming near or causing harm, *We need laws to keep poverty at bay*.
[from French]

bay⁵ *adjective*
reddish-brown. [from Latin *badius*]

bayonet *noun* (*plural* **bayonets**)
a blade that can be fixed to the end of a rifle and used for stabbing. [named after *Bayonne* in France, where it was first used]

bay window *noun* (*plural* **bay windows**)
a window that sticks out from the main wall of a house. [from *bay*²]

bazaar *noun* (*plural* **bazaars**)
1 a market place in an Eastern country.
2 a sale to raise money for a charity etc.
[from Persian *bazar* = market]

bazooka *noun* (*plural* **bazookas**)
a portable weapon for firing anti-tank rockets.
[the word originally meant a musical instrument rather like a trombone]

BBC *abbreviation*
British Broadcasting Corporation.

BC *abbreviation*
before Christ (used with dates counting back from the birth of Jesus Christ).

be *verb* (**am**, **are**, **is**; **was**, **were**; **being**, **been**)
1 exist; occupy a position, *The shop is on the corner*. 2 happen; take place, *The wedding is tomorrow*. This verb is also used 1 to join subject and complement (*He is my teacher*), 2 to form parts of other verbs (*It is raining. He was killed*).
have been have gone to or come to as a visitor etc., *We have been to Rome*.
[from Old English]

be- *prefix*
used to form verbs (as in *befriend*, *belittle*) or strengthen their meaning (as in *begrudge*). [from Old English]

beach *noun* (*plural* **beaches**)
the part of the seashore nearest to the water. [probably from Old English]

beacon *noun* (*plural* **beacons**)
a light or fire used as a signal.
[from Old English; related to *beckon*]

bead *noun* (*plural* **beads**)
1 a small piece of a hard substance with a hole in it for threading with others on a string or wire, e.g. to make a necklace.
2 a drop of liquid, *a bead of sweat*.
[from Old English *gebed* = prayer (because people kept count of the prayers they said by moving the beads on a rosary)]

beadle *noun* (*plural* **beadles**)
1 an official with ceremonial duties in a church or college. 2 (*old use*) an official of a parish. [from Old English]

beady *adjective*
(of eyes) small and bright.

beagle *noun* (*plural* **beagles**)
a small hound used for hunting hares.
beagling *noun*
[from old French; related to *bay*⁴]

beak *noun* (*plural* **beaks**)
the hard horny part of a bird's mouth.
[from Latin *beccus*, of Celtic origin]

beaker *noun* (*plural* beakers)
1 a tall drinking-mug, often without a handle. 2 a glass container used for pouring liquids in a laboratory.
[from Old Norse]

beam *noun* (*plural* beams)
1 a long thick bar of wood or metal. 2 a ray or stream of light or other radiation. 3 a happy smile.
beam *verb* (beams, beaming, beamed)
1 smile happily. 2 send out a beam of light or other radiation. [from Old English]

bean *noun* (*plural* beans)
1 a kind of plant with seeds growing in pods. 2 its seed or pod eaten as food. 3 the seed of coffee. [from Old English]

bean sprout *noun* (*plural* bean sprouts)
a sprout of a bean seed that can be eaten either cooked or raw.

bear¹ *noun* (*plural* bears)
a large heavy animal with thick fur and large teeth and claws.
[from Old English *bera*]

bear² *verb* (bears, bearing, bore, borne)
1 carry or support. 2 have a mark etc., *She still bears the scar.* 3 endure or stand, *I can't bear this pain.* 4 produce or give birth to, *She bore him two sons.* **bearer** *noun*
bear out support or confirm.
[from Old English *beran*]

bearable *adjective*
if something is bearable, you are able to endure or stand it.

beard *noun* (*plural* beards)
hair on a man's chin. **bearded** *adjective*
beard *verb* (beards, bearding, bearded)
come face to face with a person and challenge him or her boldly.
[from Old English; the verb originally = to grab someone's beard]

bearing *noun* (*plural* bearings)
1 the way a person stands, walks, behaves, etc. 2 relevance, *My friendship with Tom has no bearing on his selection for the team.* 3 the direction or position of one thing in relation to another. 4 a device for preventing friction in a machine, *ball-bearings.*

get your bearings work out where you are in relation to things.
[from *bear*²]

beast *noun* (*plural* beasts)
1 any large four-footed animal. 2 (*informal*) a cruel or vicious person.
beastly *adjective* [from Latin *bestia*]

beat *verb* (beats, beating, beat, beaten)
1 hit often, especially with a stick. 2 shape or flatten something by beating it. 3 stir vigorously. 4 make repeated movements, *The heart beats.* 5 do better than somebody; overcome. **beater** *noun*
beat *noun* (*plural* beats)
1 a regular rhythm or stroke, *the beat of your heart.* 2 emphasis in rhythm; the strong rhythm of pop music. 3 a policeman's regular route.
[from Old English]

beatific (*say* bee-a-**tif**-ik) *adjective*
showing great happiness, *a beatific smile.*
[same origin as *beatify*]

beatify (*say* bee-**at**-i-fy) *verb* (beatifies, beatifying, beatified)
(in the Roman Catholic Church) honour a person who has died by declaring that he or she is a very holy person, as a step towards declaring that person a saint.
beatification *noun*
[from Latin *beatus* = blessed]

beautiful *adjective*
attractive to your senses or your mind.
beautifully *adverb*

beautify *verb* (beautifies, beautifying, beautified)
make someone beautiful.
beautification *noun*

beauty *noun* (*plural* beauties)
1 a quality that gives pleasure to your senses or your mind. 2 a person or thing that has beauty. 3 an excellent example of something. [from old French]

beaver *noun* (*plural* beavers)
an animal with soft brown fur and strong teeth; it builds its home in a deep pool which it makes by damming a stream.
beaver *verb* (beavers, beavering, beavered)
work hard, *beavering away.*
[from Old English]

becalmed *adjective*
(in sailing) unable to move because there is
no wind.

because *conjunction*
for the reason that.
because of for the reason of, *He limped
because of his bad leg.*
[from *by* + *cause*]

beck *noun*
at someone's beck and call always ready and
waiting to do what he or she asks.
[from *beckon*]

beckon *verb* (beckons, beckoning,
beckoned)
make a sign to a person asking him or her
to come.
[from Old English; related to *beacon*]

become *verb* (becomes, becoming, became,
become)
1 come or grow to be; begin to be, *It became
dark.* **2** be suitable for; make a person look
attractive.
become of happen to, *What became of it?*
[from Old English]

bed *noun* (*plural* beds)
1 a piece of furniture that you sleep or rest
on, especially one with a mattress and
coverings. **2** a piece of a garden where
plants are grown. **3** the bottom of the sea or
of a river. **4** a flat base; a foundation. **5** a
layer of rock or soil. [from Old English]

bedclothes *plural noun*
sheets, blankets, etc.

bedding *noun*
mattresses and bedclothes.

bedlam *noun*
uproar. [from 'Bedlam', the popular name
of the Hospital of St Mary of Bethlehem, a
London mental hospital in the 14th
century]

Bedouin (*say* bed-oo-in) *noun* (*plural*
Bedouin)
a member of an Arab people living in tents
in the desert.
[from Arabic *badawi* = desert-dweller]

bedpan *noun* (*plural* bedpans)
a container for use as a lavatory by a
bedridden person.

bedraggled (*say* bid-**rag**-eld) *adjective*
very untidy; wet and dirty.
[from *be-* + *draggle* = make dirty]

bedridden *adjective*
too weak or ill to get out of bed.

bedrock *noun*
solid rock beneath soil.

bedroom *noun* (*plural* bedrooms)
a room for sleeping in.

bedsitter *noun* (*plural* bedsitters)
a room used for both living and sleeping in.

bedspread *noun* (*plural* bedspreads)
a covering spread over a bed during the
day.

bedstead *noun* (*plural* bedsteads)
the framework of a bed.
[originally the place where a bed stood;
from *bed* + *stead* = place]

bedtime *noun* (*plural* bedtimes)
the time for going to bed.

bee *noun* (*plural* bees)
a stinging insect with four wings that
makes honey. [from Old English]

beech *noun* (*plural* beeches)
a tree with smooth bark and glossy leaves.
[from Old English]

beef *noun*
meat from an ox, bull, or cow.
[from old French]

beefeater *noun* (*plural* beefeaters)
a guard at the Tower of London, wearing
Tudor dress as uniform. [originally a
scornful word for a fat, lazy servant]

beefy *adjective*
having a solid muscular body.
beefiness *noun*

beehive *noun* (*plural* beehives)
a box or other container for bees to live in.

beeline *noun*
make a beeline for go straight or quickly
towards something.
[because a bee was believed to fly in a
straight line back to its hive]

beer *noun* (*plural* beers)
an alcoholic drink made from malt and
hops. **beery** *adjective*
[from Old English]

beeswax *noun*
a yellow substance produced by bees, used
for polishing wood.

beet *noun* (*plural* beet or beets)
a plant with a thick root used as a
vegetable or for making sugar.
[from Old English]

beetle *noun* (*plural* beetles)
an insect with hard shiny wing covers.
[from Old English; related to *bite*]

beetling *adjective*
prominent; overhanging, *beetling brows*.

beetroot *noun* (*plural* beetroot)
the dark red root of beet used as a
vegetable.

befall *verb* (befalls, befalling, befell, befallen)
(*formal*)
happen to someone.
[from *be-* + *fall* = happen]

befitting *adjective*
suitable.

before *adverb*
at an earlier time, *Have you been here
before?*
before *preposition* & *conjunction*
1 earlier than, *I was here before you!*
2 in front of, *He came before the judge.*
[from Old English]

beforehand *adverb*
earlier; in readiness. [from *before* + *hand*
(with the idea of your hand doing
something before someone else's does)]

befriend *verb* (befriends, befriending,
befriended)
make friends with someone.

beg *verb* (begs, begging, begged)
1 ask to be given money, food, etc. 2 ask
earnestly or humbly or formally.
beg the question argue in an illogical way
by relying on the result that you are trying
to prove.
go begging be available.

I beg your pardon I apologize; I did not hear
what you said.
[probably from Old English]

beget *verb* (begets, begetting, begot,
begotten) (*old use*)
1 be the father of someone. 2 produce,
War begets misery.
[from Old English]

beggar *noun* (*plural* beggars)
1 a person who lives by begging.
2 (*informal*) a person, *You lucky beggar!*
beggary *noun*

begin *verb* (begins, beginning, began,
begun)
1 do the earliest or first part of something;
start speaking. 2 come into existence, *The
problem began last year.* 3 have something
as its first part, *The word begins with B.*
[from Old English]

beginner *noun* (*plural* beginners)
a person who is just beginning to learn a
subject.

begone *verb* (*old use*)
go away immediately, *Begone dull care!*
[from *be* + *gone*]

begonia (*say* big-oh-nee-a) *noun* (*plural*
begonias)
a garden plant with brightly coloured
flowers.
[named after Michel *Bégon*, a
Frenchman who encouraged the study
of plants]

begot *past tense* of **beget**.

begrudge *verb* (begrudges, begrudging,
begrudged)
resent having to give or allow something;
grudge.

beguile (*say* big I'll) *verb* (begulles,
beguiling, beguiled)
1 amuse or fascinate. 2 deceive.
[from *be-* + *guile*]

behalf *noun*
on behalf of for the benefit of someone else.

on my behalf for me.
[from an old phrase *bi halve him* = on his side]

USAGE: Do not use *on behalf of* (= for someone else) when you mean *on the part of* (= by someone). For example, do not say: *This was the worst performance on behalf of Arsenal that I can remember*.

behave *verb* (behaves, behaving, behaved)
1 act in a particular way, *They behaved badly*. 2 show good manners, *Behave yourself!* **behaviour** *noun*, **behavioural** *adjective* [from *be-* + *have*]

behead *verb* (beheads, beheading, beheaded)
cut the head off a person or thing; execute a person in this way. [from Old English]

behest *noun* (*formal*)
at a person's behest done because they have asked or commanded you to do it, *At Laura's behest we took the notice down from the window*.
[from Old English]

behind *adverb*
1 at or to the back; at a place people have left, *Don't leave it behind*. 2 not making good progress; late, *I'm behind with my rent*.
behind *preposition*
1 at or to the back of; on the further side of. 2 having made less progress than, *He is behind the others in French*. 3 supporting; causing, *What is behind all this trouble?*
behind a person's back kept secret from him or her deceitfully.
behind the times out of date.
behind *noun* (*plural* behinds) (*informal*)
a person's bottom. [from Old English]

behindhand *adverb* & *adjective*
1 late. 2 out of date. [from *behind* + *hand*, on the pattern of *beforehand*]

behold *verb* (beholds, beholding, beheld) (*old use*)
see. **beholder** *noun* [from Old English]

behove *verb* (behoves, behoving, behoved)
be a person's duty, *It behoves you to be loyal*. [from Old English]

beige (*say* bayzh) *noun* & *adjective*
a very light brown colour. [French]

being *noun* (*plural* beings)
1 existence. 2 a creature.

belated *adjective*
coming very late or too late.
belatedly *adverb*

belay *verb* (belays, belaying, belayed)
fasten a rope by winding it round a peg or spike. [from Dutch]

belch *verb* (belches, belching, belched)
1 send out wind from your stomach through your mouth noisily. 2 send out fire or smoke etc. from an opening.
belch *noun* [from Old English]

beleaguered (*say* bil-eeg-erd) *adjective*
besieged or oppressed.
[from Dutch *belegeren* = camp round]

belfry *noun* (*plural* belfries)
a tower or part of a tower in which bells hang. [from old French]

belief *noun* (*plural* beliefs)
1 believing. 2 something a person believes.
[from Old English]

believe *verb* (believes, believing, believed)
think that something is true or that someone is telling the truth. **believable** *adjective*, **believer** *noun*
believe in think that something exists or is good or can be relied on.
[from Old English]

belittle *verb* (belittles, belittling, belittled)
make something seem of little value, *Do not belittle their success*. **belittlement** *noun*

bell *noun* (*plural* bells)
1 a cup-shaped metal instrument that makes a ringing sound when struck by the clapper hanging inside it. 2 any device that makes a ringing or buzzing sound to attract attention. 3 a bell-shaped object.
[from Old English]

belle *noun* (*plural* belles)
a beautiful woman. [French]

bellicose (*say* bel-ik-ohs) *adjective*
eager to fight. [from Latin *bellum* = war]

belligerent (*say* bil-ij-er-ent) *adjective*
1 aggressive; eager to fight. 2 fighting;
engaged in a war. **belligerently** *adverb*,
belligerence *noun* [from Latin *bellum* = war
+ *gerens* = waging]

bellow *noun* (*plural* bellows)
1 the loud deep sound made by a bull or
other large animal. 2 a deep shout.
bellow *verb* (bellows, bellowing, bellowed)
give a deep shout.
[origin unknown]

bellows *plural noun*
a device for pumping air into a fire, organ-
pipes, etc. [from Old English]

belly *noun* (*plural* bellies)
the abdomen; the stomach.
[from Old English]

belong *verb* (belongs, belonging, belonged)
have a proper place, *The pans belong in the
kitchen.*
belong to be the property of; be a member
of, *We belong to the same club.*
[from *be-* + *long* = owing to, because of]

belongings *plural noun*
a person's possessions.

beloved *adjective*
dearly loved.

below *adverb*
at or to a lower position; underneath,
There's fire down below.
below *preposition*
lower than; under, *The temperature was ten
degrees below zero.*

belt *noun* (*plural* belts)
1 a strip of cloth or leather etc. worn round
the waist. 2 a band of flexible material used
in machinery. 3 a long narrow area, *a belt
of rain.*
belt *verb* (belts, belting, belted)
1 put a belt round something. 2 (*slang*) hit
or beat. 3 (*slang*) rush along.
[via Old English from Latin]

bemused *adjective*
1 puzzled or confused. 2 lost in thought.
[from *be-* + *muse*, in the sense 'wonder']

bench *noun* (*plural* benches)
1 a long seat. 2 a long table for working at.
3 the seat where judges or magistrates sit;
the judges or magistrates hearing a
lawsuit. [from Old English]

bend *verb* (bends, bending, bent)
1 change from being straight. 2 turn
downwards; stoop, *She bent to pick it up.*
bend *noun* (*plural* bends)
a place where something bends; a curve or
turn, *a bend in the road.*
[from Old English]

bene- (*say* ben-ee) *prefix*
well (as in *benefit, benevolent*).
[from Latin *bene* = well]

beneath *preposition*
1 under. 2 unworthy of, *Cheating is
beneath you.*
beneath *adverb*
underneath. [from Old English]

benediction *noun* (*plural* benedictions)
a blessing.
[from *bene-* + Latin *dicere* = to say]

benefactor *noun* (*plural* benefactors)
a person who gives money or other help.
[from *bene-* + Latin *factor* = doer]

beneficial *adjective*
having a good or helpful effect;
advantageous.
[from Latin *beneficium* = favour, support]

beneficiary (*say* ben-if-ish-er-ee) *noun*
(*plural* beneficiaries)
a person who receives benefits, especially
from a will. [same origin as *beneficial*]

benefit *noun* (*plural* benefits)
1 something that is helpful or profitable.
2 a payment to which a person is entitled
from government funds or from an
insurance policy.
benefit *verb* (benefits, benefiting, benefited)
1 do good to a person or thing. 2 receive a
benefit. [from *bene-* + Latin *facere* = do]

benevolent *adjective*
1 kind and helpful. 2 formed for charitable
purposes, *a benevolent fund.*
benevolently *adverb*, **benevolence** *noun*
[from *bene-* + Latin *volens* = wishing]

benign (*say* bin-I'n) *adjective*
1 kindly. 2 favourable. 3 (of a disease)
mild, not malignant. **benignly** *adverb*
[from Latin *benignus* = kind-hearted]

benignant (*say* bin-ig-nant) *adjective*
kindly. [same origin as *benign*]

benison *noun* (*plural* benisons) (*old use*)
a blessing. [from French]

bent *adjective*
curved or crooked.
bent on intending to do something.
bent *noun*
a talent for something.

benzene *noun*
a substance obtained from coal tar and
used as a solvent, motor fuel, and in the
manufacture of plastics. [via French from
Arabic *lubanjawi* = incense from Sumatra]

benzine *noun*
a spirit obtained from petroleum and used
in dry cleaning. [same origin as *benzene*]

bequeath *verb* (**bequeaths, bequeathing,
bequeathed**)
leave something to a person, especially in a
will. [from *be-* + Old English *cwethan* = say]

bequest *noun* (*plural* bequests)
something left to a person, especially in a
will. [from *be-* + Old English *cwiss* = saying,
a statement]

bereaved *adjective*
deprived of a relative or friend who has
died. **bereavement** *noun* [from *be-* + an old
word *reave* = take forcibly]

bereft *adjective*
deprived of something.
[old past participle of *bereave*]

beret (*say* bair-ay) *noun* (*plural* berets)
a round flat cap. [from French]

beriberi (*say* berry-berry) *noun*
a tropical disease caused by a vitamin
deficiency. [from Sinhalese (a language
spoken in Sri Lanka)]

berry *noun* (*plural* berries)
any small round juicy fruit without a
stone. [from Old English]

berserk (*say* ber-serk) *adjective*
go berserk become uncontrollably violent.
[from Icelandic *berserkr* = wild warrior,
from *ber-* = bear + *serkr* = coat]

berth *noun* (*plural* berths)
1 a sleeping place on a ship or train.
2 a place where a ship can moor.
give a wide berth keep at a safe distance
from a person or thing.
berth *verb* (**berths, berthing, berthed**)
moor in a berth. [from *bear²*]

beryl *noun* (*plural* beryls)
a pale-green precious stone. [from French]

beseech *verb* (**beseeches, beseeching,
beseeched** or **besought**)
ask earnestly; implore. [from *be-* + *seek*]

beset *verb* (**besets, besetting, beset**)
attack from all sides, *They are beset with
problems.* [from Old English]

beside *preposition*
1 by the side of; near. 2 compared with.
be beside himself or **herself** etc. be very
excited or upset.
[from Old English *be sidan* = by the side]

besides *preposition & adverb*
in addition to; also, *Who came besides you?
And besides, it's the wrong colour.*
[same origin as *beside*]

besiege *verb* (**besieges, besieging, besieged**)
1 surround a place in order to capture it.
2 crowd round, *Fans besieged the singer
after the concert.*

besotted *adjective*
too fond of something; fond in a silly way.
[from *be-* + *sot* = make stupid]

besought *past tense* of **beseech**.

best *adjective*
most excellent.
best *adverb*
1 in the best way; most. 2 most usefully;
most wisely, *We had best go.*
[from Old English]

bestial (*say* best-ee-al) *adjective*
to do with or like a beast. **bestiality** *noun*
[from Latin *bestia* = beast]

best man *noun*
the bridegroom's chief attendant at a wedding.

bestow *verb* (bestows, bestowing, bestowed)
present to someone. **bestowal** *noun*
[from *be-* + *stow*]

best-seller *noun* (*plural* best-sellers)
a book sold in large numbers.

bet *noun* (*plural* bets)
1 an agreement that you will pay money etc. if you are wrong in forecasting the result of a race etc. 2 the money that you agree to pay in this way.
bet *verb* (bets, betting, bet or betted)
1 make a bet. 2 (*informal*) think most likely; predict, *I bet he will forget.*
[origin unknown]

beta (*say* beet-a) *noun*
the second letter of the Greek alphabet, = b.

bête noire (*say* bayt nwahr) *noun*
a person or thing you greatly dislike.
[French, = black beast]

betide *verb*
woe betide you trouble will come to you.
[from *be-* + Old English *tidan* = happen]

betoken *verb* (betokens, betokening, betokened)
be a sign of. [from Old English]

betray *verb* (betrays, betraying, betrayed)
1 be disloyal to a person or country etc.
2 reveal something that should have been kept secret. **betrayal** *noun*, **betrayer** *noun*
[from *be-* + Latin *tradere* = deliver]

betrothed *adjective* (*formal*)
engaged to be married. **betroth** *verb*,
betrothal *noun* [from *be-* + *troth*]

better *adjective*
1 more excellent; more satisfactory.
2 recovered from illness.
better *adverb*
1 in a better way; more. 2 more usefully; more wisely, *We had better go.*
better *verb* (betters, bettering, bettered)
1 improve something. 2 do better than.
betterment *noun* [from Old English]

between *preposition & adverb*
1 within two or more given limits, *between the walls.* 2 connecting two or more people, places, or things, *The train runs between London and Glasgow.* 3 shared by, *Divide this money between you.* 4 separating; comparing, *Can you tell the difference between them?* [from Old English]

USAGE: The preposition *between* should be followed by the object form of the pronoun (*me*, *her*, *him*, *them*, or *us*). The expression 'between you and I' is incorrect; say *between you and me.*

betwixt *preposition & adverb* (*old use*)
between. [from Old English]

bevel *verb* (bevels, bevelling, bevelled)
give a sloping edge to something.
[from old French]

beverage *noun* (*plural* beverages)
any kind of drink. [from old French]

bevy *noun* (*plural* bevies)
a large group. [origin unknown]

bewail *verb* (bewails, bewailing, bewailed)
mourn for something.

beware *verb*
be careful, *Beware of pickpockets.*
[from *be-* + *ware* = wary]

bewilder *verb* (bewilders, bewildering, bewildered)
puzzle someone hopelessly. **bewilderment** *noun* [from *be-* + an old word *wilder* = lose your way]

bewitch *verb* (bewitches, bewitching, bewitched)
1 put a magic spell on someone. 2 delight someone very much.
[from *be-* + *witch* = put under a spell]

beyond *preposition & adverb*
1 further than; further on, *Don't go beyond the fence.* 2 outside the range of; too difficult for, *The problem is beyond me.*
[from Old English]

Bhagavadgita *noun*
the most famous book of the Hindu religion. [Sanskrit, = Song of the Lord]

bhangra *noun*
a style of music that combines traditional Punjabi music with rock music. [from Punjabi (a language spoken in the Punjab)]

bi- *prefix*
1 two (as in *bicycle*). 2 twice (as in *biannual*). [from Latin *bis* = twice]

biannual *adjective*
happening twice a year. **biannually** *adverb*

USAGE: Do not confuse this word with *biennial*.

bias *noun* (*plural* **biases**)
1 a feeling or influence for or against someone or something; a prejudice. 2 a tendency to swerve. 3 a slanting direction. [from old French]

biased *adjective*
prejudiced.

bib *noun* (*plural* **bibs**)
1 a cloth or covering put under a baby's chin during meals. 2 the part of an apron above the waist.
[probably from Latin *bibere* = to drink]

Bible *noun* (*plural* **Bibles**)
the sacred book of the Jews (the Old Testament) and of the Christians (the Old and New Testament). [from Greek *biblia* = books (originally = rolls of papyrus from Byblos, a port now in Lebanon)]

biblical *adjective*
to do with or in the Bible.

bibliography (*say* bib-lee-**og**-ra-fee) *noun* (*plural* **bibliographies**)
1 a list of books about a subject or by a particular author. 2 the study of books and their history. **bibliographical** *adjective*
[from Greek *biblion* = book, + *-graphy*]

bicarbonate *noun*
a kind of carbonate. [from *bi-* + *carbonate*]

bicentenary (*say* by-sen-**teen**-er-ee) *noun* (*plural* **bicentenaries**)
a 200th anniversary.
bicentennial (*say* by-sen-**ten**-ee-al) *adjective*
[from *bi-* + *centenary*]

biceps (*say* by-seps) *noun* (*plural* **biceps**)
the large muscle at the front of the arm above the elbow.
[Latin, = two-headed (because its end is attached at two points)]

bicker *verb* (**bickers, bickering, bickered**)
quarrel over unimportant things; squabble.
[origin unknown]

bicuspid *noun* (*plural* **bicuspids**)
a tooth with two points.
[from *bi-* + Latin *cuspis* = sharp point]

bicycle *noun* (*plural* **bicycles**)
a two-wheeled vehicle driven by pedals.
bicyclist *noun*
[from *bi-* + Greek *kyklos* = circle, wheel]

bid *noun* (*plural* **bids**)
1 the offer of an amount you are willing to pay for something, especially at an auction. 2 an attempt.

bid *verb* (**bids, bidding, bid**)
make a bid. **bidder** *noun*

bid *verb* (**bids, bidding, bid** (or *old use* **bade**), **bid** or **bidden**)
1 command, *Do as you are bid* or *bidden*. 2 say as a greeting or farewell, *bidding them good night*.
[from two Old English words; *biddan* = to ask, and *beodan* = to announce or command]

bidding *noun*
if you do someone's bidding, you do what they tell you to do.

bide *verb* (**bides, biding, bided**)
if you bide your time, you wait for the right time to do something.
[from Old English]

bidet (*say* bee-day) *noun* (*plural* **bidets**)
a low washbasin to sit on for washing the lower part of the body. [from French *bidet* = a pony (because you sit astride it)]

biennial (*say* by-en-ee-al) *adjective*
1 lasting for two years. 2 happening once every two years. **biennially** *adverb*

biennial *noun* (*plural* **biennials**)
a plant that lives for two years, flowering
and dying in the second year.
[from Latin *biennis* = of two years]

USAGE: Do not confuse this word with
biannual.

bier (*say* beer) *noun* (*plural* **biers**)
a movable stand on which a coffin or a
dead body is placed before it is buried.
[from Old English]

bifocal (*say* by-**foh**-kal) *adjective*
(of spectacle lenses) made in two sections,
with the upper part for looking at distant
objects and the lower part for reading.

bifocals *plural noun*
bifocal spectacles.

big *adjective* (**bigger, biggest**)
1 large. **2** important, *the big match*. **3** more
grown-up; elder, *my big sister*.
[origin unknown]

bigamy (*say* **big**-a-mee) *noun*
the crime of marrying a person when you
are already married to someone else.
bigamous *adjective*, **bigamist** *noun*
[from *bi-* + Greek *-gamos* = married]

bight *noun* (*plural* **bights**)
1 a loop of rope. **2** a long inward curve in a
coast. [from Old English]

bigot *noun* (*plural* **bigots**)
a bigoted person. [French]

bigoted *adjective*
narrow-minded and intolerant.
bigotry *noun*

bike *noun* (*plural* **bikes**) (*informal*)
a bicycle or motorcycle.
[abbreviation of *bicycle*]

bikini *noun* (*plural* **bikinis**)
a woman's very small two-piece swimsuit.
[named after the island of Bikini in the
Pacific Ocean, where an atomic bomb test
was carried out in 1946, at about the time
the bikini was first worn (both caused
great excitement)]

bilateral *adjective*
1 of or on two sides. **2** between two people
or groups, *a bilateral agreement*.
[from *bi-* + *lateral*]

bilberry *noun* (*plural* **bilberries**)
a small dark-blue edible berry.
[probably from Old Norse]

bile *noun*
a bitter liquid produced by the liver,
helping to digest fats. [from Latin]

bilge *noun* (*plural* **bilges**)
1 the bilges the bottom of a ship; the water
that collects there. **2** (*slang*) nonsense;
worthless ideas.
[a different spelling of *bulge*]

bilingual (*say* by-**ling**-wal) *adjective*
1 written in two languages. **2** able to speak
two languages.
[from *bi-* + Latin *lingua* = language]

bilious *adjective*
feeling sick; sickly. **biliousness** *noun*
[from *bile*]

-bility *suffix* see **-able**.

bilk *verb* (**bilks, bilking, bilked**)
cheat someone by not paying them what
you owe; defraud. [origin unknown]

bill[1] *noun* (*plural* **bills**)
1 a written statement of charges for goods
or services that have been supplied.
2 a poster. **3** a list; a programme of
entertainment. **4** the draft of a proposed
law to be discussed by Parliament.
5 (*American*) a banknote.
bill of fare a menu.
[same origin as *bull*[2]]

bill[2] *noun* (*plural* **bills**)
a bird's beak. [from Old English]

billabong *noun* (*plural* **billabongs**)
(in Australia) a backwater.
[an Aboriginal word]

billet *noun* (*plural* **billets**)
a lodging for troops, especially in a private
house.
billet *verb* (**billets, billeting, billeted**)
house someone in a billet.
[originally = an order to house troops: from
Latin *bulla* = seal, sealed letter]

billiards *noun*
a game in which three balls are struck with cues on a cloth-covered table (**billiard table**). [from French *billard* = cue]

billion *noun* (*plural* **billions**)
1 a thousand million (1,000,000,000).
2 a million million (1,000,000,000,000).
billionth *adjective* & *noun*
[French, from *bi-* + *million*]

USAGE: Although the word originally meant a million million, nowadays it usually means a thousand million.

billow *noun* (*plural* **billows**)
a huge wave.
billow *verb* (**billows**, **billowing**, **billowed**)
rise or roll like waves. [from Old Norse]

billy *noun* (*plural* **billies**)
a pot with a lid, used by campers etc. as a kettle or cooking pot. **billycan** *noun*
[from Australian Aboriginal *billa* = water]

billy goat *noun* (*plural* **billy goats**)
a male goat. (Compare *nanny goat*.)
[from the name *Billy*]

bin *noun* (*plural* **bins**)
a large or deep container.
[via Old English from a Celtic word]

binary (*say* **by-ner-ee**) *adjective*
involving sets of two; consisting of two parts. [from Latin]

binary digit *noun* (*plural* **binary digits**)
either of the two digits (0 and 1) used in the system of numbers known as binary notation or the binary scale.

bind *verb* (**binds**, **binding**, **bound**)
1 fasten material round something.
2 fasten the pages of a book into a cover.
3 tie up or tie together. 4 make somebody agree to do something. **binder** *noun*
bind a person over make him or her agree not to break the law.
bind *noun* (*slang*)
a nuisance; a bore. [from Old English]

binding *noun* (*plural* **bindings**)
something that binds, especially the covers, glue, etc. of a book.

binding *adjective*
(of an agreement or promise) that must be carried out or obeyed.

bine *noun*
the flexible stem of the hop plant.
[a different spelling of *bind*]

binge *noun* (*plural* **binges**) (*slang*)
a time spent eating a lot of food.
[origin unknown]

bingo *noun*
a game using cards on which numbered squares are crossed out as the numbers are called out at random. [origin unknown]

binoculars *plural noun*
a device with lenses for both eyes, making distant objects seem nearer. [from Latin *bini* = two together + *oculus* = eye]

bio- *prefix*
life (as in *biology*). [from Greek *bios* = life]

biochemistry *noun*
the study of the chemical composition and processes of living things.
biochemical *adjective*, **biochemist** *noun*

biodegradable *adjective*
able to be decomposed by bacteria, *This packaging is biodegradable.*

biography (*say* **by-og-ra-fee**) *noun* (*plural* **biographies**)
the story of a person's life.
biographical *adjective*, **biographer** *noun*

biology *noun*
the study of the life and structure of living things. **biological** *adjective*, **biologist** *noun*

bionic (*say* **by-on-ik**) *adjective*
(of a person or parts of the body) operated by electronic devices.
[from *bio-* + *electronic*]

biopsy (*say* **by-op-see**) *noun* (*plural* **biopsies**)
examination of tissue from a living body.
[from *bio-* + auto*psy*]

bipartite *adjective*
having two parts; involving two groups, *a bipartite agreement.*
[from *bi-* + Latin *partitum* = divided, parted]

biped (*say* by-ped) *noun* (*plural* bipeds)
a two-footed animal.
[from *bi-* + Latin *pedes* = feet]

biplane *noun* (*plural* biplanes)
an aeroplane with two sets of wings, one above the other. [from *bi-* + *plane*¹]

birch *noun* (*plural* birches)
1 a deciduous tree with slender branches.
2 a bundle of birch branches for flogging people. [from Old English]

bird *noun* (*plural* birds)
1 an animal with feathers, two wings, and two legs. 2 (*slang*) a young woman.
bird's-eye view a view from above.
[from Old English]

birdie *noun* (*plural* birdies)
1 (*informal*) a bird. 2 a score of one stroke under par for a hole at golf.

Biro *noun* (*plural* Biros) (*trade mark*)
a kind of ballpoint pen. [named after its Hungarian inventor, L. Biró]

birth *noun* (*plural* births)
1 the process by which a baby or young animal comes out from its mother's body.
2 origin; parentage, *He is of noble birth.*
[from Old Norse]

birth control *noun*
ways of avoiding conceiving a baby.

birthday *noun* (*plural* birthdays)
the anniversary of the day a person was born.

birthmark *noun* (*plural* birthmarks)
a coloured mark that has been on a person's skin since birth.

birth rate *noun* (*plural* birth rates)
the number of children born in one year for every 1,000 people.

birthright *noun*
a right or privilege to which a person is entitled through being born into a particular family or country.

biscuit *noun* (*plural* biscuits)
a small flat kind of cake that has been baked until it is crisp. [from Latin *bis* = twice + *coctus* = cooked (because

originally they were baked and then dried out in a cool oven to make them keep longer)]

bisect (*say* by-sekt) *verb* (bisects, bisecting, bisected)
divide something into two equal parts.
bisection *noun*, **bisector** *noun*
[from *bi-* + Latin *sectum* = cut]

bishop *noun* (*plural* bishops)
1 an important member of the clergy in charge of all the churches in a city or district. 2 a chess piece shaped like a bishop's mitre.
[via Old English from Latin *episcopus*]

bishopric *noun* (*plural* bishoprics)
the position or diocese of a bishop.

bismuth *noun*
1 a greyish-white metal. 2 a compound of this used in medicine.
[Latin from German]

bison (*say* by-son) *noun* (*plural* bison)
a wild ox found in North America and Europe, with a large shaggy head.
[Latin]

bistro *noun* (*plural* bistros)
a small restaurant.
[French]

bit¹ *noun* (*plural* bits)
1 a small piece or amount of something.
2 the metal part of a horse's bridle that is put into its mouth. 3 the part of a tool that cuts or grips things when twisted.
a bit 1 a short distance or time, *Wait a bit.*
2 slightly, *I'm a bit worried.*
bit by bit gradually.
[from Old English; related to *bite*]

bit² *past tense* of bite.

bit³ *noun* (*plural* bits)
the smallest unit of information in a computer, expressed as a choice between two possibilities. [from *bi*nary digi*t*]

bitch *noun* (*plural* bitches)
1 a female dog, fox, or wolf. 2 (*informal*) a spiteful woman. **bitchy** *adjective*
[from Old English]

bite *verb* (bites, biting, bit, bitten)
1 cut or take something with your teeth.
2 penetrate; sting. **3** accept bait, *The fish are biting.*
bite the dust fall wounded and die.
bite *noun* (*plural* bites)
1 biting, *She took a bite.* **2** a mark or spot made by biting, *an insect bite.* **3** a snack. [from Old English; related to *bit*[1]]

bitter *adjective*
1 tasting sharp, not sweet. **2** feeling or causing mental pain or resentment, *a bitter disappointment.* **3** very cold.
bitterly *adverb*, **bitterness** *noun*
[from Old English; related to *bite*]

bittern *noun* (*plural* bitterns)
a marsh bird, the male of which makes a booming cry. [from old French]

bitumen (*say* bit-yoo-min) *noun*
a black substance used for covering roads etc. **bituminous** (*say* bit-**yoo**-min-us) *adjective* [Latin]

bivalve *noun* (*plural* bivalves)
a shellfish (e.g. an oyster) that has a shell with two hinged parts.

bivouac (*say* biv-oo-ak) *noun* (*plural* bivouacs)
a temporary camp without tents.
bivouac *verb* (bivouacs, bivouacking, bivouacked)
camp in a bivouac. [French]

bizarre (*say* biz-**ar**) *adjective*
very odd in appearance or effect.
[from Italian *bizarro* = angry]

blab *verb* (blabs, blabbing, blabbed)
let out a secret. [imitating the sound]

Black *noun* (*plural* Blacks)
a person with a very dark or black skin.
Black *adjective*

USAGE: *Black* is the word generally preferred by African people and people of African descent.

---

black *noun* (*plural* blacks)
the very darkest colour, like coal or soot.
black *adjective*
1 of the colour black. **2** very dirty.
3 dismal; not hopeful, *The outlook is black.*

4 hostile; disapproving, *He gave me a black look.* **5** (of coffee or tea) without milk.
blackly *adverb*, **blackness** *noun*
black *verb* (blacks, blacking, blacked)
make a thing black.
black out 1 cover windows etc. so that no light can penetrate. **2** faint, lose consciousness. **blackout** *noun*
[from Old English]

blackberry *noun* (*plural* blackberries)
a sweet black berry.

blackbird *noun* (*plural* blackbirds)
a European songbird, the male of which is black.

blackboard *noun* (*plural* blackboards)
a dark board for writing on with chalk.

black box *noun* (*plural* black boxes)
a flight recorder.

black economy *noun*
employment in which payments are concealed to avoid tax.

blacken *verb* (blackens, blackening, blackened)
make or become black.

black eye *noun* (*plural* black eyes)
an eye with a bruise round it.

blackguard (*say* blag-erd) *noun* (*plural* blackguards) (*old use*)
a wicked person.
[originally the *black guard* = the servants who did the dirty jobs]

blackhead *noun* (*plural* blackheads)
a small black spot in the skin.

black hole *noun* (*plural* black holes)
a region in outer space with such a strong gravitational field that no matter or radiation can escape from it.

blackleg *noun* (*plural* blacklegs)
a person who works while their fellow workers are on strike.
[originally a disease affecting sheep]

blacklist *verb* (blacklists, blacklisting, blacklisted)
put someone on a list of those who are disapproved of.

black magic *noun*
evil magic.

blackmail *verb* (blackmails, blackmailing, blackmailed)
demand money etc. from someone by threats. **blackmail** *noun*, **blackmailer** *noun*
[from *black* + *mail*²; literally = black armour or protection]

black market *noun* (*plural* black markets)
illegal trading.

black sheep *noun*
one bad character in a well-behaved group.

blacksmith *noun* (*plural* blacksmiths)
a person who makes and repairs iron things, especially one who makes and fits horseshoes.
[because of the dark colour of iron]

black spot *noun* (*plural* black spots)
a dangerous place.

bladder *noun* (*plural* bladders)
1 the bag-like part of the body in which urine collects. 2 the inflatable bag inside a football. [from Old English]

blade *noun* (*plural* blades)
1 the flat cutting-part of a knife, sword, axe, etc. 2 the flat wide part of an oar, spade, propeller, etc. 3 a flat narrow leaf, *blades of grass.* 4 a broad flat bone, *shoulder blade.* [from Old English]

blame *verb* (blames, blaming, blamed)
1 say that somebody or something has caused what is wrong, *They blamed me.*
2 find fault with someone, *We can't blame them for wanting a holiday.*
blame *noun* (*plural* blames)
responsibility for what is wrong.
[from old French]

blameless *adjective*
deserving no blame; innocent.

blanch *verb* (blanches, blanching, blanched)
make or become white or pale, *He blanched with fear.* [from French *blanc* = white]

blancmange (*say* bla-monj) *noun* (*plural* blancmanges)
a jelly-like pudding made with milk.
[from French *blanc* = white + *mange* = eat]

bland *adjective*
1 having a mild flavour rather than a strong one. 2 gentle and casual, not irritating or stimulating, *a bland manner.*
blandly *adverb*, **blandness** *noun*
[from Latin *blandus* = soft, smooth]

blandishments *plural noun*
flattering or coaxing words.
[same origin as *bland*]

blank *adjective*
1 not written or printed on; unmarked.
2 without interest or expression, *a blank look.* 3 empty of thoughts, *My mind's gone blank.* **blankly** *adverb*, **blankness** *noun*
blank *noun* (*plural* blanks)
1 an empty space. 2 a blank cartridge.
[from French *blanc* = white]

blank cartridge *noun* (*plural* blank cartridges)
a cartridge that makes a noise but does not fire a bullet.

blank cheque *noun* (*plural* blank cheques)
a cheque with the amount not yet filled in.

blanket *noun* (*plural* blankets)
1 a warm cloth covering used on a bed etc.
2 any thick soft covering, *a blanket of snow.*
blanket *adjective*
covering a wide range of conditions etc., *a blanket agreement.*
[originally = woollen cloth which had not been dyed; from French *blanc* = white]

blank verse *noun*
poetry without rhymes.

blare *verb* (blares, blaring, blared)
make a loud harsh sound. **blare** *noun*
[imitating the sound]

blasé (*say* blah-zay) *adjective*
bored or unimpressed by things because you are used to them. [French]

blaspheme (*say* blas-feem) *verb* (blasphemes, blaspheming, blasphemed)
talk or write irreverently about sacred things.
[from Greek *blasphemos* = evil-speaking]

blasphemy (*say* blas-fim-ee) *noun* (*plural* blasphemies)
irreverent talk about sacred things.
blasphemous *adjective*

blast *noun* (*plural* blasts)
1 a strong rush of wind or air. 2 a loud noise, *the blast of the trumpets.*
blast *verb* (blasts, blasting, blasted)
blow up with explosives.
blast off launch by the firing of rockets.
blast-off *noun*
[from Old English; related to *blow¹*]

blast furnace *noun* (*plural* blast furnaces)
a furnace for smelting ore, with hot air driven in.

blatant (*say* blay-tant) *adjective*
very obvious, *a blatant lie.* **blatantly** *adverb*
[from an old word meaning 'noisy']

blaze¹ *noun* (*plural* blazes)
a very bright flame, fire, or light.
blaze *verb* (blazes, blazing, blazed)
1 burn or shine brightly. 2 show great feeling, *He was blazing with anger.*
[from Old English]

blaze² *verb* (blazes, blazing, blazed)
blaze a trail show the way for others to follow. [origin unknown]

blazer *noun* (*plural* blazers)
a kind of jacket, often with a badge or in the colours of a school or team etc.
[from *blaze¹* (because originally blazers were made in very bright colours and were thought of as shining or 'blazing')]

-ble *suffix* see **-able**.

bleach *verb* (bleaches, bleaching, bleached)
make or become white.
bleach *noun* (*plural* bleaches)
a substance used to bleach things.
[from Old English; related to *bleak*]

bleak *adjective*
1 bare and cold, *a bleak hillside.* 2 dreary or miserable, *a bleak future.* **bleakly** *adverb*,
bleakness *noun*
[from Old English; related to *bleach*]

bleary *adjective*
watery and not seeing clearly, *bleary eyes.*
blearily *adverb* [origin unknown]

bleat *noun* (*plural* bleats)
the cry of a lamb, goat, or calf.
bleat *verb* (bleats, bleating, bleated)
make a bleat. [imitating the sound]

bleed *verb* (bleeds, bleeding, bled)
1 lose blood. 2 draw blood or fluid from.
[from Old English; related to *blood*]

bleep *noun* (*plural* bleeps)
a short high sound used as a signal. **bleep** *verb* [imitating the sound]

bleeper *noun* (*plural* bleepers)
a small electronic device that bleeps when the wearer is contacted.

blemish *noun* (*plural* blemishes)
a flaw; a mark that spoils a thing's appearance. **blemish** *verb* [from old French]

blench *verb* (blenches, blenching, blenched)
flinch. [from Old English]

blend *verb* (blends, blending, blended)
mix smoothly or easily.
blend *noun* (*plural* blends)
a mixture.
[probably from a Scandinavian word]

blender *noun* (*plural* blenders)
an electric machine used to mix food or turn it into liquid.

bless *verb* (blesses, blessing, blessed)
1 make sacred or holy. 2 bring God's favour on a person or thing.
[from Old English]

blessing *noun* (*plural* blessings)
1 a prayer that blesses a person or thing; being blessed. 2 something that people are glad of.

blight *noun* (*plural* blights)
1 a disease that withers plants. 2 a bad or evil influence.
blight *verb* (blights, blighting, blighted)
1 affect with blight. 2 spoil something.
[origin unknown]

blind *adjective*
1 without the ability to see. 2 without any thought or understanding, *blind obedience.*
3 (of a tube, passage, or road) closed at one end. **blindly** *adverb*, **blindness** *noun*
blind *verb* (blinds, blinding, blinded)
make a person blind.

blind *noun* (*plural* **blinds**)
1 a screen for a window. **2** a deception; something used to hide the truth. *His journey was a blind.* [from Old English]

blind date *noun* (*plural* **blind dates**)
a date between a man and woman who have not met before.

blindfold *noun* (*plural* **blindfolds**)
a strip of cloth tied round someone's eyes so that they cannot see.
blindfold *verb* (**blindfolds, blindfolding, blindfolded**)
cover someone's eyes with a blindfold. [from Old English *blindfeld* = struck blind, from *blind* + *fell²*]

blind spot *noun* (*plural* **blind spots**)
a subject that you do not understand or know much about.

blink *verb* (**blinks, blinking, blinked**)
shut and open your eyes rapidly. **blink** *noun* [from *blench*, influenced by Dutch *blinken* = shine]

blinkers *plural noun*
leather pieces fixed on a bridle to prevent a horse from seeing sideways. **blinkered** *adjective* [originally a person who was half-blind; from *blink*]

bliss *noun*
perfect happiness.
blissful *adjective*, **blissfully** *adverb* [from Old English; related to *blithe*]

blister *noun* (*plural* **blisters**)
a swelling like a bubble, especially on skin.
blister *verb* [origin unknown]

blithe *adjective*
casual and carefree. **blithely** *adverb* [from Old English; related to *bliss*]

blitz *noun* (*plural* **blitzes**)
1 a sudden violent attack. **2** the bombing of London in 1940. [short for German *Blitzkrieg* (*Blitz* = lightning, *Krieg* = war)]

blizzard *noun* (*plural* **blizzards**)
a severe snowstorm. [origin unknown]

bloated *adjective*
swollen by fat, gas, or liquid. [from Old Norse *blautr* = soft]

bloater *noun* (*plural* **bloaters**)
a salted smoked herring. [same origin as *bloated*]

blob *noun* (*plural* **blobs**)
a small round mass of something, *blobs of paint.* [because *blob* sounds squelchy, like liquid]

bloc *noun* (*plural* **blocs**)
a group of countries that join together for a comon purpose. [French, = block]

block *noun* (*plural* **blocks**)
1 a solid piece of something. **2** an obstruction. **3** a large building divided into flats or offices. **4** a group of buildings.
block *verb* (**blocks, blocking, blocked**)
obstruct; prevent something from moving or being used. **blockage** *noun* [via French from Dutch]

blockade *noun* (*plural* **blockades**)
the blocking of a city or port etc. in order to prevent people and goods from going in or out.
blockade *verb* (**blockades, blockading, blockaded**)
set up a blockade of a place. [from *block*]

block letters *plural noun*
plain capital letters.

blond or **blonde** *adjective*
fair-haired; fair. [from Latin *blondus* = yellow]

blonde *noun* (*plural* **blondes**)
a fair-haired girl or woman.

blood *noun*
1 the red liquid that flows through veins and arteries. **2** family relationship; ancestry, *He is of royal blood.*
in cold blood deliberately and cruelly. [from Old English; related to *bleed*]

blood bank *noun* (*plural* **blood banks**)
a place where supplies of blood and plasma for transfusions are stored.

bloodbath *noun*
a massacre.

blood donor *noun* (*plural* **blood donors**)
a person who gives blood for use in transfusions.

bloodhound *noun* (*plural* **bloodhounds**)
a large dog that was used to track people by their scent.

bloodshed *noun*
the killing or wounding of people.

bloodshot *adjective*
(of eyes) streaked with red.

blood sport *noun* (*plural* **blood sports**)
a sport that involves wounding or killing animals.

bloodthirsty *adjective*
eager for bloodshed.

blood vessel *noun* (*plural* **blood vessels**)
a tube carrying blood in the body; an artery, vein, or capillary.

bloody *adjective* (**bloodier, bloodiest**)
1 bloodstained. 2 with much bloodshed, *a bloody battle*.
bloody-minded *adjective* deliberately awkward and not helpful.

bloom *noun* (*plural* **blooms**)
1 a flower. 2 the fine powder on fresh ripe grapes etc.
bloom *verb* (**blooms, blooming, bloomed**)
produce flowers. [from Old Norse]

blossom *noun* (*plural* **blossoms**)
a flower or mass of flowers, especially on a fruit tree.
blossom *verb* (**blossoms, blossoming, blossomed**)
1 produce flowers. 2 develop into something, *She blossomed into a fine singer*. [from Old English]

blot *noun* (*plural* **blots**)
1 a spot of ink. 2 a flaw or fault; something ugly, *a blot on the landscape*.
blot *verb* (**blots, blotting, blotted**)
1 make a blot or blots on something.
2 dry with blotting paper.
blot out 1 cross out thickly. 2 obscure, *Fog blotted out the view*.
[probably from a Scandinavian language]

blotch *noun* (*plural* **blotches**)
an untidy patch of colour. **blotchy** *adjective*
[related to *blot*]

blotter *noun* (*plural* **blotters**)
a pad of blotting paper; a holder for blotting paper.

blotting paper *noun*
absorbent paper for soaking up ink from writing.

blouse *noun* (*plural* **blouses**)
a woman's garment like a shirt. [from French]

blow[1] *verb* (**blows, blowing, blew, blown**)
1 send out a current of air. 2 move in or with a current of air, *His hat blew off*.
3 make or sound something by blowing, *blow bubbles*; *blow the whistle*. 4 melt with too strong an electric current, *A fuse has blown*. 5 (*slang*) damn, *Blow you!*
blow up 1 inflate. 2 explode. 3 shatter by an explosion.
blow *noun* (*plural* **blows**)
the action of blowing. [from Old English]

blow[2] *noun* (*plural* **blows**)
1 a hard knock or hit. 2 a shock; a disaster. [origin unknown]

blowlamp *noun* (*plural* **blowlamps**)
a portable device for directing a very hot flame at something.

blowpipe *noun* (*plural* **blowpipes**)
a tube for sending out a dart or pellet by blowing.

blubber *noun*
the fat of whales. [originally = sea foam; probably related to *bubble*]

bludgeon (*say* bluj-on) *noun* (*plural* **bludgeons**)
a short stick with a thickened end, used as a weapon.
bludgeon *verb* (**bludgeons, bludgeoning, bludgeoned**)
hit someone several times with a heavy stick or other object. [origin unknown]

blue *noun* (*plural* **blues**)
the colour of a cloudless sky.
out of the blue unexpectedly.
blue *adjective*
1 of the colour blue. 2 unhappy; depressed.
3 indecent; obscene, *blue films*. **blueness** *noun* [via French from Germanic]

bluebell noun (plural bluebells)
a plant with blue bell-shaped flowers.

blue blood noun
aristocratic family.

bluebottle noun (plural bluebottles)
a large bluish fly. [origin unknown]

blueprint noun (plural blueprints)
a detailed plan. [because copies of plans
were made on blue paper]

blues noun
a slow sad jazz song or tune.
the blues a very sad feeling; depression.
[short for blue devils, spiteful demons
believed to cause depression]

bluff[1] verb (bluffs, bluffing, bluffed)
deceive someone, especially by pretending
to be someone else or to be able to do
something.
bluff noun (plural bluffs)
bluffing; a threat that you make but do not
intend to carry out.
[from Dutch bluffen – boast]

bluff[2] adjective
frank and hearty in manner. **bluffness** noun
bluff noun (plural bluffs)
a cliff with a broad steep front.
[originally a sailor's word to describe a
blunt ship's bow]

bluish adjective
rather blue.

blunder noun (plural blunders)
a stupid mistake.
blunder verb (blunders, blundering,
blundered)
1 make a blunder. 2 move clumsily and
uncertainly.
[probably from a Scandinavian language]

blunderbuss noun (plural blunderbusses)
an old type of gun that fired many balls in
one shot.
[from Dutch donderbus – thunder gun]

blunt adjective
1 not sharp. 2 speaking in plain terms;
straightforward, a blunt refusal.
bluntly adverb, **bluntness** noun
blunt verb (blunts, blunting, blunted)
make a thing blunt.
[probably from a Scandinavian language]

blur verb (blurs, blurring, blurred)
make or become indistinct or smeared.
blur noun (plural blurs)
an indistinct appearance, Without his
glasses on, everything was a blur.
[origin unknown]

blurt verb (blurts, blurting, blurted)
say something suddenly or tactlessly, He
blurted it out. [origin unknown]

blush verb (blushes, blushing, blushed)
become red in the face because you are
ashamed or embarrassed.
blush noun (plural blushes)
reddening in the face. [from Old English]

bluster verb (blusters, blustering, blustered)
1 blow in gusts; be windy. 2 talk loudly and
aggressively. **blustery** adjective
[imitating the sound]

BMX abbreviation
a kind of bicycle for use in racing on a dirt
track. [short for bicycle moto-cross (x
standing for cross)]

boa (say boh-a) or **boa constrictor** noun
(plural boas, boa constrictors)
a large South American snake that
squeezes its prey so that it suffocates it.
[Latin]

boar noun (plural boars)
1 a wild pig. 2 a male pig.
[from Old English]

board noun (plural boards)
1 a flat piece of wood. 2 a flat piece of stiff
material, e.g. a chessboard. 3 daily meals
supplied in return for payment or work,
board and lodging. 4 a committee.
on board on or in a ship, aircraft, etc.
board verb (boards, boarding, boarded)
1 go on board a ship, etc. 2 give or get
meals and accommodation.
board up block with fixed boards.
[from Old English]

boarder noun (plural boarders)
1 a pupil who lives at a boarding school
during the term. 2 a lodger who receives
meals.

boarding house noun (plural boarding
houses)
a house where people obtain board and
lodging for payment.

boarding school *noun* (*plural* **boarding schools**)
a school where pupils live during the term.

boast *verb* (**boasts, boasting, boasted**)
1 speak with great pride and try to impress people. **2** have something to be proud of, *The town boasts a fine park.* **boaster** *noun*, **boastful** *adjective*, **boastfully** *adverb*
boast *noun* (*plural* **boasts**)
a boastful statement. [origin unknown]

boat *noun* (*plural* **boats**)
a vehicle built to travel on water and carry people etc.
in the same boat in the same situation; suffering the same difficulties.
[from Old English]

boater *noun* (*plural* **boaters**)
a hard flat straw hat.
[originally worn by men *boating*]

boating *noun*
going out in a boat (especially a rowing boat) for pleasure.

boatswain (*say* boh-sun) *noun* (*plural* **boatswains**)
a ship's officer in charge of rigging, boats, anchors, etc. [from *boat* + *swain* = servant]

bob *verb* (**bobs, bobbing, bobbed**)
move quickly up and down.
[origin unknown]

bobbin *noun* (*plural* **bobbins**)
a small spool holding thread or wire in a machine. [from French]

bobble *noun* (*plural* **bobbles**)
a small round ornament, often made of wool. [origin unknown]

bobsleigh or **bobsled** *noun* (*plural* **bobsleighs, bobsleds**)
a sledge with two sets of runners.
[origin unknown]

bode *verb* (**bodes, boding, boded**)
be a sign or omen of what is to come, *It bodes well.* [from Old English]

bodice *noun* (*plural* **bodices**)
the upper part of a dress. [from *body*]

bodkin *noun* (*plural* **bodkins**)
a thick blunt needle for drawing tape etc. through a hem. [origin unknown]

body *noun* (*plural* **bodies**)
1 the structure consisting of bones and flesh etc. of a person or animal; the main part of this apart from the head and limbs. **2** a corpse. **3** the main part of something. **4** a group or quantity regarded as a unit, *the school's governing body.* **5** a distinct object or piece of matter, *Stars and planets are heavenly bodies.* **bodily** *adjective* & *adverb* [from Old English]

bodyguard *noun* (*plural* **bodyguards**)
a guard to protect a person's life.

Boer (*say* boh-er) *noun* (*plural* **Boers**)
1 an Afrikaner. **2** (in history) an early Dutch inhabitant of South Africa.
[Dutch, = farmer]

bog *noun* (*plural* **bogs**)
an area of wet spongy ground. **boggy** *adjective*
bogged down stuck and unable to make any progress.
[Scottish Gaelic, = soft]

boggle *verb* (**boggles, boggling, boggled**)
be amazed or puzzled, *Our minds boggled at the idea.* [from dialect *bogle* = bogy]

bogus *adjective*
not real; sham.
[an American word; origin unknown]

bogy *noun* (*plural* **bogies**)
1 an evil spirit. **2** something that frightens people. **bogyman** *noun* [origin unknown]

boil[1] *verb* (**boils, boiling, boiled**)
1 make or become hot enough to bubble and give off steam. **2** cook or wash something in boiling water. **3** be very hot.
boil *noun*
boiling point, *bring the milk to the boil.*
[from old French]

boil[2] *noun* (*plural* **boils**)
an inflamed swelling under the skin.
[from Old English]

boiler *noun* (*plural* **boilers**)
a container in which water is heated or clothes are boiled.

boisterous *adjective*
noisy and lively. [origin unknown]

bold *adjective*
1 brave; courageous. 2 impudent. 3 (of colours) strong and vivid. **boldly** *adverb*, **boldness** *noun* [from Old English]

bole *noun* (*plural* **boles**)
the trunk of a tree. [from Old Norse]

bollard *noun* (*plural* **bollards**)
1 a short thick post to which a ship's mooring-rope may be tied. 2 a short post for directing traffic or keeping it off a pavement etc.
[probably the same origin as *bole*]

bolster *noun* (*plural* **bolsters**)
a long pillow for placing across a bed under other pillows.
bolster *verb* (**bolsters, bolstering, bolstered**)
add extra support. [from Old English]

bolt *noun* (*plural* **bolts**)
1 a sliding bar for fastening a door. 2 a thick metal pin for fastening things together. 3 a sliding bar that opens and closes the breech of a rifle. 4 a shaft of lightning. 5 an arrow shot from a crossbow. 6 the action of bolting.
a bolt from the blue a surprise, usually an unpleasant one.
bolt upright quite upright.
bolt *verb* (**bolts, bolting, bolted**)
1 fasten with a bolt or bolts. 2 run away; (of a horse) run off out of control. 3 swallow food quickly. [from Old English]

bomb *noun* (*plural* **bombs**)
an explosive device.
the bomb an atomic or hydrogen bomb.
bomb *verb* (**bombs, bombing, bombed**)
attack a place with bombs.
[probably from Greek *bombos* = booming]

bombard *verb* (**bombards, bombarding, bombarded**)
1 attack with gunfire or many missiles. 2 direct a large number of questions or comments etc. at somebody. **bombardment** *noun* [same origin as *bomb*]

bombastic (*say* bom-bast-ik) *adjective*
using pompous words. [from *bombast* = material used for padding; later 'padded' language, with long or unnecessary words]

bomber *noun* (*plural* **bombers**)
1 someone who plants or sets off a bomb. 2 an aeroplane from which bombs are dropped.

bombshell *noun* (*plural* **bombshells**)
a great shock.

bona fide (*say* boh-na fy-dee) *adjective*
genuine; without fraud, *Are they bona fide tourists or spies?* [Latin, = in good faith]

bona fides (*say* boh-na fy-deez) *plural noun*
honest intention; sincerity, *We do not doubt his bona fides.* [Latin, = good faith]

bonanza (*say* bon-an-za) *noun* (*plural* **bonanzas**)
sudden great wealth or luck.
[originally an American word; from Spanish, = good weather, prosperity]

bond *noun* (*plural* **bonds**)
1 a close friendship or connection between two or more people. 2 **bonds** ropes or chains used to tie someone up. 3 a document stating an agreement.
bond *verb* (**bonds, bonding, bonded**)
become closely linked or connected.
[a different spelling of *band*[1]]

bondage *noun*
slavery; captivity.

bone *noun* (*plural* **bones**)
one of the hard parts of a person's or animal's body (excluding teeth, nails, horns, and cartilage).
bone *verb* (**bones, boning, boned**)
remove the bones from meat or fish.
[from Old English]

bone dry *adjective*
quite dry.

bonfire *noun* (*plural* **bonfires**)
an outdoor fire to burn rubbish or celebrate something.
[originally *bone fire*, = a fire to dispose of people's or animals' bones]

bonnet *noun* (*plural* **bonnets**)
1 a hat with strings that tie under the chin. 2 a Scottish beret. 3 the hinged cover over a car engine. [from Latin *abonnis* = hat]

bonny *adjective* (**bonnier, bonniest**)
1 healthy-looking. **2** (*Scottish*) good-looking. [from French *bon* = good]

bonus (*say* boh-nus) *noun* (*plural* **bonuses**)
1 an extra payment in addition to a person's normal wages. **2** an extra benefit. [from Latin *bonus* = good]

bon voyage (*say* bawn vwah-**yah**zh) *interjection*
pleasant journey! [French]

bony *adjective*
1 with large bones; having bones with little flesh on them. **2** full of bones. **3** like bones.

boo *verb* (**boos, booing, booed**)
shout 'boo' in disapproval. **boo** *noun*

booby *noun* (*plural* **boobies**)
a babyish or stupid person. [from Spanish]

booby prize *noun* (*plural* **booby prizes**)
a prize given as a joke to someone who comes last in a contest.

booby trap *noun* (*plural* **booby traps**)
something designed to hit or injure someone unexpectedly.

book *noun* (*plural* **books**)
a set of sheets of paper, usually with printing or writing on them, fastened together inside a cover. **bookseller** *noun*, **bookshop** *noun*, **bookstall** *noun*
book *verb* (**books, booking, booked**)
1 reserve a place in a theatre, hotel, train, etc. **2** enter a person in a police record, *The police booked him for speeding.* [from Old English]

bookcase *noun* (*plural* **bookcases**)
a piece of furniture with shelves for books.

bookkeeping *noun*
recording details of the money that is spent and received by a business. **bookkeeper** *noun*

booklet *noun* (*plural* **booklets**)
a small thin book.

bookmaker *noun* (*plural* **bookmakers**)
a person whose business is taking bets. [because the bets used to be written down in a notebook]

bookmark *noun* (*plural* **bookmarks**)
something to mark a place in a book.

bookworm *noun* (*plural* **bookworms**)
1 a grub that eats holes in books. **2** a person who loves reading.

boom[1] *verb* (**booms, booming, boomed**)
1 make a deep hollow sound. **2** be growing and prospering, *Business is booming.*
boom *noun* (*plural* **booms**)
1 a deep hollow sound. **2** prosperity; growth. [imitating the sound]

boom[2] *noun* (*plural* **booms**)
1 a long pole at the bottom of a sail to keep it stretched. **2** a long pole carrying a microphone etc. **3** a chain or floating barrier that can be placed across a river or a harbour entrance.
[from Dutch, = beam, tree]

boomerang *noun* (*plural* **boomerangs**)
a curved piece of wood that can be thrown so that it returns to the thrower, originally used by Australian Aborigines.
[an Australian Aboriginal word]

boon *noun* (*plural* **boons**)
something that makes life easier.
[from Old Norse *bon* = prayer]

boon companion *noun* (*plural* **boon companions**)
a friendly companion.
[from French *bon* = good]

boor *noun* (*plural* **boors**)
an ill-mannered person. **boorish** *adjective*
[same origin as *Boer*]

boost *verb* (**boosts, boosting, boosted**)
1 increase the strength, value, or reputation of a person or thing. **2** push something upwards. **booster** *noun*
boost *noun* (*plural* **boosts**)
1 an increase. **2** an upward push.
[origin unknown]

boot *noun* (*plural* **boots**)
1 a shoe that covers the foot and ankle or leg. **2** the compartment for luggage in a car.
booted *adjective*
[via Old Norse from French]

bootee *noun* (*plural* **bootees**)
a baby's knitted boot.

booth *noun* (*plural* **booths**)
a small enclosure. [from Old Norse]

booty *noun*
valuable goods taken away by soldiers after a battle. [from old German *buite* = exchange, sharing out]

booze *verb* (**boozes, boozing, boozed**) (*slang*)
drink alcohol.
booze *noun* (*slang*)
alcoholic drink. [from old Dutch *busen* = drink too much alcohol]

borax *noun*
a soluble white powder used in making glass, detergents, etc. [via Latin and Arabic from Pahlavi (an old form of Persian)]

border *noun* (*plural* **borders**)
1 the boundary of a country; the part near this. 2 an edge. 3 something placed round an edge to strengthen or decorate it. 4 a strip of ground round a garden or part of it.
border *verb* (**borders, bordering, bordered**)
put or be a border to something.
[from old French]

borderline *noun* (*plural* **borderlines**)
a boundary.
borderline case something that is on the borderline between two different groups or kinds of things.

bore¹ *verb* (**bores, boring, bored**)
1 drill a hole. 2 get through by pushing.
bore *noun* (*plural* **bores**)
1 the width of the inside of a gun barrel. 2 a hole made by boring.
[from Old English]

bore² *verb* (**bores, boring, bored**)
make somebody feel uninterested by being dull.
bore *noun* (*plural* **bores**)
a boring person or thing. **boredom** *noun*
[origin unknown]

bore³ *noun* (*plural* **bores**)
a tidal wave with a steep front that moves up some estuaries.
[from Old Norse *bara* = wave]

bore⁴ *past tense* of **bear²**.

bored *adjective*
weary and uninterested because something is so dull.

USAGE: You can say that you are *bored with* something or *bored by* something: *I'm bored with this game*. It is not acceptable in standard English to say *bored of*.

born *adjective*
1 having come into existence by birth. (See the note on *borne*.) 2 having a certain natural quality or ability, *a born leader*. [from Old English]

borne *past participle* of **bear²**.

USAGE: The word *borne* is used before *by* or after *have*, *has*, or *had*, e.g. *children borne by Eve*; *she had borne him a son*. The word *born* is used e.g. in *a son was born*.

borough (*say* **burra**) *noun* (*plural* **boroughs**)
an important town or district. [from Old English *burg* = fortress or fortified town]

borrow *verb* (**borrows, borrowing, borrowed**)
1 get something to use for a time, with the intention to give it back afterwards.
2 obtain money as a loan. **borrower** *noun*
[from Old English]

USAGE: Do not confuse *borrow* with *lend*, which means just the opposite.

bosom *noun* (*plural* **bosoms**)
a person's breast. [from Old English]

boss¹ *noun* (*plural* **bosses**) (*informal*)
a manager; a person whose job is to give orders to workers etc.
boss *verb* (**bosses, bossing, bossed**) (*slang*)
order someone about.
[from Dutch *baas* = master]

boss² *noun* (*plural* **bosses**)
a round raised knob or stud.
[from old French]

bossy *adjective*
fond of ordering people about.
bossiness *noun*

botany *noun*
the study of plants. **botanical** *adjective*,
botanist *noun* [from Greek *botane* = a plant]

botch *verb* (botches, botching, botched)
spoil something by poor or clumsy work.
[origin unknown]

both *adjective & pronoun*
the two; not only one, *Are both films good?*
Both are old.
both *adverb*
both ... and not only ... but also, *The house
is both small and ugly.* [from Old Norse]

bother *verb* (bothers, bothering, bothered)
1 cause somebody trouble or worry; pester.
2 take trouble; feel concern, *Don't bother to
reply.*
bother *noun*
trouble or worry. [probably from Irish
bodhraim = deafen, annoy]

bottle *noun* (*plural* bottles)
1 a narrow-necked container for liquids.
2 (*slang*) courage, *She showed a lot of bottle.*
bottle *verb* (bottles, bottling, bottled)
put or store something in bottles.
bottle up if you bottle up your feelings, you
keep them to yourself.
[same origin as *butt²*]

bottle bank *noun* (*plural* bottle banks)
a large container in which used glass
bottles are collected for recycling.

bottleneck *noun* (*plural* bottlenecks)
a narrow place where something,
especially traffic, cannot flow freely.

bottom *noun* (*plural* bottoms)
1 the lowest part; the base. **2** the part
furthest away, *the bottom of the garden.* **3** a
person's buttocks.
bottom *adjective*
lowest, *the bottom shelf.* [from Old English]

bottomless *adjective*
extremely deep.

boudoir (*say* boo-dwar) *noun* (*plural*
boudoirs)
a woman's private room.
[French, = place to sulk in]

bough *noun* (*plural* boughs)
a large branch coming from the trunk of a
tree. [from Old English]

boulder *noun* (*plural* boulders)
a very large smooth stone.
[from a Scandinavian word]

boulevard (*say* bool-ev-ard) *noun* (*plural*
boulevards)
a wide street, often with trees.
[French, related to *bulwark*]

bounce *verb* (bounces, bouncing, bounced)
1 spring back when thrown against
something. **2** make a ball etc. bounce. **3** (of
a cheque) be sent back by the bank because
there is not enough money in the account.
4 jump suddenly; move in a lively manner.
bounce *noun* (*plural* bounces)
1 the action or power of bouncing. **2** a
lively confident manner, *full of bounce.*
bouncy *adjective* [origin unknown]

bouncer *noun* (*plural* bouncers)
1 a person who stands at the door of a club
etc. and stops unwanted people coming in
or makes troublemakers leave. **2** a ball in
cricket that bounces high.

bound¹ *verb* (bounds, bounding, bounded)
jump or spring; run with jumping
movements, *bounding along.*
bound *noun* (*plural* bounds)
a bounding movement.
[from old French *bondir*]

bound² *past tense* of **bind**.
bound *adjective*
obstructed or hindered by something, *We
were fogbound.*
bound to certain to, *He is bound to fail.*
bound up with closely connected with,
Happiness is bound up with success.

bound³ *adjective*
going towards something, *We are bound for
Spain.* [from Old Norse]

bound⁴ *verb* (bounds, bounding, bounded)
limit; be the boundary of, *Their land is
bounded by the river.*
[from old French *bonde*]

boundary *noun* (*plural* boundaries)
1 a line that marks a limit. **2** a hit to the
boundary of a cricket field. [from *bound⁴*]

bounden *adjective*
obligatory, *your bounden duty.* [from *bind*]

bounds *plural noun*
limits.
out of bounds where you are not allowed to go.
[from *bound⁴*]

bountiful *adjective*
1 plentiful; abundant, *bountiful harvest.*
2 giving generously.

bounty *noun* (*plural* **bounties**)
1 a generous gift. 2 generosity in giving things. 3 a reward for doing something.
[from Latin *bonitas* = goodness]

bouquet (*say* boh-**kay**) *noun* (*plural* **bouquets**)
a bunch of flowers.
[French, = group of trees]

bout *noun* (*plural* **bouts**)
1 a boxing or wrestling contest. 2 a period of exercise or work or illness, *a bout of flu.*
[probably from old German]

boutique (*say* boo-**teek**) *noun* (*plural* **boutiques**)
a small shop selling fashionable clothes.
[French]

bovine (*say* boh-vyn) *adjective*
1 to do with or like cattle. 2 stupid.
[from Latin *bovis* = of an ox]

bow¹ (rhymes with *go*) *noun* (*plural* **bows**)
1 a strip of wood curved by a tight string joining its ends, used for shooting arrows.
2 a wooden rod with horsehair stretched between its ends, used for playing a violin etc. 3 a knot made with loops.
[from Old English *boga*]

bow² (rhymes with *cow*) *verb* (**bows, bowing, bowed**)
1 bend your body forwards to show respect or as a greeting. 2 bend downwards, *bowed by the weight.*
bow *noun* (*plural* **bows**)
bowing your body.
[from Old English *bugan*]

bow³ (rhymes with *cow*) *noun* (*plural* **bows**)
the front part of a ship.
[from old German or Dutch]

bowel *noun* (*plural* **bowels**)
the intestine.
[from Latin *botellus* = little sausage]

bower *noun* (*plural* **bowers**)
a leafy shelter.
[from Old English; related to *build*]

bowl¹ *noun* (*plural* **bowls**)
1 a rounded usually deep container for food or liquid. 2 the rounded part of a spoon or tobacco pipe etc.
[from Old English]

bowl² *noun* (*plural* **bowls**)
a ball used in the game of **bowls** or in bowling, when heavy balls are rolled towards skittles.
bowl *verb* (**bowls, bowling, bowled**)
1 send a ball to be played by a batsman.
2 get a batsman out by bowling. 3 send a ball etc. rolling. [from old French]

bow-legged *adjective*
having legs that curve outwards at the knees; bandy.

bowler¹ *noun* (*plural* **bowlers**)
a person who bowls.

bowler² *noun* (also **bowler hat**) (*plural* **bowlers, bowler hats**)
a man's stiff felt hat with a rounded top.
[named after William *Bowler*, who designed it]

bowling *noun*
1 the game of bowls. 2 the game of knocking down skittles with a heavy ball.

bow tie *noun* (*plural* **bow ties**)
a man's necktie tied into a bow.

bow window *noun* (*plural* **bow windows**)
a curved window.

box¹ *noun* (*plural* **boxes**)
1 a container made of wood, cardboard, etc., usually with a top or lid. 2 a compartment in a theatre, lawcourt, etc., *witness box.* 3 a hut or shelter, *sentry box.*
4 a rectangular space to be filled in on a form or questionnaire. 5 a small evergreen shrub.
the box (*informal*) television.
box *verb* (**boxes, boxing, boxed**)
put something into a box. [from Latin]

box² *verb* (**boxes, boxing, boxed**)
fight with the fists. [origin unknown]

boxer *noun* (*plural* **boxers**)
1 a person who boxes. 2 a dog that looks
like a bulldog.

Boxing Day *noun*
the first weekday after Christmas Day.
[from the old custom of giving presents
(*Christmas boxes*) to tradesmen and
servants on that day]

box number *noun* (*plural* **box numbers**)
the number of a pigeon-hole to which
letters may be addressed in a newspaper
office or post office.

box office *noun* (*plural* **box offices**)
an office for booking seats at a theatre or
cinema etc.
[because boxes could be reserved there]

boy *noun* (*plural* **boys**)
1 a male child. 2 a young man. **boyhood**
noun, **boyish** *adjective* [origin unknown]

boycott *verb* (**boycotts, boycotting,
boycotted**)
refuse to use or have anything to do with,
*They boycotted the buses when the fares
went up.* **boycott** *noun*
[from the name of Captain Boycott, a harsh
landlord in Ireland whose tenants in 1880
refused to deal with him]

boyfriend *noun* (*plural* **boyfriends**)
a boy that a girl regularly goes out with.

bra *noun* (*plural* **bras**)
a piece of underwear worn by women to
support their breasts.
[abbreviation of French *brassière*]

brace *noun* (*plural* **braces**)
1 a device for holding things in place. 2 a
pair, *a brace of pheasants.*
brace *verb* (**braces, bracing, braced**)
support; make a thing firm against
something. [from Latin *bracchia* = arms]

bracelet *noun* (*plural* **bracelets**)
an ornament worn round the wrist.
[same origin as *brace*]

braces *plural noun*
straps to hold trousers up, passing over the
shoulders.

bracing *adjective*
making you feel refreshed and healthy, *the
bracing sea breeze.*

bracken *noun*
1 a large fern. 2 a mass of ferns.
[from Old Norse]

bracket *noun* (*plural* **brackets**)
1 a mark used in pairs to enclose words or
figures, *There are round brackets ( ) and
square brackets [ ].* 2 a support attached to
a wall etc. 3 a group or range between
certain limits, *a high income bracket.*
bracket *verb* (**brackets, bracketing,
bracketed**)
1 enclose in brackets. 2 put things together
because they are similar.
[from Latin *bracae* = breeches]

brackish *adjective*
(of water) slightly salty.
[from German or Dutch *brac* = salt water]

bradawl *noun* (*plural* **bradawls**)
a small tool for boring holes.
[from Old Norse *broddr* = spike, + *awl*]

brae (*say* bray) *noun* (*plural* **braes**)
(*Scottish*)
a hillside. [from Old Norse]

brag *verb* (**brags, bragging, bragged**)
boast. [origin unknown]

braggart *noun* (*plural* **braggarts**)
a person who brags.

brahmin *noun* (*plural* **brahmins**)
a member of the highest Hindu class,
originally priests.
[from Sanskrit *brahman* = priest]

braid *noun* (*plural* **braids**)
1 a plait of hair. 2 a strip of cloth with a
woven decorative pattern, used as
trimming.
braid *verb* (**braids, braiding, braided**)
1 plait. 2 trim with braid.
[from Old English]

Braille *noun* (rhymes with *mail*)
a system of representing letters etc. by
raised dots which blind people can read by
feeling them.
[named after Louis Braille, a blind French
teacher who invented it in about 1830]

brain *noun* (*plural* brains)
1 the organ inside the top of the head that controls the body. 2 the mind; intelligence. [from Old English]

brainwash *verb* (brainwashes, brainwashing, brainwashed)
force a person to give up one set of ideas or beliefs and accept new ones; indoctrinate.

brainwave *noun* (*plural* brainwaves)
a sudden bright idea.

brainy *adjective*
clever; intelligent.

braise *verb* (braises, braising, braised)
cook slowly in a little liquid in a closed container. [same origin as *brazier*]

brake *noun* (*plural* brakes)
a device for slowing or stopping something.
brake *verb* (brakes, braking, braked)
use a brake. [origin unknown]

bramble *noun* (*plural* brambles)
a blackberry bush or a prickly bush like it. [from Old English; related to *broom*]

bran *noun*
ground-up husks of corn. [from old French]

branch *noun* (*plural* branches)
1 a woody arm-like part of a tree or shrub. 2 a part of a railway, road, or river etc. that leads off from the main part. 3 a shop or office etc. that belongs to a large organization.
branch *verb* (branches, branching, branched)
form a branch.
branch out start something new.
[from Latin *branca* = a paw]

brand *noun* (*plural* brands)
1 a particular make of goods. 2 a mark made by branding. 3 a piece of burning wood.
brand *verb* (brands, branding, branded)
1 mark cattle or sheep etc. with a hot iron to identify them. 2 sell goods under a particular trade mark. [from Old English]

brandish *verb* (brandishes, brandishing, brandished)
wave something about. [via old French from Germanic; related to *brand*]

brand new *adjective*
completely new.

brandy *noun* (*plural* brandies)
a strong alcoholic drink, usually made from wine. [from Dutch *brandewijn* = burnt (distilled) wine]

brash *adjective*
1 impudent. 2 reckless. [origin unknown]

brass *noun* (*plural* brasses)
1 a metal that is an alloy of copper and zinc. 2 wind instruments made of brass, e.g. trumpets and trombones.
brass *adjective*, **brassy** *adjective*
[from Old English]

brassière (*say* bras-ee-air) *noun* (*plural* brassières)
a bra. [French]

brat *noun* (*plural* brats) (*contemptuous*)
a child. [origin unknown]

bravado (*say* brav-ah-doh) *noun*
a display of boldness. [from Spanish]

brave *adjective*
having or showing courage. **bravely** *adverb*, **bravery** *noun*
brave *noun* (*plural* braves)
a Native American warrior.
brave *verb* (braves, braving, braved)
face and endure something bravely. [from Latin *barbarus* = barbarous]

bravo (*say* brah-voh) *interjection*
well done! [Italian]

brawl *noun* (*plural* brawls)
a noisy quarrel or fight.
brawl *verb* (brawls, brawling, brawled)
take part in a brawl. [origin unknown]

brawn *noun*
1 muscular strength. 2 cold boiled pork or veal pressed in a mould. [via old French from Germanic]

brawny *adjective*
strong and muscular.

bray *noun* (*plural* brays)
the loud harsh cry of a donkey. **bray** *verb*
[from old French *braire* = to cry]

brazen *adjective*
1 made of brass. 2 shameless, *brazen impudence.*

brazen *verb* (**brazens, brazening, brazened**)
brazen it out behave as if there is nothing to be ashamed of when you know you have done wrong.
[from Old English]

brazier (*say* bray-zee-er) *noun* (*plural* **braziers**)
a metal framework for holding burning coals. [from French *braise* = coals, embers]

breach *noun* (*plural* **breaches**)
1 the breaking of an agreement or rule etc.
2 a broken place; a gap.

breach *verb* (**breaches, breaching, breached**)
break through; make a gap. [via old French from Germanic; related to *break*]

bread *noun* (*plural* **breads**)
a food made by baking flour and water, usually with yeast. **breadcrumbs** *noun*
[from Old English]

breadth *noun*
width; broadness. [from Old English]

breadwinner *noun* (*plural* **breadwinners**)
the member of a family who earns money to support the others.

break *verb* (**breaks, breaking, broke, broken**)
1 divide or fall into pieces by hitting or pressing. 2 fail to keep a promise or law etc. 3 stop for a time; end, *She broke her silence.* 4 change, *the weather broke.*
5 damage; stop working properly.
6 (of waves) fall in foam. 7 go suddenly or with force, *They broke through.* 8 appear suddenly, *Dawn had broken.* **breakage** *noun*
break a record do better than anyone else has done before.
break down 1 stop working properly.
2 collapse.
break out 1 begin suddenly. 2 escape.
break the news make something known.
break up 1 break into small parts.
2 separate at the end of a school term.

break *noun* (*plural* **breaks**)
1 a broken place; a gap. 2 an escape; a sudden dash. 3 a short rest from work.
4 a number of points scored continuously

in snooker etc. 5 (*informal*) a piece of luck; an opportunity.
break of day dawn.
[from Old English]

breakable *adjective*
able to be broken.

breakdown *noun* (*plural* **breakdowns**)
1 breaking down; failure. 2 a period of mental illness caused by anxiety or depression. 3 an analysis of accounts or statistics. 4 a sudden failure to work, esp. by a car, *We had a breakdown on the motorway; the breakdown of law and order.*

breaker *noun* (*plural* **breakers**)
a large wave breaking on the shore.

breakfast *noun* (*plural* **breakfasts**)
the first meal of the day.
[from *break* + *fast²*]

breakneck *adjective*
dangerously fast, *He had to drive at breakneck speed to get there on time.*

breakthrough *noun* (*plural* **breakthroughs**)
an important advance or achievement.

breakwater *noun* (*plural* **breakwaters**)
a wall built out into the sea to protect a coast from heavy waves.

bream *noun* (*plural* **bream**)
a kind of fish with an arched back.
[via old French from Germanic]

breast *noun* (*plural* **breasts**)
1 one of the two fleshy parts on the upper front of a woman's body that produce milk to feed a baby. 2 a person's or animal's chest. [from Old English]

breastbone *noun* (*plural* **breastbones**)
the flat bone down the centre of the chest or breast.

breastplate *noun* (*plural* **breastplates**)
a piece of armour covering the chest.

breath (*say* breth) *noun* (*plural* **breaths**)
1 air drawn into the lungs and sent out again. 2 a gentle blowing, *a breath of wind.*
out of breath panting.

take your breath away surprise or delight you greatly.
under your breath in a whisper.
[from Old English]

breathalyser *noun* (*plural* **breathalysers**)
a device for measuring the amount of alcohol in a person's breath.
breathalyse *verb* [from *breath* + *analyse*]

breathe (*say* bree*th*) *verb* (**breathes, breathing, breathed**)
1 take air into the body and send it out again. 2 speak or utter, *Don't breathe a word of this.* [from *breath*]

breather (*say* bree-ther) *noun* (*plural* **breathers**)
a pause for rest, *Let's take a breather.*

breathless *adjective*
out of breath.

breathtaking *adjective*
very surprising or delightful.

breech *noun* (*plural* **breeches**)
the back part of a gun barrel, where the bullets are put in.
[from Old English *brec* = hindquarters]

breeches (*say* brich-iz) *plural noun*
trousers reaching to just below the knees.
[same origin as *breech*]

breed *verb* (**breeds, breeding, bred**)
1 produce young creatures. 2 keep animals in order to produce young ones from them.
3 bring up or train. 4 create or produce, *Poverty breeds illness.* **breeder** *noun*
breed *noun* (*plural* **breeds**)
a variety of animals with qualities inherited from their parents.
[from Old English; related to *brood*]

breeze *noun* (*plural* **breezes**)
a wind. **breezy** *adjective*
[probably from Spanish]

breeze-block *noun* (*plural* **breeze-blocks**)
a lightweight building block made of cinders and cement.
[same origin as *brazier*]

brethren *plural noun* (*old use*)
brothers. [the old plural of *brother*]

breve (*say* breev) *noun* (*plural* **breves**)
a note in music, lasting eight times as long as a crochet. [same origin as *brief*]

brevity *noun*
shortness; briefness. [same origin as *brief*]

brew *verb* (**brews, brewing, brewed**)
1 make beer or tea. 2 develop, *Trouble is brewing.*
brew *noun* (*plural* **brews**)
a brewed drink. [from Old English]

brewer *noun* (*plural* **brewers**)
a person who brews beer for sale.

brewery *noun* (*plural* **breweries**)
a place where beer is brewed.

briar *noun* (*plural* **briars**)
a different spelling of *brier*.

bribe *noun* (*plural* **bribes**)
money or a gift offered to a person to influence him or her.
bribe *verb* (**bribes, bribing, bribed**)
give someone a bribe. **bribery** *noun*
[from Old French *briber* = beg]

brick *noun* (*plural* **bricks**)
1 a small hard block of baked clay etc. used to build walls. 2 a rectangular block of something.
brick *verb* (**bricks, bricking, bricked**)
close something with bricks, *We bricked up the gap in the wall.*
[from old German or Dutch]

bricklayer *noun* (*plural* **bricklayers**)
a worker who builds with bricks.

bride *noun* (*plural* **brides**)
a woman on her wedding day. **bridal** *adjective* [from Old English]

bridegroom *noun* (*plural* **bridegrooms**)
a man on his wedding day. [from Old English *brydguma* = bride's man]

bridesmaid *noun* (*plural* **bridesmaids**)
a girl or unmarried woman who attends the bride at a wedding.

bridge¹ *noun* (*plural* **bridges**)
1 a structure built over and across a river, railway, or road etc. to allow people to cross it. 2 a high platform above a ship's

deck, for the officer in charge. **3** the bony upper part of the nose. **4** something that connects things.
bridge *verb* (**bridges, bridging, bridged**)
make or form a bridge over something.
[from Old English]

bridge² *noun*
a card game rather like whist.
[origin unknown]

bridle *noun* (*plural* **bridles**)
the part of a horse's harness that fits over its head.
[from Old English; related to *braid*]

bridle path or **bridle road** *noun* (*plural* **bridle paths, bridle roads**)
a road suitable for horses but not for vehicles.

brief *adjective*
short. **briefly** *adverb*, **briefness** *noun*
in brief in a few words.
brief *noun* (*plural* **briefs**)
instructions and information given to someone, especially to a barrister.
brief *verb* (**briefs, briefing, briefed**)
1 give a brief to a barrister. **2** instruct or inform someone concisely in advance.
[from Latin *brevis* = short]

briefcase *noun* (*plural* **briefcases**)
a flat case for carrying documents etc.

briefing *noun* (*plural* **briefings**)
a meeting to give someone concise instructions or information.

briefs *plural noun*
very short knickers or underpants.

brier *noun* (*plural* **brier**)
a thorny bush, especially the wild rose.
[from Old English]

brigade *noun* (*plural* **brigades**)
1 a large unit of an army. **2** a group of people organized for a special purpose, *the fire brigade.*
[from Italian *brigata* = a troop]

brigadier *noun* (*plural* **brigadiers**)
a brigade-commander.

brigand *noun* (*plural* **brigands**)
a member of a band of robbers.
[from Italian *brigante* = foot soldier]

bright *adjective*
1 giving a strong light; shining. **2** clever. **3** cheerful. **brightly** *adverb*, **brightness** *noun*
[from Old English]

brighten *verb* (**brightens, brightening, brightened**)
make or become brighter.

brilliant *adjective*
1 very bright; sparkling. **2** very clever. **brilliantly** *adverb*, **brilliance** *noun* [from Italian *brillare* = shine]

brim *noun* (*plural* **brims**)
1 the edge of a cup etc. **2** the bottom part of a hat that sticks out.
brim-full *adjective* completely full.
brim *verb* (**brims, brimming, brimmed**)
be full to the brim.
brim over overflow.
[origin unknown]

brimstone *noun* (*old use*)
sulphur. [from Old English *brynstan* = burning stone]

brine *noun*
salt water. **briny** *adjective*
[from Old English]

bring *verb* (**brings, bringing, brought**)
cause a person or thing to come; lead; carry.
bring about cause to happen.
bring off achieve; do something successfully.
bring up 1 look after and train growing children. **2** mention a subject. **3** vomit. **4** cause to stop suddenly.
[from Old English]

brink *noun* (*plural* **brinks**)
1 the edge of a steep place or of a stretch of water. **2** the point beyond which something will happen, *We were on the brink of war.*
[from Old Norse *brekka* = hill, slope]

brisk *adjective*
quick and lively. **briskly** *adverb*, **briskness** *noun* [same origin as *brusque*]

bristle *noun* (*plural* **bristles**)
1 a short stiff hair. **2** one of the stiff pieces of hair, wire, or plastic etc. in a brush.
bristly *adjective*

bristle *verb* (bristles, bristling, bristled)
1 (of an animal) raise its bristles in anger or fear. **2** show indignation.
bristle with be full of, *The plan bristled with problems.*
[from Old English]

Britain *noun*
the island made up of England, Scotland, and Wales, with the small adjacent islands; Great Britain.

USAGE: Note the difference in use between the terms *Britain, Great Britain,* the *United Kingdom,* and the *British Isles.* Great Britain (or Britain) is used to refer to the island made up of England, Scotland, and Wales. The United Kingdom includes Great Britain and Northern Ireland. The British Isles refers to the whole of the island group which includes Great Britain, Ireland, and all the smaller nearby islands.

British Isles *plural noun*
the island group which includes Great Britain, Ireland, and all the smaller nearby islands.

USAGE: See note at *Britain.*

brittle *adjective*
hard but easy to break or snap. **brittleness** *noun* [from Old English]

broach *verb* (broaches, broaching, broached)
1 make a hole in something and draw out liquid. **2** start a discussion of something, *We were unwilling to broach the subject.*
[from old French]

broad *adjective*
1 large across; wide. **2** full and complete, *broad daylight.* **3** in general terms; not detailed, *We are in broad agreement.* **4** strong and unmistakable, *a broad hint; a broad accent.* **broadly** *adverb,* **broadness** *noun* [from Old English]

broad bean *noun* (*plural* broad beans)
a bean with large flat seeds.

broadcast *noun* (*plural* broadcasts)
a programme sent out on the radio or on television.

broadcast *verb* (broadcasts, broadcasting, broadcast)
send out a programme on the radio or on television. **broadcaster** *noun* [originally = to scatter widely: from *broad* + *cast*]

broaden *verb* (broadens, broadening, broadened)
make or become broader.

broad-minded *adjective*
tolerant; not easily shocked.

broadside *noun* (*plural* broadsides)
1 firing by all guns on one side of a ship. **2** a verbal attack.
broadside on sideways on.
[originally = the side of a ship, above the waterline]

brocade *noun*
material woven with raised patterns.
[from Italian]

broccoli *noun* (*plural* broccoli)
a kind of cauliflower with greenish flowerheads. [Italian, = cabbage-heads]

brochure (*say* broh-shoor) *noun* (*plural* brochures)
a booklet or pamphlet containing information. [from French, = stitching (because originally the pages were roughly stitched together)]

brogue[1] (rhymes with *rogue*) *noun* (*plural* brogues)
a strong kind of shoe. [via Scottish Gaelic and Irish from Old Norse]

brogue[2] *noun* (*plural* brogues)
a strong accent, *He spoke with an Irish brogue.* [origin unknown]

broil *verb* (broils, broiling, broiled)
1 cook on a fire or gridiron. **2** make or be very hot. [from French *brûler* = to burn]

broke *adjective* (*informal*)
having spent all your money.
[old past participle of *break*]

broken-hearted *adjective*
overwhelmed with grief.

broken home *noun* (*plural* broken homes)
a family lacking one parent through divorce or separation.

broker *noun* (*plural* brokers)
a person who buys and sells things,
especially shares, for other people.

brolly *noun* (*plural* brollies) (*informal*)
an umbrella.

bromide *noun*
a substance used in medicine to calm the
nerves. [from *bromine*, a chemical from
which bromide is made]

bronchial (*say* bronk-ee-al) *adjective*
to do with the tubes that lead from the
windpipe to the lungs.
[from Greek *bronchos* = windpipe]

bronchitis (*say* bronk-I-tiss) *noun*
a disease with bronchial inflammation,
which makes you cough a lot.
[from Greek *bronchos* = windpipe, + *-itis*]

brontosaurus *noun* (*plural*
brontosauruses)
a large dinosaur that fed on plants. [from
Greek *bronte* = thunder + *sauros* = lizard]

bronze *noun* (*plural* bronzes)
1 a metal that is an alloy of copper and tin.
2 something made of bronze. 3 a bronze
medal. 4 yellowish-brown. **bronze** *adjective*
[probably from Persian *birinj* = brass]

Bronze Age *noun*
the time when tools and weapons were
made of bronze.

brooch *noun* (*plural* brooches)
an ornament with a hinged pin for
fastening it on to clothes.
[a different spelling of *broach*]

brood *noun* (*plural* broods)
young birds that were hatched together.
brood *verb* (broods, brooding, brooded)
1 sit on eggs to hatch them. 2 keep
thinking about something, especially with
resentment. [from Old English]

broody *adjective*
1 (of a hen) wanting to sit on eggs.
2 thoughtful; brooding. 3 (of a woman)
longing to have children.

brook¹ *noun* (*plural* brooks)
a small stream. [from Old English *broc*]

brook² *verb* (brooks, brooking, brooked)
tolerate, *brook no delay*.
[from Old English *brucan*]

broom *noun* (*plural* brooms)
1 a brush with a long handle, for sweeping.
2 a shrub with yellow, white, or pink
flowers. [from Old English *brom* = the plant
(from which brushes used to be made)]

broomstick *noun* (*plural* broomsticks)
a broom-handle.

broth *noun* (*plural* broths)
a kind of thin soup. [from Old English]

brothel *noun* (*plural* brothels)
a house in which women work as
prostitutes. [from Old English *breothan*
= degenerate, get worse]

brother *noun* (*plural* brothers)
1 a son of the same parents as another
person. 2 a man who is a fellow member of
a Church, trade union, etc.
brotherly *adjective* [from Old English]

brotherhood *noun* (*plural* brotherhoods)
1 friendliness and companionship between
men. 2 a society or association of men.

brother-in-law *noun* (*plural* brothers-in-
law)
the brother of a married person's husband
or wife; the husband of a person's sister.

brow *noun* (*plural* brows)
1 an eyebrow. 2 the forehead. 3 the ridge
at the top of a hill; the edge of a cliff.
[from Old English]

brown *noun* (*plural* browns)
a colour between orange and black.
brown *adjective*
1 of the colour brown. 2 having a brown
skin; suntanned.
brown *verb* (browns, browning, browned)
make or become brown. [from Old English]

Brownie *noun* (*plural* Brownies)
a member of a junior branch of the Guides.

browse *verb* (browses, browsing, browsed)
1 read or look at something casually. 2 feed
on grass or leaves. [from old French]

bruise *noun* (*plural* bruises)
a dark mark made on the skin by hitting it.

bruise *verb* (bruises, bruising, bruised)
give or get a bruise or bruises.
[from Old English]

brunette *noun* (*plural* **brunettes**)
a woman with dark-brown hair.
[from French *brun* = brown, + *-ette*]

brunt *noun*
the chief impact or strain, *They bore the brunt of the attack.* [origin unknown]

brush *noun* (*plural* **brushes**)
1 an implement used for cleaning or painting things or for smoothing the hair, usually with pieces of hair, wire, or plastic etc. set in a solid base. **2** a fox's bushy tail. **3** brushing, *Give it a good brush.* **4** a short fight, *They had a brush with the enemy.*
brush *verb* (brushes, brushing, brushed)
1 use a brush on something. **2** touch gently in passing.
brush up revise a subject.
[from old French]

brusque (*say* bruusk) *adjective*
curt and offhand in manner.
brusquely *adverb*
[via French from Italian *brusco* = sour]

Brussels sprouts *plural noun*
the edible buds of a kind of cabbage.
[named after Brussels, the capital of Belgium]

brutal *adjective*
very cruel. **brutally** *adverb*, **brutality** *noun*

brute *noun* (*plural* **brutes**)
1 a brutal person. **2** an animal. **brutish** *adjective* [from Latin *brutus* = stupid]

B.Sc. *abbreviation*
Bachelor of Science.

BSE *abbreviation*
bovine spongiform encephalopathy; a fatal disease of cattle that affects the nervous system and makes the cow stagger about. BSE is sometimes known as 'mad cow disease'.

bubble *noun* (*plural* **bubbles**)
1 a thin transparent ball of liquid filled with air or gas. **2** a small ball of air in something. **bubbly** *adjective*

bubble *verb* (bubbles, bubbling, bubbled)
1 send up bubbles; rise in bubbles. **2** show great liveliness. [related to *burble*]

bubblegum *noun*
chewing gum that can be blown into large bubbles.

buccaneer *noun* (*plural* **buccaneers**)
a pirate. [from French]

buck¹ *noun* (*plural* **bucks**)
a male deer, rabbit, or hare.
buck *verb* (bucks, bucking, bucked)
(of a horse) jump with its back arched.
buck up (*informal*) **1** hurry. **2** cheer up.
[from Old English]

buck² *noun*
pass the buck (*slang*) pass the responsibility for something to another person.
buck-passing *noun* [origin unknown]

bucket *noun* (*plural* **buckets**)
a container with a handle, for carrying liquids etc. **bucketful** *noun* [from French]

buckle¹ *noun* (*plural* **buckles**)
a device through which a belt or strap is threaded to fasten it.
buckle *verb* (buckles, buckling, buckled)
fasten something with a buckle. [from Latin *buccula* = cheek-strap of a helmet]

buckle² *verb* (buckles, buckling, buckled)
bend or crumple.
buckle down to start working hard at something.
[from French *boucler* = bulge]

buckler *noun* (*plural* **bucklers**)
a small round shield. [from old French]

bucolic (*say* bew-kol-ik) *adjective*
to do with country life.
[from Greek *boukolos* = herdsman]

bud *noun* (*plural* **buds**)
a flower or leaf before it opens.
[origin unknown]

Buddhism (*say* buud-izm) *noun*
a faith that started in Asia and follows the teachings of the Indian philosopher Gautama Buddha, who lived in the 5th century BC. **Buddhist** *noun*
[from Sanskrit *Buddha* = enlightened one]

budding *adjective*
beginning to develop. [from *bud*]

buddy *noun* (*plural* **buddies**) (*informal*)
a friend. [probably from *brother*]

budge *verb* (**budges, budging, budged**)
if you cannot budge something, you cannot move it at all. [from French]

budgerigar *noun* (*plural* **budgerigars**)
an Australian bird often kept as a pet in a cage. [from Australian Aboriginal *budgeri* = good + *gar* = cockatoo]

budget *noun* (*plural* **budgets**)
1 a plan for spending money wisely. 2 an amount of money set aside for a purpose. **budgetary** *adjective*
the Budget the Chancellor of the Exchequer's statement of plans to raise money (e.g. by taxes).
budget *verb* (**budgets, budgeting, budgeted**)
plan a budget. [from old French *bougette* = small leather bag, purse]

budgie *noun* (*plural* **budgies**) (*informal*)
a budgerigar.

buff *adjective*
of a dull yellow colour.
buff *verb* (**buffs, buffing, buffed**)
polish with soft material.
[from *buff leather* = leather of buffalo hide]

buffalo *noun* (*plural* **buffalo** or **buffaloes**)
a large ox. Different kinds are found in Asia, Africa, and North America (where they are also called *bison*).
[from Portuguese]

buffer *noun* (*plural* **buffers**)
something that softens a blow, especially a device on a railway engine or wagon or at the end of a track.
[from an old word *buff* = a blow (as in *blind man's buff*): related to *buffet²*]

buffer state *noun* (*plural* **buffer states**)
a small country between two powerful ones, thought to reduce the chance of these two attacking each other.

buffet¹ (*say* buu-fay) *noun* (*plural* **buffets**)
1 a café at a station. 2 a meal where guests serve themselves. [from French = stool]

buffet² (*say* buf-it) *noun* (*plural* **buffets**)
a hit, especially with the hand.
buffet *verb* (**buffets, buffeting, buffeted**)
hit or knock, *Strong winds buffeted the aircraft.* [from old French *buffe* = a blow]

buffoon *noun* (*plural* **buffoons**)
a person who plays the fool. **buffoonery** *noun* [from Latin *buffo* = clown]

bug *noun* (*plural* **bugs**)
1 an insect. 2 an error in a computer program that prevents it working properly. 3 (*informal*) a germ or virus. 3 (*informal*) a secret hidden microphone.
bug *verb* (**bugs, bugging, bugged**) (*slang*)
1 fit with a secret hidden microphone. 2 annoy. [origin unknown]

bugbear *noun* (*plural* **bugbears**)
something you fear or dislike.
[from an old word *bug* = bogy]

buggy *noun* (*plural* **buggies**)
1 a light, horse-drawn carriage. 2 a kind of chair on wheels for pushing young children around. [origin unknown]

bugle *noun* (*plural* **bugles**)
a brass instrument like a small trumpet, used for sounding military signals.
bugler *noun* [origin unknown]

build *verb* (**builds, building, built**)
make something by putting parts together.
build in include. **built-in** *adjective*
build up 1 establish gradually.
2 accumulate. 3 cover an area with buildings. 4 make stronger or more famous, *build up a reputation.*
built-up *adjective*
build *noun* (*plural* **builds**)
the shape of someone's body, *of slender build.* [from Old English]

builder *noun* (*plural* **builders**)
someone who puts up buildings.

building *noun* (*plural* **buildings**)
1 the process of constructing houses etc. 2 a permanent built structure that people can go into.

building society *noun* (*plural* **building societies**)
an organization that accepts deposits of money and lends to people who want to buy houses etc.

bulb *noun* (*plural* **bulbs**)
1 a thick rounded part of a plant from which a stem grows up and roots grow down. **2** a rounded part of something, *the bulb of a thermometer.* **3** a glass globe that produces electric light. **bulbous** *adjective*
[from Greek *bolbos* = onion]

bulge *noun* (*plural* **bulges**)
a rounded swelling; an outward curve. **bulgy** *adjective*
bulge *verb* (**bulges, bulging, bulged**)
form or cause to form a bulge.
[from Latin *bulga* = bag]

bulk *noun* (*plural* **bulks**)
1 the size of something, especially when it is large. **2** the greater portion; the majority, *The bulk of the population voted for it.*
in bulk in large amounts.
bulk *verb* (**bulks, bulking, bulked**)
increase the size or thickness of something, *bulk it out.* [from Old English]

bulky *adjective* (**bulkier, bulkiest**)
taking up a lot of space. **bulkiness** *noun*

bull¹ *noun* (*plural* **bulls**)
the fully-grown male of cattle or of certain other large animals (e.g. elephant, whale, seal). [from Old Norse]

bull² *noun* (*plural* **bulls**)
an edict issued by the Pope.
[from Latin *bulla* = seal, sealed letter]

bulldog *noun* (*plural* **bulldogs**)
a dog of a powerful courageous breed with a short thick neck.
[because it was used for attacking tethered bulls in the sport of 'bull-baiting']

bulldoze *verb* (**bulldozes, bulldozing, bulldozed**)
clear with a bulldozer.
[originally American; origin unknown]

bulldozer *noun* (*plural* **bulldozers**)
a powerful tractor with a wide metal blade or scoop in front, used for shifting soil or clearing ground.

bullet *noun* (*plural* **bullets**)
a small lump of metal shot from a rifle or revolver. [from French *boulet* = little ball]

bulletin *noun* (*plural* **bulletins**)
a public statement giving news.
[via French from Italian; related to *bull²*]

bulletproof *adjective*
able to keep out bullets.

bullfight *noun* (*plural* **bullfights**)
a public entertainment in which bulls are tormented and killed in an arena.
bullfighter *noun*

bullfinch *noun* (*plural* **bullfinches**)
a bird with a strong beak and a pink breast.

bullion *noun*
bars of gold or silver.
[from old French *bouillon* = a mint]

bullock *noun* (*plural* **bullocks**)
a young castrated bull.
[from Old English *bulloc* = young bull]

bull's-eye *noun* (*plural* **bull's-eyes**)
1 the centre of a target. **2** a hard shiny peppermint sweet.

bully *verb* (**bullies, bullying, bullied**)
1 use strength or power to hurt or frighten a weaker person. **2** start play in hockey, when two opponents tap the ground and each other's stick, *bully off.*
bully *noun* (*plural* **bullies**)
someone who bullies people.
[probably from Dutch]

bulrush *noun* (*plural* **bulrushes**)
a tall rush with a thick velvety head.
[probably from *bull¹*, suggesting something large]

bulwark *noun* (*plural* **bulwarks**)
a wall of earth built as a defence; a protection. [from German or Dutch]

bulwarks *plural noun*
a ship's side above the level of the deck.

bum *noun* (*plural* **bums**) (*slang*)
a person's bottom. [origin unknown]

bumble *verb* (**bumbles, bumbling, bumbled**)
move or behave or speak clumsily.
[related to *boom¹*]

bumble-bee *noun* (*plural* **bumble-bees**)
a large bee with a loud hum.

bump verb (bumps, bumping, bumped)
1 knock against something. 2 move along with jolts.
bump into (informal) meet by chance.
bump off (slang) kill.
bump noun (plural bumps)
1 the action or sound of bumping. 2 a swelling or lump. **bumpy** adjective
[imitating the sound]

bumper¹ noun (plural bumpers)
1 a bar along the front or back of a motor vehicle to protect it in collisions. 2 a ball in cricket that bounces high.

bumper² adjective
unusually large or plentiful, a bumper crop.

bumpkin noun (plural bumpkins)
a country person with awkward manners.
[from Dutch]

bumptious (say bump-shus) adjective
loud and conceited. **bumptiousness** noun
[from bump; made up as a joke]

bun noun (plural buns)
1 a small round sweet cake. 2 hair twisted into a round bunch at the back of the head.
[origin unknown]

bunch noun (plural bunches)
a number of things joined or fastened together. [origin unknown]

bundle noun (plural bundles)
a number of things tied or wrapped together.
bundle verb (bundles, bundling, bundled)
1 make a number of things into a bundle.
2 push hurriedly or carelessly, They bundled him into a taxi.
[probably from old German or old Dutch]

bung noun (plural bungs)
a stopper for closing a hole in a barrel or jar.
bung verb (bungs, bunging, bunged) (slang)
throw, Bung it here.
bunged up (informal) blocked.
[from old Dutch]

bungalow noun (plural bungalows)
a house without any upstairs rooms.
[from Hindi bangla = of Bengal]

bungee jumping noun
the sport of jumping from a height with a long piece of elastic (called a **bungee**) tied to your legs to stop you from hitting the ground. [origin unknown]

bungle verb (bungles, bungling, bungled)
make a mess of doing something. **bungler** noun [because bungle sounds clumsy]

bunion noun (plural bunions)
a swelling at the side of the joint where the big toe joins the foot. [origin unknown]

bunk¹ noun (plural bunks)
a bed built like a shelf. [origin unknown]

bunk² noun
do a bunk (slang) run away. **bunk** verb
[origin unknown]

bunker noun (plural bunkers)
1 a container for storing fuel. 2 a sandy hollow built as an obstacle on a golf course.
3 an underground shelter.
[origin unknown]

bunny noun (plural bunnies) (informal)
a rabbit. [from dialect bun = rabbit]

Bunsen burner noun (plural Bunsen burners)
a small gas burner used in scientific work.
[named after a German scientist, R. W. Bunsen]

bunting¹ noun (plural buntings)
a kind of small bird. [origin unknown]

bunting² noun
strips of small flags hung up to decorate streets and buildings. [origin unknown]

buoy (say boi) noun (plural buoys)
a floating object anchored to mark a channel or underwater rocks etc.
buoy verb (buoys, buoying, buoyed)
1 keep something afloat. 2 hearten or cheer someone, They were buoyed up with new hope. [probably from old Dutch]

buoyant (say boi-ant) adjective
1 able to float. 2 light-hearted; cheerful.
buoyantly adverb, **buoyancy** noun
[from French or Spanish; related to buoy]

bur *noun* (*plural* **burs**)
a plant's seed case or flower that clings to hair or clothes.
[from a Scandinavian language]

burble *verb* (**burbles, burbling, burbled**)
make a gentle murmuring sound.
burble *noun* [imitating the sound]

burden *noun* (*plural* **burdens**)
1 a heavy load that you have to carry.
2 something troublesome that you have to bear, *Exams are a burden*.
burdensome *adjective*
burden *verb* (**burdens, burdening, burdened**)
put a burden on a person etc.
[from Old English]

bureau (*say* bewr-oh) *noun* (*plural* **bureaux**)
1 a writing desk. 2 a business office, *They will tell you at the Information Bureau.*
[French, = desk]

bureaucracy (*say* bewr-ok-ra-see) *noun*
the use of too many rules and forms by officials, especially in government departments.
bureaucratic (*say* bewr-ok-**rat**-ik) *adjective*
[from *bureau* + -*cracy*]

bureaucrat (*say* **bewr**-ok-rat) *noun* (*plural* **bureaucrats**)
a person who works in a government department.

burgeon (*say* ber-jon) *verb* (**burgeons, burgeoning, burgeoned**)
grow rapidly. [from French]

burger *noun* (*plural* **burgers**)
a hamburger. [short for *hamburger* = from *Hamburg*, a city in Germany; the first syllable was dropped because people thought it referred to ham]

burglar *noun* (*plural* **burglars**)
a person who enters a building illegally, especially in order to steal things.
burglary *noun* [from French]

burgle *verb* (**burgles, burgling, burgled**)
rob a place as a burglar. [from *burglar*]

burgundy *noun* (*plural* **burgundies**)
a rich red or white wine.
[originally made in Burgundy in France]

burial *noun* (*plural* **burials**)
burying somebody.

burlesque (*say* ber-lesk) *noun* (*plural* **burlesques**)
a comical imitation. [via French from Italian *burla* = ridicule, joke]

burly *adjective* (**burlier, burliest**)
having a strong heavy body.
[from Old English]

burn¹ *verb* (**burns, burning, burned** or **burnt**)
1 blaze or glow with fire; produce heat or light by combustion. 2 damage or destroy something by fire, heat, or chemicals. 3 be damaged or destroyed by fire etc. 4 feel very hot.

USAGE: The word *burnt* (not *burned*) is always used when an adjective is required, e.g. in *burnt wood*. As parts of the verb, either *burned* or *burnt* may be used, e.g. *the wood had burned* or *had burnt completely*.

burn *noun* (*plural* **burns**)
1 a mark or injury made by burning. 2 the firing of a spacecraft's rockets.
[from Old English *birnan*]

burn² *noun* (*plural* **burns**) (*Scottish*)
a brook. [from Old English *burna*]

burner *noun* (*plural* **burners**)
the part of a lamp or cooker that gives out the flame.

burning *adjective*
1 intense, *a burning ambition*. 2 very important; hotly discussed, *a burning question*.

burnish *verb* (**burnishes, burnishing, burnished**)
polish by rubbing. [from old French]

burr *noun* (*plural* **burrs**)
1 a bur. 2 a whirring sound. 3 a soft country accent. [a different spelling of *bur*]

burrow *noun* (*plural* **burrows**)
a hole or tunnel dug by a rabbit or fox etc. as a dwelling.
burrow *verb* (**burrows, burrowing, burrowed**)
1 dig a burrow. 2 push your way through or into something; search deeply, *She burrowed in her handbag.*
[a different spelling of *borough*]

bursar *noun* (*plural* **bursars**)
a person who manages the finances and other business of a school or college. [from Latin *bursa* = a bag]

burst *verb* (**bursts, bursting, burst**)
1 break or force apart. 2 come or start suddenly, *It burst into flame. They burst out laughing.* 3 be very full, *bursting with energy.*
burst *noun* (*plural* **bursts**)
1 bursting; a split. 2 something short and forceful, *a burst of gunfire.*
[from Old English]

bury *verb* (**buries, burying, buried**)
1 place a dead body in the earth, a tomb, or the sea. 2 put underground; cover up.
bury the hatchet agree to stop quarrelling or fighting.
[from Old English]

bus *noun* (*plural* **buses**)
a large vehicle for passengers to travel in. [short for *omnibus*]

busby *noun* (*plural* **busbies**)
a tall fur cap worn by the Guards at ceremonies. [origin unknown]

bush *noun* (*plural* **bushes**)
1 a shrub. 2 wild uncultivated land, especially in Africa and Australia. **bushy** *adjective* [from old French or Old Norse]

bushel *noun* (*plural* **bushels**)
a measure for grain and fruit (8 gallons or 4 pecks). [from old French]

busily *adverb*
in a busy way.

business (*say* biz-niss) *noun* (*plural* **businesses**)
1 a person's concern or responsibilities, *Mind your own business.* 2 an affair or subject, *I'm tired of the whole business.* 3 a shop or firm. 4 buying and selling things; trade.
businessman *noun*, **businesswoman** *noun* [from Old English *bisignis* = busyness]

businesslike *adjective*
practical; well-organized.

busker *noun* (*plural* **buskers**)
a person who entertains people in the street. **busking** *noun*
[from an old word *busk* = be a pedlar]

bust[1] *noun* (*plural* **busts**)
1 a sculpture of a person's head, shoulders, and chest. 2 the upper front part of a woman's body. [from Latin]

bust[2] *verb* (**busts, busting, bust**) (*informal*)
break something.
[a different spelling of *burst*]

bustard *noun* (*plural* **bustards**)
a large bird that can run very swiftly. [from old French]

bustle[1] *verb* (**bustles, bustling, bustled**)
hurry in a busy or excited way.
bustle *noun*
hurried or excited activity.
[probably from Old Norse]

bustle[2] *noun* (*plural* **bustles**)
padding used to puff out the top of a long skirt at the back. [origin unknown]

busy *adjective* (**busier, busiest**)
1 having much to do; occupied. 2 full of activity. **busily** *adverb*, **busyness** *noun*
busy *verb* (**busies, busying, busied**)
busy yourself occupy yourself; keep busy. [from Old English]

busybody *noun* (*plural* **busybodies**)
a person who interferes.

but *conjunction*
however; nevertheless, *I wanted to go, but I couldn't.*
but *preposition*
except, *There is no one here but me.*
but *adverb*
only; no more than, *We can but try.* [from Old English]

butcher *noun* (*plural* **butchers**)
1 a person who cuts up meat and sells it. 2 a person who kills cruelly or needlessly. **butchery** *noun*
butcher *verb* (**butchers, butchering, butchered**)
kill cruelly or needlessly.
[from old French]

butler *noun* (*plural* **butlers**)
the chief manservant of a household.
[from Old French *bouteillier* = bottler]

butt¹ *noun* (*plural* **butts**)
1 the thicker end of a weapon or tool.
2 a stub, *cigarette butts*.
[from Dutch *bot* = stumpy]

butt² *noun* (*plural* **butts**)
a large cask or barrel.
[from Latin *buttis* = cask]

butt³ *noun* (*plural* **butts**)
1 a person or thing that is a target for
ridicule or teasing, *He was the butt of their
jokes.* 2 a mound of earth behind the
targets on a shooting range.
butts *plural noun* a shooting range.
[from Old French *but* = goal]

butt⁴ *verb* (**butts, butting, butted**)
1 push or hit with the head as a ram or
goat does. 2 place the edges of things
together.
butt in interrupt or meddle.
[from Old French *buter* = hit]

butter *noun*
a soft fatty food made by churning cream.
buttery *adjective* [from Old English]

buttercup *noun* (*plural* **buttercups**)
a wild plant with bright yellow cup-shaped
flowers.

butter-fingers *noun*
a person who often drops things.

butterfly *noun* (*plural* **butterflies**)
1 an insect with large white or coloured
wings. 2 a swimming stroke in which both
arms are lifted at the same time.

buttermilk *noun*
the liquid that is left after butter has been
made.

butterscotch *noun*
a kind of hard toffee.

buttock *noun* (*plural* **buttocks**)
either of the two fleshy rounded parts of
your bottom. [from Old English]

button *noun* (*plural* **buttons**)
1 a knob or disc sewn on clothes as a
fastening or ornament. 2 a small knob,
Press the button.
button *verb* (**buttons, buttoning, buttoned**)
fasten something with a button or buttons.
[from old French]

buttonhole *noun* (*plural* **buttonholes**)
1 a slit through which a button passes to
fasten clothes. 2 a flower worn on a lapel.
buttonhole *verb* (**buttonholes,
buttonholing, buttonholed**)
stop somebody so that you can talk to him
or her.

buttress *noun* (*plural* **buttresses**)
a support built against a wall.
[same origin as *butt⁴*]

buy *verb* (**buys, buying, bought**)
get something by paying for it. **buyer** *noun*
buy *noun* (*plural* **buys**)
something that is bought.
[from Old English]

buzz *noun* (*plural* **buzzes**)
a vibrating humming sound.
buzz *verb* (**buzzes, buzzing, buzzed**)
1 make a buzz. 2 threaten an aircraft by
deliberately flying close to it.
[imitating the sound]

buzzard *noun* (*plural* **buzzards**)
a kind of hawk. [from Latin *buteo* = falcon]

buzzer *noun* (*plural* **buzzers**)
a device that makes a buzzing sound as a
signal.

by *preposition*
This word is used to show 1 closeness (*Sit
by me*), 2 direction or route (*We got here by
a short cut*), 3 time (*They came by night*),
4 manner or method (*cooking by gas*),
5 amount (*You missed it by inches*).
by the way incidentally.
by yourself alone; without help.

by *adverb*
1 past, *I can't get by.* 2 in reserve; for future
use, *Put it by.*
by and by soon; later on.
by and large on the whole.
[from Old English]

bye *noun* (*plural* **byes**)
1 a run scored in cricket when the ball goes past the batsman without being touched.
2 having no opponent for one round in a tournament and so going on to the next round as if you had won.
[from *by-* = at the side, extra]

bye-bye *interjection*
goodbye.

by-election *noun* (*plural* **by-elections**)
an election to replace a Member of Parliament who has died or resigned.
[from *by-* = extra (an 'extra' election between general elections)]

bygone *adjective*
belonging to the past.
let bygones be bygones forgive and forget.

by-law *noun* (*plural* **by-laws**)
a law that applies only to a particular town or district.
[from Old Norse *byjarlagu* = town law]

bypass *noun* (*plural* **bypasses**)
1 a road taking traffic past a city etc. **2** a channel that allows something to flow when the main route is blocked.
bypass *verb* (**bypasses, bypassing, bypassed**)
avoid something by means of a bypass.

by-product *noun* (*plural* **by-products**)
something produced while something else is being made.
[from *by-* = at the side, besides]

byre *noun* (*plural* **byres**)
a cowshed. [from Old English]

byroad *noun* (*plural* **byroads**)
a minor road.

bystander *noun* (*plural* **bystanders**)
a person standing near but not taking part in something.

byte *noun* (*plural* **bytes**)
a fixed number of bits (= binary digits) in a computer, often representing a single character. [an invented word]

byway *noun* (*plural* **byways**)
a byroad.

byword *noun* (*plural* **bywords**)
a person or thing spoken of as a famous example, *Their firm became a byword for quality*.
[from Old English *biwyrde* = proverb]

Cc

cab *noun* (*plural* **cabs**)
1 a taxi. **2** a compartment for the driver of a lorry, train, bus, or crane. [short for *cabriolet* = a light horsedrawn carriage]

cabaret (*say* **kab**-er-ay) *noun* (*plural* **cabarets**)
an entertainment, especially one provided for the customers in a restaurant or nightclub. [from old French]

cabbage *noun* (*plural* **cabbages**)
a vegetable with green or purple leaves.
[from old French *caboche* = head]

caber *noun* (*plural* **cabers**)
a tree trunk used in the sport of 'tossing the caber'. [from Scottish Gaelic or Irish]

cabin *noun* (*plural* **cabins**)
1 a hut or shelter. **2** a compartment in a ship, aircraft, or spacecraft. **3** a driver's cab. [from Latin]

Cabinet *noun*
the group of chief ministers, chosen by the Prime Minister, who meet to decide government policy.

cabinet *noun* (*plural* **cabinets**)
a cupboard or container with drawers or shelves. [from *cabin*]

cable *noun* (*plural* **cables**)
1 a thick rope of fibre or wire; a thick chain. **2** a covered group of wires laid underground for transmitting electrical signals. **3** a telegram sent overseas.
[from Latin *capulum* = halter]

cable car *noun* (*plural* **cable cars**)
a small cabin suspended on a moving cable, used for carrying people up and down a mountainside.

cable television *noun*
a broadcasting service with signals transmitted by cable to the sets of people who have paid to receive it.

cacao (*say* ka-**kay**-oh) *noun* (*plural* **cacaos**)
a tropical tree with a seed from which cocoa and chocolate are made.
[via Spanish from Nahuatl (a Central American language)]

cache (*say* kash) *noun* (*plural* **caches**)
a hiding place for treasure or stores.
[French, from *cacher* = to hide]

cackle *noun* (*plural* **cackles**)
1 a loud silly laugh. **2** noisy chatter. **3** the loud clucking noise a hen makes.
cackle *verb*
[from old German or Dutch *kake* = jaw]

cacophony (*say* kak-**off**-on-ee) *noun*
(*plural* **cacophonies**)
a loud harsh unpleasant sound.
[from Greek *kakophonia* = bad sound]

cactus *noun* (*plural* **cacti**)
a fleshy plant, usually with prickles, from a hot dry climate. [from Greek]

cad *noun* (*plural* **cads**)
a dishonourable person.
[short for *caddie* or *cadet*]

cadaverous (*say* kad-**av**-er-us) *adjective*
pale and gaunt.
[from Latin *cadaver* = corpse]

caddie *noun* (*plural* **caddies**)
a person who carries a golfer's clubs during a game. [from *cadet*]

caddy *noun* (*plural* **caddies**)
a small box for holding tea. [from Malay (a language spoken in Malaysia) or Javanese (a language spoken in Indonesia)]

cadence (*say* **kay**-denss) *noun* (*plural* **cadences**)
1 rhythm; the rise and fall of the voice in speaking. **2** the final notes of a musical phrase.
[via French from Latin *cadere* = fall]

cadenza (*say* ka-**den**-za) *noun* (*plural* **cadenzas**)
an elaborate passage for a solo instrument or singer, to show the performer's skill.
[via Italian from Latin *cadere* = fall]

cadet *noun* (*plural* **cadets**)
a young person being trained for the armed forces or the police.
[French, = younger son]

cadge *verb* (**cadges**, **cadging**, **cadged**)
get something by begging for it.
cadger *noun* [origin unknown]

cadmium *noun*
a metal that looks like tin. [from Latin]

Caesarean section (*say* siz-**air**-ee-an)
(*plural* **Caesarean sections**)
a surgical operation for taking a baby out of the mother's womb.
[so called because Julius Caesar is said to have been born in this way]

café (*say* **kaf**-ay) *noun* (*plural* **cafés**)
a small restaurant.
[French, = coffee, coffee house]

cafeteria (*say* kaf-it-**eer**-ee-a) *noun* (*plural* **cafeterias**)
a self-service café.
[American Spanish, from *café*]

caffeine (*say* **kaf**-een) *noun*
a stimulant substance found in tea and coffee. [French, from *café* = coffee]

caftan *noun* (*plural* **caftans**)
a long loose coat or dress. [from Persian]

cage *noun* (*plural* **cages**)
1 a container with bars or wires, in which birds or animals are kept. **2** the enclosed platform of a lift. [from French]

cagoule (*say* kag-**ool**) *noun* (*plural* **cagoules**)
a waterproof jacket. [French, = cowl]

cairn *noun* (*plural* **cairns**)
a pile of loose stones set up as a landmark or monument. [from Scottish Gaelic]

cajole *verb* (**cajoles**, **cajoling**, **cajoled**)
persuade someone to do something by flattering them; coax. [from French]

cake *noun* (*plural* **cakes**)
1 a baked food made from a mixture of flour, fat, eggs, sugar, etc. **2** a shaped or hardened mass, *a cake of soap*; *fish cakes*. [from a Scandinavian language]

caked *adjective*
covered with dried mud etc.

calamine *noun*
a pink powder used to make a soothing lotion for the skin. [from Latin]

calamity *noun* (*plural* **calamities**)
a disaster. **calamitous** *adjective* [from Latin]

calcium *noun*
a chemical substance found in teeth, bones, and lime. [from Latin *calx* = lime¹]

calculate *verb* (**calculates, calculating, calculated**)
1 work something out by using mathematics. **2** plan something deliberately; intend, *Her remarks were calculated to hurt me.* **calculable** *adjective*, **calculation** *noun* [same origin as *calculus*]

calculating *adjective*
planning things carefully so that you get what you want.

calculator *noun* (*plural* **calculators**)
a small electronic device for making calculations.

calculus *noun*
mathematics for working out problems about rates of change. [from Latin *calculus* = small stone (used on an abacus)]

calendar *noun* (*plural* **calendars**)
something that shows the dates of the month or year. [from Latin *kalendae* = the first day of the month]

calf¹ *noun* (*plural* **calves**)
a young cow, whale, seal, etc. [from Old English]

calf² *noun* (*plural* **calves**)
the fleshy back part of the leg below the knee. [from Old Norse]

calibre (*say* kal-**ib**-er) *noun* (*plural* **calibres**)
1 the diameter of a tube or gun barrel, or of a bullet etc. **2** ability; importance, *someone of your calibre.* [French]

calico *noun*
a kind of cotton cloth. [from Calicut, a town in India, from which the cloth was sent overseas]

caliph (*say* **kal**-if or **kay**-lif) *noun* (*plural* **caliphs**)
the former title of the ruler in certain Muslim countries. [from Arabic *khalifa* = successor of Muhammad]

call *noun* (*plural* **calls**)
1 a shout or cry. **2** a visit. **3** telephoning somebody. **4** a summons.

call *verb* (**calls, calling, called**)
1 shout or speak loudly, e.g. to attract someone's attention. **2** telephone somebody. **3** name a person or thing, *They've decided to call the baby Alexander.* **4** tell somebody to come to you; summon. **5** make a short visit. **caller** *noun*
call a person's bluff challenge a person to do what was threatened, and expose the fact that it was a bluff.
call for 1 come and collect. **2** require, *The scandal calls for investigation.*
call up summon to join the armed forces. [from Old Norse]

call box *noun* (*plural* **call boxes**)
a telephone box.

calligraphy (*say* kal-**ig**-raf-ee) *noun*
the art of beautiful handwriting. [from Greek *kalos* = beautiful, + *-graphy*]

calling *noun* (*plural* **callings**)
an occupation; a profession or trade. [from the idea that God had called·you to that occupation]

calliper *noun* (*plural* **callipers**)
a support for a weak or injured leg. [a different spelling of *calibre*]

callipers *plural noun*
compasses for measuring the width of tubes or of round objects. [from *calliper*]

callous (*say* **kal**-us) *adjective*
hard-hearted; unsympathetic. **callously** *adverb*, **callousness** *noun* [same origin as *callus*]

callow *adjective*
immature and inexperienced. **callowly** *adverb*, **callowness** *noun* [from Old English]

callus noun (plural **calluses**)
a small patch of skin that has become thick and hard through being continually pressed or rubbed.
[from Latin callum = hard skin]

calm adjective
1 quiet and still; not windy. 2 not excited or agitated. **calmly** adverb, **calmness** noun
calm verb (**calms, calming, calmed**)
make or become calm. [from Greek kauma = hot time of the day (when people rested)]

calorie noun (plural **calories**)
a unit for measuring an amount of heat or the energy produced by food. **calorific** adjective [from Latin calor = heat]

calumny (say kal-um-nee) noun (plural **calumnies**)
an untrue statement that damages a person's reputation; slander. [from Latin]

calve verb (**calves, calving, calved**)
give birth to a calf.

calypso noun (plural **calypsos**)
a West Indian song about current happenings. [origin unknown]

calyx (say kay-liks) noun (plural **calyces**)
a ring of leaves (sepals) forming the outer case of a bud. [from Greek]

camaraderie (say kam-er-ah-der-ee) noun
comradeship.
[French, from camarade = comrade]

camber noun (plural **cambers**)
a slight upward curve or arch, e.g. on a road to allow drainage.
[from Latin camurus = curved inwards]

cambric noun
thin linen or cotton cloth. [from Cambrai, a town in France, where it was first made]

camcorder noun (plural **camcorders**)
a combined video camera and sound recorder. [from camera + recorder]

camel noun (plural **camels**)
a large animal with a long neck and either one or two humps on its back, used in desert countries for riding and for carrying goods. [from Greek]

camellia noun (plural **camellias**)
a kind of evergreen flowering shrub.
[Latin, named after Joseph Camellus, a botanist]

cameo (say kam-ee-oh) noun (plural **cameos**)
1 a small hard piece of stone carved with a raised design in its upper layer. 2 a short well-performed part in a play etc.
[from old French]

camera noun (plural **cameras**)
a device for taking photographs, films, or television pictures. **cameraman** noun
in camera in a judge's private room; in private.
[Latin, = vault, chamber]

camomile noun (plural **camomiles**)
a plant with sweet-smelling daisy-like flowers. [from Greek khamaimelon = earth apple (because of the smell of the flowers)]

camouflage (say kam-off-lahzh) noun
a way of hiding things by making them look like part of their surroundings.
camouflage verb (**camouflages, camouflaging, camouflaged**)
hide by camouflage.
[from French camoufler = disguise]

camp noun (plural **camps**)
a place where people live in tents or huts etc. **campsite** noun
camp verb (**camps, camping, camped**)
make a camp; live in a camp. **camper** noun
[same origin as campus]

campaign noun (plural **campaigns**)
1 a series of battles in one area or with one purpose. 2 a planned series of actions, an advertising campaign.
campaign verb (**campaigns, campaigning, campaigned**)
take part in a campaign. **campaigner** noun
[from Latin campania = a piece of open ground]

camphor noun
a strong-smelling white substance used in medicine and mothballs and in making plastics. **camphorated** adjective
[via French, Latin, Arabic, and Malay (a language spoken in Malaysia), from Sanskrit]

campion *noun* (*plural* **campions**)
a wild plant with pink or white flowers.
[origin unknown]

campus *noun* (*plural* **campuses**)
the grounds of a university or college.
[Latin, = field]

can¹ *noun* (*plural* **cans**)
1 a sealed tin in which food or drink is
preserved. **2** a metal or plastic container
for liquids.
can *verb* (**cans, canning, canned**)
preserve in a sealed can. **canner** *noun* [from
Old English *canne* = container for liquids]

can² *auxiliary verb* (*past tense* **could**)
1 be able to, *He can play the violin.* **2** have
permission to, *You can go.* [from Old
English *cunnan* = know, know how to do]

USAGE: Some people object to *can* being
used with the meaning 'have permission
to' and insist that you should only use *may*
for this meaning. *Can* is widely used in this
meaning, however, and in most situations
there is little reason to prefer *may*. *May* is
appropriate, though, in formal or official
writing.

canal *noun* (*plural* **canals**)
1 an artificial river cut through land so
that boats can sail along it or so that it can
drain or irrigate an area. **2** a tube through
which something passes in the body, *the
alimentary canal.* [same origin as *channel*]

canary *noun* (*plural* **canaries**)
a small yellow bird that sings.
[because it came from the Canary Islands]

cancan *noun* (*plural* **cancans**)
a lively dance in which the legs are kicked
very high. [French]

cancel *verb* (**cancels, cancelling, cancelled**)
1 say that something planned will not be
done or will not take place. **2** stop an order
or instruction for something. **3** mark a
stamp or ticket etc. so that it cannot be
used again. **cancellation** *noun*
cancel out stop each other's effect, *The good
and harm cancel each other out.*
[from Latin *cancellare* = cross out]

cancer *noun* (*plural* **cancers**)
1 a disease in which harmful growths form
in the body. **2** a tumour, especially a
harmful one. **cancerous** *adjective*
[Latin, = crab, creeping ulcer]

candelabrum (*say* kan-dil-**ab**-rum) *noun*
(*plural* **candelabra**)
a candlestick with several branches for
holding candles.
[from Latin *candela* = candle]

candid *adjective*
frank. **candidly** *adverb*, **candidness** *noun*
[from Latin *candidus* = white]

candidate *noun* (*plural* **candidates**)
1 a person who wants to be elected or
chosen for a particular job or position etc.
2 a person taking an examination.
candidacy *noun*, **candidature** *noun* [from
Latin *candidus* = white (because Roman
candidates for office had to wear a pure
white toga)]

candied *adjective*
coated or preserved in sugar.
candied peel bits of the peel of citrus fruits
candied for use in cooking.
[from *candy*]

candle *noun* (*plural* **candles**)
a stick of wax with a wick through it,
giving light when burning. **candlelight**
noun [Old English from Latin, from
candere = be white, shine]

candlestick *noun* (*plural* **candlesticks**)
a holder for a candle or candles.

candour (*say* **kan**-der) *noun*
being candid; frankness.

candy *noun* (*plural* **candies**) (*American*)
sweets; a sweet.
[from Arabic *kand* = sugar]

candyfloss *noun* (*plural* **candyflosses**)
a fluffy mass of very thin strands of spun
sugar.

cane *noun* (*plural* **canes**)
1 the stem of a reed or tall grass etc. **2** a
thin stick.
cane *verb* (**canes, caning, caned**)
beat someone with a cane. [from Greek]

canine (*say* kayn-I'n) *adjective*
to do with dogs.
canine tooth a pointed tooth.
canine *noun* (*plural* canines)
1 a dog. 2 a canine tooth.
[from Latin *canis* = dog]

canister *noun* (*plural* canisters)
a metal container. [from Greek *kanastron*
= wicker basket; related to *cane*]

canker *noun*
a disease that rots the wood of trees and
plants or causes ulcers and sores on
animals. [same origin as *cancer*]

cannabis *noun*
hemp, especially when smoked as a drug.
[from *Cannabis*, the Latin name of the
hemp plant]

cannibal *noun* (*plural* cannibals)
1 a person who eats human flesh. 2 an
animal that eats animals of its own kind.
cannibalism *noun* [from Spanish *Canibales*,
the name given to the original inhabitants
of the Caribbean islands, who the Spanish
thought ate people]

cannibalize *verb* (cannibalizes,
cannibalizing, cannibalized)
take a machine or vehicle apart to provide
spare parts for others. **cannibalization** *noun*

cannon *noun*
1 (*plural* cannon) a large heavy gun.
2 (*plural* cannons) the hitting of two balls
in billiards by the third ball.
cannon *verb* (cannons, cannoning,
cannoned)
bump into something heavily. [via French
from Italian *cannone* = large tube]

USAGE: Do not confuse with *canon*.

cannon ball *noun* (*plural* cannon balls)
a large solid ball fired from a cannon.

cannot
can not.

canny *adjective* (cannier, canniest)
shrewd. **cannily** *adverb* [from *can²*]

canoe *noun* (*plural* canoes)
a narrow lightweight boat.

canoe *verb* (canoes, canoeing, canoed)
travel in a canoe. **canoeist** *noun* [via
Spanish from Carib (the language of the
original inhabitants of the Caribbean)]

canon *noun* (*plural* canons)
1 a clergyman of a cathedral. 2 a general
principle; a rule.
[from Greek *kanon* = rule]

USAGE: Do not confuse with *cannon*.

canonize *verb* (canonizes, canonizing,
canonized)
declare officially that someone is a saint.
canonization *noun*
[from *canon*, in the sense 'list of those
accepted as saints by the church']

canopy *noun* (*plural* canopies)
1 a hanging cover forming a shelter above
a throne, bed, or person etc. 2 the part of a
parachute that spreads in the air.
[from Greek *konopeion* = bed with a
mosquito net]

cant¹ *verb*
slope or tilt.
[from a Dutch word meaning 'edge']

cant² *noun*
1 insincere talk. 2 jargon.
[from Latin *cantare* = sing]

can't (*mainly spoken*)
cannot.

cantaloup *noun* (*plural* cantaloups)
a small round orange-coloured melon.
[from *Cantaluppi*, a place near Rome,
where it was first grown in Europe]

cantankerous *adjective*
bad-tempered. [origin unknown]

cantata (*say* kant-ah-ta) *noun* (*plural*
cantatas)
a musical composition for singers, like an
oratorio but shorter.
[from Italian *cantare* = sing]

canteen *noun* (*plural* canteens)
1 a restaurant for workers in a factory,
office, etc. 2 a case or box containing a set
of cutlery. 3 a soldier's or camper's water-
flask. [via French from Italian]

canter *noun*
a gentle gallop.
canter *verb* (**canters, cantering, cantered**)
go or ride at a canter.
[short for 'Canterbury gallop', the gentle
pace at which pilgrims were said to travel
to Canterbury in the Middle Ages]

canticle *noun* (*plural* **canticles**)
a religious song with words taken from the
Bible, e.g. the Magnificat.
[from Latin *canticulum* = little song]

cantilever *noun* (*plural* **cantilevers**)
a beam or girder fixed at one end only and
used to support a bridge etc.
[origin unknown]

canton *noun* (*plural* **cantons**)
each of the districts into which
Switzerland is divided. [from French]

canvas *noun* (*plural* **canvases**)
1 a kind of strong coarse cloth. 2 a piece of
canvas for painting on; a painting.
[from Latin *cannabis* = hemp, from whose
fibres cloth was made]

canvass *verb* (**canvasses, canvassing,
canvassed**)
visit people to ask for votes, opinions, etc.
canvasser *noun* [originally = to catch in a
net or bag: from *canvas*]

canyon *noun* (*plural* **canyons**)
a deep valley, usually with a river running
through it. [from Spanish *cañón* = tube]

cap *noun* (*plural* **caps**)
1 a soft hat without a brim but often with a
peak. 2 a special headdress, e.g. that worn
by a nurse. 3 a cap showing membership of
a sports team. 4 a cap-like cover or top.
5 something that makes a bang when fired
in a toy pistol.
cap *verb* (**caps, capping, capped**)
1 put a cap or cover on something; cover.
2 award a sports cap to a person chosen as
a member of a team. 3 do better than
something, *Can you cap that joke?*
[same origin as *cape*[1]]

capable *adjective*
able to do something. **capably** *adverb*,
capability *noun*
[from Latin; related to *capacity*]

capacious (*say* ka-**pay**-shus) *adjective*
roomy; able to hold a large amount.
[same origin as *capacity*]

capacity *noun* (*plural* **capacities**)
1 the amount that something can hold.
2 ability; capability. 3 the position that
someone occupies, *In my capacity as your
guardian I am responsible for you.*
[from Latin *capere* = take, hold]

cape[1] *noun* (*plural* **capes**)
a cloak. [from Latin *cappa* = hood]

cape[2] *noun* (*plural* **capes**)
a large piece of high land that sticks out
into the sea. [from Latin *caput* = head]

caper[1] *verb* (**capers, capering, capered**)
jump or run about playfully.
caper *noun* (*plural* **capers**)
1 capering. 2 (*slang*) an activity; an
adventure. [from Latin *caper* = goat]

caper[2] *noun* (*plural* **capers**)
a bud of a prickly shrub, pickled for use in
sauces etc. [from Greek]

capillary (*say* ka-**pil**-er-ee) *noun* (*plural*
capillaries)
any of the very fine blood vessels that
connect veins and arteries.
capillary *adjective*
to do with or occurring in a very narrow
tube; to do with a capillary.
[from Latin *capillus* = hair]

capital *adjective*
1 important. 2 (*informal*) excellent.
capital *noun* (*plural* **capitals**)
1 a capital city. 2 a capital letter. 3 the top
part of a pillar. 4 money or property that
can be used to produce more wealth.
[from Latin *caput* = head]

capital city *noun* (*plural* **capital cities**)
the most important city in a country.

capitalism (*say* **kap**-it-al-izm) *noun*
a system in which trade and industry are
controlled by private owners for profit.
(Compare *Communism*.)

capitalist (*say* **kap**-it-al-ist) *noun* (*plural*
capitalists)
1 a person who has much money or

property being used to make more wealth; a very rich person. **2** a person who is in favour of capitalism.

capitalize (*say* kap-it-al-I'z) *verb* (**capitalizes, capitalizing, capitalized**)
1 write or print as a capital letter. **2** change something into capital; provide with capital (= money). **capitalization** *noun*
capitalize on profit by something; use it to your own advantage, *You could capitalize on your skill at drawing.*

capital letter *noun* (*plural* **capital letters**)
a large letter of the kind used at the start of a name or sentence.

capital punishment *noun*
punishing criminals by putting them to death.

capitulate *verb* (**capitulates, capitulating, capitulated**)
admit that you are defeated and surrender. **capitulation** *noun* [from Latin]

cappuccino *noun* (*plural* **cappuccinos**)
milky coffee made frothy with pressurized steam. [Italian: named after the Capuchin monks who wore coffee-coloured habits]

caprice (*say* ka-preess) *noun* (*plural* **caprices**)
a capricious action or impulse; a whim. [via French from Italian]

capricious (*say* ka-prish-us) *adjective*
deciding or changing your mind in an impulsive way.
capriciously *adverb*, **capriciousness** *noun*

capsize *verb* (**capsizes, capsizing, capsized**)
overturn, *the boat capsized.* [origin unknown]

capstan *noun* (*plural* **capstans**)
a thick post that can be turned to pull in a rope or cable etc. that winds round it as it turns. [from Latin *capere* = seize]

capsule *noun* (*plural* **capsules**)
1 a hollow pill containing medicine. **2** a plant's seed-case that splits open when ripe. **3** a compartment that can be separated from the rest of a spacecraft. [same origin as *case¹*]

captain *noun* (*plural* **captains**)
1 a person in command of a ship, aircraft, sports team, etc. **2** an army officer ranking next below a major; a naval officer ranking next below a commodore.
captaincy *noun*

captain *verb* (**captains, captaining, captained**)
be the captain of a sports team etc. [from Latin *capitanus* = chief]

caption *noun* (*plural* **captions**)
1 the words printed with a picture to describe it. **2** a short title or heading in a newspaper or magazine. [from Latin]

captious (*say* kap-shus) *adjective*
pointing out small mistakes or faults. [same origin as *captive*]

captivate *verb* (**captivates, captivating, captivated**)
charm or delight someone. **captivation** *noun* [same origin as *captive*]

captive *noun* (*plural* **captives**)
someone taken prisoner.
captive *adjective*
taken prisoner; unable to escape. **captivity** *noun* [from Latin *capere* = take, seize]

captor *noun* (*plural* **captors**)
someone who has captured a person or animal.

capture *verb* (**captures, capturing, captured**)
1 take someone prisoner. **2** take or obtain by force, trickery, skill, or attraction, *He captured her heart.*
capture *noun*
capturing. [same origin as *captive*]

car *noun* (*plural* **cars**)
1 a motor car. **2** a carriage, *dining car.* [from old French]

carafe (*say* ka-raf) *noun* (*plural* **carafes**)
a glass bottle holding wine or water for pouring out at the table. [via French from Italian]

caramel *noun* (*plural* **caramels**)
1 a kind of toffee tasting like burnt sugar. **2** burnt sugar used for colouring and flavouring food. [via French from Spanish]

carapace (*say* ka-ra-payss) *noun* (*plural* carapaces)
the shell on the back of a tortoise or crustacean. [via French from Spanish]

carat *noun* (*plural* carats)
1 a measure of weight for precious stones. 2 a measure of the purity of gold, *Pure gold is 24 carats.*
[via French and Italian from Arabic]

caravan *noun* (*plural* caravans)
1 an enclosed carriage equipped for living in, able to be towed by a motor vehicle or a horse. 2 a group of people travelling together across desert country.
caravanning *noun*
[via French from Persian]

caraway *noun*
a plant with spicy seeds that are used for flavouring food.
[from Greek *karon* = cumin]

carbohydrate *noun* (*plural* carbohydrates)
a compound of carbon, oxygen, and hydrogen (e.g. sugar or starch). [from *carbon* + -*hydrate* = combined with water]

carbolic *noun*
a kind of disinfectant.
[from *carbon* (from which it is made)]

carbon *noun* (*plural* carbons)
1 a substance that is present in all living things and that occurs in its pure form as diamond and graphite. 2 carbon paper. 3 a carbon copy. [from Latin *carbo* = coal]

carbonate *noun* (*plural* carbonates)
a compound that gives off carbon dioxide when mixed with acid.

carbonated *adjective*
with carbon dioxide added, *Carbonated drinks are fizzy.*

carbon copy *noun* (*plural* carbon copies)
a copy made with carbon paper; an exact copy.

carbon dioxide *noun*
a gas formed when things burn, or breathed out by animals.

carboniferous *adjective*
producing coal.
[from *carbon* + Latin *ferre* = to bear]

carbon paper *noun*
thin paper with a coloured coating, placed between sheets of paper to make copies of what is written or typed on the top sheet.

carbuncle *noun* (*plural* carbuncles)
1 a bad abscess in the skin. 2 a bright-red gem. [from Latin *carbunculus* = small coal]

carburettor *noun* (*plural* carburettors)
a device for mixing fuel and air in an engine.
[from *carbon* (which the fuel contains)]

carcass *noun* (*plural* carcasses)
1 the dead body of an animal. 2 the bony part of a bird's body after the meat has been eaten. [from French]

carcinogen *noun* (*plural* carcinogens)
any substance that produces cancer.
[from Greek *karkinoma* = tumour]

card *noun* (*plural* cards)
1 a small usually oblong piece of stiff paper or of plastic. 2 a playing card. 3 cardboard.
cards *plural noun* a game using playing cards.
on the cards likely; possible.
[from Latin *charta* = papyrus leaf, paper]

cardboard *noun*
a kind of thin board made of layers of paper or wood-fibre.

cardiac (*say* kard-ee-ak) *adjective*
to do with the heart.
[from Greek *kardia* = heart]

cardigan *noun* (*plural* cardigans)
a knitted jacket. [named after the Earl of Cardigan, a commander in the Crimean War; cardigans were first worn by the troops in that war]

cardinal *noun* (*plural* cardinals)
a senior priest in the Roman Catholic Church.
cardinal *adjective*
1 chief; most important, *the cardinal features of our plan.* 2 deep scarlet (like a cardinal's cassock). [from old French]

cardinal numbers *plural noun*
the whole numbers one, two, three, etc. (Compare *ordinal*.)

cardinal points *plural noun*
the four main points of the compass
(North, South, East, West).

cardiology *noun*
the study of the structure and diseases of
the heart.
cardiological *adjective*, **cardiologist** *noun*
[from Greek *kardia* = heart, + *-logy*]

care *noun* (*plural* **cares**)
1 serious attention and thought, *Plan your
holiday with care.* **2** caution to avoid
damage or loss, *Glass—handle with care.*
3 protection; supervision, *Leave the child
in my care.* **4** worry; anxiety, *freedom from
care.*
care *verb* (**cares, caring, cared**)
1 feel interested or concerned. **2** feel
affection.
care for have in your care; be fond of.
[from Old English]

career *noun* (*plural* **careers**)
1 progress through life, especially in work.
2 an occupation with opportunities for
promotion.
career *verb* (**careers, careering, careered**)
rush along wildly.
[from Latin; related to *car*]

carefree *adjective*
without worries or responsibilities.

careful *adjective*
1 giving serious thought and attention to
something. **2** avoiding damage or danger
etc.; cautious.
carefully *adverb*, **carefulness** *noun*

careless *adjective*
not careful.
carelessly *adverb*, **carelessness** *noun*

caress *noun* (*plural* **caresses**)
a gentle loving touch.
caress *verb* (**caresses, caressing, caressed**)
touch lovingly. [from Latin *carus* = dear]

caret *noun* (*plural* **carets**)
a mark (^ or ⁁) showing where something
is to be inserted in writing or printing.
[Latin, = it is lacking]

caretaker *noun* (*plural* **caretakers**)
a person employed to look after a school,
block of flats, etc.

cargo *noun* (*plural* **cargoes**)
goods carried in a ship or aircraft.
[from Spanish]

Caribbean *adjective*
to do with or from the Caribbean Sea, a
part of the Atlantic Ocean east of Central
America.

caribou (*say* ka-rib-oo) *noun* (*plural*
caribou)
a North American reindeer. [from a Native
American word meaning 'snow-shoveller'
(because the caribou scrapes away the
snow to feed on the grass underneath)]

caricature *noun* (*plural* **caricatures**)
an amusing or exaggerated picture of
someone.
[from Italian *caricare* = exaggerate]

caries (*say* kair-eez) *noun* (*plural* **caries**)
decay in teeth or bones. [Latin]

carmine *adjective* & *noun*
deep red. [via old French from Arabic;
related to *crimson*]

carnage *noun*
the killing of many people.
[same origin as *carnal*]

carnal *adjective*
to do with the body as opposed to the spirit;
not spiritual.
[from Latin *carnis* = of flesh]

carnation *noun* (*plural* **carnations**)
a garden flower with a sweet smell.
[via Arabic from Greek]

carnival *noun* (*plural* **carnivals**)
a festival, often with a procession in fancy
dress. [from Latin *carnis* = of flesh (because
originally this meant the festivities before
Lent, when meat was given up until
Easter)]

carnivorous (*say* kar-niv-er-us) *adjective*
meat-eating. (Compare *herbivorous.*)
carnivore *noun* [from Latin *carnis* = of flesh
+ *vorare* = devour]

carol *noun* (*plural* **carols**)
a Christmas hymn. **caroller** *noun*, **carolling**
noun [from old French]

carouse *verb* (**carouses, carousing, caroused**)
if a group of people are carousing, they are enjoying themselves drinking alcohol. [from German *gar aus trinken* = drink to the bottom of the glass]

carousel (*say* ka-roo-**sel**) *noun* (*plural* **carousels**)
1 (*American*) a roundabout at a fair. 2 a rotating conveyor, e.g. for baggage at an airport. [via French from Italian]

carp¹ *noun* (*plural* **carp**)
an edible freshwater fish. [from Latin *carpa*]

carp² *verb* (**carps, carping, carped**)
keep finding fault. [from Latin *carpere* = slander]

car park *noun* (*plural* **car parks**)
an area where cars may be parked.

carpenter *noun* (*plural* **carpenters**)
a person who makes things out of wood. **carpentry** *noun* [from a Latin word meaning 'carriage-maker']

carpet *noun* (*plural* **carpets**)
a thick soft covering for a floor. **carpeted** *adjective*, **carpeting** *noun* [from old French]

carport *noun* (*plural* **carports**)
a shelter for a car.

carriage *noun* (*plural* **carriages**)
1 one of the separate parts of a train, where passengers sit. 2 a passenger vehicle pulled by horses. 3 carrying goods from one place to another; the cost of carrying goods, *Carriage is extra*. 4 a moving part carrying or holding something in a machine. [same origin as *carry*]

carriageway *noun* (*plural* **carriageways**)
the part of a road on which vehicles travel.

carrier *noun* (*plural* **carriers**)
a person or thing that carries something.

carrier bag *noun* (*plural* **carrier bags**)
a plastic or paper bag with handles.

carrion *noun*
dead and decaying flesh. [from Latin *caro* = flesh]

carrot *noun* (*plural* **carrots**)
a plant with a thick orange-coloured root used as a vegetable. [from Greek]

carry *verb* (**carries, carrying, carried**)
1 take something from one place to another. 2 support the weight of something. 3 travel clearly, *Sound carries in the mountains*. 4 if a motion is carried, it is approved by most people at the meeting, *The motion was carried by ten votes to six*.
be carried away be very excited.
carry on 1 continue. 2 (*informal*) behave excitedly. 3 (*informal*) complain. [from old French *carier*; related to *car*]

cart *noun* (*plural* **carts**)
an open vehicle for carrying loads.
cart *verb* (**carts, carting, carted**)
1 carry in a cart. 2 (*informal*) carry something heavy or tiring, *I've carted these books all round the school*. [from Old Norse]

carte blanche (*say* kart **blahnsh**) *noun*
freedom to act as you think best. [French, = blank paper]

carthorse *noun* (*plural* **carthorses**)
a large strong horse used for pulling heavy loads.

cartilage *noun*
tough white flexible tissue attached to a bone. [from Latin]

cartography *noun*
drawing maps.
cartographer *noun*, **cartographic** *adjective* [from French *carte* = map, + *-graphy*]

carton *noun* (*plural* **cartons**)
a cardboard or plastic container. [French; related to *card*]

cartoon *noun* (*plural* **cartoons**)
1 an amusing drawing. 2 a comic strip (see *comic*). 3 an animated film. **cartoonist** *noun* [originally = a drawing on stiff paper; from Italian, related to *card*]

cartridge *noun* (*plural* **cartridges**)
1 a case containing the explosive for a bullet or shell. 2 a container holding film for a camera, ink for a pen, etc. 3 the device that holds the stylus of a record player. [via French from Italian]

cartwheel *noun* (*plural* **cartwheels**)
1 the wheel of a cart. **2** a handstand balancing on each hand in turn with arms and legs spread like spokes of a wheel.

carve *verb* (**carves, carving, carved**)
1 make something by cutting wood or stone etc. **2** cut cooked meat into slices.
carver *noun* [from Old English]

cascade *noun* (*plural* **cascades**)
a waterfall.
cascade *verb* (**cascades, cascading, cascaded**)
fall like a cascade. [same origin as *case*²]

case¹ *noun* (*plural* **cases**)
1 a container. **2** a suitcase.
[from Latin *capsa* = box]

case² *noun* (*plural* **cases**)
1 an example of something existing or occurring; a situation, *In every case we found that someone had cheated.*
2 something investigated by police etc. or by a lawcourt, *a murder case.* **3** a set of facts or arguments to support something, *She put forward a good case for equality.* **4** the form of a word that shows how it is related to other words. *Fred's* is the possessive case of *Fred*; *him* is the objective case of *he*.
in any case anyway.
in case because something may happen.
[from Latin *casus* = a fall, an occasion]

casement *noun* (*plural* **casements**)
a window that opens on hinges at its side.
[same origin as *case*¹]

cash *noun*
1 money in coin or notes. **2** immediate payment for goods etc.
cash *verb* (**cashes, cashing, cashed**)
change a cheque etc. for cash. [originally = a cash box; from Latin *capsa* = box]

cash card *noun* (*plural* **cash cards**)
a plastic card used to draw money from a cash dispenser.

cash dispenser *noun* (*plural* **cash dispensers**)
a machine, usually outside a bank, from which people can draw out cash by using a cash card.

cashew *noun* (*plural* **cashews**)
a kind of small nut. [via Portuguese from Tupi (a South American language)]

cashier *noun* (*plural* **cashiers**)
a person who takes in and pays out money in a bank or takes payments in a shop.

cashmere *noun*
very fine soft wool. [from *Kashmir* in Asia, where it was first produced]

cashpoint *noun* (*plural* **cashpoints**)
a cash dispenser.

cash register *noun* (*plural* **cash registers**)
a device that registers the amount of money put in, used in a shop.

casing *noun* (*plural* **casings**)
a protective covering. [from *case*¹]

casino *noun* (*plural* **casinos**)
a public building or room for gambling.
[Italian, = little house]

cask *noun* (*plural* **casks**)
a barrel. [from French or Spanish]

casket *noun* (*plural* **caskets**)
a small box for jewellery etc.
[origin unknown]

cassava *noun*
a tropical plant with starchy roots that are an important source of food in tropical countries.
[from Taino (a South American language)]

casserole *noun* (*plural* **casseroles**)
1 a covered dish in which food is cooked and served. **2** food cooked in a casserole.
[from Greek]

cassette *noun* (*plural* **cassettes**)
a small sealed case containing recording tape, film, etc. [French, = little case]

cassock *noun* (*plural* **cassocks**)
a long garment worn by clergy and members of a church choir.
[via French from Italian]

cast *verb* (**casts, casting, cast**)
1 throw. **2** shed or throw off. **3** make a vote. **4** make something of metal or plaster in a mould. **5** choose performers for a play or film etc.

cast *noun* (*plural* casts)
1 a shape made by pouring liquid metal or plaster into a mould. 2 all the performers in a play or film. [from Old Norse]

castanets *plural noun*
two pieces of wood, ivory, etc. held in one hand and clapped together to make a clicking sound, usually for dancing. [from Spanish *castañetas* = little chestnuts]

castaway *noun* (*plural* castaways)
a shipwrecked person.
[originally = an outcast; from *cast* + *away*]

caste *noun* (*plural* castes)
(in India) one of the social classes into which Hindus are born.
[from Spanish or Portuguese *casta* = descent (from the same ancestors)]

castigate *verb* (castigates, castigating, castigated)
punish or rebuke someone severely.
castigation *noun*
[from Latin *castigare* = punish]

casting vote *noun* (*plural* casting votes)
the vote that decides which group wins when the votes on each side are equal.

cast iron *noun*
a hard alloy of iron made by casting it in a mould.

castle *noun* (*plural* castles)
1 a large old fortified building. 2 a piece in chess, also called a *rook*.
castles in the air daydreams.
[from Latin *castellum* = fort]

castor *noun* (*plural* castors)
1 a small wheel on the leg of a table, chair, etc. 2 a container with holes for sprinkling sugar. [from *cast*]

castor oil
oil from the seeds of a tropical plant, used as a laxative. [origin unknown]

castor sugar *noun*
finely-ground white sugar.

castrate *verb* (castrates, castrating, castrated)
remove the testicles of a male animal; geld. (Compare *spay*.) **castration** *noun*
[from Latin]

casual *adjective*
1 happening by chance; not planned. 2 not careful; not methodical. 3 informal; suitable for informal occasions, *casual clothes.* 4 not permanent, *casual work.*
casually *adverb*, **casualness** *noun*
[same origin as *case*²]

casualty *noun* (*plural* casualties)
a person who is killed or injured in war or in an accident.
[originally = chance; same origin as *case*²]

cat *noun* (*plural* cats)
1 a small furry domestic animal. 2 an animal of the same family as the domestic cat, *Lions and tigers are cats.* 3 (*informal*) a spiteful girl or woman.
let the cat out of the bag reveal a secret.
[from Old English]

cata- *prefix* (becoming **cat-** before a vowel; combining with an *h* to become **cath-**)
1 down (as in *catapult*). 2 thoroughly (as in *catalogue*). [from Greek *kata* = down]

cataclysm (*say* kat-a-klizm) *noun* (*plural* cataclysms)
a violent upheaval or disaster.
[from *cata-* + Greek *klyzein* = to wash]

catacombs (*say* kat-a-koomz) *plural noun*
underground passages with compartments for tombs.
[the name of a large catacomb in Rome]

catafalque (*say* kat-a-falk) *noun* (*plural* catafalques)
a decorated platform for a person's coffin. [via French from Italian]

catalogue *noun* (*plural* catalogues)
1 a list of things (e.g. of books in a library), usually arranged in order. 2 a book containing a list of things that can be bought, *Christmas catalogue.*
catalogue *verb* (catalogues, cataloguing, catalogued)
enter something in a catalogue.
[from *cata-* + Greek *legein* = choose]

catalyst (*say* kat-a-list) *noun* (*plural* catalysts)
something that starts or speeds up a change or reaction.
[from *cata-* + Greek *lysis* = loosening]

catalytic converter *noun* (*plural* **catalytic converters**)
a device fitted to a car's exhaust system, with a catalyst for converting pollutant gases into less harmful ones.

catamaran *noun* (*plural* **catamarans**)
a boat with twin hulls.
[from Tamil *kattumaram* = tied wood]

catapult *noun* (*plural* **catapults**)
1 a device with elastic for shooting small stones. 2 an ancient military device for hurling stones etc.
catapult *verb* (**catapults, catapulting, catapulted**)
hurl or rush violently.
[from *cata-* + Greek *pellein* = throw]

cataract *noun* (*plural* **cataracts**)
1 a large waterfall or rush of water. 2 a cloudy area that forms in the eye and prevents a person from seeing clearly.
[from Greek]

catarrh (*say* ka-**tar**) *noun*
inflammation in your nose that makes it drip a watery fluid.
[from Greek *katarrhein* = flow down]

catastrophe (*say* ka-**tass**-trof-ee) *noun* (*plural* **catastrophes**)
a sudden great disaster.
catastrophic (*say* kat-a-**strof**-ik) *adjective*, **catastrophically** *adverb*
[from *cata-* + Greek *strephein* = to turn]

catch *verb* (**catches, catching, caught**)
1 take and hold something. 2 capture.
3 overtake. 4 be in time to get on a bus or train etc. 5 be infected with an illness.
6 hear, *I didn't catch what he said.*
7 surprise or detect somebody, *caught in the act.* 8 trick somebody. 9 make or become fixed or unable to move; snag; entangle, *I caught my dress on a nail.*
10 hit; strike, *The blow caught him on the nose.*
catch fire start burning.
catch it (*informal*) be scolded or punished.
catch on (*informal*) 1 become popular.
2 understand.
catch *noun* (*plural* **catches**)
1 catching something. 2 something caught or worth catching. 3 a hidden difficulty.
4 a device for fastening something.
[same origin as *chase*]

catching *adjective*
infectious.

catchment area (*plural* **catchment areas**)
1 the whole area from which water drains into a river etc. 2 the area from which a school takes pupils or a hospital takes patients.

catchphrase *noun* (*plural* **catchphrases**)
a popular phrase.

catchy *adjective*
easy to remember; soon becoming popular, *a catchy tune.*

catechism (*say* **kat**-ik-izm) *noun* (*plural* **catechisms**)
a set of questions and answers that give the basic beliefs of a religion. [from Greek]

categorical (*say* kat-ig-o-**rik**-al) *adjective*
definite and absolute, *a categorical refusal.*
categorically *adverb*
[same origin as *category*]

category *noun* (*plural* **categories**)
a set of people or things classified as being similar to each other. [from Greek *kategoria* = statement, accusation]

cater *verb* (**caters, catering, catered**)
1 provide food, especially for a lot of people. 2 provide what is needed. **caterer** *noun* [from old French *acateour* = a person who buys food etc.]

caterpillar *noun* (*plural* **caterpillars**)
the creeping worm-like creature that will turn into a butterfly or moth.
[from Old French *chatepelose* = hairy cat]

cath- *prefix* see **cata-**.

cathedral *noun* (*plural* **cathedrals**)
the most important church of a district, usually containing the bishop's throne.
[from Greek *kathedra* = seat]

Catherine wheel (*plural* **Catherine wheels**)
a firework that spins round.
[named after St Catherine, who was martyred on a spiked wheel]

cathode *noun* (*plural* **cathodes**)
the electrode by which electric current leaves a device. (Compare *anode*.)
[from *cata-* = down + Greek *hodos* = way]

cathode ray tube *noun* (*plural* **cathode ray tubes**)
a tube used in televisions and computers, in which a beam of electrons from a cathode produces an image on a fluorescent screen.

Catholic *adjective*
1 of all Christians, *the Holy Catholic Church*. 2 Roman Catholic (see *Roman*). **Catholicism** *noun*
Catholic *noun* (*plural* **Catholics**)
a Roman Catholic.

catholic *adjective*
including most things, *Her taste in literature is catholic.*
[from Greek *katholikos* = universal]

catkin *noun*
a spike of small soft flowers on trees such as hazel and willow. [from Dutch]

catnap *noun* (*plural* **catnaps**)
a short sleep.

Catseye *noun* (*plural* **Catseyes**) (*trade mark*)
one of a line of reflecting studs marking the centre or edge of a road.

cattle *plural noun*
animals with horns and hoofs, kept by farmers for their milk and beef.
[same origin as *chattel*]

catty *adjective* (**cattier**, **cattiest**)
speaking or spoken spitefully.

caucus *noun* (*plural* **caucuses**)
a small group within a political party, influencing decisions and policy etc.
[from a Native American word meaning 'adviser']

cauldron *noun* (*plural* **cauldrons**)
a large deep pot for boiling things in.
[from Latin *caldarium* = hot bath]

cauliflower *noun* (*plural* **cauliflowers**)
a cabbage with a large head of white flowers. [from French *chou fleuri* = flowered cabbage]

cause *noun* (*plural* **causes**)
1 a person or thing that makes something happen or produces an effect. 2 a reason, *There is no cause for worry.* 3 a purpose for which people work; an organization or charity.
cause *verb* (**causes**, **causing**, **caused**)
be the cause of; make something happen.
[from Latin]

causeway *noun* (*plural* **causeways**)
a raised road across low or marshy ground.
[from an old word *causey* = embankment, + *way*]

caustic *adjective*
1 able to burn or wear things away by chemical action. 2 sarcastic. **caustically** *adverb* [from Greek *kaustikos* = capable of burning]

cauterize *verb* (**cauterizes**, **cauterizing**, **cauterized**)
burn the surface of flesh to destroy infection or stop bleeding.
cauterization *noun*
[from Greek *kauterion* = branding-iron]

caution *noun* (*plural* **cautions**)
1 care taken in order to avoid danger etc. 2 a warning.
caution *verb* (**cautions**, **cautioning**, **cautioned**)
warn someone.
[from Latin *cavere* = beware]

cautionary *adjective*
giving a warning.

cautious *adjective*
showing caution.
cautiously *adverb*, **cautiousness** *noun*

cavalcade *noun* (*plural* **cavalcades**)
a procession.
[from Italian *cavalcare* = ride]

Cavalier *noun* (*plural* **Cavaliers**)
a supporter of King Charles I in the English Civil War (1642–9).
[from French *chevalier* = knight, from Latin *caballus* = horse]

cavalry *noun*
soldiers who fight on horseback or in armoured vehicles. (Compare *infantry*.)
[from Latin *caballus* = horse]

cave noun (plural **caves**)
a large hollow place in the side of a hill or cliff, or underground.
cave verb (**caves, caving, caved**)
cave in fall inwards; give way in an argument.
[from Latin cavus = hollow]

caveat (say kav-ee-at) noun (plural **caveats**)
a warning. [Latin, = let a person beware]

caveman noun (plural **cavemen**)
a person living in a cave in ancient times.

cavern noun (plural **caverns**)
a large cave. **cavernous** adjective
[same origin as cave]

caviare (say kav-ee-ar) noun
the pickled roe of sturgeon or other large fish. [from Italian or French, probably from Greek]

cavil verb (**cavils, cavilling, cavilled**)
raise petty objections.
[from Latin cavilla = mockery]

caving noun
exploring caves.

cavity noun (plural **cavities**)
a hollow or hole. [same origin as cave]

cavort (say ka-vort) verb (**cavorts, cavorting, cavorted**)
jump or run about excitedly.
[originally American; origin unknown]

caw noun (plural **caws**)
the harsh cry of a crow etc.

CB abbreviation
citizens' band.

cc abbreviation
cubic centimetre(s).

CD abbreviation
compact disc.

CD-ROM abbreviation
compact disc read-only memory; a compact disc on which large amounts of data can be stored and then displayed on a computer screen.

CDT abbreviation
craft, design, and technology.

cease verb (**ceases, ceasing, ceased**)
stop or end.
cease noun
without cease not ceasing.
[from Latin; related to cede]

ceasefire noun (plural **ceasefires**)
a signal to stop firing.

ceaseless adjective
not ceasing.

cedar noun (plural **cedars**)
an evergreen tree with hard fragrant wood.
cedarwood noun [from Greek]

cede (say seed) verb (**cedes, ceding, ceded**)
give up your rights to something; surrender, They had to cede some of their territory. [from Latin cedere = yield]

cedilla (say sid-il-a) noun (plural **cedillas**)
a mark under c in certain languages to show that it is pronounced as s, e.g. in façade. [from Spanish, = a little z]

ceilidh (say kay-lee) noun (plural **ceilidhs**)
an informal gathering for music, singing, and dancing, originating from Scotland and Ireland. [from old Irish]

ceiling noun (plural **ceilings**)
1 the flat surface under the top of a room.
2 the highest limit that something can reach. [origin unknown]

celandine noun (plural **celandines**)
a small wild plant with yellow flowers.
[from Greek]

celebrate verb (**celebrates, celebrating, celebrated**)
1 do something special or enjoyable to show that a day or event is important.
2 perform a religious ceremony. **celebrant** noun, **celebration** noun [from Latin]

celebrated adjective
famous.

celebrity noun (plural **celebrities**)
1 a famous person. 2 fame; being famous.

celery noun
a vegetable with crisp white or green stems. [from Greek]

celestial (*say* sil-**est**-ee-al) *adjective*
1 to do with the sky. **2** to do with heaven; divine.
celestial bodies stars etc.
[from Latin]

celibate (*say* **sel**-ib-at) *adjective*
remaining unmarried, especially for religious reasons. **celibacy** *noun*
[from Latin *caelebs* = unmarried]

cell *noun* (*plural* **cells**)
1 a small room where a prisoner is locked up. **2** a small room in a monastery. **3** a microscopic unit of living matter. **4** a compartment of a honeycomb. **5** a device for producing electric current chemically. **6** a small group or unit in an organization etc. [from Latin *cella* = storeroom]

cellar *noun* (*plural* **cellars**)
an underground room. [same origin as *cell*]

cello (*say* **chel**-oh) *noun* (*plural* **cellos**)
a musical instrument like a large violin, placed between the knees of a player. **cellist** *noun* [from Italian *violoncello* = small double bass]

Cellophane *noun* (*trade mark*)
a thin transparent wrapping material.
[from *cellulose* + *diaphane* = a transparent substance]

cellular *adjective*
1 to do with or containing cells. **2** with an open mesh, *cellular blankets*.

celluloid *noun*
a kind of plastic.
[from *cellulose*, from which it is made]

cellulose *noun*
1 tissue that forms the main part of all plants and trees. **2** paint made from cellulose. [from Latin]

Celsius (*say* **sel**-see-us) *adjective*
(of a temperature scale) centigrade.
[named after A. Celsius, a Swedish astronomer, who invented it]

Celtic *adjective*
to do with the languages or inhabitants of ancient Britain and France before the Romans came, or of their descendants, e.g. Irish, Welsh, Gaelic.

cement *noun*
1 a mixture of lime and clay used in building, to join bricks together, etc. **2** a strong glue.

cement *verb* (**cements, cementing, cemented**)
1 put cement on something. **2** join firmly; strengthen. [from Latin]

cemetery (*say* **sem**-et-ree) *noun* (*plural* **cemeteries**)
a place where people are buried.
[from Greek *koimeterion* = dormitory]

cenotaph (*say* **sen**-o-taf) *noun* (*plural* **cenotaphs**)
a monument, especially as a war memorial, to people who are buried elsewhere. [from Greek *kenos* = empty + *taphos* = tomb]

censer *noun* (*plural* **censers**)
a container in which incense is burnt.
[same origin as *incense*]

censor *noun* (*plural* **censors**)
a person who examines films, books, letters, etc. and removes or bans anything that seems harmful. **censor** *verb*, **censorship** *noun* [Latin, = magistrate with power to ban unsuitable people from ceremonies; from *censere* = to judge]

USAGE: Do not confuse with *censure*.

censorious (*say* sen-**sor**-ee-us) *adjective*
criticizing something strongly.
[from Latin *censorius* = like a censor]

censure (*say* **sen**-sher) *noun*
strong criticism or disapproval of something. **censure** *verb*
[same origin as *census*]

USAGE: Do not confuse with *censor*.

census *noun* (*plural* **censuses**)
an official count or survey of the population of a country or area.
[from Latin *censere* = estimate, judge]

cent *noun* (*plural* **cents**)
a coin worth one-hundredth of a dollar.
[from Latin *centum* = 100]

centenarian (*say* sent-in-**air**-ee-an) *noun* (*plural* **centenarians**)
a person who is 100 years old or more.
[same origin as *centenary*]

centenary (*say* sen-teen-er-ee) *noun* (*plural* **centenaries**)
a 100th anniversary. **centennial** (*say* sen-ten-ee-al) *adjective* [from Latin *centenarius* = containing a hundred]

centi- *prefix*
1 one hundred (as in *centipede*). 2 one-hundredth (as in *centimetre*).
[from Latin *centum* = 100]

centigrade *adjective*
measuring temperature on a scale using 100 degrees, where water freezes at 0° and boils at 100°.
[from *centi-* + Latin *gradus* = step]

centimetre *noun* (*plural* **centimetres**)
one-hundredth of a metre, about four-tenths of an inch.

centipede *noun* (*plural* **centipedes**)
a small crawling creature with a long body and many legs.
[from *centi-* + Latin *pedes* = feet]

central *adjective*
1 to do with or at the centre. 2 most important. **centrally** *adverb*

central heating *noun*
a system of heating a building from one source by circulating hot water or hot air or steam in pipes or by linked radiators.

centralize *verb* (**centralizes, centralizing, centralized**)
bring under a central authority's control.
centralization *noun*

centre *noun* (*plural* **centres**)
1 the middle point or part. 2 an important place, e.g. from which things are organized; a place where certain things happen, *shopping centre*.
centre *verb* (**centres, centring, centred**)
place something at the centre.
centre on or **centre around** be concentrated in; have as its main subject or concern.
[from Greek *kentron* = sharp point, point of a pair of compasses]

centre forward *noun* (*plural* **centre forwards**)
the player in the middle of the forward line in football or hockey.

centre of gravity *noun* (*plural* **centres of gravity**)
the point in an object at which it balances perfectly.

centrifugal *adjective*
moving away from the centre; using centrifugal force. [from Latin *centrum* = centre + *fugere* = flee]

centrifugal force *noun*
a force that makes a thing that is travelling round a central point fly outwards off its circular path.

centurion (*say* sent-yoor-ee-on) *noun* (*plural* **centurions**)
an officer in the ancient Roman army. [originally he was in charge of 100 men (Latin *centum* = 100)]

century *noun* (*plural* **centuries**)
1 a period of one hundred years. 2 a hundred runs scored by a batsman in an innings at cricket.
[from Latin *centum* = 100]

cephalopod (*say* sef-al-o-pod) *noun* (*plural* **cephalopods**)
a mollusc (such as an octopus) that has a head with a ring of tentacles round the mouth. [from Greek *kephale* = head + *podos* = of a foot]

ceramic *adjective*
to do with or made of pottery. [from Greek]

ceramics *plural noun*
pottery-making.

cereal *noun* (*plural* **cereals**)
1 a grass producing seeds which are used as food, e.g. wheat, barley, rice. 2 a breakfast food made from these seeds. [from *Ceres*, the Roman goddess of farming]

USAGE: Do not confuse with *serial*.

cerebral (*say* se-rib-ral) *adjective*
to do with the brain.
[from Latin *cerebrum* = brain]

cerebral palsy *noun*
a condition caused by brain damage before birth that makes a person suffer from spasms of the muscles and jerky movements.

ceremonial *adjective*
to do with or used in a ceremony; formal.
ceremonially *adverb*

ceremonious *adjective*
full of ceremony; elaborately performed.

ceremony *noun* (*plural* **ceremonies**)
the formal actions carried out on an
important occasion, e.g. at a wedding or a
funeral.
[from Latin *caerimonia* = worship, ritual]

certain *adjective*
sure; without doubt.
a certain person or **thing** a person or thing
that is known but not named.
[from Latin *certus* = settled, sure]

certainly *adverb*
1 for certain. 2 yes.

certainty *noun* (*plural* **certainties**)
1 something that is sure to happen. 2 being
sure.

certificate *noun* (*plural* **certificates**)
an official written or printed statement
giving information about a person etc.,
a birth certificate.
[same origin as *certify*]

certify *verb* (**certifies, certifying, certified**)
declare formally that something is true.
certification *noun* [from Latin *certificare*
= make something certain]

certitude *noun*
a feeling of certainty.

cervix *noun* (*plural* **cervices,** *say* ser-vis-ees)
the entrance to the womb. **cervical** *adjective*
[Latin, = neck]

cessation *noun*
ceasing.

cesspit or **cesspool** *noun* (*plural* **cesspits,
cesspools**)
a covered pit where liquid waste or sewage
is stored temporarily. [origin unknown]

CFC *abbreviation*
chlorofluorocarbon; a gas containing
chlorine and fluorine that is thought to be
harmful to the ozone layer in the Earth's
atmosphere.

chafe *verb* (**chafes, chafing, chafed**)
1 make or become sore by rubbing.
2 become irritated or impatient, *We chafed
at the delay.*
[from French *chauffer* = make warm]

chaff¹ *noun*
husks of corn, separated from the seed.
[from Old English]

chaff² *verb*
tease someone.
[origin unknown]

chaffinch *noun* (*plural* **chaffinches**)
a kind of finch.
[from *chaff*¹ (because it searched the chaff
for seeds the threshers had missed)]

chagrin (*say* shag-rin) *noun*
a feeling of being annoyed or disappointed.
[French]

chain *noun* (*plural* **chains**)
1 a row of metal rings fastened together.
2 a connected series of things, *a chain of
mountains; a chain of events.*

chain *verb* (**chains, chaining, chained**)
fasten something with a chain or chains.
[from old French]

chain letter *noun* (*plural* **chain letters**)
a letter that you are asked to copy and send
to several other people.

chain reaction *noun* (*plural* **chain
reactions**)
a series of happenings in which each
causes the next.

chain store *noun* (*plural* **chain stores**)
one of a number of similar shops owned by
the same firm.

chair *noun* (*plural* **chairs**)
1 a movable seat, with a back, for one
person. 2 a position of authority at a
meeting, *Mr Bloggs was in the chair.*

chair *verb* (**chairs, chairing, chaired**)
be in control of a meeting, *Who will chair
this meeting?*
[from old French; related to *cathedral*]

chairman noun (plural chairmen)
the person who is in control of a meeting.
chairmanship noun

USAGE: The word chairman may be used
of a man or of a woman; they are addressed
formally as Mr Chairman and Madam
Chairman.

chairperson noun (plural chairpersons)
a chairman.

chalet (say shal-ay) noun (plural chalets)
1 a Swiss hut or cottage. 2 a hut in a
holiday camp etc. [Swiss French]

chalice noun (plural chalices)
a large goblet for holding wine, especially
one used at Holy Communion.
[from Latin calix = cup]

chalk noun (plural chalks)
1 a soft white or coloured stick used for
writing on blackboards or for drawing.
2 soft white limestone. **chalky** adjective
[from Old English]

challenge noun (plural challenges)
1 a demand to take part in a contest. 2 a
task or activity that is new and exciting
but also difficult.
challenge verb (challenges, challenging,
challenged)
1 make a challenge to someone. 2 question
whether something is true or correct.
challenger noun [from old French]

chamber noun (plural chambers)
1 (old use) a room. 2 a hall used for
meetings of a parliament etc.; the members
of the group using it. 3 a compartment in
machinery etc. [same origin as camera]

chamberlain noun (plural chamberlains)
an official who manages the household of a
sovereign or great noble. [from old French]

chambermaid noun (plural
chambermaids)
a woman employed to clean bedrooms at a
hotel etc.

chamber music noun
music for a small group of players.

chamber pot noun (plural chamber pots)
a receptacle for urine etc., used in a
bedroom.

chameleon (say kam-ee-lee-on) noun
(plural chameleons)
a small lizard that can change its colour to
that of its surroundings. [from Greek
khamaileon, literally = ground lion]

chamois noun (plural chamois)
1 (say sham-wa) a small wild antelope
living in the mountains. 2 (say sham-ee) a
piece of soft yellow leather used for
washing and polishing things. [French]

champ verb (champs, champing, champed)
munch or bite something noisily.
[imitating the sound]

champagne (say sham-payn) noun
a bubbly white wine, especially from
Champagne in France.

champion noun (plural champions)
1 a person or thing that has defeated all the
others in a sport or competition etc.
2 someone who supports a cause by
fighting, speaking, etc. **championship** noun
champion verb (champions, championing,
championed)
support a cause by fighting or speaking for
it. [from old French]

chance noun (plural chances)
1 an opportunity or possibility, Now is
your chance to escape. 2 the way things
happen without being planned, I met her by
chance.
take a chance take a risk.
chance verb (chances, chancing, chanced)
1 happen by chance, I chanced to meet her.
2 risk, Let's chance it. [from old French]

chancel noun (plural chancels)
the part of a church nearest to the altar.
[from Latin]

chancellor noun (plural chancellors)
an important official.
Chancellor of the Exchequer the
government minister in charge of a
country's finances.
[from Latin cancellarius = secretary]

chancy adjective
risky.

chandelier (*say* shand-il-**eer**) *noun* (*plural* **chandeliers**)
a support for several lights or candles that hangs from the ceiling.
[from French *chandelle* = candle]

change *verb* (**changes, changing, changed**)
1 make or become different. **2** exchange.
3 put on different clothes. **4** go from one train or bus etc. to another.

change *noun* (*plural* **changes**)
1 changing; a difference in doing something. **2** coins or notes of small values. **3** money given back to the payer when the price is less than the amount handed over. **4** a fresh set of clothes. **5** a variation in routine, *Let's walk home for a change*.
[from old French]

changeable *adjective*
likely to change; changing frequently, *changeable weather*.

changeling *noun* (*plural* **changelings**)
a child who is believed to have been substituted secretly for another, especially by fairies.

channel *noun* (*plural* **channels**)
1 a stretch of water connecting two seas.
2 a way for water to flow along. **3** the part of a river or sea etc. that is deep enough for ships. **4** a broadcasting wavelength.

channel *verb* (**channels, channelling, channelled**)
1 make a channel in something. **2** direct something through a channel or other route. [from Latin *canalis* = canal]

chant *noun* (*plural* **chants**)
1 a tune to which words with no regular rhythm are fitted, e.g. one used in singing psalms. **2** a rhythmic call or shout.

chant *verb* (**chants, chanting, chanted**)
1 sing. **2** call out words in a rhythm.
[from Latin *cantare* = sing]

chaos (*say* kay-oss) *noun*
great disorder. **chaotic** *adjective*, **chaotically** *adverb* [Greek, = bottomless pit]

chap *noun* (*plural* **chaps**) (*informal*)
a man. [short for *chapman*, an old word for a pedlar]

chapatti *noun* (*plural* **chapattis**)
a flat cake of unleavened bread, used in Indian cookery.
[Hindi, from *chapana* = flatten or roll out]

chapel *noun* (*plural* **chapels**)
1 a place used for Christian worship, other than a cathedral or parish church; a religious service in this. **2** a section of a large church, with its own altar.
[from old French]

chaperone (*say* shap-er-ohn) *noun* (*plural* **chaperones**)
an older woman in charge of a young one on social occasions. **chaperone** *verb*
[from old French]

chaplain *noun* (*plural* **chaplains**)
a member of the clergy who looks after a college or hospital or regiment etc.
[from old French]

chapped *adjective*
with skin split or cracked from cold etc.
[origin unknown]

chapter *noun* (*plural* **chapters**)
1 a division of a book. **2** the clergy of a cathedral or members of a monastery. The room where they meet is called a **chapter house**. [from Latin]

char[1] *verb* (**chars, charring, charred**)
make or become black by burning.
[from *charcoal*]

char[2] *noun* (*plural* **chars**)
a charwoman.

character *noun* (*plural* **characters**)
1 a person in a story, film, or play. **2** all the qualities that make a person or thing what he, she, or it is. **3** a letter of the alphabet.
[from Greek]

characteristic *noun* (*plural* **characteristics**)
a quality that forms part of a person's or thing's character.

characteristic *adjective*
typical of a person or thing.
characteristically *adverb*

characterize *verb* (**characterizes, characterizing, characterized**)
1 be a characteristic of. **2** describe the character of. **characterization** *noun*

charade (*say* sha-rahd) *noun* (*plural* charades)
1 a scene in the game of *charades*, in which people try to guess a word from other people's acting. 2 a pretence. [French]

charcoal *noun*
a black substance made by burning wood slowly. Charcoal can be used for drawing with. [origin unknown]

charge *noun* (*plural* charges)
1 the price asked for something. 2 a rushing attack. 3 the amount of explosive needed to fire a gun etc. 4 electricity in something. 5 an accusation that someone has committed a crime. 6 a person or thing in someone's care.
in charge in control; deciding what shall happen to a person or thing.
charge *verb* (charges, charging, charged)
1 ask a particular price. 2 rush forward in an attack. 3 give an electric charge to something. 4 accuse someone of committing a crime. 5 entrust someone with a responsibility or task.
[from Latin *carcare* = to load]

charger *noun* (*plural* chargers) (*old use*)
a cavalry horse.

chariot *noun* (*plural* chariots)
a horse-drawn vehicle with two wheels, used in ancient times for fighting, racing, etc. **charioteer** *noun*
[from old French; related to *car*]

charisma (*say* ka-riz-ma) *noun*
the special quality that makes a person attractive or influential.
[Greek, = divine favour]

charismatic (*say* ka-riz-mat-ik) *adjective*
having charisma.

charity *noun* (*plural* charities)
1 an organization set up to help people who are poor, ill, or disabled or have suffered a disaster. 2 giving money or help etc. to the needy. 3 kindness and sympathy towards others; being unwilling to think badly of people. **charitable** *adjective*, **charitably** *adverb* [from Latin *caritas* = love]

charlatan (*say* shar-la-tan) *noun* (*plural* charlatans)
a person who falsely claims to be an expert. [from Italian *ciarlatano* = babbler]

charm *noun* (*plural* charms)
1 the power to please or delight people; attractiveness. 2 a magic spell. 3 a small object believed to bring good luck. 4 an ornament worn on a bracelet etc.
charm *verb* (charms, charming, charmed)
1 give pleasure or delight to people. 2 put a spell on someone; bewitch. **charmer** *noun*
[from Latin *carmen* = song or spell]

charnel house *noun* (*plural* charnel houses)
a place in which the bodies or bones of the dead are kept. [same origin as *carnal*]

chart *noun* (*plural* charts)
1 a map for people sailing ships or flying aircraft. 2 an outline map showing special information, *a weather chart*. 3 a diagram or list etc. giving information in an orderly way.
the charts a list of the records that are most popular.
chart *verb* (charts, charting, charted)
make a chart of something; map.
[same origin as *card*]

charter *noun* (*plural* charters)
1 an official document giving somebody certain rights etc. 2 chartering an aircraft, ship, or vehicle.
charter *verb* (charters, chartering, chartered)
1 hire an aircraft, ship, or vehicle. 2 give a charter to someone. [same origin as *card*]

chartered accountant *noun* (*plural* chartered accountants)
an accountant who is qualified according to the rules of an association that has a royal charter.

charwoman *noun* (*plural* charwomen)
a woman employed as a cleaner.
[from Old English *cerr* = task]

chary (*say* chair-ee) *adjective*
cautious about doing or giving something.
[from Old English]

chase *verb* (chases, chasing, chased)
go quickly after a person or thing in order to capture or catch them up or drive them away. **chase** *noun*
[from Latin *captare* = capture]

chasm (*say* kazm) *noun* (*plural* chasms)
a deep opening in the ground.
[from Greek *chasma* = gaping hollow]

chassis (*say* shas-ee) *noun* (*plural* chassis)
the framework under a car etc., on which other parts are mounted. [originally = window frame; related to *casement*]

chaste *adjective*
not having sexual intercourse at all, or only with the person to whom you are married. **chastity** *noun*
[from Latin *castus* = pure]

chasten (*say* chay-sen) *verb* (chastens, chastening, chastened)
make someone realize that they have behaved badly or done something wrong.
[from Latin *castigare* = castigate]

chastise *verb* (chastises, chastising, chastised)
punish or scold someone severely.
chastisement *noun* [same origin as *chasten*]

chat *noun* (*plural* chats)
a friendly conversation.

chat *verb* (chats, chatting, chatted)
have a friendly conversation.
[from *chatter*]

château (*say* shat-oh) *noun* (*plural* châteaux)
a large country house in France.
[French; related to *castle*]

chattel *noun* (*plural* chattels)
(*old use*) something you own that can be moved from place to place (distinguished from a house or land).
[from old French *chatel*; related to *capital*]

chatter *verb* (chatters, chattering, chattered)
1 talk quickly about unimportant things; keep on talking. **2** if your teeth chatter, they make a rattling sound because you are cold or frightened. **chatterer** *noun*

chatter *noun*
chattering talk or sound.
[imitating the sound]

chatterbox *noun* (*plural* chatterboxes)
a talkative person.

chauffeur (*say* shoh-fer) *noun* (*plural* chauffeurs)
a person employed to drive a car.
[French, = stoker]

chauvinism (*say* shoh-vin-izm) *noun*
1 prejudiced belief that your own country is superior to others. **2** the belief of some men that men are superior to women.
chauvinist *noun*, **chauvinistic** *adjective*
[from the name of Nicolas Chauvin, a French soldier in Napoleon's army, noted for his extreme patriotism]

cheap *adjective*
1 low in price; not expensive. **2** of poor quality; of low value. **cheaply** *adverb*, **cheapness** *noun*
[from Old English *ceap* = a bargain]

cheapen *verb* (cheapens, cheapening, cheapened)
make or become cheap.

cheat *verb* (cheats, cheating, cheated)
1 trick or deceive somebody. **2** try to do well in an examination or game etc. by breaking the rules.

cheat *noun* (*plural* cheats)
a person who cheats. [from old French]

check[1] *verb* (checks, checking, checked)
1 make sure that something is correct or in good condition. **2** make something stop or go slower.

check *noun* (*plural* checks)
1 checking something. **2** stopping or slowing; a pause. **3** a receipt; a bill in a restaurant. **4** the situation in chess when a king may be captured. [from the saying of 'check' when playing chess, to show that your opponent's king is in danger: from Persian *shah* = king]

check[2] *noun* (*plural* checks)
a pattern of squares. **checked** *adjective*
[from *chequered*]

checkmate *noun*
the winning situation in chess.
checkmate *verb*
[from Persian *shah mat* = the king is dead]

checkout *noun* (*plural* checkouts)
a place where goods are paid for in a self-service shop.

Cheddar *noun*
a kind of cheese.
[named after Cheddar in Somerset]

cheek *noun* (*plural* **cheeks**)
1 the side of the face below the eye. 2 rude
or disrespectful behaviour; impudence.
[from Old English]

cheeky *adjective*
rude or disrespectful; impudent.
cheekily *adverb*, **cheekiness** *noun*

cheer *noun* (*plural* **cheers**)
1 a shout of praise or pleasure or
encouragement, especially 'hurray'.
2 cheerfulness, *full of good cheer*.
cheer *verb* (**cheers, cheering, cheered**)
1 give a cheer. 2 gladden or encourage
somebody.
cheer up make or become cheerful.
[originally = a person's expression; from
old French *chiere* = face]

cheerful *adjective*
1 looking or sounding happy. 2 pleasantly
bright or colourful.
cheerfully *adverb*, **cheerfulness** *noun*

cheerio *interjection* (*informal*)
goodbye.

cheerless *adjective*
gloomy or dreary.

cheery *adjective*
bright and cheerful.

cheese *noun* (*plural* **cheeses**)
a solid food made from milk.
[from Old English]

cheesecake *noun* (*plural* **cheesecakes**)
a dessert made of a mixture of sweetened
curds on a layer of biscuit.

cheetah *noun* (*plural* **cheetahs**)
a kind of leopard that can run extremely
fast. [from Hindi]

chef (*say* shef) *noun* (*plural* **chefs**)
the cook in a hotel or restaurant.
[French, = chief]

chemical *adjective*
to do with or produced by chemistry.

chemical *noun* (*plural* **chemicals**)
a substance obtained by or used in
chemistry.
[from Latin *alchimia* = alchemy]

chemist *noun* (*plural* **chemists**)
1 a person who makes or sells medicines.
2 an expert in chemistry.
[from Latin *alchimista* = alchemist]

chemistry *noun*
1 the way that substances combine and
react with one another. 2 the study of
substances and their reactions etc.
[from *chemist*]

chemotherapy *noun*
the treatment of disease, especially cancer,
by the use of chemical substances.

cheque *noun* (*plural* **cheques**)
a printed form on which you write
instructions to a bank to pay out money
from your account.
[a different spelling of *check*[1]]

chequered *adjective*
marked with a pattern of squares.
[same origin as *exchequer*]

cherish *verb* (**cherishes, cherishing,
cherished**)
1 look after a person or thing lovingly. 2 be
fond of. [from French *cher* = dear]

cherry *noun* (*plural* **cherries**)
a small soft round fruit with a stone.
[from old French]

cherub *noun* (*plural* **cherubim** or **cherubs**)
an angel, often pictured as a chubby child
with wings. **cherubic** (*say* che-**roo**-bik)
adjective [from Hebrew]

chess *noun*
a game for two players with sixteen pieces
each (called **chessmen**) on a board of 64
squares (a **chessboard**).
[from old French *esches* = checks]

chest *noun* (*plural* **chests**)
1 the front part of the body between the
neck and the waist. 2 a large strong box for
storing things in. [from Old English]

chestnut *noun* (*plural* **chestnuts**)
1 a tree that produces hard brown nuts.
2 the nut of this tree. 3 an old joke or story.
[from Greek]

chest of drawers *noun* (*plural* **chests of drawers**)
a piece of furniture with drawers for storing clothes etc.

chevron (*say* shev-ron) *noun* (*plural* **chevrons**)
a V-shaped stripe. [from old French]

chew *verb* (**chews, chewing, chewed**)
grind food between the teeth. **chewy** *adjective* [from Old English]

chewing gum *noun*
a sticky flavoured type of sweet for chewing.

chic (*say* sheek) *adjective*
stylish and elegant. [French]

chicanery (*say* shik-**ayn**-er-ee) *noun*
trickery. [from French *chicaner* = quibble]

chick *noun* (*plural* **chicks**)
a very young bird.
[shortened form of *chicken*]

chicken *noun* (*plural* **chickens**)
1 a young bird, especially of the domestic fowl. 2 the flesh of a domestic fowl as food.
chicken *adjective* (*slang*)
afraid to do something; cowardly.
chicken *verb* (**chickens, chickening, chickened**)
chicken out (*slang*) not take part in something because you are afraid.
[from Old English]

chickenpox *noun*
a disease that produces red spots on the skin.
[probably because the disease is mild]

chickpea *noun* (*plural* **chickpeas**)
the yellow seed of a plant of the pea family, eaten as a vegetable.
[from French *chiche* = chickpea, + *pea*]

chicory *noun*
a plant whose leaves are used as salad.
[from Greek]

chide *verb* (**chides, chiding, chided, chidden**) (*old use*)
scold. [from Old English]

chief *noun* (*plural* **chiefs**)
a person with the highest rank or authority.
chief *adjective*
most important; main. **chiefly** *adverb*
[from French]

chieftain *noun* (*plural* **chieftains**)
the chief of a tribe, band of robbers, etc.

chiffon (*say* shif-on) *noun*
a very thin almost transparent fabric.
[French]

chilblain *noun* (*plural* **chilblains**)
a sore swollen place, usually on a hand or foot, caused by cold weather.
[from *chill* + *blain* = a sore]

child *noun* (*plural* **children**)
1 a young person; a boy or girl.
2 someone's son or daughter.
[from Old English]

childhood *noun* (*plural* **childhoods**)
the time when a person is a child.

childish *adjective*
like a child; unsuitable for a grown person.
childishly *adverb*

childless *adjective*
having no children.

childminder *noun* (*plural* **childminders**)
a person who looks after children for payment.

chill *noun* (*plural* **chills**)
1 unpleasant coldness. 2 an illness that makes you shiver.
chill *verb* (**chills, chilling, chilled**)
make a person or thing cold.
[from Old English]

chilli *noun* (*plural* **chillies**)
the hot-tasting pod of a red pepper.
[via Spanish from Nahuatl (a Central American language)]

chilli con carne *noun*
a stew of chilli-flavoured minced beef and beans. [Spanish, = chilli with meat]

chilly *adjective*
1 rather cold. 2 unfriendly. **chilliness** *noun*

chime *noun* (*plural* **chimes**)
a series of notes sounded by a set of bells each making a different musical sound.
chime *verb* (**chimes, chiming, chimed**)
make a chime. [origin unknown]

chimney *noun* (*plural* **chimneys**)
a tall pipe or structure that carries smoke away from a fire. [from French]

chimney pot *noun* (*plural* **chimney pots**)
a pipe fitted to the top of a chimney.

chimney sweep *noun* (*plural* **chimney sweeps**)
a person who cleans soot from inside chimneys.

chimpanzee *noun* (*plural* **chimpanzees**)
an African ape, smaller than a gorilla. [via French from Kikongo (an African language)]

chin *noun* (*plural* **chins**)
the lower part of the face below the mouth. [from Old English]

china *noun*
thin delicate pottery. [from Persian *chini* = from China]

chink *noun* (*plural* **chinks**)
1 a narrow opening, *a chink in the curtains*. 2 a chinking sound.
chink *verb* (**chinks, chinking, chinked**)
make a sound like glasses or coins being struck together. [origin unknown]

chintz *noun*
a shiny cotton cloth used for making curtains etc. [from Hindi]

chip *noun* (*plural* **chips**)
1 a thin piece cut or broken off something hard. 2 a fried oblong strip of potato. 3 a place where a small piece has been knocked off something. 4 a small counter used in games. 5 a microchip.
a chip off the old block a child who is very like his or her father.
have a chip on your shoulder have a grievance and feel bitter or resentful.
chip *verb* (**chips, chipping, chipped**)
1 knock small pieces off something. 2 cut a potato into chips. [from Old English]

chipboard *noun*
board made from chips of wood pressed and stuck together.

chipolata *noun* (*plural* **chipolatas**)
a small spicy sausage. [via French from Italian]

chiropody (*say* ki-rop-od-ee) *noun*
medical treatment of the feet, e.g. corns. **chiropodist** *noun* [from Greek *cheir* = hand + *podos* = of the foot (because chiropodists originally treated both hands and feet)]

chirp *verb* (**chirps, chirping, chirped**)
make short sharp sounds like a small bird. **chirp** *noun* [imitating the sound]

chirpy *adjective*
lively and cheerful.

chisel *noun* (*plural* **chisels**)
a tool with a sharp end for shaping wood, stone, etc.
chisel *verb* (**chisels, chiselling, chiselled**)
shape or cut something with a chisel. [from old French]

chivalrous (*say* shiv-al-rus) *adjective*
being considerate and helpful towards people less strong than yourself. **chivalry** *noun* [= like a perfect knight (same origin as *Cavalier*)]

chive *noun* (*plural* **chives**)
a small herb with leaves that taste like onions. [from Latin *cepa* = onion]

chivvy *verb* (**chivvies, chivvying, chivvied**)
try to make someone hurry. [probably from *Chevy Chase*, the scene of a skirmish which was the subject of an old ballad]

chlorinate *verb* (**chlorinates, chlorinating, chlorinated**)
put chlorine into something. **chlorination** *noun*

chlorine (*say* klor-een) *noun*
a greenish-yellow gas used to disinfect water etc. [from Greek *chloros* = green]

chloroform (*say* klo-ro-form) *noun*
a liquid that gives off a vapour that makes people unconscious.

chlorophyll (*say* klo-ro-fil) *noun*
the substance that makes plants green.
[from Greek *chloros* = green + *phyllon*
= leaf]

choc ice *noun* (*plural* **choc ices**)
a bar of ice cream covered with chocolate.

chock *noun* (*plural* **chocks**)
a block or wedge used to prevent
something, especially an aeroplane, from
moving. [from old French]

chock-a-block *adjective*
crammed or crowded together.
[origin unknown]

chock-full *adjective*
crammed full.

chocolate *noun* (*plural* **chocolates**)
1 a solid brown food or powder made from
roasted cacao seeds. **2** a drink made with
this powder. **3** a sweet made of or covered
with chocolate.
[via French or Spanish from Nahuatl (a
Central American language)]

choice *noun* (*plural* **choices**)
1 choosing between things. **2** the range of
things from which someone can choose,
There is a wide choice of holidays. **3** a
person or thing chosen, *This is my choice.*
choice *adjective*
of the best quality, *choice bananas.*
[via old French from Germanic]

choir *noun* (*plural* **choirs**)
a group of people trained to sing together,
especially in a church. **choirboy** *noun*
[from Latin *chorus* = choir]

choke *verb* (**chokes, choking, choked**)
1 cause somebody to stop breathing
properly. **2** be unable to breathe properly.
3 clog.
choke *noun* (*plural* **chokes**)
a device controlling the flow of air into the
engine of a motor vehicle.
[from Old English]

cholera (*say* kol-er-a) *noun*
an infectious disease that is often fatal.
[from Greek]

cholesterol (*say* kol-est-er-ol) *noun*
a fatty substance that can clog the arteries.
[from Greek *chole* = bile + *stereos* = stiff]

choose *verb* (**chooses, choosing, chose,
chosen**)
decide which you are going to take from
among a number of people or things.
choosy *adjective* [from Old English]

chop *verb* (**chops, chopping, chopped**)
cut or hit something with a heavy blow.
chop *noun* (*plural* **chops**)
1 a chopping blow. **2** a small thick slice of
meat, usually on a rib. [origin unknown]

chopper *noun* (*plural* **choppers**)
1 a chopping tool; a small axe. **2** (*slang*) a
helicopter.

choppy *adjective* (**choppier, choppiest**)
(of the sea) not smooth; full of small waves.
choppiness *noun*

chopsticks *plural noun*
a pair of thin sticks used for lifting Chinese
and Japanese food to your mouth. [from
pidgin English, literally = quick sticks]

chopsuey *noun* (*plural* **chopsueys**)
a Chinese dish of meat fried with bean
sprouts and vegetables served with rice.
[from Chinese *tsaap sui* = mixed bits]

choral *adjective*
to do with or sung by a choir or chorus.
[from Latin]

chorale (*say* kor-ahl) *noun* (*plural* **chorales**)
a choral composition using the words of a
hymn. [via German from Latin]

chord[1] (*say* kord) *noun* (*plural* **chords**)
a number of musical notes sounded
together. [from *accord*]

chord[2] (*say* kord) *noun* (*plural* **chords**)
a straight line joining two points on a
curve. [a different spelling of *cord*]

USAGE: Do not confuse with *cord*.

chore (*say* chor) *noun* (*plural* **chores**)
a regular or dull task.
[a different spelling of *char*]

choreography (*say* ko-ree-og-ra-fee) *noun*
the art of writing the steps for ballets or
stage dances. **choreographer** *noun*
[from Greek *choreia* = dance, + *-graphy*]

chorister (*say* ko-rist-er) *noun* (*plural* choristers)
a member of a choir. [from Old French]

chortle *noun* (*plural* chortles)
a loud chuckle. **chortle** *verb*
[a mixture of *chuckle* and *snort*: invented by Lewis Carroll]

chorus *noun* (*plural* choruses)
1 the words repeated after each verse of a song or poem. **2** music sung by a group of people. **3** a group singing together.
chorus *verb* (choruses, chorusing, chorused)
sing or speak in chorus.
[Latin, from Greek *choros*]

chow mein *noun*
a Chinese dish of fried noodles with shredded meat or shrimps etc. and vegetables.
[from Chinese *chao mian* = fried noodles]

christen *verb* (christens, christening, christened)
1 baptize. **2** give a name or nickname to a person or thing. **christening** *noun*
[from Old English *cristnian* = make someone a Christian]

Christian *noun* (*plural* Christians)
a person who believes in Jesus Christ and his teachings.
Christian *adjective*
to do with Christians or their beliefs.
Christianity *noun*

Christian name *noun* (*plural* Christian names)
a name given to a person at his or her christening.

Christmas *noun* (*plural* Christmases)
the day (25 December) when Christians commemorate the birth of Jesus Christ; the days round it. [from Old English *Cristes maesse* = the feast day of Christ]

Christmas pudding *noun* (*plural* Christmas puddings)
a dark pudding containing dried fruit etc., eaten at Christmas.

Christmas tree *noun* (*plural* Christmas trees)
an evergreen or artificial tree decorated at Christmas.

chromatic (*say* krom-at-ik) *adjective*
to do with colours.
chromatic scale a musical scale going up or down in semitones.
[from Greek *chroma* = colour]

chrome (*say* krohm) *noun*
chromium.
[from Greek *chroma* = colour (because its compounds have brilliant colours)]

chromium (*say* kroh-mee-um) *noun*
a shiny silvery metal. [from *chrome*]

chromosome (*say* kroh-mos-ohm) *noun* (*plural* chromosomes)
a tiny thread-like part of an animal cell or plant cell, carrying genes. [from Greek *chroma* = colour + *soma* = body]

chronic *adjective*
lasting for a long time, *a chronic illness*.
chronically *adverb*
[from Greek *chronikos* = to do with time]

chronicle *noun* (*plural* chronicles)
a record of events in the order that they happened. [same origin as *chronic*]

chronological *adjective*
arranged in the order that things happened. **chronologically** *adverb*

chronology (*say* kron-ol-oj-ee) *noun*
the arrangement of events in the order in which they happened, e.g. in history or geology.
[from Greek *chronos* = time, + *-logy*]

chronometer (*say* kron-om-it-er) *noun* (*plural* chronometers)
a very exact device for measuring time.
[from Greek *chronos* = time, + *meter*]

chrysalis *noun* (*plural* chrysalises)
a caterpillar that is changing into a butterfly or moth. [from Greek *chrysos* = gold (because some are this colour)]

chrysanthemum *noun* (*plural* chrysanthemums)
a garden flower that blooms in autumn.
[originally = a kind of marigold: from Greek *chrysos* = gold + *anthemon* = flower]

chubby *adjective* (chubbier, chubbiest)
plump. **chubbiness** *noun* [origin unknown]

chuck¹ *verb* (chucks, chucking, chucked)
(*informal*)
throw. [origin unknown]

chuck² *noun* (*plural* chucks)
1 the gripping-part of a lathe. 2 the part of
a drill that holds the bit. [originally = lump
or block: a different spelling of *chock*]

chuckle *noun* (*plural* chuckles)
a quiet laugh.
chuckle *verb* (chuckles, chuckling, chuckled)
laugh quietly. [origin unknown]

chug *verb* (chugs, chugging, chugged)
make the sound of an engine.
[imitating the sound]

chum *noun* (*plural* chums) (*informal*)
a friend. **chummy** *adjective*
[short for *chamber-fellow* = a person you
share a room with]

chunk *noun* (*plural* chunks)
a thick piece of something. **chunky** *adjective*
[a different spelling of *chuck²*]

chupatty (*say* chup-at-ee) *noun* (*plural*
chupatties)
a different spelling of *chapatti*.

church *noun* (*plural* churches)
1 a public building for Christian worship.
2 a religious service in a church, *I will see
you after church.*
the Church all Christians; a group of these,
the Church of England.
[via Old English from Greek *kyriakon*
= Lord's house]

churchyard *noun* (*plural* churchyards)
the ground round a church, often used as a
graveyard.

churlish *adjective*
ill-mannered and unfriendly; surly.
[= like a *churl* = a peasant]

churn *noun* (*plural* churns)
1 a large can in which milk is carried from
a farm. 2 a machine in which milk is
beaten to make butter.
churn *verb* (churns, churning, churned)
1 make butter in a churn. 2 stir or swirl
vigorously.
churn out produce something in large
quantities.
[from Old English]

chute (*say* shoot) *noun* (*plural* chutes)
a steep channel for people or things to slide
down. [French, = a fall]

chutney *noun* (*plural* chutneys)
a strong-tasting mixture of fruit, peppers,
etc., eaten with meat. [from Hindi *chatni*]

CID *abbreviation*
Criminal Investigation Department.

-cide *suffix*
forms nouns meaning 'killing' or 'killer'
(e.g. *homicide*). [from Latin *caedere* = kill]

cider *noun* (*plural* ciders)
an alcoholic drink made from apples.
[via French and Latin from Hebrew]

cigar *noun* (*plural* cigars)
a roll of compressed tobacco leaves for
smoking. [from Spanish]

cigarette *noun* (*plural* cigarettes)
a small roll of shredded tobacco in thin
paper for smoking. [French, = little cigar]

cinder *noun* (*plural* cinders)
a small piece of partly burnt coal or wood.
[from Old English]

cine-camera (*say* sin-ee) *noun* (*plural* cine-
cameras)
a camera used for taking moving pictures.
[from Greek *kinema* = movement,
+ *camera*]

cinema *noun* (*plural* cinemas)
a place where films are shown.
[from Greek *kinema* = movement]

cinnamon (*say* sin-a-mon) *noun*
a yellowish-brown spice. [from Greek]

cipher (*say* sy-fer) *noun* (*plural* ciphers)
1 a kind of code. 2 the symbol 0,
representing nought or zero.
[from Arabic *sifr* = nought]

circle *noun* (*plural* circles)
1 a perfectly round flat shape or thing. 2 a
number of people with similar interests.
3 the balcony of a cinema or theatre.
circle *verb* (circles, circling, circled)
move in a circle; go round something.
[from Latin *circus*]

circuit (*say* ser-kit) *noun* (*plural* circuits)
1 a circular line or journey. 2 a motor-racing track. 3 the path of an electric current.
[from Latin *circum* = round + *itum* = gone]

circuitous (*say* ser-kew-it-us) *adjective*
going a long way round, not direct.

circular *adjective*
1 shaped like a circle; round. 2 moving round a circle. **circularity** *noun*

circular *noun* (*plural* circulars)
a letter or advertisement etc. sent to a number of people.

circulate *verb* (circulates, circulating, circulated)
1 go round something continuously, *Blood circulates in the body.* 2 pass from place to place. 3 send something round to a number of people. **circulation** *noun*

circum- *prefix*
around (as in *circumference*).
[from Latin *circum* = around]

circumcise *verb* (circumcises, circumcising, circumcised)
cut off the fold of skin at the tip of the penis. **circumcision** *noun*
[from *circum-* + Latin *caedere* = cut]

circumference *noun* (*plural* circumferences)
the line or distance round something, especially round a circle.
[from *circum-* + Latin *ferens* = carrying]

circumflex accent *noun* (*plural* circumflex accents)
a mark over a vowel, as over *e* in *fête*.
[from *circum-* + Latin *flectere* = bend]

circumlocution *noun* (*plural* circumlocutions)
a roundabout expression, using many words where a few would do, e.g. 'at this moment in time' for 'now'.

circumnavigate *verb* (circumnavigates, circumnavigating, circumnavigated)
sail completely round something.
circumnavigation *noun*
[from *circum-* + *navigate*]

circumscribe *verb* (circumscribes, circumscribing, circumscribed)
1 draw a line round something. 2 limit or restrict something, *Her powers are circumscribed by many regulations.*
[from *circum-* + Latin *scribere* = write]

circumspect *adjective*
cautious and watchful. **circumspection** *noun*
[from *circum-* + Latin *specere* = to look]

circumstance *noun* (*plural* circumstances)
a fact or condition connected with an event or person or action.
[from *circum-* + Latin *stans* = standing]

circumstantial (*say* ser-kum-stan-shal) *adjective*
consisting of facts that strongly suggest something but do not actually prove it, *circumstantial evidence.*

circumvent *verb* (circumvents, circumventing, circumvented)
find a way of avoiding something, *We managed to circumvent the rules.*
circumvention *noun*
[from *circum-* + Latin *ventum* = come]

circus *noun* (*plural* circuses)
a travelling show with clowns, acrobats, animals, etc. [Latin, = ring]

cistern *noun* (*plural* cisterns)
a tank for storing water. [from Latin]

citadel *noun* (*plural* citadels)
a fortress protecting a city. [from Italian]

cite (*say* sight) *verb* (cites, citing, cited)
quote as an example. **citation** *noun*
[from Latin *citare* = call]

citizen *noun* (*plural* citizens)
a person belonging to a particular city or country and having certain rights and duties because of this. **citizenship** *noun*
[same origin as *city*]

citizenry *noun*
all the citizens.

citizens' band *noun*
a range of special radio frequencies on which people can speak to one another over short distances.

citrus fruit *noun* (*plural* **citrus fruits**)
a lemon, orange, grapefruit, or other sharp-tasting fruit. [Latin]

city *noun* (*plural* **cities**)
a large important town, usually with special rights given by a charter.
the City the oldest part of London, now a centre of commerce and finance.
[from Latin *civitas* = city]

civic *adjective*
1 to do with a city of town. 2 to do with citizens. [from Latin *civis* = citizen]

civics *noun*
the study of the rights and duties of citizens.

civil *adjective*
1 to do with citizens. 2 to do with civilians; not military, *civil aviation*. 3 polite. **civilly** *adverb* [from Latin]

civil defence *noun*
protection of civilians in an air raid etc.

civil engineering *noun*
the work of designing or maintaining roads, bridges, dams, etc.
civil engineer *noun*

civilian *noun* (*plural* **civilians**)
a person who is not serving in the armed forces. [from *civil*]

civility *noun* (*plural* **civilities**)
politeness.

civilization *noun* (*plural* **civilizations**)
1 a civilized condition or society. 2 making or becoming civilized.

civilize *verb* (**civilizes, civilizing, civilized**)
bring culture and education etc. to a primitive community. [from French]

civil rights *plural noun*
the rights of citizens, especially to have freedom, equality, and the right to vote.

Civil Service *noun*
people employed by the government in various departments other than the armed forces.

civil war *noun* (*plural* **civil wars**)
war between groups of people of the same country.

clack *noun* (*plural* **clacks**)
a short sharp sound like that of plates struck together. **clack** *verb*
[imitating the sound]

clad *adjective*
clothed or covered. [old past tense of *clothe*]

claim *verb* (**claims, claiming, claimed**)
1 ask for something to which you believe you have a right. 2 declare; state something without being able to prove it.
claimant *noun*

claim *noun* (*plural* **claims**)
1 claiming. 2 something claimed. 3 a piece of ground claimed or assigned to someone for mining etc. [same origin as *clamour*]

clairvoyant *noun* (*plural* **clairvoyants**)
a person who is said to be able to predict future events or know about things that are happening out of sight. **clairvoyance** *noun* [from French *clair* = clear + *voyant* = seeing]

clam *noun* (*plural* **clams**)
a large shellfish.
[from Old English *clam* = something that grips tightly; related to *clamp*]

clamber *verb* (**clambers, clambering, clambered**)
climb with difficulty.
[from *clamb*, the old past tense of *climb*]

clammy *adjective*
damp and slimy. [from Old English *claeman* = smear, make sticky]

clamour *noun* (*plural* **clamours**)
1 a loud confused noise. 2 an outcry; a loud protest or demand. **clamorous** *adjective*

clamour *verb* (**clamours, clamouring, clamoured**)
make a loud protest or demand.
[from Latin *clamare* = call out]

clamp *noun* (*plural* **clamps**)
a device for holding things tightly.

clamp *verb* (**clamps, clamping, clamped**)
1 fix something with a clamp. 2 fix something firmly.
clamp down on 1 become stricter about

something. **2** put a stop to something. [probably from old German; related to *clam*]

clan *noun* (*plural* **clans**)
a group sharing the same ancestor, especially in Scotland. [Scottish Gaelic]

clandestine (*say* klan-dest-in) *adjective*
done secretly; kept secret. [from Latin]

clang *noun* (*plural* **clangs**)
a loud ringing sound. **clang** *verb*
[imitating the sound]

clangour *noun*
a clanging noise.
[from Latin *clangere* = resound, echo]

clank *noun* (*plural* **clanks**)
a sound like heavy pieces of metal banging together. **clank** *verb* [imitating the sound]

clap *verb* (**claps, clapping, clapped**)
1 strike the palms of the hands together loudly, especially as applause. **2** slap in a friendly way, *clapped him on the shoulder*. **3** put quickly, *They clapped him into gaol*.
clap *noun* (*plural* **claps**)
1 a sudden sharp noise, *a clap of thunder*. **2** clapping; applause. **3** a friendly slap. [from Old English]

clapper *noun* (*plural* **clappers**)
the tongue or hanging piece inside a bell that strikes against the bell to make it sound.

claptrap *noun*
insincere or foolish talk.
[originally = something done or said just to get applause]

claret *noun* (*plural* **clarets**)
a kind of red wine.
[from old French *vin claret* = clear wine]

clarify *verb* (**clarifies, clarifying, clarified**)
make or become clear or easier to understand. **clarification** *noun*
[from Latin *clarus* = clear]

clarinet *noun* (*plural* **clarinets**)
a woodwind instrument. **clarinettist** *noun*
[from French]

clarion *noun* (*plural* **clarions**)
an old type of trumpet.
[same origin as *clarify*]

clarity *noun*
clearness. [same origin as *clarify*]

clash *verb* (**clashes, clashing, clashed**)
1 make a loud sound like that of cymbals banging together. **2** conflict. **3** happen inconveniently at the same time. **4** (of colours) look unpleasant together. **clash** *noun* [imitating the sound]

clasp *noun* (*plural* **clasps**)
1 a device for fastening things, with interlocking parts. **2** a grasp.
clasp *verb* (**clasps, clasping, clasped**)
1 grasp or hold tightly. **2** fasten with a clasp. [origin unknown]

class *noun* (*plural* **classes**)
1 a group of children, students, etc. who are taught together. **2** a group of similar people, animals, or things. **3** people of the same social or economic level. **4** level of quality, *first class*.
class *verb* (**classes, classing, classed**)
arrange things in classes or groups; classify. [from Latin *classis* = a social division of the Roman people]

classic *adjective*
generally agreed to be excellent or important.
classic *noun* (*plural* **classics**)
a classic book, film, writer, etc.
[from Latin *classicus* = of the highest class]

classical *adjective*
1 to do with ancient Greek or Roman literature, art. **2** serious or conventional in style, *classical music*.

classics *noun*
the study of ancient Greek and Latin languages and literature.
[because they were considered better than modern works]

classified *adjective*
1 put into classes or groups. **2** (of information) declared officially to be secret and available only to certain people.

classify *verb* (**classifies, classifying, classified**)
arrange things in classes or groups.
classification *noun*, **classificatory** *adjective*
[from *classification*, from French]

classmate *noun* (*plural* **classmates**)
someone in the same class at school.

classroom *noun* (*plural* **classrooms**)
a room where a class of children or
students is taught.

clatter *verb* & *noun* (**clatters, clattering,
clattered**)
rattle. [imitating the sound]

clause *noun* (*plural* **clauses**)
1 a single part of a treaty, law, or contract.
2 part of a complex sentence, with its own
verb, *There are two clauses in 'We choose
what we want'*. [from Latin]

claustrophobia *noun*
fear of being inside an enclosed space.
[from Latin *claustrum* = enclosed space,
+ *phobia*]

claw *noun* (*plural* **claws**)
1 a sharp nail on a bird's or animal's foot.
2 a claw-like part or device used for
grasping things.
claw *verb* (**claws, clawing, clawed**)
grasp, pull, or scratch with a claw or hand.
[from Old English]

clay *noun*
a kind of stiff sticky earth that becomes
hard when baked, used for making bricks
and pottery. **clayey** *adjective*
[from Old English]

-cle *suffix* see **-cule**.

clean *adjective*
1 without any dirt or marks or stains.
2 fresh; not yet used. 3 honourable; not
unfair, *a clean fight*. 4 not indecent. 5 a
clean catch is one made skilfully with no
fumbling. **cleanness** *noun*
clean *verb* (**cleans, cleaning, cleaned**)
make a thing clean.
clean *adverb*
completely, *I clean forgot*.
[from Old English]

cleaner *noun* (*plural* **cleaners**)
1 a person who cleans things, especially

rooms etc. 2 something used for cleaning
things.

cleanliness (*say* klen-li-nis) *noun*
being clean.

cleanly (*say* kleen-lee) *adverb*
in a clean way.

cleanse (*say* klenz) *verb* (**cleanses,
cleansing, cleansed**)
1 clean. 2 make pure. **cleanser** *noun*
[from Old English]

clear *adjective*
1 transparent; not muddy or cloudy. 2 easy
to see or hear or understand; distinct.
3 free from obstacles or unwanted things;
free from guilt, *a clear conscience*.
4 complete, *Give three clear days' notice*.
clearly *adverb*, **clearness** *noun*
clear *adverb*
1 distinctly; clearly, *We heard you loud and
clear*. 2 completely, *He got clear away*.
3 apart; not in contact, *Stand clear of the
doors*.
clear *verb* (**clears, clearing, cleared**)
1 make or become clear. 2 show that
someone is innocent or reliable. 3 jump
over something without touching it. 4 get
approval or authorization for something,
Clear this with the headmaster.
clear away remove used plates etc. after a
meal.
clear off or **out** (*informal*) go away.
clear up 1 make things tidy. 2 become
better or brighter. 3 solve, *clear up the
mystery*.
[same origin as *clarify*]

clearance *noun* (*plural* **clearances**)
1 clearing something. 2 getting rid of
unwanted goods. 3 the space between two
things.

clearing *noun* (*plural* **clearings**)
an open space in a forest.

cleavage *noun*
the hollow between a woman's breasts.

cleave¹ *verb* (**cleaves, cleaving**; *past tense*
cleaved, clove, or **cleft**; *past participle* **cleft**
or **cloven**)
1 divide by chopping; split. 2 make a way
through, *cleaving the waves*.
[from Old English *cleofan*]

cleave² *verb* (cleaves, cleaving, cleaved) (*old use*)
cling to something.
[from Old English *cliflan*]

cleaver *noun* (*plural* cleavers)
a butcher's chopping tool.

clef *noun* (*plural* clefs)
a symbol on a stave in music, showing the pitch of the notes, *treble clef; bass clef.*
[French, = key]

cleft *past tense* of **cleave¹**.
cleft *noun* (*plural* clefts)
a split in something.

clemency *noun*
gentleness or mildness; mercy.
[from Latin]

clench *verb* (clenches, clenching, clenched)
close teeth or fingers tightly.
[from Old English]

clergy *noun*
the people who have been ordained as priests or ministers of the Christian Church. **clergyman** *noun*
[same origin as *clerical*]

clerical *adjective*
1 to do with clerks or their work. 2 to do with the clergy.
[via Latin from Greek *klerikos* = belonging to the Christian Church]

clerk (*say* klark) *noun* (*plural* clerks)
a person employed to keep records or accounts, deal with papers in an office, etc.
[originally = a Christian minister: same origin as *clerical*]

clever *adjective*
1 quick at learning and understanding things. 2 skilful. **cleverly** *adverb*, **cleverness** *noun* [origin unknown]

cliché (*say* klee-shay) *noun* (*plural* clichés)
a phrase or idea that is used too often.
[French, = stereotyped]

click *noun* (*plural* clicks)
a short sharp sound. **click** *verb*
[imitating the sound]

client *noun* (*plural* clients)
a person who gets help from a lawyer, accountant, or professional person other than a doctor; a customer.
[from Latin *cliens* = one who listens]

clientele (*say* klee-on-tel) *noun*
customers. [from French]

cliff *noun* (*plural* cliffs)
a steep rock face, especially on a coast.
[from Old English]

cliffhanger *noun* (*plural* cliffhangers)
a tense and exciting ending to an episode of a serial.

climate *noun* (*plural* climates)
the regular weather conditions of an area.
climatic (*say* kly-**mat**-ik) *adjective*
[from Greek *klima* = zone, region]

climax *noun* (*plural* climaxes)
the most interesting or important point of a story, series of events, etc.
[from Greek *klimax* = ladder]

climb *verb* (climbs, climbing, climbed)
1 go up or over or down something. 2 grow upwards. 3 go higher. **climb** *noun*, **climber** *noun*
climb down admit that you have been wrong.
[from Old English]

clinch *verb* (clinches, clinching, clinched)
1 settle something definitely, *clinch the deal.* 2 (in boxing) be clasping each other.
clinch *noun* [a different spelling of *clench*]

cling *verb* (clings, clinging, clung)
hold on tightly. [from Old English]

cling film *noun*
a thin clinging transparent film, used as a covering for food.

clinic *noun* (*plural* clinics)
a place where people see doctors etc. for treatment or advice. **clinical** *adjective*
[from Greek *klinike* = teaching (of medicine) at the bedside]

clink *noun* (*plural* clinks)
a thin sharp sound like glasses being struck together. **clink** *verb*
[probably from old Dutch]

clip¹ *noun* (*plural* clips)
a fastener for keeping things together, usually worked by a spring.
clip *verb* (clips, clipping, clipped)
fasten with a clip.
[from Old English *clyppan* = embrace, hug]

clip² *verb* (clips, clipping, clipped)
1 cut with shears or scissors etc.
2 (*informal*) hit.
clip *noun* (*plural* clips)
1 a short piece of film shown on its own.
2 (*informal*) a hit on the head.
[from Old Norse]

clipper *noun* (*plural* clippers)
an old type of fast sailing ship.
[from *clip²*, in the sense = move quickly]

clippers *plural noun*
an instrument for cutting hair.

clique (*say* kleek) *noun* (*plural* cliques)
a small group of people who stick together and keep others out. [French]

clitoris *noun* (*plural* clitorises)
the small sensitive lump of flesh near the opening of a woman's vagina.
[Latin, from Greek]

cloak *noun* (*plural* cloaks)
a sleeveless garment that hangs loosely from the shoulders.
cloak *verb* (cloaks, cloaking, cloaked)
cover or conceal. [from old French]

cloakroom *noun* (*plural* cloakrooms)
1 a place where people can leave outdoor clothes, luggage, etc. 2 a lavatory.

clobber *verb* (clobbers, clobbering, clobbered) (*slang*)
1 hit hard again and again. 2 defeat completely. [origin unknown]

cloche (*say* klosh) *noun* (*plural* cloches)
a glass or plastic cover to protect outdoor plants.
[French, = bell (because of the shape)]

clock *noun* (*plural* clocks)
1 a device (other than a watch) that shows what the time is. 2 a measuring device with a dial or showing figures.

clock *verb* (clocks, clocking, clocked)
clock in or **out** register the time you arrive at work or leave work.
clock up reach a certain speed.
[from Latin *clocca* = bell]

clockwise *adverb* & *adjective*
moving round a circle in the same direction as a clock's hands.
[from *clock* + *-wise*]

clockwork *noun*
a mechanism with a spring that has to be wound up.
like clockwork very regularly.

clod *noun* (*plural* clods)
a lump of earth or clay.
[a different spelling of *clot*]

clog *noun* (*plural* clogs)
a shoe with a wooden sole.
clog *verb* (clogs, clogging, clogged)
block up. [origin unknown]

cloister *noun* (*plural* cloisters)
a covered path along the side of a church or monastery etc., round a courtyard.
[from Latin *claustrum* = enclosed place]

clone *noun* (*plural* clones)
an animal or plant made from the cells of another animal or plant and therefore exactly like it.
[from Greek *klon* = a cutting from a plant]

close¹ (*say* klohss) *adjective*
1 near. 2 detailed or concentrated, *with close attention*. 3 tight; with little empty space, *a close fit*. 4 in which competitors are nearly equal, *a close contest*. 5 stuffy.
closely *adverb*, **closeness** *noun*
close *adverb*
closely, *close behind*.
close *noun* (*plural* closes)
1 a cul-de-sac. 2 an enclosed area, especially round a cathedral.
[same origin as *close²*]

close² (*say* klohz) *verb* (closes, closing, closed)
1 shut. 2 end.
close in 1 get nearer. 2 if the days are closing in, they are getting shorter.
close *noun*
end, *at the close of play*.
[via old French from Latin *claudere*]

closet *noun* (*plural* **closets**) (*American*)
a cupboard or storeroom.
closet *verb* (**closets, closeting, closeted**)
shut yourself away in a private room.
[old French, = small enclosed space]

close-up *noun* (*plural* **close-ups**)
a photograph or piece of film taken at close range.

closure *noun* (*plural* **closures**)
closing.

clot *noun* (*plural* **clots**)
1 a small mass of blood, cream, etc. that has become solid. 2 (*slang*) a stupid person.
clot *verb* (**clots, clotting, clotted**)
form clots. [from Old English]

cloth *noun* (*plural* **cloths**)
1 woven material or felt. 2 a piece of this material. 3 a tablecloth. [from Old English]

clothe *verb* (**clothes, clothing, clothed**)
put clothes on someone. [from *cloth*]

clothes *plural noun*
things worn to cover the body. [from *cloth*]

clothing *noun*
clothes.

clotted cream *noun*
cream thickened by being scalded.

cloud *noun* (*plural* **clouds**)
1 a mass of condensed water-vapour floating in the sky. 2 a mass of smoke, dust, etc., in the air.
cloud *verb* (**clouds, clouding, clouded**)
become cloudy. [from Old English]

cloudburst *noun* (*plural* **cloudbursts**)
a sudden heavy rainstorm.

cloudless *adjective*
without clouds.

cloudy *adjective* (**cloudier, cloudiest**)
1 full of clouds. 2 not transparent, *The liquid became cloudy.* **cloudiness** *noun*

clout *verb* (**clouts, clouting, clouted**)
(*informal*)
hit. **clout** *noun* [from Old English]

clove[1] *noun* (*plural* **cloves**)
the dried bud of a tropical tree, used as a spice. [from old French]

clove[2] *noun* (*plural* **cloves**)
one of the small bulbs in a compound bulb, *a clove of garlic*. [from Old English]

clove[3] *past tense* of **cleave**[1].

clove hitch *noun* (*plural* **clove hitches**)
a kind of knot.

cloven *past participle* of **cleave**[1].
cloven hoof a hoof that is divided, like those of cows and sheep.

clover *noun*
a small plant usually with three leaves on each stalk.
in clover in ease and luxury.
[from Old English]

clown *noun* (*plural* **clowns**)
1 a performer who does amusing tricks and actions, especially in a circus. 2 a person who does silly things.
clown *verb* (**clowns, clowning, clowned**)
do silly things, especially to amuse other people. [origin unknown]

cloying *adjective*
sickeningly sweet. [from an old word *accloy* = overfill, disgust]

club *noun* (*plural* **clubs**)
1 a heavy stick used as a weapon. 2 a stick with a shaped head used to hit the ball in golf. 3 a group of people who meet because they are interested in the same thing; the building where they meet. 4 a playing card with black clover leaves on it.
club *verb* (**clubs, clubbing, clubbed**)
hit with a heavy stick.
club together join with other people in order to pay for something, *club together to buy a boat.*
[from Old Norse]

cluck *verb* (**clucks, clucking, clucked**)
make a hen's throaty cry. **cluck** *noun*
[imitating the sound]

clue *noun* (*plural* **clues**)
something that helps a person to solve a puzzle or a mystery.
not have a clue (*informal*) be stupid or helpless.

clump [originally a ball of thread: in Greek legend, the warrior Theseus had to go into a maze (the Labyrinth); as he went in he unwound a ball of thread, and found his way out by winding it up again]

clump *noun* (*plural* **clumps**)
1 a cluster or mass of things. 2 a clumping sound.

clump *verb* (**clumps, clumping, clumped**)
1 form a cluster or mass. 2 walk with a heavy tread. [from old German]

clumsy *adjective* (**clumsier, clumsiest**)
1 heavy and ungraceful; likely to knock things over or drop things. 2 not skilful; not tactful, *a clumsy apology*.
clumsily *adverb*, **clumsiness** *noun*
[probably from a Scandinavian language]

cluster *noun* (*plural* **clusters**)
a small close group.
cluster *verb* (**clusters, clustering, clustered**)
form a cluster. [from Old English]

clutch¹ *verb* (**clutches, clutching, clutched**)
grasp tightly.
clutch *noun* (*plural* **clutches**)
1 a tight grasp. 2 a device for connecting and disconnecting the engine of a motor vehicle from its gears. [from Old English]

clutch² *noun* (*plural* **clutches**)
a set of eggs for hatching.
[from Old Norse *klekja* = to hatch]

clutter *noun*
things lying about untidily.
clutter *verb* (**clutters, cluttering, cluttered**)
fill with clutter, *Piles of books and papers cluttered her desk*.
[from an old word *clotter* = to clot]

Co. *abbreviation*
Company.

c/o *abbreviation*
care of.

co- *prefix*
1 together, jointly (as in *coexistence, cooperate*). 2 joint (as in *co-pilot*).
[same origin as *com-*]

coach *noun* (*plural* **coaches**)
1 a bus used for long journeys. 2 a carriage of a railway train. 3 a large horse-drawn carriage with four wheels. 4 an instructor in sports. 5 a teacher giving private specialized tuition.
coach *verb* (**coaches, coaching, coached**)
instruct or train somebody, especially in sports. [from Hungarian *kocsi szekér* = cart from *Kocs*, a town in Hungary]

coagulate *verb* (**coagulates, coagulating, coagulated**)
change from liquid to semi-solid; clot.
coagulant *noun*, **coagulation** *noun*
[from Latin]

coal *noun*
a hard black mineral substance used for burning to supply heat; a piece of this.
coalfield *noun* [from Old English]

coalesce (*say* koh-a-**less**) *verb* (**coalesces, coalescing, coalesced**)
combine and form one whole thing.
coalescence *noun*, **coalescent** *adjective*
[from co- + Latin *alescere* = grow up]

coalition *noun* (*plural* **coalitions**)
a temporary alliance, especially of two or more political parties in order to form a government. [same origin as *coalesce*]

coarse *adjective*
1 not smooth, not delicate; rough. 2 composed of large particles; not fine. 3 not refined; vulgar. **coarsely** *adverb*, **coarseness** *noun* [origin unknown]

coarsen *verb* (**coarsens, coarsening, coarsened**)
make or become coarse.

coast *noun* (*plural* **coasts**)
the seashore or the land close to it. **coastal** *adjective*, **coastline** *noun*
the coast is clear there is no chance of being seen or hindered.
coast *verb* (**coasts, coasting, coasted**)
ride without using power.
[from Latin *costa* = rib, side]

coastguard *noun* (*plural* **coastguards**)
a person whose job is to keep watch on the coast, detect or prevent smuggling, etc.

coat *noun* (*plural* **coats**)
1 an outdoor garment with sleeves. 2 the hair or fur on an animal's body. 3 a coating, *a coat of paint*.

coat *verb* (coats, coating, coated)
cover something with a coating.
[from old French]

coating *noun* (*plural* coatings)
a covering layer.

coat of arms *noun* (*plural* coats of arms)
a design on a shield, used as an emblem by
a family, city, etc.

coax *verb* (coaxes, coaxing, coaxed)
persuade someone gently or patiently.
[from an old word *cokes* = a stupid person]

cob *noun* (*plural* cobs)
1 the central part of an ear of maize, on
which the corn grows. 2 a sturdy horse for
riding. 3 a male swan. (The female is a
pen.) [origin unknown]

cobalt *noun*
a hard silvery-white metal.
[from German *Kobalt* = demon (because it
was believed to harm the silver ore with
which it was found)]

cobble¹ *noun* (*plural* cobbles)
a rounded stone used for paving streets etc.
cobbled *adjective*
[from *cob*, in the sense = round, stout]

cobble² *verb* (cobbles, cobbling, cobbled)
make or mend roughly. [from *cobbler*]

cobbler *noun* (*plural* cobblers)
a shoe-repairer. [origin unknown]

cobra (*say* koh-bra) *noun* (*plural* cobras)
a poisonous snake that can rear up.
[from Portuguese *cobra de capello* = snake
with a hood]

cobweb *noun* (*plural* cobwebs)
the thin sticky net made by a spider to trap
insects.
[from Old English *coppe* = spider, + *web*]

cocaine *noun*
a drug made from the leaves of a tropical
plant called *coca*.

cock *noun* (*plural* cocks)
1 a male chicken. 2 a male bird. 3 a
stopcock. 4 a lever in a gun.

cock *verb* (cocks, cocking, cocked)
1 make a gun ready to fire by raising the
cock. 2 turn something upwards or in a
particular direction, *The dog cocked its
ears*. [from Old English]

cockatoo *noun* (*plural* cockatoos)
a crested parrot. [via Dutch from Malay (a
language spoken in Malaysia)]

cocked hat *noun* (*plural* cocked hats)
a triangular hat worn with some uniforms.
[originally = a hat with the brim turned
upwards]

cockerel *noun* (*plural* cockerels)
a young male chicken. [from *cock*]

cocker spaniel *noun* (*plural* cocker
spaniels)
a kind of small spaniel.
[because they were used to hunt woodcock]

cock-eyed *adjective* (*slang*)
1 crooked; not straight. 2 absurd.
[from *cock* = turn]

cockle *noun* (*plural* cockles)
an edible shellfish.
[from old French *coquille* = shell]

cockney *noun* (*plural* cockneys)
1 a person born in the East End of London.
2 the dialect or accent of cockneys.
[originally = a small, misshapen egg,
believed to be a cock's egg (because
country people believed townspeople were
feeble)]

cockpit *noun* (*plural* cockpits)
the compartment where the pilot of an
aircraft sits.
[from the pits where cock fights took place]

cockroach *noun* (*plural* cockroaches)
a beetle-like insect. [from Spanish]

cocksure *adjective*
very sure; too confident. [from *cock* (used
to avoid saying *God* in oaths)]

cocktail *noun* (*plural* cocktails)
1 a mixed alcoholic drink. 2 a food
containing shellfish or fruit. [originally = a
racehorse that was not a thoroughbred
(because carthorses had their tails cut so
that they stood up like a cock's tail)]

cocky *adjective* (**cockier, cockiest**) (*informal*)
too self-confident. **cockiness** *noun*
[= proud as a cock]

cocoa *noun* (*plural* **cocoas**)
1 a hot drink made from a powder of
crushed cacao seeds. 2 this powder.
[a different spelling of *cacao*]

coconut *noun* (*plural* **coconuts**)
1 a large round nut that grows on a kind of
palm tree. 2 its white lining, used in sweets
and cookery. [from Spanish *coco*
= grinning face (because the base of the
nut looks like a monkey's face)]

cocoon *noun* (*plural* **cocoons**)
1 the covering round a chrysalis. 2 a
protective wrapping.
cocoon *verb* (**cocoons, cocooning,
cocooned**)
protect something by wrapping it up.
[from French]

cod *noun* (*plural* **cod**)
a large edible sea fish. [origin unknown]

coddle *verb* (**coddles, coddling, coddled**)
cherish and protect carefully.
[origin unknown]

code *noun* (*plural* **codes**)
1 a word or phrase used to represent a
message in order to keep its meaning
secret. 2 a set of signs used in sending
messages by machine etc., *the Morse code*.
3 a set of laws or rules, *the Highway Code*.
code *verb* (**codes, coding, coded**)
put a message into code.
[from Latin *codex* = book]

codicil *noun* (*plural* **codicils**)
an addition to a will.
[from Latin *codicillus* = small document]

codify *verb* (**codifies, codifying, codified**)
arrange laws or rules into a code or system.
codification *noun* [from *code*]

coeducation *noun*
educating boys and girls together.
coeducational *adjective*
[from *co-* + *education*]

coefficient *noun* (*plural* **coefficients**)
a number by which another number is
multiplied; a factor. [from *co-* + *efficient*
(because the numbers work together)]

coerce (*say* koh-**erss**) *verb* (**coerces,
coercing, coerced**)
compel someone by using threats or force.
coercion *noun* [from Latin]

coexist *verb* (**coexists, coexisting, coexisted**)
exist together or at the same time.
coexistence *noun*, **coexistent** *adjective*
[from *co-* + *exist*]

coffee *noun* (*plural* **coffees**)
1 a hot drink made from the roasted
ground seeds (*coffee beans*) of a tropical
plant. 2 these seeds. [from Arabic *kahwa*]

coffer *noun* (*plural* **coffers**)
a large strong box for holding money and
valuables.
[from Latin *cophinus* = basket, hamper]

coffin *noun* (*plural* **coffins**)
a long box in which a body is buried or
cremated. [same origin as *coffer*]

cog *noun* (*plural* **cogs**)
one of a number of tooth-like parts round
the edge of a wheel, fitting into and
pushing those on another wheel.
[origin unknown]

cogent (*say* koh-jent) *adjective*
convincing, *a cogent argument*.
[Latin, = compelling]

cogitate *verb* (**cogitates, cogitating,
cogitated**)
think deeply about something. **cogitation**
noun [from Latin]

cognac (*say* kon-yak) *noun* (*plural* **cognacs**)
brandy, especially from Cognac in France.

cogwheel *noun* (*plural* **cogwheels**)
a wheel with cogs.

cohere *verb* (**coheres, cohering, cohered**)
stick to each other in a mass. **cohesion**
noun, **cohesive** *adjective*
[from *co-* + Latin *haerere* = to stick]

coherent (*say* koh-**heer**-ent) *adjective*
clear, reasonable, and making sense.
coherently *adverb*

coil *noun* (*plural* **coils**)
something wound into a spiral.

coil *verb* (coils, coiling, coiled)
wind something into a coil.
[same origin as *collect*]

coin *noun* (*plural* coins)
a piece of metal, usually round, used as
money.
coin *verb* (coins, coining, coined)
1 manufacture coins. **2** (*informal*) make a
lot of money as profit. **3** invent a word or
phrase. [French, = die for stamping coins]

coinage *noun* (*plural* coinages)
1 coining. **2** coins; a system of money. **3** a
new word or phrase.

coincide *verb* (coincides, coinciding,
coincided)
1 happen at the same time as something
else. **2** be in the same place. **3** be the same,
My opinion coincided with hers. [from *co-*
+ Latin *incidere* = fall upon or into]

coincidence *noun* (*plural* coincidences)
the happening of similar events at the
same time by chance.

coke *noun*
the solid fuel left when gas and tar have
been extracted from coal.
[origin unknown]

col- *prefix*
with; together. see **com-**.

colander *noun* (*plural* colanders)
a bowl-shaped container with holes in it,
used for straining water from vegetables
etc. after cooking.
[from Latin *colare* = strain]

cold *adjective*
1 having or at a low temperature; not
warm. **2** not friendly or loving; not
enthusiastic. **coldly** *adverb*, **coldness** *noun*
cold shoulder deliberate unfriendliness.
cold-shoulder *verb*
get cold feet feel afraid or reluctant to do
something.
cold *noun* (*plural* colds)
1 lack of warmth; low temperature; cold
weather. **2** an infectious illness that makes
your nose run, your throat sore, etc.
[from Old English]

cold-blooded *adjective*
1 having a body temperature that changes
according to the surroundings. **2** callous;
deliberately cruel.

cold war *noun*
a situation where nations are enemies
without actually fighting.

colic *noun*
stomach-ache.
[from Latin *colicus* = to do with the colon]

collaborate *verb* (collaborates,
collaborating, collaborated)
work together on a job.
collaboration *noun*, **collaborator** *noun*
[from *col-* + Latin *laborare* = to work]

collage (*say* kol-ah*z*h) *noun* (*plural*
collages)
a picture made by fixing small objects to a
surface. [French, = gluing]

collapse *verb* (collapses, collapsing,
collapsed)
1 fall down or inwards suddenly; break.
2 become very weak or ill. **3** fold up.
collapse *noun* (*plural* collapses)
1 collapsing. **2** a breakdown.
[from *col-* + Latin *lapsum* – slipped]

collapsible *adjective*
able to be folded up, *a collapsible umbrella*.

collar *noun* (*plural* collars)
1 an upright or turned-over band round
the neck of a garment etc. **2** a band that
goes round the neck of a dog, cat, horse, etc.
collar *verb* (collars, collaring, collared)
(*informal*)
seize or catch someone.
[from Latin *collum* = neck]

collate *verb* (collates, collating, collated)
bring together and compare lists, books,
etc. **collation** *noun* [from Latin]

collateral *adjective*
additional but less important.
collateral *noun*
money or property that is used as a
guarantee that a loan will be repaid.
[from *col-* + *lateral*]

colleague *noun* (*plural* colleagues)
a person you work with. [from Latin]

collect¹ (*say* kol-ekt) *verb* (collects, collecting, collected)
1 bring people or things together from various places. **2** obtain examples of things as a hobby, *She collects stamps.* **3** come together. **4** ask for money or contributions etc. from people. **5** fetch, *Collect your coat from the cleaners.* **collector** *noun* [from *col-* + Latin *legere* = assemble, choose]

collect² (*say* kol-ekt) *noun* (*plural* collects)
a short prayer.
[from Latin *collecta* = a meeting]

collection *noun* (*plural* collections)
1 collecting. **2** things collected. **3** money collected for a charity etc.

collective *adjective*
of a group taken as a whole, *our collective opinion.*

collective noun *noun* (*plural* collective nouns)
a noun that is singular in form but refers to many individuals taken as a unit, e.g. *army*, *herd*.

college *noun* (*plural* colleges)
a place where people can continue learning something after they have left school.
[from Latin]

collide *verb* (collides, colliding, collided)
crash into something. **collision** *noun*
[from Latin *collidere* = clash together]

collie *noun* (*plural* collies)
a dog with a long pointed face.
[origin unknown]

colliery *noun* (*plural* collieries)
a coal mine and its buildings. [from *coal*]

colloquial (*say* col-oh-kwee-al) *adjective*
suitable for conversation but not for formal speech or writing. **colloquially** *adverb*, **colloquialism** *noun*
[from *col-* + Latin *loqui* = speak]

collusion *noun*
a secret agreement between two or more people who are trying to deceive or cheat someone.
[from *col-* + Latin *ludere* = to play]

cologne (*say* kol-ohn) *noun*
eau de Cologne or a similar liquid.

colon¹ *noun* (*plural* colons)
a punctuation mark (:), often used to introduce lists. [from Greek *kōlon* = clause]

colon² *noun* (*plural* colons)
the largest part of the intestine.
[from Greek *kolon*]

colonel (*say* ker-nel) *noun* (*plural* colonels)
an army officer in charge of a regiment.
[via French from Italian]

colonial *adjective*
to do with a colony.

colonialism *noun*
the policy of acquiring and keeping colonies.

colonize *verb* (colonizes, colonizing, colonized)
establish a colony in a country. **colonist** *noun*, **colonization** *noun*

colonnade *noun* (*plural* colonnades)
a row of columns. [French]

colony *noun* (*plural* colonies)
1 an area of land that the people of another country settle in and control. **2** the people of a colony. **3** a group of people or animals of the same kind living close together.
[from Latin *colonia* = farm, settlement]

coloration *noun*
colouring.

colossal *adjective*
immense; enormous.

colossus *noun* (*plural* colossi)
1 a huge statue. **2** a person of immense importance.
[from the bronze statue of Apollo at Rhodes, called the *Colossus of Rhodes*]

colour *noun* (*plural* colours)
1 the effect produced by waves of light of a particular wavelength. **2** the use of various colours, not only black and white. **3** the colour of someone's skin. **4** a substance used to colour things. **5** the special flag of a ship or regiment.
colours *plural noun* an award given to the best members of a sports team.

colour *verb* (**colours, colouring, coloured**)
1 put colour on; paint or stain. 2 blush.
3 influence what someone says or believes.
colouring *noun* [from Latin]

colour-blind *adjective*
unable to see the difference between
certain colours.

coloured *adjective*
1 having colour. 2 having a dark skin;
Black.

colourful *adjective*
1 full of colour. 2 lively; with vivid details.

colourless *adjective*
without colour.

colt *noun* (*plural* **colts**)
a young male horse. [origin unknown]

column *noun* (*plural* **columns**)
1 a pillar. 2 something long or tall and
narrow, *a column of smoke*. 3 a vertical
section of a page, *There are two columns on
this page*. 4 a regular article in a
newspaper. **columnist** *noun* [from Latin]

com- *prefix* (becoming **col-** before *l*, **cor-**
before *r*, **con-** before many other
consonants)
with; together (as in *combine, connect*).
[from Latin *cum* = with]

coma (*say* koh-ma) *noun* (*plural* **comas**)
a state of deep unconsciousness, especially
in someone who is ill or injured.
[from Greek *koma* = deep sleep]

comb *noun* (*plural* **combs**)
1 a strip of wood or plastic etc. with teeth,
used to tidy hair or hold it in place.
2 something used like this, e.g. to separate
strands of wool. 3 the red crest on a fowl's
head. 4 a honeycomb.
comb *verb* (**combs, combing, combed**)
1 tidy hair with a comb. 2 search
thoroughly. [from Old English]

combat *noun & verb* (**combats, combating,
combated**)
fight. **combatant** (*say* kom-ba-tant) *noun*
[from *com-* + Latin *batuere* – fight]

combination *noun* (*plural* **combinations**)
1 combining. 2 a number of people or
things that are combined. 3 a series of

numbers or letters used to open a
combination lock.

combination lock *noun* (*plural*
combination locks)
a lock that can be opened only by setting a
dial or dials to positions shown by
numbers or letters.

combine (*say* komb-I'n) *verb* (**combines,
combining, combined**)
join or mix together.
combine (*say* komb-I'n) *noun* (*plural*
combines)
a group of people or firms combining in
business. [from *com-* + Latin *bini* = pair]

combine harvester *noun* (*plural*
combine harvesters)
a machine that both reaps and threshes
grain.

combustible *adjective*
able to be set on fire and burn.

combustion *noun*
the process of burning, a chemical process
(accompanied by heat) in which substances
combine with oxygen in air.
[from Latin *comburere* = burn up]

come *verb* (**comes, coming, came, come**)
This word is used to show 1 movement
towards somewhere (*Come here!*), 2 arrival,
reaching a place or condition or result
(*They came to a city. We came to a decision*),
3 happening (*How did you come to lose it?*),
4 occurring (*It comes on the next page*),
5 resulting (*That's what comes of being
careless*).
come by obtain.
come in for receive a share of.
come to 1 amount to. 2 become conscious
again.
come to pass happen.
[from Old English]

comedian *noun* (*plural* **comedians**)
someone who entertains people by making
them laugh. [from French]

comedy *noun* (*plural* **comedies**)
1 a play or film etc. that makes people
laugh. 2 humour. [from Greek *komos*
= having fun + *oide* = song]

comely *adjective*
good-looking.
[from an old word *becomely* = suitable]

comet *noun* (*plural* **comets**)
an object moving across the sky with a
bright tail of light.
[from Greek *kometes* = long-haired (star)]

comfort *noun* (*plural* **comforts**)
1 a comfortable feeling or condition.
2 soothing somebody who is unhappy or in
pain. **3** a person or thing that gives
comfort.
comfort *verb* (**comforts, comforting,**
comforted)
make a person less unhappy; soothe.
[from Latin *confortare* = strengthen]

comfortable *adjective*
1 at ease; relaxed. **2** making someone feel
at ease or relaxed, *comfortable shoes*.
comfortably *adverb*

comfy *adjective* (*informal*)
comfortable.

comic *adjective*
making people laugh. **comical** *adjective*,
comically *adverb*
comic strip a series of drawings telling a
comic story or a serial.
comic *noun* (*plural* **comics**)
1 a paper full of comic strips. **2** a comedian.
[from Greek; related to *comedy*]

comma *noun* (*plural* **commas**)
a punctuation mark (,) used to mark a
pause in a sentence or to separate items in
a list. [from Greek *komma* = short clause]

command *noun* (*plural* **commands**)
1 a statement telling somebody to do
something; an order. **2** authority; control.
3 ability to use something; mastery, *She*
has a good command of Spanish.
command *verb* (**commands, commanding,**
commanded)
1 give a command to somebody; order.
2 have authority over. **3** deserve and get,
They command our respect. **commander**
noun [from *com-* + Latin *mandare* = entrust
or impose a duty]

commandant (*say* **kom-an-dant**) *noun*
(*plural* **commandants**)
a military officer in charge of a fortress etc.

commandeer *verb* (**commandeers,**
commandeering, commandeered)
take or seize something for military
purposes or for your own use.

commandment *noun* (*plural*
commandments)
a sacred command, especially one of the
Ten Commandments given to Moses.

commando *noun* (*plural* **commandos**)
a soldier trained for making dangerous
raids. [from Portuguese]

commemorate *verb* (**commemorates,**
commemorating, commemorated)
be a celebration or reminder of some past
event or person etc. **commemoration** *noun*,
commemorative *adjective*
[from *com-* + Latin *memor* = memory]

commence *verb* (**commences,**
commencing, commenced)
begin. **commencement** *noun*
[from *com-* + Latin *initiare* = initiate]

commend *verb* (**commends, commending,**
commended)
1 praise, *He was commended for bravery.*
2 entrust, *We commend him to your care.*
commendation *noun*
[same origin as *command*]

commendable *adjective*
deserving praise.

comment *noun* (*plural* **comments**)
an opinion given about an event etc. or to
explain something.
comment *verb* (**comments, commenting,**
commented)
make a comment. [from Latin]

commentary *verb* (*plural* **commentaries**)
a set of comments, especially describing a
sports event while it is happening.
commentate *verb*, **commentator** *noun*

commerce *noun*
trade and the services that assist it, e.g.
banking and insurance. [from *com-* + Latin
merx = goods for sale, merchandise]

commercial *adjective*
1 to do with commerce. **2** paid for by firms
etc. whose advertisements are included,
commercial radio. **3** profitable.
commercially *adverb*

commercial *noun* (*plural* commercials)
a broadcast advertisement.

commercialized *adjective*
altered in order to become profitable, *a commercialized resort.*
commercialization *noun*

commiserate *verb* (commiserates, commiserating, commiserated)
sympathize. **commiseration** *noun*
[from *com-* + Latin *miserari* = to pity]

commission *noun* (*plural* commissions)
1 authorization to do something; the task etc. authorized, *a commission to paint a portrait.* **2** an appointment to be an officer in the armed forces. **3** a group of people given authority to do or investigate something. **4** payment to someone for selling your goods etc.
commission *verb* (commissions, commissioning, commissioned)
give a commission to a person or for a task etc. [same origin as *commit*]

commissionaire *noun* (*plural* commissionaires)
an attendant in uniform at the entrance to a theatre, large shop, offices, etc. [French]

commissioner *noun* (*plural* commissioners)
1 an official appointed by commission. **2** a member of a commission (see *commission* 3).

commit *verb* (commits, committing, committed)
1 do or perform, *commit a crime.* **2** place in someone's care or custody, *He was committed to prison.* **3** promise that you will make your time etc. available for a particular purpose, *Don't commit all your spare time to helping him.*
[from *com-* + Latin *mittere* = put, send]

committal *noun* (*plural* committals)
1 committing a person to prison etc.
2 giving a body ceremonially for burial or cremation.

committee *noun* (*plural* committees)
a group of people appointed to deal with something.

commode *noun* (*plural* commodes)
a box or chair into which a chamber pot is fitted. [French, = convenient]

commodious *adjective*
roomy. [same origin as *commodity*]

commodity *noun* (*plural* commodities)
a useful thing; a product.
[from Latin *commodus* = convenient]

commodore *noun* (*plural* commodores)
1 a naval officer ranking next below a rear admiral. **2** the commander of part of a fleet. [probably from Dutch]

common *adjective*
1 ordinary; usual; occurring frequently, *a common weed.* **2** of all or most people, *They worked for the common good.* **3** shared, *Music is their common interest.* **4** vulgar.
commonly *adverb*, **commonness** *noun*
in common shared by two or more people or things.
common *noun* (*plural* commons)
a piece of land that everyone can use.
[same origin as *commune*[1]]

commoner *noun* (*plural* commoners)
a member of the ordinary people, not of the nobility.

Common Market *noun*
a group of European countries that trade freely together.

commonplace *adjective*
ordinary; usual.

common sense *noun*
normal good sense in thinking or behaviour.

Commonwealth *noun*
1 an association of countries, *The Commonwealth consists of Britain and various other countries, including Canada, Australia, and New Zealand.* **2** a federal association of States, *the Commonwealth of Australia.* **3** the republic set up in Britain by Cromwell, lasting from 1649 to 1660.
[from *common* + an old sense of *wealth* = welfare]

commotion *noun*
an uproar; a fuss. [from *com-* + Latin *motio* = movement, motion]

communal (*say* kom-yoo-nal) *adjective*
shared by several people. **communally**
adverb [same origin as *commune*[1]]

commune[1] (*say* kom-yoon) *noun* (*plural*
communes)
1 a group of people sharing a home, food,
etc. 2 a district of local government in
France and some other countries.
[from Latin *communis* = common]

commune[2] (*say* ko-mewn) *verb*
(**communes, communing, communed**)
talk together.
[from old French *comuner* = share]

communicant *noun* (*plural*
communicants)
1 a person who communicates with
someone. 2 a person who receives Holy
Communion.

communicate *verb* (**communicates,
communicating, communicated**)
1 pass news, information, etc. to other
people. 2 (of rooms etc.) open into each
other; connect.
[from Latin *communicare* = tell, share]

communication *noun* (*plural*
communications)
1 communicating. 2 something
communicated; a message.
communications *plural noun* links between
places (e.g. roads, railways, telephones,
radio).

communicative *adjective*
willing to talk.

communion *noun*
religious fellowship.
Communion or **Holy Communion** the
Christian ceremony in which consecrated
bread and wine are given to worshippers.
[same origin as *commune*[1]]

communiqué (*say* ko-mew-nik-ay) *noun*
(*plural* **communiqués**)
an official message giving a report.
[French, = communicated]

Communism *noun*
a political system where the State controls
property, production, trade, etc. (Compare
capitalism.) **Communist** *noun*

communism *noun*
a system where property is shared by the
community.
[French, from *commun* = common]

community *noun* (*plural* **communities**)
1 the people living in one area. 2 a group
with similar interests or origins.
[same origin as *commune*[1]]

community charge *noun*
a form of local tax.

commute *verb* (**commutes, commuting,
commuted**)
1 travel a fairly long way by train, bus, or
car to and from your daily work. 2 alter a
punishment to something less severe.
[from *com-* + Latin *mutare* = change]

commuter *noun* (*plural* **commuters**)
a person who commutes to and from work.

compact[1] *noun* (*plural* **compacts**)
an agreement or contract.
[from *com-* + *pact*]

compact[2] *adjective*
1 closely or neatly packed together.
2 concise. **compactly** *adverb*, **compactness**
noun

compact *noun* (*plural* **compacts**)
a small flat container for face powder.

compact *verb* (**compacts, compacting,
compacted**)
join or press firmly together or into a small
space.
[from Latin *compactum* = put together]

compact disc *noun* (*plural* **compact discs**)
a small disc from which recorded sound
etc. is reproduced by means of a laser
beam.

companion *noun* (*plural* **companions**)
1 a person who accompanies another.
2 one of a matching pair of things. 3 (in
book-titles) a guidebook or reference book,
The Oxford Companion to Music.
companionship *noun*
[literally = someone you eat bread with:
from *com-* + Latin *panis* = bread]

companionable *adjective*
sociable.

company *noun* (*plural* **companies**)
1 a number of people together. 2 a business firm. 3 having people with you; companionship. 4 visitors, *We've got company.* 5 a section of a battalion.
[same origin as *companion*]

comparable (*say* **kom**-per-a-bul) *adjective*
similar. **comparably** *adverb*
[same origin as *compare*]

comparative *adjective*
comparing a thing with something else, *They live in comparative comfort.*
comparatively *adverb*
comparative *noun* (*plural* **comparatives**)
the form of an adjective or adverb that expresses 'more', *The comparative of 'big' is 'bigger'.*

compare *verb* (**compares, comparing, compared**)
1 put things together so as to tell in what ways they are similar or different. 2 form the comparative and superlative of an adjective or adverb.
compare notes share information.
compare with 1 be similar to. 2 be as good as, *Our football pitch cannot compare with Wembley Stadium.*
[from *com-* + Latin *par* = equal]

USAGE: When *compare* is used with an object, it can be followed by either *to* or *with*. Traditionally, *to* is used when you are showing the similarity between two things: *She compared me to a pig.* With is used when you are looking at the similarities and differences between things: *Just compare this year's profits with last year's.*

comparison *noun* (*plural* **comparisons**)
comparing.

compartment *noun* (*plural* **compartments**)
one of the spaces into which something is divided; a separate room or enclosed space.
[from Latin *compartiri* = share with someone]

compass *noun* (*plural* **compasses**)
a device with a pointer that points north.
compasses or **pair of compasses** a device for drawing circles, usually with two rods hinged together at one end.
[from old French]

compassion *noun*
pity or mercy. **compassionate** *adjective*, **compassionately** *adverb*
[from *com-* + Latin *passum* = suffered]

compatible *adjective*
able to exist or be used together; not incompatible. **compatibly** *adverb*, **compatibility** *noun*
[from Latin *compati* = suffer together]

compel *verb* (**compels, compelling, compelled**)
force somebody to do something.
[from *com-* + Latin *pellere* = drive]

compendious *adjective*
giving much information concisely.
[same origin as *compendium*]

compendium *noun* (*plural* **compendiums** or **compendia**)
1 an encyclopedia or handbook in one volume. 2 a set of different board games in one box.
[Latin, = a saving, abbreviation]

compensate *verb* (**compensates, compensating, compensated**)
1 give a person money etc. to make up for a loss or injury. 2 have a balancing effect, *This victory compensates for our earlier defeats.* **compensation** *noun*, **compensatory** *adjective* [from Latin *compensare* = weigh one thing against another]

compère (*say* **kom**-pair) *noun* (*plural* **compères**)
a person who introduces the performers in a show or broadcast. **compère** *verb*
[French, = godfather]

compete *verb* (**competes, competing, competed**)
take part in a competition.
[from *com-* + Latin *petere* = aim at]

competent *adjective*
able to do a particular thing. **competently** *adverb*, **competence** *noun*
[from Latin, = suitable, sufficient]

competition *noun* (*plural* **competitions**)
1 a game or race or other contest in which people try to win. 2 competing. 3 the people competing with yourself.
competitive *adjective*

competitor *noun* (*plural* competitors)
someone who competes; a rival.

compile *verb* (compiles, compiling, compiled)
put things together into a list or collection, e.g. to form a book. **compiler** *noun*, **compilation** *noun* [from French]

complacent *adjective*
self-satisfied. **complacently** *adverb*, **complacency** *noun* [from Latin]

complain *verb* (complains, complaining, complained)
say that you are annoyed or unhappy about something. [from Latin]

complaint *noun* (*plural* complaints)
1 a statement complaining about something. 2 an illness.

complement *noun* (*plural* complements)
1 the quantity needed to fill or complete something, *The ship had its full complement of sailors.* 2 the word or words used after verbs such as *be* and *become* to complete the sense. In *She was brave* and *He became king of England*, the complements are *brave* and *king of England*.

complement *verb* (complements, complementing, complemented)
go well together with something else; make a thing complete, *The hat complements the outfit.* [same origin as *complete*]

USAGE: Do not confuse with *compliment*.

complementary *adjective*
completing; forming a complement.

USAGE: Do not confuse with *complimentary*.

complementary angle *noun* (*plural* complementary angles)
either of two angles that add up to 90°.

complementary medicine *noun*
alternative medicine.

complete *adjective*
1 having all its parts. 2 finished.

3 thorough; in every way, *a complete stranger*. **completely** *adverb*, **completeness** *noun*

complete *verb* (completes, completing, completed)
make a thing complete; add what is needed. **completion** *noun*
[from Latin *completum* = filled up]

complex *adjective*
1 made up of parts. 2 complicated. **complexity** *noun*

complex *noun* (*plural* complexes)
1 a set of buildings made up of related parts, *a sports complex*. 2 a group of feelings or ideas that influence a person's behaviour etc., *a persecution complex*. [from Latin *complexum* = embraced, plaited]

complexion *noun* (*plural* complexions)
1 the natural colour and appearance of the skin of the face. 2 the way things seem, *That puts a different complexion on the matter*. [from old French]

compliant *adjective*
willing to obey. **compliance** *noun*

complicate *verb* (complicates, complicating, complicated)
make a thing complex or complicated. [from *com-* + Latin *plicare* = to fold]

complicated *adjective*
1 made up of many parts. 2 difficult to understand or do.

complication *noun* (*plural* complications)
1 something that complicates things or adds difficulties. 2 a complicated condition.

complicity *noun*
being involved in a crime etc. [same origin as *complicate*]

compliment *noun* (*plural* compliments)
something said or done to show that your approve of a person or thing, *pay compliments*.
compliments *plural noun* formal greetings given in a message.

compliment *verb* (compliments, complimenting, complimented)
pay someone a compliment; congratulate.
[via French from Italian]

USAGE: Do not confuse with *complement*.

complimentary *adjective*
1 expressing a compliment. 2 given free of charge, *complimentary tickets*.

USAGE: Do not confuse with *complementary*.

comply *verb* (complies, complying, complied)
obey laws or rules.
[from Italian; related to *complete*]

component *noun* (*plural* components)
each of the parts of which a thing is made up. [same origin as *compound*[1]]

compose *verb* (composes, composing, composed)
1 form or make up, *The class is composed of 20 students.* 2 write music or poetry etc.
3 arrange in good order. 4 make calm, *compose yourself.*
[from French; related to *compound*[1]]

composed *adjective*
calm, *a composed manner.*
composedly *adverb*

composer *noun* (*plural* composers)
a person who composes music etc.

composite (*say* kom-poz-it) *adjective*
made up of a number of parts or different styles. [same origin as *compose*]

composition *noun* (*plural* compositions)
1 composing. 2 something composed, especially a piece of music. 3 an essay or story written as a school exercise. 4 the parts that make something, *the composition of the soil.*

compos mentis *adjective*
in your right mind; sane. (The opposite is **non compos mentis**.)
[Latin, = having control of the mind]

compost *noun*
1 decayed leaves and grass etc. used as a fertilizer. 2 a soil-like mixture for growing seedlings, cuttings, etc.
[same origin as *compose*]

composure *noun*
calmness of manner.

compound[1] *adjective*
made of two or more parts or ingredients.
compound *noun* (*plural* compounds)
a compound substance.
compound *verb* (compounds, compounding, compounded)
put together; combine.
[from Latin *componere* = put together]

compound[2] *noun* (*plural* compounds)
a fenced area containing buildings.
[via Portuguese or Dutch from Malay (a language spoken in Malaysia)]

comprehend *verb* (comprehends, comprehending, comprehended)
1 understand. 2 include.
[from *com-* + Latin *prehendere* = take, seize]

comprehensible *adjective*
understandable.

comprehensive *adjective*
including all or many kinds of people or things.
comprehensive *noun* (*plural* comprehensives)
a comprehensive school.

comprehensive school *noun* (*plural* comprehensive schools)
a large secondary school for all or most of the children of an area.

compress (*say* kom-**press**) *verb* (compresses, compressing, compressed)
press together or into a smaller space.
compression *noun*, **compressor** *noun*
compress (*say* kom-press) *noun* (*plural* compresses)
a soft pad or cloth pressed on the body to stop bleeding or cool inflammation etc.
[from *com-* + Latin *pressare* = to press]

comprise *verb* (comprises, comprising, comprised)
include; consist of, *The pentathlon*

comprises five events.
[from French; related to *comprehend*]

USAGE: Do not use *comprise* with *of*. It is incorrect to say 'The group was comprised of 20 men'; correct usage is 'was composed of'.

compromise (*say* kom-prom-I'z) *noun* (*plural* compromises)
settling a dispute by each side accepting less than it asked for.
compromise *verb* (compromises, compromising, compromised)
1 settle by a compromise. **2** expose someone to danger or suspicion etc., *His confession compromises his sister.*
[from *com-* + Latin *promittere* = to promise]

compulsion *noun* (*plural* compulsions)
a strong and uncontrollable desire to do something.

compulsive *adjective*
having or resulting from a strong and uncontrollable desire, *a compulsive gambler.* [same origin as *compel*]

USAGE: See *compulsory*.

compulsory *adjective*
that must be done; not optional.
[same origin as *compel*]

USAGE: Do not confuse *compulsory* with *compulsive*. An action is *compulsory* if a law or rules say that you must do it, but *compulsive* if you want to do it and cannot resist it.

compunction *noun*
a guilty feeling, *She felt no compunction about hitting the burglar.* [from *com-* + Latin *punctum* = pricked (by conscience)]

compute *verb* (computes, computing, computed)
calculate. **computation** *noun*
[from *com-* + Latin *putare* = reckon]

computer *noun* (*plural* computers)
an electronic machine for making calculations, storing and analysing information put into it, or controlling machinery automatically.

computerize *verb* (computerizes, computerizing, computerized)
equip with computers; perform or produce by computer. **computerization** *noun*

computing *noun*
the use of computers.

comrade *noun* (*plural* comrades)
a companion who shares in your activities.
comradeship *noun*
[from Spanish *camarada* = room-mate]

con[1] *verb* (cons, conning, conned) (*slang*)
swindle. [short for *confidence trick*]

con[2] *noun* (*plural* cons)
a reason against something, *There are pros and cons.* [from Latin *contra* = against]

con- *prefix*
with; together. see **com-**.

concave *adjective*
curved like the inside of a ball or circle. (The opposite is *convex.*) **concavity** *noun*
[from *con-* + Latin *cavus* = hollow]

conceal *verb* (conceals, concealing, concealed)
hide; keep something secret.
concealment *noun*
[from *con-* + Latin *celare* = hide]

concede *verb* (concedes, conceding, conceded)
1 admit that something is true. **2** grant or allow something, *They conceded us the right to cross their land.* **3** admit that you have been defeated.
[from *con-* + Latin *cedere* = cede]

conceit *noun*
being too proud of yourself; vanity.
conceited *adjective*
[originally = idea, opinion; from *conceive*]

conceivable *adjective*
able to be imagined or believed.
conceivably *adverb*

conceive *verb* (conceives, conceiving, conceived)
1 become pregnant; form a baby in the womb. **2** form an idea or plan; imagine, *I can't conceive why you want to come.*
[from Latin *concipere* = take in, contain]

concentrate *verb* (concentrates, concentrating, concentrated)
1 give your full attention or effort to something. **2** bring or come together in one place. **3** make a liquid etc. less dilute. [from French; related to *centre*]

concentration *noun* (*plural* concentrations)
1 concentrating. **2** the amount dissolved in each part of a liquid.

concentration camp *noun* (*plural* concentration camps)
a place where political prisoners etc. are brought together and confined.

concentric *adjective*
having the same centre, *concentric circles*. [from Latin; related to *centre*]

concept *noun* (*plural* concepts)
an idea. [same origin as *conceive*]

conception *noun* (*plural* conceptions)
1 conceiving. **2** an idea.

concern *verb* (concerns, concerning, concerned)
1 be important to or affect somebody. **2** worry somebody. **3** be about; have as its subject, *The story concerns a group of rabbits.*
concern *noun* (*plural* concerns)
1 something that concerns you; a responsibility. **2** worry. **3** a business. [from Latin]

concerned *adjective*
1 worried. **2** involved in or affected by something.

concerning *preposition*
on the subject of; about, *laws concerning seat belts.*

concert *noun* (*plural* concerts)
a musical entertainment. [same origin as *concerto*]

concerted *adjective*
done in cooperation with others, *We made a concerted effort.*

concertina *noun* (*plural* concertinas)
a portable musical instrument with bellows, played by squeezing. [from *concert*]

concerto (*say* kon-chert-oh) *noun* (*plural* concertos)
a piece of music for a solo instrument and an orchestra. [from Italian *concertare* = harmonize]

concession *noun* (*plural* concessions)
1 conceding. **2** something conceded. **3** a reduction in price for a certain category of person. **concessionary** *adjective* [same origin as *concede*]

conciliate *verb* (conciliates, conciliating, conciliated)
1 win over an angry or hostile person by friendliness. **2** help people who disagree to come to an agreement. **conciliation** *noun* [from Latin; related to *council*]

concise *adjective*
brief; giving much information in a few words. **concisely** *adverb*, **conciseness** *noun* [from *con-* + Latin *caedere* = cut]

conclave *noun* (*plural* conclaves)
a private meeting. [from *con-* + Latin *clavis* = key]

conclude *verb* (concludes, concluding, concluded)
1 bring or come to an end. **2** decide; form an opinion by reasoning, *The jury concluded that he was guilty.* [from *con-* + Latin *claudere* = shut]

conclusion *noun* (*plural* conclusions)
1 an ending. **2** an opinion formed by reasoning.

conclusive *adjective*
putting an end to all doubt. **conclusively** *adverb*

concoct *verb* (concocts, concocting, concocted)
1 make something by putting ingredients together. **2** invent, *concoct an excuse.* **concoction** *noun* [from *con-* + Latin *coctum* = cooked]

concord *noun*
friendly agreement or harmony. [from *con-* + Latin *cor* = heart]

concordance *noun* (*plural* concordances)
1 agreement. **2** an index of the words used in a book or an author's works.

concourse *noun* (*plural* **concourses**)
an open area through which people pass,
e.g. at an airport. [same origin as *concur*]

concrete *noun*
cement mixed with sand and gravel, used
in building.
concrete *adjective*
1 able to be touched and felt; not abstract.
2 definite, *We need concrete evidence, not
theories.* [from Latin *concretus* = stiff, hard]

concur *verb* (**concurs, concurring,
concurred**)
agree. **concurrence** *noun*
[from *con-* + Latin *currere* = run]

concurrent *adjective*
happening or existing at the same time.

concussion *noun*
a temporary injury to the brain caused by
a hard knock. **concussed** *adjective*
[from Latin *concussum* = shaken violently]

condemn *verb* (**condemns, condemning,
condemned**)
1 say that you strongly disapprove of
something. 2 convict or sentence a
criminal. 3 destine to something unhappy,
condemned to a lonely life. 4 declare that
houses etc. are not fit to be used.
condemnation *noun*
[from old French; related to *damn*]

condense *verb* (**condenses, condensing,
condensed**)
1 make a liquid denser or more compact.
2 put something into fewer words.
3 change from gas or vapour to liquid,
Steam condenses on windows. **condensation**
noun, **condenser** *noun* [from Latin
condensus = very thick or dense]

condescend *verb* (**condescends,
condescending, condescended**)
1 behave in a way which shows that you
feel superior. 2 allow yourself to do
something that seems unsuitable for a
person of your high rank. **condescension**
noun [from Latin *condescendere* = stoop,
lower yourself]

condiment *noun* (*plural* **condiments**)
a seasoning (e.g. salt or pepper) for food.
[from Latin]

condition *noun* (*plural* **conditions**)
1 the state or fitness of a person or thing,
This bicycle is in good condition. 2 the
situation or surroundings etc. that affect
something, *working conditions.*
3 something required as part of an
agreement.
on condition that only if; on the
understanding that something will be
done.
condition *verb* (**conditions, conditioning,
conditioned**)
1 put something into a proper condition.
2 train or accustom. [from Latin]

conditional *adjective*
containing a condition (see *condition* 3);
depending. **conditionally** *adverb*

conditioner *noun* (*plural* **conditioners**)
a substance you put on your hair to keep it
in good condition.

condole *verb* (**condoles, condoling,
condoled**)
express sympathy. **condolence** *noun*
[from *con-* + Latin *dolere* = grieve]

condom *noun* (*plural* **condoms**)
a rubber sheath worn on the penis as a
contraceptive. [origin unknown]

condone *verb* (**condones, condoning,
condoned**)
forgive or ignore wrongdoing, *Do not
condone violence.* **condonation** *noun*
[from Latin]

condor *noun* (*plural* **condors**)
a kind of large vulture.
[via Spanish from Quechua (a South
American language)]

conducive *adjective*
helping to cause or produce something,
*Noisy surroundings are not conducive to
work.* [same origin as *conduct*]

conduct (*say* kon-dukt) *verb* (**conducts,
conducting, conducted**)
1 lead or guide. 2 be the conductor of an
orchestra or choir. 3 manage or direct
something, *conduct an experiment.* 4 allow
heat, light, sound, or electricity to pass
along or through. 5 behave, *They conducted
themselves with dignity.*

conduct (*say* kon dukt) *noun*
behaviour.
[from con- + Latin *ducere* = to lead]

conduction *noun*
the conducting of heat or electricity etc.
(see *conduct* 4).

conductor *noun* (*plural* conductors)
1 a person who directs the performance of an orchestra or choir by movements of the arms. **2** a person who collects the fares on a bus etc. **3** something that conducts heat or electricity etc. **conductress** *noun*

conduit (*say* kon-dit) *noun* (*plural* conduits)
1 a pipe or channel for liquid. **2** a tube protecting electric wire.
[from French; related to *conduct*]

cone *noun* (*plural* cones)
1 an object that is circular at one end and narrows to a point at the other end. **2** the dry cone-shaped fruit of a pine, fir, or cedar tree. [from Greek]

confabulation *noun*
a chat. [from Latin]

confection *noun* (*plural* confections)
something made of various things, especially sweet ones, put together.
[from Latin]

confectioner *noun* (*plural* confectioners)
someone who makes or sells sweets.
confectionery *noun*

confederacy *noun* (*plural* confederacies)
a union of States; a confederation.

confederate *adjective*
allied; joined by an agreement or treaty.
confederate *noun* (*plural* confederates)
1 a member of a confederacy. **2** an ally; an accomplice.
[from con- + Latin *foederatum* = allied]

confederation *noun* (*plural* confederations)
1 the process of joining in an alliance. **2** a group of people, organizations, or States joined together by an agreement or treaty.

confer *verb* (confers, conferring, conferred)
1 grant or bestow. **2** hold a discussion before deciding something.
[from con- + Latin *ferre* = bring]

conference *noun* (*plural* conferences)
a meeting for holding a discussion.
[same origin as *confer*]

confess *verb* (confesses, confessing, confessed)
state openly that you have done something wrong or have a weakness; admit.
confession *noun* [from Latin]

confessional *noun* (*plural* confessionals)
a small room where a priest hears confessions.

confessor *noun* (*plural* confessors)
a priest who hears confessions.

confetti *noun*
tiny pieces of coloured paper thrown by wedding guests at the bride and bridegroom. [Italian, = sweets (which were traditionally thrown at Italian weddings)]

confidant *noun* (**confidante** is used of a woman) (*plural* confidants, confidantes)
a person in whom someone confides.
[a different spelling of *confident*]

confide *verb* (confides, confiding, confided)
1 tell confidentially, *confide a secret to someone* or *confide in someone*. **2** entrust.
[from con- + Latin *fidere* = to trust]

confidence *noun* (*plural* confidences)
1 firm trust. **2** a feeling of certainty or boldness; being sure that you can do something. **3** something told confidentially.
in confidence as a secret.
in a person's confidence trusted with his or her secrets.

confidence trick *noun* (*plural* confidence tricks)
swindling a person after persuading him or her to trust you.

confident *adjective*
showing or feeling confidence; bold.
confidently *adverb*
[from Latin; related to *confide*]

confidential *adjective*
something that is confidential is meant to be kept secret. **confidentially** *adverb*,
confidentiality *noun*

configuration *noun* (*plural* configurations)
1 a method of arrangement of parts etc. 2 a shape. [from Latin *configurare* = make according to a pattern]

confine *verb* (confines, confining, confined)
1 keep something within limits; restrict, *Please confine your remarks to the subject being discussed.* 2 keep somebody in a place. [from *con-* + Latin *finis* = limit, end]

confined *adjective*
narrow or restricted, *a confined space.*

confinement *noun* (*plural* confinements)
1 confining. 2 the time of giving birth to a baby.

confines (*say* kon-fynz) *plural noun*
the limits or boundaries of an area.

confirm *verb* (confirms, confirming, confirmed)
1 prove that something is true or correct. 2 make a thing definite, *Please write to confirm your booking.* 3 make a person a full member of the Christian Church. **confirmation** *noun*, **confirmatory** *adjective* [from *con-* + Latin *firmare* = strengthen]

confiscate *verb* (confiscates, confiscating, confiscated)
take something away as a punishment. **confiscation** *noun* [from Latin]

conflagration *noun* (*plural* conflagrations)
a great and destructive fire. [from *con-* + Latin *flagrare* = blaze]

conflict (*say* kon-flikt) *noun* (*plural* conflicts)
a fight, struggle, or disagreement.
conflict (*say* kon-flikt) *verb* (conflicts, conflicting, conflicted)
have a conflict; differ or disagree. [from *con-* = together + Latin *flictum* = struck]

confluence *noun* (*plural* confluences)
the place where two rivers meet. [from *con-* + Latin *fluens* = flowing]

conform *verb* (conforms, conforming, conformed)
keep to accepted rules or customs etc. **conformist** *noun*, **conformity** *noun* [from Latin *conformare* = shape evenly]

confound *verb* (confounds, confounding, confounded)
1 astonish or puzzle someone. 2 confuse. [from Latin]

confront *verb* (confronts, confronting, confronted)
1 come or bring face to face, especially in a hostile way. 2 be present and have to be dealt with, *Problems confront us.* **confrontation** *noun* [from Latin]

confuse *verb* (confuses, confusing, confused)
1 make a person puzzled or muddled. 2 mistake one thing for another. **confusion** *noun* [from old French; related to *confound*]

confute *verb* (confutes, confuting, confuted)
prove a person or statement to be wrong. **confutation** *noun* [from *con-* + Latin *refutare* = refute]

congeal (*say* kon-jeel) *verb* (congeals, congealing, congealed)
become jelly-like instead of liquid, especially in cooling, *congealed blood.* [from *con-* + Latin *gelare* = freeze]

congenial *adjective*
pleasant through being similar to yourself or suiting your tastes; agreeable, *a congenial companion.* **congenially** *adverb* [from *con-* + *genial*]

congenital (*say* kon-jen-it-al) *adjective*
existing in a person from birth. **congenitally** *adverb* [from *con-* + Latin *genitus* = born]

congested *adjective*
crowded or blocked up, *congested streets, congested lungs.* **congestion** *noun* [from Latin *congestum* = heaped up]

conglomeration *noun* (*plural* conglomerations)
a mass of different things put together. [from *con-* + Latin *glomus* = mass]

congratulate *verb* (congratulates, congratulating, congratulated)
tell a person that you are pleased about his or her success or good fortune. **congratulation** *noun*, **congratulatory** *adjective* [from *con-* + Latin *gratulari* = show joy]

congregate *verb* (congregates, congregating, congregated)
assemble; flock together.
[from con- + Latin *gregatum* = herded]

congregation *noun* (*plural* congregations)
a group who have gathered to take part in worship.

Congress *noun*
the parliament of the USA.

congress *noun* (*plural* congresses)
a conference.
[from con- + Latin *-gressus* = going]

congruent *adjective*
congruent triangles have exactly the same shape and size. **congruence** *noun*
[from Latin]

conic *adjective*
to do with a cone.

conical *adjective*
cone-shaped. **conically** *adverb*

conifer (*say* kon-if-er) *noun* (*plural* conifers)
an evergreen tree with cones. **coniferous** *adjective*
[from *cone* + Latin *ferens* = bearing]

conjecture *noun* (*plural* conjectures)
a guess. **conjecture** *verb*, **conjectural** *adjective* [from Latin]

conjugal (*say* kon-jug-al) *adjective*
to do with marriage.
[from con- + Latin *jugum* = yoke]

conjugate *verb* (conjugates, conjugating, conjugated)
give all the different forms of a verb. **conjugation** *noun*

conjunction *noun* (*plural* conjunctions)
1 a word that joins words or phrases or sentences, e.g. *and*, *but*. **2** combination, *The four armies acted in conjunction.*
[from Latin *conjunctum* = yoked together]

conjure *verb* (conjures, conjuring, conjured)
perform puzzling tricks. **conjuror** *noun*
conjure up produce in your mind, *Mention of the Arctic conjures up visions of snow.*
[from Latin]

conker *noun* (*plural* conkers)
the hard shiny brown nut of the horse chestnut tree.
conkers a game between players who each have a conker threaded on a string.
[from a dialect word = snail shell (because conkers was originally played with snail shells)]

connect *verb* (connects, connecting, connected)
1 join together; link. **2** think of as being associated with each other.
[from con- + Latin *nectere* = bind]

connection *noun* (*plural* connections)
1 a point where two things are connected; a link, *We all know there is a connection between smoking and cancer.* **2** a train, bus, etc. that leaves a station soon after another arrives, so that passengers can change from one to the other.

conning tower *noun* (*plural* conning towers)
a projecting part on top of a submarine, containing the periscope.
[from an old word *con* = guide a ship]

connive (*say* kon-I'v) *verb* (connives, conniving, connived)
connive at take no notice of wrongdoing that ought to be reported or punished. **connivance** *noun*
[from Latin *connivere* = shut the eyes]

connoisseur (*say* kon-a-ser) *noun* (*plural* connoisseurs)
a person with great experience and appreciation of something, *a connoisseur of wine.* [French, = one who knows]

conquer *verb* (conquers, conquering, conquered)
defeat or overcome. **conqueror** *noun*
[from old French]

conquest *noun* (*plural* conquests)
1 conquering. **2** conquered territory.

conscience (*say* kon-shens) *noun* (*plural* consciences)
knowing what is right and wrong, especially in your own actions.
[from Latin *conscientia* = knowledge]

conscientious (*say* kon-shee-**en**-shus) *adjective*
careful and honest, *conscientious workers.*
conscientiously *adverb*

conscientious objector *noun* (*plural* **conscientious objectors**)
a person who refuses to serve in the armed forces because he or she believes it is wrong.

conscious (*say* kon-shus) *adjective*
awake; aware of what is happening. **consciously** *adverb*, **consciousness** *noun*
[from Latin *conscius* = knowing]

conscript (*say* kon-skript) *verb* (**conscripts, conscripting, conscripted**)
make a person join the armed forces. **conscription** *noun*

conscript (*say* kon-skript) *noun* (*plural* **conscripts**)
a conscripted person. [from *con-* + Latin *scriptus* = written in a list, enlisted]

consecrate *verb* (**consecrates, consecrating, consecrated**)
officially say that a thing, especially a building, is holy. **consecration** *noun*
[from Latin]

consecutive *adjective*
following one after another. **consecutively** *adverb*
[from Latin *consequi* = follow closely]

consensus *noun* (*plural* **consensuses**)
general agreement; the opinion of most people. [same origin as *consent*]

consent *noun*
agreement to what someone wishes; permission.

consent *verb* (**consents, consenting, consented**)
say that you are willing to do or allow what someone wishes.
[from *con-* + Latin *sentire* = feel]

consequence *noun* (*plural* **consequences**)
1 something that happens as the result of an event or action. 2 importance, *It is of no consequence.*

consequent *adjective*
happening as a result. **consequently** *adverb*
[same origin as *consecutive*]

consequential *adjective*
happening as a result.

conservation *noun*
conserving; preservation, especially of the natural environment. **conservationist** *noun*

Conservative *noun* (*plural* **Conservatives**)
a person who supports the Conservative Party, a political party that favours private enterprise and freedom from State control. **Conservative** *adjective*

conservative *adjective*
1 liking traditional ways and disliking changes. 2 (of an estimate) moderate; low. **conservatively** *adverb*, **conservatism** *noun*

conservatory *noun* (*plural* **conservatories**)
a greenhouse attached to a house.
[from *conserve*]

conserve *verb* (**conserves, conserving, conserved**)
prevent something valuable from being changed, spoilt, or wasted.
[from *con-* + Latin *servare* = keep safe]

consider *verb* (**considers, considering, considered**)
1 think carefully about or give attention to something, especially in order to make a decision. 2 have an opinion; think to be, *Consider yourself lucky.* [from Latin]

considerable *adjective*
fairly great, *a considerable amount.* **considerably** *adverb*

considerate *adjective*
taking care not to inconvenience or hurt others. **considerately** *adverb*

consideration *noun* (*plural* **considerations**)
1 being considerate. 2 careful thought or attention. 3 a fact that must be kept in mind. 4 payment given as a reward. **take into consideration** allow for.

considering *preposition*
taking something into consideration, *The car runs well, considering its age.*

consign *verb* (**consigns, consigning, consigned**)
hand something over formally; entrust.
[from Latin]

consignment *noun* (*plural* consignments)
1 consigning. **2** a batch of goods etc. sent to someone.

consist *verb* (consists, consisting, consisted)
be made up or composed of, *The flat consists of three rooms.* [from Latin]

consistency *noun* (*plural* consistencies)
1 being consistent. **2** thickness or stiffness, especially of a liquid.

consistent *adjective*
1 keeping to a regular pattern or style; not changing. **2** not contradictory.
consistently *adverb*

consolation *noun* (*plural* consolations)
1 consoling. **2** something that consoles someone.

consolation prize *noun* (*plural* consolation prizes)
a prize given to a competitor who has just missed winning one of the main prizes.

console[1] (*say* kon-**sohl**) *verb* (consoles, consoling, consoled)
comfort someone who is unhappy or disappointed.
[from *con-* + Latin *solari* = soothe]

console[2] (*say* kon-**sohl**) *noun* (*plural* consoles)
1 a panel holding the controls of equipment. **2** a frame containing the keyboard and stops etc. of an organ. **3** a cabinet for a radio or television set.
[French]

consolidate *verb* (consolidates, consolidating, consolidated)
1 make or become secure and strong. **2** combine two or more organizations, funds, etc. into one. **consolidation** *noun*
[from *con-* + Latin *solidare* = make solid]

consonant *noun* (*plural* consonants)
a letter that is not a vowel, *B, c, d, f, etc. are consonants.*
[from *con-* + Latin *sonans* = sounding]

consort (*say* kon-sort) *noun* (*plural* consorts)
a husband or wife, especially of a monarch.

consort (*say* kon-sort) *verb* (consorts, consorting, consorted)
be in someone's company, *consort with criminals.* [from Latin *consors* = sharer]

consortium *noun* (*plural* consortia)
a combination of countries, companies, or other groups acting together.

conspicuous *adjective*
easily seen; noticeable. **conspicuously** *adverb*, **conspicuousness** *noun*
[from Latin *conspicere* = look at carefully]

conspiracy *noun* (*plural* conspiracies)
planning with others to do something illegal; a plot.

conspire *verb* (conspires, conspiring, conspired)
take part in a conspiracy. **conspirator** *noun*, **conspiratorial** *adjective*
[from *con-* + Latin *spirare* = breathe]

constable *noun* (*plural* constables)
a police officer of the lowest rank.
[from Latin, originally = officer in charge of the stable]

constabulary *noun* (*plural* constabularies)
a police force.

constant *adjective*
1 not changing; happening all the time. **2** faithful or loyal. **constantly** *adverb*, **constancy** *noun*
constant *noun* (*plural* constants)
1 a thing that does not vary. **2** in mathematics, a number or value that does not change.
[from *con-* + Latin *stans* = standing]

constellation *noun* (*plural* constellations)
a group of stars.
[from *con-* + Latin *stella* = star]

constipated *adjective*
unable to empty the bowels easily or regularly. **constipation** *noun*
[from Latin *constipare* = cram]

constituency *noun* (*plural* constituencies)
a district represented by a Member of Parliament elected by the people who live there.

constituent *noun* (*plural* constituents)
1 one of the parts that form a whole thing.
2 someone who lives in a particular
constituency. **constituent** *adjective*
[from Latin, = setting up, constituting]

constitute *verb* (constitutes, constituting,
constituted)
make up or form something, *Twelve
months constitute a year*.
[from *con-* + Latin *statuere* = set up]

constitution *noun* (*plural* constitutions)
1 the group of laws or principles that state
how a country is to be organized and
governed. 2 the nature of the body in
regard to healthiness, *She has a strong
constitution*. 3 constituting. 4 the
composition of something.
constitutional *adjective*

constrain *verb* (constrains, constraining,
constrained)
force someone to act in a certain way;
compel.
[from old French; related to *constrict*]

constraint *noun* (*plural* constraints)
1 constraining; compulsion. 2 a
restriction.

constrict *verb* (constricts, constricting,
constricted)
squeeze or tighten something by making it
narrower. **constriction** *noun*
[from *con-* + Latin *strictum* = bound]

construct *verb* (constructs, constructing,
constructed)
make something by placing parts together;
build. **constructor** *noun*
[from *con-* + Latin *structum* = built]

construction *noun* (*plural* constructions)
1 constructing. 2 something constructed; a
building. 3 two or more words put together
to form a phrase or clause or sentence. 4 an
explanation or interpretation, *They put a
bad construction on our refusal*.

constructive *adjective*
constructing; being helpful, *constructive
suggestions*.

construe *verb* (construes, construing,
construed)
interpret or explain.
[same origin as *construct*]

consul *noun* (*plural* consuls)
1 a government official appointed to live in
a foreign city to help people from his or her
own country who visit there. 2 either of
the two chief magistrates in ancient Rome.
consular *adjective* [Latin, related to *consult*]

consulate *noun* (*plural* consulates)
the building where a consul works.

consult *verb* (consults, consulting,
consulted)
go to a person or book etc. for information
or advice. **consultation** *noun* [from Latin
consulere = take advice or counsel]

consultant *noun* (*plural* consultants)
a person who is qualified to give expert
advice.

consultative *adjective*
for consultation, *a consultative committee*.

consume *verb* (consumes, consuming,
consumed)
1 eat or drink something. 2 use up, *Much
time was consumed in waiting*. 3 destroy,
Fire consumed the building.
[from *con-* + Latin *sumere* = take up]

consumer *noun* (*plural* consumers)
a person who buys or uses goods or
services.

consummate (*say* kon-sum-ayt) *verb*
(consummates, consummating,
consummated)
1 make complete or perfect. 2 complete a
marriage by having sexual intercourse.
consummation *noun*

consummate (*say* kon-sum-at) *adjective*
perfect; highly skilled, *a consummate artist*.
[from *con-* + Latin *summus* = highest]

consumption *noun*
1 consuming. 2 (*old use*) tuberculosis of the
lungs.

contact *noun* (*plural* contacts)
1 touching. 2 being in touch;
communication. 3 a person to
communicate with when you need
information or help.

contact *verb* (contacts, contacting,
contacted)
get in touch with a person.
[from *con-* + Latin *tactum* = touched]

contact lens noun (plural contact lenses)
a tiny lens worn against the eyeball,
instead of spectacles.

contagion noun (plural contagions)
a contagious disease.

contagious adjective
spreading by contact with an infected
person, a contagious disease.
[from con- + Latin tangere = to touch]

contain verb (contains, containing,
contained)
1 have inside, The box contains chocolates.
2 consist of, A gallon contains 8 pints.
3 restrain; hold back, Try to contain your
laughter. [from con- + Latin tenere = hold]

container noun (plural containers)
1 a box or bottle etc. designed to contain
something. 2 a large box-like object of
standard design in which goods are
transported.

contaminate verb (contaminates,
contaminating, contaminated)
make a thing dirty or impure or diseased
etc.; pollute. **contamination** noun
[from Latin; related to contagion]

contemplate verb (contemplates,
contemplating, contemplated)
1 look at something thoughtfully.
2 consider or think about doing something,
We are contemplating a visit to London.
contemplation noun, **contemplative**
adjective [from Latin]

contemporary adjective
1 belonging to the same period, Dickens
was contemporary with Thackeray.
2 modern; up-to-date, contemporary
furniture.
contemporary noun (plural
contemporaries)
a person who is contemporary with
another or who is about the same age, She
was my contemporary at college.
[from con- + Latin tempus = time]

contempt noun
a feeling of despising a person or thing.
[from Latin]

contemptible adjective
deserving contempt, Hurting her feelings
like that was a contemptible thing to do.

contemptuous adjective
feeling or showing contempt, She gave me a
contemptuous look. **contemptuously** adverb

contend verb (contends, contending,
contended)
1 struggle in a battle etc. or against
difficulties. 2 compete. 3 declare that
something is true; assert, We contend that
he is innocent. **contender** noun
[from con- + Latin tendere = strive]

content[1] (say kon-tent) adjective
contented.
content noun
contentment.
content verb (contents, contenting,
contented)
make a person contented.
[from Latin contentum = restrained]

content[2] (say kon-tent) noun or **contents**
plural noun
what something contains.
[from Latin contenta = things contained]

contented adjective
happy with what you have; satisfied.
contentedly adverb

contention noun (plural contentions)
1 contending; arguing. 2 an assertion put
forward.

contentment noun
a contented state.

contest (say kon-test) noun (plural
contests)
a competition; a struggle in which rivals
try to obtain something or to do best.
contest (say kon-test) verb (contests,
contesting, contested)
1 compete for or in, contest an election.
2 dispute; argue that something is wrong
or not legal. [from Latin]

contestant noun (plural contestants)
a person taking part in a contest; a
competitor.

context noun (plural contexts)
1 the words that come before and after a
particular word or phrase and help to fix

its meaning. **2** the background to an event that helps to explain it.
[from *con-* + Latin *textum* = woven]

contiguous *adjective*
in contact with; touching.
[same origin as *contingent*]

continent *noun* (*plural* **continents**)
one of the main masses of land in the world, *The continents are Europe, Asia, Africa, North America, South America, Australia, and Antarctica.*
continental *adjective*
the Continent the mainland of Europe, not including the British Isles.
[from Latin *terra continens* = continuous land]

contingency *noun* (*plural* **contingencies**)
something that may happen but is not intended.

contingent *adjective*
1 depending, *His future is contingent on success in this exam.* **2** possible but not certain, *other contingent events.*

contingent *noun* (*plural* **contingents**)
a group that forms part of a larger group or gathering.
[from Latin *contingere* = touch, happen to]

continual *adjective*
happening all the time, usually with breaks in between, *Stop this continual quarrelling!* **continually** *adverb*

USAGE: Do not confuse with *continuous*. *Continual* is used to describe something that happens very frequently (*there were continual interruptions*) while *continuous* is used to describe something that happens without a pause (*there was continuous rain all day*).

continuance *noun*
continuing.

continue *verb* (**continues**, **continuing**, **continued**)
1 do something without stopping. **2** begin again after stopping, *The game will continue after lunch.* **continuation** *noun*
[from Latin]

continuous *adjective*
going on and on; without a break.
continuously *adverb*, **continuity** *noun*

USAGE: See note at *continual*.

contort *verb* (**contorts**, **contorting**, **contorted**)
twist or force out of the usual shape.
contortion *noun*
[from *con-* + Latin *tortum* = twisted]

contortionist *noun* (*plural* **contortionists**)
a person who can twist his or her body into unusual positions.

contour *noun* (*plural* **contours**)
1 a line on a map joining the points that are the same height above sea level. **2** an outline.
[from Latin *contornare* = draw in outline]

contra- *prefix*
against. [Latin]

contraband *noun*
smuggled goods.
[from *contra-* + Italian *banda* = a ban]

contraception *noun*
preventing conception; birth control.
[from *contra-* + *conception*]

contraceptive *noun* (*plural* **contraceptives**)
a substance or device that prevents conception.

contract (*say* kon-trakt) *noun* (*plural* **contracts**)
1 a formal agreement to do something. **2** a document stating the terms of an agreement.

contract (*say* kon-trakt) *verb* (**contracts**, **contracting**, **contracted**)
1 make or become smaller. **2** make a contract. **3** get an illness, *She contracted measles.*
[from *con-* + Latin *tractum* = pulled]

contraction *noun* (*plural* **contractions**)
1 contracting. **2** a shortened form of a word or words. *Can't* is a contraction of *cannot*.

contractor *noun* (*plural* **contractors**)
a person who makes a contract, especially for building.

contradict *verb* (contradicts, contradicting, contradicted)
1 say that something said is not true or that someone is wrong. **2** say the opposite of, *These rumours contradict previous ones.*
contradiction *noun*, **contradictory** *adjective*
[from *contra-* + Latin *dicere* = say]

contraflow *noun* (*plural* contraflows)
a flow of road traffic travelling in the opposite direction to the usual flow and close beside it. [from *contra-* + *flow*]

contralto *noun* (*plural* contraltos)
a female singer with a low voice.
[Italian, from *contra-* + *alto*]

contraption *noun* (*plural* contraptions)
a strange-looking device or machine.
[origin unknown]

contrary *adjective*
1 (*say* kon-tra-ree) of the opposite kind or direction etc.; opposed; unfavourable.
2 (*say* kon-**trair**-ee) awkward and obstinate.
contrary (*say* kon-tra-ree) *noun*
the opposite.
on the contrary the opposite is true.
[from old French; related to *contra-*]

contrast *noun* (*plural* contrasts)
1 a difference clearly seen when things are compared. **2** something showing a clear difference.
contrast *verb* (contrasts, contrasting, contrasted)
1 compare or oppose two things in order to show that they are clearly different. **2** be clearly different when compared.
[from *contra-* + Latin *stare* = to stand]

contravene *verb* (contravenes, contravening, contravened)
act against a rule or law. **contravention** *noun* [from *contra-* + Latin *venire* = come]

contretemps (*say* kawn-tre-tahn) *noun*
an unfortunate happening.
[French, = out of time (in music)]

contribute *verb* (contributes, contributing, contributed)
1 give money or help etc. when others are doing the same. **2** write something for a newspaper or magazine etc. **3** help to cause

something. **contribution** *noun*, **contributor** *noun*, **contributory** *adjective*
[from *con-* + Latin *tribuere* = bestow]

contrite *adjective*
very sorry for having done wrong.
[from Latin *contritus* = ground down]

contrivance *noun* (*plural* contrivances)
a device.

contrive *verb* (contrives, contriving, contrived)
plan cleverly; find a way of doing or making something. [from old French]

control *verb* (controls, controlling, controlled)
1 have the power to make someone or something do what you want. **2** hold something, especially anger, in check; restrain. **controller** *noun*
control *noun*
controlling a person or thing; authority.
out of control no longer able to be controlled.
[from old French]

controls *plural noun*
the switches etc. used to control a machine.

controversial *adjective*
causing controversy.

controversy (*say* kon-tro-ver-see or kon-trov-er-see) *noun* (*plural* controversies)
a long argument or disagreement.
[from *contra-* + Latin *versum* – turned]

contusion *noun* (*plural* contusions)
a bruise. [from Latin]

conundrum *noun* (*plural* conundrums)
a riddle; a hard question. [origin unknown]

conurbation *noun* (*plural* conurbations)
a large urban area where towns have spread into each other.
[from *con-* + Latin *urbs* = city]

convalesce *verb* (convalesces, convalescing, convalesced)
be recovering from an illness.
convalescence *noun*, **convalescent** *adjective* & *noun*
[from *con-* + Latin *valescere* = grow strong]

convection *noun*
the passing on of heat within liquid, air, or gas by circulation of the warmed parts. [from *con-* + Latin *vectum* = carried]

convector *noun* (*plural* convectors)
a device that circulates warmed air.

convene *verb* (convenes, convening, convened)
summon or assemble for a meeting etc. **convener** *noun*
[from *con-* + Latin *venire* = come]

convenience *noun* (*plural* conveniences)
1 being convenient. 2 something that is convenient. 3 a public lavatory.
at your convenience whenever you find convenient; as it suits you.

convenient *adjective*
easy to use or deal with or reach. **conveniently** *adverb*
[from Latin *convenire* = to suit]

convent *noun* (*plural* convents)
a place where nuns live and work. [same origin as *convene*]

convention *noun* (*plural* conventions)
1 an accepted way of doing things. 2 a formal assembly. [from Latin *conventio* = a gathering, agreement]

conventional *adjective*
1 done or doing things in the accepted way; traditional. 2 (of weapons) not nuclear. **conventionally** *adverb*, **conventionality** *noun*

converge *verb* (converges, converging, converged)
come to or towards the same point from different directions. **convergence** *noun*, **convergent** *adjective*
[from *con-* + Latin *vergere* = turn]

conversant *adjective*
familiar with something, *Are you conversant with the rules of this game?*
[from *converse*¹]

conversation *noun* (*plural* conversations)
talk between people.
conversational *adjective*

converse¹ (*say* kon-verss) *verb* (converses, conversing, conversed)
hold a conversation.
[from Latin *conversare* = mix with people]

converse² (*say* kon-verss) *adjective*
opposite; contrary. **conversely** *adverb*
converse *noun*
an opposite idea or statement etc.
[same origin as *convert*]

conversion *noun* (*plural* conversions)
converting.

convert (*say* kon-vert) *verb* (converts, converting, converted)
1 change. 2 cause a person to change his or her beliefs. 3 kick a goal after scoring a try at Rugby football. **converter** *noun*
convert (*say* kon-vert) *noun* (*plural* converts)
a person who has changed his or her beliefs. [from *con-* + Latin *vertere* = turn]

convertible *adjective*
able to be converted. **convertibility** *noun*
convertible *noun* (*plural* convertibles)
a car with a folding roof.

convex *adjective*
curved like the outside of a ball or circle. (The opposite is *concave*.) **convexity** *noun*
[from Latin *convexus* = arched]

convey *verb* (conveys, conveying, conveyed)
1 transport. 2 communicate a message or idea etc. **conveyor** *noun*
[from old French *conveier* = lead, escort]

conveyance *noun* (*plural* conveyances)
1 conveying. 2 a vehicle for transporting people.

conveyancing *noun*
transferring the legal ownership of land etc. from one person to another.

conveyor belt (*plural* conveyor belts)
a continuous moving belt for conveying objects.

convict (*say* kon-vikt) *verb* (convicts, convicting, convicted)
prove or declare that a certain person is guilty of a crime.

convict (*say* kon-vikt) *noun* (*plural* convicts)
a convicted person who is in prison.
[from *con-* + Latin *victum* = conquered]

conviction *noun* (*plural* convictions)
1 convicting or being convicted of a crime.
2 being convinced. 3 a firm opinion or belief.
carry conviction be convincing.

convince *verb* (convinces, convincing, convinced)
make a person feel certain that something is true.
[from *con-* + Latin *vincere* = conquer]

convivial *adjective*
sociable and lively. [from Latin *convivium* = feast]

convoke *verb* (convokes, convoking, convoked)
summon people to an assembly or meeting.
[from *con-* + Latin *vocare* = to call]

convoluted *adjective*
1 coiled or twisted. 2 complicated.
convolution *noun*
[from *con-* + Latin *volutum* = rolled]

convoy *noun* (*plural* convoys)
a group of ships or lorries travelling together. [same origin as *convey*]

convulse *verb* (convulses, convulsing, convulsed)
cause violent movements or convulsions.
convulsive *adjective*
[from *con-* + Latin *vulsum* = pulled]

convulsion *noun* (*plural* convulsions)
1 a violent movement of the body. 2 a violent upheaval.

coo *verb* (coos, cooing, cooed)
make a dove's soft murmuring sound.
coo *noun*

cook *verb* (cooks, cooking, cooked)
make food ready to eat by heating it.
cook up (*informal*) if you cook up a story or plan, you invent it.
cook *noun* (*plural* cooks)
a person who cooks. [from Latin]

cooker *noun* (*plural* cookers)
a stove for cooking food.

cookery *noun*
the skill of cooking food.

cool *adjective*
1 fairly cold; not hot or warm. 2 calm; not enthusiastic. **coolly** *adverb*, **coolness** *noun*
cool *verb* (cools, cooling, cooled)
make or become cool. **cooler** *noun*
[from Old English]

coolie *noun* (*plural* coolies)
an unskilled labourer in countries of eastern Asia. [from Hindi and Telugu (a language spoken in southern India)]

coop *noun* (*plural* coops)
a cage for poultry.
[from Latin *cupa* = barrel]

cooperate *verb* (cooperates, cooperating, cooperated)
work helpfully with other people.
cooperation *noun*, **cooperative** *adjective*
[from *co-* + Latin *operari* = operate]

co-opt *verb* (co-opts, co-opting, co-opted)
invite someone to become a member of a committee etc.
[from *co-* + Latin *optare* = choose]

coordinate *verb* (coordinates, coordinating, coordinated)
organize people or things to work properly together.
coordination *noun*, **coordinator** *noun*
coordinate *noun* (*plural* coordinates)
either of the pair of numbers or letters used to fix the position of a point on a graph or map.
[from *co-* + Latin *ordinare* = arrange]

coot *noun* (*plural* coots)
a waterbird with a horny white patch on its forehead. [origin unknown]

cop *verb* (cops, copping, copped)
cop it get into trouble or be punished.
cop *noun* (*plural* cops) (*slang*)
1 a police officer. 2 a capture or arrest, *It's a fair cop!* [from dialect *cap* = capture]

cope¹ *verb* (copes, coping, coped)
manage or deal with something successfully. [from French; related to *coup*]

cope² *noun* (*plural* copes)
a long loose cloak worn by clergy in ceremonies etc. [same origin as *cape¹*]

copier *noun* (*plural* **copiers**)
a device for copying things.

coping *noun*
the top row of stones or bricks in a wall, usually slanted so that rainwater will run off. [from an old word *cope* = to cover]

copious *adjective*
plentiful; in large amounts. **copiously** *adverb* [same origin as *copy*]

copper[1] *noun* (*plural* **coppers**)
1 a reddish-brown metal used to make wire, coins, etc. **2** a reddish-brown colour. **3** a coin made of copper or metal of this colour. **copper** *adjective*
[via Old English from Latin *cyprium* = Cyprus metal (because the Romans got most of their copper from Cyprus)]

copper[2] *noun* (*plural* **coppers**) (*slang*)
a policeman. [from *cop*]

copperplate *noun*
neat handwriting. [because the books of examples of this writing for learners to copy were printed from copper plates]

coppice *noun* (*plural* **coppices**)
a small group of trees.
[from Latin *colpus* = a blow (because from time to time the trees were cut back, and allowed to grow again)]

copra *noun*
dried coconut-kernels. [via Portuguese and Spanish from Malayalam (a language spoken in southern India)]

copse *noun* (*plural* **copses**)
a small group of trees.
[a different spelling of *coppice*]

copulate *verb* (**copulates, copulating, copulated**)
have sexual intercourse with someone.
copulation *noun* [from Latin *copulare* = link or join together]

copy *noun* (*plural* **copies**)
1 a thing made to look like another.
2 something written or typed out again from its original form. **3** one of a number of specimens of the same book or newspaper etc.

copy *verb* (**copies, copying, copied**)
1 make a copy of something. **2** do the same as someone else; imitate. **copyist** *noun*
[from Latin *copia* = plenty, abundance]

copyright *noun*
the legal right to print a book, reproduce a picture, record a piece of music, etc.

coquette (*say* ko-**ket**) *noun* (*plural* **coquettes**)
a woman who flirts. **coquettish** *adjective*
[French]

cor- *prefix*
with; together. see **com-**.

coral *noun*
1 a hard red, pink, or white substance formed by the skeletons of tiny sea-creatures massed together. **2** a pink colour.
[from Greek]

corbel *noun* (*plural* **corbels**)
a piece of stone or wood that sticks out from a roof to support something.
[from old French]

cord *noun* (*plural* **cords**)
1 a long thin flexible strip of twisted threads or strands. **2** a piece of flex. **3** a cord-like structure in the body, *the spinal cord*. **4** corduroy. [from Greek]

USAGE: Do not confuse with *chord*.

cordial *noun* (*plural* **cordials**)
a fruit-flavoured drink.
cordial *adjective*
warm and friendly. **cordially** *adverb*, **cordiality** *noun* [from Latin *cordis* = of the heart (a cordial was originally a drink given to stimulate the heart)]

cordon *noun* (*plural* **cordons**)
a line of people, ships, fortifications, etc. placed round an area to guard or enclose it.
cordon *verb* (**cordons, cordoning, cordoned**)
surround with a cordon.
[from French or Italian; related to *cord*]

cordon bleu (*say* kor-dawn **bler**) *adjective*
(of cooks and cookery) first-class.
[French, = blue ribbon]

corduroy *noun*
cotton cloth with velvety ridges. [from *cord* + *duroy* = a kind of woollen material]

core *noun* (*plural* **cores**)
1 the part in the middle of something. **2** the hard central part of an apple or pear etc., containing the seeds. [origin unknown]

corgi *noun* (*plural* **corgis**)
a small dog with short legs and upright ears. [from Welsh *cor* = dwarf + *ci* = dog]

cork *noun* (*plural* **corks**)
1 the lightweight bark of a kind of oak tree. **2** a stopper for a bottle, made of cork or other material.
cork *verb* (**corks, corking, corked**)
close something with a cork.
[via Dutch and Spanish from Latin]

corkscrew *noun* (*plural* **corkscrews**)
1 a device for removing corks from bottles. **2** a spiral.

corm *noun* (*plural* **corms**)
a part of a plant rather like a bulb.
[from Greek]

cormorant *noun* (*plural* **cormorants**)
a large black seabird.
[from Latin *corvus marinus* = sea raven]

corn[1] *noun*
1 the seed of wheat and similar plants. **2** a plant, such as wheat, grown for its grain.
[from Old English]

corn[2] *noun* (*plural* **corns**)
a small hard lump on the foot.
[from Latin *cornu* = horn]

cornea *noun* (*plural* **corneas**)
the transparent covering over the pupil of the eye. **corneal** *adjective* [from Latin]

corned *adjective*
preserved with salt, *corned beef*.
[from *corn*[1] (because of the corns (= grains) of coarse salt that were used)]

corner *noun* (*plural* **corners**)
1 the angle or area where two lines or sides or walls meet or where two streets join. **2** a free hit or kick from the corner of a hockey or football field. **3** a region, *a quiet corner of the world*.
corner *verb* (**corners, cornering, cornered**)
1 drive someone into a corner or other position from which it is difficult to escape. **2** travel round a corner. **3** obtain

possession of all or most of something, *corner the market*.
[from Latin *cornu* = horn, tip]

cornerstone *noun* (*plural* **cornerstones**)
1 a stone built into the corner at the base of a building. **2** something that is a vital foundation.

cornet *noun* (*plural* **cornets**)
1 a cone-shaped wafer etc. holding ice cream. **2** a musical instrument rather like a trumpet. [French, = small horn]

cornflakes *plural noun*
toasted maize flakes eaten as a breakfast cereal.

cornflour *noun*
flour made from maize or rice, used in sauces, milk puddings, etc.

cornflower *noun* (*plural* **cornflowers**)
a plant with blue flowers that grows wild in fields of corn.

cornice *noun* (*plural* **cornices**)
a band of ornamental moulding on walls just below a ceiling or at the top of a building. [via French from Italian]

cornucopia *noun*
1 a horn-shaped container overflowing with fruit and flowers. **2** a plentiful supply of good things. [from Latin *cornu* = horn + *copiae* = of plenty]

corny *adjective* (**cornier, corniest**) (*informal*)
1 repeated so often that people are bored, *corny jokes*. **2** sentimental.
[originally = rustic, simple: from *corn*[1]]

corollary (*say* ker-ol-er-ee) *noun* (*plural* **corollaries**)
a fact etc. that logically results from another, *The work is difficult and, as a corollary, tiring*. [from Latin]

corona (*say* kor-oh-na) *noun* (*plural* **coronas**)
a circle of light round something.
[Latin, = crown]

coronary *noun* (*plural* **coronaries**)
short for **coronary thrombosis**, blockage of an artery carrying blood to the heart.
[from *corona* (because the coronary arteries encircle the heart like a crown)]

coronation *noun* (*plural* coronations)
the crowning of a king or queen.
[same origin as *corona*]

coroner *noun* (*plural* coroners)
an official who holds an inquiry into the
cause of a death thought to be from
unnatural causes. [from old French]

coronet *noun* (*plural* coronets)
a small crown. [from old French]

corporal[1] *noun* (*plural* corporals)
a soldier ranking next below a sergeant.
[via French from Italian]

corporal[2] *adjective*
to do with the body.
[from Latin *corpus* = body]

corporal punishment *noun*
punishment by being whipped or beaten.

corporate *adjective*
shared by members of a group, *corporate
responsibility*.
[from Latin *corporare* = unite in one body]

corporation *noun* (*plural* corporations)
1 a group of people elected to govern a
town. 2 a group of people legally
authorized to act as an individual in
business etc.

corps (*say* kor) *noun* (*plural* corps (*say*
korz))
1 a special army unit, *the Medical Corps*.
2 a large group of soldiers. 3 a set of people
doing the same job, *the diplomatic corps*.
[French, from Latin *corpus* = body]

corps de ballet (*say* kor der **bal**-ay) *noun*
the whole group of dancers (not the
soloists) in a ballet. [French]

corps diplomatique (*say* kor dip-lom-at-
eek) *noun*
the diplomatic service. [French]

corpse *noun* (*plural* corpses)
a dead body. [from Latin *corpus* = body]

corpulent *adjective*
having a bulky body; fat. **corpulence** *noun*
[from Latin]

corpuscle *noun* (*plural* corpuscles)
one of the red or white cells in blood.
[from Latin *corpusculum* = little body]

corral (*say* kor-ahl) *noun* (*plural* corrals)
(*American*)
an enclosure for horses, cattle, etc.
[from Spanish or Portuguese]

correct *adjective*
1 true; accurate; without any mistakes.
2 proper; done or said in an approved way.
correctly *adverb*, **correctness** *noun*

correct *verb* (corrects, correcting, corrected)
1 make a thing correct by altering or
adjusting it. 2 mark the mistakes in
something. 3 point out or punish a
person's faults. **correction** *noun*, **corrective**
adjective, **corrector** *noun*
[from *cor-* + Latin *rectus* = straight]

correlate *verb* (correlates, correlating,
correlated)
compare or connect things systematically.
correlation *noun* [from *cor-* + *relate*]

correspond *verb* (corresponds,
corresponding, corresponded)
1 write letters to each other. 2 agree;
match, *Your story corresponds with his.*
3 be similar or equivalent, *Their assembly
corresponds to our parliament.*
[from *cor-* + *respond*]

correspondence *noun*
1 letters; writing letters. 2 similarity;
agreement.

correspondent *noun* (*plural*
correspondents)
1 a person who writes letters to another.
2 a person employed to gather news and
send reports to a newspaper or radio
station etc.

corridor *noun* (*plural* corridors)
a passage in a building.
[via French from Italian]

corroborate *verb* (corroborates,
corroborating, corroborated)
help to confirm a statement etc.
corroboration *noun*
[from *cor-* + Latin *roborare* = strengthen]

corrode *verb* (corrodes, corroding, corroded)
destroy metal gradually by chemical action. **corrosion** *noun*, **corrosive** *adjective*
[from *cor-* + Latin *rodere* = gnaw]

corrugated *adjective*
shaped into alternate ridges and grooves, *corrugated iron*.
[from *cor-* + Latin *ruga* = wrinkle]

corrupt *adjective*
1 dishonest; accepting bribes. 2 wicked. 3 decaying.
corrupt *verb* (corrupts, corrupting, corrupted)
1 cause someone to become dishonest or wicked. 2 spoil; cause something to decay.
corruption *noun*, **corruptible** *adjective*
[from *cor-* + Latin *ruptum* = broken]

corsair *noun* (*plural* corsairs)
1 a pirate ship. 2 a pirate. [from French]

corset *noun* (*plural* corsets)
a piece of underwear worn to shape or support the body.
[old French, = small body]

cortège (*say* kort-ayzh) *noun* (*plural* cortèges)
a funeral procession. [French]

cosh *noun* (*plural* coshes)
a heavy weapon for hitting people.
[origin unknown]

cosine *noun* (*plural* cosines)
(in a right-angled triangle) the ratio of the length of a side adjacent to one of the acute angles to the length of the hypotenuse. (Compare *sine*.) [from *co-* + *sine*]

cosmetic *noun* (*plural* cosmetics)
a substance (e.g. face powder, lipstick) put on the skin to make it look more attractive.
[from Greek *kosmein* = arrange, decorate]

cosmetic surgery *noun*
surgery carried out to make people look more attractive.

cosmic *adjective*
1 to do with the universe. 2 to do with outer space, *cosmic rays*. [from *cosmos*]

cosmonaut *noun* (*plural* cosmonauts)
a Russian astronaut.
[from *cosmos* + *astronaut*]

cosmopolitan *adjective*
from many countries; containing people from many countries.
[from *cosmos* + Greek *polites* = citizen]

cosmos (*say* koz-moss) *noun*
the universe. [from Greek, = the world]

Cossack *noun* (*plural* Cossacks)
a member of a people of south Russia, famous as horsemen.

cosset *verb* (cossets, cosseting, cosseted)
pamper; treat someone very kindly and lovingly. [from old French]

cost *noun* (*plural* costs)
the price of something.
cost *verb* (costs, costing, cost)
1 have a certain price. 2 (*past tense* is costed) estimate the cost of something.
[from old French]

costermonger *noun* (*plural* costermongers)
a person who sells fruit etc. from a barrow in the street. [from old words *costard* = large apple + *monger* = trader]

costly *adjective* (costlier, costliest)
expensive. **costliness** *noun*

costume *noun* (*plural* costumes)
clothes, especially for a particular purpose or of a particular place or period.
[via French from Italian; related to *custom*]

cosy *adjective* (cosier, cosiest)
warm and comfortable. **cosily** *adverb*, **cosiness** *noun*
cosy *noun* (*plural* cosies)
a cover placed over a teapot or boiled egg to keep it hot. [origin unknown]

cot *noun* (*plural* cots)
a baby's bed with high sides.
[from Hindi *khat* = bedstead]

cottage *noun* (*plural* cottages)
a small simple house, especially in the country. [from Old English]

cottage cheese *noun*
soft white cheese made from curds of skimmed milk.

cottage pie *noun* (*plural* **cottage pies**)
a dish of minced meat covered with mashed potato and baked.

cottager *noun* (*plural* **cottagers**)
a person who lives in a country cottage.

cotton *noun*
1 a soft white substance covering the seeds of a tropical plant; the plant itself. 2 thread made from this substance. 3 cloth made from cotton thread.
[via French from Arabic]

cotton wool *noun*
soft fluffy wadding originally made from cotton.

couch *noun* (*plural* **couches**)
1 a long soft seat like a sofa but with only one end raised. 2 a sofa or settee.

couch *verb* (**couches, couching, couched**)
express in words of a certain kind, *The request was couched in polite terms.*
[from French *coucher* = lay down flat]

cougar (*say* koo-ger) *noun* (*plural* **cougars**)
(*American*)
a puma. [via French from Guarani (a South American language)]

cough (*say* kof) *verb* (**coughs, coughing, coughed**)
send out air from the lungs with a sudden sharp sound.

cough *noun* (*plural* **coughs**)
1 the act or sound of coughing. 2 an illness that makes you cough.
[imitating the sound]

could *past tense* of **can**².

couldn't (*mainly spoken*)
could not.

council *noun* (*plural* **councils**)
a group of people chosen or elected to organize or discuss something, especially those elected to organize the affairs of a town or county.
[from Latin *concilium* = assembly]

USAGE: Do not confuse with *counsel.*

council house *noun* (*plural* **council houses**)
a house owned and let to tenants by a town council.

councillor *noun* (*plural* **councillors**)
a member of a town or county council.

council tax *noun* (*plural* **council taxes**)
a tax paid to a local authority to pay for local services, based on the estimated value of someone's house or flat.

counsel *noun* (*plural* **counsels**)
1 advice, *give counsel.* 2 a barrister or group of barristers representing someone in a lawsuit.
take counsel with consult.

USAGE: Do not confuse with *council.*

counsel *verb* (**counsels, counselling, counselled**)
give advice to someone; recommend.
[from Latin *consulere* = consult]

counsellor *noun* (*plural* **counsellors**)
an adviser.

count¹ *verb* (**counts, counting, counted**)
1 say numbers in their proper order. 2 find the total of something by using numbers. 3 include in a total, *There are six of us, counting the dog.* 4 be important, *It's what you do that counts.* 5 regard; consider, *I should count it an honour to be invited.*
count on rely on.

count *noun* (*plural* **counts**)
1 counting. 2 a number reached by counting; a total. 3 any of the points being considered, e.g. in accusing someone of crimes, *guilty on all counts.* [via French from Latin *computare* = compute]

count² *noun* (*plural* **counts**)
a foreign nobleman. [from old French]

countdown *noun* (*plural* **countdowns**)
counting numbers backwards to zero before an event, especially the launching of a space rocket.

countenance *noun* (*plural* countenances)
a person's face; the expression on the face.
countenance *verb* (countenances,
countenancing, countenanced)
give approval to; allow, *Will they
countenance this plan?* [from old French]

counter[1] *noun* (*plural* counters)
1 a flat surface over which customers are
served in a shop, bank, etc. **2** a small round
playing piece used in certain board games.
3 a device for counting things.
under the counter sold or obtained in an
underhand way.
[same origin as *count*[1]]

counter[2] *verb* (counters, countering,
countered)
1 counteract. **2** counter-attack; return an
opponent's blow by hitting back.
counter *adverb*
contrary to something, *This is counter to
what we really want.* [via old French from
Latin *contra* = against]

counter- *prefix*
1 against; opposing; done in return (as in
counter-attack). **2** corresponding (as in
countersign). [from Latin *contra* = against]

counteract *verb* (counteracts,
counteracting, counteracted)
act against something and reduce or
prevent its effects. **counteraction** *noun*
[from *counter-* + *act*]

counter-attack *verb* (counter-attacks,
counter-attacking, counter-attacked)
attack to oppose or return an enemy's
attack. **counter-attack** *noun*

counterbalance *noun* (*plural*
counterbalances)
a weight or influence that balances
another. **counterbalance** *verb*
[from *counter-* + *balance*]

counterfeit (*say* kownt-er-feet) *adjective*
fake; not genuine.
counterfeit *noun* (*plural* counterfeits)
a forgery or imitation.
counterfeit *verb* (counterfeits,
counterfeiting, counterfeited)
forge or make an imitation of something.
[from old French *countrefait* = made in
opposition]

counterfoil *noun* (*plural* counterfoils)
a section of a cheque or receipt etc. that is
torn off and kept as a record. [from *counter-*
+ an old sense of *foil*[1] = sheet of paper]

countermand *verb* (countermands,
countermanding, countermanded)
cancel a command or instruction that has
been given. [from *counter-* + Latin *mandare*
= to command]

counterpane *noun* (*plural* counterpanes)
a bedspread. [from old French]

counterpart *noun* (*plural* counterparts)
a person or thing that corresponds to
another, *Their President is the counterpart
of our Prime Minister.*

counterpoint *noun*
a method of combining melodies in
harmony.
[from Latin *cantus contrapunctus* = song
written opposite (to the original melody)]

counterpoise *noun* & *verb* (counterpoises,
counterpoising, counterpoised)
counterbalance.

countersign *verb* (countersigns,
countersigning, countersigned)
add another signature to a document to
give it authority.

counterweight *noun* & *verb*
(counterweights, counterweighting,
counterweighted)
counterbalance.

countess *noun* (*plural* countesses)
the wife or widow of a count or earl; a
female count.

countless *adjective*
too many to count.

countrified *adjective*
like the country.

country *noun* (*plural* countries)
1 the land occupied by a nation. **2** all the
people of a country. **3** the countryside.

country dance *noun* (*plural* country
dances)
a folk dance.

countryman *noun* (*plural* **countrymen**)
1 a man who lives in the countryside. 2 a man who belongs to the same country as yourself.

countryside *noun*
an area with fields, woods, villages, etc. away from towns.

countrywoman *noun* (*plural* **countrywomen**)
1 a woman who lives in the countryside. 2 a woman who belongs to the same country as yourself.

county *noun* (*plural* **counties**)
each of the main areas that a country is divided into for local government. [originally = the land of a count (*count*²)]

coup (*say* koo) *noun* (*plural* **coups**)
a sudden action taken to win power; a clever victory. [French, = a blow]

coup de grâce (*say* koo der **grahs**) *noun*
a stroke or blow that puts an end to something. [French, = mercy-blow]

coup d'état (*say* koo day-**tah**) *noun* (*plural* **coups d'état**)
the sudden overthrow of a government. [French, = blow of State]

couple *noun* (*plural* **couples**)
two people or things considered together; a pair.
couple *verb* (**couples, coupling, coupled**)
fasten or link two things together. [same origin as *copulate*]

couplet *noun* (*plural* **couplets**)
a pair of lines in rhyming verse.

coupon *noun* (*plural* **coupons**)
a piece of paper that gives you the right to receive or do something. [French, = piece cut off]

courage *noun*
the ability to face danger or difficulty or pain even when you are afraid; bravery.
courageous *adjective*
[from Latin *cor* = heart]

courgette (*say* koor-**zhet**) *noun* (*plural* **courgettes**)
a kind of small vegetable marrow. [French, = small gourd]

courier (*say* **koor**-ee-er) *noun* (*plural* **couriers**)
1 a messenger. 2 a person employed to guide and help a group of tourists. [old French, = runner]

course *noun* (*plural* **courses**)
1 the direction in which something goes; a route, *the ship's course*. 2 a series of events or actions etc., *Your best course is to start again*. 3 a series of lessons, exercises, etc. 4 part of a meal, *the meat course*. 5 a racecourse. 6 a golf course.
of course without a doubt; as we expected.
course *verb* (**courses, coursing, coursed**)
move or flow freely, *Tears coursed down his cheeks*. [from Latin *cursus* = running]

court *noun* (*plural* **courts**)
1 the royal household. 2 a lawcourt; the judges etc. in a lawcourt. 3 an enclosed area for games such as tennis or netball. 4 a courtyard.
court *verb* (**courts, courting, courted**)
try to win somebody's love or support.
courtship *noun* [from old French]

courteous (*say* **ker**-tee-us) *adjective*
polite. **courteously** *adverb*, **courtesy** *noun* [from old French, = having manners suitable for a royal court]

courtier *noun* (*plural* **courtiers**) (*old use*)
one of a king's or queen's companions at court.

courtly *adjective*
dignified and polite.

court martial (*plural* **courts martial**)
1 a court for trying people who have broken military law. 2 a trial in this court. [originally *martial court*]

court-martial *verb* (**court-martials, court-martialling, court-martialled**)
try a person by a court martial.

courtyard *noun* (*plural* **courtyards**)
a space surrounded by walls or buildings.

cousin *noun* (*plural* **cousins**)
a child of your uncle or aunt. [from old French]

cove *noun* (*plural* **coves**)
a small bay. [from Old English *cofa* = a hollow]

coven (*say* kuv-en) *noun* (*plural* covens)
a group of witches.
[same origin as *convene*]

covenant (*say* kuv-en-ant) *noun* (*plural* covenants)
a formal agreement; a contract.
[same origin as *convene*]

Coventry *place-name*
send a person to Coventry refuse to speak to him or her.
[possibly because, during the Civil War, Cavalier prisoners were sent to Coventry (a city in the Midlands): the citizens supported the Roundheads, and would not speak to the Cavaliers]

cover *verb* (covers, covering, covered)
1 place one thing over or round another; conceal. **2** travel a certain distance, *We covered ten miles a day.* **3** aim a gun at somebody, *I've got you covered.* **4** protect by insurance or a guarantee, *These goods are covered against fire or theft.* **5** be enough money to pay for something, *£5 should cover my fare.* **6** deal with or include, *The book covers all kinds of farming.* **coverage** *noun*

cover *noun* (*plural* covers)
1 a thing used for covering something else; a lid, wrapper, envelope, etc. **2** the binding of a book. **3** something that hides or shelters or protects you. [from old French]

coverlet *noun* (*plural* coverlets)
a bedspread.
[from old French *covrir lit* = cover the bed]

covert (*say* kuv-ert) *noun* (*plural* coverts)
an area of thick bushes etc. in which birds and animals hide.
covert *adjective*
done secretly. [old French, = covered]

covet (*say* kuv-it) *verb* (covets, coveting, coveted)
wish to have something, especially a thing that belongs to someone else. **covetous** *adjective*
[from old French; related to *cupidity*]

covey (*say* kuv-ee) *noun* (*plural* coveys)
a group of partridges. [from old French]

cow[1] *noun* (*plural* cows)
the fully-grown female of cattle or of certain other large animals (e.g. elephant, whale, seal). [from Old English]

cow[2] *verb* (cows, cowing, cowed)
intimidate; subdue someone by bullying.
[from Old Norse]

coward *noun* (*plural* cowards)
a person who has no courage and shows fear in a shameful way. **cowardice** *noun*, **cowardly** *adjective* [from old French]

cowboy *noun* (*plural* cowboys)
a man in charge of grazing cattle on a ranch in the USA.

cower *verb* (cowers, cowering, cowered)
crouch or shrink back in fear.
[from old German]

cowl *noun* (*plural* cowls)
1 a monk's hood. **2** a hood-shaped covering, e.g. on a chimney.
[from Old English]

cowshed *noun* (*plural* cowsheds)
a shed for cattle.

cowslip *noun* (*plural* cowslips)
a wild plant with small yellow flowers in spring. [from Old English]

cox *noun* (*plural* coxes)
a coxswain. [abbreviation]

coxswain (*say* kok-swayn or kok-sun) *noun* (*plural* coxswains)
1 a person who steers a rowing boat. **2** a sailor with special duties. [from an old word *cock* = small boat, + *swain*]

coy *adjective*
pretending to be shy or modest; bashful.
coyly *adverb*, **coyness** *noun*
[from old French; related to *quiet*]

CPVE *abbreviation*
Certificate of Prevocational Education.

crab *noun* (*plural* crabs)
a shellfish with ten legs. [from Old English]

crab apple *noun* (*plural* crab apples)
a small sour apple.
[probably from a Scandinavian language]

crack noun (*plural* cracks)
1 a line on the surface of something where it has broken but not come completely apart. **2** a narrow gap. **3** a sudden sharp noise. **4** a knock, *a crack on the head.* **5** (*informal*) a joke; a wisecrack. **6** a drug made from cocaine.
crack adjective (*informal*)
first-class, *He is a crack shot.*
crack verb (**cracks, cracking, cracked**)
1 make or get a crack; split. **2** make a sudden sharp noise. **3** break down, *He cracked under the strain.*
crack a joke tell a joke.
crack down on (*informal*) stop something that is illegal or against rules.
get cracking (*informal*) get busy.
[from Old English]

cracker noun (*plural* crackers)
1 a paper tube that bangs when pulled apart. **2** a firework that explodes with a crack. **3** a thin biscuit.

crackle verb (**crackles, crackling, crackled**)
make small cracking sounds, *The fire crackled in the grate.* **crackle** noun
[from *crack*]

crackling noun
crisp skin on roast pork.

-cracy suffix
forms nouns meaning 'ruling' or 'government' (e.g. *democracy*).
[from Greek *-kratia* = rule]

cradle noun (*plural* cradles)
1 a small cot for a baby. **2** a supporting framework.
cradle verb (**cradles, cradling, cradled**)
hold gently. [from Old English]

craft noun (*plural* crafts)
1 a job that needs skill, especially with the hands. **2** skill. **3** cunning; trickery. **4** (*plural* is **craft**) a ship or boat; an aircraft or spacecraft. [from Old English]

craftsman noun (*plural* craftsmen)
a person who is good at a craft.
craftsmanship noun

crafty adjective (**craftier, craftiest**)
cunning. **craftily** adverb, **craftiness** noun
[originally = skilful: from *craft*]

crag noun (*plural* crags)
a steep piece of rough rock. **craggy** adjective, **cragginess** noun [a Celtic word]

cram verb (**crams, cramming, crammed**)
1 push many things into something so that it is very full. **2** learn as many facts as you can in a short time just before an examination. [from Old English]

cramp noun (*plural* cramps)
pain caused by a muscle tightening suddenly.
cramp verb (**cramps, cramping, cramped**)
1 keep in a space that is too small. **2** hinder someone's freedom or growth etc.
[via old French from Germanic]

cramped adjective
without enough room.

cranberry noun (*plural* cranberries)
a small sour red berry used for making jelly and sauce. [from German]

crane noun (*plural* cranes)
1 a machine for lifting and moving heavy objects. **2** a large wading bird with long legs and neck.
crane verb (**cranes, craning, craned**)
stretch your neck to try and see something.
[from Old English]

crane-fly noun (*plural* crane-flies)
a flying insect with very long thin legs.

cranium noun (*plural* craniums)
the skull. [from Greek]

crank noun (*plural* cranks)
1 an L-shaped part used for changing the direction of movement in machinery. **2** a person with strange or fanatical ideas.
cranky adjective
crank verb (**cranks, cranking, cranked**)
move by means of a crank.
[from Old English]

cranny noun (*plural* crannies)
a crevice. [from old French]

crash noun (*plural* crashes)
1 the loud noise of something breaking or colliding. **2** a violent collision or fall. **3** a sudden drop or failure.
crash verb (**crashes, crashing, crashed**)
1 make or have a crash; cause to crash. **2** move with a crash.

crash *adjective*
intensive, *a crash course*. [imitating the sound]

crash helmet *noun* (*plural* **crash helmets**)
a padded helmet worn to protect the head in a crash.

crash landing *noun* (*plural* **crash landings**)
an emergency landing of an aircraft, which usually damages it.

crass *adjective*
1 very obvious or shocking; gross, *crass ignorance*. 2 very stupid.
[from Latin *crassus* = thick]

-crat *suffix*
forms nouns meaning 'ruler' or 'believer in some type of government'.
[same origin as *-cracy*]

crate *noun* (*plural* **crates**)
1 a packing case made of strips of wood. 2 an open container with compartments for carrying bottles. [origin unknown]

crater *noun* (*plural* **craters**)
1 a bowl-shaped cavity or hollow. 2 the mouth of a volcano.
[from Greek *krater* = bowl]

cravat *noun* (*plural* **cravats**)
1 a short scarf. 2 a wide necktie. [from French *Cravate* = Croatian (because Croatian soldiers wore linen cravats)]

crave *verb* (**craves, craving, craved**)
1 desire strongly. 2 (*formal*) beg for something. [from Old English]

craven *adjective*
cowardly.
[from old French *cravanté* = defeated]

craving *noun* (*plural* **cravings**)
a strong desire; a longing.

crawl *verb* (**crawls, crawling, crawled**)
1 move with the body close to the ground or other surface, or on hands and knees. 2 move slowly. 3 be covered with crawling things. **crawler** *noun*
crawl *noun*
1 a crawling movement. 2 a very slow pace. 3 an overarm swimming stroke.
[origin unknown]

crayon *noun* (*plural* **crayons**)
a stick or pencil of coloured wax etc. for drawing. [French]

craze *noun* (*plural* **crazes**)
a temporary enthusiasm.
[probably from Old Norse]

crazed *adjective*
driven insane.

crazy *adjective* (**crazier, craziest**)
1 insane. 2 very foolish, *this crazy idea*.
crazily *adverb*, **craziness** *noun* [from *craze*]

crazy paving *noun*
paving made of oddly-shaped pieces of stone etc.

creak *noun* (*plural* **creaks**)
a harsh squeak like that of a stiff door-hinge. **creaky** *adjective*
creak *verb* (**creaks, creaking, creaked**)
make a creak. [imitating the sound]

cream *noun* (*plural* **creams**)
1 the fatty part of milk. 2 a yellowish-white colour. 3 a food containing or looking like cream, *chocolate cream*. 4 a soft substance, *shoe cream*. 5 the best part.
creamy *adjective*
cream *verb* (**creams, creaming, creamed**)
make creamy; beat butter etc. until it is soft like cream.
cream off remove the best part of something.
[from old French]

crease *noun* (*plural* **creases**)
1 a line made in something by folding, pressing, or crushing it. 2 a line on a cricket pitch marking a batsman's or bowler's position.
crease *verb* (**creases, creasing, creased**)
make a crease or creases in something.
[a different spelling of *crest*]

create *verb* (**creates, creating, created**)
1 bring into existence; make or produce, especially something that no one has made before. 2 (*slang*) make a fuss; grumble.
creation *noun*, **creative** *adjective*, **creativity** *noun* [from Latin]

creator *noun* (*plural* **creators**)
a person who creates something.
the Creator God.

creature *noun* (*plural* **creatures**)
a person or animal.
[from Latin *creatura* = a created being]

crèche (*say* kresh) *noun* (*plural* **crèches**)
a place where babies and young children
are looked after while their parents are at
work. [French]

credence *noun*
belief, *Don't give it any credence.*
[from Latin *credentia* = belief]

credentials *plural noun*
documents showing a person's identity,
qualifications, etc.
[same origin as *credence*]

credible *adjective*
able to be believed; convincing. **credibly**
adverb, **credibility** *noun*
[same origin as *credit*]

USAGE: Do not confuse with *creditable* or
credulous.

credit *noun* (*plural* **credits**)
1 honour; acknowledgement. 2 an
arrangement trusting a person to pay for
something later on. 3 an amount of money
in someone's account at a bank etc., or
entered in an account-book as paid in.
(Compare *debit*.) 4 belief or trust, *I put no
credit in this rumour.*
credits or **credit titles** a list of people who
have helped to produce a film or television
programme.
credit *verb* (**credits, crediting, credited**)
1 believe. 2 attribute; say that a person has
done or achieved something, *Columbus is
credited with the discovery of America.*
3 enter something as a credit in an
account-book. (Compare *debit*.)
[from Latin *credere* = believe, trust]

creditable *adjective*
deserving praise. **creditably** *adverb*

USAGE: Do not confuse with *credible*.

credit card *noun* (*plural* **credit cards**)
a card authorizing a person to buy on
credit.

creditor *noun* (*plural* **creditors**)
a person to whom money is owed.

credulous *adjective*
too ready to believe things; gullible.
[from Latin *credulus* = trusting]

USAGE: Do not confuse with *credible*.

creed *noun* (*plural* **creeds**)
a set or formal statement of beliefs.
[from Latin *credo* = I believe]

creek *noun* (*plural* **creeks**)
1 a narrow inlet. 2 (*American* &
Australian) a small stream.
up the creek (*slang*) in difficulties.
[from Old Norse]

creep *verb* (**creeps, creeping, crept**)
1 move along close to the ground. 2 move
quietly. 3 come gradually. 4 prickle with
fear, *It makes my flesh creep.*
creep *noun* (*plural* **creeps**)
1 a creeping movement. 2 (*slang*) an
unpleasant person, especially one who
seeks to win favour.
the creeps (*informal*) a nervous feeling
caused by fear or dislike.
[from Old English]

creeper *noun* (*plural* **creepers**)
a plant that grows along the ground or up a
wall etc.

creepy *adjective* (**creepier, creepiest**)
frightening and sinister.

cremate *verb* (**cremates, cremating,
cremated**)
burn a dead body to ashes. **cremation** *noun*
[from Latin *cremare* = to burn]

crematorium *noun* (*plural* **crematoria**)
a place where corpses are cremated.

crème de la crème (*say* krem der la
krem) *noun*
the very best of something.
[French, = cream of the cream]

creosote *noun*
an oily brown liquid used to prevent wood
from rotting. [via German from Greek
kreas = flesh + *soter* = saviour (because a
form of it was used as an antiseptic)]

crêpe (*say* krayp) *noun* (*plural* **crêpes**)
a thin pancake. [French]

crêpe paper *noun*
paper with a wrinkled surface.

crescendo (*say* krish-**end**-oh) *noun* (*plural* crescendos)
a gradual increase in loudness.
[Italian, = increasing]

crescent *noun* (*plural* crescents)
1 a narrow curved shape coming to a point at each end. **2** a curved street.
[originally = the new moon: from Latin *crescens* = growing]

cress *noun*
a plant with hot-tasting leaves, used in salads and sandwiches. [from Old English]

crest *noun* (*plural* crests)
1 a tuft of hair, skin, or feathers on an animal's or bird's head. **2** the top of a hill or wave etc. **3** a design used on notepaper etc. **crested** *adjective*
[from Latin *crista* = tuft, plume]

crestfallen *adjective*
disappointed or dejected.

cretin (*say* **kret**-in) *noun* (*plural* cretins)
(*slang*) a stupid person. [via French from Latin *Christianus* = Christian (as a reminder that cretins were Christian souls, and should be cared for)]

crevasse (*say* kri-**vass**) *noun* (*plural* crevasses)
a deep open crack, especially in a glacier.
[same origin as *crevice*]

crevice *noun* (*plural* crevices)
a narrow opening, especially in a rock or wall. [from old French *crever* = burst, split]

crew¹ *noun* (*plural* crews)
1 the people working in a ship or aircraft. **2** a group working together, *the camera crew*. [from old French]

crew² *past tense* of **crow²**.

crib *noun* (*plural* cribs)
1 a baby's cot. **2** a framework holding fodder for animals. **3** a model representing the Nativity of Jesus Christ. **4** something cribbed. **5** a translation for use by students.

crib *verb* (cribs, cribbing, cribbed)
copy someone else's work.
[from Old English]

cribbage *noun*
a card game. [origin unknown]

crick *noun* (*plural* cricks)
painful stiffness in the neck or back.
[origin unknown]

cricket¹ *noun*
a game played outdoors between teams with a ball, bats, and two wickets. **cricketer** *noun* [origin unknown]

cricket² *noun* (*plural* crickets)
a brown insect like a grasshopper.
[from old French *criquer* = crackle (imitating the sound it makes)]

crime *noun* (*plural* crimes)
1 an action that breaks the law. **2** law-breaking. [from Latin]

criminal *noun* (*plural* criminals)
a person who has committed a crime or crimes. **criminal** *adjective*, **criminally** *adverb*

criminology *noun*
the study of crime.
[from Latin *crimen* = offence, + *-logy*]

crimp *verb* (crimps, crimping, crimped)
press into small ridges. [origin unknown]

crimson *adjective*
deep-red. **crimson** *noun*
[from Arabic *kirmiz* = an insect which was used to make crimson dye]

cringe *verb* (cringes, cringing, cringed)
shrink back in fear; cower. [from Old English *crincan* = yield, fall in battle]

crinkle *verb* (crinkles, crinkling, crinkled)
make or become wrinkled. **crinkly** *adjective*
[same origin as *cringe*]

crinoline *noun* (*plural* crinolines)
a long skirt worn over a framework that makes it stand out. [French]

cripple *noun* (*plural* cripples)
a person who is permanently lame.

cripple *verb* (**cripples, crippling, crippled**)
1 make a person lame. **2** weaken or damage something seriously.
[from Old English]

crisis *noun* (*plural* **crises**)
an important and dangerous or difficult situation. [from Greek]

crisp *adjective*
1 very dry so that it breaks with a snap. **2** fresh and stiff, *a crisp £5 note*. **3** cold and dry, *a crisp morning*. **4** brisk and sharp, *a crisp manner*. **crisply** *adverb*, **crispness** *noun*
crisp *noun* (*plural* **crisps**)
a very thin fried slice of potato. Crisps are usually sold in packets. [from Latin]

criss-cross *adjective* & *adverb*
with crossing lines. [from *Christ-cross* (the cross on which Christ died)]

criterion (*say* kry-**teer**-ee-on) *noun* (*plural* **criteria**)
a standard by which something is judged.
[from Greek, = means of judging]

USAGE: Note that *criteria* is a plural. It is incorrect to say 'a criteria' or 'this criteria'; correct usage is *this criterion, these criteria*.

critic *noun* (*plural* **critics**)
1 a person who gives opinions on books, plays, films, music, etc. **2** a person who criticizes. [from Greek *krites* = judge]

critical *adjective*
1 criticizing. **2** to do with critics or criticism. **3** to do with or at a crisis; very serious. **critically** *adverb*

criticism *noun* (*plural* **criticisms**)
1 criticizing; pointing out faults. **2** the work of a critic.

criticize *verb* (**criticizes, criticizing, criticized**)
say that a person or thing has faults.

croak *noun* (*plural* **croaks**)
a deep hoarse sound like that of a frog.
croak *verb* [imitating the sound]

crochet (*say* **kroh**-shay) *noun*
a kind of needlework done by using a hooked needle to loop a thread into patterns. **crochet** *verb* (**crochets, crocheting, crocheted**) [from old French *croc* = hook]

crock¹ *noun* (*plural* **crocks**)
a piece of crockery. [from Old English]

crock² *noun* (*plural* **crocks**) (*informal*)
a decrepit person or thing.
[origin unknown]

crockery *noun*
household china.
[from an old word *crocker* = potter]

crocodile *noun* (*plural* **crocodiles**)
1 a large tropical reptile with a thick skin, long tail, and huge jaws. **2** a long line of schoolchildren walking in pairs.
crocodile tears sorrow that is not sincere (so called because the crocodile was said to weep while it ate its victim).
[from Greek]

crocus *noun* (*plural* **crocuses**)
a small plant with yellow, purple, or white flowers. [from Greek]

croft *noun* (*plural* **crofts**)
a small rented farm in Scotland. **crofter** *noun* [from Old English]

croissant (*say* **krwah**-sahn) *noun* (*plural* **croissants**)
a flaky crescent-shaped bread roll.
[French, = crescent]

crone *noun* (*plural* **crones**)
a very old woman. [from old French]

crony *noun* (*plural* **cronies**)
a close friend or companion. [from Greek]

crook *noun* (*plural* **crooks**)
1 a shepherd's stick with a curved end. **2** something bent or curved. **3** (*informal*) a person who makes a living dishonestly.
crook *verb* (**crooks, crooking, crooked**)
bend, *She crooked her finger*.
[from Old Norse]

crooked *adjective*
1 bent or twisted; not straight. **2** dishonest.

croon *verb* (**croons, crooning, crooned**)
sing softly and gently.
[imitating the sound]

crop *noun* (*plural* **crops**)
1 something grown for food, *a good crop of wheat.* **2** a whip with a loop instead of a lash. **3** part of a bird's throat. **4** a very short haircut.

crop *verb* (**crops, cropping, cropped**)
1 cut or bite off, *sheep were cropping the grass.* **2** produce a crop.
crop up happen unexpectedly.
[from Old English]

cropper *noun*
come a cropper (*slang*)
1 have a bad fall. **2** fail badly.
[origin unknown]

croquet (*say* kroh-kay) *noun*
a game played with wooden balls and mallets. [origin unknown]

crosier (*say* kroh-zee-er) *noun* (*plural* **crosiers**)
a bishop's staff shaped like a shepherd's crook. [from old French]

cross *noun* (*plural* **crosses**)
1 a mark or shape made like + or ×. **2** an upright post with another piece of wood across it, used in ancient times for crucifixion; **the Cross** the cross on which Christ was crucified, used as a symbol of Christianity. **3** a mixture of two different things.

cross *verb* (**crosses, crossing, crossed**)
1 go across something. **2** draw a line or lines across something. **3** make the sign or shape of a cross, *Cross your fingers for luck.* **4** produce something from two different kinds.
cross out draw a line across something because it is unwanted, wrong, etc.

cross *adjective*
1 going from one side to another. **2** annoyed; bad-tempered. **crossly** *adverb*, **crossness** *noun*
[via Old Norse and old Irish from Latin]

cross- *prefix*
1 across; crossing something (as in *crossbar*). **2** from two different kinds (as in *cross-breed*).

crossbar *noun* (*plural* **crossbars**)
a horizontal bar, especially between two uprights.

crossbow *noun* (*plural* **crossbows**)
a powerful bow with a mechanism for pulling and releasing the string.
[so called because the bow is mounted across the stock]

cross-breed *verb* (**cross-breeds, cross-breeding, cross-bred**)
breed by mating an animal with one of a different kind. **cross-breed** *noun*
(Compare *hybrid.*)

crosse *noun* (*plural* **crosses**)
a hooked stick with a net across it, used in lacrosse. [French]

cross-examine *verb* (**cross-examines, cross-examining, cross-examined**)
cross-question someone, especially in a lawcourt. **cross-examination** *noun*

cross-eyed *adjective*
with eyes that look or seem to look towards the nose.

crossfire *noun*
lines of gunfire that cross each other.

crossing *noun* (*plural* **crossings**)
a place where people can cross a road, railway, etc.

cross-legged *adjective* & *adverb*
with ankles crossed and knees spread apart.

crosspatch *noun* (*plural* **crosspatches**)
a bad-tempered person.

cross-question *verb* (**cross-questions, cross-questioning, cross-questioned**)
question someone carefully in order to test answers given to previous questions.

cross-reference *noun* (*plural* **cross-references**)
a note telling people to look at another part of a book etc. for more information.

crossroads *noun* (*plural* **crossroads**)
a place where two or more roads cross one another.

cross-section *noun* (*plural* **cross-sections**)
1 a drawing of something as if it has been cut through. **2** a typical sample.

crosswise *adverb* & *adjective*
with one thing crossing another.

crossword *noun* (*plural* crosswords)
short for **crossword puzzle**, a puzzle in
which words have to be guessed from clues
and then written into the blank squares in
a diagram.

crotch *noun* (*plural* crotches)
the part between the legs where they join
the body; a similar angle in a forked part.
[a different spelling of *crutch*]

crotchet *noun* (*plural* crotchets)
a note in music, which usually represents
one beat (written ♩).
[from French, = small hook]

crotchety *adjective*
bad-tempered.
[from an old meaning of *crotchet* = whim]

crouch *verb* (crouches, crouching, crouched)
lower your body, with your arms and legs
bent. [origin unknown]

croup (*say* kroop) *noun*
a disease causing a hard cough and
difficulty in breathing.
[imitating the sound]

crow[1] *noun* (*plural* crows)
a large black bird.
as the crow flies in a straight line.
[from Old English]

crow[2] *verb* (crows, crowing, crowed or crew)
1 make a shrill cry as a cock does. 2 boast;
be triumphant. **crow** *noun*
[imitating the sound]

crowbar *noun* (*plural* crowbars)
an iron bar used as a lever. [because the
end is shaped like a crow's beak]

crowd *noun* (*plural* crowds)
a large number of people in one place.
crowd *verb* (crowds, crowding, crowded)
1 come together in a crowd. 2 cram; fill
uncomfortably full. [from Old English]

crown *noun* (*plural* crowns)
1 an ornamental headdress worn by a king
or queen. 2 (often **Crown**) the sovereign,
This land belongs to the Crown. 3 the
highest part, *the crown of the road.* 4 a

former coin worth 5 shillings (25p).
Crown Prince or **Crown Princess** the heir to
the throne.

crown *verb* (crowns, crowning, crowned)
1 place a crown on someone as a symbol of
royal power or victory. 2 form or cover or
decorate the top of something. 3 reward;
make a successful end to something, *Our
efforts were crowned with victory.* 4 (*slang*)
hit someone on the head.
[from Latin *corona* = garland or crown]

Crown Court *noun* (*plural* Crown Courts)
a lawcourt where criminal cases are tried.

crow's nest *noun* (*plural* crow's nests)
a lookout platform high up on a ship's
mast.

crucial (*say* kroo-shal) *adjective*
most important. **crucially** *adverb*
[from Latin *crucis* = of a cross]

crucible *noun* (*plural* crucibles)
a melting pot for metals. [from Latin]

crucifix *noun* (*plural* crucifixes)
a model of the Cross or of Jesus Christ on
the Cross. [same origin as *crucify*]

crucify *verb* (crucifies, crucifying, crucified)
put a person to death by nailing or binding
the hands and feet to a cross.
crucifixion *noun*
[from Latin *crucifigere* = fix to a cross]

crude *adjective*
1 in a natural state; not yet refined, *crude
oil.* 2 not well finished; rough, *a crude
carving.* 3 vulgar. **crudely** *adverb*, **crudity**
noun [from Latin *crudus* = raw, rough]

cruel *adjective* (crueller, cruellest)
causing pain or suffering.
cruelly *adverb*, **cruelty** *noun*
[from old French; related to *crude*]

cruet *noun* (*plural* cruets)
a set of small containers for salt, pepper,
oil, etc. for use at the table.
[from old French]

cruise *noun* (*plural* cruises)
a pleasure trip in a ship.
cruise *verb* (cruises, cruising, cruised)
1 sail or travel at a moderate speed. 2 have
a cruise. [from Dutch *kruisen* = to cross]

cruiser noun (plural cruisers)
1 a fast warship. 2 a large motor boat.

crumb noun (plural crumbs)
a tiny piece of bread, etc.
[from Old English]

crumble verb (crumbles, crumbling, crumbled)
break or fall into small fragments.
crumbly adjective
[from Old English; related to crumb]

crumpet noun (plural crumpets)
a soft flat cake made with yeast, eaten toasted with butter. [origin unknown]

crumple verb (crumples, crumpling, crumpled)
1 crush or become crushed into creases.
2 collapse loosely.
[from Old English crump = crooked]

crunch verb (crunches, crunching, crunched)
crush something noisily, for example between your teeth.
crunch noun (plural crunches)
a crunching sound. **crunchy** adjective
the crunch (informal) a crucial event or turning point.
[imitating the sound]

Crusade noun (plural Crusades)
a military expedition made by Christians in the Middle Ages to recover Palestine from the Muslims who had conquered it.
Crusader noun

crusade noun (plural crusades)
a campaign against something bad.
[from Latin crux = cross]

crush verb (crushes, crushing, crushed)
1 press something so that it gets broken or harmed. 2 squeeze tightly. 3 defeat.
crush noun (plural crushes)
1 a crowd of people pressed together. 2 a drink made with crushed fruit.
[from old French]

crust noun (plural crusts)
1 the hard outer layer of something, especially bread. 2 the rocky outer layer of the earth. [from Latin crusta = rind, shell]

crustacean (say krust-ay-shon) noun (plural crustaceans)
an animal with a shell, e.g. a crab.
[same origin as crust]

crusty adjective (crustier, crustiest)
1 having a crisp crust. 2 having a harsh or irritable manner. **crustiness** noun

crutch noun (plural crutches)
a support like a long walking stick for helping a lame person to walk.
[from Old English]

cry noun (plural cries)
1 a loud wordless sound expressing pain, grief, joy, etc. 2 a shout. 3 crying, Have a good cry.
cry verb (cries, crying, cried)
1 shed tears; weep. 2 call out loudly.
[from old French]

crypt noun (plural crypts)
a room under a church.
[same origin as cryptic]

cryptic adjective
hiding its meaning in a puzzling way.
cryptically adverb
[from Greek kryptos = hidden]

cryptogram noun (plural cryptograms)
something written in cipher.
[from Greek kryptos = hidden, + -gram]

crystal noun (plural crystals)
1 a transparent colourless mineral rather like glass. 2 very clear high-quality glass.
3 a small solid piece of certain substances, crystals of snow and ice. **crystalline** adjective
[from Greek krystallos = ice]

crystallize verb (crystallizes, crystallizing, crystallized)
1 form into crystals. 2 become definite in form. **crystallization** noun

crystallized fruit noun
fruit preserved in sugar.

cub noun (plural cubs)
a young lion, tiger, fox, bear, etc.
[origin unknown]

Cub or **Cub Scout** (plural Cubs, Cub Scouts)
a member of the junior branch of the Scout Association.

cubby hole *noun* (*plural* **cubby holes**)
a small compartment.
[from an old word *cub* = coop, hutch]

cube *noun* (*plural* **cubes**)
1 something that has six equal square sides. **2** the number produced by multiplying something by itself twice, *The cube of 3 is 3 × 3 × 3 = 27.*
cube *verb* (**cubes, cubing, cubed**)
1 multiply a number by itself twice, *4 cubed is 4 × 4 × 4 = 64.* **2** cut something into small cubes. [from Greek]

cube root *noun* (*plural* **cube roots**)
the number that gives a particular number if it is multiplied by itself twice, *The cube root of 27 is 3.*

cubic *adjective*
three-dimensional.
cubic foot, cubic metre, etc., the volume of a cube with sides that are one foot or one metre etc. long.

cubicle *noun* (*plural* **cubicles**)
a compartment of a room. [originally = bedroom: from Latin *cubare* = lie down]

cuckoo *noun* (*plural* **cuckoos**)
a bird that makes a sound like 'cuck-oo'.
[imitating its call]

cucumber *noun* (*plural* **cucumbers**)
a long green-skinned vegetable eaten raw or pickled. [from Latin]

cud *noun*
half-digested food that a cow etc. brings back from its first stomach to chew again.
[from Old English]

cuddle *verb* (**cuddles, cuddling, cuddled**)
put your arms closely round a person or animal that you love. **cuddly** *adjective*
[origin unknown]

cudgel *noun* (*plural* **cudgels**)
a short thick stick used as weapon.
cudgel *verb* (**cudgels, cudgelling, cudgelled**)
beat with a cudgel.
cudgel your brains think hard about a problem.
[from Old English]

cue[1] *noun* (*plural* **cues**)
something said or done that acts as a signal for an actor etc. to say or do something.
[origin unknown]

cue[2] *noun* (*plural* **cues**)
a long stick for striking the ball in billiards or snooker. [a different spelling of *queue* (because of its long, thin shape)]

cuff *noun* (*plural* **cuffs**)
1 the end of a sleeve that fits round the wrist. **2** hitting somebody with your hand; a slap.
cuff *verb* (**cuffs, cuffing, cuffed**)
hit somebody with your hand.
[origin unknown]

cuisine (*say* kwiz-een) *noun* (*plural* **cuisines**)
a style of cooking. [French, = kitchen]

cul-de-sac *noun* (*plural* **culs-de-sac**)
a street with an opening at one end only; a dead end. [French, = bottom of a sack]

-cule *suffix*
forms diminutives (e.g. *molecule* = little mass). [from Latin]

culinary *adjective*
to do with cooking. [from Latin *culinarius* = to do with the kitchen]

cull *verb* (**culls, culling, culled**)
1 select and use, *culling lines from several poems.* **2** pick out and kill surplus animals from a flock. **cull** *noun*
[from Latin *colligere* = collect]

culminate *verb* (**culminates, culminating, culminated**)
reach its highest or last point. **culmination** *noun* [from Latin *culmen* = summit]

culpable *adjective*
deserving blame.
[from Latin *culpare* = to blame]

culprit *noun* (*plural* **culprits**)
the person who has done something wrong.
[from old French]

cult *noun* (*plural* **cults**)
1 a religious sect. **2** devotion to a person or a thing by a lot of people.
[from Latin *cultus* = worship]

cultivate verb (cultivates, cultivating, cultivated)
1 use land to grow crops. 2 grow or develop things by looking after them. **cultivation** noun, **cultivator** noun
[same origin as culture]

culture noun (plural cultures)
1 appreciation and understanding of literature, art, music, etc. 2 customs and traditions, West Indian culture.
3 improvement by care and training, physical culture. 4 cultivating things.
cultural adjective [from Latin colere = cultivate, look after, worship]

cultured adjective
educated to appreciate literature, art, music, etc.

cultured pearl noun (plural cultured pearls)
a pearl formed by an oyster when a speck of grit etc. is put into its shell.

culvert noun (plural culverts)
a drain that passes under a road or railway etc. [origin unknown]

cumbersome adjective
clumsy to carry or manage.
[from encumber + -some]

cumin noun
a plant with spicy seeds that are used for flavouring foods. [from Greek]

cummerbund noun (plural cummerbunds)
a broad sash. [from Urdu]

cumulative adjective
accumulating; increasing by continuous additions. [from Latin cumulus = heap]

cunning adjective
1 clever at deceiving people. 2 cleverly designed or planned.
cunning noun
1 skill in deceiving people; craftiness.
2 skill or ingenuity. [from Old Norse]

cup noun (plural cups)
1 a small bowl-shaped container for drinking from. 2 anything shaped like a cup. 3 a goblet-shaped ornament given as a prize. **cupful** noun

cup verb (cups, cupping, cupped)
form into the shape of a cup, cup your hands. [from Latin]

cupboard noun (plural cupboards)
a piece of furniture with a door, for storing things.
[originally = sideboard: from cup + board]

cupidity (say kew-pid-it-ee) noun
greed for gaining money or possessions.
[from Latin cupido = desire]

cupola (say kew-pol-a) noun (plural cupolas)
a small dome on a roof. [Italian]

cur noun (plural curs)
a scruffy or bad-tempered dog.
[from Old Norse]

curable adjective
able to be cured.

curate noun (plural curates)
a member of the clergy who helps a vicar.
[from Latin cura = care]

curative (say kewr-at-iv) adjective
helping to cure illness.

curator (say kewr-ay-ter) noun (plural curators)
a person in charge of a museum or other collection. [same origin as cure]

curb verb (curbs, curbing, curbed)
restrain, curb your impatience.
curb noun (plural curbs)
a restraint, Put a curb on spending.
[from old French]

USAGE: Do not confuse with kerb.

curd noun or **curds** plural noun
a thick substance formed when milk turns sour. [origin unknown]

curdle verb (curdles, curdling, curdled)
form into curds.
make someone's blood curdle horrify or terrify them.

cure verb (cures, curing, cured)
1 get rid of someone's illness. 2 stop something bad. 3 treat something in order to preserve it, Fish can be cured in smoke.

cure noun (plural cures)
1 something that cures a person or thing; a remedy. 2 curing; being cured, *We cannot promise a cure.*
[from Latin *curare* = care for, cure]

curfew noun (plural curfews)
a time or signal after which people must remain indoors until the next day.
[from old French *cuevrefeu*, literally = cover fire (from an old law saying that all fires should be covered or put out by a certain time each evening)]

curio noun (plural curios)
an object that is a curiosity.
[short for *curiosity*]

curiosity noun (plural curiosities)
1 being curious. 2 something unusual and interesting.

curious adjective
1 wanting to find out about things; inquisitive. 2 strange; unusual.
curiously adverb
[from Latin]

curl noun (plural curls)
a curve or coil, e.g. of hair.
curl verb (curls, curling, curled)
form into curls.
curl up sit or lie with knees drawn up.
[from old Dutch]

curler noun (plural curlers)
a device for curling the hair.

curlew noun (plural curlews)
a wading bird with a long curved bill.
[from old French]

curling noun
a game played on ice with large flat stones.
[from *curl* (because the stones are made to 'curl round' opponents' stones to get to the target)]

curly adjective
having curls.

currant noun (plural currants)
1 a small black dried grape used in cookery. 2 a small round red, black, or white berry.
[from old French *raisins de Courauntz* = grapes from Corinth (a city in Greece)]

USAGE: Do not confuse with *current*.

currency noun (plural currencies)
1 the money in use in a country. 2 the general use of something, *Some words have no currency now.* [from *current*]

current adjective
happening now; used now. **currently** adverb
current noun (plural currents)
1 water or air etc. moving in one direction. 2 the flow of electricity along a wire etc. or through something.
[from Latin *currens* = running]

USAGE: Do not confuse with *currant*.

curriculum noun (plural curricula)
a course of study in a school or university.
[Latin, = running, course]

curriculum vitae (*say* veet-I) noun (plural curricula vitae)
a brief account of a person's education, career, etc., which he or she sends when applying for a job. [Latin, = course of life]

curry[1] noun (plural curries)
food cooked with spices that taste hot.
curried adjective [from Tamil *kari* = sauce]

curry[2] verb (curries, currying, curried)
curry favour seek to win favour by flattering someone.
[from old French]

curse noun (plural curses)
1 a call or prayer for a person or thing to be harmed; the evil produced by this.
2 something very unpleasant. 3 an angry word or words.
curse verb (curses, cursing, cursed)
1 make a curse. 2 use a curse against a person or thing.
be cursed with something suffer from it.
[origin unknown]

cursor noun (plural cursors)
a movable indicator, usually a flashing light, on a VDU screen.
[Latin, = runner]

cursory *adjective*
hasty and not thorough, *a cursory
inspection.* **cursorily** *adverb*
[same origin as *cursor*]

curt *adjective*
brief and hasty or rude, *a curt reply.* **curtly**
adverb, **curtness** *noun*
[from Latin *curtus* = cut short]

curtail *verb* (**curtails, curtailing, curtailed**)
1 cut short, *The lesson was curtailed.*
2 reduce, *We must curtail our spending.*
curtailment *noun*
[from French; related to *curt*]

curtain *noun* (*plural* **curtains**)
1 a piece of material hung at a window or
door. 2 the large cloth screen hung at the
front of a stage. [from old French]

curtsy *noun* (*plural* **curtsies**)
a movement of respect made by women
and girls, putting one foot behind the other
and bending the knees.
curtsy *verb* (**curtsies, curtsying, curtsied**)
make a curtsy.
[a different spelling of *courtesy*]

curvature *noun* (*plural* **curvatures**)
curving; a curved shape.

curve *verb* (**curves, curving, curved**)
bend smoothly.
curve *noun* (*plural* **curves**)
a curved line or shape. **curvy** *adjective*
[from Latin]

cushion *noun* (*plural* **cushions**)
1 a bag, usually of cloth, filled with soft
material so that it is comfortable to sit on
or lean against. 2 anything soft or springy
that protects or supports something, *The
hovercraft travels on a cushion of air.*
cushion *verb* (**cushions, cushioning,
cushioned**)
1 supply with cushions, *cushioned seats.*
2 protect from the effects of a knock or
shock etc., *His fur hat cushioned the blow.*
[from old French]

cushy *adjective* (*informal*)
pleasant and easy, *a cushy job.*
[from Urdu *kushi* = pleasure]

cusp *noun* (*plural* **cusps**)
a pointed end where two curves meet, e.g.
the tips of the crescent moon.
[from Latin *cuspis* – point]

custard *noun* (*plural* **custards**)
1 a sweet yellow sauce made with milk. 2 a
pudding made with beaten eggs and milk.
[from old French]

custodian *noun* (*plural* **custodians**)
a person who has custody of something; a
keeper.

custody *noun*
1 care and supervision; guardianship.
2 imprisonment.
take into custody arrest.
[from Latin *custos* = guardian]

custom *noun* (*plural* **customs**)
1 the usual way of behaving or doing
something. 2 regular business from
customers. [from Latin *consuescere*
= become accustomed]

customary *adjective*
according to custom; usual.
customarily *adverb*

custom-built *adjective*
made according to a customer's order.

customer *noun* (*plural* **customers**)
a person who uses a shop, bank, or other
business. [originally a person who
customarily used the same shop etc.]

customs *plural noun*
1 taxes charged on goods brought into a
country. 2 the place at a port or airport
where officials examine your luggage.
[= taxes customarily charged, from *custom*]

cut *verb* (**cuts, cutting, cut**)
1 divide or wound or separate something
by using a knife, axe, scissors, etc. 2 make
a thing shorter or smaller; remove part of
something, *They are cutting all their prices.*
3 divide a pack of playing cards. 4 hit a ball
with a chopping movement. 5 go through
or across something. 6 stay away from
something deliberately, *She cut her music
lesson.* 7 make a sound recording. 8 switch
off electrical power or an engine etc.
cut a corner pass round it very closely.
cut and dried already decided.
cut in interrupt.

cut *noun* (*plural* **cuts**)
1 cutting; the result of cutting. **2** a small wound. **3** (*slang*) a share.
be a cut above something be superior.
[from a Scandinavian language]

cute *adjective* (*informal*)
1 attractive. **2** clever. **cutely** *adverb*, **cuteness** *noun* [from *acute*]

cuticle (*say* kew-tik-ul) *noun* (*plural* **cuticles**)
the skin round a nail. [from Latin]

cutlass *noun* (*plural* **cutlasses**)
a short sword with a broad curved blade. [same origin as *cutlery*]

cutlery *noun*
knives, forks, and spoons.
[from Latin *culter* = knife]

cutlet *noun* (*plural* **cutlets**)
a thick slice of meat for cooking.
[from French]

cut-out *noun* (*plural* **cut-outs**)
a shape cut out of paper, cardboard, etc.

cutter *noun* (*plural* **cutters**)
1 a person or thing that cuts. **2** a small fast sailing ship.

cutting *noun* (*plural* **cuttings**)
1 a steep-sided passage cut through high ground for a road or railway. **2** something cut out of a newspaper or magazine. **3** a piece cut from a plant to form a new plant.

cuttlefish *noun* (*plural* **cuttlefish**)
a sea creature that sends out a black liquid when attacked. [from Old English]

-cy *suffix*
forms nouns showing action or condition etc. (e.g. *piracy, infancy*).
[from Latin or Greek]

cyanide *noun*
a very poisonous chemical. [from Greek]

cycle *noun* (*plural* **cycles**)
1 a bicycle or motorcycle. **2** a series of events that are regularly repeated in the same order. **cyclic** *adjective*, **cyclical** *adjective*
cycle *verb* (**cycles, cycling, cycled**)
ride a bicycle or tricycle. **cyclist** *noun*
[from Greek *kyklos* = circle]

cyclone *noun* (*plural* **cyclones**)
a wind that rotates round a calm central area. **cyclonic** *adjective*
[from Greek *kykloma* = wheel]

cygnet (*say* sig-nit) *noun* (*plural* **cygnets**)
a young swan. [from Latin *cycnus* = swan]

cylinder *noun* (*plural* **cylinders**)
an object with straight sides and circular ends. **cylindrical** *adjective*
[from Greek *kylindros* = roller]

cymbal *noun* (*plural* **cymbals**)
a percussion instrument consisting of a metal plate that is hit to make a ringing sound. [from Greek]

USAGE: Do not confuse with *symbol*.

cynic (*say* sin-ik) *noun* (*plural* **cynics**)
a person who believes that people's reasons for doing things are selfish or bad, and shows this by sneering at them. **cynical** *adjective*, **cynically** *adverb*, **cynicism** *noun*
[from Greek *kynikos* = surly]

cypress *noun* (*plural* **cypresses**)
an evergreen tree with dark leaves.
[from Greek]

cyst (*say* sist) *noun* (*plural* **cysts**)
an abnormal swelling containing fluid or soft matter. [from Latin]

czar (*say* zar) *noun* (*plural* **czars**)
a different spelling of *tsar*.

Dd

dab *noun* (*plural* **dabs**)
1 a quick gentle touch, usually with something wet. **2** a small lump, *a dab of butter*.
dab *verb* (**dabs, dabbing, dabbed**)
touch something quickly and gently.
[imitating the sound of dabbing something wet]

dabble *verb* (**dabbles, dabbling, dabbled**)
1 splash something about in water. **2** do something as a hobby, *dabble in chemistry*.
[from *dab*]

dachshund (*say* daks-huund) *noun* (*plural* dachshunds)
a small dog with a long body and very short legs. [German, = badger-dog (because dachshunds were used to dig badgers out of their sets)]

dad or **daddy** *noun* (*plural* dads, daddies) (*informal*)
father. [imitating the sounds a child makes when it first tries to speak]

daddy-long-legs *noun* (*plural* daddy-long-legs)
a crane-fly.

daffodil *noun* (*plural* daffodils)
a yellow flower that grows from a bulb. [from *asphodel*, another plant with yellow flowers]

daft *adjective* (*informal*)
silly or stupid. [from Old English]

dagger *noun* (*plural* daggers)
a pointed knife with two sharp edges, used as a weapon. [from old French]

dahlia (*say* day-lee-a) *noun* (*plural* dahlias)
a garden plant with brightly-coloured flowers. [named after Andreas *Dahl*, a Swedish botanist]

daily *adverb* & *adjective*
every day.

dainty *adjective* (daintier, daintiest)
small, delicate, and pretty. **daintily** *adverb*, **daintiness** *noun* [via old French from Latin *dignitas* = value, beauty]

dairy *noun* (*plural* dairies)
a place where milk, butter, etc. are produced or sold. [from Old English]

dais (*say* day-iss) *noun* (*plural* daises)
a low platform, especially at the end of a room. [from old French]

daisy *noun* (*plural* daisies)
a small flower with white petals and a yellow centre.
[from *day's eye* (because the daisy opens in daylight and closes at night)]

dale *noun* (*plural* dales)
a valley. [from Old English]

dally *verb* (dallies, dallying, dallied)
dawdle or waste time. [from old French]

dam[1] *noun* (*plural* dams)
a wall built to hold water back.
dam *verb* (dams, damming, dammed)
hold water back with a dam. [from Old English]

dam[2] *noun* (*plural* dams)
the mother of a horse or dog etc. (Compare *sire*.) [from *dame*]

damage *noun*
harm or injury done to something.
damage *verb* (damages, damaging, damaged)
harm or spoil something. [from Latin *damnum* = loss]

damages *plural noun*
money paid as compensation for an injury or loss.

Dame *noun* (*plural* Dames)
the title of a lady who has been given the equivalent of a knighthood.

dame *noun* (*plural* dames)
a comic middle-aged woman in a pantomime, usually played by a man. [from Latin *domina* = lady]

damn *verb* (damns, damning, damned)
curse. [from Latin *damnare* = condemn]

damnation *noun*
being condemned to hell.

damned *adjective*
hateful or annoying.

damp *adjective*
slightly wet; not quite dry. **damply** *adverb*, **dampness** *noun*
damp *noun*
moisture in the air or on a surface or all through something.
damp *verb* (damps, damping, damped)
1 make something slightly wet. **2** reduce the strength of something, *The defeat damped their enthusiasm.*
[from a Germanic language]

damp course *noun* (*plural* damp courses)
a layer of material built into a wall to prevent dampness in the ground from rising.

dampen *verb* (dampens, dampening, dampened)
1 make something damp. 2 reduce the strength of something.

damper *noun* (*plural* dampers)
a metal plate that can be moved to increase or decrease the amount of air flowing into a fire or furnace etc.
put a damper on reduce people's enthusiasm or enjoyment.
[from *damp*]

damsel *noun* (*plural* damsels) (*old use*)
a young woman. [from old French]

damson *noun* (*plural* damsons)
a small dark-purple plum.
[from Latin *damascenum prunum* = plum from Damascus (a city in Syria)]

dance *verb* (dances, dancing, danced)
move about in time to music.
dance *noun* (*plural* dances)
1 a set of movements used in dancing. 2 a piece of music for dancing to. 3 a party or gathering where people dance. **dancer** *noun*
[from old French]

dandelion *noun* (*plural* dandelions)
a yellow wild flower with jagged leaves.
[from French *dent-de-lion* = tooth of a lion (because the jagged edges of the leaves looked like lion's teeth)]

dandruff *noun*
tiny white flakes of dead skin in a person's hair. [origin unknown]

dandy *noun* (*plural* dandies)
a man who likes to look very smart.
[origin unknown]

danger *noun* (*plural* dangers)
something that is not safe or could harm you. [from old French]

dangerous *adjective*
likely to kill or harm you.
dangerously *adverb*

dangle *verb* (dangles, dangling, dangled)
hang or swing loosely.
[from a Scandinavian language]

dank *adjective*
damp and chilly.
[from a Scandinavian language]

dapper *adjective*
dressed neatly and smartly.
[from old German or old Dutch]

dappled *adjective*
marked with patches of a different colour.
[probably from Old Norse *depill* = spot]

dare *verb* (dares, daring, dared)
1 be brave or bold enough to do something.
2 challenge a person to do something risky.
dare *noun* (*plural* dares)
a challenge to do something risky.
[from Old English]

daredevil *noun* (*plural* daredevils)
a person who is very bold and reckless.

dark *adjective*
1 with little or no light. 2 not light in colour, *a dark suit*. 3 having dark hair.
4 sinister or evil.
darkly *adverb*, **darkness** *noun*
dark *noun*
1 absence of light, *Cats can see in the dark*.
2 the time when darkness has come, *She went out after dark*. [from Old English]

darken *verb* (darkens, darkening, darkened)
make or become dark.

darkroom *noun* (*plural* darkrooms)
a room kept dark for developing and printing photographs.

darling *noun* (*plural* darlings)
someone who is loved very much.
[from Old English *deorling* = little dear]

darn *verb* (darns, darning, darned)
mend a hole by weaving threads across it.
darn *noun* (*plural* darns)
a place that has been darned.
[from Old English *diernan* = hide]

dart *noun* (*plural* darts)
1 an object with a sharp point, thrown at a target. 2 a darting movement. 3 a tapering tuck stitched in something to make it fit.
dart *verb* (darts, darting, darted)
run suddenly and quickly.
[from old French]

darts *noun*
a game in which darts are thrown at a circular board (**dartboard**).

dash verb (dashes, dashing, dashed)
1 run quickly; rush. 2 throw a thing
violently against something, *The storm
dashed the ship against the rocks.*
dash noun (*plural* dashes)
1 a short quick run; a rush. 2 energy or
liveliness. 3 a small amount, *Add a dash of
brandy.* 4 a short line (—) used in writing
or printing. [origin unknown]

dashboard noun (*plural* dashboards)
a panel with dials and controls in front of
the driver of a car etc. [originally a board
on the front of a carriage to keep out mud,
which dashed against it]

dashing adjective
lively and showy.

dastardly adjective
contemptible and cowardly.
[originally = dull, stupid: from *dazed*]

data (*say* day-ta) noun
pieces of information.

USAGE: Strictly speaking, this word is a
plural noun (the singular is *datum*), so it
should be used with a plural verb: *Here are
the data.* However, the word is widely used
nowadays as if it were a singular noun and
most people do not regard this as wrong:
Here is the data.

database noun (*plural* databases)
a store of information held in a computer.

date[1] noun (*plural* dates)
1 the time when something happens or
happened or was written, stated as the day,
month, and year (or any of these). 2 an
appointment to meet someone, especially
someone of the opposite sex.
date verb (dates, dating, dated)
1 give a date to something. 2 have existed
from a particular time, *The church dates
from 1604.* 3 seem old-fashioned. [from
Latin *data* = given (at a certain time)]

date[2] noun (*plural* dates)
a small sweet brown fruit that grows on a
kind of palm tree. [from Greek]

daub verb (daubs, daubing, daubed)
paint or smear something clumsily.
daub noun
[from Latin *dealbare* = whitewash, plaster]

daughter noun (*plural* daughters)
a girl or woman who is someone's child.
[from Old English]

daughter-in-law noun (*plural* daughters-
in-law)
a son's wife.

daunt verb (daunts, daunting, daunted)
make somebody afraid or discouraged.
[from Latin *domitare* = to tame]

dauntless adjective
brave; not to be daunted. **dauntlessly** adverb

dauphin (*say* daw-fin) noun (*plural*
dauphins)
the title of the eldest son of each of the
kings of France between 1349 and 1830.
[old French]

dawdle verb (dawdles, dawdling, dawdled)
go slowly and lazily. **dawdler** noun
[origin unknown]

dawn noun (*plural* dawns)
the time when the sun rises.
dawn verb (dawns, dawning, dawned)
1 begin to grow light in the morning.
2 begin to be realized, *The truth dawned on
them.* [from Old English]

day noun (*plural* days)
1 the 24 hours between midnight and the
next midnight. 2 the light part of this time.
3 a particular day, *sports day.* 4 a period of
time, *in Queen Victoria's day.*
[from Old English]

daybreak noun
dawn.

daydream noun (*plural* daydreams)
pleasant thoughts of something you would
like to happen.
daydream verb (daydreams, daydreaming,
daydreamed)
have daydreams.

daylight noun
1 the light of day. 2 dawn.

dazed adjective
unable to think or see clearly. **daze** noun
[from Old Norse *dasathr* = weary]

dazzle *verb* (dazzles, dazzling, dazzled)
1 make a person unable to see clearly because of too much bright light. 2 amaze or impress a person by a splendid display. [from *daze*]

de- *prefix*
1 removing (as in *defrost*). 2 down, away (as in *descend*). 3 completely (as in *denude*). [from old French; related to *dis-*]

deacon *noun* (*plural* deacons)
1 a member of the clergy ranking below bishops and priests. 2 (in some Churches) a church officer who is not a member of the clergy. **deaconess** *noun*
[from Greek *diakonos* = servant]

dead *adjective*
1 no longer alive. 2 not lively. 3 not functioning; no longer in use. 4 exact or complete, *a dead loss*. [from Old English]

deaden *verb* (deadens, deadening, deadened)
make pain or noise etc. weaker.

dead end *noun* (*plural* dead ends)
1 a road or passage with one end closed. 2 a situation where there is no chance of making progress.

dead heat *noun* (*plural* dead heats)
a race in which two or more winners finish exactly together.

deadline *noun* (*plural* deadlines)
a time limit.
[originally this meant a line round an American military prison; if prisoners went beyond it they could be shot]

deadlock *noun* (*plural* deadlocks)
a situation in which no progress can be made. [from *dead* + *lock*¹]

deadly *adjective* (deadlier, deadliest)
likely to kill.

deaf *adjective*
1 unable to hear. 2 unwilling to hear. **deafness** *noun* [from Old English]

deafen *verb* (deafens, deafening, deafened)
make somebody become deaf, especially by a very loud noise.

deal¹ *verb* (deals, dealing, dealt)
1 hand something out; give. 2 give out cards for a card game. 3 do business; trade, *He deals in scrap metal*. **dealer** *noun*
deal with 1 be concerned with, *This book deals with words and meanings*. 2 do what is needed, *deal with the problem*.

deal *noun* (*plural* deals)
1 an agreement or bargain. 2 someone's turn to deal at cards.
a good deal or **a great deal** a large amount. [from Old English *daelan* = divide, share out]

deal² *noun*
sawn fir or pine wood.
[from old Dutch *dele* = plank]

dean *noun* (*plural* deans)
1 an important member of the clergy in a cathedral etc. 2 the head of a university, college, or department. **deanery** *noun*
[from Latin]

dear *adjective*
1 loved very much. 2 a polite greeting in letters, *Dear Sir*. 3 expensive. **dearly** *adverb*
[from Old English]

dearth (*say* derth) *noun* (*plural* dearths)
a scarcity. [from *dear* (because scarcity made food etc. expensive)]

death *noun* (*plural* deaths)
dying; the end of life. [from Old English]

deathly *adjective* & *adverb*
like death.

death trap *noun* (*plural* death traps)
a very dangerous place.

debar *verb* (debars, debarring, debarred)
forbid or ban, *He was debarred from the contest*. [from *de-* + French *barrer* = to bar]

debase *verb* (debases, debasing, debased)
reduce the quality or value of something. **debasement** *noun* [from *de-* + *base*²]

debatable *adjective*
questionable; that can be argued against.

debate *noun* (*plural* debates)
a formal discussion.
debate *verb* (debates, debating, debated)
hold a debate. **debater** *noun*
[from old French]

debilitating *adjective*
causing weakness.

debility (*say* dib-il-it-ee) *noun*
weakness of the body. [from Latin]

debit *noun* (*plural* **debits**)
an entry in an account-book showing how
much money is owed. (Compare *credit*.)
debit *verb* (**debits, debiting, debited**)
enter something as a debit in an account-
book. [from Latin *debitum* = what is owed]

debonair (*say* deb-on-**air**) *adjective*
cheerful and confident. [from French *de
bon air* = of good disposition]

debris (*say* **deb**-ree) *noun*
scattered broken pieces of something;
rubbish left behind.
[from French *débris* = broken down]

debt (*say* det) *noun* (*plural* **debts**)
something that you owe someone.
in debt owing money etc.
[same origin as *debit*]

debtor (*say* **det**-or) *noun* (*plural* **debtors**)
a person who owes money to someone.

début (*say* **day**-bew) *noun* (*plural* **débuts**)
someone's first public appearance.
[from French *débuter* = begin]

deca- *prefix*
ten (as in *decathlon*). [from Greek]

decade (*say* **dek**-ayd) *noun* (*plural* **decades**)
a period of ten years. [from old French]

decadent (*say* **dek**-a-dent) *adjective*
falling to a lower standard of morality.
decadence *noun* [same origin as *decay*]

decaffeinated *adjective*
(of coffee or tea) with the caffeine removed.

decamp *verb* (**decamps, decamping,
decamped**)
1 pack up and leave a camp. **2** go away
suddenly or secretly. [from French]

decant (*say* dik-**ant**) *verb* (**decants,
decanting, decanted**)
pour wine etc. gently from one container
into another. [from Latin]

decanter (*say* dik-**ant**-er) *noun* (*plural*
decanters)
a decorative glass bottle into which wine
etc. is poured for serving. [from *decant*]

decapitate *verb* (**decapitates, decapitating,
decapitated**)
cut someone's head off; behead.
decapitation *noun*
[from *de-* + Latin *caput* = head]

decathlon *noun* (*plural* **decathlons**)
an athletic contest in which each
competitor takes part in ten events.
[from *deca-* + Greek *athlon* = contest]

decay *verb* (**decays, decaying, decayed**)
1 go bad; rot. **2** become less good or less
strong. **decay** *noun*
[from old French *decaoir* = fall down]

decease (*say* dis-**eess**) *noun*
death. [from *de-* + Latin *cedere* = go]

deceased *adjective*
dead.

deceit (*say* dis-**eet**) *noun* (*plural* **deceits**)
making a person believe something that is
not true.
deceitful *adjective*, **deceitfully** *adverb*

deceive *verb* (**deceives, deceiving, deceived**)
make a person believe something that is
not true. **deceiver** *noun* [from Latin]

decent *adjective*
1 respectable and honest. **2** reasonable or
adequate. **3** (*informal*) kind. **decently**
adverb, **decency** *noun* [from Latin]

deception *noun* (*plural* **deceptions**)
deceiving someone.
deceptive *adjective*, **deceptively** *adverb*

deci- (*say* **dess**-ee) *prefix*
one-tenth (as in *decimetre*).
[same origin as *decimal*]

decibel (*say* **dess**-ib-el) *noun* (*plural*
decibels)
a unit for measuring the loudness of sound.
[originally one-tenth of the unit called a
bel]

decide verb (decides, deciding, decided)
1 make up your mind; make a choice.
2 settle a contest or argument.
decider noun [from Latin]

decided adjective
1 having clear and definite opinions.
2 noticeable, a decided difference.
decidedly adverb

deciduous (say dis-id-yoo-us) adjective
a deciduous tree is one that loses its leaves
in autumn. [from Latin decidere = fall off]

decimal adjective
using tens or tenths.
decimal noun (plural decimals)
a decimal fraction.
[from Latin decimus = tenth]

decimal fraction noun (plural decimal
fractions)
a fraction with tenths shown as numbers
after a dot ($\frac{3}{10}$ is 0.3; $1\frac{1}{2}$ is 1.5).

decimalize verb (decimalizes, decimalizing,
decimalized)
1 express something as a decimal.
2 change something, especially coinage, to
a decimal system. **decimalization** noun

decimal point noun (plural decimal
points)
the dot in a decimal fraction.

decimate (say dess-im-ayt) verb (decimates,
decimating, decimated)
kill or destroy a large part of, The famine
decimated the population.
[from Latin decimare = kill every tenth
man (this was the ancient Roman
punishment for an army guilty of mutiny
or other serious crime)]

decipher (say dis-I-fer) verb (deciphers,
deciphering, deciphered)
1 decode. 2 work out the meaning of
something written badly.
decipherment noun

decision noun (plural decisions)
1 deciding; what you have decided.
2 determination.

decisive (say dis-I-siv) adjective
1 that settles or ends something, a decisive
battle. 2 full of determination; resolute.
decisively adverb, **decisiveness** noun

deck noun (plural decks)
1 a floor on a ship or bus. 2 a pack of
playing cards. 3 a turntable on a record
player.

deck verb (decks, decking, decked)
decorate with something, The front of the
house was decked with flags and balloons.
[from old Dutch dec = a covering]

deckchair noun (plural deckchairs)
a folding chair with a canvas or plastic
seat. [because they were used on the decks
of passenger ships]

declaim verb (declaims, declaiming,
declaimed)
make a speech etc. loudly and
dramatically. **declamation** noun
[from de- + Latin clamare = to shout]

declare verb (declares, declaring, declared)
1 say something clearly or firmly. 2 tell
customs officials that you have goods on
which you ought to pay duty. 3 end a
cricket innings before all the batsmen are
out. **declaration** noun
declare war announce that you are starting
a war against someone.
[from de- + Latin clarare = make clear]

decline verb (declines, declining, declined)
1 refuse. 2 become weaker or smaller.
3 slope downwards. 4 state the forms of a
noun, pronoun, or adjective that
correspond to particular cases, numbers,
and genders.
decline noun (plural declines)
a gradual decrease or loss of strength.
[from de- + Latin clinare = bend]

decode verb (decodes, decoding, decoded)
work out the meaning of something
written in code. **decoder** noun

decompose verb (decomposes,
decomposing, decomposed)
decay. **decomposition** noun

decompression noun
reducing air pressure.

decontamination noun
getting rid of poisonous chemicals or
radioactive material from a place, clothes,
etc.

décor (*say* day-kor) *noun*
the style of furnishings and decorations
used in a room etc.
[French, from *décorer* = decorate]

decorate *verb* (decorates, decorating,
decorated)
1 make something look more beautiful or
colourful. 2 put fresh paint or paper on
walls. 3 give somebody a medal. **decoration**
noun, **decorator** *noun*, **decorative** *adjective*
[from Latin *decor* = beauty]

decorous (*say* dek-er-us) *adjective*
polite and dignified. **decorously** *adverb*
[from Latin *decorus* = suitable, proper]

decorum (*say* dik-or-um) *noun*
polite and dignified behaviour.
[same origin as *decorous*]

decoy (*say* dee-koi) *noun* (*plural* decoys)
something used to tempt a person or
animal into a trap or into danger.
decoy (*say* dik-oi) *verb* (decoys, decoying,
decoyed)
tempt a person or animal into a trap etc.
[from Dutch]

decrease *verb* (decreases, decreasing,
decreased)
make or become smaller or fewer.
decrease *noun* (*plural* decreases)
decreasing; the amount by which
something decreases.
[from *de-* + Latin *crescere* = grow]

decree *noun* (*plural* decrees)
an official order or decision.
decree *verb* (decrees, decreeing, decreed)
make a decree. [from Latin *decretum*
= what has been decided]

decrepit (*say* dik-rep-it) *adjective*
old and weak. **decrepitude** *noun*
[from Latin *decrepitus* = creaking]

dedicate *verb* (dedicates, dedicating,
dedicated)
1 devote to a special use, *She dedicated
herself to her work.* 2 name a person as a
mark of respect, e.g. at the beginning of a
book. **dedication** *noun* [from Latin]

deduce *verb* (deduces, deducing, deduced)
work something out by reasoning.
deducible *adjective*
[from *de-* + Latin *ducere* = to lead]

deduct *verb* (deducts, deducting, deducted)
subtract part of something.
[same origin as *deduce*]

deductible *adjective*
able to be deducted.

deduction *noun* (*plural* deductions)
1 deducting; something deducted.
2 deducing; something deduced.

deed *noun* (*plural* deeds)
1 something that someone has done; an act.
2 a legal document. [from Old English]

deem *verb* (deems, deeming, deemed)
(*formal*)
consider, *I should deem it an honour to be
invited.* [from Old English]

deep *adjective*
1 going a long way down or back or in, *a
deep well*; *deep cupboards*. 2 measured from
top to bottom or front to back, *a hole six feet
deep*. 3 intense or strong, *deep colours*; *deep
feelings*. 4 low-pitched, not shrill, *a deep
voice*. **deeply** *adverb*, **deepness** *noun*
[from Old English]

deepen *verb* (deepens, deepening,
deepened)
make or become deeper.

deep-freeze *noun* (*plural* deep-freezes)
a freezer.

deer *noun* (*plural* deer)
a fast-running graceful animal, the male of
which usually has antlers.
[from Old English *deor* = an animal]

deface *verb* (defaces, defacing, defaced)
spoil the surface of something, e.g. by
scribbling on it. **defacement** *noun*
[from old French]

defame *verb* (defames, defaming, defamed)
attack a person's good reputation; slander
or libel. **defamation** (*say* def-a-may-shon)
noun, **defamatory** (*say* dif-am-a-ter-ee)
adjective
[from *de-* + Latin *fama* = fame, reputation]

default *verb* (defaults, defaulting, defaulted)
fail to do what you have agreed to do.
defaulter *noun*
default *noun* (*plural* defaults)
failure to do something. [from old French]

defeat verb (defeats, defeating, defeated)
1 win a victory over someone. 2 baffle; be too difficult for someone.

defeat noun (plural defeats)
1 defeating someone. 2 being defeated; a lost game or battle.
[from Latin disfacere = undo, destroy]

defeatist noun (plural defeatists)
a person who expects to be defeated. defeatism noun

defecate (say dee-fik-ayt) verb (defecates, defecating, defecated)
get rid of faeces from your body. defecation noun [from de- + faeces]

defect (say dif-ekt or dee-fekt) noun (plural defects)
a flaw.

defect (say dif-ekt) verb (defects, defecting, defected)
desert your own country etc. and join the enemy. defection noun, defector noun [from Latin deficere = fail, leave, undo]

defective adjective
having defects; incomplete. defectiveness noun

defence noun (plural defences)
1 defending something. 2 something that defends or protects. 3 a reply put forward by a defendant.

defenceless adjective
having no defences.

defend verb (defends, defending, defended)
1 protect, especially against an attack.
2 try to prove that a statement is true or that an accused person is not guilty. defender noun [from Latin]

defendant noun (plural defendants)
a person accused of something in a lawcourt.

defensible adjective
able to be defended. defensibility noun

defensive adjective
used or done for defence; protective. defensively adverb
on the defensive ready to defend yourself.

defer[1] verb (defers, deferring, deferred)
postpone. deferment noun, deferral noun
[from old French; related to differ]

defer[2] verb (defers, deferring, deferred)
give way to a person's wishes or authority; yield. [from Latin]

deference (say def-er-ens) noun
polite respect. deferential (say def-er-en-shal) adjective, deferentially adverb
[from defer[2]]

defiant adjective
defying; openly disobedient.
defiantly adverb, defiance noun

deficiency noun (plural deficiencies)
1 a lack or shortage. 2 a defect.
deficient adjective [same origin as defect]

deficit (say def-iss-it) noun (plural deficits)
1 the amount by which a total is smaller than what is required. 2 the amount by which spending is greater than income.
[same origin as defect]

defile verb (defiles, defiling, defiled)
make a thing dirty or impure.
defilement noun [from an old word defoul]

define verb (defines, defining, defined)
1 explain what a word or phrase means.
2 show clearly what something is; specify.
3 show a thing's outline. definable adjective
[from de- + Latin finis = limit]

definite adjective
1 clearly stated; exact, Fix a definite time.
2 certain or settled, Is it definite that we are to move? definitely adverb
definite article the word 'the'.
[from Latin definitus = defined]

definition noun (plural definitions)
1 a statement of what a word or phrase means or of what a thing is. 2 being distinct; clearness of outline (e.g. in a photograph).

definitive (say dif-in-it-iv) adjective
1 finally settling something; conclusive, a definitive victory. 2 not able to be bettered, the definitive history of the British cinema.

deflate verb (deflates, deflating, deflated)
1 let out air from a tyre or balloon etc.
2 make someone feel less proud or less

confident. **3** reduce or reverse inflation.
deflation *noun*, **deflationary** *adjective*
[from *de-* + *inflate*]

deflect *verb* (deflects, deflecting, deflected)
make something turn aside. **deflection**
noun, **deflector** *noun*
[from *de-* + Latin *flectere* = to bend]

deforest *verb* (deforests, deforesting,
deforested)
clear away the trees from an area.
deforestation *noun*

deform *verb* (deforms, deforming,
deformed)
spoil a thing's shape or appearance.
deformation *noun*
[from *de-* + Latin *forma* = shape, form]

deformed *adjective*
badly or abnormally shaped.
deformity *noun*

defraud *verb* (defrauds, defrauding,
defrauded)
take something from a person by fraud;
cheat or swindle.
[from *de-* + Latin *fraudere* = defraud]

defray *verb* (defrays, defraying, defrayed)
provide money to pay costs or expenses.
defrayal *noun*
[from *de-* + old French *frais* = cost]

defrost *verb* (defrosts, defrosting, defrosted)
thaw out something frozen.

deft *adjective*
skilful and quick. **deftly** *adverb*,
deftness *noun* [from Old English]

defunct *adjective*
no longer in use or existing.
[from Latin *defunctus* = finished]

defuse *verb* (defuses, defusing, defused)
1 remove the fuse from a bomb etc. **2** make
a situation less dangerous or tense.

defy *verb* (defies, defying, defied)
1 resist something openly; refuse to obey,
They defied the law. **2** challenge a person to
do something you believe cannot be done, *I
defy you to prove this.* **3** prevent something
being done, *The door defied all efforts to
open it.* [from *de-* + Latin *fidus* = faithful]

degenerate *verb* (degenerates,
degenerating, degenerated)
become worse, especially morally.
degeneration *noun*

degenerate *adjective*
having become immoral or bad.
degeneracy *noun* [from Latin]

degrade *verb* (degrades, degrading,
degraded)
1 humiliate or dishonour someone.
2 reduce to a simpler molecular form.
degradation (*say* deg-ra-**day**-shon) *noun*
[from *de-* + Latin *gradus* = grade]

degree *noun* (*plural* degrees)
1 a unit for measuring temperature. **2** a
unit for measuring angles. **3** extent, *to some
degree.* **4** an award to someone at a
university or college who has successfully
finished a course.
[from *de-* + Latin *gradus* = grade]

dehydrated *adjective*
dried up, with all moisture removed.
dehydration *noun*
[from *de-* + Greek *hydor* = water]

de-ice *verb* (de-ices, de-icing, de-iced)
remove ice from a windscreen etc.
de-icer *noun*

deign (*say* dayn) *verb* (deigns, deigning,
deigned)
be gracious enough to do something;
condescend. [from Latin]

deity (*say* **dee**-it-ee or **day**-it-ee) *noun*
(*plural* **deities**)
a god or goddess. [from Latin *deus* = god]

déjà vu (*say* day-zha **vew**) *noun*
a feeling that you have already
experienced what is happening now.
[French, = already seen]

dejected *adjective*
sad or depressed. **dejectedly** *adverb*,
dejection *noun*
[from *de-* + Latin *-jectum* = cast]

delay *verb* (delays, delaying, delayed)
1 make someone or something late.
2 postpone.
delay *noun* (*plural* delays)
delaying; the time for which something is
delayed, *a two-hour delay.*
[from old French]

delectable *adjective*
delightful. **delectably** *adverb*
[same origin as *delight*]

delegate (*say* del-ig-at) *noun* (*plural* delegates)
a person who represents others and acts on their instructions.
delegate (*say* del-ig-ayt) *verb* (delegates, delegating, delegated)
1 appoint someone as a delegate, *We delegated Jones to represent us.* **2** entrust, *We delegated the work to Jones.*
[from Latin *delegare* = entrust]

delegation (*say* del-ig-ay-shon) *noun* (*plural* delegations)
1 delegating. **2** a group of delegates.

delete (*say* dil-eet) *verb* (deletes, deleting, deleted)
strike out something written or printed.
deletion *noun* [from Latin]

deliberate (*say* dil-ib-er-at) *adjective*
1 done on purpose; intentional. **2** slow and careful. **deliberately** *adverb*
deliberate (*say* dil-ib-er-ayt) *verb* (deliberates, deliberating, deliberated)
discuss or think carefully. **deliberation** *noun* [from *de-* + Latin *librare* = weigh]

deliberative *adjective*
for deliberating or discussing things.

delicacy *noun* (*plural* delicacies)
1 being delicate. **2** a delicious food.

delicate *adjective*
1 fine and graceful, *delicate embroidery.* **2** fragile and easily damaged. **3** pleasant and not strong or intense. **4** becoming ill easily. **5** using or needing great care, *a delicate situation.* **delicately** *adverb*, **delicateness** *noun* [from Latin]

delicatessen *noun* (*plural* delicatessens)
a shop that sells cooked meats, cheeses, salads, etc.
[from German, = delicacies to eat]

delicious *adjective*
tasting or smelling very pleasant.
deliciously *adverb* [from Latin]

delight *verb* (delights, delighting, delighted)
1 please someone greatly. **2** take great pleasure in something.

delight *noun* (*plural* delights)
great pleasure.
delightful *adjective*, **delightfully** *adverb*
[from Latin *delectare* = entice]

delinquent (*say* dil-ing-kwent) *noun* (*plural* delinquents)
someone who breaks the law or commits an offence. **delinquent** *adjective*, **delinquency** *noun*
[from Latin *delinquere* = offend]

delirium (*say* dil-irri-um) *noun*
1 a state of mental confusion and agitation during a feverish illness. **2** wild excitement. **delirious** *adjective*, **deliriously** *adverb* [Latin, = deranged]

deliver *verb* (delivers, delivering, delivered)
1 take letters or goods etc. to someone's house or place of work. **2** give a speech or lecture etc. **3** help with the birth of a baby. **4** aim or strike a blow or an attack. **5** rescue; set free. **deliverer** *noun*, **deliverance** *noun*, **delivery** *noun*
[from *de-* + Latin *liberare* = set free]

dell *noun* (*plural* dells)
a small valley with trees.
[from Old English]

delphinium *noun* (*plural* delphiniums)
a garden plant with tall spikes of flowers, usually blue. [from Greek]

delta *noun* (*plural* deltas)
a triangular area at the mouth of a river where it spreads into branches. [shaped like the Greek letter delta (= D), written Δ]

delude *verb* (deludes, deluding, deluded)
deceive or mislead someone.
[from Latin *deludere* = play unfairly]

deluge *noun* (*plural* deluges)
1 a large flood. **2** a heavy fall of rain. **3** something coming in great numbers, *a deluge of questions.*
deluge *verb* (deluges, deluging, deluged)
overwhelm by a deluge. [from old French]

delusion *noun* (*plural* delusions)
a false belief.

de luxe *adjective*
of very high quality. [French, = of luxury]

delve *verb* (delves, delving, delved)
search deeply, e.g. for information, *delving into history*. [from Old English]

demagogue (*say* dem-a-gog) *noun* (*plural* demagogues)
a leader who wins support by making emotional speeches rather than by careful reasoning. [from Greek *demos* = people + *agogos* = leading]

demand *verb* (demands, demanding, demanded)
1 ask for something firmly or forcefully. 2 need, *It demands skill.*
demand *noun* (*plural* demands)
1 a firm or forceful request. 2 a desire to have or buy something, *There is a great demand for computers.*
in demand wanted or needed.
[from *de-* + Latin *mandare* = to order]

demarcation (*say* dee-mar-**kay**-shon) *noun*
marking the boundary or limits of something. [from Spanish]

demean *verb* (demeans, demeaning, demeaned)
lower a person's dignity, *I wouldn't demean myself to ask for it!* [from *de-* + *mean²*]

demeanour (*say* dim-**een**-er) *noun* (*plural* demeanours)
a person's behaviour or manner.
[from old French]

demented *adjective*
driven mad; crazy.
[from *de-* + Latin *mentis* = of the mind]

demerara (*say* dem-er-**air**-a) *noun*
light-brown cane sugar. [named after Demerara in Guyana, South America]

demerit *noun* (*plural* demerits)
a fault or defect. [from old French]

demi- *prefix*
half (as in *demisemiquaver*). [from French]

demigod *noun* (*plural* demigods)
a partly divine being.

demise (*say* dim-**I'z**) *noun* (*formal*)
death. [from old French]

demisemiquaver *noun* (*plural* demisemiquavers)
a note in music, equal in length to one-eighth of a crotchet.

demist *verb* (demists, demisting, demisted)
remove misty condensation from a windscreen etc. **demister** *noun*

demo *noun* (*plural* demos) (*informal*)
a demonstration.

democracy *noun* (*plural* democracies)
1 government of a country by representatives elected by the whole people. 2 a country governed in this way.
democrat *noun*, **democratic** *adjective*, **democratically** *adverb*
[from Greek *demos* = people, + *-cracy*]

Democrat *noun* (*plural* Democrats)
a member of the Democratic Party in the USA.

demolish *verb* (demolishes, demolishing, demolished)
1 knock a building down and break it up. 2 destroy something completely.
demolition *noun*
[from *de-* + Latin *moliri* = build]

demon *noun* (*plural* demons)
1 a devil; an evil spirit. 2 a fierce or forceful person. **demonic** (*say* dim-**on**-ik) *adjective* [from Greek *daimon* = a spirit]

demonstrable (*say* dem-on-**strab**-ul) *adjective*
able to be shown or proved.
demonstrably *adverb*

demonstrate *verb* (demonstrates, demonstrating, demonstrated)
1 show or prove something. 2 take part in a demonstration. **demonstrator** *noun*
[from *de-* + Latin *monstrare* = to show]

demonstration *noun* (*plural* demonstrations)
1 demonstrating; showing how to do or work something. 2 a meeting or procession etc. held to show everyone what you think about something.

demonstrative (*say* dim-on-**strat**-iv) *adjective*
1 showing or proving something.
2 showing feelings or affections openly.

3 (in grammar) pointing out the person or thing referred to. *This, that, these,* and *those* are demonstrative adjectives and pronouns. **demonstratively** *adverb,* **demonstrativeness** *noun*

demoralize *verb* (demoralizes, demoralizing, demoralized)
dishearten someone; weaken someone's confidence or morale. **demoralization** *noun* [from *de-* + *morale*]

demote *verb* (demotes, demoting, demoted)
reduce a person to a lower position or rank. **demotion** *noun* [from *de-* + *promote*]

demur (*say* dim-er) *verb* (demurs, demurring, demurred)
raise objections.
[from Latin *demorari* = delay]

demure *adjective*
shy and modest. **demurely** *adverb,* **demureness** *noun* [origin unknown]

den *noun* (*plural* dens)
1 a lair. **2** a person's private room. **3** a place where something illegal happens, *a gambling den*. [from Old English]

deniable *adjective*
able to be denied.

denial *noun* (*plural* denials)
denying or refusing something.

denier (*say* den-yer) *noun* (*plural* deniers)
a unit for measuring the fineness of silk, rayon, or nylon thread. [French]

denim *noun*
a kind of strong, usually blue, cotton cloth used to make jeans etc.
[from French *serge de Nim* = serge from Nîmes (a town in southern France)]

denizen (*say* den-iz-en) *noun* (*plural* denizens)
an inhabitant, *Lions are denizens of the jungle*. [from old French *deinz* = within]

denomination *noun* (*plural* denominations)
1 a name or title. **2** a religious group with a special name, *Baptists, Methodists, and*

other denominations. **3** a unit of weight or of money, *coins of small denomination*.
[from *de-* + Latin *nominare* = to name]

denominator *noun* (*plural* denominators)
the number below the line in a fraction, showing how many parts the whole is divided into, e.g. 4 in ¼. (Compare *numerator*.)

denote *verb* (denotes, denoting, denoted)
mean or indicate, *In road signs, P denotes a car park*. **denotation** *noun*
[from *de-* + Latin *notare* = mark out]

dénouement (*say* day-noo-mahn) *noun* (*plural* dénouements)
the final outcome of a plot or story, revealed at the end.
[French, = unravelling]

denounce *verb* (denounces, denouncing, denounced)
speak strongly against something; accuse, *They denounced him as a spy*. **denunciation** *noun*
[from *de-* + Latin *nuntiare* = announce]

dense *adjective*
1 thick; packed close together, *dense fog*. **2** stupid. **densely** *adverb* [from Latin]

density *noun* (*plural* densities)
1 thickness. **2** (in physics) the proportion of mass to volume.

dent *noun* (*plural* dents)
a hollow left in a surface where something has pressed or hit it.
dent *verb* (dents, denting, dented)
make a dent in something.
[a different spelling of *dint*]

dental *adjective*
to do with the teeth or with dentistry.
[from Latin *dentalis* = to do with a tooth]

dentist *noun* (*plural* dentists)
a person who is trained to treat teeth, fill or extract them, fit false ones, etc. **dentistry** *noun* [from French *dent* = tooth]

denture *noun* (*plural* dentures)
a set of false teeth. [French]

denude *verb* (**denudes, denuding, denuded**)
make bare or naked; strip something away.
denudation *noun*
[from *de-* + Latin *nudare* = to bare]

denunciation *noun* (*plural* **denunciations**)
denouncing.

deny *verb* (**denies, denying, denied**)
1 say that something is not true. **2** refuse to
give or allow something, *deny a request.*
[from *de-* + Latin *negare* = say no]

deodorant (*say* dee-oh-der-ant) *noun*
(*plural* **deodorants**)
a substance that removes smells.

deodorize *verb* (**deodorizes, deodorizing,
deodorized**)
remove smells. **deodorization** *noun*
[from *de-* + Latin *odor* = a smell]

depart *verb* (**departs, departing, departed**)
go away; leave.
[from old French *départir* = separate]

department *noun* (*plural* **departments**)
one section of a large organization or shop.
departmental *adjective*
[from French *département* = division]

department store *noun* (*plural*
department stores)
a large shop that sells many different kinds
of goods.

departure *noun* (*plural* **departures**)
departing.

depend *verb* (**depends, depending,
depended**)
depend on 1 rely on, *We depend on your
help.* **2** be controlled by something else,
*Whether we can picnic depends on the
weather.*
[from *de-* + Latin *pendere* = hang]

dependable *adjective*
reliable.

dependant *noun* (*plural* **dependants**)
a person who depends on another,
especially financially, *She has*

two *dependants.*

USAGE: Note that the spelling ends in *-ant*
for this noun but *-ent* for the adjective
dependent.

dependency *noun* (*plural* **dependencies**)
1 dependence. **2** a country that is
controlled by another.

dependent *adjective*
depending, *She has two dependent children;
they are dependent on her.* **dependence** *noun*

USAGE: See note at *dependant.*

depict *verb* (**depicts, depicting, depicted**)
1 show something in a painting or drawing
etc. **2** describe. **depiction** *noun*
[from *de-* + Latin *pictum* = painted]

deplete (*say* dip-leet) *verb* (**depletes,
depleting, depleted**)
reduce the amount of something by using
up large amounts. **depletion** *noun*
[from *de-* + Latin *pletum* = filled]

deplore *verb* (**deplores, deploring, deplored**)
be very upset or annoyed by something.
deplorable *adjective*, **deplorably** *adverb*
[from *de-* + Latin *plorare* = weep]

deploy *verb* (**deploys, deploying, deployed**)
place troops etc. in good positions so that
they are ready to be used effectively.
deployment *noun* [from French]

deport *verb* (**deports, deporting, deported**)
send an unwanted foreign person out of a
country. **deportation** *noun*
[from *de-* + Latin *portare* = carry]

deportment *noun*
a person's manner of standing, walking,
and behaving. [from old French]

depose *verb* (**deposes, deposing, deposed**)
remove a person from power.
[from old French *deposer* = put down]

deposit *noun* (*plural* **deposits**)
1 an amount of money paid into a bank etc.
2 money paid as a first instalment. **3** a
layer of solid matter in or on the earth.

deposit *verb* (deposits, depositing, deposited)
1 put something down. 2 pay money as a deposit. **depositor** *noun*
[from *de-* + Latin *positum* = placed]

deposition *noun* (*plural* depositions) a written piece of evidence, given under oath.

depot (*say* dep-oh) *noun* (*plural* depots)
1 a place where things are stored. 2 a headquarters. [same origin as *deposit*]

depraved *adjective*
behaving wickedly; of bad character. **depravity** *noun* [from *de-* + Latin *pravus* = perverse, wrong]

deprecate (*say* dep-rik-ayt) *verb* (deprecates, deprecating, deprecated)
say that you disapprove of something. **deprecation** *noun* [from Latin *deprecari* = keep away misfortune by prayer]

USAGE: Do not confuse with *depreciate*.

depreciate (*say* dip-ree-shee-ayt) *verb* (depreciates, depreciating, depreciated)
make or become lower in value. **depreciation** *noun*
[from *de-* + Latin *pretium* = price]

USAGE: Do not confuse with *deprecate*.

depredation (*say* dep-rid-**ay**-shon) *noun* (*plural* depredations)
the act of plundering or damaging something. (Compare *predator*.)
[from *de-* + Latin *praedere* = to plunder]

depress *verb* (depresses, depressing, depressed)
1 make somebody sad. 2 lower the value of something, *Threat of war depressed prices.* 3 press down, *Depress the lever.*
depressive *adjective*
[from Latin *depressum* = pressed down]

depression *noun* (*plural* depressions)
1 a great sadness or feeling of hopelessness. 2 a long period when trade is very slack because no one can afford to buy things. 3 a shallow hollow in the ground or on a surface. 4 an area of low air pressure which may bring rain. 5 pressing something down.

deprive *verb* (deprives, depriving, deprived)
take or keep something away from somebody. **deprival** *noun*, **deprivation** *noun*
[from *de-* + Latin *privare* = rob]

depth *noun* (*plural* depths)
1 being deep; how deep something is. 2 the deepest or lowest part.
in depth thoroughly.
out of your depth 1 in water that is too deep to stand in. 2 trying to do something that is too difficult for you.
[from *deep*]

deputation *noun* (*plural* deputations)
a group of people sent as representatives of others.

depute (*say* dip-**yoot**) *verb* (deputes, deputing, deputed)
1 appoint a person to do something, *We deputed John to take the message.* 2 assign or delegate a task to someone, *We deputed the task to him.* [from old French]

deputize *verb* (deputizes, deputizing, deputized)
act as someone's deputy.

deputy *noun* (*plural* deputies)
a person appointed to act as a substitute for another. [from French *député* = deputed]

derail *verb* (derails, derailing, derailed)
cause a train to leave the rails. **derailment** *noun* [from *de-* + French *rail* = rail]

deranged *adjective*
insane. **derangement** *noun*
[from *de-* + French *rang* = rank]

derelict (*say* **derri**-likt) *adjective*
abandoned and left to fall into ruin.
dereliction *noun*
[from *de-* + Latin *relictum* = left behind]

deride *verb* (derides, deriding, derided)
laugh at with contempt or scorn; ridicule. [from *de-* + Latin *ridere* = to laugh]

de rigueur (*say* der rig-**er**) *adjective*
proper; required by custom or etiquette.
[French, literally = of strictness]

derision *noun*
scorn or ridicule. **derisive** (*say* dir-**I**-siv) *adjective*, **derisively** *adverb*
[same origin as *deride*]

derisory *adjective*
1 scornful. 2 so small as to be ridiculous, *a derisory offer.* [same origin as *deride*]

derivation *noun* (*plural* **derivations**)
1 deriving. 2 the origin of a word from another language or from a simple word to which a prefix or suffix is added; etymology.

derivative *adjective*
derived from something. **derivative** *noun*

derive *verb* (**derives, deriving, derived**)
1 obtain something from a source, *She derived great enjoyment from music.* 2 form or originate from something, *Some English words are derived from Latin words.* [from *de-* + Latin *rivus* = a stream]

dermatology *noun*
the study of the skin and its diseases. **dermatologist** *noun*
[from Greek *derma* = skin, + *-logy*]

dermis *noun*
the layer of skin below the epidermis. [Latin, from Greek *derma* = skin]

derogatory (*say* di-**rog**-at-er-ee) *adjective*
scornful or disparaging.
[from Latin *derogare* = make smaller]

derrick *noun* (*plural* **derricks**)
1 a kind of crane for lifting things. 2 a tall framework holding the machinery used in drilling an oil well etc.
[originally a gallows; Derrick was the surname of a London hangman]

derv *noun*
diesel fuel for lorries etc. [from the initials of 'diesel-engined road vehicle']

dervish *noun* (*plural* **dervishes**)
a member of a Muslim religious group who vowed to live a life of poverty.
[from Persian *darvish* = poor]

descant *noun* (*plural* **descants**)
a tune sung or played above the main tune.
[from *dis-* + Latin *cantus* = song]

descend *verb* (**descends, descending, descended**)
go down.
be descended from have as an ancestor;

come by birth from a certain person or family.
[from *de-* + Latin *scandere* = climb]

descendant *noun* (*plural* **descendants**)
a person who is descended from someone.

descent *noun* (*plural* **descents**)
descending.

describe *verb* (**describes, describing, described**)
1 say what someone or something is like. 2 draw in outline; move in a pattern, *The orbit of the Earth around the Sun describes an ellipse.* **description** *noun*, **descriptive** *adjective* [from *de-* + Latin *scribere* = write]

desecrate (*say* **dess**-ik-rayt) *verb* (**desecrates, desecrating, desecrated**)
treat a sacred thing irreverently. **desecration** *noun* [from *de-* + *consecrate*]

desert (*say* **dez**-ert) *noun* (*plural* **deserts**)
a large area of dry often sandy land.
desert (*say* diz-ert) *verb* (**deserts, deserting, deserted**)
abandon; leave a person or place without intending to return.
deserter *noun*, **desertion** *noun*
[from Latin *desertus* = abandoned]

desert island *noun* (*plural* **desert islands**)
an uninhabited island.

deserts (*say* diz-erts) *plural noun*
what a person deserves, *He got his deserts.*
[from *deserve*]

deserve *verb* (**deserves, deserving, deserved**)
have a right to something; be worthy of something. **deservedly** *adverb* [from Latin *deservire* = serve someone well]

desiccated *adjective*
dried. [from Latin]

USAGE: Note the spelling of this word. It has one 's' and two 'c's.

design *noun* (*plural* **designs**)
1 a drawing that shows how something is to be made. 2 the way something is made or arranged. 3 lines and shapes that form a decoration; a pattern. 4 a mental plan or scheme.
have designs on plan to get hold of.

design *verb* (designs, designing, designed)
1 draw a design for something. 2 plan or intend something for a special purpose. **designer** *noun*
[from *de-* + Latin *signare* = mark out]

designate *verb* (designates, designating, designated)
mark or describe as something particular, *They designated the river as the boundary.* **designation** *noun*

designate *adjective*
appointed to a job but not yet doing it, *the bishop designate.* [same origin as *design*]

desirable *adjective*
1 causing people to desire it; worth having. 2 worth doing; advisable. **desirability** *noun*

desire *noun* (*plural* desires)
a feeling of wanting something very much. **desirous** *adjective*

desire *verb* (desires, desiring, desired)
have a desire for something. [from Latin]

desist (*say* diz-**ist**) *verb* (desists, desisting, desisted)
stop doing something. [from Latin]

desk *noun* (*plural* desks)
1 a piece of furniture with a flat top and often drawers, used when writing or reading etc. 2 a counter at which a cashier or receptionist sits. [from Latin]

desolate *adjective*
1 lonely and sad. 2 uninhabited. **desolation** *noun* [from Latin *desolare* = abandon]

despair *noun*
a feeling of hopelessness.

despair *verb* (despairs, despairing, despaired)
feel despair.
[from *de-* + Latin *sperare* = to hope]

despatch *verb* (despatches, despatching, despatched)
a different spelling of *dispatch*.
despatch *noun*

desperado (*say* dess-per-**ah**-doh) *noun* (*plural* desperadoes)
a reckless criminal. [from *desperate*]

desperate *adjective*
1 extremely serious; hopeless, *a desperate situation.* 2 reckless and ready to do anything. **desperately** *adverb*, **desperation** *noun* [same origin as *despair*]

despicable *adjective*
deserving to be despised; contemptible.

despise *verb* (despises, despising, despised)
think someone or something is inferior or worthless.
[from *de-* + Latin *-spicere* = to look]

despite *preposition*
in spite of. [same origin as *despise*]

despondent *adjective*
sad or gloomy. **despondently** *adverb*, **despondency** *noun*
[from Latin *despondere* = give up, resign]

despot (*say* dess-pot) *noun* (*plural* despots)
a tyrant. **despotism** *noun*, **despotic** (*say* dis-**pot**-ik) *adjective*
[from Greek *despotes* = master]

dessert (*say* diz-**ert**) *noun* (*plural* desserts)
fruit or a sweet food served as the last course of a meal.
[from French *desservir* = clear the table]

dessertspoon *noun* (*plural* dessertspoons)
a medium-sized spoon used for eating puddings etc.

destination *noun* (*plural* destinations)
the place to which a person or thing is travelling. [same origin as *destiny*]

destined *adjective*
having as a destiny; intended.

destiny *noun* (*plural* destinies)
what will happen or has happened to somebody or something; fate.
[from Latin *destinare* = fix, settle]

destitute *adjective*
left without anything; living in extreme poverty. **destitution** *noun*
[from Latin *destitutus* = left in the lurch]

destroy verb (destroys, destroying, destroyed)
ruin or put an end to something.
destruction noun, **destructive** adjective
[from de- + Latin struere = pile up]

destroyer noun (plural destroyers)
a fast warship.

desultory (say dess-ul-ter-ee) adjective
casual and disconnected, desultory talk.
[from Latin desultorius = like an acrobat
(someone who leaps about)]

detach verb (detaches, detaching, detached)
unfasten or separate. **detachable** adjective,
detachment noun [from de- + attach]

detached adjective
1 separated. 2 not prejudiced; not involved
in something.

detached house noun (plural detached
houses)
a house that is not joined to another.

detail noun (plural details)
1 a very small part of a design or plan
or decoration etc. 2 a small piece of
information. **detailed** adjective
[from de- + French tailler = cut in pieces]

detain verb (detains, detaining, detained)
1 keep someone waiting. 2 keep someone
at a place. **detention** noun
[from de- + Latin tenere = hold]

detainee noun (plural detainees)
a person who is officially detained or kept
in custody.

detect verb (detects, detecting, detected)
discover. **detection** noun, **detector** noun
[from de- + Latin tegere = cover]

detective noun (plural detectives)
a person who investigates crimes.

detention noun (plural detentions)
1 detaining; being detained. 2 being made
to stay late in school as a punishment.
[same origin as detain]

deter verb (deters, deterring, deterred)
discourage or prevent a person from doing
something. **determent** noun
[from de- + Latin terrere = frighten]

detergent noun (plural detergents)
a substance used for cleaning or washing
things. [from de- + Latin tergere = to clean]

deteriorate (say dit-eer-ee-er-ayt) verb
(deteriorates, deteriorating, deteriorated)
become worse. **deterioration** noun
[from Latin deterior = worse]

determination noun
1 the firm intention to achieve what you
have decided to achieve. 2 determining or
deciding something.

determine verb (determines, determining,
determined)
1 decide, determine what is to be done.
2 find out; calculate, determine the height of
the mountain.
[from de- + Latin terminare = to limit]

determined adjective
full of determination; with your mind
firmly made up.

determiner noun (plural determiners)
a word (such as a, the, many) that modifies
a noun.

deterrent noun (plural deterrents)
something that may deter people, e.g. a
nuclear weapon that deters countries from
making war on the one that has it.
deterrence noun

detest verb (detests, detesting, detested)
dislike something very much; loathe.
detestable adjective, **detestation** noun
[from Latin]

detonate (say det-on-ayt) verb (detonates,
detonating, detonated)
explode or cause something to explode.
detonation noun, **detonator** noun
[from de- + Latin tonare = to thunder]

detour (say dee-toor) noun (plural detours)
a roundabout route instead of the normal
one. [from French détourner = turn away]

detract verb (detracts, detracting,
detracted)
lessen the amount or value, It will not
detract from our pleasure. **detraction** noun
[from de- + Latin tractus = pulled]

detriment (*say* det-rim-ent) *noun*
harm or disadvantage, *She worked long
hours, to the detriment of her health.*
[from Latin *detrimentum* = worn away]

detrimental (*say* det-rim-en-tal) *adjective*
harmful or disadvantageous.
detrimentally *adverb*

de trop (*say* der **troh**) *adjective*
not wanted; unwelcome.
[French, = too much]

deuce *noun* (*plural* **deuces**)
a score in tennis where both sides have 40
points and must gain two consecutive
points to win. [from old French *deus* = two]

devalue *verb* (**devalues**, **devaluing**,
devalued)
1 reduce a thing's value. **2** reduce the value
of a country's currency in relation to other
currencies or to gold. **devaluation** *noun*

devastate *verb* (**devastates**, **devastating**,
devastated)
ruin or cause great destruction to
something. **devastation** *noun* [from Latin]

develop *verb* (**develops**, **developing**,
developed)
1 make or become bigger or better. **2** come
gradually into existence, *Storms developed.*
3 begin to have or use, *They developed bad
habits.* **4** use an area of land for building
houses, shops, factories, etc. **5** treat
photographic film with chemicals so that
pictures appear. **developer** *noun*,
development *noun* [from French]

deviate (*say* **dee**-vee-ayt) *verb* (**deviates**,
deviating, **deviated**)
turn aside from a course or from what is
usual or true. **deviation** *noun*
[from *de-* + Latin *via* = way]

device *noun* (*plural* **devices**)
1 something made for a particular
purpose, *a device for opening tins.* **2** a
design used as a decoration or emblem.
leave someone to their own devices leave
them to do as they wish.
[same origin as *devise*]

devil *noun* (*plural* **devils**)
1 an evil spirit. **2** a wicked, cruel, or
annoying person. **devilish** *adjective*, **devilry**
noun [via Old English from Latin]

devilment *noun*
mischief.

devious (*say* **dee**-vee-us) *adjective*
1 roundabout; not direct, *a devious route.*
2 not straightforward; underhand.
deviously *adverb*, **deviousness** *noun*
[same origin as *deviate*]

devise *verb* (**devises**, **devising**, **devised**)
invent or plan. [from old French]

devoid *adjective*
lacking or without something, *His work is
devoid of merit.*
[from *de-* + old French *voider* = make void]

devolution *noun*
handing over power from central
government to local or regional
government. [same origin as *devolve*]

devolve *verb* (**devolves**, **devolving**,
devolved)
pass or be passed to a deputy or successor.
[from Latin *devolvere* = roll down]

devote *verb* (**devotes**, **devoting**, **devoted**)
give completely, *He devoted his time to
sport.*
[from *de-* + Latin *vovere* = to vow]

devoted *adjective*
very loving or loyal.

devotee (*say* dev-o-**tee**) *noun* (*plural*
devotees)
a person who is devoted to something; an
enthusiast.

devotion *noun*
great love or loyalty.

devotions *plural noun*
prayers.

devour *verb* (**devours**, **devouring**, **devoured**)
eat or swallow something hungrily or
greedily.
[from *de-* + Latin *vorare* = to swallow]

devout *adjective*
earnestly religious or sincere.
devoutly *adverb*, **devoutness** *noun*
[same origin as *devote*]

dew *noun*
tiny drops of water that form during the

night on surfaces of things in the open air.
dewdrop *noun*, **dewy** *adjective*
[from Old English]

dexterity (*say* deks-**terri**-tee) *noun*
skill in handling things.
[from Latin *dexter* = on the right-hand side]

dhoti *noun* (*plural* **dhotis**)
the loincloth worn by male Hindus. [Hindi]

di-¹ *prefix*
two; double (as in *dioxide*).
[from Greek *dis* = twice]

di-² *prefix*
1 not; the reverse of. 2 apart; separated. see
dis-.

dia- *prefix*
through (as in *diarrhoea*); across (as in
diagonal). [from Greek *dia* = through]

diabetes (*say* dy-a-**bee**-teez) *noun*
a disease in which there is too much
sugar in a person's blood.
diabetic (*say* dy-a-**bet**-ik) *adjective* & *noun*
[from Greek]

diabolical *adjective*
1 like a devil; very wicked. 2 very clever or
annoying. [from Latin *diabolus* = devil]

diadem (*say* **dy**-a-dem) *noun* (*plural*
diadems)
a crown or headband worn by a royal
person. [from Greek]

diagnose *verb* (**diagnoses, diagnosing,
diagnosed**)
find out what disease a person has or what
is wrong.
diagnosis *noun*, **diagnostic** *adjective*
[from *dia-* + Greek *gignoskein* = know]

diagonal (*say* dy-**ag**-on-al) *noun* (*plural*
diagonals)
a straight line joining opposite corners.
diagonal *adjective*, **diagonally** *adverb*
[from *dia-* + Greek *gonia* = angle]

diagram *noun* (*plural* **diagrams**)
a kind of drawing or picture that shows the
parts of something or how it works.
[from *dia-* + -*gram*]

dial *noun* (*plural* **dials**)
a circular object with numbers or letters
round it.
dial *verb* (**dials, dialling, dialled**)
telephone a number by turning a telephone
dial or pressing numbered buttons. [from
Latin *diale* = clock-face, from *dies* = day]

dialect *noun* (*plural* **dialects**)
the words and pronunciations used by
people in one district but not in the rest of
a country.
[from Greek *dialektos* = way of speaking]

dialogue *noun* (*plural* **dialogues**)
a conversation. [from Greek]

dialysis (*say* dy-**al**-iss-iss) *noun*
a way of removing harmful substances
from the blood by letting it flow through a
machine.
[from *dia-* + Greek *lysis* = loosening]

diameter (*say* dy-**am**-it-er) *noun* (*plural*
diameters)
1 a line drawn straight across a circle or
sphere and passing through its centre.
2 the length of this line. [from Greek
diametros = measuring across]

diametrically *adverb*
completely, *diametrically opposite*.

diamond *noun* (*plural* **diamonds**)
1 a very hard precious stone, a form of
carbon, that looks like clear glass. 2 a
shape with four equal sides and four angles
that are not right angles. 3 a playing card
with red diamond shapes on it.
[from Greek *adamas* = adamant (= a very
hard stone)]

diaper *noun* (*plural* **diapers**)
(*American*) a baby's nappy. [from Greek
diaspros = made of white cloth]

diaphanous (*say* dy-**af**-an-us) *adjective*
(of fabric) almost transparent.
[from *dia-* + Greek *phainein* = to show]

diaphragm (*say* **dy**-a-fram) *noun* (*plural*
diaphragms)
1 the muscular layer inside the body that
separates the chest from the abdomen and
is used in breathing. 2 a dome-shaped
contraceptive device that fits over the
cervix.
[from *dia-* + Greek *phragma* = fence]

diarist *noun* (*plural* diarists)
a person who keeps a diary.

diarrhoea (*say* dy-a-**ree**-a) *noun*
too frequent and too watery emptying of
the bowels.
[from *dia-* + Greek *rhoia* = a flow]

diary *noun* (*plural* diaries)
a book in which someone writes down
what happens each day.
[from Latin *dies* = day]

diatribe *noun* (*plural* diatribes)
a strong verbal attack. [French]

dice *noun*
(strictly this is the plural of **die²**, but it is
often used as a singular, plural **dice**) a
small cube marked with dots (1 to 6) on its
sides, used in games.
dice *verb* (dices, dicing, diced)
1 play gambling games using dice. 2 cut
meat, vegetables, etc. into small cubes.
[plural of *die²*]

dictate *verb* (dictates, dictating, dictated)
1 speak or read something aloud for
someone else to write down. 2 give orders
in a bossy way. **dictation** *noun*
[from Latin *dictare* = keep saying]

dictates (*say* dik-**tayts**) *plural noun*
orders or commands.

dictator *noun* (*plural* dictators)
a ruler who has unlimited power.
dictatorial (*say* dik-ta-**tor**-ee-al) *adjective*,
dictatorship *noun*

diction *noun*
a person's way of speaking words, *clear
diction*. [from Latin *dictio* = saying, word]

dictionary *noun* (*plural* dictionaries)
a book that contains words in alphabetical
order so that you can find out how to spell
them and what they mean.
[same origin as *diction*]

didactic (*say* dy-**dak**-tik) *adjective*
having the manner of someone who is
lecturing people. **didactically** *adverb*
[from Greek *didaktikos* = teaching]

diddle *verb* (diddles, diddling, diddled)
(*slang*)
cheat or swindle. [origin unknown]

didn't (*mainly spoken*)
did not.

die¹ *verb* (dies, dying, died)
1 stop living or existing. 2 stop burning or
functioning, *The fire had died down.*
[from Old Norse]

die² *noun* singular of **dice**. [from old French]

die³ *noun* (*plural* dies)
a device that stamps a design on coins etc.
or that cuts or moulds metal.
[from old French]

diehard *noun* (*plural* diehards)
a person who obstinately refuses to give up
old ideas or policies.
[from *die hard* = die painfully]

diesel (*say* **dee**-zel) *noun* (*plural* diesels)
1 an engine that works by burning oil in
compressed air. 2 fuel for this kind of
engine. [named after R. Diesel, a German
engineer, who invented it]

diet¹ *noun* (*plural* diets)
1 special meals that someone eats in order
to be healthy or to become less fat. 2 the
sort of foods usually eaten by a person or
animal.
diet *verb* (diets, dieting, dieted)
keep to a diet.
[from Greek *diaita* = way of life]

diet² *noun* (*plural* diets)
the parliament of certain countries (e.g.
Japan). [from Latin *dieta* = day's business]

dietitian (*say* dy-it-**ish**-an) *noun* (*plural*
dietitians)
an expert in diet and nutrition.

dif- *prefix*
1 not; the reverse of. 2 apart; separated. see
dis-.

differ *verb* (differs, differing, differed)
1 be different. 2 disagree.
[from *dif-* + Latin *ferre* = carry]

difference *noun* (*plural* differences)
1 being different; the way in which things
differ. 2 the remainder left after one
number is subtracted from another, *The
difference between 8 and 3 is 5.* 3 a
disagreement.

different *adjective*
unlike; not the same. **differently** *adverb*

USAGE: It is regarded as more acceptable to say *different from* rather than *different to*, which is common in less formal use. The phrase *different than* is used in American English but not in standard British English.

differential *noun* (*plural* **differentials**)
1 a difference in wages between one group of workers and another. 2 a differential gear.

differential gear *noun* (*plural* **differential gears**)
a system of gears that makes a vehicle's driving wheels revolve at different speeds when going round corners.

differentiate *verb* (**differentiates, differentiating, differentiated**)
1 make different, *These things differentiate one breed from another.* 2 distinguish; recognize differences, *We do not differentiate between them.*
differentiation *noun*

difficult *adjective*
needing a lot of effort or skill; not easy.
difficulty *noun*
[from *dif-* + Latin *facilis* = easy]

diffident (*say* dif-id-ent) *adjective*
shy and not self-confident; hesitating to put yourself or your ideas forward.
diffidently *adverb*, **diffidence** *noun*
[from *dif-* + Latin *fidentia* = confidence]

diffract *verb* (**diffracts, diffracting, diffracted**)
break up a beam of light etc.
diffraction *noun*
[from *dif-* + Latin *fractum* = broken]

diffuse (*say* dif-yooz) *verb* (**diffuses, diffusing, diffused**)
1 spread something widely or thinly, *diffused lighting.* 2 mix slowly, *diffusing gases.* **diffusion** *noun*
diffuse (*say* dif-yooss) *adjective*
1 spread widely; not concentrated. 2 using many words; not concise.
diffusely *adverb*, **diffuseness** *noun*
[from *dif-* + Latin *fusum* = poured]

dig *verb* (**digs, digging, dug**)
1 break up soil and move it; make a hole or tunnel by moving soil. 2 poke something in, *Dig a knife into it.* 3 seek or discover by investigating, *We dug up some facts.*
digger *noun*
dig *noun* (*plural* **digs**)
1 a piece of digging, especially an archaeological excavation. 2 a poke.
[probably from Old English]

digest (*say* dy-jest) *verb* (**digests, digesting, digested**)
1 soften and change food in the stomach etc. so that the body can absorb it. 2 take information into your mind and think it over. **digestible** *adjective*, **digestion** *noun*
digest (*say* dy-jest) *noun* (*plural* **digests**)
a summary of news, information, etc.
[from Latin]

digestive *adjective*
to do with digestion, *the digestive system.*

digestive biscuit *noun* (*plural* **digestive biscuits**)
a wholemeal biscuit (because it is supposed to be easy to digest).

digit (*say* dij-it) *noun* (*plural* **digits**)
1 any of the numbers from 0 to 9. 2 a finger or toe. [from Latin *digitus* = finger or toe]

digital *adjective*
to do with or using digits.

digital clock *noun* (*plural* **digital clocks**)
a clock that shows the time with a row of figures.

digital watch *noun* (*plural* **digital watches**)
a watch that shows the time with a row of figures.

dignified *adjective*
having dignity.

dignitary *noun* (*plural* **dignitaries**)
an important official.
[same origin as *dignity*]

dignity *noun*
a calm and serious manner.
beneath your dignity not considered worthy enough for you to do.
[from Latin *dignus* = worthy]

digress *verb* (**digresses, digressing, digressed**)
stray from the main subject.
digression *noun*
[from *di-²* + Latin *gressum* = gone]

dike *noun* (*plural* **dikes**)
1 a long wall or embankment to hold back water and prevent flooding. 2 a ditch for draining water from land.
[from Old Norse]

dilapidated *adjective*
falling to pieces. **dilapidation** *noun*
[from Latin]

dilate *verb* (**dilates, dilating, dilated**)
make or become wider or larger.
[from *di-²* + Latin *latus* = wide]

dilatory (*say* dil-at-er-ee) *adjective*
slow in doing something; not prompt.
[from Latin *dilator* = someone who delays]

dilemma (*say* dil-**em**-a) *noun* (*plural* **dilemmas**)
a situation where someone has to choose between two or more possible actions, each of which will bring difficulties.
[from Greek, = double proposal]

USAGE: Do not use *dilemma* to mean simply a problem or difficult situation. There should be some idea of choosing between two (or perhaps more) things.

diligent (*say* **dil**-ij-ent) *adjective*
hard-working. **diligently** *adverb*, **diligence** *noun* [from Latin *diligens* = careful, conscientious]

dilute *verb* (**dilutes, diluting, diluted**)
make a liquid weaker by adding water or other liquid. **dilution** *noun*
dilute *adjective*
diluted, *a dilute acid*.
[from Latin *diluere* = wash away]

dim *adjective* (**dimmer, dimmest**)
1 not bright or clear; only faintly lit. 2 (*informal*) stupid. **dimly** *adverb*, **dimness** *noun*
dim *verb* (**dims, dimming, dimmed**)
make or become dim. **dimmer** *noun*
[from Old English]

dimension *noun* (*plural* **dimensions**)
1 a measurement such as length, width, area, or volume. 2 size or extent.
dimensional *adjective*
[from Latin *dimensio* = measuring out]

diminish *verb* (**diminishes, diminishing, diminished**)
make or become smaller. **diminution** *noun*
[same origin as *diminutive*]

diminutive (*say* dim-in-yoo-tiv) *adjective*
very small. [from Latin *diminuere* = lessen]

dimple *noun* (*plural* **dimples**)
a small hollow or dent, especially in the skin. **dimpled** *adjective*
[probably from Old English]

din *noun*
a loud annoying noise.
din *verb* (**dins, dinning, dinned**)
force a person to learn something by continually repeating it, *Din it into him.*
[from Old English]

dine *verb* (**dines, dining, dined**) (*formal*)
have dinner. **diner** *noun*
[from old French *disner*]

ding-dong *noun*
the sound of a bell or alternate strokes of two bells.

dinghy (*say* ding-ee) *noun* (*plural* **dinghies**)
a kind of small boat.
[from Hindi *dingi* = a small river boat]

dingle *noun* (*plural* **dingles**)
a small valley with trees. [origin unknown]

dingo *noun* (*plural* **dingoes**)
an Australian wild dog.
[from an Australian Aboriginal word]

dingy (*say* din-jee) *adjective*
dirty-looking. **dingily** *adverb*, **dinginess** *noun* [origin unknown]

dinner *noun* (*plural* **dinners**)
the main meal of the day, either at midday or in the evening. [same origin as *dine*]

dinosaur (*say* dy-noss-or) *noun* (*plural* **dinosaurs**)
a prehistoric lizard-like animal, often of enormous size. [from Greek *deinos* = terrible + *sauros* = lizard]

dint noun (plural dints)
by dint of by means of; using, *I got through the exam by dint of a good memory and a lot of luck.*
[from Old English]

diocese (say dy-oss-iss) noun (plural dioceses)
a district under the care of a bishop.
diocesan (say dy-oss-iss-an) adjective
[from Latin]

dioxide noun
an oxide with two atoms of oxygen to one of another element, *carbon dioxide.*
[from di-^{1} + oxide]

dip verb (dips, dipping, dipped)
put down or go down, especially into a liquid.
dip noun (plural dips)
1 dipping. 2 a downward slope. 3 a quick swim. 4 a substance into which things are dipped. [from Old English]

diphtheria (say dif-theer-ee-a) noun
a serious disease that causes inflammation in the throat. [from Greek *diphthera* = skin (because a tough skin forms on the throat membrane)]

diphthong (say dif-thong) noun (plural diphthongs)
a compound vowel-sound made up of two sounds, e.g. *oi* in *point* (made up of 'aw' + 'ee') or *ou* in *loud* ('ah' + 'oo').
[from di-^{1} + Greek *phthongos* = sound]

diploma noun (plural diplomas)
a certificate awarded by a college etc. for skill in a particular subject. [Latin, from Greek, literally = folded paper]

diplomacy noun
1 the work of making agreements with other countries. 2 skill in dealing with people and gently persuading them to agree to things; tact.

diplomat noun (plural diplomats)
1 a person employed in diplomacy on behalf of his or her country. 2 a tactful person.
[from Latin *diploma* = an official letter given to travellers, saying who they were]

diplomatic adjective
1 to do with diplomats or diplomacy.
2 tactful. **diplomatically** adverb

dipper noun (plural dippers)
1 a kind of bird that dives for its food. 2 a ladle. [from *dip*]

dire adjective
dreadful or serious, *dire need.* [from Latin]

direct adjective
1 as straight as possible. 2 going straight to the point; frank. 3 exact, *the direct opposite.*
directly adverb & conjunction,
directness noun
direct verb (directs, directing, directed)
1 tell someone the way. 2 guide or aim in a certain direction. 3 control or manage. 4 order, *He directed his troops to advance.*
director noun
[from Latin *directum* = kept straight]

direct current noun
electric current flowing only in one direction.

direction noun (plural directions)
1 directing. 2 the line along which something moves or faces.
directional adjective

directions plural noun
information on how to use or do something.

directive noun (plural directives)
a command.

direct object noun (plural direct objects)
the word that receives the action of the verb. In *'she hit him'*, 'him' is the direct object.

directory noun (plural directories)
a book containing a list of people with their telephone numbers, addresses, etc.
[from Latin *directorius* = guiding]

dirge noun (plural dirges)
a slow sad song. [from the first word of a song, which used to be part of the Roman Catholic service for a dead person]

dirk noun (plural dirks)
a kind of dagger. [origin unknown]

dirt *noun*
earth, soil; anything that is not clean.
[from Old Norse]

dirty *adjective* (**dirtier, dirtiest**)
1 not clean; soiled. 2 unfair;
dishonourable, *a dirty trick*. 3 indecent;
obscene. **dirtily** *adverb*, **dirtiness** *noun*

dis- *prefix* (changing to **dif-** before words
beginning with *f*, and to **di-** before some
consonants)
1 not; the reverse of (as in *dishonest*).
2 apart; separated (as in *disarm, disperse*).
[from Latin]

disabled *adjective*
unable to use part of your body properly
because of illness or injury. **disability** *noun*,
disablement *noun*

disadvantage *noun* (*plural*
disadvantages)
something that hinders or is unhelpful.
disadvantaged *adjective*,
disadvantageous *adjective*

disagree *verb* (**disagrees, disagreeing,
disagreed**)
1 have or express a different opinion from
someone. 2 have a bad effect, *Rich food
disagrees with me*. **disagreement** *noun*
[from old French]

disagreeable *adjective*
unpleasant. [from old French]

disappear *verb* (**disappears, disappearing,
disappeared**)
stop being visible; vanish.
disappearance *noun*

disappoint *verb* (**disappoints,
disappointing, disappointed**)
fail to do what someone hopes for.
disappointment *noun*
[originally = to dismiss someone from an
important position: from *dis-* + *appoint*]

disapprobation *noun*
disapproval.

disapprove *verb* (**disapproves,
disapproving, disapproved**)
have an unfavourable opinion of
something; not approve. **disapproval** *noun*

disarm *verb* (**disarms, disarming, disarmed**)
1 reduce the size of armed forces. 2 take
away someone's weapons. 3 overcome a
person's anger or doubt, *Her friendliness
disarmed their suspicions*. **disarmament**
noun [from old French]

disarray *noun*
disorder. [from old French]

disaster *noun* (*plural* **disasters**)
1 a very bad accident or misfortune. 2 a
complete failure. **disastrous** *adjective*,
disastrously *adverb*
[via French from Italian]

disband *verb* (**disbands, disbanding,
disbanded**)
break up a group. [from old French]

disbelief *noun* (*plural* **disbeliefs**)
refusal or unwillingness to believe
something.

disburse *verb* (**disburses, disbursing,
disbursed**)
pay out money. **disbursement** *noun*
[from *dis-* + French *bourse* = purse]

disc *noun* (*plural* **discs**)
1 any round flat object. 2 (in computers,
usually **disk**) a storage device consisting of
magnetically coated plates. 3 a
gramophone record.
[from Latin *discus* = disc]

discard *verb* (**discards, discarding,
discarded**)
throw something away; put something
aside because it is useless or unwanted.
[originally = to throw out an unwanted
playing card from a hand: from *dis-* + *card*]

discern (*say* dis-**sern**) *verb* (**discerns,
discerning, discerned**)
perceive; see or recognize clearly.
discernible *adjective*, **discernment** *noun*
[from *dis-* + Latin *cernere* = to separate]

discerning *adjective*
perceptive; showing good judgement.

discharge *verb* (**discharges, discharging,
discharged**)
1 release a person. 2 send something out,
discharge smoke. 3 pay or do what was
agreed, *discharge the debt*.

discharge *noun* (*plural* **discharges**)
1 discharging. 2 something that is discharged.
[from Latin *discarricare* = unload]

disciple *noun* (*plural* **disciples**)
1 a person who accepts the teachings of another whom he or she regards as a leader. 2 any of the original followers of Jesus Christ.
[from Latin *discipulus* = learner]

disciplinarian *noun* (*plural* **disciplinarians**)
a person who believes in strict discipline.

discipline *noun* (*plural* **disciplines**)
1 orderly and obedient behaviour. 2 a subject for study. **disciplinary** (*say* dis-ip-lin-er-ee) *adjective*
discipline *verb* (**disciplines, disciplining, disciplined**)
1 train to be orderly and obedient.
2 punish. [from Latin *disciplina* = training]

disc jockey *noun* (*plural* **disc jockeys**)
a person who introduces and plays records.

disclaim *verb* (**disclaims, disclaiming, disclaimed**)
disown; say that you are not responsible for something. [from old French]

disclose *verb* (**discloses, disclosing, disclosed**)
reveal. **disclosure** *noun*
[from old French *desclore* = open up]

disco *noun* (*plural* **discos**)
a place where CDs or records are played for dancing.
[from French *discothèque* = record-library]

discolour *verb* (**discolours, discolouring, discoloured**)
spoil a thing's colour; stain.
discoloration *noun*
[from *dis-* + Latin *colorare* = to colour]

discomfit *verb* (**discomfits, discomfiting, discomfited**)
make a person feel uneasy; disconcert.
discomfiture *noun*
[from old French *desconfit* = defeated]

discomfort *noun*
being uncomfortable. [from old French]

disconcert (*say* dis-kon-sert) *verb*
(**disconcerts, disconcerting, disconcerted**)
make a person feel uneasy. [from *dis-* + French *concerter* = make harmonious]

disconnect *verb* (**disconnects, disconnecting, disconnected**)
break a connection; detach.
disconnection *noun*

disconnected *adjective*
not having a connection between its parts.

disconsolate (*say* dis-kon-sol-at) *adjective*
disappointed.
[from *dis-* + Latin *consolatus* = consoled]

discontent *noun*
lack of contentment; dissatisfaction.
discontented *adjective*,
discontentment *noun*

discontinue *verb* (**discontinues, discontinuing, discontinued**)
put an end to something.
[from *dis-* + Latin *continuare* = continue]

discord *noun* (*plural* **discords**)
1 disagreement; quarrelling. 2 musical notes sounded together and producing a harsh or unpleasant sound.
discordant *adjective*
[from *dis-* + Latin *cordis* = of the heart]

discotheque (*say* dis-ko-tek) *noun* (*plural* **discotheques**)
a disco. [French, = record-library]

discount *noun* (*plural* **discounts**)
an amount by which a price is reduced.
discount *verb* (**discounts, discounting, discounted**)
ignore or disregard something, *We cannot discount the possibility.* [from old French]

discourage *verb* (**discourages, discouraging, discouraged**)
1 take away someone's enthusiasm or confidence. 2 try to persuade someone not to do something. **discouragement** *noun*
[from old French]

discourse *noun* (*plural* **discourses**)
a formal speech or piece of writing about something.

discourse *verb* (discourses, discoursing, discoursed)
speak or write at length about something. [from Latin *discursus* = running to and fro]

discourteous *adjective*
not courteous; rude. **discourteously** *adverb*, **discourtesy** *noun*

discover *verb* (discovers, discovering, discovered)
1 find. 2 be the first person to find something. **discoverer** *noun*, **discovery** *noun* [from *dis-* + Latin *cooperire* = to cover]

discredit *verb* (discredits, discrediting, discredited)
1 destroy people's confidence in a person or thing; disgrace. 2 distrust.
discredit *noun*
1 disgrace. 2 distrust. **discreditable** *adjective* [from *dis-* + *credit*]

discreet *adjective*
1 not giving away secrets. 2 not showy. **discreetly** *adverb* [from Latin *discernere* = be discerning]

USAGE: Do not confuse with *discrete*.

discrepancy (*say* dis-**krep**-an-see) *noun* (*plural* discrepancies)
difference; lack of agreement, *There are several discrepancies in the two accounts.* [from Latin *discrepantia* = discord]

discrete *adjective*
separate; distinct from each other. [from Latin *discretus* = separated]

USAGE: Do not confuse with *discreet*.

discretion (*say* dis-**kresh**-on) *noun*
1 being discreet; keeping secrets. 2 power to take action according to your own judgement, *The treasurer has full discretion.* [from *discreet*]

discriminate *verb* (discriminates, discriminating, discriminated)
1 notice the differences between things; distinguish; prefer one thing to another. 2 treat people differently or unfairly, e.g. because of their race, sex, or religion. **discrimination** *noun* [same origin as *discern*]

discus *noun* (*plural* discuses)
a thick heavy disc thrown in athletic contests. [Latin]

discuss *verb* (discusses, discussing, discussed)
talk with other people about a subject. **discussion** *noun* [from Latin]

disdain *noun*
scorn or contempt. **disdainful** *adjective*, **disdainfully** *adverb*
disdain *verb* (disdains, disdaining, disdained)
1 regard or treat with disdain. 2 not do something because of disdain, *She disdained to reply.* [from *dis-* + Latin *dignare* = deign]

disease *noun* (*plural* diseases)
an unhealthy condition; an illness. **diseased** *adjective* [from *dis-* + *ease*]

disembark *verb* (disembarks, disembarking, disembarked)
put or go ashore. **disembarkation** *noun* [from French]

disembodied *adjective*
freed from the body, *a disembodied spirit.*

disembowel *verb* (disembowels, disembowelling, disembowelled)
take out the bowels or inside parts of something. [from *dis-* + *em-* + *bowel*]

disengage *verb* (disengages, disengaging, disengaged)
disconnect or detach.

disentangle *verb* (disentangles, disentangling, disentangled)
free from tangles or confusion.

disfavour *noun*
disapproval or dislike.

disfigure *verb* (disfigures, disfiguring, disfigured)
spoil a person's or thing's appearance. **disfigurement** *noun* [from *dis-* + Latin *figura* = a shape]

disgorge *verb* (disgorges, disgorging, disgorged)
pour or send out, *The pipe disgorged its contents.* [from *dis-* + French *gorge* = throat]

disgrace *noun*
1 shame; loss of approval or respect.
2 something that causes shame.
disgraceful *adjective*, **disgracefully** *adverb*
disgrace *verb* (**disgraces, disgracing, disgraced**)
bring disgrace upon someone.
[from *dis-* + Latin *gratia* = grace]

disgruntled *adjective*
discontented or resentful. [from *dis-*
= thoroughly + *gruntle* = grunt softly]

disguise *verb* (**disguises, disguising, disguised**)
make a person or thing look different in order to deceive people.
disguise *noun* (*plural* **disguises**)
something used for disguising.
[from *dis-* + *guise*]

disgust *noun*
a feeling that something is very unpleasant or disgraceful.
disgust *verb* (**disgusts, disgusting, disgusted**)
cause disgust. **disgusted** *adjective*,
disgusting *adjective*
[from *dis-* + Latin *gustare* = to taste]

dish *noun* (*plural* **dishes**)
1 a plate or bowl for food. 2 food prepared for eating. 3 a satellite dish.
dish *verb* (**dishes, dishing, dished**) (*informal*)
dish out give out portions of something to people.
[from Old English]

dishcloth *noun* (*plural* **dishcloths**)
a cloth for washing dishes.

dishearten *verb* (**disheartens, disheartening, disheartened**)
cause a person to lose hope or confidence.

dishevelled (*say* dish-ev-eld) *adjective*
ruffled and untidy. **dishevelment** *noun*
[from *dis-* + old French *chevel* = hair]

dishonest *adjective*
not honest. **dishonestly** *adverb*,
dishonesty *noun* [from old French]

dishonour *noun* & *verb* (**dishonours, dishonouring, dishonoured**)
disgrace. **dishonourable** *adjective*
[from old French]

dishwasher *noun* (*plural* **dishwashers**)
a machine for washing dishes etc. automatically.

disillusion *verb* (**disillusions, disillusioning, disillusioned**)
get rid of someone's pleasant but wrong beliefs. **disillusionment** *noun*

disincentive *noun* (*plural* **disincentives**)
something that discourages an action or effort.

disinclination *noun*
unwillingness.

disinclined *adjective*
unwilling to do something.

disinfect *verb* (**disinfects, disinfecting, disinfected**)
destroy the germs in something.
disinfection *noun* [from French]

disinfectant *noun* (*plural* **disinfectants**)
a substance used for disinfecting things.
[from French]

disinherit *verb* (**disinherits, disinheriting, disinherited**)
deprive a person of the right to inherit something.

disintegrate *verb* (**disintegrates, disintegrating, disintegrated**)
break up into small parts or pieces.
disintegration *noun*

disinter *verb* (**disinters, disinterring, disinterred**)
dig up something that is buried.
[from French]

disinterested *adjective*
impartial; not biased; not influenced by hope of gaining something yourself. *She gave us some disinterested advice.*

USAGE: It is not accepted as part of standard English to use this word as if it meant 'not interested' or 'bored'. If this is what you mean, use *uninterested*.

disjointed *adjective*
disconnected.
[from *dis-* + Latin *jungere* = join]

disk *noun* (*plural* disks)
a disc. [the American spelling of *disc*]

dislike *noun* (*plural* dislikes)
a feeling of not liking somebody or
something.
dislike *verb* (dislikes, disliking, disliked)
not to like somebody or something.
[from *dis-* + *like*[1]]

dislocate *verb* (dislocates, dislocating,
dislocated)
1 move or force a bone from its proper
position in one of the joints. 2 disrupt, *Fog
dislocated the traffic.* **dislocation** *noun*
[from *dis-* + Latin *locare* = to place]

dislodge *verb* (dislodges, dislodging,
dislodged)
move or force something from its place.
[from French]

disloyal *adjective*
not loyal. **disloyally** *adverb*, **disloyalty** *noun*
[from French]

dismal *adjective*
1 gloomy. 2 of poor quality. **dismally** *adverb*
[from Latin *dies mali* = unlucky days]

dismantle *verb* (dismantles, dismantling,
dismantled)
take something to pieces.
[from *dis-* + old French *manteler* = fortify]

dismay *noun*
a feeling of surprise and discouragement.
dismayed *adjective* [from *dis-* + *may*[1]]

dismiss *verb* (dismisses, dismissing,
dismissed)
1 send someone away. 2 tell a person that
you will no longer employ him or her.
3 stop considering an idea etc. 4 get a
batsman or cricket side out. **dismissal** *noun*,
dismissive *adjective*
[from *dis-* + Latin *missum* = sent]

dismount *verb* (dismounts, dismounting,
dismounted)
get off a horse or bicycle.

disobedient *adjective*
not obedient. **disobediently** *adverb*,
disobedience *noun* [from old French]

disobey *verb* (disobeys, disobeying,
disobeyed)
not to obey; disregard orders.
[from old French]

disorder *noun* (*plural* disorders)
1 untidiness. 2 a disturbance. 3 an illness.
disorderly *adjective*

disorganized *adjective*
muddled and badly organized.
disorganization *noun* [from French]

disown *verb* (disowns, disowning,
disowned)
refuse to acknowledge that a person or
thing has any connection with you.

disparage (*say* dis-pa-rij) *verb* (disparages,
disparaging, disparaged)
declare that something is small or
unimportant; belittle. **disparagement** *noun*
[from *dis-* + old French *parage* = equality
in rank]

disparity *noun* (*plural* disparities)
difference or inequality.
[from *dis-* + Latin *paritas* = equality]

dispassionate *adjective*
calm and impartial. **dispassionately** *adverb*

dispatch *verb* (dispatches, dispatching,
dispatched)
1 send off to a destination. 2 kill.
dispatch *noun* (*plural* dispatches)
1 dispatching. 2 a report or message sent.
3 promptness; speed.
[from Italian or Spanish]

dispatch box *noun* (*plural* dispatch boxes)
a container for carrying official
documents.

dispatch rider *noun* (*plural* dispatch
riders)
a messenger who travels by motorcycle.

dispel *verb* (dispels, dispelling, dispelled)
drive away; scatter, *Wind dispels fog.*
[from *dis-* + Latin *pellere* = to drive]

dispensary *noun* (*plural* dispensaries)
a place where medicines are dispensed.

dispense *verb* (dispenses, dispensing,
dispensed)
1 distribute; deal out. 2 prepare medicine

according to prescriptions.
dispensation *noun*, **dispenser** *noun*
dispense with do without something.
[from Latin *dispensare* = weigh out]

disperse *verb* (disperses, dispersing,
dispersed)
scatter. **dispersal** *noun*, **dispersion** *noun*
[from Latin *dispersum* = scattered]

displace *verb* (displaces, displacing,
displaced)
1 shift from its place. 2 take a person's or
thing's place. **displacement** *noun*

display *verb* (displays, displaying, displayed)
show; arrange something so that it can be
clearly seen.
display *noun* (*plural* displays)
1 the displaying of something; an
exhibition. 2 something displayed. [from
dis- = separately + Latin *plicare* = to fold]

displease *verb* (displeases, displeasing,
displeased)
annoy or not please someone. **displeasure**
noun [from old French]

disposable *adjective*
made to be thrown away after it has been
used.

disposal *noun*
getting rid of something.
at your disposal for you to use; ready for
you.

dispose *verb* (disposes, disposing, disposed)
1 place in position; arrange, *Dispose your
troops in two lines.* 2 make a person ready
or willing to do something, *I feel disposed to
help him.*
be well disposed be friendly.
dispose of get rid of.
[from old French; related to *deposit*]

disposition *noun* (*plural* dispositions)
1 a person's nature or qualities.
2 arrangement.

disproportionate *adjective*
out of proportion; too large or too small.

disprove *verb* (disproves, disproving,
disproved)
show that something is not true.
[from old French]

disputation *noun* (*plural* disputations)
a debate or argument.

dispute *verb* (disputes, disputing, disputed)
1 argue; debate. 2 quarrel. 3 raise an
objection to, *We dispute their claim.*
dispute *noun* (*plural* disputes)
1 an argument or debate. 2 a quarrel.
in dispute being argued about.
[from *dis-* + Latin *putare* = settle]

disqualify *verb* (disqualifies, disqualifying,
disqualified)
bar someone from a competition etc.
because he or she has broken the rules or
is not properly qualified to take part.
disqualification *noun*

disquiet *noun*
anxiety or worry. **disquieting** *adjective*

disregard *verb* (disregards, disregarding,
disregarded)
ignore.
disregard *noun*
the act of ignoring something.

disrepair *noun*
bad condition caused by not doing repairs,
The old mill is in a state of disrepair.

disreputable *adjective*
not respectable. [from *disrepute*]

disrepute *noun*
bad reputation.

disrespect *noun*
lack of respect; rudeness. **disrespectful**
adjective, **disrespectfully** *adverb*

disrupt *verb* (disrupts, disrupting, disrupted)
put into disorder; interrupt a continuous
flow, *Fog disrupted traffic.* **disruption** *noun*,
disruptive *adjective*
[from *dis-* + Latin *ruptum* = broken]

dissatisfied *adjective*
not satisfied. **dissatisfaction** *noun*

dissect (*say* dis-sekt) *verb* (dissects,
dissecting, dissected)
cut something up in order to examine it.
dissection *noun*
[from *dis-* + Latin *sectum* = cut]

disseminate *verb* (disseminates, disseminating, disseminated)
spread ideas etc. widely. **dissemination** *noun* [from *dis-* + Latin *seminare* = sow (scatter seeds)]

dissent *noun*
disagreement.
dissent *verb* (dissents, dissenting, dissented)
disagree. [from *dis-* + Latin *sentire* = feel]

dissertation *noun* (*plural* dissertations)
a long essay on an academic subject, written as part of a university degree. [from Latin *dissertare* = examine, discuss]

disservice *noun*
a harmful action done by someone who was intending to help.

dissident *noun* (*plural* dissidents)
a person who disagrees, especially someone who opposes their government.
dissident *adjective*, **dissidence** *noun*
[from Latin *dissidere* = sit by yourself]

dissipate *verb* (dissipates, dissipating, dissipated)
1 disappear or scatter. **2** waste or squander something. **dissipation** *noun*
[from Latin *dissipatus* = scattered]

dissociate *verb* (dissociates, dissociating, dissociated)
separate something in your thoughts.
dissociation *noun* [from Latin]

dissolute *adjective*
having an immoral way of life.
[from Latin *dissolutus* = loose]

dissolution *noun* (*plural* dissolutions)
1 putting an end to a marriage or partnership etc. **2** formally ending a parliament or assembly. [from Latin]

dissolve *verb* (dissolves, dissolving, dissolved)
1 mix something with a liquid so that it becomes part of the liquid. **2** make or become liquid; melt. **3** put an end to a marriage or partnership etc. **4** formally end a parliament or assembly, *Parliament was dissolved and a general election was held.* [from *dis-* = separate + Latin *solvere* = loosen]

dissuade *verb* (dissuades, dissuading, dissuaded)
persuade somebody not to do something.
dissuasion *noun*
[from *dis-* + Latin *suadere* = persuade]

distaff *noun* (*plural* distaffs)
a stick holding raw wool etc. for spinning into yarn. [from Old English]

distance *noun* (*plural* distances)
the amount of space between two places.
in the distance far away.

distant *adjective*
1 far away. **2** not friendly; not sociable.
distantly *adverb*
[from *dis-* + Latin *stans* = standing]

distaste *noun*
dislike.

distasteful *adjective*
unpleasant.

distemper *noun*
1 a disease of dogs and certain other animals. **2** a kind of paint. [from Latin]

distend *verb* (distends, distending, distended)
make or become swollen because of pressure from inside. **distension** *noun*
[from *dis-* + Latin *tendere* = stretch]

distil *verb* (distils, distilling, distilled)
purify a liquid by boiling it and condensing the vapour. **distillation** *noun*
[from *dis-* + Latin *stillare* = drip down]

distiller *noun* (*plural* distillers)
a person who makes alcoholic drinks (e.g. whisky) by distillation. **distillery** *noun*

distinct *adjective*
1 easily heard or seen; noticeable. **2** clearly separate or different. **distinctly** *adverb*, **distinctness** *noun*
[from Latin *distinctus* = separated]

USAGE: See note at *distinctive*.

distinction *noun* (*plural* distinctions)
1 a difference. **2** excellence or honour. **3** an award for excellence; a high mark in an examination.

distinctive *adjective*
that distinguishes one thing from another
or others, *The school has a distinctive
uniform.* **distinctively** *adverb*

USAGE: Do not confuse this word with
distinct. A *distinct* mark is a clear mark; a
distinctive mark is one that is not found
anywhere else.

distinguish *verb* (**distinguishes,
distinguishing, distinguished**)
1 make or notice differences between
things. 2 see or hear something clearly.
3 bring honour to, *He distinguished himself
by his bravery.* **distinguishable** *adjective*
[from Latin *distinguere* = to separate]

distinguished *adjective*
excellent and famous.

distort *verb* (**distorts, distorting, distorted**)
1 pull or twist out of its normal shape.
2 misrepresent; give a false account of
something, *distort the truth.* **distortion** *noun*
[from *dis-* + Latin *tortum* = twisted]

distract *verb* (**distracts, distracting,
distracted**)
take a person's attention away from
something.
[from *dis-* + Latin *tractum* = pulled]

distracted *adjective*
greatly upset by worry or distress;
distraught.

distraction *noun* (*plural* **distractions**)
1 something that distracts a person's
attention. 2 an amusement. 3 great worry
or distress.

distraught (*say* dis-**trawt**) *adjective*
greatly upset by worry or distress.
[same origin as *distract*]

distress *noun* (*plural* **distresses**)
great sorrow, pain, or trouble.
distress *verb* (**distresses, distressing,
distressed**)
cause distress to a person.
[from old French]

distribute *verb* (**distributes, distributing,
distributed**)
1 deal or share out. 2 spread or scatter.
distribution *noun*, **distributor** *noun*
[from *dis-* = + Latin *tributum* = given]

district *noun* (*plural* **districts**)
part of a town or country. [French]

distrust *noun*
lack of trust; suspicion. **distrustful** *adjective*
distrust *verb* (**distrusts, distrusting,
distrusted**)
not to trust.

disturb *verb* (**disturbs, disturbing, disturbed**)
1 spoil someone's peace or rest. 2 cause
someone to worry. 3 move a thing from its
position. **disturbance** *noun*
[from *dis-* = thoroughly + Latin *turbare*
= confuse, upset]

disuse *noun*
the state of being no longer used.

disused *adjective*
no longer used.

ditch *noun* (*plural* **ditches**)
a trench dug to hold water or carry it away,
or to serve as a boundary.
ditch *verb* (**ditches, ditching, ditched**)
1 (*informal*) bring an aircraft down in a
forced landing on the sea. 2 (*informal*)
abandon or discard something.
[from Old English]

dither *verb* (**dithers, dithering, dithered**)
hesitate nervously. [origin unknown]

ditto *noun*
(used in lists) the same again.
[from Italian *detto* = said]

ditty *noun* (*plural* **ditties**)
a short song. [from old French]

divan *noun* (*plural* **divans**)
a bed or couch without a raised back or
sides. [Persian, = cushioned bench]

dive *verb* (**dives, diving, dived**)
1 go under water, especially head first.
2 move down quickly. **dive** *noun*
[from Old English]

diver *noun* (*plural* **divers**)
1 someone who dives. 2 a person who
works under water in a special suit with an
air supply. 3 a bird that dives for its food.

diverge *verb* (diverges, diverging, diverged)
go aside or in different directions.
divergent *adjective*, **divergence** *noun*
[from Latin]

divers (*say* dy-verz) *adjective* (*old use*)
various. [from Latin *diversus* = diverted]

diverse (*say* dy-verss) *adjective*
varied; of several different kinds. **diversity**
noun [a different spelling of *divers*]

diversify *verb* (diversifies, diversifying,
diversified)
make or become varied; involve yourself in
different kinds of things.
diversification *noun*

diversion *noun* (*plural* diversions)
1 diverting something from its course. 2 an
alternative route for traffic when a road is
closed. 3 a recreation or entertainment.
diversionary *adjective*

divert *verb* (diverts, diverting, diverted)
1 turn something aside from its course.
2 entertain or amuse.
[from *di-²* + Latin *vertere* = to turn]

divest *verb* (divests, divesting, divested)
1 strip of clothes, *He divested himself of his
robes*. 2 take away; deprive, *They divested
him of power*.
[from *di-²* + Latin *vestire* = clothe]

divide *verb* (divides, dividing, divided)
1 separate from something or into smaller
parts; split up. 2 find how many times one
number is contained in another, *Divide six
by three* (6 ÷ 3 = 2). **divider** *noun*
[from Latin]

dividend *noun* (*plural* dividends)
1 a share of a business's profit. 2 a number
that is to be divided by another. (Compare
divisor.) [from Latin *dividendum*
= something to be divided]

dividers *plural noun*
a pair of compasses for measuring
distances.

divine *adjective*
1 belonging to or coming from God. 2 like a
god. 3 (*informal*) excellent; extremely
beautiful. **divinely** *adverb*

divine *verb* (divines, divining, divined)
prophesy or guess what is about to happen.
[from Latin *divus* = god]

division *noun* (*plural* divisions)
1 dividing. 2 a dividing line; a partition.
3 one of the parts into which something is
divided. 4 (in Parliament) separation of
members into two sections for counting
votes. **divisional** *adjective*
[from Latin *dividere* = divide]

divisive (*say* div-I-siv) *adjective*
causing disagreement within a group.

divisor *noun* (*plural* divisors)
a number by which another is to be
divided. (Compare *dividend* 2.)

divorce *noun* (*plural* divorces)
the legal ending of a marriage.
divorce *verb* (divorces, divorcing, divorced)
1 end a marriage by divorce. 2 separate;
think of things separately.
[French; related to *divert*]

divulge *verb* (divulges, divulging, divulged)
reveal information. **divulgence** *noun*
[from *di-²* + Latin *vulgare* = publish]

Diwali (*say* di-wah-lee) *noun*
a Hindu religious festival at which lamps
are lit, held in October or November.
[from Sanskrit *dipavali* = row of lights]

DIY *abbreviation*
do-it-yourself.

dizzy *adjective* (dizzier, dizziest)
having or causing the feeling that
everything is spinning round; giddy. **dizzily**
adverb, **dizziness** *noun* [from Old English]

DJ *abbreviation*
disc jockey.

DNA *abbreviation*
deoxyribonucleic acid; a substance in
chromosomes that stores genetic
information.

do *verb* (does, doing, did, done)
This word has many different uses, most of
which mean performing or dealing with
something (*Do your best. I can't do this. She
is doing well at school*) or being suitable or
enough (*This will do*). The verb is also used
with other verbs 1 in questions (*Do you*

want this?), **2** in statements with 'not' (*He does not want it*), **3** for emphasis (*I do like nuts*), **4** to avoid repeating a verb that has just been used (*We work as hard as they do*).
do away with get rid of.
do up 1 fasten, *Do your coat up.* **2** repair or redecorate, *Do up the spare room.*
do *noun* (*plural* **dos**) (*informal*)
a party or other social event. [from Old English]

docile (*say* doh-syl) *adjective*
willing to obey. **docilely** *adverb*, **docility** *noun* [from Latin *docilis* = easily taught]

dock[1] *noun* (*plural* **docks**)
a part of a harbour where ships are loaded, unloaded, or repaired.
dock *verb* (**docks, docking, docked**)
1 bring or come into a dock. **2** when two spacecraft dock, they join together in space. [from old German or old Dutch]

dock[2] *noun*
an enclosure for the prisoner on trial in a lawcourt. [from Flemish *dok* = cage]

dock[3] *noun*
a weed with broad leaves.
[from Old English]

dock[4] *verb* (**docks, docking, docked**)
1 cut short an animal's tail. **2** reduce or take away part of someone's wages or supplies etc. [origin unknown]

docker *noun* (*plural* **dockers**)
a labourer who loads and unloads ships.

docket *noun* (*plural* **dockets**)
a document or label listing the contents of a package. [origin unknown]

dockyard *noun* (*plural* **dockyards**)
an open area with docks and equipment for building or repairing ships.

doctor *noun* (*plural* **doctors**)
1 a person who is trained to treat sick or injured people. **2** a person who holds an advanced degree (a **doctorate**) at a university, *Doctor of Music.*
[Latin, = teacher]

doctrine *noun* (*plural* **doctrines**)
a belief held by a religious, political, or other group. **doctrinal** *adjective*
[from Latin *doctrina* = teaching]

document *noun* (*plural* **documents**)
a written or printed paper giving information or evidence about something. **documentation** *noun*
[from Latin *documentum* = lesson, official paper]

documentary *adjective*
1 consisting of documents, *documentary evidence.* **2** showing real events or situations.
documentary *noun* (*plural* **documentaries**)
a film giving information about real events. [same origin as *document*]

dodder *verb* (**dodders, doddering, doddered**)
walk unsteadily, especially because of old age. **doddery** *adjective*
[origin unknown]

dodge *verb* (**dodges, dodging, dodged**)
move quickly to avoid someone or something.
dodge *noun* (*plural* **dodges**)
1 a dodging movement. **2** (*informal*) a trick; a clever way of doing something.
[origin unknown]

dodgem *noun* (*plural* **dodgems**)
a small electrically driven car at a funfair, in which each driver tries to bump some cars and dodge others.
[from *dodge* + *'em* (them)]

dodgy *adjective* (*informal*)
1 awkward or tricky. **2** not working properly. **3** dishonest.
[from *dodge* = a trick]

dodo *noun* (*plural* **dodos**)
a large heavy bird that used to live on an island in the Indian Ocean but has been extinct for over 200 years.
[from Portuguese *doudo* = fool (because the bird had no fear of man)]

doe *noun* (*plural* **does**)
a female deer, rabbit, or hare.
[from Old English]

doer *noun* (*plural* **doers**)
a person who does things.

doesn't (*mainly spoken*)
does not.

doff *verb* (**doffs, doffing, doffed**)
take off, *He doffed his hat.*
[from *do off*; compare *don*]

dog *noun* (*plural* **dogs**)
a four-legged animal that barks, often kept
as a pet.
dog *verb* (**dogs, dogging, dogged**)
follow closely or persistently, *Reporters
dogged his footsteps.* [from Old English]

doge (*say* dohj) *noun* (*plural* **doges**)
the elected ruler of the former republics of
Venice and Genoa.
[from Latin *dux* = leader]

dog-eared *adjective*
(of a book) having the corners of the pages
bent from constant use.

dogfish *noun* (*plural* **dogfish**)
a kind of small shark.

dogged (*say* **dog**-id) *adjective*
persistent or obstinate. **doggedly** *adverb*
[from *dog*]

doggerel *noun*
bad verse. [origin unknown]

dogma *noun* (*plural* **dogmas**)
a belief or principle that a Church or other
authority declares is true and must be
accepted. [Greek, = opinion, decree]

dogmatic *adjective*
expressing ideas in a very firm
authoritative way. **dogmatically** *adverb*
[from *dogma*]

doh *noun*
a name for the keynote of a scale in music,
or the note C. [Italian]

doily *noun* (*plural* **doilies**)
a small ornamental table-mat, made of
paper or lace. [named after a Mr *Doily* or
Doyley, who sold household linen]

do-it-yourself *adjective*
suitable for an amateur to do or make at
home.

doldrums *plural noun*
1 the ocean regions near the equator
where there is little or no wind. **2** a time of
depression or inactivity. [origin unknown]

dole *verb* (**doles, doling, doled**)
dole out distribute.
dole *noun* (*informal*)
money paid by the State to unemployed
people. [from Old English]

doleful *adjective*
sad or sorrowful. **dolefully** *adverb*
[from an old word *dole* = grief]

doll *noun* (*plural* **dolls**)
a toy model of a person.
[pet form of *Dorothy*]

dollar *noun* (*plural* **dollars**)
a unit of money in the USA and some other
countries.
[from German *thaler* = a silver coin]

dolly *noun* (*plural* **dollies**) (*informal*)
a doll.

dolphin *noun* (*plural* **dolphins**)
a sea animal like a small whale with a
beaklike snout. [from Greek]

-dom *suffix*
forms nouns showing rank, office,
territory, or condition (e.g. *kingdom,
freedom*). [from Old English]

domain (*say* dom-ayn) *noun* (*plural*
domains)
1 a kingdom. **2** an area of knowledge,
interest, etc.
[from French; related to *dominion*]

dome *noun* (*plural* **domes**)
a roof shaped like the top half of a ball.
domed *adjective* [via French from Italian]

domestic *adjective*
1 to do with the home or household. **2** (of
animals) kept by people, not wild.
domestically *adverb*, **domesticated** *adjective*
[from Latin *domesticus* = to do with the
home]

domicile (*say* dom-iss-syl) *noun* (*plural*
domiciles)
the place where someone lives; residence.
domiciled *adjective*
[from Latin *domus* = home]

dominate *verb* (**dominates, dominating,
dominated**)
1 control by being stronger or more
powerful. **2** be conspicuous or prominent,

The mountain dominated the whole landscape. **dominant** *adjective*, **dominance** *noun*, **domination** *noun* [from Latin *dominus* = master]

domineer *verb* (**domineers, domineering, domineered**)
behave in a dominating way.
domineering *adjective*
[same origin as *dominate*]

dominion *noun* (*plural* **dominions**)
1 authority to rule others; control. **2** an area over which someone rules; a domain.
[from Latin *dominium* = property]

domino *noun* (*plural* **dominoes**)
a small flat oblong piece of wood or plastic with dots (1 to 6) or a blank space at each end, used in the game of dominoes.
[French]

don *verb* (**dons, donning, donned**)
put on, *don a cloak*.
[from *do on*; compare *doff*]

donate *verb* (**donates, donating, donated**)
present money or a gift to a fund or institution etc. **donation** *noun*
[from Latin *donum* = gift]

donkey *noun* (*plural* **donkeys**)
an animal that looks like a small horse with long ears. [origin unknown]

donor *noun* (*plural* **donors**)
someone who gives something, *a blood donor*. [from old French]

don't (*mainly spoken*)
do not.

doodle *verb* (**doodles, doodling, doodled**)
scribble or draw absent-mindedly. **doodle** *noun* [from old German]

doom *noun*
a grim fate that you cannot avoid, especially death or destruction, *a sense of impending doom*.
doom *verb* (**dooms, dooming, doomed**)
destine to a grim fate. [from Old English]

doomed *adjective*
1 destined to a grim fate. **2** bound to fail or be destroyed.

doomsday *noun*
the day of the Last Judgement; the end of the world.
[from *doom* in an old sense = judgement]

door *noun* (*plural* **doors**)
a movable barrier on hinges (or one that slides or revolves), used to open or close an entrance. **doorknob** *noun*, **doormat** *noun*
[from Old English]

doorstep *noun* (*plural* **doorsteps**)
the step or piece of ground just outside a door.

door-to-door *adjective*
done at each house in turn.

doorway *noun* (*plural* **doorways**)
the opening into which a door fits.

dope *noun* (*plural* **dopes**)
1 (*informal*) a drug, especially one taken or given illegally. **2** (*informal*) a stupid person. **dopey** *adjective*
dope *verb* (**dopes, doping, doped**)
(*informal*)
give a drug to a person or animal.
[from Dutch *doop* = sauce]

dormant *adjective*
1 sleeping. **2** living or existing but not active; not extinct, *a dormant volcano*.
[French, = sleeping]

dormitory *noun* (*plural* **dormitories**)
a room for several people to sleep in, especially in a school or institution.
dormitory town or **suburb** a place from which people travel to work elsewhere.
[from Latin *dormire* = to sleep]

dormouse *noun* (*plural* **dormice**)
an animal like a large mouse that hibernates in winter. [origin unknown]

dorsal *adjective*
to do with or on the back, *Some fish have a dorsal fin*.
[from Latin *dorsum* = the back]

dosage *noun* (*plural* **dosages**)
1 the giving of medicine in doses. **2** the size of a dose.

dose *noun* (*plural* **doses**)
an amount of medicine etc. taken at one time.

dose *verb* (**doses, dosing, dosed**)
give a dose of medicine to a person or animal.
[from Greek *dosis* = something given]

dossier (*say* **doss**-ee-er or **doss**-ee-ay)
(*plural* **dossiers**)
a set of documents containing information about a person or event. [French]

dot *noun* (*plural* **dots**)
a tiny spot.
dot *verb* (**dots, dotting, dotted**)
mark something with dots.
[from Old English]

dotage (*say* **doh**-tij) *noun*
a condition of weakness of mind caused by old age, *He is in his dotage.* [from *dote*]

dote *verb* (**dotes, doting, doted**)
dote on be very fond of.
[from old Dutch *doten* = to be silly]

dotty *adjective* (**dottier, dottiest**) (*informal*)
crazy or silly. **dottiness** *noun*
[origin unknown]

double *adjective*
1 twice as much; twice as many. 2 having two things or parts that form a pair, *a double-barrelled gun.* 3 suitable for two people, *a double bed.* **doubly** *adverb*
double *noun* (*plural* **doubles**)
1 a double quantity or thing. 2 a person or thing that looks exactly like another.
double *verb* (**doubles, doubling, doubled**)
1 make or become twice as much or as many. 2 bend or fold in two. 3 turn back sharply, *The fox doubled back on its tracks.*
[from old French]

double bass *noun* (*plural* **double basses**)
a musical instrument with strings, like a large cello. [from *double* + *bass*[1]]

double-cross *verb* (**double-crosses, double-crossing, double-crossed**)
deceive or cheat someone who thinks you are working with them.

double-decker *noun* (*plural* **double-deckers**)
a bus with two decks.

double entendre *noun* (*plural* **double entendres**)
a word or phrase with two meanings, one of which is sexual or rude.
[French, = double understanding]

doublet *noun* (*plural* **doublets**)
a man's close-fitting jacket worn in the 15th–17th centuries. [from old French]

doubt *noun* (*plural* **doubts**)
a feeling of not being sure about something.
doubt *verb* (**doubts, doubting, doubted**)
feel doubt. **doubter** *noun*
[from Latin *dubitare* = hesitate]

doubtful *adjective*
1 feeling doubt. 2 making you feel doubt.
doubtfully *adverb*

doubtless *adverb*
certainly.

dough *noun*
1 a thick mixture of flour and water used for making bread, pastry, etc. 2 (*slang*) money. **doughy** *adjective*
[from Old English]

doughnut *noun* (*plural* **doughnuts**)
a round bun that has been fried and covered in sugar.

doughty (*say* **dow**-tee) *adjective*
brave. [from Old English]

dour (*say* **doo**-er) *adjective*
stern and gloomy-looking. **dourly** *adverb*
[from Scottish Gaelic *dur* = dull, obstinate]

douse *verb* (**douses, dousing, doused**)
1 put into water; pour water over something. 2 put out, *douse the light.*
[origin unknown]

dove *noun* (*plural* **doves**)
a kind of pigeon. [from Old Norse]

dovetail *noun* (*plural* **dovetails**)
a wedge-shaped joint used to join two pieces of wood.
dovetail *verb* (**dovetails, dovetailing, dovetailed**)
1 join pieces of wood with a dovetail. 2 fit neatly together, *My plans dovetailed with hers.* [because the wedge-shape looks like a dove's tail]

dowager *noun* (*plural* dowagers)
a woman who holds a title or property after her husband has died, *the dowager duchess*.
[from old French *douage* = widow's share]

dowdy *adjective* (dowdier, dowdiest)
shabby; unfashionable. **dowdily** *adverb*
[origin unknown]

dowel *noun* (*plural* dowels)
a headless wooden or metal pin for holding together two pieces of wood, stone, etc.
dowelling *noun*
[probably from old German]

down¹ *adverb*
1 to or in a lower place or position or level, *It fell down.* 2 to a source or place etc., *Track them down.* 3 in writing, *Take down these instructions.* 4 as a payment, *We will pay £5 down and the rest later.*
be down on disapprove of, *She is down on smoking.*
down *preposition*
downwards through or along or into, *Pour it down the drain.*
[from Old English *adune*]

down² *noun*
very fine soft feathers or hair. **downy** *adjective* [from Old Norse]

down³ *noun* (*plural* downs)
a grass-covered hill, *the South Downs*.
downland *noun* [from Old English *dun*]

downcast *adjective*
1 looking downwards, *downcast eyes*.
2 dejected.

downfall *noun* (*plural* downfalls)
1 a fall from power or prosperity. 2 a heavy fall of rain or snow.

downhill *adverb* & *adjective*
down a slope.

download *verb* (downloads, downloading, downloaded)
transfer data from a large computer system to a smaller one.

downpour *noun* (*plural* downpours)
a great fall of rain.

downright *adverb* & *adjective*
complete or completely, *a downright lie*.

Down's syndrome *noun*
a medical condition caused by a chromosome defect in which a baby is born with reduced intelligence and physical abnormalities.

downstairs *adverb* & *adjective*
to or on a lower floor.

downstream *adjective* & *adverb*
in the direction in which a stream flows.

downward *adjective* & *adverb*
going towards what is lower.
downwards *adverb*

dowry *noun* (*plural* dowries)
property or money brought by a bride to her husband when she marries him.
[from old French; related to *endow*]

doze *verb* (dozes, dozing, dozed)
sleep lightly.
doze *noun*
a light sleep. **dozy** *adjective*
[origin unknown]

dozen *noun* (*plural* dozens)
a set of twelve. [from old French]

USAGE: Correct use is *ten dozen* (not *ten dozens*).

drab *adjective* (drabber, drabbest)
1 not colourful. 2 dull or uninteresting, *a drab life*. **drably** *adverb*, **drabness** *noun*
[from old French]

Draconian (*say* drak-oh-nee-an) *adjective*
very harsh, *Draconian laws*.
[named after Draco, who established very severe laws in ancient Athens]

draft *noun* (*plural* drafts)
1 a rough sketch or plan. 2 a written order for a bank to pay out money.
draft *verb* (drafts, drafting, drafted)
1 prepare a draft. 2 select for a special duty, *She was drafted to our office in Paris*.
[a different spelling of *draught*]

USAGE: This is also the American spelling of *draught*.

drag *verb* (drags, dragging, dragged)
1 pull something heavy along. 2 search a river or lake etc. with nets and hooks.
3 continue slowly and dully.

drag *noun*
1 a hindrance; something boring. 2 (*slang*) women's clothes worn by men.
[from Old Norse]

dragon *noun* (*plural* **dragons**)
1 a mythological monster, usually with wings and able to breathe out fire. 2 a fierce person.
[from Greek *drakon* = serpent]

dragonfly *noun* (*plural* **dragonflies**)
an insect with a long thin body and two pairs of transparent wings.

dragoon *noun* (*plural* **dragoons**)
a member of certain cavalry regiments.
dragoon *verb* (**dragoons, dragooning, dragooned**)
force someone into doing something. [same origin as *dragon*]

drain *noun* (*plural* **drains**)
1 a pipe or ditch etc. for taking away water or other liquid. 2 something that takes away strength or resources. **drainpipe** *noun*
drain *verb* (**drains, draining, drained**)
1 take away water etc. through a drain. 2 flow or trickle away. 3 empty liquid out of a container. 4 take away strength etc.; exhaust. **drainage** *noun* [from Old English]

drake *noun* (*plural* **drakes**)
a male duck. [from West Germanic]

drama *noun* (*plural* **dramas**)
1 a play. 2 writing or performing plays. 3 a series of exciting events. [from Greek]

dramatic *adjective*
1 to do with drama. 2 exciting and impressive, *a dramatic change*.
dramatics *plural noun*, **dramatically** *adverb*

dramatis personae (*say* dram-a-tis per-sohn-I) *plural noun*
the characters in a play.
[Latin, = persons of the drama]

dramatist *noun* (*plural* **dramatists**)
a person who writes plays.

dramatize *verb* (**dramatizes, dramatizing, dramatized**)
1 make a story etc. into a play. 2 make something seem exciting.
dramatization *noun*

drape *verb* (**drapes, draping, draped**)
hang cloth etc. loosely over something. [from French *drap* = cloth]

draper *noun* (*plural* **drapers**)
a shopkeeper who sells cloth or clothes. [same origin as *drape*]

drapery *noun* (*plural* **draperies**)
1 a draper's stock. 2 cloth arranged in loose folds. [same origin as *drape*]

drastic *adjective*
having a strong or violent effect. **drastically** *adverb* [from Greek]

draught (*say* drahft) *noun* (*plural* **draughts**)
1 a current of usually cold air indoors. 2 a haul of fish in a net. 3 the depth of water needed to float a ship. 4 a swallow of liquid. **draughty** *adjective* [from Old Norse]

draughts *noun*
a game played with 24 round pieces on a chessboard. [from *draught* in an old sense = way of moving]

draughtsman *noun* (*plural* **draughtsmen**)
1 a person who makes drawings. 2 a piece used in the game of draughts.
[*draught* is an old spelling of *draft*]

draw *verb* (**draws, drawing, drew, drawn**)
1 produce a picture or outline by making marks on a surface. 2 pull. 3 take out, *draw water*. 4 attract, *The fair drew large crowds*. 5 end a game or contest with the same score on both sides. 6 move or come, *The ship drew nearer*. 7 write out a cheque to be cashed.
draw a conclusion form an opinion about something by thinking about the evidence.
draw *noun* (*plural* **draws**)
1 the drawing of lots (see *lot*). 2 the drawing out of a gun etc., *He was quick on the draw*. 3 an attraction. 4 a drawn game. [from Old English]

USAGE: Do not confuse this word with *drawer*.

drawback *noun* (*plural* **drawbacks**)
a disadvantage.
[from *draw back* = hesitate]

drawbridge *noun* (*plural* **drawbridges**)
a bridge over a moat, hinged at one end so
that it can be raised or lowered.

drawer *noun* (*plural* **drawers**)
1 a sliding box-like compartment in a piece
of furniture. **2** a person who draws
something. **3** someone who draws (= writes
out) a cheque.

drawing *noun* (*plural* **drawings**)
a picture or outline drawn.

drawing pin *noun* (*plural* **drawing pins**)
a short pin with a flat top to be pressed
with your thumb, used for fastening paper
etc. to a surface.

drawing room *noun* (*plural* **drawing
rooms**)
a sitting room. [short for *withdrawing
room* = a private room in a hotel etc., to
which guests could withdraw]

drawl *verb* (**drawls, drawling, drawled**)
speak very slowly or lazily.
drawl *noun* (*plural* **drawls**)
a drawling way of speaking. [from old
German or old Dutch *dralen* = delay]

dray *noun* (*plural* **drays**)
a strong low flat cart for carrying heavy
loads.
[from Middle English; related to *draw*]

dread *noun*
great fear.
dread *verb* (**dreads, dreading, dreaded**)
fear something greatly. [from Old English]

dreadful *adjective* (*informal*)
very bad, *dreadful weather*.
dreadfully *adverb*

dreadlocks *plural noun*
hair worn in many ringlets or plaits,
especially by Rastafarians. [from *dread*
+ *lock*² (because the style was copied from
pictures of Ethiopian warriors)]

dream *noun* (*plural* **dreams**)
1 things a person seems to see while
sleeping. **2** something imagined; an
ambition or ideal. **dreamy** *adjective*,
dreamily *adverb*
dream *verb* (**dreams, dreaming, dreamt** or
dreamed)
1 have a dream or dreams. **2** have an

ambition. **3** think something might
happen, *I never dreamt she would leave*.
dreamer *noun* [from Middle English]

dreary *adjective* (**drearier, dreariest**)
1 dull or boring. **2** gloomy. **drearily** *adverb*,
dreariness *noun* [from Old English]

dredge *verb* (**dredges, dredging, dredged**)
drag something up, especially by scooping
at the bottom of a river or the sea. **dredger**
noun [origin unknown]

dregs *plural noun*
worthless bits that sink to the bottom of a
liquid.
[from a Scandinavian language]

drench *verb* (**drenches, drenching,
drenched**)
make wet all through; soak.
[from Old English]

dress *noun* (*plural* **dresses**)
1 a woman's or girl's garment with a
bodice and skirt. **2** clothes; costume, *fancy
dress*.
dress *verb* (**dresses, dressing, dressed**)
1 put clothes on. **2** arrange a display in a
window etc.; decorate, *dress the shop
windows*. **3** prepare food for cooking or
eating. **4** put a dressing on a wound. **dresser**
noun [from French *dresser* = prepare]

dressage (*say* **dress**-ahzh) *noun*
management of a horse to show its
obedience and style. [French, = training]

dresser *noun* (*plural* **dressers**)
a sideboard with shelves at the top for
dishes etc. [same origin as *dress*]

dressing *noun* (*plural* **dressings**)
1 a bandage, plaster, or ointment etc. for a
wound. **2** a sauce of oil, vinegar, etc. for a
salad. **3** manure or other fertilizer for
spreading on the soil.

dressing gown *noun* (*plural* **dressing
gowns**)
a loose garment for wearing when you are
not fully dressed.

dressmaker *noun* (*plural* **dressmakers**)
a woman who makes women's clothes.
dressmaking *noun*

dress rehearsal *noun* (*plural* dress rehearsals)
a rehearsal at which the cast wear their costumes.

drey *noun* (*plural* dreys)
a squirrel's nest. [origin unknown]

dribble *verb* (dribbles, dribbling, dribbled)
1 let saliva trickle out of your mouth.
2 move the ball forward in football or hockey with slight touches of your feet or stick.
[from *drib*, a different spelling of *drip*]

drier *noun* (*plural* driers)
a device for drying hair, laundry, etc.

drift *verb* (drifts, drifting, drifted)
1 be carried gently along by water or air.
2 move along slowly and casually. 3 live casually with no definite objective.
drifter *noun*

drift *noun* (*plural* drifts)
1 a drifting movement. 2 a mass of snow or sand piled up by the wind. 3 the general meaning of a speech etc. [from Old Norse]

driftwood *noun*
wood floating on the sea or washed ashore by it.

drill *noun* (*plural* drills)
1 a tool for making holes; a machine for boring holes or wells. 2 repeated exercises in gymnastics, military training, etc.

drill *verb* (drills, drilling, drilled)
1 make a hole etc. with a drill. 2 do repeated exercises; make people do exercises. [from old Dutch]

drily *adverb*
in a dry way.

drink *verb* (drinks, drinking, drank, drunk)
1 swallow liquid. 2 drink a lot of alcoholic drinks. **drinker** *noun*

drink *noun* (*plural* drinks)
1 a liquid for drinking; an amount of liquid swallowed. 2 an alcoholic drink.
[from Old English]

drip *verb* (drips, dripping, dripped)
fall or let something fall in drops.

drip *noun* (*plural* drips)
1 liquid falling in drops; the sound it makes. 2 apparatus for dripping liquid into the veins of a sick person.
[from Old English]

drip-dry *adjective*
made of material that dries easily and does not need ironing.

dripping *noun*
fat melted from roasted meat and allowed to set.
[from *drip*]

drive *verb* (drives, driving, drove, driven)
1 make something or someone move.
2 operate a motor vehicle or a train etc.
3 force or compel someone to do something, *Hunger drove them to steal.*
4 force someone into a state, *She is driving me crazy.* 5 rush; move rapidly, *Rain drove against the window.* **driver** *noun*

drive *noun* (*plural* drives)
1 a journey in a vehicle. 2 a hard stroke in cricket or golf etc. 3 the transmitting of power to machinery, *four-wheel drive.*
4 energy or enthusiasm. 5 an organized effort, *a sales drive.* 6 a track for vehicles through the grounds of a house.
[from Old English]

drive-in *adjective*
that you can use without getting out of your car.

drivel *noun*
silly talk; nonsense.
[from Old English *dreflian* = dribble]

drizzle *noun*
very fine rain.
[from Old English *dreosan* = to fall]

droll *adjective*
amusing in an odd way. [from French]

dromedary *noun* (*plural* dromedaries)
a camel with one hump, bred for riding on.
[from Greek *dromas* = runner]

drone *verb* (drones, droning, droned)
1 make a deep humming sound. 2 talk in a boring voice.

drone *noun* (*plural* drones)
1 a droning sound. 2 a male bee.
[from Old English]

drool *verb* (drools, drooling, drooled)
dribble.
drool over be very emotional about liking
something.
[from *drivel*]

droop *verb* (droops, drooping, drooped)
hang down weakly. [from Old Norse]

drop *noun* (*plural* drops)
1 a tiny amount of liquid. 2 a fall or
decrease. 3 a descent. 4 a small round
sweet. 5 a hanging ornament.
drop *verb* (drops, dropping, dropped)
1 fall. 2 let something fall. 3 put down a
passenger etc., *Drop me at the station.*
drop in visit someone casually.
drop out stop taking part in something.
drop-out *noun*
[from Old English]

droplet *noun* (*plural* droplets)
a small drop.

drought (*say* drout) *noun* (*plural* droughts)
a long period of dry weather.
[from Old English]

drove *noun* (*plural* droves)
a moving herd, flock, or crowd, *droves of
people.* [from Old English; related to *drive*]

drown *verb* (drowns, drowning, drowned)
1 die or kill by suffocation under water.
2 flood or drench. 3 make so much noise
that another sound cannot be heard.
[from Old Norse]

drowsy *adjective*
sleepy. **drowsily** *adverb*, **drowsiness** *noun*
[from Old English]

drubbing *noun* (*plural* drubbings)
a severe defeat.
[from Arabic *daraba* = beat]

drudge *noun* (*plural* drudges)
a person who does dull work. **drudgery**
noun [origin unknown]

drug *noun* (*plural* drugs)
1 a substance used in medicine. 2 a
substance that affects your senses or your
mind, *a drug addict.*
drug *verb* (drugs, drugging, drugged)
give a drug to someone, especially to make
them unconscious. [from French]

Druid (*say* droo-id) *noun* (*plural* Druids)
a priest of an ancient Celtic religion in
Britain and France.

drum *noun* (*plural* drums)
1 a musical instrument made of a cylinder
with a skin or parchment stretched over
one or both ends. 2 a cylindrical object or
container, *an oil drum.*
drum *verb* (drums, drumming, drummed)
1 play a drum or drums. 2 tap repeatedly
on something. **drummer** *noun*
[imitating the sound]

drumstick *noun* (*plural* drumsticks)
1 a stick for beating a drum. 2 the lower
part of a cooked bird's leg.

drunk *adjective*
not able to control your behaviour through
drinking too much alcohol.
drunk *noun* (*plural* drunks)
a person who is drunk.
[past participle of *drink*]

drunkard *noun* (*plural* drunkards)
a person who is often drunk.

drunken *adjective*
1 drunk, *a drunken man.* 2 caused by
drinking alcohol, *a drunken brawl.*

dry *adjective* (drier, driest)
1 without water or moisture. 2 thirsty.
3 boring or dull. 4 (of remarks or
humour) said in a matter-of-fact or
ironical way, *dry wit.*
drily *adverb*, **dryness** *noun*
dry *verb* (dries, drying, dried)
make or become dry.
[from Old English]

dryad *noun* (*plural* dryads)
a wood nymph.
[from Greek *drys* = tree]

dry-cleaning *noun*
a method of cleaning clothes etc. using a
liquid that evaporates quickly.

dry dock *noun* (*plural* dry docks)
a dock that can be emptied of water so that
ships can float in and then be repaired.

dual *adjective*
composed of two parts; double.
[from Latin *duo* = two]

USAGE: Do not confuse this word with *duel*.

dual carriageway *noun* (*plural* **dual carriageways**)
a road with a dividing strip between lanes of traffic in opposite directions.

dub[1] *verb* (**dubs, dubbing, dubbed**)
1 make someone a knight by touching him on the shoulder with a sword. **2** give a person or thing a nickname. [from old French *adober* = equip with armour]

dub[2] *verb* (**dubs, dubbing, dubbed**)
change or add new sound to the soundtrack of a film or magnetic tape.
[short for *double*]

dubbin *noun*
thick grease used to soften leather and make it waterproof. [from old French]

dubious (*say* **dew**-bee-us) *adjective*
doubtful. **dubiously** *adverb*
[from Latin *dubium* = doubt]

ducal *adjective*
to do with a duke.

ducat (*say* **duk**-at) *noun* (*plural* **ducats**)
a former gold coin used in Europe.
[from Latin]

duchess *noun* (*plural* **duchesses**)
a duke's wife or widow. [from Latin]

duchy *noun* (*plural* **duchies**)
the territory of a duke, *the duchy of Cornwall*. [from old French]

duck *noun* (*plural* **ducks**)
1 a swimming bird with a flat beak; the female of this. **2** a batsman's score of nought at cricket. **3** a ducking movement.
duck *verb* (**ducks, ducking, ducked**)
1 bend down quickly to avoid something.
2 go or push quickly under water. **3** dodge; avoid doing something. [from Old English]

duckling *noun* (*plural* **ducklings**)
a young duck.

duct *noun* (*plural* **ducts**)
a tube or channel through which liquid, gas, air, or cables can pass.
[from Latin *ductus* = leading]

ductile *adjective*
(of metal) able to be drawn out into fine strands. [from Latin]

dud *noun* (*plural* **duds**) (*slang*)
something that is useless or a fake or fails to work. [origin unknown]

dudgeon (*say* **duj**-on) *noun*
in high dudgeon indignant.
[origin unknown]

due *adjective*
1 expected; scheduled to do something or to arrive, *The train is due in ten minutes.*
2 owing; needing to be paid. **3** that ought to be given; rightful, *Treat her with due respect.*
due to as a result of.

USAGE: Traditionally, correct use is as in *His lateness was due to an accident.* Some people object to the use of 'due to' without a preceding noun (e.g. 'lateness') to which it refers. However, such uses as 'He was late, due to an accident' are nowadays widely regarded as acceptable. But if you prefer, you can use *because of* or *owing to* instead.

due *adverb*
exactly, *We sailed due east.*
due *noun* (*plural* **dues**)
1 something you deserve or have a right to; proper respect, *Give him his due.* **2** a fee, *harbour dues.*
[from French *dû* = what is owed]

duel *noun* (*plural* **duels**)
a fight between two people, especially with pistols or swords. **duelling** *noun*, **duellist** *noun* [from Italian]

USAGE: Do not confuse this word with *dual*.

duet *noun* (*plural* **duets**)
a piece of music for two players or singers.
[from Italian *duo* = two]

duff *adjective* (*slang*)
worthless or broken. [origin unknown]

duffel coat (*plural* **duffel coats**)
a thick overcoat with a hood, fastened with
toggles. [named after *Duffel*, a town in
Belgium, where the cloth for it was made]

duffer *noun* (*plural* **duffers**)
a person who is stupid or not good at doing
something. [origin unknown]

dugout *noun* (*plural* **dugouts**)
1 an underground shelter. **2** a canoe made
by hollowing out a tree trunk.

duke *noun* (*plural* **dukes**)
a member of the highest rank of noblemen.
dukedom *noun* [from Latin *dux* = leader]

dulcet (*say* **dul**-sit) *adjective*
sweet-sounding.
[from Latin *dulcis* = sweet]

dulcimer *noun* (*plural* **dulcimers**)
a musical instrument with strings that are
struck by two small hammers.
[from old French]

dull *adjective*
1 not bright or clear, *dull weather*.
2 stupid. **3** boring, *a dull concert*. **4** not
sharp, *a dull pain; a dull thud*. **dully** *adverb*,
dullness *noun* [from Old English]

dullard *noun* (*plural* **dullards**)
a stupid person.

duly *adverb*
in the due or proper way. [from *due*]

dumb *adjective*
1 without the ability to speak. **2** silent.
3 (*informal*) stupid. **dumbly** *adverb*,
dumbness *noun* [from Old English]

dumbfound *verb* (**dumbfounds,
dumbfounding, dumbfounded**)
astonish; strike a person dumb with
surprise. [from *dumb* + *confound*]

dummy *noun* (*plural* **dummies**)
1 something made to look like a person or
thing. **2** an imitation teat given to a baby to
suck. [from *dumb*]

dump *noun* (*plural* **dumps**)
1 a place where something (especially
rubbish) is left or stored. **2** (*informal*) a
dull or unattractive place.

dump *verb* (**dumps, dumping, dumped**)
1 get rid of something that is not wanted.
2 put something down carelessly.
[from a Scandinavian language]

dumpling *noun* (*plural* **dumplings**)
a lump of dough cooked in a stew etc. or
baked with fruit inside.
[same origin as *dumpy*]

dumps *plural noun* (*informal*)
low spirits, *in the dumps*.
[from old Dutch *domp* = mist, dampness]

dumpy *adjective*
short and fat.
[from an old word *dump* = dumpy person]

dunce *noun* (*plural* **dunces**)
a person who is slow at learning.
[from John Duns Scotus, a Scottish
philosopher in the Middle Ages (because
his opponents said that his followers could
not understand new ideas)]

dune *noun* (*plural* **dunes**)
a mound of loose sand shaped by the wind.
[via old French from Dutch]

dung *noun*
solid waste matter excreted by an animal.
[from Old English]

dungarees *plural noun*
overalls made of thick strong cloth.
[from Hindi *dungri* = the cloth they were
made of]

dungeon (*say* **dun**-jon) *noun* (*plural*
dungeons)
an underground cell for prisoners.
[from old French]

dunk *verb* (**dunks, dunking, dunked**)
dip something into liquid. [from German]

duodenum (*say* dew-o-**deen**-um) *noun*
(*plural* **duodenums**)
the part of the small intestine that is just
below the stomach. **duodenal** *adjective*
[from Latin *duodecim* = twelve (because its
length is about twelve times the breadth of
a finger)]

dupe *verb* (**dupes, duping, duped**)
deceive. [French]

duplicate (*say* dyoop-lik-at) *noun* (*plural* duplicates)
1 something that is exactly the same as something else. 2 an exact copy.

duplicate (*say* dyoop-lik-ayt) *verb* (duplicates, duplicating, duplicated)
make or be a duplicate.
duplication *noun*, duplicator *noun*
[from Latin *duplex* = double]

duplicity (*say* dew-plis-it-ee) *noun*
deceitfulness. [same origin as *duplicate*]

durable *adjective*
strong and likely to last.
durably *adverb*, durability *noun*
[from Latin *durare* = endure]

duration *noun*
the length of time something lasts.
[same origin as *durable*]

duress (*say* dewr-ess) *noun*
the use of force or threats to get what you want. [from Latin *durus* = hard]

during *preposition*
while something else is going on.
[from Latin *durans* = lasting, enduring]

dusk *noun* (*plural* dusks)
twilight in the evening. [from Old English]

dusky *adjective*
dark or shadowy.

dust *noun*
tiny particles of earth or other solid material.
dust *verb* (dusts, dusting, dusted)
1 wipe away dust. 2 sprinkle with dust or something powdery. [from Old English]

dustbin *noun* (*plural* dustbins)
a bin for household rubbish.

duster *noun* (*plural* dusters)
a cloth for dusting things.

dustman *noun* (*plural* dustmen)
a person employed to empty dustbins and cart away rubbish.

dustpan *noun* (*plural* dustpans)
a pan into which dust is brushed from a floor.

dusty *adjective* (dustier, dustiest)
1 covered with dust. 2 like dust.

dutiful *adjective*
doing your duty; obedient. dutifully *adverb*
[from *duty* + *-ful*]

duty *noun* (*plural* duties)
1 what you ought to do or must do. 2 a task that must be done. 3 a tax charged on imports and on certain other things.
on duty actually doing what is your regular work.
[same origin as *due*]

duty-free *adjective*
(of goods) on which duty is not charged.

duvet (*say* doo-vay) *noun* (*plural* duvets)
a kind of quilt used instead of other bedclothes. [French, = down²]

dwarf *noun* (*plural* dwarfs or dwarves)
a very small person or thing.
dwarf *verb* (dwarfs, dwarfing, dwarfed)
make something seem small by contrast, *The ocean liner dwarfed the tugs that were towing it.* [from Old English]

dwell *verb* (dwells, dwelling, dwelt)
live somewhere. dweller *noun*
dwell on think or talk about something for a long time.
[from Old English]

dwelling *noun* (*plural* dwellings)
a house etc. to live in.

dwindle *verb* (dwindles, dwindling, dwindled)
get smaller gradually. [from Old English]

dye *verb* (dyes, dyeing, dyed)
colour something by putting it into a liquid. dyer *noun*
dye *noun* (*plural* dyes)
a substance used to dye things.
[from Old English]

dyke *noun* (*plural* dykes)
a different spelling of *dike*.

dynamic *adjective*
energetic or forceful. dynamically *adverb*
[from Greek *dynamis* = power]

dynamite *noun*
1 a powerful explosive. 2 something likely to make people very excited or angry. [same origin as *dynamic*]

dynamo *noun* (*plural* **dynamos**)
a machine that makes electricity.

dynasty (*say* din-a-stee) *noun* (*plural* **dynasties**)
a succession of rulers all from the same family.
dynastic *adjective*
[same origin as *dynamic*]

dys- *prefix*
bad; difficult. [from Greek]

dysentery (*say* dis-en-tree) *noun*
a disease causing severe diarrhoea. [from *dys-* + Greek *entera* = bowels]

dyslexia (*say* dis-leks-ee-a) *noun*
unusually great difficulty in being able to read and spell. **dyslexic** *adjective*
[from *dys-* + Greek *lexis* = speech (which was confused with Latin *legere* = read)]

dyspepsia (*say* dis-pep-see-a) *noun*
indigestion.
dyspeptic *adjective*
[from *dys-* + Greek *peptikos* = able to digest]

dystrophy (*say* dis-trof-ee) *noun*
a disease that weakens the muscles. [from *dys-* + Greek *-trophia* = nourishment]

Ee

E. *abbreviation*
east; eastern.

e- *prefix*
1 out; away. 2 up, upwards; thoroughly. 3 formerly. see **ex-**.

each *adjective & pronoun*
every, every one, *each child; each of you.* [from Old English]

USAGE: In standard English, the pronoun *each* should be used with a singular verb and singular pronouns: *Each has chosen her own outfit.*

eager *adjective*
strongly wanting to do something; enthusiastic. **eagerly** *adverb*, **eagerness** *noun* [from Latin]

eagle *noun* (*plural* **eagles**)
a large bird of prey with very strong sight. [from Latin]

ear¹ *noun* (*plural* **ears**)
1 the organ of the body that is used for hearing. 2 hearing ability, *She has a good ear for music.* [from Old English *eare*]

ear² *noun* (*plural* **ears**)
the spike of seeds at the top of a stalk of corn. [from Old English *ear*]

earache *noun*
pain in the ear.

eardrum *noun* (*plural* **eardrums**)
a membrane in the ear that vibrates when sounds reach it.

earl *noun* (*plural* **earls**)
a British nobleman. **earldom** *noun*
[from Old English]

early *adjective & adverb* (**earlier, earliest**)
1 before the usual or expected time. 2 near the beginning, *early in the book.*
earliness *noun* [from *ere* + *-ly*]

earmark *verb* (**earmarks, earmarking, earmarked**)
put something aside for a particular purpose. [from the custom of marking an animal's ear to identify it]

earn *verb* (**earns, earning, earned**)
get something by working or in return for what you have done. [from Old English]

earnest *adjective*
showing serious feelings or intentions.
earnestly *adverb*, **earnestness** *noun*
[from Old English]

earnings *plural noun*
money earned.

earphone *noun* (*plural* **earphones**)
a listening device that fits over the ear.
[from *ear* + Greek *phone* = sound]

earring *noun* (*plural* **earrings**)
an ornament worn on the ear.

earshot *noun*
the distance within which a sound can be
heard. [from *ear* + *shot* in the sense 'as far
as something can reach']

earth *noun* (*plural* **earths**)
1 the planet (*Earth*) that we live on. 2 the
ground; soil. 3 the hole where a fox or
badger lives. 4 connection to the ground to
complete an electrical circuit.

earth *verb* (**earths, earthing, earthed**)
connect an electrical circuit to the ground.
[from Old English]

earthenware *noun*
pottery made of coarse baked clay.

earthly *adjective*
concerned with life on earth rather than
with life after death.

earthquake *noun* (*plural* **earthquakes**)
a violent movement of part of the earth's
surface.

earthworm *noun* (*plural* **earthworms**)
a worm that lives in the soil.

earthy *adjective*
1 like earth or soil. 2 crude and vulgar.

earwig *noun* (*plural* **earwigs**)
a crawling insect with pincers at the end of
its body. [so named because it was thought
to crawl into people's ears]

ease *noun*
freedom from trouble or effort or pain, *She
climbed the tree with ease.*

ease *verb* (**eases, easing, eased**)
1 make less painful or less tight or
troublesome. 2 move gently or gradually,
ease it in. 3 become less severe, *The
pressure eased.* [from French]

easel *noun* (*plural* **easels**)
a stand for supporting a blackboard or a
painting. [from Dutch *ezel* = donkey (which
carries a load)]

easily *adverb*
1 without difficulty; with ease. 2 by far,
easily the best. 3 very likely, *He could easily
be lying.*

east *noun*
1 the direction where the sun rises. 2 the
eastern part of a country, city, etc.

east *adjective* & *adverb*
towards or in the east; coming from the
east. **easterly** *adjective*, **eastern** *adjective*,
easterner *noun*, **easternmost** *adjective*
[from Old English]

Easter *noun*
the Sunday (in March or April) when
Christians commemorate the resurrection
of Christ; the days around it. [named after
Eastre, an Anglo-Saxon goddess whose
feast was celebrated in spring]

eastward *adjective* & *adverb*
towards the east. **eastwards** *adverb*

easy *adjective* (**easier, easiest**)
able to be done or used or understood
without trouble. **easiness** *noun*

easy *adverb*
with ease; comfortably, *Take it easy!*
[from French]

easy chair *noun* (*plural* **easy chairs**)
a comfortable armchair.

eat *verb* (**eats, eating, ate, eaten**)
1 chew and swallow as food. 2 have a meal,
When do we eat? 3 use up; destroy
gradually, *Extra expenses ate up our
savings.* [from Old English]

eatable *adjective*
fit to be eaten.

eau de Cologne (*say* oh der kol-**ohn**) *noun*
a perfume first made at Cologne.
[French, = water of Cologne]

eaves *plural noun*
the overhanging edges of a roof.
[from Old English]

eavesdrop *verb* (eavesdrops,
eavesdropping, eavesdropped)
listen secretly to a private conversation.
eavesdropper *noun*
[as if you are listening outside a wall,
where water drops from the eaves]

ebb *noun* (*plural* ebbs)
1 the movement of the tide when it is going
out, away from the land. **2** a low point, *Our
courage was at a low ebb.*
ebb *verb* (ebbs, ebbing, ebbed)
1 flow away from the land. **2** weaken;
become less, *strength ebbed.*
[from Old English]

ebony *noun*
a hard black wood. [from Greek]

EC *abbreviation*
European Community.

eccentric (*say* ik-sen-trik) *adjective*
behaving strangely. **eccentrically** *adverb*,
eccentricity (*say* ek-sen-triss-it-ee) *noun*
[from Greek *ekkentros* = away from the
centre]

ecclesiastical (*say* ik-lee-zee-ast-ik-al)
adjective
to do with the Church or the clergy.
[from Greek *ekklesia* = church]

echo *noun* (*plural* echoes)
a sound that is heard again as it is reflected
off something.
echo *verb* (echoes, echoing, echoed)
1 make an echo. **2** repeat a sound or
saying. [from Greek *eche* = sound]

éclair (*say* ay-klair) *noun* (*plural* éclairs)
a finger-shaped cake of pastry with a
creamy filling. [French]

eclipse *noun* (*plural* eclipses)
the blocking of the sun's or moon's light
when the moon or the earth is in the way.
eclipse *verb* (eclipses, eclipsing, eclipsed)
1 block the light and cause an eclipse.
2 seem better or more important than
others, *Her performance eclipsed the rest of
the team.* [from Greek]

eco- *prefix*
to do with ecology or the environment.
[from *ecology*]

ecology (*say* ee-kol-o-jee) *noun*
the study of living things in relation to
each other and to where they live.
ecological *adjective*, **ecologically** *adverb*,
ecologist *noun*
[from Greek *oikos* = house, + *-logy*]

economic (*say* ee-kon-om-ik) *adjective*
1 to do with economy or economics.
2 profitable.

economical *adjective*
using as little as possible.
economically *adverb*

economics *noun*
the study of how money is used and how
goods and services are provided and used.
economist *noun*

economize *verb* (economizes,
economizing, economized)
be economical; use or spend less.

economy *noun* (*plural* economies)
1 a country's or household's income (e.g.
from what it sells or earns) and the way
this is spent (e.g. on goods and services).
2 being economical. **3** a saving, *We made
economies.* [from Greek *oikos* = house
+ *-nomia* = management]

ecstasy (*say* ek-sta-see) *noun*
1 a feeling of great delight. **2** an illegal drug
that makes people feel very energetic and
can cause hallucinations. **ecstatic** (*say* ik-
stat-ik) *adjective*, **ecstatically** *adverb*
[from Greek, = standing outside yourself]

eczema (*say* eks-im-a) *noun*
a skin disease causing rough itching
patches. [from Greek]

-ed *suffix*
can form a past tense or past participle of a
verb (e.g. *paint/painted*), or an adjective
(e.g. *diseased*). [from Old English]

eddy *noun* (*plural* eddies)
a swirling patch of water or air or smoke
etc.
eddy *verb* (eddies, eddying, eddied)
swirl. [from Old English]

edge *noun* (*plural* edges)
1 the part along the side or end of

something. **2** the sharp part of a knife or axe or other cutting instrument.
be on edge be tense and irritable.

edge *verb* (**edges, edging, edged**)
1 be the edge or border of something. **2** put a border on. **3** move gradually, *He edged away.* [from Old English]

edgeways *adverb*
with the edge forwards or outwards.

edgy *adjective*
tense and irritable. **edginess** *noun*

edible *adjective*
suitable for eating, not poisonous, *edible fruits.* [from Latin *edere* = eat]

edict (*say* ee-dikt) *noun* (*plural* **edicts**)
an official command.
[from *e-* + Latin *dictum* = said]

edifice (*say* ed-if-iss) *noun* (*plural* **edifices**)
a large building.
[from Latin *aedis* = temple]

edify *verb* (**edifies, edifying, edified**)
be an improving influence on a person's mind. **edification** *noun* [from Latin]

edit *verb* (**edits, editing, edited**)
1 be the editor of a newspaper or other publication. **2** make written material ready for publishing. **3** choose and put the parts of a film or tape recording etc. into order. [from *editor*]

edition *noun* (*plural* **editions**)
1 the form in which something is published, *a paperback edition.* **2** all the copies of a book etc. issued at the same time, *the first edition.* **3** an individual television or radio programme in a series.

editor *noun* (*plural* **editors**)
1 the person in charge of a newspaper or a section of it. **2** a person who edits something. [Latin, = producer]

editorial *adjective*
to do with editing or editors.

editorial *noun* (*plural* **editorials**)
a newspaper article giving the editor's comments on something.

educate *verb* (**educates, educating, educated**)
provide people with education. **educative** *adjective*, **educator** *noun* [from Latin]

education *noun*
the process of training people's minds and abilities so that they acquire knowledge and develop skills. **educational** *adjective*, **educationally** *adverb*, **educationist** *noun*

-ee *suffix*
forms nouns meaning 'person affected by or described as' (e.g. *absentee, employee, refugee*). [from French]

EEC *abbreviation*
European Economic Community (= the Common Market).

eel *noun* (*plural* **eels**)
a long fish that looks like a snake.
[from Old English]

eerie *adjective* (**eerier, eeriest**)
strange in a frightening or mysterious way. **eerily** *adverb*, **eeriness** *noun*
[from Old English]

ef- *prefix*
1 out; away. **2** up, upwards; thoroughly. **3** formerly. see **ex-**.

efface *verb* (**effaces, effacing, effaced**)
wipe or rub out. **effacement** *noun*
[from French]

effect *noun* (*plural* **effects**)
1 a change that is produced by an action or cause; a result. **2** an impression that is produced by something, *a cheerful effect.*

effect *verb* (**effects, effecting, effected**)
make something happen, *We want to effect a change.* [from *ef-* + Latin *-fectum* = done]

USAGE: Do not confuse with *affect.*

effective *adjective*
1 producing the effect that is wanted.
2 impressive and striking.
effectively *adverb*, **effectiveness** *noun*

effectual *adjective*
producing the result desired.
effectually *adverb*

effeminate *adjective*
(of a man) having qualities that are
thought to be feminine. **effeminacy** *noun*
[from Latin]

effervesce (*say* ef-er-**vess**) *verb* (**effervesces,
effervescing, effervesced**)
give off bubbles of gas; fizz. **effervescent**
adjective, **effervescence** *noun* [from *ef-*
+ Latin *fervescere* = come to the boil]

efficacious (*say* ef-ik-**ay**-shus) *adjective*
able to produce the result desired.
efficacy (*say* **ef**-ik-a-see) *noun*
[from Latin *efficere* = succeed in doing]

efficient *adjective*
doing work well; effective.
efficiently *adverb,* **efficiency** *noun*
[same origin as *efficacious*]

effigy *noun* (*plural* **effigies**)
a model or sculptured figure.
[from Latin *effingere* = to form]

effort *noun* (*plural* **efforts**)
1 the use of energy; the energy used.
2 something difficult or tiring. **3** an
attempt, *This painting is a good effort.*
[from old French]

effortless *adjective*
done with little or no effort.
effortlessly *adverb*

effusive *adjective*
making a great show of affection or
enthusiasm. **effusively** *adverb,* **effusiveness**
noun [from Latin *effundere* = pour out]

e.g. *abbreviation*
for example. [short for Latin *exempli gratia*
= for the sake of an example]

egalitarian (*say* ig-al-it-**air**-ee-an) *adjective*
believing that everybody is equal and that
nobody should be given special privileges.
[from French *égal* = equal]

egg[1] *noun* (*plural* **eggs**)
1 a more or less round object produced by
the female of birds, fishes, reptiles, and
insects, which may develop into a new
individual if fertilized. **2** a hen's or duck's
egg used as food. **3** an ovum.
[from Old Norse]

egg[2] *verb* (**eggs, egging, egged**)
encourage someone with taunts or dares
etc., *We egged him on.*
[from Old Norse *eggja* = sharpen]

eggplant *noun* (*plural* **eggplants**)
(*American*) an aubergine.
[because of the aubergine's shape]

ego (*say* **eeg**-oh) *noun* (*plural* **egos**)
a person's self or self-respect. [Latin, = I]

egotist (*say* **eg**-oh-tist) *noun* (*plural*
egotists)
a conceited person who is always talking
about himself or herself. **egotism** *noun,*
egotistic *adjective* [from *ego* + *-ist*]

Eid (*say* eed) *noun*
a Muslim festival. Eid ul-Fitr marks the
end of the fast of Ramadan.
[from Arabic *'id* = feast]

eiderdown *noun* (*plural* **eiderdowns**)
a quilt stuffed with soft material.
[originally the soft down of the *eider*, a kind
of duck]

eight *noun & adjective* (*plural* **eights**)
the number 8. **eighth** *adjective & noun*
[from Old English]

eighteen *noun & adjective* (*plural*
eighteens)
the number 18. **eighteenth** *adjective & noun*
[from Old English]

eighty *noun & adjective* (*plural* **eighties**)
the number 80. **eightieth** *adjective & noun*
[from Old English]

eisteddfod (*say* I-**steth**-vod) *noun* (*plural*
eisteddfods or **eisteddfodau**)
an annual Welsh gathering of poets and
musicians for competitions.
[Welsh, = session]

either *adjective & pronoun*
1 one or the other of two, *Either team can
win; either of them.* **2** both of two, *There are
fields on either side of the river.*
either *adverb*
also; similarly, *If you won't go, I won't
either.*
either *conjunction* (used with *or*)
the first of two possibilities, *He is either ill
or drunk. Either come right in or go away.*
[from Old English]

ejaculate *verb* (ejaculates, ejaculating, ejaculated)
1 (of a man) produce semen from the penis.
2 suddenly say something. **ejaculation** *noun*
[from *e-* + Latin *jacere* = to throw]

eject *verb* (ejects, ejecting, ejected)
1 send something out forcefully. **2** force someone to leave. **3** (of a pilot) be thrown out of an aircraft in a special seat in an emergency. **ejection** *noun*, **ejector** *noun*
[from *e-* + Latin *-jectum* = thrown]

eke (*say* eek) *verb* (ekes, eking, eked)
eke out manage to make something last as long as possible by only using small amounts of it.
[from Old English]

elaborate (*say* il-**ab**-er-at) *adjective*
having many parts or details; complicated.
elaborately *adverb*, **elaborateness** *noun*
elaborate (*say* il-**ab**-er-ayt) *verb*
(elaborates, elaborating, elaborated)
explain or work something out in detail.
elaboration *noun*
[from *e-* + Latin *laborare* = to work]

elapse *verb* (elapses, elapsing, elasped)
(of time) pass.
[from *e-* + Latin *lapsum* = slipped]

elastic *noun*
cord or material woven with strands of rubber etc. so that it can stretch.
elastic *adjective*
able to be stretched or squeezed and then go back to its original length or shape.
elasticity *noun* [from Greek]

elated *adjective*
feeling very pleased. **elation** *noun*
[from *e-* + Latin *latum* = carried]

elbow *noun* (*plural* elbows)
the joint in the middle of the arm.
elbow *verb* (elbows, elbowing, elbowed)
push with the elbow. [from Old English]

elder[1] *adjective*
older, *my elder brother*.
elder *noun* (*plural* elders)
1 an older person, *Respect your elders!* **2** an official in certain Churches.
[an old spelling of *older*]

elder[2] *noun* (*plural* elders)
a tree with white flowers and black berries.
elderberry *noun* [from Old English]

elderly *adjective*
rather old. [from *elder*[1] + *-ly*]

eldest *adjective*
oldest. [an old spelling of *oldest*]

elect *verb* (elects, electing, elected)
1 choose by voting. **2** choose to do something; decide.
[from *e-* + Latin *lectum* = chosen]

election *noun* (*plural* elections)
electing; the process of electing Members of Parliament.

elector *noun* (*plural* electors)
a person who has the right to vote in an election. **electoral** *adjective*

electorate *noun* (*plural* electorates)
all the electors.

electric *adjective*
1 to do with or worked by electricity.
2 causing sudden excitement, *The news had an electric effect.* **electrical** *adjective*, **electrically** *adverb*
[from Greek *elektron* = amber (which is easily given a charge of static electricity)]

electric chair *noun*
an electrified chair used for capital punishment in the USA.

electrician *noun* (*plural* electricians)
a person whose job is to deal with electrical equipment.

electricity *noun*
a form of energy carried by certain particles of matter (electrons and protons), used for lighting and heating and for making machines work.

electrify *verb* (electrifies, electrifying, electrified)
1 give an electric charge to something.
2 supply something with electric power; cause something to work with electricity.
3 thrill with sudden excitement.
electrification *noun*

electro- *prefix*
to do with or using electricity.

electrocute verb (electrocutes, electrocuting, electrocuted)
kill by electricity. **electrocution** noun
[from electro- + execute]

electrode noun (plural electrodes)
a solid conductor through which electricity enters or leaves a vacuum tube.
[from electro- + Greek hodos = way]

electromagnet noun (plural electromagnets)
a magnet worked by electricity.
electromagnetic adjective

electron noun (plural electrons)
a particle of matter with a negative electric charge. [same origin as electric]

electronic adjective
produced or worked by a flow of electrons.
electronically adverb

electronic mail noun
messages sent from one computer to others.

electronics noun
the use or study of electronic devices.

elegant adjective
graceful and dignified. **elegantly** adverb, **elegance** noun [from Latin]

elegiac adjective
expressing sadness or sorrow.

elegy (say el-ij-ee) noun (plural elegies)
a sorrowful or serious poem. [from Greek]

element noun (plural elements)
1 each of the parts that make up a whole thing. 2 each of about 100 substances composed of atoms that have the same number of protons. 3 a basic or elementary principle, the elements of algebra. 4 a wire or coil that gives out heat in an electric fire or cooker etc. 5 the environment or circumstances that suit you best, Karen is really in her element at parties.
the elements the forces of weather, such as rain, wind, and cold.
[from Latin]

elementary adjective
dealing with the simplest stages of something; easy.

elephant noun (plural elephants)
a very large animal with a trunk and tusks.
[from Greek elephas = ivory (which its tusks are made of)]

elephantine (say el-if-ant-I'n) adjective
1 very large. 2 clumsy and slow-moving.

elevate verb (elevates, elevating, elevated)
lift or raise something to a higher position.
elevation noun
[from e- + Latin levare = to lift]

elevator noun (plural elevators)
1 something that raises things. 2 (American) a lift.

eleven adjective & noun (plural elevens)
the number 11. **eleventh** adjective & noun
[from Old English]

elf noun (plural elves)
(in fairy tales) a small being with magic powers. **elfin** adjective
[from Old English]

elicit (say ill-iss-it) verb (elicits, eliciting, elicited)
draw out information by reasoning or questioning. [from Latin]

USAGE: Do not confuse with illicit.

elide verb (elides, eliding, elided)
omit part of a word by elision.

eligible (say el-ij-ib-ul) adjective
qualified or suitable for something.
eligibility noun
[from Latin eligere = choose]

eliminate verb (eliminates, eliminating, eliminated)
get rid of something. **elimination** noun
[from e- + Latin limen = entrance]

elision (say il-lizh-on) noun
omitting part of a word in pronouncing it, e.g. in saying I'm for I am.
[from Latin elidere = to push out]

élite (say ay-leet) noun
a group of people given privileges which are not given to others.
[from old French élit = chosen]

elixir (*say* il-iks-er) *noun* (*plural* elixirs)
a liquid that is believed to have magic powers, such as restoring youth to someone who is old. [from Arabic *al-iksir* = substance that would cure illness and change metals into gold]

Elizabethan (*say* il-iz-a-beeth-an) *adjective*
from the time of Queen Elizabeth I (1558–1603). **Elizabethan** *noun*

elk *noun* (*plural* elks)
a large kind of deer. [from Old English]

ellipse (*say* il-ips) *noun* (*plural* ellipses)
an oval shape. [same origin as *elliptical*]

ellipsis *noun*
omitting a word or words from a sentence, usually so that the sentence can still be understood. [same origin as *elliptical*]

elliptical (*say* il-ip-tik-al) *adjective*
1 shaped like an ellipse. 2 with some words omitted, *an elliptical phrase*. **elliptically** *adverb* [from Greek *elleipsis* = fault]

elm *noun* (*plural* elms)
a tall tree with rough leaves. [from Old English]

elocution (*say* el-o-kew-shon) *noun*
the art of speaking clearly and correctly. [same origin as *eloquent*]

elongated *adjective*
made longer; lengthened. **elongation** *noun* [from *e-* + Latin *longus* = long]

elope *verb* (elopes, eloping, eloped)
run away secretly to get married. **elopement** *noun* [from old French]

eloquent *adjective*
speaking fluently and expressing ideas vividly. **eloquently** *adverb*, **eloquence** *noun* [from *e-* + Latin *loqui* = speak]

else *adverb*
1 besides; other, *Nobody else knows*. 2 otherwise; if not, *Run or else you'll be late*. [from Old English]

elsewhere *adverb*
somewhere else.

elucidate (*say* il-oo-sid-ayt) *verb* (elucidates, elucidating, elucidated)
make something clear by explaining it. **elucidation** *noun* [from *e-* + Latin *lucidus* = clear]

elude (*say* il-ood) *verb* (eludes, eluding, eluded)
avoid being caught by someone, *The fox eluded the hounds*. **elusive** *adjective* [from *e-* + Latin *ludere* = to play]

USAGE: Do not confuse with *allude*.

em- *prefix*
1 in; into. 2 on. see **en-**.

emaciated (*say* im-ay-see-ay-tid) *adjective*
very thin from illness or starvation. **emaciation** *noun* [from *e-* + Latin *macies* = leanness]

e-mail *noun*
electronic mail.

emanate (*say* em-an-ayt) *verb* (emanates, emanating, emanated)
come from a source. [from *e-* + Latin *manare* = to flow]

emancipate (*say* im-an-sip-ayt) *verb* (emancipates, emancipating, emancipated)
set free from slavery or other restraints. **emancipation** *noun* [from *e-* + Latin *mancipium* = slave]

embalm *verb* (embalms, embalming, embalmed)
preserve a corpse from decay by using spices or chemicals. [from *em-* + *balm*]

embankment *noun* (*plural* embankments)
a long bank of earth or stone to hold back water or support a road or railway. [from *em-* + *bank*[1]]

embargo *noun* (*plural* embargoes)
a ban. [from Spanish *embargar* = restrain]

embark *verb* (embarks, embarking, embarked)
put or go on board a ship or aircraft. **embarkation** *noun*
embark on begin, *They embarked on a dangerous exercise*.
[from *em-* + French *barque* = a sailing ship]

embarrass *verb* (embarrasses,
embarrassing, embarrassed)
make someone feel awkward or ashamed.
embarrassment *noun*
[via French from Spanish]

embassy *noun* (*plural* embassies)
1 an ambassador and his or her staff.
2 the building where they work.
[from old French; related to *ambassador*]

embed *verb* (embeds, embedding,
embedded)
fix firmly in something solid.

embellish *verb* (embellishes, embellishing,
embellished)
ornament something; add details to it.
embellishment *noun*
[from em- + French *bel* = beautiful]

embers *plural noun*
small pieces of glowing coal or wood in a
dying fire. [from Old English]

embezzle *verb* (embezzles, embezzling,
embezzled)
take dishonestly money that was left in
your care. **embezzlement** *noun*
[from old French]

emblazon *verb* (emblazons, emblazoning,
emblazoned)
1 decorate something with a coat of arms.
2 decorate something with bright or eye-
catching designs or words.
[from em- + French *blason* = shield]

emblem *noun* (*plural* emblems)
a symbol that represents something, *The
crown is a royal emblem.* **emblematic**
adjective [from Latin]

embody *verb* (embodies, embodying,
embodied)
1 express principles or ideas in a visible
form, *The house embodies our idea of a
modern home.* 2 include or contain, *Parts of
the old treaty are embodied in the new one.*
embodiment *noun*

emboss *verb* (embosses, embossing,
embossed)
decorate a flat surface with a raised design.
[from em- + old French *boce* = boss²]

embrace *verb* (embraces, embracing,
embraced)
1 hold someone closely in your arms.
2 include a number of things. 3 accept or
adopt a cause or belief.
embrace *noun* (*plural* embraces)
a hug.
[from em- + Latin *bracchium* = an arm]

embrocation *noun*
a lotion for rubbing on parts of the body
that ache. [from Greek]

embroider *verb* (embroiders,
embroidering, embroidered)
1 decorate cloth with needlework. 2 add
made-up details to a story to make it more
interesting. **embroidery** *noun*
[from old French]

embroil *verb* (embroils, embroiling,
embroiled)
involve in an argument or quarrel.
[from old French]

embryo (*say* em-bree-oh) *noun* (*plural*
embryos)
1 a baby or young animal as it starts to
grow in the womb; a young bird growing in
an egg. 2 anything in its earliest stages of
development.
embryonic (*say* em-bree-on-ik) *adjective*
[from em- + Greek *bryein* = grow]

emend *verb* (emends, emending, emended)
remove errors from a piece of writing.
[from e- + Latin *menda* = a fault]

emerald *noun* (*plural* emeralds)
1 a bright-green precious stone. 2 its
colour. [from old French]

emerge *verb* (emerges, emerging, emerged)
1 come out or appear. 2 become known.
emergence *noun*, **emergent** *adjective*
[from e- + Latin *mergere* = plunge]

emergency *noun* (*plural* emergencies)
a sudden serious happening needing
prompt action. [same origin as *emerge*]

emery paper *noun*
paper with a gritty coating like sandpaper.
[from Greek]

emetic (*say* im-et-ik) *noun* (*plural* emetics)
a medicine used to make a person vomit.
[from Greek]

emigrate *verb* (emigrates, emigrating, emigrated)
leave your own country and go and live in another. **emigration** *noun*, **emigrant** *noun* [from e- + Latin *migrare* = migrate]

USAGE: People are *emigrants* from the country they leave and *immigrants* in the country where they settle.

eminence *noun*
being eminent; distinction.
His Eminence a cardinal's title.
[from Latin]

eminent *adjective*
famous and respected. **eminently** *adverb*

emir (*say* em-**eer**) *noun* (*plural* emirs)
a Muslim ruler. [from Arabic *amir* = ruler]

emission *noun* (*plural* emissions)
1 emitting something. 2 something that is emitted, especially fumes or radiation.

emit *verb* (emits, emitting, emitted)
send out light, heat, fumes, etc.
[from e- + Latin *mittere* = send]

emolument (*say* im-ol-yoo-ment) *noun*
(*plural* emoluments)
payment for work; a salary. [from Latin]

emotion *noun* (*plural* emotions)
a strong feeling in the mind, such as love or hate. **emotional** *adjective*, **emotionally** *adverb* [from French]

emotive *adjective*
causing emotion.

empathy *noun*
identifying yourself mentally with another person and understanding him or her.
[from em- + Greek *pathos* = feeling]

emperor *noun* (*plural* emperors)
a man who rules an empire.
[from Latin *imperator* = commander]

emphasis (*say* em-fa-sis) *noun* (*plural* emphases)
1 special importance given to something. 2 stress put on a word or part of a word.
[from em- + Greek *phanein* = to show]

emphasize *verb* (emphasizes, emphasizing, emphasized)
put emphasis on something.

emphatic (*say* im-**fat**-ik) *adjective*
using emphasis. **emphatically** *adverb*

empire *noun* (*plural* empires)
1 a group of countries controlled by one person or government. 2 a set of shops or firms under one control. [from Latin]

empirical *adjective*
based on observation or experiment, not on theory.
[from Greek *empeiria* = experience]

employ *verb* (employs, employing, employed)
1 pay a person to work for you. 2 make use of, *Our doctor employs the most modern methods.* **employer** *noun*, **employment** *noun* [from French]

employee *noun* (*plural* employees)
a person employed by someone (who is the *employer*).

emporium (*say* em-**por**-ee-um) *noun*
(*plural* emporias or emporiums)
a large shop.
[from Greek *emporos* = merchant]

empower *verb* (empowers, empowering, empowered)
give someone the power to do something; authorize.

empress *noun* (*plural* empresses)
1 a woman who rules an empire. 2 an emperor's wife. [from old French]

empty *adjective*
1 with nothing in it. 2 with nobody in it. 3 with no meaning or no effect, *empty promises.* **emptily** *adverb*, **emptiness** *noun*
empty *verb* (empties, emptying, emptied)
make or become empty. [from Old English]

emu *noun* (*plural* emus)
a large Australian bird rather like an ostrich. [from Portuguese]

emulate *verb* (emulates, emulating, emulated)
try to do as well as someone or something,

especially by imitating them, *He is emulating his father.* **emulation** *noun* [from Latin *aemulus* = a rival]

emulsion *noun* (*plural* **emulsions**)
1 a creamy or slightly oily liquid. 2 the coating on photographic film which is sensitive to light. [from Latin]

en- *prefix* (changing to **em-** before words beginning with *b*, *m*, or *p*)
1 in; into. 2 on. [from Latin or Greek, = in]

enable *verb* (**enables, enabling, enabled**)
give the means or ability to do something.

enact *verb* (**enacts, enacting, enacted**)
1 make a law by a formal process, *Parliament enacted new laws against drugs.* 2 perform, *enact a play.* **enactment** *noun*

enamel *noun* (*plural* **enamels**)
1 a shiny substance for coating metal. 2 paint that dries hard and shiny. 3 the shiny surface of teeth.
enamel *verb* (**enamels, enamelling, enamelled**)
coat or decorate with enamel. [from old French]

enamoured (*say* in-am-erd) *adjective*
in love with someone. [from *en-* + French *amour* = love]

en bloc (*say* ahn blok) *adverb*
all at the same time; in a block. [French]

encamp *verb* (**encamps, encamping, encamped**)
settle in a camp.

encampment *noun* (*plural* **encampments**)
a camp.

encase *verb* (**encases, encasing, encased**)
enclose something in a case. [from *en-* + *case*[1]]

enchant *verb* (**enchants, enchanting, enchanted**)
1 put someone under a magic spell. 2 fill someone with intense delight. **enchanter** *noun*, **enchantment** *noun*, **enchantress** *noun* [from old French; related to *incantation*]

encircle *verb* (**encircles, encircling, encircled**)
surround. **encirclement** *noun*

enclose *verb* (**encloses, enclosing, enclosed**)
1 put a wall or fence round; shut in on all sides. 2 put something into a box or envelope etc. [from old French; related to *include*]

enclosure *noun* (*plural* **enclosures**)
1 enclosing. 2 an enclosed area. 3 something enclosed with a letter or parcel.

encompass *verb* (**encompasses, encompassing, encompassed**)
1 surround. 2 contain or include. [from *en-* + *compass* in an old sense = circle]

encore (*say* on-kor) *noun* (*plural* **encores**)
an extra item performed at a concert etc. after previous items have been applauded. [French]

encounter *verb* (**encounters, encountering, encountered**)
1 meet someone unexpectedly. 2 experience, *We encountered some difficulties.*
encounter *noun* (*plural* **encounters**)
1 an unexpected meeting. 2 a battle. [from *en-* + Latin *contra* = against]

encourage *verb* (**encourages, encouraging, encouraged**)
1 give confidence or hope; hearten. 2 try to persuade; urge. 3 stimulate; help to develop, *Encourage healthy eating.* **encouragement** *noun* [from *en-* + old French *corage* = courage]

encroach *verb* (**encroaches, encroaching, encroached**)
intrude upon someone's rights; go further than the proper limits, *The extra work would encroach on their free time.* **encroachment** *noun* [from *en-* + French *crochier* = to hook]

encrust *verb* (**encrusts, encrusting, encrusted**)
cover with a crust or layer. **encrustation** *noun* [from Latin]

encumber *verb* (**encumbers, encumbering, encumbered**)
be a burden to; hamper. **encumbrance** *noun* [from *en-* + old French *combre* = dam]

encyclopedia *noun* (*plural* **encyclopedias**)
a book or set of books containing all kinds

of information. **encyclopedic** *adjective*
[from Greek *enkyklopaideia* = general
education]

end *noun* (*plural* **ends**)
1 the last part or extreme point of
something. 2 the half of a sports pitch or
court defended or occupied by one team or
player. 3 destruction or death. 4 purpose,
She did it to gain her own ends.
end *verb* (**ends, ending, ended**)
bring or come to an end.
[from Old English]

endanger *verb* (**endangers, endangering,
endangered**)
cause danger to.

endangered species *noun* (*plural*
endangered species)
a species in danger of extinction.

endear *verb* (**endears, endearing, endeared**)
if you endear yourself to someone, you
make them fond of you. **endearing** *adjective*

endeavour (*say* in-**dev**-er) *verb*
(**endeavours, endeavouring, endeavoured**)
attempt.
endeavour *noun* (*plural* **endeavours**)
an attempt. [from an old phrase *put
yourself in devoir* = do your best (from
French *devoir* = duty)]

endemic (*say* en-**dem**-ik) *adjective*
(of a disease) often found in a certain area
or group of people.
[from *en-* + Greek *demos* = people]

ending *noun* (*plural* **endings**)
the last part.

endless *adjective*
1 never stopping. 2 with the ends joined to
make a continuous strip for use in
machinery etc., *an endless belt.*
endlessly *adverb*

endorse *verb* (**endorses, endorsing,
endorsed**)
1 sign your name on the back of a cheque
or document. 2 make an official entry on a
licence about an offence committed by its
holder. 3 confirm or give your approval to
something. **endorsement** *noun*
[from Latin *in dorsum* = on the back]

endow *verb* (**endows, endowing, endowed**)
1 provide a source of income to establish
something, *She endowed a scholarship.*
2 provide with an ability or quality, *He
was endowed with great talent.* **endowment**
noun [from old French; related to *dowry*]

endure *verb* (**endures, enduring, endured**)
1 suffer or put up with pain or hardship
etc. 2 continue to exist; last.
endurable *adjective*, **endurance** *noun*
[from *en-* + Latin *durus* = hard]

enemy *noun* (*plural* **enemies**)
1 one who hates and opposes or seeks to
harm another. 2 a nation or army etc. at
war with another. [from old French]

energetic *adjective*
full of energy. **energetically** *adverb*

energy *noun* (*plural* **energies**)
1 strength to do things, liveliness. 2 the
ability of matter or radiation to do work.
Energy is measured in joules.
[from *en-* + Greek *ergon* = work]

enfold *verb* (**enfolds, enfolding, enfolded**)
surround or be wrapped round something.

enforce *verb* (**enforces, enforcing, enforced**)
compel people to obey a law or rule.
enforcement *noun*, **enforceable** *adjective*
[from old French]

enfranchise *verb* (**enfranchises,
enfranchising, enfranchised**)
give people the right to vote in elections.
enfranchisement *noun*
[from *en-* + old French *franc* = free]

engage *verb* (**engages, engaging, engaged**)
1 arrange to employ or use, *Engage a
typist.* 2 occupy the attention of, *They
engaged her in conversation.* 3 begin a
battle with, *We engaged the enemy.*
[from old French]

engaged *adjective*
1 having promised to marry somebody.
2 in use; occupied.

engagement *noun* (*plural* **engagements**)
1 engaging something. 2 a promise to
marry somebody. 3 an arrangement to
meet somebody or do something. 4 a battle.

engaging *adjective*
attractive or charming.

engine *noun* (*plural* engines)
1 a machine that provides power. 2 a vehicle that pulls a railway train; a locomotive.
[from old French; related to *ingenious*]

engineer *noun* (*plural* engineers)
an expert in engineering.
engineer *verb* (engineers, engineering, engineered)
plan and construct or cause to happen, *He engineered a meeting between them.*

engineering *noun*
the design and building or control of machinery or of structures such as roads and bridges.

engrave *verb* (engraves, engraving, engraved)
carve words or lines etc. on a surface.
engraver *noun*, **engraving** *noun*
[from *en-* + Old English *grafan* = carve]

engross *verb* (engrosses, engrossing, engrossed)
occupy a person's whole attention, *He was engrossed in his book.*
[originally = to buy up all of something: from French *en gros* = wholesale]

engulf *verb* (engulfs, engulfing, engulfed)
flow over and cover; swamp.

enhance *verb* (enhances, enhancing, enhanced)
make a thing more attractive; increase its value. **enhancement** *noun*
[from old French]

enigma (*say* in-**ig**-ma) *noun* (*plural* enigmas)
something very difficult to understand; a puzzle. [from Greek]

enigmatic (*say* en-ig-**mat**-ik) *adjective*
mysterious and puzzling.
enigmatically *adverb*

enjoy *verb* (enjoys, enjoying, enjoyed)
get pleasure from something.
enjoyable *adjective*, **enjoyment** *noun*
[from *en-* + old French *joir* = rejoice]

enlarge *verb* (enlarges, enlarging, enlarged)
make or become bigger. **enlargement** *noun*
[from old French]

enlighten *verb* (enlightens, enlightening, enlightened)
give more knowledge or information to a person. **enlightenment** *noun*
[from *en-* + *lighten*[1]]

enlist *verb* (enlists, enlisting, enlisted)
1 join the armed forces. 2 obtain someone's support or services etc., *enlist their help.*
enlistment *noun*
[from *en-* + *list*[1]]

enliven *verb* (enlivens, enlivening, enlivened)
make something more lively.
enlivenment *noun*

en masse (*say* ahn mass) *adverb*
all together. [French, = in a mass]

enmity *noun*
being somebody's enemy; hostility.
[from old French]

enormity *noun* (*plural* enormities)
1 great wickedness, *the enormity of this crime.* 2 great size; hugeness, *the enormity of their task.* [same origin as *enormous*]

USAGE: Many people regard the use of sense 2 as incorrect, though it is very common. In formal writing it is probably best to avoid it and to use *magnitude* instead.

enormous *adjective*
very large; huge.
enormously *adverb*, **enormousness** *noun*
[from *e-* + Latin *norma* = standard]

enough *adjective* & *noun* & *adverb*
as much or as many as necessary, *enough food; I have had enough; Are you warm enough?* [from Old English]

en passant (*say* ahn pas-ahn) *adverb*
by the way. [French, = in passing]

enquire *verb* (enquires, enquiring, enquired)
1 ask for information, *He enquired if I was*

well. **2** investigate something carefully. [same origin as *inquire*]

USAGE: See the note at *inquire*.

enquiry *noun* (*plural* enquiries)
1 a question. **2** an investigation.

enrage *verb* (enrages, enraging, enraged)
make someone very angry.
[from old French]

enrapture *verb* (enraptures, enrapturing, enraptured)
fill someone with intense delight.

enrich *verb* (enriches, enriching, enriched)
make richer. **enrichment** *noun*
[from old French]

enrol *verb* (enrols, enrolling, enrolled)
1 become a member of a society etc.
2 make someone into a member. **enrolment**
noun [from *en-* + old French *rolle* = roll]

en route (*say* ahn **root**) *adverb*
on the way. [French]

ensconce *verb* (ensconces, ensconcing, ensconced)
settle comfortably, *ensconced in a chair*.
[from *en-* + an old word *sconce* = a shelter]

ensemble (*say* on-**sombl**) *noun* (*plural* ensembles)
1 a group of things that go together. **2** a group of musicians. **3** a matching outfit of clothes. [French]

enshrine *verb* (enshrines, enshrining, enshrined)
keep as if in a shrine, *His memory is enshrined in our hearts*.

ensign *noun* (*plural* ensigns)
a military or naval flag.
[from old French; related to *insignia*]

enslave *verb* (enslaves, enslaving, enslaved)
make a slave of someone; force someone into slavery. **enslavement** *noun*

ensue *verb* (ensues, ensuing, ensued)
happen afterwards or as a result.
[from old French]

ensure *verb* (ensures, ensuring, ensured)
make certain of; guarantee, *Good food will ensure good health*. [from old French]

USAGE: Do not confuse with *insure*.

entail *verb* (entails, entailing, entailed)
make a thing necessary; involve, *This plan entails danger*. **entailment** *noun*
[from *en-* + old French *taillir* = bequeath]

entangle *verb* (entangles, entangling, entangled)
tangle. **entanglement** *noun*

entente (*say* on-**tont**) *noun* (*plural* ententes)
a friendly understanding between countries. [French]

enter *verb* (enters, entering, entered)
1 come in or go in. **2** put something into a list or book. **3** type something into a computer. **4** register as a competitor.
[from Latin *intra* = within]

enterprise *noun* (*plural* enterprises)
1 being enterprising; adventurous spirit.
2 an undertaking or project. **3** business activity, *private enterprise*.
[from *en-* + Latin *prehendere* = take]

enterprising *adjective*
willing to undertake new or adventurous projects.

entertain *verb* (entertains, entertaining, entertained)
1 amuse. **2** have people as guests and give them food and drink. **3** consider, *He refused to entertain the idea*. **entertainer** *noun*
[from old French]

entertainment *noun* (*plural* entertainments)
1 entertaining; being entertained.
2 something performed before an audience to amuse or interest them.

enthral (*say* in-**thrawl**) *verb* (enthrals, enthralling, enthralled)
hold someone spellbound; fascinate.

enthusiasm *noun* (*plural* enthusiasms)
a strong liking, interest, or excitement.
enthusiast *noun* [from Greek *enthousiazein* = be possessed by a god]

enthusiastic *adjective*
full of enthusiasm. **enthusiastically** *adverb*

entice *verb* (entices, enticing, enticed)
attract or persuade by offering something
pleasant. **enticement** *noun*
[from old French]

entire *adjective*
whole or complete. **entirely** *adverb*
[from old French; related to *integer*]

entirety (*say* int-I-rit-ee) *noun*
the whole of something.
in its entirety in its complete form.

entitle *verb* (entitles, entitling, entitled)
give the right to have something, *This
coupon entitles you to a ticket.* **entitlement**
noun [from old French]

entitled *adjective*
having as a title, *a short poem entitled
'Spring'.*

entomb (*say* in-**toom**) *verb* (entombs,
entombing, entombed)
place in a tomb. **entombment** *noun*
[from old French]

entomology (*say* en-tom-ol-ojee) *noun*
the study of insects. **entomologist** *noun*
[from Greek *entomon* = insect, + *-logy*]

entrails *plural noun*
the intestines. [from French]

entrance[1] (*say* **en**-trans) *noun* (*plural*
entrances)
1 the way into a place. 2 entering, *Her
entrance is the signal for applause.*
[from old French]

entrance[2] (*say* in-**trahns**) *verb* (entrances,
entrancing, entranced)
fill with intense delight; enchant.
[from *en-* + *trance*]

entrant *noun* (*plural* entrants)
someone who enters for an examination or
contest etc. [from French]

entreat *verb* (entreats, entreating,
entreated)
request earnestly; beg. [from old French]

entreaty *noun* (*plural* entreaties)
an earnest request.

entrench *verb* (entrenches, entrenching,
entrenched)
1 fix or establish firmly, *These ideas are
entrenched in his mind.* 2 settle in a well-
defended position. **entrenchment** *noun*

entrust *verb* (entrusts, entrusting,
entrusted)
place a person or thing in someone's care.

entry *noun* (*plural* entries)
1 an entrance. 2 something entered in a
list or in a diary etc.

entwine *verb* (entwines, entwining,
entwined)
twine round.

enumerate *verb* (enumerates,
enumerating, enumerated)
count; list one by one.
[from *e-* + Latin *numerare* = to number]

envelop (*say* en-**vel**-op) *verb* (envelops,
enveloping, enveloped)
cover or wrap round something
completely. [from old French]

envelope (*say* **en**-vel-ohp) *noun* (*plural*
envelopes)
a wrapper or covering, especially a folded
cover for a letter. [from French]

enviable *adjective*
likely to be envied.

envious *adjective*
feeling envy. **enviously** *adverb*

environment *noun* (*plural* environments)
1 surroundings, especially as they affect
people's lives. 2 the natural world of the
land, sea, and air. **environmental** *adjective*
[from old French *environer* = surround,
enclose]

environmentalist *noun* (*plural*
environmentalists)
a person who wishes to protect or improve
the environment.

environmentally-friendly *adjective*
not harmful to the environment.

environs (*say* in-**vy**-ronz) *plural noun*
the surrounding districts, *They all lived in
the environs of Liverpool.*
[same origin as *environment*]

envisage (*say* in-**viz**-ij) *verb* (**envisages, envisaging, envisaged**)
picture in the mind; imagine as being possible, *It is difficult to envisage such a change.* [from *en-* + Latin *visus* = sight]

envoy *noun* (*plural* **envoys**)
an official representative, especially one sent by one government to another. [from French *envoyé* = sent]

envy *noun*
1 a feeling of discontent you have when someone possesses things that you would like to have for yourself. **2** something causing this, *Their car is the envy of all their friends.*
envy *verb* (**envies, envying, envied**)
feel envy towards someone. [from French; related to *invidious*]

enzyme *noun* (*plural* **enzymes**)
a kind of substance that assists chemical processes. [from Greek *enzymos* = leavened]

epaulette (*say* ep-al-et) *noun* (*plural* **epaulettes**)
an ornamental flap on the shoulder of a coat. [French, = little shoulder]

ephemeral (*say* if-**em**-er-al) *adjective*
lasting only a very short time. [from Greek *ephemeros* = lasting a day]

epi- *prefix*
on; above; in addition. [from Greek *epi* = on]

epic *noun* (*plural* **epics**)
1 a long poem or story about heroic deeds or history. **2** a spectacular film. [from Greek *epos* = song]

epicentre *noun* (*plural* **epicentres**)
the point where an earthquake reaches the earth's surface. [from *epi-* + Greek *kentros* = centre]

epidemic *noun* (*plural* **epidemics**)
an outbreak of a disease that spreads quickly among the people of an area. [from *epi-* + Greek *demos* = people]

epidermis *noun*
the outer layer of the skin. [from *epi-* + Greek *derma* = skin]

epigram *noun* (*plural* **epigrams**)
a short witty saying. [from *epi-* + *-gram*]

epilepsy *noun*
a disease of the nervous system, causing convulsions. **epileptic** *adjective* & *noun* [from Greek *epilambanein* = seize, attack]

epilogue (*say* ep-il-og) *noun* (*plural* **epilogues**)
a short section at the end of a book or play etc. [from *epi-* + Greek *logos* = speech]

Epiphany (*say* ip-**if**-an-ee) *noun*
a Christian festival on 6 January, commemorating the showing of the infant Christ to the 'wise men' from the East. [from Greek *epiphanein* = to show clearly]

episcopal (*say* ip-**iss**-kop-al) *adjective*
1 to do with a bishop or bishops. **2** (of a Church) governed by bishops. [from Latin *episcopus* = bishop]

episode *noun* (*plural* **episodes**)
1 one event in a series of happenings. **2** one programme in a radio or television serial. [from Greek]

epistle *noun* (*plural* **epistles**)
a letter, especially one forming part of the New Testament. [from *epi-* + Greek *stellein* = send]

epitaph *noun* (*plural* **epitaphs**)
words written on a tomb or describing a person who has died. [from *epi-* + Greek *taphos* = tomb]

epithet *noun* (*plural* **epithets**)
an adjective; words expressing something special about a person or thing, e.g. 'the Great' in *Alfred the Great*. [from Greek *epithetos* = attributed]

epoch (*say* ee-pok) *noun* (*plural* **epochs**)
an era.
epoch-making *adjective* very important. [from Greek]

equable (*say* ek-wa-bul) *adjective*
1 calm and not likely to get annoyed, *She has an equable manner.* **2** an equable climate is a moderate one, neither too hot nor too cold. [from Latin]

equal *adjective*
1 the same in amount, size, or value etc.
2 having the necessary strength, courage, or ability etc., *She was equal to the task.*
equally *adverb*

equal *noun* (*plural* **equals**)
a person or thing that is equal to another, *She has no equal.*

equal *verb* (**equals, equalling, equalled**)
be the same in amount, size, or value etc.
[from Latin]

equality *noun*
being equal.

equalize *verb* (**equalizes, equalizing, equalized**)
make things equal. **equalization** *noun*

equalizer *noun* (*plural* **equalizers**)
a goal or point that makes the score equal.

equanimity (*say* ekwa-**nim**-it-ee) *noun*
calmness of mind or temper.
[from *equi-* + Latin *animus* = mind]

equate *verb* (**equates, equating, equated**)
say things are equal or equivalent.
[from Latin *aequus* = equal]

equation *noun* (*plural* **equations**)
a statement that two amounts etc. are equal, e.g. $3 + 4 = 2 + 5$.

equator *noun* (*plural* **equators**)
an imaginary line round the Earth at an equal distance from the North and South Poles. [from Latin *circulus aequator diei et noctis* = circle equalizing day and night]

equatorial (*say* ek-wa-**tor**-ee-al) *adjective*
to do with or near the equator.

equerry (*say* ek-**wer**-ee) *noun* (*plural* **equerries**)
a personal attendant of a member of the British royal family.
[from Latin *scutarius* = shield-bearer]

equestrian (*say* ik-**wes**-tree-an) *adjective*
to do with horse riding.
[same origin as *equine*]

equi- *prefix*
equal; equally. [from Latin *aequus* = equal]

equilateral (*say* ee-kwi-**lat**-er-al) *adjective*
(of a triangle) having all sides equal.

equilibrium (*say* ee-kwi-**lib**-ree-um) *noun*
1 a balance between different forces, influences, etc. 2 a balanced state of mind.
[from *equi-* + Latin *libra* = balance]

equine (*say* **ek**-wyn) *adjective*
to do with or like a horse.
[from Latin *equus* = horse]

equinox (*say* **ek**-win-oks) *noun* (*plural* **equinoxes**)
the time of year when day and night are equal in length (about 20 March in spring, about 22 September in autumn). **equinoctial** *adjective* [from *equi-* + Latin *nox* = night]

equip *verb* (**equips, equipping, equipped**)
supply with what is needed. [from French]

equipment *noun*
the things needed for a particular purpose.

equity (*say* **ek**-wit-ee) *noun*
fairness. **equitable** *adjective* [from Latin]

equivalent *adjective*
equal in importance, meaning, value, etc. **equivalence** *noun*
[from *equi-* + Latin *valens* = worth]

equivocal (*say* ik-**wiv**-ok-al) *adjective*
able to be interpreted in two ways and deliberately vague; ambiguous. **equivocally** *adverb* [from *equi-* + Latin *vocare* = to call]

-er¹ and **-ier** *suffix*
can form the comparative of adjectives and adverbs (e.g. *high/higher, lazy/lazier*).
[from Old English *-re*]

-er² *suffix*
can form nouns meaning 'a person or thing that does something' (e.g. *farmer, computer*).
[from Old English *-ere*; in a few words (e.g. *butler, mariner*) from Latin: compare *-or*]

era (*say* **eer**-a) *noun* (*plural* **eras**)
a period of history. [from Latin]

eradicate *verb* (**eradicates, eradicating, eradicated**)
get rid of something; remove all traces of it.
eradication *noun*
[from Latin *eradicare* = root out]

erase *verb* (**erases, erasing, erased**)
1 rub something out. **2** wipe out a recording on magnetic tape. **eraser** *noun*
[from *e-* + Latin *rasum* = scraped]

erasure *noun* (*plural* **erasures**)
1 erasing. **2** the place where something has been erased.

ere (*say* air) *preposition & conjunction* (*old use*)
before. [from Old English]

erect *adjective*
standing straight up.
erect *verb* (**erects, erecting, erected**)
set up or build something. **erection** *noun*,
erector *noun* [from Latin]

ermine *noun* (*plural* **ermines**)
1 a kind of weasel with brown fur that turns white in winter. **2** this valuable white fur. [from French]

erode *verb* (**erodes, eroding, eroded**)
wear away, *Water eroded the rocks*. **erosion**
noun [from *e-* + Latin *rodere* = gnaw]

erosion *noun*
the wearing away of the earth's surface by the action of water, wind, etc.

erotic *adjective*
arousing sexual feelings. **erotically** *adverb*
[from Greek *eros* = sexual love]

err (*say* er) *verb* (**errs, erring, erred**)
1 make a mistake. (Compare *error*.) **2** do wrong. [from Latin *errare* = wander]

errand *noun* (*plural* **errands**)
a short journey to take a message or fetch goods etc. [from Old English]

errant (*say* e-rant) *adjective*
1 misbehaving. **2** wandering; travelling in search of adventure, *a knight errant*.
[same origin as *err*]

erratic (*say* ir-at-ik) *adjective*
1 not regular. **2** not reliable. **erratically**
adverb [from Latin *erraticus* = wandering]

erroneous (*say* ir-oh-nee-us) *adjective*
incorrect. **erroneously** *adverb*
[same origin as *err*]

error *noun* (*plural* **errors**)
a mistake. [same origin as *err*]

erudite (*say* e-rew-dyt) *adjective*
having great knowledge or learning.
eruditely *adverb*, **erudition** *noun*
[from Latin *erudire* = instruct]

erupt *verb* (**erupts, erupting, erupted**)
1 burst out. **2** when a volcano erupts, it shoots out lava. **eruption** *noun*
[from *e-* + Latin *ruptum* = burst]

escalate *verb* (**escalates, escalating, escalated**)
make or become greater, more serious or more intense, *The riots escalated into a war*. **escalation** *noun* [from *escalator*]

escalator *noun* (*plural* **escalators**)
a staircase with an endless line of steps moving up or down. [from French *escalade*
= scaling a wall with ladders]

escapade (*say* eska-**payd**) *noun* (*plural* **escapades**)
a reckless adventure. [French, = an escape]

escape *verb* (**escapes, escaping, escaped**)
1 get yourself free; get out or away. **2** avoid something, *He escaped punishment*.
escape *noun* (*plural* **escapes**)
1 escaping. **2** a way to escape.
[from French]

escapist *noun* (*plural* **escapists**)
a person who likes to avoid thinking about serious matters by occupying his or her mind in entertainments, daydreams, etc.
escapism *noun*

escarpment *noun* (*plural* **escarpments**)
a steep slope at the edge of some high level ground. [from French]

escort (*say* **ess**-kort) *noun* (*plural* **escorts**)
a person or group accompanying a person or thing, especially as a protection.
escort (*say* iss-**kort**) *verb* (**escorts, escorting, escorted**)
act as an escort to somebody or something.
[from French]

Eskimo *noun* (*plural* **Eskimos** or **Eskimo**)
a member of a people living near the Arctic
coast of North America, Greenland, and
Siberia. [from a Native American word]

USAGE: It is becoming less common to
refer to these peoples as *Eskimos*. Those
who live in northern Canada and
Greenland prefer the term *Inuit*. The name
for those who live in Alaska and Asia is
Yupik.

especial *adjective*
special. [from French]

especially *adverb*
specially; more than anything else.

espionage (*say* ess-pee-on-ahzh) *noun*
spying. [from French *espion* = spy]

esplanade *noun* (*plural* **esplanades**)
a flat open area used as a promenade,
especially by the sea. [French]

espresso *noun* (*plural* **espressos**)
coffee made by forcing steam through
ground coffee beans.
[Italian, = pressed out]

esprit de corps (*say* es-pree der kor) *noun*
loyalty to your group.
[French, - spirit of the body]

espy *verb* (**espies, espying, espied**)
catch sight of. [from old French]

Esq. *abbreviation*
(short for **Esquire**) a title written after a
man's surname where no title is used
before his name. [an *esquire* was originally
a knight's attendant; from Latin *scutarius*
= shield-bearer)]

-esque *suffix*
forms adjectives meaning 'like' or 'in the
style of' (e.g. *picturesque*). [French]

-ess *suffix*
forms feminine nouns (e.g. *lioness,
princess*). [from French]

essay (*say* ess-ay) *noun* (*plural* **essays**)
1 a short piece of writing in prose. 2 an
attempt.
essay (*say* ess-ay) *verb* (**essays, essaying,
essayed**)
attempt. [from French]

essence *noun* (*plural* **essences**)
1 the most important quality or element of
something. 2 a concentrated liquid.
[from Latin *esse* = to be]

essential *adjective*
not able to be done without.
essentially *adverb*
essential *noun* (*plural* **essentials**)
an essential thing. [same origin as *essence*]

-est and **-iest** *suffix*
can form the superlative of adjectives and
adverbs (e.g. *high/highest, lazy/laziest*).
[from Old English]

establish *verb* (**establishes, establishing,
established**)
1 set up a business, government, or
relationship etc. on a firm basis. 2 show
something to be true; prove, *He established
his innocence.*
the established Church a country's national
Church, established by law.
[from old French; related to *stable*[1]]

establishment *noun* (*plural*
establishments)
1 establishing something. 2 a business
firm or other institution.
the Establishment people who are
established in positions of power and
influence.

estate *noun* (*plural* **estates**)
1 an area of land with a set of houses or
factories on it. 2 a large area of land owned
by one person. 3 all that a person owns
when he or she dies. 4 (*old use*) a condition
or status, *the holy estate of matrimony*.
[from old French; related to *state*]

estate agent *noun* (*plural* **estate agents**)
a person whose business is selling or
letting houses and land.

estate car *noun* (*plural* **estate cars**)
a car with a door or doors at the back, and
rear seats that can be removed or folded
away.

esteem *verb* (**esteems, esteeming,
esteemed**)
think that a person or thing is excellent.
esteem *noun*
respect and admiration.
[same origin as *estimate*]

ester *noun* (*plural* **esters**)
a kind of chemical compound. [German]

estimable *adjective*
worthy of esteem.

estimate (*say* ess-tim-at) *noun* (*plural* **estimates**)
a rough calculation or guess about an amount or value.

estimate (*say* ess-tim-ayt) *verb* (**estimates, estimating, estimated**)
make an estimate. **estimation** *noun* [from Latin *aestimare* = to put a value on something]

estranged *adjective*
unfriendly after having been friendly or loving. **estrangement** *noun* [from Latin *extraneare* = treat someone as a stranger]

estuary (*say* ess-tew-er-ee) *noun* (*plural* **estuaries**)
the mouth of a river where it reaches the sea and the tide flows in and out. [from Latin *aestus* = tide]

etc. *abbreviation*
(short for **et cetera**) and other similar things; and so on. [from Latin *et* = and + *cetera* = the other things]

etch *verb* (**etches, etching, etched**)
1 engrave a picture with acid on a metal plate, especially for printing. 2 if something is etched on your mind or memory, it has made a deep impression and you will never forget it. **etcher** *noun* [from Dutch]

etching *noun* (*plural* **etchings**)
a picture printed from an etched metal plate.

eternal *adjective*
lasting for ever; not ending or changing. **eternally** *adverb*, **eternity** *noun* [from old French]

ether (*say* ee-ther) *noun*
1 a colourless liquid that evaporates easily into fumes that are used as an anaesthetic. 2 the upper air. [from Greek]

ethereal (*say* ith-eer-ee-al) *adjective*
light and delicate. **ethereally** *adverb* [from Latin *aetherius* = belonging to the upper air]

ethical (*say* eth-ik-al) *adjective*
1 to do with ethics. 2 morally right; honourable. **ethically** *adverb*

ethics (*say* eth-iks) *plural noun*
standards of right behaviour; moral principles. [from Greek *ethos* = character]

ethnic *adjective*
belonging to a particular racial group within a larger set of people. [from Greek *ethnos* = nation]

ethnic cleansing *noun*
the mass killing of people from other ethnic or religious groups within a certain area.

etiquette (*say* et-ik-et) *noun*
the rules of correct behaviour. [from French]

-ette *suffix*
forms diminutives which mean 'little' (e.g. *cigarette, kitchenette*). [from French]

etymology (*say* et-im-ol-oj-ee) *noun* (*plural* **etymologies**)
1 an account of the origin of a word and its meaning. 2 the study of the origins of words. **etymological** *adjective* [from Greek *etymon* = original word, + *-logy*]

EU *abbreviation*
European Union.

eu- (*say* yoo) *prefix*
well. [from Greek]

eucalyptus (*say* yoo-kal-ip-tus) *noun* (*plural* **eucalyptuses**)
1 a kind of evergreen tree. 2 a strong-smelling oil obtained from its leaves. [from Greek]

Eucharist (*say* yoo-ker-ist) *noun*
the Christian sacrament in which bread and wine are consecrated and swallowed, commemorating the Last Supper of Christ and his disciples. [from Greek *eucharistia* = thanksgiving]

eulogy (*say* yoo-loj-ee) *noun* (*plural* **eulogies**)
a piece of praise for a person or thing. [from *eu-* + Greek *-logia* = speaking]

euphemism (*say* yoo-fim-izm) *noun*
(*plural* euphemisms)
a mild word or phrase used instead of an
offensive or frank one; *'to pass away'* is a
euphemism for *'to die'*. **euphemistic**
adjective, **euphemistically** *adverb*
[from *eu-* + Greek *pheme* = speech]

euphonium (*say* yoof-oh-nee-um) *noun*
(*plural* euphoniums)
a large brass wind instrument.
[from *eu-* + Greek *phone* = sound]

euphoria (*say* yoo-for-ee-a) *noun*
a feeling of general happiness.
[from Greek]

Eurasian *adjective*
having European and Asian parents or
ancestors. **Eurasian** *noun*
[from *Euro*pean + *Asian*]

eureka (*say* yoor-eek-a) *interjection*
I have found it! [Greek]

European *adjective*
to do with Europe or its people.
European *noun*

euthanasia (*say* yooth-an-**ay**-zee-a) *noun*
the act of causing somebody to die gently
and without pain, especially when they are
suffering from a painful incurable disease.
[from *eu-* + Greek *thanatos* = death]

evacuate *verb* (evacuates, evacuating,
evacuated)
1 move people away from a dangerous
place. 2 make a thing empty of air or other
contents. **evacuation** *noun*
[from *e-* + Latin *vacuus* = empty]

evacuee *noun* (*plural* evacuees)
a person who has been evacuated.

evade *verb* (evades, evading, evaded)
avoid a person or thing by cleverness or
trickery. [from *e-* + Latin *vadere* = go]

evaluate *verb* (evaluates, evaluating,
evaluated)
estimate the value of something; assess.
evaluation *noun* [from French]

Evangelist *noun* (*plural* Evangelists)
any of the writers (Matthew, Mark, Luke,
John) of the four Gospels.
[from Greek *euangelion* = good news]

evangelist *noun* (*plural* evangelists)
a person who preaches the Christian faith
enthusiastically.
evangelism *noun*, **evangelical** *adjective*
[from Greek, = announce good news (*eu*
= well, *angelos* = messenger)]

evaporate *verb* (evaporates, evaporating,
evaporated)
1 change from liquid into steam or vapour.
2 cease to exist, *Their enthusiasm had
evaporated.* **evaporation** *noun*
[from *e-* = out + Latin *vapor* = steam]

evasion *noun* (*plural* evasions)
1 evading. 2 an evasive answer or excuse.
[from Latin]

evasive *adjective*
evading something; not frank or
straightforward.
evasively *adverb*, **evasiveness** *noun*
[from Latin]

eve *noun* (*plural* eves)
1 the day or evening before an important
day or event, *Christmas Eve.* 2 (*old use*)
evening. [from *even²*]

even¹ *adjective*
1 level and smooth. 2 not varying. 3 calm;
not easily upset, *an even temper.* 4 equal,
Our scores were even. 5 able to be divided
exactly by two, *Six and fourteen are even
numbers.* (Compare *odd.*)
evenly *adverb*, **evenness** *noun*

even *verb* (evens, evening, evened)
make or become even.

even *adverb*
(used to emphasize a word or statement)
She ran even faster.
even so although that is correct.
[from Old English *efen*]

even² *noun* (*old use*)
evening. [from Old English *aefen*]

evening *noun* (*plural* evenings)
the time at the end of the day before most
people go to bed. [from Old English]

evensong *noun*
the service of evening prayer in the
Church of England. [from *even²* + *song*]

event *noun* (*plural* **events**)
1 something that happens, especially something important. **2** a race or competition that forms part of a sports contest. [from Latin *evenire* = happen]

eventful *adjective*
full of happenings.

eventual *adjective*
happening at last, *his eventual success.* **eventually** *adverb*
[from Latin *eventus* = result, event]

eventuality (*say* iv-en-tew-al-it-ee) *noun* (*plural* **eventualities**)
something that may happen.
[from *eventual*]

ever *adverb*
1 at any time, *the best thing I ever did.* **2** always, *ever hopeful.* **3** (*informal*, used for emphasis), *Why ever didn't you tell me?*
[from Old English]

evergreen *adjective*
having green leaves all the year.
evergreen *noun*

everlasting *adjective*
lasting for ever or for a very long time.

every *adjective*
each without any exceptions, *We enjoyed every minute.*
every one each one.
every other day or **week** etc., each alternate one; every second one.
[from Old English]

USAGE: Follow with a singular verb, e.g. *Every one of them is growing* (not 'are growing').

everybody *pronoun*
every person.

everyday *adjective*
ordinary; usual, *everyday clothes.*

everyone *pronoun*
everybody.

everything *pronoun*
1 all things; all. **2** the only or most important thing, *Beauty is not everything.*

everywhere *adverb*
in every place.

evict *verb* (**evicts, evicting, evicted**)
make people move out from where they are living. **eviction** *noun*
[from Latin *evictum* = expelled]

evidence *noun*
1 anything that gives people reason to believe something. **2** statements made or objects produced in a lawcourt to prove something. [same origin as *evident*]

evident *adjective*
obvious; clearly seen. **evidently** *adverb*
[from *e-* + Latin *videre* = see]

evil *adjective*
morally bad; wicked. **evilly** *adverb*
evil *noun* (*plural* **evils**)
1 wickedness. **2** something unpleasant or harmful. [from Old English]

evoke *verb* (**evokes, evoking, evoked**)
produce or inspire a memory or feelings etc., *The photographs evoked happy memories.* **evocation** *noun*, **evocative** *adjective* [from *e-* + Latin *vocare* = call]

evolution (*say* ee-vol-oo-shon) *noun*
1 evolving; gradual change into something different. **2** the development of animals and plants from earlier or simpler forms. **evolutionary** *adjective*

evolve *verb* (**evolves, evolving, evolved**)
develop gradually or naturally.
[from *e-* + Latin *volvere* = to roll]

ewe (*say* yoo) *noun* (*plural* **ewes**)
a female sheep. [from Old English]

ewer (*say* yoo-er) *noun* (*plural* **ewers**)
a large water jug. [from old French]

ex- *prefix* (changing to **ef-** before words beginning with *f*; shortened to **e-** before many consonants)
1 out; away (as in *extract*). **2** up, upwards; thoroughly (as in *extol*). **3** formerly (as in *ex-president*). [from Latin *ex* = out of]

exacerbate (*say* eks-**ass**-er-bayt) *verb* (**exacerbates, exacerbating, exacerbated**)
make a pain or disease or other problem worse.
[from *ex-* + Latin *acerbus* = harsh, bitter]

exact *adjective*
1 correct. 2 clearly stated; giving all details, *exact instructions.* **exactly** *adverb,* **exactness** *noun*

exact *verb* (exacts, exacting, exacted) insist on something and obtain it, *He exacted obedience from the recruits.* **exaction** *noun*
[from *ex-* + Latin *actum* = performed]

exacting *adjective*
making great demands, *an exacting task.*

exactitude *noun*
exactness.

exaggerate *verb* (exaggerates, exaggerating, exaggerated)
make something seem bigger, better, or worse etc. than it really is. **exaggeration** *noun*
[from *ex-* + Latin *aggerare* = heap up]

exalt (*say* ig-**zawlt**) *verb* (exalts, exalting, exalted)
1 raise in rank or status etc. 2 praise highly. 3 delight or elate. **exaltation** *noun*
[from *ex-* + Latin *altus* = high]

exam *noun* (*plural* exams) (*informal*)
an examination.

examination *noun* (*plural* examinations)
1 a test of a person's knowledge or skill.
2 examining something; an inspection.

examine *verb* (examines, examining, examined)
1 test a person's knowledge or skill.
2 inspect; look at something closely. **examiner** *noun*
[from Latin *examinare* = weigh accurately]

examinee *noun* (*plural* examinees)
a person being tested in an examination.

example *noun* (*plural* examples)
1 anything that shows what others of the same kind are like or how they work. 2 a person or thing good enough to be worth imitating. [from Latin]

exasperate *verb* (exasperates, exasperating, exasperated)
annoy someone greatly. **exasperation** *noun*
[from *ex-* + Latin *asper* = rough]

excavate *verb* (excavates, excavating, excavated)
dig out; uncover by digging. **excavation** *noun,* **excavator** *noun*
[from *ex-* + Latin *cavus* = hollow]

exceed *verb* (exceeds, exceeding, exceeded)
1 be greater than; surpass. 2 do more than you need or ought to do; go beyond a thing's limits, *He has exceeded his authority.* [from *ex-* + Latin *cedere* = go]

exceedingly *adverb*
very; extremely.

excel *verb* (excels, excelling, excelled)
be better than others at doing something. [from *ex-* + Latin *celsus* = lofty]

Excellency *noun* (*plural* Excellencies)
the title of high officials such as ambassadors and governors. [from Latin]

excellent *adjective*
extremely good. **excellently** *adverb,* **excellence** *noun* [from Latin]

except *preposition*
excluding; not including, *They all left except me.*

except *verb* (excepts, excepting, excepted)
exclude; leave out, *I blame you all, no one is excepted.* [from *ex-* + Latin *-ceptum* = taken]

USAGE: Do not confuse with *accept.*

excepting *preposition*
except.

exception *noun* (*plural* exceptions)
a person or thing that is left out or does not follow the general rule.
take exception raise objections to something.
with the exception of except.

exceptional *adjective*
1 forming an exception; very unusual.
2 outstandingly good. **exceptionally** *adverb*

excerpt (*say* **ek**-serpt) *noun* (*plural* excerpts)
a passage taken from a book or speech or film etc.
[from Latin *excerptum* = plucked out]

excess *noun* (*plural* **excesses**)
too much of something.
[same origin as *exceed*]

excessive *adjective*
too much or too great. **excessively** *adverb*

exchange *verb* (**exchanges, exchanging, exchanged**)
give something and receive something else for it. **exchangeable** *adjective*

exchange *noun* (*plural* **exchanges**)
1 exchanging. 2 a place where things (especially stocks and shares) are bought and sold, *a stock exchange*. 3 a place where telephone lines are connected to each other when a call is made. [from old French]

exchequer *noun* (*plural* **exchequers**)
a national treasury into which public funds (such as taxes) are paid.
[from Latin *scaccarium* = chessboard (because the Norman kings kept their accounts by means of counters placed on a chequered tablecloth)]

excise¹ (*say* eks-I'z) *noun*
a tax charged on certain goods and licences etc. [from old Dutch *excijs* = tax]

excise² (*say* iks-I'z) *verb* (**excises, excising, excised**)
remove something by cutting it away, *The surgeon excised the tumour*.
[from *ex-* + Latin *caesum* = cut]

excitable *adjective*
easily excited.

excite *verb* (**excites, exciting, excited**)
1 rouse a person's feelings; make eager, *The thought of finding gold excited them*.
2 cause a feeling; arouse, *The invention excited great interest*. **excitedly** *adverb*
[from *ex-* + Latin *citum* = woken, stirred]

excitement *noun* (*plural* **excitements**)
a strong feeling of eagerness or pleasure.

exclaim *verb* (**exclaims, exclaiming, exclaimed**)
shout or cry out in eagerness or surprise.
[from *ex-* + Latin *clamare* = cry]

exclamation *noun* (*plural* **exclamations**)
1 exclaiming. 2 a word or words cried out expressing joy or pain or surprise etc.

exclamation mark *noun* (*plural* **exclamation marks**)
the punctuation mark ! placed after an exclamation.

exclude *verb* (**excludes, excluding, excluded**)
1 keep somebody or something out. 2 leave something out, *Do not exclude the possibility of rain*. **exclusion** *noun*
[from *ex-* + Latin *claudere* = shut]

exclusive *adjective*
1 allowing only certain people to be members etc., *an exclusive club*. 2 not shared with others, *This newspaper has an exclusive report*. **exclusively** *adverb*, **exclusiveness** *noun*
exclusive of excluding, not including, *This is the price exclusive of meals*.
[same origin as *exclude*]

excommunicate *verb* (**excommunicates, excommunicating, excommunicated**)
cut off a person from membership of a Church. **excommunication** *noun*
[from Latin *excommunicare* = put out of the community]

excrement (*say* eks-krim-ent) *noun*
waste matter excreted from the bowels.
[same origin as *excrete*]

excrescence (*say* iks-kress-ens) *noun* (*plural* **excrescences**)
1 a growth or lump on a plant or animal's body. 2 an ugly addition or part.
[from *ex-* + Latin *crescens* = growing]

excrete *verb* (**excretes, excreting, excreted**)
get rid of waste matter from the body.
excretion *noun*, **excretory** *adjective*
[from *ex-* + Latin *cretum* = separated]

excruciating (*say* iks-kroo-shee-ayt-ing) *adjective*
extremely painful; agonizing.
excruciatingly *adverb*
[from *ex-* + Latin *cruciatum* = tortured]

exculpate (*say* eks-kul-payt) *verb* (**exculpates, exculpating, exculpated**)
clear a person from blame. **exculpation** *noun* [from *ex-* + Latin *culpa* = blame]

excursion *noun* (*plural* **excursions**)
a short journey made for pleasure.
[from *ex-* + Latin *cursus* = course]

excusable *adjective*
able to be excused. **excusably** *adverb*

excuse (*say* iks-**kewz**) *verb* (**excuses**, **excusing**, **excused**)
1 forgive. **2** allow someone not to do something or to leave a room etc., *Please may I be excused swimming?*
excuse (*say* iks-**kewss**) *noun* (*plural* **excuses**)
a reason given to explain why something wrong has been done.
[from *ex-* + Latin *causa* = accusation]

execrable (*say* **eks**-ik-rab-ul) *adjective*
very bad or unpleasant.
[from Latin *execrari* = to curse]

execute *verb* (**executes**, **executing**, **executed**)
1 put someone to death as a punishment. **2** perform or produce something, *She executed the somersault perfectly.* **execution** *noun* [from Latin *executare* = to carry out]

executioner *noun* (*plural* **executioners**)
an official who executes a condemned person.

executive (*say* ig-**zek**-yoo-tiv) *noun* (*plural* **executives**)
a senior person with authority in a business or government organization.
executive *adjective*
having the authority to carry out plans or laws.

executor (*say* ig-**zek**-yoo-ter) *noun* (*plural* **executors**)
a person appointed to carry out the instructions in someone's will.

exemplary (*say* ig-**zem**-pler-ee) *adjective*
very good; being an example to others, *His conduct was exemplary.*
[from Latin *exemplum* = example]

exemplify *verb* (**exemplifies**, **exemplifying**, **exemplified**)
be an example of something.
[same origin as *exemplary*]

exempt *adjective*
not having to do something that others have to do, *Charities are exempt from paying tax.*

exempt *verb* (**exempts**, **exempting**, **exempted**)
make someone or something exempt.
exemption *noun*
[from Latin *exemptus* = taken out]

exercise *noun* (*plural* **exercises**)
1 using your body to make it strong and healthy. **2** a piece of work done for practice.
exercise *verb* (**exercises**, **exercising**, **exercised**)
1 do exercises. **2** give exercise to an animal etc. **3** use, *exercise patience.* [from Latin *exercere* = keep someone working]

exert *verb* (**exerts**, **exerting**, **exerted**)
use power or influence etc., *He exerted all his strength.* **exertion** *noun*
exert yourself make an effort.
[from Latin]

exeunt (*say* **eks**-ee-unt) *verb*
(in stage directions) they leave the stage.
[Latin, = they go out]

ex gratia (*say* eks **gray**-sha) *adjective*
given without being legally obliged to be given, *an ex gratia payment.*
[Latin, = from favour]

exhale *verb* (**exhales**, **exhaling**, **exhaled**)
breathe out. **exhalation** *noun*
[from *ex-* + Latin *halare* = breathe]

exhaust *verb* (**exhausts**, **exhausting**, **exhausted**)
1 make somebody very tired. **2** use up something completely. **exhaustion** *noun*
exhaust *noun* (*plural* **exhausts**)
1 the waste gases or steam from an engine. **2** the pipe etc. through which they are sent out. [from *ex-* + Latin *haustum* = drained]

exhaustive *adjective*
thorough; trying everything possible, *We made an exhaustive search.*
exhaustively *adverb*

exhibit *verb* (**exhibits**, **exhibiting**, **exhibited**)
show or display something in public.
exhibitor *noun*
exhibit *noun* (*plural* **exhibits**)
something on display in a gallery or museum. [from *ex-* + Latin *habere* = hold]

exhibition *noun* (*plural* exhibitions)
a collection of things put on display for
people to look at.

exhibitionist *noun* (*plural* exhibitionists)
a person who behaves in a way that is
meant to attract attention.
exhibitionism *noun*

exhilarate (*say* ig-zil-er-ayt) *verb*
(exhilarates, exhilarating, exhilarated)
make someone very happy and excited.
exhilaration *noun*
[from *ex-* + Latin *hilaris* = cheerful]

exhort (*say* ig-zort) *verb* (exhorts, exhorting,
exhorted)
urge someone earnestly. **exhortation** *noun*
[from *ex-* + Latin *hortari* = encourage]

exhume (*say* ig-zewm) *verb* (exhumes,
exhuming, exhumed)
dig up a body that has been buried.
exhumation *noun*
[from *ex-* + Latin *humare* = bury]

exile *verb* (exiles, exiling, exiled)
banish.
exile *noun* (*plural* exiles)
1 a banished person. **2** having to live away
from your own country, *He was in exile for
ten years.* [from Latin]

exist *verb* (exists, existing, existed)
1 be present as part of what is real, *Do
ghosts exist?* **2** stay alive, *We cannot exist
without food.* **existence** *noun*, **existent**
adjective [from *ex-* + Latin *sistere* = stand]

exit *noun* (*plural* exits)
1 the way out of a building. **2** going off the
stage, *The actress made her exit.*
exit *verb*
(in stage directions) he or she leaves the
stage. [Latin, = he or she goes out]

exodus *noun* (*plural* exoduses)
the departure of many people.
[from Greek *exodos* = a way out]

exonerate *verb* (exonerates, exonerating,
exonerated)
declare or prove that a person is not to
blame for something. **exoneration** *noun*
[from *ex-* + Latin *onus* = a burden]

exorbitant *adjective*
much too great; excessive, *exorbitant
prices.* [from *ex-* + Latin *orbita* = orbit]

exorcize *verb* (exorcizes, exorcizing,
exorcized)
get rid of an evil spirit. **exorcism** *noun*,
exorcist *noun* [from Greek]

exotic *adjective*
1 very unusual, *exotic clothes.* **2** from
another part of the world, *exotic plants.*
exotically *adverb*
[from Greek *exo* = outside]

expand *verb* (expands, expanding,
expanded)
make or become larger or fuller.
expansion *noun*, **expansive** *adjective*
[from *ex-* + Latin *pandere* = to spread]

expanse *noun* (*plural* expanses)
a wide area. [same origin as *expand*]

expatriate (*say* eks-pat-ree-at) *noun*
(*plural* expatriates)
a person living away from his or her own
country.
[from *ex-* + Latin *patria* = native land]

expect *verb* (expects, expecting, expected)
1 think or believe that something will
happen or that someone will come. **2** think
that something ought to happen, *She
expects obedience.*
[from *ex-* + Latin *spectare* = to look]

expectant *adjective*
1 expecting something to happen; hopeful.
2 an expectant mother is a woman who is
pregnant.
expectantly *adverb*, **expectancy** *noun*

expectation *noun* (*plural* expectations)
1 expecting something; being hopeful.
2 something you expect to happen or get.

expecting *adjective* (*informal*)
(of a woman) pregnant.

expedient (*say* iks-pee-dee-ent) *adjective*
1 suitable or convenient. **2** useful and
practical though perhaps unfair.
expediently *adverb*, **expediency** *noun*
expedient *noun* (*plural* expedients)
a means of doing something, especially
when in difficulty.
[same origin as *expedite*]

expedite (*say* eks-pid-dyt) *verb* (**expedites, expediting, expedited**)
make something happen more quickly.
[from Latin *expedire* = free someone's feet]

expedition *noun* (*plural* **expeditions**)
1 a journey made in order to do something.
2 speed or promptness. **expeditionary**
adjective [from French; related to *expedite*]

expeditious (*say* eks-pid-ish-us) *adjective*
quick and efficient. **expeditiously** *adverb*

expel *verb* (**expels, expelling, expelled**)
1 send or force something out, *This fan
expels stale air*. 2 make a person leave a
school or country etc. **expulsion** *noun*
[from *ex-* + Latin *pellere* = drive]

expend *verb* (**expends, expending,
expended**)
spend; use up.
[from *ex-* + Latin *pendere* = pay]

expendable *adjective*
able to be sacrificed or got rid of in order to
gain something.

expenditure *noun* (*plural* **expenditures**)
the spending or using up of money or effort
etc.

expense *noun* (*plural* **expenses**)
the cost of doing something.
[from old French; related to *expend*]

expensive *adjective*
costing a lot. **expensively** *adverb*,
expensiveness *noun*

experience *noun* (*plural* **experiences**)
1 what you learn from doing or seeing
things. 2 something that has happened to
you.
experience *verb* (**experiences,
experiencing, experienced**)
have something happen to you.
[same origin as *experiment*]

experienced *adjective*
having great skill or knowledge from much
experience.

experiment *noun* (*plural* **experiments**)
a test made in order to find out what
happens or to prove something.
experimental *adjective*, **experimentally**
adverb

experiment *verb* (**experiments,
experimenting, experimented**)
carry out an experiment. **experimentation**
noun [from Latin *experiri* = to test]

expert *noun* (*plural* **experts**)
a person with great knowledge or skill in
something.
expert *adjective*
having great knowledge or skill.
expertly *adverb*, **expertness** *noun*
[from Latin *expertus* = experienced]

expertise (*say* eks-per-**teez**) *noun*
expert ability. [French]

expiate (*say* eks-pee-ayt) *verb* (**expiates,
expiating, expiated**)
make up for something wrong you have
done; atone for something. **expiation** *noun*
[from Latin]

expire *verb* (**expires, expiring, expired**)
1 come to an end; stop being usable, *Your
season ticket has expired*. 2 die. 3 breathe
out air. **expiration** *noun*, **expiry** *noun*
[from *ex-* + Latin *spirare* = breathe]

explain *verb* (**explains, explaining,
explained**)
1 make something clear to somebody else;
show its meaning. 2 account for
something, *That explains his absence*.
explanation *noun* [from *ex-* + Latin *planare*
= make level or plain]

explanatory (*say* iks-**plan**-at-er-ee)
adjective
giving an explanation.

explicit (*say* iks-**pliss**-it) *adjective*
stated or stating something openly and
exactly. (Compare *implicit*.) **explicitly**
adverb [from Latin *explicitus* = unfolded]

explode *verb* (**explodes, exploding,
exploded**)
1 burst or suddenly release energy with a
loud noise. 2 cause a bomb to go off.
3 increase suddenly or quickly.
[originally = to drive a player off the stage
by clapping or hissing; from *ex-* + Latin
plaudere = clap]

exploit (*say* eks-ploit) *noun* (*plural* **exploits**)
a brave or exciting deed.

exploit (*say* iks-**ploit**) *verb* (**exploits, exploiting, exploited**)
1 use or develop resources. **2** use a person or thing selfishly. **exploitation** *noun*
[from old French]

exploratory (*say* iks-**plorra**-ter-ee) *adjective*
for the purpose of exploring.

explore *verb* (**explores, exploring, explored**)
1 travel through a country etc. in order to learn about it. **2** examine a subject or idea carefully, *We explored the possibilities.* **exploration** *noun*, **explorer** *noun*
[from Latin *explorare* = search out]

explosion *noun* (*plural* **explosions**)
1 the exploding of a bomb etc.; the noise made by exploding. **2** a sudden great increase.

explosive *adjective*
able to explode.
explosive *noun* (*plural* **explosives**)
an explosive substance.

exponent *noun* (*plural* **exponents**)
1 a person who expounds something.
2 someone who uses a certain technique.
3 the raised number etc. written to the right of another (e.g. 3 in 2^3) showing how many times the first one is to be multiplied by itself; index.

export *verb* (**exports, exporting, exported**)
send goods abroad to be sold.
exportation *noun*, **exporter** *noun*
export *noun* (*plural* **exports**)
1 exporting things. **2** something exported.
[from *ex-* + Latin *portare* = carry]

expose *verb* (**exposes, exposing, exposed**)
1 reveal or uncover. **2** allow light to reach a photographic film so as to take a picture.
exposure *noun* [from old French]

expostulate *verb* (**expostulates, expostulating, expostulated**)
make a protest. **expostulation** *noun*
[from *ex-* + Latin *postulare* = demand]

expound *verb* (**expounds, expounding, expounded**)
explain something in detail.
[from Latin *exponere* = put out, publish]

express *adjective*
1 going or sent quickly. **2** clearly stated, *This was done against my express orders.*
express *noun* (*plural* **expresses**)
a fast train stopping at only a few stations.
express *verb* (**expresses, expressing, expressed**)
1 put ideas etc. into words; make your feelings known. **2** press or squeeze out, *Express the juice.* [from old French]

expression *noun* (*plural* **expressions**)
1 the look on a person's face that shows his or her feelings. **2** a word or phrase etc. **3** a way of speaking or of playing music etc. so as to show your feelings. **4** expressing, *this expression of opinion.*

expressive *adjective*
full of expression.

expressly *adverb*
1 clearly and plainly, *This was expressly forbidden.* **2** specially, *designed expressly for children.*

expulsion *noun* (*plural* **expulsions**)
expelling or being expelled.
expulsive *adjective*

expunge *verb* (**expunges, expunging, expunged**)
erase; wipe out. [from Latin]

exquisite (*say* eks-**kwiz**-it) *adjective*
very beautiful. **exquisitely** *adverb*
[from Latin *exquisitus* = sought out]

extemporize *verb* (**extemporizes, extemporizing, extemporized**)
speak or produce or do something without advance preparation. **extemporization** *noun* [from Latin *ex tempore* = on the spur of the moment]

extend *verb* (**extends, extending, extended**)
1 stretch out. **2** make something become longer or larger. **3** offer or give, *Extend a warm welcome to our friends.*
extendible *adjective*, **extensible** *adjective*
[from *ex-* + Latin *tendere* = to stretch]

extension *noun* (*plural* **extensions**)
1 extending or being extended.
2 something added on; an addition to a building. **3** one of a set of telephones in an office or house etc.

extensive *adjective*
covering a large area or range, *extensive gardens*. **extensively** *adverb*, **extensiveness** *noun*

extent *noun* (*plural* extents)
1 the area or length over which something extends. **2** the amount, level, or scope of something, *the full extent of his power*. [from Latin *extenta* = extended]

extenuating *adjective*
making a crime seem less great by providing a partial excuse, *There were extenuating circumstances*. **extenuation** *noun* [from Latin *extenuare* = reduce]

exterior *adjective*
outer.
exterior *noun* (*plural* exteriors)
the outside of something.
[Latin, = further out]

exterminate *verb* (exterminates, exterminating, exterminated)
destroy or kill all the members or examples. **extermination** *noun*, **exterminator** *noun* [originally = banish; from *ex-* + Latin *terminus* = boundary]

external *adjective*
outside. **externally** *adverb* [from Latin]

extinct *adjective*
1 not existing any more, *The dodo is an extinct bird*. **2** not burning; not active, *an extinct volcano*. [same origin as *extinguish*]

extinction *noun*
1 making or becoming extinct.
2 extinguishing; being extinguished.

extinguish *verb* (extinguishes, extinguishing, extinguished)
1 put out a fire or light. **2** put an end to; destroy, *Our hopes of victory were extinguished*.
[from *ex-* + Latin *stinguere* = quench]

extinguisher *noun* (*plural* extinguishers)
a portable device for sending out water, chemicals, or gases to extinguish a fire.

extol *verb* (extols, extolling, extolled)
praise. [from *ex-* + Latin *tollere* = raise]

extort *verb* (extorts, extorting, extorted)
obtain something by force or threats.
extortion *noun*
[from *ex-* + Latin *tortum* = twisted]

extortionate *adjective*
charging or demanding far too much.
[from *extort*]

extra *adjective*
additional; more than is usual, *extra strength*.
extra *adverb*
more than usually, *extra strong*.
extra *noun* (*plural* extras)
1 an extra person or thing. **2** a person acting as part of a crowd in a film or play. [probably from *extraordinary*]

extra- *prefix*
outside; beyond (as in *extraterrestrial*).
[from Latin]

extract (*say* iks-trakt) *verb* (extracts, extracting, extracted)
take out; remove. **extractor** *noun*
extract (*say* eks-trakt) *noun* (*plural* extracts)
1 a passage taken from a book, speech, film, etc. **2** a substance separated or obtained from another.
[from *ex-* + Latin *tractum* = pulled]

extraction *noun*
1 extracting. **2** someone's descent, *He is of Chinese extraction*.

extradite *verb* (extradites, extraditing, extradited)
hand over an accused person to the police of the country where the crime was committed. **extradition** (*say* eks-tra-**dish**-on) *noun* [from *ex-* + Latin *tradere* = hand over]

extraneous (*say* iks-**tray**-nee-us) *adjective*
1 added from outside. **2** not belonging to the matter in hand; irrelevant.
[from Latin]

extraordinary *adjective*
very unusual or strange. **extraordinarily** *adverb* [from Latin *extra ordinem* = out of the ordinary]

extrasensory *adjective*
outside the range of the known human senses.

extraterrestrial *adjective*
from beyond the earth's atmosphere; from
outer space.

extraterrestrial *noun* (*plural*
extraterrestrials)
a being from outer space.

extravagant *adjective*
spending or using too much.
extravagantly *adverb*, **extravagance** *noun*
[from *extra-* + Latin *vagans* = wandering]

extravaganza *noun* (*plural*
extravaganzas)
a very spectacular show.
[from Italian; related to *extravagant*]

extreme *adjective*
1 very great or intense, *extreme cold*.
2 furthest away, *the extreme north*. **3** going
to great lengths in actions or opinions; not
moderate. **extremely** *adverb*

extreme *noun* (*plural* **extremes**)
1 something extreme. **2** either end of
something.
[from Latin *extremus* = furthest out]

extremist *noun* (*plural* **extremists**)
a person who holds extreme (not moderate)
opinions in political or other matters.

extremity (*say* iks-**trem**-it-ee) *noun* (*plural*
extremities)
1 an extreme point; the very end. **2** an
extreme need or feeling or danger etc.

extricate (*say* eks-**trik**-ayt) *verb* (**extricates**,
extricating, **extricated**)
release from a difficult position.
extrication *noun*
[from *ex-* + Latin *tricae* = entanglements]

extrovert *noun* (*plural* **extroverts**)
a person who is generally friendly and
likes company. (The opposite is *introvert*.)
[from *extro-* = outside + Latin *vertere* = to
turn]

extrude *verb* (**extrudes**, **extruding**,
extruded)
push or squeeze out. **extrusion** *noun*
[from *ex-* + Latin *trudere* = to push]

exuberant (*say* ig-**zew**-ber-ant) *adjective*
very lively. **exuberantly** *adverb*, **exuberance**
noun [from Latin *exuberare* = grow thickly]

exude *verb* (**exudes**, **exuding**, **exuded**)
1 give off like sweat or a smell etc. **2** ooze
out. [from *ex-* + Latin *sudare* = to sweat]

exult *verb* (**exults**, **exulting**, **exulted**)
rejoice greatly.
exultant *adjective*, **exultation** *noun*
[from Latin *exsilire* = leap up]

eye *noun* (*plural* **eyes**)
1 the organ of the body that is used for
seeing. **2** the power of seeing, *She has
sharp eyes*. **3** the small hole in a needle.
4 the centre of a storm.

eye *verb* (**eyes**, **eyeing**, **eyed**)
look at something with interest.
[from Old English]

eyeball *noun* (*plural* **eyeballs**)
the ball-shaped part of the eye inside the
eyelids.

eyebrow *noun* (*plural* **eyebrows**)
the fringe of hair growing on the face
above the eye.

eye-catching *adjective*
striking or attractive.

eyelash *noun* (*plural* **eyelashes**)
one of the short hairs that grow on an
eyelid.

eyelid *noun* (*plural* **eyelids**)
either of the two folds of skin that can close
over the eyeball.

eyepiece *noun* (*plural* **eyepieces**)
the lens of a telescope or microscope etc.
that you put to your eye.

eyesight *noun*
the ability to see.

eyesore *noun* (*plural* **eyesores**)
something that is ugly to look at.

eyewitness *noun* (*plural* **eyewitnesses**)
a person who actually saw an accident or
crime etc.

eyrie (*say* **I**-ree) *noun* (*plural* **eyries**)
the nest of an eagle or other bird of prey.
[from Latin]

Ff

fable noun (plural **fables**)
a short story that teaches about behaviour,
often with animals as characters.
[from Latin fabula = story]

fabric noun (plural **fabrics**)
1 cloth. 2 the framework of a building
(walls, floors, and roof). [from Latin]

fabricate verb (**fabricates, fabricating,
fabricated**)
1 construct or manufacture something.
2 invent, fabricate an excuse.
fabrication noun
[from Latin fabricare = to make or forge]

fabulous adjective
1 wonderful. 2 incredibly great, fabulous
wealth. 3 told of in fables. **fabulously** adverb
[same origin as fable]

façade (say fas-**ahd**) noun (plural **façades**)
1 the front of a building. 2 an outward
appearance, especially a deceptive one.
[French; related to face]

face noun (plural **faces**)
1 the front part of the head. 2 the
expression on a person's face. 3 the front
or upper side of something. 4 a surface, A
cube has six faces.
face verb (**faces, facing, faced**)
1 look or have the front towards
something, Our room faced the sea. 2 meet
and have to deal with something;
encounter, Explorers face many dangers.
3 cover a surface with a layer of different
material. [from Latin facies = appearance]

facelift noun (plural **facelifts**)
surgery to remove wrinkles by tightening
the skin of the face, done to make someone
look younger.

facet (say fas-it) noun (plural **facets**)
1 one of the many sides of a cut stone or
jewel. 2 one aspect of a situation or
problem. [from French facette = small face]

facetious (say fas-**ee**-shus) adjective
trying to be funny at an unsuitable time,
facetious remarks. **facetiously** adverb
[from Latin facetus = witty]

facial (say **fay**-shal) adjective
to do with the face.

facile (say fas-I'll) adjective
done or produced easily or with little
thought or care. [from Latin facilis = easy]

facilitate (say fas-il-it-ayt) verb (**facilitates,
facilitating, facilitated**)
make something easy or easier.
facilitation noun

facility (say fas-il-it-ee) noun (plural
facilities)
1 something that provides you with the
means to do things, There are sports
facilities. 2 easiness.

facsimile (say fak-**sim**-il-ee) noun (plural
facsimiles)
1 an exact reproduction of a document etc.
2 a fax. [from Latin fac = make + simile
= a likeness]

fact noun (plural **facts**)
something that is certainly true.
the facts of life information about how
babies are conceived.
[from Latin factum = thing done]

faction noun (plural **factions**)
a small united group within a larger one,
especially in politics. [from Latin]

-faction suffix
forms nouns (e.g. satisfaction) from verbs
that end in -fy. [from Latin]

factor noun (plural **factors**)
1 something that helps to bring about a
result, Hard work was a factor in her
success. 2 a number by which a larger
number can be divided exactly, 2 and 3 are
factors of 6.
[from Latin facere = do or make]

factory noun (plural **factories**)
a large building where machines are used
to make things. [from Latin factorium
= place where things are made]

factotum (say fakt-**oh**-tum) noun (plural
factotums)
a servant or assistant who does all kinds of
work.
[from Latin fac = do + totum = everything]

factual *adjective*
based on facts; containing facts.
factually *adverb*

faculty *noun* (*plural* **faculties**)
1 any of the powers of the body or mind
(e.g. sight, speech, understanding). 2 a
department teaching a particular subject
in a university, *the faculty of music.*
[same origin as *facile*]

fad *noun* (*plural* **fads**)
1 a person's particular like or dislike.
2 a temporary fashion or craze. **faddy**
adjective [originally a dialect word; origin
unknown]

fade *verb* (**fades, fading, faded**)
1 lose or cause to lose colour or freshness
or strength. 2 disappear gradually. 3 make
a sound etc. become gradually weaker (*fade
it out*) or stronger (*fade it in* or *up*).
[from old French]

faeces (*say* fee-seez) *plural noun*
solid waste matter passed out of the body.
[plural of Latin *faex* = dregs]

fag *noun* (*plural* **fags**)
1 something that is tiring or boring.
2 (*informal*) a cigarette.
fagged out tired out; exhausted.
[origin unknown]

faggot *noun* (*plural* **faggots**)
1 a meat ball made with chopped liver and
baked. 2 a bundle of sticks bound together,
used for firewood.
[from Greek *phakelos* = bundle]

Fahrenheit *adjective*
measuring temperature on a scale where
water freezes at 32° and boils at 212°.
[named after G. D. Fahrenheit, a German
scientist, who invented the mercury
thermometer]

fail *verb* (**fails, failing, failed**)
1 try to do something but be unable to do
it. 2 become weak or useless; break down,
The brakes failed. 3 not do something, *He
failed to warn me.* 4 not get enough marks
to pass an examination. 5 judge that
someone has not passed an examination.

fail *noun* (*plural* **fails**)
not being successful in an examination,
Alex got four passes and one fail.
without fail for certain; whatever happens.
[from Latin *fallere* = disappoint, deceive]

failing *noun* (*plural* **failings**)
a weakness or a fault.

failure *noun* (*plural* **failures**)
1 not being able to do something. 2 a
person or thing that has failed.

faint *adjective*
1 pale or dim; not distinct. 2 weak or
giddy; nearly unconscious. 3 slight, *a faint
hope.* **faintly** *adverb*, **faintness** *noun*
faint *verb* (**faints, fainting, fainted**)
become unconscious. [same origin as *feint*]

USAGE: Do not confuse with *feint*.

fair[1] *adjective*
1 right or just; according to the rules, *a fair
fight.* 2 (of hair or skin) light in colour; (of
a person) having fair hair. 3 (*old use*)
beautiful. 4 fine or favourable, *fair
weather.* 5 moderate; quite good, *a fair
number of people.* **fairness** *noun*
fair *adverb*
fairly, *Play fair!* [from Old English]

fair[2] *noun* (*plural* **fairs**)
1 a group of entertainments such as
roundabouts and sideshows. 2 an
exhibition or market.
[from Latin *feriae* = holiday]

fairly *adverb*
1 justly; according to the rules.
2 moderately, *It is fairly hard.*

fairy *noun* (*plural* **fairies**)
an imaginary very small creature with
magic powers. **fairyland** *noun*, **fairy tale**
noun [from an old word *fay*, from Latin *fata*
= the Fates, three goddesses who were
believed to control people's lives]

fait accompli *noun* (*plural* **faits accomplis**)
a thing that has already been done and so
is past arguing about.
[French, = accomplished fact]

faith *noun* (*plural* **faiths**)
strong belief; trust.
in good faith with honest intentions.
[from old French; related to *fidelity*]

faithful *adjective*
1 loyal and trustworthy. 2 sexually loyal to one partner.
faithfully *adverb*, **faithfulness** *noun*
Yours faithfully see *yours*.

fake *noun* (*plural* **fakes**)
something that looks genuine but is not; a forgery.
fake *verb* (**fakes, faking, faked**)
1 make something that looks genuine, in order to deceive people. 2 pretend, *They faked illness.* **faker** *noun*
[originally slang; origin unknown]

fakir (*say* fay-keer) *noun* (*plural* **fakirs**)
a Muslim or Hindu religious beggar regarded as a holy man.
[Arabic, = a poor man]

falcon *noun* (*plural* **falcons**)
a kind of hawk often used in the sport of hunting other birds or game. **falconry** *noun*
[Latin]

fall *verb* (**falls, falling, fell, fallen**)
1 come or go down without being pushed or thrown etc. 2 decrease; become lower, *Prices fell.* 3 be captured or overthrown, *The city fell.* 4 die in battle. 5 happen, *Silence fell.* 6 become, *She fell asleep.*
fall back retreat.
fall back on use for support or in an emergency.
fall for 1 be attracted by a person.
2 be taken in by a deception.
fall out quarrel.
fall through fail, *plans fell through.*
fall *noun* (*plural* **falls**)
1 the action of falling. 2 (*American*) autumn, when leaves fall.
[from Old English]

fallacy (*say* fal-a-see) *noun* (*plural* **fallacies**)
a false idea or belief. **fallacious** (*say* fal-ay-shus) *adjective* [same origin as *fail*]

fallible (*say* fal-ib-ul) *adjective*
liable to make mistakes; not infallible, *All people are fallible.* **fallibility** *noun*
[same origin as *fail*]

Fallopian tube *noun* (*plural* **Fallopian tubes**)
one of the two tubes in a woman's body along which the eggs travel from the ovaries to the uterus.
[named after Gabriele Fallopio, a 16th-century Italian anatomist]

fallout *noun*
particles of radioactive material carried in the air after a nuclear explosion.

fallow *adjective*
(of land) ploughed but left without crops in order to restore its fertility.
[from Old English *falu* = pale brown (because of the colour of the bare earth)]

fallow deer (*plural* **fallow deer**)
a kind of light-brown deer.
[same origin as *fallow*]

falls *plural noun*
a waterfall.

false *adjective*
1 untrue or incorrect. 2 not genuine; faked.
3 treacherous or deceitful.
falsely *adverb*, **falseness** *noun*, **falsity** *noun*
[same origin as *fail*]

falsehood *noun* (*plural* **falsehoods**)
1 a lie. 2 telling lies.

falsetto *noun* (*plural* **falsettos**)
a man's voice forced into speaking or singing higher than is natural. [Italian]

falsify *verb* (**falsifies, falsifying, falsified**)
alter a thing dishonestly. **falsification** *noun*

falsity *noun*
falseness.

falter *verb* (**falters, faltering, faltered**)
1 hesitate when you move or speak.
2 become weaker; begin to give way, *His courage faltered.* [origin unknown]

fame *noun*
being famous. **famed** *adjective*
[from Latin *fama* = report, rumour]

familiar *adjective*
1 well-known; often seen or experienced.
2 knowing something well, *Are you familiar with this book?* 3 very friendly.
familiarly *adverb*, **familiarity** *noun*
[from Latin *familias* = family]

familiarize *verb* (familiarizes, familiarizing, familiarized)
make yourself familiar with something.
familiarization *noun*

family *noun* (*plural* families)
1 parents and their children, sometimes including grandchildren and other relations. 2 a group of things that are alike in some way. [from Latin]

family planning *noun*
birth control.

family tree *noun* (*plural* family trees)
a diagram showing how people in a family are related.

famine *noun* (*plural* famines)
a very bad shortage of food in an area.
[from Latin *fames* = hunger]

famished *adjective*
very hungry. **famishing** *adjective*
[same origin as *famine*]

famous *adjective*
known to very many people.
[same origin as *fame*]

famously *adverb* (*informal*)
very well, *They get on famously.*

fan¹ *noun* (*plural* fans)
an object or machine for making air move about so as to cool people or things.
fan *verb* (fans, fanning, fanned)
send a current of air on something.
fan out spread out in the shape of a fan.
[from Latin]

fan² *noun* (*plural* fans)
an enthusiast; a great admirer or supporter. [short for *fanatic*]

fanatic *noun* (*plural* fanatics)
a person who is very enthusiastic or too enthusiastic about something. **fanatical** *adjective*, **fanatically** *adverb*, **fanaticism** *noun*
[from Latin *fanaticus* = inspired by a god]

fanciful *adjective*
1 imagining things. 2 imaginary.

fancy *noun* (*plural* fancies)
1 a liking or desire for something.
2 imagination.

fancy *adjective*
decorated or elaborate; not plain.
fancy *verb* (fancies, fancying, fancied)
1 believe, *I fancy it's raining.* 2 imagine.
3 have a liking or desire for something.
[short for *fantasy*]

fancy dress *noun*
unusual costume worn for a party, often to make you look like a famous person.

fanfare *noun* (*plural* fanfares)
a short piece of loud music played on trumpets. [French]

fang *noun* (*plural* fangs)
a long sharp tooth. [from Old English]

fanlight *noun* (*plural* fanlights)
a window above a door.
[because many of these are fan-shaped]

fantasia (*say* fan-tay-zee-a) *noun* (*plural* fantasias)
an imaginative piece of music or writing.
[Italian; related to *fantastic*]

fantasize *verb* (fantasizes, fantasizing, fantasized)
imagine something pleasant or strange that you would like to happen.
[from *fantasy*]

fantastic *adjective*
1 (*informal*) excellent. 2 designed in a very fanciful way. **fantastically** *adverb*
[from Greek *phantazesthai* = imagine]

fantasy *noun* (*plural* fantasies)
something imaginary or fantastic.
[same origin as *fantastic*]

far *adverb*
1 at or to a great distance, *We didn't go far.*
2 much; by a great amount, *This is far better.*
far *adjective*
distant or remote, *On the far side of the river.* [from Old English]

farce *noun* (*plural* farces)
1 an exaggerated comedy. 2 events that are ridiculous or a pretence. **farcical** *adjective*
[French, literally = stuffing (the name given to a comic interlude between acts of a play)]

fare noun (plural fares)
1 the price charged for a passenger to travel. 2 food and drink, *There was only very plain fare.*
fare verb (fares, faring, fared)
get along; progress, *How did they fare?*
[from Old English]

farewell interjection & noun (plural farewells)
goodbye.

farm noun (plural farms)
1 an area of land where someone grows crops or keeps animals for food or other use. 2 the farmer's house. **farmhouse** noun, **farmyard** noun
farm verb (farms, farming, farmed)
1 grow crops or keep animals for food etc. 2 use land for growing crops; cultivate.
[from French]

farmer noun (plural farmers)
a person who owns or manages a farm.

farrier (say fa-ree-er) noun (plural farriers)
a smith who shoes horses. **farriery** noun
[from Latin *ferrum* = iron, an iron horseshoe]

farrow noun (plural farrows)
a litter of young pigs. [from Old English]

farther adverb & adjective
at or to a greater distance; more distant.
[a different spelling of *further*]

USAGE: *Further* and *farthest* are used only in connection with distance (e.g. *She lives farther from the school than I do*), but even in such cases many people prefer to use *further*. Only *further* can be used to mean 'additional', e.g. in *We must make further inquiries*. If you are not sure which is right, use *further*.

farthest adverb & adjective
at or to the greatest distance; most distant.

USAGE: See the note at *farther*.

farthing noun (plural farthings)
a former British coin worth one-quarter of a penny.
[from Old English *feorthing* = one-fourth]

fascinate verb (fascinates, fascinating, fascinated)
be very attractive or interesting to somebody. **fascination** noun, **fascinator** noun
[from Latin *fascinum* = a spell]

Fascist (say fash-ist) noun (plural Fascists)
a person who supports an extreme right-wing dictatorial type of government.
Fascism noun [from Latin *fasces*, the bundle of rods with an axe through it, carried before a magistrate in ancient Rome as a symbol of his power to punish people]

fashion noun (plural fashions)
1 the style of clothes or other things that most people like at a particular time. 2 a way of doing something, *Continue in the same fashion.* **fashionable** adjective, **fashionably** adverb
fashion verb (fashions, fashioning, fashioned)
make something in a particular shape or style. [via old French from Latin *facere* = make or do]

fast¹ adjective
1 moving or done quickly; rapid. 2 allowing fast movement, *a fast road.* 3 showing a time later than the correct time, *Your watch is fast.* 4 firmly fixed or attached. 5 not likely to fade, *fast colours.* **fastness** noun
fast adverb
1 quickly, *Run fast!* 2 firmly, *His leg was stuck fast in the mud.*
fast asleep in a deep sleep.
[from Old English *faest*]

fast² verb (fasts, fasting, fasted)
go without food. **fast** noun
[from Old English *faestan*]

fasten verb (fastens, fastening, fastened)
fix one thing firmly to another. **fastener** noun, **fastening** noun [from Old English]

fast food noun
restaurant food that is quickly prepared and served.

fastidious adjective
1 fussy and hard to please. 2 very careful about small details of dress or cleanliness. **fastidiously** adverb, **fastidiousness** noun
[from Latin *fastidium* = loathing]

fat noun (plural fats)
1 the white greasy part of meat. 2 oil or grease used in cooking.
the fat of the land the best food.

fat adjective (fatter, fattest)
1 having a very thick round body. 2 thick, a fat book. 3 full of fat. **fatness** noun
[from Old English]

fatal adjective
causing death or disaster, a fatal accident. **fatally** adverb [from Latin fatalis = by fate]

fatalist noun (plural fatalists)
a person who accepts whatever happens and thinks it could not have been avoided. **fatalism** noun, **fatalistic** adjective [from fatal, in an old sense = decreed by fate]

fatality (say fa-tal-it-ee) noun (plural fatalities)
a death caused by an accident, war, or other disaster.

fate noun (plural fates)
1 a power that is thought to make things happen. 2 what will happen or has happened to somebody or something; destiny. [from Latin fatum, literally = that which has been spoken]

fated adjective
destined by fate; doomed, the fated lovers, Romeo and Juliet.

fateful adjective
bringing events that are important and usually unpleasant, How well she remembered that fateful day.
fatefully adverb

father noun (plural fathers)
1 a male parent. 2 the title of certain priests. **fatherly** adjective

father verb (fathers, fathering, fathered)
be the father of, He fathered six children. [from Old English]

father-in-law noun (plural fathers-in-law)
the father of a married person's husband or wife.

fathom noun (plural fathoms)
a unit used to measure the depth of water, equal to 1.83 metres or 6 feet.

fathom verb (fathoms, fathoming, fathomed)
1 measure the depth of something. 2 get to the bottom of something; work it out. **fathomless** adjective [from Old English]

fatigue noun
1 tiredness. 2 weakness in metals, caused by stress. **fatigued** adjective
[from Latin fatigare = make weary]

fatten verb (fattens, fattening, fattened)
make or become fat.

fatty adjective
like fat; containing fat.

fatuous adjective
silly or foolish. **fatuously** adverb, **fatuousness** noun, **fatuity** noun [from Latin]

fatwa noun (plural fatwas)
a ruling on a religious matter given by an Islamic authority. [Arabic]

faucet noun (plural faucets)
(American) a tap. [from old French]

fault noun (plural faults)
1 anything that makes a person or thing imperfect; a flaw or mistake. 2 the responsibility for something wrong, It wasn't your fault. 3 a break in a layer of rock.

fault verb (faults, faulting, faulted)
1 find faults in something. 2 form a fault. [from old French; related to fail]

faultless adjective
without a fault.
faultlessly adverb, **faultlessness** noun

faulty adjective
having a fault or faults.
faultily adverb, **faultiness** noun

faun noun (plural fauns)
an ancient country god with a goat's legs, horns, and tail. [from the name of Faunus, an ancient Roman country god (see fauna)]

fauna noun
the animals of a certain area or period of time. (Compare flora.) [from the name of Fauna, an ancient Roman country goddess, sister of Faunus (see faun)]

faux pas (*say* foh **pah**) *noun* (*plural* **faux pas**)
an embarrassing blunder.
[French, = false step]

favour *noun* (*plural* **favours**)
1 a kind or helpful act. **2** approval;
goodwill. **3** friendly support shown to one
person or group but not to another, *without
fear or favour*.
favour *verb* (**favours, favouring, favoured**)
be in favour of something; show favour to a
person. [from Latin]

favourable *adjective*
1 showing approval. **2** helpful or
advantageous. **favourably** *adverb*

favourite *adjective*
liked more than others. **favourite** *noun*

favouritism *noun*
unfairly being kinder to one person than to
others.

fawn[1] *noun* (*plural* **fawns**)
1 a young deer. **2** a light-brown colour.
[from old French; related to *foetus*]

fawn[2] *verb* (**fawns, fawning, fawned**)
try to win a person's favour or affection by
flattery and humility. [from Old English]

fax *noun* (*plural* **faxes**)
1 a machine that sends an exact copy of a
document electronically. **2** a copy
produced by this.
fax *verb* (**faxes, faxing, faxed**)
send a copy of a document using a fax
machine. [from *facsimile*]

fear *noun* (*plural* **fears**)
a feeling that something unpleasant may
happen.
fear *verb* (**fears, fearing, feared**)
feel fear; be afraid of somebody or
something. [from Old English]

fearful *adjective*
1 feeling fear; afraid. **2** causing fear or
horror, *a fearful monster*. **3** (*informal*) very
great or bad. **fearfully** *adverb*

fearless *adjective*
without fear. **fearlessly** *adverb*,
fearlessness *noun*

fearsome *adjective*
frightening.

feasible *adjective*
1 able to be done; possible. **2** likely or
probable, *a feasible explanation*.
feasibly *adverb*, **feasibility** *noun*
[from French *faire* = do]

USAGE: The use of *feasible* to mean 'likely
or probable' has not become generally
accepted in standard English, so it is better
to avoid it in writing or formal situations.

feast *noun* (*plural* **feasts**)
1 a large splendid meal. **2** a religious
festival. **feast** *verb*
[from old French; related to *fête*]

feat *noun* (*plural* **feats**)
a brave or clever deed.
[from old French; related to *fact*]

feather *noun* (*plural* **feathers**)
one of the very light coverings that grow
from a bird's skin. **feathery** *adjective*
feather *verb* (**feathers, feathering,
feathered**)
cover or line something with feathers.
[from Old English]

featherweight *noun* (*plural*
featherweights)
1 a person who weighs very little. **2** a boxer
weighing between 54 and 57 kg.

feature *noun* (*plural* **features**)
1 any part of the face (e.g. mouth, nose,
eyes). **2** an important or noticeable part; a
characteristic. **3** a special newspaper
article or programme that deals with a
particular subject. **4** the main film in a
cinema programme.
feature *verb* (**features, featuring, featured**)
make or be a noticeable part of something.
[from Latin *factura* = a creation]

feckless *adjective*
not having the determination to achieve
anything in life; irresponsible.
[from Scots *feck* = effect, + *-less*]

fed *past tense* of **feed**.
fed up (*informal*) discontented.

federal *adjective*
to do with a system in which several States
are ruled by a central government but are

responsible for their own internal affairs.
federation *noun*
[from Latin *foederis* = of a treaty]

fee *noun* (*plural* **fees**)
a charge for something. [from old French]

feeble *adjective*
weak; without strength. **feebly** *adverb*,
feebleness *noun*
[from Latin *flebilis* = wept over]

feed *verb* (**feeds, feeding, fed**)
1 give food to a person or animal. **2** take
food. **3** supply something to a machine etc.
feeder *noun*
feed *noun*
food for animals or babies.
[from Old English]

feedback *noun*
1 the response you get from people to
something you have done. **2** the harsh
noise produced when some of the sound
from an amplifier goes back into it.

feel *verb* (**feels, feeling, felt**)
1 touch something to find out what it is
like. **2** be aware of something; have an
opinion. **3** experience an emotion. **4** give a
certain sensation, *It feels warm*.
feel like want.
feel *noun*
the sensation caused by feeling something,
I like the feel of silk. [from Old English]

feeler *noun* (*plural* **feelers**)
1 a long thin projection on an insect's or
crustacean's body, used for feeling; an
antenna. **2** a cautious question or
suggestion etc. to test people's reactions.

feeling *noun* (*plural* **feelings**)
1 the ability to feel things; the sense of
touch. **2** what a person feels.

feign (*say* fayn) *verb* (**feigns, feigning,
feigned**)
pretend.
[from Latin *fingere* = to form or plan]

feint (*say* faynt) *noun* (*plural* **feints**)
a pretended attack or punch meant to
deceive an opponent.

feint *verb* (**feints, feinting, feinted**)
make a feint. [old French, = feigned]

USAGE: Do not confuse with *faint*.

---

felicity *noun*
1 great happiness. **2** a pleasing manner or
style, *He expressed himself with great
felicity*. **felicitous** *adjective*, **felicitously**
adverb [from Latin *felix* = happy]

feline (*say* feel-I'n) *adjective*
to do with cats; cat-like.
[from Latin *feles* = cat]

fell[1] *past tense* of **fall**.

fell[2] *verb* (**fells, felling, felled**)
make something fall; cut or knock down,
They were felling the trees.
[from Old English]

fell[3] *noun* (*plural* **fells**)
a piece of wild hilly country, especially in
the north of England. [from Old Norse]

fellow *noun* (*plural* **fellows**)
1 a friend or companion; one who belongs
to the same group. **2** a man or boy. **3** a
member of a learned society.
fellow *adjective*
of the same group or kind, *Her fellow
teachers supported her*. [from Old Norse]

fellowship *noun* (*plural* **fellowships**)
1 friendship. **2** a group of friends; a society.

felon (*say* fel-on) *noun* (*plural* **felons**)
a criminal.
[from Latin *felo* = an evil person]

felony (*say* fel-on-ee) *noun* (*plural* **felonies**)
a serious crime. [from French]

felt[1] *past tense* of **feel**.

felt[2] *noun*
a thick fabric made of fibres of wool or fur
etc. pressed together. [from Old English]

female *adjective*
of the sex that can bear offspring or
produce eggs or fruit.
female *noun* (*plural* **females**)
a female person, animal, or plant.
[from Latin *femina* = woman]

feminine *adjective*
1 to do with or like women; suitable for women. 2 (in some languages) belonging to the class of words which includes the words referring to women. **femininity** *noun* [same origin as *female*]

feminist *noun* (*plural* feminists)
a person who believes that women should be given the same rights and status as men. **feminism** *noun*

femur (*say* fee-mer) *noun* (*plural* femurs)
the thigh bone. [Latin]

fen *noun* (*plural* fens)
an area of low-lying marshy or flooded ground.
[from Old English]

fence *noun* (*plural* fences)
1 a barrier made of wood or wire etc. round an area. 2 a structure for a horse to jump over. 3 a person who buys stolen goods and sells them again.
fence *verb* (fences, fencing, fenced)
1 put a fence round or along something. 2 fight with long narrow swords (called *foils*) as a sport. **fencer** *noun* [shortened from *defence*]

fend *verb* (fends, fending, fended)
fend for provide things for someone.
fend off keep a person or thing away from yourself.
[shortened from *defend*]

fender *noun* (*plural* fenders)
1 something placed round a fireplace to stop coals from falling into the room. 2 something hung over the side of a boat to protect it from knocks. [from *fend*]

fennel *noun*
a herb with yellow flowers.
[Old English from Latin]

feral *adjective*
wild and untamed, *feral cats*.
[from Latin *fera* = wild animal]

ferment (*say* fer-ment) *verb* (ferments, fermenting, fermented)
bubble and change chemically by the action of a substance such as yeast.
fermentation *noun*

USAGE: Do not confuse with *foment*.

ferment (*say* fer-ment) *noun*
1 fermenting. 2 an excited or agitated condition. [from Latin *fermentum* = yeast]

fern *noun* (*plural* ferns)
a plant with feathery leaves and no flowers. [from Old English]

ferocious *adjective*
fierce or savage. **ferociously** *adverb*, **ferocity** *noun* [from Latin *ferox* = fierce]

-ferous and **-iferous** *suffix*
form nouns meaning 'carrying' or 'providing' (e.g. *carboniferous*). [from Latin *ferre* = carry]

ferret *noun* (*plural* ferrets)
a small weasel-like animal used for catching rabbits and rats. **ferrety** *adjective*
ferret *verb* (ferrets, ferreting, ferreted)
1 hunt with a ferret. 2 search for something; rummage.
[from Latin *fur* = thief]

ferric or **ferrous** *adjectives*
containing iron. [from Latin *ferrum* = iron]

ferry *verb* (ferries, ferrying, ferried)
transport people or things, especially across water.
ferry *noun* (*plural* ferries)
a boat or aircraft used in ferrying.
[from Old Norse]

fertile *adjective*
1 producing good crops, *fertile soil*. 2 able to produce offspring. 3 able to produce ideas, *a fertile imagination*. **fertility** *noun* [from Latin]

fertilize *verb* (fertilizes, fertilizing, fertilized)
1 add substances to the soil to make it more fertile. 2 put pollen into a plant or sperm into an egg or female animal so that it develops seed or young.
fertilization *noun*, **fertilizer** *noun*

fervent or **fervid** *adjectives*
showing warm or strong feeling.
fervently *adverb*, **fervency** *noun*, **fervour** *noun*
[from Latin *fervens* = boiling]

fester *verb* (festers, festering, festered)
1 become septic and filled with pus.
2 cause resentment for a long time.
[from old French]

festival *noun* (*plural* festivals)
a time when people arrange special
celebrations, performances, etc.
[from Latin]

festive *adjective*
1 to do with a festival. 2 suitable for a
festival; joyful. **festively** *adverb*

festivity *noun* (*plural* festivities)
a festive occasion or celebration.

festoon *noun* (*plural* festoons)
a chain of flowers or ribbons etc. hung as a
decoration.
festoon *verb* (festoons, festooning,
festooned)
decorate something with ornaments.
[via French from Italian *festone* = festive
ornament]

fetch *verb* (fetches, fetching, fetched)
1 go for and bring back, *fetch some milk*;
fetch a doctor. 2 be sold for a particular
price, *The chairs fetched £20*.
[from Old English]

fête (*say* fayt) *noun* (*plural* fêtes)
an outdoor entertainment with stalls and
sideshows.
fête *verb* (fêtes, fêting, fêted)
honour a person with celebrations.
[from old French *feste* = feast]

fetish *noun* (*plural* fetishes)
1 an object supposed to have magical
powers. 2 something that a person has an
obsession about.
[via French from Portuguese]

fetlock *noun* (*plural* fetlocks)
the part of a horse's leg above and behind
the hoof.
[from a Germanic language; related to *foot*]

fetter *noun* (*plural* fetters)
a chain or shackle put round a prisoner's
ankle.
fetter *verb* (fetters, fettering, fettered)
put fetters on a prisoner.
[from Old English]

fettle *noun*
in fine fettle in good health.
[from Old English]

feud (*say* fewd) *noun* (*plural* feuds)
a long-lasting quarrel, especially between
two families. [via old French from
Germanic; related to *foe*]

feudal (*say* few-dal) *adjective*
to do with the system used in the Middle
Ages in which people could farm land in
exchange for work done for the owner.
feudalism *noun* [from Latin]

fever *noun* (*plural* fevers)
1 an abnormally high body temperature,
usually with an illness. 2 excitement or
agitation. **fevered** *adjective*, **feverish**
adjective, **feverishly** *adverb* [from Latin]

few *adjective*
not many. **fewness** *noun*

USAGE: Note that *fewer* means 'not so
many', while *less* means 'not so much'. It is
widely regarded as incorrect to use *less*
when you mean *fewer*.

few *noun*
a small number of people or things.
[from Old English]

fez *noun* (*plural* fezzes)
a high flat-topped red hat with a tassel,
worn by Muslim men in some countries.
[named after Fez, a town in Morocco,
where fezzes were made]

fiancé (*say* fee-ahn-say) *noun* (*plural*
fiancés)
a man who is engaged to be married.
[French, = betrothed]

fiancée (*say* fee-ahn-say) *noun* (*plural*
fiancées)
a woman who is engaged to be married.

fiasco (*say* fee-as-koh) *noun* (*plural* fiascos)
a complete failure. [Italian]

fib *noun* (*plural* fibs)
a lie about something unimportant. **fibber**
noun, **fibbing** *noun* [related to *fable*]

fibre *noun* (*plural* fibres)
1 a very thin thread. 2 a substance made of
thin threads. 3 indigestible material in

certain foods that stimulates the action of the intestines. **fibrous** *adjective* [from Latin]

fibreglass *noun*
1 fabric made from glass fibres. 2 plastic containing glass fibres.

fickle *adjective*
constantly changing; not loyal to one person or group etc. **fickleness** *noun* [from Old English]

fiction *noun* (*plural* **fictions**)
1 writings about events that have not really happened; stories and novels. 2 something imagined or untrue. **fictional** *adjective* [same origin as *feign*]

fictitious *adjective*
imagined or untrue.

fiddle *noun* (*plural* **fiddles**)
1 (*informal*) a violin. 2 (*slang*) a swindle.
fiddle *verb* (**fiddles, fiddling, fiddled**)
1 (*informal*) play the violin. 2 fidget or tinker with something, using your fingers. 3 (*slang*) swindle; get or change something dishonestly. **fiddler** *noun* [from Old English]

fiddly *adjective*
small and awkward to use or do.

fidelity *noun*
1 faithfulness or loyalty. 2 accuracy; the exactness with which sound is reproduced. [from Latin *fides* = faith]

fidget *verb* (**fidgets, fidgeting, fidgeted**)
make small restless movements.
fidgety *adjective*
fidget *noun* (*plural* **fidgets**)
a person who fidgets. [origin unknown]

field *noun* (*plural* **fields**)
1 a piece of land with grass or crops growing on it. 2 an area of interest or study, *recent advances in the field of science.* 3 those who are taking part in a race or outdoor game etc.
field *verb* (**fields, fielding, fielded**)
1 stop or catch the ball in cricket etc. 2 be on the side not batting in cricket etc. 3 put a team into a match etc., *They fielded their best players.* **fielder** *noun*, **fieldsman** *noun* [from Old English]

fieldwork *noun*
practical work or research done in various places, not in a library or museum or laboratory etc.

fiend (*say* feend) *noun* (*plural* **fiends**)
1 an evil spirit; a devil. 2 a very wicked or cruel person. 3 an enthusiast, *a fresh-air fiend.* **fiendish** *adjective* [from Old English]

fierce *adjective*
1 angry and violent or cruel. 2 intense, *fierce heat.* **fiercely** *adverb*, **fierceness** *noun* [from Latin *ferus* = untamed]

fiery *adjective*
1 full of flames or heat. 2 full of emotion. 3 easily made angry.

fife *noun* (*plural* **fifes**)
a small shrill flute.
[from German *Pfeife* = pipe]

fifteen *noun* & *adjective* (*plural* **fifteens**)
1 the number 15. 2 a team in Rugby Union football. **fifteenth** *adjective* & *noun* [from Old English]

fifth *adjective* & *noun* (*plural* **fifths**)
next after the fourth. **fifthly** *adverb* [from Old English]

fifty *noun* & *adjective* (*plural* **fifties**)
the number 50. **fiftieth** *adjective* & *noun* [from Old English]

fifty-fifty *adjective* & *adverb*
1 shared equally between two people or groups. 2 evenly balanced, *a fifty-fifty chance.*

fig *noun* (*plural* **figs**)
a soft fruit full of small seeds. [from Latin]

fight *noun* (*plural* **fights**)
1 a struggle against somebody using hands, weapons, etc. 2 an attempt to achieve or overcome something, *the fight against poverty.*
fight *verb* (**fights, fighting, fought**)
1 have a fight. 2 attempt to achieve or overcome something. **fighter** *noun* [from Old English]

figment *noun* (*plural* **figments**)
something imagined, *a figment of the imagination.* [from Latin; related to *feign*]

figurative *adjective*
using a figure of speech; metaphorical, not literal.
figuratively *adverb*

figure *noun* (*plural* **figures**)
1 the symbol of a number. **2** an amount or value. **3** a diagram or illustration. **4** a shape. **5** the shape of a person's, especially a woman's, body. **6** a person. **7** a representation of a person or animal in painting, sculpture, etc.
figure *verb* (**figures, figuring, figured**)
appear or take part in something.
figure out work something out.
[from Latin]

figurehead *noun* (*plural* **figureheads**)
1 a carved figure decorating the prow of a sailing ship. **2** a person who is head of a country or organization but has no real power.

figure of speech *noun* (*plural* **figures of speech**)
a word or phrase used for dramatic effect and not intended literally, e.g. 'a *flood of letters*'.

filament *noun* (*plural* **filaments**)
a thread or thin wire, especially one in a light bulb. [from Latin *filum* = thread]

filch *verb* (**filches, filching, filched**)
steal something slyly; pilfer.
[origin unknown]

file[1] *noun* (*plural* **files**)
a metal tool with a rough surface that is rubbed on things to shape them or make them smooth.
file *verb* (**files, filing, filed**)
shape or smooth something with a file.
[from Old English]

file[2] *noun* (*plural* **files**)
1 a folder or box etc. for keeping papers in order. **2** a collection of data stored under one name in a computer. **3** a line of people one behind the other.
file *verb* (**files, filing, filed**)
1 put something into a file. **2** walk in a file, *They filed out.* [from Latin *filum* = thread (because a string or wire was put through papers to hold them in order)]

filial (*say* fil-ee-al) *adjective*
to do with a son or daughter.
[from Latin *filius* = son, *filia* = daughter]

filibuster *verb* (**filibusters, filibustering, filibustered**)
try to delay or prevent the passing of a law by making long speeches. **filibuster** *noun*
[from Dutch *vrijbuiter* = pirate]

filigree *noun*
ornamental lace-like work of twisted metal wire. [from Latin *filum* = thread + *granum* = grain]

filings *plural noun*
tiny pieces of metal rubbed off by a file, *iron filings*.

fill *verb* (**fills, filling, filled**)
1 make or become full. **2** block up a hole or cavity. **filler** *noun*
fill *noun*
enough to fill a person or thing, *We ate our fill*. [from Old English]

fillet *noun* (*plural* **fillets**)
a piece of fish or meat without bones.
fillet *verb* (**fillets, filleting, filleted**)
remove the bones from fish or meat.
[from French]

filling *noun* (*plural* **fillings**)
1 something used to fill a hole or gap, e.g. in a tooth. **2** something put in pastry to make a pie, or between layers of bread to make a sandwich.

filly *noun* (*plural* **fillies**)
a young female horse. [from Old Norse]

film *noun* (*plural* **films**)
1 a motion picture, such as those shown in cinemas or on television. **2** a rolled strip or sheet of thin plastic coated with material that is sensitive to light, used for taking photographs or making a motion picture. **3** a very thin layer, *a film of grease*.
film *verb* (**films, filming, filmed**)
make a film of a story etc.
[from Old English *filmen* = thin skin]

filmy *adjective* (**filmier, filmiest**)
thin and almost transparent. **filminess** *noun*

filter *noun* (*plural* filters)
1 a device for holding back dirt or other unwanted material from a liquid or gas etc. that passes through it. **2** a system for filtering traffic.
filter *verb* (filters, filtering, filtered)
1 pass through a filter. **2** move gradually, *They filtered into the hall.* **3** move in a particular direction while other traffic is held up. [from old French]

filth *noun*
disgusting dirt. [from Old English]

filthy *adjective* (filthier, filthiest)
disgustingly dirty. **filthiness** *noun*

fin *noun* (*plural* fins)
1 a thin flat part sticking out from a fish's body, that helps it to swim. **2** a small part that sticks out on an aircraft or rocket etc., for helping its balance. [from Old English]

final *adjective*
1 coming at the end; last. **2** that puts an end to an argument etc., *You must go, and that's final!* **finally** *adverb*, **finality** *noun*
final *noun* (*plural* finals)
the last in a series of contests. [from Latin *finis* = end]

finale (*say* fin-ah-lee) *noun* (*plural* finales)
the final section of a piece of music or a play etc. [Italian; related to *final*]

finalist *noun* (*plural* finalists)
a competitor in a final.

finalize *verb* (finalizes, finalizing, finalized)
put something into its final form. **finalization** *noun*

finance *noun*
the use or management of money. **finances** *plural noun* money resources; funds.
finance *verb* (finances, financing, financed)
provide the money for something. **financier** *noun* [from old French *finer* – settle a debt]

financial *adjective*
to do with finance. **financially** *adverb*

finch *noun* (*plural* finches)
a small bird with a short stubby bill. [from Old English]

find *verb* (finds, finding, found)
1 get or see something by looking for it or by chance. **2** learn something by experience, *He found that digging was hard work.*
find out get or discover some information.
find *noun* (*plural* finds)
something found. [from Old English]

fine[1] *adjective*
1 of high quality; excellent. **2** dry and clear; sunny, *fine weather.* **3** very thin; consisting of small particles. **4** in good health; well, *I'm fine.* **finely** *adverb*, **fineness** *noun*
fine *adverb*
1 finely, *chop it fine.* **2** (*informal*) very well, *That will suit me fine.* [same origin as *finish*]

fine[2] *noun* (*plural* fines)
money which has to be paid as a punishment.
fine *verb* (fines, fining, fined)
make somebody pay a fine. [from Latin *finis* = end (in the Middle Ages it referred to the sum paid to settle a lawsuit)]

fine arts *plural noun*
painting, sculpture, and music.

finery *noun*
fine clothes or decorations.

finesse (*say* fin-ess) *noun*
skill and elegance in doing something. [French, = fineness]

finger *noun* (*plural* fingers)
1 one of the separate parts of the hand. **2** a narrow piece of something, *fish fingers.*
finger *verb* (fingers, fingering, fingered)
touch or feel something with your fingers. [from Old English]

fingerprint *noun* (*plural* fingerprints)
a mark made by the tiny ridges on the fingertip, used as a way of identifying someone.

fingertip *noun* (*plural* fingertips)
the tip of a finger.
have something at your fingertips be very familiar with a subject etc.

finicky *adjective*
fussy about details; hard to please.
[origin unknown]

finish *verb* (finishes, finishing, finished)
bring or come to an end.
finish *noun* (*plural* finishes)
1 the last stage of something; the end.
2 the surface or coating on woodwork etc.
[from Latin *finis* = end]

finite (*say* fy-nyt) *adjective*
limited; not infinite, *We have only a finite supply of coal.*
[from Latin *finitus* = finished]

finite verb *noun* (*plural* finite verbs)
a verb that agrees with its subject in person and number; 'was', 'went', and 'says' are finite verbs; 'going' and 'to say' are not.

fiord (*say* fee-ord) *noun* (*plural* fiords)
an inlet of the sea between high cliffs, as in Norway. [Norwegian]

fir *noun* (*plural* firs)
an evergreen tree with needle-like leaves, that produces cones. [from Old Norse]

fire *noun* (*plural* fires)
1 the process of burning that produces light and heat. 2 coal and wood etc. burning in a grate or furnace to give heat.
3 a device using electricity or gas to heat a room. 4 the shooting of guns, *Hold your fire!*
on fire burning.
set fire to start something burning.
fire *verb* (fires, firing, fired)
1 set fire to. 2 bake pottery or bricks etc. in a kiln. 3 shoot a gun; send out a bullet or missile. 4 dismiss someone from a job.
5 excite, *fire them with enthusiasm.* **firer** *noun* [from Old English]

firearm *noun* (*plural* firearms)
a small gun; a rifle, pistol, or revolver.

firebrand *noun* (*plural* firebrands)
a person who stirs up trouble.

fire brigade *noun* (*plural* fire brigades)
a team of people organized to fight fires.

fire drill *noun* (*plural* fire drills)
a rehearsal of the procedure that needs to be followed in case of a fire.

fire engine *noun* (*plural* fire engines)
a large vehicle that carries firemen and equipment to put out large fires.

fire escape *noun* (*plural* fire escapes)
a special staircase by which people may escape from a burning building etc.

fire extinguisher *noun* (*plural* fire extinguishers)
a metal cylinder from which water or foam can be sprayed to put out a fire.

firefighter *noun* (*plural* firefighters)
a member of a fire brigade.

firefly *noun* (*plural* fireflies)
a kind of beetle that gives off a glowing light.

fireman *noun* (*plural* firemen)
a member of a fire brigade.

fireplace *noun* (*plural* fireplaces)
an open structure for holding a fire in a room.

fireside *noun* (*plural* firesides)
the part of the room near a fireplace.

firewood *noun*
wood for use as fuel.

firework *noun* (*plural* fireworks)
a device containing chemicals that burn or explode attractively and noisily.

firing squad *noun* (*plural* firing squads)
a group ordered to shoot a condemned person.

firm *noun* (*plural* firms)
a business organization.
firm *adjective*
1 not giving way when pressed; hard or solid. 2 steady; not shaking or moving.
3 definite and not likely to change, *a firm belief.* **firmly** *adverb*, **firmness** *noun*
firm *adverb*
firmly, *Stand firm!*
firm *verb* (firms, firming, firmed)
make something become firm. [from Latin]

firmament *noun*
the sky with its clouds and stars.
[same origin as *firm*]

first *adjective*
coming before all others in time or order or importance. **firstly** *adverb*

first *adverb*
before everything else, *Finish this work first.*

first *noun* (*plural* **firsts**)
a person or thing that is first. [from Old English]

first aid *noun*
treatment given to an injured person before a doctor comes.

firth *noun* (*plural* **firths**)
an estuary or inlet of the sea on the coast of Scotland. [from Old Norse *fjorthr* = fiord]

fiscal *adjective*
to do with public finances. [from Latin *fiscus* = treasury]

fish *noun* (*plural* **fish** or **fishes**)
an animal with gills and fins that always lives and breathes in water.

fish *verb* (**fishes, fishing, fished**)
1 try to catch fish. 2 search for something; try to get something, *He is only fishing for praise.* [from Old English]

fisherman *noun* (*plural* **fishermen**)
a person who tries to catch fish.

fishery *noun* (*plural* **fisheries**)
1 the part of the sea where fishing is carried on. 2 the business of fishing.

fishmonger *noun* (*plural* **fishmongers**)
a shopkeeper who sells fish. [from *fish* + an old word *monger* = trader]

fishy *adjective* (**fishier, fishiest**)
1 smelling or tasting of fish. 2 (*informal*) causing doubt or suspicion, *a fishy excuse.* **fishily** *adverb*, **fishiness** *noun*

fissile *adjective*
1 likely to split. 2 capable of undergoing nuclear fission. [same origin as *fission*]

fission *noun*
1 splitting something. 2 splitting the nucleus of an atom so as to release energy. **fissionable** *adjective* [from Latin *fissum* = split]

fissure (*say* fish-er) *noun* (*plural* **fissures**)
a narrow opening made where something splits. [same origin as *fission*]

fist *noun* (*plural* **fists**)
a tightly closed hand with the fingers bent into the palm. [from Old English]

fisticuffs *noun* (*old use*)
fighting with the fists. [from *fist* + *cuff* = slap]

fit[1] *adjective* (**fitter, fittest**)
1 suitable or good enough, *a meal fit for a king.* 2 healthy, *Keep fit!* 3 ready or likely, *They worked till they were fit to collapse.* **fitly** *adverb*, **fitness** *noun*

fit *verb* (**fits, fitting, fitted**)
1 be the right size and shape for something; be suitable. 2 put something into place, *Fit a lock on the door.* 3 alter something to make it the right size and shape. 4 make suitable for something, *His training fits him for the job.* **fitter** *noun*

fit *noun*
the way something fits, *a good fit.* [origin unknown]

fit[2] *noun* (*plural* **fits**)
1 a sudden illness, especially one that makes you move violently or become unconscious. 2 an outburst, *a fit of rage.* [from Old English]

fitful *adjective*
happening in short periods, not steadily. **fitfully** *adverb* [from *fit*[2] + *-ful*]

fitment *noun* (*plural* **fitments**)
a piece of fixed furniture etc. [from *fit*[1]]

fitting *adjective*
proper or appropriate, *This statue is a fitting memorial to an extraordinary woman.*

fitting *noun* (*plural* **fittings**)
having a piece of clothing fitted, *I needed several fittings.*

fittings *plural noun*
the fixtures and fitments of a building.

five *noun* & *adjective* (*plural* **fives**)
the number 5. [from Old English]

fiver *noun* (*plural* **fivers**) (*informal*)
a five-pound note; £5.

fives *noun*
a game in which a ball is hit with gloved hands or a bat against the walls of a court. [origin unknown]

fix *verb* (**fixes, fixing, fixed**)
1 fasten or place firmly. **2** make permanent and unable to change. **3** decide or arrange, *We fixed a date for the party.* **4** repair; put into working condition, *He is fixing my bike.* **fixer** *noun*
fix up arrange or organize something.
fix *noun* (*plural* **fixes**)
1 (*informal*) an awkward situation, *I'm in a fix.* **2** finding the position of something. **3** (*slang*) an addict's dose of a drug. [from Latin]

fixation *noun* (*plural* **fixations**)
a strong interest or a concentration on one idea etc.; an obsession.

fixative *noun* (*plural* **fixatives**)
a substance used to keep something in position or make it permanent.

fixedly *adverb*
in a fixed way.

fixity *noun*
a fixed condition; permanence.

fixture *noun* (*plural* **fixtures**)
1 something fixed in its place. **2** a sports event planned for a particular day.

fizz *verb* (**fizzes, fizzing, fizzed**)
make a hissing or spluttering sound; produce a lot of small bubbles. [imitating the sound]

fizzle *verb* (**fizzles, fizzling, fizzled**)
make a slight fizzing sound.
fizzle out end feebly or unsuccessfully. [from *fizz*]

fizzy *adjective*
(of a drink) having a lot of small bubbles. **fizziness** *noun*

fjord (*say* fee-**ord**) *noun* (*plural* **fjords**)
a different spelling of *fiord*.

flabbergasted *adjective*
greatly astonished. [origin unknown]

flabby *adjective*
fat and soft, not firm. **flabbily** *adverb*, **flabbiness** *noun* [related to *flap*]

flaccid (*say* **flak**-sid or **flass**-id) *adjective*
soft and limp. **flaccidly** *adverb*, **flaccidity** *noun* [from Latin *flaccus* = flabby]

flag[1] (*plural* **flags**)
1 a piece of cloth with a coloured pattern or shape on it, used as a sign or signal. **2** a small piece of paper or plastic that looks like a flag. **flagpole** *noun*, **flagstaff** *noun*
flag *verb* (**flags, flagging, flagged**)
1 become weak; droop. **2** signal with a flag or by waving. [from an old word *flag* = drooping]

flag[2] *noun* (*plural* **flags**)
a flagstone. [from Old Norse *flaga* = slab of stone]

flagon *noun* (*plural* **flagons**)
a large bottle or container for wine or cider etc. [from Latin *flasco* = flask]

flagrant (*say* **flay**-grant) *adjective*
very bad and noticeable, *flagrant disobedience.* **flagrantly** *adverb*, **flagrancy** *noun* [from Latin *flagrans* = blazing]

flagship *noun* (*plural* **flagships**)
1 a ship that carries an admiral and flies his flag. **2** the best and most important product that a company produces.

flagstone *noun* (*plural* **flagstones**)
a flat slab of stone used for paving. [from *flag*[2] + *stone*]

flail *noun* (*plural* **flails**)
an old-fashioned tool for threshing grain.
flail *verb* (**flails, flailing, flailed**)
beat as if with a flail; wave about wildly. [from Latin *flagellum* = a whip]

flair *noun*
a natural ability or talent, *Ian has a flair for languages.*
[French, = power to smell things]

USAGE: Do not confuse with *flare.*

flak *noun*
shells fired by anti-aircraft guns. [short for German *Fliegerabwehrkanone* = aircraft-defence-cannon]

flake *noun* (*plural* flakes)
1 a very light thin piece of something.
2 a small flat piece of falling snow.
flaky *adjective*
flake *verb* (flakes, flaking, flaked)
come off in flakes. [origin unknown]

flamboyant *adjective*
very showy in appearance or manner.
[French, = blazing]

flame *noun* (*plural* flames)
a tongue-shaped portion of fire or burning
gas.
flame *verb* (flames, flaming, flamed)
1 produce flames. 2 become bright red.
[from old French]

flamingo *noun* (*plural* flamingoes)
a wading bird with long legs, a long neck,
and pinkish feathers. [from Spanish]

flammable *adjective*
able to be set on fire. **flammability** *noun*
[from Latin *flamma* = flame]

USAGE: See note at *inflammable*.

flan *noun* (*plural* flans)
a pastry or sponge shell with no cover over
the filling. [French]

flank *noun* (*plural* flanks)
the side of something, especially an
animal's body or an army.
flank *verb* (flanks, flanking, flanked)
place or be placed at the side of something
or somebody. **flanker** *noun*
[from old French]

flannel *noun* (*plural* flannels)
1 a soft cloth for washing yourself. 2 a soft
woollen material.
[from Welsh *gwlanen* = woollen]

flap *verb* (flaps, flapping, flapped)
1 wave about. 2 (*slang*) panic or fuss about
something.
flap *noun* (*plural* flaps)
1 a part that is fixed at one edge onto
something else, often to cover an opening.
2 the action or sound of flapping.
3 (*slang*) a panic or fuss, *in a flap*.
[imitating the sound]

flapjack *noun*
a cake made from oats and golden syrup.
[from *flap* + the name *Jack*]

flare *verb* (flares, flaring, flared)
1 blaze with a sudden bright flame.
2 become angry suddenly. 3 become
gradually wider, *flaring nostrils*.
flare *noun* (*plural* flares)
1 a sudden bright flame or light, especially
one used as a signal. 2 a gradual widening.
[origin unknown]

USAGE: Do not confuse with *flair*.

flash *noun* (*plural* flashes)
1 a sudden bright flame or light. 2 a device
for making a sudden bright light for taking
photographs. 3 a sudden display of anger,
wit, etc. 4 a short item of news.
flash *verb* (flashes, flashing, flashed)
1 make a flash. 2 appear suddenly; move
quickly, *The train flashed past us*.
[origin unknown]

flashback *noun* (*plural* flashbacks)
going back in a film or story to something
that happened earlier.

flashy *adjective*
gaudy or showy.

flask *noun* (*plural* flasks)
1 a bottle with a narrow neck. 2 a vacuum
flask. [via Old English from Latin; related
to *flagon*]

flat *adjective* (flatter, flattest)
1 with no curves or bumps; smooth and
level. 2 spread out; lying at full length, *Lie
flat on the ground*. 3 (of a tyre) with no air
inside. 4 (of feet) without the normal arch
underneath. 5 absolute, *a flat refusal*.
6 dull; not changing. 7 (of a drink) no
longer fizzy. 8 (of a battery) unable to
produce any more electric current. 9 (in
music) one semitone lower than the
natural note, *E flat*.
flatly *adverb*, **flatness** *noun*
flat *adverb*
1 so as to be flat, *Press it flat*. 2 (*informal*)
exactly, *in ten seconds flat*. 3 (in music)
below the correct pitch.
flat out as fast as possible.
flat *noun* (*plural* flats)
1 a set of rooms for living in, usually on
one floor of a building. 2 (in music) a note

one semitone lower than the natural note; the sign (♭) that indicates this. **3 a** punctured tyre. [from Old Norse]

flatten *verb* (**flattens, flattening, flattened**)
make or become flat.

flatter *verb* (**flatters, flattering, flattered**)
1 praise somebody more than he or she deserves. **2** make a person or thing seem better or more attractive than they really are. **flatterer** *noun*, **flattery** *noun*
[from Old French *flater* = smooth down]

flaunt *verb* (**flaunts, flaunting, flaunted**)
display something proudly in a way that annoys people; show it off, *He liked to flaunt his expensive clothes and cars.*
[origin unknown]

USAGE: Do not confuse this word with *flout*, which has a different meaning.

flavour *noun* (*plural* **flavours**)
the taste of something.
flavour *verb* (**flavours, flavouring, flavoured**)
give something a flavour; season it.
flavouring *noun* [from old French]

flaw *noun* (*plural* **flaws**)
something that makes a person or thing imperfect. **flawed** *adjective*
[origin unknown]

flawless *adjective*
without a flaw; perfect. **flawlessly** *adverb*, **flawlessness** *noun*

flax *noun*
a plant that produces fibres from which linen is made and seeds from which linseed oil is obtained. [from Old English]

flaxen *adjective*
pale-yellow like flax fibres, *flaxen hair.*

flay *verb* (**flays, flaying, flayed**)
strip the skin from an animal.
[from Old English]

flea *noun* (*plural* **fleas**)
a small jumping insect that sucks blood.
[from Old English]

flea market *noun* (*plural* **flea markets**)
a street market that sells cheap or second-hand goods.

fleck *noun* (*plural* **flecks**)
1 a very small patch of colour. **2** a particle; a speck, *flecks of dirt.* **flecked** *adjective*
[origin unknown]

fledged *adjective*
(of young birds) having grown feathers and able to fly.
fully-fledged *adjective* fully trained, *a fully-fledged engineer.*
[from Old English]

fledgeling *noun* (*plural* **fledgelings**)
a young bird that is just fledged.
[from *fledge* = become fledged, + *-ling*]

flee *verb* (**flees, fleeing, fled**)
run or hurry away from something.
[from Old English]

fleece *noun* (*plural* **fleeces**)
the woolly hair of a sheep or similar animal. **fleecy** *adjective*
fleece *verb* (**fleeces, fleecing, fleeced**)
1 shear the fleece from a sheep. **2** swindle a person out of some money.
[from Old English]

fleet[1] *noun* (*plural* **fleets**)
a number of ships, aircraft, or vehicles owned by one country or company.
[from Old English]

fleet[2] *adjective*
moving swiftly; nimble. [from Old Norse]

fleeting *adjective*
passing quickly; brief.

Flemish *adjective*
to do with Flanders in Belgium or its people or language. **Flemish** *noun*

flesh *noun*
1 the soft substance of the bodies of people and animals, consisting of muscle and fat. **2** the pulpy part of fruits and vegetables. **fleshy** *adjective* [from Old English]

flex *verb* (**flexes, flexing, flexed**)
bend or stretch something that is flexible, *flex your muscles.*
flex *noun* (*plural* **flexes**)
flexible insulated wire for carrying electric current. [from Latin *flexum* = bent]

flexible *adjective*
1 easy to bend or stretch. 2 able to be changed or adapted, *Our plans are flexible.* **flexibility** *noun*

flick *noun* (*plural* flicks)
a quick light hit or movement.
flick *verb* (flicks, flicking, flicked)
hit or move with a flick.
[from Middle English]

flicker *verb* (flickers, flickering, flickered)
1 burn or shine unsteadily. 2 move quickly to and fro.
flicker *noun* (*plural* flickers)
a flickering light or movement.
[from Old English]

flier *noun* (*plural* fliers)
a different spelling of *flyer*.

flight[1] *noun* (*plural* flights)
1 flying. 2 a journey in an aircraft etc. 3 a series of stairs. 4 the feathers or fins on a dart or arrow. [from Old English]

flight[2] *noun* (*plural* flights)
fleeing; an escape. [from Middle English]

flight recorder *noun* (*plural* flight recorders)
a device in an aircraft that records technical details during a flight. It may be used after an accident to help find the cause.

flighty *adjective* (flightier, flightiest)
silly and frivolous. **flightiness** *noun*
[from *flight*[1]]

flimsy *adjective* (flimsier, flimsiest)
made of something thin or weak. **flimsily** *adverb*, **flimsiness** *noun* [origin unknown]

flinch *verb* (flinches, flinching, flinched)
move or shrink back because you are afraid; wince. **flinch** *noun*
[via old French from Germanic]

fling *verb* (flings, flinging, flung)
throw something violently or carelessly.
fling *noun* (*plural* flings)
1 the movement of flinging. 2 a vigorous dance, *the Highland fling*. 3 a short time of enjoyment, *have a fling*. [origin unknown]

flint *noun* (*plural* flints)
1 a very hard kind of stone. 2 a piece of flint or hard metal used to produce sparks.
flinty *adjective* [from Old English]

flip *verb* (flips, flipping, flipped)
1 flick. 2 (*slang*) become crazy or very angry.
flip *noun* (*plural* flips)
a flipping movement. [origin unknown]

flippant *adjective*
not showing proper seriousness. **flippantly** *adverb*, **flippancy** *noun* [from *flip*]

flipper *noun* (*plural* flippers)
1 a limb that water-animals use for swimming. 2 a kind of flat rubber shoe, shaped like a duck's foot, that you wear on your feet to help you to swim. [from *flip*]

flirt *verb* (flirts, flirting, flirted)
behave lovingly towards somebody to amuse yourself. **flirtation** *noun*
flirt *noun* (*plural* flirts)
a person who flirts. **flirtatious** *adjective*, **flirtatiously** *adverb* [origin unknown]

flit *verb* (flits, flitting, flitted)
fly or move lightly and quickly. **flit** *noun*
[from Old Norse]

flitter *verb* (flitters, flittering, flittered)
flit about. **flitter** *noun*

float *verb* (floats, floating, floated)
1 stay or move on the surface of a liquid or in air. 2 make something float. **floater** *noun*
float *noun* (*plural* floats)
1 a device designed to float. 2 a vehicle with a platform used for delivering milk or for carrying a display in a parade etc. 3 a small amount of money kept for paying small bills or giving change etc.
[from Old English]

floating voter *noun* (*plural* floating voters)
a person who does not support any political party permanently.

flock[1] *noun* (*plural* flocks)
a group of sheep, goats, or birds.
flock *verb* (flocks, flocking, flocked)
gather or move in a crowd.
[from Old English]

flock² *noun* (*plural* **flocks**)
a tuft of wool or cotton etc. [from Latin]

floe *noun* (*plural* **floes**)
a sheet of floating ice.
[from Norwegian *flo* = layer]

flog *verb* (**flogs, flogging, flogged**)
1 beat a person or animal hard with a whip or stick as a punishment. 2 (*slang*) sell.
flogging *noun* [from Latin]

flood *noun* (*plural* **floods**)
1 a large amount of water spreading over a place that is usually dry. 2 a great amount, *a flood of requests*. 3 the movement of the tide when it is coming in towards the land.

flood *verb* (**floods, flooding, flooded**)
1 cover with a flood. 2 come in great amounts, *Letters flooded in.*
[from Old English]

floodlight *noun* (*plural* **floodlights**)
a lamp that makes a broad bright beam to light up a stage, stadium, important building, etc. **floodlit** *adjective*

floor *noun* (*plural* **floors**)
1 the part of a room that people walk on. 2 a storey of a building; all the rooms at the same level.

USAGE: In Britain, the *ground floor* of a building is the one at street level, and the one above it is the *first floor*. In the USA, the *first floor* is the one at street level, and the one above it is the *second floor*.

floor *verb* (**floors, flooring, floored**)
1 put a floor into a building. 2 knock a person down. 3 baffle somebody.
[from Old English]

floorboard *noun* (*plural* **floorboards**)
one of the boards forming the floor of a room.

flop *verb* (**flops, flopping, flopped**)
1 fall or sit down clumsily. 2 hang or sway heavily and loosely. 3 (*slang*) be a failure.

flop *noun* (*plural* **flops**)
1 a flopping movement or sound. 2 (*slang*) a failure. [a different spelling of *flap*]

floppy *adjective*
hanging loosely; not firm or rigid.
floppiness *noun*

floppy disk *noun* (*plural* **floppy disks**)
a flexible disc holding data for use in a computer.

flora *noun*
the plants of a particular area or period. (Compare *fauna*.) [from the name of *Flora*, the ancient Roman goddess of flowers; her name comes from Latin *flores* = flowers]

floral *adjective*
to do with flowers. [same orgin as *flora*]

florin *noun* (*plural* **florins**)
1 a Dutch guilder. 2 a former British coin worth two shillings (10p).
[from Italian *fiore* = flower; the name was originally given to an Italian coin which had a lily on one side]

florist *noun* (*plural* **florists**)
a shopkeeper who sells flowers.
[same origin as *flora*]

floss *noun*
silky thread or fibres. **flossy** *adjective*
[from old French]

flotation *noun* (*plural* **flotations**)
1 offering shares in a company on the stock market in order to launch or finance it. 2 floating something.

flotilla (*say* flot-il-a) *noun* (*plural* **flotillas**)
a fleet of boats or small ships.
[Spanish, = little fleet]

flotsam *noun*
wreckage or cargo found floating after a shipwreck.
flotsam and jetsam odds and ends.
[from old French *floter* = float]

flounce¹ *verb* (**flounces, flouncing, flounced**)
go in an impatient or annoyed manner, *She flounced out of the room.* **flounce** *noun*
[origin unknown]

flounce² *noun* (*plural* **flounces**)
a wide frill. [from old French]

flounder *verb* (**flounders, floundering, floundered**)
1 move clumsily and with difficulty. 2 make mistakes or become confused when trying to do something. [from old French]

flour *noun*
a fine powder of wheat or other grain, used in cooking. **floury** *adjective*
[old spelling of *flower*]

flourish *verb* (flourishes, flourishing, flourished)
1 grow or develop strongly. **2** be successful; prosper. **3** wave something about dramatically.

flourish *noun* (*plural* flourishes)
a showy or dramatic sweeping movement, curve, or passage of music.
[from Latin *florere* = to flower]

flout *verb* (flouts, flouting, flouted)
disobey a rule or instruction openly and scornfully, *She shaved her head one day, just because she loved to flout convention.*
[probably from Dutch *fluiten* = whistle, hiss]

USAGE: Do not confuse this word with *flaunt*, which has a different meaning.

flow *verb* (flows, flowing, flowed)
1 move along smoothly or continuously. **2** gush out, *Water flowed from the tap.* **3** hang loosely, *flowing hair.* **4** (of the tide) come in towards the land.

flow *noun* (*plural* flows)
1 a flowing movement or mass. **2** the movement of the tide when it is coming in towards the land, *the ebb and flow of the tide.*
[from Old English]

flower *noun* (*plural* flowers)
1 the part of a plant from which seed and fruit develops. **2** a blossom and its stem used for decoration, usually in groups. (Compare *flora.*)

flower *verb* (flowers, flowering, flowered)
produce flowers.
[from old French; related to *flora*]

flowerpot *noun* (*plural* flowerpots)
a pot in which a plant may be grown.

flowery *adjective*
1 full of flowers. **2** full of ornamental phrases.

flu *noun*
influenza.

fluctuate *verb* (fluctuates, fluctuating, fluctuated)
rise and fall; vary, *Prices fluctuated.*
fluctuation *noun*
[from Latin *fluctus* = a wave]

flue *noun* (*plural* flues)
a pipe or tube through which smoke or hot gases are drawn off. [origin unknown]

fluent (*say* floo-ent) *adjective*
1 skilful at speaking clearly and without hesitating. **2** able to speak a foreign language easily and well. **fluently** *adverb*, **fluency** *noun* [from Latin *fluens* = flowing]

fluff *noun*
a fluffy substance. [probably from Flemish]

fluffy *adjective*
having a mass of soft fur or fibres.
fluffiness *noun*

fluid *noun* (*plural* fluids)
a substance that is able to flow freely as liquids and gases do.

fluid *adjective*
1 able to flow freely. **2** not fixed, *My plans for Christmas are fluid.* **fluidity** *noun*
[from Latin *fluere* = to flow]

fluke *noun* (*plural* flukes)
a piece of good luck that makes you able to do something you thought you could not do. [origin unknown]

flummox *verb* (*informal*) (flummoxes, flummoxing, flummoxed)
baffle. [origin unknown]

fluorescent (*say* floo-er-ess-ent) *adjective*
creating light from radiation, *a fluorescent lamp.* **fluorescence** *noun*
[from *fluorspar*, a fluorescent mineral]

fluoridation *noun*
adding fluoride to drinking water in order to help prevent tooth decay.

fluoride *noun*
a chemical substance that is thought to prevent tooth decay. [from Latin]

flurry *noun* (*plural* flurries)
1 a sudden whirling gust of wind, rain, or snow. **2** an excited or flustered disturbance.
[from an old word *flurr* = to throw about]

flush¹ *verb* (flushes, flushing, flushed)
1 blush. 2 clean or remove something with a fast flow of water.
flush *noun* (*plural* flushes)
1 a blush. 2 a fast flow of water. [imitating the sound of water]

flush² *adjective*
1 level with the surrounding surface, *The doors are flush with the walls.* 2 having plenty of money. [origin unknown]

fluster *verb* (flusters, flustering, flustered)
make somebody nervous and confused. **fluster** *noun* [origin unknown]

flute *noun* (*plural* flutes)
a musical instrument consisting of a long pipe with holes that are stopped by fingers or keys. [from old French]

flutter *verb* (flutters, fluttering, fluttered)
1 flap wings quickly. 2 move or flap quickly and irregularly.
flutter *noun* (*plural* flutters)
1 a fluttering movement. 2 a nervously excited condition. 3 (*informal*) a small bet, *Have a flutter!* [from Old English]

flux *noun* (*plural* fluxes)
continual change or flow. [from Latin *fluxus* = flowing]

fly¹ *noun* (*plural* flies)
1 a small flying insect with two wings. 2 a real or artificial fly used as bait in fishing. [from Old English *flycge*]

fly² *verb* (flies, flying, flew, flown)
1 move through the air by means of wings or in an aircraft. 2 travel through the air or through space. 3 wave in the air, *Flags were flying.* 4 make something fly, *They flew model aircraft.* 5 move or pass quickly, *Time flies.* 6 flee from, *You must fly the country!* **flyer** *noun*
fly *noun* (*plural* flies)
the front opening of a pair of trousers. [from Old English *fleogan*]

flying saucer (*plural* flying saucers)
a mysterious saucer-shaped object reported to have been seen in the sky and believed by some people to be an alien spacecraft.

flying squad (*plural* flying squads)
a team of police or doctors etc. organized so that they can move rapidly.

flyleaf *noun* (*plural* flyleaves)
a blank page at the beginning or end of a book.

flyover *noun* (*plural* flyovers)
a bridge that carries one road or railway over another.

flywheel *noun* (*plural* flywheels)
a heavy wheel used to regulate machinery.

foal *noun* (*plural* foals)
a young horse.
foal *verb* (foals, foaling, foaled)
give birth to a foal. [from Old English]

foam *noun*
1 a white mass of tiny bubbles on a liquid; froth. 2 a spongy kind of rubber or plastic. **foamy** *adjective*
foam *verb* (foams, foaming, foamed)
form foam. [from Old English]

fob¹ *noun* (*plural* fobs)
1 a chain for a pocket watch. 2 a tab on a key-ring. [probably from German]

fob² *verb* (fobs, fobbing, fobbed)
fob off get rid of someone by an excuse or a trick.
[from German]

focal *adjective*
to do with or at a focus.

focus *noun* (*plural* focuses or foci)
1 the distance from an eye or lens at which an object appears clearest. 2 the point at which rays etc. seem to meet. 3 something that is a centre of interest or attention etc.
in focus appearing clearly.
out of focus not appearing clearly.
focus *verb* (focuses, focusing, focused)
1 use or adjust a lens so that objects appear clearly. 2 concentrate, *She focused her attention on it.* [Latin, = hearth (the central point of a household)]

fodder *noun*
food for horses and farm animals. [from Old English]

foe *noun* (*plural* foes) (*old use*)
an enemy. [from Old English]

foetus (*say* fee-tus) *noun* (*plural* foetuses)
a developing embryo, especially an unborn human baby. **foetal** *adjective* | Latin]

fog *noun*
thick mist. **foggy** *adjective*
[origin unknown]

foghorn *noun* (*plural* foghorns)
a loud horn for warning ships in fog.

fogy *noun* (*plural* fogies)
old fogy a person with old-fashioned ideas.
[origin unknown]

foible *noun* (*plural* foibles)
a slight peculiarity in someone's character or tastes.
[from old French; related to *feeble*]

foil¹ *noun* (*plural* foils)
1 a very thin sheet of metal. **2** a person or thing that makes another look better in contrast. [same origin as *foliage*]

foil² *noun* (*plural* foils)
a long narrow sword used in the sport of fencing. [origin unknown]

foil³ *verb* (foils, foiling, foiled)
prevent something from being successful, *We foiled his evil plan.*
[from old French *fouler* = trample]

foist *verb* (foists, foisting, foisted)
make a person accept something inferior or unwelcome, *They foisted the job on me.*
[from Dutch]

fold¹ *verb* (folds, folding, folded)
bend or move so that one part lies on another part.
fold *noun* (*plural* folds)
a line where something is folded.
[from Old English *fealdan*]

fold² *noun* (*plural* folds)
an enclosure for sheep.
[from Old English *fald*]

-fold *suffix*
forms adjectives and adverbs meaning 'multiplied by' (e.g *twofold, fourfold, manifold*). [from Old English]

folder *noun* (*plural* folders)
a folding cover for loose papers.

foliage *noun*
the leaves of a tree or plant.
[from Latin *folium* = leaf]

folk *noun*
people. [from Old English]

folk dance *nouns* (*plural* folk dances)
a dance in the traditional style of a country.

folklore *noun*
old beliefs and legends.

folk music *noun*
the traditional music of a country.

folk song *noun* (*plural* folk songs)
a song in the traditional style of a country.

follow *verb* (follows, following, followed)
1 go or come after. **2** do a thing after something else. **3** take a person or thing as a guide or example. **4** take an interest in the progress of events or a sport or team etc. **5** understand, *Did you follow what he said?* **6** result from something. **follower** *noun* [from Old English]

following *preposition*
after, as a result of, *Following the burglary, we had new locks fitted.*

folly *noun* (*plural* follies)
foolishness; a foolish action etc.
[from French *folie* = madness]

foment (*say* fo-ment) *verb* (foments, fomenting, fomented)
arouse or stimulate deliberately, *foment trouble.* [from Latin *fomentum* = poultice]

USAGE: Do not confuse with *ferment*.

fomentation *noun*
fomenting.

fond *adjective*
1 loving or liking a person or thing. **2** foolishly hopeful, *fond hopes.*
fondly *adverb*, **fondness** *noun*
[from an old word *fon* = fool]

fondle *verb* (fondles, fondling, fondled)
touch or stroke lovingly. [from *fond*]

font noun (plural **fonts**)
a basin (often of carved stone) in a church, to hold water for baptism.
[from Latin fontis = of a spring]

food noun (plural **foods**)
any substance that a plant or animal can take into its body to help it to grow and be healthy. [from Old English]

food chain noun (plural **food chains**)
a series of plants and animals each of which serves as food for the one above it in the series.

fool noun (plural **fools**)
1 a stupid person; someone who acts unwisely. 2 a jester or clown, Stop playing the fool. 3 a creamy pudding with crushed fruit in it, gooseberry fool.
fool's errand a useless errand.
fool's paradise happiness that comes only from being mistaken about something.
fool verb (**fools, fooling, fooled**)
1 behave in a joking way; play about. 2 trick or deceive someone.
[from old French]

foolery noun
foolish acts or behaviour.

foolhardy adjective
bold but foolish; reckless.
foolhardiness noun [from old French fol = foolish + hardi = bold]

foolish adjective
without good sense or judgement; unwise.
foolishly adverb, **foolishness** noun

foolproof adjective
easy to use or do correctly.

foot noun (plural **feet**)
1 lower part of the leg below the ankle. 2 any similar part, e.g. one used by certain animals to move or attach themselves to things. 3 the lowest part, the foot of the hill. 4 a measure of length, 12 inches or about 30 centimetres, a ten-foot pole; it is ten feet long. 5 a unit of rhythm in a line of poetry, e.g. each of the four divisions in Jack / and Jill / went up / the hill.
on foot walking.
[from Old English]

footage noun
a length of film.

foot-and-mouth disease noun
a serious contagious disease that affects cattle, sheep, and other animals.

football noun (plural **footballs**)
1 a game played by two teams which try to kick an inflated leather ball into their opponents' goal. 2 the ball used in this game. **footballer** noun

foothill noun (plural **foothills**)
a low hill near the bottom of a mountain or range of mountains.

foothold noun (plural **footholds**)
1 a place to put your foot when climbing. 2 a small but firm position from which you can advance in business etc.

footing noun
1 having your feet placed on something; a foothold, He lost his footing and slipped. 2 the status or nature of a relationship, We are on a friendly footing with that country.

footlights plural noun
a row of lights along the front of the floor of a stage.

footman noun (plural **footmen**)
a male servant who opens doors, serves at table, etc. [originally a servant who accompanied his master on foot]

footnote noun (plural **footnotes**)
a note printed at the bottom of the page.

footpath noun (plural **footpaths**)
a path for pedestrians.

footprint noun (plural **footprints**)
a mark made by a foot or shoe.

footsore adjective
having feet that are painful or sore from walking.

footstep noun (plural **footsteps**)
1 a step taken in walking or running. 2 the sound of this.

footstool noun (plural **footstools**)
a stool for resting your feet on when you are sitting.

for preposition
This word is used to show 1 purpose or direction (This letter is for you; We set out

for home), **2** distance or time (*Walk for six miles or two hours*), **3** price or exchange (*We bought it for £2; New lamps for old*), **4** cause (*She was fined for speeding*), **5** defence or support (*He fought for his country; Are you for us or against us?*), **6** reference (*For all her wealth, she is bored*), **7** similarity or correspondence (*We took him for a fool*),
for ever for all time; always.

for *conjunction*
because, *They hesitated, for they were afraid.* [from Old English]

for- *prefix*
1 away, off (as in *forgive*). **2** prohibiting (as in *forbid*). **3** abstaining or neglecting (as in *forgo, forsake*). [from Old English]

forage *noun*
1 food for horses and cattle. **2** the action of foraging.
forage *verb* (**forages, foraging, foraged**)
go searching for something, especially food or fuel. [via French from Germanic]

foray *noun* (*plural* **forays**)
a raid. [from old French; related to *forage*]

forbear *verb* (**forbears, forbearing, forbore, forborne**)
1 refrain from something, *We forbore to mention it.* **2** be patient or tolerant.
forbearance *noun* [from Old English]

forbid *verb* (**forbids, forbidding, forbade, forbidden**)
1 order someone not to do something.
2 refuse to allow, *We shall forbid the marriage.* [from Old English]

forbidding *adjective*
looking stern or unfriendly.

force *noun* (*plural* **forces**)
1 strength or power. **2** (in science) an influence, which can be measured, that causes something to move. **3** an organized group of police, soldiers, etc.
in or **into force** in or into effectiveness, *The new law comes into force next week.*
the forces a country's armed forces.
force *verb* (**forces, forcing, forced**)
1 use force in order to get or do something, or to make somebody obey. **2** break something open by force. **3** cause plants to

grow or bloom earlier than is normal, *You can force them in a greenhouse.*
[from Latin *fortis* = strong]

forceful *adjective*
strong and vigorous. **forcefully** *adverb*

forceps *noun* (*plural* **forceps**)
pincers or tongs used by dentists, surgeons, etc. [Latin]

forcible *adjective*
done by force; forceful. **forcibly** *adverb*

ford *noun* (*plural* **fords**)
a shallow place where you can walk across a river.
ford *verb* (**fords, fording, forded**)
cross a river at a ford. [from Old English]

fore *adjective* & *adverb*
at or towards the front, *fore and aft.*
fore *noun*
the front part.
to the fore to or at the front; in or to a prominent position.
[from Old English]

fore- *prefix*
before (as in *forecast*); in front (as in *foreleg*).

forearm[1] *noun* (*plural* **forearms**)
the arm from the elbow to the wrist or fingertips. [from *fore-* + *arm*[1]]

forearm[2] *verb* (**forearms, forearming, forearmed**)
prepare in advance against possible danger. [from *fore-* + *arm*[2]]

forebears *plural noun*
ancestors. [from *fore-* + *be-er* = someone or something that is]

foreboding *noun*
a feeling that trouble is coming.
[from *fore-* + *bode*]

forecast *noun* (*plural* **forecasts**)
a statement that tells in advance what is likely to happen.
forecast *verb* (**forecasts, forecasting, forecast**)
make a forecast. **forecaster** *noun*
[from *fore-* + *cast*]

forecastle (*say* foh-ksul) *noun* (*plural* forecastles)
the forward part of certain ships. [from *fore-* + *castle* (because originally this part was raised up like a castle to command your own or an enemy's deck)]

forecourt *noun* (*plural* forecourts)
an enclosed area in front of a building etc.

forefathers *plural noun*
ancestors.

forefinger *noun* (*plural* forefingers)
the finger next to the thumb.

forefoot *noun* (*plural* forefeet)
an animal's front foot.

forefront *noun*
the very front.

foregoing *adjective*
preceding; previously mentioned.

USAGE: Note the spelling of this word. It has an 'e' in it, whereas *forgo*, meaning 'give up', does not.

foregone conclusion (*plural* foregone conclusions)
a result that can be foreseen easily and with certainty.

foreground *noun*
the front part of a scene or view etc.

forehand *noun* (*plural* forehands)
a stroke made in tennis etc. with the palm of the hand turned forwards.

forehead (*say* forrid or for-hed) *noun* (*plural* foreheads)
the part of the face above the eyes.

foreign *adjective*
1 belonging to or in another country. 2 not belonging naturally to a place or to someone's nature, *Lying is foreign to her nature.* [from old French]

foreigner *noun* (*plural* foreigners)
a person from another country.

foreleg *noun* (*plural* forelegs)
an animal's front leg.

foreman *noun* (*plural* foremen)
1 a worker in charge of a group of other workers. 2 a member of a jury who is in charge of the jury's discussions and who speaks on its behalf.

foremost *adjective* & *adverb*
first in position or rank; most important.

forensic (*say* fer-en-sik) *adjective*
to do with or used in lawcourts. [from Latin; related to *forum*]

forensic medicine *noun*
medical knowledge needed in legal matters.

forerunner *noun* (*plural* forerunners)
a person or thing that comes before another; a sign of what is to come.

foresee *verb* (foresees, foreseeing, foresaw, foreseen)
realize what is going to happen.

foreseeable *adjective*
able to be foreseen.

foreshadow *verb* (foreshadows, foreshadowing, foreshadowed)
be a sign of something that is to come.

foreshorten *verb* (foreshortens, foreshortening, foreshortened)
show an object in a drawing etc. with some lines shortened to give an effect of distance or depth.

foresight *noun*
the ability to foresee and prepare for future needs.

foreskin *noun* (*plural* foreskins)
the fold of skin covering the end of the penis.

forest *noun* (*plural* forests)
trees and undergrowth covering a large area. **forested** *adjective* [from old French]

forestall *verb* (forestalls, forestalling, forestalled)
prevent somebody or something by taking action first.
[from Old English *foresteall* = an ambush]

forestry *noun*
planting forests and looking after them.
forester *noun*

foretaste *noun* (*plural* **foretastes**)
an experience of something that is to come
in the future.

foretell *verb* (**foretells, foretelling, foretold**)
tell in advance; prophesy.

forethought *noun*
careful thought and planning for the
future.

forewarn *verb* (**forewarns, forewarning,
forewarned**)
warn someone beforehand.

forewoman *noun* (*plural* **forewomen**)
1 a female worker in charge of other
workers. **2** a female member of a jury who
is in charge of the jury's discussions and
who speaks on its behalf.

foreword *noun* (*plural* **forewords**)
a preface.

forfeit (*say* for-fit) *verb* (**forfeits, forfeiting,
forfeited**)
pay or give up something as a penalty.
forfeiture *noun*
forfeit *noun* (*plural* **forfeits**)
something forfeited. [from old French]

forge¹ *noun* (*plural* **forges**)
a place where metal is heated and shaped; a
blacksmith's workshop.
forge *verb* (**forges, forging, forged**)
1 shape metal by heating and hammering.
2 copy something in order to deceive
people. **forger** *noun*, **forgery** *noun*
[from old French]

forge² *verb* (**forge, forging, forged**)
forge ahead move forward by a strong
effort.
[probably a different spelling of *force*]

forget *verb* (**forgets, forgetting, forgot,
forgotten**)
1 fail to remember. **2** stop thinking about,
Forget your troubles.
forget yourself behave rudely or
thoughtlessly.
[from Old English]

forgetful *adjective*
tending to forget. **forgetfully** *adverb*,
forgetfulness *noun*

forget-me-not *noun* (*plural* **forget-me-
nots**)
a plant with small blue flowers.
[because in the Middle Ages the flower was
worn by lovers]

forgive *verb* (**forgives, forgiving, forgave,
forgiven**)
stop feeling angry with somebody about
something. **forgiveness** *noun*
[from Old English]

forgo *verb* (**forgoes, forgoing, forwent,
forgone**)
give something up; go without.
[from *for-* + *go*]

USAGE: See note at *foregoing*.

fork *noun* (*plural* **forks**)
1 a small device with prongs for lifting food
to your mouth. **2** a large device with
prongs used for digging or lifting things.
3 a place where something separates into
two or more parts, *a fork in the road.*
fork *verb* (**forks, forking, forked**)
1 lift or dig with a fork. **2** form a fork by
separating into two branches. **3** follow one
of these branches, *Fork left.*
fork out (*slang*) pay out money.
[via Old English from Latin]

fork-lift truck (*plural* **fork-lift trucks**)
a truck with two metal bars at the front for
lifting and moving heavy loads.

forlorn *adjective*
left alone and unhappy.
forlorn hope the only faint hope left.
[from *for-* + an old word *lorn* = lost]

form *noun* (*plural* **forms**)
1 the shape, appearance, or condition of
something. **2** the way something exists, *Ice
is a form of water.* **3** a class in school. **4** a
bench. **5** a piece of paper with spaces to be
filled in.
form *verb* (**forms, forming, formed**)
1 shape or construct something; create.
2 come into existence; develop, *Icicles
formed.* [from Latin]

formal *adjective*
1 strictly following the accepted rules or customs; ceremonious, *a formal occasion*; *formal dress*. 2 rather serious and stiff in your manner. **formally** *adverb*
[from Latin *formalis* = having a set form]

formality *noun* (*plural* **formalities**)
1 formal behaviour. 2 something done to obey a rule or custom.

format *noun* (*plural* **formats**)
the shape and size of something; the way it is arranged.
[from Latin *formatus* = formed, shaped]

formation *noun* (*plural* **formations**)
1 the act of forming something. 2 a thing formed. 3 a special arrangement or pattern, *flying in formation*.
[from Latin *formare* = to mould]

formative *adjective*
forming or developing something.

former *adjective*
of an earlier time. **formerly** *adverb*
the former the first of two people or things just mentioned.
[from Old English; related to *fore*]

formidable (*say* for-mid-a-bul) *adjective*
1 frightening. 2 difficult to deal with or do, *a formidable task*. **formidably** *adverb*
[from Latin *formidare* = to fear]

formula *noun* (*plural* **formulae**)
1 a set of chemical symbols showing what a substance consists of. 2 a rule or statement expressed in symbols or numbers. 3 a list of substances needed for making something. 4 a fixed wording for a ceremony etc. 5 one of the groups into which racing cars are placed according to the size of their engines, *Formula One*.
[Latin, = small form]

formulate *verb* (**formulates, formulating, formulated**)
express an idea or plan clearly and exactly.
formulation *noun* [from *formula*]

fornication *noun* (*formal*)
sexual intercourse between people who are not married to each other.
[from Latin *fornix* = brothel]

forsake *verb* (**forsakes, forsaking, forsook, forsaken**)
abandon. [from Old English]

fort *noun* (*plural* **forts**)
a fortified building.
[from Latin *fortis* = strong]

forth *adverb*
1 out; into view. 2 onwards or forwards, *from this day forth*.
and so forth and so on.
[from Old English]

forthcoming *adjective*
1 happening soon, *forthcoming events*. 2 made available when needed, *Money for the trip was not forthcoming*. 3 willing to give information.

forthright *adjective*
frank and outspoken.

forthwith *adverb*
immediately.

fortification *noun* (*plural* **fortifications**)
1 fortifying something. 2 a wall or building constructed to make a place strong against attack.

fortify *verb* (**fortifies, fortifying, fortified**)
1 make a place strong against attack, especially by building fortifications. 2 strengthen. [same origin as *fort*]

fortissimo *adverb*
very loudly. [Italian]

fortitude *noun*
courage in bearing pain or trouble.
[from Latin *fortis* = strong]

fortnight *noun* (*plural* **fortnights**)
a period of two weeks.
fortnightly *adverb* & *adjective*
[from Old English *feowertene niht* = fourteen nights]

fortress *noun* (*plural* **fortresses**)
a fortified building or town.
[from French *forteresse* = strong place]

fortuitous (_say_ for-**tew**-it-us) _adjective_
happening by chance; accidental.
fortuitously _adverb_
[from Latin _forte_ = by chance]

USAGE: Note that _fortuitous_ does not mean
the same as _fortunate_.

fortunate _adjective_
lucky. **fortunately** _adverb_
[same origin as _fortune_]

fortune _noun_ (_plural_ **fortunes**)
1 luck, especially good luck. **2** a great
amount of money.
tell someone's fortune predict what will
happen to them in the future.
[from Latin _fortuna_ = luck]

forty _noun_ & _adjective_ (_plural_ **forties**)
the number 40. **fortieth** _adjective_ & _noun_
forty winks a short sleep; a nap.
[from Old English]

forum _noun_ (_plural_ **forums**)
1 the public square in an ancient Roman
city. **2** a meeting where a public discussion
is held. [Latin]

forward _adjective_
1 going forwards. **2** placed in the front.
3 having made more than the normal
progress. **4** too eager or bold.
forwardness _noun_
forward _adverb_
forwards.
forward _noun_ (_plural_ **forwards**)
a player in the front line of a team in
football, hockey, etc.
forward _verb_ (**forwards**, **forwarding**,
forwarded)
1 send on a letter etc. to a new address.
2 help something to improve or make
progress. [from Old English]

forwards _adverb_
1 to or towards the front. **2** in the direction
you are facing.

fossil _noun_ (_plural_ **fossils**)
the remains or traces of a prehistoric
animal or plant that has been buried in the
ground for a very long time and become
hardened in rock. **fossilized** _adjective_
[from Latin _fossilis_ = dug up]

fossilize _verb_ (**fossilizes**, **fossilizing**,
fossilized)
turn into a fossil. **fossilization** _noun_

foster _verb_ (**fosters**, **fostering**, **fostered**)
1 bring up someone else's child as if he or
she was your own. **2** help to grow or
develop. **foster child** _noun_, **foster father**
noun, **foster mother** _noun_
[from Old English]

foul _adjective_
1 disgusting; tasting or smelling
unpleasant. **2** (of weather) rough; stormy.
3 unfair; breaking the rules of a game.
4 colliding or entangled with something.
foully _adverb_, **foulness** _noun_
foul _noun_ (_plural_ **fouls**)
an action that breaks the rules of a game.
foul _verb_ (**fouls**, **fouling**, **fouled**)
1 make or become foul, _Smoke had fouled
the air_. **2** commit a foul against a player in
a game. [from Old English]

foul play _noun_
a violent crime, especially murder.

found¹ _past tense_ of **find**.

found² _verb_ (**founds**, **founding**, **founded**)
1 establish; provide money for starting,
They founded a hospital. **2** base, _This novel
is founded on fact_.
[from Latin _fundus_ = bottom]

foundation _noun_ (_plural_ **foundations**)
1 the founding of something. **2** a base or
basis. **3** the solid base on which a building
is built up. **foundation stone** _noun_

founder¹ _noun_ (_plural_ **founders**)
a person who founds something, _the
founder of the hospital_.

founder² _verb_ (**founders**, **foundering**,
foundered)
1 fill with water and sink, _The ship
foundered_. **2** stumble or fall. **3** fail
completely, _Their plans foundered_.
[same origin as _found²_]

foundling _noun_ (_plural_ **foundlings**)
a child found abandoned, whose parents
are not known.

foundry _noun_ (_plural_ **foundries**)
a factory or workshop where metal or glass
is made. [from _found²_]

fount *noun* (*plural* founts)
(in poetry) a fountain.

fountain *noun* (*plural* fountains)
an ornamental structure in which a jet of
water shoots up into the air.
[same origin as *font*]

fountain pen *noun* (*plural* fountain pens)
a pen that can be filled with a supply of ink.

four *noun* & *adjective* (*plural* fours)
the number 4.
on all fours on hands and knees.
[from Old English]

fourteen *noun* & *adjective* (*plural*
fourteens)
the number 14. **fourteenth** *adjective* & *noun*
[from Old English]

fourth *adjective*
next after the third. **fourthly** *adverb*
fourth *noun* (*plural* fourths)
1 the fourth person or thing. **2** one of four
equal parts; a quarter. [from Old English]

fowl *noun* (*plural* fowls)
a bird, especially one kept on a farm etc.
for its eggs or meat. [from Old English]

fox *noun* (*plural* foxes)
a wild animal that looks like a dog with a
long furry tail. **foxy** *adjective*
fox *verb* (foxes, foxing, foxed)
deceive or puzzle someone.
[from Old English]

foxglove *noun* (*plural* foxgloves)
a tall plant with flowers like the fingers of
gloves.

foyer (*say* foy-ay) *noun* (*plural* foyers)
the entrance hall of a theatre, cinema, or
hotel. [French, = hearth, home]

fraction *noun* (*plural* fractions)
1 a number that is not a whole number,
e.g. ½, 0.5. **2** a tiny part. **fractional** *adjective*,
fractionally *adverb* [Latin, = breaking]

fractious (*say* frak-shus) *adjective*
irritable. **fractiously** *adverb*, **fractiousness**
noun [from *fraction*]

fracture *noun* (*plural* fractures)
the breaking of something, especially of a
bone.

fracture *verb* (fractures, fracturing,
fractured)
break. [from Latin *fractus* = broken]

fragile *adjective*
easy to break or damage. **fragilely** *adverb*,
fragility *noun* [from Latin]

fragment *noun* (*plural* fragments)
1 a small piece broken off. **2** a small part.
fragmentary *adjective*, **fragmentation** *noun*,
fragmented *adjective* [from Latin]

fragrant *adjective*
having a pleasant smell. **fragrance** *noun*
[from Latin *fragrare* = smell sweet]

frail *adjective*
1 (of things) fragile. **2** (of people) not strong
or healthy, *a frail old man*. **frailty** *noun*
[from Latin *fragilis* = fragile]

frame *noun* (*plural* frames)
1 a holder that fits round the outside of a
picture. **2** a rigid structure that supports
something. **3** a human or animal body, *He
has a small frame*. **4** a single exposure on a
cinema film.
frame of mind the way you think or feel for
a while.
frame *verb* (frames, framing, framed)
1 put a frame on or round. **2** construct,
They framed the question badly. **3** make an
innocent person seem guilty by arranging
false evidence. **frame-up** *noun*
[from Old English]

framework *noun* (*plural* frameworks)
1 a frame supporting something. **2** a basic
plan or system.

franc *noun* (*plural* francs)
a unit of money in France, Switzerland,
and many other countries.
[from Latin *Francorum rex* = King of the
Franks, which was stamped on French gold
coins in the Middle Ages]

franchise *noun* (*plural* franchises)
1 the right to vote in elections. **2** a licence
to sell a firm's goods or services in a
certain area. [same origin as *frank*]

frank *adjective*
making your thoughts and feelings
clear to people; candid. **frankly** *adverb*,
frankness *noun*

frank verb (franks, franking, franked)
mark a letter etc. automatically in a
machine to show that postage has been
paid. [from Latin *francus* = free]

frankincense noun
a sweet-smelling gum burnt as incense.
[from old French *franc encens* = finest
incense]

frantic adjective
wildly agitated or excited. **frantically** adverb
[from old French; related to *frenzy*]

fraternal (say fra-**tern**-al) adjective
to do with brothers; brotherly. **fraternally**
adverb [from Latin *frater* = brother]

fraternity noun (plural fraternities)
1 a brotherly feeling. 2 a group of people
who have the same interests or occupation,
the medical fraternity.

fraternize verb (fraternizes, fraternizing,
fraternized)
associate with other people in a friendly
way. **fraternization** noun
[same origin as *fraternal*]

fraud noun (plural frauds)
1 a dishonest trick; a swindle. 2 an
impostor; a person or thing that is not
what it pretends to be. **fraudulent** adjective,
fraudulently adverb, **fraudulence** noun
[from Latin]

fraught adjective
1 filled with, *The situation is fraught with
danger*. 2 tense or upset, *I'm feeling rather
fraught this morning*.
[from old Dutch *vrachten* = load a ship]

fray¹ noun (plural frays)
a fight or conflict, *ready for the fray*.
[shortened from *affray*]

fray² verb (frays, fraying, frayed)
1 make or become ragged so that loose
threads show. 2 (of tempers or nerves)
become strained or upset.
[from French; related to *friction*]

freak noun (plural freaks)
a very strange or abnormal person, animal,
or thing. **freakish** adjective
[origin unknown]

freckle noun (plural freckles)
a small brown spot on the skin. **freckled**
adjective [from Old Norse]

free adjective (freer, freest)
1 able to do what you want to do or go
where you want to go. 2 not costing
anything. 3 not fixed, *Leave one end free*.
4 not having or being affected by
something, *The harbour is free of ice*.
5 available; not being used or occupied.
6 generous, *She is very free with her money*.
freely adverb

free verb (frees, freeing, freed)
set free. [from Old English]

freedom noun (plural freedoms)
being free; independence.

freehand adjective
(of a drawing) done without a ruler or
compasses etc.

freehold noun
possessing land or a house as its absolute
owner, not as a tenant renting from a
landlord.

Freemason noun (plural Freemasons)
a member of a certain secret society.
Freemasonry noun
[originally, a society of stonemasons]

free-range adjective
1 free-range hens are not kept in small
cages but are allowed to move about freely.
2 free-range eggs are ones laid by these
hens.

freewheel verb (freewheels, freewheeling,
freewheeled)
ride a bicycle without needing to pedal.

freeze verb (freezes, freezing, froze, frozen)
1 turn into ice; become covered with ice.
2 make or be very cold. 3 keep wages or
prices etc. at a fixed level. 4 suddenly stand
completely still.

freeze noun (plural freezes)
1 a period of freezing weather. 2 the
freezing of prices etc. [from Old English]

freezer noun (plural freezers)
a refrigerator in which food can be frozen
quickly and stored.

freight (*say* frayt) *noun*
goods transported as cargo.
[from old Dutch; related to *fraught*]

freighter (*say* fray-ter) *noun* (*plural* freighters)
a ship or aircraft carrying mainly cargo.

French window (*plural* French windows)
a long window that serves as a door on an outside wall.

frenzy *noun*
wild excitement or agitation.
frenzied *adjective*, frenziedly *adverb*
[from Greek *phren* = the mind]

frequency *noun* (*plural* frequencies)
1 being frequent. 2 how often something happens. 3 the number of oscillations per second of a wave of sound or light etc.

frequent (*say* freek-went) *adjective*
happening often. frequently *adverb*
frequent (*say* frik-went) *verb* (frequents, frequenting, frequented)
be in or go to a place often, *They frequented the club*. [from Latin *frequens* = crowded]

fresco *noun* (*plural* frescoes *or* frescos)
a picture painted on a wall or ceiling before the plaster is dry. [from Italian *affresco* = on the fresh (plaster)]

fresh *adjective*
1 newly made or produced or arrived; not stale, *fresh bread*. 2 not tinned or preserved, *fresh fruit*. 3 cool and clean, *fresh air*. 4 (of water) not salty. freshly *adverb*, freshness *noun* [from Old English]

freshen *verb* (freshens, freshening, freshened)
make or become fresh.

freshwater *adjective*
of fresh water not sea water; living in rivers or lakes.

fret[1] *verb* (frets, fretting, fretted)
worry or be upset about something.
fretful *adjective*, fretfully *adverb*
[from Old English]

fret[2] *noun* (*plural* frets)
a bar or ridge on the fingerboard of a guitar etc. [origin unknown]

fretsaw *noun* (*plural* fretsaws)
a very narrow saw used for making fretwork.

fretwork *noun*
cutting decorative patterns in wood; wood cut in this way. [from French *frete* = trellis]

friable *adjective*
easily crumbled. [from Latin]

friar *noun* (*plural* friars)
a man who is a member of certain Roman Catholic religious orders, who has vowed to live a life of poverty. friary *noun*
[from French *frère* = brother]

friction *noun*
1 rubbing. 2 bad feeling between people; quarrelling. frictional *adjective*
[from Latin *fricare* = to rub]

fridge *noun* (*plural* fridges) (*informal*)
a refrigerator.

friend *noun* (*plural* friends)
1 a person you like who likes you.
2 a helpful or kind person.
[from Old English]

friendless *adjective*
without a friend.

friendly *adjective*
behaving like a friend. friendliness *noun*

friendship *noun* (*plural* friendships)
being friends.

frieze (*say* freez) *noun* (*plural* friezes)
a strip of designs or pictures round the top of a wall. [from Latin]

frigate *noun* (*plural* frigates)
a small warship. [via French from Italian]

fright *noun* (*plural* frights)
1 sudden great fear. 2 a person or thing that looks ridiculous. [from Old English]

frighten *verb* (frightens, frightening, frightened)
make or become afraid.
be frightened of be afraid of.

frightful *adjective*
awful; very great or bad. frightfully *adverb*

frigid *adjective*
1 extremely cold. 2 unfriendly; not affectionate. **frigidly** *adverb*, **frigidity** *noun*
[from Latin *frigidus* = cold]

frill *noun* (*plural* **frills**)
1 a decorative gathered or pleated trimming on a dress, curtain, etc.
2 something extra that is pleasant but unnecessary, *a simple life with no frills*.
frilled *adjective*, **frilly** *adjective*
[from Flemish]

fringe *noun* (*plural* **fringes**)
1 a decorative edging with many threads hanging down loosely. 2 a straight line of hair hanging down over the forehead. 3 the edge of something. **fringed** *adjective*
[from old French]

frisk *verb* (**frisks, frisking, frisked**)
1 jump or run about playfully. 2 search somebody by running your hands over his or her clothes. **frisky** *adjective*, **friskily** *adverb*, **friskiness** *noun*
[from old French *frisque* = lively]

fritter[1] *noun* (*plural* **fritters**)
a slice of meat or fruit or potato etc. coated in batter and fried.
[from Latin *frictum* = fried]

fritter[2] *verb* (**fritters, frittering, frittered**)
waste something gradually; spend money or time on trivial things.
[from an old word *fritters* = fragments]

frivolous *adjective*
seeking pleasure in a light-hearted way; not serious. **frivolously** *adverb*, **frivolity** *noun* [from Latin]

frizzle *verb* (**frizzles, frizzling, frizzled**)
1 fry with a spluttering noise. 2 shrivel something by burning it. [from *fry*[1]]

frizzy *adjective*
(of hair) in tight curls. **frizziness** *noun*
[from French]

fro *adverb*
to and fro backwards and forwards.
[from Old Norse]

frock *noun* (*plural* **frocks**)
a girl's or woman's dress.
[from old French]

frog *noun* (*plural* **frogs**)
a small jumping animal that can live both in water and on land.
a frog in your throat hoarseness.
[from Old English]

frogman *noun* (*plural* **frogmen**)
a swimmer equipped with a rubber suit, flippers, and breathing-apparatus for swimming and working underwater.

frolic *noun* (*plural* **frolics**)
a lively cheerful game or entertainment.
frolicsome *adjective*

frolic *verb* (**frolics, frolicking, frolicked**)
play about in a lively cheerful way.
[from Dutch *vrolijk* = joyously]

from *preposition*
This word is used to show 1 starting point in space or time or order (*We flew from London to Paris. We work from 9 to 5 o'clock. Count from one to ten*), 2 source or origin (*Get water from the tap*),
3 separation or release (*Take the gun from him. She was freed from prison*),
4 difference (*Can you tell margarine from butter?*), 5 cause (*I suffer from headaches*).
[from Old English]

frond *noun* (*plural* **fronds**)
a leaf-like part of a fern, palm tree, etc.
[from Latin *frondis* = of a leaf]

front *noun* (*plural* **fronts**)
1 the part or side that comes first or is the most important or furthest forward. 2 a road or promenade along the seashore.
3 the place where fighting is happening in a war. **frontal** *adjective*

front *adjective*
of the front; in front.
[from Latin *frons* = forehead, front]

frontage *noun* (*plural* **frontages**)
the front of a building; the land beside this.

frontier *noun* (*plural* **frontiers**)
the boundary between two countries or regions. [from old French; related to *front*]

frontispiece *noun* (*plural* **frontispieces**)
an illustration opposite the title-page of a book. [from French]

frost *noun* (*plural* frosts)
1 powdery ice that forms on things in freezing weather. 2 weather with a temperature below freezing point.
frost *verb* (frosts, frosting, frosted)
cover with frost or frosting.
[from Old English]

frostbite *noun*
harm done to the body by very cold weather. **frostbitten** *adjective*

frosted glass *noun*
glass made cloudy so that you cannot see through it.

frosting *noun*
sugar icing for cakes.

frosty *adjective*
1 cold with frost. 2 unfriendly and unwelcoming, *a frosty look*.
frostily *adverb*

froth *noun*
a white mass of tiny bubbles on a liquid.
frothy *adjective* [from Old Norse]

frown *verb* (frowns, frowning, frowned)
wrinkle your forehead because you are angry or worried.
frown *noun* (*plural* frowns)
a frowning movement or look.
[from old French]

frugal (*say* froo-gal) *adjective*
1 spending very little money. 2 costing very little money; not plentiful, *a frugal meal*. **frugally** *adverb*, **frugality** *noun*
[from Latin]

fruit *noun* (*plural* fruits or fruit)
1 the seed-container that grows on a tree or plant and is often used as food. 2 the result of doing something, *the fruits of his efforts*.
fruity *adjective*
fruit *verb* (fruits, fruiting, fruited)
produce fruit. [same origin as *fruition*]

fruitful *adjective*
producing good results, *fruitful discussions*.
fruitfully *adverb*

fruition (*say* froo-ish-on) *noun*
the achievement of what was hoped or worked for, *Our plans never came to fruition*. [from Latin *frui* = enjoy]

fruitless *adjective*
producing no results. **fruitlessly** *adverb*

fruit machine *noun* (*plural* fruit machines)
a gambling machine worked by putting a coin in a slot.

frustrate *verb* (frustrates, frustrating, frustrated)
prevent somebody from doing something; prevent something from being successful, *frustrate their wicked plans*. **frustration** *noun* [from Latin *frustra* = in vain]

fry[1] *verb* (fries, frying, fried)
cook something in very hot fat. **fryer** *noun*
[from Latin]

fry[2] *plural noun*
very young fishes. [from Old Norse]

frying pan *noun* (*plural* frying pans)
a shallow pan for frying things.

fuchsia (*say* few-sha) *noun* (*plural* fuchsias)
an ornamental plant with flowers that hang down. [named after Leonard *Fuchs*, a German botanist]

fudge *noun*
a soft sugary sweet. [origin unknown]

fuel *noun* (*plural* fuels)
something that is burnt to produce heat or power.
fuel *verb* (fuels, fuelling, fuelled)
supply something with fuel.
[from old French; related to *focus*]

fug *noun* (*informal*)
a stuffy atmosphere. **fuggy** *adjective*, **fugginess** *noun*
[originally slang: origin unknown]

fugitive (*say* few-jit-iv) *noun* (*plural* fugitives)
a person who is running away from something. [from Latin *fugere* = flee]

fugue (*say* fewg) *noun* (*plural* fugues)
a piece of music in which tunes are repeated in a pattern.
[via French from Italian]

-ful *suffix*
forms 1 adjectives meaning 'full of' or 'having this quality' (e.g. *beautiful*,

truthful), **2** nouns meaning 'the amount required to fill something' (e.g. *handful*). [from *full*]

fulcrum *noun* (*plural* **fulcrums** or **fulcra**)
the point on which a lever rests. [Latin]

fulfil *verb* (**fulfils, fulfilling, fulfilled**)
1 do what is required; satisfy; carry out, *You must fulfil your promises.* **2** make something come true, *It fulfilled an ancient prophecy.* **3** give you satisfaction. **fulfilment** *noun* [from Old English *fullfyllan* = fill up, satisfy]

full *adjective*
1 containing as much or as many as possible. **2** having many people or things, *full of ideas.* **3** complete, *the full story.* **4** the greatest possible, *at full speed.* **5** fitting loosely; with many folds, *a full skirt.* **6** when there is a full moon, you can see its whole disc.
fully *adverb*, **fullness** *noun*
full *adverb*
completely and directly, *It hit him full in the face.* [from Old English]

full-blown *adjective*
fully developed.

full stop *noun* (*plural* **full stops**)
the dot used as a punctuation mark at the end of a sentence or an abbreviation.

fully *adverb*
completely.

fulsome *adjective*
praising something or thanking someone too much or too emotionally; excessive. [Middle English, = plentiful, from *full*]

USAGE: Note that *fulsome praise* does not mean 'generous praise', but rather 'excessive praise'.

fumble *verb* (**fumbles, fumbling, fumbled**)
hold or handle something clumsily. [from German or Dutch]

fume *noun* or **fumes** *plural noun*
strong-smelling smoke or gas.
fume *verb* (**fumes, fuming, fumed**)
1 give off fumes. **2** be very angry. [from Latin *fumus* = smoke]

fumigate (*say* **few**-mig-ayt) *verb* (**fumigates, fumigating, fumigated**)
disinfect something by fumes.
fumigation *noun*

fun *noun*
amusement or enjoyment.
make fun of make people laugh at a person or thing.
[origin unknown]

function *noun* (*plural* **functions**)
1 what somebody or something is there to do, *The function of a knife is to cut things.* **2** an important event or party. **3** a basic operation in a computer. **4** a variable quantity whose value depends on the value of other variable quantities, *X is a function of Y and Z.*
function *verb* (**functions, functioning, functioned**)
perform a function; work properly. [from Latin *functum* = performed]

functional *adjective*
1 working properly. **2** practical without being decorative or luxurious.
functionally *adverb*

fund *noun* (*plural* **funds**)
1 money collected or kept for a special purpose. **2** a stock or supply.
fund *verb* (**funds, funding, funded**)
supply with money. [same origin as *found*[2]]

fundamental *adjective*
basic. **fundamentally** *adverb*
[from Latin *fundamentum* = foundation]

funeral *noun* (*plural* **funerals**)
the ceremony when a dead person is buried or cremated.
[from Latin *funeris* = of a burial]

funereal (*say* few-**neer**-ee-al) *adjective*
gloomy or depressing.
[same origin as *funeral*]

fungus *noun* (*plural* **fungi**, *say* fung-I)
a plant without leaves or flowers that grows on other plants or on decayed material, *Mushrooms are fungi.* [Latin]

funk[1] *noun* (*slang*)
fear.
funk *verb* (**funks, funking, funked**) (*slang*)
be afraid of doing something and avoid it.
[origin unknown]

funk² *noun*
a style of popular music with a strong rhythm, based on jazz and African music. [origin unknown]

funnel *noun* (*plural* funnels)
1 a metal chimney on a ship or steam engine. 2 a tube that is wide at the top and narrow at the bottom to help you pour things into a narrow opening.
[from Latin *fundere* = pour]

funny *adjective* (funnier, funniest)
1 that makes you laugh or smile. 2 strange or odd, *a funny smell*. **funnily** *adverb*

fur *noun* (*plural* furs)
1 the soft hair that covers some animals. 2 animal skin with the fur on it, used for clothing; fabric that looks like animal fur. [from old French]

furbish *verb* (furbishes, furbishing, furbished)
polish or clean; renovate.
[via old French from Germanic]

furious *adjective*
1 very angry. 2 violent or intense, *furious heat*. **furiously** *adverb* [from Latin]

furl *verb* (furls, furling, furled)
roll up a sail, flag, or umbrella.
[from old French *ferlier* = bind firmly]

furlong *noun* (*plural* furlongs)
one-eighth of a mile, 220 yards.
[from Old English *furlang* = 'furrow long'; the length of a furrow in a common field]

furlough (*say* ferl-oh) *noun* (*plural* furloughs)
a time when a soldier is not on duty and is allowed to return to his or her own country. [from Dutch]

furnace *noun* (*plural* furnaces)
a device in which great heat can be produced, e.g. for melting metals or making glass. [from Latin *furnus* = oven]

furnish *verb* (furnishes, furnishing, furnished)
1 provide a place with furniture. 2 provide or supply with something.
[via old French from Germanic]

furnishings *plural noun*
furniture and fittings, curtains, etc.

furniture *noun*
tables, chairs, and other movable things that you need in a house or school or office etc.

furore (*say* few-ror-ee) *noun*
an excited or angry uproar.
[from Latin *furor* = madness]

furrow *noun* (*plural* furrows)
1 a long cut in the ground made by a plough or other implement. 2 a groove. 3 a deep wrinkle in the skin.
furrow *verb* (furrows, furrowing, furrowed)
make furrows in something.
[from Old English]

furry *adjective*
like fur; covered with fur.

further *adverb* & *adjective*
1 at or to a greater distance; more distant. 2 more; additional, *We made further enquiries.*

USAGE: See the note at *farther*.

further *verb* (furthers, furthering, furthered)
help something to progress, *This success will further your career.* **furtherance** *noun*
[from Old English]

further education *noun*
education for people above school age.

furthermore *adverb*
also; moreover.

furthest *adverb* & *adjective*
at or to the greatest distance; most distant.

USAGE: See the note at *farther*.

furtive *adjective*
stealthy; trying not to be seen.
furtively *adverb*, **furtiveness** *noun*
[from Latin *furtivus* = stolen]

fury *noun*
wild anger; rage. [from Latin *furia* = rage; an avenging spirit]

furze *noun*
gorse. [from Old English]

fuse¹ *noun* (*plural* **fuses**)
a safety device containing a short piece of wire that melts if too much electricity is passed through it.
fuse *verb* (**fuses, fusing, fused**)
1 stop working because a fuse has melted. **2** blend together, especially through melting. [from Latin *fusum* = melted]

fuse² *noun* (*plural* **fuses**)
a length of material that burns easily, used for setting off an explosive.
[from Latin *fusus* = spindle (because originally the material was put in a tube)]

fuselage (*say* **few**-zel-ah*zh*) *noun* (*plural* **fuselages**)
the body of an aircraft.
[French, = shaped like a spindle]

fusillade (*say* few-zil-**ayd**) *noun* (*plural* **fusillades**)
a great outburst of firing guns or questions etc. [French, from *fusiller* = shoot]

fusion *noun*
1 the action of blending or uniting things. **2** the uniting of atomic nuclei, usually releasing energy.

fuss *noun* (*plural* **fusses**)
1 unnecessary excitement or bustle. **2** an agitated protest.
fuss *verb* (**fusses, fussing, fussed**)
make a fuss about something.
[origin unknown]

fussy *adjective* (**fussier, fussiest**)
1 fussing; inclined to make a fuss. **2** choosing very carefully; hard to please. **3** full of unnecessary details or decorations. **fussily** *adverb*, **fussiness** *noun*

fusty *adjective* (**fustier, fustiest**)
smelling stale or stuffy. **fustiness** *noun*
[from old French]

futile (*say* **few**-tyl) *adjective*
useless; having no result. **futility** *noun*
[from Latin *futilis* = leaking]

future *noun*
the time that will come; what is going to happen then.
future *adjective*
belonging or referring to the future.
[from Latin]

futuristic *adjective*
very modern, as if belonging to the future rather than the present, *futuristic buildings.*

fuzz *noun*
something fluffy or frizzy.
[probably from Dutch]

fuzzy *adjective*
1 like fuzz; covered with fuzz. **2** blurred; not clear. **fuzzily** *adverb*, **fuzziness** *noun*

-fy *suffix*
forms verbs meaning 'make' or 'bring into a certain condition' (e.g. *beautify, purify*).
[from Latin *-ficare* = make]

Gg

gabardine *noun*
a strong fabric woven in a slanting pattern.
[from old French *gauvardine*, a kind of cloak]

gabble *verb* (**gabbles, gabbling, gabbled**)
talk so quickly that it is difficult to know what is being said. [from old Dutch]

gable *noun* (*plural* **gables**)
the pointed part at the top of an outside wall, between two sloping roofs. **gabled** *adjective* [from Old Norse]

gad *verb* (**gads, gadding, gadded**)
gad about go about in search of pleasure; gallivant. **gadabout** *noun*
[from Old English]

gadget *noun* (*plural* **gadgets**)
any small useful tool. **gadgetry** *noun*
[originally a sailors' word; origin unknown]

Gaelic (*say* **gay**-lik) *noun*
the Celtic languages of Scotland and Ireland.

gaff *noun* (*plural* **gaffs**)
a stick with a metal hook for landing large fish. [from French]

gag *noun* (*plural* **gags**)
1 something put into a person's mouth or tied over it to prevent him or her speaking. **2** a joke.

gag *verb* (**gags, gagging, gagged**)
1 put a gag on a person. **2** prevent someone from making comments, *We cannot gag the press.* **3** retch.
[imitating the sound of someone retching]

gaiety *noun*
1 cheerfulness. **2** brightly coloured appearance.
(see *gay* for origin and usage note.)

gaily *adverb*
in a cheerful way.

gain *verb* (**gains, gaining, gained**)
1 get something that you did not have before; obtain. **2** a clock or watch gains when it becomes ahead of the correct time. **3** reach; arrive at, *At last we gained the shore.*
gain on come closer to a person or thing when chasing them or in a race.

gain *noun* (*plural* **gains**)
something gained; a profit or improvement. **gainful** *adjective*
[via old French from Germanic]

gait *noun* (*plural* **gaits**)
a way of walking or running, *He walked with a shuffling gait.*
[from Old Norse *gata* = a road]

gaiter *noun* (*plural* **gaiters**)
a leather or cloth covering for the lower part of the leg. [from French]

gala (*say* **gah**-la) *noun* (*plural* **galas**)
1 a festival or celebration. **2** a set of sports contests.
[from old French *galer* = celebrate]

galaxy *noun* (*plural* **galaxies**)
a very large group of stars.
galactic (*say* ga-**lak**-tik) *adjective*
[originally = the Milky Way: from Greek *galaxias* = milky]

gale *noun* (*plural* **gales**)
a very strong wind. [origin unknown]

gall¹ (*say* gawl) *noun*
1 bile. **2** bitterness of feeling. **3** (*informal*) impudence. [from Old English *gealla*]

gall² (*say* gawl) *noun* (*plural* **galls**)
a sore spot on an animal's skin.
gall *verb* (**galls, galling, galled**)
1 rub a sore. **2** annoy or humiliate someone. [from Old English *gealle*]

gallant (*say* **gal**-lant) *adjective*
1 brave or chivalrous. **2** fine and stately, *our gallant ship.* **gallantly** *adverb*, **gallantry** *noun* [originally = spendidly dressed: from old French *galant* = celebrating]

galleon *noun* (*plural* **galleons**)
a large Spanish sailing ship used in the 16th–17th centuries. [same origin as *galley*]

gallery *noun* (*plural* **galleries**)
1 a platform jutting out from the wall in a church or hall. **2** the highest balcony in a cinema or theatre. **3** a long room or passage. **4** a room or building for showing works of art. [from Italian *galleria* = gallery, church porch, perhaps from *Galilee* (a church porch furthest from the altar was called a *galilee*, as Galilee was the province furthest from Jerusalem)]

galley *noun* (*plural* **galleys**)
1 an ancient type of ship driven by oars. **2** the kitchen in a ship or aircraft.
[from Latin or Greek *galea*]

galling (*say* **gawl**-ing) *adjective*
annoying or humiliating. [from *gall*²]

gallivant *verb* (**gallivants, gallivanting, gallivanted**)
go out or wander about in search of pleasure. [origin unknown]

gallon (*plural* **gallons**)
a unit used to measure liquids, 8 pints or 4.546 litres. [from old French]

gallop *noun* (*plural* **gallops**)
1 the fastest pace that a horse can go. **2** a fast ride on a horse.
gallop *verb* (**gallops, galloping, galloped**)
go or ride at a gallop.
[from old French; related to *wallop*]

gallows *noun* (*plural* **gallows** or **gallowses**)
a framework with a noose for hanging criminals. [from Old English]

galore *adverb*
in great numbers; in a large amount, *bargains galore.* [from Irish]

galoshes *plural noun*
a pair of waterproof shoes worn over ordinary shoes. [from old French]

galvanize *verb* (galvanizes, galvanizing, galvanized)
1 stimulate someone into sudden activity. 2 coat iron with zinc to protect it from rust. **galvanization** *noun*
[named after an Italian scientist, Luigi Galvani, who discovered that muscles move because of electricity in the body]

gambit *noun* (*plural* gambits)
1 a kind of opening move in chess. 2 an action or remark intended to gain an advantage.
[from Italian *gambetto* = tripping up]

gamble *verb* (gambles, gambling, gambled)
1 bet on the result of a game, race, or other event. 2 take great risks in the hope of gaining something. **gambler** *noun*
gamble *noun* (*plural* gambles)
1 a bet or chance, *a gamble on the lottery.* 2 a risky attempt.
[from Old English *gamenian* = play games]

gambol *verb* (gambols, gambolling, gambolled)
jump or skip about in play. [from French]

game *noun* (*plural* games)
1 a form of play or sport, especially one with rules, *a game of football*, *a computer game.* 2 a section of a long game such as tennis or whist. 3 a scheme or plan; a trick, *Whatever his game is, he won't succeed.* 4 wild animals or birds hunted for sport or food.
give the game away reveal a secret.
game *adjective*
1 able and willing to do something, *'Shall we swim to the island?' 'I'm game!'* 2 brave.
gamely *adverb* [from Old English]

gamekeeper *noun* (*plural* gamekeepers)
a person employed to protect game birds and animals, especially from poachers.

gaming *noun*
gambling.

gamma *noun*
the third letter of the Greek alphabet, = g.

gamma rays *plural noun*
very short X-rays.

gammon *noun*
a kind of ham. [from old French]

gander *noun* (*plural* ganders)
a male goose. [from Old English]

gang *noun* (*plural* gangs)
a number of people who do things together, *a gang of criminals, a roadmending gang.*
gang *verb* (gangs, ganging, ganged)
join in a gang, *gang up.* [from Old Norse]

gangling *adjective*
tall, thin, and awkward-looking.
[from Old English]

gangplank *noun* (*plural* gangplanks)
a plank placed so that people can walk into or out of a boat.
[from Old Norse *gangr* = walking, going]

gangrene (*say* gang-green) *noun*
decay of body tissue in a living person.
[from Greek]

gangster *noun* (*plural* gangsters)
a member of a gang of violent criminals.

gangway *noun* (*plural* gangways)
1 a gap left for people to pass between rows of seats or through a crowd. 2 a movable bridge placed so that people can walk into or out of a ship. [same origin as *gangplank*]

gannet *noun* (*plural* gannets)
a large seabird which catches fish by flying above the sea and then diving in.
[from Old English]

gaol (*say* jayl) *noun* (*plural* gaols)
a different spelling of *jail.*
gaol *verb*, **gaoler** *noun*

gap *noun* (*plural* gaps)
1 a break or opening in something continuous such as a hedge or fence. 2 an interval. 3 a wide difference in ideas.
[from Old Norse]

gape *verb* (gapes, gaping, gaped)
1 have your mouth open. 2 stare with your mouth open. 3 be open wide.
[from Old Norse]

garage (*say* ga-rahzh or ga-rij) *noun*
(*plural* garages)
1 a building in which a motor vehicle or vehicles may be kept. 2 a place where

motor vehicles are repaired or serviced and where petrol is sold. [French, = a shelter]

garb *noun*
special clothing.
garb *verb* (**garbs, garbing, garbed**)
(*old use* or *poetic*) dress. [via old French and Italian from Germanic]

garbage *noun*
rubbish, especially household rubbish. [from old French]

garble *verb* (**garbles, garbling, garbled**)
give a confused account of a story or message so that it is misunderstood. [from Arabic *garbala* = sift, select (because the real facts are 'sifted out')]

garden *noun* (*plural* **gardens**)
a piece of ground where flowers, fruit, or vegetables are grown.
gardener *noun*, **gardening** *noun*
[via old French from Germanic]

gargantuan (*say* gar-gan-tew-an) *adjective*
gigantic. [from *Gargantua*, the name of a giant in a book by Rabelais]

gargle *verb* (**gargles, gargling, gargled**)
hold a liquid at the back of the mouth and breathe air through it to wash the inside of the throat. **gargle** *noun*
[from French *gargouille* = throat]

gargoyle *noun* (*plural* **gargoyles**)
an ugly or comical face or figure carved on a building, especially on a waterspout. [from French *gargouille* = throat (because the water passes through the throat of the figure)]

garish (*say* gair-ish) *adjective*
too bright or highly coloured; gaudy.
garishly *adverb* [origin unknown]

garland *noun* (*plural* **garlands**)
a wreath of flowers worn or hung as a decoration. **garland** *verb* [from old French]

garlic *noun*
a plant with a bulb divided into smaller bulbs (cloves), which have a strong smell and taste and are used for flavouring food. [from Old English]

garment *noun* (*plural* **garments**)
a piece of clothing. [from French *garnement* = equipment]

garner *verb* (**garners, garnering, garnered**)
(*formal* or *poetic*)
store up; gather or collect. [from Latin *granarium* = granary]

garnet *noun* (*plural* **garnets**)
a dark-red stone used as a gem. [from old Dutch]

garnish *verb* (**garnishes, garnishing, garnished**)
decorate something, especially food.
garnish *noun*
something used to decorate food or give it extra flavour. [via old French from Germanic]

garret *noun* (*plural* **garrets**)
an attic. [from old French *garite* = watchtower]

garrison *noun* (*plural* **garrisons**)
1 troops who stay in a town or fort to defend it. 2 the building they occupy.
garrison *verb*
[from old French *garison* = defence]

garrotte (*say* ga-rot) *noun* (*plural* **garrottes**)
1 a metal collar for strangling a person condemned to death, formerly used in Spain. 2 a cord or wire used for strangling a victim.
garrotte *verb* (**garrottes, garrotting, garrotted**)
strangle with a garrotte. [from Spanish]

garrulous (*say* ga-rool-us) *adjective*
talkative. **garrulousness** *noun*
[from Latin *garrire* = to chatter]

garter *noun* (*plural* **garters**)
a band of elastic to hold up a sock or stocking. [from old French]

gas¹ *noun* (*plural* **gases**)
1 a substance that (like air) can move freely and is not liquid or solid at ordinary temperatures. 2 a gas that can be burned, used for lighting, heating, or cooking.

gas verb (**gasses, gassing, gassed**)
1 kill or injure someone with gas.
2 (*informal*) talk idly for a long time.
[an invented word suggested by the Greek word *chaos*]

gas² noun (*American*)
gasoline. [abbreviation]

gaseous (*say* gas-ee-us) adjective
in the form of a gas.

gash noun (*plural* **gashes**)
a long deep cut or wound.
gash verb (**gashes, gashing, gashed**)
make a gash in something.
[from old French]

gasket noun (*plural* **gaskets**)
a flat ring or strip of soft material for sealing a joint between metal surfaces. [origin unknown]

gasoline noun (*American*)
petrol. [from *gas* + Latin *oleum* = oil]

gasometer (*say* gas-**om**-it-er) noun (*plural* **gasometers**)
a large round tank in which gas is stored. [from French *gazomètre* = a container for measuring gas]

gasp verb (**gasps, gasping, gasped**)
1 breathe in suddenly when you are shocked or surprised. 2 struggle to breathe with your mouth open when you are tired or ill. 3 speak in a breathless way. **gasp** noun [from Old Norse]

gassy adjective
fizzy.

gastric adjective
to do with the stomach.
[from Greek *gaster* = stomach]

gastronomy (*say* gas-**tron**-om-ee) noun
the art of science of good eating.
gastronomic adjective [from Greek *gaster* = stomach + *-nomia* = management]

gastropod noun (*plural* **gastropods**)
an animal (e.g. a snail) that moves by means of a fleshy 'foot' on its stomach. [from Greek *gaster* – stomach + *podos* = of the foot]

gate noun (*plural* **gates**)
1 a movable barrier, usually on hinges, used as a door in a wall or fence. 2 the opening it covers. 3 a barrier for controlling the flow of water in a dam or lock. 4 the number of people attending a football match etc. [from Old English]

gateau (*say* gat-oh) noun (*plural* **gateaus** or **gateaux**)
a large rich cream cake. [French]

gatecrash verb (**gatecrashes, gatecrashing, gatecrashed**)
go to a private party without being invited.
gatecrasher noun

gateway noun (*plural* **gateways**)
1 an opening containing a gate. 2 a way to reach something, *The gateway to success.*

gather verb (**gathers, gathering, gathered**)
1 come or bring together. 2 collect; obtain gradually, *gather information.* 3 collect as harvest; pluck, *Gather the corn when it is ripe*; *gather flowers.* 4 understand or learn, *We gather you have been on holiday.* 5 pull cloth into folds by running a thread through it. 6 a sore gathers when it swells up and forms pus. [from Old English]

gathering noun (*plural* **gatherings**)
1 an assembly of people. 2 a swelling that forms pus.

gaudy adjective
too showy and bright.
gaudily adverb, **gaudiness** noun
[from Latin *gaudere* = rejoice]

gauge (*say* gayj) noun (*plural* **gauges**)
1 a standard measurement. 2 the distance between a pair of rails on a railway. 3 a measuring instrument.
gauge verb (**gauges, gauging, gauged**)
1 measure. 2 estimate; form a judgement. [from old French]

gaunt adjective
1 a gaunt person is lean and haggard. 2 a gaunt place is grim or desolate-looking.
gauntness noun [origin unknown]

gauntlet¹ noun (*plural* **gauntlets**)
a glove with a wide cuff covering the wrist. [from French *gant* = glove]

gauntlet[2] *noun*
run the gauntlet have to suffer continuous severe criticism or risk.
[from a former military and naval punishment in which the victim was made to pass between two rows of men who struck him as he passed; the word is from Swedish *gatlopp* = passage]

gauze *noun*
1 thin transparent woven material. 2 fine wire mesh. **gauzy** *adjective* [from *Gaza*, a town in Palestine, where it was first made]

gay *adjective*
1 homosexual. 2 cheerful. 3 brightly coloured. **gayness** *noun* [from French]

USAGE: Nowadays the most common meaning of *gay* is 'homosexual'. The older meanings 'cheerful' and 'brightly coloured' can still be used but are becoming less and less common in everyday use. *Gayness* is the noun from meaning 1 of *gay*. The noun that relates to the other two meanings is *gaiety*.

gaze *verb* (**gazes, gazing, gazed**)
look at something steadily for a long time.
gaze *noun* (*plural* **gazes**)
a long steady look. [origin unknown]

gazelle *noun* (*plural* **gazelles** or **gazelle**)
a small antelope, usually fawn and white, from Africa or Asia.
[via old French from Arabic]

gazette *noun* (*plural* **gazettes**)
1 a newspaper. 2 an official journal.
[from Italian *gazetta de la novità* = a halfpenny worth of news (a *gazetta* was a Venetian coin of small value)]

gazetteer (*say* gaz-it-**eer**) *noun* (*plural* **gazetteers**)
a list of place names.
[originally = journalist; the first gazetteer was intended to help journalists]

GCSE *abbreviation*
General Certificate of Secondary Education.

gear *noun* (*plural* **gears**)
1 a cogwheel, especially one of a set in a motor vehicle that turn power from the engine into movement of the wheels.
2 equipment or apparatus, *camping gear*.
gear *verb* (**gears, gearing, geared**)
gear to make something match something else, *Health care should be geared to people's needs, not to whether they can pay*.
gear up get ready for, *We were all geared up to play cricket, but then it rained*.
[from Old Norse]

gearbox *noun* (*plural* **gearboxes**)
a case enclosing gears.

Geiger counter (*say* gy-ger) *noun* (*plural* **Geiger counters**)
an instrument that detects and measures radioactivity.
[named after a German scientist, H. W. Geiger, who helped to develop it]

gelatine *noun*
a clear jelly-like substance made by boiling animal tissue and used to make jellies and other foods and in photographic film.
gelatinous (*say* jil-**at**-in-us) *adjective*
[from Italian *gelata* = jelly]

geld *verb* (**gelds, gelding, gelded**)
castrate or spay an animal.
[from Old Norse]

gelding *noun* (*plural* **geldings**)
a castrated horse or other male animal.

gelignite (*say* jel-ig-nyt) *noun*
a kind of explosive.
[from *gelatine* + Latin *lignum* = wood (because gelignite contains wood pulp)]

gem *noun* (*plural* **gems**)
1 a precious stone. 2 an excellent person or thing. [via Old English from Latin]

-gen *suffix*
used in scientific language to form nouns meaning 'producing' or 'produced' (e.g. *oxygen, hydrogen*).

gender *noun* (*plural* **genders**)
1 the group in which a noun is classed in the grammar of some languages (e.g. *masculine, feminine, neuter*). 2 a person's sex, *Jobs should be open to all, regardless of race or gender*.
[from Latin *genus* = a kind]

gene (*say* jeen) *noun* (*plural* **genes**)
the part of a living cell that controls which characteristics (such as the colour of hair or eyes) are inherited from parents.
[from Greek *genos* = kind, race]

genealogy (*say* jeen-ee-**al**-o-jee) *noun* (*plural* **genealogies**)
1 a statement or diagram showing how people are descended from an ancestor; a pedigree. **2** the study of family history and ancestors. **genealogical** (*say* jeen-ee-a-**loj**-ik-al) *adjective*
[from Greek *genea* = race of people, + *-logy*]

genera (*say* **jen**-e-ra)
plural of **genus**.

general *adjective*
1 to do with or involving most people or things, *This drug is now in general use.* **2** not detailed; broad, *I've got the general idea.* **3** chief or head, *the general manager.*
general *noun* (*plural* **generals**)
a senior army officer. [from Latin]

general election *noun* (*plural* **general elections**)
an election of Members of Parliament for the whole country.

generality *noun* (*plural* **generalities**)
1 being general. **2** a general statement without exact details.

generalize *verb* (**generalizes**, **generalizing**, **generalized**)
1 make a statement that is true in most cases. **2** bring into general use.
generalization *noun*

generally *adverb*
1 usually. **2** in a general sense; without regard to details, *I was speaking generally.*

general practitioner *noun* (*plural* **general practitioners**)
a doctor who treats all kinds of diseases. He or she is the first doctor that people see when they are ill.

generate *verb* (**generates**, **generating**, **generated**)
produce or create.
[from Latin *generatus* = fathered]

generation *noun* (*plural* **generations**)
1 generating. **2** a single stage in a family, *Three generations were included: children, parents, and grandparents.* **3** all the people born at about the same time, *our parents' generation.*

generator *noun* (*plural* **generators**)
1 an apparatus for producing gases or steam. **2** a machine for converting mechanical energy into electricity.

generic (*say* jin-e-rik) *adjective*
belonging to a whole genus or kind.
generically *adverb*

generous *adjective*
1 willing to give things or share them. **2** given freely; plentiful, *a generous helping.* **generously** *adverb*, **generosity** *noun*
[from Latin *generosus* = noble]

genesis *noun*
the beginning or origin of something.
[Greek, = creation or origin]

genetic (*say* jin-et-ik) *adjective*
1 to do with genes. **2** to do with characteristics inherited from parents or ancestors. **genetically** *adverb* [from *genesis*]

genial (*say* **jee**-nee-al) *adjective*
kindly and cheerful. **genially** *adverb*, **geniality** (*say* jee-nee-**al**-it-ee) *noun*
[from Latin *genialis* = joyous]

genie (*say* **jee**-nee) *noun* (*plural* **genii**, *say* **jee**-nee-y)
(in Arabian tales) a spirit with strange powers. [same origin as *genius*]

genital (*say* **jen**-it-al) *adjective*
to do with animal reproduction or reproductive organs.
[from old French; related to *generate*]

genitals (*say* **jen**-it-alz) *plural noun*
external sexual organs.

genius *noun* (*plural* **geniuses**)
1 an unusually clever person. **2** a very great natural ability, *He has a real genius for music.* [Latin, = a spirit]

genocide (*say* **jen**-o-syd) *noun*
deliberate extermination of a race of people.
[from Greek *genos* = kind, race, + *-cide*]

gent *noun* (*plural* **gents**) (*informal*)
a gentleman; a man.

genteel (*say* jen-**teel**) *adjective*
trying to seem polite and refined. **genteelly**
adverb, **gentility** (*say* jen-**til**-it-ee) *noun*
[from French; related to *gentle*]

gentile *noun* (*plural* **gentiles**)
a person who is not Jewish.
[from Latin *gens* = clan or race]

gentle *adjective*
kind and quiet; not rough or severe.
gently *adverb*, **gentleness** *noun*
[from Latin *gentilis* = from a good family]

gentlefolk *noun* (*old use*)
upper-class people.

gentleman (*plural* **gentlemen**)
1 a well-mannered or honourable man. **2** a
man of good social position. **3** (*in polite use*)
a man.

gentry *noun* (*old use*)
upper-class people.

genuine *adjective*
real; not faked or pretending. **genuinely**
adverb, **genuineness** *noun*
[from Latin *genu* = knee (because a father
would take a baby onto his knee to show
that he accepted it as his)]

genus (*say* **jee**-nus) *noun* (*plural* **genera**,
say **jen**-er-a)
a group of similar animals or plants, *Lions
and tigers belong to the same genus.*
[Latin, = family or race]

geo- *prefix*
earth. [from Greek *ge* = earth]

geography (*say* jee-**og**-ra-fee) *noun*
the study of the earth's surface and of its
climate, peoples, and products. **geographer**
noun, **geographical** *adjective*, **geographically**
adverb [from *geo-* + *-graphy*]

geology (*say* jee-**ol**-o-jee) *noun*
the study of the structure of the earth's
crust and its layers. **geological** *adjective*,
geologically *adverb*, **geologist** *noun*
[from *geo-* + *-logy*]

geometry (*say* jee-**om**-it-ree) *noun*
the study of lines, angles, surfaces, and
solids in mathematics. **geometric** *adjective*,
geometrical *adjective*, **geometrically** *adverb*
[from *geo-* + Greek *-metria* = measurement]

Georgian *adjective*
belonging to the time of the kings George I–
IV (1714–1830) or George V–VI (1910–52).

geranium *noun* (*plural* **geraniums**)
1 a garden plant with red, pink, or white
flowers. **2** a wild plant whose seeds have a
long, pointed end, like a bird's beak.
[from Greek]

gerbil (*say* **jer**-bil) *noun* (*plural* **gerbils**)
a small brown animal with long hind legs,
from Africa and Asia. One sort of gerbil,
which originally came from Mongolia, is
often kept as a pet. [from Latin]

geriatric (*say* je-ree-**at**-rik) *adjective*
to do with the care of old people and their
health. [from Greek *geras* = old age
+ *iatros* = doctor]

germ *noun* (*plural* **germs**)
1 a micro-organism, especially one that
can cause disease. **2** a tiny living structure
from which a plant or animal may develop.
3 part of the seed of a cereal plant.
[from Latin *germen* = seed or sprout]

Germanic *noun*
1 a group of languages spoken in northern
Europe and Scandinavia. **2** an unrecorded
language believed to be the ancestor of this
group.

German measles *noun*
rubella.

German shepherd dog *noun* (*plural*
German shepherd dogs)
a large strong dog, often used by the police.

germicide *noun* (*plural* **germicides**)
a substance that kills germs.
[from *germ* + *-cide*]

germinate *verb* (**germinates, germinating,
germinated**)
when a seed germinates, it begins to
develop, and roots and shoots grow from it.
germination *noun* [same origin as *germ*]

gesticulate (*say* jes-tik-yoo-layt) *verb*
(**gesticulates, gesticulating, gesticulated**)
make expressive movements with your
hands and arms.
gesticulation *noun*
[same origin as *gesture*]

gesture (*say* jes-cher) *noun* (*plural*
gestures)
1 a movement that expresses what a
person feels. **2** an action that shows
goodwill, *It would be a nice gesture to send
her some flowers.*
gesture *verb* (**gestures, gesturing, gestured**)
tell a person something by making a
gesture, *She gestured me to be quiet.*
[from Latin *gestus* = action, way of
standing or moving]

get *verb* (**gets, getting, got**)
This word has many different uses,
including **1** obtain or receive, *She got first
prize.* **2** become, *Don't get angry!* **3** reach a
place, *We got there by midnight.* **4** put or
move, *I can't get my shoe on.* **5** prepare, *Will
you get the tea?* **6** persuade or order, *Get
him to wash up.* **7** catch or suffer from an
illness. **8** (*informal*) understand, *Do you get
what I mean?*
get away with 1 escape with something.
2 avoid being punished for what you have
done.
get by (*informal*) manage.
get on 1 make progress. **2** be friendly with
somebody.
get over recover from an illness etc.
get up 1 stand up. **2** get out of your bed in
the morning. **3** prepare or organize, *We got
up a concert.*
get your own back (*informal*) have your
revenge.
have got to must.
[from Old Norse]

getaway *noun* (*plural* **getaways**)
an escape after committing a crime, *They
made their getaway in a stolen car.*

geyser (*say* gee-zer or gy-zer) *noun* (*plural*
geysers)
1 a natural spring that shoots up columns
of hot water. **2** a kind of water heater.
[from *Geysir* = gusher, the name of a geyser
in Iceland]

ghastly *adjective*
1 very unpleasant or bad. **2** looking pale

and ill. **ghastliness** *noun*
[from Old English *gaestan* = terrify]

gherkin (*say* ger-kin) *noun* (*plural*
gherkins)
a small cucumber used for pickling.
[via Dutch from Greek]

ghetto (*say* get-oh) *noun* (*plural* **ghettos**)
an area of a city, often a slum area, where a
group of people live who are treated
unfairly in comparison with others.
[probably from Italian *getto* = foundry
(because the first ghetto was established in
1516 in the site of a foundry in Venice)]

ghost *noun* (*plural* **ghosts**)
the spirit of a dead person that appears to
the living. **ghostly** *adjective*
[from Old English]

ghoulish (*say* gool-ish) *adjective*
enjoying things that are grisly or
unpleasant. **ghoulishly** *adverb*, **ghoulishness**
noun [from Arabic *gul* = a demon that eats
dead bodies]

giant *noun* (*plural* **giants**)
1 (in myths or fairy tales) a creature like a
huge man. **2** a man, animal, or plant that is
much larger than the usual size.
[from Greek]

gibber (*say* jib-er) *verb* (**gibbers, gibbering,
gibbered**)
make quick meaningless sounds, especially
when shocked or terrified.
[imitating the sound]

gibberish (*say* jib-er-ish) *noun*
meaningless speech; nonsense.
[probably from *gibber* + *-ish*]

gibbet (*say* jib-it) *noun* (*plural* **gibbets**)
1 a gallows. **2** an upright post with an arm
from which a criminal's body was hung
after execution, as a warning to others.
[from old French]

gibbon *noun* (*plural* **gibbons**)
a small ape from south-east Asia. Gibbons
have very long arms to help them swing
through the trees where they live. [French]

gibe (*say* jyb) *noun* (*plural* **gibes**)
a remark that is meant to hurt someone's
feelings or make them look silly.

gibe *verb* (gibes, gibing, gibed)
make a hurtful remark; taunt, mock.
[origin unknown]

giblets (*say* jib-lits) *plural noun*
the parts of the inside of a bird, such as the
heart, liver, etc., that are taken out before
it is cooked. [from old French]

giddy *adjective*
1 feeling that everything is spinning round
and that you might fall. 2 causing this
feeling, *We looked down from the giddy
height of the cliff.* **giddily** *adverb*, **giddiness**
noun [from Old English]

gift *noun* (*plural* gifts)
1 a present. 2 a talent, *She has a gift for
music.* [from Old Norse]

gifted *adjective*
talented.

gig *noun* (*plural* gigs) (*informal*)
a show when a musician or band plays pop
music in public. [origin unknown]

gigantic (*say* jy-gan-tik) *adjective*
extremely large; huge.
[from Latin *gigantis* = of a giant]

giggle *verb* (giggles, giggling, giggled)
laugh in a silly way.
giggle *noun* (*plural* giggles)
1 a silly laugh. 2 (*informal*) something
amusing; a bit of fun. [imitating the sound]

gild *verb* (gilds, gilding, gilded)
cover something with a thin layer of gold
or gold paint. [from Old English]

gills *plural noun*
1 the part of the body through which fishes
and certain other water animals breathe.
2 the thin upright parts under the cap of a
mushroom, that come out from the centre
like the spokes of a wheel. [from Old Norse]

gilt *noun*
a thin covering of gold or gold paint.
gilt *adjective*
gilded; gold-coloured.
[the old past tense of *gild*]

gimlet *noun* (*plural* gimlets)
a small tool with a screw-like tip for boring
holes. [via old French from Germanic]

gimmick *noun* (*plural* gimmicks)
something unusual or silly done or used
just to attract people's attention.
[originally American; origin unknown]

gin¹ *noun*
a colourless alcoholic drink flavoured with
juniper berries. [from the name of Geneva,
a city in Switzerland]

gin² *noun* (*plural* gins)
1 a kind of trap for catching animals. 2 a
machine for separating the fibres of the
cotton plant from its seeds.
[from old French *engin* = engine]

ginger *noun*
1 the hot-tasting root of a tropical plant, or
a flavouring made from this root, used
especially in drinks and Eastern cooking.
2 liveliness or energy. 3 a reddish-yellow
colour. **ginger** *adjective*
ginger *verb* (gingers, gingering, gingered)
make something more lively, *This will
ginger things up!* [via Old English, Latin,
and Greek from Dravidian (a group of
languages spoken in southern India)]

gingerbread *noun*
a ginger-flavoured cake or biscuit.

gingerly *adverb*
cautiously. [origin unknown]

gipsy *noun* (*plural* gipsies)
a different spelling of *gypsy*.

giraffe *noun* (*plural* giraffe or giraffes)
an African animal, the world's tallest
mammal, which reaches up to 5.5 metres in
height. The giraffe's neck makes up nearly
half its height. [from Arabic]

gird *verb* (girds, girding, girded)
1 fasten with a belt or band, *He girded on
his sword.* 2 prepare for an effort, *gird
yourself for action.* [from Old English]

girder *noun* (*plural* girders)
a metal beam supporting part of a building
or a bridge. [from an old meaning of *gird*
= brace or strengthen]

girdle¹ *noun* (*plural* girdles)
a belt or cord worn round the waist.
[from Old English]

girdle² *noun* (*plural* **girdles**) (*Scottish* and *Northern English*)
a griddle. [from old French]

girl *noun* (*plural* **girls**)
1 a female child. **2** a young woman.
girlhood *noun*, **girlish** *adjective*
[origin unknown]

girlfriend *noun* (*plural* **girlfriends**)
a girl that a boy regularly goes out with.

giro (*say* jy-roh) *noun*
a system of arranging payment for customers, run by a post office or bank.
[via German from Italian]

girt *adjective* (*old use*)
girded. [old past tense of *gird*]

girth *noun* (*plural* **girths**)
1 the distance round something. **2** a band passing under a horse's body to hold the saddle in place. [from Old Norse]

gist (*say* jist) *noun*
the essential points or general sense of a speech, conversation, etc.
[from old French]

give *verb* (**gives, giving, gave, given**)
1 let someone have something. **2** make or do something, *He gave a laugh.* **3** be flexible or springy; bend or collapse when pressed. **giver** *noun*
give in acknowledge that you are defeated; yield.
give up 1 stop trying. **2** end a habit.
[from Old English]

given *adjective*
named or stated in advance, *All the people in a given area.*

gizzard *noun* (*plural* **gizzards**)
a bird's second stomach, in which food is ground up. [from old French]

glacé (*say* glas-ay) *adjective*
iced with sugar; crystallized.
[French, = iced]

glacial (*say* glay-shal) *adjective*
icy; made of or produced by ice. **glacially** *adverb* [from Latin *glacies* = ice]

glacier (*say* glas-ee-er) *noun* (*plural* **glaciers**)
a mass of ice that moves very slowly down a mountain valley. [same origin as *glacial*]

glad *adjective*
1 pleased; expressing joy. **2** giving pleasure, *We brought the glad news.*
gladly *adverb*, **gladness** *noun*
glad of grateful for or pleased with something.
[from Old English]

gladden *verb* (**gladdens, gladdening, gladdened**)
make a person glad.

glade *noun* (*plural* **glades**)
an open space in a forest. [origin unknown]

gladiator (*say* glad-ee-ay-ter) *noun* (*plural* **gladiators**)
a man trained to fight for public entertainment in ancient Rome.
gladiatorial (*say* glad-ee-at-or-ee-al) *adjective* [from Latin *gladius* = sword]

glamorize *verb* (**glamorizes, glamorizing, glamorized**)
make something glamorous or romantic.

glamorous *adjective*
excitingly attractive.

glamour *noun*
attractiveness, romantic charm. [from an old meaning of *grammar* = magic]

glance *verb* (**glances, glancing, glanced**)
1 look at something briefly. **2** strike something at an angle and slide off it, *The ball glanced off his bat.* **glance** *noun*
[origin unknown]

gland *noun* (*plural* **glands**)
an organ of the body that separates substances from the blood so that they can be used or secreted (passed out of the body). **glandular** *adjective* [from Latin]

glare *verb* (**glares, glaring, glared**)
1 shine with an unpleasant dazzling light. **2** stare angrily or fiercely. **glare** *noun*
[from old German or old Dutch]

glaring *adjective*
very obvious, *a glaring error.*

glasnost *noun*
the open reporting of news or giving of
information, especially in the former
Soviet Union. [Russian, = openness]

glass *noun* (*plural* **glasses**)
1 a hard brittle substance that is usually
transparent. **2** a container made of glass
for drinking from. **3** a mirror. **4** a lens.
glassy *adjective* [from Old English]

glasses *plural noun*
1 spectacles. **2** binoculars.

glaze *verb* (**glazes, glazing, glazed**)
1 fit a window or building with glass.
2 give a shiny surface to something.
3 become glassy.
glaze *noun* (*plural* **glazes**)
a shiny surface or coating, especially on
pottery. [from *glass*]

glazier (*say* glay-zee-er) *noun* (*plural*
glaziers)
a person whose job is to fit glass in
windows.

gleam *noun* (*plural* **gleams**)
1 a beam of soft light, especially one that
comes and goes. **2** a small amount of hope,
humour, etc.
gleam *verb* (**gleams, gleaming, gleamed**)
shine brightly, especially after cleaning or
polishing. [from Old English]

glean *verb* (**gleans, gleaning, gleaned**)
1 pick up grain left by harvesters. **2** gather
bit by bit, *glean some information.* **gleaner**
noun [via Latin from a Celtic language]

glee *noun*
lively or triumphant delight.
gleeful *adjective*, **gleefully** *adverb*
[from Old English]

glen *noun* (*plural* **glens**)
a narrow valley.
[from Scottish Gaelic or Irish]

glib *adjective*
speaking or writing readily but not
sincerely or thoughtfully. **glibly** *adverb*,
glibness *noun*
[from an old word *glibbery* = slippery]

glide *verb* (**glides, gliding, glided**)
1 move along smoothly. **2** fly without using
an engine. **3** birds glide when they fly
without beating their wings. **glide** *noun*
[from Old English]

glider *noun* (*plural* **gliders**)
an aeroplane without an engine that flies
by floating on warm air currents called
thermals.

glimmer *noun* (*plural* **glimmers**)
1 a faint light. **2** a small sign or trace of
something, *a glimmer of hope.*
glimmer *verb* (**glimmers, glimmering,
glimmered**)
shine with a faint, flickering light.
[probably from a Scandinavian language]

glimpse *noun* (*plural* **glimpses**)
a brief view.
glimpse *verb* (**glimpses, glimpsing,
glimpsed**)
see something briefly.
[probably from Old English]

glint *noun* (*plural* **glints**)
a very brief flash of light.
glint *verb* (**glints, glinting, glinted**)
shine with a flash of light.
[probably from a Scandinavian language]

glisten (*say* glis-en) *verb* (**glistens,
glistening, glistened**)
shine like something wet or oily.
[from Old English]

glitter *verb* (**glitters, glittering, glittered**)
shine with tiny flashes of light; sparkle.
glitter *noun*
tiny sparkling pieces used for decoration.
[from Old Norse]

gloaming *noun* (*Scottish*)
the evening twilight. [from Old English]

gloat *verb* (**gloats, gloating, gloated**)
be pleased in an unkind way that you have
succeeded or that someone else has been
hurt or upset. [origin unknown]

global *adjective*
1 to do with the whole world; worldwide.
2 to do with the whole of a system. **globally**
adverb [from *globe*]

global warming *noun*
the increase in the temperature of the earth's atmosphere, caused by the greenhouse effect.

globe *noun* (*plural* **globes**)
1 something shaped like a ball, especially one with a map of the whole world on it. 2 the world, *She has travelled all over the globe.* 3 a hollow round glass object. [from Latin]

globular (*say* glob-yoo-ler) *adjective*
shaped like a globe.
[same origin as *globule*]

globule (*say* glob-yool) *noun* (*plural* **globules**)
a small rounded drop.
[from Latin *globulus* = small globe]

gloom *noun*
1 darkness. 2 sadness or despair.
[origin unknown]

gloomy *adjective* (**gloomier, gloomiest**)
1 almost dark. 2 depressed or depressing. **gloomily** *adverb*, **gloominess** *noun*

glorify *verb* (**glorifies, glorifying, glorified**)
1 give great praise or great honour to.
2 make a thing seem more splendid or attractive than it really is, *It is a film that glorifies war.* **glorification** *noun*

glorious *adjective*
splendid or magnificent. **gloriously** *adverb*

glory *noun* (*plural* **glories**)
1 fame and honour. 2 praise. 3 beauty or magnificence.
glory *verb* (**glories, glorying, gloried**)
rejoice; pride yourself, *They gloried in victory.* [from Latin]

gloss¹ *noun* (*plural* **glosses**)
the shine on a smooth surface.
gloss *verb* (**glosses, glossing, glossed**)
make a thing glossy. [origin unknown]

gloss² *verb* (**glosses, glossing, glossed**)
gloss over mention a fault or mistake etc. only briefly to make it seem less serious than it really is.
[from old French *gloser* = flatter or deceive]

glossary *noun* (*plural* **glossaries**)
a list of difficult words with their meanings explained.
[from Greek *glossa* = tongue, language]

glossy *adjective* (**glossier, glossiest**)
smooth and shiny. **glossily** *adverb*, **glossiness** *noun*

glove *noun* (*plural* **gloves**)
a covering for the hand, usually with separate divisions for each finger and thumb. **gloved** *adjective* [from Old English]

glow *noun*
1 brightness and warmth without flames.
2 a warm or cheerful feeling, *We felt a glow of pride.*
glow *verb* (**glows, glowing, glowed**)
shine with a soft, warm light.
[from Old English]

glower (rhymes with *flower*) *verb* (**glowers, glowering, glowered**)
stare angrily; scowl. [origin unknown]

glow-worm *noun* (*plural* **glow-worms**)
a kind of beetle whose tail gives out a green light.

glucose *noun*
a form of sugar found in fruit juice and honey. [same origin as *glycerine*]

glue *noun* (*plural* **glues**)
a sticky substance used for joining things together. **gluey** *adjective*
glue *verb* (**glues, gluing, glued**)
1 stick with glue. 2 attach or hold closely, *His ear was glued to the keyhole.*
[from French; related to *gluten*]

glum *adjective*
miserable or depressed. **glumly** *adverb*, **glumness** *noun*
[from dialect *glum* = to frown]

glut *noun* (*plural* **gluts**)
an excessive supply.
[from Latin *gluttire* = to swallow]

gluten (*say* gloo-ten) *noun*
a sticky protein substance in flour.
[Latin, = glue]

glutinous (*say* gloo-tin-us) *adjective*
glue-like or sticky. [same origin as *gluten*]

glutton *noun* (*plural* **gluttons**)
a person who eats too much.
gluttonous *adjective*, **gluttony** *noun*
glutton for punishment a person who seems
to enjoy doing something difficult or
unpleasant.
[from old French; related to *glut*]

glycerine (*say* glis-er-een) *noun*
a thick sweet colourless liquid used in
ointments and medicines and in
explosives. [from Greek *glykys* = sweet]

gm *abbreviation*
gram.

GMT *abbreviation*
Greenwich Mean Time.

gnarled (*say* narld) *adjective*
twisted and knobbly, like an old tree.
[from old German or old Dutch]

gnash (*say* nash) *verb* (**gnashes**, **gnashing**,
gnashed)
grind your teeth together.
[origin unknown]

gnat (*say* nat) *noun* (*plural* **gnats**)
a tiny fly that bites. [from Old English]

gnaw (*say* naw) *verb* (**gnaws**, **gnawing**,
gnawed)
keep on biting something hard so that it
wears away. [from Old English]

gnome (*say* nohm) *noun* (*plural* **gnomes**)
a kind of dwarf in fairy tales, usually living
underground. [from Latin]

gnu (*say* noo) *noun* (*plural* **gnu** or **gnus**)
a large ox-like antelope.
[from Khoisan (a group of languages
spoken in southern Africa)]

go *verb* (**goes**, **going**, **went**, **gone**)
This word is used to show **1** movement,
especially away from somewhere (*Where
are you going?*), **2** direction (*The road goes
to Bristol*), **3** change (*Milk went sour*),
4 progress or result (*The gun went bang*),
5 place (*Plates go on that shelf*), **6** sale (*The
house went very cheaply*).
go off 1 explode. **2** become stale. **3** stop
liking something.
go on continue.
go out stop burning or shining.

go *noun* (*plural* **goes**)
1 a turn or try, *May I have a go?*
2 (*informal*) energy or liveliness, *She is full
of go.*
make a go of make a success of something.
on the go active; always working or
moving.
[from Old English]

goad *noun* (*plural* **goads**)
a stick with a pointed end for prodding
cattle to move onwards.
goad *verb* (**goads**, **goading**, **goaded**)
stir into action by being annoying, *He
goaded me into fighting*. [from Old English]

go-ahead *noun*
permission to proceed.
go-ahead *adjective*
energetic; willing to try new methods.

goal *noun* (*plural* **goals**)
1 the place where a ball must go to score a
point in football, hockey, etc. **2** a point
scored in this way. **3** something that you
are trying to reach or achieve.
[origin unknown]

goalkeeper *noun* (*plural* **goalkeepers**)
the player who stands in the goal to try and
keep the ball from entering.

goat *noun* (*plural* **goats**)
a mammal with horns and a beard, closely
related to the sheep. Domestic goats are
kept for their milk. [from Old English]

gobble *verb* (**gobbles**, **gobbling**, **gobbled**)
eat quickly and greedily.
[from old French *gober* = to swallow]

gobbledegook *noun* (*slang*)
the pompous and technical language that is
often used by officials and is difficult to
understand. [imitation of the sound a
turkeycock makes]

go-between *noun* (*plural* **go-betweens**)
a person who acts as a messenger or
negotiator between others.

goblet *noun* (*plural* **goblets**)
a drinking glass with a stem and a foot.
[from French *gobelet* = little cup]

goblin *noun* (*plural* **goblins**)
a mischievous ugly elf. [from old French]

God *noun*
the creator of the universe in Christian, Jewish, and Muslim belief.
[from Old English]

god *noun* (*plural* **gods**)
a male being that is worshipped, *Mars was a Roman god.*

goddess *noun* (*plural* **goddesses**)
a female being that is worshipped.

godhead *noun*
the divine nature of God.
[from *god* + Old English *-had* = -hood]

godly *adjective* (**godlier, godliest**)
sincerely religious. **godliness** *noun*

godparent *noun* (*plural* **godparents**)
a person at a child's christening who promises to see that it is brought up as a Christian. **godchild** *noun*, **god-daughter** *noun*, **godfather** *noun*, **godmother** *noun*, **godson** *noun*

godsend *noun* (*plural* **godsends**)
a piece of unexpected good luck. [from an old phrase *God's send* = what God has sent]

goggle *verb* (**goggles, goggling, goggled**)
stare with wide-open eyes.
[origin unknown]

goggles *plural noun*
large spectacles for protecting your eyes from wind, water, dust, etc.
[from *goggle*]

going *present participle* of **go**.
be going to do something be ready or likely to do it.

gold *noun* (*plural* **golds**)
1 a precious yellow metal. **2** a deep yellow colour. **3** a gold medal, usually given as first prize. **gold** *adjective*
[from Old English]

golden *adjective*
1 made of gold. **2** coloured like gold. **3** precious or excellent, *a golden opportunity.*

golden wedding *noun* (*plural* **golden weddings**)
a couple's fiftieth wedding anniversary.

goldfinch *noun* (*plural* **goldfinches**)
a bird with yellow feathers in its wings.

goldfish *noun* (*plural* **goldfish**)
a small red or orange fish, often kept as a pet.

goldsmith *noun* (*plural* **goldsmiths**)
a person who makes things in gold.

golf *noun*
an outdoor game played by hitting a small white ball with a club into a series of holes on a specially prepared ground (a **golf course** or **golf links**) and taking as few strokes as possible.
golfer *noun*, **golfing** *noun*
[origin unknown]

-gon *suffix*
used to form nouns meaning 'having a certain number of angles (and sides)' (e.g. *hexagon*).
[from Greek *gonia* = angle]

gondola (*say* gond-ol-a) *noun* (*plural* **gondolas**)
a boat with high pointed ends used on the canals in Venice.
[Italian]

gondolier *noun* (*plural* **gondoliers**)
the person who moves a gondola along with a pole.

gong *noun* (*plural* **gongs**)
a large metal disc that makes an echoing sound when it is hit.
[from Malay (a language spoken in Maylasia)]

good *adjective* (**better, best**)
1 having the right qualities; of the kind that people like, *a good book.* **2** kind, *It was good of you to help us.* **3** well-behaved, *Be a good boy.* **4** skilled or talented, *a good pianist.* **5** healthy; giving benefit, *Exercise is good for you.* **6** thorough, *Give it a good clean.* **7** large; considerable, *It's a good distance from the shops.*

good *noun*
1 something good, *Do good to others.* **2** benefit, *It's for your own good.*
for good for ever.

no good useless.
[from Old English]

USAGE: In standard English, *good* cannot be used as an adverb. You can say *She's a good player* but not *She played good.* The adverb that goes with *good* is *well.*

goodbye *interjection*
a word used when you leave somebody or at the end of a phone call.
[short for *God be with you*]

Good Friday *noun*
the Friday before Easter, when Christians commemorate the Crucifixion of Christ.

goodness *noun*
1 being good. 2 the good part of something.

goods *plural noun*
1 things that are bought and sold. 2 things that are carried on trains or lorries.

goodwill *noun*
a kindly feeling towards another person.

goody *noun* (*plural* **goodies**) (*informal*)
1 something good or attractive, especially to eat. 2 a good person, especially one of the heroes in a story.

goose *noun* (*plural* **geese**)
a long-necked water bird with webbed feet, larger than a duck. [from Old English]

gooseberry *noun* (*plural* **gooseberries**)
1 a small green fruit that grows on a prickly bush. 2 (*informal*) an unwanted extra person.
[probably from French dialect *gozell*]

goose-flesh *noun* or **goose pimples** *plural noun*
skin that has turned rough with small bumps on it because a person is cold or afraid. [because it looks like the skin of a plucked goose]

gore[1] *verb* (**gores, goring, gored**)
wound by piercing with a horn or tusk.
[origin unknown]

gore[2] *noun*
thickened blood from a cut or wound.
[from Old English *gor* = filth or slime]

gorge *noun* (*plural* **gorges**)
a narrow valley with steep sides.

gorge *verb* (**gorges, gorging, gorged**)
eat greedily; stuff with food.
[French, = throat]

gorgeous *adjective*
magnificent or beautiful. **gorgeously** *adverb* [from old French]

gorilla *noun* (*plural* **gorillas**)
an African ape, the largest of all the apes. Males are about 1.8 metres tall and can weigh up to 300kg. [from Latin, probably from an African word = hairy woman]

USAGE: Do not confuse with *guerrilla*, which can be pronounced in the same way.

gorse *noun*
a prickly bush with small yellow flowers.
[from Old English]

gory *adjective*
1 covered with blood. 2 with much bloodshed, *a gory battle.*

gosh *interjection*
an exclamation of surprise.
[used to avoid saying 'God']

gosling *noun* (*plural* **goslings**)
a young goose. [from Old Norse]

gospel *noun*
1 the teachings of Jesus Christ.
2 something you can safely believe to be true.
the Gospels the first four books of the New Testament, telling of the life and teachings of Jesus Christ.
[from Old English *god* = good + *spel* = news]

gossamer *noun*
1 fine cobwebs made by small spiders.
2 any fine delicate material.
[from *goose summer*, a period of fine weather in the autumn (when geese were eaten), when gossamer is very common]

gossip *verb* (**gossips, gossiping, gossiped**)
talk a lot about other people.
gossip *noun* (*plural* **gossips**)
1 talk, especially rumours, about other people. 2 a person who enjoys gossiping.

gossipy *adjective* [from Old English *godsibb* = close friend (literally = god-brother or sister), someone to gossip with]

got *past tense* of **get**.
have got possess, *Have you got a car?*
have got to must.

Gothic *noun*
the style of building common in the 12th–16th centuries, with pointed arches and much decorative carving.
[from the Goths, whom the Romans regarded as barbarians (because some people thought this style was barbaric compared to Greek or Roman styles)]

gouge (*say* gowj) *verb* (**gouges, gouging, gouged**)
scoop or force out by pressing.
[from Latin *gubia* = a kind of chisel]

goulash (*say* goo-lash) *noun*
a Hungarian meat stew seasoned with paprika. [from Hungarian *gulyáshús* = herdsman's meat]

gourd (*say* goord) *noun* (*plural* **gourds**)
the rounded hard-skinned fruit of a climbing plant. [from old French]

gourmet (*say* goor-may) *noun* (*plural* **gourmets**)
a person who understands and appreciates good food and drink.
[French, = wine taster]

gout *noun*
a disease that causes painful inflammation (heat and swelling) of the toes, knees, and fingers. **gouty** *adjective*
[from old French or Latin]

govern *verb* (**governs, governing, governed**)
be in charge of the public affairs of a country or region.
[from Latin *gubernare* = steer or direct]

governess *noun* (*plural* **governesses**)
a woman employed to teach children in a private household.

government *noun* (*plural* **governments**)
1 the group of people who are in charge of the public affairs of a country. 2 the process of governing.
governmental *adjective*

governor *noun* (*plural* **governors**)
1 a person who governs a State or a colony etc. 2 a member of the governing body of a school or other institution. 3 the person in charge of a prison.

gown *noun* (*plural* **gowns**)
a loose flowing garment.
[from Latin *gunna* = a fur-lined robe]

GP *abbreviation*
general practitioner.

grab *verb* (**grabs, grabbing, grabbed**)
take hold of something suddenly or greedily. [from old German or old Dutch]

grace *noun*
1 beauty, especially of movement.
2 goodwill or favour. 3 dignity or good manners, *At least he had the grace to apologize.* 4 a short prayer of thanks before or after a meal. 5 the title of a duke, duchess, or archbishop, *His Grace the Duke of Kent.*
grace *verb* (**graces, gracing, graced**)
bring honour or dignity to something, *The mayor himself graced us with his presence.*
[from Latin *gratus* = pleasing]

graceful *adjective*
beautiful and elegant in movement or shape. **gracefully** *adverb*, **gracefulness** *noun*

gracious *adjective*
behaving kindly and honourably.
graciously *adverb*, **graciousness** *noun*

grade *noun* (*plural* **grades**)
1 a step in a scale of quality or value or rank. 2 a mark showing the quality of a student's work.
grade *verb* (**grades, grading, graded**)
arrange in grades.
[from Latin *gradus* = a step]

gradient (*say* gray-dee-ent) *noun* (*plural* **gradients**)
a slope or the steepness of a slope.
[from *grade*]

gradual *adjective*
happening slowly but steadily.
gradually *adverb*

graduate (*say* grad-yoo-ayt) *verb* (**graduates, graduating, graduated**)
1 get a university or college degree.

2 divide something into graded sections; mark something with units of measurement.

graduate (*say* grad-yoo-at) *noun* (*plural* graduates)
a person who has a university or college degree. [same origin as *grade*]

graffiti *noun*
words or drawings scribbled or sprayed on a wall. [Italian, = scratchings]

USAGE: Strictly speaking, this word is a plural noun (the singular is *graffito*), so it should be used with a plural verb: *There are graffiti all over the wall.* However, the word is widely used nowadays as if it were a singular noun and most people do not regard this as wrong: *There is graffiti all over the wall.*

graft *noun* (*plural* grafts)
1 a shoot from one plant or tree fixed into another to form a new growth. 2 a piece of living tissue transplanted by a surgeon to replace what is diseased or damaged, *a skin graft*.

graft *verb* (grafts, grafting, grafted)
insert or transplant as a graft.
[from Greek *grapheion* = pointed writing stick (because of the pointed shape of the end of the shoot)]

grain *noun* (*plural* grains)
1 a small hard seed or similar particle. 2 cereal plants when they are growing or after being harvested. 3 a very small amount, *a grain of truth*. 4 the pattern of lines made by the fibres in a piece of wood or paper. **grainy** *adjective* [from Latin]

gram *noun* (*plural* grams)
a unit of mass or weight in the metric system.
[from Latin *gramma* = a small weight]

-gram *suffix*
used to form nouns meaning something written or drawn etc. (e.g. *diagram*).
[from Greek *gramma* = thing written]

grammar *noun* (*plural* grammars)
1 the rules for using words correctly. 2 a book about these rules.
[from Greek, = the art of letters]

grammar school *noun* (*plural* grammar schools)
a secondary school for children with academic ability.

grammatical *adjective*
according to the rules of grammar.
grammatically *adverb*

gramophone *noun* (*plural* gramophones)
(*old use*) a record player.
[altered from 'phonogram' (the name given to the first record player, from Greek *phone* = a sound, + *-gram*)]

grampus *noun* (*plural* grampuses)
a large dolphin-like sea animal.
[from Latin *craspiscis* = fat fish]

granary *noun* (*plural* granaries)
a storehouse for grain. [from Latin]

grand *adjective*
1 splendid and impressive. 2 most important or highest-ranking. 3 including everything; complete. **grandly** *adverb*, **grandness** *noun*
[from Latin *grandis* = fully-grown]

grandad (*informal*)
grandfather.

grandchild *noun* (*plural* grandchildren)
the child of a person's son or daughter.
granddaughter *noun*, **grandson** *noun*

grandeur (*say* grand-yer) *noun*
impressive beauty; splendour.
[from French]

grandfather *noun* (*plural* grandfathers)
the father of a person's father or mother.

grandfather clock *noun* (*plural* grandfather clocks)
a clock in a tall wooden case.

grandiose (*say* grand-ee-ohss) *adjective*
large and impressive; trying to seem impressive. [via French from Italian]

grandma *noun* (*informal*)
grandmother.

grandmother *noun* (*plural* grandmothers)
the mother of a person's father or mother.

grandpa *noun* (*informal*)
grandfather.

grandparent *noun* (*plural* **grandparents**)
a grandfather or grandmother.

grand piano *noun* (*plural* **grand pianos**)
a large piano with the strings fixed
horizontally.

grandstand *noun* (*plural* **grandstands**)
a building with a roof and rows of seats for
spectators at a racecourse or sports
ground.

grand total *noun*
the sum of other totals.

grange *noun* (*plural* **granges**)
a large country house. [originally = barn:
from French, related to *grain*]

granite *noun*
a very hard kind of rock used for building.
[from Italian *granito* = granular (because
of the small particles you can see in the
rock)]

granny *noun* (*plural* **grannies**) (*informal*)
grandmother.

granny knot *noun* (*plural* **granny knots**)
a reef knot with the strings crossed the
wrong way.

grant *verb* (**grants, granting, granted**)
1 give or allow someone what he or she has
asked for, *grant a request*. **2** admit; agree
that something is true.
take for granted assume that something is
true or will always be available.
grant *noun* (*plural* **grants**)
something granted, especially a sum of
money. [from old French]

Granth (*say* grunt) *noun*
the sacred scriptures of the Sikhs.
[from Sanskrit]

granular *adjective*
like grains. [from *granule*]

granulated *adjective*
in grains, *granulated sugar*.

granule *noun* (*plural* **granules**)
a small grain. [from Latin]

grape *noun* (*plural* **grapes**)
a small green or purple berry that grows in
bunches on a vine. Grapes are used to
make wine. [from old French]

grapefruit *noun* (*plural* **grapefruit**)
a large round yellow citrus fruit.
[because they grow in clusters, like grapes]

grapevine *noun* (*plural* **grapevines**)
1 a vine on which grapes grow. **2** a way by
which news spreads unofficially, with
people passing it on from one to another.

graph *noun* (*plural* **graphs**)
a diagram showing how two quantities or
variables are related.
[from Greek *graphein* = to write or draw]

-graph *suffix*
used to form nouns and verbs meaning
1 something written, drawn, or recorded in
some way (e.g. *photograph*). **2** a machine
which records (e.g. *telegraph*,
seismograph). [same origin as *graph*]

graphic *adjective*
1 to do with drawing or painting, *a graphic
artist*. **2** giving a lively description.
graphically *adverb* [same origin as *graph*]

graphics *plural noun*
diagrams, lettering, and drawings,
especially pictures that are produced by a
computer.

graphite *noun*
a soft black form of carbon used for the
lead in pencils, as a lubricant, and in
nuclear reactors.
[from Greek *graphein* = to write or draw
(because pencil lead is made of graphite)]

graph paper *noun*
paper printed with small squares, used for
drawing graphs.

-graphy *suffix*
used to form names of **1** sciences (e.g.
geography), **2** methods of writing, drawing,
or recording (e.g. *photography*).
[same origin as *graph*]

grapnel *noun* (*plural* **grapnels**)
a heavy metal device with claws for
hooking things.
[via old French from Germanic]

grapple *verb* (**grapples, grappling, grappled**)
1 struggle or wrestle. **2** seize or hold firmly. **3** try to deal with a problem etc., *I've been grappling with this essay all day.*
[from old French; related to *grapnel*]

grasp *verb* (**grasps, grasping, grasped**)
1 seize and hold firmly. **2** understand.
grasp *noun*
1 the power of understanding something. **2** a firm hold.
[origin unknown]

grasping *adjective*
greedy for money or possessions.

grass *noun* (*plural* **grasses**)
1 a plant with green blades and stalks that are eaten by animals. **2** ground covered with grass; lawn.
grassy *adjective*
[from Old English]

grasshopper *noun* (*plural* **grasshoppers**)
a jumping insect that makes a shrill noise.

grassland *noun* (*plural* **grasslands**)
a wide area covered in grass with few trees.

grass roots *plural noun*
the ordinary people in a political party or other group.

grate[1] *noun* (*plural* **grates**)
1 a metal framework that keeps fuel in a fireplace. **2** a fireplace.
[from old French or Spanish]

grate[2] *verb* (**grates, grating, grated**)
1 shred something into small pieces by rubbing it on a rough surface. **2** make an unpleasant noise by rubbing. **3** sound harshly.
grate on have an irritating effect.
[via old French from Germanic]

grateful *adjective*
feeling or showing that you are thankful for something that has been done for you.
gratefully *adverb*
[from Latin *gratus* = thankful, pleasing]

grater *noun* (*plural* **graters**)
a device with a jagged surface for grating food.

gratify *verb* (**gratifies, gratifying, gratified**)
1 give pleasure. **2** satisfy a feeling or desire, *Please gratify our curiosity.*
gratification *noun*
[from Latin *gratus* = pleasing]

grating *noun* (*plural* **gratings**)
a framework of metal bars placed across an opening. [from *grate*[1]]

gratis (*say* **gray**-tiss) *adverb & adjective*
free of charge, *You can have the leaflet gratis.* [Latin, = out of kindness]

gratitude *noun*
being grateful.

gratuitous (*say* gra-**tew**-it-us) *adjective*
1 given or done without payment. **2** done without good reason; uncalled for.
gratuitously *adverb*

gratuity (*say* gra-**tew**-it-ee) *noun* (*plural* **gratuities**)
money given in gratitude; a tip.
[from Latin *gratuitas* = gift]

grave[1] *noun* (*plural* **graves**)
the place where a corpse is buried.
[from Old English]

grave[2] *adjective*
serious or solemn. **gravely** *adverb*
[from Latin *gravis* = heavy]

grave accent (rhymes with *starve*) *noun* (*plural* **grave accents**)
a mark over a vowel, as over *a* in *vis-à-vis*.
[from French; related to *grave*[2]]

gravel *noun*
small stones mixed with coarse sand, used to make paths. **gravelled** *adjective*, **gravelly** *adjective* [from old French]

graven (*say* **gray**-ven) *adjective*
(*old use*) carved.
[from Old English *grafan* = dig out]

gravestone *noun* (*plural* **gravestones**)
a stone monument over a grave.

graveyard *noun* (*plural* **graveyards**)
a burial ground.

gravitate *verb* (**gravitates, gravitating, gravitated**)
move or be attracted towards something.

gravitation *noun*
1 gravitating. 2 the force of gravity.
gravitational *adjective*

gravity *noun*
1 the force that pulls all objects in the
universe towards each other. 2 the force
that pulls everything towards the earth.
3 seriousness. [same origin as *grave²*]

gravy *noun*
a hot brown sauce made from meat juices.
[from old French]

graze *verb* (**grazes, grazing, grazed**)
1 feed on growing grass. 2 scrape your skin
slightly, *I grazed my elbow on the wall.*
3 touch something lightly in passing.
graze *noun* (*plural* **grazes**)
a raw place where skin has been scraped.
[from Old English *graes* = grass]

grease *noun*
melted fat; any thick oily substance.
greasy *adjective*
grease *verb* (**greases, greasing, greased**)
put grease on something.
[from Latin *crassus* = thick, fat]

great *adjective*
1 very large; much above average. 2 very
important or talented, *a great composer.*
3 (*informal*) very good or enjoyable, *It's
great to see you again.* 4 older or younger
by one generation, *great-grandfather.*
greatly *adverb*, **greatness** *noun*
[from Old English]

Great Britain *noun*
the island made up of England, Scotland,
and Wales, with the small adjacent islands.

USAGE: See the note at *Britain.*

grebe (*say* greeb) *noun* (*plural* **grebes**)
a kind of diving bird. [from French]

greed *noun*
being greedy. [from *greedy*]

greedy *adjective*
wanting more food, money, or other things
than you need. **greedily** *adverb*, **greediness**
noun [from Old English]

green *noun* (*plural* **greens**)
1 the colour of grass, leaves, etc. 2 an area
of grassy land, *the village green; a putting
green.*
green *adjective*
1 of the colour green. 2 concerned with
protecting the natural environment.
3 inexperienced and likely to make
mistakes. **greenness** *noun*
[from Old English]

green belt *noun* (*plural* **green belts**)
an area kept as open land round a city.

greenery *noun*
green leaves or plants.

greenfly *noun* (*plural* **greenfly**)
a small green insect that sucks the juices
from plants.

greengrocer *noun* (*plural* **greengrocers**)
a person who keeps a shop that sells fruit
and vegetables. **greengrocery** *noun*

greenhouse *noun* (*plural* **greenhouses**)
a glass building where plants are protected
from cold.

greenhouse effect *noun*
the warming up of the earth's surface when
radiation from the sun is trapped by the
atmosphere.

greenhouse gas *noun* (*plural* **greenhouse
gases**)
any of the gases, especially carbon dioxide
and methane, that are found in the earth's
atmosphere and contribute to the
greenhouse effect.

greens *plural noun*
green vegetables, such as cabbage and
spinach.

Greenwich Mean Time (*say* gren-ich)
the time on the line of longitude which
passes through Greenwich in London, used
as a basis for calculating time throughout
the world.

greet *verb* (**greets, greeting, greeted**)
1 speak to a person who arrives. 2 receive,
They greeted the song with applause.
3 present itself to, *A strange sight greeted
our eyes.* [from Old English]

greeting *noun*
words or actions used to greet somebody.

greetings *plural noun*
good wishes, *a greetings card*.

gregarious (*say* grig-air-ee-us) *adjective*
1 fond of company. 2 living in flocks or
communities.
gregariously *adverb*, **gregariousness** *noun*
[from Latin *gregis* = of a herd]

grenade (*say* grin-**ayd**) *noun* (*plural*
grenades)
a small bomb, usually thrown by hand.
[from old French *pome grenate*
= pomegranate (because of the shape
of the grenade)]

grey *noun* (*plural* **greys**)
the colour between black and white, like
ashes or dark clouds. **grey** *adjective*,
greyness *noun* [from Old English]

greyhound *noun* (*plural* **greyhounds**)
a slender dog with smooth hair, used in
racing. [from Old English *grighund*,
probably = bitch-hound]

grid *noun* (*plural* **grids**)
a framework or pattern of bars or lines
crossing each other. [from *gridiron*]

griddle *noun* (*plural* **griddles**)
a round iron plate for cooking things on
(also called a *girdle*).
[from old French *gredil* = gridiron]

gridiron *noun* (*plural* **gridirons**)
a framework of bars for cooking on.
[from *griddle*]

grid reference *noun* (*plural* **grid
references**)
a set of numbers that allows you to
describe the exact position of something on
a map.

grief *noun*
deep sorrow, especially at a person's death.
come to grief suffer a disaster.
[same origin as *grieve*]

grievance *noun* (*plural* **grievances**)
something that people are discontented
about. [old French, = injury or hardship]

grieve *verb* (**grieves**, **grieving**, **grieved**)
1 feel deep sorrow, especially at a person's
death. 2 make a person feel very sad.
[from old French *grever* = to burden;
related to *grave*²]

grievous (*say* **gree**-vus) *adjective*
1 causing grief. 2 serious.
grievously *adverb*

griffin *noun* (*plural* **griffins**)
a creature in fables, with an eagle's head
and wings on a lion's body.
[from old French]

grill *noun* (*plural* **grills**)
1 a heated element on a cooker, for sending
heat downwards. 2 food cooked under this.
3 a grille.
grill *verb* (**grills**, **grilling**, **grilled**)
1 cook under a grill. 2 question closely and
severely, *The police grilled him for an hour*.
[same origin as *griddle*]

grille *noun* (*plural* **grilles**)
a metal grating covering a window or
similar opening. [from French]

grim *adjective* (**grimmer**, **grimmest**)
1 stern or severe. 2 unpleasant or
unattractive, *a grim prospect*. **grimly**
adverb, **grimness** *noun* [from Old English]

grimace (*say* grim-**ayss** or **grim**-as) *noun*
(*plural* **grimaces**)
a twisted expression on the face made in
pain or disgust.
grimace *verb* (**grimaces**, **grimacing**,
grimaced)
make a grimace.
[from Spanish *grima* = fright]

grime *noun*
dirt in a layer on a surface or on the skin.
grimy *adjective*
[from old German or old Dutch]

grin *noun* (*plural* **grins**)
a broad smile showing your teeth.
grin *verb* (**grins**, **grinning**, **grinned**)
smile broadly showing your teeth.
[from Old English]

grind *verb* (**grinds**, **grinding**, **ground**)
1 crush something into tiny pieces or
powder. 2 sharpen or smooth something by
rubbing it on a rough surface. 3 rub
harshly together, *He ground his teeth in*

fury. **4** move with a harsh grating noise, *The bus ground to a halt.* **grinder** *noun*
[from Old English]

grindstone *noun* (*plural* **grindstones**)
a thick round rough revolving stone for sharpening or grinding things.

grip *verb* (**grips, gripping, gripped**)
1 hold something firmly. **2** hold a person's attention, *The opening chapter really gripped me.*
grip *noun* (*plural* **grips**)
1 a firm hold. **2** a handle, especially on a sports racket, bat, etc. **3** (*American*) a travelling bag. **4** control or power, *The country is in the grip of lottery fever.*
get to grips with begin to deal with successfully.
[from Old English]

gripe *verb* (**gripes, griping, griped**)
(*informal*)
grumble or complain.
gripe *noun* (*plural* **gripes**)
a complaint. [from Old English]

grisly *adjective* (**grislier, grisliest**)
causing horror or disgust; gruesome.
[from Old English]

grist *noun*
corn for grinding.
grist to the mill experience or knowledge that you can make use of.
[from Old English]

gristle *noun*
tough rubbery tissue in meat. **gristly** *adjective* [from Old English]

grit *noun*
1 tiny pieces of stone or sand. **2** courage and endurance.
gritty *adjective*, **grittiness** *noun*
grit *verb* (**grits, gritting, gritted**)
1 spread a road or path with grit. **2** clench your teeth when in pain or trouble.
[from Old English]

grizzle *verb* (**grizzles, grizzling, grizzled**)
whimper or whine. [origin unknown]

grizzled *adjective*
streaked with grey hairs.
[from old French *grisel* = grey]

grizzly *adjective*
grey-haired.

grizzly bear *noun* (*plural* **grizzly bears**)
a large fierce bear of North America.
[from *grizzled* (the bear has brown fur with white-tipped hairs)]

groan *verb* (**groans, groaning, groaned**)
1 make a long deep sound in pain, distress, or disapproval. **2** creak loudly under a heavy load. **groan** *noun*, **groaner** *noun*
[from Old English]

grocer *noun* (*plural* **grocers**)
a person who keeps a shop that sells food and household goods.
[originally = wholesaler; from Latin *grossus* = gross (because a wholesaler buys goods *in the gross* = in large quantities)]

groceries *plural noun*
goods sold by a grocer.

grocery *noun* (*plural* **groceries**)
a grocer's shop.

grog *noun*
a drink of alcoholic spirits, usually rum, mixed with water, formerly given to sailors in the Royal Navy.
[from *Old Grog*, the nickname of Admiral Vernon, who ordered that sailors should be issued with grog instead of neat rum]

groggy *adjective* (**groggier, groggiest**)
dizzy and unsteady, especially after illness.
groggily *adverb*, **grogginess** *noun*
[originally = drunk; from *grog*]

groin *noun*
the hollow between your thigh and the trunk of the body. [origin unknown]

groom *noun* (*plural* **grooms**)
1 a person whose job is to look after horses. **2** a bridegroom.
groom *verb* (**grooms, grooming, groomed**)
1 clean and brush a horse or other animal. **2** make something neat and trim. **3** train a person for a certain job or position, *Evans is being groomed for the captaincy.*
[origin unknown]

groove *noun* (*plural* **grooves**)
a long narrow furrow or channel cut in the surface of something. **grooved** *adjective*
[from old Dutch *groeve* = furrow or ditch]

grope *verb* (gropes, groping, groped)
feel about for something you cannot see.
[from Old English]

gross (*say* grohss) *adjective*
1 fat and ugly. 2 having bad manners;
vulgar. 3 very obvious or shocking,
gross stupidity. 4 total; without anything
being deducted, *our gross income.*
(Compare *net²*.)
grossly *adverb*, **grossness** *noun*

gross *noun* (*plural* gross)
twelve dozen (144) of something, *ten gross
= 1440.* [from Latin]

grotesque (*say* groh-tesk) *adjective*
fantastically ugly or very strangely shaped.
grotesquely *adverb*, **grotesqueness** *noun*
[via French from Italian]

grotto *noun* (*plural* grottoes)
1 an attractive cave. 2 an artificial cave,
especially one that is brightly decorated.
[from Italian; related to *crypt*]

ground¹ *past tense* of **grind**.

ground² *noun* (*plural* grounds)
1 the solid surface of the earth. 2 a sports
field.

ground *verb* (grounds, grounding,
grounded)
1 prevent a plane from flying, *All aircraft
are grounded because of the fog.* 2 give a
good basic training, *Ground them in the
rules of spelling.* 3 base, *This theory is
grounded on reliable evidence.*
[from Old English]

ground control *noun*
the people and machinery that control and
monitor an aircraft, spacecraft, etc. from
the ground.

grounding *noun*
basic training.

groundless *adjective*
without reason, *Your fears are groundless.*

grounds *plural noun*
1 the gardens of a large house. 2 solid
particles that sink to the bottom, *coffee
grounds.* 3 reasons, *There are grounds for
suspicion.*

groundsheet *noun* (*plural* groundsheets)
a piece of waterproof material for
spreading on the ground, especially in a
tent.

groundsman *noun* (*plural* groundsmen)
a person whose job is to look after a sports
ground.

groundwork *noun*
work that lays the basis for something.

group *noun* (*plural* groups)
1 a number of people, animals, or things
that come together or belong together in
some way. 2 a band of musicians.

group *verb* (groups, grouping, grouped)
put together or come together in a group or
groups.
[via French and Italian from Germanic]

grouse¹ *noun* (*plural* grouse)
a bird with feathered feet, hunted as game.
[origin unknown]

grouse² *verb* (grouses, grousing, groused)
(*informal*)
grumble or complain. **grouse** *noun*, **grouser**
noun [origin unknown]

grove *noun* (*plural* groves)
a group of trees; a small wood.
[from Old English]

grovel *verb* (grovels, grovelling, grovelled)
1 crawl on the ground, especially in a show
of fear or humility. 2 act in an excessively
humble way, for example by apologizing a
lot. **groveller** *noun*
[from Old Norse *a grufu* = face downwards]

grow *verb* (grows, growing, grew, grown)
1 become bigger or greater. 2 develop.
3 cultivate; plant and look after, *She grows
roses.* 4 become, *He grew rich.* **grower** *noun*
[from Old English]

growl *verb* (growls, growling, growled)
make a deep angry sound in the throat.
growl *noun* [imitating the sound]

grown-up *noun* (*plural* grown-ups)
an adult person.
grown-up *adjective* like or suitable for an
adult.

growth *noun* (*plural* **growths**)
1 growing or developing. 2 something that has grown. 3 a lump that has grown on or inside a person's body; a tumour.

grub *noun* (*plural* **grubs**)
1 a tiny worm-like creature that will become an insect; a larva. 2 (*slang*) food.
grub *verb* (**grubs, grubbing, grubbed**)
1 dig up by the roots. 2 turn things over or move them about while looking for something; rummage. [origin unknown]

grubby *adjective* (**grubbier, grubbiest**)
rather dirty. **grubbiness** *noun*

grudge *noun* (*plural* **grudges**)
a feeling of resentment or ill will, *She isn't the sort of person who bears a grudge.*
grudge *verb* (**grudges, grudging, grudged**)
resent having to give or allow something. [from old French *grouchier* = grumble]

gruelling *adjective*
exhausting. [from old French]

gruesome *adjective*
horrible or disgusting.
[from an old word *grue* = to shudder]

gruff *adjective*
having a rough unfriendly voice or manner. **gruffly** *adverb*, **gruffness** *noun*
[from Dutch *grof* = coarse or rude]

grumble *verb* (**grumbles, grumbling, grumbled**)
complain in a bad-tempered way. **grumble** *noun*, **grumbler** *noun* [origin unknown]

grumpy *adjective*
bad-tempered. **grumpily** *adverb*, **grumpiness** *noun* [imitating the muttering noises made by a grumpy person]

grunt *verb* (**grunts, grunting, grunted**)
1 make a pig's gruff snort. 2 speak or say gruffly. **grunt** *noun* [from Old English *grunnettan*, imitating the sound]

guarantee *noun* (*plural* **guarantees**)
a formal promise to do something or to repair an object if it breaks or goes wrong.
guarantee *verb* (**guarantees, guaranteeing, guaranteed**)
give a guarantee; promise. **guarantor** *noun*
[from Spanish]

guard *verb* (**guards, guarding, guarded**)
1 protect; keep safe. 2 watch over and prevent from escaping.
guard *noun* (*plural* **guards**)
1 guarding; protection, *Keep the prisoners under close guard.* 2 someone who guards a person or place. 3 a group of soldiers or police officers etc. acting as a guard. 4 a railway official in charge of a train. 5 a protecting device, *a fireguard.* [via old French from Germanic; related to *ward*]

guardian *noun* (*plural* **guardians**)
1 someone who guards. 2 a person who is legally in charge of a child whose parents cannot look after him or her. **guardianship** *noun* [via old French from Germanic; related to *warden*]

guerrilla (*say* ger-il-a) *noun* (*plural* **guerrillas**)
a member of a small unofficial army who fights by making surprise attacks.
[Spanish, = little war]

USAGE: Do not confuse with *gorilla.*

guess *noun* (*plural* **guesses**)
an opinion or answer that you give without making careful calculations or without certain knowledge.
guess *verb* (**guesses, guessing, guessed**)
make a guess. **guesser** *noun*
[probably from old German or old Dutch]

guest *noun* (*plural* **guests**)
1 a person who is invited to visit or stay at another's house. 2 a person staying at a hotel. 3 a person who takes part in another's show as a visiting performer.
[from Old Norse]

guffaw *verb* (**guffaws, guffawing, guffawed**)
laugh noisily. **guffaw** *noun*
[imitating the sound]

guidance *noun*
1 guiding. 2 advising or advice on problems.

Guide *noun* (*plural* **Guides**)
a member of the Girl Guides Association, an organization for girls.

guide *noun* (*plural* **guides**)
1 a person who shows others the way or

points out interesting sights. **2** a book giving information about a place or subject.

guide *verb* (**guides, guiding, guided**)
show someone the way or how to do something. [via old French from Germanic; related to *wit*]

guidebook *noun* (*plural* **guidebooks**)
a book of information about a place, for travellers or visitors.

guide dog *noun* (*plural* **guide dogs**)
a dog trained to lead a blind person.

guidelines *plural noun*
statements that give general advice about how something should be done.

guild (*say* gild) *noun* (*plural* **guilds**)
a society of people with similar skills or interests. [from old German or old Dutch]

guilder (*say* gild-er) *noun* (*plural* **guilders**)
a Dutch coin. [from Dutch]

guile (rhymes with *mile*) *noun*
craftiness. [via old French from Old Norse]

guillotine (*say* gil-ot-een) *noun* (*plural* **guillotines**)
1 a machine with a heavy blade for beheading criminals, used in France. **2** a machine with a long blade for cutting paper or metal.
guillotine *verb* (**guillotines, guillotining, guillotined**)
cut with a guillotine.
[named after Dr Guillotin, who suggested its use in France in 1789]

guilt *noun*
1 the fact that you have committed an offence. **2** a feeling that you are to blame for something that has happened.
[from Old English *gylt* = a crime or sin]

guilty *adjective*
1 having done wrong. **2** feeling or showing guilt. **guiltily** *adverb*

guinea (*say* gin-ee) *noun* (*plural* **guineas**)
1 a former British gold coin worth 21 shillings (£1.05). **2** this amount of money. [originally = a coin used by British traders in Africa: named after *Guinea* in west Africa]

guinea pig *noun* (*plural* **guinea pigs**)
1 a small furry animal without a tail. **2** a person who is used as the subject of an experiment.
[from *Guinea* in west Africa, probably by mistake for Guiana, in South America, where the guinea pig comes from]

guise (*say* guys) *noun* (*plural* **guises**)
an outward disguise or pretence. [via old French from Germanic; related to *wise*]

guitar *noun* (*plural* **guitars**)
a musical instrument played by plucking its strings. **guitarist** *noun*
[from Greek *kithara*, a small harp]

gulf *noun* (*plural* **gulfs**)
1 a large area of the sea that is partly surrounded by land. **2** a wide gap; a great difference. [from Greek]

gull *noun* (*plural* **gulls**)
a seagull. [a Celtic word]

gullet *noun* (*plural* **gullets**)
the tube from the throat to the stomach. [from old French *gole* = throat]

gullible *adjective*
easily deceived.
[from an old word *gull* = fool or deceive]

gully *noun* (*plural* **gullies**)
a narrow channel that carries water. [same origin as *gullet*]

gulp *verb* (**gulps, gulping, gulped**)
1 swallow hastily or greedily. **2** make a loud swallowing noise, especially because of fear.
gulp *noun* (*plural* **gulps**)
1 the act of gulping. **2** a large mouthful of liquid. [imitating the sound]

gum¹ *noun* (*plural* **gums**)
the firm flesh in which your teeth are rooted. [from Old English]

gum² *noun* (*plural* **gums**)
1 a sticky substance produced by some trees and shrubs, used as glue. **2** a sweet made with gum or gelatine, *a fruit gum*. **3** chewing gum. **4** a gum tree.
gummy *adjective*
gum *verb* (**gums, gumming, gummed**)
cover or stick something with gum. [via old French, Latin, and Greek from Egyptian]

gumption *noun* (*informal*)
common sense. [origin unknown]

gum tree *noun* (*plural* **gum trees**)
a eucalyptus.

gun *noun* (*plural* **guns**)
1 a weapon that fires shells or bullets from
a metal tube. **2** a starting pistol. **3** a device
that forces a substance out of a tube, *a
grease gun*. **gunfire** *noun*, **gunshot** *noun*
gun *verb* (**guns, gunning, gunned**)
gun down shoot someone with a gun.
[probably from the Swedish girl's name
Gunnhildr, from *gunnr* = war]

gunboat *noun* (*plural* **gunboats**)
a small warship.

gunman *noun* (*plural* **gunmen**)
a criminal with a gun.

gunner *noun* (*plural* **gunners**)
a person in the armed forces who operates
a large gun.

gunnery *noun*
the making or use of guns.

gunpowder *noun*
an explosive made from a powdered
mixture of potassium nitrate, charcoal,
and sulphur.

gunwale (*say* **gun**-al) *noun* (*plural*
gunwales)
the upper edge of a small ship's or boat's
side. [from *gun* + *wale* = a ridge (because it
was formerly used to support guns)]

gurdwara *noun* (*plural* **gurdwaras**)
a Sikh temple. [from Sanskrit *guru*
= teacher + *dvara* = door]

gurgle *verb* (**gurgles, gurgling, gurgled**)
make a low bubbling sound. **gurgle** *noun*
[imitating the sound]

guru *noun* (*plural* **gurus**)
1 a Hindu religious leader. **2** an influential
teacher; a mentor. [from Sanskrit]

gush *verb* (**gushes, gushing, gushed**)
1 flow suddenly or quickly. **2** talk too
enthusiastically or emotionally. **gush** *noun*
[imitating the sound]

gust *noun* (*plural* **gusts**)
a sudden rush of wind, rain, or smoke.
gusty *adjective*, **gustily** *adverb*
gust *verb* (**gusts, gusting, gusted**)
blow in gusts. [from Old Norse]

gusto *noun*
great enjoyment; zest.
[Italian, from Latin *gustus* = a taste]

gut *noun* (*plural* **guts**)
the lower part of the digestive system; the
intestine.
gut *verb* (**guts, gutting, gutted**)
1 remove the guts from a dead fish or other
animal. **2** remove or destroy the inside of
something, *The fire gutted the factory*.
[from Old English]

guts *plural noun*
1 the digestive system; the inside parts of a
person or thing. **2** (*informal*) courage.

gutted *adjective* (*informal*)
extremely disappointed or upset.

gutter *noun* (*plural* **gutters**)
a long narrow channel at the side of a
street, or along the edge of a roof, for
carrying away rainwater.
gutter *verb* (**gutters, guttering, guttered**)
a candle gutters when it burns unsteadily
so that melted wax runs down.
[from Latin *gutta* = a drop]

guttersnipe *noun* (*plural* **guttersnipes**)
a poor child who plays in the streets in a
slum. [from *gutter* + *snipe*, which used to be
used as an insult]

guttural (*say* **gut**-er-al) *adjective*
throaty and harsh-sounding, *a guttural
voice*. [from Latin *guttur* = throat]

guy¹ *noun* (*plural* **guys**)
1 a figure representing Guy Fawkes, burnt
on 5 November in memory of the
Gunpowder Plot which planned to blow up
Parliament on that day in 1605.
2 (*informal*) a man.

guy² or **guy-rope** *noun* (*plural* **guys, guy-
ropes**)
a rope used to hold something in place,
especially a tent.
[probably from old German]

guzzle *verb* (**guzzles, guzzling, guzzled**)
eat or drink greedily. **guzzler** *noun*
[from old French]

gym (*say* jim) *noun* (*plural* **gyms**)
(*informal*)
1 a gymnasium. **2** gymnastics.

gymkhana (*say* jim-kah-na) *noun* (*plural*
gymkhanas)
a series of horse-riding contests and other
sports events. [from Urdu]

gymnasium *noun* (*plural* **gymnasia,
gymnasiums**)
a place equipped for gymnastics.
[from Greek *gymnos* = naked (because
Greek men exercised naked)]

gymnast *noun* (*plural* **gymnasts**)
an expert in gymnastics.

gymnastics *plural noun*
exercises performed to develop the muscles
or to show the performer's agility.
gymnastic *adjective*

gynaecology (*say* guy-ni-kol-o-ji) *noun*
the branch of medicine concerned with
the diseases and disorders of women's
bodies, especially with the reproductive
system.
[from Greek *gynaikos* = of a woman,
+ *-ology*]

gypsy *noun* (*plural* **gypsies**)
a member of a people who live in caravans
and wander from place to place, especially
a Romany.
[from *Egyptian*, because gypsies were
originally thought to have come from
Egypt]

gyrate (*say* jy-rayt) *verb* (**gyrates, gyrating,
gyrated**)
revolve; move in circles or spirals.
gyration *noun*
[from Greek *gyros* = a ring or circle]

gyroscope (*say* jy-ro-skohp) *noun* (*plural*
gyroscopes)
a device that keeps steady because of a
heavy wheel spinning inside it.
[same origin as *gyrate*]

Hh

ha *interjection*
an exclamation of triumph or surprise.

haberdashery *noun*
small articles used in sewing, e.g. ribbons,
buttons, thread. [origin unknown]

habit *noun* (*plural* **habits**)
1 something that you do without thinking
because you have done it so often; a settled
way of behaving. **2** the long dress worn by
a monk or nun. **habitual** *adjective*, **habitually**
adverb [from Latin]

habitat *noun* (*plural* **habitats**)
where an animal or plant lives naturally.
[Latin, literally = inhabits]

habitation *noun* (*plural* **habitations**)
1 a dwelling. **2** inhabiting a place.
[from Latin *habitare* = inhabit]

hack¹ *verb* (**hacks, hacking, hacked**)
1 chop or cut roughly. **2** (*informal*) break
into a computer system. [from Old English]

hack² *noun* (*plural* **hacks**)
a horse for ordinary riding. [from
Hackney, in London (because many horses
used to be kept on Hackney Marshes)]

hacker *noun* (*plural* **hackers**)
a person who breaks into a computer
system.

hackles *plural noun*
with his or **her hackles up** angry and ready
to fight.
[*hackles* are the long feathers on some
birds' necks]

hackneyed *adjective*
used so often that it is no longer
interesting. [same origin as *hack²*: hack or
hackney was used to mean a hired horse,
one that everyone used]

hacksaw *noun* (*plural* **hacksaws**)
a saw for cutting metal.

haddock *noun* (*plural* **haddock**)
a sea fish like cod but smaller, used as food.
[from old French]

hadn't (*mainly spoken*)
had not.

haemoglobin (*say* heem-a-**gloh**-bin) *noun*
the red substance that carries oxygen in
the blood. [from Greek *haima* = blood
+ *globule* (because of the shape of
haemoglobin cells)]

haemophilia (*say* heem-o-fil-ee-a) *noun*
a disease that causes people to bleed
dangerously from even a slight cut.
haemophiliac *noun* [from Greek *haima*
= blood + *philia* = loving]

haemorrhage (*say* hem-er-ij) *noun*
bleeding, especially inside a person's body.
[from Greek *haima* = blood + *rhegnunai*
= burst]

hag *noun* (*plural* hags)
an ugly old woman. [from Old English]

haggard *adjective*
looking ill or very tired. [from old French]

haggis *noun* (*plural* haggises)
a Scottish food made from sheep's offal.
[probably from Old Norse]

haggle *verb* (haggles, haggling, haggled)
argue about a price or agreement.
[from Old Norse]

ha ha *interjection*
laughter.

haiku (*say* hy-koo) *noun* (*plural* haiku)
a Japanese form of poem, written in three
lines. [from Japanese *haikai no ku* = light
or comic verse]

hail¹ *noun*
frozen drops of rain. **hail** *verb*, **hailstone**
noun, **hailstorm** *noun* [from Old English]

hail² *interjection*
an exclamation of greeting.
hail *verb* (hails, hailing, hailed)
call out to somebody.
hail from come from, *He hails from Ireland.*
[from Old Norse]

hair *noun* (*plural* hairs)
1 a soft covering that grows on the heads
and bodies of people and animals. **2** one of
the threads that make up this covering.
hairbrush *noun*, **haircut** *noun*

keep your hair on (*informal*) do not lose
your temper.
split hairs make petty or unimportant
distinctions of meaning. **hair-splitting** *noun*
[from Old English]

hairdresser *noun* (*plural* hairdressers)
a person whose job is to cut and arrange
people's hair.

hairpin *noun* (*plural* hairpins)
a U-shaped pin for keeping hair in place.

hairpin bend *noun* (*plural* hairpin bends)
a sharp bend in a road.

hair-raising *adjective*
terrifying.

hairstyle *noun* (*plural* hairstyles)
a particular way of arranging your hair.

hairy *adjective*
1 with a lot of hair. **2** (*informal*) dangerous
or risky.

haj *noun*
the annual Muslim pilgrimage to Mecca.
[Arabic, = pilgrimage]

hake *noun* (*plural* hake)
a sea fish used as food. [from Old English]

halal *noun*
meat prepared according to Muslim law.
[Arabic, = according to religious law]

halcyon (*say* **hal**-see-on) *adjective*
happy and peaceful, *halcyon days.*
[from Greek *alkyon* = a bird which was
once believed to build its nest on the sea,
which magically stayed calm]

hale *adjective*
strong and healthy, *hale and hearty.*
[from Old English *hal* = whole]

half *noun* (*plural* halves)
one of the two equal parts or amounts into
which something is or can be divided.
half *adverb*
partly; not completely, *This meat is only
half cooked.*
not half (*slang*) extremely, *Was she cross?
Not half!*
[from Old English]

half-baked *adjective* (*informal*)
not well planned or thought out.

half-brother *noun* (*plural* **half-brothers**)
a brother to whom you are related by one parent but not by both parents.

half-hearted *adjective*
not very enthusiastic. **half-heartedly** *adverb*

half-life *noun* (*plural* **half-lives**)
the time taken for the radioactivity of a substance to fall to half its original value.

halfpenny (*say* **hayp**-nee) *noun* (*plural* **halfpennies** for separate coins, **halfpence** for a sum of money)
a former coin worth half a penny.

half-sister *noun* (*plural* **half-sisters**)
a sister to whom you are related by one parent but not by both parents.

half-term *noun* (*plural* **half-terms**)
a short holiday in the middle of a term.

half-time *noun*
the point or interval halfway through a game.

halfway *adjective* & *adverb*
between two others and equally distant from each.

half-witted *adjective*
stupid. **half-wit** *noun*

halibut *noun* (*plural* **halibut**)
a large flat fish used as food.
[from *holy* + *butt*, a dialect word = flatfish (because it was eaten on Christian holy days, when meat was forbidden)]

hall *noun* (*plural* **halls**)
1 a space or passage into which the front entrance of a house etc. opens. 2 a very large room or building used for meetings, concerts, etc. [from Old English]

hallelujah *interjection* & *noun* (*plural* **hallelujahs**)
alleluia.

hallmark *noun* (*plural* **hallmarks**)
an official mark made on gold, silver, and platinum to show its quality.
[because the first such marks were made at the Goldsmiths' Hall in London]

hallo *interjection*
hello. [origin unknown]

hallowed *adjective*
honoured as being holy. [from Old English]

Hallowe'en *noun*
31 October, traditionally a time when ghosts and witches are believed to appear. [from *All Hallow Even*, the evening before the Christian festival honouring all the *hallows* = saints]

hallucination *noun* (*plural* **hallucinations**)
something you think you can see or hear that is not really there. [from Latin *alucinari* = wander in your mind]

halo *noun* (*plural* **haloes**)
a circle of light round something, especially round the head of a saint etc. in paintings. [from Greek]

halt *verb* (**halts, halting, halted**)
stop.
halt *noun* (*plural* **halts**)
1 a stop, *Work came to a halt.* 2 a small stopping place on a railway.
[from German]

halter *noun* (*plural* **halters**)
a rope or strap put round a horse's head so that it can be led or fastened to something. [from Old English]

halve *verb* (**halves, halving, halved**)
1 divide something into halves. 2 reduce something to half its size. [from *half*]

ham *noun* (*plural* **hams**)
1 meat from a pig's leg. 2 (*slang*) an actor who overacts. 3 (*informal*) someone who operates a radio to send and receive messages as a hobby. [from Old English]

hamburger *noun* (*plural* **hamburgers**)
a flat round cake of minced beef served fried, often in a bread roll. [named after Hamburg in Germany (not after *ham*)]

hamlet *noun* (*plural* **hamlets**)
a small village.
[via old French from old German]

hammer *noun* (*plural* **hammers**)
a tool with a heavy metal head used for driving nails in, breaking things, etc.

hammer *verb* (hammers, hammering, hammered)
1 hit something with a hammer. 2 strike loudly. 3 (*informal*) defeat.
[from Old English]

hammock *noun* (*plural* hammocks)
a bed made of a strong net or piece of cloth hung by cords. [via Spanish from Taino (a South American language)]

hamper¹ *noun* (*plural* hampers)
a large box-shaped basket with a lid.
[from old French]

hamper² *verb* (hampers, hampering, hampered)
hinder; prevent from moving or working freely. [origin unknown]

hamster *noun* (*plural* hamsters)
a small furry animal with cheek pouches for carrying grain. [from German]

hand *noun* (*plural* hands)
1 the end part of the arm below the wrist. 2 a pointer on a clock or dial. 3 a worker; a member of a ship's crew, *All hands on deck!* 4 the cards held by one player in a card game. 5 side or direction, *on the other hand.* 6 help or aid, *Give me a hand with these boxes.*
at hand near.
by hand using your hand or hands.
give or **receive a big hand** applaud or be applauded.
hands down winning easily.
in good hands in the care or control of someone who can be trusted.
in hand in your possession; being dealt with.
on hand available.
out of hand out of control.

hand *verb* (hands, handing, handed)
give or pass something to somebody, *Hand it over.*
hand down pass something from one generation to another.
[from Old English]

handbag *noun* (*plural* handbags)
a small bag for holding a purse and personal articles.

handbook *noun* (*plural* handbooks)
a small book that gives useful facts about something.

handcuff *noun* (*plural* handcuffs)
one of a pair of metal rings linked by a chain, for fastening wrists together.
handcuff *verb* (handcuffs, handcuffing, handcuffed)
fasten with handcuffs.

handful *noun* (*plural* handfuls)
1 as much as can be carried in one hand. 2 a few people or things. 3 (*informal*) a troublesome person or task.

handicap *noun* (*plural* handicaps)
1 a disadvantage. 2 a physical or mental disability. **handicapped** *adjective* [from *hand in cap* (from an old game in which forfeit money was deposited in a cap)]

handicraft *noun* (*plural* handicrafts)
artistic work done with the hands, e.g. woodwork, needlework.

handily *adverb*
in a handy way.

handiwork *noun*
1 something made by hand. 2 something done, *Is this mess your handiwork?*

handkerchief *noun* (*plural* handkerchiefs)
a small square of cloth for wiping the nose or face. [from *hand* + *kerchief*]

handle *noun* (*plural* handles)
the part of a thing by which it is carried or controlled.
handle *verb* (handles, handling, handled)
1 touch or feel something with your hands. 2 deal with; manage, *Will you handle the catering?* **handler** *noun* [from Old English]

handlebar *noun* or **handlebars** *plural noun*
the bar, with a handle at each end, that steers a bicycle or motorcycle etc.

handout *noun* (*plural* handouts)
1 money etc. given to a needy person. 2 a sheet of information given out in a lesson, lecture, etc.

handrail *noun* (*plural* handrails)
a narrow rail for people to hold as a support.

handshake *noun* (*plural* handshakes)
shaking hands with someone as a greeting etc.

handsome *adjective*
1 good-looking. 2 generous.
handsomely *adverb* [originally = easy to
handle or use: from *hand* + *-some*]

handstand *noun* (*plural* **handstands**)
balancing on your hands with your feet in
the air.

handwriting *noun*
writing done by hand.
handwritten *adjective*

handy *adjective* (**handier, handiest**)
1 convenient or useful. 2 good at using the
hands. **handily** *adverb*, **handiness** *noun*

handyman *noun* (*plural* **handymen**)
a person who does household repairs or
odd jobs.

hang *verb* (**hangs, hanging, hung**)
1 fix the top or side of something to a hook
or nail etc.; be supported in this way.
2 stick wallpaper to a wall. 3 decorate
with drapery or hanging ornaments etc.,
The tree was hung with lights. 4 droop or
lean, *People hung over the gate.* 5 (with *past
tense & past participle* **hanged**) execute
someone by hanging them from a rope that
tightens round the neck, *He was hanged in
1950.*
hang about 1 loiter. 2 not go away.
hang back hesitate to go forward or to do
something.
hang on 1 hold tightly. 2 (*informal*) wait.
hang up end a telephone conversation by
putting back the receiver.
hang *noun*
get the hang of (*informal*) learn how to do
or use something.
[from Old English]

hangar *noun* (*plural* **hangars**)
a large shed where aircraft are kept.
[French, originally = a shed]

hanger *noun* (*plural* **hangers**)
a device on which to hang things, *a coat-
hanger*.

hang-glider *noun* (*plural* **hang-gliders**)
a framework in which a person can glide
through the air. **hang-gliding** *noun*

hangman *noun* (*plural* **hangmen**)
a man whose job it is to hang people
condemned to death.

hangover *noun* (*plural* **hangovers**)
an unpleasant feeling after drinking too
much alcohol.

hank *noun* (*plural* **hanks**)
a coil or piece of wool, thread, etc.
[from Old Norse]

hanker *verb* (**hankers, hankering, hankered**)
feel a longing for something.
[origin unknown]

hanky *noun* (*plural* **hankies**) (*informal*)
a handkerchief.

Hanukkah (*say* hah-noo-ka) *noun*
the eight-day Jewish festival of lights
beginning in December.
[Hebrew, = consecration]

haphazard *adjective*
done or chosen at random, not by planning.
[from an old word *hap* = luck, + *hazard*]

hapless *adjective*
having no luck.
[from an old word *hap* = luck, + *-less*]

happen *verb* (**happens, happening,
happened**)
1 take place; occur. 2 do something by
chance, *I happened to see him.*
[from an old word *hap* = luck]

happening *noun* (*plural* **happenings**)
something that happens; an event.

happy *adjective* (**happier, happiest**)
1 pleased or contented. 2 fortunate, *a
happy coincidence.* **happily** *adverb*,
happiness *noun* [same origin as *happen*]

hara-kiri *noun*
a form of suicide formerly used by
Japanese officers when in disgrace. [from
Japanese *hara* = belly + *kiri* = cutting]

harangue (*say* ha-rang) *verb* (**harangues,
haranguing, harangued**)
make a long speech to somebody. **harangue**
noun [from Latin]

harass (*say* ha-ras) *verb* (**harasses,
harassing, harassed**)
trouble or annoy somebody often.
harassment (*say* ha-ras-ment) *noun*
[from French *harer* = set a dog on
someone]

harbour *noun* (*plural* harbours)
a place where ships can shelter or unload.
harbour *verb* (**harbours, harbouring, harboured**)
1 give shelter to somebody, *harbouring a criminal*. **2** keep in your mind, *harbouring a grudge*. [from Old English]

hard *adjective*
1 firm or solid; not soft. **2** difficult, *hard sums*. **3** severe or stern. **4** causing suffering, *hard luck*. **5** using great effort, *a hard worker*. **6** hard drugs are strong and addictive ones. **hardness** *noun*
hard of hearing slightly deaf.
hard up (*informal*) short of money.
hard *adverb*
1 so as to be hard, *The ground froze hard*.
2 with great effort; intensively, *We worked hard. It is raining hard*. **3** with difficulty, *hard-earned*. [from Old English]

hardboard *noun*
stiff board made of compressed wood pulp.

hard disk *noun* (*plural* hard disks)
a disk fixed inside a computer, able to store large amounts of data.

harden *verb* (**hardens, hardening, hardened**)
make or become hard or hardy.
hardener *noun*

hard-hearted *adjective*
unsympathetic.

hardly *adverb*
only just; only with difficulty, *She can hardly walk*.

USAGE: It is not acceptable in standard English to use 'not' with *hardly*, as in 'she can't hardly walk'.

hardship *noun* (*plural* hardships)
difficult conditions that cause discomfort or suffering, *a life of hardship*.

hardware *noun*
1 metal implements and tools etc.; machinery. **2** the machinery of a computer as opposed to the software. (Compare *software*.)

hard water *noun*
water containing minerals that prevent soap from making much lather.

hardwood *noun* (*plural* hardwoods)
hard heavy wood from deciduous trees, e.g. oak and teak.

hardy *adjective* (**hardier, hardiest**)
able to endure cold or difficult conditions.
hardiness *noun*
[from French *hardi* = bold or daring]

hare *noun* (*plural* hares)
an animal like a rabbit but larger.
[from Old English]

harem (*say* har-eem) *noun* (*plural* harems)
the part of a Muslim palace or house where the women live; the women living there.
[from Arabic *harim* = forbidden]

hark *verb* (**harks, harking, harked**)
listen.
hark back return to an earlier subject.
[probably from Old English; *hark back* from a call telling hounds to retrace their steps to find a lost scent]

harlequin *adjective*
in mixed colours. [from *Arlecchino*, the name of a character in Italian comedies whose clothes were of several colours]

harm *verb* (**harms, harming, harmed**)
damage or injure.
harm *noun*
damage or injury. **harmful** *adjective*,
harmless *adjective* [from Old English]

harmonic *adjective*
to do with harmony in music.

harmonica *noun* (*plural* harmonicas)
a mouth organ. [from Latin *harmonicus* = to do with melody]

harmonious *adjective*
1 combining together in a pleasant and attractive way. **2** peaceful and friendly.

harmonize *verb* (**harmonizes, harmonizing, harmonized**)
combine together in a pleasant and attractive way. **harmonization** *noun*

harmony *noun* (*plural* harmonies)
1 a pleasant combination, especially of musical notes. **2** being friendly to each other and not quarrelling.
[from Latin *harmonia* = agreement]

harness *noun* (*plural* harnesses)
the straps put round a horse's head and
neck for controlling it.
harness *verb* (harnesses, harnessing,
harnessed)
1 put a harness on a horse. **2** control and
use something, *Could we harness the power
of the wind?* [via French from Old Norse]

harp *noun* (*plural* harps)
a musical instrument made of strings
stretched across a frame and plucked by
the fingers. **harpist** *noun*
harp *verb* (harps, harping, harped)
keep on talking about something in a
tiresome way, *He is always harping on his
misfortunes.* [from Old English]

harpoon *noun* (*plural* harpoons)
a spear attached to a rope, used for
catching whales etc. **harpoon** *verb*
[from French]

harpsichord *noun* (*plural* harpsichords)
an instrument like a piano but with strings
that are plucked (not struck) by a
mechanism. [from Latin *harpa* = harp
+ *chorda* = string]

harrow *noun* (*plural* harrows)
a heavy device pulled over the ground to
break up the soil. [from Old Norse]

harrowing *adjective*
very upsetting or distressing.
[as if a harrow had been pulled over you]

harry *verb* (harries, harrying, harried)
harass or worry. [from Old English]

harsh *adjective*
1 rough and unpleasant. **2** severe or cruel.
harshly *adverb*, **harshness** *noun*
[from old German *horsch* = rough or hairy]

hart *noun* (*plural* harts)
a male deer. (Compare *hind*².)
[from Old English]

harvest *noun* (*plural* harvests)
1 the time when farmers gather in the
corn, fruit, or vegetables that they have
grown. **2** the crop that is gathered in.
harvest *verb* (harvests, harvesting,
harvested)
gather in a crop; reap. **harvester** *noun*
[from Old English]

hash *noun*
a mixture of small pieces of meat and
vegetables, usually fried.
make a hash of (*informal*) make a mess of
something; bungle.
[from French *hacher* = cut up small]

hashish *noun*
a drug made from hemp. [from Arabic]

hasn't (*mainly spoken*)
has not.

hassle *noun* (*informal*)
something that is difficult or troublesome.
[origin unknown]

hassock *noun* (*plural* hassocks)
a small thick cushion for kneeling on in
church. [origin unknown]

haste *noun*
a hurry.
make haste act quickly.
[via old French from Germanic]

hasten *verb* (hastens, hastening, hastened)
hurry.

hasty *adjective*
hurried; done too quickly. **hastily** *adverb*,
hastiness *noun*

hat *noun* (*plural* hats)
a shaped covering for the head.
keep it under your hat keep it secret.
[from Old English]

hatch¹ *noun* (*plural* hatches)
an opening in a floor, wall, or door, usually
with a covering. [from Old English]

hatch² *verb* (hatches, hatching, hatched)
1 break out of an egg. **2** keep an egg warm
until a baby bird comes out. **3** plan, *They
hatched a plot.* [origin unknown]

hatchback *noun* (*plural* hatchbacks)
a car with a sloping back hinged at the top.

hatchet *noun* (*plural* hatchets)
a small axe.
[via old French and Latin from Germanic]

hate *verb* (hates, hating, hated)
dislike very strongly.
hate *noun*
extreme dislike. [from Old English]

hateful *adjective*
arousing hatred.

hatred *noun*
extreme dislike.

hatter *noun* (*plural* **hatters**)
a person who makes hats.

hat-trick *noun* (*plural* **hat-tricks**)
getting three goals, wickets, victories, etc.
one after the other.

haughty *adjective*
proud of yourself and looking down on
other people. **haughtily** *adverb*, **haughtiness**
noun [from French *haut* = high]

haul *verb* (**hauls, hauling, hauled**)
pull or drag with great effort. **haulage** *noun*
haul *noun* (*plural* **hauls**)
1 hauling. 2 the amount obtained by an
effort; booty, *The robbers made a good haul.*
3 a distance to be covered, *a long haul.*
[via old French from Old Norse]

haulage *noun*
1 transporting goods. 2 a charge for this.

haunch *noun* (*plural* **haunches**)
the buttock and top part of the thigh.
[via old French from Germanic]

haunt *verb* (**haunts, haunting, haunted**)
1 (of ghosts) appear often in a place or to a
person. 2 visit a place often. 3 stay in your
mind, *Memories haunt me.*
haunt *noun* (*plural* **haunts**)
a place that you often visit.
[via old French from Germanic]

have *verb* (**has, having, had**)
This word has many uses, including
1 possess or own, *We have two dogs.*
2 contain, *This tin has sweets in it.*
3 experience, *He had a shock.* 4 be obliged
to do something, *We have to go now.*
5 allow, *I won't have him bullied.* 6 receive
or accept, *Will you have a sweet?* 7 get
something done, *I'm having my watch
mended.* 8 (*slang*) cheat or deceive, *We've
been had!*
have somebody on (*informal*) fool him or
her.
have *auxiliary verb*
used to form the past tense of verbs, e.g. *He
has gone.* [from Old English]

haven *noun* (*plural* **havens**)
a refuge. [from Old Norse]

haven't (*mainly spoken*)
have not.

haversack *noun* (*plural* **haversacks**)
a strong bag carried on your back or over
your shoulder.
[from old German *Habersack* = oat-bag
(in which the German cavalry carried oats
for their horses)]

havoc *noun*
great destruction or disorder. [from old
French *havot*, an order to begin looting]

haw *noun* (*plural* **haws**)
a hawthorn berry.
[from Old English]

hawk[1] *noun* (*plural* **hawks**)
a bird of prey with very strong eyesight.
[from Old English]

hawk[2] *verb* (**hawks, hawking, hawked**)
carry goods about and try to sell them.
hawker *noun* [from Dutch]

hawthorn *noun* (*plural* **hawthorns**)
a thorny tree with small red berries (called
haws).

hay *noun*
dried grass for feeding to animals.
[from Old English]

hay fever *noun*
irritation of the nose, throat, and eyes,
caused by pollen or dust.

haystack or **hayrick** *noun* (*plural*
haystacks, hayricks)
a large neat pile of hay packed for storing.

haywire *adjective* (*informal*)
out of control.
[because wire for tying up hay bales was
often used for makeshift repairs]

hazard *noun* (*plural* **hazards**)
1 a danger or risk. 2 an obstacle.
hazardous *adjective*
[via French from Persian or Turkish
zar = dice]

haze *noun*
thin mist. [origin unknown]

hazel *noun* (*plural* hazels)
1 a bush with small nuts. 2 a light brown colour. **hazelnut** *noun* [from Old English]

hazy *adjective*
1 misty. 2 vague or uncertain.
hazily *adverb*, **haziness** *noun*

H-bomb *noun* (*plural* H-bombs)
a hydrogen bomb.

he *pronoun*
1 the male person or animal being talked about. 2 a person (male or female), *He who hesitates is lost.* [from Old English]

head *noun* (*plural* heads)
1 the part of the body containing the brains, eyes, and mouth. 2 your brains or mind; intelligence, *Use your head!* 3 a talent or ability, *She has a good head for figures.* 4 the side of a coin on which someone's head is shown. 5 a person, *It costs £2 per head.* 6 the top, *a pinhead*; the leading part of something, *at the head of the procession.* 7 the chief; the person in charge. 8 a headteacher.
come to a head reach a crisis point.
keep your head stay calm.

head *verb* (heads, heading, headed)
1 be at the top or front of something. 2 hit a ball with your head. 3 move in a particular direction, *We headed for the coast.* 4 force someone to turn by getting in front, *head him off.* [from Old English]

headache *noun* (*plural* headaches)
1 a pain in the head. 2 (*informal*) a worrying problem.

headdress *noun* (*plural* headdresses)
a covering or decoration for the head.

header *noun* (*plural* headers)
heading the ball in football.

heading *noun* (*plural* headings)
a word or words put at the top of a piece of printing or writing.

headland *noun* (*plural* headlands)
a large piece of high land that sticks out into the sea; a promontory.

headlight *noun* (*plural* headlights)
a powerful light at the front of a car, engine, etc.

headline *noun* (*plural* headlines)
a heading in a newspaper.
the headlines the main items of news.

headlong *adverb* & *adjective*
1 head first. 2 in a hasty or thoughtless way.

headmaster *noun* (*plural* headmasters)
a male headteacher.

headmistress *noun* (*plural* headmistresses)
a female headteacher.

head-on *adverb* & *adjective*
with the front parts colliding, *a head-on collision.*

headphones *plural noun*
a pair of earphones on a band that fits over the head.

headquarters *noun* or *plural noun*
the place from which an organization is controlled.

headstrong *adjective*
determined to do as you want.

headteacher *noun* (*plural* headteachers)
the person in charge of a school.

headway *noun*
make headway make progress.

heal *verb* (heals, healing, healed)
1 make or become healthy flesh again, *The wound healed.* 2 (*old use*) cure, *healing the sick.*
[from Old English]

health *noun*
1 the condition of a person's body or mind, *His health is bad.* 2 being healthy, *in sickness and in health.*
[from Old English]

health food *noun* (*plural* health foods)
food that contains only natural substances and is thought to be good for your health.

healthy *adjective* (healthier, healthiest)
1 being well; free from illness. 2 producing good health, *Fresh air is healthy.*
healthily *adverb*, **healthiness** *noun*

heap *noun* (*plural* **heaps**)
a pile, especially an untidy one.
heaps *plural noun* (*informal*) a great
amount; plenty, *There's heaps of time.*
heap *verb* (**heaps, heaping, heaped**)
1 make things into a heap. **2** put on large
amounts, *She heaped the plate with food.*
[from Old English]

hear *verb* (**hears, hearing, heard**)
1 take in sounds through the ears.
2 receive news or information etc.
hearer *noun*
hear! hear! (in a debate) I agree.
[from Old English]

hearing *noun* (*plural* **hearings**)
1 the ability to hear. **2** a chance to be
heard; a trial in a lawcourt.

hearing aid *noun* (*plural* **hearing aids**)
a device to help a deaf person to hear.

hearsay *noun*
something heard, e.g. in a rumour or
gossip.

hearse *noun* (*plural* **hearses**)
a vehicle for taking the coffin to a funeral.
[from old French]

heart *noun* (*plural* **hearts**)
1 the organ of the body that makes the
blood circulate. **2** a person's feelings or
emotions; sympathy. **3** enthusiasm;
courage, *Take heart.* **4** the middle or most
important part. **5** a curved shape
representing a heart. **6** a playing card with
red heart shapes on it.
break a person's heart make him or her
very unhappy. **heartbroken** *adjective*
by heart memorized.
[from Old English]

heart attack *noun* (*plural* **heart attacks**)
a sudden failure of the heart to work
properly, which results in great pain or
sometimes death.

hearten *verb* (**heartens, heartening,
heartened**)
make a person feel encouraged.

heart failure *noun*
a gradual failure of the heart to work
properly.

heartfelt *adjective*
felt deeply.

hearth *noun* (*plural* **hearths**)
the floor of or near a fireplace.
[from Old English]

heartland *noun*
the central or most important region.

heartless *adjective*
without pity or sympathy.

hearty *adjective*
1 strong and vigorous. **2** enthusiastic and
sincere, *hearty congratulations.* **3** (of a
meal) large.
heartily *adverb*, **heartiness** *noun*

heat *noun* (*plural* **heats**)
1 hotness or (in scientific use) the form of
energy causing this. **2** hot weather. **3** a
race or contest to decide who will take part
in the final.
heat *verb* (**heats, heating, heated**)
make or become hot. [from Old English]

heater *noun* (*plural* **heaters**)
a device for heating something.

heath *noun* (*plural* **heaths**)
flat land with low shrubs.
[from Old English]

heathen *noun* (*plural* **heathens**)
a person who does not believe in one of the
chief religions. [from Old English]

heather *noun*
an evergreen plant with small purple, pink,
or white flowers. [from Old English]

heatwave *noun* (*plural* **heatwaves**)
a long period of hot weather.

heave *verb* (**heaves, heaving, heaved** (in
sense 5 **hove**))
1 lift or move something heavy.
2 (*informal*) throw. **3** rise and fall. **4** if
your stomach heaves, you feel like
vomiting. **5** (of ships) **heave into view**
appear; **heave to** stop without mooring or
anchoring, *The ships hove to.*
heave *noun*
heave a sigh utter a deep sigh.
[from Old English]

heaven *noun* (*plural* heavens)
1 the place where God and angels are
thought to live. 2 a very pleasant place or
condition.
the heavens the sky.
[from Old English]

heavenly *adjective*
1 to do with heaven. 2 in the sky, *Stars are*
heavenly bodies. 3 (*informal*) very pleasing.

heavy *adjective* (heavier, heaviest)
1 having great weight; difficult to lift or
carry. 2 great in amount or force etc.,
heavy rain; a heavy penalty. 3 needing
much effort, *heavy work.* 4 full of sadness
or worry, *with a heavy heart.* heavily
adverb, heaviness *noun* [from Old English]

heavy industry *noun* (*plural* heavy
industries)
machines producing metal, machines, etc.

heavyweight *noun* (*plural* heavyweights)
1 a heavy person. 2 a boxer of the heaviest
weight. heavyweight *adjective*

Hebrew *noun*
the language of the Jews in ancient
Palestine and modern Israel.

heckle *verb* (heckles, heckling, heckled)
interrupt a speaker with awkward
questions. heckler *noun* [originally, to use a
heckle = a steel comb for hemp or flax]

hectare (*say* hek-tar) *noun* (*plural* hectares)
a unit of area equal to 10,000 square metres
or nearly 2½ acres.
[from Greek *hekaton* = hundred, + French
are = a hundred square metres]

hectic *adjective*
full of activity. [from Greek]

hecto- *prefix*
one hundred (as in *hectogram* = 100 grams).
[from Greek]

hector *verb* (hectors, hectoring, hectored)
frighten someone by bullying talk.
[from a gang of young bullies in London in
the 17th century who named themselves
after Hector, a hero in Greek legend]

hedge *noun* (*plural* hedges)
a row of bushes forming a barrier or
boundary.

hedge *verb* (hedges, hedging, hedged)
1 surround with a hedge or other barrier.
2 make or trim a hedge. 3 avoid giving a
definite answer. hedger *noun*
[from Old English]

hedgehog *noun* (*plural* hedgehogs)
a small animal covered with long prickles.
[because of the grunting noises it makes]

hedgerow *noun* (*plural* hedgerows)
a hedge round a field etc.

heed *verb* (heeds, heeding, heeded)
pay attention to.
heed *noun*
take or pay heed give attention to
something. heedful *adjective*, heedless
adjective [from Old English]

hee-haw *noun* (*plural* hee-haws)
a donkey's bray. [imitating the sound]

heel¹ *noun* (*plural* heels)
1 the back part of the foot. 2 the part round
or under the heel of a sock or shoe etc.
take to your heels run away.
[from Old English *hela*]

heel² *verb* (heels, heeling, heeled)
lean over to one side; tilt.
[from Old English *hieldan*]

hefty *adjective* (heftier, heftiest)
large and strong. heftily *adverb*
[probably from a Scandinavian language]

Hegira (*say* hej-ir-a) *noun*
the flight of Muhammad from Mecca in
AD 622. The Muslim era is reckoned from
this date. [from Arabic *hijra* = departure
from your home or country]

heifer (*say* hef-er) *noun* (*plural* heifers)
a young cow. [from Old English]

height *noun* (*plural* heights)
1 how high something is; the distance from
the base to the top or from head to foot. 2 a
high place. 3 the highest or most intense
part, *at the height of the holiday season.*
[from Old English]

heighten *verb* (heightens, heightening,
heightened)
make or become higher or more intense.

heir (*say as* air) *noun* (*plural* heirs)
a person who inherits something.
[from Latin]

heir apparent *noun* (*plural* heirs
apparent)
an heir whose right to inherit cannot be
cancelled.

heiress (*say* air-ess) *noun* (*plural* heiresses)
a female heir, especially to great wealth.

heirloom (*say* air-loom) *noun* (*plural*
heirlooms)
a valued possession that has been handed
down in a family for several generations.
[from *heir* + Old English *geloma* = tool]

heir presumptive *noun* (*plural* heirs
presumptive)
an heir whose right to inherit will be
cancelled if someone with a stronger right
is born.

helicopter *noun* (*plural* helicopters)
a kind of aircraft with a large horizontal
propeller or rotor.
[from *helix* + Greek *pteron* = wing]

heliotrope *noun* (*plural* heliotropes)
a plant with small fragrant purple flowers.
[from Greek *helios* = sun + *trope* = turning
(because the plant turns its flowers to the
sun)]

helium (*say* hee-lee-um) *noun*
a light colourless gas that does not burn.
[from Greek *helios* = sun]

helix (*say* hee-liks) *noun* (*plural* helices, *say*
hee-liss-eez)
a spiral. [Greek, = coil]

hell *noun*
1 a place where wicked people are thought
to be punished after they die. 2 a very
unpleasant place. 3 (*informal*) an
exclamation of anger.
hell for leather (*informal*) at high speed.
[from Old English]

hello *interjection*
a word used to greet somebody or to attract
their attention.

helm *noun* (*plural* helms)
the handle or wheel used to steer a ship.
helmsman *noun* [from Old English]

helmet *noun* (*plural* helmets)
a strong covering worn to protect the head.
[old French, from Old English]

help *verb* (helps, helping, helped)
1 do part of another person's work for him
or her. 2 benefit; make something better or
easier, *This will help you to sleep.* 3 if you
cannot help doing something, you cannot
avoid doing it, *I can't help coughing.*
4 serve food etc. to somebody. **helper** *noun*,
helpful *adjective*, **helpfully** *adverb*
help *noun*
1 helping somebody. 2 a person or thing
that helps. [from Old English]

helping *noun* (*plural* helpings)
a portion of food.

helpless *adjective*
not able to do things. **helplessly** *adverb*,
helplessness *noun*

helpline *noun* (*plural* helplines)
a telephone service providing help with
problems.

helpmate *noun* (*plural* helpmates)
a helper.

helter-skelter *adverb*
in great haste.
helter-skelter *noun* (*plural* helter-skelters)
a spiral slide at a fair. [vaguely imitating
the sound of many running feet]

hem *noun* (*plural* hems)
the edge of a piece of cloth that is folded
over and sewn down.
hem *verb* (hems, hemming, hemmed)
put a hem on something.
hem in surround and restrict.
[from Old English]

hemisphere *noun* (*plural* hemispheres)
1 half a sphere. 2 half the earth.
hemispherical *adjective*
[from Greek *hemi-* = half, + *sphere*]

hemlock *noun*
a poisonous plant or poison made from it.
[from Old English]

hemp *noun*
1 a plant that produces coarse fibres from
which cloth and ropes are made. 2 a drug
made from this plant. **hempen** *adjective*
[from Old English]

hen *noun* (*plural* hens)
1 a female bird. 2 a female fowl.
[from Old English]

hence *adverb*
1 henceforth. 2 therefore. 3 (*old use*) from
here. [from Old English]

henceforth *adverb*
from now on.

henchman *noun* (*plural* henchmen)
a trusty supporter. [origin unknown]

henna *noun*
a reddish-brown dye. [from Arabic]

hepatitis *noun*
inflammation of the liver.
[from Greek *hepar* = liver, + *-itis*]

hepta- *prefix*
seven. [from Greek]

heptagon *noun* (*plural* heptagons)
a flat shape with seven sides and seven
angles. **heptagonal** *adjective*
[from *hepta-* + Greek *gonia* = angle]

heptathlon *noun* (*plural* heptathlons)
an athletic contest in which each
competitor takes part in seven events.

her *pronoun*
the form of *she* used as the object of a verb
or after a preposition.
her *adjective*
belonging to her, *her book*.
[from Old English]

herald *noun* (*plural* heralds)
1 an official in former times who made
announcements and carried messages for a
king or queen. 2 a person or thing that
heralds something.
herald *verb* (heralds, heralding, heralded)
show that something is coming.
[via old French from Germanic]

heraldry *noun*
the study of coats of arms. **heraldic**
(*say* hir-**al**-dik) *adjective* [because a herald
(sense 1) decided who could have a coat of
arms and what should be on it]

herb *noun* (*plural* herbs)
a plant used for flavouring or for making
medicine. **herbal** *adjective* [from Latin]

herbaceous (*say* her-**bay**-shus) *adjective*
1 containing many flowering plants, *a
herbaceous border*. 2 to do with or like
herbs.

herbivorous (*say* her-**biv**-er-us) *adjective*
plant-eating. (Compare *carnivorous*.)
herbivore *noun*
[from Latin *herba* = grass, + *-vorous*]

herculean (*say* her-kew-**lee**-an) *adjective*
needing great strength or effort, *a
herculean task*.
[from *Hercules*, a hero in ancient Greek
legend]

herd *noun* (*plural* herds)
1 a group of cattle or other animals that
feed together. 2 a mass of people; a mob.
herdsman *noun*
herd *verb* (herds, herding, herded)
1 gather or move or send in a herd, *We all
herded into the dining room*. 2 look after a
herd of animals.
[from Old English]

here *adverb*
in or to this place etc.
here and there in various places or
directions.
[from Old English]

hereafter *adverb*
from now on; in future.

hereby *adverb*
by this act or decree etc.

hereditary *adjective*
1 inherited, *a hereditary disease*.
2 inheriting a position, *Our Queen is a
hereditary monarch*.
[from Latin]

heredity (*say* hir-**ed**-it-ee) *noun*
inheriting characteristics from parents or
ancestors.
[from Latin *heredis* = to do with an heir]

heresy (*say* **herri**-see) *noun* (*plural*
heresies)
an opinion that disagrees with the beliefs
accepted by the Christian Church or other
authority.
[from Greek *hairesis* = choice]

heretic (*say* herri-tik) *noun* (*plural* heretics)
a person who supports a heresy.
heretical (*say* hi-ret-ik-al) *adjective*
[from Greek]

heritage *noun*
the things that someone has inherited.
[from Latin *hereditare* = inherit]

hermetically *adverb*
so as to be airtight, *The tin is hermetically sealed.* [from Latin]

hermit *noun* (*plural* hermits)
a person who lives alone and keeps away from people.
[from Greek *eremos* = alone or deserted]

hermitage *noun* (*plural* hermitages)
a hermit's home.

hernia *noun* (*plural* hernias)
a condition in which an internal part of the body pushes through another part; a rupture. [Latin]

hero *noun* (*plural* heroes)
1 a man or boy who is admired for doing something very brave or great. **2** the chief male character in a story etc. **heroic** *adjective*, **heroically** *adverb*, **heroism** *noun*
[from Greek *heros* = a very strong or brave man, whom the gods love]

heroin *noun*
a very strong drug, made from morphine.
[from Greek]

heroine *noun* (*plural* heroines)
1 a woman or girl who is admired for doing something very brave or great. **2** the chief female character in a story etc.
[Greek, feminine of *heros* = hero]

heron *noun* (*plural* herons)
a wading bird with long legs and a long neck. [via old French from Germanic]

herring *noun* (*plural* herring or herrings)
a sea fish used as food.
[from Old English]

herringbone *noun*
a zigzag pattern. [because it looks like the spine and ribs of a herring]

hers *possessive pronoun*
belonging to her, *Those books are hers.*
[from *her*]

USAGE: It is incorrect to write *her's*.

herself *pronoun*
she or her and nobody else. The word is used to refer back to the subject of a sentence (e.g. *She cut herself*) or for emphasis (e.g. *She herself has said it*).
by herself alone; on her own.

hertz *noun* (*plural* hertz)
a unit of frequency of electromagnetic waves, = one cycle per second.
[named after a German scientist, H. R. Hertz, who discovered radio waves]

hesitant *adjective*
hesitating.
hesitantly *adverb*, **hesitancy** *noun*

hesitate *verb* (hesitates, hesitating, hesitated)
be slow or uncertain in speaking, moving, etc. **hesitation** *noun*
[from Latin *haesitare* = get stuck]

hessian *noun*
sackcloth. [named after *Hesse*, in Germany, where it was made]

hetero- *prefix*
other; different.
[from Greek *heteros* = other]

heterogeneous (*say* het-er-o-jeen-ee-us) *adjective*
composed of people or things of different kinds.
[from *hetero-* + Greek *genos* = a kind]

heterosexual *adjective*
attracted to people of the opposite sex; not homosexual. **heterosexual** *noun*

hew *verb* (hews, hewing, hewn)
chop or cut with an axe or sword etc.
[from Old English]

hexa- *prefix*
six. [from Greek]

hexagon *noun* (*plural* hexagons)
a flat shape with six sides and six angles.
hexagonal *adjective*
[from *hexa-* + Greek *gonia* = angle]

hey *interjection*
an exclamation calling attention or expressing surprise or enquiry.

heyday *noun*
the time of a thing's greatest success or prosperity.
[from *hey-day*, an expression of joy]

hi *interjection*
an exclamation calling attention or expressing a greeting.

hiatus (*say* hy-**ay**-tus) *noun* (*plural* hiatuses)
a gap in something that is otherwise continuous. [Latin, = gaping]

hibernate *verb* (hibernates, hibernating, hibernated)
spend the winter in a state like deep sleep. **hibernation** *noun*
[from Latin *hibernus* = wintry]

hiccup *noun* (*plural* hiccups)
1 a high gulping sound made when your breath is briefly interrupted. **2** a brief hitch. **hiccup** *verb* [imitating the sound]

hickory *noun* (*plural* hickories)
a tree rather like the walnut tree.
[from a Native American language]

hide¹ *verb* (hides, hiding, hid, hidden)
1 keep a person or thing from being seen; conceal. **2** get into a place where you cannot be seen. **3** keep a thing secret.
[from Old English *hydan*]

hide² *noun* (*plural* hides)
an animal's skin. [from Old English *hyd*]

hide-and-seek *noun*
a game in which one person looks for others who are hiding.

hidebound *adjective*
narrow-minded. [originally used of underfed cattle, with skin stretched tight over their bones, later of a tree whose bark was so tight it could not grow]

hideous *adjective*
very ugly or unpleasant. **hideously** *adverb*
[from old French]

hideout *noun* (*plural* hideouts)
a place where somebody hides.

hiding¹ *noun*
being hidden, *She went into hiding.*
hiding place *noun*

hiding² *noun* (*plural* hidings)
a thrashing or beating. [from an old word *hide* = to beat the hide (skin)]

hierarchy (*say* **hyr**-ark-ee) *noun* (*plural* hierarchies)
an organization that ranks people one above another according to the power or authority that they hold.
[from Greek *hieros* = sacred, + *-archy*]

hieroglyphics (*say* hyr-o-**glif**-iks) *plural noun*
pictures or symbols used in ancient Egypt to represent words. [from Greek *hieros* = sacred + *glyphe* = carving]

hi-fi *noun* (*plural* hi-fis) (*informal*)
1 high fidelity. **2** equipment for reproducing recorded sound with very little distortion.

higgledy-piggledy *adverb* & *adjective*
completely mixed up; in great disorder.
[nonsense word based on *pig* (because of the way pigs huddle together)]

high *adjective*
1 reaching a long way upwards, *high hills.* **2** far above the ground or above sea level, *high clouds.* **3** measuring from top to bottom, *two metres high.* **4** above average level in importance, quality, amount, etc., *high rank*; *high prices.* **5** (of meat) beginning to go bad. **6** (*slang*) affected by a drug.
high time fully time, *it's high time we left.*
high *adverb*
at or to a high level or position etc., *They flew high above us.* [from Old English]

highbrow *adjective*
intellectual.
[from *highbrowed* = having a high forehead (thought to be a sign of intelligence)]

higher *adjective* & *adverb*
more high.

higher education *noun*
education at a university, polytechnic, or college.

high explosive *noun* (*plural* **high explosives**)
a powerful explosive.

high fidelity *noun*
reproducing recorded sound with very little distortion.

high jump *noun*
an athletic contest in which competitors try to jump over a high bar.

highlands *plural noun*
mountainous country.
highland *adjective*, **highlander** *noun*

highlight *noun* (*plural* **highlights**)
1 the most interesting part of something, *The highlight of the holiday was the trip to Pompeii.* **2** a light area in a painting etc. **3** a light-coloured streak in a person's hair.
highlight *verb* (**highlights**, **highlighting**, **highlighted**)
draw special attention to something.

highly *adverb*
1 extremely, *highly amusing.* **2** very favourably, *We think highly of her.*

Highness *noun* (*plural* **Highnesses**)
the title of a prince or princess.

high-rise *adjective*
with many storeys.

high road *noun* (*plural* **high roads**)
the main road.

high school *noun* (*plural* **high schools**)
a secondary school.

high street *noun* (*plural* **high streets**)
a town's main street.

high tea *noun*
an evening meal with tea and meat or other cooked food.

highway *noun* (*plural* **highways**)
a main road or route.

highwayman *noun* (*plural* **highwaymen**)
a man who robbed travellers on highways in former times.

hijack *verb* (**hijacks**, **hijacking**, **hijacked**)
seize control of an aircraft or vehicle during a journey. **hijack** *noun*, **hijacker** *noun*
[origin unknown]

hike *noun* (*plural* **hikes**)
a long walk. **hike** *verb*, **hiker** *noun*
[origin unknown]

hilarious *adjective*
very funny. **hilariously** *adverb*, **hilarity** *noun*
[from Greek *hilaros* = cheerful]

hill *noun* (*plural* **hills**)
a piece of land that is higher than the ground around it. **hillside** *noun*, **hilly** *adjective* [from Old English]

hillock *noun* (*plural* **hillocks**)
a small hill; a mound.
[from *hill* + Old English *-oc* = small]

hilt *noun* (*plural* **hilts**)
the handle of a sword or dagger etc.
to the hilt completely.
[from Old English]

him *pronoun*
the form of *he* used as the object of a verb or after a preposition. [from Old English]

himself *pronoun*
he or him and nobody else. (Compare *herself.*)

hind¹ *adjective*
at the back, *the hind legs.*
[probably from *behind*]

hind² *noun* (*plural* **hinds**)
a female deer. (Compare *hart.*)
[from Old English]

hinder *verb* (**hinders**, **hindering**, **hindered**)
get in someone's way; make it difficult for a person to do something quickly or for something to happen. **hindrance** *noun*
[from Old English]

Hindi *noun*
one of the languages of India.

hindmost *adjective*
furthest behind.

hindquarters *plural noun*
an animal's hind legs and rear parts.

hindsight *noun*
looking back on an event with knowledge or understanding that you did not have at the time.

Hindu *noun* (*plural* Hindus)
a person who believes in Hinduism, which is one of the religions of India.

hinge *noun* (*plural* hinges)
a joining device on which a lid or door etc. turns when it opens.
hinge *verb* (hinges, hinging, hinged)
1 fix something with a hinge. 2 depend, *Everything hinges on this meeting.*
[Middle English, related to *hang*]

hint *noun* (*plural* hints)
1 a slight indication or suggestion, *Give me a hint of what you want.* 2 a useful suggestion, *household hints.*
hint *verb* (hints, hinting, hinted)
make a hint. [from an old word *hent* = getting hold, especially of an idea]

hinterland *noun* (*plural* hinterlands)
the district lying inland beyond a coast or port etc. [German, = land behind]

hip¹ *noun* (*plural* hips)
the bony part at the side of the body between the waist and the thigh.
[from Old English *hype*]

hip² *noun* (*plural* hips)
the fruit of the wild rose.
[from Old English *heope*]

hip³ *interjection*
part of a cheer, *Hip, hip, hooray!*
[origin unknown]

hippie *noun* (*plural* hippies) (*slang*)
a young person who joins with others to live in an unconventional way, often based on ideas of peace and love. Hippies first appeared in the 1960s. [from American slang *hip* = aware of and understanding new music, fashions, and attitudes]

hippo *noun* (*plural* hippos) (*informal*)
a hippopotamus.

hippopotamus *noun* (*plural* hippopotamuses)
a very large African animal that lives near water. [from Greek *hippos ho potamios* = horse of the river]

hire *verb* (hires, hiring, hired)
1 pay to borrow something. 2 lend for payment, *He hires out bicycles.* **hirer** *noun*
hire *noun*
hiring, *for hire.* [from Old English]

hire purchase *noun*
buying something by paying in instalments.

hirsute (*say* herss-yoot) *adjective*
hairy.
[from Latin *hirsutus* = rough or shaggy]

his *adjective* & *possessive pronoun*
belonging to him, *That is his book. That book is his.* [from Old English]

hiss *verv* (hisses, hissing, hissed)
make a sound like an *s*, *The snakes were hissing.* **hiss** *noun* [imitating the sound]

histogram *noun* (*plural* histograms)
a chart consisting of rectangles of varying sizes. [from Greek *histos* = mast, + *-gram*]

historian *noun* (*plural* historians)
a person who writes or studies history.

historic *adjective*
famous or important in history; likely to be remembered, *a historic town; a historic meeting.*

USAGE: Do not confuse with *historical.*

historical *adjective*
1 to do with history. 2 that actually existed or took place in the past, *The novel is based on historical events.*

USAGE: Do not confuse with *historic.*

history *noun* (*plural* histories)
1 what happened in the past. 2 study of past events. 3 a description of important events.
[from Greek *historia* = learning or finding out]

hit *verb* (hits, hitting, hit)
1 come forcefully against a person or thing; knock or strike. 2 have a bad effect on, *Famine has hit the poor countries.* 3 reach, *I can't hit that high note.*
hit on discover something by chance.

hit *noun* (*plural* hits)
1 hitting; a knock or stroke. **2** a shot that hits the target. **3** a success. **4** a successful song, show, etc. [from Old Norse]

hit-and-run *adjective*
a hit-and-run driver is one who injures someone in an accident and drives off without stopping.

hitch *verb* (hitches, hitching, hitched)
1 raise or pull with a slight jerk. **2** fasten with a loop or hook etc. **3** hitch-hike.
hitch *noun* (*plural* hitches)
1 a hitching movement. **2** a knot. **3** a difficulty causing delay. [origin unknown]

hitch-hike *verb* (hitch-hikes, hitch-hiking, hitch-hiked)
travel by getting lifts from passing vehicles.
hitch-hiker *noun*

hi-tech *adjective*
using the most advanced technology, especially electronic devices and computers.

hither *adverb*
to or towards this place. [from Old English]

hitherto *adverb*
until this time.

HIV *abbreviation*
human immunodeficiency virus; a virus that causes Aids. [from the initial letters of *human immunodeficiency virus*]

hive *noun* (*plural* hives)
1 a beehive. **2** the bees living in a beehive. **hive of industry** a place full of people working busily. [from Old English]

ho *interjection*
an exclamation of triumph, surprise, etc.

hoard *noun* (*plural* hoards)
a carefully saved store of money, treasure, food, etc.

hoard *verb* (hoards, hoarding, hoarded)
store something away. **hoarder** *noun* [from Old English]

USAGE: Do not confuse with *horde*.

hoarding *noun* (*plural* hoardings)
a tall fence covered with advertisements. [from old French]

hoar frost *noun*
a white frost. [from Old English *har* = grey-haired, + *frost*]

hoarse *adjective*
with a rough voice. **hoarsely** *adverb*, **hoarseness** *noun* [from Old English]

hoary *adjective*
1 white or grey from age, *hoary hair*. **2** old, *hoary jokes*. [from Old English]

hoax *verb* (hoaxes, hoaxing, hoaxed)
deceive somebody as a joke. **hoax** *noun*, **hoaxer** *noun* [probably from *hocus-pocus*, used by conjurors as a 'magic' word]

hob *noun* (*plural* hobs)
a flat surface on a cooker or beside a fireplace, where food etc. can be cooked or kept warm. [a different spelling of *hub*]

hobble *verb* (hobbles, hobbling, hobbled)
limp. [probably from old German]

hobby *noun* (*plural* hobbies)
something you do for pleasure in your spare time. [from *hobby horse*]

hobby horse *noun* (*plural* hobby horses)
1 a stick with a horse's head, used as a toy. **2** a subject that a person likes to talk about whenever he or she gets the chance. [from *hobby*, a pet form of the name Robert, often used for ponies, + *horse*]

hobgoblin *noun* (*plural* hobgoblins)
a mischievous or evil spirit. [from *hob*, a pet form of the name Robert, + *goblin*]

hobnob *verb* (hobnobs, hobnobbing, hobnobbed)
spend time together in a friendly way, *hobnobbing with rock stars*. [from an old phrase *drink hob and nob* = drink to each other]

hock *noun* (*plural* hocks)
the middle joint of an animal's hind leg.
[from Old English]

hockey *noun*
a game played by two teams with curved
sticks and a hard ball. [origin unknown]

hoe *noun* (*plural* hoes)
a tool for scraping up weeds.
hoe *verb* (hoes, hoeing, hoed)
scrape or dig with a hoe.
[via old French from Germanic]

hog *noun* (*plural* hogs)
1 a male pig. 2 (*informal*) a greedy person.
go the whole hog (*slang*) do something
completely or thoroughly.
hog *verb* (hogs, hogging, hogged)
(*informal*)
take more than your fair share of
something.
[probably from a Celtic language]

Hogmanay *noun*
New Year's Eve in Scotland.
[from old French]

hoi polloi *noun*
the ordinary people; the masses.
[Greek, = the many]

hoist *verb* (hoists, hoisting, hoisted)
lift; raise something by using ropes and
pulleys etc. [probably from Dutch]

hold *verb* (holds, holding, held)
This word has many uses, including 1 have
and keep, especially in your hands, 2 have
room for (*The jug holds two pints*),
3 support (*This plank won't hold my
weight*), 4 stay unbroken; continue (*Will
the fine weather hold?*), 5 believe or
consider (*We shall hold you responsible*),
6 cause something to take place (*hold a
meeting*), 7 restrain or stop (*Hold
everything!*).
hold forth make a long speech.
hold out refuse to give in.
hold up 1 hinder. 2 stop and rob somebody
by threats or force.
hold with approve of, *We don't hold with
bullying.*
hold your tongue (*informal*) stop talking.
hold *noun* (*plural* holds)
1 holding something; a grasp. 2 something
to hold on to for support. 3 the part of a

ship where cargo is stored, below the deck.
get hold of 1 grasp. 2 obtain. 3 make
contact with a person.
[from Old English]

holdall *noun* (*plural* holdalls)
a large portable bag or case.

holder *noun* (*plural* holders)
a person or thing that holds something.

hold-up *noun* (*plural* hold-ups)
1 a delay. 2 a robbery with threats or force.

hole *noun* (*plural* holes)
1 a hollow place; a gap or opening. 2 a
burrow. 3 one of the small holes into which
you have to hit the ball in golf. 4 (*informal*)
an unpleasant place. **holey** *adjective*
in a hole in an awkward situation.
hole *verb* (holes, holing, holed)
1 make a hole or holes in something. 2 hit
a golf ball into one of the holes.
[from Old English]

Holi *noun*
a Hindu festival held in the spring. [Hindi]

holiday *noun* (*plural* holidays)
1 a day or week etc. when people do not go
to work or to school. 2 a time when you go
away to enjoy yourself.
[from *holy* + *day* (because holidays were
originally religious festivals)]

holiness *noun*
being holy or sacred.
His Holiness the title of the pope.

hollow *adjective*
with an empty space inside; not solid.
hollowly *adverb*
hollow *adverb*
completely, *We beat them hollow.*
hollow *noun* (*plural* hollows)
a hollow or sunken place.
hollow *verb* (hollows, hollowing, hollowed)
make a thing hollow. [from Old English]

holly *noun* (*plural* hollies)
an evergreen bush with shiny prickly
leaves and red berries. [from Old English]

hollyhock *noun* (*plural* hollyhocks)
a plant with large flowers on a very tall
stem. [from Old English]

holocaust *noun* (*plural* holocausts)
an immense destruction, especially by fire,
the nuclear holocaust.
the Holocaust the mass murder of the Jews
by the Nazis from 1939 to 1945.
[from Greek *holos* = whole + *kaustos*
= burnt]

hologram *noun* (*plural* holograms)
a type of photograph made by laser beams
that produces a three-dimensional image.
[from Greek *holos* = whole, + *-gram*]

holster *noun* (*plural* holsters)
a leather case in which a pistol or revolver
is carried. [probably from Dutch]

holy *adjective* (holier, holiest)
1 belonging or devoted to God.
2 consecrated, *holy water*. **holiness** *noun*
[from Old English]

homage *noun* (*plural* homages)
an act or expression of respect or honour,
We paid homage to his achievements.
[from old French]

home *noun* (*plural* homes)
1 the place where you live. **2** the place
where you were born or where you feel you
belong. **3** a place where those who need
help are looked after, *an old people's home.*
4 the place to be reached in a race or in
certain games.
home *adjective*
1 of a person's own home or country, *home
industries.* **2** played on a team's own
ground, *a home match.*
home *adverb*
1 to or at home, *Is she home yet?* **2** to the
point aimed at, *Push the bolt home.*
bring something home to somebody make
him or her realize it.
home *verb* (homes, homing, homed)
make for a target, *The missile homed in.*
[from Old English]

home economics *noun*
the study of household management.

homeless *adjective*
having no home.

homely *adverb*
simple and ordinary, *a homely meal.*
homeliness *noun*

home-made *adjective*
made at home, not bought from a shop.

homeopath *noun* (*plural* homeopaths)
a person who practises homeopathy.

homeopathy *noun*
the treatment of disease by tiny doses of
drugs that in a healthy person would
produce symptoms of the disease.
homeopathic *adjective* [from Greek *homoios*
= similar + *-pathos* = suffering]

homesick *adjective*
sad because you are away from home.
homesickness *noun*

homestead *noun* (*plural* homesteads)
a farmhouse, usually with the land and
buildings round it. [from *home* + Old
English *stede* = a place]

homeward *adjective* & *adverb*
going towards home. **homewards** *adverb*

homework *noun*
school work that has to be done at home.

homicide *noun* (*plural* homicides)
the killing of one person by another.
homicidal *adjective*
[from Latin *homo* = person, + *-cide*]

homily *noun* (*plural* homilies)
a lecture about behaviour.
[from Greek *homilia* = sermon]

homing *adjective*
trained to fly home, *a homing pigeon.*

homo- *prefix*
same. [from Greek]

homogeneous (*say* hom-o-**jeen**-ee-us)
adjective
composed of people or things of the same
kind. [from *homo-* + Greek *genos* = a kind]

homograph *noun* (*plural* homographs)
a word that is spelt like another but has a
different meaning or origin, e.g. *bat* (a
flying animal) and *bat* (for hitting a ball).
[from *homo-* + *-graph*]

homonym (*say* **hom**-o-nim) *noun* (*plural*
homonyms)
a homograph or homophone.
[from *homo-* + Greek *onyma* = name]

homophone *noun* (*plural* homophones)
a word with the same sound as another,
e.g. *son, sun*.
[from *homo-* + Greek *phone* = sound]

Homo sapiens *noun*
human beings regarded as a species of
animal. [Latin, = wise man or person]

homosexual *adjective*
attracted to people of the same sex.
homosexual *noun*, homosexuality *noun*

honest *adjective*
not stealing or cheating or telling lies;
truthful. honestly *adverb*, honesty *noun*
[from old French; related to *honour*]

honey *noun*
a sweet sticky food made by bees.
[from Old English]

honeycomb *noun* (*plural* honeycombs)
a wax structure of small six-sided sections
made by bees to hold their honey and eggs.

honeycombed *adjective*
with many holes or tunnels.

honeymoon *noun* (*plural* honeymoons)
a holiday spent together by a newly-
married couple. [from *honey* + *moon*
(because the first intensely passionate
feelings gradually wane)]

honeysuckle *noun*
a climbing plant with fragrant yellow or
pink flowers. [because people sucked the
flowers for their sweet nectar]

honk *noun* (*plural* honks)
a loud sound like that made by a goose or
an old-fashioned car horn. honk *verb*
[imitating the sound]

honorary *adjective*
1 given or received as an honour, *an
honorary degree*. 2 unpaid, *the honorary
treasurer of the club*.

USAGE: Do not confuse with *honourable*.

honour *noun* (*plural* honours)
1 great respect. 2 a person or thing that
brings honour. 3 honesty and loyalty, *a
man of honour*. 4 an award for distinction.

honour *verb* (honours, honouring,
honoured)
1 feel or show honour for a person.
2 acknowledge and pay a cheque etc.
3 keep to the terms of an agreement or
promise. [from Latin]

honourable *adjective*
deserving honour; honest and loyal.
honourably *adverb*

USAGE: Do not confuse with *honorary*.

hood *noun* (*plural* hoods)
1 a covering of soft material for the head
and neck. 2 a folding roof or cover.
hooded *adjective*
[from Old English *hod*]

-hood *suffix*
forms nouns meaning condition or quality
(e.g. *childhood*). [from Old English]

hoodwink *verb* (hoodwinks, hoodwinking,
hoodwinked)
deceive. [originally = to blindfold with a
hood: from *hood* + an old sense of *wink*
= close the eyes]

hoof *noun* (*plural* hoofs or hooves)
the horny part of the foot of a horse etc.
[from Old English]

hook *noun* (*plural* hooks)
a bent or curved piece of metal etc. for
hanging things on or for catching hold of
something.
hook *verb* (hooks, hooking, hooked)
1 catch something with a hook. 2 fasten
something with or on a hook. 3 send a ball
in a curving direction.
be hooked on something (*slang*) be addicted
to it.
[from Old English]

hookah *noun* (*plural* hookahs)
an oriental tobacco pipe with a long tube
passing through a jar of water.
[via Urdu from Arabic *hukka* = box or jar]

hooked *adjective*
hook-shaped.

hooligan *noun* (*plural* hooligans)
a rough and violent young person.
hooliganism *noun* [the surname of a rowdy
Irish family in a cartoon]

hoop *noun* (*plural* **hoops**)
a ring made of metal or wood.
[from Old English]

hoopla *noun*
a game in which people try to throw hoops
round objects.

hooray *interjection*
a different spelling of *hurray*.

hoot *noun* (*plural* **hoots**)
1 the sound made by an owl or a vehicle's
horn or a steam whistle. **2** a cry of scorn or
disapproval. **3** laughter. **4** something
funny. **hoot** *verb*, **hooter** *noun*
[imitating the sound]

hop[1] *verb* (**hops, hopping, hopped**)
1 jump on one foot. **2** (of an animal) spring
from all feet at once. **3** (*informal*) move
quickly, *Here's the car—hop in!*
hop it (*slang*) go away.
hop *noun* (*plural* **hops**)
a hopping movement.
[from Old English]

hop[2] *noun* (*plural* **hops**)
a climbing plant used to give beer its
flavour. [from old German or old Dutch]

hope *noun* (*plural* **hopes**)
1 a wish for something to happen. **2** a
person or thing that gives hope, *You are
our only hope.*
hope *verb* (**hopes, hoping, hoped**)
feel hope; want and expect something.
[from Old English]

hopeful *adjective*
1 feeling hope. **2** likely to be good or
successful.

hopefully *adverb*
1 it is to be hoped; I hope that. **2** in a
hopeful way.

USAGE: Some people say it is incorrect to
use *hopefully* to mean 'I hope that' or 'let's
hope', and say that it should only be used to
mean 'in a hopeful way'. This first use is
very common in informal language but
you should probably avoid it when you are
writing or speaking formally.

hopeless *adjective*
1 without hope. **2** very bad at something.
hopelessly *adverb*, **hopelessness** *noun*

hopper *noun* (*plural* **hoppers**)
a large funnel-shaped container.

hopscotch *noun*
a game of hopping into squares drawn on
the ground. [from *hop* + an old word *scotch*
= a cut or scratch]

horde *noun* (*plural* **hordes**)
a large group or crowd. [via Polish from
Turkish *ordu* = royal camp]

USAGE: Do not confuse with *hoard*.

horizon *noun* (*plural* **horizons**)
the line where the earth and the sky seem
to meet.
[from Greek *horizein* = form a boundary]

horizontal *adjective*
level, so as to be parallel to the horizon;
going across from left to right. (The
opposite is *vertical*.) **horizontally** *adverb*

hormone *noun* (*plural* **hormones**)
a substance that stimulates an organ of the
body or of a plant. **hormonal** *adjective*
[from Greek *horman* = set something
going]

horn *noun* (*plural* **horns**)
1 a hard substance that grows into a point
on the head of a bull, cow, ram, etc. **2** a
pointed part. **3** a brass instrument played
by blowing. **4** a device for making a
warning sound. **horned** *adjective*, **horny**
adjective [from Old English]

hornet *noun* (*plural* **hornets**)
a large kind of wasp. [from Old English]

hornpipe *noun* (*plural* **hornpipes**)
a sailors' dance.
[originally = a wind instrument made of
horn, which was played to dance to]

horoscope *noun* (*plural* **horoscopes**)
an astrologer's forecast of future events.
[from Greek *hora* = hour (of birth) + *skopos*
= observer]

horrendous *adjective*
horrifying. [from Latin *horrendus*
= making your hair stand on end]

horrible *adjective*
1 horrifying. **2** very unpleasant. **horribly**
adverb [from Latin]

horrid *adjective*
horrible. **horridly** *adverb* [from Latin
horridus = rough, shaggy, or wild]

horrific *adjective*
horrifying. **horrifically** *adverb*
[from Latin]

horrify *verb* (**horrifies, horrifying, horrified**)
1 make somebody feel great fear and
dislike. **2** shock. [from Latin *horrificare*
= make someone shiver with cold or fear]

horror *noun* (*plural* **horrors**)
1 great fear and dislike or dismay.
2 a person or thing causing horror.
[from Latin]

hors-d'oeuvre (*say* or-**dervr**) *noun* (*plural*
hors-d'oeuvres) food served as an appetizer
at the start of a meal.
[French, = outside the work]

horse *noun* (*plural* **horses**)
1 a large four-legged animal used for riding
on and for pulling carts etc. **2** a framework
for hanging clothes on to dry. **3** a vaulting
horse.
on horseback mounted on a horse.
[from Old English]

horse chestnut *noun* (*plural* **horse
chestnuts**)
a large tree that produces dark-brown nuts
(conkers).

horseman *noun* (*plural* **horsemen**)
a man who rides a horse, especially a
skilled rider. **horsemanship** *noun*

horseplay *noun*
rough play.

horsepower *noun*
a unit for measuring the power of an
engine. [because the unit was based on the
amount of work a horse could do]

horseshoe *noun* (*plural* **horseshoes**)
a U-shaped piece of metal nailed to a
horse's hoof.

horsewoman *noun* (*plural* **horsewomen**)
a woman who rides a horse, especially a
skilled rider.

horticulture *noun*
the art of cultivating gardens.
horticultural *adjective*
[from Latin *hortus* = garden, + *culture*]

hose *noun* (*plural* **hoses**)
1 (also **hosepipe**) a flexible tube for taking
water to something. **2** (*old use*) breeches,
doublet and hose.
hose *verb* (**hoses, hosing, hosed**)
water or spray with a hose.
[from Old English]

hosiery *noun*
(in shops) socks and stockings. [from *hose*]

hospice (*say* **hosp**-iss) *noun* (*plural*
hospices)
a nursing home for people who are very ill.
[from Latin *hospitium* = hospitality or
lodgings]

hospitable *adjective*
welcoming; liking to give hospitality.
hospitably *adverb* [from Latin]

hospital *noun* (*plural* **hospitals**)
a place providing medical and surgical
treatment for people who are ill or injured.
[from Latin *hospitalis* = hospitable]

hospitality *noun*
welcoming people and giving them food
and entertainment. [from Latin]

host[1] *noun* (*plural* **hosts**)
a person who has guests and looks after
them.
host *verb* (**hosts, hosting, hosted**)
organize a party, event, etc. and look after
the people who come. [from Latin *hospes*]

host[2] *noun* (*plural* **hosts**)
a large number of people or things.
[from Latin *hostis* = enemy or army]

host[3] *noun* (*plural* **hosts**)
the bread consecrated at Holy Communion.
[from Latin *hostia* = sacrifice]

hostage *noun* (*plural* **hostages**)
a person who is held prisoner until the
holder gets what he or she wants.
[from old French]

hostel *noun* (*plural* hostels)
a building where travellers, students, or other groups can stay or live.
[from old French; related to *hospital*]

hostess *noun* (*plural* hostesses)
a woman who has guests and looks after them. [from old French]

hostile *adjective*
1 to do with an enemy. 2 unfriendly, *a hostile glance.* **hostility** *noun*
[same origin as *host*²]

hot *adjective* (hotter, hottest)
1 having great heat or a high temperature. 2 giving a burning sensation when tasted. 3 passionate or excitable, *a hot temper.*
hotly *adverb*, **hotness** *noun*
in hot water (*informal*) in trouble or disgrace.
hot *verb* (hots, hotting, hotted)
hot up (*informal*) make or become hot or hotter or more exciting.
[from Old English]

hot cross bun *noun* (*plural* hot cross buns)
a fresh spicy bun marked with a cross, usually eaten at Easter.

hot dog *noun* (*plural* hot dogs)
a hot sausage in a bread roll.

hotel *noun* (*plural* hotels)
a building where people pay to have meals and stay for the night.
[from French; related to *hostel*]

hotfoot *adverb*
in eager haste.

hothead *noun* (*plural* hotheads)
an impetuous person.

hothouse *noun* (*plural* hothouses)
a heated greenhouse.

hotplate *noun* (*plural* hotplates)
a heated surface for cooking food etc. or keeping it hot.

hotpot *noun* (*plural* hotpots)
a stew.

hound *noun* (*plural* hounds)
a dog used in hunting or racing.

hound *verb* (hounds, hounding, hounded)
pursue or harass someone.
[from Old English]

hour *noun* (*plural* hours)
1 one twenty-fourth part of a day and night; sixty minutes. 2 a time, *Why are you up at this hour?*
hours *plural noun* a fixed period for work, *Office hours are 9 a.m. to 5 p.m.*
[from Greek]

hourglass *noun* (*plural* hourglasses)
a glass container with a very narrow part in the middle through which sand runs from the top half to the bottom half, taking one hour.

hourly *adverb* & *adjective*
every hour.

house (*say* howss) *noun* (*plural* houses)
1 a building made for people to live in, usually designed for one family. 2 a building or establishment for a special purpose, *the opera house.* 3 a building for a government assembly; the assembly itself, *the House of Commons; the House of Lords.* 4 each of the divisions of a school for sports competitions etc. 5 a family or dynasty, *the royal house of Tudor.*
house (*say* howz) *verb* (houses, housing, housed)
provide accommodation or room for someone or something.
[from Old English]

houseboat *noun* (*plural* houseboats)
a barge-like boat for living in.

household *noun* (*plural* households)
all the people who live together in the same house.
[from *house* + an old sense of *hold* = possession]

householder *noun* (*plural* householders)
a person who owns or rents a house.

housekeeper *noun* (*plural* housekeepers)
a person employed to look after a household.

housekeeping *noun*
1 looking after a household. 2 (*informal*) the money for a household's food and other necessities.

housemaid *noun* (*plural* **housemaids**)
a woman servant in a house, especially one who cleans rooms.

house plant *noun* (*plural* **house plants**)
a plant grown indoors.

house-proud *adjective*
very careful to keep a house clean and tidy.

house-trained *adjective*
(of an animal) trained to be clean in the house.

house-warming *noun* (*plural* **house-warmings**)
a party to celebrate moving into a new home.

housewife *noun* (*plural* **housewives**)
a woman who does the housekeeping for her family.

housework *noun*
the cleaning and cooking etc. done in housekeeping.

housing *noun* (*plural* **housings**)
1 accommodation; houses. 2 a stiff cover or guard for a piece of machinery.

housing estate *noun* (*plural* **housing estates**)
a set of houses planned and built together in one area.

hove *past tense* of **heave** (when used of ships).

hovel *noun* (*plural* **hovels**)
a small shabby house. [origin unknown]

hover *verb* (**hovers, hovering, hovered**)
1 stay in one place in the air. 2 wait about near someone or something; linger.
[origin unknown]

hovercraft *noun* (*plural* **hovercraft**)
a vehicle that travels just above the surface of land or water, supported by a strong current of air sent downwards from its engines.

how *adverb*
1 in what way; by what means, *How did you do it?* 2 to what extent or amount etc., *How high can you jump?* 3 in what condition, *How are you?*

how about would you like, *How about a game of football?*
how do you do? a formal greeting.
[from Old English]

however *adverb*
1 in whatever way; to whatever extent, *You will never catch him, however hard you try.*
2 all the same; nevertheless, *Later, however, he decided to go.*

howl *noun* (*plural* **howls**)
a long loud sad-sounding cry or sound, such as that made by a dog or wolf.

howl *verb* (**howls, howling, howled**)
1 make a howl. 2 weep loudly.
[imitating the sound]

howler *noun* (*plural* **howlers**)
(*informal*) a foolish mistake.

hub *noun* (*plural* **hubs**)
1 the central part of a wheel. 2 the central point of interest or activity.
[origin unknown]

hubbub *noun*
a loud confused noise of voices.
[probably from Irish]

huddle *verb* (**huddles, huddling, huddled**)
1 crowd together into a small space. 2 curl your body closely. **huddle** *noun*
[origin unknown]

hue¹ *noun* (*plural* **hues**)
a colour or tint. [from Old English]

hue² *noun*
hue and cry a general outcry of demand, alarm, or protest.
[from old French *huer* = to shout]

huff *noun*
in a huff offended or sulking about something, *She went away in a huff.*
huffy *adjective*

huff *verb* (**huffs, huffing, huffed**)
blow, *huffing and puffing.*
[imitating the sound]

hug *verb* (**hugs, hugging, hugged**)
1 clasp someone tightly in your arms; embrace. 2 keep close to something, *The ship hugged the shore.*

hug *noun* (*plural* **hugs**)
a tight embrace.
[probably from a Scandinavian language]

huge *adjective*
extremely large; enormous. **hugely** *adverb*,
hugeness *noun* [from old French]

hulk *noun* (*plural* **hulks**)
1 the body or wreck of an old ship. 2 a
large clumsy person or thing. **hulking**
adjective [from Old English]

hull *noun* (*plural* **hulls**)
the framework of a ship.
[from Old English]

hullabaloo *noun* (*plural* **hullabaloos**)
an uproar. [origin unknown]

hullo *interjection*
hello.

hum *verb* (**hums, humming, hummed**)
1 sing a tune with your lips closed. 2 make
a low continuous sound as some flying
insects do.
hum *noun* (*plural* **hums**)
a humming sound. [imitating the sound]

human *adjective*
to do with human beings.
human *noun* (*plural* **humans**)
a human being. [from Latin]

human being *noun* (*plural* **human beings**)
a creature distinguished from other
animals by its better mental development,
power of speech, and upright posture.

humane (*say* hew-**mayn**) *adjective*
kind-hearted and merciful. **humanely**
adverb [old spelling of *human*]

humanist *noun* (*plural* **humanists**)
a person who is concerned with people's
needs and with finding rational ways to
solve human problems, rather than using
religious belief. **humanism** *noun*

humanitarian *adjective*
concerned with people's welfare and the
reduction of suffering. **humanitarian** *noun*

humanity *noun*
1 human beings; people. 2 being human.
3 being humane.
humanities *plural noun* arts subjects.

humanize *verb* (**humanizes, humanizing,**
humanized)
make human or humane.
humanization *noun*

humble *adjective*
1 modest; not proud or showy. 2 of low
rank or importance. **humbly** *adverb*,
humbleness *noun*
humble *verb* (**humbles, humbling, humbled**)
make someone feel humble. [from Latin
humilis = near the ground, low]

humbug *noun* (*plural* **humbugs**)
1 insincere or dishonest talk or behaviour.
2 a hard peppermint sweet.
[origin unknown]

humdrum *adjective*
dull and not exciting; commonplace.
[origin unknown]

humid (*say* hew-mid) *adjective*
(of air) moist. **humidity** *noun* [from Latin]

humiliate *verb* (**humiliates, humiliating,**
humiliated)
make a person feel disgraced. **humiliation**
noun [same origin as *humble*]

humility *noun*
being humble. [same origin as *humble*]

hummingbird *noun* (*plural*
hummingbirds)
a small tropical bird that makes a
humming sound by moving its wings
rapidly.

hummock *noun* (*plural* **hummocks**)
a hump in the ground. [origin unknown]

humorist *noun* (*plural* **humorists**)
a humorous writer.

humorous *adjective*
full of humour.

humour *noun*
1 being amusing; what makes people
laugh. 2 the ability to enjoy comical things,
a sense of humour. 3 a mood, *in a good*
humour.
humour *verb* (**humours, humouring,**
humoured)
keep a person contented by doing what he
or she wants. [from Latin]

hump *noun* (*plural* humps)
1 a rounded lump or mound. 2 an
abnormal outward curve at the top of a
person's back.
hump *verb* (humps, humping, humped)
carry something heavy with difficulty.
[probably from old German or Dutch]

humpback bridge *noun* (*plural*
humpback bridges) a small bridge that
steeply curves upwards in the middle.

humus (*say* hew-mus) *noun*
rich earth made by decayed plants.
[Latin, = soil]

hunch¹ *noun* (*plural* hunches)
a feeling that you can guess what will
happen. [origin unknown]

hunch² *verb* (hunches, hunching, hunched)
bend into a hump, *He hunched his
shoulders.* [origin unknown]

hunchback *noun* (*plural* hunchbacks)
someone with a hump on their back.
hunchbacked *adjective*

hundred *noun* & *adjective* (*plural*
hundreds)
the number 100. **hundredth** *adjective* &
noun [from Old English]

hundredfold *adjective* & *adverb*
one hundred times as much or as many.

hundredweight *noun* (*plural*
hundredweight)
a unit of weight, 112 pounds (= 50.8
kilograms).
[probably originally = 100 pounds]

hunger *noun*
the feeling that you have when you have
not eaten for some time; need for food.
[from Old English]

hunger strike *noun* (*plural* hunger strikes)
refusing to eat, as a way of making a
protest.

hungry *adjective* (hungrier, hungriest)
feeling hunger. **hungrily** *adverb*

hunk *noun* (*plural* hunks)
1 a large piece of something. 2 (*informal*) a
muscular, good-looking man.
[probably from old Dutch]

hunt *verb* (hunts, hunting, hunted)
1 chase and kill animals for food or as a
sport. 2 search for something. **hunter** *noun*,
huntsman *noun*
hunt *noun* (*plural* hunts)
1 hunting. 2 a group of hunters.
[from Old English]

hurdle *noun* (*plural* hurdles)
1 an upright frame to be jumped over in
hurdling. 2 an obstacle. [from Old English]

hurdling *noun*
racing in which the runners jump over
hurdles. **hurdler** *noun*

hurl *verb* (hurls, hurling, hurled)
throw something violently.
[origin unknown]

hurly-burly *noun*
a rough bustle of activity. [from *hurl*]

hurrah or **hurray** *interjection*
a shout of joy or approval; a cheer.
[origin unknown]

hurricane *noun* (*plural* hurricanes)
a storm with violent wind.
[via Spanish and Portuguese from Taino
(a South American language)]

hurry *verb* (hurries, hurrying, hurried)
1 move quickly; do something quickly.
2 try to make somebody or something be
quick. **hurried** *adjective*, **hurriedly** *adverb*
hurry *noun*
hurrying; a need to hurry.
[origin unknown]

hurt *verb* (hurts, hurting, hurt)
cause pain or damage or injury.
hurt *noun*
pain or injury. **hurtful** *adjective*
[from old French]

hurtle *verb* (hurtles, hurtling, hurtled)
move rapidly, *The train hurtled along.*
[from an old sense of *hurt* = knock or dash
against something]

husband *noun* (*plural* husbands)
the man to whom a woman is married.
husband *verb* (husbands, husbanding,
husbanded)
manage money, strength, etc. economically
and try to save it. [from Old Norse
husbondi = master of the house]

husbandry *noun*
1 farming. 2 management of resources.
[from *husband*]

hush *verb* (**hushes, hushing, hushed**)
make or become silent or quiet.
hush *noun*
silence. [imitating the soft hissing sound
you make to get someone to be quiet]

husk *noun* (*plural* **husks**)
the dry outer covering of some seeds and
fruits. [probably from old German]

husky[1] *adjective* (**huskier, huskiest**)
1 hoarse. 2 big and strong; burly.
huskily *adverb*, **huskiness** *noun*
[from *husk*]

husky[2] *noun* (*plural* **huskies**)
a large dog used in the Arctic for pulling
sledges. [from a Native American word
meaning 'Eskimo']

hustings *plural noun*
political speeches and campaigning just
before an election. [from Old Norse]

hustle *verb* (**hustles, hustling, hustled**)
hurry or bustle. **hustle** *noun*, **hustler** *noun*
[from Dutch *husselen* = shake or toss]

hut *noun* (*plural* **huts**)
a small roughly-made house or shelter.
[via French from old German]

hutch *noun* (*plural* **hutches**)
a box-like cage for a pet rabbit etc.
[from Latin]

hyacinth *noun* (*plural* **hyacinths**)
a fragrant flower that grows from a bulb.
[because, in Greek legend, the flower
sprang from the blood of Hyacinthus, a
youth who was accidentally killed by
Apollo]

hybrid *noun* (*plural* **hybrids**)
1 a plant or animal produced by combining
two different species or varieties.
2 something that combines parts or
characteristics of two different things.
[from Latin]

hydr- *prefix*
1 water. 2 contaning hydrogen. see **hydro-**.

hydra *noun* (*plural* **hydras** or **hydrae**)
a microscopic freshwater animal with a
tubular body. [Greek, = water-snake]

hydrangea (*say* hy-drayn-ja) *noun* (*plural*
hydrangeas)
a shrub with pink, blue, or white flowers
growing in large clusters. [from *hydr-*
+ Greek *angeion* = container (because the
seed capsule is shaped like a cup)]

hydrant *noun* (*plural* **hydrants**)
a special water-tap to which a large hose
can be attached for fire-fighting or street-
cleaning etc. [same origin as *hydro-*]

hydraulic *adjective*
worked by the force of water or other fluid,
hydraulic brakes.
[from *hydr-* + Greek *aulos* = pipe]

hydro- *prefix* (**hydr-** before a vowel)
1 water (as in *hydroelectric*). 2 (in chemical
names) containing hydrogen (as in
hydrochloric). [from Greek *hydor* = water]

hydrochloric acid *noun*
a colourless acid containing hydrogen and
chlorine.

hydroelectric *adjective*
using water-power to produce electricity.
hydroelectricity *noun*

hydrofoil *noun* (*plural* **hydrofoils**)
a boat designed to skim over the surface of
water. [from *hydro-* + *foil*[1]]

hydrogen *noun*
a lightweight gas that combines with
oxygen to form water.
[from *hydro-* + *-gen* = producing]

hydrogen bomb *noun* (*plural* **hydrogen
bombs**)
a very powerful bomb using energy created
by the fusion of hydrogen nuclei.

hydrolysis *noun*
the chemical reaction of a substance with
water, usually resulting in decomposition.
[from *hydro-* + Greek *lysis* = loosening]

hydrophobia *noun*
abnormal fear of water, as in someone
suffering from rabies.
[from *hydro-* + *phobia*]

hyena noun (plural **hyenas**)
a wild animal that looks like a wolf and makes a shrieking howl. [from Greek]

hygiene (say hy-jeen) noun
keeping things clean in order to remain healthy and prevent disease.
hygienic adjective, **hygienically** adverb [from Greek hygies = healthy]

hymn noun (plural **hymns**)
a religious song, usually of praise to God.
hymn book noun [from Greek]

hymnal noun (plural **hymnals**)
a hymn book.

hyper- prefix
over or above; excessive.
[from Greek hyper = over]

hyperbola (say hy-**per**-bol-a) noun (plural **hyperbolas**)
a kind of curve. [same origin as hyperbole]

hyperbole (say hy-**per**-bol-ee) noun (plural **hyperboles**)
a dramatic exaggeration that is not meant to be taken literally, e.g. 'I've got a stack of work a mile high'.
[from hyper- + Greek bole = a throw]

hypermarket noun (plural **hypermarkets**)
a very large supermarket, usually outside a town.

hyphen noun (plural **hyphens**)
a short dash used to join words or parts of words together (e.g. in hitch-hiker).
[from Greek, = together]

hyphenate verb (**hyphenates, hyphenating, hyphenated**)
join with a hyphen. **hyphenation** noun

hypnosis (say hip-**noh**-sis) noun
a condition like a deep sleep in which a person's actions may be controlled by someone else.
[from Greek hypnos = sleep]

hypnotize verb (**hypnotizes, hypnotizing, hypnotized**)
produce hypnosis in somebody.
hypnotism noun, **hypnotic** adjective, **hypnotist** noun

hypo- prefix
below; under. [from Greek hypo = under]

hypochondriac (say hy-po-**kon**-dree-ak) noun (plural **hypochondriacs**)
a person who constantly imagines that he or she is ill. **hypochondria** noun [from Greek hypochondrios = under the breastbone (because the organs there were once thought to be the source of depression and anxiety)]

hypocrite (say **hip**-o-krit) noun (plural **hypocrites**)
a person who pretends to be more virtuous than he or she really is.
hypocrisy (say hip-**ok**-riss-ee) noun, **hypocritical** adjective
[from Greek hypokrites = actor or pretender]

hypodermic adjective
injecting something under the skin, a hypodermic syringe.
[from hypo- + Greek derma = skin]

hypotenuse (say hy-**pot**-i-newz) noun (plural **hypotenuses**)
the side opposite the right angle in a right-angled triangle. [from Greek]

hypothermia noun
being too cold; the condition in which someone's temperature is below normal.
[from hypo- + Greek therme = heat]

hypothesis (say hy-**poth**-i-sis) noun (plural **hypotheses**)
a suggestion or guess that tries to explain something. **hypothetical** adjective
[from hypo- + Greek thesis = placing]

hysterectomy (say hist-er-**ek**-tom-ee) noun (plural **hysterectomies**)
surgical removal of the womb. [from Greek hystera = womb, + -ectomy = cutting out]

hysteria noun
wild uncontrollable excitement, panic, or emotion. **hysterics** noun
[from Greek hystera = womb (once thought to be the cause of hysteria)]

hysterical adjective
1 in a state of hysteria. 2 (informal) extremely funny. **hysterically** adverb

Ii

I *pronoun*
a word used by a person to refer to himself or herself. [from Old English]

-ible see **-able**.

-ic *suffix*
forms **1** adjectives, some of which are used as nouns (e.g. *comic, domestic, public*), **2** names of arts (e.g. *music, magic*). [from Latin *-icus* or Greek *-ikos*]

-ical *suffix*
forms adjectives from or similar to words ending in *-ic* (e.g. *comical, musical*).

ice *noun* (*plural* ices)
1 frozen water, a brittle transparent solid substance. **2** an ice cream.
ice *verb* (ices, icing, iced)
1 make or become icy. **2** put icing on a cake. [from Old English]

ice age *noun* (*plural* ice ages)
a period in the past when most of the earth's surface was covered with ice.

iceberg *noun* (*plural* icebergs)
a large mass of ice floating in the sea with most of it under water. [from Dutch]

ice cap *noun* (*plural* ice caps)
a permanent covering of ice and snow at the North or South Pole.

ice cream *noun* (*plural* ice creams)
a sweet creamy frozen food.

ice hockey *noun*
a form of hockey played on ice.

ice lolly *noun* (*plural* ice lollies)
frozen juice on a small stick.

ice rink *noun* (*plural* ice rinks)
a place made for skating.

-ician *suffix*
forms nouns meaning 'person skilled in something' (e.g. *musician*).

icicle *noun* (*plural* icicles)
a pointed hanging piece of ice formed when dripping water freezes. [from Old English]

icing *noun*
a sugary substance for decorating cakes.

-icity *suffix*
forms nouns (e.g. *publicity*) from words ending in *-ic*.

icon (*say* I-kon) *noun* (*plural* icons)
1 a sacred painting or mosaic etc. **2** a small symbol or picture on a computer screen, representing a program, window, etc. that you can select [from Greek *eikon* = image]

-ics *suffix*
forms nouns which are plural in form but are often used with a singular verb (e.g. *mathematics, gymnastics*).

icy *adjective* (icier, iciest)
1 covered with ice. **2** very cold.
icily *adverb*, **iciness** *noun*

Id *noun*
a different spelling of *Eid*.

idea *noun* (*plural* ideas)
1 a plan or thought formed in the mind. **2** an opinion or belief. [Greek]

ideal *adjective*
perfect; completely suitable. **ideally** *adverb*
ideal *noun* (*plural* ideals)
a person or thing regarded as perfect or as worth trying to achieve.
[from Latin, related to *idea*]

idealist *noun* (*plural* idealists)
a person who has high ideals and wishes to achieve them.
idealism *noun*, **idealistic** *adjective*

identical *adjective*
exactly the same. **identically** *adverb*
[same origin as *identity*]

identify *verb* (identifies, identifying, identified)
1 recognize as being a certain person or thing. **2** treat something as being identical to something else, *Don't identify wealth with happiness.* **3** think of yourself as sharing someone's feelings etc., *We can identify with the hero of this play.*
identification *noun*

identity *noun* (*plural* identities)
1 who or what a person or thing is. 2 being identical; sameness. 3 distinctive character.
[from Latin *idem* = same]

ideology (*say* I-dee-ol-o-jee) *noun* (*plural* ideologies)
a set of beliefs and aims, especially in politics, *a socialist ideology.*
ideological *adjective*
[from *idea* + *-ology*]

idiocy *noun*
1 being an idiot. 2 stupid behaviour.

idiom *noun* (*plural* idioms)
a phrase that means something different from the meanings of the words in it, e.g. *in hot water* (= in disgrace), *hell for leather* (= at high speed).
idiomatic *adjective*, **idiomatically** *adverb*
[from Greek *idios* = your own]

idiosyncrasy (*say* id-ee-o-sink-ra-see) *noun* (*plural* idiosyncrasies)
one person's own way of behaving or doing something.
[from Greek *idios* = your own + *syn-* + *krasis* = mixture]

idiot *noun* (*plural* idiots)
1 a stupid or foolish person. 2 a person who is mentally deficient. **idiocy** *noun*, **idiotic** *adjective*, **idiotically** *adverb*
[from Greek *idiotes* = private citizen, uneducated person]

idle *adjective*
1 doing no work; lazy. 2 not in use, *The machines were idle.* 3 useless; with no special purpose, *idle gossip.* **idly** *adverb*, **idleness** *noun*

idle *verb* (idles, idling, idled)
1 be idle. 2 (of an engine) work slowly. **idler** *noun* [from Old English]

idol *noun* (*plural* idols)
1 a statue or image that is worshipped as a god. 2 a person who is admired intensely.
[from Greek *eidolon* = image]

idolatry *noun*
1 worship of idols. 2 idolizing someone.
idolatrous *adjective*
[from *idol* + Greek *latreia* = worship]

idolize *verb* (idolizes, idolizing, idolized)
admire someone intensely. **idolization** *noun*

idyll (*say* id-il) *noun* (*plural* idylls)
a poem describing a peaceful or romantic scene. **idyllic** (*say* id-il-ik) *adjective*
[from Greek *eidyllion* = little picture]

i.e. *abbreviation*
that is, *The world's highest mountain (i.e. Mount Everest) is in the Himalayas.*
[short for Latin *id est* = that is]

USAGE: Do not confuse with *e.g.*

-ie see -y.

-ier see -er.

-iest see -est.

if *conjunction*
1 on condition that; supposing that, *He will do it if you pay him.* 2 even though, *I'll finish this job if it kills me.* 3 whether, *Do you know if dinner is ready?*
if only I wish, *If only I were rich!*
[from Old English]

-iferous see -ferous.

-ification *suffix*
forms nouns of action (e.g. *purification*) from verbs that end in *-ify.*
[from Latin *-ficare* = make]

igloo *noun* (*plural* igloos)
an Inuit round house built of blocks of hard snow. [from Inuit *iglu* = house]

igneous *adjective*
formed by the action of a volcano, *igneous rocks.* [from Latin *igneus* = fiery]

ignite *verb* (ignites, igniting, ignited)
1 set fire to something. 2 catch fire.
[from Latin *ignis* = fire]

ignition *noun* (*plural* ignitions)
1 igniting. 2 the part of a motor engine that starts the fuel burning.

ignoble *adjective*
not noble; shameful. [from Latin]

ignominious *adjective*
humiliating; with disgrace. **ignominy** *noun*
[from Latin]

ignoramus *noun* (*plural* ignoramuses)
an ignorant person.
[Latin, = we do not know]

ignorant *adjective*
not knowing about something or about
many things. **ignorantly** *adverb*, **ignorance**
noun [same origin as *ignore*]

ignore *verb* (ignores, ignoring, ignored)
take no notice of a person or thing.
[from Latin *ignorare* = not know]

iguana (*say* ig-**wah**-na) *noun* (*plural*
iguanas)
a large tree-climbing tropical lizard.
[via Spanish from Arawak (a South
American language)]

il- *prefix*
1 in; into. **2** on; towards. **3** not. see **in-**.

ilk *noun*
of that ilk (*informal*) of that kind.
[from Old English *ilca* = same]

ill *adjective*
1 unwell; in bad health. **2** bad or harmful,
There were no ill effects.
ill *adverb*
badly, *She was ill-treated.*
ill at ease uncomfortable or embarrassed.
[from Old Norse]

illegal *adjective*
not legal; against the law.
illegally *adverb*, **illegality** *noun*

illegible *adjective*
impossible to read.
illegibly *adverb*, **illegibility** *noun*

illegitimate *adjective*
born when the parents are not married to
each other.
illegitimately *adverb*, **illegitimacy** *noun*

illicit *adjective*
done in a way that is against the law; not
allowed. **illicitly** *adverb*
[from *il-* + Latin *licitus* = allowed]

USAGE: Do not confuse with *elicit*.

illiterate *adjective*
unable to read or write.
illiterately *adverb*, **illiteracy** *noun*

illness *noun* (*plural* illnesses)
1 being ill. **2** a particular form of bad
health; a disease.

illogical *adjective*
not logical; not reasoning correctly.
illogically *adverb*, **illogicality** *noun*

illuminate *verb* (illuminates, illuminating,
illuminated)
1 light something up. **2** decorate streets
etc. with lights. **3** decorate a manuscript
with coloured designs. **4** clarify or help to
explain something. **illumination** *noun*
[from *il-* + Latin *lumen* = light]

illusion *noun* (*plural* illusions)
something unreal or imaginary; a false
impression, *The train went so fast that we
had the illusion that it was flying.* (Compare
delusion.) **illusive** *adjective*, **illusory** *adjective*
[from Latin *illudere* = mock]

illusionist *noun* (*plural* illusionists)
a conjuror.

illustrate *verb* (illustrates, illustrating,
illustrated)
1 show something by pictures, examples,
etc. **2** put illustrations in a book. **illustrator**
noun [from Latin *illustrare* = add light or
brilliance]

illustration *noun* (*plural* illustrations)
1 a picture in a book etc. **2** illustrating
something. **3** an example that helps to
explain something.

illustrious *adjective*
famous and distinguished. [from Latin]

ill will *noun*
unkind feelings towards a person.

im- *prefix*
1 in; into. **2** on; towards. **3** not. see **in-**.

image *noun* (*plural* images)
1 a picture or statue of a person or thing.
2 the appearance of something as seen in a
mirror or through a lens etc. **3** a person or
thing that is very much like another, *He is
the image of his father.* **4** a person's public
reputation. [from Latin]

imagery *noun*
a writer's or speaker's use of words to
produce effects.

imaginable *adjective*
able to be imagined.

imaginary *adjective*
existing only in the imagination; not real.

imagination *noun* (*plural* imaginations)
the ability to imagine things, especially in a creative or inventive way.
imaginative *adjective*

imagine *verb* (imagines, imagining, imagined)
form pictures or ideas in your mind.
[from Latin]

imam *noun* (*plural* imams)
a Muslim religious leader.
[Arabic, = leader]

imbalance *noun*
lack of balance.

imbecile (*say* imb-i-seel) *noun* (*plural* imbeciles)
an idiot. **imbecile** *adjective*, **imbecility** *noun*
[from Latin]

imbibe *verb* (imbibes, imbibing, imbibed)
drink. [from *im-* + Latin *bibere* = drink]

imitate *verb* (imitates, imitating, imitated)
copy or mimic something. **imitation** *noun*, **imitator** *noun*, **imitative** *adjective*
[from Latin]

immaculate *adjective*
1 perfectly clean; spotless. 2 without any fault or blemish. **immaculately** *adverb*
[from *im-* + Latin *macula* = spot or blemish]

immaterial *adjective*
1 having no material body, *as immaterial as a ghost*. 2 unimportant; not mattering, *It is immaterial whether he goes or stays*.

immature *adjective*
not mature. **immaturity** *noun*

immediate *adjective*
1 happening or done without any delay. 2 nearest; with nothing or no one between, *our immediate neighbours*.
immediately *adverb*, **immediacy** *noun*
[from *im-* + Latin *mediatus* = coming between]

immemorial *adjective*
going further back in time than what can be remembered, *from time immemorial*.
[from *im-* + Latin *memoria* = memory]

immense *adjective*
exceedingly great; huge. **immensely** *adverb*, **immensity** *noun*
[from *im-* + Latin *mensum* = measured]

immerse *verb* (immerses, immersing, immersed)
1 put something completely into a liquid. 2 absorb or involve deeply, *She was immersed in her work*. **immersion** *noun*
[from *im-* + Latin *mersum* = dipped]

immersion heater *noun* (*plural* immersion heaters)
a device that heats up water by means of an electric element immersed in the water in a tank etc.

immigrate *verb* (immigrates, immigrating, immigrated)
come into a country to live there.
immigration *noun*, **immigrant** *noun*

USAGE: See the note at *emigrate*.

imminent *adjective*
likely to happen at any moment, *an imminent storm*. **imminence** *noun*
[from Latin *imminere* = hang over]

immobile *adjective*
not moving; immovable. **immobility** *noun*

immobilize *verb* (immobilizes, immobilizing, immobilized)
stop a thing from moving or working.
immobilization *noun*

immodest *adjective*
1 without modesty; indecent. 2 conceited.

immoral *adjective*
morally wrong; wicked.
immorally *adverb*, **immorality** *noun*

immortal *adjective*
1 living for ever; not mortal. 2 famous for all time. **immortal** *noun*, **immortality** *noun*, **immortalize** *verb*

immovable *adjective*
unable to be moved. **immovably** *adverb*

immune *adjective*
safe from or protected against something, *immune from* (or *against* or *to*) *infection* etc.
immunity *noun*
[from Latin *immunis* = exempt]

immunize *verb* (immunizes, immunizing, immunized)
make a person immune from a disease etc., e.g. by vaccination. **immunization** *noun*

immutable (*say* i-mewt-a-bul) *adjective*
unchangeable. **immutably** *adverb*

imp *noun* (*plural* imps)
1 a small devil. **2** a mischievous child.
impish *adjective* [from Old English]

impact *noun* (*plural* impacts)
1 a collision; the force of a collision. **2** an influence or effect, *the impact of computers on our lives.*
[from *im-* + Latin *pactum* = driven]

impair *verb* (impairs, impairing, impaired)
damage or weaken something, *Smoking impairs health.* **impairment** *noun*
[from *im-* + Latin *pejor* = worse]

impala (*say* im-pah-la) *noun* (*plural* impala)
a small African antelope. [from Zulu]

impale *verb* (impales, impaling, impaled)
pierce or fix something on a sharp pointed object. **impalement** *noun*
[from *im-* + Latin *palus* = a stake]

impart *verb* (imparts, imparting, imparted)
1 tell, *She imparted the news to her brother.*
2 give, *Lemon imparts a sharp flavour to drinks.* [from Latin *impartire* = give someone part of something]

impartial *adjective*
not favouring one side more than the other; not biased. **impartially** *adverb*, **impartiality** *noun*

impassable *adjective*
not able to be travelled along or over, *The roads are impassable because of floods.*

impasse (*say* am-pahss) *noun* (*plural* impasses)
a situation in which no progress can be made; a deadlock.
[French, = impassable place]

impassive *adjective*
not showing any emotion, *His face remained impassive as the charges were read out.* **impassively** *adverb* [from *im-* + an old sense of *passive* = suffering]

impatient *adjective*
not patient.
impatiently *adverb*, **impatience** *noun*

impeach *verb* (impeaches, impeaching, impeached)
bring a person to trial for a serious crime against his or her country.
impeachment *noun*
[from old French; related to *impede*]

impeccable *adjective*
faultless. **impeccably** *adverb*
[from *im-* + Latin *peccare* = to sin]

impede *verb* (impedes, impeding, impeded)
hinder.
[from Latin *impedire* = shackle the feet]

impediment *noun* (*plural* impediments)
1 a hindrance. **2** a defect, *He has a speech impediment* (= a lisp or stammer).
[same origin as *impede*]

impel *verb* (impels, impelling, impelled)
1 urge or drive someone to do something, *Curiosity impelled her to investigate.* **2** drive forward; propel.
[from *im-* + Latin *pellere* = to drive]

impending *adjective*
soon to happen; imminent.
[from *im-* + Latin *pendere* = hang]

impenetrable *adjective*
1 impossible to get through. **2** incomprehensible.

impenitent *adjective*
not regretting at all something wrong you have done; unrepentant.

imperative *adjective*
1 expressing a command. **2** essential, *Speed is imperative.*

imperative *noun* (*plural* imperatives)
a command; the form of a verb used in making commands (e.g. 'come' in *Come here!*). [from Latin *imperare* = to command]

imperceptible *adjective*
if something is imperceptible it is so slight or gradual that it is almost impossible to notice.

imperfect *adjective*
1 not perfect. 2 (of a tense of a verb) showing a continuous action, e.g. *She was singing.*
imperfectly *adverb*, **imperfection** *noun*

imperial *adjective*
1 to do with an empire or its rulers. 2 (of weights and measures) fixed by British law; non-metric, *an imperial gallon.*
imperially *adverb*
[from Latin *imperium* = supreme power]

imperialism *noun*
the policy of extending a country's empire or its influence; colonialism.
imperialist *noun*

imperious *adjective*
haughty and bossy.
[same origin as *imperial*]

impermeable *adjective*
not allowing liquid to pass through it.

impersonal *adjective*
1 not affected by personal feelings; showing no emotion. 2 not referring to a particular person. **impersonally** *adverb*

impersonal verb *noun* (*plural* **impersonal verbs**)
a verb used only with 'it', e.g. in *It is raining* or *It is hard to find one.*

impersonate *verb* (**impersonates, impersonating, impersonated**)
pretend to be another person.
impersonation *noun*, **impersonator** *noun*
[from *im-* + Latin *persona* = person]

impertinent *adjective*
insolent; not showing proper respect.
impertinently *adverb*, **impertinence** *noun*

imperturbable *adjective*
not excitable; calm. **imperturbably** *adverb*

impervious *adjective*
1 not allowing water, heat, etc. to pass through, *impervious to water.* 2 not able to be affected by something, *impervious*

to criticism.
[from *im-* + Latin *per* = through + *via* = way]

impetuous *adjective*
acting hastily without thinking; rash.
[same origin as *impetus*]

impetus *noun*
1 the force that makes an object start moving and that keeps it moving. 2 the influence that causes something to develop more quickly. [Latin, = an attack]

impiety *noun*
lack of reverence.
impious (*say* imp-ee-us) *adjective*

impinge *verb* (**impinges, impinging, impinged**)
1 have an impact on; influence, *The economic recession impinged on all aspects of our lives.* 2 encroach or trespass.
[from *im-* + Latin *pangere* = drive in]

implacable *adjective*
not able to be placated; relentless.
implacably *adverb*
[from *im-* + *placate* + *-able*]

implant *verb* (**implants, implanting, implanted**)
insert; fix something in. **implantation** *noun*

implant *noun* (*plural* **implants**)
an organ or piece of tissue inserted in the body. [from *im-* + Latin *plantare* = to plant]

implement *noun* (*plural* **implements**)
a tool.

implement *verb* (**implements, implementing, implemented**)
put into action, *We shall implement these plans next month.* **implementation** *noun*
[from Latin]

implicate *verb* (**implicates, implicating, implicated**)
involve a person in a crime etc.; show that a person is involved, *His evidence implicates his sister.*
[from Latin *implicare* = to fold in]

implication *noun* (*plural* **implications**)
1 implicating. 2 implying; something that is implied.

implicit (*say* im-pliss-it) *adjective*
1 implied but not stated openly. (Compare *explicit*.) 2 absolute; unquestioning, *She expects implicit obedience.* **implicitly** *adverb*
[from Latin *implicitus* = entangled]

implore *verb* (implores, imploring, implored)
beg somebody to do something; entreat.
[from Latin *implorare* = ask tearfully]

imply *verb* (implies, implying, implied)
suggest something without actually saying it. **implication** *noun*
[from old French; related to *implicate*]

USAGE: See note at *infer*.

impolite *adjective*
not polite.

imponderable *adjective*
not able to be judged or estimated.
[from *im-* + Latin *ponderabilis* = able to be weighed]

import *verb* (imports, importing, imported)
bring in goods etc. from another country.
import *noun* (*plural* imports)
1 importing; something imported.
2 (*formal*) meaning or importance, *The message was of great import.*
[from *im-* + Latin *portare* = carry]

important *adjective*
1 having or able to have a great effect.
2 having great authority or influence.
importantly *adverb*, **importance** *noun*
[from Latin]

impose *verb* (imposes, imposing, imposed)
put or inflict, *It imposes a strain upon us.*
impose on somebody put an unfair burden on him or her.
[from *im-* + Latin *positum* = placed]

imposing *adjective*
impressive.

imposition *noun* (*plural* impositions)
1 something imposed; an unfair burden or inconvenience. 2 imposing something.

impossible *adjective*
1 not possible. 2 (*informal*) very annoying; unbearable, *He really is impossible!*
impossibly *adverb*, **impossibility** *noun*

impostor *noun* (*plural* impostors)
a person who dishonestly pretends to be someone else. [from French]

imposture *noun* (*plural* impostures)
a dishonest pretence.

impotent *adjective*
1 powerless; unable to take action. 2 (of a man) unable to have sexual intercourse.
impotently *adverb*, **impotence** *noun*

impound *verb* (impounds, impounding, impounded)
confiscate; take possession of.
[from *im-* + *pound*^{2}]

impoverish *verb* (impoverishes, impoverishing, impoverished)
1 make a person poor. 2 make a thing poor in quality, *impoverished soil.*
impoverishment *noun*
[from *im-* + old French *povre* = poor]

impracticable *adjective*
not able to be done in practice.

impractical *adjective*
not practical.

imprecise *adjective*
not precise.

impregnable *adjective*
strong enough to be safe against attack.
[from *im-* + old French *prendre* = take]

impregnate *verb* (impregnates, impregnating, impregnated)
1 fertilize; make pregnant. 2 saturate; fill throughout, *The air was impregnated with the scent.* **impregnation** *noun*
[from *im-* + Latin *pregnare* = be pregnant]

impresario *noun* (*plural* impresarios)
a person who organizes concerts, shows, etc.
[Italian, from *impresa* = an undertaking]

impress *verb* (impresses, impressing, impressed)
1 make a person admire something or think it is very good. 2 fix something firmly in the mind, *He impressed on them the need for secrecy.* 3 press a mark into something.
[from *im-* + old French *presser* = to press]

impression *noun* (*plural* impressions)
1 an effect produced on the mind. 2 a vague idea. 3 an imitation of a person or a sound etc. 4 a reprint of a book.

impressionable *adjective*
easily influenced or affected.

impressionism *noun*
a style of painting that gives the general effect of a scene etc. but without details. **impressionist** *noun*

impressive *adjective*
making a strong impression; seeming to be very good.

imprint *noun* (*plural* imprints)
a mark pressed into or on something.
[from Latin *imprimere* = press in]

imprison *verb* (imprisons, imprisoning, imprisoned)
put someone in prison; shut someone up in a place. **imprisonment** *noun*
[from old French]

improbable *adjective*
unlikely.
improbably *adverb*, **improbability** *noun*

impromptu *adjective* & *adverb*
done without any rehearsal or preparation.
[from Latin *in promptu* = in readiness]

improper *adjective*
1 unsuitable or wrong. 2 indecent.
improperly *adverb*, **impropriety** (*say* im-pro-pry-it-ee) *noun*

improper fraction *noun* (*plural* improper fractions)
a fraction that is greater than 1, with the numerator greater than the denominator, e.g. $\frac{5}{3}$.

improve *verb* (improves, improving, improved)
make or become better. **improvement** *noun*
[from old French *emprouer* = make a profit]

improvident *adjective*
not providing or planning for the future; not thrifty.

improvise *verb* (improvises, improvising, improvised)
1 compose or perform something without any rehearsal or preparation. 2 make something quickly with whatever is available. **improvisation** *noun*
[from im- + Latin *provisus* = provided for]

imprudent *adjective*
unwise.

impudent *adjective*
cheeky or disrespectful.
impudently *adverb*, **impudence** *noun*
[from im- + Latin *pudens* = ashamed]

impulse *noun* (*plural* impulses)
1 a sudden desire to do something. 2 a push; impetus. 3 (in physics) a force acting for a very short time, *electrical impulses*.
[same origin as *impel*]

impulsive *adjective*
done or acting on impulse, not after careful thought.
impulsively *adverb*, **impulsiveness** *noun*

impunity (*say* im-pewn-it-ee) *noun*
freedom from punishment or injury.
[from im- + Latin *poena* = penalty]

impure *adjective*
not pure. **impurity** *noun*

impute *verb* (imputes, imputing, imputed)
(*formal*) regard someone as being responsible for something; attribute.
imputation *noun* [from old French]

in *preposition*
This word is used to show position or condition, e.g. 1 at or inside; within the limits of something (*in a box*; *in two hours*), 2 into (*He fell in a puddle*), 3 arranged as; consisting of (*a serial in four parts*), 4 occupied with; a member of (*He is in the army*), 5 by means of (*We paid in cash*).
in all in total number; altogether.

in *adverb*
1 so as to be in something or inside (*Get in*), 2 inwards (*The top caved in*), 3 at home; indoors (*Is anybody in?*), 4 in action; (in cricket) batting; (of a fire) burning, 5 having arrived (*The train is in*).
in for likely to get, *You're in for a shock.*
in on (*informal*) aware of or sharing in, *I want to be in on this project.*
[from Old English]

in- *prefix* (changing to **il-** before *l*, **im-** before *b*, *m*, *p*, **ir-** before *r*)
1 in; into; on; towards (as in *include*, *invade*). [from Latin] **2** not (as in *incorrect*, *indirect*). [usually from Latin; in a few words from Germanic *un-*]

inability *noun*
being unable.

inaccessible *adjective*
not accessible.

inaccurate *adjective*
not accurate.

inactive *adjective*
not active. **inaction** *noun*, **inactivity** *noun*

inadequate *adjective*
1 not enough. **2** not capable enough.
inadequately *adverb*, **inadequacy** *noun*

inadvertent *adjective*
unintentional. [from *in-* + Latin *advertentia* = directing towards]

inadvisable *adjective*
not advisable.

inalienable *adjective*
that cannot be taken away, *an inalienable right*. [from *in-* + *alienate* + *-able*]

inane *adjective*
silly; without sense. **inanely** *adverb*, **inanity** *noun* [from Latin *inanis* = empty]

inanimate *adjective*
1 not living. **2** not moving.

inappropriate *adjective*
not appropriate.

inarticulate *adjective*
1 not able to speak or express yourself clearly, *inarticulate with rage*. **2** not expressed in words, *an inarticulate cry*.

inattention *noun*
not being attentive; not listening.
inattentive *adjective*

inaudible *adjective*
unable to be heard.
inaudibly *adverb*, **inaudibility** *noun*

inaugurate *verb* (**inaugurates**, **inaugurating**, **inaugurated**)
1 start or introduce something new and important. **2** formally establish a person in office, *inaugurate a new President*.
inaugural *adjective*, **inauguration** *noun*, **inaugurator** *noun* [from Latin]

inauspicious *adjective*
not auspicious; unlikely to be successful.

inborn *adjective*
present in a person or animal from birth, *an inborn ability*.

inbred *adjective*
1 inborn. **2** produced by inbreeding.

inbreeding *noun*
breeding from closely related individuals.

incalculable *adjective*
not able to be calculated or predicted.
[from *in-* + *calculate* + *-able*]

in camera *adverb*
in a judge's private room, not in public.
[Latin, = in the room]

incandescent *adjective*
giving out light when heated; shining.
incandescence *noun* [from *in-* + Latin *candescere* = become white]

incantation *noun* (*plural* **incantations**)
a spoken spell or charm; the chanting of this. [from *in-* = in + Latin *cantare* = sing]

incapable *adjective*
not able to do something, *incapable of working alone*.

incapacitate *verb* (**incapacitates**, **incapacitating**, **incapacitated**)
make a person or thing unable to do something; disable.
[from *in-* + *capacity* + *-ate*]

incapacity *noun*
inability; lack of sufficient strength or power.

incarcerate *verb* (**incarcerates**, **incarcerating**, **incarcerated**)
shut in or imprison a person. **incarceration** *noun* [from *in-* + Latin *carcer* = prison]

incarnate *adjective*
having a body or human form, *a devil incarnate.* **incarnation** *noun*
the Incarnation the embodiment of God in human form as Jesus Christ.
[from *in-* + Latin *carnis* = of flesh]

incautious *adjective*
rash.

incendiary *adjective*
starting or designed to start a fire, *an incendiary bomb.* [same origin as *incense*]

incense (*say* in-sens) *noun*
a substance making a spicy smell when it is burnt.
incense (*say* in-sens) *verb* (**incenses, incensing, incensed**)
make a person angry.
[from Latin *incendere* = set fire to]

incentive *noun* (*plural* **incentives**)
something that encourages a person to do something or to work harder.
[from Latin *incentivus* = setting the tune]

inception *noun*
the beginning of something.
[same origin as *incipient*]

incessant *adjective*
continuing without a pause; unceasing.
[from *in-* + Latin *cessare* = cease]

incest *noun*
sexual intercourse between two people who are so closely related that they cannot marry each other. **incestuous** *adjective*
[from *in-* + Latin *castus* = pure]

inch *noun* (*plural* **inches**)
a measure of length, one-twelfth of a foot (about 2½ centimetres). [from Old English]

incidence *noun*
the extent or frequency of something, *Study the incidence of the disease.*
[from Latin *incidens* = happening]

incident *noun* (*plural* **incidents**)
an event. [from Latin *incidere* = fall upon or happen to]

incidental *adjective*
happening as a minor part of something else, *incidental expenses.* [from *incident*]

incidentally *adverb*
by the way.

incinerate *verb* (**incinerates, incinerating, incinerated**)
destroy something by burning. **incineration** *noun* [from *in-* + Latin *cineris* = of ashes]

incinerator *noun* (*plural* **incinerators**)
a device for burning rubbish.

incipient (*say* in-**sip**-ee-ent) *adjective*
just beginning, *incipient decay.*
[from Latin *incipere* = begin]

incise *verb* (**incises, incising, incised**)
cut or engrave something into a surface.
[from *in-* + Latin *caesum* = cut]

incision *noun* (*plural* **incisions**)
a cut, especially one made in a surgical operation.

incisive *adjective*
clear and sharp, *incisive comments.*
[same origin as *incise*]

incisor (*say* in-**sy**-zer) *noun* (*plural* **incisors**)
each of the sharp-edged front teeth in the upper and lower jaws.
[same origin as *incise*]

incite *verb* (**incites, inciting, incited**)
urge a person to do something; stir up, *They incited a riot.* **incitement** *noun*
[from *in-* = towards + Latin *citare* = rouse]

incivility *noun*
rudeness or discourtesy.
[from *in-* + *civility*]

inclement *adjective* (*formal*)
cold, wet, or stormy, *inclement weather.*
[from *in-* + Latin *clemens* = mild]

inclination *noun* (*plural* **inclinations**)
1 a tendency. 2 a liking or preference.
3 a slope or slant.

incline *verb* (**inclines, inclining, inclined**)
1 lean or slope. 2 bend the head or body forward, as in a nod or bow. 3 cause or influence, *Her frank manner inclines me to believe her.*
be inclined have a tendency, *The door is inclined to bang.*
incline *noun* (*plural* **inclines**)
a slope. [from Latin *inclinare* = to bend]

include *verb* (includes, including, included)
make or consider something as part of a group of things.
[from Latin *includere* = enclose]

inclusive *adjective*
including everything.

incognito (*say* in-kog-**neet**-oh or in-**kog**-nit-oh) *adjective & adverb*
with your name or identity concealed, *The film star was travelling incognito.*
[Italian, from *in-* + Latin *cognitus* = known]

incoherent *adjective*
not speaking or reasoning in an orderly way.

incombustible *adjective*
unable to be set on fire. [from *in-* + Latin *combustibilis* = combustible]

income *noun* (*plural* incomes)
money received regularly from wages, investments, etc. [from *in* (adverb) + *come*]

income tax *noun*
tax charged on income.

incoming *adjective*
1 coming in, *incoming telephone calls.*
2 about to take over from someone else, *the incoming chairman.*

incomparable *adjective*
without an equal; unsurpassed, *incomparable beauty.* [from *in-* + Latin *comparabilis* = comparable]

incompatible *adjective*
not compatible.

incompetent *adjective*
not competent.

incomplete *adjective*
not complete.

incomprehensible *adjective*
not able to be understood. **incomprehension** *noun* [from *in-* + Latin *comprehensibilis* = comprehensible]

inconceivable *adjective*
not able to be imagined; most unlikely.

inconclusive *adjective*
not conclusive.

incongruous *adjective*
out of place or unsuitable. **incongruously** *adverb*, **incongruity** *noun* [from *in-* + Latin *congruus* = agreeing or suitable]

inconsiderable *adjective*
of small value.

inconsiderate *adjective*
not considerate.

inconsistent *adjective*
not consistent. **inconsistently** *adverb*, **inconsistency** *noun*

inconsolable *adjective*
not able to be consoled; very sad.

inconspicuous *adjective*
not conspicuous. **inconspicuously** *adverb*

incontinent *adjective*
not able to control the bladder or bowels.
incontinence *noun* [from *in-* + Latin *continentia* = restraining, keeping in]

incontrovertible *adjective*
unable to be denied; indisputable.
[from *in-* + Latin *controversus* = disputed]

inconvenience *noun* (*plural* inconveniences)
being inconvenient.
inconvenience *verb* (inconveniences, inconveniencing, inconvenienced)
cause inconvenience or slight difficulty to someone.

inconvenient *adjective*
not convenient.

incorporate *verb* (incorporates, incorporating, incorporated)
include something as a part. **incorporation** *noun* [from *in-* + Latin *corpus* = body]

incorporated *adjective*
(of a business firm) formed into a legal corporation.

incorrect *adjective*
not correct. **incorrectly** *adverb*

incorrigible *adjective*
not able to be reformed, *an incorrigible liar.*
[from *in-* + Latin *corrigere* = to correct]

incorruptible *adjective*
1 not able to decay. 2 not able to be bribed.

increase *verb* (increases, increasing, increased)
make or become larger or more.

increase *noun* (*plural* increases)
increasing; the amount by which a thing increases.
[from *in-* + Latin *crescere* = grow]

incredible *adjective*
unbelievable.
incredibly *adverb*, **incredibility** *noun*

USAGE: Do not confuse with *incredulous*.

incredulous *adjective*
not believing somebody; showing disbelief.
incredulously *adverb*, **incredulity** *noun*

USAGE: Do not confuse with *incredible*.

increment (*say* in-krim-ent) *noun* (*plural* increments)
an increase; an added amount.
[from Latin *incrementum* = growth]

incriminate *verb* (incriminates, incriminating, incriminated)
show a person to have been involved in a crime etc. **incrimination** *noun* [from *in-* + Latin *criminare* = accuse of a crime]

incrustation *noun* (*plural* incrustations)
encrusting; a crust or deposit that forms on a surface.
[from *in-* + Latin *crustare* = form a crust]

incubate *verb* (incubates, incubating, incubated)
1 hatch eggs by keeping them warm.
2 cause bacteria or a disease etc. to develop. **incubation** *noun*
[from *in-* + Latin *cubare* = lie]

incubator *noun* (*plural* incubators)
1 a device for incubating eggs etc. 2 a device in which a baby born prematurely can be kept warm and supplied with oxygen.

incumbent *adjective*
if it is incumbent on you to do something, it is your duty to do it, *It is incumbent on you to warn people of the danger.*

incumbent *noun* (*plural* incumbents)
a person who holds a particular office or position.
[from *in-* + Latin *-cumbens* = lying]

incur *verb* (incurs, incurring, incurred)
bring something on yourself, *incur expense*.
[from *in-* + Latin *currere* = to run]

incurable *adjective*
not able to be cured. **incurably** *adverb*

incurious *adjective*
feeling or showing no curiosity about something.

incursion *noun* (*plural* incursions)
a raid or brief invasion.
[same origin as *incur*]

indebted *adjective*
owing money or gratitude to someone.
[from old French]

indecent *adjective*
not decent; improper.
indecently *adverb*, **indecency** *noun*

indecipherable *adjective*
not able to be deciphered.

indecision *noun*
being unable to make up your mind; hesitation.

indecisive *adjective*
not decisive.

indeed *adverb*
1 really; truly, *I am indeed surprised*; (used to strengthen a meaning), *very nice indeed.*
2 admittedly, *It is, indeed, his first attempt.*
[from *in deed* = in action or fact]

indefensible *adjective*
unable to be defended or justified, *an indefensible decision.*

indefinable *adjective*
unable to be defined or described clearly.

indefinite *adjective*
not definite; vague.
indefinite article the word 'a' or 'an'.

indefinitely *adverb*
for an indefinite or unlimited time.

indelible *adjective*
impossible to rub out or remove. **indelibly**
adverb [from *in-* + Latin *delere* = destroy]

indelicate *adjective*
1 slightly indecent. **2** tactless.
indelicacy *noun*

indent *verb* (indents, indenting, indented)
1 make notches or recesses in something.
2 start a line of writing or printing further
in from the margin than other lines,
*Always indent the first line of a new
paragraph.* **3** place an official order for
goods or stores, *Indent for a new office desk.*
indentation *noun*
[from *in-* + Latin *dens* = tooth (because the
indentations looked like teeth)]

indenture *noun* or **indentures** *plural
noun*
an agreement binding an apprentice to
work for a certain employer. **indentured**
adjective [same origin as *indent* (because
each copy of the agreement had notches cut
into it, so that the copies could be fitted
together to show that they were genuine)]

independent *adjective*
1 not dependent; not controlled by any
other person or thing. **2** (of a country)
governing itself. **3** (of broadcasting) not
financed by money from licences.
independently *adverb*, **independence** *noun*

indescribable *adjective*
unable to be described. **indescribably** *adverb*

indestructible *adjective*
unable to be destroyed. **indestructibility**
noun [from *in-* + Latin *destruere* = destroy]

indeterminate *adjective*
not fixed or decided exactly; left vague.
[from *in-* + Latin *determinare* = define or
determine]

index *noun*
1 (*plural* indexes) an alphabetical list of
things, especially at the end of a book. **2** a
number showing how prices or wages have
changed from a previous level. **3** (*plural*
indices) the raised number etc. written to
the right of another (e.g. 3 in 2^3) showing
how many times the first one is to be
multiplied by itself.

index *verb* (indexes, indexing, indexed)
make an index to a book etc.; put
something into an index. [Latin, = pointer]

index finger *noun* (*plural* index fingers)
the forefinger.

Indian *adjective*
1 to do with India or its people. **2** to do with
Native Americans. **Indian** *noun*

USAGE: The preferred term for the
descendants of the original inhabitants of
North and South America is *Native
American. American Indian* is usually
acceptable but the term *Red Indian* is now
regarded as offensive and should not be
used.

Indian summer *noun* (*plural* Indian
summers)
a warm period in late autumn (originally
in North America).

india rubber *noun* (*plural* india rubbers)
a rubber.
[because it was made of rubber from India]

indicate *verb* (indicates, indicating,
indicated)
1 point something out or make it known.
2 be a sign of. **3** when drivers indicate,
they signal which direction they are
turning by using their indicators.
indication *noun*
[from Latin; related to *index*]

indicative *adjective*
giving an indication.
indicative *noun*
the form of a verb used in making a
statement (e.g. 'he said' or 'he is coming'),
not in a command or question etc.

indicator *noun* (*plural* indicators)
1 a thing that indicates or points to
something. **2** a flashing light used to signal
that a motor vehicle is turning.

indict (*say* ind-I't) *verb* (indicts, indicting,
indicted)
charge a person with having committed a
crime. **indictment** *noun*
[from Latin *indicere* = proclaim]

indifferent *adjective*
1 not caring about something; not
interested. **2** not very good, *an indifferent*

cricketer. **indifferently** *adverb*, **indifference**
noun [from *in-* + Latin *differre* = recognize
differences]

indigenous (*say* in-dij-in-us) *adjective*
growing or originating in a particular
country; native, *The koala bear is
indigenous to Australia.*
[from Latin *indigena* = born in a country]

indigent (*say* in-dij-ent) *adjective*
needy. [from Latin]

indigestible *adjective*
difficult or impossible to digest.

indigestion *noun*
pain caused by difficulty in digesting food.
[from *in-* + Latin *digerere* = digest]

indignant *adjective*
angry at something that seems unfair or
wicked. **indignantly** *adverb*, **indignation**
noun [from Latin *indignari* = regard as
unworthy]

indignity *noun* (*plural* **indignities**)
treatment that makes a person feel
undignified or humiliated; an insult.
[from *in-* + Latin *dignus* worthy]

indigo *noun*
a deep-blue colour. [from Greek *indikon*
= something from India]

indirect *adjective*
not direct. **indirectly** *adverb*

indiscreet *adjective*
1 not discreet; revealing secrets. **2** not
cautious; rash. **indiscreetly** *adverb*,
indiscretion *noun*

indiscriminate *adjective*
showing no discrimination; not making a
careful choice. **indiscriminately** *adverb*

indispensable *adjective*
not able to be dispensed with; essential.
indispensability *noun*

indisposed *adjective*
1 slightly unwell. **2** unwilling, *They seem
indisposed to help us.* **indisposition** *noun*

indisputable *adjective*
undeniable.
[from *in-* + Latin *disputare* = dispute]

indistinct *adjective*
not distinct.
indistinctly *adverb*, **indistinctness** *noun*

indistinguishable *adjective*
not able to be told apart; not
distinguishable.

individual *adjective*
1 of or for one person. **2** single or separate,
Count each individual word.
individually *adverb*

individual *noun* (*plural* **individuals**)
one person, animal, or plant.
[from *in-* + Latin *dividuus* = able to be
divided]

individuality *noun*
the things that make one person or thing
different from another; distinctive
identity.

indivisible *adjective*
not able to be divided or separated.
indivisibly *adverb*
[from *in-* + Latin *divisum* = divided]

indoctrinate *verb* (**indoctrinates,
indoctrinating, indoctrinated**)
fill a person's mind with particular ideas
or beliefs, especially so that he or she
comes to accept them without thinking.
indoctrination *noun*
[from *in-* = in, + *doctrine*]

indolent *adjective*
lazy. **indolently** *adverb*, **indolence** *noun*
[from *in-* + Latin *dolere* = suffer pain or
trouble]

indomitable *adjective*
not able to be overcome or conquered.
[from *in-* + Latin *domitare* = to tame]

indoor *adjective*
used or placed or done etc. inside a
building, *indoor games.*

indoors *adverb*
inside a building.

indubitable (*say* in-**dew**-bit-a-bul) *adjective*
not able to be doubted; certain.
indubitably *adverb*
[from *in-* + Latin *dubitare* = to doubt]

induce *verb* (**induces, inducing, induced**)
1 persuade. **2** produce or cause, *Some substances induce sleep.* **3** if a pregnant woman is induced, labour is brought on artificially with the use of drugs. **induction** *noun* [from *in-* + Latin *ducere* = to lead]

inducement *noun* (*plural* **inducements**)
an incentive.

indulge *verb* (**indulges, indulging, indulged**)
allow a person to have or do what he or she wishes.
indulgence *noun*, **indulgent** *adjective*
indulge in allow yourself to have or do something that you like.
[from Latin]

industrial *adjective*
to do with industry; working or used in industry. **industrially** *adverb*

industrial action *noun*
striking or working to rule.

industrialist *noun* (*plural* **industrialists**)
a person who owns or manages an industrial business.

industrialized *adjective*
(of a country or district) having many industries. **industrialization** *noun*

Industrial Revolution *noun*
the expansion of British industry by the use of machines in the late 18th and early 19th century.

industrious *adjective*
working hard. **industriously** *adverb*

industry *noun* (*plural* **industries**)
1 making or producing goods etc., especially in factories. **2** a particular branch of this, *the motor industry.* **3** being industrious.
[from Latin *industria* = hard work]

inebriated *adjective*
drunk. [from *in-* + Latin *ebrius* = drunk]

inedible *adjective*
not edible.

ineffective *adjective*
not effective; inefficient.
ineffectively *adverb*

ineffectual *adjective*
not achieving anything.

inefficient *adjective*
not efficient.
inefficiently *adverb*, **inefficiency** *noun*

inelegant *adjective*
not elegant.

ineligible *adjective*
not eligible.

inept *adjective*
lacking any skill; bungling.
ineptly *adverb*, **ineptitude** *noun*
[from *in-* + Latin *aptus* = apt]

inequality *noun* (*plural* **inequalities**)
not being equal.

inequity *noun* (*plural* **inequities**)
unfairness. **inequitable** *adjective*

inert *adjective*
not moving or reacting. **inertly** *adverb*
[from Latin *iners* = idle]

inert gas *noun* (*plural* **inert gases**)
a gas that almost never combines with other substances.

inertia (*say* in-er-sha) *noun*
1 inactivity; being inert or slow to take action. **2** the tendency for a moving thing to keep moving in a straight line.
[same origin as *inert*]

inescapable *adjective*
unavoidable.

inessential *adjective*
not essential.

inestimable *adjective*
too great or precious to be able to be estimated.

inevitable *adjective*
unavoidable; sure to happen.
inevitably *adverb*, **inevitability** *noun*
[from *in-* + Latin *evitare* = avoid]

inexact *adjective*
not exact.

inexcusable *adjective*
not excusable.

inexhaustible *adjective*
so great that it cannot be used up completely, *Ben has an inexhaustible supply of jokes.*

inexorable (*say* in-eks-er-a-bul) *adjective*
1 relentless. 2 not able to be persuaded by requests or entreaties. **inexorably** *adverb*
[from *in-* + Latin *exorare* = plead]

inexpensive *adjective*
not expensive; cheap. **inexpensively** *adverb*

inexperience *noun*
lack of experience. **inexperienced** *adjective*

inexpert *adjective*
unskilful.
[from Latin *inexpertus* = inexperienced]

inexplicable *adjective*
impossible to explain. **inexplicably** *adverb*
[from *in-* + Latin *explicare* = unfold]

in extremis (*say* eks-**treem**-iss) *adverb*
at the point of death; in very great difficulties.
[Latin, = in the greatest danger]

infallible *adjective*
1 never wrong. 2 never failing, *an infallible remedy.*
infallibly *adverb*, **infallibility** *noun*
[from *in-* + Latin *fallere* = deceive]

infamous (*say* in-fam-us) *adjective*
having a bad reputation; wicked.
infamously *adverb*, **infamy** *noun* [from *in-* + Latin *fama* = good reputation, fame]

infancy *noun*
1 early childhood; babyhood. 2 an early stage of development.

infant *noun* (*plural* **infants**)
a baby or young child.
[from Latin *infans* = unable to speak]

infantile *adjective*
1 to do with infants. 2 very childish.

infantry *noun*
soldiers who fight on foot. (Compare *cavalry.*) [from Italian *infante* = a youth]

infatuated *adjective*
filled with foolish or unreasoning love.
infatuation *noun*
[from *in-* + Latin *fatuus* = foolish]

infect *verb* (**infects, infecting, infected**)
pass on a disease or bacteria etc. to a person, animal, or plant.
[from Latin *infectum* = tainted]

infection *noun* (*plural* **infections**)
1 infecting. 2 an infectious disease or condition.

infectious *adjective*
1 (of a disease) able to be spread by air or water etc. (Compare *contagious.*) 2 quickly spreading to others, *His fear was infectious.*

infer *verb* (**infers, inferring, inferred**)
form an opinion or work something out from what someone says or does, even though they do not actually say it, *I infer from your luggage that you are going on holiday.* **inference** *noun*
[from *in-* + Latin *ferre* = bring]

USAGE: Do not confuse with *imply.*
Remember that *imply* and *infer* are a pair of words with opposite meanings, in the same way that *lend* means the opposite of *borrow* and *teach* the opposite of *learn.*
Don't say 'What exactly are you inferring?' when you mean 'What exactly are you implying?'

inferior *adjective*
less good or less important; low or lower in position, quality, etc. **inferiority** *noun*
[Latin, = lower]

infernal *adjective*
1 to do with or like hell, *the infernal regions.* 2 (*informal*) detestable or tiresome, *that infernal noise.*
infernally *adverb*
[from Latin *infernus* = below, used by Christians to mean 'hell']

inferno *noun* (*plural* **infernos**)
a terrifying fire.
[same origin as *infernal*]

infertile *adjective*
not fertile. **infertility** *noun*

infest *verb* (infests, infesting, infested)
(of pests) be numerous and troublesome in a place. **infestation** *noun*
[from Latin *infestus* = hostile]

infidel (*say* in-fid-el) *noun* (*plural* infidels)
a person who does not believe in a religion.
[from *in-* + Latin *fidelis* = faithful]

infidelity *noun*
unfaithfulness.
[same origin as *infidel*]

infiltrate *verb* (infiltrates, infiltrating, infiltrated)
get into a place or organization gradually and without being noticed.
infiltration *noun*, **infiltrator** *noun*
[from *in-* + Latin *filtrare* = to filter]

infinite *adjective*
1 endless; without a limit. 2 too great to be measured. **infinitely** *adverb*
[from Latin *infinitus* = unlimited]

infinitesimal *adjective*
extremely small. **infinitesimally** *adverb*
[from Latin]

infinitive *noun* (*plural* infinitives)
a form of a verb that does not indicate a particular tense or number or person, in English used with or without *to*, e.g. *go* in 'Let him go' or 'Allow him to go'.
[from *in-* + Latin *finitivus* = definite]

infinity *noun*
an infinite number or distance or time.

infirm *adjective*
weak, especially from old age or illness.
infirmity *noun*
[from *in-* + Latin *firmus* = firm]

infirmary *noun* (*plural* infirmaries)
1 a hospital. 2 a place where sick people are cared for in a school or monastery etc.

inflame *verb* (inflames, inflaming, inflamed)
1 produce strong feelings or anger in people. 2 cause redness, heat, and swelling in a part of the body.
[from *in-* + Latin *flamma* = flame]

inflammable *adjective*
able to be set on fire.
[same origin as *inflame*]

USAGE: This word means the same as *flammable*. If you want to say that something is not able to be set on fire, use *non-flammable*.

---

inflammation *noun*
painful redness or swelling in a part of the body.

inflammatory *adjective*
likely to make people angry, *inflammatory leaflets*.

inflatable *adjective*
able to be inflated.

inflate *verb* (inflates, inflating, inflated)
1 fill something with air or gas so that it expands. 2 increase something too much. 3 raise prices or wages etc. more than is justifiable.
[from *in-* + Latin *flatum* = blown]

inflation *noun*
1 inflating. 2 a general rise in prices and fall in the purchasing power of money.
inflationary *adjective*

inflect *verb* (inflects, inflecting, inflected)
1 change the ending or form of a word to show its tense or its grammatical relation to other words, e.g. *sing* changes to *sang* or *sung*, *child* changes to *children*. 2 alter the voice in speaking. [originally = bend inwards: from *in-* + Latin *flectere* = to bend]

inflection *noun* (*plural* inflections)
an ending or form of a word used to inflect, e.g. *-ed*.

inflexible *adjective*
not able to be bent or changed or persuaded. **inflexibly** *adverb*, **inflexibility** *noun* [from *in-* + Latin *flexibilis* = flexible]

inflexion *noun* (*plural* inflexions)
a different spelling of *inflection*.

inflict *verb* (inflicts, inflicting, inflicted)
make a person suffer something, *She inflicted a severe blow on him*.
infliction *noun*
[from *in-* + Latin *flictum* = struck]

inflow *noun*
flowing in; what flows in.

influence *noun* (*plural* **influences**)
1 the power to produce an effect. 2 a person or thing with this power.

influence *verb* (**influences, influencing, influenced**)
have influence on a person or thing; affect.
[from *in-* + Latin *fluentia* = flowing]

influential *adjective*
having influence.

influenza *noun*
an infectious disease that causes fever, catarrh, and pain.
[Italian, literally = influence]

influx *noun*
a flowing in, especially of people or things coming in. [from Latin]

inform *verb* (**informs, informing, informed**)
give information to somebody. **informant** *noun* [from Latin *informare* = form an idea of something]

informal *adjective*
not formal.
informally *adverb*, **informality** *noun*

USAGE: In this dictionary, words marked *informal* are used in talking but not when you are writing or speaking formally.

information *noun*
facts told or heard or discovered, or put into a computer etc.
[from Latin *informatio* = idea]

information technology *noun*
the study or use of ways of storing, arranging, and giving out information, especially computers and telecommunications.

informative *adjective*
giving a lot of useful information.

informed *adjective*
knowing about something.

informer *noun* (*plural* **informers**)
a person who gives information against someone, especially to the police.

infra- *prefix*
below. [Latin]

infra-red *adjective*
below or beyond red in the spectrum.

infrequent *adjective*
not frequent.

infringe *verb* (**infringes, infringing, infringed**)
break a rule or an agreement etc.; violate.
infringement *noun*
[from *in-* + Latin *frangere* = break]

infuriate *verb* (**infuriates, infuriating, infuriated**)
make a person very angry; enrage.
infuriation *noun*
[from *in-* + Latin *furia* = fury]

infuse *verb* (**infuses, infusing, infused**)
1 add or inspire with a feeling etc., *infuse them with courage*; *infuse courage into them.* 2 soak or steep tea or herbs etc. in a liquid to extract the flavour. **infusion** *noun*
[from Latin *infusum* = poured in]

-ing *suffix*
forms nouns and adjectives showing the action of a verb (e.g. *hearing, tasting, telling*).

ingenious *adjective*
1 clever at inventing things. 2 cleverly made. **ingeniously** *adverb*, **ingenuity** *noun*
[from Latin *ingenium* = genius]

USAGE: Do not confuse with *ingenuous*.

ingenuous *adjective*
naive. **ingenuously** *adverb*, **ingenuousness** *noun* [from Latin *ingenuus* = inborn]

USAGE: Do not confuse with *ingenious*.

ingot *noun* (*plural* **ingots**)
a lump of gold or silver etc. that is cast in a brick shape.
[from *in-* + Old English *geotan* = pour]

ingrained *adjective*
1 (of dirt) marking a surface deeply. 2 (of feelings or habits etc.) firmly fixed.
[from *in the grain* (of wood)]

ingratiate *verb* (ingratiates, ingratiating, ingratiated)
ingratiate yourself get yourself into favour with someone, especially by flattering them or always agreeing with them.
ingratiation *noun*
[from Latin *in gratiam* = into favour]

ingratitude *noun*
lack of gratitude.

ingredient *noun* (*plural* ingredients)
one of the parts of a mixture; one of the things used in a recipe.
[from Latin *ingrediens* = going in]

inhabit *verb* (inhabits, inhabiting, inhabited)
live in a place. **inhabitant** *noun*
[from *in-* + Latin *habitare* = occupy]

inhale *verb* (inhales, inhaling, inhaled)
breathe in. **inhalation** *noun*
[from *in-* + Latin *halare* = breathe]

inhaler *noun* (*plural* inhalers)
a device used for relieving asthma etc. by inhaling.

inharmonious *adjective*
not harmonious.

inherent (*say* in-**heer**-ent) *adjective*
existing in something as one of its natural or permanent qualities.
inherently *adverb*, **inherence** *noun*
[from *in-* + Latin *haerere* = to stick]

inherit *verb* (inherits, inheriting, inherited)
1 receive money, property, or a title etc. when its previous owner dies. 2 get certain qualities etc. from parents or predecessors.
inheritance *noun*, **inheritor** *noun*
[from *in-* + Latin *heres* = heir]

inhibit *verb* (inhibits, inhibiting, inhibited)
hinder or restrain something.

inhibition *noun* (*plural* inhibitions)
a feeling of embarrassment or worry that prevents you from doing something or expressing your emotions. **inhibited**
adjective [from *in-* + Latin *habere* = to hold]

inhospitable *adjective*
not hospitable.

inhuman *adjective*
cruel; without pity or kindness.
inhumanity *noun*
[from *in-* + Latin *humanus* = human]

inhumane *adjective*
not humane.

inimitable *adjective*
impossible to imitate.

iniquitous *adjective*
very unjust. **iniquity** *noun*
[from *in-* + Latin *aequus* = equal or fair]

initial *noun* (*plural* initials)
the first letter of a word or name.
initial *verb* (initials, initialling, initialled)
mark or sign something with the initials of your names.
initial *adjective*
at the beginning, *the initial stages*.
initially *adverb*
[from Latin *initium* = the beginning]

initiate *verb* (initiates, initiating, initiated)
1 start something. 2 admit a person as a member of a society or group, often with special ceremonies. **initiation** *noun*, **initiator** *noun* [same origin as *initial*]

initiative (*say* in-**ish**-a-tiv) *noun*
the power or courage to get something started; enterprising ability.
take the initiative take action to start something happening.

inject *verb* (injects, injecting, injected)
1 put a medicine or drug into the body by means of a hollow needle. 2 put liquid into something by means of a syringe etc. 3 add a new quality, *Inject some humour into the story*. **injection** *noun*
[from *in-* + Latin *jacere* = to throw]

injudicious *adjective*
unwise.

injunction *noun* (*plural* injunctions)
a command given with authority, e.g. by a lawcourt. [from Latin]

injure *verb* (injures, injuring, injured)
harm or hurt someone. **injury** *noun*,
injurious (*say* in-**joor**-ee-us) *adjective*
[originally = treat someone unfairly: from *in-* + Latin *juris* = of right]

injustice noun (plural injustices)
1 lack of justice. 2 an unjust action or treatment.

ink noun (plural inks)
a black or coloured liquid used in writing and printing. [from Greek]

inkling noun (plural inklings)
a hint; a slight knowledge or suspicion, I had no inkling of your artistic talents. [origin unknown]

inky adjective
1 stained with ink. 2 black like ink, inky darkness.

inland adjective & adverb
in or towards the interior of a country; away from the coast.

Inland Revenue noun
the government department responsible for collecting taxes and similar charges inland (not at a port).

in-laws plural noun (informal)
relatives by marriage. [from French en loi de mariage = in law of marriage]

inlay verb (inlays, inlaying, inlaid)
set pieces of wood or metal etc. into a surface to form a design. **inlay** noun
[from in- + lay¹]

inlet noun (plural inlets)
1 a strip of water reaching into the land from a sea or lake. 2 a passage that lets something in (e.g. to a tank).

inmate noun (plural inmates)
one of the occupants of a prison, hospital, or other institution.
[originally = a lodger: from inn + mate¹]

in memoriam preposition
in memory of. [Latin]

inmost adjective
most inward.

inn noun (plural inns)
a hotel or public house, especially in the country. **innkeeper** noun
[from Old English]

innate adjective
inborn. [from in- + Latin natus = born]

inner adjective
inside; nearer to the centre.
innermost adjective

innings noun (plural innings)
the time when a cricket team or player is batting.
[from an old verb in = put or get in, + -ing]

innocent adjective
1 not guilty. 2 not wicked. 3 harmless.
innocently adverb, **innocence** noun
[from in- + Latin nocens = doing harm]

innocuous adjective
harmless.
[from in- + Latin nocuus = harmful]

innovation noun (plural innovations)
1 introducing new things or new methods. 2 something newly introduced.
innovative adjective, **innovator** noun
[from in- + Latin novus = new]

innuendo noun (plural innuendoes)
indirect reference to something insulting or rude.
[Latin, = by nodding at or pointing to]

Innuit noun (plural Innuit)
a different spelling of Inuit.

innumerable adjective
countless. [from in- + Latin numerare = to count or number]

inoculate verb (inoculates, inoculating, inoculated)
inject or treat someone with a vaccine or serum as a protection against a disease.
inoculation noun
[from Latin inoculare = implant]

USAGE: Note the spelling of this word. It has one 'n' and one 'c'.

inoffensive adjective
harmless.

inordinate adjective
excessive. **inordinately** adverb
[from in- + Latin ordinare = ordain]

inorganic adjective
not of living organisms; of mineral origin.

input noun
what is put into something (e.g. data into a computer). **input** verb

inquest noun (plural inquests)
an official inquiry to find out how a person died.
[from old French; related to inquire]

inquire verb (inquires, inquiring, inquired)
1 investigate something carefully. 2 ask for information.
[from in- + Latin quaerere = seek]

USAGE: You can spell this word inquire or enquire in either of its meanings. It is probably more common for inquire to be used for 'investigate' and enquire to be used for 'ask for information', but there is no real need to follow this distinction.

inquiry noun (plural inquiries)
1 an investigation. 2 a question.

inquisition noun (plural inquisitions)
a detailed questioning or investigation. **inquisitor** noun
the Inquisition a council of the Roman Catholic Church in the Middle Ages set up to discover and punish heretics.
[same origin as inquire]

inquisitive adjective
always asking questions or trying to look at things; prying. **inquisitively** adverb
[same origin as inquire]

inroads plural noun
make inroads on or **into** use up large quantities of stores etc.
[from in (adverb) + an old sense of road = riding]

inrush noun (plural inrushes)
a sudden rushing in.

insane adjective
not sane; mad.
insanely adverb, **insanity** noun

insanitary adjective
unclean and likely to be harmful to health.

insatiable (say in-say-sha-bul) adjective
impossible to satisfy, an insatiable appetite.
[from in- + Latin satiare = satiate]

inscribe verb (inscribes, inscribing, inscribed)
write or carve words etc. on something.
[from in- + Latin scribere = write]

inscription noun (plural inscriptions)
1 words or names inscribed on a monument, coin, stone, etc. 2 inscribing.

inscrutable adjective
mysterious; impossible to interpret, an inscrutable smile.
[from in- + Latin scrutari = to search]

insect noun (plural insects)
a small animal with six legs, no backbone, and a body divided into three parts (head, thorax, abdomen).
[from Latin insectum = cut up]

insecticide noun (plural insecticides)
a substance for killing insects.
[from insect + -cide]

insectivorous adjective
feeding on insects and other small invertebrate creatures. **insectivore** noun

insecure adjective
not secure; unsafe.
insecurely adverb, **insecurity** noun

inseminate verb (inseminates, inseminating, inseminated)
insert semen into the womb. **insemination** noun [from in- + Latin seminare = to sow]

insensible adjective
1 unconscious. 2 unaware of something, He was insensible of her needs.

insensitive adjective
not sensitive.
insensitively adverb, **insensitivity** noun

inseparable adjective
1 not able to be separated. 2 liking to be constantly together, inseparable friends.
inseparably adverb

insert verb (inserts, inserting, inserted)
put a thing into something else. **insertion** noun [from in- + Latin serere = to plant]

inshore adverb & adjective
near or nearer to the shore.

inside *noun* (*plural* **insides**)
1 the inner side, surface, or part.
2 (*informal*) the organs in the abdomen; the stomach and bowels.
inside out with the inside turned to face outwards.

inside *adjective*
on or coming from the inside; in or nearest to the middle.

inside *adverb* & *preposition*
on or to the inside of something; in, *Come inside. It's inside that box.*

insider *noun* (*plural* **insiders**)
a member of a certain group, especially someone with access to private information.

insidious *adjective*
unnoticed but harmful. **insidiously** *adverb*
[from Latin *insidiae* = an ambush]

insight *noun* (*plural* **insights**)
being able to perceive the truth about things; understanding.

insignia *singular* or *plural noun*
a badge or symbol that shows that you belong to something or hold a particular office. [from Latin; related to *sign*]

insignificant *adjective*
not important or influential.
insignificance *noun*

insincere *adjective*
not sincere.
insincerely *adverb*, **insincerity** *noun*

insinuate *verb* (**insinuates, insinuating, insinuated**)
1 hint something unpleasant. 2 introduce a thing or yourself gradually or craftily into a place. **insinuation** *noun*
[from *in-* + Latin *sinuare* = to curve]

insipid *adjective*
1 lacking flavour. 2 not lively or interesting. **insipidity** *noun*
[from *in-* + Latin *sapidus* = having flavour]

insist *verb* (**insists, insisting, insisted**)
be very firm in saying or asking for something. **insistent** *adjective*, **insistence** *noun* [from *in-* + Latin *sistere* = to stand]

in situ (*say* in sit-yoo) *adverb*
in its original place. [Latin]

insolent *adjective*
very impudent; insulting.
insolently *adverb*, **insolence** *noun*
[from Latin *insolentia* = pride]

insoluble *adjective*
1 impossible to solve, *an insoluble problem.*
2 impossible to dissolve. **insolubility** *noun*
[from *in-* + Latin *solubilis* = soluble]

insolvent *adjective*
unable to pay your debts. **insolvency** *noun*

insomnia *noun*
being unable to sleep. **insomniac** *noun*
[from *in-* + Latin *somnus* = sleep]

inspect *verb* (**inspects, inspecting, inspected**)
examine something carefully and critically. **inspection** *noun*
[from *in-* + Latin *specere* = to look]

inspector *noun* (*plural* **inspectors**)
1 a person whose job is to inspect or supervise things. 2 a police officer ranking next above a sergeant.

inspiration *noun* (*plural* **inspirations**)
1 a sudden brilliant idea. 2 inspiring; an inspiring influence.

inspire *verb* (**inspires, inspiring, inspired**)
fill a person with enthusiasm or creative feelings or ideas, *The applause inspired us with confidence.*
[from *in-* + Latin *spirare* = breathe]

instability *noun*
lack of stability.

install *verb* (**installs, installing, installed**)
1 put something in position and ready to use, *They installed central heating.* 2 put a person into an important position with a ceremony, *He was installed as pope.*
installation *noun* [from *in-* + Latin *stallum* = a place or position]

instalment *noun* (*plural* **instalments**)
each of the parts in which something is given or paid for gradually, *an instalment of a serial.* [from old French]

instance *noun* (*plural* **instances**)
an example, *for instance.* [from Latin]

instant *adjective*
1 happening immediately, *instant success*.
2 (of food) designed to be prepared quickly
and easily, *instant coffee*. **instantly** *adverb*
instant *noun* (*plural* instants)
a moment, *not an instant too soon*.
[from Latin *instans* = urgent]

instantaneous *adjective*
happening immediately.
instantaneously *adverb*

instead *adverb*
in place of something else.
[from *in-* + *stead* = a place]

instep *noun* (*plural* insteps)
the top of the foot between the toes and the
ankle. [origin unknown]

instigate *verb* (instigates, instigating,
instigated)
stir up; cause something to be done,
instigate a rebellion. **instigation** *noun*,
instigator *noun* [same origin as *instinct*]

instil *verb* (instils, instilling, instilled)
put ideas into a person's mind gradually.
[from *in-* + Latin *stilla* = a drop]

instinct *noun* (*plural* instincts)
a natural tendency or ability, *Birds fly by
instinct*. **instinctive** *adjective*, **instinctively**
adverb [from Latin *instinguere* = urge on]

institute *noun* (*plural* institutes)
a society or organization; the building used
by this.
institute *verb* (institutes, instituting,
instituted)
establish or found something; start an
inquiry or custom etc.
[from *in-* + Latin *statuere* = set up]

institution *noun* (*plural* institutions)
1 an institute; a public organization, e.g. a
hospital or university. 2 a habit or custom.
3 instituting something.
institutional *adjective*

instruct *verb* (instructs, instructing,
instructed)
1 teach a person a subject or skill.
2 inform. 3 tell a person what he or she
must do. **instruction** *noun*,
instructional *adjective*, **instructor** *noun*
[from Latin *instruere* = to build up or
prepare]

instructive *adjective*
giving knowledge.

instrument *noun* (*plural* instruments)
1 a device for producing musical sounds.
2 a tool used for delicate or scientific work.
3 a measuring-device.
[same origin as *instruct*]

instrumental *adjective*
1 performed on musical instruments,
without singing. 2 being the means of
doing something, *She was instrumental in
getting me a job.*

instrumentalist *noun* (*plural*
instrumentalists)
a person who plays a musical instrument.

insubordinate *adjective*
disobedient or rebellious.
insubordination *noun*

insufferable *adjective*
unbearable.

insufficient *adjective*
not sufficient.

insular *adjective*
1 to do with or like an island. 2 narrow-
minded. [same origin as *insulate*]

insulate *verb* (insulates, insulating,
insulated)
cover or protect something to prevent heat,
cold, or electricity etc. from passing in or
out. **insulation** *noun*, **insulator** *noun*
[from Latin *insula* = island]

insulin *noun*
a substance that controls the amount of
sugar in the blood. The lack of insulin
causes diabetes. [from Latin]

insult (*say* in-sult) *verb* (insults, insulting,
insulted)
hurt a person's feelings or pride.
insult (*say* in-sult) *noun* (*plural* insults)
an insulting remark or action. [from Latin]

insuperable *adjective*
unable to be overcome, *an insuperable
difficulty*.
[from *in-* + Latin *superare* = to overcome]

insurance *noun*
an agreement to compensate someone for a loss, damage, or injury etc., in return for a payment (called a *premium*) made in advance.

insure *verb* (insures, insuring, insured)
protect with insurance, *Is your jewellery insured?* [a different spelling of *ensure*]

USAGE: Do not confuse with *ensure*.

insurgent *noun* (*plural* insurgents)
a rebel. **insurgent** *adjective* [from *in-* = against + Latin *surgere* = to rise]

insurmountable *adjective*
unable to be overcome.

insurrection *noun* (*plural* insurrections)
a rebellion. [same origin as *insurgent*]

intact *adjective*
not damaged; complete. [from *in-* + Latin *tactum* = touched]

intake *noun* (*plural* intakes)
1 taking something in. **2** the number of people or things taken in.

intangible *adjective*
not able to be touched; not solid.

integer *noun* (*plural* integers)
a whole number (e.g. 0, 3, 19), not a fraction. [Latin, = whole]

integral (*say* in-tig-ral) *adjective*
1 being an essential part of a whole thing, *An engine is an integral part of a car.* **2** whole or complete. [same origin as *integer*]

integrate *verb* (integrates, integrating, integrated)
1 make parts into a whole; combine. **2** join together harmoniously into a single community. **integration** *noun* [from Latin *integrare* = make whole]

integrity (*say* in-**teg**-rit-ee) *noun*
honesty. [from Latin *integritas* = wholeness or purity]

intellect *noun* (*plural* intellects)
the ability to think (contrasted with *feeling* and *instinct*). [same origin as *intelligent*]

intellectual *adjective*
1 to do with or using the intellect. **2** having a good intellect and a liking for knowledge. **intellectually** *adverb*

intellectual *noun* (*plural* intellectuals)
an intellectual person.

intelligence *noun*
1 being intelligent. **2** information, especially of military value; the people who collect and study this information.

intelligent *adjective*
able to learn and understand things; having great mental ability. **intelligently** *adverb* [from Latin *intelligere* = understand]

intelligentsia *noun*
intellectual people regarded as a group. [via Russian and Polish from Latin]

intelligible *adjective*
able to be understood. **intelligibly** *adverb*, **intelligibility** *noun* [same origin as *intelligent*]

intend *verb* (intends, intending, intended)
have something in mind as what you want to do; plan. [from Latin *intendere* = stretch, aim]

intense *adjective*
1 very strong or great. **2** feeling things very strongly and seriously, *He's a very intense young man.* **intensely** *adverb*, **intensity** *noun* [from Latin *intensus* = stretched tight]

intensify *verb* (intensifies, intensifying, intensified)
make or become more intense. **intensification** *noun*

intensive *adjective*
concentrated; using a lot of effort over a short time. **intensively** *adverb*

intent *noun* (*plural* intents)
intention.

intent *adjective*
with concentrated attention; very interested. **intently** *adverb* [same origin as *intend*]

intention *noun* (*plural* intentions)
what a person intends; a purpose or plan.

intentional *adjective*
deliberate, not accidental.
intentionally *adverb*

inter *verb* (inters, interring, interred)
bury. [from *in-* + Latin *terra* = earth]

inter- *prefix*
between; among. [from Latin]

interact *verb* (interacts, interacting,
interacted)
have an effect upon one another.
Interaction *noun*

interbreed *verb* (interbreeds,
interbreeding, interbred)
breed with each other; cross-breed.

intercede *verb* (intercedes, interceding,
interceded)
intervene on behalf of another person or as
a peacemaker. **intercession** *noun*
[from *inter-* + Latin *cedere* = go]

intercept *verb* (intercepts, intercepting,
intercepted
stop or catch a person or thing that is going
from one place to another. **interception**
noun [from *inter-* + Latin *captum* = seized]

interchange *verb* (interchanges,
interchanging, interchanged)
1 put each of two things into the other's
place. 2 exchange things. 3 alternate.
interchangeable *adjective*

interchange *noun* (*plural* interchanges)
1 interchanging. 2 a road junction where
vehicles can move from one motorway etc.
to another.

intercom *noun* (*plural* intercoms)
(*informal*)
a system of communication between rooms
or compartments, operating rather like a
telephone. [short for *intercommunication*]

intercourse *noun*
1 communication or dealings between
people. 2 sexual intercourse.
[from Latin *intercursus* = running
between]

interdependent *adjective*
dependent upon each other.

interdict *noun* (*plural* interdicts)
an order that forbids something; a
prohibition.
[from Latin *interdicere* = stop by
interrupting, from *inter-* + *dicere* = speak]

interest *noun* (*plural* interests)
1 a feeling of wanting to know about or
help with something. 2 a thing that
interests somebody, *Science fiction is one of
my interests.* 3 an advantage or benefit, *She
looks after her own interests.* 4 money paid
regularly in return for money lent or
deposited.

interest *verb* (interests, interesting,
interested)
attract a person's interest.
interested *adjective*, **interesting** *adjective*
[Latin, = it matters]

interfere *verb* (interferes, interfering,
interfered)
1 take part in something that has nothing
to do with you. 2 get in the way; obstruct.
interference *noun*
[from *inter-* + Latin *ferire* = to strike]

interim *noun*
an interval of time between two events.

interim *adjective*
in the interim; temporary, *an interim
arrangement.* [Latin, = meanwhile]

interior *adjective*
inner.

interior *noun* (*plural* interiors)
the inside of something; the central or
inland part of a country.
[Latin, = further in]

interject *verb* (interjects, interjecting,
interjected)
break in with a remark while someone is
speaking.
[from *inter-* + Latin *jactum* = thrown]

interjection *noun* (*plural* interjections)
a word or words exclaimed expressing joy
or pain or surprise, such as *oh!* or *wow!* or
good heavens!

interlock *verb* (interlocks, interlocking,
interlocked)
fit into each other.
[from *inter-* + *lock*[1]]

interloper *noun* (*plural* **interlopers**)
an intruder.
[from *inter-* + Dutch *loper* = runner]

interlude *noun* (*plural* **interludes**)
1 an interval. 2 something happening in an interval or between other events.
[from *inter-* + Latin *ludus* = game]

intermediary *noun* (*plural* **intermediaries**)
someone who tries to settle a dispute by negotiating with both sides; a mediator.
[from French; related to *intermediate*]

intermediate *adjective*
coming between two things in time, place, or order.
[from *inter-* + Latin *medius* = middle]

interment *noun* (*plural* **interments**)
burial.

USAGE: Do not confuse with *internment*.

interminable *adjective*
endless; long and boring. **interminably** *adverb* [from *in-* + Latin *terminare* = to limit or end]

intermission *noun* (*plural* **intermissions**)
an interval, especially between parts of a film. [same origin as *intermittent*]

intermittent *adjective*
happening at intervals; not continuous.
intermittently *adverb*
[from *inter-* + Latin *mittere* = to let go]

intern *verb* (**interns, interning, interned**)
imprison in a special camp or area, usually in wartime. [from French]

internal *adjective*
inside. **internally** *adverb* [from Latin]

internal-combustion engine *noun*
(*plural* **internal-combustion engines**)
an engine that produces power by burning fuel inside the engine itself.

international *adjective*
to do with or belonging to more than one country; agreed between nations.
internationally *adverb*
international *noun* (*plural* **internationals**)
1 a sports contest between teams representing different countries. 2 a sports player who plays for his or her country.

Internet *noun*
an international computer network that allows users all over the world to interchange information.

internment *noun*
being interned.

USAGE: Do not confuse with *interment*.

interplanetary *adjective*
between planets.

interplay *noun*
the way two things have an effect on each other.

interpolate *verb* (**interpolates, interpolating, interpolated**)
1 interject a remark in a conversation.
2 insert words; put terms into a mathematical series. **interpolation** *noun*
[from Latin *interpolare* = redecorate or smarten up]

interpose *verb* (**interposes, interposing, interposed**)
place something between two things.
[from *inter-* + Latin *positum* = put]

interpret *verb* (**interprets, interpreting, interpreted**)
1 explain what something means.
2 translate what someone says into another language orally.
interpretation *noun*, **interpreter** *noun*
[from Latin]

interregnum *noun* (*plural* **interregnums** or **interregna**)
an interval between the reign of one ruler and that of his or her successor.
[from *inter-* + Latin *regnum* = reign]

interrogate *verb* (**interrogates, interrogating, interrogated**)
question someone closely or formally.
interrogation *noun*, **interrogator** *noun*
[from *inter-* + Latin *rogare* = ask]

interrogative *adjective*
questioning; expressing a question.
interrogatory *adjective*

interrupt *verb* (**interrupts, interrupting, interrupted**)
1 break in on a person's speech etc. by

Inserting a remark. 2 prevent something from continuing. **interruption** noun
[from *inter-* + Latin *ruptum* = broken]

intersect verb (intersects, intersecting, intersected)
1 divide a thing by passing or lying across it. 2 (of lines or roads etc.) cross each other. **intersection** noun
[from *inter-* + Latin *sectum* = cut]

intersperse verb (intersperses, interspersing, interspersed)
insert things here and there in something.
[from *inter-* + Latin *sparsum* = scattered]

interval noun (*plural* intervals)
1 a time between two events or parts of a play etc. 2 a space between two things.
at intervals with some time or distance between each one.
[from Latin *intervallum* = space between ramparts]

intervene verb (intervenes, intervening, intervened)
1 come between two events, *in the intervening years*. 2 interrupt a discussion or fight etc. to try and stop it or change its result. **intervention** noun
[from *inter-* + Latin *venire* = come]

interview noun (*plural* interviews)
a formal meeting with someone to ask him or her questions or to obtain information.
interview verb (interviews, interviewing, interviewed)
hold an interview with someone.
interviewer noun
[from *inter-* + French *voir* = see]

intestine noun (*plural* intestines)
the long tube along which food passes while being absorbed by the body, between the stomach and the anus. **intestinal** *adjective* [from Latin *intestinus* = internal]

intimate (*say* in-tim-at) *adjective*
1 very friendly with someone. 2 private and personal, *intimate thoughts*. 3 detailed, *an intimate knowledge of the country.*
intimately *adverb*, **intimacy** noun
intimate (*say* in-tim-ayt) *verb* (intimates, intimating, intimated)
hint at something. **intimation** noun
[from Latin *intimus* = close friend]

intimidate verb (intimidates, intimidating, intimidated)
frighten a person by threats into doing something. **intimidation** noun
[from *in-* + Latin *timidus* = timid]

into preposition
used to express 1 movement to the inside (*Go into the house*), 2 change of condition or occupation etc. (*It broke into pieces. She went into politics*), 3 (in division) *4 into 20 = 20 divided by 4.*

intolerable *adjective*
unbearable. **intolerably** *adverb*

intolerant *adjective*
not tolerant.
intolerantly *adverb*, **intolerance** noun

intonation noun (*plural* intonations)
1 the tone or pitch of the voice in speaking. 2 intoning.

intone verb (intones, intoning, intoned)
recite in a chanting voice.
[from *in-* + Latin *tonus* = tone]

intoxicate verb (intoxicates, intoxicating, intoxicated)
make a person drunk or very excited.
intoxication noun
[from *in-* + Latin *toxicum* = poison]

intra- *prefix*
within. [from Latin]

intractable *adjective*
unmanageable; difficult to deal with or control. **intractability** noun
[from *in-* + Latin *tractare* = to handle]

intransigent *adjective*
stubborn. **intransigence** noun
[from *in-* + Latin *transigere* = come to an understanding]

intransitive *adjective*
(of a verb) used without a direct object after it, e.g. *hear* in *we can hear* (but not in *we can hear you*). Compare *transitive.*
intransitively *adverb* [from *in-* + Latin *transitivus* = passing over]

intravenous (*say* in-tra-**veen**-us) *adjective*
into a vein.
[from *intra-* + Latin *vena* = vein]

intrepid *adjective*
fearless and brave.
intrepidly *adverb*, **intrepidity** *noun*
[from *in-* + Latin *trepidus* = alarmed]

intricate *adjective*
very complicated.
intricately *adverb*, **intricacy** *noun*
[from Latin *intricatus* = entangled]

intrigue (*say* in-**treeg**) *verb* (**intrigues,
intriguing, intrigued**)
1 plot with someone in an underhand way.
2 interest someone very much, *The subject
intrigues me.*
intrigue *noun* (*plural* **intrigues**)
1 plotting; an underhand plot. **2** (*old use*) a
secret love affair.
[from Italian; related to *intricate*]

intrinsic *adjective*
belonging naturally in something;
inherent. **intrinsically** *adverb* [from Latin
intrinsecus = inwardly or inwards]

intro- *prefix*
into; inwards. [from Latin]

introduce *verb* (**introduces, introducing,
introduced**)
1 make a person known to other people.
2 announce a broadcast, speaker, etc.
3 bring something into use or for
consideration.
[from *intro-* + Latin *ducere* = to lead]

introduction *noun* (*plural* **introductions**)
1 introducing somebody or something.
2 an explanation put at the beginning of a
book or speech etc. **introductory** *adjective*

introspective *adjective*
examining your own thoughts and feelings.
introspection *noun*
[from *intro-* + Latin *specere* = to look]

introvert *noun* (*plural* **introverts**)
a shy person who does not like to talk
about his or her own thoughts and feelings
with other people. (The opposite is
extrovert.) **introverted** *adjective*
[from *intro-* + Latin *vertere* = to turn]

intrude *verb* (**intrudes, intruding, intruded**)
come in or join in without being wanted.
intrusion *noun*, **intrusive** *adjective*
[from *in-* + Latin *trudere* = to push]

intruder *noun* (*plural* **intruders**)
1 someone who intrudes. **2** a burglar.

intuition *noun*
the power to know or understand things
without having to think hard or without
being taught. **intuitive** *adjective*, **intuitively**
adverb [from *in-* + Latin *tueri* = to look]

Inuit (*say* in-yoo-it) *noun* (*plural* **Inuit**)
1 a member of a people living in northern
Canada and Greenland; an Eskimo. **2** the
language of the Inuit. [Inuit, = people]

USAGE: See note at *Eskimo*.

inundate *verb* (**inundates, inundating,
inundated**)
flood or overwhelm a place, *We've been
inundated with letters about the
programme.* **inundation** *noun*
[from *in-* + Latin *unda* = a wave]

inure (*say* in-**yoor**) *verb* (**inures, inuring,
inured**)
accustom someone to something
unpleasant, *I've become inured to criticism
by now.* [from old French]

invade *verb* (**invades, invading, invaded**)
1 attack and enter a country etc. **2** crowd
into a place, *Tourists invade Oxford in
summer.* **invader** *noun*
[from *in-* + Latin *vadere* = go]

invalid (*say* in-va-leed) *noun* (*plural*
invalids)
a person who is ill or who is weakened by
illness.
invalid (*say* in-**val**-id) *adjective*
not valid, *This passport is invalid.* **invalidity**
noun [from *in-* + Latin *validus* = strong or
powerful]

invalidate *verb* (**invalidates, invalidating,
invalidated**)
make a thing invalid. **invalidation** *noun*

invaluable *adjective*
having a value that is too great to be
measured; extremely valuable.
[from *in-* + *value* + *-able*]

invariable *adjective*
not variable; never changing.
invariably *adverb*

invasion *noun* (*plural* invasions)
attacking and entering a country etc.
[same origin as *invade*]

invective *noun*
abusive words.
[from Latin *invehere* = attack in words]

inveigle (*say* in-**vay**-gul) *verb* (inveigles,
inveigling, inveigled)
entice. **inveiglement** *noun*
[from old French *aveugler* = to blind]

invent *verb* (invents, inventing, invented)
1 be the first person to make or think of a
particular thing. **2** make up a false story
etc., *invent an excuse*. **invention** *noun*,
inventor *noun*, **inventive** *adjective*
[from *in-* + Latin *venire* = come]

inventory (*say* in-ven-ter-ee) *noun* (*plural*
inventories)
a detailed list of goods or furniture. [from
Latin *inventarium* = list of things found]

inverse *adjective*
opposite or reverse. **inversely** *adverb*
[same origin as *invert*]

invert *verb* (inverts, inverting, inverted)
turn something upside down. **inversion**
noun [from *in-* + Latin *vertere* = to turn]

invertebrate *noun* (*plural* invertebrates)
an animal without a backbone.
invertebrate *adjective*

inverted commas *plural noun*
punctuation marks " " or ' ' put round
quotations and spoken words.

invest *verb* (invests, investing, invested)
1 use money to make a profit, e.g. by
lending it in return for interest to be paid,
or by buying stocks and shares or
property. **2** give somebody a rank, medal,
etc. in a formal ceremony.
investment *noun*, **investor** *noun*
[from Latin *investire* = to clothe]

investigate *verb* (investigates,
investigating, investigated)
find out as much as you can about
something; make a systematic inquiry.
investigation *noun*, **investigator** *noun*,
investigative *adjective* [from Latin]

investiture *noun* (*plural* investitures)
the process of investing someone with an
honour etc.

inveterate *adjective*
firmly established; habitual, *an inveterate
gambler*.
[from Latin *inveterare* = to make old]

invidious *adjective*
causing resentment because of unfairness.
[from Latin *invidia* = bad feeling or envy]

invigilate *verb* (invigilates, invigilating,
invigilated)
supervise candidates at an examination.
invigilation *noun*, **invigilator** *noun*
[from *in-* + Latin *vigilare* = to watch]

invigorate *verb* (invigorates, invigorating,
invigorated)
give a person strength or courage.
(Compare *vigour*.)
[from *in-* + Latin *vigor* = vigour]

invincible *adjective*
not able to be defeated; unconquerable.
invincibly *adverb*, **invincibility** *noun*
[from *in-* + Latin *vincere* = conquer]

invisible *adjective*
not visible; not able to be seen.
invisibly *adverb*, **invisibility** *noun*

invite *verb* (invites, inviting, invited)
1 ask a person to come or do something.
2 be likely to cause something to happen,
You are inviting disaster. **invitation** *noun*
[from Latin]

inviting *adjective*
attractive or tempting. **invitingly** *adverb*

invoice *noun* (*plural* invoices)
a list of goods sent or work done, with the
prices charged.
[from French *envoyer* = send]

invoke *verb* (invokes, invoking, invoked)
1 call upon a god in prayer asking for help
etc. **2** appeal to a law or someone's
authority for help or protection. **invocation**
noun [from *in-* + Latin *vocare* = to call]

involuntary *adjective*
not deliberate; unintentional.
involuntarily *adverb*

involve *verb* (involves, involving, involved)
1 have as a part; make a thing necessary, *The job involves hard work.* **2** make someone share in something, *They involved us in their charity work.* **involvement** *noun* [from *in-* + Latin *volvere* = to roll]

involved *adjective*
1 complicated. **2** concerned; sharing in something.

invulnerable *adjective*
not vulnerable.

inward *adjective*
1 on the inside. **2** going or facing inwards.
inward *adverb*
inwards. [from Old English]

inwards *adverb*
towards the inside.

iodine *noun*
a chemical substance used as an antiseptic. [from Greek *iodes* = violet-coloured (because it gives off violet-coloured vapour)]

ion *noun* (*plural* ions)
an electrically charged particle. [from Greek]

-ion, **-sion**, **-tion**, and **-xion** *suffixes*
form nouns meaning 'condition or action' (e.g. *dominion, dimension, attraction, pollution, inflexion*).

ionosphere (*say* I-on-os-feer) *noun*
a region of the upper atmosphere, containing ions.

iota *noun* (*plural* iotas)
a tiny amount of something, *There's not an iota of truth in what she says.* [the name of *i*, the ninth and smallest letter of the Greek alphabet]

IQ *abbreviation*
intelligence quotient; a number showing how a person's intelligence compares with that of an average person.

ir- *prefix*
1 in; into. **2** on; towards. **3** not. see **in-**.

IRA *abbreviation*
Irish Republican Army.

irascible (*say* ir-as-ib-ul) *adjective*
easily becoming angry; irritable. [from Latin *irasci* = become angry]

irate (*say* I-rayt) *adjective*
angry. [from Latin *ira* = anger]

iridescent *adjective*
showing rainbow-like colours. **iridescence** *noun* [from Greek *iris* = iris or rainbow]

iris *noun* (*plural* irises)
1 a plant with long pointed leaves and large flowers. **2** the coloured part of the eyeball. [from Greek]

irk *verb* (irks, irking, irked)
annoy. [probably from a Scandinavian language]

irksome *adjective*
annoying or tiresome.

iron *noun* (*plural* irons)
1 a hard grey metal. **2** a device with a flat base that is heated for smoothing clothes or cloth. **3** a tool etc. made of iron.
iron *adjective*
iron *verb* (irons, ironing, ironed)
smooth clothes or cloth with an iron. [from Old English]

Iron Age *noun*
the time when tools and weapons were made of iron.

ironic (*say* I-ron-ik) *adjective*
using irony; full of irony.
ironical *adjective*, **ironically** *adverb*

ironmonger *noun* (*plural* ironmongers)
a shopkeeper who sells tools and other metal objects. **ironmongery** *noun* [from *iron* + an old word *monger* = trader]

irons *plural noun*
fetters.

irony (*say* I-ron-ee) *noun* (*plural* ironies)
1 saying the opposite of what you mean in order to emphasize it, e.g. saying 'What a lovely day' when it is pouring with rain. **2** an oddly contradictory situation, *The irony of it is that I tripped while telling someone else to be careful.* [from Greek *eiron* = someone who pretends not to know]

irrational *adjective*
not rational; illogical. **Irrationally** *adverb*

irreducible *adjective*
unable to be reduced, *an irreducible minimum.*

irrefutable (*say* ir-ef-yoo-ta-bul) *adjective*
unable to be refuted.

irregular *adjective*
1 not regular; uneven. 2 against the rules or usual custom. 3 (of troops) not in the regular armed forces.
irregularly *adverb*, **irregularity** *noun*

irrelevant (*say* ir-el-iv-ant) *adjective*
not relevant.
irrelevantly *adverb*, **irrelevance** *noun*

irreparable (*say* ir-ep-er-a-bul) *adjective*
unable to be repaired or replaced.
irreparably *adverb*
[from *ir-* + Latin *reparare* = repair]

irreplaceable *adjective*
unable to be replaced.

irrepressible *adjective*
unable to be repressed; always lively and cheerful. **irrepressibly** *adverb*

irreproachable *adjective*
blameless or faultless.
irreproachably *adverb*
[from *ir-* + French *reprocher* = reproach]

irresistible *adjective*
unable to be resisted; very attractive.
irresistibly *adverb*

irresolute *adjective*
feeling uncertain; hesitant.
irresolutely *adverb*

irrespective *adjective*
not taking something into account, *Prizes are awarded to winners, irrespective of age.*

irresponsible *adjective*
not showing a proper sense of responsibility.
irresponsibly *adverb*, **irresponsibility** *noun*

irretrievable *adjective*
not able to be retrieved. **irretrievably** *adverb*

irreverent *adjective*
not reverent; not respectful.
irreverently *adverb*, **irreverence** *noun*

irrevocable (*say* ir-ev-ok-a-bul) *adjective*
unable to be revoked or altered.
irrevocably *adverb*

irrigate *verb* (irrigates, irrigating, irrigated)
supply land with water so that crops etc. can grow. **irrigation** *noun*
[from *ir-* + Latin *rigare* = to water]

irritable *adjective*
easily annoyed; bad-tempered.
irritably *adverb*, **irritability** *noun*

irritate *verb* (irritates, irritating, irritated)
1 annoy. 2 cause itching. **irritation** *noun*,
irritant *adjective* & *noun* [from Latin]

irrupt *verb* (irrupts, irrupting, irrupted)
enter forcibly or violently. **irruption** *noun*
[from *ir-* + Latin *ruptum* = burst]

USAGE: Do not confuse with *erupt.*

-ise *suffix* see -ize.

-ish *suffix*
forms nouns meaning 1 'of a certain nature' (e.g. *foolish*), 2 'rather' (e.g. *greenish, yellowish*).

Islam *noun*
the religion of Muslims. **Islamic** *adjective*
[Arabic, = submission to God]

island *noun* (*plural* islands)
1 a piece of land surrounded by water.
2 something that resembles an island because it is isolated. [from Old English]

islander *noun* (*plural* islanders)
an inhabitant of an island.

isle (*say as* I'll) *noun* (*plural* isles) (*poetic & in names*)
an island. [from Latin *insula* – island]

-ism *suffix*
forms nouns showing action from verbs ending in *-ize* (e.g. *baptism, criticism*), or condition (e.g. *heroism*).

isn't (*mainly spoken*)
is not.

iso- *prefix*
equal (as in *isobar*). [from Greek]

isobar (*say* I-so-bar) *noun* (*plural* **isobars**)
a line (on a map) connecting places that
have the same atmospheric pressure.
[from *iso-* + Greek *baros* = weight]

isolate *verb* (**isolates, isolating, isolated**)
place a person or thing apart or alone;
separate. **isolation** *noun* [from Latin
insulatus = made into an island]

isosceles (*say* I-soss-il-eez) *adjective*
an isosceles triangle has two sides of equal
length. [from *iso-* + Greek *skelos* = leg]

isotope *noun* (*plural* **isotopes**)
a form of an element that differs from other
forms in its nuclear properties but not in
its chemical properties.
[from *iso-* + Greek *topos* = place (because
they appear in the same place in the table
of chemical elements)]

issue *verb* (**issues, issuing, issued**)
1 come or go out; flow out. **2** supply; give
out, *We issued one blanket to each refugee.*
3 put out for sale; publish. **4** send out, *They
issued a gale warning.* **5** result.
issue *noun* (*plural* **issues**)
1 a subject for discussion or concern, *What
are the real issues?* **2** a result, *Await the
issue of the trial.* **3** a particular edition of a
newspaper or magazine, *The Christmas
issue of Radio Times.* **4** issuing something,
The issue of passports is held up. [from old
French; related to *exit*]

-ist *suffix*
forms nouns meaning 'person who does
something or believes in or supports
something' (e.g. *cyclist, Communist*).

isthmus (*say* iss-mus) *noun* (*plural*
isthmuses)
a narrow strip of land connecting two
larger pieces of land. [from Greek]

IT *abbreviation*
information technology.

it *pronoun*
1 the thing being talked about. **2** the player
who has to catch others in a game. The
word is also used **3** in statements about the
weather (*It is raining*) or about
circumstances etc. (*It is six miles to York*),

4 as an indefinite object (*Run for it!*),
5 to refer to a phrase (*It is unlikely that
she will fail*).
[from Old English]

italic (*say* it-al-ik) *adjective*
printed with sloping letters (called **italics**)
like this.
[because this style was first used in Italy]

itch *verb* (**itches, itching, itched**)
1 have or feel a tickling sensation in the
skin that makes you want to scratch it.
2 long to do something.
itch *noun* (*plural* **itches**)
1 an itching feeling. **2** a longing. **itchy**
adjective, **itchiness** *noun* [from Old English]

-ite *suffix*
(in scientific use) forms names of minerals
(e.g. *anthracite*), explosives (e.g. *dynamite*),
and salts of certain acids (e.g. *nitrite*;
compare *-ate*).

item *noun* (*plural* **items**)
1 one thing in a list or group of things.
2 one piece of news, article etc. in a
newspaper or bulletin.
[Latin, = just so, similarly (used to
introduce each item on a list)]

itinerant (*say* it-in-er-ant) *adjective*
travelling from place to place, *an itinerant
preacher.* [same origin as *itinerary*]

itinerary (*say* I-tin-er-er-ee) *noun* (*plural*
itineraries)
a list of places to be visited on a journey; a
route. [from Latin *itinerari* = travel from
place to place]

-itis *suffix*
forms nouns meaning inflammation of part
of the body (as in *bronchitis*). [Greek]

its *possessive pronoun*
belonging to it, *The cat hurt its paw.*

USAGE: Do not put an apostrophe into *its*
unless you mean 'it is' or 'it has' (see the
next entry).

it's (*mainly spoken*)
1 it is, *It's very hot.* **2** it has, *It's broken all
records.*

USAGE: Do not confuse with *its*.

itself *pronoun*
it and nothing else. (Compare *herself*.)
by itself on its own; alone.

ITV *abbreviation*
Independent Television.

-ive *suffix*
forms adjectives, chiefly from verbs (e.g.
active, explosive).

ivory *noun*
1 the hard creamy-white substance that
forms elephants' tusks. 2 a creamy-white
colour. [from Latin]

ivy *noun* (*plural* **ivies**)
a climbing evergreen plant with shiny
leaves. [from Old English]

-ize or **-ise** *suffix*
forms verbs meaning 'bring or come into a
certain condition' (e.g. *civilize*), or 'treat in
a certain way' (e.g. *pasteurize*), or 'have a
certain feeling' (e.g. *sympathize*). [from the
Greek verb-ending *-izein*, or French *-iser*]

Jj

jab *verb* (**jabs, jabbing, jabbed**)
poke roughly; push a thing into something.
jab *noun* (*plural* **jabs**)
1 a jabbing movement. 2 (*informal*) an
injection. [originally Scots]

jabber *verb* (**jabbers, jabbering, jabbered**)
speak quickly and not clearly; chatter.
jabber *noun* [imitating the sound]

jack *noun* (*plural* **jacks**)
1 a device for lifting something heavy off
the ground. 2 a playing card with a picture
of a young man. 3 a small white ball aimed
at in bowls.
jack of all trades someone who can do many
different kinds of work.
jack *verb* (**jacks, jacking, jacked**)
lift something with a jack.
jack it in (*slang*) give up or abandon an
attempt etc.
[the name *Jack*, used for various sorts

of tool (as though it was a person
helping you)]

jackal *noun* (*plural* **jackals**)
a wild animal rather like a dog.
[from Persian]

jackass *noun* (*plural* **jackasses**)
1 a male donkey. 2 a stupid person.
[from the name *Jack* + *ass*]

jackdaw *noun* (*plural* **jackdaws**)
a kind of small crow. [from the name *Jack*
+ Middle English *dawe* = jackdaw]

jacket *noun* (*plural* **jackets**)
1 a short coat, usually reaching to the hips.
2 a cover to keep the heat in a water-tank
etc. 3 a paper wrapper for a book. 4 the
skin of a potato that is baked without being
peeled. [from old French]

jack-in-the-box *noun* (*plural* **jack-in-the-boxes**)
a toy figure that springs out of a box when
the lid is lifted.

jackknife *verb* (**jackknifes, jackknifing,
jackknifed**)
if an articulated lorry jackknifes, it folds
against itself in an accidental skidding
movement. [from *jackknife*, a folding knife]

jackpot *noun* (*plural* **jackpots**)
an amount of prize money that increases
until someone wins it.
hit the jackpot 1 win a large prize. 2 have
remarkable luck or sucess.
[originally = a kitty which could be won
only by playing a pair of jacks or cards of
higher value: from *jack* + *pot*[1]]

Jacobean *adjective*
from the reign of James I of England
(1603–25). [from Latin *Jacobus* = James]

Jacobite *noun* (*plural* **Jacobites**)
a supporter of the exiled Stuarts after the
abdication of James II (1688).
[same origin as *Jacobean*]

jade *noun*
a green stone that is carved to make
ornaments. [from Spanish *piedra de ijada*
= colic stone (because it was believed to
cure diseases of the stomach)]

jaded *adjective*
tired and bored.
[from an old word *jade* = a worn-out horse]

jagged (*say* jag-id) *adjective*
having an uneven edge with sharp points.
[from Scots *jag* = stab]

jaguar *noun* (*plural* jaguars)
a large fierce South American animal
rather like a leopard. [via Portuguese from
a South American language]

jail *noun* (*plural* jails)
a prison.
jail *verb* (jails, jailing, jailed)
put into prison. **jailer** *noun*
[from old French *jaiole* = cage or prison]

Jain (*say as* jine) *noun* (*plural* Jains)
a believer in an Indian religion rather like
Buddhism. [from Sanskrit]

jam *noun* (*plural* jams)
1 a sweet food made of fruit boiled with
sugar until it is thick. **2** a lot of people,
cars, or logs etc. crowded together so that
movement is difficult.
in a jam in a difficult situation.
jam *verb* (jams, jamming, jammed)
1 crowd or squeeze into a space. **2** make or
become fixed and difficult to move. **3** push
something forcibly, *jam the brakes on.*
4 block a broadcast by causing
interference with the transmission.
[origin unknown]

jamb (*say* jam) *noun* (*plural* jambs)
a side post of a doorway or window frame.
[from French *jambe* = leg]

jamboree *noun* (*plural* jamborees)
a large party or celebration.
[origin unknown]

jangle *verb* (jangles, jangling, jangled)
make a loud harsh ringing sound.
jangle *noun* [from old French]

janitor *noun* (*plural* janitors)
a caretaker. [originally = doorkeeper: from
Latin *janua* = door]

jar¹ *noun* (*plural* jars)
a container made of glass or pottery.
[via French from Arabic]

jar² *verb* (jars, jarring, jarred)
1 cause an unpleasant jolt or shock.
2 sound harshly.
jar *noun* (*plural* jars)
a jarring effect. [imitating the sound]

jargon *noun*
special words used by a group of people,
scientists' jargon. [from French]

jasmine *noun*
a shrub with yellow or white flowers.
[via French from Arabic]

jaundice *noun*
a disease in which the skin becomes
yellow. [from French *jaune* = yellow]

jaunt *noun* (*plural* jaunts)
a short trip. **jaunting** *noun*
[origin unknown]

jaunty *adjective* (jauntier, jauntiest)
lively and cheerful. **jauntily** *adverb*,
jauntiness *noun* [originally = stylish,
elegant: from French, related to *gentle*]

javelin *noun* (*plural* javelins)
a lightweight spear. [from French]

jaw *noun* (*plural* jaws)
1 either of the two bones that form the
framework of the mouth. **2** the lower part
of the face. **3** something shaped like the
jaws or used for gripping things. **4** (*slang*)
talking. [from old French]

jay *noun* (*plural* jays)
a noisy brightly-coloured bird.
[from French]

jaywalker *noun* (*plural* jaywalkers)
a person who dangerously walks across a
road without looking out for traffic.
jaywalking *noun*
[from an American meaning of *jay* = fool]

jazz *noun*
a kind of music with strong rhythm.
jazzy *adjective*
[probably a Black American word]

jealous *adjective*
1 unhappy or resentful because you feel
that someone is your rival or is better or
luckier than yourself. **2** careful in keeping

something, *He is very jealous of his own rights.* **jealously** *adverb,* **jealousy** *noun* [from French]

jeans *plural noun*
trousers made of strong cotton fabric. [from *Genoa*, a city in Italy, where such a cloth was once made]

jeer *verb* (jeers, jeering, jeered)
laugh or shout at somebody rudely or scornfully. **jeer** *noun* [origin unknown]

jelly *noun* (*plural* jellies)
1 a soft transparent food. 2 any soft slippery substance. **jellied** *adjective* [from Latin *gelare* = freeze]

jellyfish *noun* (*plural* jellyfish)
a sea animal with a body like jelly.

jemmy *noun* (*plural* jemmies)
a burglar's crowbar. [from the name *Jimmy* (compare *jack*)]

jeopardize (*say* jep-er-dyz) *verb* (jeopardizes, jeopardizing, jeopardized)
put someone in danger; put something at risk.

jeopardy (*say* jep-er-dee) *noun*
danger of harm or failure. [from old French]

jerk *verb* (jerks, jerking, jerked)
1 make a sudden sharp movement. 2 pull something suddenly.
jerk *noun* (*plural* jerks)
1 a sudden sharp movement. 2 (*slang*) a stupid person. **jerky** *adjective,* **jerkily** *adverb* [origin unknown]

jerkin *noun* (*plural* jerkins)
a sleeveless jacket. [origin unknown]

jerry-built *adjective*
built badly and with poor materials. [origin unknown]

jersey *noun* (*plural* jerseys)
1 a pullover with sleeves. 2 a plain machine-knitted material used for making clothes. [originally = a woollen cloth made in *Jersey*, one of the Channel Islands]

jest *noun* (*plural* jests)
a joke.

jest *verb* (jests, jesting, jested)
make jokes. [from Middle English *gest* = a story]

jester *noun* (*plural* jesters)
a professional entertainer at a royal court in the Middle Ages.

Jesuit *noun* (*plural* Jesuits)
a member of the Society of Jesus (a Roman Catholic religious order). [from Latin *Jesuita* = follower of Jesus]

jet¹ *noun* (*plural* jets)
1 a stream of water, gas, flame, etc. shot out from a narrow opening. 2 a spout or nozzle from which a jet comes. 3 an aircraft driven by engines that send out a high-speed jet of hot gases at the back.
jet *verb* (jets, jetting, jetted)
1 come or send out in a strong stream. 2 (*informal*) travel in a jet aircraft. [from French *jeter* = to throw]

jet² *noun*
1 a hard black mineral substance. 2 a deep glossy black colour. [from old French]

jet lag *noun*
extreme tiredness that a person feels after a long flight between different time zones.

jetsam *noun*
goods thrown overboard and washed ashore from a ship in distress. [from *jettison*]

jettison *verb* (jettisons, jettisoning, jettisoned)
1 throw something overboard. 2 get rid of something that is no longer wanted. 3 release or drop something from an aircraft or spacecraft in flight. [same origin as *jet¹*]

jetty *noun* (*plural* jetties)
a small landing stage. [same origin as *jet¹*]

Jew *noun* (*plural* Jews)
a member of a people descended from the ancient tribes of Israel, or who believes in the religion of this people. **Jewish** *adjective* [from Hebrew *yehudi* = belonging to the tribe of Judah (the founder of one of the ten tribes of ancient Israel)]

jewel *noun* (*plural* **jewels**)
1 a precious stone. **2** an ornament containing precious stones.
jewelled *adjective* [from old French]

jeweller *noun* (*plural* **jewellers**)
a person who sells or makes jewellery.

jewellery *noun*
jewels and similar ornaments for wearing.

jib¹ *noun* (*plural* **jibs**)
1 a triangular sail stretching forward from a ship's front mast. **2** the arm of a crane. [origin unknown]

jib² *verb* (**jibs, jibbing, jibbed**)
be reluctant or unwilling to do something. [origin unknown]

jiffy *noun* (*informal*)
a moment. [origin unknown]

jig *noun* (*plural* **jigs**)
1 a lively jumping dance. **2** a device that holds something in place while you work on it with tools.
jig *verb* (**jigs, jigging, jigged**)
move up and down quickly and jerkily. [origin unknown]

jiggle *verb* (**jiggles, jiggling, jiggled**)
rock or jerk something lightly. [from *jig*]

jigsaw *noun* (*plural* **jigsaws**)
1 a saw that can cut curved shapes. **2** a jigsaw puzzle.

jigsaw puzzle *noun* (*plural* **jigsaw puzzles**)
a picture cut into irregular pieces which are then shuffled and fitted together again for amusement.

jihad *noun* (*plural* **jihads**)
(in Islam) a holy war. [Arabic]

jilt *verb* (**jilts, jilting, jilted**)
abandon a boyfriend or girlfriend, especially after promising to marry him or her. [origin unknown]

jingle *verb* (**jingles, jingling, jingled**)
make or cause to make a tinkling sound.
jingle *noun* (*plural* **jingles**)
1 a jingling sound. **2** a very simple verse or tune, especially one used in advertising. [imitating the sound]

jingoism *noun*
an extremely strong and unreasonable belief that your country is superior to others. **jingoistic** *adjective*
[from the saying *by jingo!*, used in a warlike popular song in the 19th century]

jitters *plural noun* (*informal*)
nervousness. **jittery** *adjective*
[origin unknown]

job *noun* (*plural* **jobs**)
1 work that someone does regularly to earn a living. **2** a piece of work to be done. **3** (*informal*) a difficult task, *You'll have a job to lift that box.* **4** (*informal*) a thing; a state of affairs, *It's a good job you're here.* [origin unknown]

jobcentre *noun* (*plural* **jobcentres**)
a government office with information about available jobs.

jockey *noun* (*plural* **jockeys**)
a person who rides horses in races. [pet form of the name *Jock*]

jocular *adjective*
joking. **jocularly** *adverb*, **jocularity** *noun*
[from Latin *jocus* = a joke]

jodhpurs (*say* jod-perz) *plural noun*
trousers for horse riding, fitting closely from the knee to the ankle.
[named after *Jodhpur*, a city in India, where similar trousers are worn]

jog *verb* (**jogs, jogging, jogged**)
1 run or trot slowly, especially for exercise. **2** give something a slight push. **jogger** *noun*
jog someone's memory help him or her to remember something.
jog *noun* (*plural* **jogs**)
1 a slow run or trot. **2** a slight knock or push. [same origin as *jagged*]

joggle *verb* (**joggles, joggling, joggled**)
shake slightly or move jerkily. **joggle** *noun*
[from *jog*]

jogtrot *noun*
a slow steady trot.

joie de vivre (*say* zhwah der **veevr**) *noun*
a feeling of great enjoyment of life.
[French, = joy of life]

join *verb* (joins, joining, joined)
1 put or come together; fasten or connect.
2 do something together with others, *We all joined in the chorus.* **3** become a member of a group or organization etc., *Join the Navy.*
join up enlist in the armed forces.
join *noun* (*plural* joins)
a place where things join. [from French]

joiner *noun* (*plural* joiners)
a person whose job is to make doors, window frames, etc. and furniture out of wood. **joinery** *noun*

joint *noun* (*plural* joints)
1 a join. **2** the place where two bones fit together. **3** a large piece of meat cut ready for cooking.
joint *adjective*
shared or done by two or more people, nations, etc., *a joint project.* **jointly** *adverb* [from French]

joist *noun* (*plural* joists)
any of the long beams supporting a floor or ceiling. [from old French]

joke *noun* (*plural* jokes)
something said or done to make people laugh.
joke *verb* (jokes, joking, joked)
make jokes. [originally slang: probably from Latin]

joker *noun* (*plural* jokers)
1 someone who jokes. **2** an extra playing card with a jester on it.

jolly *adjective* (jollier, jolliest)
cheerful and good-humoured. **jollity** *noun*
jolly *adverb* (*informal*)
very, *jolly good.*
jolly *verb* (jollies, jollying, jollied) (*informal*)
jolly along keep someone in a good humour. [from old French]

jolt *verb* (jolts, jolting, jolted)
1 shake or dislodge something with a sudden sharp movement. **2** move along jerkily, e.g. on a rough road. **3** give someone a shock.
jolt *noun* (*plural* jolts)
1 a jolting movement. **2** a shock. [origin unknown]

jostle *verb* (jostles, jostling, jostled)
push roughly, especially in a crowd. [from *joust*]

jot *verb* (jots, jotting, jotted)
write something quickly, *jot it down.* [from Greek]

jotter *noun* (*plural* jotters)
a notepad or notebook.

joule (*say* jool) *noun* (*plural* joules)
a unit of work or energy. [named after an English scientist, James Joule]

journal *noun* (*plural* journals)
1 a newspaper or magazine. **2** a diary. [from Latin, = by day]

journalist *noun* (*plural* journalists)
a person who writes for a newspaper or magazine.
journalism *noun*, **journalistic** *adjective*

journey *noun* (*plural* journeys)
1 going from one place to another. **2** the distance or time taken to travel somewhere, *two days' journey.*
journey *verb* (journeys, journeying, journeyed)
make a journey. [from French *journée* = a day's travel, from *jour* = day]

joust (*say* jowst) *verb* (jousts, jousting, jousted)
fight on horseback with lances. [from old French *juster* = bring together]

jovial *adjective*
cheerful and good-humoured.
jovially *adverb*, **joviality** *noun*
[from Latin *jovialis* = to do with Jupiter (because people born under its influence were said to be cheerful)]

jowl *noun* (*plural* jowls)
1 the jaw or cheek. **2** loose skin on the neck. [from Old English]

joy *noun* (*plural* joys)
1 a feeling of great pleasure; gladness. **2** a thing that causes joy.
joyful *adjective*, **joyfully** *adverb*, **joyfulness** *noun*, **joyous** *adjective*, **joyously** *adverb* [from old French]

joyride *noun* (*plural* **joyrides**)
a drive in a stolen car for amusement.
joyrider *noun*, **joyriding** *noun*

joystick *noun* (*plural* **joysticks**)
1 the control lever of an aircraft. 2 a device
for moving a cursor etc. on a VDU screen.

JP *abbreviation*
Justice of the Peace.

jubilant *adjective*
rejoicing or triumphant.
jubilantly *adverb*, **jubilation** *noun*
[from Latin *jubilans* = shouting for joy]

jubilee (*say* joo-bil-ee) *noun* (*plural* **jubilees**)
a special anniversary, *silver* (25th), *golden*
(50th), *and diamond* (60th) *jubilee*. [from
Hebrew *yobel* = a year when slaves were
freed and property returned to its owners,
held in ancient Israel every 50 years]

Judaism (*say* joo-day-izm) *noun*
the religion of the Jewish people.
[from Greek *Ioudaios* = Jew]

judder *verb* (**judders, juddering, juddered**)
shake noisily or violently.
[imitating the sound]

judge *noun* (*plural* **judges**)
1 a person appointed to hear cases in a
lawcourt and decide what should be done.
2 a person deciding who has won a contest
or competition, or the value or quality of
something.
judge *verb* (**judges, judging, judged**)
1 act as a judge. 2 form and give an
opinion. 3 estimate, *He judged the
distance carefully*.
[from Latin *judex* = a judge, from *jus* = law
+ *-dicus* = saying]

judgement *noun* (*plural* **judgements**)
1 judging. 2 the decision made by a
lawcourt. 3 someone's opinion. 4 the
ability to judge wisely. 5 something
considered as a punishment from God, *It's
a judgement on you!*

judicial *adjective*
to do with lawcourts, judges, or

judgements, *the British judicial system*.
judicially *adverb*

USAGE: Do not confuse with *judicious*.

judiciary (*say* joo-dish-er-ee) *noun* (*plural*
judiciaries)
all the judges in a country.

judicious (*say* joo-dish-us) *adjective*
having or showing good sense or good
judgement. **judiciously** *adverb*
[same origin as *judge*]

USAGE: Do not confuse with *judicial*.

judo *noun*
a Japanese method of self-defence without
using weapons.
[from Japanese *ju* = gentle + *do* = way]

jug *noun* (*plural* **jugs**)
a container for holding and pouring
liquids, with a handle and a lip.
[pet form of *Joan* or *Jenny*]

juggernaut *noun* (*plural* **juggernauts**)
a huge lorry. [named after a Hindu god
whose image was dragged in procession on
a huge wheeled vehicle]

juggle *verb* (**juggles, juggling, juggled**)
1 toss and keep a number of objects in the
air, for entertainment. 2 rearrange or alter
things skilfully or in order to deceive
people. **juggler** *noun* [from old French]

jugular *adjective*
to do with the throat or neck, *the jugular
veins*. [from Latin *jugulum* = throat]

juice *noun* (*plural* **juices**)
1 the liquid from fruit, vegetables, or other
food. 2 a liquid produced by the body, *the
digestive juices*. **juicy** *adjective* [from Latin]

jukebox *noun* (*plural* **jukeboxes**)
a machine that automatically plays a
record you have selected when you put a
coin in.
[probably from a West African word]

jumble *verb* (**jumbles, jumbling, jumbled**)
mix things up into a confused mass.
jumble *noun*
a confused mixture of things; a muddle.
[origin unknown]

jumble sale *noun* (*plural* jumble sales)
a sale of second-hand goods.

jumbo *noun* (*plural* jumbos)
1 something very large; a jumbo jet. **2** an elephant. [the name of a very large elephant in London Zoo]

jumbo jet *noun* (*plural* jumbo jets)
a very large jet aircraft.

jump *verb* (jumps, jumping, jumped)
1 move up suddenly from the ground into the air. **2** go over something by jumping, *jump the fence*. **3** pass over something; miss out part of a book etc. **4** move suddenly in surprise. **5** pass quickly to a different place or level.
jump at (*informal*) accept something eagerly.
jump the gun start before you should.
jump the queue not wait your turn.
jump *noun* (*plural* jumps)
1 a jumping movement. **2** an obstacle to jump over. **3** a sudden rise or change. [origin unknown]

jumper *noun* (*plural* jumpers)
a jersey. [from French *jupe* = tunic]

jumpy *adjective*
nervous.

junction *noun* (*plural* junctions)
1 a join. **2** a place where roads or railway lines meet. [from Latin *junctum* = joined]

juncture *noun* (*plural* junctures)
1 a point of time, especially in a crisis. **2** a place where things join. [from Latin *junctura* = joint]

jungle *noun* (*plural* jungles)
a thick tangled forest, especially in the tropics. **jungly** *adjective* [from Hindi]

junior *adjective*
1 younger. **2** for young children, *a junior school*. **3** lower in rank or importance, *junior officers*.
junior *noun* (*plural* juniors)
a junior person. [Latin, = younger]

juniper *noun* (*plural* junipers)
an evergreen shrub. [from Latin]

junk¹ *noun*
rubbish; things of no value.
[origin unknown]

junk² *noun* (*plural* junks)
a Chinese sailing boat.
[via Portuguese or French from Malay (a language spoken in Malaysia)]

junk food *noun*
food that is not nourishing.

junkie *noun* (*plural* junkies) (*slang*)
a drug addict. [from an American meaning of *junk¹* = heroin]

jurisdiction *noun*
authority; official power, especially to interpret and apply the law.
[from old French; related to *judge*]

juror *noun* (*plural* jurors)
a member of a jury.

jury *noun* (*plural* juries)
a group of people (usually twelve) appointed to give a verdict about a case in a lawcourt. **juryman** *noun*, **jurywoman** *noun*
[from Latin *jurare* = take an oath]

just *adjective*
1 giving proper consideration to everyone's claims. **2** deserved; right in amount etc., *a just reward*.
justly *adverb*, **justness** *noun*
just *adverb*
1 exactly, *It's just what I wanted*. **2** only; simply, *I just wanted to see him*. **3** barely; by only a small amount, *just below the knee*. **4** at this moment or only a little while ago, *She has just gone*.
[from Latin *justus* = rightful]

justice *noun* (*plural* justices)
1 being just; fair treatment. **2** legal proceedings, *a court of justice*. **3** a judge or magistrate.

justify *verb* (justifies, justifying, justified)
show that something is fair, just, or reasonable. **justification** *noun*

jut *verb* (juts, jutting, jutted)
stick out. [a different spelling of *jet¹*]

jute *noun*
fibre from tropical plants, used for making
sacks etc. [from Bengali (a language spoken
in Bangladesh and West Bengal)]

juvenile *adjective*
to do with or for young people.
[from Latin *juvenis* = young person]

juvenile delinquent *noun* (*plural* **juvenile
delinquents**)
a young person who has broken the law.

juxtapose *verb* (**juxtaposes, juxtaposing,
juxtaposed**)
put things side by side. **juxtaposition** *noun*
[from Latin *juxta* = next + *positum* = put]

Kk

kale *noun*
a kind of cabbage. [from Old English]

kaleidoscope (*say* kal-I-dos-kohp) *noun*
(*plural* **kaleidoscopes**)
a tube that you look through to see brightly
coloured patterns which change as you
turn the end of the tube. **kaleidoscopic**
adjective [from Greek *kalos* = beautiful
+ *eidos* = form + *skopein* = look at]

kangaroo *noun* (*plural* **kangaroos**)
an Australian animal that jumps along on
its strong hind legs. (See *marsupial*.)
[an Australian Aboriginal word]

kaolin *noun*
fine white clay used in making porcelain
and in medicine. [from Chinese *gao ling*
= high hill (because it was first found on a
hill in northern China)]

karaoke *noun*
a form of entertainment in which people
sing well-known songs against a pre-
recorded backing. [Japanese]

karate (*say* ka-**rah**-tee) *noun*
a Japanese method of self-defence in which
the hands and feet are used as weapons.
[from Japanese *kara* = empty + *te* = hand]

kayak *noun* (*plural* **kayaks**)
a small canoe with a covering that fits
round the canoeist's waist. [an Inuit word]

kebab *noun* (*plural* **kebabs**)
small pieces of meat or vegetables cooked
on a skewer. [from Arabic]

keel *noun* (*plural* **keels**)
the long piece of wood or metal along the
bottom of a boat.
on an even keel steady.

keel *verb* (**keels, keeling, keeled**)
keel over fall down or overturn, *The ship
keeled over.*
[from Old Norse]

keen[1] *adjective*
1 enthusiastic; very interested in or eager
to do something, *a keen swimmer.* 2 sharp,
a keen edge. 3 piercingly cold, *a keen wind.*
keenly *adverb*, **keenness** *noun*
[from Old English]

keen[2] *verb* (**keens, keening, keened**)
wail, especially in mourning. [from Irish]

keep *verb* (**keeps, keeping, kept**)
This word has many uses, including 1 have
something and look after it or not get rid of
it, 2 stay or cause to stay in the same
condition etc. (*keep still; keep it hot*), 3 do
something continually (*She keeps
laughing*), 4 respect and not break (*keep a
promise*), 5 make entries in (*keep a diary*).
keep up 1 make the same progress as
others. 2 continue something.

keep *noun* (*plural* **keeps**)
1 maintenance; the food etc. that you need
to live, *She earns her keep.* 2 a strong tower
in a castle.
for keeps (*informal*) permanently; to keep,
Is this football mine for keeps?
[origin unknown]

keeper *noun* (*plural* **keepers**)
1 a person who looks after an animal,
building, etc., *the park keeper.* 2 a
goalkeeper or wicketkeeper.

keeping *noun*
care; looking after something, *in safe
keeping.*
in keeping with conforming to; suiting,
*Modern furniture is not in keeping with an
old house.*

keepsake *noun* (*plural* **keepsakes**)
a gift to be kept in memory of the person who gave it.

keg *noun* (*plural* **kegs**)
a small barrel. [from Old Norse]

kelp *noun*
a large seaweed. [origin unknown]

kelvin *noun* (*plural* **kelvins**)
the SI unit of thermodynamic temperature. [named after a British scientist, Lord Kelvin, who invented it]

kennel *noun* (*plural* **kennels**)
a shelter for a dog. [from Latin *canis* = dog]

kennels *noun*
a place where dogs are bred or where they can be looked after while their owners are away.

kerb *noun* (*plural* **kerbs**)
the edge of a pavement.
[a different spelling of *curb*]

kerchief *noun* (*plural* **kerchiefs**) (*old use*)
1 a square scarf worn on the head. 2 a handkerchief. [from old French *couvre* = cover + *chief* = head]

kernel *noun* (*plural* **kernels**)
the part inside the shell of a nut etc. [from Old English]

kestrel *noun* (*plural* **kestrels**)
a small falcon. [probably from French]

ketchup *noun*
a thick sauce made from tomatoes and vinegar etc. [probably from Chinese *k'e chap* = tomato juice]

kettle *noun* (*plural* **kettles**)
a container with a spout and handle, for boiling water in. [from Old English]

kettledrum *noun* (*plural* **kettledrums**)
a drum consisting of a large metal bowl with skin or plastic over the top.

key *noun* (*plural* **keys**)
1 a piece of metal shaped so that it will open a lock. 2 a device for winding up a clock or clockwork toy etc. 3 a small lever to be pressed by a finger, e.g. on a piano, typewriter, or computer. 4 a system of

notes in music, *the key of C major.* 5 a fact or clue that explains or solves something, *the key to the mystery.*

key *verb* (**keys, keying, keyed**)
key in type information into a computer using a keyboard.
[from Old English]

keyboard *noun* (*plural* **keyboards**)
the set of keys on a piano, typewriter, computer, etc.

keyhole *noun* (*plural* **keyholes**)
the hole through which a key is put into a lock.

keynote *noun* (*plural* **keynotes**)
1 the note on which a key in music is based, *The keynote of C major is C.* 2 the main idea in something said, written, or done; a theme.

keystone *noun* (*plural* **keystones**)
the central wedge-shaped stone in an arch, locking the others together.

kg *abbreviation*
kilogram.

khaki *noun*
a dull yellowish-brown colour, used for military uniforms.
[from Urdu *khaki* = dust-coloured]

kibbutz *noun* (*plural* **kibbutzim**)
a commune in Israel, especially for farming. [from Hebrew *qibbus* = gathering]

kick *verb* (**kicks, kicking, kicked**)
1 hit or move a person or thing with your foot. 2 move your legs about vigorously. 3 (of a gun) recoil when fired.
kick out get rid of; dismiss.
kick up (*informal*) make a noise or fuss.

kick *noun* (*plural* **kicks**)
1 a kicking movement. 2 the recoiling movement of a gun. 3 (*informal*) a thrill. 4 (*informal*) an interest or activity, *He's on a health kick.* [origin unknown]

kid *noun* (*plural* **kids**)
1 (*informal*) a child. 2 a young goat. 3 fine leather made from goat's skin.

kid *verb* (**kids, kidding, kidded**) (*informal*)
deceive someone in fun. [from Old Norse]

kiddie *noun* (*plural* **kiddies**) (*informal*)
a child.

kidnap *verb* (kidnaps, kidnapping, kidnapped)
take someone away by force, especially in order to obtain a ransom. **kidnapper** *noun*
[from *kid* + an old word *napper* = thief]

kidney *noun* (*plural* kidneys)
either of the two organs in the body that remove waste products from the blood and excrete urine into the bladder.
[origin unknown]

kidney bean *noun* (*plural* kidney beans)
a dark red bean with a curved shape like a kidney.

kill *verb* (kills, killing, killed)
1 make a person or thing die. 2 destroy or put an end to something. **killer** *noun*
kill time occupy time idly while waiting.
kill *noun* (*plural* kills)
1 killing an animal. 2 the animal or animals killed by a hunter.
[probably from Old English]

killing *adjective* (*informal*)
very amusing.

kiln *noun* (*plural* kilns)
an oven for hardening pottery or bricks, for drying hops, or for burning lime.
[from Latin *culina* = cooking-stove]

kilo *noun* (*plural* kilos)
a kilogram.

kilo- *prefix*
one thousand (as in *kilolitre* = 1,000 litres, *kilohertz* = 1,000 hertz).
[from Greek *chilioi* = thousand]

kilogram *noun* (*plural* kilograms)
a unit of mass or weight equal to 1,000 grams (about 2.2 pounds).

kilometre (*say* kil-o-meet-er or kil-**om**-it-er) *noun* (*plural* kilometres)
a unit of length equal to 1,000 metres (about ⅗ of a mile).

kilowatt *noun* (*plural* kilowatts)
a unit of electrical power equal to 1,000 watts.

kilt *noun* (*plural* kilts)
a kind of pleated skirt worn especially by Scotsmen. **kilted** *adjective*
[probably from a Scandinavian language]

kimono *noun* (*plural* kimonos)
a long loose Japanese robe. [from Japanese *ki* = wearing + *mono* = thing]

kin *noun*
a person's relatives.
kinsman *noun*, **kinswoman** *noun*
next of kin a person's closest relative.
[from Old English]

-kin *suffix*
forms diminutives (e.g. *lambkin* = little lamb). [from old Dutch]

kind¹ *noun* (*plural* kinds)
a class of similar things or animals; a sort or type.
payment in kind payment in goods not in money.
[from Old English *cynd* = nature]

USAGE: Correct use is *this kind of thing* or *these kinds of things* (not 'these kind of things').

kind² *adjective*
friendly and helpful; considerate.
kind-hearted *adjective*, **kindness** *noun*
[from Old English *gecynd* = natural or proper]

kindergarten *noun* (*plural* kindergartens)
a school or class for very young children.
[from German *Kinder* = children + *Garten* = garden]

kindle *verb* (kindles, kindling, kindled)
1 start a flame; set light to something.
2 begin burning. [from Old Norse]

kindling *noun*
small pieces of wood used for lighting fires.

kindly *adjective* (kindlier, kindliest)
kind, *a kindly smile*. **kindliness** *noun*

kindred *noun*
kin.
kindred *adjective*
related or similar, *chemistry and kindred subjects*.

kinetic *adjective*
to do with or produced by movement, *kinetic energy*.
[from Greek *kinetikos* = moving]

king *noun* (*plural* **kings**)
1 a man who is the ruler of a country through inheriting the position. **2** a person or thing regarded as supreme, *the lion is the king of beasts.* **3** the most important piece in chess. **4** a playing card with a picture of a king. **kingly** *adjective*, **kingship** *noun* [from Old English]

kingdom *noun* (*plural* **kingdoms**)
a country ruled by a king or queen.

kingfisher *noun* (*plural* **kingfishers**)
a small bird with blue feathers that dives to catch fish.

kink *noun* (*plural* **kinks**)
1 a short twist in a rope, wire, piece of hair, etc. **2** a peculiarity. [from old German]

kinky *adjective*
involving peculiar sexual behaviour.

kiosk *noun* (*plural* **kiosks**)
1 a telephone box. **2** a small hut or stall where newspapers, sweets, etc. are sold. [via French and Turkish from Persian]

kipper *noun* (*plural* **kippers**)
a smoked herring. [from Old English]

kirk *noun* (*plural* **kirks**) (*Scottish*)
a church. [from Old Norse]

kiss *noun* (*plural* **kisses**)
touching somebody with your lips as a sign of affection.
kiss *verb* (**kisses, kissing, kissed**)
give somebody a kiss. [from Old English]

kiss of life *noun*
blowing air from your mouth into another person's to help the other person to start breathing again, especially after an accident.

kit *noun* (*plural* **kits**)
1 equipment or clothes for a particular occupation. **2** a set of parts sold ready to be fitted together. [from old Dutch]

kitchen *noun* (*plural* **kitchens**)
a room in which meals are prepared and cooked. [from Old English]

kitchenette *noun* (*plural* **kitchenettes**)
a small kitchen.

kite *noun* (*plural* **kites**)
1 a light framework covered with cloth, paper, etc. and flown in the wind on the end of a long piece of string. **2** a large hawk. [from Old English]

kith and kin
friends and relatives. [from Old English *cyth* = what or who you know, + *kin*]

kitten *noun* (*plural* **kittens**)
a very young cat.
[from old French *chitoun* = small cat]

kitty *noun* (*plural* **kitties**)
1 an amount of money that you can win in a card game. **2** a fund for use by several people. [origin unknown]

kiwi (*say* **kee-wee**) *noun* (*plural* **kiwis**)
a New Zealand bird that cannot fly.
[a Maori word]

kiwi fruit *noun* (*plural* **kiwi fruits**)
a fruit with thin hairy skin, green flesh, and black seeds.
[named after the kiwi, because the fruit was exported from New Zealand]

kleptomania *noun*
an uncontrollable urge to steal things.
kleptomaniac *noun*
[from Greek *kleptes* = thief, + *mania*]

km *abbreviation*
kilometre.

knack *noun*
a special skill, *There's a knack to putting up a deckchair.*
[origin unknown]

knacker *noun*
a person who buys and slaughters horses and sells the meat and hides.
[origin unknown]

knapsack *noun* (*plural* **knapsacks**)
a bag carried on the back by soldiers, hikers, etc. [from Dutch]

knave *noun* (*plural* **knaves**)
1 (*old use*) a dishonest man; a rogue. **2** a jack in playing cards. [from Old English *cnafa* = a boy or male servant]

knead *verb* (kneads, kneading, kneaded)
press and stretch something soft
(especially dough) with your hands.
[from Old English]

knee *noun* (*plural* knees)
the joint in the middle of the leg.
[from Old English]

kneecap *noun* (*plural* kneecaps)
the small bone covering the front of the
knee joint.

kneel *verb* (kneels, kneeling, knelt)
be or get yourself in a position on your
knees. [from Old English]

knell *noun* (*plural* knells)
the sound of a bell rung solemnly after a
death or at a funeral. [from Old English]

knickerbockers *plural noun*
loose-fitting short trousers gathered in at
the knees. [from D. Knickerbocker, the
imaginary author of a book in which
people were shown wearing
knickerbockers]

knickers *plural noun*
a woman's or girl's undergarment worn on
the lower part of the body.
[from *knickerbockers*]

knick-knack *noun* (*plural* knick-knacks)
a small ornament.
[probably from old Dutch]

knife *noun* (*plural* knives)
a cutting instrument consisting of a sharp
blade set in a handle.
knife *verb* (knifes, knifing, knifed)
stab with a knife. [from Old English]

knight *noun* (*plural* knights)
1 a man who has been given the rank that
allows him to put 'Sir' before his name. **2** a
piece in chess, with a horse's head.
knighthood *noun*
knight *verb* (knights, knighting, knighted)
make someone a knight.
[from Old English *cniht* = young man]

knit *verb* (knits, knitting, knitted or knit)
make something by looping together wool
or other yarn, using long needles or a
machine. **knitter** *noun*, **knitting needle** *noun*
knit your brow frown.
[from Old English *cnyttan* = tie in knots]

knob *noun* (*plural* knobs)
1 the round handle of a door, drawer, etc.
2 a round lump on something. **3** a small
round piece of something, *a knob of butter*.
knobbly *adjective*, **knobby** *adjective*
[from old German]

knock *verb* (knocks, knocking, knocked)
1 hit a thing hard or so as to make a noise.
2 produce by hitting, *knock a hole in it*.
3 (*slang*) criticize unfavourably, *Stop
knocking Britain!*
knock off 1 (*informal*) stop working.
2 deduct something from a price. **3** (*slang*)
steal.
knock out make a person unconscious,
especially by a blow to the head.
knock *noun* (*plural* knocks)
the act or sound of knocking.
[from Old English]

knocker *noun* (*plural* knockers)
a hinged metal device for knocking on a
door.

knockout *noun* (*plural* knockouts)
1 knocking somebody out. **2** a contest in
which the loser in each round has to drop
out. **3** (*slang*) an amazing person or thing.

knoll *noun* (*plural* knolls)
a small round hill; a mound.
[from Old English]

knot *noun* (*plural* knots)
1 a place where a piece of string, rope, or
ribbon etc. is twisted round itself or
another piece. **2** a tangle; a lump. **3** a round
spot on a piece of wood where a branch
joined it. **4** a cluster of people or things. **5** a
unit for measuring the speed of ships and
aircraft, 2,025 yards (= 1,852 metres or 1
nautical mile) per hour.
knot *verb* (knots, knotting, knotted)
1 tie or fasten with a knot. **2** entangle.
[from Old English]

knotty *adjective* (knottier, knottiest)
1 full of knots. **2** difficult or puzzling, *a
knotty problem*.

know *verb* (knows, knowing, knew, known)
1 have something in your mind that you
have learnt or discovered. **2** recognize or
be familiar with a person or place, *I've
known him for years*. **3** understand, *She
knows how to please us*. [from Old English]

know-all *noun* (*plural* **know-alls**)
a person who behaves as if he or she knows everything.

know-how *noun*
skill; ability for a particular job.

knowing *adjective*
showing that you know something, *a knowing look*.

knowingly *adverb*
1 in a knowing way. **2** deliberately.

knowledge *noun*
1 knowing. **2** all that a person knows. **3** all that is known.
to my knowledge as far as I know.
[from *know* + Old English *lac* = practice]

knowledgeable *adjective*
well-informed. **knowledgeably** *adverb*

knuckle *noun* (*plural* **knuckles**)
a joint in the finger.
knuckle *verb* (**knuckles, knuckling, knuckled**)
knuckle down to buckle down to.
knuckle under be submissive.
[from old German]

koala (*say* koh-ah-la) *noun* (*plural* **koalas**)
an Australian animal that looks like a small bear.
[an Australian Aboriginal word]

Koran (*say* kor-ahn) *noun*
the sacred book of Islam, written in Arabic, believed by Muslims to contain the words of Allah revealed to the prophet Muhammad.
[from Arabic *kur'an* = reading]

kosher *adjective*
keeping to Jewish laws about food, *kosher meat*.
[from Hebrew *kasher* = suitable or proper]

kremlin *noun* (*plural* **kremlins**)
a citadel in a Russian city.
the Kremlin the government of the USSR, in Moscow.
[from Russian]

krill *noun*
a mass of tiny shrimp-like creatures, the chief food of certain whales.
[from Norwegian *kril* = fish fry]

krypton *noun*
an inert gas that is present in the earth's atmosphere and is used in fluorescent lamps. [from Greek *kryptos* = hidden]

kudos (*say* kew-doss) *noun*
honour and glory. [Greek, = praise]

kung fu *noun*
a Chinese method of self-defence, rather like karate.
[from Chinese *kung* = merit + *fu* = master]

kw *abbreviation*
kilowatt.

Ll

L *abbreviation*
learner, a person learning to drive a car.

lab *noun* (*plural* **labs**) (*informal*)
a laboratory.

label *noun* (*plural* **labels**)
a small piece of paper, cloth, or metal etc. fixed on or beside something to show what it is or what it costs, or its owner or destination, etc.
label *verb* (**labels, labelling, labelled**)
put a label on something. [from old French]

labial (*say* lay-hee-al) *adjective*
to do with the lips. [from Latin *labia* = lips]

laboratory *noun* (*plural* **laboratories**)
a room or building equipped for scientific experiments.
[from Latin *laboratorium* = workplace]

laborious *adjective*
1 needing or using a lot of hard work.
2 explaining something at great length and with obvious effort. **laboriously** *adverb*

Labour *noun*
the Labour Party, a socialist political party.

labour *noun* (*plural* **labours**)
1 hard work. **2** a task. **3** the contractions of the womb when a baby is being born.

labour *verb* (labours, labouring, laboured)
1 work hard. **2** explain something at great
length and with obvious effort, *Don't
labour the point.* [from Latin *labor* = work,
trouble, or suffering]

labourer *noun* (*plural* labourers)
a person who does hard manual work,
especially outdoors.

Labrador *noun* (*plural* Labradors)
a large black or light-brown dog.
[named after Labrador, a district in
Canada, where it was bred]

laburnum *noun* (*plural* laburnums)
a tree with hanging yellow flowers. [Latin]

labyrinth *noun* (*plural* labyrinths)
a complicated arrangement of passages or
paths; a maze. [from Greek]

lace *noun* (*plural* laces)
1 net-like material with decorative
patterns of holes in it. **2** a piece of thin cord
or leather for fastening a shoe, etc.
lacy *adjective*
lace *verb* (laces, lacing, laced)
1 fasten with a lace. **2** thread a cord etc.
through something. **3** add spirits to a
drink. [from old French]

lacerate *verb* (lacerates, lacerating,
lacerated)
injure flesh by cutting or tearing it.
laceration *noun* [from Latin]

lachrymal (*say* lak-rim-al) *adjective*
to do with tears; producing tears,
lachrymal ducts.
[from Latin *lacrima* = a tear]

lachrymose *adjective* (*formal*)
tearful.

lack *noun*
being without something.
lack *verb* (lacks, lacking, lacked)
be without something, *He lacks courage.*
[probably from Old English]

lackadaisical *adjective*
lacking vigour or determination; careless.
[from *lack-a-day*, an old phrase expressing
grief or surprise]

lackey *noun* (*plural* lackeys)
a footman. [from French]

laconic *adjective*
using few words; terse, *a laconic reply.*
laconically *adverb*
[from Greek *Lakon* = a native of Laconia,
an area in Greece (because the Laconians
were famous for their terse speech)]

lacquer *noun*
a hard glossy varnish. **lacquered** *adjective*
[via French from Portuguese]

lacrosse *noun*
a game using a stick with a net on it
(a *crosse*) to catch and throw a ball.
[from French *la crosse* = the crosse]

lactate *verb* (lactates, lactating, lactated)
(of mammals) produce milk.
[from Latin *lac* = milk]

lacy *adjective*
made of lace or like lace.

lad *noun* (*plural* lads)
a boy or youth. [origin unknown]

ladder *noun* (*plural* ladders)
1 two upright pieces of wood or metal etc.
and crosspieces (*rungs*), for use in
climbing. **2** a vertical ladder-like flaw in a
stocking etc. where a stitch has become
undone.
ladder *verb* (ladders, laddering, laddered)
get a ladder in a stocking etc.
[from Old English]

laden *adjective*
carrying a heavy load.
[from Old English *hladan* = load a ship]

ladle *noun* (*plural* ladles)
a large deep spoon with a long handle, used
for lifting and pouring liquids.
ladle *verb* (ladles, ladling, ladled)
lift and pour a liquid with a ladle.
[from Old English]

lady *noun* (*plural* ladies)
1 a well-mannered woman. **2** a woman of
good social position. **3** (in polite use) a
woman. **ladylike** *adjective*, **ladyship** *noun*
Lady *noun* the title of a noblewoman.
[from Old English *hlaefdige* = person who
makes the bread (compare *lord*)]

ladybird *noun* (*plural* ladybirds)
a small flying beetle, usually red with black
spots.

lady-in-waiting *noun* (*plural* **ladies-in-waiting**)
a woman of good social position who attends a queen or princess.

lag[1] *verb* (**lags, lagging, lagged**)
go too slowly and fail to keep up with others.
lag *noun* (*plural* **lags**)
a delay. [origin unknown]

lag[2] *verb* (**lags, lagging, lagged**)
wrap pipes or boilers etc. in insulating material (**lagging**) to keep them warm. [probably from a Scandinavian language]

lager (*say* **lah**-ger) *noun* (*plural* **lagers**)
a light beer.
[from German *Lager* = storehouse (because the beer was kept to mature)]

laggard *noun* (*plural* **laggards**)
a person who lags behind.

lagoon *noun* (*plural* **lagoons**)
a salt-water lake separated from the sea by sandbanks or reefs.
[from Latin *lacuna* = pool]

laid *past tense* of **lay**.

lain *past participle* of **lie**[2].

lair *noun* (*plural* **lairs**)
a sheltered place where a wild animal lives. [from Old English]

laissez-faire (*say* lay-say-**fair**) *noun*
a government's policy of not interfering. [French, = let (them) act]

laity (*say* **lay**-it-ee) *noun*
lay people, not the clergy.

lake *noun* (*plural* **lakes**)
a large area of water entirely surrounded by land. [from Latin]

lama *noun* (*plural* **lamas**)
a Buddhist priest or monk in Tibet and Mongolia. [from Tibetan]

lamb *noun* (*plural* **lambs**)
1 a young sheep. 2 meat from a lamb.
lambswool *noun* [from Old English]

lame *adjective*
1 unable to walk normally. 2 weak; not convincing, *a lame excuse*. **lamely** *adverb*, **lameness** *noun* [from Old English]

lament *noun* (*plural* **laments**)
a statement, song, or poem expressing grief or regret.
lament *verb* (**laments, lamenting, lamented**)
express grief or regret about something.
lamentation *noun*
[from Latin *lamentari* = weep]

lamentable (*say* **lam**-in-ta-bul) *adjective*
regrettable or deplorable.

laminated *adjective*
made of layers joined together.
[from Latin *lamina* = layer]

lamp *noun* (*plural* **lamps**)
a device for producing light from electricity, gas, or oil.
lamplight *noun*, **lampshade** *noun*
[from Greek *lampas* = torch]

lamp-post *noun* (*plural* **lamp-posts**)
a tall post in a street etc., with a lamp at the top.

lamprey *noun* (*plural* **lampreys**)
a small eel-like water animal. [from Latin]

lance *noun* (*plural* **lances**)
a long spear.
lance *verb* (**lances, lancing, lanced**)
cut open a boil etc. with a surgeon's lancet.
[from Latin]

lance corporal *noun* (*plural* **lance corporals**)
a soldier ranking between a private and a corporal. [origin unknown]

lancet *noun* (*plural* **lancets**)
1 a pointed two-edged knife used by surgeons. 2 a tall narrow pointed window or arch.
[from French *lancette* = small lance]

land *noun* (*plural* **lands**)
1 the part of the earth's surface not covered by sea. 2 the ground or soil; an area of country, *forest land*. 3 the area occupied by a nation; a country.
land *verb* (**lands, landing, landed**)
1 arrive or put on land from a ship or aircraft etc. 2 reach the ground after

jumping or falling. **3** bring a fish out of the water. **4** obtain, *She landed an excellent job.* **5** arrive or cause to arrive at a certain place or position etc., *They landed up in gaol.* **6** present with a problem, *He landed me with this task.* [from Old English]

landed *adjective*
1 owning land. **2** consisting of land, *landed estates.*

landing *noun* (*plural* landings)
1 bringing or coming to land. **2** a place where people can get on and off a boat. **3** the level area at the top of stairs.

landing stage *noun* (*plural* landing stages)
a platform on which people and goods are taken on and off a boat.

landlady *noun* (*plural* landladies)
1 a woman who lets rooms to lodgers. **2** a woman who looks after a public house.

landlord *noun* (*plural* landlords)
1 a person who lets a house, room, or land to a tenant. **2** a person who looks after a public house.

landlubber *noun* (*plural* landlubbers) (*informal*)
a person who is not used to the sea. [from *land* + an old word *lubber* = an awkward, clumsy person]

landmark *noun* (*plural* landmarks)
1 an object that is easily seen in a landscape. **2** an important event in the history of something.

landowner *noun* (*plural* landowners)
a person who owns a large amount of land.

landscape *noun* (*plural* landscapes)
the scenery or a picture of the countryside. [from Dutch]

landscape gardening *noun*
laying out a garden to imitate natural scenery.

landslide *noun* (*plural* landslides)
1 a landslip. **2** an overwhelming victory in an election, *She won the General Election by a landslide.*

landslip *noun* (*plural* landslips)
a huge mass of soil and rocks sliding down a slope.

landward *adjective* & *adverb*
towards the land. **landwards** *adverb*

lane *noun* (*plural* lanes)
1 a narrow road, especially in the country. **2** a strip of road for a single line of traffic. **3** a strip of track or water for one runner, swimmer, etc. in a race. [from Old English]

language *noun* (*plural* languages)
1 words and their use. **2** the words used in a particular country or by a particular group of people.
[from Latin *lingua* = tongue]

language laboratory *noun* (*plural* language laboratories)
a room equipped with tape recorders etc. for learning a foreign language.

languid *adjective*
slow because of tiredness, weakness, or laziness. **languidly** *adverb*, **languor** *noun*
[same origin as *languish*]

languish *verb* (languishes, languishing, languished)
1 become weak or listless and depressed. **2** live in miserable conditions; be neglected.
[from Latin *languere* = be faint or weak]

lank *adjective*
(of hair) long and limp. [from Old English]

lanky *adjective* (lankier, lankiest)
awkwardly thin and tall. **lankiness** *noun*

lanolin *noun*
a kind of ointment, made of fat from sheep's wool.
[from Latin *lana* = wool + *oleum* = oil]

lantern *noun* (*plural* lanterns)
a transparent case for holding a light and shielding it from the wind.
[from Latin; related to *lamp*]

lanyard *noun* (*plural* lanyards)
a short cord for fastening or holding something. [from old French]

lap¹ *noun* (*plural* **laps**)
1 the level place formed by the front of the legs above the knees when a person is sitting down. **2** going once round a racecourse. **3** one section of a journey, *the last lap.*
lap *verb* (**laps, lapping, lapped**)
be a lap ahead of someone in a race.
[from Old English *laeppa*]

lap² *verb* (**laps, lapping, lapped**)
1 take up liquid by moving the tongue, as a cat does. **2** make a gentle splash against something, *Waves lapped the shore.*
[from Old English *lapian*]

lapel (*say* la-**pel**) *noun* (*plural* **lapels**)
a flap folded back at the front edge of a coat etc. [from *lap¹*]

lapse *noun* (*plural* **lapses**)
1 a slight mistake or failure, *a lapse of memory.* **2** an amount of time elapsed, *after a lapse of six months.*
lapse *verb* (**lapses, lapsing, lapsed**)
1 pass or slip gradually, *He lapsed into unconsciousness.* **2** be no longer valid, through not being renewed, *My insurance policy has lapsed.*
[from Latin *lapsus* = sliding]

lapwing *noun* (*plural* **lapwings**)
a black and white bird with a crested head and a shrill cry. [from Old English]

larceny *noun*
stealing possessions.
[from Latin *latro* = robber]

larch *noun* (*plural* **larches**)
a tall deciduous tree that bears small cones. [via old German from Latin]

lard *noun*
a white greasy substance prepared from pig-fat and used in cooking.
[French, = bacon]

larder *noun* (*plural* **larders**)
a cupboard or small room for storing food.
[from Latin]

large *adjective*
of more than the ordinary or average size; big. **largeness** *noun*
at large 1 free to roam about, not captured, *The escaped prisoners are still at large.* **2** in general, as a whole, *She is respected by the country at large.*
[from Latin *largus* = abundant or generous]

largely *adverb*
to a great extent, *You are largely responsible for the accident.*

largesse (*say* lar-**jess**) *noun*
money or gifts generously given.
[French, related to *large*]

lark¹ *noun* (*plural* **larks**)
a small sandy-brown bird; the skylark.
[from Old English]

lark² *noun* (*plural* **larks**) (*informal*)
something amusing; a bit of fun, *We did it for a lark.*
lark *verb* (**larks, larking, larked**)
lark about have fun; play tricks.
[origin unknown]

larva *noun* (*plural* **larvae**)
an insect in the first stage of its life, after it comes out of the egg. **larval** *adjective*
[Latin, = ghost or mask]

laryngitis *noun*
inflammation of the larynx, causing hoarseness.

larynx (*say* **la**-rinks) *noun* (*plural* **larynxes**)
the part of the throat that contains the vocal cords. [from Greek]

lasagne (*say* laz-**an**-ya) *noun*
pasta in the form of sheets, usually cooked with minced meat and cheese sauce.
[Italian]

laser *noun* (*plural* **lasers**)
a device that makes a very strong narrow beam of light or other electromagnetic radiation.
[from the initials of 'light amplification (by) stimulated emission (of) radiation']

lash *noun* (*plural* **lashes**)
1 a stroke with a whip etc. **2** the cord or cord-like part of a whip. **3** an eyelash.
lash *verb* (**lashes, lashing, lashed**)
1 strike with a whip; beat violently. **2** tie with cord etc., *Lash the sticks together.*
lash down (of rain or wind) pour or beat down forcefully.

lash out 1 speak or hit out angrily. **2** spend money extravagantly.
[origin unknown]

lashings *plural noun*
plenty, *lashings of custard.*

lass *noun* (*plural* **lasses**)
a girl or young woman. **lassie** *noun*
[from Old Norse]

lassitude *noun*
tiredness; lack of energy.
[from Latin *lassus* = weary]

lasso *noun* (*plural* **lassoes** or **lassos**)
a rope with a sliding noose at the end, used for catching cattle etc.

lasso *verb* (**lassoes, lassoing, lassoed**)
catch an animal with a lasso.
[from Spanish]

last¹ *adjective* & *adverb*
1 coming after all others; final. **2** latest; most recent, *last night.* **3** least likely, *She is the last person I'd have chosen.*
the last straw a final thing that makes problems unbearable.

last *noun*
1 a person or thing that is last. **2** the end, *He was brave to the last.*
at last or **at long last** finally; after much delay.
[from Old English *latost*]

last² *verb* (**lasts, lasting, lasted**)
1 continue; go on existing or living or being usable. **2** be enough for, *The food will last us for three days.*
[from Old English *laestan*]

last³ *noun* (*plural* **lasts**)
a block of wood or metal shaped like a foot, used in making and repairing shoes.
[from Old English *laeste*]

lasting *adjective*
able to last for a long time, *a lasting peace.*

lastly *adverb*
in the last place; finally.

last post *noun*
a military bugle call sounded at sunset and at military funerals etc.

latch *noun* (*plural* **latches**)
a small bar fastening a door or gate, lifted by a lever or spring. **latchkey** *noun*

latch *verb* (**latches, latching, latched**)
fasten with a latch.
latch onto 1 meet someone and follow them around all the time. **2** understand something.
[from Old English]

late *adjective* & *adverb*
1 after the usual or expected time. **2** near the end, *late in the afternoon.* **3** recent, *the latest news.* **4** who has died recently, *the late king.*
of late recently.
[from Old English]

lately *adverb*
recently.

latent (*say* **lay**-tent) *adjective*
existing but not yet developed or active or visible. [from Latin *latens* = lying hidden]

latent heat *noun*
the heat needed to change a solid into a liquid or vapour, or a liquid into a vapour, without a change in temperature.

lateral *adjective*
1 to do with the side or sides. **2** sideways, *lateral movement.* **laterally** *adverb*
[from Latin *lateris* = of a side]

lateral thinking *noun*
solving problems by thinking about them in an indirect, and apparently illogical, way.

latex *noun*
the milky juice of various plants and trees, especially the rubber tree.

lath *noun* (*plural* **laths**)
a narrow thin strip of wood.
[from Old English]

lathe (*say* layth) *noun* (*plural* **lathes**)
a machine for holding and turning pieces of wood while they are being shaped.
[from Old English]

lather *noun*
a mass of froth.

lather *verb* (**lathers, lathering, lathered**)
1 cover with lather. **2** form a lather.
[from Old English]

Latin *noun*
the language of the ancient Romans.
[from *Latium*, an ancient district of Italy including Rome]

Latin America *noun*
the parts of Central and South America where the main language is Spanish or Portuguese. [because these languages developed from Latin]

latitude *noun* (*plural* **latitudes**)
1 the distance of a place from the equator, measured in degrees. 2 freedom from restrictions on what people can do or believe. [from Latin *latitudo* = breadth]

latrine (*say* la-treen) *noun* (*plural* **latrines**)
a lavatory in a camp or barracks etc. [French, related to *lavatory*]

latter *adjective*
later, *the latter part of the year.*
the latter the second of two people or things just mentioned. (Compare *former*.)
[from Old English]

latterly *adverb*
recently.

lattice *noun* (*plural* **lattices**)
a framework of crossed laths or bars with spaces between. [from French]

laud *verb* (**lauds, lauding, lauded**) (*formal*)
praise.
laudatory (*say* law-dat-er-ee) *adjective*
[from Latin]

laudable *adjective*
praiseworthy. **laudably** *adverb*

laugh *verb* (**laughs, laughing, laughed**)
make the sounds that show you think something is funny.
laugh *noun* (*plural* **laughs**)
the sound of laughing. [from Old English]

laughable *adjective*
deserving to be laughed at.

laughing stock *noun* (*plural* **laughing stocks**)
a person or thing that is the object of ridicule and scorn.

laughter *noun*
the act, sound, or manner of laughing. [from Old English]

launch[1] *verb* (**launches, launching, launched**)
1 send a ship from the land into the water. 2 set a thing moving by throwing or pushing it. 3 send a rocket etc. into space. 4 start into action, *launch an attack.*
launch *noun* (*plural* **launches**)
the launching of a ship or spacecraft. [from old French]

launch[2] *noun* (*plural* **launches**)
a large motor boat. [from Spanish]

launder *verb* (**launders, laundering, laundered**)
wash and iron clothes etc. [same origin as *laundry*]

launderette *noun* (*plural* **launderettes**)
a place fitted with washing machines that people pay to use. [from *laundry* + *-ette*]

laundry *noun* (*plural* **laundries**)
1 a place where clothes etc. are washed and ironed for customers. 2 clothes etc. sent to or from a laundry. [from Latin *lavandaria* = things to be washed]

laureate (*say* lorri-at) *adjective*
Poet Laureate a person appointed to write poems for national occasions.
[from *laurel*, because a laurel wreath was worn in ancient times as a sign of victory]

laurel *noun* (*plural* **laurels**)
an evergreen shrub with smooth shiny leaves. [from Latin]

lava *noun*
molten rock that flows from a volcano; the solid rock formed when it cools.
[from Latin *lavare* = to wash]

lavatory *noun* (*plural* **lavatories**)
1 a toilet. 2 a room containing a toilet. [from Latin *lavatorium* = a basin or bath for washing]

lavender *noun*
1 a shrub with sweet-smelling purple flowers. 2 light-purple colour. [from Latin]

lavish *adjective*
1 generous. 2 plentiful.
lavishly *adverb*, **lavishness** *noun*

lavish *verb* (lavishes, lavishing, lavished)
give generously, *They lavished praise upon him*.
[from Old French *lavasse* = heavy rain]

law *noun* (*plural* laws)
1 a rule or set of rules that everyone must obey. 2 (*informal*) the police. 3 a scientific statement of something that always happens, *the law of gravity*.
[via Old English from Old Norse]

law-abiding *adjective*
obeying the law.

lawcourt *noun* (*plural* lawcourts)
a room or building in which a judge or magistrate hears evidence and decides whether someone has broken the law.

lawful *adjective*
allowed or accepted by the law.
lawfully *adverb*

lawless *adjective*
1 not obeying the law. 2 without proper laws, *a lawless country*.
lawlessly *adverb*, **lawlessness** *noun*

lawn[1] *noun* (*plural* lawns)
an area of closely-cut grass in a garden or park. [from old French]

lawn[2] *noun*
very fine cotton material.
[probably from *Laon*, a town in France where cloth was made]

lawnmower *noun* (*plural* lawnmowers)
a machine for cutting the grass of lawns.

lawn tennis *noun*
tennis played on an outdoor grass or hard court.

lawsuit *noun* (*plural* lawsuits)
a dispute or claim etc. that is brought to a lawcourt to be settled.

lawyer *noun* (*plural* lawyers)
a person who is qualified to give advice in matters of law.

lax *adjective*
slack; not strict, *discipline was lax*.
laxly *adverb*, **laxity** *noun*
[from Latin *laxus* = loose]

laxative *noun* (*plural* laxatives)
a medicine that stimulates the bowels to empty. [from Latin *laxare* = loosen]

lay[1] *verb* (lays, laying, laid)
1 put something down in a particular place or way. 2 arrange things, especially for a meal, *lay the table*. 3 place, *He laid the blame on his sister*. 4 prepare or arrange, *We laid our plans*. 5 produce an egg.
lay off 1 stop employing somebody for a while. 2 (*informal*) stop doing something.
lay on supply or provide.
lay out 1 arrange or prepare. 2 knock a person unconscious. 3 prepare a corpse for burial.
[from Old English]

USAGE: Do not confuse *lay/laid/laying* = 'put down', with *lie/lay/lain/lying* = 'be in a flat position'. Correct uses are as follows: *Go and lie down*; *she went and lay down*; *please lay it on the floor*. 'Go and lay down' is incorrect.

lay[2] *past tense* of **lie**[2].

lay[3] *noun* (*plural* lays) (*old use*)
a poem meant to be sung; a ballad.
[from old French]

lay[4] *adjective*
1 not belonging to the clergy, *a lay preacher*. 2 not professionally qualified, *lay opinion*. [from Greek *laos* = people]

layabout *noun* (*plural* layabouts)
a person who lazily avoids working for a living.

lay-by *noun* (*plural* lay-bys)
a place where vehicles can stop beside a main road.

layer *noun* (*plural* layers)
a single thickness or coating. [from *lay*[1]]

layman *noun* (*plural* laymen)
1 a person who does not have specialized knowledge or training (e.g. as a doctor or lawyer). 2 a person who is not ordained as a member of the clergy. [from *lay*[4] + *man*]

layout *noun* (*plural* layouts)
an arrangement of parts of something according to a plan.

laywoman *noun* (*plural* **laywomen**)
1 a woman who does not have specialized knowledge or training (e.g. as a doctor or lawyer). 2 a woman who is not ordained as a member of the clergy.

laze *verb* (**lazes, lazing, lazed**)
spend time in a lazy way. [from *lazy*]

lazy *adjective* (**lazier, laziest**)
not wanting to work; doing little work.
lazily *adverb*, **laziness** *noun*
[probably from old Dutch]

lea *noun* (*plural* **leas**) (*poetic*)
a meadow. [from Old English]

lead¹ (*say* leed) *verb* (**leads, leading, led**)
1 take or guide someone, especially by going in front. 2 be winning in a race or contest etc.; be ahead. 3 be in charge of a group of people. 4 be a way or route, *This path leads to the beach.* 5 play the first card in a card game. 6 live or experience, *He leads a dull life.*
lead to result in; cause.

lead (*say* leed) *noun* (*plural* **leads**)
1 guidance or example, *Give us a lead.* 2 a leading place or part or position, *She took the lead.* 3 a strap or cord for leading a dog or other animal. 4 an electrical wire attached to something.
[from Old English *laedan*]

lead² (*say* led) *noun* (*plural* **leads**)
1 a soft heavy grey metal. 2 the writing substance (graphite) in a pencil. **lead** *adjective* [from Old English *lead*]

leaden (*say* led-en) *adjective*
1 made of lead. 2 heavy and slow.
3 lead-coloured; dark grey, *leaden skies.*

leader *noun* (*plural* **leaders**)
1 the person in charge of a group of people; a chief. 2 the person who is winning.
leadership *noun*

leaf *noun* (*plural* **leaves**)
1 a flat usually green part of a plant, growing out from its stem, branch, or root. 2 the paper forming one page of a book. 3 a very thin sheet of metal, *gold leaf.* 4 a flap that makes a table larger.
leafy *adjective*, **leafless** *adjective*
turn over a new leaf make a fresh start and improve your behaviour.
[from Old English]

leaflet *noun* (*plural* **leaflets**)
1 a piece of paper printed with information. 2 a small leaf.

league¹ *noun* (*plural* **leagues**)
1 a group of people or nations who agree to work together. 2 a group of teams who compete against each other for a championship.
in league with working or plotting together.
[from Latin *legare* = bind]

league² *noun* (*plural* **leagues**)
an old measure of distance, about 3 miles.
[from Greek]

leak *noun* (*plural* **leaks**)
1 a hole or crack etc. through which liquid or gas accidentally escapes. 2 the revealing of secret information. **leaky** *adjective*

leak *verb* (**leaks, leaking, leaked**)
1 get out or let out through a leak. 2 reveal secret information. **leakage** *noun*
[probably from old German or Dutch]

lean¹ *adjective*
1 with little or no fat, *lean meat.* 2 thin, *a lean body.*
[from Old Engligh *hlaene*]

lean² *verb* (**leans, leaning, leaned** or **leant**)
1 bend your body towards or over something. 2 put or be in a sloping position. 3 rest against something.
[from Old English *hleonian*]

leaning *noun* (*plural* **leanings**)
a tendency or preference.

leap *verb* (**leaps, leaping, leaped** or **leapt**)
jump vigorously. **leap** *noun*
[from Old English]

leapfrog *noun*
a game in which each player jumps with legs apart over another who is bending down.

leap year *noun* (*plural* **leap years**)
a year with an extra day in it (29 February). [probably because the dates from March onwards 'leap' a day of the week; a date which would fall on a Monday in an ordinary year will be on Tuesday in a leap year]

learn *verb* (**learns, learning, learned** or **learnt**)
get knowledge or skill; find out about something. [from Old English]

USAGE: It is not acceptable in standard English to use *learn* to mean 'to teach'.

---

learned (*say* ler-nid) *adjective*
having much knowledge obtained by study.

learner *noun* (*plural* **learners**)
a person who is learning something, especially to drive a car.

learning *noun*
knowledge obtained by study.

lease *noun* (*plural* **leases**)
an agreement to allow someone to use a building or land etc. for a fixed period in return for payment. **leaseholder** *noun*
lease *verb* (**leases, leasing, leased**)
allow or obtain the use of something by lease. [from old French]

leash *noun* (*plural* **leashes**)
a dog's lead. [from old French]

least *adjective* & *adverb*
very small in amount etc., *the least bit*; *the least expensive bike*.
least *noun*
the smallest amount etc.
[from Old English]

leather *noun*
material made from animal skins.
leathery *adjective* [from Old English]

leave *verb* (**leaves, leaving, left**)
1 go away from a person or place. **2** stop belonging to a group. **3** cause or allow something to stay where it is or as it is, *You left the door open.* **4** go away without taking something, *I left my book at home.* **5** put something to be collected or passed on, *leave a message.*
leave off cease.
leave out omit; not include.
leave *noun*
1 permission. **2** official permission to be away from work; the time for which this permission lasts, *three days leave.*
[from Old English]

leaven (*say* lev-en) *noun*
a substance (e.g. yeast) used to make dough rise.
leaven *verb* (**leavens, leavening, leavened**)
add leaven to dough.
[from Latin *levare* = to lighten or raise]

lechery *noun*
excessive sexual lust. **lecherous** *adjective*
[via old French from Germanic]

lectern *noun* (*plural* **lecterns**)
a stand to hold a Bible or other large book or notes for reading.
[same origin as *lecture*]

lecture *noun* (*plural* **lectures**)
1 a talk about a subject to an audience or a class. **2** a long serious warning or rebuke.
lecture *verb* (**lectures, lecturing, lectured**)
give a lecture. **lecturer** *noun* [from Latin *lectura* = reading, or something to be read]

led *past tense* of **lead**[1].

ledge *noun* (*plural* **ledges**)
a narrow shelf, *a window ledge*; *a mountain ledge*. [origin unknown]

ledger *noun* (*plural* **ledgers**)
an account-book. [probably from Dutch]

lee *noun* (*plural* **lees**)
the sheltered side or part of something, away from the wind. [from Old English]

leech *noun* (*plural* **leeches**)
a small blood-sucking worm that lives in water. [from Old English]

leek *noun* (*plural* **leeks**)
a long green and white vegetable of the onion family. [from Old English]

leer *verb* (**leers, leering, leered**)
look at someone in an insulting, sly, or unpleasant way. **leer** *noun*
[origin unknown]

leeward *adjective*
on the lee side.

leeway *noun*
1 extra space or time available. **2** a drift to leeward or off course.
make up leeway make up lost time; regain a lost position.

left¹ *adjective & adverb*
1 on or towards the west if you think of yourself as facing north. **2** (of political groups) in favour of socialist reforms.
left-hand *adjective*
left *noun*
the left-hand side or part etc.
[from Old English *lyft* = weak]

left² *past tense* of **leave**.

left-handed *adjective*
using the left hand in preference to the right hand.
[same origin as *left¹*]

leftovers *plural noun*
food not eaten.

leg *noun* (*plural* **legs**)
1 one of the limbs on a person's or animal's body, on which it stands or moves. **2** the part of a piece of clothing covering a leg. **3** each of the supports of a chair or other piece of furniture. **4** one part of a journey. **5** one of a pair of matches between the same teams. [from Old Norse]

legacy *noun* (*plural* **legacies**)
something left to a person in a will.
[from Latin]

legal *adjective*
1 lawful. **2** to do with the law or lawyers.
legally *adverb*, **legality** *noun* [from Latin]

legalize *verb* (**legalizes, legalizing, legalized**)
make a thing legal. **legalization** *noun*

legate *noun* (*plural* **legates**)
an official representative, especially of the pope. [from Latin]

legend *noun* (*plural* **legends**)
an old story handed down from the past, which may or may not be true. (Compare *myth*.) **legendary** *adjective*
[from Latin *legenda* = things to be read]

leggings *plural noun*
an outer covering for each leg.

legible *adjective*
clear enough to read. **legibly** *adverb*,
legibility *noun* [from Latin *legere* = to read]

legion *noun* (*plural* **legions**)
1 a division of the ancient Roman army.
2 a group of soldiers or former soldiers.
[from Latin]

legionnaire *noun* (*plural* **legionnaires**)
a member of an association of former soldiers.

legionnaires' disease *noun*
a serious form of pneumonia caused by bacteria. [so-called because of an outbreak at a meeting of the American Legion of ex-servicemen in 1976]

legislate *verb* (**legislates, legislating, legislated**)
make laws. **legislation** *noun*, **legislator** *noun*
[from Latin *legis* = of a law + *latio* = proposing]

legislative *adjective*
making laws, *a legislative assembly*.

legislature *noun* (*plural* **legislatures**)
a country's parliament or law-making assembly.

legitimate *adjective*
1 lawful. **2** born when parents are married to each other. **legitimately** *adverb*,
legitimacy *noun* [from Latin *legitimare* = make something lawful]

leisure *noun*
time that is free from work, when you can do what you like. **leisured** *adjective*, **leisurely** *adjective*
at leisure having leisure; not hurried.
at your leisure when you have time.
[from old French]

lemming *noun* (*plural* **lemmings**)
a small mouse-like animal of Arctic regions that migrates in large numbers and is said to run headlong into the sea and drown.
[from Norwegian or Danish]

lemon *noun* (*plural* **lemons**)
1 an oval yellow citrus fruit with a sour taste. **2** pale-yellow colour.
[same origin as *lime²*]

lemonade *noun*
a lemon-flavoured drink.

lemur (*say* lee-mer) *noun* (*plural* **lemurs**)
a monkey-like animal. [from Latin]

lend *verb* (**lends, lending, lent**)
1 allow a person to use something of yours for a short time. **2** provide someone with money that they must repay, usually in return for payments (called *interest*).
lender *noun*
lend a hand help somebody.
[from Old English]

USAGE: Do not confuse *lend* with *borrow*, which means just the opposite.

length *noun* (*plural* **lengths**)
1 how long something is. **2** a piece of cloth, rope, wire, etc. cut from a larger piece.
3 the amount of thoroughness in an action, *They went to great lengths to make us comfortable.*
at length 1 after a long time. **2** taking a long time; in detail.
[from Old English]

lengthen *verb* (**lengthens, lengthening, lengthened**)
make or become longer.

lengthways or **lengthwise** *adverb*
from end to end; along the longest part.

lengthy *adjective*
1 very long. **2** long and boring.
lengthily *adverb*

lenient (*say* **lee-nee-ent**) *adjective*
merciful; not severe. **leniently** *adverb*,
lenience *noun* [from Latin *lenis* = gentle]

lens *noun* (*plural* **lenses**)
1 a curved piece of glass or plastic used to focus things. **2** the transparent part of the eye, immediately behind the pupil.
[Latin, = lentil (because of its shape)]

Lent *noun*
a time of fasting and penitence observed by Christians for about six weeks before Easter. **Lenten** *adjective*
[from Old English *lencten* = the spring]

lent *past tense* of **lend.**

lentil *noun* (*plural* **lentils**)
a kind of small bean.
[from old French; related to *lens*]

leopard (*say* **lep-erd**) *noun* (*plural* **leopards**)
a large lion-like spotted wild animal, also called a panther. **leopardess** *noun*
[from Greek]

leotard (*say* **lee-o-tard**) *noun* (*plural* **leotards**)
a close-fitting garment worn by acrobats and dancers. [named after a French trapeze artist, J. Leotard, who designed it]

leper *noun* (*plural* **lepers**)
a person who has leprosy.

lepidopterous *adjective*
of the group of insects that includes butterflies and moths.
[from Greek *lepis* = scale^2 + *pteron* = wing]

leprechaun (*say* **lep-rek-awn**) *noun* (*plural* **leprechauns**)
(in Irish folklore) an elf who looks like a little old man. [from Irish, = a small body]

leprosy *noun*
an infectious disease that makes parts of the body waste away. **leprous** *adjective*
[from Greek *lepros* = scaly (because white scales form on the skin)]

lesbian *noun* (*plural* **lesbians**)
a homosexual woman.
[named after the Greek island of Lesbos (because Sappho, a poetess who lived there about 600 BC, was said to be homosexual)]

less *adjective* & *adverb*
smaller in amount; not so much, *Make less noise. It is less important.*

USAGE: Do not use *less* when you mean *fewer*. You should use *fewer* when you are talking about a number of individual things, and *less* when you are talking about a quantity or mass of something: *The less batter you make, the fewer pancakes you'll get.*

less *noun*
a smaller amount.
less *preposition*
minus; deducting, *She earned £100, less tax.*
[from Old English]

-less *suffix*
forms adjectives meaning 'without' (e.g. *colourless*) or 'unable to be ...' (e.g. *countless*). [from Old English]

lessen *verb* (lessens, lessening, lessened)
make or become less.

lesser *adjective*
not so great as the other, *the lesser evil.*

lesson *noun* (*plural* lessons)
1 an amount of teaching given at one time.
2 something to be learnt by a pupil. **3** an example or experience from which you should learn, *Let this be a lesson to you!* **4** a passage from the Bible read aloud as part of a church service.
[from old French; related to *lecture*]

lest *conjunction* (*old use*)
so that something should not happen, *Remind us, lest we forget.*
[from Old English]

let *verb* (lets, letting, let)
1 allow somebody or something to do something; not prevent or forbid, *Let me see it.* **2** cause to, *Let us know what happens.* **3** allow or cause to come or go or pass, *Let me out!* **4** allow someone to use a house or building etc. in return for payment (*rent*).
5 leave, *Let it alone.*
let down 1 deflate. **2** disappoint somebody.
let off 1 cause to explode. **2** excuse somebody from a duty or punishment etc.
let up (*informal*) relax. **let-up** *noun*
[from Old English]

lethal (*say* lee-thal) *adjective*
deadly; causing death. **lethally** *adverb*
[from Latin *letum* = death]

lethargy (*say* leth-er-jee) *noun*
extreme lack of energy or vitality; sluggishness. **lethargic** (*say* lith-ar-jik) *adjective* [from Greek *lethargos* = forgetful]

letter *noun* (*plural* letters)
1 a symbol representing a sound used in speech. **2** a written message, usually sent by post. [from Latin]

letter box *noun* (*plural* letter boxes)
1 a slot in a door, through which letters are delivered. **2** a postbox.

lettering *noun*
letters drawn or painted.

lettuce *noun* (*plural* lettuces)
a garden plant with broad crisp leaves used in salads. [from Latin]

leukaemia (*say* lew-kee-mee-a) *noun*
a disease in which there are too many white corpuscles in the blood. [from Greek *leukos* = white + *haima* = blood]

level *adjective*
1 flat or horizontal. **2** at the same height or position etc. as others.

level *noun* (*plural* levels)
1 height, depth, position, or value etc., *Fix the shelves at eye level.* **2** a level surface. **3** a device that shows whether something is level.
on the level (*informal*) honest.

level *verb* (levels, levelling, levelled)
1 make or become level. **2** aim a gun or missile. **3** direct an accusation at a person.
[from Latin *libra* = balance]

level crossing *noun* (*plural* level crossings)
a place where a road crosses a railway at the same level.

lever *noun* (*plural* levers)
1 a bar that turns on a fixed point (the *fulcrum*) in order to lift something or force something open. **2** a bar used as a handle to operate machinery etc., *a gear lever.*

lever *verb* (levers, levering, levered)
lift or move something by means of a lever.
[from Latin *levare* = raise]

leverage *noun*
1 the force you need when you use a lever.
2 influence.

leveret *noun* (*plural* leverets)
a young hare. [from French *lièvre* = hare]

levitation *noun*
rising into the air and floating there.
[same origin as *levity*]

levity *noun*
being humorous, especially at an unsuitable time; frivolity.
[from Latin *levis* = lightweight]

levy *verb* (levies, levying, levied)
1 impose or collect a tax or other payment by the use of authority or force. **2** enrol, *levy an army.*

levy *noun* (*plural* levies)
an amount of money paid in tax.
[same origin as *lever*]

lewd *adjective*
indecent or crude. **lewdly** *adverb*, **lewdness**
noun [origin unknown]

lexicography *noun*
the writing of dictionaries. **lexicographer**
noun [from Greek *lexis* = word, + *-graphy*]

liability *noun* (*plural* liabilities)
1 being liable. 2 a debt or obligation. 3 a
disadvantage or handicap.

liable *adjective*
1 likely to do or get something, *She is liable
to colds. The cliff is liable to crumble.*
2 legally responsible for something.
[probably from old French]

liaise (*say* lee-**ayz**) *verb* (liaises, liaising,
liaised) (*informal*)
act as a liaison or go-between.
[from *liaison*]

liaison (*say* lee-**ay**-zon) *noun* (*plural*
liaisons)
1 communication and cooperation
between people or groups. 2 a person who
is a link or go-between.
[from French *lier* = bind]

liar *noun* (*plural* liars)
a person who tells lies. [from Old English]

libel (*say* **ly**-bel) *noun* (*plural* libels)
an untrue written, printed, or broadcast
statement that damages a person's
reputation. (Compare *slander*.)
libellous *adjective*
libel *verb* (libels, libelling, libelled)
make a libel against someone.
[from Latin *libellus* = little book]

Liberal *noun* (*plural* Liberals)
a member of the Liberal Party, a political
party favouring moderate reforms.

liberal *adjective*
1 giving generously. 2 given in large
amounts. 3 not strict; tolerant.
liberally *adverb*, **liberality** *noun*
[same origin as *liberty*]

Liberal Democrat *noun* (*plural* Liberal
Democrats)
a member of the Liberal Democrat political
party.

liberalize *verb* (liberalizes, liberalizing,
liberalized)
make less strict. **liberalization** *noun*

liberate *verb* (liberates, liberating, liberated)
set free. **liberation** *noun*, **liberator** *noun*
[same origin as *liberty*]

liberty *noun* (*plural* liberties)
freedom.
take liberties behave too casually or in too
familiar a way.
[from Latin *liber* = free]

librarian *noun* (*plural* librarians)
a person in charge of or assisting in a
library. **librarianship** *noun*

library (*say* **ly**-bra-ree) *noun* (*plural*
libraries)
1 a place where books are kept for people
to use or borrow. 2 a collection of books,
records, films, etc.
[from Latin *libraria* = bookshop]

libretto *noun* (*plural* librettos)
the words of an opera or other long musical
work. [Italian, = little book]

lice *plural* of **louse**.

licence *noun* (*plural* licences)
1 an official permit to do or use or own
something, *a driving licence.* 2 special
freedom to avoid the usual rules or
customs. [from Latin *licere* = be allowed]

license *verb* (licenses, licensing, licensed)
give a licence to a person; authorize, *We are
licensed to sell tobacco.*

licensee *noun* (*plural* licensees)
a person who holds a licence, especially to
sell alcohol.

licentious (*say* ly-**sen**-shus) *adjective*
breaking the rules of conduct; immoral.
licentiousness *noun*
[from Latin *licentiosus* = not restrained]

lichen (*say* **ly**-ken or **lich**-en) *noun* (*plural*
lichens)
a dry-looking plant that grows on rocks,
walls, trees, etc.
[from Greek]

lick *verb* (licks, licking, licked)
1 move your tongue over something. **2** (of a wave or flame) move like a tongue; touch lightly. **3** (*slang*) defeat.
lick *noun* (*plural* licks)
1 licking. **2** a slight application of paint etc. **3** (*slang*) a fast pace. [from Old English]

lid *noun* (*plural* lids)
1 a cover for a box or pot etc. **2** an eyelid. [from Old English]

lido (*say* leed-oh) *noun* (*plural* lidos)
a public open-air swimming pool or pleasure beach. [from Lido, the name of a beach near Venice]

lie¹ *noun* (*plural* lies)
a statement that the person who makes it knows to be untrue.
lie *verb* (lies, lying, lied)
tell a lie or lies; be deceptive. [from Old English *leogan*]

lie² *verb* (lays, lying, lay, lain)
1 be or get in a flat or resting position, *He lay on the grass. The cat has lain here all night.* **2** be or remain, *The island lies near the coast. The machinery lay idle.*
lie low keep yourself hidden.
lie *noun* (*plural* lies)
the way something lies, *the lie of the land.* [from Old English *licgan*]

USAGE: See the note at **lay¹**.

liege (*say* leej) *noun* (*plural* lieges) (*old use*)
a person who is entitled to receive feudal service or allegiance (*a liege lord*) or bound to give it (*a liege man*). [from old French]

lieu (*say* lew) *noun*
in lieu instead, *He accepted a cheque in lieu of cash.* [French, = place]

lieutenant (*say* lef-ten-ant) *noun* (*plural* lieutenants)
1 an officer in the army or navy. **2** a deputy or chief assistant. [from French *lieu* = place + *tenant* = holding]

life *noun* (*plural* lives)
1 the ability to function and grow. **2** the period between birth and death. **3** living things, *Is there life on Mars?* **4** liveliness, *full of life.* **5** a biography. [from Old English]

lifebelt *noun* (*plural* lifebelts)
a ring of material that will float, used to support someone's body in water.

lifeboat *noun* (*plural* lifeboats)
a boat for rescuing people at sea.

lifebuoy *noun* (*plural* lifebuoys)
a device to support someone's body in water.

life cycle *noun* (*plural* life cycles)
the series of changes in the life of a living thing.

lifeguard *noun* (*plural* lifeguards)
someone whose job is to rescue swimmers who are in difficulty.

life jacket *noun* (*plural* life jackets)
a jacket of material that will float, used to support someone's body in water.

lifeless *adjective*
1 without life. **2** unconscious.
lifelessly *adverb*

lifelike *adjective*
looking exactly like a real person or thing.

lifelong *adjective*
continuing for the whole of someone's life.

lifespan *noun* (*plural* lifespans)
the length of someone's life.

lifetime *noun* (*plural* lifetimes)
the time for which someone is alive.

lift *verb* (lifts, lifting, lifted)
1 raise or pick up something. **2** rise or go upwards. **3** (*informal*) steal. **4** remove or abolish something, *The ban has been lifted.*
lift *noun* (*plural* lifts)
1 lifting. **2** a device for taking people or goods from one floor or level to another in a building. **3** a free ride in somebody else's vehicle, *Can you give me a lift to the station?* [from Old Norse]

lift-off *noun* (*plural* lift-offs)
the vertical take-off of a rocket or spacecraft.

ligament *noun* (*plural* ligaments)
a piece of the tough flexible tissue that holds your bones together. [from Latin *ligare* = bind]

ligature *noun* (*plural* **ligatures**)
a thing used in tying something, especially in surgical operations.
[same origin as *ligament*]

light¹ *noun* (*plural* **lights**)
1 radiation that stimulates the sense of sight and makes things visible.
2 something that provides light, especially an electric lamp. **3** a flame.
bring or **come to light** make or become known.
light *adjective*
1 full of light; not dark. **2** pale, *light blue*.
light *verb* (**lights, lighting, lit** or **lighted**)
1 start a thing burning; kindle. **2** provide the light.
light up 1 put lights on, especially at dusk.
2 make or become light or bright.
[from Old English *leoht*]

USAGE: Say *He lit the lamps*; *the lamps were lit* (not 'lighted'), but *She carried a lighted torch* (not 'a lit torch').

light² *adjective*
1 having little weight; not heavy. **2** small in amount or force etc., *light rain*; *a light punishment*. **3** needing little effort, *light work*. **4** cheerful, not sad, *with a light heart*. **5** not serious or profound, *light music*.
lightly *adverb*, **lightness** *noun*
light *adverb*
lightly; with only a small load, *We were travelling light*. [from Old English *liht*]

lighten¹ *verb* (**lightens, lightening, lightened**)
make or become lighter or brighter.

lighten² *verb* (**lightens, lightening, lightened**)
make or become lighter or less heavy.

lighter *noun* (*plural* **lighters**)
a device for lighting cigarettes etc.

light-hearted *adjective*
1 cheerful and free from worry. **2** not serious.

lighthouse *noun* (*plural* **lighthouses**)
a tower with a bright light at the top to guide or warn ships.

light industry *noun* (*plural* **light industries**)
an industry producing small or light articles.

lighting *noun*
lamps, or the light they provide.

lightning *noun*
a flash of bright light produced by natural electricity during a thunderstorm.
like lightning with very great speed.

lightning conductor *noun* (*plural* **lightning conductors**)
a metal rod or wire fixed on a building to divert lightning into the earth.

lightweight *noun* (*plural* **lightweights**)
1 a person who is not heavy. **2** a boxer weighing between 57.1 and 59 kg.
lightweight *adjective*

light year *noun* (*plural* **light years**)
the distance that light travels in one year (about 9.5 million million km).

like¹ *verb* (**likes, liking, liked**)
1 think a person or thing is pleasant or satisfactory. **2** wish, *I should like to come*.
[from Old English]

like² *adjective*
similar; having some or all of the qualities of another person or thing, *They are as like as two peas*.
like *noun*
a similar person or thing, *We shall not see his like again*.
like *preposition*
1 similar to; in the manner of, *He swims like a fish*. **2** in a suitable state for, *It looks like rain. I feel like a cup of tea*.
[from Old Norse]

likeable *adjective*
easy to like; pleasant.

likelihood *noun*
being likely; probability.

likely *adjective* (**likelier, likeliest**)
1 probable; expected to happen or be true etc., *Rain is likely*. **2** expected to be successful, *a likely lad*; *a likely spot*.
[from *like²*]

liken *verb* (likens, likening, likened)
compare, *He likened the human heart to a pump.*

likeness *noun* (*plural* likenesses)
1 a similarity in appearance; a resemblance. 2 a portrait

likewise *adverb*
similarly.

liking *noun*
a feeling that you like something, *She has a liking for ice cream.*

lilac *noun*
1 a bush with fragrant purple or white flowers. 2 pale purple.
[from Persian *lilak* = bluish]

lilt *noun* (*plural* lilts)
a light pleasant rhythm. **lilting** *adjective*
[from old German or Dutch]

lily *noun* (*plural* lilies)
a garden plant with trumpet-shaped flowers, growing from a bulb. [from Greek]

limb *noun* (*plural* limbs)
1 a leg, arm, or wing. 2 a large branch of a tree.
out on a limb isolated; without any support.
[from Old English]

limber *verb* (limbers, limbering, limbered)
limber up exercise in preparation for an athletic activity.
[origin unknown]

limbo¹ *noun*
in limbo in an uncertain situation where you are waiting for something to happen, *Lack of money has left our plans in limbo.*
[the name of a place formerly believed by Christians to exist on the borders of hell, where the souls of people who were not baptized waited for God's judgement]

limbo² *noun*
a West Indian dance in which you bend backwards to pass under a low bar.

lime¹ *noun*
a white substance (calcium oxide) used in making cement and as a fertilizer.
[from Old English *lim*]

lime² *noun* (*plural* limes)
a green fruit like a small round lemon.
lime juice *noun*
[from Arabic *lima* = citrus fruit]

lime³ *noun* (*plural* limes)
a tree with yellow flowers.
[from Old English *lind*]

limelight *noun*
in the limelight receiving a lot of publicity and attention.
[from *lime¹* which gives a bright light when heated, formerly used to light up the stage of a theatre]

limerick *noun* (*plural* limericks)
a type of amusing poem with five lines.
[named after Limerick, a town in Ireland]

limestone *noun*
a kind of rock from which lime (calcium oxide) is obtained.

limit *noun* (*plural* limits)
1 a line, point, or level where something ends. 2 the greatest amount allowed, *the speed limit.*
limit *verb* (limits, limiting, limited)
1 keep something within certain limits.
2 be a limit to something. **limitation** *noun*
[from Latin *limes* = boundary]

limited *adjective*
kept within limits; not great, *a limited choice; limited experience.*

limited company *noun* (*plural* limited companies)
a business company whose shareholders would have to pay only some of its debts.

limousine (*say* lim-oo-zeen) *noun* (*plural* limousines)
a luxurious car. [originally, a hooded cape worn in Limousin, a district in France; the name given to the cars because early ones had a canvas roof to shelter the driver]

limp¹ *verb* (limps, limping, limped)
walk lamely.
limp *noun* (*plural* limps)
a limping walk. [origin unknown]

limp² *adjective*
1 not stiff or firm. 2 without strength or energy. **limply** *adverb*, **limpness** *noun*
[origin unknown]

limpet *noun* (*plural* limpets)
a small shellfish that attaches itself firmly
to rocks. [via Old English from Latin]

limpid *adjective*
(of liquids) clear; transparent.
limpidity *noun* [from Latin]

linchpin *noun* (*plural* linchpins)
1 a pin passed through the end of an axle to
keep a wheel in position. 2 the person or
thing that is vital to the success of
something. [from Old English]

line¹ *noun* (*plural* lines)
1 a long thin mark. 2 a row or series of
people or things; a row of words. 3 a length
of rope, string, wire, etc. used for a special
purpose, *a fishing line*. 4 a railway; a line of
railway track. 5 a system of ships, aircraft,
buses, etc. 6 a way of doing things or
behaving; a type of business.
in line 1 forming a straight line.
2 conforming.
line *verb* (lines, lining, lined)
1 mark something with lines, *Use lined
paper*. 2 form something into a line or
lines, *Line them up*.
[from Old English]

line² *verb* (lines, lining, lined)
cover the inside of something.
[from *linen* (used for linings)]

lineage (*say* lin-ee-ij) *noun* (*plural* lineages)
ancestry; a line of descendants from an
ancestor.

lineal (*say* lin-ee-al) *adjective*
in the direct line of descent or ancestry.

linear (*say* lin-ee-er) *adjective*
1 arranged in a line. 2 to do with a line or
length.

linen *noun*
1 cloth made from flax. 2 shirts, sheets,
and tablecloths etc. (which were formerly
made of linen). [from Latin *linum* = flax]

liner *noun* (*plural* liners)
a large ship or aircraft on a regular route,
usually carrying passengers. [from *line*¹]

linesman *noun* (*plural* linesmen)
an official in football or tennis etc. who
decides whether the ball has crossed a line.

-ling *suffix*
forms nouns meaning 'having a certain
quality' (e.g. *weakling*) or diminutives
meaning 'little' (e.g. *duckling*).
[from Old English]

linger *verb* (lingers, lingering, lingered)
stay for a long time, as if unwilling to
leave; be slow to leave. [from Old English]

lingerie (*say* lan-zher-ee) *noun*
women's underwear.
[French, from *linge* = linen]

linguist *noun* (*plural* linguists)
an expert in languages.
[same origin as *language*]

linguistics *noun*
the study of languages. linguistic *adjective*

liniment *noun*
a lotion for rubbing on parts of the body
that ache; embrocation.
[from Latin *linire* = to smear]

lining *noun* (*plural* linings)
a layer that covers the inside of something.
[from *line*²]

link *noun* (*plural* links)
1 one ring or loop of a chain. 2 a
connection.
link *verb* (links, linking, linked)
join things together; connect. linkage *noun*
[from Old Norse]

links *noun* or *plural noun*
a golf course. [from Old English *hlinc*
= sandy ground near the seashore (where
golf was often played)]

linnet *noun* (*plural* linnets)
a kind of finch. [from old French (named
because the bird feeds on linseed)]

lino *noun*
linoleum.

linocut *noun* (*plural* linocuts)
a print made from a design cut into a block
of thick linoleum.

linoleum *noun*
a stiff shiny floor covering. [from Latin
linum = flax + *oleum* = oil (because linseed
oil is used to make linoleum)]

linseed *noun*
the seed of flax, from which oil is obtained.
[from Latin *linum* = flax, + *seed*]

lint *noun*
a soft material for covering wounds.
[probably from old French *lin* = flax (from
which lint was originally made)]

lintel *noun* (*plural* **lintels**)
a horizontal piece of wood or stone etc.
above a door or other opening.
[from old French]

lion *noun* (*plural* **lions**)
a large strong flesh-eating animal found in
Africa and India. **lioness** *noun* [from Greek]

lip *noun* (*plural* **lips**)
1 either of the two fleshy edges of the
mouth. 2 the edge of something hollow,
such as a cup or crater. 3 the pointed part
at the top of a jug etc., from which you pour
things. [from Old English]

lip-reading *noun*
understanding what a person says by
watching the movements of his or her lips,
not by hearing.

lip-service *noun*
pay lip-service to something say that you
approve of it but do nothing to support it.

lipstick *noun* (*plural* **lipsticks**)
a stick of a waxy substance for colouring
the lips.

liquefy *verb* (**liquefies, liquefying, liquefied**)
make or become liquid. **liquefaction** *noun*

liqueur (*say* lik-yoor) *noun* (*plural* **liqueurs**)
a strong sweet alcoholic drink.
[French, = liquor]

liquid *noun* (*plural* **liquids**)
a substance (such as water or oil) that
flows freely but is not a gas.
liquid *adjective*
1 in the form of a liquid; flowing freely.
2 easily converted into cash, *the firm's
liquid assets.* **liquidity** *noun*
[from Latin *liquidus* = flowing]

liquidate *verb* (**liquidates, liquidating,
liquidated**)
1 pay off or settle a debt. 2 close down a
business and divide its value between its

creditors. 3 got rid of someone, especially
by killing them.
liquidation *noun*, **liquidator** *noun*

liquidize *verb* (**liquidizes, liquidizing,
liquidized**)
make something, especially food, into a
liquid or pulp. **liquidizer** *noun*

liquor *noun*
1 alcoholic drink. 2 juice produced in
cooking; liquid in which food has been
cooked. [from Latin]

liquorice (*say* lick-er-iss) *noun*
1 a black substance used in medicine and
as a sweet. 2 the plant from whose root this
substance is obtained.
[from Greek *glykys* = sweet + *rhiza* = root]

lisp *noun* (*plural* **lisps**)
a fault in speech in which *s* and *z* are
pronounced like *th*. **lisp** *verb*
[from Old English]

list[1] *noun* (*plural* **lists**)
a number of names, items, or figures etc.
written or printed one after another.
list *verb* (**lists, listing, listed**)
make a list of people or things.
[from old French]

list[2] *verb* (**lists, listing, listed**)
(of a ship) lean over to one side; tilt.
list *noun* [origin unknown]

listed *adjective*
(of a building) protected from being
demolished or altered because of its
historical importance.

listen *verb* (**listens, listening, listened**)
pay attention in order to hear something.
listener *noun* [from Old English]

listless *adjective*
too tired to be active or enthusiastic.
listlessly *adverb*, **listlessness** *noun*
[from an old word *list* = desire, + *-less*]

lit *past tense* of **light**[1].

litany *noun* (*plural* **litanies**)
a formal prayer with fixed responses.
[from Greek *litaneia* = prayer]

literacy *noun*
the ability to read and write.

literal *adjective*
1 meaning exactly what is said, not metaphorical or exaggerated. 2 word for word, *a literal translation*.
[from Latin *littera* = letter]

literally *adverb*
really; exactly as stated, *The noise made me literally jump out of my seat*.

literary (say lit-er-er-i) *adjective*
to do with literature; interested in literature. [same origin as *literal*]

literate *adjective*
able to read and write.
[same origin as *literal*]

literature *noun*
books and other writings, especially those considered to have been written well.
[same origin as *literal*]

lithe *adjective*
flexible and supple. [from Old English]

litigant *noun* (*plural* litigants)
a person who is involved in a lawsuit.
[from Latin *litigare* = start a lawsuit]

litigation *noun* (*plural* litigations)
a lawsuit; the process of carrying on a lawsuit. [same origin as *litigant*]

litmus *noun*
a blue substance that is turned red by acids and can be turned back to blue by alkalis.
[from Old Norse *litr* = dye + *mosi* = moss (because litmus is obtained from some kinds of moss)]

litmus paper *noun*
paper stained with litmus.

litre *noun* (*plural* litres)
a measure of liquid, about $1\frac{3}{4}$ pints.
[French]

litter *noun* (*plural* litters)
1 rubbish or untidy things left lying about. 2 straw etc. put down as bedding for animals. 3 the young animals born to one mother at one time. 4 a kind of stretcher.

litter *verb* (litters, littering, littered)
1 make a place untidy with litter. 2 spread straw etc. for animals.
[from old French *litière* = bed]

little *adjective* (less, least)
small in amount or size or intensity etc.; not great or big or much.
little by little gradually; by a small amount at a time.

little *adverb*
not much, *I eat very little*.
[from Old English]

liturgy *noun* (*plural* liturgies)
a fixed form of public worship used in churches. **liturgical** *adjective*
[from Greek *leitourgia* = worship]

live¹ (rhymes with *give*) *verb* (lives, living, lived)
1 have life; be alive. 2 have your home, *She lives in Glasgow*. 3 pass your life in a certain way, *He lived as a hermit*.
live down if you cannot live down a mistake or embarrassment, you cannot make people forget it.
live on use something as food; depend on for your living.
[from Old English]

live² (rhymes with *hive*) *adjective*
1 alive. 2 burning, *live coals*. 3 carrying electricity. 4 broadcast while it is actually happening, not from a recording.
[from *alive*]

livelihood *noun* (*plural* livelihoods)
a way of earning money or providing enough food to support yourself. [from Old English *lif* = life + *lad* = course or way]

lively *adjective* (livelier, liveliest)
full of life or action; vigorous and cheerful.
liveliness *noun*

liven *verb* (livens, livening, livened)
make or become lively, *liven things up*.

liver *noun* (*plural* livers)
1 a large organ of the body, found in the abdomen, that processes digested food and purifies the blood. 2 an animal's liver used as food. [from Old English]

livery *noun* (*plural* liveries)
1 a uniform worn by male servants in a household. 2 the distinctive colours used by a railway or bus company etc.
[originally = the giving of food or clothing: from Latin *librare* = to set free or hand over]

livery stables noun (plural livery stables)
a place where horses are kept for their
owner or where horses may be hired.

livestock noun
farm animals.

live wire noun (plural live wires)
a forceful energetic person.

livid adjective
1 bluish-grey, a livid bruise. 2 furiously
angry. [from Latin]

living noun
1 being alive. 2 the way that a person lives,
a good standard of living. 3 a way of
earning money or providing enough food
to support yourself.

living room noun (plural living rooms)
a room for general use during the day.

lizard noun (plural lizards)
a reptile with a rough or scaly skin, four
legs, and a long tail. [from Latin]

llama (say lah-ma) noun (plural llamas)
a South American animal with woolly fur,
like a camel but with no hump.
[via Spanish from Quechua (a South
American language)]

lo interjection (old use)
see, behold. [from Old English]

load noun (plural loads)
1 something carried; a burden. 2 the
quantity that can be carried. 3 the total
amount of electric current supplied.
4 (informal) a large amount, It's a load of
nonsense. You could earn loads of money.

load verb (loads, loading, loaded)
1 put a load in or on something. 2 fill
heavily. 3 weight with something heavy,
loaded dice. 4 put a bullet or shell into a
gun; put a film into a camera. 5 enter data
etc. into a computer. [from Old English]

loaf¹ noun (plural loaves)
1 a shaped mass of bread baked in one
piece. 2 minced or chopped meat etc.
moulded into an oblong shape.
use your loaf think; use common sense.
[from Old English]

loaf² verb (loafs, loafing, loafed)
spend time idly; loiter or stand about.
loafer noun [probably from German
Landläufer = a tramp]

loam noun
rich soil containing clay, sand, and
decayed leaves etc. **loamy** adjective
[from Old English]

loan noun (plural loans)
1 something lent, especially money.
2 lending; being lent, These books are on
loan from the library.

loan verb (loans, loaning, loaned)
lend. [from Old Norse]

USAGE: Some people dislike the use of this
verb except when it means to lend money,
but it is now well established in standard
English.

loath (rhymes with both) adjective
unwilling, I was loath to go. [from Old
English lath = angry or repulsive]

loathe (rhymes with clothe) verb (loathes,
loathing, loathed)
feel great hatred and disgust for
something; detest. **loathing** noun
[same origin as loath]

loathsome adjective
making you feel great hatred and disgust;
detestable.

lob verb (lobs, lobbing, lobbed)
send a ball in a high curve into the air.

lob noun (plural lobs)
a lobbed ball. [probably from Dutch]

lobby noun (plural lobbies)
1 an entrance hall. 2 a group who lobby
Members of Parliament etc.

lobby verb (lobbies, lobbying, lobbied)
try to influence a Member of Parliament
etc. in favour of a special interest.
[same origin as lodge: the lobby of the
Houses of Parliament is where members of
the public can meet Members]

lobe noun (plural lobes)
1 a rounded fairly flat part of a leaf or an
organ of the body. 2 the rounded soft part
at the bottom of an ear. **lobar** adjective,
lobed adjective [from Greek]

lobster *noun* (*plural* **lobsters**)
a large shellfish with eight legs and two long claws. [via Old English from Latin]

lobster pot *noun* (*plural* **lobster pots**)
a basket for catching lobsters.

local *adjective*
belonging to a particular place or a small area. **locally** *adverb*
local *noun* (*plural* **locals**) (*informal*)
1 someone who lives in a particular district. 2 a public house near a person's home. [from Latin *locus* = a place]

local anaesthetic *noun* (*plural* **local anaesthetics**)
an anaesthetic affecting only the part of the body where it is applied.

local government *noun*
the organization of the affairs of a town or county etc. by people elected by those who live there.

locality *noun* (*plural* **localities**)
a district or location.

localized *adjective*
restricted to a particular place, *localized showers*.

locate *verb* (**locates, locating, located**)
1 discover where something is, *locate the electrical fault*. 2 situate something in a particular place, *The cinema is located in High Street*. [from Latin *locare* = to place]

location *noun* (*plural* **locations**)
1 the place where something is situated. 2 discovering where something is; locating.
on location filmed in natural surroundings, not in a studio.

loch *noun* (*plural* **lochs**)
a lake in Scotland. [Scottish Gaelic]

lock¹ *noun* (*plural* **locks**)
1 a fastening that is opened with a key or other device. 2 a section of a canal or river fitted with gates and sluices so that boats can be raised or lowered to the level beyond each gate. 3 a wrestling-hold that keeps an opponent's arm or leg from moving.
lock, stock, and barrel completely.

lock *verb* (**locks, locking, locked**)
1 fasten or secure something by means of a lock. 2 store something away securely. 3 become fixed in one place; jam.
[from Old English *loc*]

lock² *noun* (*plural* **locks**)
a clump of hair. [from Old English *locc*]

locker *noun* (*plural* **lockers**)
a small cupboard or compartment where things can be stowed safely.

locket *noun* (*plural* **lockets**)
a small ornamental case for holding a portrait or lock of hair etc., worn on a chain round the neck. [from old French *locquet* = small latch or lock]

locks *plural noun*
the hair of the head.

locksmith *noun* (*plural* **locksmiths**)
a person whose job is to make and mend locks.

locomotive *noun* (*plural* **locomotives**)
a railway engine.
locomotive *adjective*
to do with movement or the ability to move, *locomotive power*. **locomotion** *noun*
[from Latin *locus* = place + *motivus* = moving]

locum *noun* (*plural* **locums**)
a doctor or member of the clergy who takes the place of another who is temporarily away. [short for Latin *locum tenens* = person holding the place]

locus (*say* loh-kus) *noun* (*plural* **loci**, *say* loh-sy)
1 the exact place of something. 2 (in geometry) the path traced by a moving point, or made by points placed in a certain way. [Latin, = place]

locust *noun* (*plural* **locusts**)
a kind of grasshopper that travels in large swarms which eat all the plants in an area. [from Latin]

locution *noun* (*plural* **locutions**) (*formal*)
a word or phrase.
[from Latin *locutum* = spoken]

lodestone *noun* (*plural* lodestones)
a kind of stone that can be used as a
magnet.
[from Old English *lad* = way (because it
was used in compasses to guide travellers)]

lodge *noun* (*plural* lodges)
1 a small house, especially at the gates of a
park. 2 a porter's room at the entrance to a
college, factory, etc. 3 a beaver's or otter's
lair.
lodge *verb* (lodges, lodging, lodged)
1 stay somewhere as a lodger. 2 provide a
person with somewhere to live
temporarily. 3 become stuck or caught
somewhere, *The ball lodged in the tree.*
lodging house *noun*
lodge a complaint complain formally.
[from old French *loge* = hut, from
Germanic]

lodger *noun* (*plural* lodgers)
a person who pays to live in another
person's house.

lodgings *plural noun*
a room or rooms (not in a hotel) rented for
living in.

loft *noun* (*plural* lofts)
a room or storage space under the roof of a
house or barn etc. [from Old Norse]

lofty *adjective*
1 tall. 2 noble. 3 haughty.
loftily *adverb*, **loftiness** *noun*
[from an old sense of *loft* = sky]

log¹ *noun* (*plural* logs)
1 a large piece of a tree that has fallen or
been cut down; a piece cut off this. 2 a
detailed record of a ship's voyage,
aircraft's flight, etc. kept in a **logbook**.
log *verb* (logs, logging, logged)
enter facts in a logbook.
log in (or **on**), **log out** (or **off**) connect and
disconnect a terminal correctly to or from
a computer system.
[origin unknown]

log² *noun* (*plural* logs)
a logarithm, *log tables.*

loganberry *noun* (*plural* loganberries)
a dark-red fruit like a blackberry.
[named after an American lawyer
H. R. Logan, who first grew it]

logarithm *noun* (*plural* logarithms)
one of a series of numbers set out in tables
which make it possible to do sums by
adding and subtracting instead of
multiplying and dividing. [from Greek
logos = reckoning + *arithmos* = number]

log cabin *noun* (*plural* log cabins)
a hut built of logs.

loggerheads *plural noun*
at loggerheads disagreeing or quarrelling.
[from an old word *loggerhead* = a stupid
person]

logic *noun*
1 reasoning; a system of reasoning. 2 the
principles used in designing a computer;
the circuits involved in this.
[from Greek *logos* = word, reason]

logical *adjective*
using logic; reasoning or reasoned
correctly. **logically** *adverb*, **logicality** *noun*

-logical *suffix*
forms adjectives (e.g. *biological*) from
nouns ending in *-logy*.

-logist *suffix*
forms nouns meaning 'an expert in or
student of something' (e.g. *biologist*).
[same origin as *-logy*]

logo (*say* loh-goh *or* log-oh) *noun* (*plural*
logos)
a printed symbol used by a business
company etc. as its emblem.
[short for *logograph*, from Greek *logos*
= word, + *-graph*]

-logy and **-ology** *suffixes*
form nouns meaning a subject of study (e.g.
biology). [from Greek *-logia* = study]

loin *noun* (*plural* loins)
the side and back of the body between the
ribs and the hip bone.
[from old French; related to *lumbar*]

loincloth *noun* (*plural* loincloths)
a piece of cloth worn round the hips as a
garment.

loiter *verb* (loiters, loitering, loitered)
linger or stand about idly. **loiterer** *noun*
[probably from old Dutch]

loll *verb* (lolls, lolling, lolled)
lean lazily against something.
[origin unknown]

lollipop *noun* (*plural* lollipops)
a large round hard sweet on a stick.
[origin unknown]

lollipop woman or **man** *noun* (*plural*
lollipop women, lollipop men)
an official who uses a circular sign on a
stick to signal traffic to stop so that
children can cross a road.

lolly *noun* (*plural* lollies) (*informal*)
1 a lollipop. 2 (*slang*) money.
[short for *lollipop*]

lone *adjective*
solitary. [from *alone*]

lonely *adjective* (lonelier, loneliest)
1 sad because you are on your own.
2 solitary. 3 far from inhabited places; not
often visited or used, *a lonely road.*
loneliness *noun* [from *lone*]

lonesome *adjective*
lonely.

long¹ *adjective*
1 measuring a lot from one end to the
other. 2 taking a lot of time, *a long holiday.*
3 having a certain length, *The river is 10
miles long.*
long *adverb*
1 for a long time, *Have you been waiting
long?* 2 at a long time before or after, *They
left long ago.* 3 throughout a time, *all night
long.*
as long as or **so long as** provided that; on
condition that.
[from Old English *lang*]

long² *verb* (longs, longing, longed)
feel a strong desire.
[from Old English *langian*]

long division *noun*
dividing one number by another and
writing down all the calculations.

longevity (*say* lon-**jev**-it-ee) *noun*
long life.
[from Latin *longus* = long + *aevum* = age]

longhand *noun*
ordinary writing, contrasted with
shorthand or typing.

longing *noun* (*plural* longings)
a strong desire.

longitude *noun* (*plural* longitudes)
the distance east or west, measured in
degrees, from the Greenwich meridian.
[from Latin *longitudo* = length]

longitudinal *adjective*
1 to do with longitude. 2 to do with length;
measured lengthways.

long jump *noun*
an athletic contest in which competitors
jump as far as possible along the ground in
one leap.

long-sighted *adjective*
able to see distant things clearly but not
things close to you.

long-suffering *adjective*
putting up with things patiently.

long-winded *adjective*
talking or writing at great length.

loo *noun* (*plural* loos) (*informal*)
a toilet. [origin unknown]

loofah *noun* (*plural* loofahs)
a rough sponge made from a dried gourd.
[from Arabic]

look *verb* (looks, looking, looked)
1 use your eyes; turn your eyes in a
particular direction. 2 face in a particular
direction. 3 have a certain appearance;
seem, *You look sad.*
look after 1 protect or take care of someone.
2 be in charge of something.
look down on despise.
look forward to be waiting eagerly for
something you expect.
look into investigate.
look out be careful.
look up 1 search for information about
something. 2 improve in prospects, *Things
are looking up.*
look up to admire or respect.
look *noun* (*plural* looks)
1 the act of looking; a gaze or glance.
2 appearance, *I don't like the look of this
place.* [from Old English]

looker-on *noun* (*plural* **lookers on**)
a spectator; someone who sees what happens but takes no part in it.

looking-glass *noun* (*plural* **looking-glasses**)
a glass mirror.

lookout *noun* (*plural* **lookouts**)
1 looking out or watching for something. 2 a place from which you can keep watch. 3 a person whose job is to keep watch. 4 a future prospect, *It's a poor lookout for us.* 5 (*informal*) a person's own concern, *If he wastes his money, that's his lookout.*

loom¹ *noun* (*plural* **looms**)
a machine for weaving cloth. [from Old English]

loom² *verb* (**looms, looming, loomed**)
appear suddenly; seem large or close and threatening, *An iceberg loomed up through the fog.* [probably from old Dutch]

loony *adjective* (**loonier, looniest**) (*slang*)
crazy. [short for *lunatic*]

loop *noun* (*plural* **loops**)
the shape made by a curve crossing itself; a piece of string, ribbon, wire, etc. made into this shape.

loop *verb* (**loops, looping, looped**)
1 make string etc. into a loop. 2 enclose something in a loop. [origin unknown]

loophole *noun* (*plural* **loopholes**)
1 a way of avoiding a law or rule or promise etc. without actually breaking it. 2 a narrow opening in the wall of a fort etc.

loose *adjective*
1 not tight; not firmly fixed, *a loose tooth.* 2 not tied up or shut in, *There's a lion loose!* 3 not packed in a box or packet etc. 4 not exact, *a loose translation.*
loosely *adverb*, **looseness** *noun*
at a loose end with nothing to do.

loose *verb* (**looses, loosing, loosed**)
1 loosen. 2 untie or release. [from Old Norse]

loose-leaf *adjective*
with each leaf or page removable, *a loose-leaf notebook.*

loosen *verb* (**loosens, loosening, loosened**)
make or become loose or looser.

loot *noun*
stolen things; goods taken from an enemy.

loot *verb* (**loots, looting, looted**)
1 rob a place or an enemy, especially in a time of war or disorder. 2 take something as loot. **looter** *noun* [from Hindi]

lop *verb* (**lops, lopping, lopped**)
cut away branches or twigs; cut off. [origin unknown]

lope *verb* (**lopes, loping, loped**)
run with a long jumping stride. **lope** *noun* [from Old Norse *hlaupa* = to leap]

lop-eared *adjective*
with drooping ears. [from an old word *lop* = droop]

lopsided *adjective*
with one side lower than the other; uneven. [same origin as *lop-eared*]

loquacious (*say* lok-**way**-shus) *adjective*
talkative. **loquacity** (*say* lok-**wass**-it-ee) *noun* [from Latin *loqui* = speak]

lord *noun* (*plural* **lords**)
1 a nobleman, especially one who is allowed to use the title 'Lord' in front of his name. 2 a master or ruler.
lordly *adjective*, **lordship** *noun*
Lord Mayor the mayor of a large city.
Our Lord Jesus Christ.
the Lord God.

lord *verb* (**lords, lording, lorded**)
behave in a masterful or domineering way, *lording it over the whole club.* [from Old English *hlaford* = person who keeps the bread (compare *lady*)]

lore *noun*
a set of traditional facts or beliefs, *gypsy lore.* [from Old English]

lorgnette (*say* lorn-**yet**) *noun* (*plural* **lorgnettes**)
a pair of spectacles held on a long handle. [French, from *lorgner* = to squint]

lorry *noun* (*plural* **lorries**)
a large strong motor vehicle for carrying heavy goods or troops. [origin unknown]

lose *verb* (**loses, losing, lost**)
1 be without something that you once had, especially because you cannot find it. 2 fail to keep or obtain something, *We lost*

control. **3** be defeated in a contest or argument etc. **4** cause the loss of, *That fall lost us the game.* **5** (of a clock or watch) become behind the correct time. **loser** *noun*
be lost or **lose your way** not know where you are or which is the right path.
lose your life be killed.
lost cause an idea or policy etc. that is failing.
[from Old English]

loss *noun* (*plural* **losses**)
1 losing something. **2** something lost.
be at a loss not know what to do or say.
[from Old English]

lot *noun* (*plural* **lots**)
1 a number of people or things. **2** one of a set of objects used in choosing or deciding something by chance, *We drew lots to see who should go first.* **3** a person's share or fate. **4** something for sale at an auction. **5** a piece of land.
the lot or **the whole lot** everything; all.
[from Old English]

loth *adjective*
a different spelling of *loath.*

lotion *noun* (*plural* **lotions**)
a liquid for putting on the skin.
[from Latin *lotio* = washing]

lottery *noun* (*plural* **lotteries**)
a way of raising money by selling numbered tickets and giving prizes to people who hold winning numbers, which are chosen by a method depending on chance (compare *lot* 2).
[probably from Dutch]

lotto *noun*
a game like bingo. [Italian]

lotus *noun* (*plural* **lotuses**)
a kind of tropical water lily. [from Greek]

loud *adjective*
1 easily heard; producing much noise.
2 unpleasantly bright; gaudy, *loud colours.*
loudly *adverb*, **loudness** *noun*
[from Old English]

loudspeaker *noun* (*plural* **loudspeakers**)
a device that changes electrical signals into sound.

lounge *noun* (*plural* **lounges**)
a sitting room.

lounge *verb* (**lounges, lounging, lounged**)
sit or stand in a lazy and relaxed way.
[originally Scots; origin unknown]

louring (rhymes with *flowering*) *adjective*
looking dark and threatening, *a louring sky.* [origin unknown]

louse *noun* (*plural* **lice**)
a small insect that lives as a parasite on animals or plants. [from Old English]

lousy *adjective* (**lousier, lousiest**)
1 full of lice. **2** (*slang*) very bad or unpleasant.

lout *noun* (*plural* **louts**)
a bad-mannered man. [origin unknown]

lovable *adjective*
easy to love.

love *noun* (*plural* **loves**)
1 great liking or affection. **2** sexual affection or passion. **3** a loved person; a sweetheart. **4** (in tennis) no score; nil.
in love feeling strong love.
make love have sexual intercourse.

love *verb* (**loves, loving, loved**)
feel love for a person or thing. **lover** *noun*, **lovingly** *adverb* [from Old English]

love affair *noun* (*plural* **love affairs**)
a romantic or sexual relationship between two people in love.

loveless *adjective*
without love.

lovelorn *adjective*
pining with love, especially when abandoned by a lover.
[from *love* + an old word *lorn* = abandoned]

lovely *adjective* (**lovelier, loveliest**)
1 beautiful. **2** very pleasant or enjoyable.
loveliness *noun*

lover *noun* (*plural* **lovers**)
a person who someone is having a sexual relationship with but is not married to.

lovesick *adjective*
longing for someone you love, especially someone who does not love you.

low[1] *adjective*
not high. **lowness** *noun*

low *adverb*
at or to a low level or position etc., *The plane was flying low*. [from Old Norse]

low[2] *verb* (**lows, lowing, lowed**)
moo like a cow. [from Old English]

lower *adjective & adverb*
less high.

lower *verb* (**lowers, lowering, lowered**)
make or become lower.

lowlands *plural noun*
low-lying country.
lowland *adjective*, **lowlander** *noun*

lowly *adjective* (**lowlier, lowliest**)
humble. **lowliness** *noun*

loyal *adjective*
always firmly supporting your friends or group or country etc. **loyally** *adverb*, **loyalty** *noun* [from old French]

Loyalist *noun* (*plural* **Loyalists**)
(in Northern Ireland) a person who is in favour of keeping Northern Ireland's link with Britain.

loyalist *noun* (*plural* **loyalists**)
a person who is loyal to the government during a revolt.

lozenge *noun* (*plural* **lozenges**)
1 a small flavoured tablet, especially one containing medicine. 2 a diamond shape. [from old French]

Ltd. *abbreviation*
limited.

lubricant *noun* (*plural* **lubricants**)
a lubricating substance.

lubricate *verb* (**lubricates, lubricating, lubricated**)
oil or grease something so that it moves smoothly. **lubrication** *noun*
[from Latin *lubricus* = slippery]

lucid *adjective*
1 clear and easy to understand. 2 sane. **lucidly** *adverb*, **lucidity** *noun*
[from Latin *lucidus* = bright]

luck *noun*
1 the way things happen without being planned; chance. 2 good fortune, *It will bring you luck*. [from old German]

luckless *adjective*
unlucky.

lucky *adjective* (**luckier, luckiest**)
having or bringing or resulting from good luck. **luckily** *adverb*

lucrative (*say* loo-kra-tiv) *adjective*
profitable; earning you a lot of money. [same origin as *lucre*]

lucre (*say* loo-ker) *noun* (*contemptuous*)
money. [from Latin *lucrum* = profit]

Luddite *noun* (*plural* **Luddites**)
a person who opposes new kinds of machinery or methods, like the English workers who in 1811–16 destroyed the new machinery because they thought it would take their jobs.
[named after one of them, Ned Lud]

ludicrous *adjective*
ridiculous. **ludicrously** *adverb*
[from Latin *ludere* = to play or have fun]

ludo *noun*
a game played with dice and counters on a board. [Latin, = I play]

lug *verb* (**lugs, lugging, lugged**)
drag or carry something heavy.

lug *noun* (*plural* **lugs**)
1 an ear-like part on an object, by which it may be carried or fixed. 2 (*slang*) an ear. [probably from a Scandinavian language]

luggage *noun*
suitcases and bags etc. holding things for taking on a journey. [from *lug*]

lugubrious (*say* lug-oo-bree-us) *adjective*
gloomy or mournful. **lugubriously** *adverb*
[from Latin *lugubris* = mourning]

lukewarm *adjective*
1 only slightly warm; tepid. 2 not very enthusiastic, *lukewarm applause*. [from an old word *luke* = tepid, + *warm*]

lull *verb* (**lulls, lulling, lulled**)
soothe or calm; send someone to sleep.

lull *noun* (*plural* lulls)
a short period of quiet or inactivity.
[imitating the sounds you make to soothe a child]

lullaby *noun* (*plural* lullabies)
a song that is sung to send a baby to sleep.
[from *lull* + *bye* as in *bye-byes*, a child's word for bed or sleep]

lumbago *noun*
pain in the muscles of the lower back.
[same origin as *lumbar*]

lumbar *adjective*
to do with the lower back area.
[from Latin *lumbus* = loin]

lumber *noun*
1 unwanted furniture etc.; junk.
2 (*American*) timber.
lumber *verb* (lumbers, lumbering, lumbered)
1 leave someone with an unwanted or unpleasant task. 2 move in a heavy clumsy way. [origin unknown]

lumberjack *noun* (*plural* lumberjacks)
(*American*)
a person whose job is to cut or carry timber.

luminescent *adjective*
giving out light. **luminescence** *noun*
[from Latin *lumen* = light]

luminous *adjective*
glowing in the dark. **luminosity** *noun*
[same origin as *luminescent*]

lump¹ *noun* (*plural* lumps)
1 a solid piece of something. 2 a swelling.
lumpy *adjective*
lump *verb* (lumps, lumping, lumped)
put or treat things together in a group because you regard them as alike in some way. [origin unknown]

lump² *verb* (lumps, lumping, lumped)
lump it (*informal*) put up with something you dislike.
[from an old word *lump* = look sulky]

lump sum *noun* (*plural* lump sums)
a single payment, especially one covering a number of items.

lunacy *noun* (*plural* lunacies)
insanity or great foolishness.
[from *lunatic*]

lunar *adjective*
to do with the moon.
[from Latin *luna* = moon]

lunar month *noun* (*plural* lunar months)
the period between new moons; four weeks.

lunatic *noun* (*plural* lunatics)
an insane person. **lunatic** *adjective*
[from Latin *luna* = moon (because formerly people were thought to be affected by changes of the moon)]

lunch *noun* (*plural* lunches)
a meal eaten in the middle of the day.
lunch *verb* [short for *luncheon*]

luncheon *noun* (*plural* luncheons)
(*formal*)
lunch. [origin unknown]

lung *noun* (*plural* lungs)
either of the two parts of the body, in the chest, used in breathing.
[from Old English]

lunge *verb* (lunges, lunging, lunged)
thrust the body forward suddenly.
lunge *noun*
[from French *allonger* = lengthen]

lupin *noun* (*plural* lupins)
a garden plant with tall spikes of flowers.
[from Latin]

lurch¹ *verb* (lurches, lurching, lurched)
stagger; lean suddenly to one side. **lurch** *noun* [originally a sailor's word: origin unknown]

lurch² *noun*
leave somebody in the lurch leave somebody in difficulties.
[from old French]

lure *verb* (lures, luring, lured)
tempt a person or animal into a trap; entice. **lure** *noun*
[via old French from Germanic]

lurid (*say* lewr-id) *adjective*
1 in very bright colours; gaudy.

2 sensational and shocking, *the lurid details of the murder.* **luridly** *adverb,* **luridness** *noun* [from Latin]

lurk *verb* (lurks, lurking, lurked)
wait where you cannot be seen.
[origin unknown]

luscious (*say* lush-us) *adjective*
delicious. **lusciously** *adverb,* **lusciousness** *noun* [origin unknown]

lush *adjective*
1 growing thickly and strongly, *lush grass.* **2** luxurious. **lushly** *adverb,* **lushness** *noun* [origin unknown]

lust *noun* (*plural* lusts)
powerful desire, especially sexual desire. **lustful** *adjective*

lust *verb* (lusts, lusting, lusted)
have a powerful desire for a person or thing, *people who lust after power.* [Old English, = pleasure]

lustre *noun*
brightness or brilliance. **lustrous** *adjective* [from Latin *lustrare* = illuminate]

lusty *adjective* (lustier, lustiest)
strong and vigorous. **lustily** *adverb,* **lustiness** *noun* [originally = lively and cheerful: same origin as *lust*]

lute *noun* (*plural* lutes)
a musical instrument rather like a guitar, popular in the 14th–17th centuries. [via French from Arabic]

luxuriant *adjective*
growing abundantly.
[same origin as *luxury*]

USAGE: Do not confuse with *luxurious.*

luxuriate *verb* (luxuriates, luxuriating, luxuriated)
enjoy something as a luxury, *luxuriating in the warm sunshine.*

luxury *noun* (*plural* luxuries)
1 something expensive that you enjoy but do not really need. **2** expensive and comfortable surroundings, *a life of luxury.* **luxurious** *adjective,* **luxuriously** *adverb* [from Latin *luxus* = plenty]

-ly *suffix*
forms **1** adjectives (e.g. *friendly, heavenly, sickly*), **2** adverbs from adjectives (e.g. *boldly, sweetly, thoroughly*).
[from Old English]

lych-gate *noun* (*plural* lych-gates)
a churchyard gate with a roof over it. [from Old English *lic* = corpse (because the coffin-bearers would shelter there until it was time to enter the church)]

lying *present participle* of **lie**[1] and **lie**[2].

lymph (*say* limf) *noun*
a colourless fluid from the flesh or organs of the body, containing white blood cells. **lymphatic** *adjective* [from Latin]

lynch *verb* (lynches, lynching, lynched)
join together to execute or punish someone violently without a proper trial, especially by hanging them. [named after William Lynch, an American judge who allowed this kind of punishment in about 1780]

lynx *noun* (*plural* lynxes)
a wild animal like a very large cat with thick fur and very sharp sight.
[from Greek]

lyre *noun* (*plural* lyres)
an ancient musical instrument like a small harp. [from Greek]

lyric (*say* li-rik) *noun* (*plural* lyrics)
1 a short poem that expresses thoughts and feelings. **2** the words of a song. **lyrical** *adjective,* **lyrically** *adverb* [from Greek *lyrikos* = to be sung to the lyre]

Mm

MA *abbreviation*
Master of Arts.

ma *noun* (*slang*)
mother. [short for *mama*]

ma'am (*say* mam) *noun*
madam.

mac *noun* (*plural* macs) (*informal*)
a mackintosh.

macabre (*say* mak-ahbr) *adjective*
gruesome; strange and horrible.
[from French]

macadam *noun*
layers of broken stone rolled flat to make a
firm road-surface. **macadamized** *adjective*
[named after a Scottish engineer,
J. McAdam, who first laid such roads]

macaroni *noun*
flour-paste (*pasta*) formed into tubes.
[via Italian from Greek]

macaroon *noun* (*plural* macaroons)
a small sweet cake or biscuit made with
ground almonds.

macaw (*say* ma-kaw) *noun* (*plural* macaws)
a brightly coloured parrot from Central
and South America. [from Portuguese]

mace *noun* (*plural* maces)
an ornamental staff carried or placed in
front of an official. [from old French]

mach (*say* mahk) *noun*
mach number the ratio of the speed of a
moving object to the speed of sound, *Mach
one is the speed of sound.* [named after the
Austrian scientist Ernst Mach (1838–1916)]

machete (*say* mash-et-ee) *noun* (*plural*
machetes)
a broad heavy knife used as a tool or
weapon. [from Spanish]

machiavellian (*say* mak-ee-a-**vel**-ee-an)
adjective
very cunning or deceitful. [named after an
unscrupulous Italian statesman, Niccolo
dei Machiavelli (1469–1527)]

machinations (*say* mash-in-**ay**-shonz)
plural noun
clever schemes or plots.
[from Latin *machinare* = devise or plot;
related to *machine*]

machine *noun* (*plural* machines)
something with parts that work together to
do a job.

machine *verb* (machines, machining,
machined)
make something with a machine.
[from Greek *mechane* = device]

machine-gun *noun* (*plural* machine-guns)
a gun that can keep firing bullets quickly
one after another.

machine-readable *adjective*
(of data) in a form that a computer can
process.

machinery *noun*
1 machines. 2 mechanism. 3 an organized
system for doing something.

macho (*say* mach-oh) *adjective*
showing off masculine strength.
[Spanish, = male]

mackerel *noun* (*plural* mackerel)
a sea fish used as food. [from old French]

mackintosh *noun* (*plural* mackintoshes)
a raincoat.
[named after the Scottish inventor of a
waterproof material, C. Macintosh]

mad *adjective* (madder, maddest)
1 having something wrong with the mind;
insane. 2 extremely foolish. 3 very keen,
He is mad about football. 4 (*informal*) very
excited or annoyed. **madly** *adverb*, **madness**
noun, **madman** *noun*
like mad (*informal*) with great speed,
energy, or enthusiasm.
[from Old English]

madam *noun*
a word used when speaking politely to a
woman, *Can I help you, madam?*
[from French *ma dame* = my lady]

madcap *noun* (*plural* madcaps)
a wildly impulsive person.

mad cow disease *noun*
BSE.

madden *verb* (maddens, maddening,
maddened)
make a person mad or angry.

madonna *noun* (*plural* madonnas)
a picture or statue of the Virgin Mary.
[from old Italian *ma donna* = my lady]

madrigal *noun* (*plural* **madrigals**)
a song for several voices singing different
parts together. [from Italian]

maelstrom (*say* mayl-strom) *noun* (*plural*
maelstroms)
a great whirlpool. [originally the name of a
whirlpool off the Norwegian coast: from
Dutch *malen* = whirl + *stroom* = stream]

maestro (*say* my-stroh) *noun* (*plural*
maestros)
a master, especially a musician.
[Italian, = master]

mafia *noun*
1 a large organization of criminals in Italy,
Sicily, and the United States of America.
2 any group of people believed to act
together in a sinister way.
[Italian, = bragging]

magazine *noun* (*plural* **magazines**)
1 a paper-covered publication that comes
out regularly, with articles or stories etc.
by a number of writers. 2 the part of a gun
that holds the cartridges. 3 a store for
weapons and ammunition or for
explosives. 4 a device that holds film for a
camera or slides for a projector.
[from Arabic *makhazin* = storehouses]

magenta (*say* ma-jen-ta) *noun*
a colour between bright red and purple.
[named after Magenta, a town in north
Italy, where Napoleon III won a battle in
the year when the dye was discovered
(1859)]

maggot *noun* (*plural* **maggots**)
the larva of some kinds of fly. **maggoty**
adjective [origin unknown]

Magi (*say* mayj-I) *plural noun*
the 'wise men' from the East who brought
offerings to the infant Jesus at Bethlehem.
[from old Persian *magus* = priest; later
= astrologer or wizard]

magic *noun*
the art or pretended art of making things
happen by secret or unusual powers. **magic**
adjective, **magical** *adjective*, **magically**
adverb [same origin as *Magi*]

magician *noun* (*plural* **magicians**)
1 a person who does magic tricks. 2 a
wizard.

magisterial *adjective*
1 to do with a magistrate. 2 masterful or
imperious. [same origin as *magistrate*]

magistrate *noun* (*plural* **magistrates**)
an official who hears and judges minor
cases in a local court. **magistracy** *noun*
[from Latin *magister* = master]

magma *noun*
a molten substance beneath the earth's
crust. [from Greek]

magnanimous (*say* mag-nan-im-us)
adjective
generous and forgiving, not petty-minded.
magnanimously *adverb*, **magnanimity** *noun*
[from Latin *magnus* = great + *animus*
= mind]

magnate *noun* (*plural* **magnates**)
a wealthy influential person, especially in
business. [from Latin *magnus* = great]

magnesia *noun*
a white powder that is a compound of
magnesium, used in medicine.
[from Greek *Magnesia lithos* = stone from
Magnesia (now part of Turkey)]

magnesium *noun*
a silvery-white metal that burns with a
very bright flame. [from *magnesia*]

magnet *noun* (*plural* **magnets**)
a piece of iron or steel that can attract iron
and that points north and south when it is
hung up. **magnetism** *noun*
[same origin as *magnesia*]

magnetic *adjective*
having the powers of a magnet.
magnetically *adverb*

magnetic tape *noun* (*plural* **magnetic
tapes**)
a plastic strip coated with a magnetic
substance for recording sound.

magnetize *verb* (**magnetizes, magnetizing,
magnetized**)
1 make into a magnet. 2 attract like a
magnet. **magnetization** *noun*

magneto (*say* mag-neet-oh) *noun* (*plural*
magnetos)
a small electric generator using magnets.

magnificent *adjective*
1 grand or splendid in appearance etc.
2 excellent.
magnificently *adverb*, **magnificence** *noun*
[from Latin *magnificus* = splendid]

magnify *verb* (**magnifies, magnifying, magnified**)
make something look or seem bigger than it really is. **magnification** *noun*, **magnifier** *noun* [from Latin *magnus* = great + *facere* = make]

magnifying glass *noun* (*plural* **magnifying glasses**)
a lens that magnifies things.

magnitude *noun* (*plural* **magnitudes**)
1 size or extent. 2 importance.
[from Latin *magnus* = great]

magnolia *noun* (*plural* **magnolias**)
a tree with large white or pale-pink flowers.
[named after a French botanist, P. Magnol]

magnum *noun* (*plural* **magnums**)
a large wine bottle of about twice the standard size (about 1.5 litres).
[Latin, = large thing]

magpie *noun* (*plural* **magpies**)
a noisy bird with black and white feathers, related to the crow. [from *Mag* (short for Margaret) + an old word *pie* = magpie]

maharajah *noun* (*plural* **maharajahs**)
the title of certain Indian princes.
[from Sanskrit *maha* = great + *raja* = rajah]

mah-jong *noun*
a Chinese game for four people, played with pieces called tiles. [from Chinese]

mahogany *noun*
a hard brown wood. [origin unknown]

maid *noun* (*plural* **maids**)
1 a female servant. 2 (*old use*) a girl.
maidservant *noun* [short for *maiden*]

maiden *noun* (*plural* **maidens**) (*old use*)
a girl. **maidenhood** *noun*
maiden *adjective*
1 not married, *a maiden aunt*. 2 first, *a maiden voyage*. [from Old English]

maiden name *noun* (*plural* **maiden names**)
a woman's family name before she married.

maiden over *noun* (*plural* **maiden overs**)
a cricket over in which no runs are scored.

mail¹ *noun*
letters or parcels etc. sent by post.
mail order ordering goods by post.
mail *verb* (**mails, mailing, mailed**)
send by post.
[from old French *male* = a bag]

mail² *noun*
armour made of metal rings joined together, *a suit of chain mail*.
[from Latin *macula* = mesh]

mailing list *noun* (*plural* **mailing lists**)
a list of names and addresses of people to whom an organization sends information from time to time.

mail order *noun*
a system for buying and selling goods by post.

maim *verb* (**maims, maiming, maimed**)
injure a person so that part of his or her body will never work again.
[from old French]

main *adjective*
largest or most important.
main *noun*
1 the main pipe or cable in a public system carrying water, gas, or (usually called **mains**) electricity to a building. 2 (*old use*) the seas, *Drake sailed the Spanish main*.
[from Old English]

main clause *noun* (*plural* **main clauses**)
a clause that can be used as a complete sentence. (Compare *subordinate clause*.)

mainland *noun*
the main part of a country or continent, not the islands round it.

mainly *adverb*
1 chiefly. 2 almost completely. 3 usually.

mainmast *noun* (*plural* **mainmasts**)
the tallest and most important mast on a ship.

mainstay *noun*
the chief support. [from *main* + *stay*²]

mainstream *noun*
the most widely accepted ideas or opinions about something, *Fascism is not in the mainstream of British politics.*

maintain *verb* (**maintains, maintaining, maintained**)
1 cause something to continue; keep in existence. 2 keep a thing in good condition. 3 provide money for a person to live on. 4 state that something is true. **maintenance** *noun* [from Latin *manu* = by hand + *tenere* = to hold]

maisonette *noun* (*plural* **maisonettes**)
1 a small house. 2 part of a house used as a separate dwelling. [from French]

maître d'hôtel (*say* metr doh-**tel**) *noun* (*plural* **maîtres d'hôtel**)
a head waiter. [French, = master of house]

maize *noun*
a tall kind of corn with large seeds on cobs. [via French and Spanish from Taino (a South American language)]

majestic *adjective*
1 stately and dignified. 2 imposing. **majestically** *adverb*

majesty *noun* (*plural* **majesties**)
1 the title of a king or queen, *Her Majesty the Queen.* 2 being majestic. [from old French; related to *major*]

major *adjective*
1 greater; very important, *major roads.* 2 of the musical scale that has a semitone after the 3rd and 7th notes. (Compare *minor.*)
major *noun* (*plural* **majors**)
an army officer ranking next above a captain. [Latin, = larger, greater]

majority *noun* (*plural* **majorities**)
1 the greatest part of a group of people or things. (Compare *minority.*) 2 the difference between numbers of votes, *She had a majority of 25 over her opponent.* 3 the age at which a person becomes an adult according to the law (now 18, formerly 21 years of age), *He attained his majority.* [same origin as *major*]

make *verb* (**makes, making, made**)
1 bring something into existence, especially by putting things together. 2 gain or earn, *She makes £5,000 a year.* 3 cause or compel, *Make him repeat it.* 4 achieve, *The swimmer just made the shore.* 5 reckon, *What do you make the time?* 6 perform an action etc., *make an effort.* 7 arrange for use, *make the beds.* 8 cause to be successful or happy, *Her visit made my day.*
make do manage with something that is not what you really want.
make for go towards.
make love 1 have sexual intercourse. 2 (*old use*) try to win someone's love.
make off go away quickly.
make out 1 manage to see, hear, or understand something. 2 claim or pretend that something is true.
make up 1 build or put together. 2 invent a story etc. 3 compensate for something. 4 put on make-up.
make up your mind decide.
make *noun* (*plural* **makes**)
1 making; how something is made. 2 a brand of goods; something made by a particular firm.
[from Old English]

make-believe *noun*
pretending or imagining things.

make-over *noun* (*plural* **make-overs**)
changes in your make-up, hairstyle, and the way you dress to make you look and feel more attractive.

maker *noun* (*plural* **makers**)
the person or firm that has made something.

makeshift *adjective*
improvised or used because you have nothing better, *We used a box as a makeshift table.*
[from an old phrase *make shift* = manage somehow, put up with]

make-up *noun*
1 cosmetics. 2 the way something is made up. 3 a person's character.

mal- *prefix*
1 bad. 2 badly (as in *malnourished*). [from Latin *male* = badly]

maladjusted *adjective*
unable to fit in or cope with other people or
your own circumstances.
[from *mal-* + *adjust*]

maladministration *noun*
bad administration, especially of business
affairs.

malady *noun* (*plural* **maladies**)
an illness or disease.
[from French *malade* = ill]

malapropism *noun* (*plural* **malapropisms**)
a comical confusion of words, e.g. using
hooligan instead of *hurricane*. [named after
Mrs Malaprop in Sheridan's play *The
Rivals*, who made mistakes of this kind]

malaria *noun*
a feverish disease spread by mosquitoes.
malarial *adjective*
[from Italian *mala aria* = bad air, which
was once thought to cause the disease]

malcontent *noun* (*plural* **malcontents**)
a discontented person who is likely to
make trouble.

male *adjective*
1 belonging to the sex that reproduces by
fertilizing egg-cells produced by the female.
2 of men, *a male voice choir*.
male *noun* (*plural* **males**)
a male person, animal, or plant.
[from old French; related to *masculine*]

male chauvinist *noun* (*plural* **male
chauvinists**)
a man who thinks that women are not as
good as men.

malefactor (*say* mal-if-ak-ter) *noun* (*plural*
malefactors)
a criminal or wrongdoer.
[from *mal-* + Latin *factor* = doer]

malevolent (*say* ma-lev-ol-ent) *adjective*
wishing to harm people.
malevolently *adverb*, **malevolence** *noun*
[from *mal-* + Latin *volens* = wishing]

malformed *adjective*
faultily formed.

malfunction *noun* (*plural* **malfunctions**)
faulty functioning, *a malfunction in the
computer*.

malfunction *verb* (**malfunctions,
malfunctioning, malfunctioned**)
fail to work properly.

malice *noun*
the desire to harm others or to tease.
malicious *adjective*, **maliciously** *adverb*
[from Latin *malus* = evil]

malign (*say* mal-I'n) *adjective*
1 harmful, *a malign influence*. **2** showing
malice. **malignity** (*say* mal-ig-nit-ee) *noun*
malign *verb* (**maligns, maligning, maligned**)
say unpleasant and untrue things about
somebody.
[from Latin *malignare* = plot wickedly]

malignant *adjective*
1 (of a tumour) growing uncontrollably.
2 full of malice. **malignantly** *adverb*,
malignancy *noun* [same origin as *malign*]

malinger *verb* (**malingers, malingering,
malingered**)
pretend to be ill in order to avoid work.
malingerer *noun* [from old French]

mallard *noun* (*plural* **mallard** or **mallards**)
a kind of wild duck of North America,
Europe, and parts of Asia.
[from old French]

malleable *adjective*
1 able to be pressed or hammered into
shape. **2** easy to influence; adaptable.
malleability *noun*
[from Latin *malleare* = to hammer]

mallet *noun* (*plural* **mallets**)
1 a large hammer, usually made of wood.
2 an implement with a long handle, used in
croquet or polo for striking the ball.
[from Latin *malleus* = a hammer]

malnutrition *noun*
bad health because you do not have enough
food or the right kind of food.
malnourished *adjective*

malpractice *noun*
wrongdoing by a professional person such
as a doctor or lawyer.

malt *noun*
dried barley used in brewing, making
vinegar, etc. **malted** *adjective*
[from Old English]

maltreat *verb* (maltreats, maltreating, maltreated)
ill-treat. **maltreatment** *noun*

mama or **mamma** *noun* (*old use*)
mother. [imitating the sounds a child makes when it first tries to speak]

mammal *noun* (*plural* mammals)
any animal which gives birth to live babies which are fed with milk from the mother's body. **mammalian** (*say* mam-**ay**-lee-an) *adjective* [from Latin *mamma* = breast]

mammoth *noun* (*plural* mammoths)
an extinct elephant with a hairy skin and curved tusks.
mammoth *adjective*
huge. [from Russian]

man *noun* (*plural* men)
1 a grown-up male human being. 2 an individual person. 3 mankind. 4 a piece used in chess etc.
man *verb* (mans, manning, manned)
supply with people to work something, *Man the pumps!* [from Old English]

manacle *noun* (*plural* manacles)
a fetter or handcuff.
manacle *verb* (manacles, manacling, manacled)
fasten with manacles.
[from Latin *manus* = hand]

manage *verb* (manages, managing, managed)
1 be able to cope with something difficult. 2 be in charge of a shop, factory, etc.
manageable *adjective*
[from Italian *maneggiare* = to handle]

management *noun*
1 managing. 2 managers; the people in charge.

management buyout *noun* (*plural* management buyouts)
the buying of most or all of a company's shares by its management.

manager *noun* (*plural* managers)
a person who manages something.
manageress *noun*, **managerial** (*say* man-a-jeer-ee-al) *adjective*

mandarin *noun* (*plural* mandarins)
1 an important official. 2 a kind of small orange.
[via Portuguese and Malay (a language spoken in Malaysia) from Sanskrit]

mandate *noun* (*plural* mandates)
authority given to someone to carry out a certain task or policy, *An elected government has a mandate to govern the country.*
[from Latin *mandatum* = commanded]

mandatory *adjective*
obligatory or compulsory.
[same origin as *mandate*]

mandible *noun* (*plural* mandibles)
1 a jaw, especially the lower one. 2 either part of a bird's beak or the similar part in insects etc. (Compare *maxilla*.)
[from Latin *mandere* = chew]

mandolin *noun* (*plural* mandolins)
a musical instrument rather like a guitar.
[via French from Italian]

mane *noun* (*plural* manes)
the long hair on a horse's or lion's neck.
[from Old English]

manful *adjective*
brave or determined. **manfully** *adverb*

manganese *noun*
a hard brittle metal. [via French from Italian; related to *magnesia*]

mange *noun*
a skin disease of dogs etc.
[from old French]

mangel-wurzel *noun* (*plural* mangel-wurzels)
a large beet used as cattle food. [from German *Mangold* = beet + *Wurzel* = root]

manger *noun* (*plural* mangers)
a trough in a stable etc., for horses or cattle to feed from. [from French *manger* = eat]

mangle *verb* (mangles, mangling, mangled)
damage something by crushing or cutting it roughly. [from old French]

mango *noun* (*plural* mangoes)
a tropical fruit with yellow pulp.
[via Portuguese and Malay (a language
spoken in Malaysia) from Tamil]

mangold *noun* (*plural* mangolds)
a mangel-wurzel. [from German]

mangrove *noun* (*plural* mangroves)
a tropical tree growing in mud and
swamps, with many tangled roots above
the ground. [probably from a South
American language]

mangy *adjective*
1 having mange. 2 scruffy or dirty.

manhandle *verb* (manhandles,
manhandling, manhandled)
treat or push roughly.

manhole *noun* (*plural* manholes)
a space or opening, usually with a cover, by
which a person can get into a sewer or
boiler etc. to inspect or repair it.

manhood *noun*
1 the condition of being a man. 2 manly
qualities.

mania *noun* (*plural* manias)
1 violent madness. 2 great enthusiasm, *a
mania for sport*. **manic** *adjective*
[Greek, = madness]

maniac *noun* (*plural* maniacs)
a person with mania.

manicure *noun* (*plural* manicures)
care and treatment of the hands and nails.
manicure *verb*, **manicurist** *noun*
[from Latin *manus* = hand + *cura* = care]

manifest *adjective*
clear and obvious. **manifestly** *adverb*
manifest *verb* (manifests, manifesting,
manifested)
show a thing clearly. **manifestation** *noun*
[from Latin]

manifesto *noun* (*plural* manifestos)
a public statement of a group's or person's
policy or principles.
[Italian; related to *manifest*]

manifold *adjective*
of many kinds; very varied.
[from *many* + *-fold*]

manioc *noun*
1 cassava. 2 the flour made from this.
[via French from Tupi (a South American
language)]

manipulate *verb* (manipulates,
manipulating, manipulated)
handle or arrange something cleverly or
cunningly. **manipulation** *noun*, **manipulator**
noun [from Latin *manus* = hand]

mankind *noun*
human beings in general.

manly *adjective*
1 suitable for a man. 2 brave and strong.
manliness *noun*

manner *noun*
1 the way something happens or is done.
2 a person's way of behaving. 3 sort, *all
manner of things*. [from old French]

mannerism *noun* (*plural* mannerisms)
a person's own particular gesture or way of
speaking.

manners *plural noun*
how a person behaves with other people;
politeness.

mannish *adjective*
like a man.

manœuvre (*say* man-oo-ver) *noun* (*plural*
manœuvres)
a difficult or skilful or cunning action.
manœuvre *verb* (manœuvres,
manœuvring, manœuvred)
move carefully and skilfully. **manœuvrable**
adjective [via French from Latin *manu
operari* = work by hand]

man-of-war *noun* (*plural* men-of-war)
a warship.

manor *noun* (*plural* manors)
1 a manor house. 2 the land belonging to a
manor house. **manorial** *adjective*
[from old French; related to *mansion*]

manor house *noun* (*plural* manor houses)
a large important house in the country.

manpower *noun*
the number of people who are working or
needed or available for work on something.

manse *noun* (*plural* **manses**)
a church minister's house, especially in
Scotland. [same origin as *mansion*]

mansion *noun* (*plural* **mansions**)
a large stately house. [from Latin *mansio*
= a place to stay, a dwelling]

manslaughter *noun*
killing a person unlawfully but without
meaning to.

mantelpiece *noun* (*plural* **mantelpieces**)
a shelf above a fireplace. [same origin as
mantle (because it goes over the fireplace)]

mantilla *noun* (*plural* **mantillas**)
a lace veil worn by Spanish women over
the hair and shoulders.
[Spanish, = little mantle]

mantle *noun* (*plural* **mantles**)
1 a cloak. **2** a covering, *a mantle of snow*.
[from Latin]

mantra *noun* (*plural* **mantras**)
a word or phrase that is constantly
repeated to help people meditate,
originally in Hinduism and Buddhism.
[Sanskrit, = thought]

manual *adjective*
worked by or done with the hands,
a manual typewriter, *manual work*.
manually *adverb*
manual *noun* (*plural* **manuals**)
a handbook. [from Latin *manus* = hand]

manufacture *verb* (**manufactures,**
manufacturing, manufactured)
make things. **manufacture** *noun*,
manufacturer *noun* [from Latin *manu* = by
hand + *facere* = make]

manure *noun*
fertilizer, especially dung.
[from old French]

manuscript *noun* (*plural* **manuscripts**)
something written or typed but not
printed. [from Latin *manu* = by hand
+ *scriptum* = written]

Manx *adjective*
to do with the Isle of Man.

many *adjective* (**more, most**)
great in number; numerous, *many people*.

many *noun*
many people or things, *Many were found*.
[from Old English]

Maori (rhymes with *flowery*) *noun* (*plural*
Maoris)
1 a member of the aboriginal people of
New Zealand. **2** their language.

map *noun* (*plural* **maps**)
a diagram of part or all of the earth's
surface or of the sky.
map *verb* (**maps, mapping, mapped**)
make a map of an area.
map out plan the details of something.
[from Latin *mappa mundi* = sheet of the
world]

maple *noun* (*plural* **maples**)
a tree with broad leaves.
[from Old English]

maple syrup *noun*
a sweet substance made from the sap of
some kinds of maple.

mar *verb* (**mars, marring, marred**)
spoil. [from Old English]

marathon *noun* (*plural* **marathons**)
a long-distance race for runners. [named
after Marathon in Greece, from which a
messenger is said to have run to Athens
(about 40 kilometres) to announce that the
Greeks had defeated the Persian army]

marauding *adjective*
going about in search of plunder or prey.
marauder *noun*
[from French *maraud* = rogue]

marble *noun* (*plural* **marbles**)
1 a small glass ball used in games. **2** a kind
of limestone polished and used in sculpture
or building.
[from Greek *marmaros* = shining stone]

march *verb* (**marches, marching, marched**)
1 walk with regular steps. **2** make
somebody walk somewhere, *He marched
them up the hill*. **marcher** *noun*
march *noun* (*plural* **marches**)
1 marching. **2** music suitable for marching
to. [from old French]

marchioness *noun* (*plural* **marchionesses**)
the wife or widow of a marquis.
[from Latin]

mare *noun* (*plural* mares)
a female horse or donkey.
[from Old English]

mare's nest *noun*
a discovery that seems interesting but
turns out to be false or worthless.

margarine (*say* mar-ja-**reen** or mar-ga-
reen) *noun*
a substance used like butter, made from
animal or vegetable fats. [from French]

marge *noun* (*informal*)
margarine.

margin *noun* (*plural* margins)
1 an edge or border. 2 the blank space
between the edge of a page and the writing
or pictures etc. on it. 3 the difference
between two scores or prices etc., *She won
by a narrow margin.* [from Latin]

marginal *adjective*
1 in a margin, *marginal notes.* 2 very
slight, *a marginal difference.*
marginally *adverb*

marginal seat *noun* (*plural* marginal
seats)
a constituency where a Member of
Parliament was elected with only a small
majority and may be defeated in the next
election.

marigold *noun* (*plural* marigolds)
a yellow or orange garden flower.
[from the name *Mary* + *gold*]

marijuana (*say* ma-ri-**hwah**-na) *noun*
a drug made from hemp.
[an American Spanish word]

marina *noun* (*plural* marinas)
a harbour for yachts, motor boats, etc.
[same origin as *marine*]

marinade *noun* (*plural* marinades)
a flavoured liquid in which meat or fish is
soaked before being cooked. **marinade** *verb*
[via French from Spanish]

marinate *verb* (marinates, marinating,
marinated)
soak in a marinade.
[via French from Italian]

marine (*say* ma-**reen**) *adjective*
of or concerned with the sea.

marine *noun* (*plural* marines)
a member of the troops who are trained to
serve at sea as well as on land.
[from Latin *mare* = sea]

mariner (*say* ma-**rin**-er) *noun* (*plural*
mariners)
a sailor.

marionette *noun* (*plural* marionettes)
a puppet worked by strings or wires.
[French, = little Mary]

marital *adjective*
to do with marriage.
[from Latin *maritus* = husband]

maritime *adjective*
1 to do with the sea or ships. 2 found near
the sea. [same origin as *marine*]

marjoram *noun*
a herb with a mild flavour, used in
cooking. [from old French]

mark¹ *noun* (*plural* marks)
1 a spot, dot, line, or stain etc. on
something. 2 a number or letter etc. put on
a piece of work to show how good it is. 3 a
distinguishing feature. 4 a symbol, *They
all stood as a mark of respect.* 5 a target.
on your marks! a command to runners to
get ready to begin a race.
up to the mark of the normal or expected
standard.
mark *verb* (marks, marking, marked)
1 put a mark on something. 2 give a mark
to a piece of work; correct. 3 pay attention
to something, *Mark my words!* 4 keep close
to an opposing player in football etc.
marker *noun* [from Old English *merc*]

mark² *noun* (*plural* marks)
a German unit of money.

marked *adjective*
noticeable, *a marked improvement.*
markedly *adverb*

market *noun* (*plural* markets)
1 a place where things are bought and sold,
usually from stalls in the open air.
2 demand for things; trade.
market place *noun*

market *verb* (markets, marketing, marketed)
offer things for sale. **marketable** *adjective*
[via Old English from Latin *merx* = goods,
merchandise]

marketing *noun*
the branch of business concerned with
advertising and selling the product.

market research *noun*
the study of what people need or want to
buy.

marksman *noun* (*plural* marksmen)
an expert in shooting at a target.
marksmanship *noun*

mark time *verb*
1 march on one spot without moving
forward. 2 occupy your time without
making any progress.

marmalade *noun*
jam made from oranges, lemons, or other
citrus fruit. [via French from Portuguese
marmelo = quince (from which marmalade
was first made)]

marmoset *noun* (*plural* marmosets)
a kind of small monkey. [from French]

maroon¹ *verb* (maroons, marooning,
marooned)
abandon or isolate somebody in a deserted
place; strand. [via French from Spanish
cimarrón = runaway slave]

maroon² *noun*
dark red. [from French *marron* = chestnut]

marquee (*say* mar-kee) *noun* (*plural*
marquees)
a large tent used for a party or exhibition
etc. [from French; related to *marquis*]

marquis *noun* (*plural* marquises)
a nobleman ranking next above an earl.
[from old French]

marriage *noun* (*plural* marriages)
1 the state of being married. 2 a wedding.

marrow *noun* (*plural* marrows)
1 a large gourd eaten as a vegetable. 2 the
soft substance inside bones.
[from Old English]

marry *verb* (marries, marrying, married)
1 become a person's husband or wife.
2 unite a man and woman legally for the
purpose of living together.
[from Latin *maritus* = husband]

marsh *noun* (*plural* marshes)
an area of very wet ground. **marshy**
adjective [from Old English]

marshal *noun* (*plural* marshals)
1 an official who supervises a contest or
ceremony etc. 2 an officer of very high
rank, *a Field Marshal*.
marshal *verb* (marshals, marshalling,
marshalled)
1 arrange neatly. 2 usher or escort.
[via old French from Germanic]

marshmallow *noun* (*plural*
marshmallows)
a soft spongy sweet, usually pink or white.
[originally made from the root of the
marshmallow, a pink flower that grows in
marshes]

marsupial (*say* mar-soo-pee-al) *noun*
(*plural* marsupials)
an animal such as a kangaroo or wallaby.
The female has a pouch on the front of its
body in which its babies are carried.
[from Greek *marsypion* = pouch]

martial *adjective*
to do with war; warlike.
[Latin, = belonging to Mars, the Roman
god of war]

martial arts *plural noun*
fighting sports, such as judo and karate.

martial law *noun*
government of a country by the armed
forces during a crisis.

martin *noun* (*plural* martins)
a bird rather like a swallow. [probably
after St Martin of Tours, who gave half his
cloak to a beggar (because of the bird's
markings, which look like a torn cloak)]

martinet *noun* (*plural* martinets)
a very strict person. [named after a French
army officer, J. Martinet, who imposed
harsh discipline on his troops]

martyr *noun* (*plural* martyrs)
a person who is killed or made to suffer
because of his or her beliefs.
martyrdom *noun*
martyr *verb* (martyrs, martyring, martyred)
kill or torment someone as a martyr.
[via Old English from Greek]

marvel *noun* (*plural* marvels)
a wonderful thing.
marvel *verb* (marvels, marvelling, marvelled)
be filled with wonder.
[from old French; related to *miracle*]

marvellous *adjective*
wonderful.

Marxism *noun*
the Communist theories of the German
writer Karl Marx (1818–83).
Marxist *noun* & *adjective*

marzipan *noun*
a soft sweet food made of ground almonds,
eggs, and sugar. [via German from Italian]

mascara *noun*
a cosmetic for darkening the eyelashes.
[Italian, = mask]

mascot *noun* (*plural* mascots)
a person, animal, or thing that is believed
to bring good luck. [from French]

masculine *adjective*
1 to do with men. 2 typical of or suitable
for men. 3 (in some languages) belonging
to the class of words which includes the
words referring to men, such as *garçon* and
livre in French. **masculinity** *noun*
[from Latin *masculus* = male]

mash *verb* (mashes, mashing, mashed)
crush into a soft mass.
mash *noun* (*plural* mashes)
1 a soft mixture of cooked grain or bran
etc. 2 (*informal*) mashed potatoes.
[from Old English]

mask *noun* (*plural* masks)
a covering worn over the face to disguise
or protect it.
mask *verb* (masks, masking, masked)
1 cover with a mask. 2 disguise; screen;
conceal. [via French from Italian]

masochist (*say* mas-ok-ist) *noun* (*plural*
masochists)
a person who enjoys things that seem
painful or tiresome. **masochism** *noun*
[named after an Austrian novelist, L. von
Sacher-Masoch, who wrote about
masochism]

Mason *noun* (*plural* Masons)
a Freemason.

mason *noun* (*plural* masons)
a person who builds or works with stone.
[from old French]

masonry *noun*
1 the stone parts of a building; stonework.
2 a mason's work.

masquerade *noun* (*plural* masquerades)
a pretence.
masquerade *verb* (masquerades,
masquerading, masqueraded)
pretend to be something, *He masqueraded
as a policeman.*
[via French from Italian *mascara* = mask]

Mass *noun* (*plural* masses)
the Communion service in a Roman
Catholic church.
[via Old English from Latin]

mass *noun* (*plural* masses)
1 a large amount. 2 a heap or other
collection of matter. 3 (in scientific use)
the quantity of matter that a thing
contains. In non-scientific use this is called
weight.
mass *adjective*
involving a large number of people, *mass
murder.*
mass *verb* (masses, massing, massed)
collect into a mass. [from Greek]

massacre *noun* (*plural* massacres)
the killing of a large number of people.
massacre *verb* [from French, = butchery]

massage (*say* mas-ah*zh*) *verb* (massages,
massaging, massaged)
rub and press the body to make it less stiff
or less painful. **massage** *noun*, **masseur**
noun, **masseuse** *noun* [from French]

massive *adjective*
large and heavy; huge.
[from French; related to *mass*]

mass media *noun*
the media.

mass production *noun*
manufacturing goods in large quantities.
mass-produced *adjective*

mast *noun* (*plural* **masts**)
a tall pole that holds up a ship's sails or a flag or an aerial. [from Old English]

master *noun* (*plural* **masters**)
1 a man who is in charge of something. 2 a male teacher. 3 a great artist, composer, sportsman, etc. 4 something from which copies are made. 5 **Master** a title put before a boy's name.
master *verb* (**masters, mastering, mastered**)
1 learn a subject or a skill thoroughly.
2 overcome; bring under control.
[same origin as *magistrate*]

masterful *adjective*
1 domineering. 2 very skilful.
masterfully *adverb*

master key *noun* (*plural* **master keys**)
a key that will open several different locks.

masterly *adjective*
very skilful.

mastermind *noun* (*plural* **masterminds**)
1 a very clever person. 2 the person who is planning and organizing a scheme etc.
mastermind *verb* (**masterminds, masterminding, masterminded**)
plan and organize a scheme etc.

Master of Arts *noun* (*plural* **Masters of Arts**)
a person who has taken the next degree after Bachelor of Arts.

master of ceremonies *noun* (*plural* **masters of ceremonies**)
a person who introduces the speakers at a formal event, or the entertainers at a variety show.

Master of Science *noun* (*plural* **Masters of Science**)
a person who has taken the next degree after Bachelor of Science.

masterpiece *noun* (*plural* **masterpieces**)
1 an excellent piece of work. 2 a person's best piece of work.

mastery *noun*
complete control or thorough knowledge or skill in something.

masticate *verb* (**masticates, masticating, masticated**)
chew food. **mastication** *noun*
[from Greek *mastichan* = gnash the teeth]

mastiff *noun* (*plural* **mastiffs**)
a large kind of dog. [from old French]

masturbate *verb* (**masturbates, masturbating, masturbated**)
excite yourself by fingering your genitals.
masturbation *noun* [from Latin]

mat *noun* (*plural* **mats**)
1 a small carpet. 2 a doormat. 3 a small piece of material put on a table to protect the surface. [from Old English]

matador *noun* (*plural* **matadors**)
a bullfighter who fights on foot.
[Spanish, from *matar* = kill]

match¹ *noun* (*plural* **matches**)
a small thin stick with a head made of a substance that gives a flame when rubbed on something rough. **matchbox** *noun*,
matchstick *noun* [from old French]

match² *noun* (*plural* **matches**)
1 a game or contest between two teams or players. 2 one person or thing that matches another. 3 a marriage.
match *verb* (**matches, matching, matched**)
1 be equal or similar to another person or thing. 2 put teams or players to compete against each other. 3 find something that is similar or corresponding.
[from Old English]

matchboard *noun* (*plural* **matchboards**)
a piece of board that fits into a groove in a similar piece.

mate¹ *noun* (*plural* **mates**)
1 a companion or friend. 2 one of a mated pair. 3 an officer on a merchant ship.
mate *verb* (**mates, mating, mated**)
1 come or put together so as to have offspring. 2 put things together as a pair or because they correspond.
[from old German]

mate² *noun* & *verb* (*in chess*)
checkmate.

material *noun* (*plural* **materials**)
1 anything used for making something else. 2 cloth or fabric.
[from Latin *materia* = matter]

materialism *noun*
the belief that possessions are very important. **materialist** *noun*, **materialistic** *adjective* [same origin as *material*]

materialize *verb* (**materializes, materializing, materialized**)
1 become visible; appear, *The ghost didn't materialize.* 2 become a fact; happen, *The trip did not materialize.*
materialization *noun*
[same origin as *material*]

maternal *adjective*
1 to do with a mother. 2 motherly.
maternally *adverb*
[from Latin *mater* = mother]

maternity *noun*
motherhood.
maternity *adjective*
to do with having a baby, *maternity ward.* [same origin as *maternal*]

matey *adjective*
friendly and sociable.

mathematics *noun*
the study of numbers, measurements, and shapes. **mathematical** *adjective*,
mathematically *adverb*, **mathematician** *noun*
[from Greek *mathema* = science]

maths *noun* (*informal*)
mathematics.

matinée *noun* (*plural* **matinées**)
an afternoon performance at a theatre or cinema. [French, literally = morning]

matins *noun*
the church service of morning prayer.
[from Latin *matutinus* = belonging to the morning]

matriarch (*say* **may**-tree-ark) *noun* (*plural* **matriarchs**)
a woman who is head of a family or tribe. (Compare *patriarch*.) **matriarchal** *adjective*,
matriarchy *noun*
[from Latin *mater* = mother, + *-arch*]

matrimony *noun*
marriage. **matrimonial** *adjective*
[from Latin *mater* = mother]

matrix (*say* **may**-triks) *noun* (*plural* **matrices**, *say* **may**-tri-seez)
1 an array of mathematical quantities etc. in rows and columns. 2 a mould or framework in which something is made or allowed to develop. [from Latin]

matron *noun* (*plural* **matrons**)
1 a mature married woman. 2 a woman in charge of nursing in a school etc. or (formerly) of the nursing staff in a hospital.
matronly *adjective*
[same origin as *matrimony*]

matt *adjective*
not shiny, *matt paint*. [from French]

matted *adjective*
tangled into a mass. [from *mat*]

matter *noun* (*plural* **matters**)
1 something you can touch or see, not spirit or mind or qualities etc. 2 things of a certain kind, *printed matter*. 3 something to be thought about or done, *It's a serious matter*. 4 a quantity, *in a matter of minutes*.
no matter it does not matter.
what is the matter? what is wrong?
matter *verb* (**matters, mattering, mattered**)
be important. [same origin as *material*]

matter of course *noun*
the natural or expected thing, *I always lock my bike up, as a matter of course.*

matter-of-fact *adjective*
keeping to facts; not imaginative or emotional, *She talked about death in a very matter-of-fact way.*

matting *noun*
rough material for covering floors.

mattress *noun* (*plural* **mattresses**)
soft or springy material in a fabric covering, used on or as a bed.
[via French from Arabic]

mature *adjective*
1 fully grown or developed. 2 grown-up.
maturely *adverb*, **maturity** *noun*
mature *verb* (**matures, maturing, matured**)
make or become mature.
[from Latin *maturus* = ripe]

maudlin *adjective*
sentimental in a silly or tearful way.
[from an old pronunciation of St Mary
Magdalen (because pictures usually show
her weeping)]

maul *verb* (**mauls, mauling, mauled**)
injure by handling or clawing, *He was
mauled by a lion.*
[originally = knock down: from Latin
malleus = a hammer]

mausoleum (*say* maw-sol-**ee**-um) *noun*
(*plural* **mausoleums**)
a magnificent tomb.
[named after the tomb of Mausolus, a king
in the 4th century BC in what is now
Turkey]

mauve (*say* mohv) *noun*
pale purple.
[from Latin *malva* = a plant with mauve
flowers]

maverick *noun* (*plural* **mavericks**)
a person who belongs to a group but often
disagrees with its beliefs.
[originally = an unbranded calf: named
after an American rancher, S. A. Maverick,
who did not brand his cattle]

maw *noun* (*plural* **maws**)
the jaws, mouth, or stomach of a hungry or
fierce animal. [from Old English]

maxilla *noun* (*plural* **maxillae**, *say* mak-si-
lee)
the upper jaw; a similar part in a bird or
insect etc. (Compare *mandible*.)
[Latin, = jaw]

maxim *noun* (*plural* **maxims**)
a short saying giving a general truth or
rule of behaviour, e.g. 'Waste not, want
not'. [from Latin *maxima propositio*
= greatest statement]

maximize *verb* (**maximizes, maximizing,
maximized**)
increase something to a maximum.

maximum *noun* (*plural* **maxima** or
maximums)
the greatest possible number or amount.
(The opposite is *minimum*.)
[Latin, = greatest thing]

may¹ *auxiliary verb* (**may, might**)
used to express **1** permission (*You may go
now*), **2** possibility (*It may be true*), **3** wish
(*Long may she reign*), **4** uncertainty
(*whoever it may be*). [from Old English]

USAGE: See note at *can*.

may² *noun*
hawthorn blossom. [because the hawthorn
blooms in the month of May]

maybe *adverb*
perhaps; possibly.

mayday *noun* (*plural* **maydays**)
an international radio signal calling for
help. [from French *m'aider* = help me]

mayfly *noun* (*plural* **mayflies**)
an insect that lives for only a short time, in
spring.

mayhem *noun*
violent confusion or damage, *The mob
caused mayhem.*
[from old French; related to *maim*]

mayonnaise *noun*
a creamy sauce made from eggs, oil,
vinegar, etc., eaten with salad.
[French, named after Mahón on Minorca,
which the French had just captured when
mayonnaise was invented]

mayor *noun* (*plural* **mayors**)
the person in charge of the council in a
town or city. **mayoral** *adjective*, **mayoress**
noun [from old French; related to *major*]

maypole *noun* (*plural* **maypoles**)
a decorated pole round which people dance
on 1 May.

maze *noun* (*plural* **mazes**)
a network of paths, especially one designed
as a puzzle in which to try and find your
way. [from *amaze*]

MC *abbreviation*
master of ceremonies.

ME *noun*
long-lasting fever, weakness, and pain in
the muscles following a viral infection.
[abbreviation of the scientific name,
myalgic encephalomyelitis]

me *pronoun*
the form of *I* used as the object of a verb or after a preposition. [from Old English]

mead *noun*
an alcoholic drink made from honey and water. [from Old English]

meadow (*say* med-oh) *noun* (*plural* meadows)
a field of grass. [from Old English]

meagre *adjective*
scanty in amount; barely enough, *a meagre diet*. [from French]

meal[1] *noun* (*plural* meals)
food served and eaten at one sitting. [from Old English *mael*]

meal[2] *noun*
coarsely-ground grain. **mealy** *adjective* [from Old English *melu*]

mealtime *noun* (*plural* mealtimes)
a regular time for having a meal.

mealy-mouthed *adjective*
too polite or timid to say what you really mean. [from *meal*[2] (because of the softness of meal)]

mean[1] *verb* (means, meaning, meant (*say* ment))
1 have as an equivalent, *'Maybe' means 'perhaps'*. 2 have as a purpose; intend, *I mean to win*. 3 indicate, *Dark clouds mean rain*. [from Old English *maenan*]

mean[2] *adjective* (meaner, meanest)
1 not generous; miserly. 2 unkind or spiteful, *a mean trick*. 3 poor in quality or appearance, *a mean little house*. **meanly** *adverb*, **meanness** *noun* [from Old English *maene*]

mean[3] *noun* (*plural* means)
a middle point or condition.
mean *adjective*
average.
[from old French; related to *medial*]

meander (*say* mee-an-der) *verb* (meanders, meandering, meandered)
take a winding course; wander. **meander** *noun* [named after the Meander, a river in Turkey (now Mendere or Menderes)]

meaning *noun* (*plural* meanings)
what something means.
meaningful *adjective*, **meaningless** *adjective*

means *noun*
a way of achieving something or producing a result, *a means of transport*.
by all means certainly.
by means of by this method; using this.
by no means not at all.
means *plural noun*
money or other wealth.
live beyond your means spend more than you can afford.
[from *mean*[3], in an old sense = someone in the middle, a go-between]

means test *noun* (*plural* means tests)
an inquiry into how much money etc. a person has, in order to decide whether he or she is entitled to get help from public funds.

meantime *noun*
in the meantime the time between two events or while something else is happening.
[from *mean*[3] + *time*]

meanwhile *adverb*
in the time between two events or while something else is happening.
[from *mean*[3] + *while*]

measles *noun*
an infectious disease that causes small red spots on the skin. [probably from old German *masele* = pimple]

measly *adjective* (*informal*)
not adequate or generous, *He paid me a measly £2 for a whole day's work*.
[originally = infected with measles; later = blotchy, marked, of poor quality]

measure *verb* (measures, measuring, measured)
1 find how big or heavy something is by comparing it with a unit of standard size or weight. 2 be a certain size, *The room measures 3×4 metres*.
measurable *adjective*, **measurement** *noun*
measure *noun* (*plural* measures)
1 a unit used for measuring, *A kilometre is a measure of length*. 2 a device used in measuring. 3 the size or quantity of

something. 4 something done for a particular purpose, *We took measures to stop vandalism.* [from Latin]

meat *noun*
animal flesh used as food. **meaty** *adjective*
[from Old English *mete* = food]

mecca *noun*
a place which attracts people with a particular interest, *Wimbledon is a mecca for tennis fans.*
[from *Mecca* in Saudi Arabia, a holy city and place of pilgrimage for Muslims]

mechanic *noun* (*plural* **mechanics**)
a person who maintains or repairs machinery.

mechanical *adjective*
1 to do with machines. 2 produced or worked by machines. 3 done or doing things without thought. **mechanically** *adverb* [from Greek *mechane* = machine]

mechanics *noun*
1 the study of movement and force. 2 the study or use of machines.

mechanism *noun* (*plural* **mechanisms**)
1 the moving parts of a machine. 2 the way a machine works.

mechanized *adjective*
equipped with machines.
mechanization *noun*

medal *noun* (*plural* **medals**)
a piece of metal shaped like a coin, star, or cross, given to a person for bravery or for achieving something. [from French]

medallion *noun* (*plural* **medallions**)
a large medal, usually worn round the neck as an ornament. [via French from Italian]

medallist *noun* (*plural* **medallists**)
a winner of a medal.

meddle *verb* (**meddles, meddling, meddled**)
1 interfere. 2 tinker, *Don't meddle with it.*
meddler *noun*, **meddlesome** *adjective*
[from old French; related to *mix*]

media *plural* of **medium** *noun*
the **media** newspapers, radio, and

television, which convey information and ideas to the public. (See *medium.*)

USAGE: This word is a plural. Although it is commonly used with a singular verb, this is not generally approved of. Say *The media are* (not 'is') *very influential.* It is incorrect to speak of one of them (e.g. television) as 'this media'.

medial *adjective*
1 in the middle. 2 average.
[from Latin *medius* = middle]

median *adjective*
in the middle.
median *noun* (*plural* **medians**)
1 a median point or line. 2 a median number or position.
[same origin as *medial*]

mediate *verb* (**mediates, mediating, mediated**)
negotiate between the opposing sides in a dispute. **mediation** *noun*, **mediator** *noun*
[same origin as *medial*]

medical *adjective*
to do with the treatment of disease.
medically *adverb*
[from Latin *medicus* = doctor]

medicament *noun* (*plural* **medicaments**)
a medicine or ointment etc.
[same origin as *medicated*]

medicated *adjective*
treated with a medicinal substance.
[from Latin *medicare* = give medicine]

medication *noun*
1 a medicine. 2 treatment using medicine.

medicine *noun* (*plural* **medicines**)
1 a substance, usually swallowed, used to try to cure a disease. 2 the study and treatment of diseases. **medicinal** (*say* med-iss-in-al) *adjective*, **medicinally** *adverb*
[same origin as *medical*]

medieval (*say* med-ee-ee-val) *adjective*
belonging to or to do with the Middle Ages.
[from Latin *medius* = middle + *aevum* = age]

mediocre (*say* mee-dee-oh-ker) *adjective*
not very good; of only medium quality.

mediocrity *noun*
[from Latin *mediocris* = of medium height]

meditate *verb* (**meditates, meditating, meditated**)
think deeply and quietly. **meditation** *noun*, **meditative** *adjective* [from Latin]

Mediterranean *adjective*
to do with the Mediterranean Sea (which lies between Europe and Africa) or the countries round it. [from Latin *Mare Mediterraneum* = sea in the middle of land, from *medius* = middle + *terra* = land]

medium *adjective*
neither large or small; moderate.

medium *noun* (*plural* **media**)
1 a thing in which something exists, moves, or is expressed, *Air is the medium in which sound travels. Television is used as a medium for advertising.* (See *media*.)
2 (with plural **mediums**) a person who claims to be able to communicate with the dead. [Latin, = middle thing]

medley *noun* (*plural* **medleys**)
an assortment or mixture of things. [from old French]

meek *adjective* (**meeker, meekest**)
quiet and obedient. **meekly** *adverb*, **meekness** *noun* [from Old Norse]

meet[1] *verb* (**meets, meeting, met**)
1 come together from different places. 2 get to know someone, *We met at a party.* 3 come into contact; touch. 4 go to receive an arrival, *We will meet your train.* 5 pay a bill or the cost of something. 6 satisfy, *I hope this meets your needs.*

meet *noun* (*plural* **meets**)
a gathering of riders and hounds for a hunt. [from Old English *metan*]

meet[2] *adjective* (*old use*)
proper or suitable.
[from Old English *gemaete*]

meeting *noun* (*plural* **meetings**)
1 coming together. 2 a number of people who have come together for a discussion, contest, etc.

mega- *prefix*
1 large or great (as in *megaphone*). 2 one million (as in *megahertz* = one million hertz). [from Greek *megas* = great]

megalomania *noun*
an exaggerated idea of your own importance. **megalomaniac** *noun*
[from *mega-* + *mania*]

megaphone *noun* (*plural* **megaphones**)
a funnel-shaped device for amplifying a person's voice.
[from *mega-* + Greek *phone* = voice]

melamine *noun*
a strong kind of plastic. [from *melam*, a chemical used to make melamine]

melancholy *adjective*
sad; gloomy.

melancholy *noun*
sadness or depression.
[from Greek *melas* = black + *chole* = bile (because black bile in the body was once thought to cause melancholy)]

mêlée (*say* mel-ay) *noun* (*plural* **mêlées**)
1 a confused fight. 2 a muddle.
[French, = medley]

mellow *adjective* (**mellower, mellowest**)
1 not harsh; soft and rich in flavour, colour, or sound. 2 kindly and genial.
mellowness *noun*

mellow *verb* (**mellows, mellowing, mellowed**)
make or become mellow. [origin unknown]

melodic *adjective*
to do with melody.

melodious *adjective*
like a melody; pleasant to listen to.

melodrama *noun* (*plural* **melodramas**)
a play full of dramatic excitement and emotion. **melodramatic** *adjective*
[from Greek *melos* = music + French *drame* = drama (because melodramas were originally musicals)]

melody *noun* (*plural* **melodies**)
a tune, especially a pleasing tune.
[from Greek *melos* = music + *oide* = song]

melon *noun* (*plural* **melons**)
a large sweet fruit with a yellow or green skin. [from French]

melt *verb* (**melts, melting, melted**)
1 make or become liquid by heating.
2 disappear slowly. **3** soften.
[from Old English]

melting pot *noun* (*plural* **melting pots**)
a place where people of many different
races and cultures live and influence each
other.

member *noun* (*plural* **members**)
1 a person or thing that belongs to a
particular society or group. **2** a part of
something. **membership** *noun*
[from Latin *membrum* = limb]

membrane *noun* (*plural* **membranes**)
a thin skin or similar covering.
membranous *adjective* [from Latin]

memento *noun* (*plural* **mementoes**)
a souvenir. [Latin, = remember]

memo (*say* mem-oh) *noun* (*plural* **memos**)
(*informal*)
a memorandum.

memoir (*say* mem-wahr) *noun* (*plural*
memoirs)
a biography, especially one written by
someone who knew the person.
[from French *mémoire* = memory]

memoirs *plural noun*
an autobiography.

memorable *adjective*
1 worth remembering. **2** easy to
remember. **memorably** *adverb*

memorandum *noun* (*plural* **memoranda**
or **memorandums**)
1 a note to remind yourself of something.
2 a note from one person to another in the
same firm.
[Latin, = thing to be remembered]

memorial *noun* (*plural* **memorials**)
something to remind people of a person or
event, *a war memorial*. **memorial** *adjective*
[from Latin *memoria* = memory]

memorize *verb* (**memorizes, memorizing,
memorized**)
get something into your memory.
[from *memory*]

memory *noun* (*plural* **memories**)
1 the ability to remember things.
2 something that you remember. **3** the part
of a computer where information is stored.
[from Latin *memor* = remembering]

menace *noun* (*plural* **menaces**)
1 a threat or danger. **2** a troublesome
person or thing.
menace *verb* (**menaces, menacing,
menaced**)
threaten with harm or danger.
[from Latin *minax* = threatening]

menagerie *noun* (*plural* **menageries**)
a small zoo. [from French]

mend *verb* (**mends, mending, mended**)
1 repair. **2** make or become better;
improve. **mender** *noun*
mend *noun* (*plural* **mends**)
a repair. [from *amend*]

mendacious (*say* men-**day**-shus) *adjective*
1 untruthful; telling lies. **2** untrue.
mendaciously *adverb*, **mendacity** *noun*
[from Latin]

menial (*say* **meen**-ee-al) *adjective*
needing little or no skill or thought, *menial
tasks*. **menially** *adverb*
menial *noun* (*plural* **menials**)
a person who does menial work; a servant.
[from old French]

meningitis *noun*
a disease causing inflammation of the
membranes (*meninges*) round the brain
and spinal cord.

menopause *noun*
the time of life when a woman gradually
ceases to menstruate. [from Greek *menos*
= of a month + *pausis* = stopping]

menstruate *verb* (**menstruates,
menstruating, menstruated**)
bleed from the womb about once a month,
as girls and women normally do from their
teens until middle age. **menstruation** *noun*,
menstrual *adjective*
[from Latin *menstruus* = monthly]

mental *adjective*
1 to do with or in the mind. **2** (*informal*)
mad. **mentally** *adverb*
[from Latin *mentis* = of the mind]

mentality *noun* (*plural* mentalities)
a person's mental ability or attitude.

menthol *noun*
a solid white peppermint-flavoured
substance. [from Latin *mentha* = mint[1]]

mention *verb* (mentions, mentioning,
mentioned)
speak or write about a person or thing
briefly; refer to.

mention *noun* (*plural* mentions)
an example of mentioning something, *Our
school got a mention in the local paper.*
[from Latin]

mentor *noun* (*plural* mentors)
an experienced and trusted adviser.
[named after Mentor in Greek legend, who
advised Odysseus' son]

menu (*say* men-yoo) *noun* (*plural* menus)
1 a list of the food available in a restaurant
or served at a meal. 2 a list of things,
shown on a screen, from which you decide
what you want a computer to do.
[from French]

MEP *abbreviation*
Member of the European Parliament.

mercantile *adjective*
to do with trade or trading.
[from Italian *mercante* = merchant]

mercenary *adjective*
working only for money or some other
reward.

mercenary *noun* (*plural* mercenaries)
a soldier hired to serve in a foreign army.
[from Latin *merces* = wages]

merchandise *noun*
goods for sale.
[from French *marchand* = merchant]

merchant *noun* (*plural* merchants)
a person involved in trade.
[from Latin *mercari* = to trade]

merchant bank *noun* (*plural* merchant
banks)
a bank that gives loans and advice to
businesses.

merchant navy *noun*
the ships and sailors that carry goods for
trade.

merciful *adjective*
showing mercy. **mercifully** *adverb*

merciless *adjective*
showing no mercy; cruel. **mercilessly** *adverb*

mercurial *adjective*
1 to do with mercury. 2 having sudden
changes of mood.

mercury *noun*
a heavy silvery metal (also called
quicksilver) that is usually liquid, used in
thermometers. **mercuric** *adjective*
[from the name of the planet Mercury]

mercy *noun* (*plural* mercies)
1 kindness or pity shown in not punishing
a wrongdoer severely or not harming a
defeated enemy etc. 2 something to be
thankful for. [from old French]

mere[1] *adjective*
not more than, *He's a mere child.*
[from old French]

mere[2] *noun* (*plural* meres) (*poetic*)
a lake. [from Old English]

merely *adverb*
only; simply.

merest *adjective*
very small, *the merest trace of colour.*

merge *verb* (merges, merging, merged)
combine or blend.
[from Latin *mergere* = dip]

merger *noun* (*plural* mergers)
the combining of two business companies
etc. into one.

meridian *noun* (*plural* meridians)
a line on a map or globe from the North
Pole to the South Pole. The meridian that
passes through Greenwich is shown on
maps as 0° longitude. [from Latin]

meringue (*say* mer-ang) *noun* (*plural*
meringues)
a crisp cake made from egg white and
sugar. [French]

merino *noun* (*plural* merinos)
a kind of sheep with fine soft wool.
[Spanish]

merit *noun* (*plural* merits)
1 a quality that deserves praise.
2 excellence. **meritorious** *adjective*
merit *verb* (merits, meriting, merited)
deserve. [from Latin *meritum* = value]

mermaid *noun* (*plural* mermaids)
a mythical sea creature with a woman's
body but with a fish's tail instead of legs.
merman *noun*
[from Old English *mere* = sea, + *maid*]

merry *adjective* (merrier, merriest)
cheerful and lively. **merrily** *adverb*,
merriment *noun* [from Old English]

merry-go-round *noun* (*plural* merry-go-
rounds)
a roundabout at a fair.

mesh *noun* (*plural* meshes)
1 the open spaces in a net, sieve, or other
criss-cross structure. 2 material made like
a net; network.
mesh *verb* (meshes, meshing, meshed)
(of gears) engage.
[probably from old Dutch]

mesmerize *verb* (mesmerizes,
mesmerizing, mesmerized)
1 (*old use*) hypnotize. 2 fascinate or hold a
person's attention completely. **mesmerism**
noun [named after an Austrian doctor, F.
A. Mesmer, who made hypnosis famous]

mess *noun* (*plural* messes)
1 a dirty or untidy condition or thing. 2 a
difficult or confused situation; trouble.
3 (in the armed forces) a dining room.
make a mess of bungle.
mess *verb* (messes, messing, messed)
mess about 1 behave stupidly. 2 potter.
mess up 1 make a thing dirty or untidy.
2 bungle; spoil by muddling, *They messed
up our plans.*
mess with interfere or tinker with.
[from old French *mes* = a portion of food]

message *noun* (*plural* messages)
a piece of information etc. sent from one
person to another.
[from old French; related to *missile*]

messenger *noun* (*plural* messengers)
a person who carries a message.

Messiah (*say* mis-I-a) *noun* (*plural*
Messiahs)
1 the saviour expected by the Jews. 2 Jesus
Christ, who Christians believe was this
saviour. **Messianic** *adjective*
[from Hebrew *mashiah* = anointed]

Messrs *plural* of **Mr**.
[abbreviation of French *messieurs*
= gentlemen]

messy *adjective* (messier, messiest)
dirty and untidy.
messily *adverb*, **messiness** *noun*

metabolism (*say* mit-ab-ol-izm) *noun*
the process by which food is built up into
living material in a plant or animal, or
used to supply it with energy.
metabolic *adjective*, **metabolize** *verb*
[from Greek *metabole* = change]

metal *noun* (*plural* metals)
a hard mineral substance (e.g. gold, silver,
copper, iron) that melts when it is heated.
metallic *adjective* [from Latin]

metallurgy (*say* mit-al-er-jee) *noun*
1 the study of metals. 2 the craft of making
and using metals.
metallurgical *adjective*, **metallurgist** *noun*
[from *metal* + Greek *-ourgia* = working]

metamorphic *adjective*
formed or changed by heat or pressure,
Marble is a metamorphic rock.
[from Greek *meta-* = change + *morphe*
= form]

metamorphosis (*say* met-a-mor-fo-sis)
noun (*plural* **metamorphoses**, *say* met-a-
mor-fo-seez)
a change of form or character.
metamorphose *verb*
[same origin as *metamorphic*]

metaphor *noun* (*plural* metaphors)
using a word or phrase in a way that is not
literal, e.g. 'The pictures of starving people
touched our hearts'. **metaphorical** *adjective*,
metaphorically *adverb*
[from Greek *metapherein* = transfer]

mete *verb* (metes, meting, meted)
mete out deal out or allot, usually
something unpleasant, *mete out
punishment.* [from Old English]

meteor (*say* meet-ee-er) *noun* (*plural* meteors)
a piece of rock or metal that moves through space and burns up when it enters the earth's atmosphere.
[from Greek *meteoros* = high in the air]

meteoric (*say* meet-ee-o-rik) *adjective*
1 to do with meteors. 2 like a meteor in brilliance or sudden appearance, *a meteoric career*.

meteorite *noun* (*plural* meteorites)
the remains of a meteor that has landed on the earth.

meteorology *noun*
the study of the conditions of the atmosphere, especially in order to forecast the weather. **meteorological** *adjective*, **meteorologist** *noun* [from Greek *meteoros* = high in the air, + -*logy*]

meter *noun* (*plural* meters)
a device for measuring something, e.g. the amount supplied, *a gas meter*. **meter** *verb*
[from *mete*]

USAGE: Do not confuse with *metre*.

methane (*say* mee-thayn) *noun*
an inflammable gas produced by decaying matter. [from *methyl*, a chemical which methane contains]

method *noun* (*plural* methods)
1 a procedure or way of doing something.
2 methodical behaviour; orderliness. [from Greek *methodos* = pursuit of knowledge]

methodical *adjective*
doing things in an orderly or systematic way. **methodically** *adverb*

Methodist *noun* (*plural* Methodists)
a member of a Christian religious group started by John and Charles Wesley in the 18th century. **Methodism** *noun*

meths *noun* (*informal*)
methylated spirit.

methylated spirit or **spirits** *noun*
a liquid fuel made from alcohol.
[from *methyl*, a chemical added to make alcohol nasty to drink]

meticulous *adjective*
very careful and exact. **meticulously** *adverb*
[from Latin]

metre *noun* (*plural* metres)
1 a unit of length in the metric system, about $39\frac{1}{2}$ inches. 2 rhythm in poetry.
[from Greek *metron* = a measure]

USAGE: Do not confuse with *meter*.

metric *adjective*
1 to do with the metric system. 2 to do with metre in poetry. **metrically** *adverb*

metrical *adjective*
in, or to do with, rhythmic metre, not prose, *metrical psalms*.

metrication *noun*
changing to the metric system.

metric system *noun*
a measuring system based on decimal units (the metre, litre, and gram).

metric ton *noun* (*plural* metric tons)
1,000 kilograms.

metronome *noun* (*plural* metronomes)
a device that makes a regular clicking noise to help a person keep in time when practising music. [from Greek *metron* = measure + *nomos* = law]

metropolis *noun* (*plural* metropolises)
the chief city of a country or region.
[from Greek *meter* = mother + *polis* = city]

metropolitan *adjective*
1 to do with a metropolis. 2 to do with a city and its suburbs.

mettle *noun*
courage or strength of character.
mettlesome *adjective*
be on your mettle be determined to show your courage or ability.
[a different spelling of *metal*]

mew *verb* (mews, mewing, mewed)
make a cat's cry. **mew** *noun*
[imitating the sound]

mews *noun* (*plural* mews)
a group of what were once stables, rebuilt

or converted into garages or small houses. [first used of royal stables in London, built on the site of hawks' cages (called *mews*)]

miaow *verb & noun*
mew. [imitating the sound]

miasma (*say* mee-**az**-ma) *noun* (*plural* miasmas)
unpleasant or unhealthy air. [Greek, = pollution]

mica *noun*
a mineral substance used to make electrical insulators. [Latin]

mice *plural* of mouse.

micro- *prefix*
very small (as in *microfilm*). [from Greek *mikros* = small]

microbe *noun* (*plural* microbes)
a micro-organism. [from *micro-* + Greek *bios* = life]

microchip *noun* (*plural* microchips)
a very small piece of silicon etc. made to work like a complex wired electric circuit.

microcomputer *noun* (*plural* microcomputers)
a very small computer.

microcosm *noun* (*plural* microcosms)
a world in miniature; something regarded as resembling something else on a very small scale. [from Greek *mikros kosmos* = little world]

microfiche *noun* (*plural* microfiches)
a piece of film on which pages of information are photographed in greatly reduced size. [from *micro-* + French *fiche* = slip of paper]

microfilm *noun*
a length of film on which written or printed material is photographed in greatly reduced size.

micron *noun* (*plural* microns)
a unit of measurement, one millionth of a metre. [same origin as *micro-*]

micro-organism *noun* (*plural* micro-organisms)
a microscopic creature, e.g. a bacterium or virus.

microphone *noun* (*plural* microphones)
an electrical device that picks up sound waves for recording, amplifying, or broadcasting. [from *micro-* + Greek *phone* = sound]

microprocessor *noun* (*plural* microprocessors)
a miniature computer (or a unit of this) consisting of one or more microchips.

microscope *noun* (*plural* microscopes)
an instrument with lenses that magnify tiny objects or details. [from *micro-* + Greek *skopein* = look at]

microscopic *adjective*
1 extremely small; too small to be seen without the aid of a microscope. 2 to do with a microscope.

microwave *noun* (*plural* microwaves)
1 a very short electromagnetic wave. 2 a microwave oven.
microwave *verb* (microwaves, microwaving, microwaved)
cook in a microwave oven.

microwave oven *noun* (*plural* microwave ovens)
an oven that uses microwaves to heat or cook food very quickly.

mid *adjective*
1 in the middle of. 2 middle, *He's in his mid thirties*. [from Old English]

midday *noun*
the middle of the day; noon.

middle *noun* (*plural* middles)
1 the place or part of something that is at the same distance from all its sides or edges or from both its ends. 2 someone's waist.
middle *adjective*
1 placed or happening in the middle. 2 moderate in size or rank etc. [from Old English]

Middle Ages *noun*
the period in history from about AD 1000 to 1400.

middle class or **classes** *noun*
the class of people between the upper class and the working class, including business and professional people such as teachers, doctors, and lawyers. **middle-class** *adjective*

Middle East *noun*
the countries from Egypt to Iran inclusive.

Middle English *noun*
the English language from about 1150 to 1500.

middleman *noun* (*plural* **middlemen**)
1 a trader who buys from a producer and sells to a consumer. 2 a go-between or intermediary.

middle school *noun* (*plural* **middle schools**)
a school for children aged from about 9 to 13.

middling *adjective*
of medium size or quality.
middling *adverb*
fairly or moderately.

midge *noun* (*plural* **midges**)
a small insect like a gnat.
[from Old English]

midget *noun* (*plural* **midgets**)
an extremely small person or thing. **midget** *adjective* [from *midge*]

midland *adjective*
1 to do with the middle part of a country.
2 to do with the Midlands.

Midlands *plural noun*
the central part of England.

midnight *noun*
twelve o'clock at night.

midriff *noun* (*plural* **midriffs**)
the front part of the body just above the waist. [from *mid* + Old English *hrif* = stomach]

midshipman *noun* (*plural* **midshipmen**)
a sailor ranking next above a cadet. [because they were stationed in the middle part of the ship]

midst *noun*
in the midst of in the middle of or surrounded by.
in our midst among us.

midsummer *noun*
the middle of summer, about 21 June in the northern hemisphere.

Midsummer's Day *noun*
24 June.

midway *adverb*
halfway.

midwife *noun* (*plural* **midwives**)
a person trained to look after a woman who is giving birth to a baby. **midwifery** *noun* [from Old English *mid* = with + *wif* = woman]

mien (*say* meen) *noun*
a person's manner and expression. [origin unknown]

might[1] *noun*
great strength or power.
with all your might using all your strength and determination.
[from Old English]

might[2] *auxiliary verb*
used 1 as the past tense of *may*[1] (*We told her she might go*), 2 to express possibility (*It might be true*).

mighty *adjective*
very strong or powrful.
mightily *adverb*, **mightiness** *noun*

mignonette (*say* min-yon-et) *noun* (*plural* **mignonettes**)
a plant with fragrant leaves. [from French]

migraine (*say* mee-grayn or my-grayn) *noun* (*plural* **migraines**)
a severe kind of headache. [French]

migrant *noun* (*plural* **migrants**)
a person or animal that migrates or has migrated.

migrate *verb* (**migrates**, **migrating**, **migrated**)
1 leave one place or country and settle in another. 2 (of birds or animals) move

periodically from one area to another.
migration *noun*, **migratory** *adjective*
[from Latin]

mike *noun* (*plural* **mikes**) (*informal*)
a microphone.

mild *adjective* (**milder**, **mildest**)
1 gentle; not harsh or severe. 2 not
strongly flavoured. **mildly** *adverb*, **mildness**
noun [from Old English]

mildew *noun*
a tiny fungus that forms a white coating on
things kept in damp conditions. **mildewed**
adjective [from Old English]

mile *noun* (*plural* **miles**)
a measure of distance, 1,760 yards (about
1.6 kilometres).
[from Latin *mille* = thousand (paces)]

mileage *noun* (*plural* **mileages**)
the number of miles travelled.

milestone *noun* (*plural* **milestones**)
1 a stone of a kind that used to be fixed
beside a road to mark the distance between
towns. 2 an important event in life or
history.

milieu (*say* meel-yer) *noun* (*plural* **milieus**
or **milieux**)
environment or surroundings.
[French, from *mi* = mid + *lieu* = place]

militant *adjective*
1 eager to fight. 2 forceful or aggressive, *a
militant protest*. **militant** *noun*, **militancy**
noun [same origin as *militate*]

militarism *noun*
belief in the use of military strength and
methods.
militarist *noun*, **militaristic** *adjective*

military *adjective*
to do with soldiers or the armed forces.
[from Latin *miles* = soldier]

militate *verb* (**militates**, **militating**, **militated**)
have a strong effect or influence, *The
weather militated against the success of*

our plans.
[from Latin *militare* = be a soldier]

USAGE: Do not confuse with *mitigate*.

militia (*say* mil-ish-a) *noun* (*plural* **militias**)
a military force, especially one raised from
civilians. [Latin, = military service]

milk *noun*
1 a white liquid that female mammals
produce in their bodies to feed their babies.
2 the milk of cows, used as food by human
beings. 3 a milky liquid, e.g. that in a
coconut.
milk *verb* (**milks**, **milking**, **milked**)
get the milk from a cow or other animal.
[from Old English]

milkman *noun* (*plural* **milkmen**)
a man who delivers milk to customers'
houses.

milk tooth *noun* (*plural* **milk teeth**)
one of the first set of teeth of a child or
animal, which will be replaced by adult
teeth.

milky *adjective* (**milkier**, **milkiest**)
1 like milk. 2 white.

Milky Way *noun*
the broad band of stars formed by our
galaxy.

mill *noun* (*plural* **mills**)
1 machinery for grinding corn to make
flour; a building containing this
machinery. 2 a grinding machine, *a coffee
mill*. 3 a factory for processing certain
materials, *a paper mill*.
mill *verb* (**mills**, **milling**, **milled**)
1 grind or crush in a mill. 2 cut markings
round the edge of a coin. 3 move in a
confused crowd, *The animals were milling
around*. **miller** *noun*
[via Old English from Latin *molere* = grind]

millennium *noun* (*plural* **millenniums**)
a period of 1,000 years. [from Latin *mille*
= thousand + *annus* = year]

millepede *noun* (*plural* **millepedes**)
a small crawling creature like a centipede,
with many legs. [from Latin *mille*
= thousand + *pedes* = feet]

millet *noun*
a kind of cereal with tiny seeds.
[from Latin]

milli- *prefix*
1 one thousand (as in *millepede*). 2 one-thousandth (as in *milligram, millilitre, millimetre*). [from Latin *mille* = thousand]

milliner *noun* (*plural* **milliners**)
a person who makes or sells women's hats.
millinery *noun* [originally = a person from Milan, an Italian city where fashionable accessories and hats were made]

million *noun* (*plural* **millions**)
one thousand thousand (1,000,000).
millionth *adjective* & *noun*
[French, related to *milli-*]

USAGE: Say *a few million*, not 'a few millions'.

millionaire *noun* (*plural* **millionaires**)
an extremely rich person.

millstone *noun* (*plural* **millstones**)
either of a pair of large circular stones between which corn is ground.
a millstone around someone's neck a heavy responsibility or burden.

milometer *noun* (*plural* **milometers**)
an instrument for measuring how far a vehicle has travelled. [from *mile* + *meter*]

milt *noun*
a male fish's sperm. [from Old English]

mime *noun* (*plural* **mimes**)
acting with movements of the body, not using words. **mime** *verb*
[from Greek *mimos* = a mimic]

mimic *verb* (**mimics, mimicking, mimicked**)
imitate. **mimicry** *noun*
mimic *noun* (*plural* **mimics**)
a person who mimics others, especially to amuse people. [same origin as *mime*]

mimosa *noun* (*plural* **mimosas**)
a tropical tree or shrub with small ball-shaped flowers. [from Latin]

minaret *noun* (*plural* **minarets**)
the tall tower of a mosque.
[from Arabic *manara* = lighthouse]

mince *verb* (**minces, mincing, minced**)
1 cut into very small pieces in a machine. 2 walk in an affected way. **mincer** *noun*
not to mince matters speak bluntly.
mince *noun*
minced meat.
[from French; related to *minute*^{2}]

mincemeat *noun*
a sweet mixture of currants, raisins, apple, etc. used in pies.
[from *mince* + an old sense of *meat* = food]

mince pie *noun* (*plural* **mince pies**)
a pie containing mincemeat.

mind *noun* (*plural* **minds**)
1 the ability to think, feel, understand, and remember, originating in the brain. 2 a person's thoughts and feelings or opinion, *I changed my mind.*
mind *verb* (**minds, minding, minded**)
1 look after, *He was minding the baby.* 2 be careful about, *Mind the step.* 3 be sad or upset about something; object to, *We don't mind waiting.* **minder** *noun*
[from Old English]

mindful *adjective*
taking thought or care, *He was mindful of his reputation.*

mindless *adjective*
without intelligence or thought.

mine^1 *possessive pronoun*
belonging to me.
[from Old English]

mine^2 *noun* (*plural* **mines**)
1 a place where coal, metal, precious stones, etc. are dug out of the ground. 2 an explosive placed in or on the ground or in the sea etc. to destroy people or things that come close to it.
mine *verb* (**mines, mining, mined**)
1 dig from a mine. 2 lay explosive mines in a place.
[from old French]

minefield *noun* (*plural* **minefields**)
1 an area where explosive mines have been laid. 2 something with hidden dangers or problems.

miner *noun* (*plural* **miners**)
a person who works in a mine.

mineral *noun* (*plural* minerals)
1 a hard inorganic substance found in the ground. 2 a cold fizzy non-alcoholic drink. [from Latin *minera* = ore]

mineralogy (*say* min-er-al-o-jee) *noun*
the study of minerals. **mineralogist** *noun* [from *mineral* + *-logy*]

minestrone (*say* mini-stroh-nee) *noun*
an Italian soup containing vegetables and pasta. [Italian, from *ministrare* = to serve up a dish]

mingle *verb* (mingles, mingling, mingled)
mix. [from Old English]

mingy *adjective* (mingier, mingiest) (*informal*)
not generous; mean. [probably from *mean*² + *stingy*]

mini- *prefix*
miniature; very small. [short for *miniature*]

miniature *adjective*
1 very small. 2 copying something on a very small scale, *a miniature railway*.
miniature *noun* (*plural* miniatures)
1 a very small portrait. 2 a small-scale model. [from Italian]

minibus *noun* (*plural* minibuses)
a small bus, seating about ten people.

minicomputer *noun* (*plural* minicomputers)
a small computer.

minim *noun* (*plural* minims)
a note in music, lasting twice as long as a crotchet (written ♩). [same origin as *minimum*]

minimal *adjective*
very little; as little as possible.

minimize *verb* (minimizes, minimizing, minimized)
reduce something to a minimum.

minimum *noun* (*plural* minima or minimums)
the lowest possible number or amount. (The opposite is *maximum*.) **minimal** *adjective* [Latin, = least thing]

minion *noun* (*plural* minions) (*contemptuous*)
a very humble or obedient assistant or servant. [from French]

minister *noun* (*plural* ministers)
1 a person in charge of a government department. 2 a member of the clergy. **ministerial** *adjective*
minister *verb* (ministers, ministering, ministered)
attend to people's needs. [Latin, = servant]

ministry *noun* (*plural* ministries)
1 a government department, *the Ministry of Defence*. 2 the work of the clergy. [same origin as *minister*]

mink *noun* (*plural* mink or minks)
1 an animal rather like a stoat. 2 this animal's valuable brown fur. 3 a coat etc. made of mink fur. [origin unknown]

minnow *noun* (*plural* minnows)
a tiny freshwater fish. [probably from Old English]

minor *adjective*
1 not very important, especially when compared to something else. 2 to do with the musical scale that has a semitone after the second note. (Compare *major*.) [Latin, = smaller, lesser]

minority *noun* (*plural* minorities)
1 the smallest part of a group of people or things. 2 a small group that is different from others. (Compare *majority*.) [same origin as *minor*]

minstrel *noun* (*plural* minstrels)
a travelling singer and musician in the Middle Ages. [from old French; related to *minister*]

mint¹ *noun* (*plural* mints)
1 a plant with fragrant leaves that are used for flavouring things. 2 peppermint or a sweet flavoured with this. [from Latin *mentha* = mint]

mint² *noun* (*plural* mints)
the place where a country's coins are made. **in mint condition** in perfect condition, as though it had never been used.
mint *verb* (mints, minting, minted)
make coins. [from Latin *moneta* = coins; a mint]

minuet *noun* (*plural* minuets)
a slow stately dance.
[from French *menuet* = small or delicate]

minus *preposition*
with the next number or thing subtracted,
Ten minus four equals six (10 − 4 = 6).
minus *adjective*
less than zero, *temperatures of minus ten
degrees* (−10˚). [Latin, = less]

minuscule *adjective*
extremely small.

minute¹ (*say* min-it) *noun* (*plural* minutes)
1 one-sixtieth of an hour. **2** a very short
time; a moment. **3** a particular time, *Come
here this minute!* **4** one-sixtieth of a degree
(used in measuring angles). [from Latin
pars minuta prima = first little part]

minute² (*say* my-**newt**) *adjective*
1 very small, *a minute insect.* **2** very
detailed, *a minute examination.* **minutely**
adverb [from Latin *minutus* = little]

minutes *plural noun*
a written summary of what was said at a
meeting. [probably from Latin *minuta
scriptura* = small writing]

minx *noun* (*plural* minxes) (*old use*)
a cheeky or mischievous girl.
[origin unknown]

miracle *noun* (*plural* miracles)
something wonderful and good that
happens, especially something believed to
have a supernatural or divine cause.
miraculous *adjective*, **miraculously** *adverb*
[same origin as *mirror*]

mirage (*say* mi-rah*zh*) *noun* (*plural*
mirages)
an illusion; something that seems to be
there but is not, especially when a lake
seems to appear in a desert. [French, from
se mirer = be reflected or mirrored]

mire *noun*
1 a swamp. **2** deep mud. [from Old Norse]

mirror *noun* (*plural* mirrors)
a device or surface of reflecting material,
usually glass.
mirror *verb* (mirrors, mirroring, mirrored)
reflect in or like a mirror. [from Latin
mirari = to look at or wonder at]

mirth *noun*
merriment or laughter. **mirthful** *adjective*,
mirthless *adjective* [from Old English]

mis- *prefix*
badly or wrongly. (Compare *amiss*.)
[from Old English *mis-* (related to *amiss*,
or old French *mes-* (related to *minus*)]

misadventure *noun* (*plural*
misadventures)
a piece of bad luck. [from old French
mesavenir = to turn out badly]

misanthropy *noun*
dislike of people. **misanthropist** *noun*,
misanthropic *adjective* [from Greek *misos*
= hatred + *anthropos* = human being]

misapprehend *verb* (misapprehends,
misapprehending, misapprehended)
misunderstand something.
misapprehension *noun*

misappropriate *verb* (misappropriates,
misappropriating, misappropriated)
take something dishonestly.
misappropriation *noun*

misbehave *verb* (misbehaves, misbehaving,
misbehaved)
behave badly. **misbehaviour** *noun*

miscalculate *verb* (miscalculates,
miscalculating, miscalculated)
calculate incorrectly. **miscalculation** *noun*

miscarriage *noun* (*plural* miscarriages)
1 the birth of a baby before it has
developed enough to live. **2** failure to
achieve the right result, *a miscarriage of
justice.* [from *miscarry* = to be lost,
destroyed, or badly managed]

miscellaneous (*say* mis-el-**ay**-nee-us)
adjective
of various kinds; mixed.
miscellany (*say* mis-**el**-an-ee) *noun*
[from Latin *miscellus* = mixed]

mischance *noun*
misfortune.

mischief *noun*
1 naughty or troublesome behaviour.
2 trouble caused by this. **mischievous**
adjective, **mischievously** *adverb* [from old
French *meschever* = come to a bad end]

misconception noun (plural misconceptions)
a mistaken idea.

misconduct noun
bad behaviour by someone in a responsible position, professional misconduct.

misconstrue verb (misconstrues, misconstruing, misconstrued)
to understand or interpret something wrongly. misconstruction noun

miscreant (say mis-kree-ant) noun (plural miscreants)
a wrongdoer or criminal.
[originally = heretic: from old French mescreance = false belief]

misdeed noun (plural misdeeds)
a wrong or improper action.

misdemeanour noun (plural misdemeanours)
an action which is wrong or illegal, but not very serious; a petty crime.

miser noun (plural misers)
a person who hoards money and spends as little as possible. miserly adjective, miserliness noun [same origin as misery]

miserable adjective
1 full of misery; very unhappy, poor, or uncomfortable. 2 disagreeable or unpleasant, miserable weather. miserably adverb [same origin as misery]

misery noun (plural miseries)
1 great unhappiness or discomfort or suffering, especially lasting for a long time. 2 (informal) a discontented or disagreeable person. [from Latin miser = wretched]

misfire verb (misfires, misfiring, misfired)
1 fail to fire. 2 fail to function correctly or to have the required effect, The joke misfired.

misfit noun (plural misfits)
a person who does not fit in well with other people or who is not well suited to his or her work.

misfortune noun (plural misfortunes)
1 bad luck. 2 an unlucky event or accident.

misgiving noun (plural misgivings)
a feeling of doubt or slight fear or mistrust.
[from an old word misgive = give someone bad feelings about something]

misguided adjective
guided by mistaken ideas or beliefs.

mishap (say mis-hap) noun (plural mishaps)
an unlucky accident.
[from mis- + Middle English hap = luck]

misinterpret verb (misinterprets, misinterpreting, misinterpreted)
interpret incorrectly. misinterpretation noun

misjudge verb (misjudges, misjudging, misjudged)
judge wrongly; form a wrong opinion or estimate. misjudgement noun

mislay verb (mislays, mislaying, mislaid)
lose something for a short time because you cannot remember where you put it.

mislead verb (misleads, misleading, misled)
give somebody a wrong idea; deceive.

mismanagement noun
bad management.

misnomer noun (plural misnomers)
an unsuitable name for something.
[from mis- + Latin nomen = name]

misogynist (say mis-oj-in-ist) noun (plural misogynists)
a person who hates women. misogyny noun
[from Greek misos = hatred + gyne = woman]

misplaced adjective
1 placed wrongly. 2 inappropriate, misplaced sympathy. misplacement noun

misprint noun (plural misprints)
a mistake in printing.

mispronounce verb (mispronounces, mispronouncing, mispronounced)
pronounce incorrectly. mispronunciation noun

misquote verb (misquotes, misquoting, misquoted)
quote incorrectly. misquotation noun

misread *verb* (**misreads, misreading, misread** (*say* mis-**red**))
read or interpret incorrectly.

misrepresent *verb* (**misrepresents, misrepresenting, misrepresented**)
represent in a false or misleading way.
misrepresentation *noun*

misrule *noun*
bad government.

Miss *noun* (*plural* **Misses**)
a title put before a girl's or unmarried woman's name. [short for *mistress*]

miss *verb* (**misses, missing, missed**)
1 fail to hit, reach, catch, see, hear, or find something. 2 be sad because someone or something is not with you. 3 notice that something has gone.
miss *noun* (*plural* **misses**)
missing something, *Was that shot a hit or a miss?* [from Old English]

misshapen *adjective*
badly shaped. [from *mis-* + *shapen*, the old past participle of *shape*]

missile *noun* (*plural* **missiles**)
a weapon or other object for firing or throwing at a target.
[from Latin *missum* = sent]

missing *adjective*
1 lost; not in the proper place. 2 absent.

mission *noun* (*plural* **missions**)
1 an important job that somebody is sent to do or feels he or she must do. 2 a place or building where missionaries work.
[from Latin *missio* = sending someone out]

missionary *noun* (*plural* **missionaries**)
a person who is sent to another country to spread a religious faith.

mist *noun* (*plural* **mists**)
1 damp cloudy air near the ground. 2 condensed water vapour on a window, mirror, etc. [from Old English]

mistake *noun* (*plural* **mistakes**)
1 something done wrongly. 2 an incorrect opinion.
mistake *verb* (**mistakes, mistaking, mistook, mistaken**)
1 misunderstand, *Don't mistake my*

meaning. 2 choose or identify wrongly, *We mistook her for her sister*.
[from *mis-* + Old Norse *taka* = take]

mistaken *adjective*
1 incorrect. 2 having an incorrect opinion.

mistime *verb* (**mistimes, mistiming, mistimed**)
do or say something at a wrong time.

mistletoe *noun*
a plant with white berries that grows as a parasite on trees. [from Old English]

mistreat *verb* (**mistreats, mistreating, mistreated**)
treat badly.

mistress *noun* (*plural* **mistresses**)
1 a woman who is in charge of something. 2 a woman teacher. 3 a woman who is a man's lover but not his wife.
[from old French *maistresse*, feminine form of *maistre* = master]

mistrust *verb* (**mistrusts, mistrusting, mistrusted**)
feel no trust in somebody or something.
mistrust *noun*

misty *adjective* (**mistier, mistiest**)
1 full of mist. 2 not clear or distinct.
mistily *adverb*, **mistiness** *noun*

misunderstand *verb* (**misunderstands, misunderstanding, misunderstood**)
get a wrong idea or impression of something.

misuse *verb* (**misuses, misusing, misused**)
1 use incorrectly. 2 treat badly.
misuse *noun*

mite *noun* (*plural* **mites**)
1 a tiny spider-like creature found in food, *cheese-mites*. 2 a small child.
[from Old English]

mitigate *verb* (**mitigates, mitigating, mitigated**)
make a thing less intense or less severe.
mitigation *noun*
[from Latin *mitigare* = make mild]

USAGE: Do not confuse with *militate*.

mitigating circumstances *plural noun*
facts that may partially excuse
wrongdoing.

mitre *noun* (*plural* mitres)
1 the tall tapering hat worn by a bishop.
2 a mitred join.

mitre *verb* (mitres, mitring, mitred)
join two tapered pieces of wood or cloth etc.
so that they form a right angle.
[from Greek *mitra* = turban]

mitten *noun* (*plural* mittens)
a kind of glove without separate parts for
the fingers. [from French]

mix *verb* (mixes, mixing, mixed)
1 put different things together so that the
substances etc. are no longer distinct;
blend or combine. 2 (of a person) get
together with others. **mixer** *noun*
mix up 1 mix thoroughly. 2 confuse.

mix *noun* (*plural* mixes)
a mixture. [from *mixed*]

mixed *adjective*
containing two or more kinds of things or
people. [from Latin *mixtus* = mingled]

mixed blessing *noun* (*plural* mixed
blessings)
something that has disadvantages as well
as advantages.

mixed farming *noun*
farming of both crops and animals.

mixture *noun* (*plural* mixtures)
1 something made of different things
mixed together. 2 the process of mixing.

mizzen-mast *noun* (*plural* mizzen-masts)
the mast nearest to and behind the
mainmast. [via French from Italian]

mnemonic (*say* nim-on-ik) *noun* (*plural*
mnemonics)
a verse or saying that helps you to
remember something. [from Greek
mnemonikos = for the memory]

moan *verb* (moans, moaning, moaned)
1 make a long low sound of pain or
suffering. 2 grumble. **moan** *noun*
[probably from Old English]

moat *noun* (*plural* moats)
a deep wide ditch round a castle, usually
filled with water. **moated** *adjective*
[from old French]

mob *noun* (*plural* mobs)
1 a large disorderly crowd; a rabble. 2 a
gang.

mob *verb* (mobs, mobbing, mobbed)
crowd round somebody. [from Latin *mobile
vulgus* = excitable crowd]

mobile *adjective*
moving easily. **mobility** *noun*

mobile *noun* (*plural* mobiles)
a decoration for hanging up so that its
parts move in currents of air.
[from Latin *movere* = move]

mobile home *noun* (*plural* mobile homes)
a large caravan permanently parked and
used for living in.

mobilize *verb* (mobilizes, mobilizing,
mobilized)
assemble people or things for a particular
purpose, especially for war.
mobilization *noun*

moccasin *noun* (*plural* moccasins)
a soft leather shoe.
[a Native American word]

mock *verb* (mocks, mocking, mocked)
1 make fun of a person or thing. 2 imitate
someone or something to make people
laugh. **mockery** *noun*

mock *adjective*
imitation, not real, *mock exams*.
[from old French]

mock-up *noun* (*plural* mock-ups)
a model of something, made in order to test
or study it.

mode *noun* (*plural* modes)
1 the way a thing is done. 2 what is
fashionable. [from Latin]

model *noun* (*plural* models)
1 a copy of an object, usually on a smaller
scale. 2 a particular design. 3 a person who
poses for an artist or displays clothes by
wearing them. 4 a person or thing that is
worth copying.

model *verb* (models, modelling, modelled)
1 make a model of something. 2 make
according to a model. 3 work as an artist's
model or a fashion model.
[from Latin *modulus* = a small measure]

modem (*say* moh-dem) *noun* (*plural*
modems)
a device that links a computer to a
telephone line.
[from *mo*dulator + *de*modulator]

moderate *adjective*
1 medium; not extremely small or great or
hot etc., *a moderate climate*. 2 not extreme
or unreasonable, *moderate opinions*.
moderately *adverb*
moderate (*say* mod-er-ayt) *verb*
(moderates, moderating, moderated)
make or become moderate.
moderation *noun*
in moderation in moderate amounts.
[from Latin *moderari* = restrain]

modern *adjective*
1 belonging to the present or recent times.
2 in fashion now. **modernity** *noun*
[from Latin *modo* = just now]

modernize *verb* (modernizes, modernizing,
modernized)
make a thing more modern.
modernization *noun*

modest *adjective*
1 not vain or boastful. 2 moderate, *a
modest income*. 3 not showy or splendid.
4 behaving or dressing decently or
decorously. **modestly** *adverb*, **modesty** *noun*
[from Latin, = keeping the proper
measure]

modicum *noun*
a small amount.
[Latin, from *modicus* = moderate]

modify *verb* (modifies, modifying, modified)
1 change something slightly. 2 describe a
word or limit its meaning, *Adjectives
modify nouns*. **modification** *noun*
[from Latin *modificare* = to limit]

modulate *verb* (modulates, modulating,
modulated)
1 adjust or regulate. 2 vary in pitch or tone
etc. 3 alter an electronic wave to allow
signals to be sent. **modulation** *noun*,
modulator *noun* [same origin as *model*]

module *noun* (*plural* modules)
1 an independent part of a spacecraft,
building, etc. 2 a unit; a section of a course
of study. **modular** *adjective*
[same origin as *model*]

modus operandi (*say* moh-dus op-er-and-
ee) *noun*
1 a person's way of working. 2 the way a
thing works. [Latin, = way of working]

mogul (*say* moh-gul) *noun* (*plural* moguls)
(*informal*)
an important or influential person.
[the Moguls were the ruling family in
northern India in the 16th–19th centuries]

mohair *noun*
fine silky wool from an angora goat.
[from Arabic]

moist *adjective*
slightly wet; damp. **moistly** *adverb*,
moistness *noun* [from old French]

moisten *verb* (moistens, moistening,
moistened)
make or become moist.

moisture *noun*
water in the air or making a thing moist.

molar *noun* (*plural* molars)
any of the wide teeth at the back of the jaw,
used in chewing.
[from Latin *mola* = millstone]

molasses *noun*
dark syrup from raw sugar.
[from Latin *mellaceus* = like honey]

mole¹ *noun* (*plural* moles)
1 a small furry animal that burrows under
the ground. 2 a person who secretly gives
confidential information to an enemy or
rival. [probably from old Dutch]

mole² *noun* (*plural* moles)
a small dark spot on skin.
[from Old English]

molecule *noun* (*plural* molecules)
the smallest part into which a substance
can be divided without changing its
chemical nature; a group of atoms.
molecular *adjective*
[from Latin *molecula* = little mass]

molehill *noun* (*plural* **molehills**)
a small pile of earth thrown up by a burrowing mole.

molest *verb* (**molests, molesting, molested**)
1 attack and harm. 2 abuse someone sexually. **molestation** *noun*
[from Latin *molestus* = troublesome]

mollify *verb* (**mollifies, mollifying, mollified**)
make a person less angry. **mollification** *noun* [from Latin *mollificare* = soften]

mollusc *noun* (*plural* **molluscs**)
an animal with no backbone and a soft body protected by a shell; snails and many shellfish are molluscs.
[from Latin *molluscus* = soft thing]

molten *adjective*
melted; made liquid by great heat.
[the old past participle of *melt*]

moment *noun* (*plural* **moments**)
1 a very short time. 2 a particular time, *Call me the moment she arrives.*
[from Latin *movere* = move]

momentary *adjective*
lasting for only a moment.
momentarily *adverb*

momentous (*say* mo-ment-us) *adjective*
very important. [from an old sense of *moment* = importance]

momentum *noun*
amount or force of movement, *The stone gathered momentum as it rolled downhill.*
[Latin, = movement]

monarch *noun* (*plural* **monarchs**)
a king, queen, emperor, or empress ruling a country. **monarchic** *adjective* [from Greek *monos* = alone + *archein* = to rule]

monarchy *noun* (*plural* **monarchies**)
a country ruled by a monarch.
monarchist *noun*

monastery *noun* (*plural* **monasteries**)
a building where monks live and work.
monastic *adjective*
[from Greek *monazein* = live alone]

monetary *adjective*
to do with money.

money *noun*
1 coins and banknotes. 2 wealth.
[same origin as *mint*[2]]

mongoose *noun* (*plural* **mongooses**)
a small tropical animal rather like a stoat, that can kill snakes.
[from a southern Indian language]

mongrel (*say* mung-rel) *noun* (*plural* **mongrels**)
a dog of mixed breeds. [related to *mingle*]

monitor *noun* (*plural* **monitors**)
1 a device for watching or testing how something is working. 2 a pupil who is given a special responsibility in a school.
monitor *verb* (**monitors, monitoring, monitored**)
watch or test how something is working.
[from Latin *monere* = warn]

monk *noun* (*plural* **monks**)
a member of a community of men who live according to the rules of a religious organization. (Compare *nun*.)
[via Old English from Greek *monachos* = single or solitary]

monkey *noun* (*plural* **monkeys**)
1 an animal with long arms, hands with thumbs, and often a tail. 2 a mischievous person. [origin unknown]

mono- *prefix*
1 one. 2 single. [from Greek *monos* = alone]

monochrome *adjective*
done in one colour or in black and white.
[from *mono-* + Greek *chroma* = colour]

monocle *noun* (*plural* **monocles**)
a lens worn over one eye, like half of a pair of spectacles.
[from *mono-* + Latin *oculus* = eye]

monogamy *noun*
the custom of being married to only one person at a time. (Compare *polygamy*.)
monogamous *adjective*
[from *mono-* + Greek *gamos* = marriage]

monogram *noun* (*plural* **monograms**)
a design made up of a letter or letters, especially a person's initials.
monogrammed *adjective*
[from *mono-* + -*gram*]

monograph *noun* (*plural* **monographs**)
a scholarly book or article on one
particular subject. [from *mono-* + *-graph*]

monolith *noun* (*plural* **monoliths**)
a large single upright block of stone.
[from *mono-* + Greek *lithos* = stone]

monolithic *adjective*
1 consisting of monoliths. 2 to do with or
like a monolith. 3 huge and difficult to
move or change.

monologue *noun* (*plural* **monologues**)
a speech by one person.
[from *mono-* + Greek *logos* = word]

monoplane *noun* (*plural* **monoplanes**)
a type of aeroplane with only one set of
wings.

monopolize *verb* (**monopolizes**,
monopolizing, **monopolized**)
take the whole of something for yourself,
One girl monopolized my attention.
monopolization *noun* [from *monopoly*]

monopoly *noun* (*plural* **monopolies**)
complete possession or control of
something by one group, *The company had
a monopoly in supplying electricity.*
[from *mono-* + Greek *polein* = sell]

monorail *noun* (*plural* **monorails**)
a railway that uses a single rail, not a pair
of rails.

monosyllable *noun* (*plural* **monosyllables**)
a word with only one syllable.
monosyllabic *adjective*

monotheism (*say* mon-oth-ee-izm) *noun*
the belief that there is only one god.
monotheist *noun*
[from *mono-* + Greek *theos* = god]

monotone *noun*
a level unchanging tone of voice in
speaking or singing.

monotonous *adjective*
boring because it does not change.
monotonously *adverb*, **monotony** *noun*
[from *mono-* + Greek *tonos* = tone]

monoxide *noun* (*plural* **monoxides**)
an oxide with one atom of oxygen.

monsoon *noun* (*plural* **monsoons**)
1 a strong wind in and near the Indian
Ocean, bringing heavy rain in summer.
2 the rainy season brought by this wind.
[via Dutch from Arabic *mawsim* = a
season]

monster *noun* (*plural* **monsters**)
1 a large frightening creature. 2 a huge
thing. 3 a wicked or cruel person.
monster *adjective*
huge. [from Latin *monstrum* = marvel]

monstrosity *noun* (*plural* **monstrosities**)
a monstrous thing.

monstrous *adjective*
1 like a monster; huge. 2 very shocking or
outrageous.

month *noun* (*plural* **months**)
each of the twelve parts into which a year
is divided. [from Old English; related to
moon (because time was measured by the
changes in the moon's appearance)]

monthly *adjective* & *adverb*
happening or done once a month.

monument *noun* (*plural* **monuments**)
a statue, building, or column etc. put up as
a memorial of some person or event.
[from Latin *monumentum* = a memorial]

monumental *adjective*
1 built as a monument. 2 very large or
important.

moo *verb* (**moos**, **mooing**, **mooed**)
make the low deep sound of a cow. **moo**
noun [imitating the sound]

mood *noun* (*plural* **moods**)
the way someone feels, *She is in a cheerful
mood.* [from Old English]

moody *adjective* (**moodier**, **moodiest**)
1 gloomy or sullen. 2 having sudden
changes of mood for no apparent reason.
moodily *adverb*, **moodiness** *noun*

moon *noun* (*plural* **moons**)
1 the natural satellite of the earth that can
be seen in the sky at night. 2 a satellite of
any planet. **moonbeam** *noun*, **moonlight**
noun, **moonlit** *adjective*

moon *verb* (**moons, mooning, mooned**)
go about in a dreamy or listless way.
[from Old English]

Moor *noun* (*plural* **Moors**)
a member of a Muslim people of north-west
Africa. **Moorish** *adjective* [from Greek]

moor[1] *noun* (*plural* **moors**)
an area of rough land covered with
heather, bracken, and bushes. **moorland**
noun [from Old English]

moor[2] *verb* (**moors, mooring, moored**)
fasten a boat etc. to a fixed object by means
of a cable. [probably from old German]

moorhen *noun* (*plural* **moorhens**)
a small waterbird.
[from an old sense of *moor*[1] = fen]

mooring *noun* (*plural* **moorings**)
a place where a boat can be moored.

moose *noun* (*plural* **moose**)
a North American elk. [from Abnaki, a
Native American language]

moot *adjective*
a moot point a question that is undecided
or debatable.
[from Old English *mot* = a meeting]

mop *noun* (*plural* **mops**)
1 a bunch or pad of soft material fastened
on the end of a stick, used for cleaning
floors etc. **2** a thick mass of hair.
mop *verb* (**mops, mopping, mopped**)
clean or wipe with a mop etc.
mop up 1 wipe or soak up liquid. **2** deal
with the last parts of something, *The army
is mopping up the last of the rebels.*
[origin unknown]

mope *verb* (**mopes, moping, moped**)
be sad.
[probably from a Scandinavian language]

moped (*say* moh-ped) *noun* (*plural*
mopeds)
a kind of small motorcycle that can be
pedalled. [from *motor* + *ped*al]

moraine *noun* (*plural* **moraines**)
a mass of stones and earth etc. carried
down by a glacier. [from French]

moral *adjective*
1 connected with what is right and wrong
in behaviour. **2** virtuous.
morally *adverb*, **morality** *noun*
moral support encouragement.
moral *noun* (*plural* **morals**)
a lesson in right behaviour taught by a
story or event.
[from Latin *mores* = customs]

USAGE: Do not confuse with *morale*.

morale (*say* mor-ahl) *noun*
the level of confidence and good spirits in a
person or group of people, *Morale was high
after the victory.* [same origin as *moral*]

USAGE: Do not confuse with *moral*.

moralize *verb* (**moralizes, moralizing,
moralized**)
talk or write about right and wrong
behaviour. **moralist** *noun*

morals *plural noun*
standards of behaviour.

morass (*say* mo-rass) *noun* (*plural*
morasses)
1 a marsh or bog. **2** a confused mass.
[via Dutch from French *marais* = marsh]

moratorium *noun* (*plural* **moratoriums**)
a temporary ban.
[from Latin *morari* = to delay]

morbid *adjective*
1 thinking about gloomy or unpleasant
things. **2** unhealthy.
morbidly *adverb*, **morbidity** *noun*
[from Latin *morbus* = disease]

more *adjective* (comparative of **much** and
many)
greater in amount etc.
more *noun*
a greater amount.
more *adverb*
1 to a greater extent, *more beautiful.*
2 again, *once more.*
more or less 1 approximately. **2** nearly or
practically.
[from Old English]

moreover *adverb*
besides; in addition to what has been said.

Mormon *noun* (*plural* **Mormons**)
a member of a religious group founded in the USA. [the name of a prophet who they believe wrote their sacred book]

morn *noun* (*poetic*)
morning. [from Old English]

morning *noun* (*plural* **mornings**)
the early part of the day, before noon or before lunchtime. [from *morn*]

morocco *noun*
a kind of leather originally made in Morocco from goatskins.

moron *noun* (*plural* **morons**) (*informal*)
a very stupid person. **moronic** *adjective*
[from Greek *moros* = foolish]

morose (*say* mo-rohss) *adjective*
bad-tempered and miserable. **morosely** *adverb*, **moroseness** *noun* [from Latin]

morphia or **morphine** (*say* mor-feen) *noun*
a drug made from opium, used to lessen pain. [named after Morpheus, the Roman god of dreams]

morris dance *noun* (*plural* **morris dances**)
a traditional English dance performed in costume by men with ribbons and bells. [originally *Moorish dance* (because it was thought to have come from the Moors)]

morrow *noun* (*poetic*)
the following day. [same origin as *morn*]

Morse code
a signalling code using short and long sounds or flashes of light (dots and dashes) to represent letters. [named after its American inventor, S. F. B. Morse]

morsel *noun* (*plural* **morsels**)
a small piece of food. [from old French]

mortal *adjective*
1 not living for ever, *All of us are mortal.*
2 causing death; fatal, *a mortal wound.*
3 deadly, *mortal enemies.*
mortally *adverb*, **mortality** *noun*
mortal *noun* (*plural* **mortals**)
a human being, as compared to a god or immortal spirit.
[from Latin *mortis* = of death]

mortar *noun* (*plural* **mortars**)
1 a mixture of sand, cement, and water used in building to stick bricks together.
2 a hard bowl in which substances are pounded with a pestle. 3 a short cannon. [from old French]

mortarboard *noun* (*plural* **mortarboards**)
an academic cap with a stiff square top. [because it looks like the board used by workmen to hold mortar]

mortgage (*say* mor-gij) *noun* (*plural* **mortgages**)
an arrangement to borrow money to buy a house, with the house as security for the loan.
mortgage *verb* (**mortgages, mortgaging, mortgaged**)
offer a house etc. as security in return for a loan. [from old French]

mortify *verb* (**mortifies, mortifying, mortified**)
humiliate someone or make them feel very ashamed. **mortification** *noun*
[originally = kill or destroy: from Latin *mors* = death]

mortise *noun* (*plural* **mortises**)
a hole made in a piece of wood for another piece to be joined to it. (Compare *tenon*.) [from old French]

mortise lock *noun* (*plural* **mortise locks**)
a lock set into a door.

mortuary *noun* (*plural* **mortuaries**)
a place where dead bodies are kept before being buried. [from Latin *mortuus* = dead]

mosaic (*say* mo-zay-ik) *noun* (*plural* **mosaics**)
a picture or design made from small coloured pieces of stone or glass. [via old French from Italian]

mosque (*say* mosk) *noun* (*plural* **mosques**)
a building where Muslims worship. [via French and Italian from Arabic]

mosquito *noun* (*plural* **mosquitoes**)
a kind of gnat that sucks blood. [Spanish or Portuguese, = little fly]

moss *noun* (*plural* mosses)
a plant that grows in damp places and has no flowers. **mossy** *adjective*
[from Old English]

most *adjective* (superlative of **much** and **many**)
greatest in amount etc., *Most people came by bus.*
most *noun*
the greatest amount, *Most of the food was eaten.*
most *adverb*
1 to the greatest extent; more than any other, *most beautiful.* **2** very or extremely, *most impressive.* [from Old English]

-most *suffix*
forms superlative adjectives (e.g. *hindmost, uppermost*). [from Old English *-mest*]

mostly *adverb*
mainly.

motel *noun* (*plural* motels)
a hotel providing accommodation for motorists and their cars.
[from *motor* + ho*tel*]

moth *noun* (*plural* moths)
an insect rather like a butterfly, that usually flies at night. [from Old English]

mother *noun* (*plural* mothers)
a female parent. **motherhood** *noun*
mother *verb* (mothers, mothering, mothered)
look after someone in a motherly way.
[from Old English]

Mothering Sunday *noun*
Mother's Day.

mother-in-law *noun* (*plural* mothers-in-law)
the mother of a married person's husband or wife.

motherly *adjective*
kind and gentle like a mother.
motherliness *noun*

mother-of-pearl *noun*
a pearly substance lining the shells of mussels etc.

Mother's Day *noun*
the fourth Sunday in Lent, when many people give cards or presents to their mothers.

motif (*say* moh-teef) *noun* (*plural* motifs)
a repeated design or theme. [French]

motion *noun* (*plural* motions)
1 a way of moving; movement. **2** a formal statement to be discussed and voted on at a meeting.
motion *verb* (motions, motioning, motioned)
signal by a gesture, *She motioned him to sit beside her.* [from Latin *motio* = movement]

motionless *adjective*
not moving.

motivate *verb* (motivates, motivating, motivated)
give a person a motive or incentive to do something. **motivation** *noun*

motive *noun* (*plural* motives)
what makes a person do something, *a motive for murder.*
motive *adjective*
producing movement, *The engine provides motive power.*
[from Latin *motivus* = moving]

motley *adjective*
1 multicoloured. **2** made up of various sorts of things. [origin unknown]

motor *noun* (*plural* motors)
a machine providing power to drive machinery etc.; an engine.
motor *verb* (motors, motoring, motored)
go or take someone in a car.
[Latin, = mover]

motorcade *noun* (*plural* motorcades)
a procession of cars.
[from *motor* + cavalcade]

motorist *noun* (*plural* motorists)
a person who drives a car.

motorized *adjective*
equipped with a motor or with motor vehicles.

motor neurone disease *noun*
a disease of the nerves that control

movement, so that the muscles get weaker and weaker until the person dies.

motorway noun (plural motorways)
a wide road for fast long-distance traffic.

mottled adjective
marked with spots or patches of colour.
[probably from motley]

motto noun (plural mottoes)
1 a short saying used as a guide for behaviour, Their motto is 'Who dares, wins'. 2 a short verse or riddle etc. found inside a cracker. [Italian]

mould[1] noun (plural moulds)
a hollow container of a particular shape, in which a liquid or soft substance is put to set into this shape.
mould verb (moulds, moulding, moulded)
make something have a particular shape or character.
[from Latin modulus = little measure]

mould[2] noun
a fine furry growth of very small fungi.
mouldy adjective
[from Old Norse]

moulder verb (moulders, mouldering, mouldered)
rot away or decay into dust.
[origin unknown]

moult verb (moults, moulting, moulted)
shed feathers, hair, or skin etc. while a new growth forms. [from Latin mutari = to change, probably via Old English]

mound noun (plural mounds)
1 a pile of earth or stones etc. 2 a small hill.
[origin unknown]

mount verb (mounts, mounting, mounted)
1 climb or go up; ascend. 2 get on a horse or bicycle etc. 3 increase in amount, Our costs mounted. 4 place or fix in position for use or display, Mount your photos in an album.
mount noun (plural mounts)
1 a mountain, Mount Everest. 2 something on which an object is mounted. 3 a horse etc. for riding.
[from Latin mons = mountain]

mountain noun (plural mountains)
1 a very high hill. 2 a large heap or pile or quantity. **mountainous** adjective
[from old French; related to mount]

mountaineer noun (plural mountaineers)
a person who climbs mountains.
mountaineering noun

mounted adjective
serving on horseback, mounted police.

mourn verb (mourns, mourning, mourned)
be sad, especially because someone has died. **mourner** noun [from Old English]

mournful adjective
sad and sorrowful. **mournfully** adverb

mouse noun (plural mice)
1 a small animal with a long thin tail and a pointed nose. 2 (plural mouses or mice) a small device which you move around on a mat to control a computer. **mousetrap** noun, **mousy** adjective [from Old English]

moussaka noun
a dish of minced meat, aubergine, etc., with a cheese sauce. [from Arabic]

mousse (say mooss) noun (plural mousses)
1 a creamy pudding flavoured with fruit or chocolate. 2 a frothy creamy substance put on the hair so that it can be styled more easily. [French, = froth]

moustache (say mus-tahsh) noun (plural moustaches)
hair allowed to grow on a man's upper lip.
[via French from Italian]

mouth noun (plural mouths)
1 the opening through which food is taken into the body. 2 the place where a river enters the sea. 3 an opening or outlet. **mouthful** noun
mouth verb (mouths, mouthing, mouthed)
form words carefully with your lips, especially without saying them aloud.
[from Old English]

mouth organ noun (plural mouth organs)
a small musical instrument that you play by blowing and sucking while passing it along your lips.

mouthpiece *noun* (*plural* mouthpieces)
the part of a musical or other instrument
that you put to your mouth.

movable *adjective*
able to be moved.

move *verb* (moves, moving, moved)
1 take or go from one place to another;
change a person's or thing's position.
2 affect a person's feelings, *Their sad story
moved us deeply.* 3 put forward a formal
statement (a *motion*) to be discussed and
voted on at a meeting.
mover *noun*

move *noun* (*plural* moves)
1 a movement. 2 a player's turn to move a
piece in chess etc.
get a move on (*informal*) hurry up.
on the move moving or making progress.
[from Latin]

movement *noun* (*plural* movements)
1 moving or being moved. 2 a group of
people working together to achieve
something. 3 one of the main divisions of a
symphony or other long musical work.

movie *noun* (*plural* movies) (*American
informal*)
a cinema film. [short for *moving picture*]

mow *verb* (mows, mowing, mowed, mown)
cut down grass etc.
mower *noun*
mow down knock down and kill.
[from Old English]

mozzarella *noun*
a kind of Italian cheese used in cooking,
originally made from buffalo's milk.

MP *abbreviation*
Member of Parliament.

Mr (*say* mist-er) *noun* (*plural* Messrs)
a title put before a man's name
[short for *mister*]

Mrs (*say* mis-iz) *noun* (*plural* Mrs)
a title put before a married woman's name.
[short for *mistress*]

MS *abbreviation*
multiple sclerosis.

Ms (*say* miz) *noun*
a title put before a woman's name.
[from *Mrs* and *Miss*]

USAGE: You put *Ms* before the name of a
woman if she does not wish to be called
'Miss' or 'Mrs', or if you do not know
whether she is married.

M.Sc. *abbreviation*
Master of Science.

Mt *abbreviation*
mount or mountain.

much *adjective* (more, most)
existing in a large amount, *much noise.*
much *noun*
a large amount of something.
much *adverb*
1 greatly or considerably, *much to my
surprise.* 2 approximately, *It is much the
same.* [from Old English]

muck *noun*
1 farmyard manure. 2 (*informal*) dirt or
filth. 3 (*informal*) a mess. **mucky** *adjective*
muck *verb*
muck about (*informal*) mess about.
muck out clean out the place where an
animal is kept.
muck up (*informal*) 1 make dirty. 2 make a
mess of; spoil.
[probably from a Scandinavian language]

mucous (*say* mew-kus) *adjective*
1 like mucus. 2 covered with mucus, *a
mucous membrane.*

mucus (*say* mew-kus) *noun*
the moist sticky substance on the inner
surface of the throat etc. [Latin]

mud *noun*
wet soft earth. **muddy** *adjective*, **muddiness**
noun [probably from old German]

muddle *verb* (muddles, muddling, muddled)
1 jumble or mix things up. 2 confuse.
muddler *noun*
muddle *noun* (*plural* muddles)
a muddled condition or thing; confusion or
disorder. [origin unknown]

mudguard *noun* (*plural* mudguards)
a curved cover over the top part of the

wheel of a bicycle etc. to protect the rider from the mud and water thrown up by the wheel.

muesli (*say* mooz-lee) *noun*
a breakfast food made of mixed cereals, dried fruit, nuts, etc. [Swiss German]

muezzin (*say* moo-ez-een) *noun* (*plural* **muezzins**)
a Muslim crier who calls the hours of prayer from a minaret. [from Arabic *mu'addin* = calling to prayer]

muff¹ *noun* (*plural* **muffs**)
a short tube-shaped piece of warm material into which the hands are pushed from opposite ends. [from Dutch]

muff² *verb* (**muffs, muffing, muffed**)
(*informal*)
bungle. [origin unknown]

muffin *noun* (*plural* **muffins**)
1 a flat bun eaten toasted and buttered. 2 a small sponge cake, usually containing fruit, chocolate chips, etc.
[origin unknown]

muffle *verb* (**muffles, muffling, muffled**)
1 cover or wrap something to protect it or keep it warm. 2 deaden the sound of something, *a muffled scream*.
[probably from old French]

muffler *noun* (*plural* **mufflers**)
a warm scarf. [from *muffle*]

mufti *noun*
ordinary clothes worn by someone who usually wears a uniform.
[probably from Arabic]

mug *noun* (*plural* **mugs**)
1 a kind of large cup, usually used without a saucer. 2 (*slang*) a fool; a person who is easily deceived. 3 (*slang*) a person's face.
mug *verb* (**mugs, mugging, mugged**)
attack and rob somebody in the street.
mugger *noun*
[probably from a Scandinavian language]

muggy *adjective* (**muggier, muggiest**)
(of the weather) unpleasantly warm and damp. **mugginess** *noun*
[probably from a Scandinavian language]

mulberry *noun* (*plural* **mulberries**)
a purple or white fruit rather like a blackberry. [from Old English]

mule *noun* (*plural* **mules**)
an animal that is the offspring of a donkey and a mare, known for being stubborn.
mulish *adjective* [from Old English]

mull¹ *verb* (**mulls, mulling, mulled**)
heat wine or beer with sugar and spices, as a drink, *mulled ale*. [origin unknown]

mull² *verb* (**mulls, mulling, mulled**)
mull something over think about something carefully; ponder.
[probably related to *mill*]

mullet *noun* (*plural* **mullet**)
a kind of fish used as food. [from Greek]

multi- *prefix*
many (as in *multicoloured* = with many colours). [from Latin *multus* = many]

multicultural *adjective*
made up of people of many different races, religions, and cultures.

multifarious (*say* multi-fair-ee-us) *adjective*
of many kinds; very varied. [from Latin]

multilateral *adjective*
(of an agreement or treaty) made between three or more people or countries etc.
[from Latin *multilaterus* = many sided]

multimedia *adjective*
using more than one medium, *a multimedia show with pictures, lights, and music*.
multimedia *noun*
a computer program with sound and still and moving pictures linked to the text.

multimillionaire *noun* (*plural* **multimillionaires**)
a person with a fortune of several million pounds.

multinational *noun* (*plural* **multinationals**)
a large business company which works in several countries.

multiple *adjective*
having many parts.

multiple *noun* (*plural* multiples)
a number that contains another number (a *factor*) an exact amount of times with no remainder, *8 and 12 are multiples of 4.* [same origin as *multiply*]

multiple sclerosis *noun*
a disease of the nervous system which makes a person unable to control their movements, and may affect their sight.

multiplex *noun* (*plural* multiplexes)
a large cinema complex that has many screens. [from *multi-* + Latin *-plex* = -fold]

multiplicity *noun*
a great variety or large number.

multiply *verb* (multiplies, multiplying, multiplied)
1 take a number a given quantity of times, *Five multiplied by four equals twenty* (5 × 4 = 20). 2 make or become many; increase. **multiplication** *noun*, **multiplier** *noun* [from Latin *multiplex* = many-sided]

multiracial *adjective*
consisting of people of many different races.

multitude *noun* (*plural* multitudes)
a great number of people or things. **multitudinous** *adjective* [from Latin *multus* = many]

mum[1] *noun* (*plural* mums) (*informal*)
mother. [short for *mummy*[1]]

mum[2] *adjective* (*informal*)
silent, *keep mum.* [imitating a sound made with closed lips]

mumble *verb* (mumbles, mumbling, mumbled)
speak indistinctly so that you are not easy to hear. **mumble** *noun*, **mumbler** *noun* [from *mum*[2]]

mumbo-jumbo *noun*
talk or ceremony that has no real meaning. [probably from a West African language]

mummy[1] *noun* (*plural* mummies) (*informal*)
mother. [from *mama*]

mummy[2] *noun* (*plural* mummies)
a corpse wrapped in cloth and treated with oils etc. before being buried so that it does not decay, as was the custom in ancient Egypt. **mummify** *verb* [from Arabic]

mumps *noun*
an infectious disease that causes the neck to swell painfully. [from an old word *mump* = pull a face (because the glands in the face sometimes swell)]

munch *verb* (munches, munching, munched)
chew vigorously. [imitating the sound]

mundane *adjective*
1 ordinary, not exciting. 2 concerned with practical matters, not ideals. [from Latin *mundus* = world]

municipal (*say* mew-**nis**-ip-al) *adjective*
to do with a town or city. [from Latin *municipium* = a town whose citizens had the same privileges as Roman citizens]

municipality *noun* (*plural* municipalities)
a town or city that has its own local government.

munificent *adjective*
extremely generous. **munificently** *adverb*, **munificence** *noun* [from Latin *munus* = gift]

munitions *plural noun*
military weapons and ammunition etc. [from Latin *munitum* = fortified]

muntjac *noun* (*plural* muntjacs)
a kind of small deer, originally from southern Asia but now also found in western Europe. [from Sundanese (a language spoken in Indonesia)]

mural *adjective*
on or to do with a wall.
mural *noun* (*plural* murals)
a wall painting. [from Latin *murus* = wall]

murder *verb* (murders, murdering, murdered)
kill a person unlawfully and deliberately. **murderer** *noun*, **murderess** *noun*
murder *noun* (*plural* murders)
the murdering of somebody. **murderous** *adjective* [from Old English]

murky *adjective* (murkier, murkiest)
dark and gloomy. **murk** *noun*, **murkiness** *noun* [from Old English]

murmur *verb* (**murmurs, murmuring, murmured**)
1 make a low continuous sound. 2 speak in a soft voice. **murmur** *noun* [from Latin]

muscle *noun* (*plural* **muscles**)
1 a band or bundle of fibrous tissue that can contract and relax and so produce movement in parts of the body. 2 the power of muscles; strength. **muscular** *adjective*, **muscularity** *noun* [from Latin]

muse *verb* (**muses, musing, mused**)
think deeply about something; ponder or meditate. [from old French]

museum *noun* (*plural* **museums**)
a place where interesting, old, or valuable objects are displayed for people to see. [from Greek *mouseion* = place of Muses (goddesses of the arts and sciences)]

mush *noun*
soft pulp. **mushy** *adjective*
[different spelling of *mash*]

mushroom *noun* (*plural* **mushrooms**)
an edible fungus with a stem and a dome-shaped top.
mushroom *verb* (**mushrooms, mushrooming, mushroomed**)
grow or appear suddenly in large numbers, *Blocks of flats mushroomed in the city.* [from old French]

music *noun*
1 a pattern of pleasant or interesting sounds made by instruments or by the voice. 2 printed or written symbols which stand for musical sounds. [from Greek *mousike* = of the Muses (see *museum*)]

musical *adjective*
1 to do with music. 2 producing music. 3 good at music or interested in it. **musically** *adverb*
musical *noun* (*plural* **musicals**)
a play or film containing a lot of songs.

musician *noun* (*plural* **musicians**)
someone who plays a musical instrument.

musk *noun*
a strong-smelling substance used in perfumes. **musky** *adjective* [from Persian]

musket *noun* (*plural* **muskets**)
a kind of gun with a long barrel, formerly used by soldiers. [via French from Italian]

musketeer *noun* (*plural* **musketeers**)
a soldier armed with a musket.

Muslim *noun* (*plural* **Muslims**)
a person who follows the religious teachings of Muhammad (who lived in about 570–632), set out in the Koran. [Arabic, = someone who submits to God]

muslin *noun*
very thin cotton cloth. [named after Mosul, a city in Iraq, where it was first made]

mussel *noun* (*plural* **mussels**)
a black shellfish. [from Old English]

must *auxiliary verb*
used to express 1 necessity or obligation (*You must go*), 2 certainty (*You must be joking!*) [from Old English]

mustang *noun* (*plural* **mustangs**)
a wild horse of the United States of America and Mexico. [from Spanish]

mustard *noun*
a yellow paste or powder used to give food a hot taste.
mustard and cress small green plants eaten in salads.
[from old French]

muster *verb* (**musters, mustering, mustered**)
assemble or gather together.
muster *noun* (*plural* **musters**)
an assembly of people or things.
pass muster be up to the required standard. [from Latin *monstrare* = to show]

mustn't (*mainly spoken*)
must not.

musty *adjective* (**mustier, mustiest**)
smelling or tasting mouldy or stale. **mustiness** *noun* [probably from *moist*]

mutable (*say* mew-ta-bul) *adjective*
able or likely to change. **mutability** *noun* [from Latin *mutare* = to change]

mutation *noun* (*plural* **mutations**)
a change in the form of a living creature because of changes in its genes. [same origin as *mutable*]

mute *adjective*
1 silent; not speaking or able to speak.
2 not pronounced, *The g in 'gnat' is mute.*
mutely *adverb*, **muteness** *noun*
mute *noun* (*plural* **mutes**)
a person who cannot speak.
mute *verb* (**mutes, muting, muted**)
make a thing quieter or less intense.
[from Latin]

mutilate *verb* (**mutilates, mutilating, mutilated**)
damage something by breaking or cutting off part of it. **mutilation** *noun*
[from Latin *mutilus* = maimed]

mutineer *noun* (*plural* **mutineers**)
a person who mutinies.

mutiny *noun* (*plural* **mutinies**)
rebellion against authority, especially refusal by members of the armed forces to obey orders. **mutinous** *adjective*, **mutinously** *adverb*
mutiny *verb* (**mutinies, mutinying, mutinied**)
take part in a mutiny. [from old French]

mutter *verb* (**mutters, muttering, muttered**)
1 speak in a low voice. 2 grumble. **mutter** *noun* [related to *mute*]

mutton *noun*
meat from a sheep. [from old French]

mutual (*say* **mew**-tew-al) *adjective*
1 given or done to each other, *mutual destruction.* 2 felt by each for the other, *mutual affection.* **mutually** *adverb*
[from Latin]

muzzle *noun* (*plural* **muzzles**)
1 an animal's nose and mouth. 2 a cover put over an animal's nose and mouth so that it cannot bite. 3 the open end of a gun.
muzzle *verb* (**muzzles, muzzling, muzzled**)
1 put a muzzle on an animal. 2 silence; prevent a person from expressing opinions. [from old French]

my *adjective*
belonging to me. [originally, the form of *mine*[1] used before consonants]

myriad (*say* **mirri**-ad) *adjective*
innumerable. [from Greek *myrioi* = 10,000]

myriads *plural noun*
a very great number, *myriads of gnats.*

myrrh (*say* mer) *noun*
a substance used in perfumes and incense and medicine.
[from Old English]

myrtle *noun* (*plural* **myrtles**)
an evergreen shrub with dark leaves and white flowers.
[from Greek]

myself *pronoun*
I or me and nobody else. (Compare *herself.*)

mysterious *adjective*
full of mystery; puzzling.
mysteriously *adverb*

mystery *noun* (*plural* **mysteries**)
something that cannot be explained or understood; something puzzling.
[from Greek *mysterion* = a secret thing or ceremony]

mystic *adjective*
1 having a spiritual meaning.
2 mysterious and filling people with wonder. **mystical** *adjective*, **mystically** *adverb*, **mysticism** *noun*
mystic *noun* (*plural* **mystics**)
a person who seeks to obtain spiritual contact with God by deep religious meditation. [from Greek *mystikos* = secret]

mystify *verb* (**mystifies, mystifying, mystified**)
puzzle or bewilder. **mystification** *noun*
[from French]

mystique (*say* mis-**teek**) *noun*
an air of mystery or secret power. [French, = mystic]

myth (*say* mith) *noun* (*plural* **myths**)
1 an old story containing ideas about ancient times or about supernatural beings. (Compare *legend.*) 2 an untrue story or belief.
[from Greek *mythos* = story]

mythical *adjective*
imaginary; found only in myths, *a mythical animal.*

mythology *noun*
myths or the study of myths.
mythological *adjective*

myxomatosis (*say* miks-om-at-oh-sis)
noun
a disease that kills rabbits.
[from Greek *myxa* = mucus (because the mucous membranes swell up)]

Nn

N. *abbreviation*
1 north. 2 northern.

nab *verb* (nabs, nabbing, nabbed) (*slang*)
catch or arrest (a wrongdoer); seize.
[origin unknown]

nag[1] *verb* (nags, nagging, nagged)
1 pester a person by keeping on criticizing, complaining, or asking for things. 2 keep on hurting, *a nagging pain*.
[origin unknown]

nag[2] *noun* (*plural* nags) (*informal*)
a horse. [origin unknown]

nail *noun* (*plural* nails)
1 the hard covering over the end of a finger or toe. 2 a small sharp piece of metal hammered in to fasten pieces of wood etc. together.
nail *verb* (nails, nailing, nailed)
1 fasten with a nail or nails. 2 catch; arrest. [from Old English]

naive or **naïve** (*say* nah-eev) *adjective*
showing a lack of experience or good judgement; innocent and trusting.
naively *adverb*, **naivety** *noun*
[French; related to *native*]

naked *adjective*
without any clothes or coverings on.
nakedly *adverb*, **nakedness** *noun*
[from Old English]

naked eye *noun*
the eye when it is not helped by a telescope or microscope etc.

name *noun* (*plural* names)
1 the word or words by which a person, animal, place, or thing is known. 2 a reputation.

name *verb* (names, naming, named)
1 give a name to. 2 state the name or names of.
name the day decide when something, especially a wedding, is to take place or happen, *Have you two named the day yet?*
[from Old English]

nameless *adjective*
without a name.

namely *adverb*
that is to say, *My two favourite subjects are sciences, namely chemistry and biology.*

namesake *noun* (*plural* namesakes)
a person or thing with the same name as another.

nanny *noun* (*plural* nannies)
1 a nurse who looks after young children.
2 (*informal*) grandmother.
[pet form of *Ann*]

nanny goat *noun* (*plural* nanny goats)
a female goat. (Compare *billy goat*.)

nap[1] *noun* (*plural* naps)
a short sleep.
catch a person napping catch a person unprepared for something or not alert.
[from Old English]

nap[2] *noun*
short raised fibres on the surface of cloth or leather. [from old German or Dutch]

napalm (*say* nay-pahm) *noun*
a substance made of petrol, used in some incendiary bombs.
[from *naphtha* and *palmitic acid* (two chemicals from which it is made)]

napkin *noun* (*plural* napkins)
1 a piece of cloth or paper used to keep your clothes clean or to wipe your lips or fingers; a serviette, *a table napkin*. 2 a nappy.
[from French *nappe* = tablecloth, + -*kin*]

nappy *noun* (*plural* nappies)
a piece of cloth or other fabric put round a baby's bottom.

narcissistic *adjective*
extremely vain.
[from *Narcissus*, a youth in Greek legend
who fell in love with his own reflection and
was turned into a flower]

narcissus *noun* (*plural* narcissi)
a garden flower like a daffodil.
[same origin as *narcissistic*]

narcotic *noun* (*plural* narcotics)
a drug that makes a person sleepy or
unconscious. **narcotic** *adjective*, **narcosis**
noun [from Greek *narke* = numbness]

narrate *verb* (narrates, narrating, narrated)
tell a story or give an account of
something. **narration** *noun*, **narrator** *noun*
[from Latin]

narrative *noun* (*plural* narratives)
a spoken or written account of something.

narrow *adjective*
1 not wide or broad. 2 uncomfortably
close; with only a small margin of safety, *a
narrow escape*. **narrowly** *adverb*
narrow *verb* (narrows, narrowing,
narrowed)
make or become narrower.
[from Old English]

narrow-minded *adjective*
not tolerant of other people's beliefs and
ways.

nasal *adjective*
1 of the nose. 2 sounding as if the breath
comes out through the nose, *a nasal voice*.
nasally *adverb* [from Latin *nasus* = nose]

nasturtium (*say* na-ster-shum) *noun*
(*plural* nasturtiums)
a garden plant with round leaves and red,
yellow, or orange flowers.
[from Latin *nasus* = nose + *torquere* = to
twist (because of its sharp smell)]

nasty *adjective* (nastier, nastiest)
1 unpleasant. 2 unkind. **nastily** *adverb*,
nastiness *noun* [origin unknown]

natal (*say* nay-tal) *adjective*
1 to do with birth. 2 from or since birth.
[from Latin *natus* = born]

nation *noun* (*plural* nations)
a large community of people most of whom
have the same ancestors, language,
history, and customs, and who usually live
in the same part of the world under one
government.
national *adjective* & *noun*, **nationally** *adverb*
[from Latin *natio* = birth or race]

national anthem *noun* (*plural* national
anthems)
a nation's official song, which is played or
sung on important occasions.

national curriculum *noun*
the subjects that must be taught by state
schools in England and Wales.

nationalist *noun* (*plural* nationalists)
1 a person who is very patriotic. 2 a person
who wants his or her country to be
independent and not to form part of
another country, *Scottish Nationalists*.
nationalism *noun*, **nationalistic** *adjective*

nationality *noun* (*plural* nationalities)
the condition of belonging to a particular
nation, *What is his nationality?*

nationalize *verb* (nationalizes,
nationalizing, nationalized)
put an industry etc. under public
ownership. **nationalization** *noun*

national park *noun* (*plural* national parks)
an area of natural beauty which is
protected by the government and which
the public may visit.

native *noun* (*plural* natives)
a person born in a particular place, *He is a
native of Sweden*.
native *adjective*
1 belonging to a person because of the
place of his or her birth, *my native country*.
2 natural; belonging to a person by nature,
native ability.
[from Latin *nativus* = natural or innate]

Native American *noun* (*plural* Native
Americans)
one of the original inhabitants of North
and South America.

USAGE: See note at **Indian**.

nativity *noun* (*plural* **nativities**)
a person's birth.
the Nativity the birth of Jesus Christ.

natty *adjective* (**nattier, nattiest**)
neat and trim; dapper. **nattily** *adverb*
[probably from *neat*]

natural *adjective*
1 produced or done by nature, not by
people or machines. 2 normal; not
surprising. 3 (of a note in music) neither
sharp nor flat.
naturally *adverb*, **naturalness** *noun*

natural *noun* (*plural* **naturals**)
1 a person who is naturally good at
something. 2 a natural note in music; a
sign (♮) that shows this.

natural gas *noun*
gas found underground or under the sea,
not made from coal.

natural history *noun*
the study of plants and animals.

naturalist *noun* (*plural* **naturalists**)
an expert in natural history.

naturalize *verb* (**naturalizes, naturalizing,
naturalized**)
1 give a person full rights as a citizen of a
country although they were not born there.
2 cause a plant or animal to grow or live
naturally in a country that is not its own.
naturalization *noun*

natural science *noun*
the study of physics, chemistry, and
biology.

natural selection *noun*
Charles Darwin's theory that only the
plants and animals best suited to their
surroundings will survive and breed.

nature *noun* (*plural* **natures**)
1 everything in the world that was not
made by people. 2 the qualities and
characteristics of a person or thing, *She
has a loving nature.* 3 a kind or sort of
thing, *He likes things of that nature.*
[from Latin]

nature reserve *noun* (*plural* **nature
reserves**)
an area of land which is managed so as to
preserve the wild animals and plants that
live there.

nature trail *noun* (*plural* **nature trails**)
a path in a country area with signs telling
you about the plants and animals that live
there.

naturist *noun* (*plural* **naturists**)
a person who believes that going naked is
enjoyable and good for the health.
naturism *noun*

naught *noun* (*old use*)
nothing. [from Old English]

naughty *adjective* (**naughtier, naughtiest**)
1 badly behaved or disobedient. 2 slightly
rude or indecent, *naughty pictures.*
naughtily *adverb*, **naughtiness** *noun*
[originally = poor: from *naught*]

nausea (*say* naw-zee-a) *noun*
a feeling of sickness or disgust.
nauseous *adjective*, **nauseating** *adjective*
[from Greek *nausia* = seasickness]

nautical *adjective*
of ships or sailors.
[from Greek *nautes* = sailor]

nautical mile *noun* (*plural* **nautical miles**)
a measure of distance used at sea, 2025
yards (1.852 kilometres).

naval *adjective*
to do with a navy. [from Latin *navis* = ship]

nave *noun* (*plural* **naves**)
the main central part of a church (the other
parts are the chancel, aisles, and
transepts). [from Latin]

navel *noun* (*plural* **navels**)
the small hollow in the centre of the
abdomen, where the umbilical cord was
attached. [from Old English]

navigable *adjective*
1 suitable for ships to sail in, *a navigable
river.* 2 able to be steered. **navigability** *noun*

navigate *verb* (**navigates, navigating,
navigated**)
1 sail in or through a river or sea etc., *The*

ship navigated the Suez Canal. 2 make sure that a ship, aircraft, or vehicle is going in the right direction.
navigation *noun*, **navigator** *noun*
[from Latin *navis* = ship + *agere* = to drive]

navvy *noun* (*plural* navvies)
a labourer digging a road, railway, canal, etc. [short for 'navigator', = person who constructs a 'navigation' (= canal)]

navy *noun* (*plural* navies)
1 a country's warships and the people trained to use them. 2 (also **navy blue**) very dark blue, the colour of naval uniform. [from old French *navie* = a ship or fleet; related to *naval*]

nay *adverb* (*old use*)
no. [from Old Norse]

Nazi (*say* nah-tsee) *noun* (*plural* Nazis)
a member of the National Socialist Party in Germany in Hitler's time, with Fascist beliefs. **Nazism** *noun* [from the German pronunciation of *Nationalsozialist*]

NB *abbreviation*
take note that (Latin *nota bene* = note well).

NCO *abbreviation*
non-commissioned officer.

NE *abbreviation*
1 north-east. 2 north-eastern.

Neanderthal (*say* nee-an-der-tahl) *noun*
an early type of human who lived in Europe during the Stone Age. [named after Neanderthal, an area in Germany where fossil remains have been found]

near *adverb* & *adjective*
not far away.
near by not far away, *They live near by.*
near *preposition*
not far away from, *near the shops.*
near *verb* (nears, nearing, neared)
come near to, *The ship neared the harbour.*
[from Old Norse]

nearby *adjective*
near, *a nearby house.*

nearly *adverb*
1 almost, *We have nearly finished.* 2 closely, *They are nearly related.*

neat *adjective* (neater, neatest)
1 simple and clean and tidy. 2 skilful. 3 undiluted, *neat whisky.*
neatly *adverb*, **neatness** *noun*
[from Latin *nitidus* = clean, shining]

neaten *verb* (neatens, neatening, neatened)
make or become neat.

nebula *noun* (*plural* nebulae)
a bright or dark patch in the sky, caused by a distant galaxy or a cloud of dust or gas. [Latin, = mist]

nebulous *adjective*
indistinct or vague, *nebulous ideas.*
[same origin as *nebula*]

necessary *adjective*
not able to be done without; essential.
necessarily *adverb* [from Latin]

necessitate *verb* (necessitates, necessitating, necessitated)
make a thing necessary.

necessitous *adjective*
needy.

necessity *noun* (*plural* necessities)
1 need, *the necessity of buying food and clothing.* 2 something necessary.

neck *noun* (*plural* necks)
1 the part of the body that joins the head to the shoulders. 2 the part of a garment round the neck. 3 a narrow part of something, especially of a bottle. [from Old English]

necklace *noun* (*plural* necklaces)
an ornament worn round the neck.

necklet *noun* (*plural* necklets)
1 a necklace. 2 a small fur worn round the neck.

necktie *noun* (*plural* neckties)
a strip of material worn passing under the collar of a shirt and knotted in front.

nectar *noun*
1 a sweet liquid collected by bees from flowers. 2 a delicious drink. [from Greek]

nectarine *noun* (*plural* nectarines)
a kind of peach with a thin, smooth skin.

nectary *noun* (*plural* **nectaries**)
the nectar-producing part of a plant.

née (*say* nay) *adjective*
born (used in giving a married woman's
maiden name), *Mrs Smith, née Jones.*
[French]

need *verb* (**needs, needing, needed**)
1 be without something you should have;
require, *We need two more chairs.* 2 (as an
auxiliary verb) have to do something, *You
need not answer.*
need *noun* (*plural* **needs**)
1 something needed; a necessary thing. 2 a
situation where something is necessary,
There is no need to cry. 3 great poverty or
hardship. **needful** *adjective*, **needless**
adjective [from Old English]

needle *noun* (*plural* **needles**)
1 a very thin pointed piece of steel used in
sewing. 2 something long and thin and
sharp, *a knitting needle, pine needles.* 3 the
pointer of a meter or compass.
[from Old English]

needlework *noun*
sewing or embroidery.

needy *adjective* (**needier, neediest**)
very poor; lacking things necessary for life.
neediness *noun*

ne'er *adverb* (*poetic*)
never.

nefarious (*say* nif-air-ee-us) *adjective*
wicked. [from Latin *nefas* = wickedness]

negate *verb* (**negates, negating, negated**)
1 make a thing ineffective. 2 disprove or
deny. **negation** *noun*
[from Latin *negare* = deny]

negative *adjective*
1 that says 'no', *a negative answer.* 2 not
definite or positive. 3 less than nought;
minus. 4 to do with the kind of electric
charge carried by electrons.
negatively *adverb*

USAGE: The opposite of sense 1 is
affirmative, and of senses 2, 3, 4 *positive.*

---

negative *noun* (*plural* **negatives**)
1 a negative statement. 2 a photograph on
film with the dark parts light and the light
parts dark, from which a positive print
(with the dark and light or colours correct)
can be made. [same origin as *negate*]

neglect *verb* (**neglects, neglecting,
neglected**)
1 not look after or attend to a person or
thing. 2 not do something; forget, *He
neglected to shut the door.*
neglect *noun*
neglecting or being neglected.
neglectful *adjective*
[from Latin *nec* = not + *legere* = choose]

negligence *noun*
lack of proper care or attention;
carelessness. **negligent** *adjective*,
negligently *adverb* [same origin as *neglect*]

negligible *adjective*
not big enough or important enough to be
worth bothering about.
[from French *négliger* = neglect]

negotiable *adjective*
1 able to be changed after being discussed,
The salary is negotiable. 2 (of a cheque)
able to be changed for cash or transferred
to another person. [from *negotiate*]

negotiate *verb* (**negotiates, negotiating,
negotiated**)
1 bargain or discuss with others in order to
reach an agreement. 2 arrange after
discussion, *They negotiated a treaty.* 3 get
over an obstacle or difficulty.
negotiation *noun*, **negotiator** *noun*
[from Latin *negotium* = business]

Negro *noun* (*plural* **Negroes**)
a member of the black-skinned race of
people originally from Africa.
[from Latin *niger* = black]

USAGE: This word is usually considered to
be offensive. *Black* is the term that is
generally preferred.

---

neigh *verb* (**neighs, neighing, neighed**)
make the high-pitched cry of a horse.
neigh *noun*
[from Old English; imitating the sound]

neighbour *noun* (*plural* **neighbours**)
a person who lives next door or near to

another. **neighbouring** *adjective*, **neighbourly** *adjective* [from Old English *neahgebur* = near dweller]

neighbourhood *noun* (*plural* **neighbourhoods**)
1 the surrounding district or area. 2 a part of a town where people live, *a quiet neighbourhood*.

neither (*say* ny-*th*er or nee-*th*er) *adjective* & *pronoun*
not either.

USAGE: Correct use is *Neither of them likes it. Neither he nor his children like it.* Use a singular verb (e.g. *likes*) unless one of its subjects is plural (e.g. *children*).

neither *adverb* & *conjunction*
neither ... nor not one thing and not the other, *She neither knew nor cared.* [from Old English]

USAGE: Say *I don't know that either* (not 'neither').

nemesis (*say* nem-i-sis) *noun*
retribution; justifiable punishment that comes upon somebody who hoped to escape it. [named after Nemesis, goddess of retribution in Greek mythology]

neo- *prefix*
new. [from Greek]

neolithic (*say* nee-o-lith-ik) *adjective*
belonging to the later part of the Stone Age. [from *neo-* + Greek *lithos* = stone]

neon *noun*
a gas that glows when electricity passes through it, used in glass tubes to make illuminated signs. [from Greek *neos* = new]

nephew *noun* (*plural* **nephews**)
the son of a person's brother or sister. [same origin as *nepotism*]

nepotism (*say* nep-ot-izm) *noun*
showing favouritism to relatives in appointing them to jobs. [from Latin *nepos* = nephew]

nerve *noun* (*plural* **nerves**)
1 any of the fibres in the body that carry messages to and from the brain, so that parts of the body can feel and move. 2 courage; calmness in a dangerous situation, *Don't lose your nerve.* 3 impudence, *You've got a nerve!* **nerves** *plural noun* nervousness.

nerve *verb* (**nerves, nerving, nerved**)
give strength or courage to someone. [from Latin *nervus* = sinew]

nerve centre *noun* (*plural* **nerve centres**)
1 a cluster of neurons. 2 the place from which a system or organization is controlled.

nervous *adjective*
1 easily upset or agitated; excitable. 2 slightly afraid; timid. 3 of the nerves, *a nervous illness.*
nervously *adverb*, **nervousness** *noun*

nervous breakdown *noun* (*plural* **nervous breakdowns**)
a state of severe depression and anxiety, so that the person cannot cope with life.

nervous system *noun* (*plural* **nervous systems**)
the system, consisting of the brain, spinal cord, and nerves, which sends electrical messages from one part of the body to another.

nervy *adjective* (**nervier, nerviest**)
nervous.

-ness *suffix*
forming nouns from adjectives (e.g. *kindness, sadness*). [from Old English]

nest *noun* (*plural* **nests**)
1 a structure or place in which a bird lays its eggs and feeds its young. 2 a place where some small creatures (e.g. mice, wasps) live. 3 a set of similar things that fit inside each other, *a nest of tables*.
nest *verb* (**nests, nesting, nested**)
1 have or make a nest. 2 fit inside something. [from Old English]

nest egg *noun* (*plural* **nest eggs**)
a sum of money saved up for future use. [originally – an egg left in the nest to encourage a hen to lay more]

nestle *verb* (**nestles, nestling, nestled**)
curl up comfortably. [from Old English *nestlian* = to nest]

nestling *noun* (*plural* **nestlings**)
a bird that is too young to leave the nest.

net¹ *noun* (*plural* **nets**)
1 material made of pieces of thread, cord, or wire etc. joined together in a criss-cross pattern with holes between. 2 something made of this.
net *verb* (**nets, netting, netted**)
cover or catch with a net.
[from Old English]

net² *adjective*
remaining when nothing more is to be deducted, *The net weight, without the box, is 100 grams.* (Compare *gross.*)
net *verb* (**nets, netting, netted**)
obtain or produce as net profit.
[from French *net* = neat]

netball *noun*
a game in which two teams try to throw a ball into a high net hanging from a ring.

nether *adjective*
lower, *the nether regions.*
[from Old English]

netting *noun*
a piece of net.

nettle *noun* (*plural* **nettles**)
a wild plant with leaves that sting when they are touched.
nettle *verb* (**nettles, nettling, nettled**)
annoy or provoke someone.
[from Old English]

network *noun* (*plural* **networks**)
1 a net-like arrangement of connected lines or parts, *the railway network.* 2 a group of radio or television stations which broadcast the same programmes. 3 a set of computers which are linked to each other.

neuralgia (*say* newr-al-ja) *noun*
pain along a nerve, especially in your face or head.
[from Greek *neuron* = nerve + *algos* = pain]

neurology *noun*
the study of nerves and their diseases.
neurological *adjective*, **neurologist** *noun*
[from Greek *neuron* = nerve, + *-logy*]

neuron *noun* (*plural* **neurons**)
a cell that is part of the nervous system and sends impulses to and from the brain.

neurotic (*say* newr-ot-ik) *adjective*
always very worried about something.
[from Greek *neuron* = nerve]

neuter *adjective*
1 neither masculine nor feminine. 2 (in some languages) belonging to the class of words which are neither masculine nor feminine, such as *Fenster* in German.
neuter *verb* (**neuters, neutering, neutered**)
remove an animal's sex organs so that it cannot breed. [Latin, = neither]

neutral *adjective*
1 not supporting either side in a war or quarrel. 2 not very distinctive, *a neutral colour such as grey.* 3 neither acid nor alkaline. **neutrally** *adverb*, **neutrality** *noun*
[same origin as *neuter*]

neutral gear *noun*
a gear that is not connected to the driving parts of an engine.

neutralize *verb* (**neutralizes, neutralizing, neutralized**)
make a thing neutral or ineffective.
neutralization *noun*

neutron *noun* (*plural* **neutrons**)
a particle with no electric charge.
[from *neutral*]

never *adverb*
1 at no time; not ever. 2 not at all.
[from Old English *naefre* = not ever]

nevertheless *adverb* & *conjunction*
in spite of this; although this is a fact.

new *adjective*
not existing before; just made, invented, discovered, or received etc.
newly *adverb*, **newness** *noun*
new *adverb*
newly, *newborn; new-laid.*
[from Old English]

New Age *adjective*
to do with a way of living and thinking that includes belief in astrology and alternative medicine, and concern for environmental and spiritual matters rather than possessions.

newcomer *noun* (*plural* **newcomers**)
a person who has arrived recently.

newel *noun* (*plural* newels)
the upright post to which the handrail of a stair is fixed, or that forms the centre pillar of a winding stair. [from old French]

newfangled *adjective*
disliked because it is new in method or style.
[from *new* + Middle English *fang* = seize]

newly *adverb*
1 recently. 2 in a new way.

new moon *noun* (*plural* new moons)
the moon at the beginning of its cycle, when only a thin crescent can be seen.

news *noun*
1 information about recent events or a broadcast report of this. 2 a piece of new information.

newsagent *noun* (*plural* newsagents)
a shopkeeper who sells newspapers.

newsflash *noun* (*plural* newsflashes)
a short news broadcast which interrupts a programme because something important has happened.

newsletter *noun* (*plural* newsletters)
a short, informal report sent regularly to members of an organization.

newspaper *noun* (*plural* newspapers)
1 a daily or weekly publication on large sheets of paper, containing news reports, articles, etc. 2 the sheets of paper forming a newspaper, *Wrap it in newspaper.*

newsy *adjective* (*informal*)
full of news.

newt *noun* (*plural* newts)
a small animal rather like a lizard, that lives near or in water.
[from Old English: originally *an ewt*]

newton *noun* (*plural* newtons)
a unit for measuring force. [named after an English scientist, Isaac Newton]

New Year's Day *noun*
1 January.

next *adjective*
nearest; coming immediately after, *on the next day.*

next *adverb*
1 in the next place. 2 on the next occasion, *What happens next?* [from Old English]

next door *adverb* & *adjective*
in the next house or room.

nib *noun* (*plural* nibs)
the pointed metal part of a pen.
[from old German or old Dutch]

nibble *verb* (nibbles, nibbling, nibbled)
take small, quick, or gentle bites.
[probably from old Dutch]

nice *adjective* (nicer, nicest)
1 pleasant or kind. 2 precise or careful, *Dictionaries make nice distinctions between meanings of words.* **nicely** *adverb*, **niceness** *noun* [originally = stupid: from Latin *nescius* = ignorant]

nicety (*say* ny-sit-ee) *noun* (*plural* niceties)
1 precision. 2 a small detail or difference pointed out. [from *nice*]

niche (*say* nich or neesh) *noun* (*plural* niches)
1 a small recess, especially in a wall, *The vase stood in a niche.* 2 a suitable place or position, *She found her niche in the drama club.*
[old French, from *nichier* = make a nest]

nick *noun* (*plural* nicks)
1 a small cut or notch. 2 (*slang*) a police station or prison.
in good nick (*informal*) in good condition.
in the nick of time only just in time.
nick *verb* (nicks, nicking, nicked)
1 make a nick in something. 2 (*slang*) steal. 3 (*slang*) catch; arrest. [origin unknown]

nickel *noun* (*plural* nickels)
1 a silvery-white metal. 2 (*American*) a 5-cent coin. [from German]

nickname *noun* (*plural* nicknames)
a name given to a person instead of his or her real name.
[originally *an eke-name*: from Middle English *eke* = addition, + *name*]

nicotine *noun*
a poisonous substance found in tobacco. [from the name of J. Nicot, who introduced tobacco into France in 1560]

niece noun (plural **nieces**)
the daughter of a person's brother or sister.
[from French; related to nephew]

niggardly adjective
mean or stingy. **niggardliness** noun [from
Middle English nig = a mean person]

niggle verb (**niggles, niggling, niggled**)
fuss over details or very small faults.
[probably from a Scandinavian language]

nigh adverb & preposition (poetic)
near. [from Old English]

night noun (plural **nights**)
1 the dark hours between sunset and
sunrise. 2 a particular night or evening,
the first night of the play.
[from Old English]

nightcap noun (plural **nightcaps**)
1 (old use) a knitted cap worn in bed. 2 a
drink, especially an alcoholic one, which
you have before going to bed.

nightclub noun (plural **nightclubs**)
a place that is open at night where people
go to drink and dance.

nightdress noun (plural **nightdresses**)
a loose dress that girls or women wear in
bed.

nightfall noun
the coming of darkness at the end of the
day.

nightie noun (plural **nighties**)
a nightdress.

nightingale noun (plural **nightingales**)
a small brown bird that sings sweetly.
[from Old English nihtegala = night-singer
(because it often sings until late in the
evening)]

nightlife noun
the places of entertainment that you can go
to at night, a popular resort with plenty of
nightlife.

nightly adjective & adverb
happening every night.

nightmare noun (plural **nightmares**)
1 a frightening dream. 2 an unpleasant

experience, the journey was a nightmare.
nightmarish adjective [from night + Middle
English mare = an evil spirit]

nil noun
nothing or nought.
[from Latin nihil = nothing]

nimble adjective
able to move quickly; agile. **nimbly** adverb
[from Old English]

nine noun & adjective (plural **nines**)
the number 9. **ninth** adjective & noun
[from Old English]

ninepins noun
the game of skittles played with nine
objects.

nineteen noun & adjective
the number 19. **nineteenth** adjective & noun
[from Old English]

ninety noun & adjective (plural **nineties**)
the number 90. **ninetieth** adjective & noun
[from Old English]

nip verb (**nips, nipping, nipped**)
1 pinch or bite quickly. 2 (informal) go
quickly.

nip noun (plural **nips**)
1 a quick pinch or bite. 2 sharp coldness,
There's a nip in the air. 3 a small drink of a
spirit, a nip of brandy.
[probably from old Dutch]

nipper noun (plural **nippers**) (informal)
a young child.

nippers plural noun
pincers.

nipple noun (plural **nipples**)
a small projecting part, especially at the
front of a person's breast.
[origin unknown]

nippy adjective (**nippier, nippiest**) (informal)
1 quick or nimble. 2 cold.

nirvana noun
(in Buddhism and Hinduism) the highest
state of knowledge and understanding,
achieved by meditation. [Sanskrit]

nit *noun* (*plural* **nits**)
a parasitic insect or its egg, found in people's hair. [from Old English]

nit-picking *noun*
pointing out very small faults.

nitrate *noun* (*plural* **nitrates**)
1 a chemical compound containing nitrogen. 2 potassium or sodium nitrate, used as a fertilizer.

nitric acid (*say* ny-trik)
a very strong colourless acid containing nitrogen.

nitrogen (*say* ny-tro-jen) *noun*
a gas that makes up about four-fifths of the air. [from *nitre* = a substance once thought to be a vital part of the air]

nitwit *noun* (*plural* **nitwits**) (*informal*)
a stupid person. **nitwitted** *adjective*
[origin unknown]

no *adjective*
not any, *We have no money.*

no *adverb*
1 used to deny or refuse something, *Will you come? No.* 2 not at all, *She is no better.*
[from *none*]

No. or **no.** *abbreviation* (*plural* **Nos.** or **nos.**)
number. [from Latin *numero* = by number]

noble *adjective* (**nobler**, **noblest**)
1 of high social rank; aristocratic. 2 having a very good character or qualities, *a noble king.* 3 stately or impressive, *a noble building.* **nobly** *adverb*, **nobility** *noun*
noble *noun* (*plural* **nobles**)
a person of high social rank. **nobleman** *noun*, **noblewoman** *noun* [from Latin]

nobody *pronoun*
no person; no one.

nobody *noun* (*plural* **nobodies**) (*informal*)
an unimportant or unimpressive person; a nonentity.

nocturnal *adjective*
1 happening at night. 2 active at night, *nocturnal animals.*
[from Latin *noctis* = of night]

nocturne *noun* (*plural* **nocturnes**)
a piece of music with the quiet dreamy feeling of night.
[French; related to *nocturnal*]

nod *verb* (**nods**, **nodding**, **nodded**)
1 move the head up and down, especially as a way of agreeing with somebody or as a greeting. 2 be drowsy. **nod** *noun*
[origin unknown]

node *noun* (*plural* **nodes**)
a swelling like a small knob.
[from Latin *nodus* = knot]

nodule *noun* (*plural* **nodules**)
a small node.

noise *noun* (*plural* **noises**)
a sound, especially one that is loud or unpleasant. **noisy** *adjective*, **noisily** *adverb*, **noiseless** *adjective* [from French]

noisome (*say* noi-sum) *adjective*
smelling unpleasant; harmful.
[from *annoy* + *-some*]

nomad *noun* (*plural* **nomads**)
a member of a tribe that moves from place to place looking for pasture for their animals. **nomadic** *adjective*
[from Greek *nomas* = roaming]

no man's land *noun*
an area that does not belong to anybody, especially the land between opposing armies.

nom de plume *noun* (*plural* **noms de plume**)
a writer's pseudonym.
[French, = pen-name (this phrase is not used in French)]

nominal *adjective*
1 in name, *He is the nominal ruler, but the real power is held by the generals.* 2 small, *We charged them only a nominal fee.*
nominally *adverb*
[from Latin *nomen* = name]

nominate *verb* (**nominates**, **nominating**, **nominated**)
name a person or thing to be appointed or chosen. **nomination** *noun*, **nominator** *noun*
[from Latin *nominare* = to name]

nominee *noun* (*plural* **nominees**)
a person who is nominated.

non- *prefix*
not. [from Latin]

nonagenarian *noun* (*plural*
nonagenarians)
a person aged between 90 and 99.
[from Latin *nonageni* = 90 each]

nonchalant (*say* non-shal-ant) *adjective*
calm and casual; showing no anxiety or
excitement. **nonchalantly** *adverb*,
nonchalance *noun* [from *non-* + French
chalant = being concerned]

non-commissioned officer *noun*
(*plural* **non-commissioned officers**)
a member of the armed forces, such as a
corporal or sergeant, who has not been
commissioned as an officer but has been
promoted from the ranks of ordinary
soldiers.

non-committal *adjective*
not committing yourself; not showing what
you think.

Nonconformist *noun* (*plural*
Nonconformists)
a member of a Church (e.g. Baptist,
Methodist) that does not conform to all the
customs of the Church of England.

nondescript *adjective*
having no special or distinctive qualities
and therefore difficult to describe.

none *pronoun*
1 not any. **2** no one, *None can tell.*

USAGE: It is better to use a singular verb
(e.g. *None of them is here*), but the plural is
not incorrect (e.g. *None of them are here*).

none *adverb*
not at all, *He is none too bright.*
[from Old English *nan* = not one]

nonentity (*say* non-en-tit-ee) *noun* (*plural*
nonentities)
an unimportant person.
[from *non-* + *entity*]

non-existent *adjective*
not existing or unreal.

non-fiction *noun*
writings that are not fiction; books about
real people and things and true events.

non-flammable *adjective*
not able to be set on fire.

USAGE: See note at *inflammable*.

nonplussed *adjective*
puzzled or confused.
[from Latin *non plus* = not further]

nonsense *noun*
1 words put together in a way that does not
mean anything. **2** stupid ideas or
behaviour. **nonsensical** (*say* non-**sens**-ik-al)
adjective [from *non-* + *sense*]

non sequitur (*say* non **sek**-wit-er) *noun*
(*plural* **non sequiturs**)
a conclusion that does not follow from the
evidence given. [Latin, = it does not follow]

non-stop *adjective* & *adverb*
1 not stopping, *They talked non-stop for
hours.* **2** not stopping between two main
stations, *a non-stop train.*

noodles *plural noun*
pasta made in narrow strips, used in soups
etc. [from German]

nook *noun* (*plural* **nooks**)
a sheltered corner; a recess.
[origin unknown]

noon *noun*
twelve o'clock midday.
[via Old English from Latin]

no one *noun*
no person; nobody.

noose *noun* (*plural* **nooses**)
a loop in a rope that gets smaller when the
rope is pulled. [origin unknown]

nor *conjunction*
and not, *She cannot do it; nor can I.*
[from Old English]

norm *noun* (*plural* **norms**)
1 a standard or average type, amount,
level, etc. **2** normal or expected behaviour,
social norms.
[from Latin *norma* = a pattern or rule]

normal *adjective*
1 usual or ordinary. 2 natural and healthy; without a physical or mental illness.
normally *adverb*, **normality** *noun*
[same origin as *norm*]

Norman *noun* (*plural* **Normans**)
a member of the people of Normandy in northern France, who conquered England in 1066. **Norman** *adjective*
[from Old Norse *northmathr* = man from the north (because the Normans were partly descended from the Vikings)]

north *noun*
1 the direction to the left of a person who faces east. 2 the northern part of a country, city, etc.
north *adjective* & *adverb*
towards or in the north. **northerly** *adjective*, **northern** *adjective*, **northerner** *noun*, **northernmost** *adjective* [from Old English]

north-east *noun*, *adjective*, & *adverb*
midway between north and east. **north-easterly** *adjective*, **north-eastern** *adjective*

northward *adjective* & *adverb*
towards the north. **northwards** *adverb*

north-west *noun*, *adjective*, & *adverb*
midway between north and west. **north-westerly** *adjective*, **north-western** *adjective*

Nos. or **nos.** *plural* of **No.** or **no.**

nose *noun* (*plural* **noses**)
1 the part of the face that is used for breathing and for smelling things. 2 the front end or part.
nose *verb* (**noses, nosing, nosed**)
1 push the nose into or near something. 2 go forward cautiously, *Ships nosed through the ice.* [from Old English]

nosebag *noun* (*plural* **nosebags**)
a bag containing fodder, for hanging on a horse's head.

nosedive *noun* (*plural* **nosedives**)
a steep downward dive, especially of an aircraft. **nosedive** *verb*

nosegay *noun* (*plural* **nosegays**)
a small bunch of flowers. [from *nose* + Middle English *gay* = an ornament]

nostalgia (*say* nos-tal-ja) *noun*
sentimental remembering or longing for the past. **nostalgic** *adjective*, **nostalgically** *adverb* [originally = homesickness: from Greek *nostos* = return home + *algos* = pain]

nostril *noun* (*plural* **nostrils**)
either of the two openings in the nose. [from Old English *nosthryl* = nose-hole]

nosy *adjective* (**nosier, nosiest**)
inquisitive. **nosily** *adverb*, **nosiness** *noun* [from *sticking your nose in* = being inquisitive]

not *adverb*
used to change the meaning of something to its opposite or absence. [from *nought*]

notable *adjective*
worth noticing; remarkable or famous. **notably** *adverb*, **notability** *noun*

notation *noun* (*plural* **notations**)
a system of symbols representing numbers, quantities, musical notes, etc.

notch *noun* (*plural* **notches**)
a small V-shape cut into a surface.
notch *verb* (**notches, notching, notched**)
cut a notch or notches in.
notch up score.
[from old French]

note *noun* (*plural* **notes**)
1 something written down as a reminder or as a comment or explanation. 2 a short letter. 3 a banknote, *a £5 note.* 4 a single sound in music. 5 any of the black or white keys on a piano etc. (see *key* 3). 6 a sound or quality that indicates something, *a note of warning.* 7 notice or attention, *Take note.*
note *verb* (**notes, noting, noted**)
1 make a note about something; write down. 2 notice or pay attention to, *Note what we say.* [from Latin *nota* = a mark]

notebook *noun* (*plural* **notebooks**)
a book with blank pages on which to write notes.

noted *adjective*
famous, especially for a particular reason, *an area noted for its mild climate.*

notepaper *noun*
paper for writing letters.

nothing *noun*
1 no thing; not anything. 2 no amount; nought.
for nothing 1 without payment, free.
2 without a result.

nothing *adverb*
1 not at all. 2 in no way, *It's nothing like as good.* [from *no thing*]

notice *noun* (*plural* **notices**)
1 something written or printed and displayed for people to see. 2 attention, *It escaped my notice.* 3 information that something is going to happen; warning that you are about to end an agreement or a person's employment etc., *We gave him a month's notice.*
notice *verb* (**notices, noticing, noticed**)
see or become aware of something.
[from Latin *notus* = known]

noticeable *adjective*
easily seen or noticed. **noticeably** *adverb*

noticeboard *noun* (*plural* **noticeboards**)
a board on which notices may be displayed.

notifiable *adjective*
that must be reported, *Cholera is a notifiable disease.*

notify *verb* (**notifies, notifying, notified**)
tell someone formally or officially, *Notify the police.* **notification** *noun*
[from Latin *notificare* = make known]

notion *noun* (*plural* **notions**)
an idea, especially one that is vague or incorrect.
[from Latin *notio* = getting to know]

notional *adjective*
guessed and not definite. **notionally** *adverb*

notorious *adjective*
well-known for something bad. **notoriously** *adverb*, **notoriety** (*say* noh-ter-I-it-ee) *noun*
[same origin as *notice*]

notwithstanding *preposition*
in spite of.

nougat (*say* noo-gah) *noun*
a chewy sweet made from nuts, sugar or honey, and egg white. [French]

nought (*say* nawt) *noun*
1 the figure 0. 2 nothing.
[from Old English *nowiht* = not anything]

noun *noun* (*plural* **nouns**)
a word that stands for a person, place, or thing. *Common nouns* are words such as *boy, dog, river, sport, table*, which are used of a whole kind of people or things; *proper nouns* are words such as *Charles, Thames*, and *London* which name a particular person or thing.
[from Latin *nomen* = name]

nourish *verb* (**nourishes, nourishing, nourished**)
keep a person, animal, or plant alive and well by means of food. **nourishment** *noun*
[from old French; related to *nutrient*]

nouveau riche (*say* noo-voh **reesh**) *noun* (*plural* **nouveaux riches**)
a person who has only recently become rich. [French, = new rich]

novel *noun* (*plural* **novels**)
a story that fills a whole book.
novel *adjective*
of a new and unusual kind, *a novel experience.*
[from Latin *novus* = new]

novelist *noun* (*plural* **novelists**)
a person who writes novels.

novelty *noun* (*plural* **novelties**)
1 newness and originality. 2 something new and unusual. 3 a small and unusual object, suitable as a small gift.

novice *noun* (*plural* **novices**)
1 a beginner. 2 a person preparing to be a monk or nun.
[from French; related to *novel*]

now *adverb*
1 at this time. 2 by this time.
3 immediately, *You must go now.* 4 I wonder, or I am telling you, *Now why didn't I think of that?*
now and again or **now and then** sometimes; occasionally.
now *conjunction*
as a result of or at the same time as something, *Now that you have come, we'll start.*

now *noun*
this moment, *They will be at home by now.*
[from Old English]

nowadays *adverb*
at the present time, as contrasted with
years ago.

nowhere *adverb*
not anywhere.
nowhere *noun*
no place, *Nowhere is as beautiful as
Scotland.*

noxious *adjective*
unpleasant and harmful. [from Latin]

nozzle *noun* (*plural* **nozzles**)
the spout of a hose or pipe etc.
[= little nose]

nuance (*say* new-ahns) *noun* (*plural*
nuances)
a slight difference or shade of meaning.
[from French]

nub *noun* (*plural* **nubs**)
1 a small knob or lump. 2 the central point
of a problem. [from old German]

nuclear *adjective*
1 to do with a nucleus or nuclei. 2 using
the energy that is created by reactions in
the nuclei of atoms.

nucleus *noun* (*plural* **nuclei**)
1 the part in the centre of something,
round which other things are grouped.
2 the central part of an atom or of a seed or
a biological cell. [Latin, = kernel]

nude *adjective*
not wearing any clothes; naked. **nudity**
noun [from Latin *nudus* = bare]

nudge *verb* (**nudges, nudging, nudged**)
1 poke a person gently with your elbow.
2 push slightly or gradually. **nudge** *noun*
[origin unknown]

nudist *noun* (*plural* **nudists**)
a naturist. **nudism** *noun*

nugget *noun* (*plural* **nuggets**)
a rough lump of gold or platinum found in
the earth. [origin unknown]

nuisance *noun* (*plural* **nuisances**)
an annoying person or thing.
[from French *nuire* = to hurt someone]

null *adjective*
not valid, *null and void.*
[from Latin *nullus* = none]

nullify *verb* (**nullifies, nullifying, nullified**)
make a thing null. **nullification** *noun*

numb *adjective*
unable to feel or move.
numbly *adverb*, **numbness** *noun*
numb *verb* (**numbs, numbing, numbed**)
make numb. [from Old English]

number *noun* (*plural* **numbers**)
1 a symbol or word indicating how many; a
numeral or figure. 2 a numeral given to a
thing to identify it, *a telephone number.* 3 a
quantity of people or things, *the number of
people present.* 4 one issue of a magazine or
newspaper. 5 a song or piece of music.

USAGE: Note that *a number of*, meaning
'several', should be followed by a plural
verb: *A number of problems remain.*

number *verb* (**numbers, numbering,
numbered**)
1 mark with numbers. 2 count. 3 amount
to, *The crowd numbered 10,000.*
[from old French; related to *numeral*]

numberless *adjective*
too many to count.

numeral *noun* (*plural* **numerals**)
a symbol that represents a certain number;
a figure. [from Latin *numerus* = number]

numerate (*say* new-mer-at) *adjective*
having a good basic knowledge of
mathematics. **numeracy** *noun*
[same origin as *numeral*]

numeration *noun*
numbering.
[from Latin *numerare* = to number]

numerator *noun* (*plural* **numerators**)
the number above the line in a fraction,
showing how many parts are to be taken,
e.g. 2 in ⅔. (Compare *denominator*.)
[same origin as *numeration*]

numerical (*say* new-**merri**-kal) *adjective*
of a number or series of numbers, *in numerical order*. **numerically** *adverb*
[same origin as *numeral*]

numerous *adjective*
many. [same origin as *numeral*]

numismatics (*say* new-miz-**mat**-iks) *noun*
the study of coins. **numismatist** *noun*
[from Greek *nomisma* = coin]

nun *noun* (*plural* **nuns**)
a member of a community of women who live according to the rules of a religious organization. (Compare *monk*.)
[via Old English from Latin *nonna*, feminine of *nonnus* = monk]

nunnery *noun* (*plural* **nunneries**)
a convent.

nuptial *adjective*
1 to do with marriage. 2 to do with a wedding. [from Latin *nuptiae* = a wedding]

nuptials *plural noun*
a wedding.

nurse *noun* (*plural* **nurses**)
1 a person trained to look after people who are ill or injured. 2 a woman employed to look after young children.
nurse *verb* (**nurses, nursing, nursed**)
1 look after someone who is ill or injured.
2 hold carefully. 3 feed a baby.
[from *nourish*]

nursemaid *noun* (*plural* **nursemaids**)
a young woman employed to look after young children.

nursery *noun* (*plural* **nurseries**)
1 a place where young children are looked after or play. 2 a place where young plants are grown and usually for sale.

nursery rhyme *noun* (*plural* **nursery rhymes**)
a simple rhyme or song of the kind that young children like.

nursery school *noun* (*plural* **nursery schools**)
a school for children below primary school age.

nursing home *noun* (*plural* **nursing homes**)
a small hospital or home for invalids.

nurture *verb* (**nurtures, nurturing, nurtured**)
1 nourish. 2 train and educate; bring up.
nurture *noun*
1 nurturing. 2 nourishment.
[from old French *nourture* = nourishment]

nut *noun* (*plural* **nuts**)
1 a fruit with a hard shell. 2 a kernel. 3 a small piece of metal with a hole in the middle, for screwing onto a bolt. 4 (*slang*) the head. 5 (*slang*) a mad or eccentric person. **nutty** *adjective* [from Old English]

nutcrackers *plural noun*
pincers for cracking nuts.

nutmeg *noun*
the hard seed of a tropical tree, grated and used in cooking.
[from Latin *nux muscata* = spicy nut]

nutrient (*say* new-**tree**-ent) *noun* (*plural* **nutrients**)
a nourishing substance. **nutrient** *adjective*
[from Latin *nutrire* = nourish]

nutriment (*say* new-**trim**-ent) *noun*
nourishing food. [same origin as *nutrient*]

nutrition (*say* new-**trish**-on) *noun*
1 nourishment. 2 the study of what nourishes people.
nutritional *adjective*, **nutritionally** *adverb*
[same origin as *nutrient*]

nutritious (*say* new-**trish**-us) *adjective*
nourishing; giving good nourishment.
nutritiousness *noun*
[same origin as *nutrient*]

nutritive (*say* new-**trit**-iv) *adjective*
nourishing. [same origin as *nutrient*]

nutshell *noun* (*plural* **nutshells**)
the shell of a nut.
in a nutshell stated very briefly.

nuzzle *verb* (**nuzzles, nuzzling, nuzzled**)
rub gently with the nose. [from *nose*]

NW *abbreviation*
1 north-west. 2 north-western.

nylon *noun*
a synthetic, strong, lightweight cloth or fibre.
[invented to go with *rayon* and *cotton*]

nymph (*say* nimf) *noun* (*plural* **nymphs**)
1 (in myths) a young goddess living in the sea or woods etc. **2** the immature form of insects such as the dragonfly. [from Greek]

NZ *abbreviation*
New Zealand.

Oo

O *interjection*
oh.

oaf *noun* (*plural* **oafs**)
a stupid lout. [from Old Norse]

oak *noun* (*plural* **oaks**)
a large deciduous tree with seeds called acorns. **oaken** *adjective* [from Old English]

OAP *abbreviation*
old-age pensioner.

oar *noun* (*plural* **oars**)
a pole with a flat blade at one end, used for rowing a boat. **oarsman** *noun*, **oarsmanship** *noun* [from Old English]

oasis (*say* oh-ay-sis) *noun* (*plural* **oases**)
a fertile place in a desert, with a spring or well of water. [from Greek]

oath *noun* (*plural* **oaths**)
1 a solemn promise to do something or that something is true, appealing to God or a holy person as witness. **2** a swear word. [from Old English]

oatmeal *noun*
ground oats.

oats *plural noun*
a cereal used to make food (*oats* for horses, *oatmeal* for people). [from Old English]

ob- *prefix* (changing to **oc-** before *c*, **of-** before *f*, **op-** before *p*)
1 to; towards (as in *observe*). **2** against (as

in *opponent*). **3** in the way; blocking (as in *obstruct*).
[from Latin *ob* = towards, against]

obedient *adjective*
doing what you are told; willing to obey.
obediently *adverb*, **obedience** *noun*
[from Latin]

obeisance (*say* o-bay-sans) *noun* (*plural* **obeisances**)
a deep bow or curtsy showing respect.
[French, from *obéissant* = obeying]

obelisk *noun* (*plural* **obelisks**)
a tall pillar set up as a monument.
[from Greek *obeliskos* = small pillar]

obese (*say* o-beess) *adjective*
very fat. **obesity** (*say* o-beess-it-ee) *noun*
[from Latin *obesus* = having overeaten]

obey *verb* (**obeys**, **obeying**, **obeyed**)
do what you are told to do by a person, law, etc.
[from *ob-* + Latin *audire* = listen or hear]

obituary *noun* (*plural* **obituaries**)
a notice in a newspaper of a person's death, often with a short account of his or her life.
[from Latin *obitus* = death]

object (*say* ob-jikt) *noun* (*plural* **objects**)
1 something that can be seen or touched. **2** a purpose or intention. **3** (in grammar) the word or words naming who or what is acted upon by a verb or by a preposition, e.g. *him* in *the dog bit him* and *against him*.
object (*say* ob-jekt) *verb* (**objects**, **objecting**, **objected**)
say that you are not in favour of something or do not agree; protest. **objector** *noun*
[from *ob-* + Latin *-jectum* = thrown]

objection *noun* (*plural* **objections**)
1 objecting to something. **2** a reason for objecting.

objectionable *adjective*
unpleasant or nasty. **objectionably** *adverb*

objective *noun* (*plural* **objectives**)
what you are trying to reach or do; an aim.
objective *adjective*
1 real or actual, *Dreams have no objective existence.* **2** not influenced by personal

feelings or opinions, *an objective account of the quarrel.* (Compare *subjective.*)
objectively *adverb*, **objectivity** *noun*

objet d'art (*say* ob-zhay dar) *noun* (*plural* objets d'art)
a small artistic object.
[French, = object of art]

obligation *noun* (*plural* obligations)
1 being obliged to do something. 2 what you are obliged to do; a duty.
under an obligation owing gratitude to someone who has helped you.

obligatory (*say* ob-lig-a-ter-ee) *adjective*
compulsory, not optional.

oblige *verb* (obliges, obliging, obliged)
1 force or compel. 2 help and please someone, *Can you oblige me with a loan?*
be obliged to someone feel gratitude to a person who has helped you.
[from *ob-* + Latin *ligare* = bind]

obliging *adjective*
polite and helpful.

oblique (*say* ob-leek) *adjective*
1 slanting. 2 not saying something straightforwardly, *an oblique reply.*
obliquely *adverb* [from Latin]

obliterate *verb* (obliterates, obliterating, obliterated)
blot out; destroy and remove all traces of something. **obliteration** *noun*
[from Latin *obliterare* = cross out, from *ob-* + *littera* = letter]

oblivion *noun*
1 being forgotten. 2 being unconscious.

oblivious *adjective*
completely unaware of something, *oblivious to the danger.*
[from Latin *oblivisci* = forget]

oblong *adjective*
rectangular in shape and longer than it is wide. **oblong** *noun* [from Latin]

obnoxious *adjective*
very unpleasant; objectionable.
[from *ob-* + Latin *noxa* = harm]

oboe *noun* (*plural* oboes)
a high-pitched woodwind instrument.
oboist *noun*
[from French *haut* = high + *bois* = wood]

obscene (*say* ob-seen) *adjective*
indecent in a very offensive way. **obscenely** *adverb*, **obscenity** *noun* [from Latin]

obscure *adjective*
1 difficult to see or to understand; not clear. 2 not well-known.
obscurely *adverb*, **obscurity** *noun*
obscure *verb* (obscures, obscuring, obscured)
make a thing obscure; darken or conceal, *Clouds obscured the sun.*
[from Latin *obscurus* = dark]

obsequious (*say* ob-seek-wee-us) *adjective*
respectful in an excessive or sickening way; servile.
obsequiously *adverb*, **obsequiousness** *noun*
[from *ob-* + Latin *sequi* = follow]

observance *noun*
obeying or keeping a law, custom, religious festival, etc.

observant *adjective*
quick at observing or noticing things.
observantly *adverb*

observation *noun* (*plural* observations)
1 observing or watching. 2 a comment or remark.

observatory *noun* (*plural* observatories)
a building with telescopes etc. for observing the stars or weather.

observe *verb* (observes, observing, observed)
1 see and notice; watch carefully. 2 obey a law. 3 keep or celebrate a custom or religious festival etc. 4 make a remark.
observer *noun* [from *ob-* + Latin *servare* = to watch or keep]

obsess *verb* (obsesses, obsessing, obsessed)
occupy a person's thoughts continually.
obsession *noun*, **obsessive** *adjective* [from Latin *obsessum* = haunted or besieged]

obsolescent *adjective*
becoming obsolete; going out of use or fashion. **obsolescence** *noun*

obsolete *adjective*
not used any more; out of date.
[from Latin *obsoletus* = worn out]

obstacle *noun* (*plural* obstacles)
something that stands in the way or
obstructs progress.
[from *ob-* + Latin *stare* = to stand]

obstetrics *noun*
the branch of medicine and surgery that
deals with the birth of babies.
[from Latin *obstetrix* = midwife]

obstinate *adjective*
keeping firmly to your own ideas or ways,
even though they may be wrong.
obstinately *adverb*, **obstinacy** *noun*
[from Latin *obstinare* = keep on, persist]

obstreperous (*say* ob-strep-er-us) *adjective*
noisy and unruly.
[from *ob-* + Latin *strepere* = make a noise]

obstruct *verb* (obstructs, obstructing,
obstructed)
stop a person or thing from getting past;
hinder. **obstruction** *noun*, **obstructive**
adjective [from *ob-* + Latin *structum* = built]

obtain *verb* (obtains, obtaining, obtained)
get something by buying, taking, or being
given it. **obtainable** *adjective*
[from *ob-* + Latin *tenere* = to hold]

obtrude *verb* (obtrudes, obtruding,
obtruded)
force yourself or your ideas on someone; be
obtrusive. **obtrusion** *noun*
[from *ob-* + Latin *trudere* = to push]

obtrusive *adjective*
unpleasantly noticeable. **obtrusiveness**
noun [same origin as *obtrude*]

obtuse *adjective*
slow to understand.
obtusely *adverb*, **obtuseness** *noun*
[from *ob-* + Latin *tusum* = blunted]

obtuse angle *noun* (*plural* obtuse angles)
an angle of more than 90° but less than
180°. (Compare *acute angle*.)

obverse *noun*
the side of a coin or medal showing the
head or chief design (the other side is the
reverse). [from *ob-* + Latin *versum* = turned]

obvious *adjective*
easy to see or understand. **obviously** *adverb*
[from Latin *ob viam* = in the way]

oc- *prefix*
1 to; towards. 2 against. 3 in the way;
blocking. see **ob-**.

occasion *noun* (*plural* occasions)
1 the time when something happens. 2 a
special event. 3 a suitable time; an
opportunity.
occasion *verb* (occasions, occasioning,
occasioned)
cause. [from Latin]

occasional *adjective*
1 happening at intervals. 2 for special
occasions, *occasional music*.
occasionally *adverb*

Occident (*say* ok-sid-ent) *noun*
the West as opposed to the Orient.
occidental *adjective* [from Latin, = sunset]

occult *adjective*
to do with the supernatural or magic,
occult powers.
[from Latin *occultum* = hidden]

occupant *noun* (*plural* occupants)
someone who occupies a place.
occupancy *noun*

occupation *noun* (*plural* occupations)
1 a person's job or profession. 2 something
you do to pass your time. 3 capturing a
country etc. by military force.

occupational *adjective*
caused by an occupation, *an occupational
disease.*

occupational therapy *noun*
creative work designed to help people to
recover from certain illnesses.

occupy *verb* (occupies, occupying, occupied)
1 live in a place; inhabit. 2 fill a space or
position. 3 capture a country etc. and place
troops there. 4 keep somebody busy.
occupier *noun* [from Latin]

occur *verb* (occurs, occurring, occurred)
1 happen or exist. 2 be found; appear,
These plants occur in ponds. 3 come into a
person's mind, *An idea occurred to me.*
[from Latin]

occurrence *noun* (*plural* occurrences)
1 occurring. **2** an incident or event; a happening.

ocean *noun* (*plural* oceans)
the seas that surround the continents of the earth, especially one of the large named areas of this, *the Pacific Ocean*.
oceanic *adjective*
[from Oceanus, the river that the ancient Greeks thought surrounded the world]

ocelot (*say* oss-il-ot) *noun* (*plural* ocelots)
a leopard-like animal of Central and South America. [via French from Nahuatl (a Central American language)]

ochre (*say* oh-ker) *noun*
1 a mineral used as a pigment. **2** pale brownish-yellow. [via French from Greek *ochros* = pale yellow]

o'clock *adverb*
by the clock, *Lunch is at one o'clock*.
[short for *of the clock*]

octa- or **octo-** *prefix*
eight. [from Greek]

octagon *noun* (*plural* octagons)
a flat shape with eight sides and eight angles. **octagonal** *adjective*
[from *octa-* + Greek *gonia* = angle]

octave *noun* (*plural* octaves)
the interval of eight steps between one musical note and the next note of the same name above or below it.
[from Latin *octavus* = eighth]

octet *noun* (*plural* octets)
a group of eight instruments or singers.
[from *octo-*]

octo- *prefix*
eight. see **octa-**.

octogenarian *noun* (*plural* octogenarians)
a person aged between 80 and 89. [from Latin *octogeni* = 80 each]

octopus *noun* (*plural* octopuses)
a sea creature with eight long tentacles.
[from *octo-* + Greek *pous* = foot]

ocular *adjective*
to do with or for the eyes.
[from Latin *oculus* = eye]

oculist *noun* (*plural* oculists)
a doctor who treats diseases of the eye.
[same origin as *ocular*]

odd *adjective*
1 strange or unusual. **2** (of a number) not able to be divided exactly by 2; not even. **3** left over from a pair or set, *I've got one odd sock*. **4** of various kinds; not regular, *odd jobs*. **oddly** *adverb*, **oddness** *noun*, **oddity** *noun* [from Old Norse]

oddments *plural noun*
small things of various kinds.

odds *plural noun*
the chances that a certain thing will happen; a measure of this, *When the odds are 10 to 1, you will win £10 if you bet £1*.
odds and ends oddments.

ode *noun* (*plural* odes)
a poem addressed to a person or thing.
[from Greek *oide* = song]

odious (*say* oh-dee-us) *adjective*
hateful. **odiously** *adverb*, **odiousness** *noun*
[same origin as *odium*]

odium (*say* oh-dee-um) *noun*
general hatred or disgust felt towards a person or actions. [Latin, = hatred]

odour *noun* (*plural* odours)
a smell. **odorous** *adjective*, **odourless** *adjective* [Latin *odor* = smell]

odyssey (*say* od-iss-ee) *noun* (*plural* odysseys)
a long adventurous journey. [named after the *Odyssey*, a Greek poem telling of the wanderings of Odysseus]

o'er *preposition* & *adverb* (*poetic*)
over.

oesophagus (*say* ee-sof-a-gus) *noun* (*plural* oesophagi)
the tube from the throat to the stomach; the gullet. [from Greek]

of *preposition*
(used to indicate relationships)
1 belonging to, *the mother of the child*. **2** concerning; about, *news of the disaster*. **3** made from, *built of stone*. **4** from, *north of the town*. [from Old English]

of- *prefix*
1 to; towards. 2 against. 3 in the way; blocking. see **ob-**.

off *preposition*
1 not on; away or down from, *He fell off the ladder.* 2 not taking or wanting, *She is off her food.* 3 deducted from, *£5 off the price.*

off *adverb*
1 away or down from something, *His hat blew off.* 2 not working or happening, *The heating is off. The match is off because of snow.* 3 to the end; completely, *Finish it off.* 4 as regards money or supplies, *How are you off for cash?* 5 behind or at the side of a stage, *There were noises off.* 6 (of food) beginning to go bad.
[from Old English]

offal *noun*
the organs of an animal (e.g. liver, kidneys) sold as food. [originally = waste products: from *off* + *fall*]

offence *noun* (*plural* **offences**)
1 an illegal action. 2 a feeling of annoyance or resentment.

offend *verb* (**offends, offending, offended**)
1 cause offence to someone; hurt a person's pride. 2 do wrong, *offend against the law.*
offender *noun*
[from *ob-* + Latin *fendere* = to strike]

offensive *adjective*
1 causing offence; insulting. 2 disgusting, *an offensive smell.* 3 used in attacking, *offensive weapons.*
offensively *adverb*, **offensiveness** *noun*

offensive *noun* (*plural* **offensives**)
an attack.
take the offensive be the first to attack.

offer *verb* (**offers, offering, offered**)
1 present something so that people can accept it if they want to. 2 say that you are willing to do or give something or to pay a certain amount.

offer *noun* (*plural* **offers**)
1 offering something. 2 an amount offered.
[from Old English]

offering *noun* (*plural* **offerings**)
what is offered.

offhand *adjective*
1 said or done without preparation. 2 rather casual and rude; curt.
offhanded *adjective*

office *noun* (*plural* **offices**)
1 a room or building used for business, especially for clerical work; the people who work there. 2 a government department, *the Foreign and Commonwealth Office.* 3 an important job or position.
be in office hold an official position.
[from Latin *officium* = a service or duty]

officer *noun* (*plural* **officers**)
1 a person who is in charge of others, especially in the armed forces. 2 an official. 3 a member of the police.

official *adjective*
1 done or said by someone with authority. 2 done as part of your job or position, *official duties.* **officially** *adverb*

USAGE: Do not confuse with *officious.*

official *noun* (*plural* **officials**)
a person who holds a position of authority.
[from Latin]

officiate *verb* (**officiates, officiating, officiated**)
be in charge of a meeting, event, etc.
[from Latin *officiare* = hold a service]

officious *adjective*
too ready to give orders; bossy. **officiously** *adverb* [from Latin *officiosus* = ready to do your duty]

USAGE: Do not confuse with *official.*

offing *noun*
in the offing likely to happen soon.

off-licence *noun* (*plural* **off-licences**)
a shop with a licence to sell alcohol to be drunk somewhere else.

offset *verb* (**offsets, offsetting, offset**)
cancel out or make up for something, *Defeats are offset by successes.*

offshoot *noun* (*plural* **offshoots**)
1 a side shoot on a plant. 2 a by-product.

offshore *adjective*
1 from the land towards the sea, *an offshore breeze.* 2 in the sea some distance from the shore, *an offshore island.*

offside *adjective & adverb*
(of a player in football etc.) in a position where the rules do not allow him or her to play the ball.

offspring *noun* (*plural* **offspring**)
a person's child or children; the young of an animal.

oft *adverb* (*old use*)
often. [from Old English]

often *adverb*
many times; in many cases. [from *oft*]

ogle *verb* (**ogles, ogling, ogled**)
stare at someone whom you find attractive. [probably from old Dutch]

ogre *noun* (*plural* **ogres**)
1 a cruel giant in fairy tales. 2 a terrifying person. [French]

oh *interjection*
an exclamation of pain, surprise, delight, etc., or used for emphasis (*Oh yes I will!*).

ohm *noun* (*plural* **ohms**)
a unit of electrical resistance. [named after a German scientist, G. S. Ohm, who studied electric currents]

OHMS *abbreviation*
On Her (or His) Majesty's Service.

oil *noun* (*plural* **oils**)
1 a thick slippery liquid that will not dissolve in water. 2 a kind of petroleum used as fuel. **oil well** *noun*
oil *verb* (**oils, oiling, oiled**)
put oil on something, especially to make it work smoothly. [from Latin]

oilfield *noun*
an area where oil is found.

oil paint *noun* (*plural* **oil paints**)
paint made with oil.

oil painting *noun* (*plural* **oil paintings**)
a painting done with oil colours.

oilskin *noun* (*plural* **oilskins**)
cloth made waterproof by treatment with oil.

oily *adjective*
1 containing or like oil; covered or soaked with oil. 2 behaving in an insincerely polite way. **oiliness** *noun*

ointment *noun* (*plural* **ointments**)
a cream or slippery paste for putting on sore skin and cuts. [from old French]

OK or **okay** *adverb & adjective* (*informal*)
all right. [perhaps from the initials of *oll* (or *orl*) *korrect*, a humorous spelling of *all correct*, first used in the USA in 1839]

old *adjective*
1 not new; born or made or existing from a long time ago. 2 of a particular age, *I'm ten years old.* 3 former or original, *in its old place.* 4 (*informal*, used casually or for emphasis), *good old mum!* **oldness** *noun* [from Old English]

olden *adjective* (*old use*)
of former times.

Old English *noun*
the English language from about 700 to 1150, also called *Anglo-Saxon.*

old-fashioned *adjective*
of the kind that was usual a long time ago; no longer fashionable.

Old Norse *noun*
the language spoken by the Vikings, the ancestor of modern Scandinavian languages.

olfactory *adjective*
to do with the sense of smell. [from Latin *olfacere* = to smell]

oligarchy *noun* (*plural* **oligarchies**)
a country ruled by a small group of people. **oligarch** *noun*, **oligarchic** *adjective* [from Greek *oligoi* = few, + *-archy*]

olive *noun* (*plural* **olives**)
1 an evergreen tree with a small bitter fruit. 2 this fruit, from which an oil (*olive oil*) is made. 3 a shade of green like an unripe olive. [from Greek]

olive branch *noun* (*plural* olive branches)
something you do or offer that shows you
want to make peace.
[from a story in the Bible, where the dove
brings Noah an olive branch as a sign that
God is no longer angry with man]

-ology *suffix* see -logy.

Olympic Games or **Olympics** *plural
noun*
a series of international sports contests
held every fourth year in a different part of
the world. [from the name of Olympia, a
city in Greece where they were held in
ancient times]

ombudsman *noun* (*plural* ombudsmen)
an official whose job is to investigate
complaints against government
organizations etc. [from Swedish *ombud*
= legal representative]

omega (*say* oh-meg-a) *noun*
the last letter of the Greek alphabet, a long
o. [from Greek *o mega* = big O]

omelette *noun* (*plural* omelettes)
eggs beaten together and cooked in a pan,
often with a filling. [French]

omen *noun* (*plural* omens)
an event regarded as a sign of what is going
to happen. [Latin]

ominous *adjective*
suggesting that trouble is coming.
ominously *adverb*
[from Latin *ominosus* = acting as an omen]

omission *noun* (*plural* omissions)
1 omitting. 2 something that has been
omitted or not done.

omit *verb* (omits, omitting, omitted)
1 miss something out. 2 fail to do
something. [from Latin]

omni- *prefix*
all. [from Latin]

omnibus *noun* (*plural* omnibuses)
1 a book containing several stories or
books that were previously published
separately. 2 (*old use*) a bus.
[Latin, = for everybody]

omnipotent *adjective*
having unlimited power or very great
power.
[from *omni-* + Latin *potens* = potent, able]

omniscient (*say* om-niss-ee-ent) *adjective*
knowing everything. **omniscience** *noun*
[from *omni-* + Latin *sciens* = knowing]

omnivorous (*say* om-niv-er-us) *adjective*
feeding on all kinds of food. (Compare
carnivorous, herbivorous.)
[from *omni-* + Latin *vorare* = devour]

on *preposition*
1 supported by; covering; added or
attached to, *the sign on the door*. 2 close to;
towards, *The army advanced on Paris*.
3 during; at the time of, *on my birthday*.
4 by reason of, *Arrest him on suspicion*.
5 concerning, *a book on butterflies*. 6 in a
state of; using or showing, *The house was
on fire*.

on *adverb*
1 so as to be on something, *Put it on*.
2 further forward, *Move on*. 3 working; in
action, *Is the heater on?*
on and off not continually.
[from Old English]

once *adverb*
1 for one time or on one occasion only,
They came only once. 2 formerly, *They once
lived here*.

once *noun*
one time, *Once is enough*.

once *conjunction*
as soon as, *You can go once I have taken
your names*. [from *one*]

oncoming *adjective*
approaching; coming towards you,
oncoming traffic.

one *adjective*
1 single. 2 individual or united.

one *noun*
1 the smallest whole number, 1. 2 a person
or thing alone.
one another each other.

one *pronoun*
a person; any person, *One likes to help*.
oneself *pronoun*
[from Old English]

onerous (*say* ohn-er-us or on-er-us)
adjective
difficult to bear or do; burdensome.
[from Latin *onus* = burden]

one-sided *adjective*
1 with one side or person in a contest,
conversation etc. being much stronger or
doing a lot more than the other, *a one-sided
match*. 2 showing only one point of view in
an unfair way, *This is a very one-sided
account of the conflict*.

one-way *adjective*
where traffic is allowed to travel in one
direction only.

onion *noun* (*plural* **onions**)
a round vegetable with a strong flavour.
oniony *adjective* [from old French]

onlooker *noun* (*plural* **onlookers**)
a spectator.

only *adjective*
being the one person or thing of a kind;
sole, *my only wish*.
only child a child who has no brothers or
sisters.
only *adverb*
no more than; and that is all, *There are only
three cakes left*.
only *conjunction*
but then; however, *He makes promises, only
he never keeps them*. [from Old English]

onomatopoeia (*say* on-om-at-o-**pee**-a)
noun
the formation of words that imitate what
they stand for, e.g. *cuckoo, plop*.
onomatopoeic *adjective* [from Greek *onoma*
= name + *poiein* = make]

onrush *noun*
an onward rush.

onset *noun*
1 a beginning, *the onset of winter*. 2 an
attack.

onshore *adjective*
from the sea towards the land, *an onshore
breeze*.

onslaught *noun* (*plural* **onslaughts**)
a fierce attack.
[from old Dutch *aan* = on + *slag* = a blow]

onto *preposition*
to a position on.

onus (*say* oh-nus) *noun*
the duty or responsibility of doing
something, *The onus is on the prosecution to
prove he did it*. [Latin, = burden]

onward *adverb* & *adjective*
going forward; further on. **onwards** *adverb*

onyx *noun*
a stone rather like marble, with different
colours in layers. [from Greek]

ooze *verb* (**oozes, oozing, oozed**)
1 flow out slowly; trickle. 2 allow
something to flow out slowly, *The wound
oozed blood*.
ooze *noun*
mud at the bottom of a river or sea.
[from Old English]

op- *prefix*
1 to; towards. 2 against. 3 in the way;
blocking. see **ob-**.

opal *noun* (*plural* **opals**)
a kind of stone with a rainbow sheen.
opalescent *adjective*
[via French or Latin from Sanskrit]

opaque (*say* o-**payk**) *adjective*
not able to be seen through; not
transparent or translucent.
[from Latin *opacus* = shady or dark]

OPEC *abbreviation*
Organization of Petroleum Exporting
Countries.

open *adjective*
1 allowing people or things to go in and
out; not closed or fastened. 2 not covered or
blocked up. 3 spread out; unfolded. 4 not
limited or restricted, *an open
championship*. 5 letting in visitors or
customers. 6 with wide empty spaces, *open
country*. 7 honest and frank; not secret or
secretive, *Be open about the danger*. 8 not
decided, *an open mind*. **openness** *noun*
in the open air not inside a house or
building. **open-air** *adjective*
open *verb* (**opens, opening, opened**)
1 make or become open or more open.
2 begin. **opener** *noun* [from Old English]

opencast *adjective*
(of a mine) worked by removing layers of earth from the surface, not underground.

opening *noun* (*plural* openings)
1 a space or gap; a place where something opens. 2 the beginning of something. 3 an opportunity.

openly *adverb*
without secrecy.

opera[1] *noun* (*plural* operas)
a play in which all or most of the words are sung. **operatic** *adjective* [Latin, = work]

opera[2] *plural* of **opus**.

operate *verb* (operates, operating, operated)
1 make a machine work. 2 be in action; work. 3 perform a surgical operation on somebody. **operable** *adjective*
[from Latin *operari* = to work]

operation *noun* (*plural* operations)
1 a piece of work or method of working. 2 something done to the body to take away or repair a part of it. 3 a planned military activity.
in operation working or in use, *When does the new system come into operation?*
operational *adjective*

operative *adjective*
1 working or functioning. 2 to do with surgical operations.

operator *noun* (*plural* operators)
a person who works something, especially a telephone switchboard or exchange.

operetta *noun* (*plural* operettas)
a short light opera. [Italian, = little opera]

ophthalmic (*say* off-thal-mik) *adjective*
to do with or for the eyes.
[from Greek *ophthalmos* = eye]

ophthalmic optician *noun* (*plural* ophthalmic opticians)
a person who is qualified to test people's eyesight and prescribe spectacles etc.

opinion *noun* (*plural* opinions)
what you think of something; a belief or judgement. [from Latin *opinari* = believe]

opinionated *adjective*
having strong opinions and holding them whatever anybody says.

opinion poll *noun* (*plural* opinion polls)
an estimate of what people think, made by questioning a sample of them.

opium *noun*
a drug made from the juice of certain poppies, used in medicine.
[from Greek *opion* = poppy juice]

opossum *noun* (*plural* opossums)
a small furry marsupial that lives in trees, with different kinds in America and Australia.
[from a Native American language]

opponent *noun* (*plural* opponents)
a person or group opposing another in a contest or war.
[from Latin *opponere* = to set against]

opportune *adjective*
1 (of time) suitable for a purpose. 2 done or happening at a suitable time. **opportunely** *adverb* [from *op-* + Latin *portus* = harbour (originally used of wind blowing a ship towards a harbour)]

opportunist *noun* (*plural* opportunists)
a person who is quick to seize opportunities.

opportunity *noun* (*plural* opportunities)
a good chance to do a particular thing.
[same origin as *opportune*]

oppose *verb* (opposes, opposing, opposed)
1 argue or fight against; resist. 2 contrast, *'Soft' is opposed to 'hard'.*
[from French; related to *opponent*]

opposite *adjective*
1 placed on the other or further side; facing, *on the opposite side of the road.* 2 moving away from or towards each other, *The trains were travelling in opposite directions.* 3 completely different, *opposite characters.*

opposite *noun* (*plural* opposites)
an opposite person or thing.

opposite *adverb*
in an opposite position or direction, *I'll sit opposite.*

opposite *preposition*
opposite to, *They live opposite the school.*
[from Latin *oppositus* = set or placed
against]

opposition *noun*
1 opposing something; resistance. 2 the
people who oppose something; **the
Opposition** the chief political party
opposing the one that is in power.

oppress *verb* (**oppresses, oppressing,
oppressed**)
1 govern or treat somebody cruelly or
unjustly. 2 weigh somebody down with
worry or sadness.
oppression *noun*, **oppressor** *noun*
[from *op-* + Latin *pressus* = pressed]

oppressive *adjective*
1 cruel or harsh, *an oppressive regime.*
2 worrying and difficult to bear. 3 (of
weather) unpleasantly hot and humid.

opt *verb* (**opts, opting, opted**)
choose.
opt out decide not to take part in
something.
[from Latin *optare* = wish for]

optic *adjective*
to do with the eye or sight.
[from Greek *optos* = seen]

optical *adjective*
to do with sight; aiding sight, *optical
instruments.* **optically** *adverb* [from *optic*]

optical illusion *noun* (*plural* **optical
illusions**)
a deceptive appearance that makes you see
something wrongly.

optician *noun* (*plural* **opticians**)
a person who makes or sells spectacles etc.
[from French, related to *optic*]

optics *noun*
the study of sight and of light as connected
with this.

optimist *noun* (*plural* **optimists**)
a person who expects that things will turn
out well. (Compare *pessimist.*) **optimism**
noun, **optimistic** *adjective*, **optimistically**
adverb [from French, related to *optimum*]

optimum *adjective*
best; most favourable. **optimum** *noun*,
optimal *adjective* [Latin, = best thing]

option *noun* (*plural* **options**)
1 the right or power to choose something.
2 something chosen or that may be chosen.
[same origin as *opt*]

optional *adjective*
that you can choose, not compulsory.
optionally *adverb*

opulent *adjective*
1 wealthy or luxurious. 2 plentiful.
opulently *adverb*, **opulence** *noun*
[from Latin *opes* = wealth]

opus (*say* oh-pus) *noun* (*plural* **opuses** or
opera)
a numbered musical composition,
Beethoven opus 15. [Latin, = work]

or *conjunction*
used to show that there is a choice or an
alternative, *Do you want a bun or a biscuit?*
[from *other*]

-or *suffix*
forms nouns meaning 'a person or thing
that does something' (e.g. *tailor,
refrigerator*). [from Latin or old French]

oracle *noun* (*plural* **oracles**)
1 a shrine where the ancient Greeks
consulted one of their gods for advice or a
prophecy. 2 a wise or knowledgeable
adviser. **oracular** (*say* or-ak-yoo-ler)
adjective [from Latin *orare* = speak]

oracy (*say* or-a-see) *noun*
the ability to express yourself well in
speaking. [same origin as *oral*]

oral *adjective*
1 spoken, not written. 2 to do with or using
the mouth. **orally** *adverb*
[from Latin *oris* = of the mouth]

USAGE: Do not confuse with *aural.*

orange *noun* (*plural* **oranges**)
1 a round juicy citrus fruit with reddish-
yellow peel. 2 a reddish-yellow colour.
[via French, Arabic, and Persian from
Sanskrit]

orangeade *noun*
an orange-flavoured drink.

orang-utan *noun* (*plural* orang-utans)
a large ape of Borneo and Sumatra.
[from Malay *orang hutan* = man of the
forest (Malay is spoken in Malaysia)]

oration *noun* (*plural* orations)
a long formal speech.
[from Latin *orare* = speak]

orator *noun* (*plural* orators)
a person who makes speeches.
oratorical *adjective*

oratorio *noun* (*plural* oratorios)
a piece of music for voices and an
orchestra, usually on a religious subject.
[Italian, related to *oration*]

oratory *noun*
the art of making speeches in public.

orb *noun* (*plural* orbs)
a sphere or globe.
[from Latin *orbis* = circle]

orbit *noun* (*plural* orbits)
1 the curved path taken by something
moving round a planet etc. in space. **2** the
range of someone's influence or control.
orbital *adjective*

orbit *verb* (orbits, orbiting, orbited)
move in an orbit round something, *The
spacecraft orbited the earth.*
[same origin as *orb*]

orchard *noun* (*plural* orchards)
a piece of ground planted with fruit trees.
[from Old English]

orchestra *noun* (*plural* orchestras)
a large group of people playing various
musical instruments together. **orchestral**
adjective [Greek, = the space where the
chorus danced during a play]

orchestrate *verb* (orchestrates,
orchestrating, orchestrated)
1 compose or arrange music for an
orchestra. **2** coordinate things
deliberately, *They orchestrated their
campaigns.* **orchestration** *noun*
[from *orchestra*]

orchid *noun* (*plural* orchids)
a kind of flower, often with unevenly
shaped petals. [from Latin]

ordain *verb* (ordains, ordaining, ordained)
1 make a person a member of the clergy in
the Christian Church, *He was ordained in
1981.* **2** declare or order something by law.
[from old French; related to *order*]

ordeal *noun* (*plural* ordeals)
a difficult or horrific experience.
[from Old English]

order *noun* (*plural* orders)
1 a command. **2** a request for something to
be supplied. **3** the way things are arranged,
in alphabetical order. **4** a neat
arrangement; a proper arrangement or
condition, *in working order.* **5** obedience to
rules or laws, *law and order.* **6** a kind or
sort, *She showed courage of the highest
order.* **7** a group of monks or nuns who live
by certain religious rules.
in order that or **in order to** for the purpose of.

order *verb* (orders, ordering, ordered)
1 command. **2** ask for something to be
supplied. **3** put something into order;
arrange neatly. [from Latin *ordo* = a row,
series, or arrangement]

orderly *adjective*
1 arranged neatly or well; methodical.
2 well-behaved and obedient.
orderliness *noun*

orderly *noun* (*plural* orderlies)
1 a soldier whose job is to assist an officer.
2 an assistant in a hospital.

ordinal number *noun* (*plural* ordinal
numbers)
a number that shows a thing's position in a
series, e.g. *first, fifth, twentieth.* (Compare
cardinal numbers.)
[from Latin *ordinalis* = showing the order]

ordinance *noun* (*plural* ordinances)
a command or decree.
[from Latin *ordinare* = put in order]

ordinary *adjective*
normal or usual; not special.
ordinarily *adverb*
[from Latin *ordinarius* = orderly or usual]

ordination *noun* (*plural* ordinations)
ordaining or being ordained as a member
of the clergy.

ordnance *noun*
weapons and other military equipment.
[from old French *ordenance* = ordinance]

Ordnance Survey *noun*
an official survey organization that makes
detailed maps of the British Isles.
[because the maps were originally made
for the army]

ore *noun* (*plural* ores)
rock with metal or other useful substances
in it, *iron ore*. [from Old English]

oregano *noun*
the dried leaves of wild marjoram used as a
herb in cooking. [via Spanish from Greek]

organ *noun* (*plural* organs)
1 a musical instrument from which sounds
are produced by air forced through pipes,
played by keys and pedals. 2 a part of the
body with a particular function, *the
digestive organs*.
[from Greek *organon* = tool]

organdie *noun*
a kind of thin fabric, usually stiffened.
[from French]

organic *adjective*
1 to do with the organs of the body, *organic
diseases*. 2 to do with or formed from living
things, *organic matter*. 3 organic food is
grown or produced without the use of
chemical fertilizers, pesticides, etc.,
organic farming. **organically** *adverb*

organism *noun* (*plural* organisms)
a living thing; an individual animal or
plant. [from Greek]

organist *noun* (*plural* organists)
a person who plays the organ.

organization *noun* (*plural* organizations)
1 an organized group of people, such as a
business, charity, government department,
etc. 2 the organizing of something.
organizational *adjective*

organize *verb* (organizes, organizing,
organized)
1 plan and prepare something, *We
organized a picnic*. 2 form people into a
group to work together. 3 put things in
order. **organizer** *noun*
[same origin as *organ*]

orgasm *noun* (*plural* orgasms)
the climax of sexual excitement.
[from Greek]

orgy *noun* (*plural* orgies)
1 a wild party that involves a lot of
drinking and sex. 2 an extravagant
activity, *an orgy of spending*.
[from Latin *orgia* = secret rites (held in
honour of Bacchus, the Greek and Roman
god of wine)]

Orient *noun*
the East; oriental countries. (Compare
Occident.) [from Latin, = sunrise]

orient *verb* (orients, orienting, oriented)
place something or face in a certain
direction; orientate.

oriental *adjective*
to do with the countries east of the
Mediterranean Sea, especially China and
Japan.

orientate *verb* (orientates, orientating,
orientated)
place something or face in a certain
direction. **orientation** *noun*
[originally = turn to face the east: same
origin as *Orient*]

orienteering *noun*
the sport of finding your way across rough
country with a map and compass.
[from Swedish *orientering* = orientating]

orifice (*say* o-rif-iss) *noun* (*plural* orifices)
an opening in your body.
[from Latin *oris* = of the mouth]

origami (*say* o-rig-ah-mee) *noun*
folding paper into decorative shapes.
[from Japanese *ori* = fold + *kami* = paper]

origin *noun* (*plural* origins)
1 the start of something; the point or cause
from which something began. 2 the point
where two or more axes on a graph meet.
[from Latin *oriri* = to rise]

original *adjective*
1 existing from the start; earliest, *the
original inhabitants*. 2 new in its design
etc.; not a copy. 3 producing new ideas;
inventive.
originally *adverb*, **originality** *noun*

original *noun* (*plural* originals)
a document, painting etc. which was the
first one made and is not a copy.

originate *verb* (originates, originating,
originated)
1 cause something to begin; create. **2** have
its origin, *The quarrel originated in rivalry.*
origination *noun*, originator *noun*

ornament *noun* (*plural* ornaments)
an object displayed or worn as a
decoration. ornamental *adjective*

ornament *verb* (ornaments, ornamenting,
ornamented)
decorate something with beautiful things.
ornamentation *noun*
[from Latin *ornare* = adorn]

ornate *adjective*
elaborately decorated. ornately *adverb*
[from Latin *ornatum* = adorned]

ornithology *noun*
the study of birds.
ornithologist *noun*, ornithological *adjective*
[from Greek *ornithos* = of a bird, + *-logy*]

orphan *noun* (*plural* orphans)
a child whose parents are dead.
orphaned *adjective*
[from Greek]

orphanage *noun* (*plural* orphanages)
a home for orphans.

ortho- *prefix*
right; straight; correct.
[from Greek *orthos* = straight]

orthodox *adjective*
holding beliefs that are correct or
generally accepted. orthodoxy *noun*
[from *ortho-* + Greek *doxa* = opinion]

Orthodox Church *noun*
the Christian Churches of eastern Europe.

orthopaedics (*say* orth-o-pee diks) *noun*
the treatment of deformities and injuries
to bones and muscles. orthopaedic *adjective*
[from *ortho-* + Greek *paideia* = rearing of
children (because the treatment was
originally of children)]

oscillate *verb* (oscillates, oscillating,
oscillated)
1 move to and fro like a pendulum; vibrate.
2 waver or vary. oscillation *noun*, oscillator
noun [from Latin *oscillare* = to swing]

osier (*say* oh-zee-er) *noun* (*plural* osiers)
a willow with flexible twigs used in making
baskets. [from old French]

-osis *suffix*
1 a diseased condition (as in *tuberculosis*).
2 an action or process (as in
metamorphosis). [from Latin or Greek]

osmosis *noun*
the passing of fluid through a porous
partition into another more concentrated
fluid. [from Greek *osmos* = a push]

ostensible *adjective*
apparent, but actually concealing the true
reason, *Their ostensible reason for
travelling was to visit friends.* ostensibly
adverb [from Latin *ostendere* = to show]

ostentatious *adjective*
making a showy display of something to
impress people. ostentatiously *adverb*,
ostentation *noun* [same origin as *ostensible*]

osteopath *noun* (*plural* osteopaths)
a person who treats certain diseases etc. by
manipulating a patient's bones and
muscles. osteopathy *noun*, osteopathic
adjective [from Greek *osteon* = bone
+ *-patheia* = suffering]

ostracize *verb* (ostracizes, ostracizing,
ostracized)
exclude someone from your group and
completely ignore them. ostracism *noun*
[from Greek *ostrakon* = piece of pottery
(because people voted to banish someone
by writing his name on this)]

ostrich *noun* (*plural* ostriches)
a large long-legged African bird that can
run very fast but cannot fly. It was said to
bury its head in the sand when pursued,
believing that it cannot then be seen.
[from old French]

other *adjective*
1 different, *some other tune.* **2** remaining,
Try the other shoe. **3** additional, *my other
friends.* **4** just recent or past, *I saw him the
other day.*

other *noun & pronoun* (*plural* others)
the other person or thing, *Where are the others?* [from Old English]

otherwise *adverb*
1 if things happen differently; if you do not, *Write it down, otherwise you'll forget.* 2 in other ways, *It rained, but otherwise the holiday was good.* 3 differently, *We could not do otherwise.* [from *other* + *-wise*]

otter *noun* (*plural* otters)
a fish-eating animal with webbed feet, a flat tail, and thick brown fur, living near water. [from Old English]

ottoman *noun* (*plural* ottomans)
1 a long padded seat. 2 a storage box with a padded top. [from *Ottomanus*, the Latin name of the family who ruled Turkey from the 14th to the 20th century (because the ottoman originated in Turkey)]

ought *auxiliary verb*
expressing duty (*We ought to feed them*), rightness or advisability (*You ought to take more exercise*), or probability (*At this speed, we ought to be there by noon*).
[from Old English *ahte* = owed]

oughtn't (*mainly spoken*)
ought not.

ounce *noun* (*plural* ounces)
a unit of weight equal to $\frac{1}{16}$ of a pound (about 28 grams). [from Latin]

our *adjective*
belonging to us. [from Old English]

ours *possessive pronoun*
belonging to us, *These seats are ours.*
[from *our*]

USAGE: It is incorrect to write *our's*.

---

ourselves *pronoun*
we or us and nobody else. (Compare *herself.*)

oust *verb* (ousts, ousting, ousted)
drive a person out from a position or employment etc. [from old French]

out *adverb*
1 away from or not in a particular place or position or state etc.; not at home. 2 into the open; into existence or sight etc., *The*
sun came out. 3 not in action or use etc.; (of a batsman) having had the innings ended; (of a fire) not burning. 4 to or at an end; completely, *sold out; tired out.* 5 without restraint; boldly or loudly, *Speak out!*
be out for or **out to** be seeking or wanting, *They are out to make trouble.*
out of date 1 old-fashioned. 2 not valid any more.
out of doors in the open air.
out of the way remote.
[from Old English]

out- *prefix*
1 out of; away from (as in *outcast*).
2 external; separate (as in *outhouse*).
3 more than; so as to defeat or exceed (as in *outdo*).

out and out *adjective*
thorough or complete, *an out and out villain.*

outback *noun*
the remote inland districts of Australia.

outboard motor *noun* (*plural* outboard motors)
a motor fitted to the outside of a boat's stern.

outbreak *noun* (*plural* outbreaks)
the start of a disease or war or anger etc.

outburst *noun* (*plural* outbursts)
the bursting out of anger or laughter etc.

outcast *noun* (*plural* outcasts)
a person who has been rejected by family, friends, or society.

outcome *noun* (*plural* outcomes)
the result of what happens or has happened.

outcrop *noun* (*plural* outcrops)
a piece of rock from a lower level that sticks out on the surface of the ground.
[from *out*, + *crop* = outcrop]

outcry *noun* (*plural* outcries)
a strong protest.

outdated *adjective*
out of date.

outdistance *verb* (outdistances, outdistancing, outdistanced)
get far ahead of someone in a race etc.

outdo *verb* (outdoes, outdoing, outdid, outdone)
do better than another person etc.

outdoor *adjective*
done or used outdoors.

outdoors *adverb*
in the open air.

outer *adjective*
outside or external; nearer to the outside.
outermost *adjective*

outer space *noun*
the universe beyond the earth's atmosphere.

outfit *noun* (*plural* outfits)
1 a set of clothes worn together. 2 a set of equipment. 3 (*informal*) a team or organization.

outflow *noun* (*plural* outflows)
1 flowing out; what flows out. 2 a pipe for liquid flowing out.

outgoing *adjective*
1 going out; retiring from office, *the outgoing chairman*. 2 sociable and friendly.

outgoings *plural noun*
expenditure.

outgrow *verb* (outgrows, outgrowing, outgrew, outgrown)
1 grow out of clothes or habits etc. 2 grow faster or larger than another person or thing.

outgrowth *noun* (*plural* outgrowths)
something that grows out of another thing, *Feathers are outgrowths on a bird's skin.*

outhouse *noun* (*plural* outhouses)
a small building (e.g. a shed or barn) that belongs to a house but is separate from it.

outing *noun* (*plural* outings)
a journey for pleasure.

outlandish *adjective*
looking or sounding strange or foreign.
[from Old English *utland* = a foreign land]

outlast *verb* (outlasts, outlasting, outlasted)
last longer than something else.

outlaw *noun* (*plural* outlaws)
a person who is punished by being excluded from legal rights and the protection of the law.
outlaw *verb* (outlaws, outlawing, outlawed)
1 make a person an outlaw. 2 declare something to be illegal; forbid.

outlay *noun* (*plural* outlays)
what is spent on something.

outlet *noun* (*plural* outlets)
1 a way for something to get out. 2 a market for goods.

outline *noun* (*plural* outlines)
1 a line round the outside of something, showing its boundary or shape. 2 a summary.
outline *verb* (outlines, outlining, outlined)
1 make an outline of something. 2 summarize.

outlive *verb* (outlives, outliving, outlived)
live or last longer than another person etc.

outlook *noun* (*plural* outlooks)
1 a view on which people look out. 2 a person's mental attitude to something. 3 future prospects, *The outlook is bleak.*

outlying *adjective*
far from the centre; remote, *the outlying districts.*

outmanoeuvre *verb* (outmanoeuvres, outmanoeuvring, outmanoeuvred)
use skill or cunning to gain an advantage over someone.

outmoded *adjective*
out of date.

outnumber *verb* (outnumbers, outnumbering, outnumbered)
be more numerous than another group.

outpatient *noun* (*plural* outpatients)
a person who visits a hospital for treatment but does not stay there.

outpost *noun* (*plural* outposts)
a distant settlement. [from *out* + *post*³]

output *noun* (*plural* **outputs**)
1 the amount produced. 2 the information or results produced by a computer.

outrage *noun* (*plural* **outrages**)
1 something that shocks people by being very wicked or cruel. 2 great anger.
outrageous *adjective*, **outrageously** *adverb*
outrage *verb* (**outrages, outraging, outraged**)
shock and anger people greatly.
[from old French *outrer* = go beyond, exaggerate, influenced by *rage*]

outrider *noun* (*plural* **outriders**)
a person riding on a motorcycle as an escort or guard.

outrigger *noun* (*plural* **outriggers**)
a framework attached to the side of a boat, e.g. to prevent a canoe from capsizing.
[origin unknown]

outright *adverb*
1 completely; not gradually, *This drug should be banned outright.* 2 frankly, *We told him this outright.*
outright *adjective*
thorough or complete, *an outright fraud.*

outrun *verb* (**outruns, outrunning, outran, outrun**)
1 run faster or further than another. 2 go on for longer than it should.

outset *noun*
the beginning of something, *from the outset of his career.*

outside *noun* (*plural* **outsides**)
the outer side, surface, or part.
at the outside at the most, *a mile at the outside.*
outside *adjective*
1 on or coming from the outside, *the outside edge.* 2 greatest possible, *the outside price.* 3 remote or slight, *an outside chance.*
outside *adverb*
on or to the outside; outdoors, *Leave it outside. It's cold outside.*
outside *preposition*
on or to the outside of, *Leave it outside the door.*

outside broadcast *noun* (*plural* **outside broadcasts**)
a broadcast made on location and not in a studio.

outsider *noun* (*plural* **outsiders**)
1 a person who does not belong to a certain group. 2 a horse or person thought to have no chance of winning a race or competition.

outsize *adjective*
much larger than average.

outskirts *plural noun*
the outer parts or districts, especially of a town.

outspoken *adjective*
speaking or spoken very frankly.

outspread *adjective*
spread out.

outstanding *adjective*
1 extremely good or distinguished. 2 not yet paid or dealt with.

outstretched *adjective*
stretched out.

outstrip *verb* (**outstrips, outstripping, outstripped**)
1 run faster or further than another; outrun. 2 surpass in achievement or success. [from *out-* + Middle English *strypen* = move quickly]

outvote *verb* (**outvotes, outvoting, outvoted**)
defeat someone by a majority of votes.

outward *adjective*
1 going outwards. 2 on the outside.
outwardly *adverb*, **outwards** *adverb*

outweigh *verb* (**outweighs, outweighing, outweighed**)
be greater in weight or importance than something else.

outwit *verb* (**outwits, outwitting, outwitted**)
deceive somebody by being crafty.

ova *plural* of **ovum.**

oval *adjective*
shaped like a 0, rounded and longer than it is broad. **oval** *noun*
[from Latin *ovum* = egg]

ovary *noun* (*plural* **ovaries**)
1 either of the two organs in which ova or egg-cells are produced in a woman's or female animal's body. **2** part of the pistil in a plant, from which fruit is formed.
[from Latin *ovum* = egg]

ovation *noun* (*plural* **ovations**)
enthusiastic applause.
[from Latin *ovare* = rejoice]

oven *noun* (*plural* **ovens**)
a closed space in which things are cooked or heated.
[from Old English]

over *preposition*
1 above. **2** more than, *It's over a mile away.* **3** concerning, *They quarrelled over money.* **4** across the top of; on or to the other side of, *They rowed the boat over the lake.* **5** during, *We can talk over dinner.* **6** in superiority or preference to, *their victory over United.*

over *adverb*
1 out and down from the top or edge; from an upright position, *He fell over.* **2** so that a different side shows, *Turn it over.* **3** at or to a place; across, *Walk over to our house.* **4** remaining, *There is nothing left over.* **5** all through; thoroughly, *Think it over.* **6** at an end, *The lesson is over.*
over and over many times; repeatedly.

over *noun* (*plural* **overs**)
a series of six balls bowled in cricket.
[from Old English]

over- *prefix*
1 over (as in *overturn*). **2** too much; too (as in *over-anxious*).

overact *verb* (**overacts, overacting, overacted**)
(of an actor) act in an exaggerated manner.

overall *adjective*
including everything; total, *the overall cost.*
overall *noun* (*plural* **overalls**)
a type of coat worn over other clothes to protect them when working.

overalls *plural noun*
a garment, like a shirt and trousers combined, worn over other clothes to protect them.

overarm *adjective* & *adverb*
with the arm lifted above shoulder level and coming down in front of the body, *bowling overarm.*

overawe *verb* (**overawes, overawing, overawed**)
overcome a person with awe.

overbalance *verb* (**overbalances, overbalancing, overbalanced**)
lose balance and fall over.

overbearing *adjective*
domineering.

overblown *adjective*
1 exaggerated or pretentious. **2** (of a flower) too fully open; past its best.

overboard *adverb*
from in or on a ship into the water, *She jumped overboard.*

overcast *adjective*
covered with cloud.

overcoat *noun* (*plural* **overcoats**)
a warm outdoor coat.

overcome *verb* (**overcomes, overcoming, overcame, overcome**)
1 win a victory over somebody; defeat. **2** make a person helpless, *He was overcome by the fumes.* **3** find a way of dealing with a problem etc.

overcrowd *verb* (**overcrowds, overcrowding, overcrowded**)
crowd too many people into a place or vehicle etc. **overcrowded** *adjective*

overdo *verb* (**overdoes, overdoing, overdid, overdone**)
1 do something too much. **2** cook food for too long.

overdose *noun* (*plural* **overdoses**)
too large a dose of a drug.

overdraft *noun* (*plural* **overdrafts**)
the amount by which a bank account is overdrawn.

overdraw *verb* (overdraws, overdrawing, overdrew, overdrawn)
draw more money from a bank account than the amount you have in it.

overdue *adjective*
late; not paid or arrived etc. by the proper time.

overestimate *verb* (overestimates, overestimating, overestimated)
estimate something too highly.

overflow *verb* (overflows, overflowing, overflowed)
flow over the edge or limits of something. **overflow** *noun*

overgrown *adjective*
covered with weeds or unwanted plants.

overhang *verb* (overhangs, overhanging, overhung)
jut out over something. **overhang** *noun*

overhaul *verb* (overhauls, overhauling, overhauled)
1 examine something thoroughly and repair it if necessary. 2 overtake. **overhaul** *noun*

overhead *adjective* & *adverb*
1 above the level of your head. 2 in the sky.

overheads *plural noun*
the expenses of running a business.

overhear *verb* (overhears, overhearing, overheard)
hear something accidentally or without the speaker intending you to hear it.

overjoyed *adjective*
filled with great joy.

overland *adjective* & *adverb*
travelling over the land, not by sea or air.

overlap *verb* (overlaps, overlapping, overlapped)
1 lie across part of something. 2 happen partly at the same time. **overlap** *noun*
[from *over* + *lap*[1]]

overlay *verb* (overlays, overlaying, overlaid)
cover with a layer; lie on top of something.
overlay *noun* (*plural* overlays)
a thing laid over another.

overlie *verb* (overlies, overlying, overlay, overlain)
lie over something.

overlook *verb* (overlooks, overlooking, overlooked)
1 not notice or consider something. 2 not punish an offence. 3 have a view over something.

overlord *noun* (*plural* overlords)
a supreme lord.

overnight *adjective* & *adverb*
of or during a night, *an overnight stop in Rome.*

overpower *verb* (overpowers, overpowering, overpowered)
overcome.

overpowering *adjective*
very strong.

overrate *verb* (overrates, overrating, overrated)
have too high an opinion of something.

overreach *verb* (overreaches, overreaching, overreached)
overreach yourself fail through being too ambitious.

override *verb* (overrides, overriding, overrode, overridden)
1 overrule. 2 be more important than, *Safety overrides all other considerations.*

overripe *adjective*
too ripe.

overrule *verb* (overrules, overruling, overruled)
reject a suggestion etc. by using your authority, *We voted for having a disco but the headteacher overruled the idea.*

overrun *verb* (overruns, overrunning, overran, overrun)
1 spread over and occupy or harm something, *Mice overran the place.* 2 go on for longer than it should, *The broadcast overran its time.*

overseas *adverb*
across or beyond the sea; abroad.

oversee *verb* (oversees, overseeing, oversaw, overseen)
watch over or supervise people working.
overseer *noun*

overshadow *verb* (overshadows, overshadowing, overshadowed)
1 cast a shadow over something. **2** make a person or thing seem unimportant in comparison.

overshoot *verb* (overshoots, overshooting, overshot)
go beyond a target or limit, *The plane overshot the runway.*

oversight *noun* (*plural* oversights)
a mistake made by not noticing something.

oversleep *verb* (oversleeps, oversleeping, overslept)
sleep for longer than you intended.

overspill *noun*
what spills over; the extra population of a town, who take homes in nearby districts.

overstep *verb* (oversteps, overstepping, overstepped)
go beyond a limit.

overt *adjective*
done or shown openly, *overt hostility.*
overtly *adverb* [from old French, = open]

overtake *verb* (overtakes, overtaking, overtook, overtaken)
1 pass a moving vehicle or person etc. **2** catch up with someone.

overtax *verb* (overtaxes, overtaxing, overtaxed)
1 tax too heavily. **2** put too heavy a burden or strain on someone.

overthrow *verb* (overthrows, overthrowing, overthrew, overthrown)
remove someone from power by force, *They overthrew the king.*
overthrow *noun* (*plural* overthrows)
1 overthrowing. **2** throwing a ball too far.

overtime *noun*
time spent working outside the normal hours; payment for this.

overtone *noun* (*plural* overtones)
a feeling or quality that is suggested but not expressed directly, *There were overtones of envy in his speech.*

overture *noun* (*plural* overtures)
1 a piece of music written as an introduction to an opera, ballet, etc. **2** a friendly attempt to start a discussion, *They made overtures of peace.*
[from old French, = opening]

overturn *verb* (overturns, overturning, overturned)
1 turn over or upside down. **2** reverse a legal decision.

overweight *adjective*
too heavy.

overwhelm *verb* (overwhelms, overwhelming, overwhelmed)
1 bury or drown beneath a huge mass. **2** overcome completely.
[from *over* + Middle English *whelm* = turn upside down]

overwork *verb* (overworks, overworking, overworked)
1 work or make someone work too hard. **2** use something too often, *'Nice' is an overworked word.*
overwork *noun*

overwrought *adjective*
very upset and nervous or worried.

ovoid *adjective*
egg-shaped. [from French, related to *ovum*]

ovulate *verb* (ovulates, ovulating, ovulated)
produce an ovum from an ovary.
[from French, related to *ovum*]

ovum (*say* oh-vum) *noun* (*plural* ova)
a female cell that can develop into a new individual when it is fertilized.
[Latin, = egg]

owe *verb* (owes, owing, owed)
1 have a duty to pay or give something to someone, especially money. **2** have something because of the action of another person or thing, *They owed their lives to the pilot's skill.*

owing to because of; caused by.
[from Old English]

USAGE: The use of *owing to* as a preposition meaning 'because of' is entirely acceptable, unlike this use of *due to*, which some people object to. See note at *due*.

owl *noun* (*plural* **owls**)
a bird of prey with large eyes, usually flying at night.
[from Old English]

own *adjective*
belonging to yourself or itself.
get your own back get revenge.
on your own alone.
own *verb* (**owns, owning, owned**)
1 possess; have something as your property. 2 acknowledge or admit something, *I own that I made a mistake.*
own up confess; admit guilt.
[from Old English]

owner *noun* (*plural* **owners**)
the person who owns something.
ownership *noun*

ox *noun* (*plural* **oxen**)
a large animal kept for its meat and for pulling carts.
[from Old English]

oxide *noun* (*plural* **oxides**)
a compound of oxygen and one other element.
[from French]

oxidize *verb* (**oxidizes, oxidizing, oxidized**)
1 combine or cause to combine with oxygen. 2 coat with an oxide.
oxidation *noun*

oxtail *noun* (*plural* **oxtails**)
the tail of an ox, used to make soup or stew.

oxygen *noun*
a colourless odourless tasteless gas that exists in the air and is essential for living things. [from French]

oyster *noun* (*plural* **oysters**)
a kind of shellfish whose shell sometimes contains a pearl.
[from Greek]

ozone *noun*
a form of oxygen with a sharp smell.
[from Greek *ozein* = to smell]

ozone layer *noun*
a layer of ozone high in the atmosphere, protecting the world from harmful amounts of the sun's rays.

Pp

p *abbreviation*
penny or pence.

p. *abbreviation* (*plural* **pp.**)
page.

pa *noun* (*slang*)
father. [short for *papa*]

pace *noun* (*plural* **paces**)
1 one step in walking, marching, or running. 2 speed, *He set a fast pace.*
pace *verb* (**paces, pacing, paced**)
1 walk with slow or regular steps.
2 measure a distance in paces, *pace it out.* [from Latin *passus*, literally = a stretch of the leg]

pacemaker *noun* (*plural* **pacemakers**)
1 a person who sets the pace for another in a race. 2 an electrical device to keep the heart beating.

pacific (*say* pa-**sif**-ik) *adjective*
peaceful; making or loving peace.
pacifically *adverb*

pacifist (*say* **pas**-if-ist) *noun* (*plural* **pacifists**)
a person who believes that war is always wrong. **pacifism** *noun*

pacify *verb* (**pacifies, pacifying, pacified**)
1 calm a person down. 2 bring peace to a country etc. **pacification** *noun*
[from Latin *pacis* = of peace]

pack *noun* (*plural* **packs**)
1 a bundle; a collection of things wrapped or tied together. 2 a set of playing cards (usually 52). 3 a group of hounds or wolves etc. 4 a group of people; a group of

Brownies or Cub Scouts. **5** a large amount, *a pack of lies.* **6** a mass of pieces of ice floating in the sea, *pack ice.*
pack *verb* (packs, packing, packed)
1 put things into a suitcase, bag, or box etc. in order to move or store them. **2** crowd together; fill tightly.
pack off send a person away.
send a person packing dismiss him or her.
[from old German or Dutch]

package *noun* (*plural* packages)
1 a parcel or packet. **2** a number of things offered or accepted together. **packaging** *noun* [from *pack*]

package holiday *noun* (*plural* package holidays)
a holiday with everything arranged and included in the price.

packet *noun* (*plural* packets)
a small parcel. [from *pack*]

pact *noun* (*plural* pacts)
an agreement or treaty. [from Latin]

pad[1] *noun* (*plural* pads)
1 a soft thick mass of material, used e.g. to protect or stuff something. **2** a piece of soft material worn to protect your leg in cricket and other games. **3** a set of sheets of paper fastened together at one edge. **4** the soft fleshy part under an animal's foot or the end of a finger or toe. **5** a flat surface from which rockets are launched or where helicopters take off and land.
pad *verb* (pads, padding, padded)
put a pad on or in something.
[probably from old Dutch]

pad[2] *verb* (pads, padding, padded)
walk softly. [from Dutch *pad* = path]

padding *noun*
material used to pad things.

paddle[1] *verb* (paddles, paddling, paddled)
walk about in shallow water. **paddle** *noun*
[probably from old Dutch]

paddle[2] *noun* (*plural* paddles)
a short oar with a broad blade; something shaped like this.
paddle *verb* (paddles, paddling, paddled)
move a boat along with a paddle or paddles; row gently. [origin unknown]

paddock *noun* (*plural* paddocks)
a small field where horses are kept.
[from Old English]

paddy[1] *noun* (*plural* paddies)
a field where rice is grown. **paddy field** *noun* [from Malay *padi* = rice (Malay is spoken in Malaysia)]

paddy[2] *noun* (*plural* paddies) (*informal*)
a fit of temper. [pet form of *Patrick*]

padlock *noun* (*plural* padlocks)
a detachable lock with a metal loop that passes through a ring or chain etc.
[origin unknown]

padre (*say* pah-dray) *noun* (*plural* padres) (*informal*)
a chaplain in the armed forces.
[Italian, Spanish, and Portuguese, = father]

paean (*say* pee-an) *noun* (*plural* paeans)
a song of praise or triumph.
[from Greek, = hymn]

paediatrics (*say* peed-ee-at-riks) *noun*
the study of children's diseases. **paediatric** *adjective*, **paediatrician** *noun* [from Greek *paidos* = of a child + *iatros* = doctor]

pagan (*say* pay-gan) *noun* (*plural* pagans)
a person who does not believe in one of the chief religions; a heathen. **pagan** *adjective*
[same origin as *peasant*]

page[1] *noun* (*plural* pages)
a piece of paper that is part of a book or newspaper etc.; one side of this.
[from Latin]

page[2] *noun* (*plural* pages)
a boy or man employed to go on errands or be an attendant.
[from Greek *paidion* = small boy]

pageant *noun* (*plural* pageants)
1 a play or entertainment about historical events and people. **2** a procession of people in costume as an entertainment. **pageantry** *noun* [origin unknown]

pagoda (*say* pag-oh-da) *noun* (*plural* pagodas)
a Buddhist tower, or a Hindu temple shaped like a pyramid, in India and the Far East. [via Portuguese from Persian]

paid *past tense* of **pay**.
put paid to (*informal*) put an end to someone's activity or hope etc.

pail *noun* (*plural* **pails**)
a bucket. [from Old English]

pain *noun* (*plural* **pains**)
1 an unpleasant feeling caused by injury or disease. 2 suffering in the mind. **painful** *adjective*, **painfully** *adverb*, **painless** *adjective*
take pains make a careful effort with work etc.
pain *verb* (**pains, paining, pained**)
cause suffering or distress to someone. [from Latin *poena* = punishment]

painkiller *noun* (*plural* **painkillers**)
a medicine or drug that relieves pain.

painstaking *adjective*
very careful and thorough.

paint *noun* (*plural* **paints**)
a liquid substance put on something to colour it. **paintbox** *noun*, **paintbrush** *noun*
paint *verb* (**paints, painting, painted**)
1 put paint on something. 2 make a picture with paints. [from Latin]

painter¹ *noun* (*plural* **painters**)
a person who paints.

painter² *noun* (*plural* **painters**)
a rope used to tie up a boat.
[from old French *penteur* = rope]

painting *noun* (*plural* **paintings**)
a painted picture.

pair *noun* (*plural* **pairs**)
1 a set of two things or people; a couple. 2 something made of two joined parts, *a pair of scissors*.
pair *verb* (**pairs, pairing, paired**)
put two things together as a pair. [from Latin *paria* = equal things]

pal *noun* (*plural* **pals**) (*informal*)
a friend. [Romany, = brother]

palace *noun* (*plural* **palaces**)
a mansion where a king, queen, or other important person lives. [from *Palatium*, the name of a hill on which the house of the emperor Augustus stood in ancient Rome]

palaeolithic (*say* pal-ee-o-lith-ik) *adjective*
belonging to the early part of the Stone Age.
[from Greek *palaios* = old + *lithos* = stone]

palaeontology (*say* pal-ee-on-tol-o-jee) *noun*
the study of fossils. [from Greek *palaios* = ancient + *onta* = beings, + *-ology*]

palatable *adjective*
tasting pleasant.

palate *noun* (*plural* **palates**)
1 the roof of your mouth. 2 a person's sense of taste. [from Latin]

USAGE: Do not confuse with *palette* and *pallet*.

palatial (*say* pa-lay-shal) *adjective*
like a palace; large and splendid.
[same origin as *palace*]

pale¹ *adjective*
1 almost white, *a pale face*. 2 not bright in colour or light, *pale green; the pale moonlight*. **palely** *adverb*, **paleness** *noun*
[from Latin *pallidus* = pallid]

pale² *noun* (*plural* **pales**)
a boundary.
beyond the pale beyond the limits of good taste or behaviour etc.
[from Latin *palus* = a stake or fence post]

palette *noun* (*plural* **palettes**)
a board on which an artist mixes colours ready for use. [French]

USAGE: Do not confuse with *palate* and *pallet*.

palindrome *noun* (*plural* **palindromes**)
a word or phrase that reads the same backwards as forwards, e.g. *radar*. [from Greek *palindromos* = running back again]

paling *noun* (*plural* **palings**)
a fence made of wooden posts or railings; one of its posts. [from *pale²*]

palisade *noun* (*plural* **palisades**)
a fence of pointed sticks or boards.
[French, related to *pale²*]

pall¹ (*say* pawl) *noun* (*plural* **palls**)
1 a cloth spread over a coffin. 2 a dark

covering, *A pall of smoke lay over the town.*
[from Latin *pallium* = cloak]

pall² (*say* pawl) *verb* (**palls, palling, palled**)
become uninteresting or boring to
someone, *The novelty of the new computer
game soon began to pall.* [from *appal*]

pallbearer *noun* (*plural* **pallbearers**)
a person helping to carry the coffin at a
funeral.

pallet *noun* (*plural* **pallets**)
1 a mattress stuffed with straw. 2 a hard
narrow bed.
[from old French *paille* = straw]

USAGE: Do not confuse with *palate* and
palette.

palliate *verb* (**palliates, palliating, palliated**)
make a thing less serious or less severe.
palliation *noun* [same origin as *pall¹*]

palliative *noun* (*plural* **palliatives**)
something that lessens pain or suffering.
palliative *adjective*

pallid *adjective*
pale, especially because of illness.
[from Latin]

pallor *noun*
paleness in a person's face, especially
because of illness.

palm *noun* (*plural* **palms**)
1 the inner part of the hand, between the
fingers and the wrist. 2 a palm tree.

palm *verb* (**palms, palming, palmed**)
pick up something secretly and hide it in
the palm of your hand.
palm off deceive a person into accepting
something.
[from Latin]

palmistry *noun*
fortune-telling by looking at the creases in
the palm of a person's hand. **palmist** *noun*

Palm Sunday *noun*
the Sunday before Easter, commemorating
Jesus Christ's entry into Jerusalem when
people spread palm leaves in his path.

palm tree *noun* (*plural* **palm trees**)
a tropical tree with large leaves and no
branches.

palpable *adjective*
1 able to be touched or felt. 2 obvious, *a
palpable lie.* **palpably** *adverb*
[from Latin *palpare* = to touch]

palpitate *verb* (**palpitates, palpitating,
palpitated**)
1 (of the heart) beat hard and quickly. 2 (of
a person) quiver with fear or excitement.
palpitation *noun* [from Latin]

palsy (*say* pawl-zee) *noun* (*old use*)
paralysis. [same origin as *paralysis*]

paltry (*say* pol-tree) *adjective*
very small and almost worthless, *a paltry
amount.* [origin unknown]

pampas *noun*
wide grassy plains in South America.
[via Spanish from Quechua (a South
American language)]

pampas grass *noun*
a tall grass with long feathery flowers.

pamper *verb* (**pampers, pampering,
pampered**)
treat or look after someone very kindly and
indulgently; coddle.
[probably from old German or old Dutch]

pamphlet *noun* (*plural* **pamphlets**)
a leaflet or booklet giving information on a
subject. [from *Pamphilet*, the name of a
long 12th-century poem in Latin]

pan *noun* (*plural* **pans**)
1 a wide container with a flat base, used for
cooking etc. 2 something shaped like this.
3 the bowl of a lavatory. [from Old English]

pan- *prefix*
1 all (as in *panorama*). 2 to do with the
whole of a continent or group etc. (as in
pan-African). [from Greek]

panacea (*say* pan-a-see-a) *noun* (*plural*
panaceas)
a cure for all kinds of diseases or troubles.
[from *pan-* + Greek *akos* = remedy]

panama *noun* (*plural* **panamas**)
a hat made of a fine straw-like material.
[from Panama in Central America
(because the hats were originally made
from the leaves of a plant which grows
there)]

pancake *noun* (*plural* pancakes)
a thin round cake of batter fried on both
sides. [from *pan* + *cake*]

Pancake Day *noun*
Shrove Tuesday, when people often eat
pancakes.

pancreas (*say* pan-kree-as) *noun*
a gland near the stomach, producing
insulin and digestive juices. [from Greek]

panda *noun* (*plural* pandas)
a large bear-like black-and-white animal
found in China. [from the name given to a
related animal in Nepal]

panda car *noun* (*plural* panda cars)
a police patrol car, originally white with
black stripes on the doors.

pandemonium *noun*
uproar and complete confusion.
[from *pan-* + *demon*]

pander *verb* (panders, pandering, pandered)
pander to indulge someone by giving them
whatever they want, *Don't pander to his
taste for sweet things!*
[from *Pandare*, a character in an old poem
who acted as go-between for two lovers]

pane *noun* (*plural* panes)
a sheet of glass in a window. [from Latin]

panegyric (*say* pan-i-jirrik) *noun* (*plural*
panegyrics)
a speech praising somone; a eulogy.
[from Greek]

panel *noun* (*plural* panels)
1 a long flat piece of wood, metal, etc. that
is part of a door, wall, piece of furniture,
etc. **2** a group of people chosen to discuss or
decide something.
panelled *adjective*, **panelling** *noun*
[from old French, related to *pane*]

pang *noun* (*plural* pangs)
a sudden sharp pain. [from *prong*]

panic *noun*
sudden uncontrollable fear.
panic-stricken *adjective*, **panicky** *adjective*
panic *verb* (panics, panicking, panicked)
fill or be filled with panic. [from the name
of Pan, an ancient Greek god thought to be
able to cause sudden fear]

pannier *noun* (*plural* panniers)
a large bag or basket hung on one side of a
bicycle or horse etc.
[from Latin *panarium* = breadbasket]

panoply *noun* (*plural* panoplies)
a splendid display or collection of things.
[from *pan-* + Greek *hopla* = weapons]

panorama *noun* (*plural* panoramas)
a view or picture of a wide area.
panoramic *adjective*
[from *pan-* + Greek *horama* = view]

pansy *noun* (*plural* pansies)
a small brightly coloured garden flower
with velvety petals.
[from French *pensée* = thought]

pant *verb* (pants, panting, panted)
take short quick breaths, usually after
running or working hard.
[from old French]

pantaloons *plural noun*
wide trousers.
[from *Pantalone*, a character in old Italian
comedies who wore these]

pantechnicon *noun* (*plural*
pantechnicons)
a kind of large lorry, used for carrying
furniture. [originally the name of a large
art and craft gallery in London, which was
later used for storing furniture: from *pan-*
+ Greek *techne* = art]

panther *noun* (*plural* panthers)
a leopard. [from Greek]

panties *plural noun* (*informal*)
short knickers. [from *pants*]

pantile *noun* (*plural* pantiles)
a curved tile for a roof. [because the curved
shape reminded people of a pan]

pantomime *noun* (*plural* pantomimes)
1 a Christmas entertainment, usually
based on a fairy tale. **2** mime. [from *pan-*
+ *mime* (because in its most ancient form
an actor mimed the different parts)]

pantry *noun* (*plural* pantries)
a small room for storing food; a larder.
[from old French *paneterie*, literally
= bread-store]

pants *plural noun* (*informal*)
1 trousers. 2 underpants or knickers.
[short for *pantaloons*]

pap *noun*
1 soft food suitable for babies. 2 trivial
entertainment; nonsense. [probably via old
German from Latin *pappare* = eat]

papa *noun* (*old use*)
father. [from Greek *pappas* = father]

papacy (*say* pay-pa-see) *noun* (*plural*
papacies)
the position of pope.
[from Latin *papa* = pope]

papal (*say* pay-pal) *adjective*
to do with the pope.

paper *noun* (*plural* **papers**)
1 a substance made in thin sheets from
wood, rags, etc. and used for writing or
printing or drawing on or for wrapping
things. 2 a newspaper. 3 wallpaper. 4 a
document.
paper *verb* (**papers, papering, papered**)
cover a wall or room with wallpaper.
[from old French, related to *papyrus*]

paperback *noun* (*plural* **paperbacks**)
a book with a thin flexible cover.

paperweight *noun* (*plural* **paperweights**)
a small heavy object used for holding down
loose papers.

paperwork *noun*
all the writing of reports, keeping of
records etc. that someone has to do as part
of their job.

papier mâché (*say* pap-yay **mash**-ay)
paper made into pulp and moulded to make
models, ornaments, etc.
[French, = chewed paper]

paprika (*say* pap-rik a) *noun*
red pepper. [Hungarian]

papyrus (*say* pap-I-rus) *noun* (*plural*
papyri)
1 a kind of paper made from the stems of a
plant like a reed, used in ancient Egypt. 2 a
document written on this paper.
[Greek, = paper-reed]

par *noun*
1 an average or normal amount or
condition, *I'm feeling below par today.* 2 in
golf, the number of strokes that a good
player should normally take for a
particular hole or course.
on a par with equal to in amount or quality.
[Latin, = equal]

para-¹ *prefix*
1 beside (as in *parallel*). 2 beyond (as in
paradox). [from Greek]

para-² *prefix*
protecting from (as in *parasol*).
[from Italian]

parable *noun* (*plural* **parables**)
a story told to teach people something,
especially one of those told by Jesus Christ.
[from Greek *paraballein* = put beside or
compare: related to *parabola*]

parabola (*say* pa-rab-ol-a) *noun* (*plural*
parabolas)
a curve like the path of an object thrown
into the air and falling down again.
parabolic *adjective*
[from *para-¹* + Greek *bole* = a throw]

parachute *noun* (*plural* **parachutes**)
an umbrella-like device on which people or
things can float slowly to the ground from
an aircraft. **parachuting** *noun*, **parachutist**
noun [from *para-²* + French *chute* = a fall]

parade *noun* (*plural* **parades**)
1 a procession that displays people or
things. 2 an assembly of troops for
inspection, drill, etc.; a ground for this. 3 a
public square, promenade, or row of shops.
parade *verb* (**parades, parading, paraded**)
1 move in a parade. 2 assemble for a
parade. [from Spanish or Italian, = display]

paradise *noun*
1 heaven; a heavenly place. 2 the Garden
of Eden.
[from ancient Persian *pairidaeza* = garden]

paradox *noun* (*plural* **paradoxes**)
a statement that seems to contradict itself
but which contains a truth, e.g. 'More
haste, less speed'.
paradoxical *adjective*, **paradoxically** *adverb*
[from *para-¹* + Greek *doxa* = opinion]

paraffin *noun*
a kind of oil used as fuel.
[via German from Latin *parum* = hardly + *affinis* = related (because paraffin does not combine readily with other substances)]

paragliding *noun*
the sport of being towed through the air while being supported by a kind of parachute.

paragon *noun* (*plural* **paragons**)
a person or thing that seems to be perfect. [from Italian *paragone* = touchstone]

paragraph *noun* (*plural* **paragraphs**)
one or more sentences on a single subject, forming a section of a piece of writing and beginning on a new line, usually slightly in from the margin of the page.
[from *para-*[1] + *-graph*]

parakeet *noun* (*plural* **parakeets**)
a kind of small parrot. [from old French]

parallax *noun*
what seems to be a change in the position of something when you look at it from a different place. [from *para-*[1] + Greek *allassein* = to change]

parallel *adjective*
1 (of lines etc.) always at the same distance from each other, like the rails on which a train runs. 2 similar or corresponding, *When petrol prices rise there is a parallel rise in bus fares.* **parallelism** *noun*

parallel *noun* (*plural* **parallels**)
1 something similar or corresponding. 2 a comparison, *You can draw a parallel between the two situations.* 3 a line etc. that is parallel to another. 4 a line of latitude.

parallel *verb* (**parallels**, **paralleling**, **paralleled**)
find or be a parallel to something.
[from *para-*[1] + Greek *allelos* = one another]

USAGE: Take care with the spelling of this word: one 'r', two 'l's, then one 'l'.

parallelogram *noun* (*plural* **parallelograms**)
a quadrilateral with its opposite sides equal and parallel. [from *parallel* + *-gram*]

paralyse *verb* (**paralyses**, **paralysing**, **paralysed**)
1 cause paralysis in a person etc. 2 make something be unable to move, *She was paralysed with fear.*
[from French, related to *paralysis*]

paralysis *noun*
being unable to move, especially because of a disease or an injury to the nerves.
paralytic (*say* pa-ra-**lit**-ik) *adjective*
[from Greek *para* = on one side + *lysis* = loosening]

paramedic *noun* (*plural* **paramedics**)
a person who is trained to help doctors and nurses. [from *para-*[1] + *medical*]

parameter (*say* pa-**ram**-it-er) *noun* (*plural* **parameters**)
a quantity or quality etc. that is variable and affects other things by its changes.
[from *para-*[1] + Greek *metron* = measure]

USAGE: Do not confuse with *perimeter*.

paramilitary *adjective*
organized like a military force but not part of the armed services.
[from *para-*[1] + *military*]

paramount *adjective*
more important than anything else, *Secrecy is paramount.*
[from old French *paramont* = above]

paranoia *noun*
a mental illness in which a person has delusions or suspects and distrusts people.
paranoid *adjective*
[from *para-*[1] + Greek *noos* = the mind]

paranormal *adjective*
beyond what is normal and can be rationally explained; supernatural.

parapet *noun* (*plural* **parapets**)
a low wall along the edge of a balcony, bridge, roof, etc. [via French from Italian]

paraphernalia *noun*
numerous pieces of equipment, belongings, etc. [originally = the personal belongings a woman could keep after her marriage (as opposed to her dowry, which went to her husband): from *para-*[1] + Greek *pherne* = dowry]

paraphrase *verb* (**paraphrases,
paraphrasing, paraphrased**)
give the meaning of something by using
different words. **paraphrase** *noun*
[from *para-*¹ + *phrase*]

paraplegia *noun*
paralysis of the lower half of the body.
paraplegic *noun* & *adjective*
[from *para-*¹ + Greek *plessein* = strike]

parasite *noun* (*plural* **parasites**)
an animal or plant that lives in or on
another, from which it gets its food.
parasitic *adjective*
[from Greek *parasitos* = guest at a meal]

parasol *noun* (*plural* **parasols**)
a lightweight umbrella used to shade
yourself from the sun.
[from *para-*² + Italian *sole* = sun]

paratroops *plural noun*
troops trained to be dropped from aircraft
by parachute. **paratrooper** *noun*
[from *para*chute + *troops*]

parboil *verb* (**parboils, parboiling, parboiled**)
boil food until it is partly cooked.
[from Latin *per-* = thoroughly + *bullire* = to
boil (*per-* was later confused with *part*)]

parcel *noun* (*plural* **parcels**)
something wrapped up to be sent by post or
carried.
parcel *verb* (**parcels, parcelling, parcelled**)
1 wrap something up as a parcel. **2** divide
something into portions, *parcel out the
work.* [from old French, related to *particle*]

parched *adjective*
very dry or thirsty. [origin unknown]

parchment *noun* (*plural* **parchments**)
a kind of heavy paper, originally made
from animal skins. [from the city of
Pergamum, now in Turkey, where
parchment was made in ancient times]

pardon *noun*
forgiveness.
pardon *verb* (**pardons, pardoning,
pardoned**)
1 forgive somebody. **2** excuse somebody
kindly.
pardonable *adjective*, **pardonably** *adverb*

pardon *interjection*
used to mean 'I didn't hear or understand
what you said' or 'I apologize'.
[from old French]

pare (*say as* pair) (**pares, paring, pared**)
1 trim something by cutting away the
edges. **2** reduce something gradually, *We
had to pare down our expenses.*
[from Latin *parare* = prepare]

parent *noun* (*plural* **parents**)
1 a father or mother; a living thing that has
produced others of its kind. **2** a source
from which others are derived, *the parent
company.* **parenthood** *noun*, **parenting**
noun, **parental** (*say* pa-**rent**-al) *adjective*
[from Latin *parens* = producing offspring]

parentage *noun*
who your parents are.

parenthesis (*say* pa-ren-thi-sis) (*plural*
parentheses)
1 something extra that is inserted in a
sentence, usually between brackets or
dashes. **2** either of the pair of brackets (like
these) used to mark off words from the rest
of a sentence. **parenthetical** *adjective*
[Greek, = putting in besides]

par excellence (*say* par eks-el-**ahns**)
adverb
more than all the others; to the greatest
degree.
[French, = because of special excellence]

pariah (*say* pa-**ry**-a) *noun* (*plural* **pariahs**)
an outcast. [from Tamil]

parish *noun* (*plural* **parishes**)
a district with its own church.
parishioner *noun*
[from Greek *paroikia* = neighbourhood,
from *para*-¹ = beside + *oikos* = house]

parity *noun*
equality. [same origin as *par*]

park *noun* (*plural* **parks**)
1 a large garden or recreation ground for
public use. **2** an area of grassland or
woodland belonging to a country house.
park *verb* (**parks, parking, parked**)
leave a vehicle somewhere for a time.
[from French]

parka *noun* (*plural* **parkas**)
a warm jacket with a hood attached.
[via an Eskimo language from Russian]

Parkinson's disease *noun*
a disease that makes a person's arms and
legs shake and the muscles become stiff.
[named after an English doctor, James
Parkinson]

parley *verb* (**parleys, parleying, parleyed**)
hold a discussion with someone. **parley**
noun [from French *parler* = speak]

parliament *noun* (*plural* **parliaments**)
the assembly that makes a country's laws.
parliamentary *adjective*
[same origin as *parley*]

parliamentarian *noun* (*plural*
parliamentarians)
a person who is good at debating things in
parliament.

parlour *noun* (*plural* **parlours**) (*old use*)
a sitting room. [originally = a room in a
monastery where the monks were allowed
to talk: from French *parler* = speak]

parochial (*say* per-oh-kee-al) *adjective*
1 to do with a parish. 2 local; interested
only in your own area, *a narrow parochial
attitude.*

parody *noun* (*plural* **parodies**)
an imitation that makes fun of a person or
thing.
parody *verb* (**parodies, parodying, parodied**)
make or be a parody of a person or thing.
[from *para-*¹ + Greek *oide* = song]

parole *noun*
the release of a prisoner before the end of
his or her sentence on condition of good
behaviour, *He was on parole.*
[French, = word of honour]

paroxysm (*say* pa-roks-izm) *noun* (*plural*
paroxysms)
a sudden outburst of rage, jealousy,
laughter, etc. [from Greek *paroxynein* = to
annoy or exasperate]

parquet (*say* par-kay) *noun*
wooden blocks arranged in a pattern to
make a floor. [French]

parrot *noun* (*plural* **parrots**)
a brightly-coloured tropical bird that can
learn to repeat words etc. [from French]

parry *verb* (**parries, parrying, parried**)
1 turn aside an opponent's weapon or blow
by using your own to block it. 2 avoid an
awkward question skilfully.
[from Italian *parare* = defend]

parse *verb* (**parses, parsing, parsed**)
state what is the grammatical form and
function of a word or words in a sentence.
[origin unknown]

parsimonious *adjective*
stingy; very sparing in the use of
something. **parsimony** *noun* [from Latin]

parsley *noun*
a plant with crinkled green leaves used to
flavour and decorate food.
[via Old English from Latin]

parsnip *noun* (*plural* **parsnips**)
a plant with a pointed pale-yellow root
used as a vegetable. [from old French]

parson *noun* (*plural* **parsons**)
a member of the clergy, especially a rector
or vicar.
[from old French *persone* = person]

parsonage *noun* (*plural* **parsonages**)
a rectory or vicarage.

part *noun* (*plural* **parts**)
1 some but not all of a thing or number of
things; anything that belongs to something
bigger. 2 the character played by an actor
or actress. 3 the words spoken by a
character in a play. 4 one side in an
agreement or in a dispute or quarrel.
take in good part not be offended at
something.
take part join in an activity.
part *verb* (**parts, parting, parted**)
separate or divide.
part with give away or get rid of something.
[from Latin]

partake *verb* (**partakes, partaking, partook,
partaken**)
1 participate. 2 eat or drink something, *We
all partook of the food.* [from *part* + *take*]

part exchange *noun*
giving something that you own, as part of
the price of what you are buying.

Parthian shot *noun* (*plural* **Parthian shots**)
a sharp remark made by a person who is
just leaving. [named after the horsemen of
Parthia (an ancient kingdom in what is
now Iran), who were famous for shooting
arrows at the enemy while retreating]

partial *adjective*
1 not complete or total, *a partial eclipse*.
2 favouring one side more than the other;
biased or unfair.
partially *adverb*, **partiality** *noun*
be partial to be fond of something.

participate *verb* (**participates, participating,
participated**)
take part or have a share in something.
participant *noun*, **participation** *noun*,
participator *noun*
[from Latin *pars* = part + *capere* = take]

participle *noun* (*plural* **participles**)
a word formed from a verb (e.g. *gone, going;
guided, guiding*) and used with an
auxiliary verb to form certain tenses (e.g. *It
has gone. It is going*) or the passive (e.g. *We
were guided to our seats*), or as an adjective
(e.g. *a guided missile; a guiding light*). The
past participle (e.g. *gone, guided*) describes a
completed action or past condition. The
present participle (which ends in *-ing*)
describes a continuing action or condition.
[from Latin *particeps* = taking part]

particle *noun* (*plural* **particles**)
a very small portion or amount.
[from Latin, = little part]

particoloured *adjective*
partly of one colour and partly of another;
variegated.

particular *adjective*
1 of this one and no other; individual, *This
particular stamp is very rare*. 2 special,
Take particular care of it. 3 giving
something close attention; choosing
carefully, *He is very particular about his
clothes*.
particularly *adverb*, **particularity** *noun*
particular *noun* (*plural* **particulars**)
a single fact; a detail, *Can you give me the
particulars of the case?*

in particular 1 especially, *We liked this one
in particular*. 2 special, *We did nothing in
particular*.
[same origin as *particle*]

parting *noun* (*plural* **partings**)
1 leaving or separation. 2 a line where hair
is combed away in different directions.

partisan *noun* (*plural* **partisans**)
1 a strong supporter of a party or group
etc. 2 a member of an organization
resisting the authorities in a conquered
country.
partisan *adjective*
strongly supporting a particular cause.
[via French from Italian]

partition *noun* (*plural* **partitions**)
1 a thin wall that divides a room or space.
2 dividing something, especially a country,
into separate parts.
partition *verb* (**partitions, partitioning,
partitioned**)
1 divide something into separate parts.
2 divide a room or space by means of a
partition. [from Latin *partitio* = division]

partly *adverb*
to some extent but not completely.

partner *noun* (*plural* **partners**)
1 one of a pair of people who do something
together, e.g. in business or dancing or
playing a game. 2 the person that someone
is married to or is having a sexual
relationship with. **partnership** *noun*
partner *verb* (**partners, partnering,
partnered**)
be a person's partner.
[from Latin *partiri* = to divide or share]

part of speech *noun* (*plural* **parts of
speech**)
any of the groups into which words are
divided in grammar (noun, pronoun,
adjective, verb, adverb, preposition,
conjunction, interjection).

partook *past tense* of **partake**.

partridge *noun* (*plural* **partridges**)
a game bird with brown feathers.
[from old French]

part-time *adjective* & *adverb*
working for only some of the normal
hours. **part-timer** *noun*

party noun (plural parties)
1 a gathering of people to enjoy themselves, a birthday party. 2 a group working or travelling together. 3 an organized group of people with similar political beliefs, the Labour Party. 4 a person who is involved in an action or lawsuit etc., the guilty party.
[from old French; related to part]

pas de deux (say pah der der) noun
(plural pas de deux)
a dance (e.g in a ballet) for two persons.
[French, = step of two]

pass verb (passes, passing, passed)
1 go past something; go onwards. 2 move something in a certain direction, Pass the cord through the ring. 3 give or transfer something to another person, Pass the butter to your father. 4 be successful in a test or examination. 5 approve or accept, They passed a law. 6 occupy time.
7 happen, We heard what passed when they met. 8 come to an end. 9 utter, Pass a remark. 10 let your turn go by at cards or in a competition etc., Pass!
pass out 1 complete your military training. 2 faint.

pass noun (plural passes)
1 passing something. 2 a permit to go in or out of a place. 3 a route through a gap in a range of mountains. 4 a critical state of affairs, Things have come to a pretty pass!
[from Latin passus = pace]

passable adjective
1 able to be passed. 2 satisfactory but not especially good. **passably** adverb

passage noun (plural passages)
1 a way through something; a corridor. 2 a journey by sea or air. 3 a section of a piece of writing or music. 4 passing, the passage of time. **passageway** noun
[old French, = passing]

passbook noun (plural passbooks)
a special notebook in which a bank or building society writes down how much a customer has paid in or drawn out.

passé (say pas-say) adjective
no longer fashionable.
[French, = passed]

passenger noun (plural passengers)
a person who is driven or carried in a car, train, ship, or aircraft etc.
[same origin as passage]

passer-by noun (plural passers-by)
a person who happens to be going past something.

passion noun (plural passions)
1 strong emotion. 2 great enthusiasm.
the Passion the sufferings of Jesus Christ at the Crucifixion.
[from Latin passio = suffering]

passionate adjective
full of passion. **passionately** adverb

passive adjective
1 not resisting or fighting against something. 2 acted upon and not active.
3 (of a form of a verb) used when the subject of the sentence receives the action, e.g. was hit in 'She was hit on the head'. (Compare active.) **passively** adverb,
passiveness noun, **passivity** noun
[from Latin passivus = capable of suffering]

Passover noun
a Jewish religious festival commemorating the freeing of the Jews from slavery in Egypt. [from pass over, because God spared the Jews from the fate which affected the Egyptians]

passport noun (plural passports)
an official document that entitles the person holding it to travel abroad.
[from pass + port¹]

password noun (plural passwords)
1 a secret word or phrase used to distinguish friends from enemies. 2 a word you need to key in to gain access to certain computer files.

past adjective
of the time gone by, during the past week.
past noun
the time gone by.
past preposition
1 beyond, Walk past the school. 2 after, It is past midnight.
past it (slang) too old to be able to do something.
[the old past participle of pass]

pasta *noun*
an Italian food consisting of a dried paste made from flour and shaped into macaroni, spaghetti, etc. [Italian, = paste]

paste *noun* (*plural* **pastes**)
1 a soft and moist or gluey substance. 2 a hard glassy substance used to make imitation jewellery.
paste *verb* (**pastes, pasting, pasted**)
1 stick something onto a surface by using paste. 2 coat something with paste. 3 (*slang*) beat or thrash someone. [from Greek]

pastel *noun* (*plural* **pastels**)
1 a crayon that is like chalk. 2 a light delicate colour. [from Latin *pastellus* = woad]

pastern *noun* (*plural* **pasterns**)
the part of a horse's foot between the fetlock and the hoof. [from old French]

pasteurize *verb* (**pasteurizes, pasteurizing, pasteurized**)
purify milk by heating and then cooling it. [named after a French scientist, Louis Pasteur, who invented the process]

pastille *noun* (*plural* **pastilles**)
a small flavoured sweet for sucking. [from Latin *pastillus* = lozenge]

pastime *noun* (*plural* **pastimes**)
something you do to make time pass pleasantly; a hobby or game.

pastor *noun* (*plural* **pastors**)
a member of the clergy who is in charge of a church or congregation. [Latin, = shepherd]

pastoral *adjective*
1 to do with country life, *a pastoral scene*. 2 to do with a pastor or a pastor's duties.

pastry *noun* (*plural* **pastries**)
1 dough made with flour, fat, and water, rolled flat and baked. 2 something made of pastry. [from *paste*]

pasture *noun* (*plural* **pastures**)
land covered with grass etc. that cattle, sheep, or horses can eat.
pasture *verb* (**pastures, pasturing, pastured**)
put animals to graze in a pasture. [from Latin *pastum* = fed]

pasty[1] (*say* pas-tee) *noun* (*plural* **pasties**)
pastry with a filling of meat and vegetables, baked without a dish to shape it. [from old French *pasté* = paste or pastry]

pasty[2] (*say* pay-stee) *adjective*
looking pale and unhealthy. [from *paste*]

pat *verb* (**pats, patting, patted**)
tap gently with the open hand or with something flat.
pat *noun* (*plural* **pats**)
1 a patting movement or sound. 2 a small piece of butter or other soft substance.
a pat on the back praise.
[probably from the sound]

patch *noun* (*plural* **patches**)
1 a piece of material or metal etc. put over a hole or damaged place. 2 an area that is different from its surroundings. 3 a piece of ground, *the cabbage patch*. 4 a small area or piece of something, *There are patches of fog*.
not a patch on (*informal*) not nearly as good as.
patch *verb* (**patches, patching, patched**)
put a patch on something.
patch up 1 repair something roughly. 2 settle a quarrel. [probably from old French *pieche* = piece]

patchwork *noun*
needlework in which small pieces of different cloth are sewn edge to edge.

patchy *adjective*
occurring in patches; uneven.
patchily *adverb*, **patchiness** *noun*

pate *noun* (*plural* **pates**) (*old use*)
the top of a person's head, *his bald pate*. [origin unknown]

pâté (*say* pat-ay) *noun* (*plural* **pâtés**)
paste made of meat or fish. [French]

pâté de foie gras (*say* pat-ay der fwah grah) *noun*
a paste or pie of goose-liver. [French, = paste of fat liver]

patent (*say* pat-ent or pay-tent) *noun* (*plural* **patents**)
the official right given to an inventor to make or sell his or her invention and to prevent other people from copying it.

patent (*say* pay-tent) *adjective*
1 protected by a patent, *patent medicines.*
2 obvious. **patently** *adverb*
patent *verb* (**patents, patenting, patented**)
get a patent for something.
[originally, in *letters patent*, an open letter
from a monarch or government recording
a contract or granting a right: from Latin
patens = lying open]

patentee (*say* pay-ten-**tee** or pat-en-**tee**)
noun (*plural* **patentees**)
a person who holds a patent.

patent leather *noun*
glossy leather.

paternal *adjective*
1 to do with a father. 2 fatherly. **paternally**
adverb [from Latin *pater* = father]

paternalistic *adjective*
treating people in a paternal way,
providing for their needs but giving them
no responsibility. **paternalism** *noun*

paternity *noun*
1 fatherhood. 2 being the father of a
particular baby. [same origin as *paternal*]

path *noun* (*plural* **paths**)
1 a narrow way along which people or
animals can walk. 2 a line along which a
person or thing moves. [from Old English]

pathetic *adjective*
1 making you feel pity or sympathy.
2 miserably inadequate or useless, *a
pathetic attempt.* **pathetically** *adverb*
[same origin as *pathos*]

pathology *noun*
the study of diseases of the body.
pathological *adjective*, **pathologist** *noun*
[from Greek *pathos* = suffering, + *-logy*]

pathos (*say* pay-thoss) *noun*
a quality of making people feel pity or
sympathy. [Greek, = feeling or suffering]

-pathy *suffix*
forms nouns meaning 'feeling or suffering
something' (e.g. *sympathy, telepathy*).
[from Greek *patheia* = feeling or suffering]

patience *noun*
1 being patient. 2 a card game for one
person.

patient *adjective*
1 able to wait or put up with annoyances
without becoming angry. 2 able to
persevere. **patiently** *adverb*
patient *noun* (*plural* **patients**)
a person who has treatment from a doctor
or dentist etc.
[from Latin *patiens* = suffering]

patio *noun* (*plural* **patios**)
a paved area beside a house.
[Spanish, = courtyard]

patriarch (*say* pay-tree-ark) *noun* (*plural*
patriarchs)
1 the male who is head of a family or tribe.
2 a bishop of high rank in the Orthodox
Christian churches. **patriarchal** *adjective*
[from Greek *patria* = family + *archein* = to
rule]

patrician *noun* (*plural* **patricians**)
an ancient Roman noble. (Compare
plebeian.)
patrician *adjective*
from a noble family; aristocratic. [from
Latin *patricius* = having a noble father]

patriot (*say* pay-tree-ot or pat-ree-ot) *noun*
(*plural* **patriots**)
a person who loves his or her country and
supports it loyally. **patriotic** *adjective*,
patriotically *adverb*, **patriotism** *noun*
[from Greek *patris* = fatherland]

patrol *verb* (**patrols, patrolling, patrolled**)
walk or travel regularly over an area in
order to guard it and see that all is well.
patrol *noun* (*plural* **patrols**)
1 a patrolling group of people, ships,
aircraft, etc. 2 a group of Scouts or Guides.
on patrol patrolling.
[from French *patrouiller* = paddle in mud]

patron (*say* pay-tron) *noun* (*plural* **patrons**)
1 someone who supports a person or cause
with money or encouragement. 2 a regular
customer. **patronage** (*say* pat-ron-ij) *noun*
[from Latin *patronus* = protector]

patronize (*say* pat-ron-I'z) *verb* (**patronizes,
patronizing, patronized**)
1 be a regular customer of a particular
shop, restaurant, etc. 2 talk to someone in
a way that shows you think they are stupid
or inferior to you.

patron saint *noun* (*plural* **patron saints**)
a saint who is thought to protect a
particular place or activity.

patter¹ *noun*
a series of light tapping sounds.
patter *verb* (**patters, pattering, pattered**)
make light tapping sounds, *Rain pattered
on the window panes.* [from *pat*]

patter² *noun*
the quick talk of a comedian, conjuror,
salesperson, etc.
[originally = recite a prayer: from Latin
pater noster = Our Father, the first words
of a Christian prayer]

pattern *noun* (*plural* **patterns**)
1 a repeated arrangement of lines, shapes,
or colours etc. **2** a thing to be copied in
order to make something, *a dress pattern.*
3 the regular way in which something
happens, *James Bond films follow a set
pattern.* **4** an excellent example or model.
[same origin as *patron*]

patty *noun* (*plural* **patties**)
a small pie or pasty. [from *pâté*]

paucity *noun* (*formal*)
smallness of number or quantity; scarcity.
[from Latin *pauci* = few]

paunch *noun* (*plural* **paunches**)
a large belly. [from old French]

pauper *noun* (*plural* **paupers**)
a person who is very poor. [Latin, = poor]

pause *noun* (*plural* **pauses**)
a temporary stop in speaking or doing
something.
pause *verb* (**pauses, pausing, paused**)
stop speaking or doing something for a
short time. [from Greek *pauein* = to stop]

pave *verb* (**paves, paving, paved**)
lay a hard surface on a road or path etc.
paving-stone *noun*
pave the way prepare for something.
[from Latin *pavire* = ram down]

pavement *noun* (*plural* **pavements**)
a paved path along the side of a street.

pavilion *noun* (*plural* **pavilions**)
1 a building for use by players and
spectators etc., especially at a cricket

ground. **2** an ornamental building or
shelter used for dances, concerts,
exhibitions, etc.
[from French *pavillon* = tent]

paw *noun* (*plural* **paws**)
the foot of an animal that has claws.
paw *verb* (**paws, pawing, pawed**)
touch or scrape something with a hand or
foot. [from old French]

pawl *noun* (*plural* **pawls**)
a bar with a catch that fits into the notches
of a ratchet. [origin unknown]

pawn¹ *noun* (*plural* **pawns**)
1 the least valuable piece in chess. **2** a
person whose actions are controlled by
somebody else.
[from Latin *pedo* = foot-soldier]

pawn² *verb* (**pawns, pawning, pawned**)
leave something with a pawnbroker as
security for a loan.
[from old French *pan* = pledge]

pawnbroker *noun* (*plural* **pawnbrokers**)
a shopkeeper who lends money to people in
return for objects that they leave as
security. **pawnshop** *noun*

pawpaw *noun* (*plural* **pawpaws**)
an orange-coloured tropical fruit used as
food. [via Spanish and Portuguese from a
South American language]

pay *verb* (**pays, paying, paid**)
1 give money in return for goods or
services. **2** give what is owed, *pay your
debts; pay the rent.* **3** be profitable or
worthwhile, *It pays to advertise.* **4** give or
express, *pay attention; pay them a visit; pay
compliments.* **5** suffer a penalty. **6** let out a
rope by loosening it gradually. **payer** *noun*
pay off 1 pay in full what you owe. **2** be
worthwhile or have good results, *All the
preparation she did really paid off.*
pay up pay the full amount you owe.
pay *noun*
salary or wages.
[from Latin *pacare* = appease]

payable *adjective*
that must be paid.

PAYE *abbreviation*
pay-as-you-earn; a method of collecting

income tax by deducting it from wages before these are paid to people who earn them.

payee *noun* (*plural* **payees**)
a person to whom money is paid or is to be paid.

paymaster *noun* (*plural* **paymasters**)
an official who pays troops or workmen etc.

payment *noun* (*plural* **payments**)
1 paying. 2 money paid.

PC *abbreviation*
1 personal computer. 2 police constable.

PE *abbreviation*
physical education.

pea *noun* (*plural* **peas**)
the small round green seed of a climbing plant, growing inside a pod and used as a vegetable. [via Old English from Greek]

peace *noun*
1 a time when there is no war, violence, or disorder. 2 quietness and calm. [from Latin]

peaceable *adjective*
fond of peace; not quarrelsome or warlike. **peaceably** *adverb*

peaceful *adjective*
quiet and calm.
peacefully *adverb*, **peacefulness** *noun*

peach *noun* (*plural* **peaches**)
1 a round soft juicy fruit with a pinkish or yellowish skin and a large stone. 2 (*informal*) a thing of great quality, *a peach of a shot*. [from old French]

peacock *noun* (*plural* **peacocks**)
a male bird with a long brightly-coloured tail that it can spread out like a fan. **peahen** *noun* [via Old English from Latin]

peak *noun* (*plural* **peaks**)
1 a pointed top, especially of a mountain. 2 the highest or most intense part of something, *Traffic reaches its peak at 5 p.m.* 3 the part of a cap that sticks out in front. **peaked** *adjective*

peak *verb* (**peaks**, **peaking**, **peaked**)
reach its highest point or value. [origin unknown]

peaky *adjective*
looking pale and ill.
[from Middle English *peak* = mope]

peal *noun* (*plural* **peals**)
1 the loud ringing of a bell or set of bells. 2 a loud burst of thunder or laughter.
peal *verb* (**peals**, **pealing**, **pealed**)
(of bells) ring loudly. [from *appeal*]

peanut *noun* (*plural* **peanuts**)
a small round nut that grows in a pod in the ground.

peanut butter *noun*
roasted peanuts crushed into a paste.

pear *noun* (*plural* **pears**)
a juicy fruit that gets narrower near the stalk. [via Old English from Latin]

pearl *noun* (*plural* **pearls**)
a small shiny white ball found in the shells of some oysters and used as a jewel. **pearly** *adjective* [from French]

pearl barley *noun*
grains of barley made small by grinding.

peasant *noun* (*plural* **peasants**)
a person who belongs to a farming community, especially in poor areas of the world. **peasantry** *noun*
[from Latin *paganus* = villager]

peat *noun*
rotted plant material that can be dug out of the ground and used as fuel or in gardening. **peaty** *adjective* [from Latin *peta*, probably from a Celtic word]

pebble *noun* (*plural* **pebbles**)
a small round stone. **pebbly** *adjective* [origin unknown]

peccadillo *noun* (*plural* **peccadilloes**)
a small and unimportant fault or offence. [Spanish, = little sin]

peck[1] *verb* (**pecks**, **pecking**, **pecked**)
1 bite at something quickly with the beak. 2 kiss someone lightly on the cheek.

peck *noun* (*plural* pecks)
1 a quick bite by a bird. 2 a light kiss on the cheek. [probably from old German]

peck² *noun* (*plural* pecks)
a measure of grain or fruit etc., *4 pecks = 1 bushel.* [from old French]

peckish *adjective* (*informal*)
hungry. [from peck¹ + -ish]

pectin *noun*
a substance found in ripe fruits, causing jam to set firmly.
[from Greek *pektos* = fixed or set]

pectoral *adjective*
to do with the chest or breast, *pectoral muscles.* [from Latin *pectus* = breast]

peculiar *adjective*
1 strange or unusual. 2 belonging to a particular person, place, or thing; restricted, *This custom is peculiar to this tribe.* 3 special, *This point is of peculiar interest.* **peculiarly** *adverb*, **peculiarity** *noun*
[from Latin *peculium* = private property]

pecuniary *adjective*
to do with money, *pecuniary aid.*
[from Latin *pecunia* = money (from *pecu* = cattle, because in early times wealth consisted in cattle and sheep)]

pedagogue (*say* ped-a-gog) *noun* (*plural* pedagogues)
a teacher, especially one who teaches in a pedantic way. [from Greek *paidagogos* = a slave who took a boy to school]

pedal *noun* (*plural* pedals)
a lever pressed by the foot to operate a bicycle, car, machine, etc. or in certain musical instruments.
pedal *verb* (pedals, pedalling, pedalled)
use a pedal; move or work something, especially a bicycle, by means of pedals.
[from Latin *pedis* = of a foot]

pedant *noun* (*plural* pedants)
a pedantic person.
[from French *pédant* = schoolteacher]

pedantic *adjective*
being very careful and strict about exact meanings and facts etc. in learning.
pedantically *adverb*

peddle *verb* (peddles, peddling, peddled)
1 go from house to house selling small things. 2 sell illegal drugs. 3 try to get people to accept an idea, way of life, etc.
[from *pedlar*]

pedestal *noun* (*plural* pedestals)
the raised base on which a statue or pillar etc. stands.
put someone on a pedestal admire him or her greatly.
[from Italian *piede* = foot, + *stall¹*]

pedestrian *noun* (*plural* pedestrians)
a person who is walking.
pedestrian *adjective*
ordinary and dull. [same origin as *pedal*]

pedestrian crossing *noun* (*plural* pedestrian crossings)
a place where pedestrians can cross the road safely.

pedigree *noun* (*plural* pedigrees)
a list of a person's or animal's ancestors, especially to show how well an animal has been bred. [from old French *pé de grue* = crane's foot (from the shape made by the lines on a family tree)]

pediment *noun* (*plural* pediments)
a wide triangular part decorating the top of a building. [origin unknown]

pedlar *noun* (*plural* pedlars)
a person who goes from house to house selling small things. [from Middle English *ped* = a hamper or basket (in which a pedlar carried his goods)]

peek *verb* (peeks, peeking, peeked)
have a quick or sly look at something.
peek *noun* [origin unknown]

peel *noun* (*plural* peels)
the skin of certain fruits and vegetables.
peel *verb* (peels, peeling, peeled)
1 remove the peel or covering from something. 2 come off in strips or layers. 3 lose a covering or skin. [Middle English; related to Latin *pilare* = cut off the hair]

peelings *plural noun*
strips of skin peeled from potatoes etc.

peep *verb* (peeps, peeping, peeped)
1 look quickly or secretly. 2 look through a narrow opening. 3 come slowly or briefly

into view, *The moon peeped out from behind the clouds.* peep *noun,* peephole *noun*
[origin unknown]

peer[1] *verb* (peers, peering, peered)
look at something closely or with difficulty. [origin unknown]

peer[2] *noun* (*plural* peers)
1 a noble. 2 someone who is equal to another in rank, merit, or age etc., *She had no peer.* peeress *noun*
[from Latin *par* = equal]

peerage *noun* (*plural* peerages)
1 peers. 2 the rank of peer, *He was raised to the peerage.*

peerless *adjective*
without an equal; better than the others.

peeved *adjective* (*informal*)
annoyed. [from *peevish*]

peevish *adjective*
irritable. [origin unknown]

peewit *noun* (*plural* peewits)
a lapwing. [imitating its call]

peg *noun* (*plural* pegs)
a piece of wood or metal or plastic for fastening things together or for hanging things on.
peg *verb* (pegs, pegging, pegged)
1 fix something with pegs. 2 keep wages or prices at a fixed level.
peg away work diligently; persevere.
peg out (*slang*) die.
[probably from old Dutch]

pejorative (*say* pij-orra-tiv) *adjective*
showing disapproval; insulting or derogatory. [from Latin *pejor* = worse]

peke *noun* (*plural* pekes) (*informal*)
a Pekingese.

Pekingese *noun* (*plural* Pekingese)
a small kind of dog with short legs, a flat face, and long silky hair. [from *Peking*, the old name of Beijing, the capital of China (where the breed came from)]

pelican *noun* (*plural* pelicans)
a large bird with a pouch in its long beak for storing fish. [from Greek]

pelican crossing *noun* (*plural* pelican crossings)
a place where pedestrians can cross a street safely by operating lights that signal traffic to stop.

pellet *noun* (*plural* pellets)
a tiny ball of metal, food, paper, etc.
[from Latin *pila* = ball]

pell-mell *adverb* & *adjective*
in a hasty untidy way. [from old French]

pelmet *noun* (*plural* pelmets)
an ornamental strip of wood or material etc. above a window, used to conceal a curtain rail. [probably from French]

pelt[1] *verb* (pelts, pelting, pelted)
1 throw a lot of things at someone. 2 run fast. 3 rain very hard. [origin unknown]

pelt[2] *noun* (*plural* pelts)
an animal skin, especially with the fur still on it. [from Latin *pellis* = skin or leather]

pelvis *noun* (*plural* pelvises)
the round framework of bones at the lower end of the spine. pelvic *adjective*
[Latin, = basin (because of its shape)]

pen[1] *noun* (*plural* pens)
an instrument with a point for writing with ink.
[from Latin *penna* = feather (because a pen was originally a sharpened quill)]

pen[2] *noun* (*plural* pens)
an enclosure for cattle, sheep, hens, or other animals.
pen *verb* (pens, penning, penned)
shut animals etc. into a pen or other enclosed space. [from Old English]

pen[3] *noun* (*plural* pens)
a female swan. (Compare *cob.*)
[origin unknown]

penal (*say* peen-al) *adjective*
to do with the punishment of criminals, especially in prisons.
[from Latin *poena* = punishment]

penalize *verb* (penalizes, penalizing, penalized)
punish; put a penalty on someone.
penalization *noun*

penalty *noun* (*plural* penalties)
1 a punishment. 2 a point or advantage given to one side in a game when a member of the other side has broken a rule.

penance *noun*
a punishment that you willingly suffer to show that you regret something wrong that you have done.
[from Latin *poenitentia* = penitence]

pence *plural noun* see **penny**.
[from *pennies*]

pencil *noun* (*plural* pencils)
an instrument for drawing or writing, made of a thin stick of graphite or coloured chalk etc. enclosed in a cylinder of wood or metal.
pencil *verb* (pencils, pencilling, pencilled)
write, draw, or mark with a pencil.
[from Latin *penicillum* = paintbrush]

pendant *noun* (*plural* pendants)
an ornament worn hanging on a cord or chain round the neck.
[from Latin *pendens* = hanging]

pendent *adjective*
hanging. [same origin as *pendant*]

pending *preposition*
1 until, *Please take charge, pending his return.* 2 during, *pending these discussions.*
pending *adjective*
waiting to be decided or settled.
[same origin as *pendant*]

pendulous *adjective*
hanging down. [from Latin]

pendulum *noun* (*plural* pendulums)
a weight hung so that it can swing to and fro, especially in the works of a clock.
[from Latin, = something hanging down]

penetrable *adjective*
able to be penetrated.

penetrate *verb* (penetrates, penetrating, penetrated)
make or find a way through or into something; pierce.
penetration *noun*, **penetrative** *adjective*
[from Latin *penitus* = inside]

penfriend *noun* (*plural* penfriends)
a friend to whom you write without meeting.

penguin *noun* (*plural* penguins)
an Antarctic seabird that cannot fly but uses its wings as flippers for swimming.
[origin unknown]

penicillin *noun*
an antibiotic obtained from mould.
[from the Latin name of the mould used]

peninsula *noun* (*plural* peninsulas)
a piece of land that is almost surrounded by water. **peninsular** *adjective* [from Latin *paene* = almost + *insula* = island]

penis (*say* peen-iss) *noun* (*plural* penises)
the part of the body with which a male urinates and has sexual intercourse.
[Latin, = tail]

penitence *noun*
regret for having done wrong. **penitent** *adjective*, **penitently** *adverb* [from Latin *paenitere* = to make someone sorry]

penknife *noun* (*plural* penknives)
a small folding knife.
[originally used for sharpening quill pens]

pen-name *noun* (*plural* pen-names)
a name used by an author instead of his or her real name.

pennant *noun* (*plural* pennants)
a long pointed flag. [a mixture of *pendant* and *pennon* = the flag on a knight's lance]

penniless *adjective*
having no money; very poor.

penny *noun* (*plural* pennies for separate coins, pence for a sum of money)
1 a British coin worth $\frac{1}{100}$ of a pound. 2 a former coin worth $\frac{1}{12}$ of a shilling.
[from Old English]

pension *noun* (*plural* pensions)
an income consisting of regular payments made by a government or firm to someone who is retired, widowed, or disabled.
pension *verb* (pensions, pensioning, pensioned)
pay a pension to someone.
[from Latin *pensio* = payment]

pensioner *noun* (*plural* pensioners)
a person who receives a pension.

pensive *adjective*
deep in thought. **pensively** *adverb*
[from Latin *pensare* = consider]

penta- *prefix*
five. [from Greek]

pentagon *noun* (*plural* pentagons)
a flat shape with five sides and five angles.
pentagonal (*say* pent-ag-on-al) *adjective*
the Pentagon a five-sided building in
Washington, headquarters of the leaders of
the American armed forces.
[from *penta-* + Greek *gonia* = angle]

pentameter *noun* (*plural* pentameters)
a line of verse with five rhythmic beats.
[from *penta-* + Greek *metron* = measure]

pentathlon *noun* (*plural* pentathlons)
an athletic contest consisting of five
events.
[from *penta-* + Greek *athlon* = contest]

Pentecost *noun*
1 the Jewish harvest festival, fifty days
after Passover. 2 Whit Sunday.
[from Greek *pentekoste* = fiftieth (day)]

penthouse *noun* (*plural* penthouses)
a flat at the top of a tall building.
[from Latin *appendicium* = something
added on, later confused with French *pente*
= slope and with *house*]

pent-up *adjective*
shut in, *pent-up feelings*.
[old past participle of *pen*²]

penultimate *adjective*
last but one.
[from Latin *paene* = almost, + *ultimate*]

penumbra *noun* (*plural* penumbras or
penumbrae)
an area that is partly but not fully shaded,
e.g. during an eclipse. [from Latin *paene*
= almost + *umbra* = shade]

penurious (*say* pin-yoor-ee-us) *adjective*
(*formal*)
1 in great poverty. 2 mean or stingy.
[from Latin *penuria* = poverty]

penury (*say* pen-yoor-ee) *noun* (*formal*)
great poverty.

peony *noun* (*plural* peonies)
a plant with large round red, pink, or white
flowers. [named after Paion, physician of
the Greek gods (because the plant was once
used in medicines)]

people *plural noun*
human beings; persons, especially those
belonging to a particular country, area, or
group etc.
people *noun* (*plural* peoples)
a community or nation, *a warlike people*;
the English-speaking peoples.
people *verb* (peoples, peopling, peopled)
fill a place with people; populate.
[from Latin]

pep *noun* (*slang*)
vigour or energy. [from *pepper*]

pepper *noun* (*plural* peppers)
1 a hot-tasting powder used to flavour food.
2 a bright green, red, or yellow vegetable.
peppery *adjective*
pepper *verb* (peppers, peppering, peppered)
1 sprinkle with pepper. 2 pelt with many
small objects. [from Old English]

peppercorn *noun* (*plural* peppercorns)
the dried black berry from which pepper is
made.

peppermint *noun* (*plural* peppermints)
1 a kind of mint used for flavouring. 2 a
sweet flavoured with this mint.
[because of its sharp taste]

pepperoni *noun*
beef and pork sausage seasoned with
pepper. [from Italian *peperone* = chilli]

per *preposition*
for each, *The charge is £2 per person*.
[from Latin, = through]

per- *prefix*
1 through (as in *perforate*). 2 thoroughly
(as in *perturb*). 3 away entirely; towards
badness (as in *pervert*). [from Latin]

perambulate *verb* (perambulates,
perambulating, perambulated) (*formal*)
walk through or round an area.
perambulation *noun*
[from *per-* + Latin *ambulare* = to walk]

perambulator *noun* (*plural* perambulators) (*formal*)
a baby's pram.

per annum *adverb*
for each year; yearly.
[from *per* + Latin *annus* = year]

per capita (*say* kap-it-a) *adverb* & *adjective*
for each person. [Latin, = for heads]

perceive *verb* (perceives, perceiving, perceived)
see, notice, or understand something.
[from Latin *percipere* = seize, understand]

per cent *adverb*
for or in every hundred, *three per cent* (3%).
[from *per* + Latin *centum* = hundred]

percentage *noun* (*plural* percentages)
an amount or rate expressed as a
proportion of 100.

perceptible *adjective*
able to be seen or noticed.
perceptibly *adverb*, **perceptibility** *noun*

perception *noun* (*plural* perceptions)
the ability to see, notice, or understand
something. [same origin as *perceive*]

perceptive *adjective*
quick to notice or understand things.

perch[1] *noun* (*plural* perches)
1 a place where a bird sits or rests. 2 a seat
high up.
perch *verb* (perches, perching, perched)
rest or place on a perch.
[from Latin *pertica* = pole]

perch[2] *noun* (*plural* perch)
an edible freshwater fish. [from Greek]

percipient *adjective* (*formal*)
quick to notice or understand things;
perceptive. **percipience** *noun*
[same origin as *perceive*]

percolate *verb* (percolates, percolating, percolated)
flow through small holes or spaces.
percolation *noun*
[from *per-* + Latin *colum* = strainer]

percolator *noun* (*plural* percolators)
a pot for making coffee, in which boiling
water percolates through coffee grounds.

percussion *noun*
1 musical instruments (e.g. drums,
cymbals) played by being struck or shaken.
2 the striking of one thing against another.
percussive *adjective*
[from Latin *percussum* = hit]

perdition *noun*
eternal damnation.
[from Latin *perditum* = destroyed]

peregrination *noun* (*plural* peregrinations) (*formal*)
travelling about; a journey.
[from *per-* + Latin *ager* = field]

peregrine *noun* (*plural* peregrines)
a kind of falcon. [from Latin *peregrinus*
= travelling (because it migrates)]

peremptory *adjective*
giving commands and expecting to be
obeyed at once.
[from Latin *peremptorius* = final, decisive]

perennial *adjective*
lasting for many years; keeping on
recurring. **perennially** *adverb*
perennial *noun* (*plural* perennials)
a plant that lives for many years.
[from *per-* + Latin *annus* = year]

perestroika (*say* peri-stroik-a) *noun*
restructuring a system, especially the
political and economic system of the
former Soviet Union.
[Russian, = restructuring]

perfect (*say* per-fikt) *adjective*
1 so good that it cannot be made any better.
2 complete, *a perfect stranger*.
perfectly *adverb*
perfect (*say* per-fekt) *verb* (perfects,
perfecting, perfected)
make a thing perfect. **perfection** *noun*
to perfection perfectly.
[from Latin *perfectum* = completed]

perfectionist *noun* (*plural* perfectionists)
a person who likes everything to be done
perfectly.

perfect tense *noun*
a tense of a verb showing a completed action, e.g. *He has arrived.*

perfidious *adjective*
treacherous or disloyal. **perfidiously** *adverb*, **perfidy** *noun* [from *per-* = becoming bad + Latin *fides* = faith]

perforate *verb* (perforates, perforating, perforated)
1 make tiny holes in something, especially so that it can be torn off easily. 2 pierce. **perforation** *noun*
[from *per-* + Latin *forare* = bore through]

perforce *adverb* (*old use*)
by necessity; unavoidably.
[from old French *par force* = by force]

perform *verb* (performs, performing, performed)
1 do something in front of an audience, *perform a play.* 2 do something, *perform an operation.* **performance** *noun*, **performer** *noun* [from old French]

perfume *noun* (*plural* perfumes)
1 a pleasant smell. 2 a liquid for giving something a pleasant smell; scent.
perfume *verb*, **perfumery** *noun*
[originally used of smoke from something burning: via French from old Italian *parfumare* = to smoke through]

perfunctory *adjective*
done without much care or interest, *a perfunctory glance.* **perfunctorily** *adverb*
[from Latin]

pergola *noun* (*plural* pergolas)
an arch formed by climbing plants growing over trellis-work. [Italian]

perhaps *adverb*
it may be; possibly.
[from *per* + Middle English *hap* = luck]

peri- *prefix*
around (as in *perimeter*). [from Greek]

peril *noun* (*plural* perils)
danger. **perilous** *adjective*, **perilously** *adverb*
[from Latin *periculum* = danger]

perimeter *noun* (*plural* perimeters)
1 the outer edge or boundary of something.

2 the distance round the edge.
[from *peri-* + Greek *metron* = measure]

USAGE: Do not confuse with *parameter.*

period *noun* (*plural* periods)
1 a length of time. 2 the time when a woman menstruates. 3 (in punctuation) a full stop. [from Greek *periodos* = course or cycle (of events)]

periodic *adjective*
occurring at regular intervals.
periodically *adverb*

periodical *noun* (*plural* periodicals)
a magazine published at regular intervals (e.g. monthly).

periodic table *noun*
a table in which the chemical elements are arranged in order of increasing atomic number.

peripatetic *adjective*
going from place to place.
[from *peri-* + Greek *patein* = to walk]

peripheral *adjective*
1 of minor importance. 2 at the edge or boundary.

periphery (*say* per-if-er-ee) *noun* (*plural* peripheries)
the part at the edge or boundary.
[from Greek, = circumference]

periphrasis (*say* per-if-ra-sis) *noun* (*plural* periphrases)
a roundabout way of saying something; a circumlocution.
[from *peri-* + Greek *phrasis* = speech]

periscope *noun* (*plural* periscopes)
a device with a tube and mirrors with which a person in a trench or submarine etc. can see things that are otherwise out of sight.
[from *peri-* + Greek *skopein* = look at]

perish *verb* (perishes, perishing, perished)
1 die; be destroyed. 2 rot, *The rubber ring has perished.* **perishable** *adjective*
[from *per-* + Latin *ire* = go]

perished *adjective* (*informal*)
feeling very cold.

perishing *adjective* (*informal*)
freezing cold, *It's perishing outside!*

periwinkle[1] *noun* (*plural* **periwinkles**)
a trailing plant with blue or white flowers.
[from Latin]

periwinkle[2] *noun* (*plural* **periwinkles**)
a winkle. [origin unknown]

perjure *verb* (**perjures, perjuring, perjured**)
perjure yourself commit perjury.

perjury *noun*
telling a lie while you are on oath to speak
the truth.
[from Latin *perjurare* = break an oath]

perk[1] *verb* (**perks, perking, perked**)
perk up make or become more cheerful.
[from *perch*[1]]

perk[2] *noun* (*plural* **perks**) (*informal*)
something extra given to a worker, *Free
bus travel is one of the perks of the job.*
[from *perquisite*]

perky *adjective*
lively and cheerful. **perkily** *adverb*
[from *perk*[1]]

perm *noun* (*plural* **perms**)
a permanent wave. **perm** *verb*

permanent *adjective*
lasting for always or for a very long time.
permanently *adverb*, **permanence** *noun*
[from *per-* + Latin *manens* = remaining]

permanent wave *noun* (*plural*
permanent waves)
treatment of the hair to give it long-lasting
waves.

permeable *adjective*
able to be permeated by fluids etc.
permeability *noun*

permeate *verb* (**permeates, permeating,
permeated**)
spread into every part of something;
pervade, *Smoke had permeated the hall.*
permeation *noun*
[from *per-* + Latin *meare* = to pass]

permissible *adjective*
allowable.

permission *noun*
the right to do something, given by
someone in authority; authorization.
[same origin as *permit*]

permissive *adjective*
letting people do what they wish; tolerant
or liberal.

permit (*say* per-mit) *verb* (**permits,
permitting, permitted**)
give permission or consent or a chance to
do something; allow.

permit (*say* per-mit) *noun* (*plural* **permits**)
written or printed permission to do
something or go somewhere.
[from *per-* + Latin *mittere* = send or let go]

permutation *noun* (*plural* **permutations**)
1 changing the order of a set of things. **2** a
changed order, *3, 1, 2 is a permutation of 1,
2, 3.* [from *per-* + Latin *mutare* = to change]

pernicious *adjective*
very harmful.
[from Latin *pernicies* = destruction]

peroration *noun* (*plural* **perorations**)
an elaborate ending to a speech.
[from *per-* + Latin *oratio* = speech, oration]

peroxide *noun*
a chemical used for bleaching hair.
[from *per-* + *oxide*]

perpendicular *adjective*
upright; at a right angle (90°) to a line or
surface.
[from Latin *perpendiculum* = plumb line]

perpetrate *verb* (**perpetrates, perpetrating,
perpetrated**)
commit or be guilty of, *perpetrate a crime
or an error.* **perpetration** *noun*, **perpetrator**
noun [from *per-* + Latin *patrare* = make
something happen]

perpetual *adjective*
lasting for a long time; continual.
perpetually *adverb*
[from Latin *perpes* = uninterrupted]

perpetuate *verb* (**perpetuates,
perpetuating, perpetuated**)
cause to continue or be remembered for a
long time, *The statue will perpetuate his
memory.* **perpetuation** *noun*

perpetuity *noun*
being perpetual.
in perpetuity for ever.

perplex *verb* (perplexes, perplexing,
perplexed)
bewilder or puzzle somebody. **perplexity**
noun [from *per-* + Latin *plexus* = twisted
together]

perquisite (*say* per-kwiz-it) *noun* (*plural*
perquisites)
something extra given to a worker; a perk,
*Use of the firm's car is a perquisite of this
job.* [originally = property that you got
yourself, as opposed to property left to you:
from *per-* + Latin *quaerere* = seek]

perry *noun*
a drink rather like cider, made from pears.
[from old French; related to *pear*]

persecute *verb* (persecutes, persecuting,
persecuted)
be continually cruel to somebody,
especially because you disagree with his or
her beliefs. **persecution** *noun*, **persecutor**
noun [from Latin *persecutum* = pursued]

persevere *verb* (perseveres, persevering,
persevered)
go on doing something even though it is
difficult. **perseverance** *noun*
[from *per-* + Latin *severus* = strict]

Persian *adjective*
to do with or belonging to Persia, a country
in the Middle East now called Iran.
Persian *noun*
the language of Persia.

persist *verb* (persists, persisting, persisted)
1 continue firmly or obstinately, *She
persists in breaking the rules.* **2** continue to
exist, *The custom persists in some countries.*
persistent *adjective*, **persistently** *adverb*,
persistence *noun*, **persistency** *noun*
[from *per-* + Latin *sistere* = to stand]

person *noun* (*plural* people or persons)
1 a human being; a man, woman, or child.
2 (in grammar) any of the three groups of
personal pronouns and forms taken by
verbs. The **first person** (= *I, me, we, us*)
refers to the person(s) speaking; the **second
person** (= *you*) refers to the person(s)
spoken to; the **third person** (= *he, him, she,*

her, it, they, them) refers to the person(s)
spoken about.
in person being actually present oneself,
She was there in person.
[from Latin *persona* = mask used by an
actor]

personable *adjective*
pleasing in appearance and behaviour.

personage *noun* (*plural* personages)
an important person.

personal *adjective*
1 belonging to, done by, or concerning a
particular person, *personal belongings.*
2 criticizing a person, *making personal
remarks.* **personally** *adverb*

USAGE: Do not confuse with *personnel.*

personality *noun* (*plural* personalities)
1 a person's character, *She has a cheerful
personality.* **2** a well-known person, *a TV
personality.*

personal stereo *noun* (*plural* personal
stereos)
a small portable cassette player with
headphones.

personify *verb* (personifies, personifying,
personified)
represent a quality or idea etc. as a person.
personification *noun*

personnel *noun*
the people employed by a firm or other
large organization. [French, = personal]

USAGE: Do not confuse with *personal.*

perspective *noun* (*plural* perspectives)
the impression of depth and space in a
picture or scene.
in perspective giving a well-balanced view
of things.
[from Latin *perspicere* = look at closely]

Perspex *noun* (*trade mark*)
a tough transparent plastic used instead of
glass.
[from Latin *perspectum* = looked through]

perspicacious *adjective*
quick to notice or understand things.
perspicacity *noun*
[same origin as *perspective*]

perspire *verb* (perspires, perspiring, perspired)
sweat. **perspiration** *noun*
[from *per-* + Latin *spirare* = breathe]

persuade *verb* (persuades, persuading, persuaded)
make someone believe or agree to do something. **persuasion** *noun*, **persuasive** *adjective* [from *per-* + Latin *suadere* = advise or induce]

pert *adjective*
cheeky. **pertly** *adverb*, **pertness** *noun*
[from old French]

pertain *verb* (pertains, pertaining, pertained)
be relevant to something, *evidence pertaining to the crime.*
[from Latin *pertinere* = belong]

pertinacious *adjective* (*formal*)
persistent and determined.
pertinaciously *adverb*, **pertinacity** *noun*
[from *per-* + Latin *tenax* = holding fast, tenacious]

pertinent *adjective*
relevant to what you are talking about.
pertinently *adverb*, **pertinence** *noun*

perturb *verb* (perturbs, perturbing, perturbed)
worry someone. **perturbation** *noun*
[from *per-* + Latin *turbare* = disturb]

peruse (*say* per-ooz) *verb* (peruses, perusing, perused)
read something carefully. **perusal** *noun*
[from *per-* + Latin *usitari* = use often]

pervade *verb* (pervades, pervading, pervaded)
spread all through something; permeate.
pervasion *noun*, **pervasive** *adjective*
[from *per-* + Latin *vadere* = go]

perverse *adjective*
obstinately doing something different from what is reasonable or required.
perversely *adverb*, **perversity** *noun*
[same origin as *pervert*]

pervert (*say* per-vert) *verb* (perverts, perverting, perverted)
1 turn something from the right course of action, *By false evidence they perverted the course of justice.* **2** cause a person to behave wickedly or abnormally. **perversion** *noun*

pervert (*say* per-vert) *noun* (*plural* perverts)
a person whose sexual behaviour is thought to be unnatural or disgusting.
[from *per-* + Latin *vertere* = to turn]

Pesach *noun*
the Passover festival. [Hebrew]

pessimist *noun* (*plural* pessimists)
a person who expects that things will turn out badly. (Compare *optimist*.) **pessimism** *noun*, **pessimistic** *adjective*, **pessimistically** *adverb* [from Latin *pessimus* = worst]

pest *noun* (*plural* pests)
1 a destructive insect or animal, such as a locust or a mouse. **2** a nuisance.
[from Latin *pestis* = plague]

pester *verb* (pesters, pestering, pestered)
keep annoying someone by frequent questions or requests. [from French *empestrer* = infect with plague]

pesticide *noun* (*plural* pesticides)
a substance for killing harmful insects and other pests. [from *pest* + *-cide*]

pestiferous *adjective*
troublesome or harmful.
[from *pest* + Latin *ferre* = carry]

pestilence *noun* (*plural* pestilences)
a deadly epidemic. [same origin as *pest*]

pestilential *adjective*
troublesome or harmful.
[same origin as *pest*]

pestle *noun* (*plural* pestles)
a tool with a heavy rounded end for pounding substances in a mortar.
[from Latin]

pet *noun* (*plural* pets)
1 a tame animal kept for companionship and pleasure. **2** a person treated as a favourite, *teacher's pet.*
pet *adjective*
favourite, *Science fiction is my pet subject.*
pet *verb* (pets, petting, petted)
treat or fondle someone affectionately.
[origin unknown]

petal *noun* (*plural* petals)
one of the separate coloured outer parts of a flower. [from Greek *petalos* = spread out, unfolded]

peter *verb* (peters, petering, petered)
peter out become gradually less and cease to exist.
[origin unknown]

petition *noun* (*plural* petitions)
a formal request for something, especially a written one signed by many people.
petition *verb* (petitions, petitioning, petitioned)
request something by a petition. **petitioner** *noun* [from Latin *petere* = claim or ask for]

petrel *noun* (*plural* petrels)
a kind of seabird. [perhaps named after St Peter, who tried to walk on the water (because the bird flies just over the waves with its legs dangling)]

petrify *verb* (petrifies, petrifying, petrified)
1 make someone so terrified that he or she cannot move. **2** turn to stone. **petrifaction** *noun* [from Greek *petra* = rock]

petrochemical *noun* (*plural* petrochemicals)
a substance obtained from petroleum or natural gas.

petrol *noun*
a liquid made from petroleum, used as fuel for engines.

petroleum *noun*
an oil found underground that is refined to make fuel (e.g. petrol, paraffin) or for use in dry-cleaning etc. [from Greek *petra* = rock + Latin *oleum* = oil]

petticoat *noun* (*plural* petticoats)
a woman's or girl's dress-length undergarment. [from *petty* = little, + *coat*]

pettifogging *adjective*
paying too much attention to unimportant details. [from an old slang word *pettifogger* = a lawyer who dealt with trivial cases]

petting *noun*
affectionate touching or fondling.

pettish *adjective*
irritable or bad-tempered; peevish.

petty *adjective* (pettier, pettiest)
1 unimportant or trivial, *petty regulations*. **2** mean and small-minded.
pettily *adverb*, **pettiness** *noun*
[from French *petit* = small]

petty cash *noun*
cash kept by an office for small payments.

petty officer *noun* (*plural* petty officers)
an NCO in the navy.

petulant *adjective*
irritable or bad-tempered, especially in a childish way; peevish.
petulantly *adverb*, **petulance** *noun*
[from old French]

petunia *noun* (*plural* petunias)
a garden plant with funnel-shaped flowers. [from *petun*, an old word for tobacco (because it is related to the tobacco plant)]

pew *noun* (*plural* pews)
a long wooden seat, usually fixed in rows, in a church.
[from old French; related to *podium*]

pewter *noun*
a grey alloy of tin and lead.
[from old French]

pH *noun*
a measure of the acidity or alkalinity of a solution. Pure water has a pH of 7, acids have a pH between 0 and 7, and alkalis have a pH between 7 and 14.
[from the initial letter of German *Potenz* = power, + H, the symbol for hydrogen]

phalanx *noun* (*plural* phalanxes)
a number of people or soldiers in a close formation. [from Greek]

phantasm *noun* (*plural* phantasms)
a phantom.
[from Greek *phantasma* = a vision, a ghost]

phantom *noun* (*plural* phantoms)
a ghost; something that is not real.
[from old French; related to *phantasm*]

Pharaoh (*say* fair-oh) *noun* (*plural* Pharaohs)
the title of the king of ancient Egypt.
[from ancient Egyptian *pr-'o* = great house]

pharmaceutical (*say* farm-as-**yoot**-ik-al)
adjective
to do with pharmacy; to do with medicines,
the pharmaceutical industry.
[from Greek *pharmakeutes* = pharmacist]

pharmacist *noun* (*plural* **pharmacists**)
a person who is trained to prepare and sell
medicines. [from *pharmacy*]

pharmacology *noun*
the study of medicinal drugs.
pharmacological *adjective*,
pharmacologist *noun*
[from Greek *pharmakon* = drug, + *-logy*]

pharmacy *noun* (*plural* **pharmacies**)
1 a shop selling medicines; a dispensary.
2 the job of preparing medicines.
[from Greek *pharmakon* = drug]

pharynx (*say* **fa**-rinks) *noun* (*plural*
pharynges)
the cavity at the back of the mouth and
nose. [Greek, = throat]

phase *noun* (*plural* **phases**)
a stage in the progress or development of
something.
phase *verb* (**phases, phasing, phased**)
do something in stages, not all at once, *a
phased withdrawal*. [from Latin]

Ph.D. *abbreviation*
Doctor of Philosophy; a university degree
awarded to someone who has done
advanced research in their subject.

pheasant (*say* **fez**-ant) *noun* (*plural*
pheasants)
a game bird with a long tail. [from Greek]

phenomenal *adjective*
amazing or remarkable.
phenomenally *adverb*

phenomenon *noun* (*plural* **phenomena**)
an event or fact, especially one that is
remarkable. [from Greek *phainomenon*
= something appearing]

USAGE: Note that *phenomena* is a plural. It
is incorrect to say 'this phenomena' or
'these phenomenas'.

phial *noun* (*plural* **phials**)
a small glass bottle. [from Greek]

phil- *prefix*
1 fond of. 2 a lover of. see **philo-**

philander *verb* (**philanders, philandering,
philandered**)
flirt or have casual affairs with women.
philanderer *noun* [from Greek]

philanthropy *noun*
love of mankind, especially as shown by
kind and generous acts that benefit large
numbers of people. **philanthropist** *noun*,
philanthropic *adjective*
[from *phil-* + Greek *anthropos* = mankind]

philately (*say* fil-**at**-il-ee) *noun*
stamp-collecting. **philatelist** *noun*
[from *phil-* + Greek *ateleia* = not needing to
pay (because postage has been paid for by
buying a stamp)]

philharmonic *adjective*
(in names of orchestras etc.) devoted to
music. [from *phil-* + French *harmonique*
= harmonic]

philistine (*say* **fil**-ist-I'n) *noun* (*plural*
philistines)
a person who dislikes art, poetry, etc.
[from the Philistines in the Bible, who
were enemies of the Israelites]

philo- *prefix*
1 fond of. 2 a lover of.
[from Greek *philein* = to love]

philology *noun*
the study of words and their history.
philological *adjective*, **philologist** *noun*
[from *philo-* + Greek *logos* = word]

philosopher *noun* (*plural* **philosophers**)
an expert in philosophy.

philosophical *adjective*
1 to do with philosophy. 2 calm and not
upset after a misfortune or
disappointment, *Be philosophical about
losing.* **philosophically** *adverb*

philosophy *noun* (*plural* **philosophies**)
1 the study of truths about life, morals, etc.
2 a set of ideas or principles or beliefs.
[from *philo-* + Greek *sophia* = wisdom]

philtre (*say* **fil**-ter) *noun* (*plural* **philtres**)
a magic drink, especially a love potion.
[from Greek *philein* = to love]

phlegm (*say* flem) *noun*
thick mucus that forms in the throat and lungs when you have a bad cold. [from Greek]

phlegmatic (*say* fleg-**mat**-ik) *adjective*
not easily excited or worried.
phlegmatically *adverb* [same origin as *phlegm* (because too much phlegm in the body was believed to make you sluggish)]

phobia (*say* foh-bee-a) *noun* (*plural* phobias)
great or abnormal fear of something. [from Greek *phobos* = fear]

-phobia *suffix*
forms nouns meaning 'fear or great dislike of something' (e.g. *hydrophobia*).

phoenix (*say* feen-iks) *noun* (*plural* phoenixes)
a mythical bird that was said to burn itself to death in a fire and be born again from the ashes. [from Greek]

phone *noun* (*plural* phones)
a telephone.
phone *verb* (phones, phoning, phoned)
telephone. [short for *telephone*]

phonecard *noun* (*plural* phonecards)
a plastic card that you can use to work some public telephones instead of money.

phone-in *noun* (*plural* phone-ins)
a broadcast in which people phone the studio and take part in a discussion.

phonetic (*say* fon-**et**-ik) *adjective*
1 to do with speech-sounds. 2 representing speech-sounds. **phonetically** *adverb* [from Greek *phonein* = speak]

phoney *adjective* (*informal*)
sham; not genuine. [origin unknown]

phosphate *noun* (*plural* phosphates)
a substance containing phosphorus.

phosphorescent (*say* fos-fer-**ess**-ent) *adjective*
glowing in the dark; luminous.
phosphorescence *noun* [from *phosphorus*]

phosphorus *noun*
a chemical substance that glows in the dark. [from Greek *phos* = light + -*phoros* = bringing]

photo *noun* (*plural* photos)
a photograph.

photo- *prefix*
light (as in *photograph*). [from Greek]

photocopy *noun* (*plural* photocopies)
a copy of a document or page etc. made by photographing it on special paper.
photocopy *verb*, **photocopier** *noun*

photoelectric *adjective*
using the electrical effects of light.

photogenic *adjective*
looking attractive in photographs. [from *photo-* + -*genic* = producing]

photograph *noun* (*plural* photographs)
a picture made by the effect of light or other radiation on film or special paper.
photograph *verb* (photographs, photographing, photographed)
take a photograph of a person or thing.
photographer *noun*

photography *noun*
taking photographs. **photographic** *adjective*

photosynthesis *noun*
the process by which green plants use sunlight to turn carbon dioxide and water into complex substances, giving off oxygen.

phrase *noun* (*plural* phrases)
1 a group of words that form a unit in a sentence or clause, e.g. *in the garden* in 'The Queen was in the garden'. 2 a short section of a tune.
phrase *verb* (phrases, phrasing, phrased)
1 put something into words. 2 divide music into phrases.
[from Greek *phrazein* = declare]

phrase book *noun* (*plural* phrase books)
a book which lists useful words and expressions in a foreign language, with their translations.

phraseology (*say* fray-zee-**ol**-o-jee) *noun* (*plural* phraseologies)
wording; the way something is worded. [from *phrase* + -*ology*]

physical *adjective*
1 to do with the body rather than the mind or feelings. 2 to do with things that you can touch or see. 3 to do with physics.
physically *adverb* [same origin as *physics*]

physical education or **physical training** *noun*
gymnastics or other exercises done to keep the body healthy.

physician *noun* (*plural* physicians)
a doctor, especially one who is not a surgeon.
[from old French *fisicien* = physicist]

physicist (*say* fiz-i-sist) *noun* (*plural* physicists)
an expert in physics.

physics (*say* fiz-iks) *noun*
the study of the properties of matter and energy (e.g. heat, light, sound, movement).
[from Greek *physikos* = natural]

physiognomy (*say* fiz-ee-on-o-mee) *noun* (*plural* physiognomies)
the features of a person's face. [from Greek *physis* = nature + *gnomon* – indicator]

physiology (*say* fiz-ee-ol-o-jee) *noun*
the study of the body and its parts and how they function.
physiological *adjective*, **physiologist** *noun*
[from Greek *physis* = nature, + *-ology*]

physiotherapy (*say* fiz-ee-o-th'erra-pee) *noun*
the treatment of a disease or weakness by massage, exercises, etc.
physiotherapist *noun*
[from Greek *physis* = nature, + *therapy*]

physique (*say* fiz-eek) *noun* (*plural* physiques)
a person's build. [French, = physical]

pi *noun*
the symbol (π) of the ratio of the circumference of a circle to its diameter. The value of pi is approximately 3.142.
[the name of the sixteenth letter (π) of the Greek alphabet]

pianist *noun* (*plural* pianists)
a person who plays the piano.

piano *noun* (*plural* pianos)
a large musical instrument with a keyboard. [short for *pianoforte*, from Italian *piano* – soft + *forte* = loud (because it can produce soft notes and loud notes)]

piccolo *noun* (*plural* piccolos)
a small high-pitched flute. [Italian, – small]

pick[1] *verb* (picks, picking, picked)
1 separate a flower or fruit from its plant, *We picked apples.* 2 choose; select carefully. 3 pull bits off or out of something. 4 open a lock by using something pointed, not with a key.
pick a quarrel deliberately provoke a quarrel with somebody.
pick holes in find fault with.
pick on keep criticizing or harassing a particular person.
pick someone's pocket steal from it.
pick up 1 lift or take up. **2** collect. **3** take someone into a vehicle. **4** manage to hear something. **5** get better or recover.

pick *noun*
1 choice, *take your pick.* 2 the best of a group. [origin unknown]

pick[2] *noun* (*plural* picks)
1 a pickaxe. 2 a plectrum.
[a different spelling of *pike*]

pickaxe *noun* (*plural* pickaxes)
a heavy pointed tool with a long handle, used for breaking up hard ground etc.
[from old French *picois*, later confused with *axe*]

picket *noun* (*plural* pickets)
1 a striker or group of strikers who try to persuade other people not to go into a place of work during a strike. 2 a pointed post as part of a fence.
picket *verb* (pickets, picketing, picketed)
stand outside a place of work to try to persuade other people not to go in during a strike. [from French *picquet* = small pike]

pickle *noun* (*plural* pickles)
1 a strong-tasting food made of pickled vegetables. 2 (*informal*) a mess.
pickle *verb* (pickles, pickling, pickled)
preserve food in vinegar or salt water.
[from old German or old Dutch]

pickpocket *noun* (*plural* pickpockets)
a thief who steals from people's pockets or
bags.

pick-up *noun* (*plural* pick-ups)
1 the part of a record player that holds the
stylus. 2 an open truck for carrying small
loads.

picnic *noun* (*plural* picnics)
a meal eaten in the open air away from
home.
picnic *verb* (picnics, picnicking, picnicked)
have a picnic. **picnicker** *noun* [from French]

Pict *noun* (*plural* Picts)
a member of an ancient people of north
Britain. **Pictish** *adjective* [from Latin
Picti = painted or tattooed people]

pictorial *adjective*
with or using pictures. **pictorially** *adverb*

picture *noun* (*plural* pictures)
1 a representation of a person or thing
made by painting, drawing, or
photography. 2 a film at the cinema. 3 how
something seems; an impression.
picture *verb* (pictures, picturing, pictured)
1 show in a picture. 2 imagine.
[from Latin *pictum* = painted]

picturesque *adjective*
1 forming an attractive scene, *a
picturesque village*. 2 vividly described;
expressive, *picturesque language*.
picturesquely *adverb*

pidgin *noun* (*plural* pidgins)
a simplified form of a language used by
people who do not speak the same
language.
[from the Chinese pronunciation of
business (because it was used by traders)]

pie *noun* (*plural* pies)
a baked dish of meat, fish, or fruit covered
with pastry.
[perhaps from *magpie* (because the
contents of a pie look like the bits and
pieces a magpie collects in its nest)]

piebald *adjective*
with patches of black and white, *a piebald
donkey*. [from *pie* = magpie, + *bald*]

piece *noun* (*plural* pieces)
1 a part or portion of something; a
fragment. 2 a separate thing or example, *a
fine piece of work*. 3 something written,
composed, or painted etc., *a piece of music*.
4 one of the objects used to play a game on
a board, *a chess-piece*.
piece *verb* (pieces, piecing, pieced)
put pieces together to make something.
[from old French]

pièce de résistance (*say* pee-ess der ray-
zees-**tahns**) *noun* (*plural* pièces de
résistance)
the most important item. [French]

piecemeal *adjective* & *adverb*
done or made one piece at a time. [from
piece + Old English *mael* = a measure]

pie chart *noun* (*plural* pie charts)
a circle divided into sectors to represent
the way in which a quantity is divided up.

pier *noun* (*plural* piers)
1 a long structure built out into the sea for
people to walk on. 2 a pillar supporting a
bridge or arch. [from Latin]

pierce *verb* (pierces, piercing, pierced)
make a hole through something; penetrate.
[from old French]

piercing *adjective*
1 very loud and high-pitched.
2 penetrating; very strong, *a piercing wind*.

piety *noun*
being very religious and devout; piousness.
[from Latin *pietas* = dutiful behaviour]

piffle *noun* (*slang*)
nonsense. [originally a dialect word]

pig *noun* (*plural* pigs)
1 a fat animal with short legs and a blunt
snout, kept for its meat. 2 (*informal*)
someone greedy, dirty, or unpleasant.
piggy *adjective* & *noun* [origin unknown]

pigeon¹ *noun* (*plural* pigeons)
a bird with a fat body and a small head.
[from old French *pijon* = young bird]

pigeon² *noun* (*informal*)
a person's business or responsibility,
That's your pigeon. [same origin as *pidgin*]

pigeon-hole *noun* (*plural* pigeon-holes)
a small compartment above a desk etc.,
used for holding letters or papers.

pigeon-hole *verb* (pigeon-holes, pigeon-
holing, pigeon-holed)
decide that a person belongs to a particular
category, *She doesn't want to be pigeon-
holed simply as a pop singer.*

piggery *noun* (*plural* piggeries)
a place where pigs are bred or kept.

piggyback *adverb*
carried on somebody else's back or
shoulders. **piggyback** *noun*
[from *pick-a-back*]

piggy bank *noun* (*plural* piggy banks)
a money box made in the shape of a hollow
pig.

pig-headed *adjective*
obstinate.

pig-iron *noun*
iron that has been processed in a smelting
furnace. [because the blocks of iron
reminded people of pigs]

piglet *noun* (*plural* piglets)
a young pig.

pigment *noun* (*plural* pigments)
a substance that colours something.
pigmented *adjective*, **pigmentation** *noun*
[from Latin *pingere* = to paint]

pigsty *noun* (*plural* pigsties)
1 a partly-covered pen for pigs. 2 a filthy
room or house.

pigtail *noun* (*plural* pigtails)
a plait of hair worn hanging at the back of
the head.

pike *noun* (*plural* pikes)
1 a heavy spear. 2 (*plural* pike) a large
freshwater fish. [origin unknown]

pilau *noun*
an Indian dish of spiced rice with meat and
vegetables. [from Turkish]

pilchard *noun* (*plural* pilchards)
a small sea fish. [origin unknown]

pile¹ *noun* (*plural* piles)
1 a number of things on top of one another.
2 (*informal*) a large quantity; a lot of
money. 3 a tall building.

pile *verb* (piles, piling, piled)
put things into a pile; make a pile.
[from Latin *pila* = pillar]

pile² *noun* (*plural* piles)
a heavy beam made of metal, concrete, or
timber driven into the ground to support
something. [from Old English]

pile³ *noun*
a raised surface on fabric, made of upright
threads, *a carpet with a thick pile.*
[from Latin *pilus* = hair]

pile-up *noun* (*plural* pile-ups)
a road accident that involves a number of
vehicles.

pilfer *verb* (pilfers, pilfering, pilfered)
steal small things. **pilferer** *noun*,
pilferage *noun* [from old French]

pilgrim *noun* (*plural* pilgrims)
a person who travels to a holy place for
religious reasons. **pilgrimage** *noun*
[same origin as *peregrine*]

pill *noun* (*plural* pills)
a small solid piece of medicine for
swallowing.
the pill a contraceptive pill.
[from Latin *pila* = ball]

pillage *verb* (pillages, pillaging, pillaged)
carry off goods using force, especially in a
war; plunder. **pillage** *noun*
[from Latin *pilare* = cut the hair from]

pillar *noun* (*plural* pillars)
a tall stone or wooden post.
[same origin as *pile¹*]

pillar box *noun* (*plural* pillar boxes)
a postbox standing in a street.
[because many of them are shaped like a
short pillar]

pillion *noun* (*plural* pillions)
a seat behind the driver on a motorcycle.
[from Scottish Gaelic *pillean* = cushion]

pillory *noun* (*plural* **pillories**)
a wooden framework with holes for a person's head and hands, in which offenders were formerly made to stand and be ridiculed by the public as a punishment.

pillory *verb* (**pillories, pillorying, pilloried**)
expose a person to public ridicule and scorn, *He was pilloried in the newspapers for what he had done.* [from old French]

pillow *noun* (*plural* **pillows**)
a cushion for a person's head to rest on, especially in bed.

pillow *verb* (**pillows, pillowing, pillowed**)
rest the head on a pillow or something soft, *He pillowed his head on his arms.* [from Old English]

pillowcase or **pillowslip** *noun* (*plural* **pillowcases, pillowslips**)
a cloth cover for a pillow.

pilot *noun* (*plural* **pilots**)
1 a person who works the controls for flying an aircraft. 2 a person qualified to steer a ship in and out of a port or through a difficult stretch of water. 3 a guide.

pilot *verb* (**pilots, piloting, piloted**)
1 be pilot of an aircraft or ship. 2 guide or steer.

pilot *adjective*
testing on a small scale how something will work, *a pilot scheme.*
[from Greek *pedon* = oar or rudder]

pilot light *noun* (*plural* **pilot lights**)
1 a small flame that lights a larger burner on a gas cooker etc. 2 an electric indicator light.

pimp *noun* (*plural* **pimps**)
a man who gets clients for prostitutes and lives off their earnings. [origin unknown]

pimpernel (*say* pimp-er-nel) *noun* (*plural* **pimpernels**)
a plant with small red, blue, or white flowers that close in cloudy weather. [from old French]

pimple *noun* (*plural* **pimples**)
a small round raised spot on the skin.
pimply *adjective*
[via Old English from Latin]

PIN *abbreviation*
personal identification number; a number used as a person's password so that he or she can use a cash dispenser, computer, etc.

pin *noun* (*plural* **pins**)
1 a short thin piece of metal with a sharp point and a rounded head, used to fasten pieces of cloth or paper etc. together. 2 a pointed device for fixing or marking something.
pins and needles a prickling feeling.

pin *verb* (**pins, pinning, pinned**)
1 fasten something with a pin or pins. 2 make a person or thing unable to move, *He was pinned under the wreckage.* 3 fix, *They pinned the blame on her.* [via Old English from Latin]

pinafore *noun* (*plural* **pinafores**)
an apron. [from *pin* + *afore* = in front (because originally the bib of the apron was pinned to the front of the dress)]

pinball *noun* (*plural* **pinballs**)
a game in which you shoot small metal balls across a special table and score points when they strike pins with lights etc.

pincer *noun* (*plural* **pincers**)
the claw of a shellfish such as a lobster. [from old French *pincier* = to pinch]

pincers *plural noun*
a tool with two parts that are pressed together for gripping and holding things.

pinch *verb* (**pinches, pinching, pinched**)
1 squeeze something tightly or painfully between two things, especially between the finger and thumb. 2 (*informal*) steal.

pinch *noun* (*plural* **pinches**)
1 a pinching movement. 2 the amount that can be held between the tips of the thumb and forefinger, *a pinch of salt.*
at a pinch in time of difficulty; if necessary.
feel the pinch suffer from lack of money. [same origin as *pincer*]

pincushion *noun* (*plural* **pincushions**)
a small pad into which pins are stuck to keep them ready for use.

pine¹ *noun* (*plural* **pines**)
an evergreen tree with needle-shaped leaves. [from Latin]

pine² *verb* (**pines, pining, pined**)
1 feel an intense longing for somebody or

something. **2** become weak through longing for somebody or something. [from Old English]

pineapple *noun* (*plural* pineapples)
a large tropical fruit with a tough prickly skin and yellow flesh. [from *pine*¹ + *apple* (because it looks like a pine cone)]

ping *noun* (*plural* pings)
a short sharp ringing sound. **ping** *verb* [imitating the sound]

ping-pong *noun*
table tennis.
[from the sound of the bats hitting the ball]

pinion¹ *noun* (*plural* pinions)
a bird's wing, especially the outer end.
pinion *verb* (pinions, pinioning, pinioned)
1 clip a bird's wings to prevent it from flying. **2** hold or fasten someone's arms or legs in order to prevent them from moving. [from Latin *pinna* = pin, arrow, or feather]

pinion² *noun* (*plural* pinions)
a small cogwheel that fits into another or into a rod (called a *rack*). [from Latin *pinus* = pine tree (because the wheel's teeth reminded people of a pine cone)]

pink¹ *adjective*
pale red. **pinkness** *noun*
pink *noun* (*plural* pinks)
1 pink colour. **2** a garden plant with fragrant flowers, often pink or white. [origin unknown]

pink² *verb* (pinks, pinking, pinked)
1 pierce slightly. **2** cut a zigzag edge on cloth. [probably from old Dutch]

pinnacle *noun* (*plural* pinnacles)
1 a pointed ornament on a roof. **2** a high mountain top. **3** the highest point of something, *It was the pinnacle of her career.* [from old French]

pinpoint *adjective*
exact or precise, *with pinpoint accuracy.*
pinpoint *verb* (pinpoints, pinpointing, pinpointed)
find or identify something precisely.

pinprick *noun* (*plural* pinpricks)
a small annoyance.

pinstripe *noun* (*plural* pinstripes)
one of the very narrow stripes that form a pattern in cloth. **pinstriped** *adjective*

pint *noun* (*plural* pints)
a measure for liquids, one-eighth of a gallon. [from old French]

pin-up *noun* (*plural* pin-ups) (*informal*)
a picture of an attractive or famous person for pinning on a wall.

pioneer *noun* (*plural* pioneers)
one of the first people to go to a place or do or investigate something. **pioneer** *verb* [from French *pionnier* = foot soldier, later = one of the troops who went ahead of the army to prepare roads etc.]

pious *adjective*
very religious; devout.
piously *adverb*, **piousness** *noun*
[from Latin *pius* = dutiful]

pip *noun* (*plural* pips)
1 a small hard seed of an apple, pear, orange, etc. **2** one of the stars on the shoulder of an army officer's uniform. **3** a short high-pitched sound, *She heard the six pips of the time signal on the radio.*
pip *verb* (pips, pipping, pipped) (*informal*)
defeat someone by a small amount. [short for *pippin*]

pipe *noun* (*plural* pipes)
1 a tube through which water or gas etc. can flow from one place to another. **2** a short narrow tube with a bowl at one end in which tobacco can burn for smoking. **3** a tube forming a musical instrument or part of one.
the pipes bagpipes.
pipe *verb* (pipes, piping, piped)
1 send something along pipes. **2** transmit music or other sound by wire or cable. **3** play music on a pipe or the bagpipes. **4** decorate a cake with thin lines of icing, cream, etc.
pipe down (*informal*) be quiet.
pipe up begin to say something.
[from Old English]

pipe dream *noun* (*plural* pipe dreams)
an impossible wish. [perhaps from dreams produced by smoking opium]

pipeline *noun* (*plural* pipelines)
a pipe for carrying oil or water etc. a long distance.
in the pipeline in the process of being made or organized.

piper *noun* (*plural* pipers)
a person who plays a pipe or bagpipes.

pipette *noun* (*plural* pipettes)
a small glass tube used in a laboratory, usually filled by suction.
[French, = little pipe]

piping *noun*
1 pipes; a length of pipe. 2 a decorative line of icing, cream, etc. on a cake or other dish. 3 a long narrow pipe-like fold decorating clothing, upholstery, etc.
piping *adjective*
shrill, *a piping voice.*
piping hot very hot.

pipit *noun* (*plural* pipits)
a small songbird. [imitating its call]

pippin *noun* (*plural* pippins)
a kind of apple. [from French]

piquant (*say* pee-kant) *adjective*
1 pleasantly sharp and appetizing, *a piquant smell.* 2 pleasantly stimulating.
piquancy *noun* [same origin as *pique*]

pique (*say* peek) *noun*
a feeling of hurt pride. **pique** *verb*
[from French *piquer* = to prick]

piranha *noun* (*plural* piranhas)
a South American freshwater fish that has sharp teeth and eats flesh.
[via Portuguese from Tupi (a South American language)]

pirate *noun* (*plural* pirates)
1 a person on a ship who robs other ships at sea or makes a plundering raid on the shore. 2 someone who produces or publishes or broadcasts without authorization, *a pirate radio station*; *pirate videos.* **piratical** *adjective*, **piracy** *noun*
[from Greek *peiraein* = to attack]

pirouette (*say* pir-oo-et) *noun* (*plural* pirouettes)
a spinning movement of the body made while balanced on the point of the toe or on one foot. **pirouette** *verb*
[French, = spinning top]

pistachio *noun* (*plural* pistachios)
a nut with an edible green kernel.
[from Greek]

pistil *noun* (*plural* pistils)
the part of a flower that produces the seed, consisting of the ovary, style, and stigma.
[from Latin *pistillum* = pestle (because of its shape)]

pistol *noun* (*plural* pistols)
a small handgun.
[via French and German from Czech]

piston *noun* (*plural* pistons)
a disc or cylinder that fits inside a tube in which it moves up and down as part of an engine or pump etc.
[via French from Italian *pestone* = pestle]

pit *noun* (*plural* pits)
1 a deep hole. 2 a hollow. 3 a coal mine. 4 the part of a racecourse where racing cars are refuelled and repaired during a race.
pit *verb* (pits, pitting, pitted)
1 make holes or hollows in something, *The ground was pitted with holes.* 2 put somebody in competition with somebody else, *He was pitted against the champion.*
[from Old English]

pit bull terrier *noun* (*plural* pit bull terriers)
a small strong and fierce breed of dog.

pitch¹ *noun* (*plural* pitches)
1 a piece of ground marked out for cricket, football, or another game. 2 the highness or lowness of a voice or a musical note. 3 intensity or strength, *Excitement was at fever pitch.* 4 the steepness of a slope, *the pitch of the roof.*
pitch *verb* (pitches, pitching, pitched)
1 throw or fling. 2 fix a tent etc. 3 fall heavily, *He pitched forward as the bus braked suddenly.* 4 move up and down on a rough sea. 5 set something at a particular level, *They pitched their hopes high.* 6 (of a bowled ball in cricket) strike the ground.
pitch in (*informal*) start working or eating vigorously.
[origin unknown]

pitch² *noun*
a black sticky substance rather like tar.
pitch-black or **pitch-dark** *adjectives* very
black or very dark.
[from Old English]

pitchblende *noun*
a mineral ore (uranium oxide) from which
radium is obtained.
[from *pitch²* + German *blenden* = deceive
(because it looks like pitch)]

pitched battle *noun* (*plural* **pitched
battles**)
a battle between troops in prepared
positions.

pitcher *noun* (*plural* **pitchers**)
a large jug. [from old French *pichier* = pot]

pitchfork *noun* (*plural* **pitchforks**)
a large fork with two prongs, used for
lifting hay.
pitchfork *verb* (**pitchforks, pitchforking,
pitchforked**)
1 lift something with a pitchfork. 2 put a
person somewhere suddenly.
[originally *pickfork*: from *pick¹*]

piteous *adjective*
making you feel pity. **piteously** *adverb*

pitfall *noun* (*plural* **pitfalls**)
an unsuspected danger or difficulty.

pith *noun*
the spongy substance in the stems of
certain plants or lining the rind of oranges
etc. [from Old English]

pithy *adjective*
1 like pith; containing much pith. 2 short
and full of meaning, *pithy comments.*

pitiable *adjective*
making you feel pity; pitiful.

pitiful *adjective*
making you feel pity; pathetic.
pitifully *adverb*

pitiless *adjective*
showing no pity. **pitilessly** *adverb*

pittance *noun*
a very small allowance of money.
[originally = a 'pious gift' (one given to a
church): same origin as *piety*]

pity *noun*
1 the feeling of being sorry because
someone is in pain or trouble. 2 a cause for
regret, *It's a pity that you can't come.*
take pity on feel sorry for someone and help
them.

pity *verb* (**pities, pitying, pitied**)
feel pity for someone. [same origin as *piety*]

pivot *noun* (*plural* **pivots**)
a point or part on which something turns
or balances. **pivotal** *adjective*
pivot *verb* (**pivots, pivoting, pivoted**)
turn or place something to turn on a pivot.
[from French]

pixie *noun* (*plural* **pixies**)
a small fairy; an elf. [origin unknown]

pizza (*say* **peets**-a) *noun* (*plural* **pizzas**)
an Italian food that consists of a layer of
dough baked with a savoury topping.
[Italian, = pie]

pizzicato (*say* pits-i-**kah**-toh) *adjective* &
adverb
plucking the strings of a musical
instrument.
[Italian, = pinched or twitched]

placard *noun* (*plural* **placards**)
a poster or notice, especially one carried at
a demonstration.
[from old French *plaquier* = to lay flat]

placate *verb* (**placates, placating, placated**)
make someone feel less angry; pacify.
placatory *adjective*
[from Latin *placare* = please or appease]

place *noun* (*plural* **places**)
1 a particular part of space, especially
where something belongs; an area or
position. 2 a seat, *Save me a place.* 3 a job;
employment. 4 a building; a home, *Come
round to our place.* 5 a duty or function, *It's
not my place to interfere.* 6 a point in a
series of things, *In the first place, the date is
wrong.*
in place 1 in the right position. 2 suitable.
out of place 1 in the wrong position.
2 unsuitable.
place *verb* (**places, placing, placed**)
put something in a particular place.
placement *noun*
[from Greek *plateia* = broad way]

placebo (*say* plas-**ee**-boh) *noun* (*plural* placebos)
a harmless substance given as if it were a medicine, usually to reassure a patient. [Latin, = I shall be pleasing]

placenta *noun*
a piece of body tissue that forms in the womb during pregnancy and supplies the foetus with nourishment. [from Greek *plakous* = flat cake (because of its shape)]

placid *adjective*
calm and peaceful; not easily made anxious or upset. **placidly** *adverb*, **placidity** *noun* [from Latin *placidus* = gentle]

placket *noun* (*plural* plackets)
an opening in a skirt to make it easy to put on and take off. [same origin as *placard*]

plagiarize (*say* play-jee-er-I'z) *verb* (plagiarizes, plagiarizing, plagiarized)
copy and use someone else's writings or ideas etc. as if they were your own. **plagiarism** *noun*, **plagiarist** *noun* [from Latin *plagiarius* = kidnapper]

plague *noun* (*plural* plagues)
1 a dangerous illness that spreads very quickly. 2 a large number of pests, *a plague of locusts*.
plague *verb* (plagues, plaguing, plagued)
pester or annoy, *We've been plagued by wasps all afternoon.* [from Latin]

plaice *noun* (*plural* plaice)
a flat edible sea fish. [from Greek *platys* = broad]

plaid (*say* plad) *noun*
cloth with a tartan or similar pattern. [from Scottish Gaelic]

plain *adjective*
1 simple; not decorated or elaborate. 2 not beautiful. 3 easy to see or hear or understand. 4 frank and straightforward. **plainly** *adverb*, **plainness** *noun*
plain *noun* (*plural* plains)
a large area of flat country. [from Latin *planus* = flat]

USAGE: Do not confuse with *plane*.

plain clothes *noun*
civilian clothes worn instead of a uniform, e.g. by police.

plaintiff *noun* (*plural* plaintiffs)
the person who brings a complaint against somebody else to a lawcourt. (Compare *defendant.*) [same origin as *plaintive*]

plaintive *adjective*
sounding sad. [from French *plaintif* = grieving or complaining]

plait (*say* plat) *verb* (plaits, plaiting, plaited)
weave three or more strands of hair or rope to form one length.
plait *noun* (*plural* plaits)
a length of hair or rope that has been plaited. [from Latin *plicatum* = folded]

plan *noun* (*plural* plans)
1 a way of doing something thought out in advance. 2 a drawing showing the arrangement of parts of something. 3 a map of a town or district.
plan *verb* (plans, planning, planned)
make a plan for something. **planner** *noun* [French, = flat surface, plan of a building: related to *plain*]

plane[1] *noun* (*plural* planes)
1 an aeroplane. 2 a tool for making wood smooth by scraping its surface. 3 a flat or level surface.
plane *verb* (planes, planing, planed)
smooth wood with a plane.
plane *adjective*
flat or level, *a plane surface.* [same origin as *plain*]

USAGE: Do not confuse with *plain*.

plane[2] *noun* (*plural* planes)
a tall tree with broad leaves. [from Greek]

planet *noun* (*plural* planets)
one of the bodies that move in an orbit round the sun, *The main planets are Mercury, Venus, Earth, Mars, Jupiter, Saturn, Uranus, Neptune, and Pluto.* **planetary** *adjective* [from Greek *planetes* = wanderer (because planets seem to move in relation to the stars)]

plank *noun* (*plural* planks)
a long flat piece of wood. [from Latin]

plankton *noun*
microscopic plants and animals that float in the sea, lakes, etc. [Greek, = wandering or drifting]

plant *noun* (*plural* **plants**)
1 a living thing that cannot move and that makes its food from chemical substances, *Flowers, trees, and shrubs are plants.* **2** a small plant, not a tree or shrub. **3** a factory or its equipment. **4** (*slang*) something planted to deceive people (see *plant* verb 3).

plant *verb* (**plants, planting, planted**)
1 put something in soil for growing. **2** fix something firmly in place. **3** place something where it will be found, usually to mislead people or cause trouble. **planter** *noun* [from Latin]

plantation *noun* (*plural* **plantations**)
1 a large area of land where cotton, tobacco, or tea etc. is planted. **2** a group of planted trees.

plaque (*say* plak) *noun* (*plural* **plaques**)
1 a flat piece of metal or porcelain fixed on a wall as an ornament or memorial. **2** a filmy substance that forms on teeth and gums, where bacteria can live.
[via French from Dutch]

plasma *noun*
the colourless liquid part of blood, carrying the corpuscles. [from Greek]

plaster *noun* (*plural* **plasters**)
1 a mixture of lime, sand, and water etc. for covering walls and ceilings. **2** plaster of Paris. **3** a piece of sticking plaster.

plaster *verb* (**plasters, plastering, plastered**)
1 cover a wall etc. with plaster. **2** cover something thickly; daub.
[via Old English from Latin]

plaster of Paris *noun*
a white paste used for making moulds or for casts round a broken limb etc.

plastic *noun* (*plural* **plastics**)
a strong light synthetic substance that can be moulded into a permanent shape.

plastic *adjective*
1 made of plastic. **2** soft and easy to mould, *Clay is a plastic substance.*
plasticity *noun*
[from Greek *plastos* = moulded or formed]

plastic surgery *noun*
surgery to repair deformed or injured parts of the body. **plastic surgeon** *noun*

plate *noun* (*plural* **plates**)
1 an almost flat usually circular object from which food is eaten or served. **2** a thin flat sheet of metal, glass, or other hard material. **3** an illustration on special paper in a book. **plateful** *noun*

plate *verb* (**plates, plating, plated**)
1 coat metal with a thin layer of gold, silver, tin, etc. **2** cover something with sheets of metal.
[from Latin *platus* = broad or flat]

plateau (*say* plat-oh) *noun* (*plural* **plateaux**, *say* plat-ohz)
a flat area of high land.
[French, related to *plate*]

platform *noun* (*plural* **platforms**)
1 a flat surface that is above the level of the ground or the rest of the floor, e.g. in a hall or beside a railway line at a station. **2** the policies that a political party puts forward when there is an election.
[from French *plateforme* = a flat surface]

platinum *noun*
a valuable silver-coloured metal that does not tarnish. [from Spanish *plata* = silver]

platitude *noun* (*plural* **platitudes**)
a trite or hackneyed remark. **platitudinous** *adjective* [French, from *plat* = flat]

platoon *noun* (*plural* **platoons**)
a small group of soldiers.
[from French *peloton* = little ball]

platter *noun* (*plural* **platters**)
a flat dish or plate.
[from old French; related to *plate*]

platypus *noun* (*plural* **platypuses**)
an Australian animal with a beak like that of a duck, that lays eggs like a bird but is a mammal and suckles its young.
[from Greek *platys* = broad + *pous* = foot]

plaudits *plural noun*
applause; expressions of approval. [from Latin *plaudere* = to clap]

plausible *adjective*
seeming to be honest or worth believing but perhaps deceptive, *a plausible excuse.*
plausibly *adverb*, **plausibility** *noun* [from Latin *plausibilis* = deserving applause]

play *verb* (plays, playing, played)
1 take part in a game, sport, or other amusement. 2 make music or sound with a musical instrument, record player, etc. 3 perform a part in a play or film.
player *noun*
play down give people the impression that something is not important.
play up (*informal*) be mischievous or annoying.

play *noun* (*plural* plays)
1 a story acted on a stage or on radio or television. 2 playing. [from Old English]

playback *noun* (*plural* playbacks)
playing back something that has been recorded.

playful *adjective*
1 wanting to play; full of fun. 2 done in fun; not serious.
playfully *adverb*, **playfulness** *noun*

playground *noun* (*plural* playgrounds)
a piece of ground for children to play on.

playgroup *noun* (*plural* playgroups)
a group of very young children who play together regularly, supervised by adults.

playing card *noun* (*plural* playing cards)
each of a set of cards (usually 52) used for playing games.

playing field *noun* (*plural* playing fields)
a field used for outdoor games.

playmate *noun* (*plural* playmates)
a person you play games with.

play-off *noun* (*plural* play-offs)
a match that is played to decide a draw or tie.

plaything *noun* (*plural* playthings)
a toy.

playtime *noun*
the time when young schoolchildren may go out to play.

playwright *noun* (*plural* playwrights)
a dramatist. [from *play* + *wright* = maker]

PLC or **p.l.c.** *abbreviation*
public limited company.

plea *noun* (*plural* pleas)
1 a request or appeal, *a plea for mercy*. 2 an excuse, *He stayed at home on the plea of a headache*. 3 a formal statement of 'guilty' or 'not guilty' made in a lawcourt by someone accused of a crime.
[from old French]

plead *verb* (pleads, pleading, pleaded)
1 beg someone to do something. 2 state formally in a lawcourt that you are guilty or not guilty of a crime. 3 give something as an excuse, *She didn't come on holiday with us, pleading poverty*.

pleasant *adjective*
pleasing; giving pleasure.
pleasantly *adverb*, **pleasantness** *noun*
[from French *plaisant* = pleasing]

pleasantry *noun* (*plural* pleasantries)
a friendly or good-humoured remark.

please *verb* (pleases, pleasing, pleased)
1 make a person feel satisfied or glad. 2 (used to make a request or an order polite), *Please ring the bell*. 3 like; think suitable, *Do as you please*.
[from Latin *placere* = satisfy]

pleasurable *adjective*
causing pleasure.

pleasure *noun* (*plural* pleasures)
1 a feeling of satisfaction or gladness; enjoyment. 2 something that pleases you.
[from French *plaisir* = to please]

pleat *noun* (*plural* pleats)
a flat fold made by doubling cloth upon itself. **pleated** *adjective* [from *plait*]

plebeian (*say* plib-ee-an) *noun* (*plural* plebeians)
a member of the common people in ancient Rome. (Compare *patrician*.)
plebeian *adjective*
[from Latin *plebs* = the common people]

plebiscite (*say* pleb-iss-it) *noun* (*plural* plebiscites)
a referendum. [from Latin *plebs* = the common people + *scitum* = decree]

plectrum *noun* (*plural* plectra)
a small piece of metal or bone etc. for

plucking the strings of a musical instrument. [from Greek *plektron* = something to strike with]

pledge *noun* (*plural* pledges)
1 a solemn promise. 2 a thing handed over as security for a loan or contract.
pledge *verb* (pledges, pledging, pledged)
1 promise solemnly to do or give something. 2 hand something over as security. [from old French]

plenary (*say* pleen-er-ee) *adjective*
attended by all members, *a plenary session of the council.* [from Latin *plenus* = full]

plenipotentiary (*say* plen-i-pot-**en**-sher-ee) *adjective*
having full authority to make decisions on behalf of a government, *Our ambassador has plenipotentiary power.*
plenipotentiary *noun* [from Latin *plenus* = full + *potentia* = power]

plentiful *adjective*
quite enough in amount; abundant.
plentifully *adverb*

plenty *noun*
quite enough; as much as is needed or wanted.
plenty *adverb* (*informal*)
quite or fully, *It's plenty big enough.*
[from Latin *plenitas* = fullness]

plethora *noun*
too large a quantity of something.
[from Greek]

pleurisy (*say* **ploor**-i-see) *noun*
inflammation of the membrane round the lungs. [from Greek *pleura* = ribs]

pliable *adjective*
1 easy to bend; flexible. 2 easy to influence or control. **pliability** *noun*
[French, from *plier* = to bend]

pliant *adjective*
pliable [French, = bending]

pliers *plural noun*
pincers that have jaws with flat surfaces for gripping things. [from *ply*²]

plight¹ *noun* (*plural* plights)
a difficult situation. [from old French]

plight² *verb* (plights, plighting, plighted) (*old use*)
pledge or promise solemnly.
[from Old English]

plimsoll *noun* (*plural* plimsolls)
a canvas sports shoe with a rubber sole.
[same origin as *Plimsoll line* (because the thin sole reminded people of a Plimsoll line)]

Plimsoll line *noun* (*plural* Plimsoll lines)
a mark on a ship's side showing how deeply it may legally go down in the water when loaded. [named after an English politician, S. Plimsoll, who in the 1870s protested about ships being overloaded]

plinth *noun* (*plural* plinths)
a block or slab forming the base of a column or a support for a statue or vase etc. [from Greek]

PLO *abbreviation*
Palestine Liberation Organization.

plod *verb* (plods, plodding, plodded)
1 walk slowly and heavily. 2 work slowly but steadily. **plodder** *noun*
[origin unknown]

plonk *noun* (*informal*)
cheap wine.
plonk *verb* (plonks, plonking, plonked) (*informal*)
put something down clumsily or heavily.
[originally Australian; probably from French *blanc* = white, in *vin blanc* = white wine]

plop *noun* (*plural* plops)
the sound of something dropping into water. **plop** *verb* [imitating the sound]

plot *noun* (*plural* plots)
1 a secret plan. 2 the story in a play, novel, or film. 3 a small piece of land.
plot *verb* (plots, plotting, plotted)
1 make a secret plan. 2 make a chart or graph of something, *We plotted the ship's route on our map.* [origin unknown]

plough *noun* (*plural* ploughs)
a farming implement for turning the soil over.
plough *verb* (ploughs, ploughing, ploughed)
1 turn over soil with a plough. 2 go through something with great effort or

difficulty, *He ploughed through the book.*
ploughman *noun*
plough back reinvest profits in the business
that produced them.
[from Old Norse]

ploughshare *noun* (*plural* **ploughshares**)
the cutting blade of a plough.
[from *plough* + Old English *scaer* = blade]

plover (*say* pluv-er) *noun* (*plural* **plovers**)
a kind of wading bird.
[from Latin *pluvia* = rain]

ploy *noun* (*plural* **ploys**)
a cunning manoeuvre to gain an
advantage; a ruse.
[originally Scots: origin unknown]

pluck *verb* (**plucks, plucking, plucked**)
1 pick a flower or fruit. **2** pull the feathers
off a bird. **3** pull something up or out.
4 pull a string (e.g. on a guitar) and let it go
again.
pluck up courage summon up courage and
overcome fear.
pluck *noun*
1 courage or spirit. **2** plucking.
[from Old English]

plucky *adjective* (**pluckier, pluckiest**)
brave or spirited. **pluckily** *adverb*

plug *noun* (*plural* **plugs**)
1 something used to stop up a hole. **2** a
device that fits into a socket to connect
wires to a supply of electricity.
3 (*informal*) a piece of publicity for
something.
plug *verb* (**plugs, plugging, plugged**)
1 stop up a hole. **2** (*informal*) publicize
something.
plug in put a plug into an electrical socket.
[from old German or old Dutch]

plum *noun* (*plural* **plums**)
1 a soft juicy fruit with a pointed stone in
the middle. **2** (*old use*) a dried grape or
raisin used in cooking, *plum pudding.*
3 reddish-purple colour. **4** (*informal*)
something good, *a plum job.*
[via Old English from Latin]

plumage (*say* ploom-ij) *noun* (*plural*
plumages)
a bird's feathers. [same origin as *plume*]

plumb *verb* (**plumbs, plumbing, plumbed**)
1 measure how deep something is. **2** get to
the bottom of a matter, *We could not plumb
the mystery.* **3** fit a room or building with a
plumbing system.
plumb *adjective*
exactly upright; vertical, *The wall was
plumb.*
plumb *adverb* (*informal*)
exactly, *It fell plumb in the middle.*
[from Latin *plumbum* = lead² (originally
plumb = the lead weight on a plumb line)]

plumber *noun* (*plural* **plumbers**)
a person who fits and mends plumbing.

plumbing *noun*
1 the water pipes, water tanks, and
drainage pipes in a building. **2** the work of
a plumber. [from *plumb* (because water
pipes used to be made of lead)]

plumb line *noun* (*plural* **plumb lines**)
a cord with a weight on the end, used to
find how deep something is or whether a
wall etc. is vertical.

plume *noun* (*plural* **plumes**)
1 a large feather. **2** something shaped like
a feather, *a plume of smoke.*
plume *verb* (**plumes, pluming, plumed**)
if a bird plumes its feathers, it smooths
them with its beak; preen.
[from Latin *pluma* = feather]

plumed *adjective*
decorated with plumes, *a plumed helmet.*

plummet *noun* (*plural* **plummets**)
a plumb line or the weight on its end.
plummet *verb* (**plummets, plummeting,
plummeted**)
drop downwards quickly.
[from old French; related to *plumb*]

plump¹ *adjective*
slightly fat; rounded. **plumpness** *noun*
plump *verb* (**plumps, plumping, plumped**)
make something rounded, *plump up a
cushion.*
[from old German *plumpich* = bulky]

plump² *verb* (**plumps, plumping, plumped**)
plump for (*informal*) choose.
[from old German *plompen* = to plop]

plunder *verb* (plunders, plundering, plundered)
rob a person or place using force; loot.
plunderer *noun*
plunder *noun*
1 plundering. 2 goods etc. that have been plundered; loot. [from old German]

plunge *verb* (plunges, plunging, plunged)
1 go or push forcefully into something; dive. 2 fall or go downwards suddenly. 3 go or force into action etc., *They plunged the world into war.*
plunge *noun* (*plural* plunges)
a sudden fall or dive.
take the plunge start a bold course of action.
[from old French; related to *plumb*]

plunger *noun* (*plural* plungers)
a rubber cup on a handle used for clearing blocked pipes.

plural *noun* (*plural* plurals)
the form of a noun or verb used when it stands for more than one person or thing, *The plural of 'child' is 'children'.* (Compare *singular*.) **plural** *adjective*, **plurality** *noun*
[from Latin *pluralis* = of many]

plus *preposition*
with the next number or thing added, *2 plus 2 equals four* (2 + 2 = 4).
[Latin, = more]

plush *noun*
a thick velvety cloth used in furnishings.
plushy *adjective* [from Latin *pilus* = hair]

plutocrat *noun* (*plural* plutocrats)
a person who is powerful because of his or her wealth.
[from Greek *ploutos* = wealth, + -*crat*]

plutonium *noun*
a radioactive substance used in nuclear weapons and reactors.
[named after the planet Pluto]

ply¹ *noun* (*plural* plies)
1 a thickness or layer of wood or cloth etc. 2 a strand in yarn, *4-ply wool.*
[from French *pli* = a fold]

ply² *verb* (plies, plying, plied)
1 use or wield a tool or weapon. 2 work at, *Tailors plied their trade.* 3 keep offering, *They plied her with food or with questions.*
4 go regularly, *The boat plies between the two harbours.* 5 drive or wait about looking for custom, *Taxis are allowed to ply for hire.* [from *apply*]

plywood *noun*
strong thin board made of layers of wood glued together.

PM *abbreviation*
Prime Minister.

p.m. *abbreviation*
post meridiem (Latin, = after noon).

pneumatic (*say* new-mat-ik) *adjective*
filled with or worked by compressed air, *a pneumatic drill.* **pneumatically** *adverb*
[from Greek *pneuma* = wind]

pneumonia (*say* new-moh-nee-a) *noun*
a serious illness caused by inflammation of one or both lungs.
[from Greek *pneumon* = lung]

PO *abbreviation*
1 Post Office. 2 postal order.

poach *verb* (poaches, poaching, poached)
1 cook an egg (removed from its shell) in or over boiling water. 2 cook fish or fruit etc. in a small amount of liquid. 3 steal game or fish from someone else's land or water. 4 take something unfairly, *One club was poaching members from another.*
poacher *noun*
[same origin as *pouch*]

pocket *noun* (*plural* pockets)
1 a small bag-shaped part, especially in a garment. 2 a person's supply of money, *The expense is beyond my pocket.* 3 an isolated part or area, *small pockets of rain.*
pocketful *noun*
be out of pocket have spent more money than you have gained.
pocket *adjective*
small enough to carry in a pocket, *a pocket calculator.*
pocket *verb* (pockets, pocketing, pocketed)
put something into a pocket.
[from Old French *pochet* = little pouch]

pocket money *noun*
money given to a child to spend as he or she likes.

pod *noun* (*plural* **pods**)
a long seed-container of the kind found on a pea or bean plant. [origin unknown]

podgy *adjective* (**podgier, podgiest**)
short and fat. [origin unknown]

podium (*say* poh-dee-um) *noun* (*plural* **podiums** or **podia**)
a small platform on which a music conductor or someone making a speech stands. [from Greek *podion* = little foot]

poem *noun* (*plural* **poems**)
a piece of poetry.
[from Greek *poiema* = thing made]

poet *noun* (*plural* **poets**)
a person who writes poetry. **poetess** *noun*
[from Greek *poietes* = maker]

poetry *noun*
writing arranged in short lines, usually with a particular rhythm and sometimes with rhymes. **poetic** *adjective*,
poetical *adjective*, **poetically** *adverb*

pogrom *noun* (*plural* **pogroms**)
an organized massacre.
[Russian, = destruction]

poignant (*say* poin-yant) *adjective*
very distressing; affecting the feelings, *poignant memories*. **poignancy** *noun*
[from French, = pricking]

point *noun* (*plural* **points**)
1 the narrow or sharp end of something.
2 a dot, *the decimal point*. 3 a particular place or time, *At this point she was winning*. 4 a detail or characteristic, *He has his good points*. 5 the important or essential idea, *Keep to the point!* 6 purpose or value, *There is no point in hurrying*. 7 an electrical socket. 8 a device for changing a train from one track to another.

point *verb* (**points, pointing, pointed**)
1 aim or direct, *She pointed a gun at me*.
2 show where something is, especially by holding out a finger etc. towards it. 3 fill in the parts between bricks with mortar or cement.
point out draw attention to something.
[from Latin *punctum* = pricked]

point-blank *adjective*
1 aimed or fired from close to the target.

2 direct and straightforward, *a point-blank refusal*.

point-blank *adverb*
in a point-blank manner, *He refused point-blank*. [from to *point* + *blank* = the white centre of a target]

point duty *noun*
being stationed at a road junction to control the movement of traffic.
[because the person stays at one point, rather than patrolling]

pointed *adjective*
1 with a point at the end. 2 clearly directed at a person, *a pointed remark*.
pointedly *adverb*

pointer *noun* (*plural* **pointers**)
1 a stick, rod, or mark etc. used to point at something. 2 a dog that points with its muzzle towards birds that it scents. 3 an indication or hint.

pointless *adjective*
without a point; with no purpose.
pointlessly *adverb*

point of view *noun* (*plural* **points of view**)
a way of looking or thinking of something.

poise *verb* (**poises, poising, poised**)
balance.
poise *noun*
1 a dignified self-confident manner.
2 balance. [from old French]

poison *noun* (*plural* **poisons**)
a substance that can harm or kill a living thing. **poisonous** *adjective*
poison *verb* (**poisons, poisoning, poisoned**)
1 give poison to; kill somebody with poison. 2 put poison in something.
3 corrupt or spoil something, *He poisoned their minds*. **poisoner** *noun*
[same origin as *potion*]

poke¹ *verb* (**pokes, poking, poked**)
1 prod or jab. 2 push out or forward; stick out. 3 search, *I was poking about in the attic*.
poke fun at ridicule.
poke *noun* (*plural* **pokes**)
a poking movement; a prod.
[from old German or old Dutch]

poke² *noun*
buy a pig in a poke buy something without
seeing it.
[same origin as *pouch*]

poker¹ *noun* (*plural* pokers)
a stiff metal rod for poking a fire.

poker² *noun*
a card game in which players bet on who
has the best cards.
[probably from German *pochen* = to brag]

poky *adjective* (pokier, pokiest)
small and cramped, *poky little rooms.*
[from *poke¹*]

polar *adjective*
1 to do with or near the North Pole or
South Pole. 2 to do with either pole of a
magnet. **polarity** *noun*

polar bear *noun* (*plural* polar bears)
a white bear living in Arctic regions.

polarize *verb* (polarizes, polarizing,
polarized)
1 keep vibrations of light-waves etc. to a
single direction. 2 divide into two groups
of completely opposite extremes of feeling
or opinion, *Opinions had polarized.*
polarization *noun* [from *pole²*]

Polaroid *noun* (*trade mark*)
a type of plastic, used in sunglasses, which
reduces the brightness of light passing
through it. [originally = a material which
polarizes light passing through it: from
polarize + *-oid*]

Polaroid camera *noun* (*plural* Polaroid
cameras) (*trade mark*)
a camera that takes a picture and produces
the finished photograph a few seconds
later.

pole¹ *noun* (*plural* poles)
a long slender rounded piece of wood or
metal. [same origin as *pale²*]

pole² *noun* (*plural* poles)
1 a point on the earth's surface that is as
far north (**North Pole**) or as far south (**South
Pole**) as possible. 2 either of the ends of a
magnet. 3 either terminal of an electric cell
or battery. [from Greek *polos* – axis]

polecat *noun* (*plural* polecats)
an animal of the weasel family with an
unpleasant smell. [origin unknown]

polemic (*say* pol-em-ik) *noun* (*plural*
polemics)
an attack in words against someone's
opinion or actions. **polemical** *adjective*
[from Greek *polemos* = war]

pole star *noun*
the star above the North Pole.

pole vault *noun*
an athletic contest in which competitors
jump over a high bar with the help of a
long pole.

police *noun*
the people whose job is to catch criminals
and make sure that the law is kept.
policeman *noun*, **policewoman** *noun*
police *verb* (polices, policing, policed)
keep order in a place by means of police.
[same origin as *political*]

police officer *noun* (*plural* police officers)
a policeman or policewoman.

policy¹ *noun* (*plural* policies)
the aims or plan of action of a person or
group. [same origin as *political*]

policy² *noun* (*plural* policies)
a document stating the terms of a contract
of insurance.
[from Greek *apodeixis* – evidence]

polio *noun*
poliomyelitis.

poliomyelitis (*say* poh-lee-oh-my-il-I-tiss)
noun
a disease that can cause paralysis.
[from Greek]

polish *verb* (polishes, polishing, polished)
1 make a thing smooth and shiny by
rubbing. 2 make a thing better by making
corrections and alterations. **polisher** *noun*
polish off finish off.
polish *noun* (*plural* polishes)
1 a substance used in polishing. 2 a shine.
3 elegance of manner. [from Latin]

polite *adjective*
having good manners. **politely** *adverb*,
politeness *noun*
[from Latin *politus* = polished]

politic (*say* pol-it-ik) *adjective*
prudent or wise. [same origin as *political*]

political *adjective*
connected with the governing of a country,
city, or county. **politically** *adverb*
[from Greek *politeia* = citizenship or
government]

politician *noun* (*plural* **politicians**)
a person who is involved in politics.

politics *noun*
political matters.

polka *noun* (*plural* **polkas**)
a lively dance for couples.
[via German and French from Czech]

poll (*say as* pole) *noun* (*plural* **polls**)
1 voting or votes at an election. **2** an
opinion poll. **3** (*old use*) the head.
poll *verb* (**polls, polling, polled**)
1 vote at an election. **2** receive a stated
number of votes in an election.
polling booth *noun*, **polling station** *noun*
[probably from old Dutch word *polle*
= head. In some polls those voting yes
stand apart from those voting no, and the
decision is reached by counting the heads
in the two groups]

pollarded *adjective*
(of trees) with the tops trimmed so that
young shoots start to grow thickly there.
[from *poll* 3]

polled *adjective*
(of cattle) with the horns trimmed.
[from *poll* 3]

pollen *noun*
powder produced by the anthers of flowers,
containing male cells for fertilizing other
flowers. [Latin, = fine flour]

pollen count *noun* (*plural* **pollen counts**)
a measurement of the amount of pollen in
the air, given as a warning for people who
are allergic to pollen.

pollinate *verb* (**pollinates, pollinating,
pollinated**)
fertilize a plant with pollen.
pollination *noun*

pollster *noun* (*plural* **pollsters**)
a person who conducts an opinion poll.

poll tax *noun* (*plural* **poll taxes**)
a tax on each person; the community
charge.

pollute *verb* (**pollutes, polluting, polluted**)
make a place or thing dirty or impure.
pollutant *noun*, **pollution** *noun* [from Latin]

polo *noun*
a game rather like hockey, with players on
horseback. [from Tibetan]

polo neck *noun* (*plural* **polo necks**)
a high round turned-over collar.
polo-necked *adjective*

poltergeist *noun* (*plural* **poltergeists**)
a ghost or spirit that throws things about
noisily. [from German *poltern* = make a
disturbance + *Geist* = ghost]

poly *noun* (*plural* **polys**) (*informal*)
a polytechnic.

poly- *prefix*
many (as in *polytechnic*). [from Greek]

polyanthus *noun* (*plural* **polyanthuses**)
a kind of cultivated primrose.
[from *poly-* + Greek *anthos* = flower]

polychromatic or **polychrome** *adjective*
having many colours.
[from *poly-* + Greek *chroma* = colour]

polyester *noun*
a synthetic material, often used to make
clothing. [from *polymer* + *ester*]

polygamy (*say* pol-ig-a-mee) *noun*
having more than one wife at a time.
polygamous *adjective*
[from *poly-* + Greek *gamos* = marriage]

polyglot *adjective*
knowing or using several languages.
[from *poly-* + Greek *glotta* = language]

polygon *noun* (*plural* polygons)
a shape with many sides, *Hexagons and octagons are polygons.* **polygonal** *adjective*
[from *poly-* + Greek *gonia* = corner]

polyhedron *noun* (*plural* polyhedrons)
a solid shape with many sides.
[from *poly-* + Greek *hedra* = base]

polymer *noun* (*plural* polymers)
a substance whose molecule is formed from a large number of simple molecules combined.
[from *poly-* + Greek *meros* = part]

polyp (*say* pol-ip) *noun* (*plural* polyps)
1 a tiny creature with a tube-shaped body. **2** a small abnormal growth. [from Latin]

polystyrene *noun*
a kind of plastic used for insulating or packing things. [from *polymer* + *styrene*, the name of a resin]

polytechnic *noun* (*plural* polytechnics)
a college giving instruction in many subjects at degree level or below. In 1992 the British polytechnics were able to change their names and call themselves universities.
[from *poly-* + Greek *techne* = skill]

polytheism (*say* pol-ith-ee-izm) *noun*
belief in more than one god. **polytheist** *noun*
[from *poly-* + Greek *theos* = god]

polythene *noun*
a lightweight plastic used to make bags, wrappings, etc. [from *polyethylene*, a polymer from which it is made]

pomegranate *noun* (*plural* pomegranates)
a tropical fruit with many seeds.
[from Latin *pomum* = apple + *granatum* = having many seeds]

pommel *noun* (*plural* pommels)
1 a knob on the handle of a sword. **2** the raised part at the front of a saddle.
[from Latin *pomum* = apple]

pomp *noun*
the ceremonial splendour that is traditional on important public occasions.
[from Greek *pompe* = solemn procession]

pompon *noun* (*plural* pompons)
a ball of coloured threads used as a decoration. [French]

pompous *adjective*
full of excessive dignity and self-importance.
pompously *adverb*, **pomposity** *noun*
[from *pomp*]

pond *noun* (*plural* ponds)
a small lake. [from *pound*²]

ponder *verb* (ponders, pondering, pondered)
think deeply and seriously; muse.
[from Latin *ponderare* = weigh]

ponderous *adjective*
1 heavy and awkward. **2** laborious and dull, *He writes in a ponderous style.*
ponderously *adverb*
[from Latin *ponderis* = of weight]

pontiff *noun* (*plural* pontiffs)
the Pope.
[from Latin *pontifex* = chief priest]

pontifical *adjective*
1 to do with a pontiff. **2** speaking or writing pompously. **pontifically** *adverb*

pontificate *verb* (pontificates, pontificating, pontificated)
speak or write pompously. **pontification** *noun* [literally = behave like a pontiff]

pontoon¹ *noun* (*plural* pontoons)
a boat or float used to support a bridge (a **pontoon bridge**) over a river.
[from Latin *pontis* = of a bridge]

pontoon² *noun*
1 a card game in which players try to get cards whose value totals 21. **2** a score of 21 from two cards in this game.
[from a bad English pronunciation of French *vingt-et-un* = 21]

pony *noun* (*plural* ponies)
a small horse.
[from French *poulenet* = small foal]

ponytail *noun* (*plural* ponytails)
a bunch of long hair tied at the back of the head.

pony-trekking *noun*
travelling across country on a pony for
pleasure. **pony-trekker** *noun*

poodle *noun* (*plural* **poodles**)
a dog with thick curly hair.
[from German *Pudelhund* = water-dog]

pooh *interjection*
an exclamation of contempt.

pool[1] *noun* (*plural* **pools**)
1 a pond. 2 a puddle. 3 a swimming pool.
[from Old English]

pool[2] *noun* (*plural* **pools**)
1 the fund of money staked in a gambling
game. 2 a group of things shared by several
people.
the pools gambling based on the results of
football matches.
pool *verb* (**pools, pooling, pooled**)
put money or things together for sharing.
[from French]

poop *noun* (*plural* **poops**)
the stern of a ship. [from Latin]

poor *adjective*
1 with very little money or other
resources. 2 not good; inadequate, *a poor
piece of work*. 3 unfortunate; deserving
pity, *Poor fellow!* **poorness** *noun*
[from old French; related to *pauper*]

poorly *adverb*
1 in a poor way, *We've played poorly this
season*. 2 rather ill.

pop[1] *noun* (*plural* **pops**)
1 a small explosive sound. 2 a fizzy drink.
pop *verb* (**pops, popping, popped**)
1 make a pop. 2 (*informal*) go or put
quickly, *Pop down to the shop. I'll just pop
this pie into the microwave.*
[imitating the sound]

pop[2] *noun*
modern popular music. [short for *popular*]

popcorn *noun*
maize heated to burst and form fluffy balls.

Pope *noun* (*plural* **Popes**)
the leader of the Roman Catholic Church.
[from Greek *papas* = father]

pop-eyed *adjective*
with bulging eyes.

popgun *noun* (*plural* **popguns**)
a toy gun that shoots a cork etc. with a
popping sound.

poplar *noun* (*plural* **poplars**)
a tall slender tree. [from Latin]

poplin *noun*
a plain woven cotton material.
[from old French]

poppadam *noun* (*plural* **poppadams**)
a thin crisp biscuit made of lentil-flour,
eaten with Indian food. [from Tamil]

poppy *noun* (*plural* **poppies**)
a plant with large red flowers.
[via Old English from Latin]

populace *noun*
the general public.
[same origin as *popular*]

popular *adjective*
1 liked or enjoyed by many people.
2 intended for the general public.
popularly *adverb*, **popularity** *noun*
[from Latin *populus* = people]

popularize *verb* (**popularizes, popularizing,
popularized**)
make a thing generally liked or known.
popularization *noun*

populate *verb* (**populates, populating,
populated**)
supply with a population; inhabit.
[same origin as *popular*]

population *noun* (*plural* **populations**)
the people who live in a district or country;
the total number of these people.

porcelain *noun*
the finest kind of china. [from French]

porch *noun* (*plural* **porches**)
a shelter outside the entrance to a building.
[same origin as *portico*]

porcupine *noun* (*plural* **porcupines**)
a small animal covered with long prickles.
[from old French *porc espin* = spiny pig]

pore¹ *noun* (*plural* pores)
a tiny opening on the skin through which moisture can pass in or out.
[from Greek *poros* = passage]

pore² *verb* (pores, poring, pored)
pore over study with close attention, *He was poring over his books.*
[origin unknown]

USAGE: Do not confuse with *pour.*

pork *noun*
meat from a pig. [from Latin *porcus* = pig]

pornography (*say* porn-og-ra-fee) *noun*
obscene pictures or writings.
pornographic *adjective*
[from Greek *porne* = prostitute, + *-graphy*]

porous *adjective*
allowing liquid or air to pass through.
porosity *noun* [same origin as *pore¹*]

porphyry (*say* por-fir-ee) *noun*
a kind of rock containing crystals of minerals.
[from Greek *porphyrites* = purple stone]

porpoise (*say* por-pus) *noun* (*plural* porpoises)
a sea animal rather like a small whale. [from Latin *porcus* = pig + *piscis* = fish]

porridge *noun*
a food made by boiling oatmeal to a thick paste. [from an old word *pottage* = soup]

porringer *noun* (*plural* porringers)
a small bowl for holding porridge.

port¹ *noun* (*plural* ports)
1 a harbour. 2 a city or town with a harbour. 3 the left-hand side of a ship or aircraft when you are facing forward. (Compare *starboard.*)
[from Latin *portus* = harbour]

port² *noun*
a strong red Portuguese wine.
[from the city of Oporto in Portugal]

portable *adjective*
able to be carried.
[from Latin *portare* = carry]

portal *noun* (*plural* portals)
a doorway or gateway.
[from Latin *porta* = gate]

portcullis *noun* (*plural* portcullises)
a strong heavy vertical grating that can be lowered in grooves to block the gateway to a castle. [from old French *porte coleice* = sliding door]

portend *verb* (portends, portending, portended)
be a sign or warning that something will happen, *Dark clouds portend a storm.* [from Latin *pro-* = forwards + *tendere* = stretch]

portent *noun* (*plural* portents)
an omen; a sign that something will happen. **portentous** *adjective*
[same origin as *portend*]

porter¹ *noun* (*plural* porters)
a person whose job is to carry luggage or other goods. [from Latin *portare* = carry]

porter² *noun* (*plural* porters)
a person whose job is to look after the entrance to a large building.
[from Latin *porta* = gate]

portfolio *noun* (*plural* portfolios)
1 a case for holding documents or drawings. 2 a government minister's special responsibility. [from Italian *portare* = carry + *foglio* = sheet of paper]

porthole *noun* (*plural* portholes)
a small window in the side of a ship or aircraft. [from Latin *porta* = gate, + *hole*]

portico *noun* (*plural* porticoes)
a roof supported on columns, usually forming a porch to a building.
[from Latin *porticus* = porch]

portion *noun* (*plural* portions)
a part or share given to somebody.
portion *verb* (portions, portioning, portioned)
divide something into portions, *Portion it out.* [from Latin]

portly *adjective* (portlier, portliest)
stout and dignified. **portliness** *noun*
[originally = dignified: from Middle English *port* = bearing, deportment]

portmanteau (*say* port-**mant**-oh) *noun*
(*plural* **portmanteaus**)
a trunk that opens into two equal parts for
holding clothes etc. [from French *porter*
= carry + *manteau* = coat]

portmanteau word *noun* (*plural*
portmanteau words)
a word made from the sounds and
meanings of two others, e.g. *motel* (from
*mo*tor + ho*tel*).

portrait *noun* (*plural* **portraits**)
a picture of a person or animal.

portray *verb* (**portrays, portraying,
portrayed**)
1 make a picture of a person or scene etc.
2 describe or show, *The play portrays the
king as a kindly man.* **portrayal** *noun*
[from old French]

pose *noun* (*plural* **poses**)
1 a position or posture of the body, e.g. for
a portrait or photograph. 2 a pretence;
unnatural and affected behaviour to
impress people.

pose *verb* (**poses, posing, posed**)
1 take up a pose. 2 put someone into a
pose. 3 pretend. 4 put forward or present,
It poses several problems for us.
[from French]

poser *noun* (*plural* **posers**)
1 a puzzling question or problem. 2 a
person who behaves in an affected way in
order to impress other people.

posh *adjective* (*informal*)
1 very smart; high-class, *a posh restaurant.*
2 upper-class, *a posh accent.*
[origin unknown]

position *noun* (*plural* **positions**)
1 the place where something is or should
be. 2 the way a person or thing is placed or
arranged, *in a sitting position.* 3 a situation
or condition, *I am in no position to help you.*
4 paid employment; a job.
positional *adjective*

position *verb* (**positions, positioning,
positioned**)
place a person or thing in a certain
position. [from Latin *positio* = placing]

positive *adjective*
1 definite or certain, *We have positive proof
that he is guilty.* 2 agreeing; saying 'yes',
We received a positive reply. 3 greater than
nought. 4 of the kind of electric charge that
lacks electrons. 5 (of an adjective or
adverb) in the simple form, not
comparative or superlative, *The positive
form is 'big', the comparative is 'bigger', the
superlative is 'biggest'.* **positively** *adverb*

USAGE: The opposite of senses 1–4 is
negative.

positive *noun* (*plural* **positives**)
a photograph with the light and dark parts
or colours as in the thing photographed.
(Compare *negative.*)
[from Latin *positivus* = settled]

positron *noun* (*plural* **positrons**)
a particle of matter with a positive electric
charge. [from *positive* + *electron*]

posse (*say* **poss**-ee) *noun* (*plural* **posses**)
a group of people, especially one that helps
a sheriff. [from Latin *posse comitatus*
= force of the county]

possess *verb* (**possesses, possessing,
possessed**)
1 have or own something. 2 control
someone's thoughts or behaviour, *I don't
know what possessed you to do such a thing!*
possessor *noun* [from Latin]

possessed *adjective*
seeming to be controlled by strong emotion
or an evil spirit, *He fought like a man
possessed.*

possession *noun* (*plural* **possessions**)
1 something you possess or own.
2 possessing.

possessive *adjective*
1 wanting to possess and keep things for
yourself. 2 showing that somebody owns
something, *a possessive pronoun* (see
pronoun).

possibility *noun* (*plural* **possibilities**)
1 being possible. 2 something that may
exist or happen etc.

possible *adjective*
able to exist, happen, be done, or be used.
[from Latin *posse* = be able]

possibly *adverb*
1 in any way, *I can't possibly do it.*
2 perhaps.

possum *noun* (*plural* possums)
an opossum.

post¹ *noun* (*plural* posts)
1 an upright piece of wood, concrete, or metal etc. set in the ground. 2 the starting point or finishing point of a race, *He was left at the post.*
post *verb* (posts, posting, posted)
put up a notice or poster etc. to announce something. [from Latin *postis* = post]

post² *noun*
1 the collecting and delivering of letters, parcels, etc. 2 these letters and parcels etc.
post *verb* (posts, posting, posted)
put a letter or parcel etc. into a postbox for collection.
keep me posted keep me informed.
[from French; related to *post³* (because originally mail was carried in relays by riders posted along the route)]

post³ *noun* (*plural* posts)
1 a position of paid employment; a job.
2 the place where someone is on duty, *a sentry-post.* 3 a place occupied by soldiers, traders, etc.
post *verb* (posts, posting, posted)
place someone on duty, *We posted sentries.*
[from Latin *positum* = placed]

post- *prefix*
after (as in *post-war*). [from Latin]

postage *noun*
the charge for sending something by post.

postage stamp *noun* (*plural* postage stamps)
a stamp for sticking on things to be posted, showing the amount paid.

postal *adjective*
to do with or by the post.

postal order *noun* (*plural* postal orders)
a document bought from a post office for sending money by post.

postbox *noun* (*plural* postboxes)
a box into which letters are put for collection.

postcard *noun* (*plural* postcards)
a card for sending messages by post without an envelope.

postcode *noun* (*plural* postcodes)
a group of letters and numbers included in an address to help in sorting the post.

poster *noun* (*plural* posters)
a large sheet of paper announcing or advertising something, for display in a public place. [from *post¹*]

poste restante (*say* rest-ahnt) *noun*
a part of a post office where letters etc. are kept until called for.
[French, = letters remaining]

posterior *adjective*
situated at the back of something. (The opposite is *anterior*.)
posterior *noun* (*plural* posteriors)
the buttocks. [Latin, = further back]

posterity *noun*
future generations of people, *These letters and diaries should be preserved for posterity.*
[from Latin *posterus* = following, future]

postern *noun* (*plural* posterns)
a small entrance at the back or side of a fortress etc.
[from old French; related to *posterior*]

post-haste *adverb*
with great speed or haste.
[from *post²* + *haste* (because post was the quickest way of communication)]

posthumous (*say* poss-tew-mus) *adjective*
happening after a person's death.
posthumously *adverb*
[from Latin *postumus* = last]

postilion (*say* poss-til-yon) *noun* (*plural* postilions)
a person riding one of the horses pulling a carriage.
[from Italian *postiglione* = post-boy]

postman *noun* (*plural* postmen)
a person who delivers or collects letters etc.

postmark *noun* (*plural* postmarks)
an official mark put on something sent by post to show where and when it was posted.

post-mortem *noun* (*plural* post-mortems)
an examination of a dead body to discover
the cause of death. [Latin, = after death]

post office *noun* (*plural* post offices)
a building or room where postal business
is carried on.

postpone *verb* (postpones, postponing,
postponed)
fix a later time for something, *They
postponed the meeting for a fortnight.*
postponement *noun*
[from *post-* + Latin *ponere* = to place]

postscript *noun* (*plural* postscripts)
something extra added at the end of a letter
(after the writer's signature) or at the end
of a book.
[from *post-* + Latin *scriptum* = written]

postulant *noun* (*plural* postulants)
a person who applies to be admitted to an
order of monks or nuns.
[from Latin, = claiming]

postulate *verb* (postulates, postulating,
postulated)
assume that something is true and use it in
reasoning. **postulation** *noun*
postulate *noun* (*plural* postulates)
something postulated.
[from Latin *postulare* = to claim]

posture *noun* (*plural* postures)
the way a person stands, sits, or walks; a
pose.
posture *verb* (postures, posturing, postured)
pose, especially to impress people. [from
Latin *positura* = position or situation]

post-war *adjective*
happening during the time after a war.

posy *noun* (*plural* posies)
a small bunch of flowers.
[from French *poésie* = poetry]

pot[1] *noun* (*plural* pots)
1 a deep usually round container.
2 (*informal*) a lot of something, *He has got
pots of money.*
go to pot (*informal*) lose quality; be ruined.
take pot luck (*informal*) take whatever is
available.
pot *verb* (pots, potting, potted)
put into a pot. [from Old English]

pot[2] *noun* (*slang*)
marijuana. [short for Spanish *potiguaya*
= drink of grief]

potash *noun*
potassium carbonate. [from Dutch *potasch*
= pot ash (because it was first obtained
from vegetable ashes washed in a pot)]

potassium *noun*
a soft silvery-white metal substance that is
essential for living things. [from *potash*]

potato *noun* (*plural* potatoes)
a starchy white tuber growing
underground, used as a vegetable.
[via Spanish from Taino (a South
American language)]

potent (*say* poh-tent) *adjective*
powerful. **potency** *noun*
[from Latin *potens* = able]

potentate (*say* poh-ten-tayt) *noun* (*plural*
potentates)
a powerful monarch or ruler.
[from Latin *potentatus* = power or rule]

potential (*say* po-ten-shal) *adjective*
capable of happening or being used or
developed, *a potential winner.*
potentially *adverb*, **potentiality** *noun*
potential *noun*
the ability of a person or thing to develop
in the future. [from Latin *potentia* = power]

pothole *noun* (*plural* potholes)
1 a deep natural hole in the ground. 2 a
hole in a road.

potholing *noun*
exploring underground potholes.
potholer *noun*

potion *noun* (*plural* potions)
a liquid for drinking as a medicine etc.
[from Latin *potio* = a drink]

pot-pourri (*say* poh-poor-ee) *noun* (*plural*
pot-pourris)
a scented mixture of dried petals and
spices. [French, = rotten pot]

potted *adjective*
shortened or abridged, *a potted account of
the story.*

potter¹ *noun* (*plural* **potters**)
a person who makes pottery.

potter² *verb* (**potters, pottering, pottered**)
work or move about in a leisurely way, *I spent the afternoon pottering around in the garden.*
[from an old word *pote* = push or poke]

pottery *noun* (*plural* **potteries**)
1 cups, plates, ornaments, etc. made of baked clay. 2 a place where a potter works.

potty¹ *adjective* (*slang*)
mad or foolish. [origin unknown]

potty² *noun* (*plural* **potties**) (*informal*)
a child's chamber pot. [from *pot¹*]

pouch *noun* (*plural* **pouches**)
1 a small bag. 2 something shaped like a bag. [from French *poche* = bag or pocket]

pouffe (*say* poof) *noun* (*plural* **pouffes**)
a low padded stool. [French]

poultice *noun* (*plural* **poultices**)
a soft hot dressing put on a sore or inflamed place.
[from Latin *pultes* = soft food, pap]

poultry *noun*
birds (e.g. chickens, geese, turkeys) kept for their eggs and meat.
[from old French *poulet* = pullet]

pounce *verb* (**pounces, pouncing, pounced**)
jump or swoop down quickly on something. **pounce** *noun* [from old French]

pound¹ *noun* (*plural* **pounds**)
1 a unit of money (in Britain = 100 pence). 2 a unit of weight equal to 16 ounces or about 454 grams. [from Old English *pund*]

pound² *noun* (*plural* **pounds**)
1 a place where stray animals are taken. 2 a public enclosure for vehicles officially removed. [origin unknown]

pound³ *verb* (**pounds, pounding, pounded**)
1 hit something often, especially in order to crush it. 2 run or go heavily, *pounding along.* 3 thump, *My heart was pounding.* [from Old English *punian*]

poundage *noun*
a payment or charge of so much for each pound.

pour *verb* (**pours, pouring, poured**)
1 flow or make something flow. 2 rain heavily, *It poured all day.* 3 come or go in large amounts, *Letters poured in.* **pourer** *noun* [origin unknown]

USAGE: Do not confuse with *pore.*

pout *verb* (**pouts, pouting, pouted**)
push out your lips when you are annoyed or sulking. **pout** *noun*
[probably from a Scandinavian language]

poverty *noun*
being poor.
[from old French; related to *pauper*]

powder *noun* (*plural* **powders**)
1 a mass of fine dry particles of something. 2 a medicine or cosmetic etc. made as a powder. 3 gunpowder, *Keep your powder dry.* **powdery** *adjective*
powder *verb* (**powders, powdering, powdered**)
1 put powder on something. 2 make something into powder.
[from old French; related to *pulverize*]

powder room *noun* (*plural* **powder rooms**)
a women's toilet in a public building.

power *noun* (*plural* **powers**)
1 strength or energy. 2 the ability to do something, *the power of speech.* 3 political authority or control. 4 a powerful country, person, or organization. 5 mechanical or electrical energy; the electricity supply, *There was a power failure after the storm.* 6 (in mathematics) the product of a number multiplied by itself a given number of times, *The third power of $2 = 2 \times 2 \times 2 = 8$.*
powered *adjective*, **powerless** *adjective*
[from old French]

powerboat *noun* (*plural* **powerboats**)
a powerful motor boat.

powerful *adjective*
having great power, strength, or influence.
powerfully *adverb*

powerhouse *noun* (*plural* **powerhouses**)
1 a person with great strength and energy.
2 a power station.

power station *noun* (*plural* **power stations**)
a building where electricity is produced.

pp. *abbreviation*
pages.

practicable *adjective*
able to be done. [French, from *pratiquer* = put into practice]

USAGE: Do not confuse with *practical*.

practical *adjective*
1 able to do useful things, *a practical person.* 2 likely to be useful, *a very practical invention.* 3 actually doing something, *She has had practical experience.* **practicality** *noun*

USAGE: Do not confuse with *practicable*.

practical *noun* (*plural* **practicals**)
a lesson or examination in which you actually do or make something rather than reading or writing about it, *a chemistry practical.* [from Greek *prattein* = do]

practical joke *noun* (*plural* **practical jokes**)
a trick played on somebody.

practically *adverb*
1 in a practical way. 2 almost, *I've practically finished.*

practice *noun* (*plural* **practices**)
1 practising, *Have you done your piano practice?* 2 actually doing something; action, not theory, *It works well in practice.* 3 the professional business of a doctor, dentist, lawyer, etc. 4 a habit or custom, *It is his practice to work until midnight.*
out of practice no longer skilful because you have not practised recently.
[from *practise*]

USAGE: See the note on *practise*.

practise *verb* (**practises, practising, practised**)
1 do something repeatedly in order to become better at it. 2 do something actively or habitually, *Practise what you*

preach. 3 work as a doctor, dentist, or lawyer.
[from Latin *practicare* = carry out, perform]

USAGE: Note the spelling: *practice* is a noun, *practise* is a verb.

practised *adjective*
experienced or expert.

practitioner *noun* (*plural* **practitioners**)
a professional worker, especially a doctor.
[from old French]

pragmatic *adjective*
treating things in a practical way, *Take a pragmatic approach to the problem.*
pragmatically *adverb*, **pragmatism** *noun*, **pragmatist** *noun*
[from Greek *pragmatikos* = businesslike]

prairie *noun* (*plural* **prairies**)
a large area of flat grass-covered land in North America.
[French, from Latin *pratum* = meadow]

praise *verb* (**praises, praising, praised**)
1 say that somebody or something is very good. 2 honour God in words.
praise *noun*
words that praise somebody or something.
praiseworthy *adjective*
[from Latin *pretium* = value]

pram *noun* (*plural* **prams**)
a four-wheeled carriage for a baby, pushed by a person walking.
[short for *perambulator*]

prance *verb* (**prances, prancing, pranced**)
move about in a lively or happy way.
[origin unknown]

prank *noun* (*plural* **pranks**)
a trick played for mischief; a practical joke.
prankster *noun*
[probably from German or Dutch]

prattle *verb* (**prattles, prattling, prattled**)
chatter like a young child. **prattle** *noun*
[from old German]

prawn *noun* (*plural* **prawns**)
an edible shellfish like a large shrimp.
[origin unknown]

pray *verb* (**prays, praying, prayed**)
1 talk to God. 2 ask earnestly for
something. 3 (*formal*) please, *Pray be
seated.* [from old French]

prayer *noun* (*plural* **prayers**)
praying; words used in praying.

pre- *prefix*
before (as in *prehistoric*). [from Latin]

preach *verb* (**preaches, preaching, preached**)
give a religious or moral talk. **preacher**
noun [from old French]

preamble *noun* (*plural* **preambles**)
the introduction to a speech or book or
document etc.
[from *pre-* + Latin *ambulare* = go]

pre-arranged *adjective*
arranged beforehand.
pre-arrangement *noun*

precarious (*say* pri-**kair**-ee-us) *adjective*
not very safe or secure. **precariously** *adverb*
[from Latin *precarius* = uncertain]

precaution *noun* (*plural* **precautions**)
something done to prevent future trouble
or danger. **precautionary** *adjective*
[from *pre-* + Latin *cavere* = take care]

precede *verb* (**precedes, preceding,
preceded**)
come or go before or in front of another
thing. [from *pre-* + Latin *cedere* = go]

USAGE: Do not confuse with *proceed.*

precedence (*say* **press**-i-dens) *noun*
the right of something to be put first
because it is more important; priority.

precedent (*say* **press**-i-dent) *noun* (*plural*
precedents)
a previous case that is taken as an example
to be followed.

precept (*say* **pree**-sept) *noun* (*plural*
precepts)
a rule for action or conduct; an instruction.
[from *pre-* + Latin *-ceptum* = taken]

precinct (*say* **pree**-sinkt) *noun* (*plural*
precincts)
1 the area round a place, especially round

a cathedral. 2 a part of a town where traffic
is not allowed, *a shopping precinct.*
[from *pre-* + Latin *cinctum* = surrounded]

precious *adjective*
1 very valuable. 2 greatly loved.
preciousness *noun*
precious *adverb* (*informal*)
very, *We have precious little time.*
[from Latin *pretium* = value]

precipice *noun* (*plural* **precipices**)
a very steep place, such as the face of a cliff.
[from Latin *praeceps* = headlong]

precipitate *verb* (**precipitates, precipitating,
precipitated**)
1 make something happen suddenly or
soon, *The insult precipitated a quarrel.*
2 throw or send something down; make
something fall, *The push precipitated him
through the window.* 3 cause a solid
substance to separate chemically from a
solution. **precipitation** *noun*
precipitate *noun* (*plural* **precipitates**)
a substance precipitated from a solution.
precipitate *adjective*
hurried or hasty, *a precipitate departure.*
[same origin as *precipice*]

precipitous *adjective*
like a precipice; steep. **precipitously** *adverb*

précis (*say* **pray**-see) *noun* (*plural* **précis**, *say*
pray-seez)
a summary. [French, = precise]

precise *adjective*
exact; clearly stated.
precisely *adverb*, **precision** *noun*
[from Latin *praecisum* = cut short]

preclude *verb* (**precludes, precluding,
precluded**)
prevent.
[from *pre-* + Latin *claudere* = shut]

precocious (*say* prik-**oh**-shus) *adjective*
(of a child) very advanced or developed for
his or her age.
precociously *adverb*, **precocity** *noun*
[from Latin *praecox* = ripe very early]

preconceived *adjective*
(of an idea) formed in advance, before full
information is available. **preconception**
noun [from *pre-* + *conceive*]

precursor *noun* (*plural* precursors)
something that was an earlier form of
something that came later; a forerunner.
[from *pre-* + Latin *cursor* = runner]

predator (*say* pred-a-ter) *noun* (*plural*
predators)
an animal that hunts or preys upon others.
predatory *adjective*
[from Latin *praedator* = plunderer]

predecessor (*say* pree-dis-ess-er) *noun*
(*plural* predecessors)
an earlier person or thing, e.g. an ancestor
or the former holder of a job. [from *pre-*
+ Latin *decessor* = person departed]

predestine *verb* (predestines, predestining,
predestined)
determine something beforehand.
predestination *noun*

predicament (*say* prid-ik-a-ment) *noun*
(*plural* predicaments)
a difficult or unpleasant situation.
[from Latin]

predicate *noun* (*plural* predicates)
the part of a sentence that says something
about the subject, e.g. 'is short' in *life is
short*. [from Latin *praedicare* = proclaim]

predicative (*say* prid-ik-a-tiv) *adjective*
forming part of the predicate, e.g. *old* in
The dog is old. (Compare *attributive*.)
predicatively *adverb*

predict *verb* (predicts, predicting, predicted)
say what will happen in the future; foretell
or prophesy. **predictable** *adjective*,
prediction *noun*, **predictor** *noun*
[from *pre-* + Latin *dicere* = say]

predispose *verb* (predisposes,
predisposing, predisposed)
influence you in advance so that you are
likely to do or be in favour of something,
We are predisposed to pity the refugees.
predisposition *noun*

predominate *verb* (predominates,
predominating, predominated)
be the largest or most important or most
powerful. **predominant** *adjective*,
predominance *noun* [from *pre-* + Latin
dominari = rule, dominate]

pre-eminent *adjective*
excelling others; outstanding.
pre-eminently *adverb*, **pre-eminence** *noun*

preen *verb* (preens, preening, preened)
1 (of a bird) smooth its feathers with its
beak. 2 (of a person) smarten.
preen yourself congratulate yourself.
[origin unknown]

prefab *noun* (*plural* prefabs) (*informal*)
a prefabricated building.

prefabricated *adjective*
made in sections ready to be assembled on
a site. **prefabrication** *noun*
[from *pre-* + *fabricate*]

preface (*say* pref-as) *noun* (*plural* prefaces)
an introduction at the beginning of a book
or speech. **preface** *verb* [from Latin
praefatio = something said beforehand]

prefect *noun* (*plural* prefects)
1 a school pupil given authority to help to
keep order. 2 a district official in France,
Japan, and other countries.
[from Latin *praefectus* = overseer]

prefer *verb* (prefers, preferring, preferred)
1 like one person or thing more than
another. 2 put forward, *They preferred
charges of forgery against him*.
preference *noun*
[from *pre-* + Latin *ferre* = carry]

preferable (*say* pref-er-a-bul) *adjective*
liked better; more desirable.
preferably *adverb*

preferential (*say* pref-er-en-shal) *adjective*
being favoured above others, *preferential
treatment*.

preferment *noun*
promotion.

prefix *noun* (*plural* prefixes)
a word or syllable joined to the front of a
word to change or add to its meaning, as in
*dis*order, *out*stretched, *un*happy.
[from Latin]

pregnant *adjective*
having a baby developing in the womb.
pregnancy *noun*
[from *pre-* + Latin *gnasci* = be born]

prehensile *adjective*
(of an animal's foot or tail etc.) able to grasp things.
[from Latin *prehendere* = seize]

prehistoric *adjective*
belonging to very ancient times, before written records of events were made.
prehistory *noun*

prejudice *noun* (*plural* prejudices)
a fixed opinion formed without examining the facts fairly. **prejudiced** *adjective*
[from *pre-* + Latin *judicium* = judgement]

prelate (*say* prel-at) *noun* (*plural* prelates)
an important member of the clergy.
[from Latin *praelatus* = preferred]

preliminary *adjective*
coming before an important action or event and preparing for it.
[from *pre-* + Latin *limen* = threshold]

prelude *noun* (*plural* preludes)
1 a thing that introduces or leads up to something else. 2 a short piece of music.
[from *pre-* + Latin *ludere* = to play]

premature *adjective*
too early; coming before the usual or proper time. **prematurely** *adverb*
[from *pre-* + Latin *maturus* = mature]

premeditated *adjective*
planned beforehand, *a premeditated crime.*
[from *pre-* + Latin *meditare* = meditate]

premier (*say* prem-ee-er) *adjective*
first in importance, order, or time.
premier *noun* (*plural* premiers)
a prime minister or other head of government. [French, = first]

première (*say* prem-yair) *noun* (*plural* premières)
the first public performance of a play or film. [French, feminine of *premier* = first]

premises *plural noun*
a building and its grounds. [originally, the buildings etc. previously mentioned on a deed: from Latin *praemittere* = put before]

premiss (*say* prem-iss) *noun* (*plural* premisses)
a statement used as the basis for a piece of reasoning. [same origin as *premises*]

premium *noun* (*plural* premiums)
1 an amount or instalment paid to an insurance company. 2 an extra payment; a bonus.
at a premium above the normal price; highly valued.
[from Latin *praemium* = reward]

Premium Bond *noun* (*plural* Premium Bonds)
a savings certificate that gives the person who holds it a chance to win a prize of money.

premonition *noun* (*plural* premonitions)
a feeling that something is about to happen, especially something bad.
[from *pre-* + Latin *monere* = warn]

preoccupied *adjective*
having your thoughts completely busy with something. **preoccupation** *noun*

prep *noun*
homework. [short for *preparation*]

preparation *noun* (*plural* preparations)
1 preparing. 2 something prepared.

preparatory *adjective*
preparing for something.

preparatory school *noun* (*plural* preparatory schools)
a school that prepares pupils for a higher school.

prepare *verb* (prepares, preparing, prepared)
make ready; get ready.
be prepared to be ready and willing to do something.
[from *pre-* + Latin *parare* = get something ready]

preponderate *verb* (preponderates, preponderating, preponderated)
be more than others or more powerful.
preponderance *noun*,
preponderant *adjective*
[from Latin *praeponderare* = outweigh]

preposition *noun* (*plural* prepositions)
a word used with a noun or pronoun to show place, position, time, or means, e.g. *at* home, *in* the hall, *on* Sunday, *by* train.
[from *pre-* + Latin *positio* = placing]

prepossessing *adjective*
attractive, *Its appearance is not very prepossessing.* [from *pre-* + *possess*]

preposterous *adjective*
very absurd; outrageous.
[from Latin *praeposterus* = back to front, from *prae* = before + *posterus* = behind]

prep school *noun* (*plural* **prep schools**)
a preparatory school.

prerequisite *noun* (*plural* **prerequisites**)
something required as a condition or in preparation for something else, *The ability to swim is a prerequisite for learning to sail.*
prerequisite *adjective*

prerogative *noun* (*plural* **prerogatives**)
a right or privilege that belongs to one person or group. [from Latin *praerogativa* = the people who vote first]

Presbyterian (*say* prez-bit-**eer**-ee-an) *noun*
(*plural* **Presbyterians**)
a member of a Church that is governed by people called *elders* or *presbyters* who are chosen by the congregation.
[from Greek *presbyteros* = elder]

presbytery *noun* (*plural* **presbyteries**)
the house of a Roman Catholic priest.

pre-school *adjective*
to do with the time before a child is old enough to attend school.

prescribe *verb* (**prescribes, prescribing, prescribed**)
1 advise a person to use a particular medicine or treatment etc. 2 say what should be done.
[from *pre-* + Latin *scribere* = write]

USAGE: Do not confuse with *proscribe.*

prescription *noun* (*plural* **prescriptions**)
1 a doctor's written order for a medicine. 2 the medicine prescribed. 3 prescribing.

presence *noun*
1 being present in a place, *Your presence is required.* 2 if someone has presence, they have an impressive personality or manner.

presence of mind *noun*
the ability to act quickly and sensibly in an emergency.

present[1] *adjective*
1 in a particular place, *No one else was present.* 2 belonging or referring to what is happening now; existing now, *the present Queen.*

present *noun*
present times or events.
[from Latin *praesens* = being at hand]

present[2] *noun* (*plural* **presents**)
something given or received without payment; a gift.

present (*say* priz-**ent**) *verb* (**presents, presenting, presented**)
1 give something, especially with a ceremony, *Who is to present the prizes?*
2 introduce someone to another person or to an audience. 3 put on a play or other entertainment. 4 show. 5 cause or provide something, *Writing a dictionary presents many problems.* **presentation** *noun*, **presenter** *noun* [from Latin *praesentare* = place before someone]

presentable *adjective*
fit to be presented to other people; looking good.

presentiment *noun* (*plural* **presentiments**)
a feeling that something bad is about to happen; a foreboding. [from *pre-* + old French *sentement* = feeling]

presently *adverb*
1 soon, *I shall be with you presently.* 2 now, *the person who is presently in charge.*
[from *present*[1]]

preserve *verb* (**preserves, preserving, preserved**)
keep something safe or in good condition.
preserver *noun*, **preservation** *noun*, **preservative** *adjective* & *noun*

preserve *noun* (*plural* **preserves**)
1 jam. 2 an activity that belongs to a particular person or group.
[from *pre-* + Latin *servare* = keep]

preside *verb* (**presides, presiding, presided**)
be in charge of a meeting etc.
[from *pre-* + Latin *-sidere* = sit]

president *noun* (*plural* **presidents**)
1 the person in charge of a club, society, or

council etc. **2** the head of a republic.
presidency *noun*, **presidential** *adjective*
[from Latin *praesidens* = sitting in front]

press *verb* (**presses, pressing, pressed**)
1 put weight or force steadily on
something; squeeze. **2** make something by
pressing. **3** make clothes smooth by
ironing them. **4** urge; make demands, *They
pressed for an increase in wages.*
press *noun* (*plural* **presses**)
1 a device for pressing things, *a trouser
press.* **2** a machine for printing things. **3** a
firm that prints or publishes books etc.,
Oxford University Press. **4** newspapers;
journalists.
[from Latin *pressum* = squeezed]

press conference *noun* (*plural* **press
conferences**)
an interview with a group of journalists.

press-gang *noun* (*plural* **press-gangs**)
(in history) a group of men whose job was
to force people to serve in the army or
navy.

pressure *noun* (*plural* **pressures**)
1 continuous pressing. **2** the force with
which something presses. **3** an influence
that persuades or compels you to do
something. [from Latin]

pressure cooker *noun* (*plural* **pressure
cookers**)
a large air-tight pan used for cooking food
quickly under steam pressure.

pressurize *verb* (**pressurizes, pressurizing,
pressurized**)
1 keep a compartment at the same air-
pressure all the time. **2** try to compel a
person to do something.
pressurization *noun*

prestige (*say* pres-**teej**) *noun*
good reputation. **prestigious** *adjective*
[from Latin *praestigium* = an illusion]

presumably *adverb*
according to what you may presume.

presume *verb* (**presumes, presuming,
presumed**)
1 suppose; assume something to be true.
2 take the liberty of doing something;

venture, *May we presume to advise you?*
presumption *noun*
[from *pre-* + Latin *sumere* = take]

presumptive *adjective*
presuming something.
heir presumptive see *heir.*

presumptuous *adjective*
too bold or confident.
presumptuously *adverb*

presuppose *verb* (**presupposes,
presupposing, presupposed**)
suppose or assume something beforehand.
presupposition *noun* [from French]

pretence *noun* (*plural* **pretences**)
an attempt to pretend that something is
true.
false pretences pretending to be something
that you are not, in order to deceive people,
You've invited me here under false pretences.

pretend *verb* (**pretends, pretending,
pretended**)
1 behave as if something is true or real
when you know that it is not, either in play
or so as to deceive people. **2** put forward a
claim, *The son of King James II was called
the Old Pretender because he pretended to
the British throne.* **pretender** *noun* [from
Latin *praetendere* = put forward or claim]

pretension *noun* (*plural* **pretensions**)
1 a doubtful claim. **2** pretentious or showy
behaviour.

pretentious *adjective*
1 showy or ostentatious. **2** claiming to
have great merit or importance.
pretentiously *adverb*, **pretentiousness** *noun*
[from French; related to *pretend*]

pretext *noun* (*plural* **pretexts**)
a reason put forward to conceal the true
reason. [from Latin *praetextus* = an
outward display]

pretty *adjective* (**prettier, prettiest**)
attractive in a delicate way. **prettily** *adverb*,
prettiness *noun*
pretty *adverb*
quite, *It's pretty cold.* [from Old English]

prevail *verb* (**prevails, prevailing, prevailed**)
1 be the most frequent or general, *The*

prevailing wind is from the south-west.
2 be victorious.
[from *pre-* + Latin *valere* = have power]

prevalent (*say* prev-a-lent) *adjective*
most frequent or common; widespread.
prevalence *noun* [same origin as *prevail*]

prevaricate *verb* (prevaricates,
prevaricating, prevaricated)
say something that is not actually a lie but
is evasive or misleading.
prevarication *noun*
[from Latin *praevaricari* = go crookedly]

prevent *verb* (prevents, preventing,
prevented)
1 stop something from happening. **2** stop a
person from doing something.
preventable *adjective*, **prevention** *noun*,
preventive or **preventative** *adjective* & *noun*
[from Latin *praevenire* = come first,
anticipate]

preview *noun* (*plural* previews)
a showing of a film or play etc. before it is
shown to the general public.

previous *adjective*
coming before this; preceding.
previously *adverb*
[from *pre-* + Latin *via* = way]

prey (*say as* pray) *noun*
an animal that is hunted or killed by
another for food.
bird or **beast of prey** one that kills and eats
other birds or four-footed animals.
prey *verb* (preys, preying, preyed)
prey on 1 hunt or take as prey. **2** cause to
worry, *The problem preyed on his mind.*
[from old French]

price *noun* (*plural* prices)
1 the amount of money for which
something is bought or sold. **2** what must
be given or done in order to achieve
something.
price *verb* (prices, pricing, priced)
decide the price of something.
[from old French: related to *praise*]

priceless *adjective*
1 very valuable. **2** (*informal*) very
amusing.

prick *verb* (pricks, pricking, pricked)
1 make a tiny hole in something. **2** hurt

somebody with a pin or needle etc.
prick *noun*
prick up your ears start listening suddenly.
[from Old English]

prickle *noun* (*plural* prickles)
1 a small thorn. **2** a sharp spine on a
hedgehog or cactus etc. **3** a feeling that
something is pricking you. **prickly** *adjective*
prickle *verb* (prickles, prickling, prickled)
feel or cause a pricking feeling.
[from Old English]

pride *noun* (*plural* prides)
1 being proud. **2** something that makes you
feel proud. **3** a group of lions.
pride of place the most important or most
honoured position.
pride *verb* (prides, priding, prided)
pride yourself on be proud of.
[from *proud*]

priest *noun* (*plural* priests)
1 a member of the clergy. **2** a person who
conducts religious ceremonies. **priestess**
noun, **priesthood** *noun*, **priestly** *adjective*
[via Old English from Latin]

prig *noun* (*plural* prigs)
a self-righteous person. **priggish** *adjective*
[origin unknown]

prim *adjective* (primmer, primmest)
formal and correct in manner; disliking
anything rough or rude. **primly** *adverb*,
primness *noun* [origin unknown]

primacy (*say* pry-ma-see) *noun*
1 being the first or most important. **2** the
position of primate (= archbishop).

prima donna (*say* preem-a) *noun* (*plural*
prima donnas)
the chief female singer in an opera.
[Italian, = first lady]

prima facie (*say* pry-ma fay-shee) *adverb* &
adjective
at first sight; judging by the first
impression. [Latin, = on first appearance]

primary *adjective*
first; most important. (Compare
secondary.) **primarily** (*say* pry-mer-il-ee)
adverb [same origin as *prime*]

primary colour noun (*plural* primary colours)
one of the colours from which all others can be made by mixing (red, yellow, and blue for paint; red, green, and blue for light).

primary school noun (*plural* primary schools)
a school for the first stage of a child's education.

primate (*say* pry-mat) noun (*plural* primates)
1 an archbishop. 2 an animal of the group that includes human beings, apes, and monkeys.
[from Latin *primas* = of the first rank]

prime adjective
1 chief; most important, *the prime cause.* 2 excellent; first-rate, *prime beef.*

prime noun
the best time or stage of something, *in the prime of life.*

prime verb (primes, priming, primed)
1 prepare something for use or action. 2 put a coat of liquid on something to prepare it for painting. 3 equip a person with information.
[from Latin *primus* = first]

prime minister noun (*plural* prime ministers)
the leader of a government.

prime number noun (*plural* prime numbers)
a number (e.g. 2, 3, 5, 7, 11) that can be divided exactly only by itself and one.

primer noun (*plural* primers)
1 a liquid for priming a surface. 2 an elementary textbook.

primeval (*say* pry-mee-val) adjective
belonging to the earliest times of the world.
[from Latin *primus* = first + *aevum* = age]

primitive adjective
1 at an early stage of civilization. 2 at an early stage of development; not complicated or sophisticated.

primogeniture noun
being a first-born child; the custom by which an eldest son inherits all his parents' property.
[from Latin *primo* = first + *genitus* = born]

primordial adjective
belonging to the earliest times of the world; primeval.
[from Latin *primus* = first + *ordiri* = begin]

primrose noun (*plural* primroses)
a pale-yellow flower that blooms in spring.
[from Latin *prima rosa* = first rose]

prince noun (*plural* princes)
1 the son of a king or queen. 2 a man or boy in a royal family. **princely** adjective
[from Latin *princeps* = chieftain]

princess noun (*plural* princesses)
1 the daughter of a king or queen. 2 a woman or girl in a royal family. 3 the wife of a prince. [from French]

principal adjective
chief; most important. **principally** adverb

principal noun (*plural* principals)
the head of a college or school.
[from Latin *principalis* = first or chief]

USAGE: Do not confuse with *principle.*

principality noun (*plural* principalities)
a country ruled by a prince.
the Principality Wales.

principle noun (*plural* principles)
1 a general truth, belief, or rule, *She taught me the principles of geometry.* 2 a rule of conduct, *Cheating is against his principles.*
in principle in general, not in details.
on principle because of your principles of behaviour.
[from Latin *principium* = source]

USAGE: Do not confuse with *principal.*

print verb (prints, printing, printed)
1 put words or pictures on paper by using a machine. 2 write with letters that are not joined together. 3 press a mark or design etc. on a surface. 4 make a picture from the negative of a photograph. **printer** noun

print *noun* (*plural* **prints**)
1 printed lettering or words. 2 a mark made by something pressing on a surface. 3 a printed picture, photograph, or design. [from old French *priente* = pressed]

printed circuit *noun* (*plural* **printed circuits**)
an electric circuit made by pressing thin metal strips on to a surface.

printout *noun* (*plural* **printouts**)
information etc. produced in printed form by a computer.

prior *adjective*
earlier or more important than something else, *a prior engagement*.
prior *noun* (*plural* **priors**)
a monk who is the head of a religious house or order. **prioress** *noun*
[Latin, = former, more important]

priority *noun* (*plural* **priorities**)
1 being earlier or more important than something else; precedence. 2 something considered more important than other things, *Safety is a priority*.
[from French; related to *prior*]

priory *noun* (*plural* **priories**)
a religious house governed by a prior or prioress.

prise *verb* (**prises, prising, prised**)
lever something out or open, *Prise the lid off the crate*. [French, = seized]

prism (*say* prizm) *noun* (*plural* **prisms**)
1 a solid shape with ends that are triangles or polygons which are equal and parallel. 2 a glass prism that breaks up light into the colours of the rainbow. **prismatic** *adjective* [from Greek]

prison *noun* (*plural* **prisons**)
a place where criminals are kept as a punishment. [from old French]

prisoner *noun* (*plural* **prisoners**)
1 a person kept in prison. 2 a captive.

pristine *adjective*
in its original condition; unspoilt.
[from Latin *pristinus* = former]

private *adjective*
1 belonging to a particular person or group, *private property*. 2 confidential, *private talks*. 3 secluded. 4 not holding public office, *a private citizen*. 5 independent; not organized by a government, *private medicine*; *a private detective*. **privately** *adverb*, **privacy** (*say* priv-a-see) *noun*
in private where only particular people can see or hear; not in public.
private *noun* (*plural* **privates**)
a soldier of the lowest rank.
[from Latin *privus* = single or individual]

privation *noun* (*plural* **privations**)
loss or lack of something; lack of necessities.
[from Latin *privatus* = deprived]

privatize *verb* (**privatizes, privatizing, privatized**)
transfer a nationalized industry etc. to a private organization. **privatization** *noun*

privet *noun* (*plural* **privets**)
an evergreen shrub with small leaves, used to make hedges. [origin unknown]

privilege *noun* (*plural* **privileges**)
a special right or advantage given to one person or group. **privileged** *adjective*
[from Latin *privus* = an individual + *legis* = of law]

privy *adjective* (*old use*)
secret and private.
be privy to be sharing in the secret of someone's plans etc.
privy *noun* (*plural* **privies**) (*old use*)
an outside toilet.
[from Latin *privatus* = private]

Privy Council *noun*
a group of distinguished people who advise the sovereign.

privy purse *noun*
an allowance made to the sovereign from public funds.

prize *noun* (*plural* **prizes**)
an award given to the winner of a game or competition etc.
prize *verb* (**prizes, prizing, prized**)
value something greatly.
[a different spelling of *price*]

pro *noun* (*plural* **pros**) (*informal*)
a professional.

pro- *prefix*
1 favouring or supporting (as in *pro-British*). 2 deputizing or substituted for (as in *pronoun*). 3 onwards; forwards (as in *proceed*). [from Latin *pro* = for; in front of]

pro and con
for and against.
pros and cons reasons for and against something.
[from Latin *pro* = for + *contra* = against]

probable *adjective*
likely to happen or be true.
probably *adverb*, **probability** *noun*
[from Latin *probare* = prove]

probate *noun*
the official process of proving that a person's will is valid.
[from Latin *probatum* = tested, proved]

probation *noun*
the testing of a person's character and abilities. **probationary** *adjective*
on probation being supervised by a probation officer instead of being sent to prison.
[same origin as *prove*]

probationer *noun* (*plural* **probationers**)
a person at an early stage of training, e.g. as a nurse.

probation officer *noun* (*plural* **probation officers**)
an official who supervises the behaviour of a convicted criminal who is not in prison.

probe *noun* (*plural* **probes**)
1 an instrument for exploring something. 2 an investigation.
probe *verb* (**probes, probing, probed**)
1 explore something with a probe. 2 investigate. [from Latin *proba* = proof]

probity (*say* proh-bit-ee) *noun*
honesty.
[from Latin *probus* = good, honest]

problem *noun* (*plural* **problems**)
1 something difficult to deal with or understand. 2 something that has to be done or answered. **problematic** or **problematical** *adjective* [from Greek]

proboscis (*say* pro-boss-iss) *noun* (*plural* **proboscises**)
1 a long flexible snout. 2 an insect's long mouthpart. [from Greek]

procedure *noun* (*plural* **procedures**)
an orderly way of doing something.
[French, from *procéder* = proceed]

proceed *verb* (**proceeds, proceeding, proceeded**)
1 go forward or onward. 2 continue; go on to do something, *She proceeded to explain the plan.* [from *pro-* + Latin *cedere* = go]

USAGE: Do not confuse with *precede*.

proceedings *plural noun*
1 things that happen; activities. 2 a lawsuit.

proceeds *plural noun*
the money made from a sale or show etc.; profit.

process[1] (*say* proh-sess) *noun* (*plural* **processes**)
a series of actions for making or doing something.
in the process of in the course of doing something.
process *verb* (**processes, processing, processed**)
put something through a manufacturing or other process, *processed cheese.*
[same origin as *proceed*]

process[2] (*say* pro-sess) *verb* (**processes, processing, processed**)
go in procession. [from *procession*]

procession *noun* (*plural* **processions**)
a number of people or vehicles etc. moving steadily forward following each other.
[from Latin *processio* = an advance]

processor *noun* (*plural* **processors**)
1 a machine that processes things. 2 the part of a computer that controls all its operations.

proclaim *verb* (**proclaims, proclaiming, proclaimed**)
announce something officially or publicly.
proclamation *noun*
[from *pro-* + Latin *clamare* = to shout]

procrastinate *verb* (procrastinates, procrastinating, procrastinated)
put off doing something.
procrastination *noun*, procrastinator *noun*
[from *pro-* + Latin *crastinus* = of tomorrow]

procreate *verb* (procreates, procreating, procreated)
produce offspring by the natural process of reproduction. procreation *noun*
[from *pro-* + Latin *creare* = to produce]

procure *verb* (procures, procuring, procured)
obtain or acquire something.
procurement *noun*
[from *pro-* + Latin *curare* = look after]

prod *verb* (prods, prodding, prodded)
1 poke. 2 stimulate someone into action.
prod *noun* [origin unknown]

prodigal *adjective*
wasteful or extravagant.
prodigally *adverb*, prodigality *noun*
[from Latin *prodigus* = lavish, generous]

prodigious *adjective*
wonderful or enormous. prodigiously
adverb [same origin as *prodigy*]

prodigy *noun* (*plural* prodigies)
1 a person with wonderful abilities. 2 a wonderful thing.
[from Latin *prodigium* = good omen]

produce *verb* (produces, producing, produced)
1 make or create something; bring something into existence. 2 bring something out so that it can be seen. 3 organize the performance of a play, making of a film, etc. 4 extend a line further, *Produce the base of the triangle.*
producer *noun*

produce (*say* prod-yooss) *noun*
things produced, especially by farmers.
[from *pro-* + Latin *ducere* = to lead]

product *noun* (*plural* products)
1 something produced. 2 the result of multiplying two numbers. (Compare *quotient.*)
[from Latin *productum* = produced]

production *noun* (*plural* productions)
1 producing. 2 the thing or amount produced.

productive *adjective*
producing a lot of things. productivity *noun*

profane *adjective*
showing disrespect for religion; blasphemous. profanely *adverb*

profane *verb* (profanes, profaning, profaned)
treat something, especially religion, with disrespect.
[from Latin *profanus* = outside the temple]

profanity *noun* (*plural* profanities)
words or language that show disrespect for religion.

profess *verb* (professes, professing, professed)
1 declare or express something. 2 claim to have something, *She professed interest in our work.* professedly *adverb*
[from Latin *professus* = declared publicly]

profession *noun* (*plural* professions)
1 an occupation that needs special education and training, *The professions include being a doctor, nurse, or lawyer.* 2 a declaration, *They made professions of loyalty.*
[from Latin *professio* = public declaration]

professional *adjective*
1 to do with a profession. 2 doing a certain kind of work as a full-time job for payment, not as an amateur, *a professional footballer.*
professional *noun*, professionally *adverb*

professor *noun* (*plural* professors)
a university lecturer of the highest rank.
professorship *noun* [same origin as *profess*]

proffer *verb* (proffers, proffering, proffered)
offer. [from *pro-* + French *offrir* = to offer]

proficient *adjective*
doing something properly because of training or practice; skilled.
proficiency *noun*
[from Latin *proficiens* = making progress]

profile *noun* (*plural* profiles)
1 a side view of a person's face. 2 a short description of a person's character or career.
keep a low profile not make yourself noticeable.
[from old Italian *profilare* = draw in outline]

profit *noun* (*plural* **profits**)
1 the extra money obtained by selling something for more than it cost to buy or make. 2 an advantage gained by doing something.
profitable *adjective*, **profitably** *noun*
profit *verb* (**profits, profiting, profited**)
gain an advantage or benefit from something. [from old French]

profiteer *noun* (*plural* **profiteers**)
a person who makes a great profit unfairly.
profiteering *noun*

profligate *adjective*
wasteful and extravagant. **profligacy** *noun*
[from Latin *profligare* = to ruin]

profound *adjective*
1 very deep or intense, *We take a profound interest in it.* 2 showing or needing great study. **profoundly** *adverb*, **profundity** *noun*
[from *pro-* + Latin *fundus* = bottom]

profuse *adjective*
lavish or plentiful. **profusely** *adverb*, **profuseness** *noun*, **profusion** *noun*
[from Latin *profusus* = poured out]

progenitor *noun* (*plural* **progenitors**)
an ancestor. [same origin as *progeny*]

progeny (*say* proj-in-ee) *noun*
offspring or descendants.
[from *pro-* + Latin *gignere* = create, father]

prognosis (*say* prog-**noh**-sis) *noun* (*plural* **prognoses**)
a forecast or prediction, especially about a disease. **prognostication** *noun* [from Greek *pro-* = before + *gnosis* = knowing]

program *noun* (*plural* **programs**)
a series of coded instructions for a computer to carry out.
program *verb* (**programs, programming, programmed**)
prepare a computer by means of a program. **programmer** *noun*
[the American spelling of *programme*]

programme *noun* (*plural* **programmes**)
1 a list of planned events. 2 a leaflet giving details of a play, concert, etc. 3 a show, play or talk etc. on radio or television.
[from Greek *programma* = public notice]

progress (*say* **proh**-gress) *noun*
1 forward movement; an advance. 2 a development or improvement.
progress (*say* pro-**gress**) *verb* (**progresses, progressing, progressed**)
1 move forward. 2 improve.
progression *noun*, **progressive** *adjective*
[from *pro-* + Latin *gressus* = going]

prohibit *verb* (**prohibits, prohibiting, prohibited**)
forbid or ban, *Smoking is prohibited.*
prohibition *noun* [from Latin]

prohibitive *adjective*
1 prohibiting. 2 (of prices) so high that people will not buy things.

project (*say* **proj**-ekt) *noun* (*plural* **projects**)
1 a plan or scheme. 2 the task of finding out as much as you can about something and writing about it.
project (*say* pro-**jekt**) *verb* (**projects, projecting, projected**)
1 stick out. 2 show a picture on a screen. 3 give people a particular impression, *He likes to project an image of absent-minded brilliance.* **projection** *noun*
[from *pro-* + Latin *-jectum* = thrown]

projectile *noun* (*plural* **projectiles**)
a missile.

projectionist *noun* (*plural* **projectionists**)
a person who works a projector.

projector *noun* (*plural* **projectors**)
a machine for showing films or photographs on a screen.

proletariat (*say* proh-lit-**air**-ee-at) *noun*
working people. [from Latin]

proliferate *verb* (**proliferates, proliferating, proliferated**)
increase rapidly in numbers. **proliferation** *noun* [from Latin *proles* = offspring + *ferre* = to bear]

prolific *adjective*
producing a lot, *a prolific author.*
prolifically *adverb*
[same origin as *proliferate*]

prologue (*say* **proh**-log) *noun* (*plural* **prologues**)
an introduction to a poem or play etc.
[from Greek *pro-* = before + *logos* = speech]

prolong *verb* (prolongs, prolonging, prolonged)
make a thing longer or make it last for a long time. **prolongation** *noun*
[from *pro-* + Latin *longus* = long]

prom *noun* (*plural* proms) (*informal*)
1 a promenade. 2 a promenade concert.

promenade (*say* prom-in-ahd) *noun* (*plural* promenades)
1 a place suitable for walking, especially beside the seashore. 2 a leisurely walk.
promenade *verb*
[French, from *se promener* = to walk]

promenade concert (*plural* promenade concerts)
a concert where part of the audience may stand or walk about.

prominent *adjective*
1 sticking out; projecting. 2 conspicuous. 3 important. **prominently** *adverb*,
prominence *noun* [from Latin]

promiscuous *adjective*
1 having many casual sexual relationships. 2 indiscriminate.
promiscuously *adverb*, **promiscuity** *noun*
[from Latin]

promise *noun* (*plural* promises)
1 a statement that you will definitely do or not do something. 2 an indication of future success or good results, *His work shows promise.*
promise *verb* (promises, promising, promised)
make a promise. [from Latin]

promising *adjective*
likely to be good or successful, *a promising pianist.*

promontory *noun* (*plural* promontories)
a piece of high land that sticks out into a sea or lake. [from Latin]

promote *verb* (promotes, promoting, promoted)
1 move a person to a higher rank or position. 2 help the progress or sale of something, *He has done much to promote the cause of peace.*
promoter *noun*, **promotion** *noun*
[from *pro-* + Latin *motum* = moved]

prompt *adjective*
1 without delay, *a prompt reply.* 2 punctual. **promptly** *adverb*,
promptness *noun*, **promptitude** *noun*

prompt *verb* (prompts, prompting, prompted)
1 cause or encourage a person to do something. 2 remind an actor or speaker of words when he or she has forgotten them.
prompter *noun*
[from Latin *promptum* = produced]

promulgate *verb* (promulgates, promulgating, promulgated)
make something known to the public; proclaim. **promulgation** *noun*
[from Latin]

prone *adjective*
lying face downwards. (The opposite is *supine.*)
be prone to be likely to do or suffer something, *He is prone to jealousy.*
[from Latin *pro* = forwards]

prong *noun* (*plural* prongs)
one of the spikes on a fork.
pronged *adjective*
[origin unknown]

pronoun *noun* (*plural* pronouns)
a word used instead of a noun.
demonstrative pronouns are *this, that, these, those;* **interrogative pronouns** are *who? what? which?,* etc.; **personal pronouns** are *I, me, we, us, thou, thee, you, ye, he, him, she, her, it, they, them;* **possessive pronouns** are *mine, yours, theirs,* etc.; **reflexive pronouns** are *myself, yourself,* etc.; **relative pronouns** are *who, what, which, that.*
[from *pro-* = in place of + *noun*]

pronounce *verb* (pronounces, pronouncing, pronounced)
1 say a sound or word in a particular way, *'Two' is pronounced like 'too'.* 2 declare something formally, *I now pronounce you man and wife.*
[from *pro-* + Latin *nuntiare* = announce]

pronounced *adjective*
noticeable, *This street has a pronounced slope.*

pronouncement *noun* (*plural* pronouncements)
a declaration.

pronunciation noun (plural
pronunciations)
1 the way a word is pronounced. 2 the way
a person pronounces words.

USAGE: Note the spelling; this word
should not be written or spoken as
'pronounciation'.

proof noun (plural proofs)
1 a fact or thing that shows something is
true. 2 a printed copy of a book or
photograph etc. made for checking before
other copies are printed.
proof adjective
able to resist something or not be
penetrated, a bulletproof jacket.
[from old French; related to prove]

prop¹ noun (plural props)
a support, especially one made of a long
piece of wood or metal.
prop verb (props, propping, propped)
support something by leaning it against
something else. [probably from old Dutch]

prop² noun (plural props)
an object or piece of furniture used on a
theatre stage or in a film. [from property]

propaganda noun
publicity intended to make people believe
something.
[Italian, = propagating, spreading]

propagate verb (propagates, propagating,
propagated)
1 breed or reproduce. 2 spread an idea or
belief to a lot of people. **propagation** noun,
propagator noun [from Latin]

propel verb (propels, propelling, propelled)
push something forward.
[from pro- + Latin pellere = to drive]

propellant noun (plural propellants)
a substance that propels things, Liquid fuel
is the propellant used in these rockets.

propeller noun (plural propellers)
a device with blades that spin round to
drive an aircraft or ship.

propensity noun (plural propensities)
a tendency. [from Latin propendere = lean
forward or hang down]

proper adjective
1 suitable or right, the proper way to hold a
bat. 2 respectable, prim and proper.
3 (informal) complete or thorough, You're
a proper nuisance! **properly** adverb
[from Latin proprius = your own, special]

proper fraction noun (plural proper
fractions)
a fraction that is less than 1, with the
numerator less than the denominator, e.g. $\frac{3}{8}$.

proper noun noun (plural proper nouns)
the name of one person or thing, e.g. Mary,
London, Spain.

property noun (plural properties)
1 a thing or things that belong to
somebody. 2 a building or someone's land.
3 a quality or characteristic, It has the
property of becoming soft when heated.
[same origin as proper]

prophecy noun (plural prophecies)
1 a statement that prophesies something.
2 the action of prophesying.

prophesy verb (prophesies, prophesying,
prophesied)
say what will happen in the future; foretell.
[from Greek pro = before + phanai = speak]

prophet noun (plural prophets)
1 a person who makes prophecies. 2 a
religious teacher who is believed to be
inspired by God.
prophetess noun, **prophetic** adjective
the Prophet Muhammad, who founded the
Muslim faith.
[from Greek prophetes = someone who
speaks for a god]

propinquity noun
nearness.
[from Latin propinquus = neighbouring]

propitiate (say pro-pish-ee-ayt) verb
(propitiates, propitiating, propitiated)
win a person's favour or forgiveness.
propitiation noun, **propitiatory** adjective
[same origin as propitious]

propitious (say pro-pish-us) adjective
favourable. [from Latin propitius]

proponent (*say* prop-oh-nent) *noun*
(*plural* proponents)
the person who puts forward a proposal.
[from *pro-* + Latin *ponere* = to place]

proportion *noun* (*plural* proportions)
1 a part or share of a whole thing. 2 a ratio.
3 the correct relationship in size, amount,
or importance between two things, *You've
drawn his head out of proportion.*
proportional *adjective*, proportionally
adverb, proportionate *adjective*
proportions *plural noun* size, *a ship of large
proportions.*
[from *pro-* + Latin *portio* = portion or
share]

proportional representation *noun*
a system in which each political party has
a number of Members of Parliament in
proportion to the number of votes for all its
candidates.

propose *verb* (proposes, proposing,
proposed)
1 suggest an idea or plan etc. 2 ask a
person to marry you. proposal *noun*
[from old French; related to *proponent*]

proposition *noun* (*plural* propositions)
1 a suggestion or offer. 2 a statement.
3 (*informal*) an undertaking or problem, *a
difficult proposition.*
[same origin as *proponent*]

propound *verb* (propounds, propounding,
propounded)
put forward an idea for consideration.
[same origin as *proponent*]

proprietary (*say* pro-pry-it-er-ee) *adjective*
1 made or sold by one firm; branded,
proprietary medicines. 2 to do with an
owner or ownership.
[same origin as *proper*]

proprietor *noun* (*plural* proprietors)
the owner of a shop or business.
proprietress *noun* [from *proprietary*]

propriety (*say* pro-pry-it-ee) *noun* (*plural*
proprieties)
1 being proper. 2 correct behaviour.
[same origin as *proper*]

propulsion *noun*
propelling something.

prorogue *verb* (prorogues, proroguing,
prorogued)
stop the meetings of Parliament
temporarily without dissolving it.
prorogation *noun*
[from Latin *prorogare* = prolong]

prosaic *adjective*
plain or dull and ordinary. prosaically
adverb [from *prose*]

proscribe *verb* (proscribes, proscribing,
proscribed)
forbid by law.
[from Latin *proscribere* = to outlaw]

USAGE: Do not confuse with *prescribe*.

prose *noun*
writing or speech that is not in verse.
[from Latin *prosa* = straightforward, plain]

prosecute *verb* (prosecutes, prosecuting,
prosecuted)
1 make someone go to a lawcourt to be
tried for a crime. 2 continue with
something; pursue, *prosecuting their trade.*
prosecution *noun*, prosecutor *noun*
[from Latin *prosecutus* = pursued]

proselyte *noun* (*plural* proselytes)
a person who has been converted to the
Jewish faith or from one religion, opinion,
etc. to another.
[from Greek *proselythos* = stranger]

proselytize *verb* (proselytizes,
proselytizing, proselytized)
convert people from one religion, opinion,
etc. to another.

prosody (*say* pross-od-ee) *noun*
the study of verse and its structure.
[from Greek *prosodia* = song]

prospect *noun* (*plural* prospects)
1 a possibility or expectation of something,
There is no prospect of success. 2 a wide
view.
prospect (*say* pro-spekt) *verb* (prospects,
prospecting, prospected)
explore in search of something, *prospecting
for gold.* prospector *noun*
[from *pro-* + Latin *-spicere* = to look]

prospective *adjective*
expected to be or to happen; possible,
prospective customers.

prospectus *noun* (*plural* **prospectuses**)
a booklet describing and advertising a
school, business company, etc.
[Latin, = view or prospect]

prosper *verb* (**prospers, prospering,
prospered**)
be successful. [from Latin]

prosperous *adjective*
successful or rich. **prosperity** *noun*

prostitute *noun* (*plural* **prostitutes**)
a person who takes part in sexual acts for
payment. **prostitution** *noun*
[from Latin *prostitutus* = for sale]

prostrate *adjective*
lying face downwards.
prostrate *verb* (**prostrates, prostrating,
prostrated**)
if you prostrate yourself, you lie face
downwards, usually in submission.
prostration *noun*
[from Latin *prostratum* = laid flat]

protagonist *noun* (*plural* **protagonists**)
1 the main character in a play. **2** a person
competing against another.
[from *proto-* + Greek *agonistes* – actor]

protect *verb* (**protects, protecting,
protected**)
keep safe from harm or injury. **protection**
noun, **protective** *adjective*, **protector** *noun*
[from *pro-* + Latin *tectum* = covered]

protectorate *noun* (*plural* **protectorates**)
a country that is under the official
protection of a stronger country.

protégé (*say* prot-ezh-ay) *noun* (*plural*
protégés)
a person who is given helpful protection or
encouragement by another.
[French, = protected]

protein *noun* (*plural* **proteins**)
a substance that is found in all living
things and is an essential part of the food of
animals. [from Greek *proteios* = primary,
most important]

protest (*say* proh-test) *noun* (*plural*
protests)
a statement or action showing that you
disapprove of something.

protest (*say* pro-test) *verb* (**protests,
protesting, protested**)
1 make a protest. **2** declare firmly, *They
protested their innocence.* **protestation** *noun*
[from *pro-* + Latin *testari* = say on oath]

Protestant *noun* (*plural* **Protestants**)
a member of any of the western Christian
Churches separated from the Roman
Catholic Church.
[because in the 16th century many people
protested (= declared firmly) their
opposition to the Catholic Church]

proto- *prefix*
1 first. **2** at an early stage of development.
[from Greek *protos* = first or earliest]

protocol *noun*
etiquette connected with people's rank.
[from Greek]

proton *noun* (*plural* **protons**)
a particle of matter with a positive electric
charge. [same origin as *proto-*]

prototype *noun* (*plural* **prototypes**)
the first model of something, from which
others are copied or developed.

protract *verb* (**protracts, protracting,
protracted**)
make something last longer than usual;
prolong.
protracted *adjective*, **protraction** *noun*
[from *pro-* + Latin *tractum* = drawn out]

protractor *noun* (*plural* **protractors**)
a device for measuring angles, usually a
semicircle marked off in degrees.

protrude *verb* (**protrudes, protruding,
protruded**)
stick out; project. **protrusion** *noun*
[from *pro-* + Latin *trudere* = push]

protuberance *noun* (*plural*
protuberances)
a part that bulges out from a surface.

protuberant *adjective*
bulging out from a surface.
[from *pro-* + Latin *tuber* = a swelling]

proud *adjective*
1 very pleased with yourself or with
someone else who has done well. **2** causing
pride, *This is a proud moment for us.* **3** full

of self-respect and independence, *They were too proud to ask for help.*
proudly *adverb*
[via Old English from old French *prud* = brave]

prove *verb* (proves, proving, proved)
1 show that something is true. **2** turn out, *The forecast proved to be correct.*
provable *adjective*
[from Latin *probare* = to test]

proven (*say* proh-ven) *adjective*
proved, *a man of proven ability.*

provender *noun*
food, especially for animals.
[from old French *provendre* = provide]

proverb *noun* (*plural* proverbs)
a short well-known saying that states a truth, e.g. 'Many hands make light work'.
[from *pro-* + Latin *verbum* = word]

proverbial *adjective*
1 referred to in a proverb. **2** well-known.

provide *verb* (provides, providing, provided)
1 make something available; supply.
2 prepare for something, *Try to provide against emergencies.* **provider** *noun*
[from Latin *providere* = foresee]

provided *conjunction*
on condition, *You can stay provided that you help.*

providence *noun*
1 being provident. **2** God's or nature's care and protection.

provident *adjective*
wisely providing for the future; thrifty.
[same origin as *provide*]

providential *adjective*
happening very luckily. **providentially** *adverb* [from *providence*]

providing *conjunction*
provided.

province *noun* (*plural* provinces)
1 a section of a country. **2** the area of a person's special knowledge or responsibility, *Repairing stereos is outside my province, I'm afraid.* **provincial** *adjective*

the provinces the parts of a country outside its capital city.
[from Latin]

provision *noun* (*plural* provisions)
1 providing something. **2** a statement in a document, *the provisions of the treaty.*
[from Latin *provisum* = provided]

provisional *adjective*
arranged or agreed upon temporarily but possibly to be altered later.
provisionally *adverb*

provisions *plural noun*
supplies of food and drink.

proviso (*say* prov-I-zoh) *noun* (*plural* provisos)
a condition inisisted on beforehand; a stipulation.
[from Latin *proviso quod* = provided that]

provoke *verb* (provokes, provoking, provoked)
1 make a person angry. **2** cause or give rise to something, *The joke provoked laughter.*
provocation *noun*, **provocative** *adjective*
[from *pro-* + Latin *vocare* = summon]

provost *noun* (*plural* provosts)
a Scottish official similar to a mayor in England and Wales. [from Old English]

prow *noun* (*plural* prows)
the front end of a ship. [from French]

prowess *noun*
great ability or daring. [from old French; related to *proud*]

prowl *verb* (prowls, prowling, prowled)
move about quietly or cautiously, like a hunter. **prowl** *noun*, **prowler** *noun*
[origin unknown]

proximity *noun*
nearness. [from Latin *proximus* = nearest]

proxy *noun* (*plural* proxies)
a person authorized to represent or act for another person, *I will be abroad, so I have arranged to vote by proxy.* [from Latin]

prude *noun* (*plural* prudes)
a person who is easily shocked. **prudish** *adjective*, **prudery** *noun* [from old French]

prudent *adjective*
careful, not rash or reckless. **prudently**
adverb, **prudence** *noun*, **prudential** *adjective*
[from French; related to *provide*]

prune¹ *noun* (*plural* **prunes**)
a dried plum. [from Greek]

prune² *verb* (**prunes, pruning, pruned**)
cut off unwanted parts of a tree or bush etc.
[from old French]

pry *verb* (**pries, prying, pried**)
look or ask inquisitively.
[origin unknown]

PS *abbreviation*
postscript.

psalm (*say* sahm) *noun* (*plural* **psalms**)
a religious song, especially one from the
Book of Psalms in the Bible. **psalmist** *noun*
[via Old English from Greek *psalmos*
= song sung to the harp]

pseudo- (*say* s'yood-oh) *prefix*
false; pretended. [from Greek]

pseudonym *noun* (*plural* **pseudonyms**)
a false name used by an author.
[from *pseudo-* + Greek *onyma* = name]

psychedelic *adjective*
having vivid colours and patterns, *a
psychedelic design*. [from Greek *psyche*
= life, soul + *deloun* = reveal]

psychiatrist (*say* sy-ky-a-trist) *noun*
(*plural* **psychiatrists**)
a doctor who treats mental illnesses.
psychiatry *noun*, **psychiatric** *adjective*
[from *psycho-* + Greek *iatreia* = healing]

psychic (*say* sy-kik) *adjective*
1 supernatural. **2** having supernatural
powers, especially being able to predict the
future. **3** to do with the mind or soul.
psychical *adjective* [same origin as *psycho-*]

psycho- *prefix*
to do with the mind.
[from Greek *psyche* = life or soul]

psychoanalysis *noun*
investigation of a person's mental
processes, especially in psychotherapy.

psychology *noun*
the study of the mind and how it works.
psychological *adjective*, **psychologist** *noun*
[from *psycho-* + *-logy*]

psychotherapy *noun*
treatment of mental illness by
psychological methods.

PT *abbreviation*
physical training.

PTA *abbreviation*
parent-teacher association; an
organization that arranges discussions
between teachers and parents about school
business, and raises money for the school.

ptarmigan (*say* tar-mig-an) *noun* (*plural*
ptarmigans)
a bird of the grouse family.
[from Scottish Gaelic]

pterodactyl (*say* te-ro-dak-til) *noun* (*plural*
pterodactyls)
an extinct flying reptile.
[from Greek *pteron* = wing + *daktylos*
= finger (because one of the 'fingers' on its
front leg was enlarged to support its wing)]

PTO *abbreviation*
please turn over.

pub *noun* (*plural* **pubs**) (*informal*)
a public house.

puberty (*say* pew-ber-tee) *noun*
the time when a young person is
developing physically into an adult.
[same origin as *pubic*]

pubic (*say* pew-bik) *adjective*
to do with the lower front part of the
abdomen.
[from Latin *pubes* = an adult, the genitals]

public *adjective*
belonging to or known by everyone, not
private. **publicly** *adverb*
public *noun*
people in general.
in public openly, not in private.
[from Latin *publicus* = of the people]

publican *noun* (*plural* **publicans**)
the person in charge of a public house.

publication *noun* (*plural* **publications**)
1 publishing. 2 a published book or newspaper etc.

public house *noun* (*plural* **public houses**)
a building licensed to serve alcoholic drinks to the public.

publicity *noun*
public attention; doing things (e.g. advertising) to draw people's attention to something.

publicize *verb* (**publicizes, publicizing, publicized**)
bring something to people's attention; advertise. [from *public*]

public school *noun* (*plural* **public schools**)
1 a secondary school that charges fees. 2 (in Scotland and the USA) a school run by a local authority or by the State.

publish *verb* (**publishes, publishing, published**)
1 have something printed and sold to the public. 2 announce something in public.
publisher *noun*
[from Latin *publicare* = make public]

puce *noun*
brownish-purple colour. [from French *couleur puce* = the colour of a flea]

puck *noun* (*plural* **pucks**)
a hard rubber disc used in ice hockey. [origin unknown]

pucker *verb* (**puckers, puckering, puckered**)
wrinkle. [origin unknown]

pudding *noun* (*plural* **puddings**)
1 a food made in a soft mass, especially in a mixture of flour and other ingredients. 2 the sweet course of a meal. [from French]

puddle *noun* (*plural* **puddles**)
a shallow patch of liquid, especially of rainwater on a road. [from Old English]

pudgy *adjective*
short and fat, *pudgy fingers*. [origin unknown]

puerile (*say* pew-er-I'll) *adjective*
silly and childish. **puerility** *noun*
[from Latin *puer* = boy]

puff *noun* (*plural* **puffs**)
1 a short blowing of breath, wind, or smoke etc. 2 a soft pad for putting powder on the skin. 3 a cake of very light pastry filled with cream.
puff *verb* (**puffs, puffing, puffed**)
1 blow out puffs of smoke etc. 2 breathe with difficulty; pant. 3 inflate or swell something, *He puffed out his chest.* [imitating the sound]

puffin *noun* (*plural* **puffins**)
a seabird with a large striped beak. [origin unknown]

puffy *adjective*
puffed out; swollen. **puffiness** *noun*

pug *noun* (*plural* **pugs**)
a small dog with a flat face like a bulldog. [probably from old Dutch]

pugilist (*say* pew-jil-ist) *noun* (*plural* **pugilists**)
a boxer. [from Latin]

pugnacious *adjective*
wanting to fight; aggressive.
pugnaciously *adverb*, **pugnacity** *noun*
[from Latin *pugnare* = to fight]

pull *verb* (**pulls, pulling, pulled**)
1 make a thing come towards or after you by using force on it. 2 move by a driving force, *The car pulled out into the road.*
pull *noun*
pull a face make a strange face.
pull off achieve something.
pull somebody's leg tease him or her.
pull through recover from an illness.
pull yourself together become calm or sensible.
[from Old English]

pullet *noun* (*plural* **pullets**)
a young hen. [from French]

pulley *noun* (*plural* **pulleys**)
a wheel with a rope, chain, or belt over it, used for lifting or moving heavy things. [from old French]

pullover *noun* (*plural* **pullovers**)
a knitted piece of clothing for the top half of the body.

pulmonary (*say* pul-mon-er-ee) *adjective*
to do with the lungs.
[from Latin *pulmo* = lung]

pulp *noun*
1 the soft moist part of fruit. 2 any soft
moist mass. **pulpy** *adjective* [from Latin]

pulpit *noun* (*plural* **pulpits**)
a small enclosed platform for the preacher
in a church or chapel. [from Latin
pulpitum = a platform, stage, or scaffold]

pulsate *verb* (**pulsates, pulsating, pulsated**)
expand and contract rhythmically; vibrate.
pulsation *noun* [from Latin]

pulse¹ *noun* (*plural* **pulses**)
1 the rhythmical movement of the arteries
as blood is pumped through them by the
beating of the heart, *The pulse can be felt in
a person's wrists.* 2 a throb.
pulse *verb* (**pulses, pulsing, pulsed**)
throb or pulsate.
[from Latin *pulsum* = driven, beaten]

pulse² *noun* (*plural* **pulses**)
the edible seed of peas, beans, lentils, etc.
[from Latin]

pulverize *verb* (**pulverizes, pulverizing,
pulverized**)
crush something into powder. **pulverization**
noun [from Latin *pulveris* = of dust]

puma (*say* pew-ma) *noun* (*plural* **pumas**)
a large brown animal of western America,
also called a cougar or mountain lion.
[via Spanish from Quechua (a South
American language)]

pumice *noun*
a kind of porous stone used for rubbing
stains from the skin or as powder for
polishing things. [from Latin]

pummel *verb* (**pummels, pummelling,
pummelled**)
keep on hitting something.
[a different spelling of *pommel*]

pump¹ *noun* (*plural* **pumps**)
a device that pushes air or liquid into or
out of something, or along pipes.
pump *verb* (**pumps, pumping, pumped**)
1 move air or liquid with a pump.
2 (*informal*) question a person to obtain
information.

pump up inflate.
[originally a sailors' word: origin
unknown]

pump² *noun* (*plural* **pumps**)
a canvas sports shoe with a rubber sole.
[origin unknown]

pumpkin *noun* (*plural* **pumpkins**)
a very large round fruit with a hard orange
skin.
[from Greek *pepon*, a kind of large melon]

pun *noun* (*plural* **puns**)
a joking use of a word sounding the same
as another, e.g. 'Deciding where to bury
him was a *grave* decision'.
[origin unknown]

punch¹ *verb* (**punches, punching, punched**)
1 hit someone with your fist. 2 make a hole
in something.
punch *noun* (*plural* **punches**)
1 a hit with a fist. 2 a device for making
holes in paper, metal, leather, etc. 3 vigour.
[same origin as *puncture*]

punch² *noun*
a drink made by mixing wine or spirits and
fruit juice in a bowl.
[from Sanskrit *pañca* = five (the number of
ingredients in the traditional recipe:
spirits, fruit juice, water, sugar, and spice)]

punchline *noun* (*plural* **punchlines**)
words that give the climax of a joke or
story.

punch-up *noun* (*plural* **punch-ups**)
(*informal*)
a fight.

punctilious *adjective*
very careful about details; conscientious.
punctiliously *adverb*, **punctiliousness** *noun*
[from Latin *punctillum* = little point]

punctual *adjective*
doing things exactly at the time arranged;
not late. **punctually** *adverb*, **punctuality** *noun*
[from Latin *punctum* = a point]

punctuate *verb* (**punctuates, punctuating,
punctuated**)
1 put punctuation marks into something.
2 put something in at intervals, *His speech
was punctuated with cheers.* [from Latin
punctuare = mark with points or dots]

punctuation *noun*
marks such as commas, full stops, and brackets put into a piece of writing to make it easier to read.

puncture *noun* (*plural* **punctures**)
a small hole made by something sharp, especially in a tyre.
puncture *verb* (**punctures, puncturing, punctured**)
make a puncture in something.
[from Latin]

pundit *noun* (*plural* **pundits**)
a person who is an authority on something. [from Sanskrit *pandita* = learned]

pungent (*say* pun-jent) *adjective*
1 having a strong taste or smell. 2 (of remarks) sharp.
pungently *adverb*, **pungency** *noun*
[from Latin *pungere* = to prick]

punish *verb* (**punishes, punishing, punished**)
make a person suffer because he or she has done something wrong.
punishable *adjective*, **punishment** *noun*
[same origin as *pain*]

punitive (*say* pew-nit-iv) *adjective*
inflicting punishment.

punk *noun* (*plural* **punks**)
1 (also **punk rock**) a loud aggressive style of rock music. 2 a person who likes this music. [origin unknown]

punnet *noun* (*plural* **punnets**)
a small container for soft fruit such as strawberries. [origin unknown]

punt[1] *noun* (*plural* **punts**)
a flat-bottomed boat, usually moved by pushing a pole against the bottom of a river while standing in the punt.
punt *verb* (**punts, punting, punted**)
move a punt with a pole.
[from Latin *ponto* = pontoon[1]]

punt[2] *verb* (**punts, punting, punted**)
kick a football after dropping it from your hands and before it touches the ground. [origin unknown]

punt[3] *verb* (**punts, punting, punted**)
gamble; bet on a horse race. **punt** *noun*
[from French]

punter *noun* (*plural* **punters**)
1 a person who lays a bet. 2 (*informal*) a customer.

puny (*say* pew-nee) *adjective*
small or undersized; feeble.
[from old French *puisne* = a younger or inferior person]

pup *noun* (*plural* **pups**)
1 a puppy. 2 a young seal. [from *puppy*]

pupa (*say* pew-pa) *noun* (*plural* **pupae**)
a chrysalis. [from Latin; related to *pupil*]

pupate (*say* pew-payt) *verb* (**pupates, pupating, pupated**)
become a pupa. **pupation** *noun*

pupil *noun* (*plural* **pupils**)
1 someone who is being taught by another person, especially at school. 2 the opening in the centre of the eye. [from Latin *pupilla* = little girl or doll (the use in sense 2 refers to the tiny images of people and things that can be seen in the eye)]

puppet *noun* (*plural* **puppets**)
1 a kind of doll that can be made to move by fitting it over your hand or working it by strings or wires. 2 a person whose actions are controlled by someone else.
puppetry *noun*
[probably related to *pupil*]

puppy *noun* (*plural* **puppies**)
a young dog.
[from old French; related to *pupil*]

purchase *verb* (**purchases, purchasing, purchased**)
buy. **purchaser** *noun*
purchase *noun* (*plural* **purchases**)
1 something bought. 2 buying. 3 a firm hold to pull or raise something.
[from old French]

purdah *noun*
the Muslim or Hindu custom of keeping women from the sight of men or strangers. [from Persian or Urdu *parda* = veil or curtain]

pure *adjective*
1 not mixed with anything else; clean. 2 mere; nothing but, *pure nonsense*. **purely** *adverb*, **pureness** *noun* [from Latin]

purée (*say* pewr-ay) *noun* (*plural* purées)
fruit or vegetables made into pulp.
[French, = squeezed]

purgative *noun* (*plural* purgatives)
a strong laxative. [same origin as *purge*]

purgatory *noun*
1 a state of temporary suffering. 2 (in
Roman Catholic belief) a place in which
souls are purified by punishment before
they can enter heaven.
[same origin as *purge*]

purge *verb* (purges, purging, purged)
get rid of unwanted people or things.
purge *noun* (*plural* purges)
1 purging. 2 a purgative.
[from Latin *purgare* = make pure]

purify *verb* (purifies, purifying, purified)
make a thing pure.
purification *noun*, **purifier** *noun*

purist *noun* (*plural* purists)
a person who likes things to be exactly
right, especially in people's use of words.

Puritan *noun* (*plural* Puritans)
a Protestant in the 16th and 17th centuries
who wanted simpler religious ceremonies
and strictly moral behaviour.

puritan *noun* (*plural* puritans)
a person with very strict morals.
puritanical *adjective*
[from Latin *puritas* = purity]

purity *noun*
pureness.

purl[1] *noun* (*plural* purls)
a knitting stitch that makes a ridge
towards the knitter. **purl** *verb*
[from Scottish *pirl* = twist]

purl[2] *verb* (purls, purling, purled)
(of a stream) ripple with a murmuring
sound.
[probably from a Scandinavian language]

purloin *verb* (purloins, purloining,
purloined)
take something without permission.
[from old French]

purple *noun*
deep reddish blue colour.
[via Old English from Latin]

purport (*say* per-port) *verb* (purports,
purporting, purported)
claim, *The letter purports to be from the
council.* **purportedly** *adverb*
purport (*say* per-port) *noun*
meaning, *The purport of the letter could not
be clearer.* [from old French]

purpose *noun* (*plural* purposes)
1 what you intend to do; a plan or aim.
2 determination.
purposeful *adjective*, **purposefully** *adverb*
on purpose by intention, not by accident.
[from old French; related to *propose*]

purposely *adverb*
on purpose.

purr *verb* (purrs, purring, purred)
make the low murmuring sound that a cat
does when it is pleased. **purr** *noun*
[imitating the sound]

purse *noun* (*plural* purses)
a small pouch for carrying money.
purse *verb* (purses, pursing, pursed)
draw something into folds, *She pursed up
her lips.* [from Latin *bursa* = a bag]

purser *noun* (*plural* pursers)
a ship's officer in charge of accounts.
[from *purse*]

pursuance *noun*
performing or carrying out an intention
etc., *in pursuance of my duties.*

pursue *verb* (pursues, pursuing, pursued)
1 chase someone in order to catch them.
2 continue with something; work at, *We
are pursuing our enquiries.* **pursuer** *noun*
[from old French; related to *prosecute*]

pursuit *noun* (*plural* pursuits)
1 pursuing. 2 a regular activity.

purvey *verb* (purveys, purveying, purveyed)
supply food etc. as a trade. **purveyor** *noun*
[from old French; related to *provide*]

pus *noun*
a thick yellowish substance produced in
inflamed or infected tissue, e.g. in an
abscess or boil. [Latin]

push *verb* (**pushes, pushing, pushed**)
1 make a thing go away from you by using force on it. **2** move yourself by using force, *He pushed in front of me.* **3** try to force someone to do or use something; urge. **push off** (*slang*) go away.

push *noun* (*plural* **pushes**)
a pushing movement or effort.
at a push if necessary but only with difficulty.
[from French; related to *pulse*¹]

pushchair *noun* (*plural* **pushchairs**)
a folding chair on wheels, in which a child can be pushed along.

pusher *noun* (*plural* **pushers**)
a person who sells illegal drugs.

pushy *adjective*
unpleasantly self-confident and eager to do things.

pusillanimous (*say* pew-zil-**an**-im-us) *adjective*
timid or cowardly. [from Latin *pusillus* = small + *animus* = mind]

puss *noun* (*informal*)
a cat.
[probably from old German or old Dutch]

pussy *noun* (*plural* **pussies**) (*informal*)
a cat.

pussyfoot *verb* (**pussyfoots, pussyfooting, pussyfooted**)
act too cautiously and timidly.

pussy willow *noun* (*plural* **pussy willows**)
a willow with furry catkins.

pustule *noun* (*plural* **pustules**)
a pimple containing pus. [from Latin]

put *verb* (**puts, putting, put**)
This word has many uses, including **1** move a person or thing to a place or position (*Put the lamp on the table*), **2** cause a person or thing to do or experience something or be in a certain condition (*Put the light on. Put her in a good mood*), **3** express in words (*She put it tactfully*).
be hard put have difficulty in doing something.
put off 1 postpone. **2** dissuade. **3** stop someone wanting something, *The smell puts me off.*

put out 1 stop a fire from burning or a light from shining. **2** annoy or inconvenience, *Our lateness has put her out.*
put up 1 build. **2** raise. **3** give someone a place to sleep; provide, *Who will put up the money?*
put up with endure or tolerate.
[from Old English]

putrefy (*say* pew-trif-I) *verb* (**putrefies, putrefying, putrefied**)
decay or rot. **putrefaction** *noun*
[from Latin *puter* = rotten]

putrid (*say* pew-trid) *adjective*
1 rotting. **2** smelling bad.
[same origin as *putrefy*]

putt *verb* (**putts, putting, putted**)
hit a golf ball gently towards the hole.
putt *noun*, **putter** *noun*, **putting green** *noun*
[a different spelling of *put*]

putty *noun*
a soft paste that sets hard, used for fitting the glass into a window frame.
[from French]

puzzle *noun* (*plural* **puzzles**)
1 a difficult question or problem. **2** a game or toy that sets a problem or difficult task. **3** a jigsaw puzzle.
puzzle *verb* (**puzzles, puzzling, puzzled**)
1 give someone a problem so that they have to think hard. **2** think patiently about how to solve something. **puzzlement** *noun*
[origin unknown]

PVC *abbreviation*
polyvinyl chloride, a plastic used to make clothing, pipes, flooring, etc.
[the initial letters of *polyvinyl chloride*, a polymer of vinyl, from which it is made]

pygmy (*say* pig-mee) *noun* (*plural* **pygmies**)
1 a very small person or thing. **2** a member of a race of very small people in Central Africa. [from Greek]

pyjamas *plural noun*
a loose jacket and trousers worn in bed.
[from Persian or Urdu *pay* = leg + *jamah* = clothing]

pylon *noun* (*plural* **pylons**)
a tall framework made of strips of steel, supporting electric cables. [from Greek]

pyramid *noun* (*plural* **pyramids**)
1 a structure with a square base and with sloping sides that meet in a point at the top.
2 an ancient Egyptian tomb shaped like this. **pyramidal** (*say* pir-am-id-al) *adjective*
[from Greek]

pyre *noun* (*plural* **pyres**)
a pile of wood etc. for burning a dead body as part of a funeral ceremony.
[from Greek *pyr* = fire]

python *noun* (*plural* **pythons**)
a large snake that kills its prey by coiling round and crushing it.
[the name of a large serpent or monster in Greek legend, killed by Apollo]

Qq

QC *abbreviation*
Queen's Counsel.

QED *abbreviation*
quod erat demonstrandum (Latin, = which was the thing that had to be proved).

quack¹ *verb* (**quacks, quacking, quacked**)
make the harsh cry of a duck. **quack** *noun*
[imitating the sound]

quack² *noun* (*plural* **quacks**)
a person who falsely claims to have medical skill or have remedies to cure diseases. [from Dutch *quacken* = to boast]

quad (*say* kwod) *noun* (*plural* **quads**)
1 a quadrangle. 2 a quadruplet.

quadrangle *noun* (*plural* **quadrangles**)
a rectangular courtyard with large buildings round it. [from *quadri-* + *angle*]

quadrant *noun* (*plural* **quadrants**)
a quarter of a circle.
[from Latin *quadrare* = to make square]

quadratic equation *noun* (*plural* **quadratic equations**)
an equation that involves quantities or variables raised to the power of two, but no higher than two.
[from Latin *quadrare* = to square]

quadri- *prefix*
four. [from Latin]

quadrilateral *noun* (*plural* **quadrilaterals**)
a flat geometric shape with four sides.

quadruped *noun* (*plural* **quadrupeds**)
an animal with four feet.
[from *quadri-* + Latin *pedis* = of a foot]

quadruple *adjective*
1 four times as much or as many. 2 having four parts.

quadruple *verb* (**quadruples, quadrupling, quadrupled**)
make or become four times as much or as many. [from Latin]

quadruplet *noun* (*plural* **quadruplets**)
each of four children born to the same mother at one time. [from *quadruple*]

quadruplicate *noun* (*plural* **quadruplicates**)
each of four things that are exactly alike.
[from Latin]

quaff (*say* kwof) *verb* (**quaffs, quaffing, quaffed**)
drink. [probably from old German]

quagmire *noun* (*plural* **quagmires**)
a bog or marsh.
[from an old word *quag* = marsh, + *mire*]

quail¹ *noun* (*plural* **quail** or **quails**)
a bird related to the partridge.
[from old French]

quail² *verb* (**quails, quailing, quailed**)
flinch; feel or show fear. [origin unknown]

quaint *adjective*
attractively odd or old-fashioned.
quaintly *adverb*, **quaintness** *noun*
[from old French]

quake *verb* (**quakes, quaking, quaked**)
tremble; shake with fear.
[from Old English]

Quaker *noun* (*plural* **Quakers**)
a member of a religious group called the Society of Friends, founded by George Fox in the 17th century.
[originally an insult, probably from George Fox's saying that people should 'tremble at the name of the Lord']

qualify verb (qualifies, qualifying, qualified)
1 make or become able to do something through having certain qualities or training, or by passing a test. **2** make a statement less extreme; limit its meaning. **3** (of an adjective) add meaning to a noun. **qualification** noun [from Latin qualis = of what kind?, of a particular kind]

quality noun (plural qualities)
1 how good or bad something is. **2** a characteristic; something that is special in a person or thing. [same origin as qualify]

qualm (say kwahm) noun (plural qualms)
a misgiving or scruple. [origin unknown]

quandary noun (plural quandaries)
a difficult situation where you are uncertain what to do. [origin unknown]

quantity noun (plural quantities)
1 how much there is of something; how many things there are of one sort. **2** a large amount. [from Latin quantus = how big?, how much?]

quantum noun (plural quanta)
a quantity or amount.
[same origin as quantity]

quantum leap or **jump** noun (plural quantum leaps, quantum jumps)
a sudden large increase or advance.

quarantine noun
keeping a person or animal isolated in case they have a disease which could spread to others. [from Italian quaranta = forty (the original period of isolation was 40 days)]

quarrel noun (plural quarrels)
an angry disagreement.
quarrel verb (quarrels, quarrelling, quarrelled)
have a quarrel. **quarrelsome** adjective
[from Latin querela = complaint]

quarry¹ noun (plural quarries)
an open place where stone or slate is dug or cut out of the ground.
quarry verb (quarries, quarrying, quarried)
dig or cut from a quarry. [from Latin]

quarry² noun (plural quarries)
an animal etc. being hunted or pursued. [from old French]

quart noun (plural quarts)
two pints, a quarter of a gallon.
[from old French; related to quarter]

quarter noun (plural quarters)
1 each of four equal parts into which a thing is or can be divided. **2** three months one-fourth of a year. **3** a district or region. People came from every quarter.
at close quarters very close together.
give no quarter show no mercy.
quarter verb (quarters, quartering, quartered)
1 divide something into quarters. **2** put soldiers etc. into lodgings.
[from Latin quartus = fourth]

quarterdeck noun (plural quarterdecks)
the part of a ship's upper deck nearest the stern, usually reserved for the officers.

quarterly adjective & adverb
happening or produced once in every three months.
quarterly noun (plural quarterlies)
a quarterly magazine etc.

quarters plural noun
lodgings.

quartet noun (plural quartets)
1 a group of four musicians. **2** a piece of music for four musicians. **3** a set of four people or things.
[via French from Italian quarto = fourth]

quartz noun
a hard mineral. [via German from Polish]

quash verb (quashes, quashing, quashed)
cancel or annul something, The judges quashed his conviction.
[from Latin cassus = null, not valid]

quasi- (say kwayz-I) prefix
seeming to be something but not really so, a quasi-scientific explanation.
[from Latin quasi = as if]

quatrain noun (plural quatrains)
a stanza with four lines.
[French, from quatre = four]

quaver verb (quavers, quavering, quavered)
tremble or quiver.

quaver *noun* (*plural* quavers)
1 a quavering sound. 2 a note in music (♪) lasting half as long as a crotchet.
[from Old English]

quay (*say* kee) *noun* (*plural* quays)
a landing-place where ships can be tied up for loading and unloading; a wharf.
quayside *noun* [from old French]

queasy *adjective*
feeling slightly sick. **queasily** *adverb*, **queasiness** *noun* [origin unknown]

queen *noun* (*plural* queens)
1 a woman who is the ruler of a country through inheriting the position. 2 the wife of a king. 3 a female bee or ant that produces eggs. 4 an important piece in chess. 5 a playing card with a picture of a queen on it. **queenly** *adjective*
[from Old English]

queen mother *noun* (*plural* queen mothers)
a king's widow who is the mother of the present king or queen.

Queen's Counsel *noun* (*plural* Queen's Counsels)
a senior barrister.

queer *adjective*
1 strange or eccentric. 2 slightly ill or faint. **queerly** *adverb*, **queerness** *noun*
queer *verb* (queers, queering, queered)
queer a person's pitch spoil his or her chances beforehand.
[origin unknown]

quell *verb* (quells, quelling, quelled)
1 crush a rebellion. 2 stop yourself from feeling fear, anger etc.; suppress.
[from Old English]

quench *verb* (quenches, quenching, quenched)
1 satisfy your thirst by drinking. 2 put out a fire or flame. [from Old English]

quern *noun* (*plural* querns)
a hand-operated device for grinding corn or pepper. [from Old English]

querulous (*say* kwe-rew-lus) *adjective*
complaining all the time. **querulously** *adverb* [same origin as *quarrel*]

query (*say* kweer-ee) *noun* (*plural* queries)
1 a question. 2 a question mark.
[from Latin *quaere* = ask!]

quest *noun* (*plural* quests)
a long search for something, *the quest for gold*. [same origin as *question*]

question *noun* (*plural* questions)
1 a sentence asking something. 2 a problem to be discussed or solved, *Parliament debated the question of education.* 3 doubt, *Whether we shall win is open to question.*
in question being discussed or disputed, *His honesty is not in question.*
out of the question impossible.
question *verb* (questions, questioning, questioned)
1 ask someone questions. 2 say that you are doubtful about something. **questioner** *noun* [from Latin *quaesitum* = sought for]

questionable *adjective*
causing doubt; not certainly true or honest or advisable.

question mark *noun* (*plural* question marks)
the punctuation mark ? placed after a question.

questionnaire *noun* (*plural* questionnaires)
a list of questions.

queue (*say* kew) *noun* (*plural* queues)
a line of people or vehicles waiting for something.
queue *verb* (queues, queueing, queued)
wait in a queue. [French]

quibble *noun* (*plural* quibbles)
a trivial complaint or objection.
quibble *verb* (quibbles, quibbling, quibbled)
make trivial complaints or objections.
[probably from Latin *quibus* = what?, for which, for whom (because *quibus* often appeared in legal documents)]

quiche (*say* keesh) *noun* (*plural* quiches)
an open tart with a savoury filling.
[French]

quick *adjective*
1 taking only a short time to do something. 2 done in a short time. 3 able to notice or

learn or think quickly. **4** (*old use*) alive, *the quick and the dead*. **quickly** *adverb*, **quickness** *noun* [from Old English]

quicken *verb* (**quickens, quickening, quickened**)
1 make or become quicker. **2** stimulate; make or become livelier.

quicksand *noun* (*plural* **quicksands**)
an area of loose wet sand which is so deep that heavy objects sink into it.
[from *quick* in sense 4 (because the sand moves as if it were alive and 'eats' things)]

quicksilver *noun*
mercury.

quid *noun* (*plural* **quid**) (*slang*)
£1. [origin unknown]

quid pro quo (*say* kwoh) *noun* (*plural* **quid pro quos**)
something given or done in return for something.
[Latin, = something for something]

quiescent (*say* kwee-ess-ent) *adjective*
inactive or quiet. **quiescence** *noun*
[from Latin *quiescens* = becoming quiet]

quiet *adjective*
1 silent, *Be quiet!* **2** with little sound; not loud or noisy. **3** calm and peaceful; without disturbance, *a quiet life*. **4** (of colours) not bright. **quietly** *adverb*, **quietness** *noun*
quiet *noun*
quietness. [from Latin *quietus* = calm]

quieten *verb* (**quietens, quietening, quietened**)
make or become quiet.

quiff *noun* (*plural* **quiffs**)
an upright tuft of hair. [origin unknown]

quill *noun* (*plural* **quills**)
1 a large feather. **2** a pen made from a large feather. **3** one of the spines on a hedgehog.
[probably from old German]

quilt *noun* (*plural* **quilts**)
a padded bedcover.
quilt *verb* (**quilts, quilting, quilted**)
line material with padding and fix it with lines of stitching.
[from Latin *culcita* = mattress or cushion]

quin *noun* (*plural* **quins**)
a quintuplet.

quince *noun* (*plural* **quinces**)
a hard pear-shaped fruit used for making jam. [from Latin]

quincentenary *noun* (*plural* **quincentenaries**)
the 500th anniversary of something.
[from Latin *quinque* = five, + *centenary*]

quinine (*say* kwin-een) *noun*
a bitter-tasting medicine used to cure malaria. [via Spanish from Quechua (a South American language)]

quintessence *noun*
1 the most essential part of something. **2** a perfect example of a quality. [from Latin *quinta essentia* = the fifth essence (after earth, air, fire, and water, which the alchemists thought everything contained)]

quintet *noun* (*plural* **quintets**)
1 a group of five musicians. **2** a piece of music for five musicians.
[from Italian *quinto* = fifth]

quintuplet *noun* (*plural* **quintuplets**)
each of five children born to the same mother at one time.
[from Latin *quintus* = fifth]

quip *noun* (*plural* **quips**)
a witty remark. [origin unknown]

quirk *noun* (*plural* **quirks**)
1 a peculiarity of a person's behaviour. **2** a trick of fate. [origin unknown]

quit *verb* (**quits, quitting, quitted** or **quit**)
1 leave or abandon. **2** (*informal*) stop doing something. **quitter** *noun*
[same origin as *quiet*]

quite *adverb*
1 completely or entirely, *I am quite all right*. **2** somewhat; to some extent, *She is quite a good swimmer*. **3** really, *It's quite a change*. [same origin as *quiet*]

quits *adjective*
even or equal after retaliating or paying someone, *I think you and I are quits now*.

quiver¹ *noun* (*plural* quivers)
a container for arrows.
[via old French from Germanic]

quiver² *verb* (quivers, quivering, quivered)
tremble. **quiver** *noun* [from Old English]

quixotic (*say* kwiks-ot-ik) *adjective*
very chivalrous and unselfish, often to an
impractical extent. **quixotically** *adverb*
[named after Don Quixote, hero of a
Spanish story]

quiz *noun* (*plural* quizzes)
a series of questions, especially as an
entertainment or competition.
quiz *verb* (quizzes, quizzing, quizzed)
question someone closely.
[origin unknown]

quizzical *adjective*
1 in a questioning way. 2 gently amused.
quizzically *adverb* [from *quiz*]

quoit (*say* koit) *noun* (*plural* quoits)
a ring thrown at a peg in the game of
quoits. [origin unknown]

quorum *noun*
the smallest number of people needed to
make a meeting of a committee etc. valid.
[Latin, = of which people]

quota *noun* (*plural* quotas)
1 a fixed share that must be given or
received or done. 2 a limited amount.
[from Latin *quot* = how many?]

quotation *noun* (*plural* quotations)
1 quoting. 2 something quoted. 3 a
statement of the price.

quotation marks *plural noun*
inverted commas.

quote *verb* (quotes, quoting, quoted)
1 repeat words that were first written or
spoken by someone else. 2 mention
something as proof. 3 state the price of
goods or services that you can supply.
quote *noun* (*plural* quotes)
a quotation.
[from Latin *quotare* = to number]

quoth *verb* (*old use*)
said. [from Old English]

quotient (*say* kwoh-shent) *noun* (*plural*
quotients)
the result of dividing one number by
another. (Compare *product*.)
[from Latin *quotiens* = how many times?]

Rr

rabbi (*say* rab-I) *noun* (*plural* rabbis)
a Jewish religious leader.
[Hebrew, = my master]

rabbit *noun* (*plural* rabbits)
a furry animal with long ears that digs
burrows. [origin unknown]

rabble *noun* (*plural* rabbles)
a disorderly crowd; a mob.
[probably from old German or old Dutch]

rabid (*say* rab-id) *adjective*
1 fanatical, *a rabid tennis fan*. 2 suffering
from rabies.

rabies (*say* ray-beez) *noun*
a fatal disease that affects dogs, cats, etc.
and can infect people.
[Latin, from *rabere* = to be mad]

raccoon *noun* (*plural* raccoons or raccoon)
a North American animal with a bushy,
striped tail.
[from a Native American language]

race¹ *noun* (*plural* races)
1 a competition to be the first to reach a
particular place or to do something. 2 a
strong fast current of water, *the tidal race*.
race *verb* (races, racing, raced)
1 compete in a race. 2 move very fast. **racer**
noun [from Old Norse]

race² *noun* (*plural* races)
a very large group of people thought to
have the same ancestors and with physical
characteristics (e.g. colour of skin and
hair, shape of eyes and nose) that differ
from those of other groups. **racial** *adjective*
[via French from Italian]

racecourse *noun* (*plural* racecourses)
a place where horse races are run.

race relations *noun*
relationships between people of different
races in the same country.

racialism (*say* ray-shal-izm) *noun*
racism. **racialist** *noun*

racism (*say* ray-sizm) *noun*
1 belief that a particular race of people is
better than others. 2 hostility towards
people of other races. **racist** *noun*

rack¹ *noun* (*plural* **racks**)
1 a framework used as a shelf or container.
2 a bar or rail with cogs into which the
cogs of a gear or wheel etc. fit. 3 an ancient
device for torturing people by stretching
them.
rack *verb* (**racks, racking, racked**)
torment, *He was racked with pain.*
rack your brains think hard in trying to
solve a problem.
[from old German or old Dutch]

rack² *noun*
destruction, *The place has gone to rack and
ruin.* [a different spelling of *wreck*]

racket¹ *noun* (*plural* **rackets**)
a bat with strings stretched across a frame,
used in tennis and similar games.
[from Arabic *rahat* = palm of the hand]

racket² *noun* (*plural* **rackets**)
1 a loud noise; a din. 2 a dishonest
business; a swindle. [origin unknown]

racketeer *noun* (*plural* **racketeers**)
a person involved in a dishonest business.
racketeering *noun*

racoon *noun* (*plural* **racoons** or **racoon**)
a different spelling of *raccoon*.

racy *adjective* (**racier, raciest**)
lively and slightly shocking in style, *She
gave a racy account of her travels.*
[originally = having a particular quality:
from *race²*]

radar *noun*
a system or apparatus that uses radio
waves to show on a screen etc. the position
of objects that cannot be seen because of
darkness, fog, distance, etc.
[from the initial letters of *radio detection
and ranging*]

radar trap *noun* (*plural* **radar traps**)
a system using radar that the police use to
catch drivers who are going too fast.

radial *adjective*
1 to do with rays or radii. 2 having spokes
or lines that radiate from a central point.
radially *adverb*

radiant *adjective*
1 radiating light or heat etc. 2 radiated,
radiant heat. 3 looking very bright and
happy. **radiantly** *adverb*, **radiance** *noun*

radiate *verb* (**radiates, radiating, radiated**)
1 send out light, heat, or other energy in
rays. 2 spread out from a central point like
the spokes of a wheel.
[same origin as *radium*]

radiation *noun*
1 the process of radiating. 2 light, heat, or
other energy radiated. 3 the energy or
particles sent out by a radioactive
substance.

radiator *noun* (*plural* **radiators**)
1 a device that gives out heat, especially a
metal case that is heated electrically or
through which steam or hot water flows.
2 a device that cools the engine of a motor
vehicle. [from *radiate*]

radical *adjective*
1 basic and thorough, *radical changes.*
2 wanting to make great reforms, *a radical
politician.* **radically** *adverb*
radical *noun* (*plural* **radicals**)
a person who wants to make great reforms.
[from Latin *radicis* = of a root]

radicchio (*say* ra-**dee**-ki-oh) *noun*
a kind of chicory with dark red leaves.
[Italian, = chicory]

radicle *noun* (*plural* **radicles**)
a root that forms in the seed of a plant.
[from Latin *radicula* = little root]

radio *noun* (*plural* **radios**) (also called
wireless)
1 the process of sending and receiving
sound or pictures by means of
electromagnetic waves without a
connecting wire. 2 an apparatus for
receiving sound (a *receiver*) or sending it
out (a *transmitter*) in this way. 3 sound
broadcasting. [same origin as *radium*]

radio- *prefix*
1 to do with rays or radiation. 2 to do with radio.

radioactive *adjective*
having atoms that break up and send out radiation which produces electrical and chemical effects and penetrates things.
radioactivity *noun*

radio beacon *noun* (*plural* **radio beacons**)
an instrument that sends out radio signals, which aircraft use to find their way.

radiocarbon dating *noun*
the use of a kind of radioactive carbon that decays at a steady rate, to find out how old something is.

radiography *noun*
the production of X-ray photographs.
radiographer *noun*

radiology *noun*
the study of X-rays and similar radiation, especially in treating diseases.
radiologist *noun*

radio telescope *noun* (*plural* **radio telescopes**)
an instrument that can detect radio waves from space.

radiotherapy *noun*
the use of radioactive substances in treating diseases.

radish *noun* (*plural* **radishes**)
a small hard round red vegetable, eaten raw in salads. [from Latin *radix* = root]

radium *noun*
a radioactive substance found in pitchblende, often used in radiotherapy. [from Latin *radius* = a spoke or ray]

radius *noun* (*plural* **radii** or **radiuses**)
1 a straight line from the centre of a circle or sphere to the circumference; the length of this line. 2 a range or distance from a central point, *The school takes pupils living within a radius of ten kilometres.*
[Latin, = a spoke or ray]

radon *noun*
a radioactive gas used in radiotherapy. [from *radium*]

RAF *abbreviation*
Royal Air Force.

raffia *noun*
soft fibre from the leaves of a kind of palm tree. [from Malagasy (the language of Madagascar)]

raffish *adjective*
cheerfully disreputable. [from *riff-raff*]

raffle *noun* (*plural* **raffles**)
a kind of lottery, usually to raise money for a charity.
raffle *verb* (**raffles, raffling, raffled**)
offer something as a prize in a raffle. [probably from French]

raft *noun* (*plural* **rafts**)
a flat floating structure made of wood etc., used as a boat. [from Old Norse]

rafter *noun* (*plural* **rafters**)
any of the long sloping pieces of wood that hold up a roof. [from Old English]

rag[1] *noun* (*plural* **rags**)
1 an old or torn piece of cloth. 2 a piece of ragtime music. [from *ragged*]

rag[2] *noun* (*plural* **rags**)
a carnival held by students to collect money for charity.
rag *verb* (**rags, ragging, ragged**) (*slang*)
tease. [origin unknown]

rage *noun* (*plural* **rages**)
1 great or violent anger. 2 a craze, *Skateboarding was all the rage.*
rage *verb* (**rages, raging, raged**)
1 be very angry. 2 be violent or noisy, *A storm was raging.*
[from old French; related to *rabies*]

ragged *adjective*
1 torn or frayed. 2 wearing torn clothes. 3 jagged. 4 irregular or uneven, *a ragged performance.*
[from Old Norse *roggvathr* = tufted]

raglan *adjective*
(of a sleeve) joined to a garment by sloping seams. [named after Lord Raglan, British military commander (died 1855), who wore a coat with raglan sleeves]

ragtime *noun*
a kind of jazz music.
[perhaps from *ragged time*]

raid *noun* (*plural* **raids**)
1 a sudden attack. 2 a surprise visit by
police etc. to arrest people or seize illegal
goods.
raid *verb* (**raids, raiding, raided**)
make a raid on a place. **raider** *noun*
[from Old English]

rail¹ *noun* (*plural* **rails**)
1 a level or sloping bar for hanging things
on or forming part of a fence, banisters, etc.
2 a long metal bar forming part of a
railway track.
by rail on a train.
[from old French; related to *rule*]

rail² *verb* (**rails, railing, railed**)
protest angrily or bitterly.
[via French from Portuguese]

railings *plural noun*
a fence made of metal bars.

railway *noun*
1 the parallel metal bars that trains travel
on. 2 (*plural* **railways**) a system of
transport using rails.

raiment *noun* (*old use*)
clothing. [from *array*]

rain *noun*
drops of water that fall from the sky.
rainy *adjective*
rain *verb* (**rains, raining, rained**)
1 fall as rain or like rain. 2 send down like
rain, *They rained blows on him.*
[from Old English]

rainbow *noun* (*plural* **rainbows**)
a curved band of colours seen in the sky
when the sun shines through rain.

raincoat *noun* (*plural* **raincoats**)
a waterproof coat.

raindrop *noun* (*plural* **raindrops**)
a single drop of rain.

rainfall *noun*
the amount of rain that falls in a particular
place or time.

rainforest *noun* (*plural* **rainforests**)
a dense tropical forest in an area of very
heavy rainfall.

raise *verb* (**raises, raising, raised**)
1 move something to a higher place or an
upright position. 2 increase the amount or
level of something. 3 collect; manage to
obtain, *They raised £100 for Oxfam.* 4 bring
up young children or animals, *raise a
family.* 5 rouse or cause, *She raised a laugh
with her joke.* 6 put forward, *We raised
objections.* 7 end a siege. [from Old Norse]

raisin *noun* (*plural* **raisins**)
a dried grape. [French, = grape]

raison d'être (*say* ray-zawn **detr**) *noun*
(*plural* **raisons d'être**)
the purpose of a thing's existence.
[French, = reason for being]

raj (*say* rahj) *noun*
the period of Indian history when the
country was ruled by Britain.
[Hindi, = reign]

rajah *noun* (*plural* **rajahs**)
an Indian king or prince. (Compare *ranee*.)
[from Sanskrit]

rake¹ *noun* (*plural* **rakes**)
a gardening tool with a row of short spikes
fixed to a long handle.
rake *verb* (**rakes, raking, raked**)
1 gather or smooth with a rake. 2 search.
3 gather; collect, *raking it in.*
rake up 1 collect. 2 remind people of an old
scandal etc., *Don't rake that up.*
[from Old English]

rake² *noun* (*plural* **rakes**)
a man who lives an irresponsible and
immoral life. [from an old word *rakehell*]

rakish (*say* ray-kish) *adjective*
1 immoral or irresponsible. 2 jaunty.
[from *rake²*]

rally *noun* (*plural* **rallies**)
1 a large meeting to support something or
share an interest. 2 a competition to test
skill in driving, *the Monte Carlo Rally.* 3 a
series of strokes in tennis before a point is
scored. 4 a recovery.

rally *verb* (**rallies, rallying, rallied**)
1 bring or come together for a united effort, *They rallied support. People rallied round.* 2 revive; recover strength.
[from French]

RAM *abbreviation*
random-access memory (in a computer), with contents that can be retrieved or stored directly without having to read through items already stored.

ram *noun* (*plural* **rams**)
1 a male sheep. 2 a device for ramming things.
ram *verb* (**rams, ramming, rammed**)
push one thing hard against another.
[from Old English]

Ramadan *noun*
the ninth month of the Muslim year, when Muslims do not eat or drink between sunrise and sunset.
[Arabic, from *ramida* = to be parched]

ramble *noun* (*plural* **rambles**)
a long walk in the country.
ramble *verb* (**rambles, rambling, rambled**)
1 go for a ramble; wander. 2 talk or write a lot without keeping to the subject. **rambler** *noun* [origin unknown]

ramifications *plural noun*
1 the branches of a structure. 2 the many effects of a plan or action.
[from Latin *ramificare* = to branch out]

ramp *noun* (*plural* **ramps**)
a slope joining two different levels.
[from French *ramper* = to climb]

rampage *verb* (**rampages, rampaging, rampaged**)
rush about wildly or destructively.
on the rampage rampaging.
[origin unknown]

rampant *adjective*
1 growing or increasing unrestrained, *Disease was rampant in the poorer districts.* 2 (of an animal on coats of arms) standing upright on a hind leg, *a lion rampant.*
[same origin as *ramp*]

rampart *noun* (*plural* **ramparts**)
a wide bank of earth built as a fortification or a wall on top of this.
[from French *remparer* = fortify]

ramrod *noun* (*plural* **ramrods**)
a straight rod formerly used for ramming an explosive into a gun.
like a ramrod very stiff and straight.

ramshackle *adjective*
badly made and rickety, *a ramshackle hut.*
[from *ransack*]

ranch *noun* (*plural* **ranches**)
a large cattle-farm in America.
[from Spanish]

rancid *adjective*
smelling or tasting unpleasant like stale fat. [from Latin]

rancour (*say* rank-er) *noun*
bitter resentment or ill will.
rancorous *adjective*
[from old French; related to *rancid*]

random *noun*
at random using no particular order or method, *In bingo, numbers are chosen at random.*
random *adjective*
done or taken at random, *a random sample.*
[via old French from Germanic]

ranee (*say* rah-nee) *noun* (*plural* **ranees**)
a rajah's wife or widow.
[from Sanskrit]

range *noun* (*plural* **ranges**)
1 a line or series of things, *a range of mountains.* 2 the limits between which things exist or are available; an extent, *a wide range of goods.* 3 the distance that a gun can shoot, an aircraft can travel, a sound can be heard, etc. 4 a place with targets for shooting-practice. 5 a large open area of grazing-land or hunting-ground. 6 a kitchen fireplace with ovens.
range *verb* (**ranges, ranging, ranged**)
1 exist between two limits; extend, *Prices ranged from £1 to £50.* 2 arrange. 3 move over a wide area; wander.
[from old French; related to *rank¹*]

Ranger *noun* (*plural* **Rangers**)
a senior Guide.

ranger *noun* (*plural* **rangers**)
someone who looks after or patrols a park, forest, etc. [from *range*]

rank¹ *noun* (*plural* ranks)
1 a line of people or things. 2 a place where taxis stand to await customers. 3 a position in a series of different levels, *He holds the rank of sergeant.*
rank *verb* (ranks, ranking, ranked)
1 arrange in a rank or ranks. 2 have a certain rank or place, *She ranks among the greatest novelists.*
[via old French from Germanic]

rank² *adjective* (ranker, rankest)
1 growing too thickly and coarsely.
2 smelling very unpleasant.
3 unmistakably bad, *rank injustice.*
rankly *adverb*, **rankness** *noun*
[from Old English]

rank and file *noun*
the ordinary people or soldiers, not the leaders.

rankle *verb* (rankles, rankling, rankled)
cause lasting annoyance or resentment.
[from old French]

ransack *verb* (ransacks, ransacking, ransacked)
1 search thoroughly or roughly. 2 rob or pillage a place. [from Old Norse]

ransom *noun* (*plural* ransoms)
money that has to be paid for a prisoner to be set free.
hold to ransom hold someone captive or in your power and demand ransom.
ransom *verb* (ransoms, ransoming, ransomed)
1 free someone by paying a ransom. 2 get a ransom for someone.
[from old French; related to *redeem*]

rant *verb* (rants, ranting, ranted)
speak loudly and violently. [from Dutch]

rap *verb* (raps, rapping, rapped)
1 knock loudly. 2 (*informal*) reprimand.
3 (*slang*) chat. 4 speak rhymes with a backing of rock music.
rap *noun* (*plural* raps)
1 a rapping movement or sound.
2 (*informal*) blame or punishment, *take the rap.* 3 (*slang*) a chat. 4 rhymes spoken with a backing of rock music.
[imitating the sound]

rapacious (*say* ra-pay-shus) *adjective*
1 greedy. 2 using threats or force to get everything you can.
rapaciously *adverb*, **rapacity** *noun*
[from Latin *rapax* = grasping]

rape¹ *noun* (*plural* rapes)
the act of having sexual intercourse with a person without her or his consent.
rape *verb* (rapes, raping, raped)
force someone to have sexual intercourse.
rapist *noun*
[from Latin *rapere* = take by force]

rape² *noun*
a plant grown as food for sheep and for its seed from which oil is obtained.
[from Latin *rapum* = turnip (to which it is related)]

rapid *adjective*
moving very quickly; swift. **rapidly** *adverb*, **rapidity** *noun* [from Latin]

rapids *plural noun*
part of a river where the water flows very quickly.

rapier *noun* (*plural* rapiers)
a thin lightweight sword.
[probably from Dutch]

rapt *adjective*
very intent and absorbed; enraptured.
raptly *adverb* [from Latin *raptum* = seized]

rapture *noun*
very great delight.
rapturous *adjective*, **rapturously** *adverb*
[from old French; related to *rapt*]

rare¹ *adjective* (rarer, rarest)
1 unusual; not often found or happening.
2 (of air) thin; below normal pressure.
rarely *adverb*, **rareness** *noun*, **rarity** *noun*
[from Latin]

rare² *adjective*
(of meat) only lightly cooked; undercooked.
[from Old English]

rarefied *adjective*
1 (of air) rare. 2 remote from everyday life, *the rarefied atmosphere of the university.*

rascal *noun* (*plural* rascals)
a dishonest or mischievous person; a rogue. **rascally** *adjective* [from old French]

rash¹ *adjective*
doing something or done without thinking
of the possible risks or effects.
rashly *adverb*, **rashness** *noun*
[probably from Old English]

rash² *noun* (*plural* **rashes**)
1 an outbreak of spots or patches on the
skin. **2** a number of (usually unwelcome)
events happening in a short time, *a rash of
accidents*. [probably from old French]

rasher *noun* (*plural* **rashers**)
a slice of bacon. [origin unknown]

rasp *noun* (*plural* **rasps**)
1 a file with sharp points on its surface. **2** a
rough grating sound.
rasp *verb* (**rasps, rasping, rasped**)
1 scrape roughly. **2** make a rough grating
sound or effect.
[via old French from Germanic]

raspberry *noun* (*plural* **raspberries**)
a small soft red fruit. [origin unknown]

Rastafarian *noun* (*plural* **Rastafarians**)
a member of a religious group that started
in Jamaica. [from *Ras Tafari* (*ras* = chief),
the title of a former Ethiopian king whom
the group reveres]

rat *noun* (*plural* **rats**)
1 an animal like a large mouse. **2** an
unpleasant or treacherous person.
[from Old English]

ratchet *noun* (*plural* **ratchets**)
a row of notches on a bar or wheel in which
a device (a *pawl*) catches to prevent it
running backwards. [from French]

rate *noun* (*plural* **rates**)
1 speed, *The train travelled at a great rate.*
2 a measure of cost, value, etc., *Postage
rates went up.* **3** quality or standard, *first-
rate.*
at any rate anyway.
rate *verb* (**rates, rating, rated**)
1 put a value on something. **2** regard as, *He
rated me among his friends.*
[from Latin *ratum* = reckoned]

rather *adverb*
1 slightly or somewhat, *It's rather dark.*
2 preferably or more willingly, *I would
rather not go.* **3** more exactly, *He is lazy*

rather than stupid. **4** (*informal*) definitely,
yes, *'Will you come?' 'Rather!'*
[from Old English]

ratify *verb* (**ratifies, ratifying, ratified**)
confirm or agree to something officially,
They ratified the treaty. **ratification** *noun*
[from Latin *ratus* = fixed or established]

rating *noun* (*plural* **ratings**)
1 the way something is rated. **2** a sailor
who is not an officer. [from *rate*]

ratio (*say* ray-shee-oh) *noun* (*plural* **ratios**)
1 the relationship between two numbers,
given by the quotient, *The ratio of 2 to 10*
= $2:10 = \frac{2}{10} = \frac{1}{5}$. **2** proportion, *Mix flour and
butter in the ratio of two to one* (= two
measures of flour to one measure of
butter). [Latin, = reasoning, reckoning]

ration *noun* (*plural* **rations**)
an amount allowed to one person.
ration *verb* (**rations, rationing, rationed**)
share something out in fixed amounts.
[French; related to *ratio*]

rational *adjective*
1 reasonable or sane. **2** able to reason,
Plants are not rational. **rationally** *adverb*,
rationality *noun* [same origin as *ratio*]

rationalize *verb* (**rationalizes, rationalizing,
rationalized**)
1 make a thing logical and consistent,
*Attempts to rationalize English spelling
have failed.* **2** invent a reasonable
explanation of something, *She rationalized
her meanness by calling it economy.* **3** make
an industry etc. more efficient by
reorganizing it. **rationalization** *noun*

rations *plural noun*
a fixed daily amount of food issued to a
soldier etc.

rat race *noun*
a continuous struggle for success in a
career, business, etc.

rattle *verb* (**rattles, rattling, rattled**)
1 make a series of short sharp hard sounds.
2 make a person nervous or flustered.
rattle off say or recite rapidly.
rattle *noun* (*plural* **rattles**)
1 a rattling sound. **2** a device or baby's toy
that rattles. [imitating the sound]

rattlesnake *noun* (*plural* **rattlesnakes**)
a poisonous American snake with a tail
that rattles.

rattling *adjective*
1 that rattles. **2** vigorous or brisk, *a
rattling pace.*

ratty *adjective* (**rattier, rattiest**) (*informal*)
angry or irritable. [from *rat*]

raucous (*say* raw-kus) *adjective*
loud and harsh, *a raucous voice.*
[from Latin *raucus* = hoarse]

ravage *verb* (**ravages, ravaging, ravaged**)
do great damage to something; devastate.

ravages *plural noun*
damaging effects, *the ravages of war.*
[same origin as *ravine*]

rave *verb* (**raves, raving, raved**)
1 talk wildly or angrily or madly. **2** talk
rapturously about something.
rave *noun* (*plural* **raves**)
a big party or event with loud fast music
and flashing lights. [from old French]

raven *noun* (*plural* **ravens**)
a large black bird, related to the crow.
[from Old English]

ravenous *adjective*
very hungry. **ravenously** *adverb*
[from French *raviner* = rush, ravage]

ravine (*say* ra-veen) *noun* (*plural* **ravines**)
a deep narrow gorge or valley.
[French, = a rush of water (because a
ravine is cut by rushing water)]

ravish *verb* (**ravishes, ravishing, ravished**)
1 rape. **2** enrapture.
[from old French; related to *rape*[1]]

ravishing *adjective*
very beautiful.

raw *adjective*
1 not cooked. **2** in the natural state; not yet
processed, *raw materials.* **3** without
experience, *raw recruits.* **4** with the skin
removed, *a raw wound.* **5** cold and damp, *a
raw morning.* **rawness** *noun*
[from Old English]

raw deal *noun*
unfair treatment.

raw material *noun* (*plural* **raw materials**)
natural substances used in industry, *rich
in iron ore, coal, and other raw materials.*

ray[1] *noun* (*plural* **rays**)
1 a thin line of light, heat, or other
radiation. **2** each of a set of lines or parts
extending from a centre.
[from Latin *radius*]

ray[2] *noun* (*plural* **ray** or **rays**)
a large sea fish with a flat body and a long
tail. [from Latin *raia*]

rayon *noun*
a synthetic fibre or cloth made from
cellulose. [a made-up word, probably based
on French *rayon* = a ray of light (because of
its shiny surface)]

raze *verb* (**razes, razing, razed**)
destroy a building or town completely, *raze
it to the ground.*
[from Latin *rasum* = scraped]

razor *noun* (*plural* **razors**)
a device with a very sharp blade, especially
one used for shaving. [same origin as *raze*]

razzmatazz *noun* (*informal*)
showy publicity. [origin unknown]

RC *abbreviation*
Roman Catholic.

re- *prefix*
1 again (as in *rebuild*). **2** back again, to an
earlier condition (as in *reopen*). **3** in
return; to each other (as in *react*). **4** against
(as in *rebel*). **5** away or down (as in *recede*).
[from Latin]

reach *verb* (**reaches, reaching, reached**)
1 go as far as; arrive at a place or thing.
2 stretch out your hand to get or touch
something. **reachable** *adjective*
reach *noun* (*plural* **reaches**)
1 the distance a person or thing can reach.
2 a distance you can easily travel, *We live
within reach of the sea.* **3** a straight stretch
of a river or canal. [from Old English]

react *verb* (**reacts, reacting, reacted**)
respond to something; have a reaction.
[from *re-* + Latin *agere* = act or do]

reaction *noun* (*plural* **reactions**)
1 an effect or feeling etc. produced in one person or thing by another. **2** a chemical change caused when substances act upon each other.

reactionary *adjective*
opposed to progress or reform.

reactor *noun* (*plural* **reactors**)
an apparatus for producing nuclear power in a controlled way.

read *verb* (**reads, reading, read** (*say as* red))
1 look at something written or printed and understand it or say it aloud. **2** (of a computer) copy, search, or extract data. **3** indicate or register, *The thermometer reads 20° Celsius.* **readable** *adjective*
[from Old English]

reader *noun* (*plural* **readers**)
1 a person who reads. **2** a book that helps you learn to read.

readily (*say* red-il-ee) *adverb*
1 willingly. **2** easily; without any difficulty.

reading *noun* (*plural* **readings**)
1 reading books. **2** the figure shown on a meter or gauge. **3** a gathering of people at which something is read aloud, *a poetry reading.*

ready *adjective* (**readier, readiest**)
able or willing to do something or be used immediately; prepared. **readiness** *noun*
at the ready ready for use or action.
ready *adverb*
beforehand, *This meat is ready cooked.*
ready-made *adjective* [from Old English]

reagent *noun* (*plural* **reagents**)
a substance used in a chemical reaction, especially to detect another substance.
[from *re-* + *agent*]

real *adjective*
1 existing or true; not imaginary. **2** genuine, not an imitation, *real pearls.* **3** (of food) regarded as superior because it is produced by traditional methods, *real ale.* [from Latin]

realism *noun*
seeing or showing things as they really are.
realist *noun*, **realistic** *adjective*,
realistically *adverb*

reality *noun* (*plural* **realities**)
1 what is real, *You must face reality.*
2 something real, *Her worst fears had become a reality.*

realize *verb* (**realizes, realizing, realized**)
1 be fully aware of something; accept something as true. **2** make a hope or plan etc. happen, *She realized her ambition to become a racing driver.* **3** obtain money in exchange for something by selling it.
realization *noun* [from *real* + *-ize*]

really *adverb*
1 truly or in fact. **2** very, *She's really clever.*

realm (*say* relm) *noun* (*plural* **realms**)
1 a kingdom. **2** an area of knowledge, interest, etc., *in the realms of science.*
[from old French; related to *regiment*]

ream *noun* (*plural* **reams**)
500 (originally 480) sheets of paper.
[via French from Arabic *rizma* = bundle]

reams *plural noun*
a large quantity of writing.

reap *verb* (**reaps, reaping, reaped**)
1 cut down and gather corn when it is ripe.
2 obtain as the result of something done, *They reaped great benefit from their training.* **reaper** *noun* [from Old English]

reappear *verb* (**reappears, reappearing, reappeared**)
appear again.

reappraise *verb* (**reappraises, reappraising, reappraised**)
think about or examine something again.
reappraisal *noun* [from *re-* + *appraise*]

rear[1] *noun*
the back part.
rear *adjective*
placed at the rear.
[from Latin *retro-* = back]

rear[2] *verb* (**rears, rearing, reared**)
1 bring up young children or animals.
2 rise up; raise itself on hind legs, *The horse reared in fright.* **3** build or set up a monument etc. [from Old English]

rearguard *noun* (*plural* **rearguards**)
troops protecting the rear of an army.

fight a rearguard action go on defending or resisting something even though you are losing.

rearrange *verb* (**rearranges, rearranging, rearranged**)
arrange in a different way or order.
rearrangement *noun*

reason *noun* (*plural* **reasons**)
1 a cause or explanation of something.
2 reasoning; common sense, *Listen to reason.*

USAGE: Do not use the phrase *the reason is* with the word *because* (which means the same thing). Correct usage is *We cannot come. The reason is that we both have flu* (not 'The reason is because ...').

reason *verb* (**reasons, reasoning, reasoned**)
1 use your ability to think and draw conclusions. **2** try to persuade someone by giving reasons, *We reasoned with the rebels.*
[from old French; related to *ratio*]

reasonable *adjective*
1 ready to use or listen to reason; sensible or logical. **2** fair or moderate; not expensive, *reasonable prices.* **3** acceptable or fairly good, *a reasonable standard of living.* **reasonably** *adverb*

reassure *verb* (**reassures, reassuring, reassured**)
restore someone's confidence by removing doubts and fears.
reassurance *noun*

rebate *noun* (*plural* **rebates**)
a reduction in the amount to be paid; a partial refund.
[from *re-* + French *abattre* = abate]

rebel (*say* rib-el) *verb* (**rebels, rebelling, rebelled**)
refuse to obey someone in authority, especially the government; fight against the rulers of your own country.
rebel (*say* reb-el) *noun* (*plural* **rebels**)
someone who rebels against the government, or against accepted standards of behaviour.
rebellion *noun*, **rebellious** *adjective*
[from *re-* + Latin *bellum* = war (originally referring to a defeated enemy who began to fight again)]

rebirth *noun*
a return to life or activity; a revival of something.

rebound *verb* (**rebounds, rebounding, rebounded**)
bounce back after hitting something.
rebound *noun*

rebuff *noun* (*plural* **rebuffs**)
an unkind refusal; a snub. **rebuff** *verb*
[from *re-* + Italian *buffo* = a gust]

rebuild *verb* (**rebuilds, rebuilding, rebuilt**)
build something again after it has been destroyed.

rebuke *verb* (**rebukes, rebuking, rebuked**)
speak severely to a person who has done wrong. **rebuke** *noun*
[originally = to force back: from *re-* + old French *buker* = to hit]

rebut *verb* (**rebuts, rebutting, rebutted**)
prove that something said about you is not true. **rebuttal** *noun*
[from *re-* + French *boter* = to butt]

recalcitrant *adjective*
disobedient or uncooperative.
recalcitrance *noun*
[from Latin *recalcitrare* = to kick back]

recall *verb* (**recalls, recalling, recalled**)
1 ask a person to come back. **2** ask for something to be returned. **3** bring back into the mind; remember.
recall *noun*
1 an order to return. **2** the ability to remember; remembering.

recant *verb* (**recants, recanting, recanted**)
state formally and publicly that you no longer believe something. **recantation** *noun*
[from *re-* + Latin *cantare* = sing]

recap *verb* (**recaps, recapping, recapped**)
(*informal*)
recapitulate. **recap** *noun*

recapitulate *verb* (**recapitulates, recapitulating, recapitulated**)
state again the main points of what has been said. **recapitulation** *noun*
[from *re-* + Latin *capitulare* = arrange under headings]

recapture *verb* (recaptures, recapturing, recaptured)
1 capture again; recover. 2 bring or get back a mood or feeling. **recapture** *noun*

recede *verb* (recedes, receding, receded)
go back from a certain point, *The floods receded.* [from re- + Latin *cedere* = go]

receipt (*say* ris-**eet**) *noun* (*plural* receipts)
1 a written statement that money has been paid or something has been received.
2 receiving something.

receive *verb* (receives, receiving, received)
1 take or get something that is given or sent. 2 greet someone who comes.
[from re- + Latin *capere* = take]

receiver *noun* (*plural* receivers)
1 a person or thing that receives something. 2 a person who buys and sells stolen goods. 3 an official who takes charge of a bankrupt person's property. 4 a radio or television set that receives broadcasts. 5 the part of a telephone that receives the sound and is held to a person's ear.

recent *adjective*
happening or made or done a short time ago. **recently** *adverb* [from Latin]

receptacle *noun* (*plural* receptacles)
something for holding or containing what is put into it. [same origin as *receive*]

reception *noun* (*plural* receptions)
1 the way a person or thing is received. 2 a formal party to receive guests, *a wedding reception.* 3 a place in a hotel or office etc. where visitors are received and registered.

receptionist *noun* (*plural* receptionists)
a person whose job is to receive and direct visitors, patients, etc.

receptive *adjective*
quick or willing to receive ideas etc.

recess (*say* ris-**ess**) *noun* (*plural* recesses)
1 an alcove. 2 a time when work or business is stopped for a while.
[same origin as *recede*]

recession *noun* (*plural* recessions)
1 receding from a point. 2 a reduction in trade or prosperity.

recharge *verb* (recharges, recharging, recharged)
1 reload or refill. 2 put an electric charge in a used battery so that it will work again. 3 accuse again. **rechargeable** *adjective*

recipe (*say* ress-ip-ee) *noun* (*plural* recipes)
instructions for preparing or cooking food.
[Latin, = take (used at the beginning of a list of ingredients)]

recipient *noun* (*plural* recipients)
a person who receives something.

reciprocal (*say* ris-**ip**-rok-al) *adjective*
given and received; mutual, *reciprocal help.* **reciprocally** *adverb*, **reciprocity** *noun*
reciprocal *noun* (*plural* reciprocals)
a reversed fraction, $\frac{3}{2}$ *is the reciprocal of* $\frac{2}{3}$.
[from Latin *reciprocus* = moving backwards and forwards]

reciprocate *verb* (reciprocates, reciprocating, reciprocated)
give and receive; do the same thing in return, *She did not reciprocate his love.*
reciprocation *noun*
[same origin as *reciprocal*]

recital *noun* (*plural* recitals)
1 reciting something. 2 a musical entertainment given by one performer or group.

recitative (*say* res-it-a-**teev**) *noun* (*plural* recitatives)
a speech sung to music in an oratorio or opera.
[from Italian *recitativo* = something recited]

recite *verb* (recites, reciting, recited)
say a poem etc. aloud from memory.
recitation *noun*
[from Latin *recitare* = to read aloud]

reckless *adjective*
rash; ignoring risk or danger.
recklessly *adverb*, **recklessness** *noun*
[from an old word *reck* = heed, + -*less*]

reckon *verb* (reckons, reckoning, reckoned)
1 calculate or count up. 2 have as an opinion; feel confident, *I reckon we shall win.*
reckon with think about or deal with, *We didn't reckon with the train strike when we planned our journey.*
[from Old English]

reclaim *verb* (reclaims, reclaiming, reclaimed)
1 claim or get something back. 2 make a thing usable again, *reclaimed land.*
reclamation *noun*

recline *verb* (reclines, reclining, reclined)
lean or lie back.
[from *re-* + Latin *-clinare* = to lean]

recluse *noun* (*plural* recluses)
a person who lives alone and avoids mixing with people.
[from *re-* + Latin *clausum* = shut]

recognize *verb* (recognizes, recognizing, recognized)
1 know who someone is or what something is because you have seen that person or thing before. 2 realize, *We recognize the truth of what you said.* 3 accept something as genuine, welcome, or lawful etc., *Nine countries recognized the island's new government.*
recognition *noun*, recognizable *adjective*
[from *re-* + Latin *cognoscere* = know]

recoil *verb* (recoils, recoiling, recoiled)
1 move back suddenly in shock or disgust. 2 (of a gun) jerk backwards when it is fired.
[from French]

recollect *verb* (recollects, recollecting, recollected)
remember. recollection *noun*
[from *re-* + Latin *colligere* = collect]

recommend *verb* (recommends, recommending, recommended)
say that a person or thing would be a good one to do a job or achieve something.
recommendation *noun*
[from *re-* + Latin *commendare* = commend]

recompense *verb* (recompenses, recompensing, recompensed)
repay or reward someone; compensate.
recompense *noun* [from *re-* + Latin *compensare* = compensate]

reconcile *verb* (reconciles, reconciling, reconciled)
1 make people who have quarrelled become friendly again. 2 persuade a person to put up with something, *New frames reconciled him to wearing glasses.* 3 make things agree, *I cannot reconcile*
what you say with what you do.
reconciliation *noun*
[from *re-* + Latin *conciliare* = conciliate]

recondition *verb* (reconditions, reconditioning, reconditioned)
overhaul and repair.

reconnaissance (*say* rik-on-i-sans) *noun*
an exploration of an area, especially in order to gather information about it for military purposes. [French, = recognition]

reconnoitre *verb* (reconnoitres, reconnoitring, reconnoitred)
make a reconnaissance of an area.
[old French, = recognize]

reconsider *verb* (reconsiders, reconsidering, reconsidered)
consider something again and perhaps change an earlier decision.
reconsideration *noun*

reconstitute *verb* (reconstitutes, reconstituting, reconstituted)
1 to form something again, especially in a different way. 2 to make dried food edible again by adding water.

reconstruct *verb* (reconstructs, reconstructing, reconstructed)
1 construct or build something again. 2 create or act past events again, *Police reconstructed the robbery.*
reconstruction *noun*

record (*say* rek-ord) *noun* (*plural* records)
1 information kept in a permanent form, e.g. written or printed. 2 a disc on which sound has been recorded. 3 facts known about a person's past life or career etc., *She has a good school record.* 4 the best performance in a sport etc., or the most remarkable event of its kind, *He holds the record for the high jump.*
record (*say* rik-ord) *verb* (records, recording, recorded)
1 put something down in writing or other permanent form. 2 store sounds or scenes (e.g. television pictures) on a disc or magnetic tape etc. so that you can play or show them later. [from French]

recorder *noun* (*plural* recorders)
1 a kind of flute held downwards from the player's mouth. 2 a person or thing that records something.

record player noun (plural record players)
a device for reproducing sound from
records.

recount verb (recounts, recounting,
recounted)
give an account of, We recounted our
adventures.
[from old French reconter = tell]

re-count verb (re-counts, re-counting,
re-counted)
count something again.

recoup (say ri-koop) verb (recoups,
recouping, recouped)
recover the cost of an investment etc. or of
a loss. [from old French]

USAGE: Note that this word does not mean
recuperate.

recourse noun
a source of help.
have recourse to go to a person or thing for
help.
[from old French]

recover verb (recovers, recovering,
recovered)
1 get something back again after losing it;
regain. 2 get well again after being ill or
weak. **recovery** noun
[from old French; related to recuperate]

re-cover verb (re-covers, re-covering,
re-covered)
put a new cover on something.

recreation noun (plural recreations)
1 refreshing your mind or body after work
through an enjoyable pastime. 2 a game or
hobby etc. that is an enjoyable pastime.
recreational adjective
[from re- + Latin creatio = creation]

recrimination noun (plural
recriminations)
an angry retort or accusation made against
a person who has criticized or blamed you.
[from re- + Latin criminare = accuse]

recrudescence (say rek-roo-dess-ens)
noun
a fresh outbreak of a disease or trouble etc.
[from re- + Latin crudescens = becoming
raw]

recruit noun (plural recruits)
1 a person who has just joined the armed
forces. 2 a new member of a society or
group etc.
recruit verb (recruits, recruiting, recruited)
enlist recruits. **recruitment** noun
[from French recroître = to increase again]

rectangle noun (plural rectangles)
a shape with four sides and four right
angles. **rectangular** adjective [from Latin
rectus = straight or right, + angle]

rectify verb (rectifies, rectifying, rectified)
correct or put something right. **rectification**
noun [from Latin rectus = right]

rectilinear adjective
with straight lines, Squares and triangles
are rectilinear figures.
[from Latin rectus = straight, + linear]

rectitude noun
moral goodness; honest or straightforward
behaviour. [same origin as rectify]

rectum noun (plural rectums or recta)
the last part of the large intestine, ending
at the anus. [Latin, = straight (intestine)]

recumbent adjective
lying down.
[from re- + Latin cumbens = lying]

recuperate verb (recuperates, recuperating,
recuperated)
get better after an illness. **recuperation**
noun [from Latin]

recur verb (recurs, recurring, recurred)
happen again; keep on happening.
recurrent adjective, **recurrence** noun
[from re- + Latin currere = to run]

recycle verb (recycles, recycling, recycled)
convert waste material into a form in
which it can be reused.

red adjective (redder, reddest)
1 of the colour of blood or a colour rather
like this. 2 to do with Communists;
favouring Communism. **redness** noun
red noun
1 red colour. 2 a Communist.
in the red in debt (because debts were
entered in red in account-books).
[from Old English]

red deer *noun* (*plural* **red deer**)
a kind of large deer with a reddish-brown coat, found in Europe and Asia.

redden *verb* (**reddens, reddening, reddened**)
make or become red.

reddish *adjective*
rather red.

redeem *verb* (**redeems, redeeming, redeemed**)
1 buy something back or pay off a debt. 2 save a person from damnation, *Christians believe that Christ redeemed us all.* 3 make up for faults, *His one redeeming feature is his kindness.*
redeemer *noun*, **redemption** *noun*
[from *re-* + Latin *emere* = buy]

redevelop *verb* (**redevelops, redeveloping, redeveloped**)
develop land etc. in a different way.
redevelopment *noun*

red-handed *adjective*
catch red-handed catch while actually committing a crime.

redhead *noun* (*plural* **redheads**)
a person with reddish hair.

red herring *noun* (*plural* **red herrings**)
something that draws attention away from the main subject; a misleading clue. [because a red herring (= a kipper) drawn across a fox's path put hounds off the scent]

red-hot *adjective*
very hot; so hot that it has turned red.

Red Indian *noun* (*plural* **Red Indians**)
(*old use*) a Native American from North America.

USAGE: see note at *Indian*.

red-light district *noun* (*plural* **red-light districts**)
an area in a city where there are many prostitutes, strip clubs, etc.

red meat *noun*
meat, such as beef, lamb, or mutton, which is red when raw.

redolent (*say* red-ol-ent) *adjective*
1 having a strong smell, *redolent of onions.* 2 full of memories, *a castle redolent of romance.*
[from *re-* + Latin *olens* = giving off a smell]

redoubtable *adjective*
formidable.
[from French *redouter* = to fear]

redound *verb* (**redounds, redounding, redounded**)
come back as an advantage or disadvantage, *This will redound to our credit.* [from Latin *redundare* = overflow]

redress *verb* (**redresses, redressing, redressed**)
set right or rectify, *redress the balance.*
redress *noun*
1 redressing. 2 compensation, *You should seek redress for this damage.* [from French]

red tape *noun*
use of too many rules and forms in official business. [because bundles of official papers are tied up with red or pink tape]

reduce *verb* (**reduces, reducing, reduced**)
1 make or become smaller or less. 2 force someone into a condition or situation, *He was reduced to borrowing the money.*
reduction *noun*
[from *re-* + Latin *ducere* = bring]

redundant *adjective*
not needed, especially for a particular job.
redundancy *noun* [same origin as *redound*]

re-echo *verb* (**re-echoes, re-echoing, re-echoed**)
echo; go on echoing.

reed *noun* (*plural* **reeds**)
1 a tall plant that grows in water or marshy ground. 2 a thin strip that vibrates to make the sound in a clarinet, saxophone, oboe, etc. [from Old English]

reedy *adjective* (**reedier, reediest**)
1 full of reeds. 2 (of a voice) having a thin high tone like a reed instrument.
reediness *noun*

reef¹ *noun* (*plural* **reefs**)
a ridge of rock or sand etc., especially one near the surface of the sea. [via old German or old Dutch from Old Norse]

reef² *verb* (**reefs, reefing, reefed**)
shorten a sail by drawing in a strip (called a *reef*) at the top or bottom to reduce the area exposed to the wind.
[via Dutch from Old Norse]

reef knot *noun*
a symmetrical double knot that is very secure. [from *reef²*]

reek *verb* (**reeks, reeking, reeked**)
smell strongly or unpleasantly. **reek** *noun*
[from Old English]

reel *noun* (*plural* **reels**)
1 a spool. 2 a lively Scottish dance.
reel *verb* (**reels, reeling, reeled**)
1 wind something onto or off a reel.
2 stagger.
reel off say something quickly.
[from Old English]

re-elect *verb* (**re-elects, re-electing, re-elected**)
elect again.

re-enter *verb* (**re-enters, re-entering, re-entered**)
enter again.

re-examine *verb* (**re-examines, re-examining, re-examined**)
examine again.

ref *noun* (*plural* **refs**) (*informal*)
a referee.

refectory *noun* (*plural* **refectories**)
the dining room of a monastery etc.
[from Latin *refectum* = refreshed]

refer *verb* (**refers, referring, referred**)
pass a problem etc. to someone else, *My doctor referred me to a specialist.*
referral *noun*
refer to 1 mention or speak about, *I wasn't referring to you.* 2 look in a book etc. for information, *We referred to our dictionary.*
[from *re-* + Latin *ferre* = bring]

referee *noun* (*plural* **referees**)
someone appointed to see that people keep to the rules of a game.
referee *verb* (**referees, refereeing, refereed**)
act as a referee; umpire.
[literally = someone who is referred to]

reference *noun* (*plural* **references**)
1 referring to something, *There was no reference to recent events.* 2 a direction to a book or page or file etc. where information can be found. 3 a testimonial.
in or **with reference to** concerning or about.

reference book *noun* (*plural* **reference books**)
a book (such as a dictionary or encyclopedia) that gives information systematically.

reference library *noun* (*plural* **reference libraries**)
a library where books can be used but not taken away.

referendum *noun* (*plural* **referendums** or **referenda**)
voting by all the people of a country (not by Parliament) to decide whether something shall be done. It is also called a *plebiscite*.
[Latin, = referring]

refill *verb* (**refills, refilling, refilled**)
fill again.
refill *noun* (*plural* **refills**)
a container holding a substance which is used to refill something, *this pen needs another refill.*

refine *verb* (**refines, refining, refined**)
1 purify. 2 improve something, especially by making small changes. [from *re-* + Middle English *fine* = make pure]

refined *adjective*
1 purified. 2 cultured; having good taste or good manners.

refinement *noun* (*plural* **refinements**)
1 the action of refining. 2 being refined.
3 something added to improve a thing.

refinery *noun* (*plural* **refineries**)
a factory for refining something, *an oil refinery.*

reflect *verb* (**reflects, reflecting, reflected**)
1 send back light, heat, or sound etc. from a surface. 2 form an image of something as a mirror does. 3 think something over; consider. 4 be influenced by something, *Prices reflect the cost of producing things.*
reflection *noun*, **reflective** *adjective*, **reflector** *noun*
[from *re-* + Latin *flectere* = to bend]

reflex *noun* (*plural* **reflexes**)
a movement or action done without any
conscious thought. [same origin as *reflect*]

reflex angle *noun* (*plural* **reflex angles**)
an angle of more than 180°.

reflexive pronoun *noun* (*plural* **reflexive
pronouns**)
any of the pronouns *myself, herself, himself,*
etc. (as in 'She cut *herself*'), which refer
back to the subject of the verb.

reflexive verb *noun* (*plural* **reflexive
verbs**)
a verb where the subject and the object are
the same person or thing, as in 'She *cut
herself*', 'The cat *washed itself*'.

reform *verb* (**reforms, reforming, reformed**)
make or become better by removing faults.
reformer *noun,* **reformative** *adjective,*
reformatory *adjective*
reform *noun* (*plural* **reforms**)
1 reforming. 2 a change made in order to
improve something.
[from *re-* + Latin *formare* = to form]

reformation *noun*
reforming.
the Reformation a religious movement in
Europe in the 16th century intended to
reform certain teachings and practices of
the Roman Catholic Church, which
resulted in the establishment of the
Reformed or Protestant Churches.

refract *verb* (**refracts, refracting, refracted**)
bend a ray of light at the point where it
enters water or glass etc. at an angle.
refraction *noun,* **refractor** *noun,*
refractive *adjective*
[from *re-* + Latin *fractum* = broken]

refractory *adjective*
1 difficult to control; stubborn. 2 (of
substances) resistant to heat.
[from *re-* + Latin *frangere* = break]

refrain¹ *verb* (**refrains, refraining, refrained**)
stop yourself from doing something,
Refrain from talking.
[from Latin *refrenare* = to bridle]

refrain² *noun* (*plural* **refrains**)
the chorus of a song. [from French]

refresh *verb* (**refreshes, refreshing,
refreshed**)
make a tired person etc. feel fresh and
strong again.

refresher course *noun* (*plural* **refresher
courses**)
a training course to bring people's
knowledge up to date.

refreshing *adjective*
1 producing new strength, *a refreshing
sleep.* 2 pleasantly different or unusual,
refreshing honesty.

refreshment *noun* (*plural* **refreshments**)
1 being refreshed. 2 food and drink.

refreshments *plural noun*
drinks and snacks provided at an event.

refrigerate *verb* (**refrigerates, refrigerating,
refrigerated**)
make a thing extremely cold, especially in
order to preserve it and keep it fresh.
refrigeration *noun*
[from *re-* + Latin *frigus* = cold]

refrigerator *noun* (*plural* **refrigerators**)
a cabinet or room in which food is stored at
a very low temperature.

refuel *verb* (**refuels, refuelling, refuelled**)
supply a ship or aircraft with more fuel.

refuge *noun* (*plural* **refuges**)
a place where a person is safe from pursuit
or danger.
take refuge go somewhere or do something
so that you are protected.
[from *re-* + Latin *fugere* = flee]

refugee *noun* (*plural* **refugees**)
a person who has had to leave home and
seek refuge somewhere, e.g. because of war
or persecution or famine.

refund *verb* (**refunds, refunding, refunded**)
pay money back.
refund *noun*
money paid back. [from Latin *refundere*
= pour back]

refurbish *verb* (**refurbishes, refurbishing,
refurbished**)
freshen something up; redecorate and
repair.

refuse (*say* ri-**fewz**) *verb* (**refuses, refusing, refused**)
say that you are unwilling to do or give or accept something. **refusal** *noun*

refuse (*say* ref-**yooss**) *noun*
waste material, *Lorries collected the refuse.*
[from French]

refute *verb* (**refutes, refuting, refuted**)
prove that a person or statement etc. is wrong. **refutation** *noun*
[from Latin *refutare* = repel]

USAGE: This word is sometimes used as if it meant 'deny', but this meaning is not fully accepted as part of standard English and should be avoided.

regain *verb* (**regains, regaining, regained**)
1 get something back after losing it.
2 reach a place again.

regal (*say* **ree**-gal) *adjective*
1 by or to do with a monarch. 2 dignified and splendid; fit for a king or queen. [from Latin *regis* = of a king]

regale (*say* rig-**ayl**) *verb* (**regales, regaling, regaled**)
feed or entertain well, *They regaled us with stories.* [from French]

regalia (*say* rig-**ayl**-i-a) *plural noun*
the emblems of royalty or rank, *The royal regalia include the crown, sceptre, and orb.*

regard *verb* (**regards, regarding, regarded**)
1 look or gaze at. 2 think of in a certain way; consider to be, *We regard the matter as serious.*
regard *noun*
1 a gaze. 2 consideration; heed, *You acted without regard to people's safety.* 3 respect, *We have a great regard for her.*
with regard to concerning.
[from re- + French *garder* = to guard]

regarding *preposition*
concerning, *There are laws regarding drugs.*

regardless *adverb*
without considering something, *Do it, regardless of the cost.*

regards *plural noun*
kind wishes sent in a message, *Give him my regards.*

regatta *noun* (*plural* **regattas**)
a meeting for boat or yacht races
[from Italian]

regency *noun* (*plural* **regencies**)
1 being a regent. 2 a period when a country is ruled by a regent.

regenerate *verb* (**regenerates, regenerating, regenerated**)
give new life or strength to something.
regeneration *noun*

regent *noun* (*plural* **regents**)
a person appointed to rule a country while the monarch is too young or unable to rule.
[from Latin *regens* = ruling]

reggae (*say* **reg**-ay) *noun*
a West Indian style of music with a strong beat. [origin unknown]

regime (*say* ray-**zheem**) *noun* (*plural* **regimes**)
a system of government or organization, *a Communist regime.*
[French; related to *regiment*]

regiment *noun* (*plural* **regiments**)
an army unit, usually divided into battalions or companies.
regimental *adjective*
[from Latin *regimentum* = rule, governing]

region *noun* (*plural* **regions**)
an area; a part of a country or of the world, *in tropical regions.*
regional *adjective*, **regionally** *adverb*
in the region of near, *The cost will be in the region of £100.*
[from Latin *regio* = boundary]

register *noun* (*plural* **registers**)
1 an official list of things or names etc. 2 a book in which information about school attendances is recorded. 3 the range of a voice or musical instrument.
register *verb* (**registers, registering, registered**)
1 list something in a register. 2 indicate; show, *The thermometer registered 100°.*
3 make an impression on someone's mind.
4 pay extra for a letter or parcel to be sent with special care. **registration** *noun*
[from Latin]

register office noun (plural register offices)
an office where marriages are performed and records of births, marriages, and deaths are kept.

registrar noun (plural registrars)
an official whose job is to keep written records or registers.

registry noun (plural registries)
a place where registers are kept.

registry office noun (plural registry offices)
(informal) a register office.

regress verb (regresses, regressing, regressed)
return to an earlier condition or way of behaving, especially a worse one. **regressive** adjective
[from re- + Latin gressus = gone]

regret noun (plural regrets)
a feeling of sorrow or disappointment about something that has happened or been done.
regretful adjective, **regretfully** adverb
regret verb (regrets, regretting, regretted)
feel regret about something.
regrettable adjective, **regrettably** adverb
[from old French regreter = mourn for the dead]

regular adjective
1 always happening or doing something at certain times. 2 even or symmetrical, regular teeth. 3 normal, standard, or correct, the regular procedure. 4 belonging to a country's permanent armed forces, a regular soldier. **regularly** adverb, **regularity** noun [from Latin regula = a rule]

regulate verb (regulates, regulating, regulated)
1 control, especially by rules. 2 make a machine work at a certain speed. **regulator** noun [same origin as regular]

regulation noun
1 regulating. 2 a rule or law.

regurgitate verb (regurgitates, regurgitating, regurgitated)
bring swallowed food up again into the mouth. **regurgitation** noun
[from re- + Latin gurgitare = to swallow]

rehabilitation noun
restoring a person to a normal life or a building etc. to a good condition.
rehabilitate verb
[from re- + Latin habilitare = enable]

rehash verb (rehashes, rehashing, rehashed) (informal)
repeat something without changing it very much.
[from re- + hash = to make into hash]

rehearse verb (rehearses, rehearsing, rehearsed)
practice something before performing to an audience. **rehearsal** noun
[from old French]

reign verb
1 rule a country as king or queen. 2 be supreme; be the strongest influence, Silence reigned.
reign noun
the time when someone reigns.
[from Latin regnum = royal authority]

reimburse verb (reimburses, reimbursing, reimbursed)
repay money that has been spent, Your travelling expenses will be reimbursed.
reimbursement noun
[from re- + an old word imburse = pay]

rein noun (plural reins)
a strap used to guide a horse.
[from old French; related to retain]

reincarnation noun
being born again into a new body.
[from re- + incarnation (see incarnate)]

reindeer noun (plural reindeer)
a kind of deer that lives in Arctic regions.
[from Old Norse]

reinforce verb (reinforces, reinforcing, reinforced)
strengthen by adding extra people or supports etc.
[from re- + old French enforcer = enforce]

reinforced concrete noun
concrete containing metal bars or wires to strengthen it.

reinforcement noun (plural reinforcements)
1 reinforcing. 2 something that reinforces.

reinforcements *plural noun*
extra troops or ships etc. sent to strengthen a force.

reinstate *verb* (reinstates, reinstating, reinstated)
put a person or thing back into a former position. **reinstatement** *noun*
[from *re-* + *in-* + *state*]

reiterate *verb* (reiterates, reiterating, reiterated)
say something again and again. **reiteration** *noun* [from *re-* + Latin *iterare* = repeat]

reject *verb* (rejects, rejecting, rejected)
1 refuse to accept a person or thing.
2 throw away or discard. **rejection** *noun* [from *re-* + Latin *-jectum* = thrown]

rejoice *verb* (rejoices, rejoicing, rejoiced)
feel or show great joy. [from old French]

rejoin *verb* (rejoins, rejoining, rejoined)
join again.

rejoinder *noun* (*plural* rejoinders)
an answer or retort. [old French, = rejoin]

rejuvenate *verb* (rejuvenates, rejuvenating, rejuvenated)
make a person seem young again.
rejuvenation *noun*
[from *re-* + Latin *juvenis* = young]

relapse *verb* (relapses, relapsing, relapsed)
return to a previous condition; become worse after improving. **relapse** *noun*
[from *re-* + Latin *lapsum* = slipped]

relate *verb* (relates, relating, related)
1 narrate. 2 connect or compare one thing with another. 3 understand and get on well with, *Some people cannot relate to animals.* [from Latin]

related *adjective*
belonging to the same family.

relation *noun* (*plural* relations)
1 a relative. 2 the way one thing is related to another.

relationship *noun* (*plural* relationships)
1 how people or things are related. 2 how people get on with each other. 3 a close association with strong feelings.

relative *noun* (*plural* relatives)
a person who is related to another.
relative *adjective*
connected or compared with something; compared with the average, *They live in relative comfort.* **relatively** *adverb*
relative pronoun see *pronoun.*

relax *verb* (relaxes, relaxing, relaxed)
1 become less strict or stiff. 2 stop working; rest. **relaxation** *noun*
[from *re-* + Latin *laxus* = loose]

relay (*say* ri-lay) *verb* (relays, relaying, relayed)
pass on a message or broadcast.
relay *noun* (*say* re-lay) (*plural* relays)
1 a fresh group taking the place of another, *The firemen worked in relays.* 2 a relay race. 3 a device for relaying a broadcast. [from old French]

relay race *noun* (*plural* relay races)
a race between teams in which each person covers part of the distance.

release *verb* (releases, releasing, released)
1 set free or unfasten. 2 let a thing fall or fly or go out. 3 make a film or record etc. available to the public.
release *noun* (*plural* releases)
1 being released. 2 something released.
3 a device that unfastens something.
[from old French; related to *relax*]

relegate *verb* (relegates, relegating, relegated)
1 put into a less important place. 2 put a sports team into a lower division of a league. **relegation** *noun*
[from *re-* + Latin *legatum* = sent]

relent *verb* (relents, relenting, relented)
become less severe or more merciful.
[from *re-* + Latin *lentare* = bend, soften]

relentless *adjective*
not stopping or relenting; pitiless.
relentlessly *adverb*

relevant *adjective*
connected with what is being discussed or dealt with. (The opposite is *irrelevant.*)
relevance *noun* [from Latin]

reliable *adjective*
able to be relied on; trustworthy.
reliably *adverb*, **reliability** *noun*

reliance *noun*
1 relying or depending. 2 trust.
reliant *adjective*

relic *noun* (*plural* relics)
something that has survived from an
earlier time.
[from Latin *reliquus* = remaining]

relief *noun* (*plural* reliefs)
1 the ending or lessening of pain, trouble,
boredom, etc. 2 something that gives relief
or help. 3 a person who takes over a turn of
duty when another finishes. 4 a method of
making a design etc. that stands out from a
surface.

relief map *noun* (*plural* relief maps)
a map that shows hills and valleys by
shading or moulding.

relieve *verb* (relieves, relieving, relieved)
give relief to a person or thing.
relieve of take something from a person,
The thief relieved him of his wallet.
[from *re-* + Latin *levare* = raise, lighten]

religion *noun* (*plural* religions)
1 what people believe about God or gods,
and how they worship. 2 a particular
system of beliefs and worship.
[from Latin *religio* = reverence]

religious *adjective*
1 to do with religion. 2 believing firmly in
a religion and taking part in its customs.
religiously *adverb*

relinquish *verb* (relinquishes, relinquishing,
relinquished)
give something up; let go.
relinquishment *noun*
[from *re-* + Latin *linquere* = to leave]

relish *noun* (*plural* relishes)
1 great enjoyment. 2 something tasty that
adds flavour to plainer food.
relish *verb* (relishes, relishing, relished)
enjoy greatly. [from old French]

relive *verb* (relives, reliving, relived)
remember something that happened very
vividly, as though it was happening again.

relocate *verb* (relocates, relocating,
relocated)
move or be moved to a new place.

reluctant *adjective*
unwilling or not keen.
reluctantly *adverb*, **reluctance** *noun*
[from *re-* + Latin *luctatus* = struggling]

rely *verb* (relies, relying, relied)
rely on trust a person or thing to help or
support you.
[from old French *relier* = bind together]

remain *verb* (remains, remaining, remained)
1 be there after other parts have gone or
been dealt with; be left over. 2 continue to
be in the same place or condition; stay.
[from *re-* + Latin *manere* = to stay]

remainder *noun*
1 the remaining part or people or things.
2 the number left after subtraction or
division.

remains *plural noun*
1 all that is left over after other parts have
been removed or destroyed. 2 ancient
ruins or objects; relics. 3 a dead body.

remand *verb* (remands, remanding,
remanded)
send a prisoner back into custody while
further evidence is sought. **remand** *noun*
on remand in prison while waiting for a
trial.
[from *re-* + Latin *mandare* = entrust]

remark *noun* (*plural* remarks)
something said; a comment.
remark *verb* (remarks, remarking, remarked)
1 make a remark; say. 2 notice.
[from French]

remarkable *adjective*
unusual or extraordinary. **remarkably**
adverb [from *remark*]

remedial *adjective*
1 helping to cure an illness or deficiency.
2 helping to overcome a difficulty or
disability. [same origin as *remedy*]

remedy *noun* (*plural* remedies)
something that cures or relieves a disease
etc. or that puts a matter right.
remedy *verb* (remedies, remedying,
remedied)
be a remedy for something; put right.
[from *re-* + Latin *mederi* = heal]

remember *verb* (remembers, remembering, remembered)
1 keep something in your mind. 2 bring something back into your mind.
remembrance *noun*
[from re- + Latin *memor* = mindful, remembering]

remind *verb* (reminds, reminding, reminded)
help or make a person remember something. reminder *noun*
[from re- + an old sense of *mind* = put into someone's mind, mention]

reminisce (*say* rem-in-iss) *verb* (reminisces, reminiscing, reminisced)
think or talk about things that you remember.
reminiscence *noun*, reminiscent *adjective*
[from Latin *reminisci* = remember]

remiss *adjective*
negligent; careless about doing what you ought to do. [same origin as *remit*]

remission *noun*
1 remitting. 2 reduction of a prison sentence, especially for good behaviour while in prison.

remit *verb* (remits, remitting, remitted)
1 send, especially money. 2 forgive; reduce or cancel a punishment etc. 3 make or become less intense; slacken, *We must not remit our efforts.*
[from re- + Latin *mittere* = send]

remittance *noun* (*plural* remittances)
1 sending money. 2 the money sent.

remnant *noun* (*plural* remnants)
a part or piece left over from something. [from old French; related to *remain*]

remonstrate *verb* (remonstrates, remonstrating, remonstrated)
make a protest, *We remonstrated with him about his behaviour.*
[from re- + Latin *monstrare* = to show]

remorse *noun*
deep regret for having done wrong.
remorseful *adjective*, remorsefully *adverb*
[from re- + Latin *morsum* = bitten]

remorseless *adjective*
relentless.

remote *adjective*
1 far away or isolated. 2 some but very little; unlikely, *a remote chance.*
remotely *adverb*, remoteness *noun*
[from Latin *remotum* = removed]

remote control *noun*
controlling something from a distance, usually by electricity or radio.

remould *noun* (*plural* remoulds)
a used tyre that has been given a new tread.

removable *adjective*
able to be removed.

removal *noun*
removing or moving something.

remove *verb* (removes, removing, removed)
take something away or off.

remove *noun* (*plural* removes)
a distance or degree away from something, *That is several removes from the truth.*
[from re- + Latin *movere* = move]

remunerate *verb* (remunerates, remunerating, remunerated)
pay or reward someone.
remuneration *noun*, remunerative *adjective*
[from re- + Latin *muneris* = of a gift]

Renaissance (*say* ren-ay-sans) *noun*
the revival of classical styles of art and literature in Europe in the 14th–16th centuries. [French, = rebirth]

renal (*say* reen-al) *adjective*
to do with the kidneys.
[from Latin]

rend *verb* (rends, rending, rent) (*poetic*)
rip or tear. [from Old English]

render *verb* (renders, rendering, rendered)
1 (*formal*) give or perform something, *render help to the victims.* 2 cause to become, *The shock rendered us speechless.*
[from French]

rendezvous (*say* rond-ay-voo) *noun*
(*plural* rendezvous, *say* rond-ay-vooz)
1 a meeting with somebody. 2 a place arranged for this.
[French, = present yourselves]

renegade (*say* ren-ig-ayd) *noun* (*plural* renegades)
a person who deserts a group or religion etc. [from *re-* + Latin *negare* = deny]

renege (*say* re-nayg) *verb* (reneges, reneging, reneged)
break your word or an agreement.

renew *verb* (renews, renewing, renewed)
1 restore something to its original condition or replace it with something new. 2 begin or make or give again, *We renewed our request.* **renewal** *noun*

renewable *adjective*
able to be renewed.

renewable resource *noun* (*plural* renewable resources)
a resource (such as power from the sun, wind, or waves) that can never be used up, or which can be renewed.

rennet *noun*
a substance used to curdle milk in making cheese or junket.
[probably from Old English]

renounce *verb* (renounces, renouncing, renounced)
give up or reject. **renunciation** *noun*
[from *re-* + Latin *nuntiare* = announce]

renovate *verb* (renovates, renovating, renovated)
repair a thing and make it look new.
renovation *noun*
[from *re-* + Latin *novus* = new]

renowned *adjective*
well-known because of something good.
[from *re-* + French *nomer* = to name]

rent¹ *noun* (*plural* rents)
a regular payment for the use of something, especially a house that belongs to another person.

rent *verb* (rents, renting, rented)
have or allow the use of something in return for rent. [from French]

rent² *past tense* of **rend**.

rent³ *noun* (*plural* rents)
a torn place; a split. [from *rend*]

rental *noun*
the amount paid as rent.

renunciation *noun*
renouncing something.

repair¹ *verb* (repairs, repairing, repaired)
put something into good condition after it has been damaged or broken etc.
repairable *adjective*

repair *noun* (*plural* repairs)
1 repairing, *closed for repair.* 2 a mended place, *the repair is hardly visible.*
in good repair in good condition; well maintained.
[from *re-* + Latin *parare* = get something ready]

repair² *verb* (repairs, repairing, repaired) (*formal*)
go, *The guests repaired to the dining room.*
[from old French; related to *repatriate*]

reparation *noun* (*plural* reparations) (*formal*)
compensate; pay for damage or loss.
make reparations compensate.
[same origin as *repair¹*]

reparations *plural noun*
compensation for war damage paid by the defeated nation.

repartee *noun*
witty replies and remarks.
[from French *repartir* = answer back]

repast *noun* (*plural* repasts) (*formal*)
a meal. [from *re-* + Latin *pascere* = to feed]

repatriate *verb* (repatriates, repatriating, repatriated)
send a person back to his or her own country. **repatriation** *noun*
[from *re-* + Latin *patria* = native country]

repay *verb* (repays, repaying, repaid)
pay back, especially money.
repayable *adjective*, **repayment** *noun*
[from old French]

repeal *verb* (repeals, repealing, repealed)
cancel a law officially. **repeal** *noun*
[from *re-* + French *appeler* = to appeal]

repeat *verb* (repeats, repeating, repeated)
say or do the same thing again.
repeatedly *adverb*

repeat *noun* (*plural* **repeats**)
1 the action of repeating. **2** something that is repeated. [from *re-* + Latin *petere* = seek]

repel *verb* (**repels, repelling, repelled**)
1 drive away or repulse, *repel the attack*.
2 disgust somebody. **repellent** *adjective* &
noun [from *re-* + Latin *pellere* = to drive]

repent *verb* (**repents, repenting, repented**)
be sorry for what you have done.
repentance *noun*, **repentant** *adjective*
[from old French; related to *penitent*]

repercussion *noun* (*plural* **repercussions**)
a result or reaction produced indirectly by something.
[from *re-* + Latin *percutere* = to strike]

repertoire (*say* rep-er-twahr) *noun*
a stock of songs or plays etc. that a person or company knows and can perform.
[French; related to *repertory*]

repertory *noun* (*plural* **repertories**)
a repertoire. [from Latin *repertorium*
= a list or catalogue]

repertory company or **theatre** *noun*
(*plural* **repertory companies** or **theatres**)
a company or theatre giving performances of various plays for short periods.

repetition *noun* (*plural* **repetitions**)
1 repeating. **2** something repeated.
repetitious *adjective*

repetitive *adjective*
full of repetitions. **repetitively** *adverb*

replace *verb* (**replaces, replacing, replaced**)
1 put a thing back in its place. **2** take the place of another person or thing. **3** put a new or different thing in place of something. **replacement** *noun*

replay *verb* (**replays, replaying, replayed**)
play a sports match or a recording again.
replay *noun*

replenish *verb* (**replenishes, replenishing, replenished**)
1 fill again. **2** add a new supply of something. **replenishment** *noun*
[from *re-* + Latin *plenus* = full]

replete *adjective*
1 well supplied. **2** feeling full after eating.
[from *re-* + Latin *pletum* = filled]

replica *noun* (*plural* **replicas**)
an exact copy. [from Italian]

reply *noun* (*plural* **replies**)
something said or written to deal with a question, letter, etc.; an answer.
reply *verb* (**replies, replying, replied**)
give a reply to; answer. [from old French]

report *verb* (**reports, reporting, reported**)
1 describe something that has happened or that you have done or studied. **2** make a complaint or accusation against somebody.
3 go and tell somebody that you have arrived or are ready for work.
report *noun* (*plural* **reports**)
1 a description or account of something.
2 a regular statement of how someone has worked or behaved, e.g. at school. **3** an explosive sound.
[from *re-* + Latin *portare* = carry]

reporter *noun* (*plural* **reporters**)
a person whose job is to collect and report news for a newspaper, radio or television programme, etc.

repose *noun*
calm, rest, or sleep.
repose *verb* (**reposes, reposing, reposed**)
rest or lie somewhere. [from *re-* + Latin *pausare* = to pause]

repository *noun* (*plural* **repositories**)
a place where things are stored.
[from Latin]

repossess *verb* (**repossesses, repossessing, repossessed**)
take something back because it has not been paid for.

reprehensible *adjective*
extremely bad and deserving blame or rebuke.
[from Latin *reprehendere* = blame, rebuke]

represent *verb* (**represents, representing, represented**)
1 show a person or thing in a picture or play etc. **2** symbolize or stand for, *In Roman numerals, V represents 5*. **3** be an example or equivalent of something. **4** help

someone by speaking or doing something on their behalf. **representation** *noun*
[from *re-* + Latin *praesentare* = to present]

representative *noun* (*plural* **representatives**)
a person or thing that represents another or others.
representative *adjective*
1 representing others. 2 typical of a group.

repress *verb* (**represses, repressing, repressed**)
1 keep down; control by force. 2 restrain or suppress. **repression** *noun*, **repressive** *adjective* [from Latin]

reprieve *noun* (*plural* **reprieves**)
postponement or cancellation of a punishment etc., especially the death penalty.
reprieve *verb* (**reprieves, reprieving, reprieved**)
give a reprieve to. [from old French]

reprimand *noun* (*plural* **reprimands**)
a rebuke, especially a formal or official one.
reprimand *verb* (**reprimands, reprimanding, reprimanded**)
give someone a reprimand.
[from French; related to *repress*]

reprisal *noun* (*plural* **reprisals**)
an act of revenge. [from old French]

reproach *verb* (**reproaches, reproaching, reproached**)
tell someone you are upset and disappointed by something he or she has done. **reproach** *noun*, **reproachful** *adjective*, **reproachfully** *adverb* [from old French]

reproduce *verb* (**reproduces, reproducing, reproduced**)
1 cause to be seen or heard or happen again. 2 make a copy of something. 3 produce offspring.
reproduction *noun*, **reproductive** *adjective*

reprove *verb* (**reproves, reproving, reproved**)
rebuke or reproach. **reproof** *noun*
[from Latin *reprobare* = disapprove]

reptile *noun* (*plural* **reptiles**)
a cold-blooded animal that has a backbone and very short legs or no legs at all, e.g. a snake, lizard, crocodile, or tortoise.
[from Latin *reptilis* = crawling]

republic *noun* (*plural* **republics**)
a country that has a president, especially one who is elected. (Compare *monarchy*.)
republican *adjective*
[from Latin *res publica* = public affairs]

repudiate *verb* (**repudiates, repudiating, repudiated**)
reject or deny. **repudiation** *noun*
[from Latin *repudiare* = to divorce]

repugnant *adjective*
distasteful; very unpleasant or disgusting.
repugnance *noun*
[from *re-* + Latin *pugnans* = fighting]

repulse *verb* (**repulses, repulsing, repulsed**)
1 drive away or repel. 2 reject an offer etc.; rebuff. [same origin as *repel*]

repulsion *noun*
1 repelling or repulsing. 2 a feeling of disgust. (The opposite is *attraction*.)

repulsive *adjective*
1 disgusting. 2 repelling things. (The opposite is *attractive*.)
repulsively *adverb*, **repulsiveness** *noun*

reputable (*say* rep-yoo-ta-bul) *adjective*
having a good reputation; respected.
reputably *adverb*

reputation *noun* (*plural* **reputations**)
what people say about a person or thing.
[from Latin *reputare* = consider]

repute *noun*
reputation.

reputed *adjective*
said or thought to be something, *This is reputed to be the best hotel.* **reputedly** *adverb*

request *verb* (**requests, requesting, requested**)
1 ask for a thing. 2 ask a person to do something.
request *noun* (*plural* **requests**)
1 asking for something. 2 a thing asked for.
[from old French; related to *require*]

requiem (*say* rek-wee-em) *noun* (*plural* requiems)
1 a special Mass for someone who has died.
2 music for the words of this.
[Latin, = rest]

require *verb* (requires, requiring, required)
1 need. 2 make somebody do something;
oblige, *Drivers are required to pass a test.*
[from re- + Latin *quaerere* = seek]

requirement *noun* (*plural* requirements)
what is required; a need.

requisite (*say* rek-wiz-it) *adjective*
required or needed.
requisite *noun* (*plural* requisites)
a thing needed for something.
[same origin as *require*]

requisition *verb* (requisitions,
requisitioning, requisitioned)
take something over for official use.
[same origin as *require*]

rescue *verb* (rescues, rescuing, rescued)
save from danger, harm, etc.; free from
captivity. **rescuer** *noun*
rescue *noun* (*plural* rescues)
the action of rescuing. [from old French]

research *noun*
careful study or investigation to discover
facts or information.
research (*say* ri-serch) *verb* (researches,
researching, researched)
do research into something.
[from old French *recerche* = careful search]

resemblance *noun* (*plural* resemblances)
likeness or similarity.

resemble *verb* (resembles, resembling,
resembled)
be like another person or thing.
[from old French; related to *similar*]

resent *verb* (resents, resenting, resented)
feel indignant about or insulted by
something. **resentful** *adjective*,
resentfully *adverb*, **resentment** *noun*
[from re- + Latin *sentire* = feel]

reservation *noun* (*plural* reservations)
1 reserving. 2 something reserved. 3 an
area of land kept for a special purpose. 4 a
limit on how far you agree with something,
*I believe most of his story, but I have some
reservations.*

reserve *verb* (reserves, reserving, reserved)
1 keep or order something for a particular
person or a special use. 2 postpone, *reserve
judgement.*
reserve *noun* (*plural* reserves)
1 a person or thing kept ready to be used if
necessary. 2 an area of land kept for a
special purpose, *a nature reserve.*
3 shyness; being reserved.
[from re- + Latin *servare* = keep]

reserved *adjective*
1 kept for someone's use, *reserved seats.*
2 shy or unwilling to show your feelings.

reservoir (*say* rez-er-vwar) *noun* (*plural*
reservoirs)
a place where water is stored, especially an
artificial lake.
[from French *réservoir*; related to *reserve*]

reshuffle *noun* (*plural* reshuffles)
a rearrangement, especially an exchange of
jobs between members of a group, *a
Cabinet reshuffle.* **reshuffle** *verb*

reside *verb* (resides, residing, resided)
live in a particular place; dwell.
[from re- + Latin *-sidere* = sit]

residence *noun* (*plural* residences)
1 a place where a person lives. 2 residing.

resident *noun* (*plural* residents)
a person living or residing in a particular
place. **resident** *adjective*
[from re- + Latin *-sidens* = sitting]

residential *adjective*
1 containing people's homes, *a residential
area.* 2 making it necessary to live in a
particular place, *residential care.*

residue *noun* (*plural* residues)
what is left over. **residual** *adjective*
[from Latin *residuus* = remaining]

resign *verb* (resigns, resigning, resigned)
give up your job or position.
resignation *noun*
be resigned or **resign yourself** to something
accept that you must put up with it.
[from Latin *resignare* = unseal]

resilient *adjective*
1 springy. 2 recovering quickly from illness or trouble. **resilience** *noun*
[from Latin *resilire* = jump back]

resin *noun* (*plural* resins)
a sticky substance that comes from plants or is manufactured, used in varnish, plastics, etc. **resinous** *adjective* [from Latin]

resist *verb* (resists, resisting, resisted)
oppose; fight or act against something.
[from *re-* + Latin *sistere* = stand firmly]

resistance *noun*
1 resisting. 2 the ability of a substance to hinder the flow of electricity.
resistant *adjective*

resistor *noun* (*plural* resistors)
a device that increases the resistance to an electric current.

resit *verb* (resits, resitting, resat)
to sit an examination again because you did not do well enough the first time.
resit *noun*

resolute *adjective*
showing great determination. **resolutely** *adverb* [same origin as *resolve*]

resolution *noun* (*plural* resolutions)
1 being resolute. 2 something you have resolved to do, *New Year resolutions*. 3 a formal decision made by a committee etc. 4 the solving of a problem etc.

resolve *verb* (resolves, resolving, resolved)
1 decide firmly or formally. 2 solve a problem etc. 3 overcome doubts or disagreements.
resolve *noun*
1 something you have decided to do; a resolution. 2 great determination.
[from *re-* + Latin *solvere* = loosen]

resonant *adjective*
resounding or echoing. **resonance** *noun*
[from *re-* + Latin *sonans* = sounding]

resort *verb* (resorts, resorting, resorted)
turn to or make use of something, *They resorted to violence.*
resort *noun* (*plural* resorts)
1 a place where people go for relaxation or holidays. 2 resorting, *without resort to cheating.*

the last resort something to be tried when everything else has failed.
[from *re-* + French *sortir* = go out]

resound *verb* (resounds, resounding, resounded)
fill a place with sound; echo.
[from *re-* + Latin *sonare* = to sound]

resounding *adjective*
1 loud and echoing. 2 very great; outstanding, *a resounding victory.*

resource *noun* (*plural* resources)
1 something that can be used; an asset, *The country's natural resources include coal and oil.* 2 an ability; ingenuity.
resource *verb* (resources, resourcing, resourced)
provide money or other resources for.
[from old French; related to *resurgence*]

resourceful *adjective*
clever at finding ways of doing things.
resourcefully *adverb*, **resourcefulness** *noun*

respect *noun* (*plural* respects)
1 admiration for a person's or thing's good qualities. 2 politeness or consideration, *Have respect for people's feelings.* 3 a detail or aspect, *In this respect he is like his sister.* 4 reference, *The rules with respect to bullying are quite clear.*
respect *verb* (respects, respecting, respected)
have respect for a person or thing. [from Latin *respicere* = look back at, consider]

respectable *adjective*
1 having good manners and character etc. 2 fairly good, *a respectable score.*
respectably *adverb*, **respectability** *noun*

respectful *adjective*
showing respect.
respectfully *adverb*

respecting *preposition*
concerning.

respective *adjective*
of or for each individual, *We went to our respective rooms.* **respectively** *adverb*

respiration *noun*
breathing. **respiratory** *adjective*

respirator *noun* (*plural* respirators)
1 a device that fits over a person's nose and mouth to purify air before it is breathed.
2 an apparatus for giving artificial respiration.

respire *verb* (respires, respiring, respired)
breathe.
[from re- + Latin *spirare* = breathe]

respite *noun* (*plural* respites)
an interval of rest, relief, or delay.
[from old French]

resplendent *adjective*
brilliant with colour or decorations.
[from re- + Latin *splendens* = glittering]

respond *verb* (responds, responding, responded)
1 reply. 2 act in answer to, or because of, something; react.
[from re- + Latin *spondere* = to promise]

respondent *noun* (*plural* respondents)
the person answering.

response *noun* (*plural* responses)
1 a reply. 2 a reaction.

responsibility *noun* (*plural* responsibilities)
1 being responsible. 2 something for which a person is responsible.

responsible *adjective*
1 looking after a person or thing and having to take the blame if something goes wrong. 2 reliable and trustworthy. 3 with important duties, *a responsible job*.
4 causing something, *His carelessness was responsible for their deaths.* **responsibly** *adverb* [same origin as *respond*]

responsive *adjective*
responding well.

rest¹ *noun* (*plural* rests)
1 a time of sleep or freedom from work as a way of regaining strength. 2 a support, *an armrest*. 3 an interval of silence between notes in music.
rest *verb* (rests, resting, rested)
1 have a rest; be still. 2 allow to rest, *Sit down and rest your feet.* 3 support; be supported. 4 be left without further investigation etc., *And there the matter rests.* [from Old English]

rest² *noun*
the rest the remaining part; the others.
rest *verb* (rests, resting, rested)
remain, *Rest assured, it will be a success.*
rest with be left to someone to deal with, *It rests with you to suggest a date.*
[from Latin *restare* = stay behind]

restaurant *noun* (*plural* restaurants)
a place where you can buy a meal and eat it. [French, literally = restoring]

restaurateur (*say* rest-er-a-tur) *noun*
(*plural* restaurateurs)
a person who owns or manages a restaurant.

USAGE: Note the spelling of this word. Unlike 'restaurant' there is no 'n' in it.

restful *adjective*
giving rest or a feeling of rest.

restitution *noun*
1 restoring something. 2 compensation.
[from re- + Latin *statutum* = established]

restive *adjective*
restless or impatient because of delay, boredom, etc. [earlier (of a horse) = refusing to move: from *rest¹*]

restless *adjective*
unable to rest or keep still. **restlessly** *adverb*

restore *verb* (restores, restoring, restored)
put something back to its original place or condition. **restoration** *noun* [from Latin]

restrain *verb* (restrains, restraining, restrained)
hold a person or thing back; keep under control. **restraint** *noun* [from Latin *restringere* = tie up firmly, confine]

restrict *verb* (restricts, restricting, restricted)
limit or control.
restriction *noun*, **restrictive** *adjective*
[from Latin *restrictus* = restrained]

result *noun* (*plural* results)
1 something produced by an action or condition etc.; an effect or consequence.
2 the score or situation at the end of a game, competition, or race etc. 3 the answer to a sum or calculation.

result *verb* (results, resulting, resulted)
1 happen as a result. 2 have a particular result. **resultant** *adjective* [from Latin]

resume *verb* (resumes, resuming, resumed)
1 begin again after stopping for a while. 2 take or occupy again, *After the interval we resumed our seats.* **resumption** *noun*
[from *re-* + Latin *sumere* = take up]

résumé (*say* rez-yoo-may) *noun* (*plural* résumés)
a summary. [French, = summed up]

resurgence *noun* (*plural* resurgences)
a rise or revival of something, *a resurgence of interest in grammar*.
[from *re-* + Latin *surgens* = rising]

resurrect *verb* (resurrects, resurrecting, resurrected)
bring back into use or existence, *resurrect an old custom*. [from *resurrection*]

resurrection *noun*
1 coming back to life after being dead. 2 the revival of something.
the Resurrection in the Christian religion, the resurrection of Jesus Christ three days after his death.
[same origin as *resurgence*]

resuscitate *verb* (resuscitates, resuscitating, resuscitated)
revive a person from unconsciousness or apparent death. **resuscitation** *noun*
[from *re-* + Latin *suscitare* = revive]

retail *verb* (retails, retailing, retailed)
1 sell goods to the general public. 2 tell what happened; recount or relate.
retailer *noun*
retail *noun*
selling to the general public. (Compare *wholesale*.)
[from old French *retaille* = a piece cut off]

retain *verb* (retains, retaining, retained)
1 continue to have something; keep in your possession or memory etc. 2 hold something in place.
[from *re-* + Latin *tenere* = to hold]

retainer *noun* (*old use*) (*plural* retainers)
1 an attendant of a person of high rank. 2 a sum of money regularly paid to someone so that he or she will work for you when needed.

retaliate *verb* (retaliates, retaliating, retaliated)
repay an injury or insult etc. with a similar one; counter-attack. **retaliation** *noun*
[from *re-* + Latin *talis* = the same kind]

retard *verb* (retards, retarding, retarded)
slow down or delay the progress or development of something.
retarded *adjective*, **retardation** *noun*
[from *re-* + Latin *tardus* = slow]

retch *verb* (retches, retching, retched)
strain your throat as if being sick.
[from Old English]

USAGE: Do not confuse with *wretch*.

retention *noun*
retaining or keeping. **retentive** *adjective*

reticent (*say* ret-i-sent) *adjective*
not telling people what you feel or think; discreet. **reticence** *noun*
[from Latin *reticere* = keep silent]

retina *noun* (*plural* retinas)
a layer of membrane at the back of the eyeball, sensitive to light. [from Latin]

retinue *noun* (*plural* retinues)
a group of people accompanying an important person. [from old French *retenue* = restrained, in someone's service]

retire *verb* (retires, retiring, retired)
1 give up your regular work because you are getting old. 2 retreat. 3 go to bed or to your private room. **retirement** *noun*
[from *re-* + French *tirer* = to draw]

retiring *adjective*
shy; avoiding company.

retort *noun* (*plural* retorts)
1 a quick or witty or angry reply. 2 a glass bottle with a long downward-bent neck, used in distilling liquids. 3 a receptacle used in making steel etc.
retort *verb* (retorts, retorting, retorted)
make a quick, witty, or angry reply.
[from *re-* + Latin *tortum* = twisted]

retrace *verb* (retraces, retracing, retraced)
go back over something, *We retraced our steps and returned to the ferry.*
[from French]

retract *verb* (retracts, retracting, retracted)
1 pull back or in, *The snail retracts its horns.* 2 withdraw an offer or statement. retraction *noun*, retractable *adjective*, retractile *adjective*
[from re- + Latin *tractum* = pulled]

retread *noun* (*plural* retreads)
a remould.

retreat *verb* (retreats, retreating, retreated)
go back after being defeated or to avoid danger or difficulty etc.; withdraw.
retreat *noun* (*plural* retreats)
1 retreating. 2 a quiet place to which someone can withdraw.
[from old French; related to *retract*]

retrench *verb* (retrenches, retrenching, retrenched)
reduce costs or economize. retrenchment *noun* [from French; related to *truncate*]

retribution *noun* (*plural* retributions)
a deserved punishment.
[from re- + Latin *tributum* = assigned]

retrieve *verb* (retrieves, retrieving, retrieved)
1 bring or get something back. 2 rescue.
retrievable *adjective*, retrieval *noun*
[from Old French *retrover* = find again]

retriever *noun* (*plural* retrievers)
a kind of dog that is often trained to retrieve game.

retro- *prefix*
1 back. 2 backward (as in *retrograde*).
[from Latin]

retrograde *adjective*
1 going backwards. 2 becoming less good.
[from retro- + Latin *gradus* = a step]

retrogress *verb* (retrogresses, retrogressing, retrogressed)
1 move backwards. 2 become worse; deteriorate.
retrogression *noun*, retrogressive *adjective*
[from retro- + *progress*]

retrospect *noun*
in retrospect when you look back at what has happened.
[from retro- + *prospect*]

retrospective *adjective*
1 looking back on the past. 2 applying to the past as well as the future, *The law could not be made retrospective.*
retrospection *noun*

return *verb* (returns, returning, returned)
1 come back or go back. 2 bring, give, put, or send back.
return *noun* (*plural* returns)
1 returning. 2 something returned. 3 profit, *He gets a good return on his savings.* 4 a return ticket.
[from re- + Latin *tornare* = to turn]

return match *noun* (*plural* return matches)
a second match played between the same teams.

return ticket *noun* (*plural* return tickets)
a ticket for a journey to a place and back again.

reunify *verb* (reunifies, reunifying, reunified)
make a divided country into one again, *Can Ireland ever be reunified?*
reunification *noun*

reunion *noun* (*plural* reunions)
1 reuniting. 2 a meeting of people who have not met for some time.

reunite *verb* (reunites, reuniting, reunited)
unite again after being separated.

reuse *verb* (reuses, reusing, reused)
use again. reusable *adjective*
reuse *noun*
using again.

Rev. *abbreviation*
Reverend.

rev *verb* (revs, revving, revved) (*informal*)
make an engine run quickly, especially when starting.
rev *noun* (*plural* revs) (*informal*)
a revolution of an engine.
[short for *revolution*]

reveal *verb* (reveals, revealing, revealed)
let something be seen or known.
[from Latin *revelare* = unveil]

reveille (*say* riv-al-ee) *noun* (*plural* reveilles)
a military waking-signal sounded on a bugle or drums.
[from French *réveillez* = wake up!]

revel *verb* (revels, revelling, revelled)
1 take great delight in something. 2 hold revels. **reveller** *noun*
[from old French; related to *rebel*]

revelation *noun* (*plural* revelations)
1 revealing. 2 something revealed, especially something surprising.

revelry *noun*
1 revelling. 2 revels.

revels *plural noun*
noisy festivities.

revenge *noun*
harming somebody in return for harm that they have caused.

revenge *verb* (revenges, revenging, revenged)
avenge; take vengeance.
[from old French; related to *vindicate*]

revenue *noun* (*plural* revenues)
1 a country's income from taxes etc., used for paying public expenses. 2 a company's income. [French, = returned]

reverberate *verb* (reverberates, reverberating, reverberated)
resound or re-echo. **reverberation** *noun*
[from *re-* + Latin *verberare* = to beat]

revere (*say* riv-eer) *verb* (reveres, revering, revered)
respect deeply or with reverence.
[from Latin]

reverence *noun*
a feeling of awe and deep or religious respect.

Reverend *noun*
the title of a member of the clergy, *the Reverend John Smith.* [from Latin *reverendus* = someone to be revered]

USAGE: Do not confuse with *reverent.*

reverent *adjective*
feeling or showing reverence.
reverently *adverb*

USAGE: Do not confuse with *Reverend.*

reverie (*say* rev-er-ee) *noun* (*plural* reveries)
a daydream. [from French]

revers (*say* riv-eer) *noun* (*plural* revers, *say* riv-eerz)
a folded-back part of a garment, as in a lapel. [French; related to *revert*]

reversal *noun* (*plural* reversals)
1 reversing or being reversed. 2 a piece of bad luck; a reverse.

reverse *adjective*
opposite in direction, order, or manner etc.

reverse *noun* (*plural* reverses)
1 the reverse side, order, manner, etc. 2 a piece of misfortune, *They suffered several reverses.*
in reverse the opposite way round.

reverse *verb* (reverses, reversing, reversed)
1 turn in the opposite direction or order etc.; turn something inside out or upside down. 2 move backwards. 3 cancel a decision or decree. **reversible** *adjective*
[same origin as *revert*]

reverse gear *noun*
a gear that allows a vehicle to be driven backwards.

revert *verb* (reverts, reverting, reverted)
return to a former condition, habit, or subject etc. **reversion** *noun*
[from *re-* + Latin *vertere* = to turn]

review *noun* (*plural* reviews)
1 an inspection or survey. 2 a published description and opinion of a book, film, play, etc.

review *verb* (reviews, reviewing, reviewed)
make a review of something.
reviewer *noun*

USAGE: Do not confuse with *revue.*

revile *verb* (reviles, reviling, reviled)
criticize angrily; abuse. **revilement** *noun*
[from *re-* + old French *vil* = vile]

revise *verb* (revises, revising, revised)
1 go over work that you have already done, especially in preparing for an examination. 2 alter or correct something.
revision *noun*
[from *re-* + Latin *visere* = examine]

revitalize *verb* (revitalizes, revitalizing, revitalized)
put new strength or vitality into something. [from *re-* + *vital* + *-ize*]

revive *verb* (revives, reviving, revived)
come or bring back to life, strength, activity, or use etc. **revival** *noun*
[from *re-* + Latin *vivere* = to live]

revoke *verb* (revokes, revoking, revoked)
withdraw or cancel a decree or licence etc.
[from *re-* + Latin *vocare* = to call]

revolt *verb* (revolts, revolting, revolted)
1 rebel. 2 disgust somebody.
revolt *noun* (*plural* revolts)
1 a rebellion. 2 a feeling of disgust.
[same origin as *revolve*]

revolting *adjective*
disgusting.

revolution *noun* (*plural* revolutions)
1 a rebellion that overthrows the government. 2 a complete change.
3 revolving; rotation; one complete turn of a wheel, engine, etc.

revolutionary *adjective*
1 involving a great change. 2 to do with a political revolution.

revolutionize *verb* (revolutionizes, revolutionizing, revolutionized)
make a great change in something.

revolve *verb* (revolves, revolving, revolved)
turn or keep on turning round.
[from *re-* + Latin *volvere* = to roll]

revolver *noun* (*plural* revolvers)
a pistol with a revolving mechanism that makes it possible to fire it a number of times without reloading.

revue *noun* (*plural* revues)
an entertainment consisting of songs, sketches, etc., often about current events.
[French, = review]

USAGE: Do not confuse with *review*.

---

revulsion *noun*
1 strong disgust. 2 a sudden violent change of feeling. [from *re-* + Latin *vulsus* = pulled]

reward *noun* (*plural* rewards)
something given in return for a useful action or a merit.
reward *verb* (rewards, rewarding, rewarded)
give a reward to someone. [originally = consider, take notice: related to *regard*]

rewarding *adjective*
giving satisfaction and a feeling of achievement, *a rewarding job.*

rewrite *verb* (rewrites, rewriting, rewrote, rewritten)
write something again or differently.

rhapsody (*say* rap-so-dee) *noun* (*plural* rhapsodies)
1 a statement of great delight about something. 2 a romantic piece of music.
rhapsodize *verb* [from Greek *rhapsoidos* = someone who stitches songs together]

rhesus monkey *noun* (*plural* rhesus monkeys)
a kind of small monkey from Northern India, often used in experiments.
[from Latin]

rhesus positive *adjective*
having a substance (*rhesus factor*) found in the red blood cells of many humans and some other primates, first found in the rhesus monkey.
rhesus negative *adjective* without rhesus factor.

rhetoric (*say* ret-er-ik) *noun*
1 the act of using words impressively, especially in public speaking. 2 affected or exaggerated expressions used because they sound impressive.
rhetorical *adjective*, **rhetorically** *adverb*
[from Greek *rhetor* = orator]

rhetorical question *noun* (*plural* rhetorical questions)
something put as a question so that it sounds dramatic, not to get an answer, e.g. 'Who cares?' (= nobody cares).

rheumatism *noun*
a disease that causes pain and stiffness in joints and muscles.
rheumatic *adjective*, **rheumatoid** *adjective*
[from Greek *rheuma*, a substance in the body which was once believed to cause rheumatism]

rhinoceros *noun* (*plural* **rhinoceros** or **rhinoceroses**)
a large heavy animal with a horn or two horns on its nose.
[from Greek *rhinos* = of the nose + *keras* = horn]

rhizome *noun* (*plural* **rhizomes**)
a thick underground stem which produces roots and new plants. [from Greek]

rhododendron *noun* (*plural* **rhododendrons**)
an evergreen shrub with large trumpet-shaped flowers.
[from Greek *rhodon* = rose + *dendron* = tree]

rhombus *noun* (*plural* **rhombuses**)
a shape with four equal sides but no right angles, like the diamond on playing cards.
[from Greek]

rhubarb *noun*
a plant with thick reddish stalks that are used as fruit. [from Latin]

rhyme *noun* (*plural* **rhymes**)
1 a similar sound in the endings of words, e.g. *bat/fat/mat, batter/fatter/matter*. 2 a poem with rhymes. 3 a word that rhymes with another.
rhyme *verb* (**rhymes, rhyming, rhymed**)
1 form a rhyme. 2 have rhymes.
[from old French; related to *rhythm* (originally used of a kind of rhythmic verse which also usually rhymed)]

rhythm *noun* (*plural* **rhythms**)
a regular pattern of beats, sounds, or movements. **rhythmic** *adjective*, **rhythmical** *adjective*, **rhythmically** *adverb* [from Greek]

rib *noun* (*plural* **ribs**)
1 each of the curved bones round the chest. 2 a curved part that looks like a rib or supports something, *the ribs of an umbrella*. **ribbed** *adjective*
[from Old English]

ribald (*say* rib-ald) *adjective*
funny in a rude or disrespectful way.
ribaldry *noun*
[via old French from Germanic]

riband *noun* (*plural* **ribands**)
a ribbon. [from old French]

ribbon *noun* (*plural* **ribbons**)
1 a narrow strip of silk or nylon etc. used for decoration or for tying something. 2 a long narrow strip of inked material used in a typewriter etc.
[a different spelling of *riband*]

rice *noun*
a cereal plant grown in flooded fields in hot countries, or its seeds. [from Greek]

rich *adjective*
1 having a lot of money or property or resources etc.; wealthy. 2 full of goodness, quality, etc. 3 expensive or luxurious.
richly *adverb*, **richness** *noun*
[from Old English]

riches *plural noun*
wealth.

Richter scale *noun*
a scale (from 0–10) used to show the force of an earthquake.
[named after an American scientist, C. F. Richter, who studied earthquakes]

rick¹ *noun* (*plural* **ricks**)
a large neat stack of hay or straw.
[from Old English]

rick² *verb* (**ricks, ricking, ricked**)
sprain or wrench. [origin unknown]

rickets *noun*
a disease caused by lack of vitamin D, causing deformed bones. [origin unknown]

rickety *adjective*
shaky; likely to break or fall down.
[from *rickets*]

rickshaw *noun* (*plural* **rickshaws**)
a two-wheeled carriage pulled by one or more people, used in the Far East.
[from Japanese *jin-riki-sha* = person-power-vehicle]

ricochet (*say* rik-osh-ay) *verb* (**ricochets, ricocheting, ricocheted**)
bounce off something; rebound, *The bullets ricocheted off the wall.* **ricochet** *noun*
[French, = the skipping of a flat stone on water]

ricotta *noun*
a kind of soft Italian cheese made from sheep's milk. [Italian]

rid *verb* (**rids, ridding, rid**)
make a person or place free from something unwanted, *He rid the town of rats.*
get rid of cause to go away.
[from Old Norse]

riddle[1] *noun* (*plural* **riddles**)
a puzzling question, especially as a joke.
[from Old English *raedels*]

riddle[2] *noun* (*plural* **riddles**)
a coarse sieve.
riddle *verb* (**riddles, riddling, riddled**)
1 pass gravel etc. through a riddle. **2** pierce with many holes, *They riddled the target with bullets.* [from Old English *hridder*]

ride *verb* (**rides, riding, rode, ridden**)
1 sit on a horse, bicycle, etc. and be carried along on it. **2** travel in a car, bus, train, etc. **3** float or be supported on something, *The ship rode the waves.*
ride *noun* (*plural* **rides**)
1 a journey on a horse, bicycle, etc. or in a vehicle. **2** a roundabout etc. that you ride on at a fair. [from Old English]

rider *noun* (*plural* **riders**)
1 someone who rides. **2** an extra comment or statement.

ridge *noun* (*plural* **ridges**)
a long narrow part higher than the rest of something. **ridged** *adjective*
[from Old English]

ridicule *verb* (**ridicules, ridiculing, ridiculed**)
make fun of a person or thing. **ridicule** *noun*
[from Latin *ridere* = to laugh]

ridiculous *adjective*
so silly that it makes people laugh or despise it. **ridiculously** *adverb*

rife *adjective*
widespread; happening frequently, *Crime was rife in the town.*
[probably from Old Norse]

riff-raff *noun*
the rabble; disreputable people.
[from old French *rif et raf* = everybody or everything]

rifle *noun* (*plural* **rifles**)
a long gun with spiral grooves (called *rifling*) inside the barrel that make the bullet spin and so travel more accurately.
rifle *verb* (**rifles, rifling, rifled**)
search and rob, *They rifled his desk.*
[from French]

rift *noun* (*plural* **rifts**)
1 a crack or split. **2** a disagreement that separates friends. [a Scandinavian word]

rift valley *noun* (*plural* **rift valleys**)
a steep-sided valley formed where the land has sunk.

rig *verb* (**rigs, rigging, rigged**)
1 provide a ship with ropes, spars, sails, etc. **2** set something up quickly or out of makeshift materials.
rig out provide with clothes or equipment.
rig-out *noun*
rig *noun* (*plural* **rigs**)
1 a framework supporting the machinery for drilling an oil well. **2** the way a ship's masts and sails etc. are arranged.
3 (*informal*) an outfit of clothes.
[probably from a Scandinavian language]

rigging *noun*
the ropes etc. that support a ship's mast and sails.

right *adjective*
1 on or towards the east, if you think of yourself as facing north. **2** correct; true, *the right answer.* **3** morally good; fair or just, *Is it right to cheat?* **4** (of political groups) conservative; not in favour of socialist reforms. **right-hand** *adjective*, **rightly** *adverb*, **rightness** *noun*
right *adverb*
1 on or towards the right-hand side, *Turn right.* **2** straight, *Go right on.* **3** completely, *Go right round it.* **4** exactly, *right in the middle.* **5** rightly, *You did right to tell me.*
right away immediately.

right *noun* (*plural* **rights**)
1 the right-hand side or part etc. 2 what is morally good or fair or just. 3 something that people are allowed to do or have, *People over 18 have the right to vote in elections.*

right *verb* (**rights, righting, righted**)
make a thing right or upright, *They righted the boat.* [from Old English]

right angle *noun*
an angle of 90°.

righteous *adjective*
doing what is right; virtuous.
righteously *adverb*, **righteousness** *noun*

rightful *adjective*
deserved or proper, *in her rightful place.*
rightfully *adverb*

right hand *noun* (*plural* **right hands**)
1 the hand that most people use more than the left, on the right side of the body. 2 a right-hand man.

right-handed *adjective*
using the right hand in preference to the left hand.

right-hand man *noun* (*plural* **right-hand men**)
a trusted and impartial assistant.

right-minded *adjective*
having ideas and opinions which are sensible and morally good.

right of way *noun* (*plural* **rights of way**)
1 a public path across private land. 2 the right of one vehicle to pass or cross a junction etc. before another.

rigid *adjective*
1 stiff or firm; not bending, *a rigid support.* 2 strict, *rigid rules.* **rigidly** *adverb*, **rigidity** *noun* [from Latin]

rigmarole *noun* (*plural* **rigmaroles**)
1 a long rambling statement. 2 a complicated procedure. [from Middle English *ragman* = a legal document]

rigor mortis (*say* ry-ger mor-tis) *noun*
stiffening of the body after death. [Latin, = stiffness of death]

rigorous *adjective*
1 strict or severe. 2 careful and thorough. **rigorously** *adverb*

rigour *noun* (*plural* **rigours**)
1 strictness or severity. 2 harshness of weather or conditions, *the rigours of winter.* [from Latin *rigor* = stiffness]

rile *verb* (**riles, riling, riled**) (*informal*)
annoy. [probably from old French]

rill *noun* (*plural* **rills**)
a very small stream.
[probably from old Dutch]

rim *noun* (*plural* **rims**)
the outer edge of a cup, wheel, or other round object. [from Old English]

rimmed *adjective*
edged.

rind *noun*
the tough skin on bacon, cheese, or fruit. [from Old English]

ring[1] *noun* (*plural* **rings**)
1 a circle. 2 a thin circular piece of metal worn on a finger. 3 the space where a circus performs. 4 a square area in which a boxing match or wrestling match takes place.

ring *verb* (**rings, ringing, ringed**)
put a ring round something; encircle. [from Old English *hring*]

ring[2] *verb* (**rings, ringing, rang, rung**)
1 cause a bell to sound. 2 make a loud clear sound like that of a bell. 3 be filled with sound, *The hall rang with cheers.* 4 telephone, *Please ring me tomorrow.* **ringer** *noun*

ring *noun* (*plural* **rings**)
the act or sound of ringing.
give someone a ring (*informal*) telephone someone.
[from Old English *hringan*]

ringleader *noun* (*plural* **ringleaders**)
a person who leads others in rebellion, mischief, crime, etc. [from *ring*[1]]

ringlet *noun* (*plural* **ringlets**)
a tube-shaped curl.

ringmaster *noun* (*plural* ringmasters)
the person in charge of a performance in a
circus ring.

ring road *noun* (*plural* ring roads)
a road that runs around the edge of a town
so that traffic does not have to go through
the centre.

ringworm *noun*
a fungal skin infection that causes itchy
circular patches, especially on the scalp.

rink *noun* (*plural* rinks)
a place made for skating. [origin unknown]

rinse *verb* (rinses, rinsing, rinsed)
1 wash something lightly. 2 wash in clean
water to remove soap.
rinse *noun* (*plural* rinses)
1 rinsing. 2 a liquid for colouring the hair.
[from French]

riot *noun* (*plural* riots)
wild or violent behaviour by a crowd of
people.
riot *verb* (riots, rioting, rioted)
take part in a riot.
[from old French *rihoter* = to quarrel]

riot gear *noun*
protective clothing, helmets, shields, etc.
worn or carried by the police or army if
rioting is expected.

riotous *adjective*
1 disorderly or unruly. 2 boisterous,
riotous laughter.

RIP *abbreviation*
may he or she (or they) rest in peace.
[short for Latin *requiescat* (or *requiescant*)
in pace]

rip *verb* (rips, ripping, ripped)
1 tear roughly. 2 rush.
rip *noun*
a torn place. [origin unknown]

ripe *adjective* (riper, ripest)
1 ready to be harvested or eaten. 2 ready
and suitable, *The time is ripe for revolution.*
ripeness *noun*
a ripe old age a great age.
[from Old English]

ripen *verb* (ripens, ripening, ripened)
make or become ripe.

rip-off *noun* (*plural* rip-offs)
(*informal*) a fraud or swindle. **rip off** *verb*

riposte (*say* rip-ost) *noun* (*plural* ripostes)
1 a quick counterstroke in fencing. 2 a
quick retort.
[from Italian; related to *respond*]

ripple *noun* (*plural* ripples)
a small wave or series of waves.
ripple *verb* (ripples, rippling, rippled)
form ripples. [origin unknown]

rise *verb* (rise, rising, rose, risen)
1 go upwards. 2 get up from lying, sitting,
or kneeling. 3 get out of bed. 4 rebel, *They
rose in revolt against the tyrant.* 5 (of a
river) begin its course. 6 (of the wind)
begin to blow more strongly.
rise *noun* (*plural* rises)
1 the action of rising; an upward
movement. 2 an increase in amount etc. or
in wages. 3 an upward slope.
give rise to cause.
[from Old English]

rising *noun* (*plural* risings)
a revolt.

risk *noun* (*plural* risks)
a chance of danger or loss.
risk *verb* (risks, risking, risked)
take the chance of damaging or losing
something. [via French from Italian]

risky *adjective* (riskier, riskiest)
full of risk.

risotto *noun*
an Italian dish of rice cooked with
vegetables and, usually, meat. [Italian,
from *riso* = rice]

rissole *noun* (*plural* rissoles)
a fried cake of minced meat or fish.
[French]

rite *noun* (*plural* rites)
a religious ceremony; a solemn ritual.
[from Latin]

ritual *noun* (*plural* rituals)
the series of actions used in a religious or
other ceremony. **ritual** *adjective*, **ritually**
adverb [from Latin *ritus* = rite]

rival *noun* (*plural* rivals)
a person or thing that competes with another or tries to do the same thing.
rivalry *noun*

rival *verb* (rivals, rivalling, rivalled)
be a rival of a person or thing.
[from Latin *rivalis* = someone using the same stream (from *rivus* = stream)]

river *noun* (*plural* rivers)
a large stream of water flowing in a natural channel. [from Latin *ripa* = bank]

rivet *noun* (*plural* rivets)
a strong nail or bolt for holding pieces of metal together. The end opposite the head is flattened to form another head when it is in place.

rivet *verb* (rivets, riveting, riveted)
1 fasten with rivets. 2 hold firmly, *He stood riveted to the spot.* 3 fascinate, *The concert was riveting.* **riveter** *noun* [from old French]

rivulet *noun* (*plural* rivulets)
a small stream. [from Latin *rivus* = stream]

RN *abbreviation*
Royal Navy.

roach *noun* (*plural* roach)
a small freshwater fish. [from old French]

road *noun* (*plural* roads)
1 a level way with a hard surface made for traffic to travel on. 2 a way or course, *the road to success.* [from Old English]

roadblock *noun* (*plural* roadblocks)
a barrier across a road, set up by the police or army to stop and check vehicles.

road-holding *adjective*
the ability of a vehicle to remain stable and under control when cornering, especially when travelling fast.

road rage *noun*
abuse, violence, or aggressive behaviour by a driver towards other drivers.

roadway *noun*
the middle part of the road, used by traffic.

roadworthy *adjective*
safe to be used on roads.

roam *verb* (roams, roaming, roamed)
wander. **roam** *noun* [origin unknown]

roan *adjective*
(of a horse) brown or black with many white hairs. [from old French]

roar *noun* (*plural* roars)
a loud deep sound like that made by a lion.

roar *verb* (roars, roaring, roared)
make a roar.
a roaring trade brisk selling of something. [from Old English]

roast *verb* (roasts, roasting, roasted)
1 cook meat etc. in an oven or by exposing it to heat. 2 make or be very hot.

roast *adjective*
roasted, *roast beef.*

roast *noun* (*plural* roasts)
1 meat for roasting. 2 roast meat. [via old French from Germanic]

rob *verb* (robs, robbing, robbed)
take or steal from somebody, *He robbed me of my watch.* **robber** *noun*, **robbery** *noun* [via old French from Germanic]

robe *noun* (*plural* robes)
a long loose garment.

robe *verb* (robes, robing, robed)
dress in a robe or ceremonial robes. [via old French from Germanic]

robin *noun* (*plural* robins)
a small brown bird with a red breast. [from old French, = Robert]

robot *noun* (*plural* robots)
1 a machine that looks or acts like a person. 2 a machine operated by remote control. **robotic** *adjective* [from Czech *robota* = forced labour]

robust *adjective*
strong and vigorous.
robustly *adverb*, **robustness** *noun* [from Latin *robur* = strength, an oak tree]

rock¹ *noun* (*plural* rocks)
1 a large stone or boulder. 2 the hard part of the earth's crust, under the soil. 3 a hard sweet usually shaped like a stick and sold at the seaside. [from old French]

rock² *verb* (rocks, rocking, rocked)
1 move gently backwards and forwards while supported on something. 2 shake violently, *The earthquake rocked the city.*

rock *noun*
1 a rocking movement. 2 rock music.
[from Old English]

rock-bottom *adjective*
at the lowest level, *rock-bottom prices.*

rocker *noun* (*plural* **rockers**)
1 a thing that rocks something or is
rocked. 2 a rocking chair.
off your rocker (*slang*) mad.

rockery *noun* (*plural* **rockeries**)
a mound or bank in a garden, where plants
are made to grow between large rocks.

rocket *noun* (*plural* **rockets**)
1 a firework that shoots high into the air.
2 a structure that flies by expelling
burning gases, used to send up a missile or
a spacecraft. **rocketry** *noun*
rocket *verb* (**rockets, rocketing, rocketed**)
move quickly upwards or away.
[from Italian *rocchetto* = small distaff
(because of the shape)]

rocking chair *noun* (*plural* **rocking chairs**)
a chair that can be rocked by a person
sitting in it.

rocking horse *noun* (*plural* **rocking
horses**)
a model of a horse that can be rocked by a
child sitting on it.

rock music *noun*
popular music with a heavy beat.

rocky¹ *adjective* (**rockier, rockiest**)
1 like rock. 2 full of rocks.

rocky² *adjective* (**rockier, rockiest**)
unsteady. **rockiness** *noun*

rod *noun* (*plural* **rods**)
1 a long thin stick or bar. 2 a stick with a
line attached for fishing.
[from Old English]

rodent *noun* (*plural* **rodents**)
an animal that has large front teeth for
gnawing things, *Rats, mice, and squirrels
are rodents.* [from Latin *rodens* = gnawing]

rodeo (*say* roh-**day**-oh) *noun* (*plural* **rodeos**)
a display of cowboys' skill in riding,
controlling horses, etc.
[Spanish, from *rodear* = go round]

roe¹ *noun*
a mass of eggs or reproductive cells in a
fish's body.
[from old German or old Dutch]

roe² *noun* (*plural* **roes** or **roe**)
a kind of small deer of Europe and Asia.
The male is called a **roebuck**.
[from Old English]

rogue *noun* (*plural* **rogues**)
1 a dishonest person. 2 a mischievous
person. **roguery** *noun* [origin unknown]

roguish *adjective*
playful and mischievous.

roister *verb* (**roisters, roistering, roistered**)
make merry noisily.
[from old French *rustre* = ruffian]

role *noun* (*plural* **roles**)
1 a performer's part in a play or film etc.
2 someone's or something's purpose or
function, *the role of computers in education.*
[from French *rôle* = roll (originally the roll
of paper on which an actor's part was
written)]

role model *noun* (*plural* **role models**)
a person who is regarded as an example of
how to behave, *fathers are role models to
their sons.*

roll *verb* (**rolls, rolling, rolled**)
1 move along by turning over and over,
like a ball or wheel. 2 form something into
the shape of a cylinder or ball. 3 flatten
something by rolling a rounded object over
it. 4 rock from side to side. 5 pass steadily,
The years rolled on. 6 make a long
vibrating sound, *The thunder rolled.*
roll *noun* (*plural* **rolls**)
1 a cylinder made by rolling something up.
2 a small individual portion of bread baked
in a rounded shape. 3 an official list of
names. 4 a long vibrating sound, *a drum
roll.* [from Latin *rotula* = little wheel]

roll-call *noun* (*plural* **roll-calls**)
the calling of a list of names to check that
everyone is present.

roller *noun* (*plural* **rollers**)
1 a cylinder for rolling over things, or on
which something is wound. 2 a long
swelling sea-wave.

rollerball *noun* (*plural* **rollerballs**)
a ballpoint pen using a smaller ball and
thinner ink so that it writes very smoothly.

Rollerblade *noun* (*plural* **Rollerblades**)
(*trade mark*) a boot like an ice-skating boot,
with a line of wheels in place of the skate,
for rolling smoothly on hard ground.
rollerblading *noun*

roller coaster *noun* (*plural* **roller coasters**)
a switchback at a fair etc.

roller skate *noun* (*plural* **roller skates**)
a framework with wheels, fitted under a
shoe so that the wearer can roll smoothly
over the ground. **roller-skating** *noun*

rollicking *adjective*
boisterous and full of fun.
[from *romp* + *frolic*]

rolling pin *noun*
a heavy cylinder for rolling over pastry to
flatten it.

rolling stock *noun*
railway engines and carriages and wagons
etc.

roly-poly *noun* (*plural* **roly-polies**)
a pudding of paste covered with jam, rolled
up and boiled.
[a nonsense word based on *roll*]

ROM *abbreviation*
read-only memory (in a computer), with
contents that can be searched or copied but
not changed.

Roman *adjective*
1 of ancient or modern Rome or its people.
2 Roman Catholic. **Roman** *noun*

Roman alphabet *noun*
this alphabet, in which most European
languages are written.

Roman candle *noun* (*plural* **Roman candles**)
a tubular firework that sends out coloured
fireballs.

Roman Catholic *adjective*
belonging to or to do with the Church that
has the Pope (bishop of Rome) as its leader.

Roman Catholic *noun* (*plural* **Roman Catholics**)
a member of this Church.

romance (*say* ro-manss) *noun* (*plural* **romances**)
1 tender feelings, experiences, and
qualities connected with love. 2 a love
story. 3 a love affair. 4 an imaginative
story about the adventures of heroes, *a
romance of King Arthur's court*.
[from old French]

Roman numerals *plural noun*
letters that represent numbers (I = 1, V = 5,
X = 10, etc.), used by the ancient Romans.
(Compare *arabic numerals*.)

romantic *adjective*
1 to do with romance. 2 sentimental or
idealistic; not realistic or practical.
romantically *adverb*

Romany *noun* (*plural* **Romanies**)
1 a gypsy. 2 the language of gypsies.
[from a Romany word *rom* = man]

romp *verb* (**romps, romping, romped**)
play in a lively way. **romp** *noun*
[origin unknown]

rompers *plural noun*
a piece of clothing for a baby or young
child, covering the body and legs.

rondo *noun* (*plural* **rondos**)
a piece of music whose first part recurs
several times.
[Italian, from French *rondeau* = circle]

roof *noun* (*plural* **roofs**)
1 the part that covers the top of a building,
shelter, or vehicle. 2 the top inside surface
of something, *the roof of the mouth*.
[from Old English]

roof-rack *noun* (*plural* **roof-racks**)
a framework for carrying luggage on top of
a vehicle.

rook[1] *noun* (*plural* **rooks**)
a black crow that nests in large groups.

rook *verb* (**rooks, rooking, rooked**)
(*informal*)
swindle; charge people an unnecessarily
high price. [from Old English]

rook² *noun* (*plural* rooks)
a chess piece shaped like a castle.
[from Arabic]

rookery *noun* (*plural* rookeries)
a place where many rooks nest.

room *noun* (*plural* rooms)
1 a part of a building with its own walls
and ceiling. 2 enough space, *Is there room
for me?* **roomful** *noun* [from Old English]

roomy *adjective* (roomier, roomiest)
containing plenty of room; spacious.

roost *verb* (roosts, roosting, roosted)
(of birds) perch or settle for sleep.
roost *noun* (*plural* roosts)
a place where birds roost.
[from Old English]

rooster *noun* (*plural* roosters) (*American*)
a cockerel.

root¹ *noun* (*plural* roots)
1 that part of a plant that grows under the
ground and absorbs water and
nourishment from the soil. 2 a source or
basis, *The love of money is the root of all
evil.* 3 a number in relation to the number
it produces when multiplied by itself, *9 is
the square root of 81* (9 × 9 = 81).
take root 1 grow roots. 2 become
established.
root *verb* (roots, rooting, rooted)
1 take root; cause something to take root.
2 fix firmly, *Fear rooted us to the spot.*
root out get rid of something.
[from Old Norse]

root² *verb* (roots, rooting, rooted)
rummage; (of an animal) turn up ground in
search of food. [from Old English]

rope *noun* (*plural* ropes)
a strong thick cord made of twisted strands
of fibre.
show someone the ropes show him or her
how to do something.
rope *verb* (ropes, roping, roped)
fasten with a rope.
rope in persuade a person to take part in
something.
[from Old English]

rosary *noun* (*plural* rosaries)
a string of beads for keeping count of a set
of prayers as they are said. [from Latin]

rose¹ *noun* (*plural* roses)
1 a shrub that has showy flowers often
with thorny stems. 2 deep pink colour. 3 a
sprinkling-nozzle with many holes, e.g. on
a watering can or hosepipe.
[via Old English from Greek]

rose² *past tense* of **rise**.

rosemary *noun*
an evergreen shrub with fragrant leaves,
used in cooking. [from Latin]

rosette *noun* (*plural* rosettes)
a large circular badge or ornament, made
of ribbon. [French, = little rose]

Rosh Hashanah or Rosh Hashana
noun
the Jewish New Year.
[Hebrew, = head of the year]

roster *noun* (*plural* rosters)
a list showing people's turns to be on duty
etc.
roster *verb* (rosters, rostering, rostered)
place on a roster. [from Dutch]

rostrum *noun* (*plural* rostra)
a platform for one person. [Latin, = beak,
prow of a warship (because a rostrum in
ancient Rome was decorated with the
prows of captured enemy ships)]

rosy *adjective* (rosier, rosiest)
1 deep pink. 2 hopeful or cheerful, *a rosy
future.* **rosiness** *noun*

rot *verb* (rots, rotting, rotted)
go soft or bad and become useless; decay.
rot *noun*
1 rotting or decay. 2 (*informal*) nonsense.
[from Old English]

rota (*say* roh-ta) *noun* (*plural* rotas)
a list of people to do things or of things to
be done in turn. [Latin, = wheel]

rotate *verb* (rotates, rotating, rotated)
1 go round like a wheel; revolve. 2 arrange
or happen in a series; take turns at doing
something. **rotation** *noun*, **rotary** *adjective*,
rotatory *adjective* [same origin as *rota*]

rote *noun*
by rote from memory or by routine,

without full understanding of the meaning, *We used to learn French songs by rote.* [origin unknown]

rotor *noun* (*plural* **rotors**)
a rotating part of a machine or helicopter. [from *rotate*]

rotten *adjective*
1 rotted, *rotten apples.* 2 (*informal*) worthless or unpleasant. **rottenness** *noun*

rottweiler *noun* (*plural* **rottweilers**)
a German breed of powerful black-and-tan working dog, sometimes used as guard dogs. [German, from *Rottweil*, a town in Germany where the dog was bred]

rotund *adjective*
rounded or plump. **rotundity** *noun* [from Latin *rotundus* = round]

rouble (*say* roo-bul) *noun* (*plural* **roubles**)
the unit of money in Russia. [via French from Russian]

rouge (*say* roozh) *noun*
a reddish cosmetic for colouring the cheeks. **rouge** *verb* [French, = red]

rough *adjective* (**rougher, roughest**)
1 not smooth; uneven. 2 not gentle or careful; violent, *a rough push.* 3 not exact, *a rough guess.*
roughly *adverb*, **roughness** *noun*
rough *verb* (**roughs, roughing, roughed**)
rough it do without ordinary comforts.
rough out draw or plan something roughly.
rough up (*slang*) treat a person violently.
[from Old English]

roughage *noun*
fibre in food, which helps digestion.

roughen *verb* (**roughens, roughening, roughened**)
make or become rough.

roulette (*say* roo-let) *noun*
a gambling game where players bet on where the ball in a rotating disc will come to rest. [French, = little wheel]

round *adjective*
1 shaped like a circle or ball or cylinder; curved. 2 full or complete, *a round dozen.* 3 returning to the start, *a round trip.*

roundness *noun*
in round figures approximately, without giving exact units.

round *adverb*
1 in a circle or curve; round something, *Go round to the back of the house.* 2 in every direction, *Hand the cakes round.* 3 in a new direction, *Turn your chair round.* 4 to someone's house or office etc., *Go round after dinner.*
come round become conscious again.
round about 1 near by. 2 approximately.

round *preposition*
1 on all sides of, *Put a fence round the field.* 2 in a curve or circle at an even distance from, *The earth moves round the sun.* 3 to all parts of, *Show them round the house.* 4 on the further side of, *The shop is round the corner.*

round *noun* (*plural* **rounds**)
1 a round object. 2 a whole slice of bread; a sandwich made with two slices of bread. 3 a series of visits made by a doctor, postman, etc. 4 one section or stage in a competition, *Winners go on to the next round.* 5 a shot or volley of shots from a gun; ammunition for this. 6 a song in which people sing the same words but start at different times.

round *verb* (**rounds, rounding, rounded**)
1 make or become round. 2 travel round, *The car rounded the corner.*
round off finish something.
round up gather people or animals together.
[from old French; related to *rotund*]

roundabout *noun* (*plural* **roundabouts**)
1 a road junction where traffic has to pass round a circular structure in the road. 2 a circular revolving ride at a fair.

roundabout *adjective*
indirect; not using the shortest way of going or of saying or doing something, *I heard the news in a roundabout way.*

rounders *noun*
a game in which players try to hit a ball and run round a circuit.

Roundhead *noun* (*plural* **Roundheads**)
an opponent of King Charles I in the English Civil War (1642–9). [so called because many of them wore their hair cut short at a time when long hair was in fashion for men]

roundly *adverb*
1 thoroughly or severely, *We were roundly told off for being late.* **2** in a rounded shape.

round-shouldered *adjective*
with the shoulders bent forward, so that the back is rounded.

roundsman *noun* (*plural* **roundsmen**)
a tradesman's employee who delivers goods on a regular round.

round-the-clock *adjective*
lasting or happening all day and all night.

round trip *noun* (*plural* **round trips**)
a trip to one or more places and back to where you started.

round-up *noun* (*plural* **round-ups**)
1 a gathering up of cattle or people, *a police round-up of suspects.* **2** a summary, *a round-up of the news.*

roundworm *noun* (*plural* **roundworms**)
a kind of worm that lives as a parasite in the intestines of animals and birds.

rouse *verb* (**rouses, rousing, roused**)
1 make or become awake. **2** cause to become active or excited.
[probably from old French]

rousing *adjective*
loud or exciting, *three rousing cheers.*

rout *verb* (**routs, routing, routed**)
defeat and chase away an enemy. **rout** *noun*
[from old French]

route (*say as* root) *noun* (*plural* **routes**)
the way taken to get to a place.
[from old French]

routine (*say* roo-**teen**) *noun* (*plural* **routines**)
a regular way of doing things. **routinely** *adverb* [French; related to *route*]

rove *verb* (**roves, roving, roved**)
roam. **rover** *noun* [probably from a Scandinavian language]

row[1] (rhymes with *go*) *noun* (*plural* **rows**)
a line of people or things.
[from Old English *raw*]

row[2] (rhymes with *go*) *verb* (**rows, rowing, rowed**)
make a boat move by using oars.
rower *noun*, **rowing boat** *noun*
[from Old English *rowan*]

row[3] (rhymes with *cow*) *noun* (*plural* **rows**)
1 a loud noise. **2** a quarrel. **3** a scolding.
[origin unknown]

rowan (*say* roh-an) *noun* (*plural* **rowans**)
a tree that bears hanging bunches of red berries. [a Scandinavian word]

rowdy *adjective* (**rowdier, rowdiest**)
noisy and disorderly. **rowdiness** *noun*
[originally American; origin unknown]

rowlock (*say* rol-ok) *noun* (*plural* **rowlocks**)
a device on the side of a boat, keeping an oar in place. [from an earlier word *oarlock*, with *row*[2] in place of *oar*]

royal *adjective*
to do with a king or queen. **royally** *adverb*
[from old French; related to *regal*]

royalty *noun*
1 being royal. **2** a royal person or persons, *in the presence of royalty.* **3** (*plural* **royalties**) a payment made to an author or composer etc. for each copy of a work sold or for each performance.

RSVP *abbreviation*
répondez s'il vous plaît (French, = please reply).

rub *verb* (**rubs, rubbing, rubbed**)
move something backwards and forwards while pressing it on something else.
rub *noun*
rub out remove something by rubbing.
[origin unknown]

rubber *noun* (*plural* **rubbers**)
1 a strong elastic substance used for making tyres, balls, hoses, etc. **2** a piece of rubber for rubbing out pencil or ink marks. **rubbery** *adjective*

rubber plant *noun* (*plural* **rubber plants**)
1 a tall evergreen plant with tough shiny leaves, often grown as a house plant. **2** a rubber tree.

rubber stamp *noun* (*plural* **rubber stamps**)
a small device with lettering or a design on it, which is inked and used to mark paper etc.

rubber-stamp *verb* (**rubber-stamps, rubber-stamping, rubber-stamped**)
give official approval to a decision without thinking about it.

rubber tree *noun* (*plural* **rubber trees**)
a tropical tree from which rubber is obtained.

rubbish *noun*
1 things that are worthless or not wanted. 2 nonsense. [from old French]

rubble *noun*
broken pieces of brick or stone. [from old French]

rubella *noun*
an infectious disease which causes a red rash, and which can damage a baby if the mother catches it early in pregnancy. [from Latin *rubellus* = reddish]

rubric *noun*
a set of instructions at the beginning of an official document or an examination paper. [from Latin *rubeus* = red (because rubrics used to be written in red)]

ruby *noun* (*plural* **rubies**)
a red jewel. [from Latin *rubeus* = red]

ruby wedding *noun*
a couple's fortieth wedding anniversary.

ruck *noun* (*plural* **rucks**)
a dense crowd. [probably from a Scandinavian language]

rucksack *noun* (*plural* **rucksacks**)
a bag on straps for carrying on the back. [from German *Rücken* = back + *Sack* = sack[1]]

ructions *plural noun* (*informal*)
protests and noisy argument. [origin unknown]

rudder *noun* (*plural* **rudders**)
a hinged upright piece at the back of a ship or aircraft, used for steering. [from Old English]

ruddy *adjective* (**ruddier, ruddiest**)
red and healthy-looking, *a ruddy complexion*. [from Old English]

rude *adjective* (**ruder, rudest**)
1 impolite. 2 indecent or improper. 3 roughly made; crude, *a rude shelter*. 4 vigorous and hearty, *in rude health*. **rudely** *adverb*, **rudeness** *noun*
[from Latin *rudis* = raw, wild]

rudimentary *adjective*
1 to do with rudiments; elementary. 2 not fully developed, *Penguins have rudimentary wings*.

rudiments (*say* rood-i-ments) *plural noun*
the elementary principles of a subject, *Learn the rudiments of chemistry*. [same origin as *rude*]

rueful *adjective*
regretful. **ruefully** *adverb*
[from Old English]

ruff *noun* (*plural* **ruffs**)
1 a starched pleated frill worn round the neck in the 16th century. 2 a collar-like ring of feathers or fur round a bird's or animal's neck. [a different spelling of *rough*]

ruffian *noun* (*plural* **ruffians**)
a violent lawless person. **ruffianly** *adjective*
[via French and Italian from Germanic]

ruffle *verb* (**ruffles, ruffling, ruffled**)
1 disturb the smoothness of a thing. 2 upset or annoy someone.
ruffle *noun* (*plural* **ruffles**)
a gathered ornamental frill. [origin unknown]

rug *noun* (*plural* **rugs**)
1 a thick mat for the floor. 2 a piece of thick fabric used as a blanket. [probably from a Scandinavian language]

Rugby or **Rugby football** *noun*
a kind of football game using an oval ball that players may carry or kick. [named after Rugby School in Warwickshire, where it was first played]

rugged *adjective*
1 having an uneven surface or outline; craggy. 2 sturdy. [probably from a Scandinavian language]

rugger *noun*
Rugby football.

ruin *noun* (*plural* **ruins**)
1 severe damage or destruction to something. 2 a building that has fallen down.
ruin *verb* (**ruins, ruining, ruined**)
damage a thing so severely that it is useless; destroy. **ruination** *noun*
[from Latin *ruere* = to fall]

ruinous *adjective*
1 causing ruin. 2 in ruins; ruined.

rule *noun* (*plural* **rules**)
1 something that people have to obey.
2 ruling; governing, *under French rule.* 3 a carpenter's ruler.
as a rule usually; more often than not.
rule *verb* (**rules, ruling, ruled**)
1 govern; reign. 2 make a decision, *The referee ruled that it was a foul.* 3 draw a straight line with a ruler or other straight edge. [from old French; related to *regulate*]

ruler *noun* (*plural* **rulers**)
1 a person who governs. 2 a strip of wood, metal, or plastic with straight edges, used for measuring and drawing straight lines.

ruling *noun* (*plural* **rulings**)
a judgement.

rum *noun*
a strong alcoholic drink made from sugar or molasses.
[origin unknown]

rumble *verb* (**rumbles, rumbling, rumbled**)
make a deep heavy continuous sound like thunder. **rumble** *noun*
[probably from old Dutch]

rumble strip *noun* (*plural* **rumble strips**)
a series of raised strips on a road that warns drivers of the edge of the roadway, or tells them to slow down, by making vehicles vibrate.

ruminant *adjective*
ruminating.
ruminant *noun* (*plural* **ruminants**)
an animal that chews the cud (see *cud*).

ruminate *verb* (**ruminates, ruminating, ruminated**)
1 chew the cud. 2 meditate or ponder.
rumination *noun*, **ruminative** *adjective*
[from Latin]

rummage *verb* (**rummages, rummaging, rummaged**)
turn things over or move them about while looking for something. **rummage** *noun*
[from old French]

rummy *noun*
a card game in which players try to form sets or sequences of cards.
[originally American: origin unknown]

rumour *noun* (*plural* **rumours**)
information that spreads to a lot of people but may not be true.
rumour *verb*
be rumoured be spread as a rumour.
[from Latin *rumor* = noise]

rump *noun* (*plural* **rumps**)
the hind part of an animal.
[probably from a Scandinavian language]

rumple *verb* (**rumples, rumpling, rumpled**)
crumple; make a thing untidy.
[from Dutch]

rump steak *noun* (*plural* **rump steaks**)
a piece of meat from the rump of a cow.

rumpus *noun* (*plural* **rumpuses**) (*informal*)
an uproar; an angry protest.
[origin unknown]

run *verb* (**runs, running, ran, run**)
1 move with quick steps so that both or all feet leave the ground at each stride. 2 go or travel; flow, *Tears ran down his cheeks.*
3 produce a flow of liquid, *Run some water into it.* 4 work or function, *The engine was running smoothly.* 5 manage or organize, *She runs a grocery shop.* 6 compete in a contest, *He ran for President.* 7 extend, *A fence runs round the estate.* 8 go or take in a vehicle, *I'll run you to the station.*
run away leave a place secretly or quickly.
run down 1 run over. 2 stop gradually; decline. 3 (*informal*) say unkind or unfair things about someone.
run into 1 collide with. 2 happen to meet.
run out 1 have used up your stock of something. 2 knock over the wicket of a running batsman.

run over knock down or crush with a moving vehicle.
run through examine or rehearse.
run noun (plural **runs**)
1 the action of running; a time spent running, *Go for a run.* 2 a point scored in cricket or baseball. 3 a continuous series of events, etc., *She had a run of good luck.*
4 an enclosure for animals, *a chicken run.*
5 a track, *a ski run.*
on the run running away from pursuit or capture.
[from Old English]

runaway noun (plural **runaways**)
someone who has run away.
runaway adjective
1 having run away or out of control. 2 won easily, *a runaway victory.*

rundown adjective
1 tired and in bad health. 2 in bad condition; dilapidated.

rung[1] noun (plural **rungs**)
a crosspiece in a ladder.
[from Old English]

rung[2] past participle of **ring**[2].

runner noun (plural **runners**)
1 a person or animal that runs, especially in a race. 2 a stem that grows away from a plant and roots itself. 3 a groove, rod, or roller for a thing to move on; each of the long strips under a sledge. 4 a long narrow strip of carpet or covering.

runner bean noun (plural **runner beans**)
a kind of climbing bean with long green pods which are eaten.

runner-up noun (plural **runners-up**)
someone who comes second in a competition.

running present participle of **run**.
in the running competing and with a chance of winning.
running adjective
continuous or consecutive; without an interval, *It rained for four days running.*

runny adjective (**runnier**, **runniest**)
1 flowing like liquid, *runny honey.*
2 producing a flow of liquid, *a runny nose.*

runway noun (plural **runways**)
a long hard surface on which aircraft take off and land.

rupee noun (plural **rupees**)
the unit of money in India and Pakistan.
[from Sanskrit *rupya* = wrought silver]

rupture verb (**ruptures**, **rupturing**, **ruptured**)
break or burst. **rupture** noun
[from Latin *ruptum* = broken]

rural adjective
to do with or belonging to the countryside.
[from Latin *ruris* = of the country]

ruse noun (plural **ruses**)
a deception or trick. [from French]

rush[1] verb (**rushes**, **rushing**, **rushed**)
1 hurry. 2 move or flow quickly. 3 attack or capture by rushing.
rush noun (plural **rushes**)
1 a hurry. 2 a sudden movement towards something. 3 a sudden great demand for something. [from old French]

rush[2] noun (plural **rushes**)
a plant with a thin stem that grows in marshy places. [from Old English]

rush hour noun (plural **rush hours**)
the time when traffic is busiest.

rusk noun (plural **rusks**)
a kind of hard, dry biscuit, especially for feeding babies.
[from Spanish or Portuguese]

russet noun
reddish-brown colour.
[from Latin *russus* = red]

rust noun
1 a red or brown substance that forms on iron or steel exposed to damp and corrodes it. 2 reddish-brown colour.
rust verb (**rusts**, **rusting**, **rusted**)
make or become rusty. [from Old English]

rustic adjective
1 rural. 2 made of rough timber or branches, *a rustic bridge.*
[same origin as *rural*]

rustle verb (**rustles**, **rustling**, **rustled**)
1 make a sound like paper being crumpled.
2 (*American*) steal horses or cattle, *cattle*

rustling. rustle *noun*, **rustler** *noun*
rustle up (*informal*) produce, *rustle up a meal*.
[imitating the sound]

rusty *adjective* (**rustier, rustiest**)
1 coated with rust. 2 weakened by lack of use or practice, *My French is a bit rusty*.
rustiness *noun*

rut *noun* (*plural* **ruts**)
1 a deep track made by wheels in soft ground. 2 a settled and usually dull way of life, *We are getting into a rut*. **rutted** *adjective* [probably related to *route*]

ruthless *adjective*
pitiless, merciless, or cruel.
ruthlessly *adverb*, **ruthlessness** *noun*
[from Middle English *ruth* = pity]

rye *noun*
a cereal used to make bread, biscuits, etc.
[from Old English]

Ss

S. *abbreviation*
1 south. 2 southern.

sabbath *noun* (*plural* **sabbaths**)
a weekly day for rest and prayer, Saturday for Jews, Sunday for Christians.
[from Hebrew *shabat* = rest]

sable *noun*
1 a kind of dark fur. 2 (*poetic*) black.
[via old French and Latin from a Slavonic language]

sabotage *noun*
deliberate damage or disruption to hinder an enemy, employer, etc.
sabotage *verb*, **saboteur** *noun*
[from French *saboter* = make a noise with *sabots* (= wooden clogs)]

sabre *noun* (*plural* **sabres**)
1 a heavy sword with a curved blade. 2 a light fencing-sword. [from Hungarian]

sac *noun* (*plural* **sacs**)
a bag-shaped part in an animal or plant.
[French, from Latin *saccus* = sack[1]]

saccharin (*say* sak-er-in) *noun*
a very sweet substance used as a substitute for sugar. [from Greek *saccharon* = sugar]

saccharine (*say* sak-er-een) *adjective*
unpleasantly sweet, *a saccharine smile*.

sachet (*say* sash-ay) *noun* (*plural* **sachets**)
a small sealed bag or packet holding a scented substance or a single portion of something. [French, = little sack]

sack[1] *noun* (*plural* **sacks**)
a large bag made of strong material.
sacking *noun*
the sack (*informal*) dismissal from a job, *He got the sack*.
sack *verb* (*informal*) (**sacks, sacking, sacked**)
dismiss someone from a job.
[via Old English from Latin]

sack[2] *verb* (**sacks, sacking, sacked**) (*old use*)
plunder a captured town in a violent destructive way. **sack** *noun*
[from French *mettre à sac* = put in a sack]

sacrament *noun* (*plural* **sacraments**)
an important Christian religious ceremony such as baptism or Holy Communion.
[same origin as *sacred*]

sacred *adjective*
holy; to do with God or a god. [from Latin]

sacrifice *noun* (*plural* **sacrifices**)
1 giving something that you think will please a god. 2 giving up a thing you value, so that something good may happen. 3 a thing sacrificed. **sacrificial** *adjective*
sacrifice *verb* (**sacrifices, sacrificing, sacrificed**)
give something as a sacrifice. [from Latin *sacrificare* = make something holy]

sacrilege (*say* sak-ril-ij) *noun*
disrespect or damage to something people regard as sacred. **sacrilegious** *adjective*
[from Latin *sacer* = sacred + *legere* = take away]

sacrosanct *adjective*
sacred or respected and therefore not to be harmed. [from Latin *sacro* = by a sacred rite + *sanctus* = holy]

sad *adjective* (sadder, saddest)
unhappy; showing or causing sorrow. **sadly**
adverb, **sadness** *noun* [from Old English]

sadden *verb* (saddens, saddening,
saddened)
make a person sad.

saddle *noun* (*plural* saddles)
1 a seat for putting on the back of a horse
or other animal. 2 the seat of a bicycle. 3 a
ridge of high land between two peaks.
saddle *verb* (saddles, saddling, saddled)
put a saddle on a horse etc.
[from Old English]

sadist (*say* say-dist) *noun* (*plural* sadists)
a person who enjoys hurting or
humiliating other people.
sadism *noun*, **sadistic** *adjective*
[named after a French novelist, the
Marquis de Sade, noted for the cruelties in
his stories]

s.a.e. *abbreviation*
stamped addressed envelope.

safari *noun* (*plural* safaris)
an expedition to see or hunt wild animals.
[from Arabic *safar* = a journey]

safari park *noun* (*plural* safari parks)
a park where wild animals are kept in
large enclosures to be seen by visitors.

safe *adjective*
1 not in danger. 2 not dangerous.
safely *adverb*, **safeness** *noun*, **safety** *noun*
safe *noun* (*plural* safes)
a strong cupboard or box in which
valuables can be locked safely.
[from old French; related to *save*]

safeguard *noun* (*plural* safeguards)
a protection.
safeguard *verb* (safeguards, safeguarding,
safeguarded)
protect.

safe sex *noun*
sexual activity in which precautions, such
as using a condom, are taken to prevent the
spread of Aids or other infections.

safety pin *noun* (*plural* safety pins)
a U-shaped pin with a clip fastening over
the point.

saffron *noun*
1 deep yellow colour. 2 a kind of crocus
with orange-coloured stigmas. 3 these
stigmas dried and used to colour or flavour
food. [from Arabic]

sag *verb* (sags, sagging, sagged)
go down in the middle because something
heavy is pressing on it; droop. **sag** *noun*
[from old German]

saga (*say* sah-ga) *noun* (*plural* sagas)
a long story with many episodes.
[from Old Norse]

sagacious (*say* sa-gay-shus) *adjective*
shrewd and wise. **sagaciously** *adverb*,
sagacity *noun* [from Latin]

sage[1] *noun*
a kind of herb used in cooking and
formerly used in medicine.
[from Latin *salvia* = healing plant]

sage[2] *adjective*
wise. **sagely** *adverb*
sage *noun* (*plural* sages)
a wise and respected person.
[from Latin *sapere* = to be wise]

sago *noun*
a starchy white food used to make
puddings. [from Malay (a language spoken
in Malaysia)]

said past tense of **say**.

sail *noun* (*plural* sails)
1 a large piece of strong cloth attached to a
mast etc. to catch the wind and make a ship
or boat move. 2 a short voyage. 3 an arm of
a windmill.
sail *verb* (sails, sailing, sailed)
1 travel in a ship or boat. 2 start a voyage,
We sail at noon. 3 control a ship or boat.
4 move quickly and smoothly. **sailing ship**
noun [from Old English]

sailboard *noun* (*plural* sailboards)
a flat board with a mast and sail, used in
windsurfing.

sailor *noun* (*plural* sailors)
a person who sails; a member of a ship's
crew or of a navy.

saint noun (plural saints)
a holy or very good person.
saintly adverb, **saintliness** noun
[via Old English from Latin sanctus = holy]

sake noun
for the sake of so as to help or please a
person, get a thing, etc.
[from Old English]

salad noun (plural salads)
a mixture of vegetables eaten raw or cold.
[from French]

salamander noun (plural salamanders)
a lizard-like amphibian formerly thought
to live in fire. [from Greek]

salami noun
a spiced sausage, originally made in Italy.
[Italian]

salary noun (plural salaries)
a regular wage, usually for a year's work,
paid in monthly instalments.
salaried adjective
[from Latin salarium = salt-money, money
given to Roman soldiers to buy salt]

sale noun (plural sales)
1 selling. 2 a time when things are sold at
reduced prices. [from Old Norse]

salesperson noun (plural salespersons)
a person employed to sell goods.
salesman noun (plural salesmen),
saleswoman noun (plural saleswomen)

salient (say say-lee-ent) adjective
1 jutting out; projecting. 2 most noticeable,
the salient features of the plan.
salient noun (plural salients)
a part of a fortification or battle-line that
juts out. [from Latin saliens = leaping]

saline adjective
containing salt. [from Latin sal = salt]

saliva noun
the natural liquid in a person's or animal's
mouth. **salivary** adjective [Latin]

salivate (say sal-iv-ayt) verb (salivates,
salivating, salivated)
form saliva, especially a large amount.
salivation noun

sallow adjective
(of the skin) slightly yellow. **sallowness**
noun [from Old English]

sally noun (plural sallies)
1 a sudden rush forward. 2 an excursion.
3 a lively or witty remark.
sally verb (sallies, sallying, sallied)
make a sudden attack or an excursion.
[same origin as salient]

salmon (say sam-on) noun (plural salmon)
a large edible fish with pink flesh.
[from Latin]

salmonella (say sal-mon-el-a) noun
a bacterium that can cause food poisoning.
[named after an American scientist, Elmer
Salmon, who studied the causes of disease]

salon noun (plural salons)
1 a large elegant room. 2 a room or shop
where a hairdresser etc. receives
customers. [French]

saloon noun (plural saloons)
1 a car with a hard roof and a separate
boot. 2 a room where people can sit, drink,
etc. [from French salon]

salsa noun
1 a hot spicy sauce. 2 a kind of modern
Latin American dance music; a dance to
this. [Spanish, = sauce]

salt noun (plural salts)
1 sodium chloride, the white substance
that gives sea water its taste and is used for
flavouring food. 2 a chemical compound of
a metal and an acid. **salty** adjective
salt verb (salts, salting, salted)
flavour or preserve food with salt.
[from Old English]

salt cellar noun (plural salt cellars)
a small dish or perforated pot holding salt
for use at meals.
[cellar from old French salier = salt-box]

salts plural noun
a substance that looks like salt, especially a
laxative.

salubrious adjective
good for people's health. **salubrity** noun
[from Latin salus = health]

salutary *adjective*
beneficial; having a good effect, *She gave us some salutary advice.*
[same origin as *salubrious*]

salutation *noun* (*plural* salutations)
a greeting.

salute *verb* (salutes, saluting, saluted)
1 raise your right hand to your forehead as a sign of respect. **2** greet. **3** say that you respect or admire something, *We salute this achievement.*
salute *noun* (*plural* salutes)
1 the act of saluting. **2** the firing of guns as a sign of greeting or respect.
[same origin as *salubrious*]

salvage *verb* (salvages, salvaging, salvaged)
save or rescue something so that it can be used again. **salvage** *noun*
[from Latin *salvare* = save]

salvation *noun*
1 saving from loss or damage etc. **2** (in Christian teaching) saving the soul from sin and its consequences.
[same origin as *salvage*]

salve *noun* (*plural* salves)
1 a soothing ointment. **2** something that soothes.
salve *verb* (salves, salving, salved)
soothe a person's conscience or wounded pride. [from Old English]

salver *noun* (*plural* salvers)
a small tray, usually of metal.
[via French from Spanish]

salvo *noun* (*plural* salvoes or salvos)
a volley of shots or of applause.
[from Italian *salva* = salutation]

same *adjective*
1 of one kind, exactly alike or equal. **2** not changing; not different. **sameness** *noun*
[from Old Norse]

samosa *noun* (*plural* samosas)
a triangular, thin pastry case filled with spicy meat or vegetables, fried and eaten as a snack. [from Urdu]

samovar *noun* (*plural* samovars)
a Russian tea-urn. [Russian, = self-boiler]

sampan *noun* (*plural* sampans)
a small flat-bottomed boat used in China.
[from Chinese *sanpan* (*san* = three, *pan* = boards)]

sample *noun* (*plural* samples)
a small amount that shows what something is like; a specimen.
sample *verb* (samples, sampling, sampled)
take a sample of something.
[from old French *essample* = example]

sampler *noun* (*plural* samplers)
a piece of embroidery worked in various stitches to show skill in needlework.
[same origin as *sample*]

samurai (*say* sam-oor-eye or sam-yoor-eye) *noun* (*plural* samurai)
a member of an ancient Japanese warrior caste. [Japanese]

sanatorium *noun* (*plural* sanatoriums or sanatoria)
a hospital for treating chronic diseases or convalescents. [from Latin *sanare* = heal]

sanctify *verb* (sanctifies, sanctifying, sanctified)
make holy or sacred. **sanctification** *noun*
[from Latin *sanctus* = holy]

sanctimonious *adjective*
making a show of being virtuous or pious.
[from Latin *sanctimonia* = holiness, piety]

sanction *noun* (*plural* sanctions)
1 permission or authorization. **2** action taken against a nation that is considered to have broken an international law etc., *Sanctions against that country include refusing to trade with it.*
sanction *verb* (sanctions, sanctioning, sanctioned)
permit or authorize.
[from Latin *sancire* = make holy]

sanctity *noun*
being sacred; holiness.
[same origin as *sanctify*]

sanctuary *noun* (*plural* sanctuaries)
1 a safe place; a refuge. **2** a sacred place; the part of a church where the altar stands.
[same origin as *sanctify*]

sanctum *noun* (*plural* sanctums)
a person's private room.
[Latin, = holy thing]

sand *noun*
the tiny particles that cover the ground in deserts, seashores, etc.
sand *verb* (sands, sanding, sanded)
smooth or polish with sandpaper or some other rough material. **sander** *noun*
[from Old English]

sandal *noun* (*plural* sandals)
a lightweight shoe with straps over the foot. **sandalled** *adjective*
[from Greek *sandalon* = wooden shoe]

sandalwood *noun*
a scented wood from a tropical tree. [via Latin, Greek, and Persian from Sanskrit]

sandbag *noun* (*plural* sandbags)
a bag filled with sand, used to build defences.

sandbank *noun* (*plural* sandbanks)
a bank of sand under water.

sandpaper *noun*
strong paper coated with sand or a similar substance, rubbed on rough surfaces to make them smooth.

sands *plural noun*
a beach or sandy area.

sandstone *noun*
rock made of compressed sand.

sandwich *noun* (*plural* sandwiches)
two or more slices of bread with jam, meat, or cheese etc. between them.
sandwich *verb* (sandwiches, sandwiching, sandwiched)
put a thing between two other things.
[invented by the Earl of Sandwich (1718–92) so that he could eat while gambling]

sandwich course *noun* (*plural* sandwich courses)
a college or university course which includes periods in industry or business.

sandy *adjective*
1 like sand. 2 covered with sand.
3 yellowish-red, *sandy hair*. **sandiness** *noun*

sane *adjective*
1 having a healthy mind; not mad.
2 sensible. **sanely** *adverb*, **sanity** *noun*
[from Latin *sanus* = healthy]

sang-froid (*say* sahn-frwah) *noun*
calmness in danger or difficulty.
[French, = cold blood]

sanguinary *adjective*
1 bloodthirsty. 2 involving much violence and slaughter. [from Latin *sanguis* = blood]

sanguine (*say* sang-gwin) *adjective*
hopeful; cheerful and optimistic.
[same origin as *sanguinary* (because good blood was believed to be the cause of cheerfulness)]

sanitary *adjective*
1 free from germs and dirt; hygienic. 2 to do with sanitation.
[from Latin *sanitas* = health]

sanitary towel *noun* (*plural* sanitary towels)
an absorbent pad worn during menstruation.

sanitation *noun*
arrangements for drainage and the disposal of sewage. [from *sanitary*]

sanitize *verb* (sanitizes, sanitizing, sanitized)
1 make sanitary; clean and disinfect.
2 make less unpleasant by taking out anything that might shock or offend, *sanitized stories of 'the good old days'*.

sanity *noun*
being sane.

Sanskrit *noun*
the ancient and sacred language of the Hindus in India.

sap *noun*
the liquid inside a plant, carrying food to all its parts.
sap *verb* (saps, sapping, sapped)
take away a person's strength gradually.
[from Old English]

sapling *noun* (*plural* saplings)
a young tree. [from *sap*]

sapphire *noun* (*plural* sapphires)
a bright-blue jewel. [from Latin]

Saracen noun (plural Saracens)
an Arab or Muslim of the time of the
Crusades.

sarcastic adjective
saying amusing or contemptuous things
that hurt someone's feelings.
sarcastically adverb, **sarcasm** noun
[from Greek sarkazein = tear the flesh]

sarcophagus noun (plural sarcophagi)
a stone coffin, often decorated with
carvings. [from Greek sarkos = of flesh
+ -phagos = eating]

sardine noun (plural sardines)
a small sea fish, usually sold in tins, packed
tightly in oil. [from French]

sardonic adjective
funny in a grim or sarcastic way.
sardonically adverb
[from French]

sari noun (plural saris)
a length of cloth worn wrapped round the
body as a dress, especially by Indian
women and girls. [from Hindi]

sarong noun (plural sarongs)
a strip of cloth worn like a kilt by men and
women of Malaya and Java. [from Malay (a
language spoken in Malaysia)]

sartorial adjective
to do with clothes.
[from Latin sartor = tailor]

sash noun (plural sashes)
a strip of cloth worn round the waist or
over one shoulder.
[from Arabic shash = turban]

sash window (plural sash windows)
a window that slides up and down.
[from chassis]

satanic (say sa-tan-ik) adjective
to do with or like Satan, the Devil in
Jewish and Christian teaching.

satchel noun (plural satchels)
a bag worn on the shoulder or the back,
especially for carrying books to and from
school. [from Latin saccellus = little sack]

sate verb (sates, sating, sated)
satiate. [from Old English]

sateen noun
a cotton material that looks like satin.
[from satin]

satellite noun (plural satellites)
1 a planet or spacecraft etc. that moves in
an orbit round a planet, The moon is a
satellite of the earth. 2 a country that is
under the influence of a more powerful
country; a hanger-on.
[from Latin satelles = a guard]

satiate (say say-shee-ayt) verb (satiates,
satiating, satiated)
satisfy an appetite or desire etc. fully; glut.
[from Latin satis = enough]

satiety (say sat-I-it-ee) noun
being or feeling satiated.

satin noun
a silky material that is shiny on one side.
satiny adjective
[via old French from Arabic]

satire noun (plural satires)
1 using humour or exaggeration to show
what is bad about a person or thing. 2 a
play or poem etc. that does this. **satirical**
adjective, **satirically** adverb, **satirist** noun,
satirize verb [from Latin]

USAGE: Do not confuse with satyr.

satisfaction noun
1 satisfying. 2 being satisfied and pleased
because of this. 3 something that satisfies a
desire etc.
[from Latin satis = enough + facere = make]

satisfactory adjective
good enough; sufficient.
satisfactorily adverb

satisfy verb (satisfies, satisfying, satisfied)
1 give a person etc. what is needed or
wanted. 2 make someone feel certain;
convince, The firemen were satisfied that
the fire was out.
[same origin as satisfaction]

satsuma noun (plural satsumas)
a kind of mandarin orange originally
grown in Japan.
[named after Satsuma, a province of
Japan]

saturate *verb* (**saturates, saturating, saturated**)
1 make a thing very wet. **2** make something take in as much as possible of a substance or goods etc. **saturation** *noun* [from Latin *satur* = full, satiated]

saturnine *adjective*
looking gloomy and forbidding, *a saturnine face.* [because people born under the influence of the planet Saturn were believed to be gloomy]

satyr (*say* sat-er) *noun* (*plural* **satyrs**)
(in Greek myths) a woodland god with a man's body and a goat's ears, tail, and legs.

USAGE: Do not confuse with *satire.*

sauce *noun* (*plural* **sauces**)
1 a thick liquid served with food to add flavour. **2** (*informal*) being cheeky; impudence. [from Latin *salsus* = salted]

saucepan *noun* (*plural* **saucepans**)
a metal cooking pan with a handle at the side.

saucer *noun* (*plural* **saucers**)
a small shallow object on which a cup etc. is placed. [from old French *saussier* = container for sauce]

saucy *adjective* (**saucier, sauciest**)
cheeky or impudent.
saucily *adverb*, **sauciness** *noun*

sauerkraut (*say* sour-krowt) *noun*
chopped and pickled cabbage, originally made in Germany. [from German *sauer* = sour + *Kraut* = cabbage]

sauna *noun* (*plural* **saunas**)
a room or compartment filled with steam, used as a kind of bath. [Finnish]

saunter *verb* (**saunters, sauntering, sauntered**)
walk slowly and casually. **saunter** *noun* [origin unknown]

sausage *noun* (*plural* **sausages**)
a tube of skin or plastic stuffed with minced meat and other filling. [from old French; related to *sauce*]

savage *adjective*
wild and fierce; cruel **savagely** *adverb*, **savageness** *noun*, **savagery** *noun*

savage *noun* (*plural* **savages**)
1 a savage person. **2** (*old use*) a member of a primitive people.

savage *verb* (**savages, savaging, savaged**)
attack by biting, scratching, or trampling, *The sheep was savaged by a dog.* [from Latin *silvaticus* = of the woods, wild]

savannah or **savanna** *noun* (*plural* **savannahs** or **savannas**)
a grassy plain in a hot country, with few or no trees. [via Spanish from Taino (a South American language)]

save *verb* (**saves, saving, saved**)
1 keep safe; free a person or thing from danger or harm. **2** keep something, especially money, so that it can be used later. **3** avoid wasting something, *This will save time.* **4** (in sports) prevent an opponent from scoring.
save *noun*, **saver** *noun*

save *preposition*
except, *All the trains save one were late.* [from old French; related to *salvage*]

savings *plural noun*
money saved.

saviour *noun* (*plural* **saviours**)
a person who saves someone.
the or **our Saviour** (in Christianity) Jesus Christ.

savoir faire (*say* sav-wahr **fair**) *noun*
knowledge of how to behave socially. [French, = knowing how to do]

savour *noun* (*plural* **savours**)
the taste or smell of something.

savour *verb* (**savours, savouring, savoured**)
1 taste or smell. **2** enjoy or relish. [from Latin *sapor* = flavour]

savoury *adjective*
1 tasty but not sweet. **2** having an appetizing taste or smell.

savoury *noun* (*plural* **savouries**)
a savoury dish.

savoy *noun* (*plural* **savoys**)
a kind of cabbage with wrinkled leaves. [named after Savoie, a region in France]

saw¹ noun (plural saws)
a tool with a zigzag edge for cutting wood
or metal etc.
saw verb (saws, sawing, sawed, sawn)
1 cut something with a saw. 2 move to and
fro as a saw does. [from Old English]

saw² past tense of see¹.

sawdust noun
powder that comes from wood cut by a saw.

sawmill noun (plural sawmills)
a mill where timber is cut into planks etc.
by machinery.

Saxon noun (plural Saxons)
1 a member of a people who came from
Europe and occupied parts of England in
the 5th–6th centuries. 2 an Anglo-Saxon.

saxophone noun (plural saxophones)
a brass wind instrument with a reed in the
mouthpiece. **saxophonist** noun
[named after a Belgian instrument maker,
Adolphe Sax, who invented it]

say verb (says, saying, said)
1 speak or express something in words.
2 give an opinion.
say noun
the power to decide something, I have no
say in the matter. [from Old English]

saying noun (plural sayings)
a well-known phrase or proverb or other
statement.

scab noun (plural scabs)
1 a hard crust that forms over a cut or
graze while it is healing. 2 (offensive) a
blackleg. **scabby** adjective [from Old Norse]

scabbard noun (plural scabbards)
the sheath of a sword or dagger.
[from old French]

scabies (say skay-beez) noun
a contagious skin disease with severe
itching, caused by a parasite.
[Latin, from scabere = to scratch]

scaffold noun (plural scaffolds)
a platform on which criminals are
executed.
[from old French; related to catafalque]

scaffolding noun
a structure of poles or tubes and planks
making platforms for workers to stand on
while building or repairing a house etc.

scald verb (scalds, scalding, scalded)
1 burn yourself with very hot liquid or
steam. 2 heat milk until it is nearly
boiling. 3 clean pans etc. with boiling
water. **scald** noun
[from Latin excaldare = wash in hot water]

scale¹ noun (plural scales)
1 a series of units, degrees, or qualities etc.
for measuring something. 2 a series of
musical notes going up or down in a fixed
pattern. 3 proportion or ratio, The scale of
this map is one centimetre to the kilometre.
4 the relative size or importance of
something, They entertain friends on a
large scale.
to scale with the parts in the same
proportions as those of an original, The
architect's plans were drawn to scale.
scale verb (scales, scaling, scaled)
climb, She scaled the ladder.
scale down or **up** reduce or increase at a
fixed rate, or in proportion to something
else.
[from Latin scala = ladder]

scale² noun (plural scales)
1 each of the thin overlapping parts on the
outside of fish, snakes, etc.; a thin flake or
part like this. 2 a hard substance formed in
a kettle or boiler by hard water, or on
teeth.
scale verb (scales, scaling, scaled)
remove scales or scale from something.
[from old French; related to scales]

scale model noun (plural scale models)
a model of something, made to scale.

scales plural noun
a device for weighing things.
[from Old Norse skal = bowl]

scallop noun (plural scallops)
1 a shellfish with two hinged fan-shaped
shells. 2 each curve in an ornamental wavy
border. **scalloped** adjective
[from old French]

scalp noun (plural scalps)
the skin on the top of the head.

scalp verb (scalps, scalping, scalped)
cut or tear the scalp from.
[probably from a Scandinavian language]

scalpel noun (plural scalpels)
a small knife with a thin, sharp blade, used by a surgeon or artist. [from Latin]

scaly adjective (scalier, scaliest)
covered in scales or scale.

scam noun (plural scams) (slang)
a dishonest scheme; a swindle.
[originally American; origin unknown]

scamp noun (plural scamps)
a rascal. [same origin as scamper]

scamper verb (scampers, scampering, scampered)
run quickly, lightly, or playfully. **scamper** noun [originally = run away, decamp; probably via old Dutch from Latin ex-
= away + campus = field]

scampi plural noun
large prawns. [Italian]

scan verb (scans, scanning, scanned)
1 look at every part of something. 2 glance at something. 3 count the beats of a line of poetry; be correct in rhythm, This line doesn't scan. 4 sweep a radar or electronic beam over an area to examine it or in search of something.
scan noun (plural scans)
1 scanning. 2 an examination using a scanner. [from Latin]

scandal noun (plural scandals)
1 something shameful or disgraceful.
2 gossip about people's faults and wrongdoing. **scandalous** adjective
[from Greek skandalon = stumbling block]

scandalize verb (scandalizes, scandalizing, scandalized)
shock a person by something considered shameful or disgraceful.

scandalmonger noun (plural scandalmongers)
a person who invents or spreads scandal.
[from scandal + an old word monger
= trader]

Scandinavian adjective
from or to do with Scandinavia (= Norway, Sweden, and Denmark; sometimes also Finland and Iceland). **Scandinavian** noun

scanner noun (plural scanners)
1 a machine that examines things by means of light or other rays. 2 a machine that converts printed text, pictures, etc. into machine-readable form.

scansion noun
the scanning of verse.

scant adjective
scanty.

scanty adjective (scantier, scantiest)
small in amount or extent; meagre, a scanty harvest. **scantily** adverb, **scantiness** noun
[from Old Norse]

scapegoat noun (plural scapegoats)
a person who is made to bear the blame or punishment for what others have done.
[named after the goat which the ancient Jews allowed to escape into the desert after the priest had symbolically laid the people's sins upon it]

scar[1] noun (plural scars)
the mark left by a cut or burn etc. after it has healed.
scar verb (scars, scarring, scarred)
make a scar or scars on skin etc.
[from Latin]

scar[2] noun (plural scars)
a steep craggy place. [from Old Norse]

scarab noun (plural scarabs)
an ancient Egyptian ornament or symbol carved in the shape of a beetle.
[from Latin scarabaeus = beetle]

scarce adjective (scarcer, scarcest)
1 not enough to supply people. 2 rare.
scarcity noun
make yourself scarce (informal) go away; keep out of the way.
[from old French]

scarcely adverb
only just; only with difficulty, She could scarcely walk.

scare verb (scares, scaring, scared)
frighten.

scare noun (plural scares)
1 a fright. 2 alarm, mistaken or unnecessary anxiety. [from Old Norse]

scarecrow noun (plural scarecrows)
a figure of a person dressed in old clothes, set up to frighten birds away from crops.

scaremonger noun (plural scaremongers)
a person who spreads scare stories. [from scare + an old word monger = trader]

scare story noun (plural scare stories)
an inaccurate or exaggerated account of something which makes people worry unnecessarily.

scarf noun (plural scarves)
a strip of material worn round the neck or head. [from old French]

scarlet adjective & noun
bright red. [via old French and Arabic from Latin]

scarlet fever noun
an infectious fever producing a scarlet rash.

scarp noun (plural scarps)
a steep slope on a hill. [from Italian]

scarper verb (scarpers, scarpering, scarpered) (slang)
run away. [probably from Italian scappare = escape]

scary adjective (informal)
frightening.

scathing (say skayth-ing) adjective
severely criticizing a person or thing. [from Old Norse skatha = injure or damage]

scatter verb (scatters, scattering, scattered)
throw or send or move in various directions. [a different spelling of shatter]

scatterbrain noun (plural scatterbrains)
a careless forgetful person.
scatterbrained adjective

scavenge verb (scavenges, scavenging, scavenged)
1 search for useful things amongst rubbish. 2 (of a bird or animal) search for decaying flesh as food. **scavenger** noun
[from old French]

scenario noun (plural scenarios)
1 a summary of the plot of a play etc. 2 an imagined series of events or set of circumstances. [Italian]

USAGE: Note that this word does not mean the same as scene.

scene noun (plural scenes)
1 the place where something has happened, the scene of the crime. 2 a part of a play or film. 3 a view as seen by a spectator. 4 an angry or noisy outburst, He made a scene about the money. 5 stage scenery.
[from Greek skene = stage]

scenery noun
1 the natural features of a landscape. 2 things put on a stage to make it look like a place.

scenic adjective
having fine natural scenery, a scenic road along the coast.

scent noun (plural scents)
1 a pleasant smell. 2 a liquid perfume. 3 an animal's smell that other animals can detect.

scent verb (scents, scenting, scented)
1 discover something by its scent; detect. 2 put scent on or in something; make fragrant, scented soap. **scented** adjective
[from Latin]

sceptic (say skep-tik) noun (plural sceptics)
a sceptical person.

sceptical (say skep-tik-al) adjective
inclined to question things; not believing easily. **sceptically** adverb, **scepticism** noun
[from Greek skeptikos = thoughtful]

sceptre noun (plural sceptres)
a rod carried by a king or queen as a symbol of power. [from old French]

schedule (say shed-yool) noun (plural schedules)
a programme or timetable of planned events or work.

schedule *verb* (schedules, scheduling, scheduled)
put into a schedule; plan. [from Latin *scedula* = little piece of paper]

schematic (*say* skee-mat-ik) *adjective*
in the form of a diagram or chart.
[same origin as *scheme*]

scheme *noun* (*plural* schemes)
a plan of action.
scheme *verb* (schemes, scheming, schemed)
make plans; plot. **schemer** *noun*
[from Greek *schema* = form]

scherzo (*say* skairts-oh) *noun* (*plural* scherzos)
a lively piece of music. [Italian, = joke]

schism (*say* sizm) *noun* (*plural* schisms)
the splitting of a group into two opposing sections because they disagree about something important.
[from Greek *schisma* = a split]

schizophrenia (*say* skid-zo-free-nee-a) *noun*
a kind of mental illness in which people cannot relate their thoughts and feelings to reality. **schizophrenic** *adjective* & *noun*
[from Greek *schizein* = to split + *phren* = mind]

scholar *noun* (*plural* scholars)
1 a person who has studied a subject thoroughly. 2 a person who has been awarded a scholarship. **scholarly** *adjective*
[from Latin *scholaris* = to do with a school]

scholarship *noun* (*plural* scholarships)
1 a grant of money given to someone to help to pay for his or her education.
2 scholars' knowledge or methods; advanced study.

scholastic *adjective*
to do with schools or education; academic.
[from Greek *scholastikos* = studious]

school[1] *noun* (*plural* schools)
1 a place where teaching is done, especially of pupils aged 5–18. 2 the pupils in a school.
3 the time when teaching takes place in a school, *School begins at 9 a.m.* 4 a group of people who have the same beliefs or style of work etc.

school *verb* (schools, schooling, schooled)
train, *She was schooling her horse for the competition.* [from Greek]

school[2] *noun* (*plural* schools)
a shoal of fish or whales etc. [from old German or old Dutch *schole* = a troop]

schoolchild *noun* (*plural* schoolchildren)
a child who goes to school.
schoolboy *noun*, **schoolgirl** *noun*

schooling *noun*
1 training. 2 education, especially in a school.

schoolteacher *noun* (*plural* schoolteachers)
a person who teaches in a school.
schoolmaster *noun*, **schoolmistress** *noun*

schooner (*say* skoon-er) *noun* (*plural* schooners)
1 a sailing ship with two or more masts and with sails rigged along its length, not crosswise. 2 a tall glass for serving sherry.
[origin unknown]

sciatica (*say* sy-at-ik-a) *noun*
pain in the sciatic nerve (a large nerve in the hip and thigh). [Latin]

science *noun*
the study of chemistry, physics, plants and animals, etc.
[from Latin *scientia* = knowledge]

science fiction *noun*
stories about imaginary scientific discoveries or space travel and life on other planets.

science park *noun* (*plural* science parks)
an area set up for industries using science or for organizations doing scientific research.

scientific *adjective*
1 to do with science or scientists.
2 studying things systematically and testing ideas carefully. **scientifically** *adverb*

scientist *noun* (*plural* scientists)
1 an expert in science. 2 someone who uses scientific methods.

scimitar (*say* sim-it-ar) *noun* (*plural* scimitars)
a curved oriental sword.
[from French or Italian]

scintillate *verb* (scintillates, scintillating, scintillated)
1 sparkle. 2 be lively and witty. **scintillation** *noun* [from Latin *scintilla* = spark]

scion (*say* sy-on) *noun* (*plural* scions)
a descendant, especially of a noble family.
[from Old French *cion* = a twig or shoot]

scissors *plural noun*
a cutting instrument used with one hand, with two blades pivoted so that they can close against each other.
[from Latin *scissum* = cut]

scoff¹ *verb* (scoffs, scoffing, scoffed)
jeer; speak contemptuously. **scoffer** *noun*
[probably from a Scandinavian language]

scoff² *verb* (scoffs, scoffing, scoffed)
(*informal*) eat greedily; eat up.
[from a dialect word *scaff* = food]

scold *verb* (scolds, scolding, scolded)
to speak angrily; to tell someone off.
scolding *noun* [probably from Old Norse]

scone (*say* skon *or* skohn) *noun* (*plural* scones)
a soft flat cake, usually eaten with butter.
[origin unknown]

scoop *noun* (*plural* scoops)
1 a kind of deep spoon for serving ice cream etc. 2 a deep shovel for lifting grain, sugar, etc. 3 a scooping movement. 4 an important piece of news published by only one newspaper.
scoop *verb* (scoops, scooping, scooped)
lift or hollow something out with a scoop.
[from old German or old Dutch]

scoot *verb* (scoots, scooting, scooted)
1 propel a bicycle or scooter by sitting or standing on it and pushing it along with one foot. 2 run or go away quickly.
[origin unknown]

scooter *noun* (*plural* scooters)
1 a kind of motorcycle with small wheels. 2 a board with wheels and a long handle, which you ride on by scooting. [from *scoot*]

scope *noun*
1 opportunity to work, *This job gives scope for your musical abilities.* 2 the range or extent of a subject.
[from Greek *skopos* = target]

scorch *verb* (scorches, scorching, scorched)
make something go brown by burning it slightly. [origin unknown]

scorched-earth policy *noun*
the burning of crops and destruction of anything that might be useful to an opposing army.

scorching *adjective* (*informal*)
very hot.

score *noun* (*plural* scores or, in sense 2, score)
1 the number of points or goals made in a game; a result. 2 (*old use*) twenty, *'Three score years and ten' means 3 × 20 + 10 = 70 years.* 3 written or printed music.
on that score for that reason, because of that, *You needn't worry on that score.*
score *verb* (scores, scoring, scored)
1 get a point or goal in a game. 2 keep a count of the score. 3 mark with lines or cuts. 4 write out a musical score. **scorer** *noun* [from Old Norse]

scores *plural noun*
many; a large number.

scorn *noun*
contempt.
scornful *adjective*, **scornfully** *adverb*
scorn *verb* (scorns, scorning, scorned)
1 treat someone with contempt. 2 refuse something scornfully.
[via old French from Germanic]

scorpion *noun* (*plural* scorpions)
an animal that looks like a tiny lobster, with a poisonous sting. [from Greek]

Scot *noun* (*plural* Scots)
a person who comes from Scotland.

scotch¹ *noun*
whisky made in Scotland. [from *Scottish*]

scotch² *verb* (scotches, scotching, scotched)
put an end to an idea or rumour etc.
[origin unknown]

Scotch egg *noun* (*plural* Scotch eggs)
a hard-boiled egg enclosed in sausage meat
and fried.

Scotch terrier *noun* (*plural* Scotch
terriers)
a breed of terrier with rough hair.

scot-free *adjective*
without harm or punishment.
[from *scot* = a form of tax + *free*]

Scots *adjective*
from or belonging to Scotland.

USAGE: See note at *Scottish*.

Scottish *adjective*
to do with or belonging to Scotland.

USAGE: *Scottish* is the most widely used
word for describing things to do with
Scotland: *Scottish education, Scottish
mountains*. *Scots* is less common and is
mainly used to describe people: *a Scots girl*.
Scotch is only used in fixed expressions
like *Scotch egg* and *Scotch terrier*.

scoundrel *noun* (*plural* scoundrels)
a wicked or dishonest person.
[origin unknown]

scour[1] *verb* (scours, scouring, scoured)
1 rub something until it is clean and
bright. **2** clear a channel or pipe by the
force of water flowing through it.
scourer *noun*
[from *ex-* + *curare* = take care of, clean]

scour[2] *verb* (scours, scouring, scoured)
search thoroughly. [origin unknown]

scourge (*say* skerj) *noun* (*plural* scourges)
1 a whip for flogging people. **2** something
that inflicts suffering or punishment.
[from *ex-* + Latin *corrigia* = whip]

Scout *noun* (*plural* Scouts)
a member of the Scout Association, an
organization for boys.

scout *noun* (*plural* scouts)
someone sent out to collect information.
scout *verb* (scouts, scouting, scouted)
1 act as a scout. **2** search an area
thoroughly.
[from Latin *auscultare* = listen]

scowl *noun* (*plural* scowls)
a bad-tempered frown.
scowl *verb* (scowls, scowling, scowled)
make a scowl.
[probably from a Scandinavian language]

Scrabble *noun* (*trade mark*)
a game played on a board, in which words
are built up from single letters.

scrabble *verb* (scrabbles, scrabbling,
scrabbled)
1 scratch or claw at something with the
hands or feet. **2** grope or struggle to get
something. [from old Dutch]

scraggy *adjective*
thin and bony. [origin unknown]

scram *verb* (*slang*)
go away! [probably from *scramble*]

scramble *verb* (scrambles, scrambling,
scrambled)
1 move quickly and awkwardly. **2** struggle
to do or get something. **3** (of aircraft or
their crew) hurry and take off quickly.
4 cook eggs by mixing them up and heating
them in a pan. **5** mix things together.
6 alter a radio or telephone signal so that it
cannot be used without a decoding device.
scrambler *noun*
scramble *noun* (*plural* scrambles)
1 a climb or walk over rough ground. **2** a
struggle to do or get something. **3** a motorcycle race over rough ground.
[origin unknown]

scrap[1] *noun* (*plural* scraps)
1 a small piece. **2** rubbish; waste material,
especially metal that is suitable for
reprocessing.
scrap *verb* (scraps, scrapping, scrapped)
get rid of something that is useless or
unwanted. [from Old Norse]

scrap[2] *noun* (*plural* scraps) (*informal*)
a fight.
scrap *verb* (scraps, scrapping, scrapped)
(*informal*)
fight. [probably from *scrape*]

scrape *verb* (scrapes, scraping, scraped)
1 clean or smooth or damage something by
passing something hard over it. **2** remove
by scraping, *Scrape the mud off your shoes*.
3 pass with difficulty, *We scraped through*.

4 get something by great effort or care, *They scraped together enough money for a holiday.* **scraper** *noun*

scrape *noun* (*plural* **scrapes**)
1 a scraping movement or sound. **2** a mark etc. made by scraping. **3** an awkward situation caused by mischief or foolishness. [from Old English]

scrappy *adjective*
1 made of scraps or bits or disconnected things. **2** carelessly done. **scrappiness** *noun*

scratch *verb* (**scratches, scratching, scratched**)
1 mark or cut the surface of a thing with something sharp. **2** rub the skin with fingernails or claws because it itches. **3** withdraw from a race or competition.
scratch *noun* (*plural* **scratches**)
1 a mark made by scratching. **2** the action of scratching. **scratchy** *adjective*
start from scratch start from the beginning or with nothing prepared.
up to scratch up to the proper standard. [origin unknown]

scratch card *noun* (*plural* **scratch cards**)
a card you buy as part of a lottery; you scratch off part of the surface to see whether you have won a prize.

scrawl *noun* (*plural* **scrawls**)
untidy handwriting.
scrawl *verb* (**scrawls, scrawling, scrawled**)
write in a scrawl. [origin unknown]

scrawny *adjective*
scraggy.
[originally American; origin unknown]

scream *noun* (*plural* **screams**)
1 a loud cry of pain, fear, anger, or excitement. **2** a loud piercing sound. **3** (*informal*) a very amusing person or thing.
scream *verb* (**screams, screaming, screamed**)
make a scream. [origin unknown]

scree *noun*
a mass of loose stones on the side of a mountain. [from Old Norse]

screech *noun* (*plural* **screeches**)
a harsh high-pitched scream or sound.
screech *verb* [imitating the sound]

screed *noun* (*plural* **screeds**)
a very long piece of writing.
[probably from Old English]

screen *noun* (*plural* **screens**)
1 a thing that protects, hides, or divides something. **2** a surface on which films or television pictures are shown. **3** a windscreen.
screen *verb* (**screens, screening, screened**)
1 protect, hide, or divide with a screen. **2** show a film or television pictures on a screen. **3** examine carefully, e.g. to check whether a person is suitable for a job or whether a substance is present in something. **4** sift gravel etc.
[from old French]

screenplay *noun* (*plural* **screenplays**)
the script of a film, with instructions to the actors etc.

screw *noun* (*plural* **screws**)
1 a metal pin with a spiral ridge (the *thread*) round it, holding things together by being twisted in. **2** a twisting movement. **3** something twisted. **4** a propeller, especially for a ship or motor boat.
screw *verb* (**screws, screwing, screwed**)
1 fasten with a screw or screws. **2** twist. [from old French]

screwdriver *noun* (*plural* **screwdrivers**)
a tool for turning screws.

scribble *verb* (**scribbles, scribbling, scribbled**)
1 write quickly or untidily or carelessly. **2** make meaningless marks. **scribble** *noun*
[same origin as *scribe*]

scribe *noun* (*plural* **scribes**)
1 a person who made copies of writings before printing was invented. **2** (in biblical times) a professional religious scholar.
scribal *adjective*
[from Latin *scribere* = write]

scrimmage *noun* (*plural* **scrimmages**)
a confused struggle. [from *skirmish*]

scrimp *verb* (**scrimps, scrimping, scrimped**)
skimp, *scrimp and save*. [origin unknown]

script *noun* (*plural* **scripts**)
1 handwriting. **2** the text of a play, film,

broadcast talk, etc.
[from Latin *scriptum* = written]

scripture *noun* (*plural* **scriptures**)
1 sacred writings. 2 (in Christianity)
the Bible. [same origin as *script*]

scroll *noun* (*plural* **scrolls**)
1 a roll of paper or parchment used for
writing on. 2 a spiral design.
scroll *verb* (**scrolls, scrolling, scrolled**)
move the display on a computer screen up
or down to see what comes before or after
it. [from old French]

scrotum (*say* skroh-tum) *noun* (*plural*
scrota or **scrotums**)
the pouch of skin behind the penis,
containing the testicles. **scrotal** *adjective*
[Latin]

scrounge *verb* (**scrounges, scrounging,
scrounged**)
cadge. **scrounger** *noun* [from an old word
scringe = squeeze roughly]

scrub[1] *verb* (**scrubs, scrubbing, scrubbed**)
1 rub with a hard brush, especially to clean
something. 2 (*informal*) cancel.
scrub *noun*
[probably from old German or old Dutch]

scrub[2] *noun*
1 low trees and bushes. 2 land covered
with these. [from *shrub*]

scrubby *adjective*
undersized and shabby or wretched.
[from *scrub*[2]]

scruff *noun*
the back of the neck. [from Old Norse]

scruffy *adjective*
shabby and untidy.
scruffily *adverb*, **scruffiness** *noun*
[a different spelling of *scurfy*]

scrum *noun* (*plural* **scrums**)
1 (also **scrummage**) a group of players
from each side in Rugby football who
push against each other and try to heel
out the ball which is thrown between
them. 2 a crowd pushing against each
other.
[a different spelling of *scrimmage*]

scrumptious *adjective* (*informal*)
delicious. [origin unknown]

scrunch *verb* (**scrunches, scrunching,
scrunched**)
1 crunch. 2 crush or crumple.
[imitating the sound]

scrunchy or **scrunchie** *noun* (*plural*
scrunchies)
a band of elastic covered in fabric, used to
tie up your hair. [from *scrunch*]

scruple *noun* (*plural* **scruples**)
a feeling of doubt or hesitation when your
conscience tells you that an action would
be wrong.
scruple *verb* (**scruples, scrupling, scrupled**)
have scruples, *He would not scruple to
betray us*. [from Latin]

scrupulous *adjective*
1 very careful and conscientious. 2 strictly
honest or honourable. **scrupulously** *adverb*
[from *scruple*]

scrutinize *verb* (**scrutinizes, scrutinizing,
scrutinized**)
examine or look at something carefully.
scrutiny *noun* [from Latin *scrutari*
= examine, (originally) = sort rags]

scuba diving *noun*
swimming underwater using a tank of air
strapped to your back.
[from the initials of *self-contained
underwater breathing apparatus*]

scud *verb* (**scuds, scudding, scudded**)
move quickly and lightly; skim along,
Clouds scudded across the sky.
[origin unknown]

scuff *verb* (**scuffs, scuffing, scuffed**)
1 drag your feet while walking. 2 scrape
with your foot; mark or damage something
by doing this. [origin unknown]

scuffle *noun* (*plural* **scuffles**)
a confused fight or struggle.
scuffle *verb* (**scuffles, scuffling, scuffled**)
take part in a scuffle.
[probably from a Scandinavian language]

scull *noun* (*plural* **sculls**)
a small or lightweight oar.
scull *verb* (**sculls, sculling, sculled**)
row with sculls. [origin unknown]

scullery noun (plural sculleries)
a room where dishes etc. are washed up.
[from Latin scutella = small dish]

sculpt verb (sculpts, sculpting, sculpted)
sculpture; make sculptures.

sculptor noun (plural sculptors)
a person who makes sculptures.

sculpture noun (plural sculptures)
1 making shapes by carving wood or stone
or casting metal. 2 a shape made in this
way. **sculpture** verb
[from Latin sculpere = carve]

scum noun
1 froth or dirt on top of a liquid.
2 worthless people.
[from old German or old Dutch]

scupper noun (plural scuppers)
an opening in a ship's side to let water
drain away.
scupper verb (scuppers, scuppering,
scuppered)
1 sink a ship deliberately. 2 (informal)
wreck, It scuppered our plans.
[probably from old French]

scurf noun
flakes of dry skin. **scurfy** adjective
[from Old English]

scurrilous adjective
rude, insulting, and probably untrue,
scurrilous attacks in the newspapers.
scurrilously adverb [from Latin]

scurry verb (scurries, scurrying, scurried)
run with short steps; hurry.
[origin unknown]

scurvy noun
a disease caused by lack of vitamin C in
food. [a different spelling of scurfy]

scut noun (plural scuts)
the short tail of a rabbit, hare, or deer.
[origin unknown]

scutter verb (scutters, scuttering, scuttered)
scurry. [probably from scuttle²]

scuttle¹ noun (plural scuttles)
a bucket or container for coal in a house.
[via Old Norse from Latin scutella = dish]

scuttle² verb (scuttles, scuttling, scuttled)
scurry; hurry away. [from scud]

scuttle³ noun (plural scuttles)
a small opening with a lid in a ship's deck
or side.
scuttle verb (scuttles, scuttling, scuttled)
sink a ship deliberately by letting water
into it.
[probably from Spanish escotar = cut out]

scythe noun (plural scythes)
a tool with a long curved blade for cutting
grass or corn.
scythe verb (scythes, scything, scythed)
cut with a scythe. [from Old English]

SE abbreviation
1 south-east. 2 south-eastern.

se- prefix
1 apart or aside (as in secluded). 2 without
(as in secure). [Latin]

sea noun (plural seas)
1 the salt water that covers most of the
earth's surface; a part of this. 2 a large
lake, the Sea of Galilee. 3 a large area of
something, a sea of faces.
at sea 1 on the sea. 2 not knowing what to
do.
[from Old English]

sea anemone noun (plural sea anemones)
a sea creature with short tentacles round
its mouth.

seaboard noun (plural seaboards)
a coastline or coastal region.

sea breeze noun (plural sea breezes)
a breeze blowing from the sea onto the
land.

sea change noun (plural sea changes)
a dramatic change.

seafaring adjective & noun
working or travelling on the sea.
seafarer noun

seafood noun
fish or shellfish from the sea eaten as food.

seagull noun (plural seagulls)
a seabird with long wings.

sea horse *noun* (*plural* sea horses)
a small fish that swims upright, with a head rather like a horse's head.

seal[1] *noun* (*plural* seals)
a sea mammal with thick fur or bristles, that breeds on land. [from Old English]

seal[2] *noun* (*plural* seals)
1 a piece of metal with an engraved design for pressing on a soft substance to leave an impression. 2 this impression.
3 something designed to close an opening and prevent air or liquid etc. from getting in or out. 4 a small decorative sticker, *Christmas seals*.
seal *verb* (seals, sealing, sealed)
1 close something by sticking two parts together. 2 close securely; stop up. 3 press a seal on something.
seal off prevent people getting to an area. [from old French; related to *sign*]

sea level *noun*
the level of the sea halfway between high and low tide.

sealing-wax *noun*
a substance that is soft when heated but hardens when cooled, used for sealing documents or for marking with a seal.

sea lion *noun* (*plural* sea lions)
a kind of large seal that lives in the Pacific Ocean.

seam *noun* (*plural* seams)
1 the line where two edges of cloth or wood etc. join. 2 a layer of coal in the ground. [from Old English]

seaman *noun* (*plural* seamen)
a sailor.

seamanship *noun*
skill in seafaring.

seamy *adjective*
seamy side the less attractive side or part, *Police see a lot of the seamy side of life.*
[originally, the 'wrong' side of a piece of sewing, where the rough edges of the seams show]

seance (*say* say-ahns) *noun* (*plural* seances)
a spiritualist meeting. [French, = a sitting]

seaplane *noun* (*plural* seaplanes)
an aeroplane that can land on and take off from water.

seaport *noun* (*plural* seaports)
a port on the coast.

sear *verb* (sears, searing, seared)
scorch or burn the surface of something. [from Old English]

search *verb* (searches, searching, searched)
look very carefully in a place etc. in order to find something. **search** *noun*, **searcher** *noun* [from old French]

searchlight *noun* (*plural* searchlights)
a light with a strong beam that can be turned in any direction.

search party *noun* (*plural* search parties)
a group of people organized to search for a missing person or thing.

search warrant *noun* (*plural* search warrants)
an official document giving the police permission to search private property.

seascape *noun* (*plural* seascapes)
a picture or view of the sea.
[from *sea* + *-scape* as in *landscape*]

seasick *adjective*
sick because of the movement of a ship. **seasickness** *noun*

seaside *noun*
a place by the sea where people go for holidays.

season *noun* (*plural* seasons)
1 each of the four main parts of the year (spring, summer, autumn, winter). 2 the time of year when something happens, *the football season.*
in season available and ready for eating, *Strawberries are in season in the summer.*

season *verb* (seasons, seasoning, seasoned)
1 give extra flavour to food by adding salt, pepper, or other strong-tasting substances.
2 dry and treat timber etc. to make it ready for use.
[from Latin *satio* = time for sowing seed]

seasonable *adjective*
suitable for the season, *Hot weather is seasonable in summer.* **seasonably** *adverb*

USAGE: Do not confuse with *seasonal.*

seasonal *adjective*
1 for or to do with a season. **2** happening in a particular season, *Fruit-picking is seasonal work.* **seasonally** *adverb*

USAGE: Do not confuse with *seasonable.*

seasoning *noun* (*plural* **seasonings**)
a substance used to season food.

season ticket *noun* (*plural* **season tickets**)
a ticket that can be used as often as you like throughout a period of time.

seat *noun* (*plural* **seats**)
1 a thing made or used for sitting on. **2** the right to be a member of a council, committee, parliament, etc., *She won the seat ten years ago.* **3** the buttocks; the part of a skirt or trousers covering these. **4** the place where something is based or located, *London is the seat of our government.*
seat *verb* (**seats, seating, seated**)
1 place in or on a seat. **2** have seats for, *The theatre seats 3,000 people.*
[from Old Norse]

seat belt *noun* (*plural* **seat belts**)
a strap to hold a person securely in a seat.

seating *noun*
1 the seats in a place, *seating for 400.* **2** the arrangement of seats, *a seating plan.*

sea urchin *noun* (*plural* **sea urchins**)
a sea animal with a spherical shell covered in sharp spikes.
[from an old meaning of *urchin* = hedgehog]

seaward *adjective* & *adverb*
towards the sea.
seawards *adverb*

seaweed *noun*
a plant or plants that grow in the sea.

seaworthy *adjective*
(of a ship) fit for a sea voyage.
seaworthiness *noun*

sebum *noun*
the natural oil produced by glands (*sebaceous glands*) in the skin to lubricate the skin and hair.
[Latin, = grease or tallow]

secateurs *plural noun*
clippers held in the hand for pruning plants. [French, from Latin *secare* = to cut]

secede (*say* sis-**seed**) *verb* (**secedes, seceding, seceded**)
withdraw from being a member of a political or religious organization.
secession *noun* [from se- + Latin *cedere* = go]

secluded *adjective*
screened or sheltered from view. **seclusion** *noun* [from se- + Latin *claudere* = shut]

second¹ *adjective*
1 next after the first. **2** another, *a second chance.* **3** less good, *second quality.*
secondly *adverb*
second *noun* (*plural* **seconds**)
1 a person or thing that is second. **2** an attendant of a fighter in a boxing match, duel, etc. **3** a thing that is of second (not the best) quality. **4** one-sixtieth of a minute of time or of a degree used in measuring angles.
second *verb* (**seconds, seconding, seconded**)
1 assist someone. **2** support a proposal, motion, etc. **seconder** *noun*
[from Latin *secundus* = next]

second² (*say* sik-**ond**) *verb* (**seconds, seconding, seconded**)
transfer a person temporarily to another job or department etc. **secondment** *noun* [from French *en second* = in the second rank (because officers seconded to another company served under officers who belonged to that company)]

secondary *adjective*
1 coming after or from something. **2** less important. **3** (of education etc.) for children of more than about 11 years old, *a secondary school.* (Compare *primary.*)

secondary colour *noun* (*plural* **secondary colours**)
a colour made by mixing two primary colours.

second-hand *adjective*
1 bought or used after someone else has owned it. 2 selling used goods, *a second-hand shop.*

second nature *noun*
behaviour that has become automatic or a habit, *Lying is second nature to him.*

second-rate *adjective*
inferior; not very good.

second sight *noun*
the ability to foresee the future.

secret *adjective*
1 that must not be told or shown to other people. 2 not known by everybody. 3 working secretly.
secretly *adverb,* secrecy *noun*
secret *noun* (*plural* secrets)
something secret.
[from Latin *secretum* = set apart]

secretariat *noun* (*plural* secretariats)
an administrative department of a large organization such as the United Nations.
[same origin as *secretary*]

secretary (*say* sek-rit-ree) *noun* (*plural* secretaries)
1 a person whose job is to help with letters, answer the telephone, and make business arrangements for a person or organization. 2 the chief assistant of a government minister or ambassador.
secretarial *adjective*
[from Latin *secretarius* = an officer or servant allowed to know your secrets]

secrete (*say* sik-reet) *verb* (secretes, secreting, secreted)
1 hide something. 2 produce a substance in the body, *Saliva is secreted in the mouth.*
secretion *noun* [same origin as *secret*]

secretive (*say* seek-rit-iv) *adjective*
liking or trying to keep things secret.
secretively *adverb,* secretiveness *noun*

secret police *noun*
a police force which works in secret for political purposes, not to deal with crime.

secret service *noun*
a government department responsible for espionage.

sect *noun* (*plural* sects)
a group whose beliefs differ from those of others in the same religion; a faction.
[from Latin]

sectarian (*say* sekt-air-ee-an) *adjective*
belonging to or supporting a sect.

section *noun* (*plural* sections)
1 a part of something. 2 a cross-section.
[from Latin *sectum* = cut]

sectional *adjective*
1 made in sections that can be put together and taken apart. 2 concerned with only one group within a community.

sector *noun* (*plural* sectors)
1 one part of an area. 2 a part of something, *the private sector of industry.*
[from Latin *secare* = to cut]

secular *adjective*
to do with worldly affairs, not spiritual or religious matters.
[from Latin *saecularis* = worldly]

secure *adjective*
1 safe, especially against attack. 2 certain not to slip or fail. 3 reliable. securely *adverb*
secure *verb* (secures, securing, secured)
1 make a thing secure. 2 obtain, *We secured two tickets for the show.*
[from se- + Latin *cura* = care]

security *noun* (*plural* securities)
1 being secure; safety. 2 precautions against theft or spying etc. 3 something given as a guarantee that a promise will be kept or a debt repaid. 4 investments such as stocks and shares.

security guard *noun* (*plural* security guards)
a person employed to guard a building or its contents against theft and vandalism.

security risk *noun* (*plural* security risks)
a person or situation thought likely to threaten the security of a country.

sedan chair *noun* (*plural* sedan chairs)
an enclosed chair for one person, mounted on two horizontal poles and carried by two men, used in the 17th–18th centuries.
[origin unknown]

sedate *adjective*
calm and dignified.
sedately *adverb*, **sedateness** *noun*
sedate *verb* (sedates, sedating, sedated)
give a sedative to. **sedation** *noun*
[from Latin *sedatum* = made calm]

sedative (*say* sed-a-tiv) *noun* (*plural*
sedatives)
a medicine that makes a person calm.
[from Latin *sedare* = settle]

sedentary (*say* sed-en-ter-ee) *adjective*
done sitting down, *sedentary work.*
[from Latin *sedens* = sitting]

Seder *noun* (*plural* **Seders**)
(in Judaism) a ritual and a ceremonial
meal to mark the beginning of Passover.
[Hebrew, = order, procedure]

sedge *noun*
a grass-like plant growing in marshes or
near water. [from Old English]

sediment *noun*
fine particles of solid matter that float in
liquid or sink to the bottom of it.
[from Latin *sedere* = sit]

sedimentary *adjective*
formed from particles that have settled on
a surface, *sedimentary rocks.*

sedition *noun*
speeches or actions intended to make
people rebel against the authority of the
State. **seditious** *adjective*
[from *se-* + Latin *itio* = going]

seduce *verb* (seduces, seducing, seduced)
1 persuade a person to have sexual
intercourse. **2** attract or lead astray by
offering temptations. **seducer** *noun*,
seduction *noun*, **seductive** *adjective*
[from *se-* + Latin *ducere* = to lead]

sedulous *adjective*
diligent and persevering. **sedulously** *adverb*
[from Latin]

see[1] *verb* (sees, seeing, saw, seen)
1 perceive with the eyes. *See a doctor about your cough.*
3 understand, *She saw what I meant.*
4 imagine, *Can you see yourself as a
teacher?* **5** consider, *I will see what can be
done.* **6** make sure, *See that the windows are*

shut. **7** discover, *See who is at the door.*
8 escort, *See her to the door.*
see through not be deceived by something.
see to attend to.
[from Old English]

see[2] *noun* (*plural* **sees**)
the district of which a bishop or
archbishop is in charge, *the see of
Canterbury.* [from Latin *sedes* = seat]

seed *noun* (*plural* **seeds** or **seed**)
1 a fertilized part of a plant, capable of
growing into a new plant. **2** (*old use*)
descendants. **3** a seeded player.
seed *verb* (seeds, seeding, seeded)
1 plant or sprinkle seeds in something.
2 name the best players and arrange for
them not to play against each other in the
early rounds of a tournament. [from Old
English]

seedling *noun* (*plural* **seedlings**)
a very young plant growing from a seed.

seedy *adjective* (seedier, seediest)
1 full of seeds. **2** shabby and disreputable.
seediness *noun*

seeing *conjunction*
considering, *Seeing that we have all
finished, let's go.*

seek *verb* (seeks, seeking, sought)
1 search for. **2** try to obtain.
[from Old English]

seem *verb* (seems, seeming, seemed)
give the impression of being something,
She seems worried about her work.
seemingly *adverb* [from Old Norse]

seemly *adjective* (*old use*)
(of behaviour etc.) proper or suitable.
seemliness *noun*
[from an old sense of *seem* = be suitable]

seep *verb* (seeps, seeping, seeped)
ooze slowly out or through something.
seepage *noun* [probably from Old English]

seer *noun* (*plural* **seers**)
a prophet. [from *see*[1] + *-er*[2]]

seersucker *noun*
fabric woven with a puckered surface.
[from Persian *shir o shakar*, literally
= milk and sugar, also = striped cloth]

see-saw *noun* (*plural* see-saws)
a plank balanced in the middle so that two people can sit, one on each end, and make it go up and down.
[from an old rhyme which imitated the rhythm of a saw going to and fro, later used by children on a see-saw]

seethe *verb* (seethes, seething, seethed)
1 bubble and surge like water boiling. 2 be very angry or excited. [from Old English]

segment *noun* (*plural* segments)
a part that is cut off or separates naturally from other parts, *the segments of an orange.*
segmented *adjective* [from Latin]

segregate *verb* (segregates, segregating, segregated)
1 separate people of different religions, races, etc. 2 isolate a person or thing.
segregation *noun*
[from *se-* + Latin *gregis* = from a flock]

seismic (*say* sy-zmik) *adjective*
to do with earthquakes or other vibrations of the earth.
[from Greek *seismos* = earthquake]

seismograph (*say* sy-zmo-grahf) *noun*
(*plural* seismographs)
an instrument for measuring the strength of earthquakes. [from Greek *seismos* = earthquake, + *-graph*]

seize *verb* (seizes, seizing, seized)
1 take hold of a person or thing suddenly or forcibly. 2 take eagerly, *Seize your chance!* 3 have a sudden effect on, *Panic seized us.*
seize up become jammed, especially because of friction or overheating.
[via old French from Germanic]

seizure *noun* (*plural* seizures)
1 seizing. 2 a sudden fit, as in epilepsy or a heart attack.

seldom *adverb*
rarely; not often. [from Old English]

select *verb* (selects, selecting, selected)
choose a person or thing. **selector** *noun*
select *adjective*
1 carefully chosen, *a select group of pupils.* 2 (of a club etc.) choosing its members carefully; exclusive.
[from *se-* + Latin *lectus* = collected]

selection *noun* (*plural* selections)
1 selecting; being selected. 2 a person or thing selected. 3 a group selected from a larger group. 4 a range of goods from which to choose.

selective *adjective*
choosing or chosen carefully.
selectively *adverb*, **selectivity** *noun*

self *noun* (*plural* selves)
1 a person as an individual. 2 a person's particular nature, *She has recovered and is her old self again.* 3 a person's own advantage, *He always puts self first.*
[from Old English]

self- *prefix*
1 of or to or done by yourself or itself. 2 automatic (as in *self-loading*).

self-addressed *adjective*
addressed to yourself.

self-assured *adjective*
confident.

self-catering *noun*
catering for yourself (instead of having meals provided).

self-centred *adjective*
selfish.

self-confident *adjective*
confident of your own abilities.

self-conscious *adjective*
embarrassed or unnatural because you know that people are watching you.

self-contained *adjective*
(of accommodation) complete in itself; containing all the necessary facilities.

self-control *noun*
the ability to control your own behaviour.
self-controlled *adjective*

self-defence *noun*
1 defending yourself. 2 techniques for doing this.

self-denial *noun*
deliberately going without things you would like to have.

self-determination *noun*
a country's right to rule itself and choose its own government.

self-employed *adjective*
working independently, not for an employer.

self-esteem *noun*
your own opinion of yourself and your own worth.

self-evident *adjective*
obvious and not needing proof or explanation.

self-help group *noun* (*plural* **self-help groups**)
a group of people with similar problems who help each other.

self-image *noun* (*plural* **self-images**)
your own idea of your appearance, personality, and abilities.

self-important *adjective*
pompous.

self-interest *noun*
your own advantage.

selfish *adjective*
doing what you want and not thinking of other people; keeping things for yourself.
selfishly *adverb*, **selfishness** *noun*

selfless *adjective*
unselfish.

self-made *adjective*
rich or successful because of your own efforts.

self-pity *noun*
too much sorrow and pity for yourself and your own problems.

self-possessed *adjective*
calm and dignified.

self-raising *adjective*
(of flour) making cakes rise without needing to have baking powder etc. added.

self-respect *noun*
your own proper respect for yourself.

self-righteous *adjective*
smugly sure that you are behaving virtuously.

selfsame *adjective*
the very same.

self-satisfied *adjective*
very pleased with yourself.

self-seeking *adjective*
selfishly trying to benefit yourself.

self-service *adjective*
where customers help themselves to things and pay a cashier for what they have taken.

self-sufficient *adjective*
able to produce or provide what you need without help from others.

self-supporting *adjective*
earning enough to keep yourself without needing money from others.

self-willed *adjective*
obstinately doing what you want; stubborn.

sell *verb* (**sells, selling, sold**)
exchange something for money. **seller** *noun*
sell out 1 sell all your stock of something. **2** (*informal*) betray someone.

sell *noun*
1 (*informal*) a deception. **2** the manner of selling something.
hard sell *noun* forceful selling; putting pressure on someone to buy.
soft sell selling by suggestion or gentle persuasion.
[from Old English]

sell-by date *noun* (*plural* **sell-by dates**)
a date marked on the packaging of food etc. by which it must be sold.

sell-out *noun* (*plural* **sell-outs**)
an entertainment, sporting event, etc. for which all the tickets have been sold.

selvage *noun* (*plural* **selvages**)
an edge of cloth woven so that it does not unravel. [from *self* + *edge*]

selves *plural* of **self**.

semaphore *noun*
a system of signalling by holding the arms in positions that indicate letters of the alphabet. [from Greek *sema* = sign + *-phoros* = carrying]

semblance *noun*
an outward appearance or apparent likeness.
[from old French; related to *similar*]

semen (*say* seem-en) *noun*
a white liquid produced by males and containing sperm.
[Latin, from *semere* = to sow]

semi *noun* (*plural* semis) (*informal*)
a semi-detached house.

semi- *prefix*
1 half. 2 partly. [from Latin]

semibreve *noun* (*plural* semibreves)
the longest musical note normally used (○), lasting four times as long as a crotchet.

semicircle *noun* (*plural* semicircles)
half a circle. **semicircular** *adjective*

semicolon *noun* (*plural* semicolons)
a punctuation mark (;) used to mark a break that is more than that marked by a comma.

semiconductor *noun* (*plural* semiconductors)
a substance that can conduct electricity but not as well as most metals do.

semi-detached *adjective*
(of a house) joined to another house on one side only.

semifinal *noun* (*plural* semifinals)
a match or round whose winner will take part in the final.

seminar *noun* (*plural* seminars)
a meeting for advanced discussion and research on a subject.
[German; related to *seminary*]

seminary *noun* (*plural* seminaries)
a training college for priests or rabbis.
[from Latin *seminarium* = seedbed]

semiquaver *noun* (*plural* semiquavers)
a note in music (♪), equal in length to one quarter of a crotchet.

semi-skimmed *adjective*
(of milk) having had some of the cream taken out.

Semitic (*say* sim-it-ik) *adjective*
to do with the Semites, the group of people that includes the Jews and Arabs. **Semite** (*say* see-my't) *noun*

semitone *noun* (*plural* semitones)
half a tone in music.

semolina *noun*
hard round grains of wheat used to make milk puddings and pasta.
[from Italian *semola* = bran]

senate *noun* (*plural* senates)
1 the governing council in ancient Rome. 2 the upper house of the parliament of the United States, France, and certain other countries. **senator** *noun*
[from Latin *senatus* = council of elders]

send *verb* (sends, sending, sent)
1 make a person or thing go somewhere. 2 cause to become, *It sent them mad.*
sender *noun*
send for order a person or thing to come or be brought to you.
send up (*informal*) make fun of something by imitating it.
[from Old English]

senile (*say* seen-I'll) *adjective*
weak or confused and forgetful because of old age. **senility** *noun*
[from Latin *senilis* = old]

senior *adjective*
1 older than someone else. 2 higher in rank. 3 for older children, *a senior school.* **seniority** *noun*
senior *noun* (*plural* seniors)
1 a person who is older or higher in rank than you are, *He is my senior.* 2 a member of a senior school. [Latin, = older]

senior citizen *noun* (*plural* senior citizens)
an elderly person, especially a pensioner.

senna *noun*
the dried pods or leaves of a tropical tree, used as a laxative. [via Latin from Arabic]

sensation *noun* (*plural* sensations)
1 a feeling, *a sensation of warmth.* 2 a very excited condition; something causing this, *The news caused a great sensation.*
[from Latin *sensus* = sense]

sensational *adjective*
1 causing great excitement, interest, or shock. 2 (*informal*) very good; wonderful.
sensationally *adverb*

sensationalism *noun*
deliberate use of dramatic words or style etc. to arouse excitement.
sensationalist *noun*

sense *noun* (*plural* senses)
1 the ability to see, hear, smell, touch, or taste things. 2 the ability to feel or appreciate something; awareness, *a sense of humour.* 3 the power to think or make wise decisions, *He hasn't got the sense to come in out of the rain.* 4 meaning, *The word 'run' has many senses.*
make sense 1 have a meaning. 2 be a sensible idea.

sense *verb* (senses, sensing, sensed)
1 feel; get an impression, *I sensed that she did not like me.* 2 detect something, *This device senses radioactivity.* [from Latin]

senseless *adjective*
1 stupid; not showing good sense.
2 unconscious.

senses *plural noun*
sanity, *He is out of his senses.*

sensibility *noun* (*plural* sensibilities)
sensitiveness or delicate feeling, *The criticism hurt the artist's sensibilities.*

USAGE: Note that this word does not mean 'being sensible' or 'having good sense'.

sensible *adjective*
wise; having or showing good sense.
sensibly *adverb*

sensitive *adjective*
1 receiving impressions quickly and easily, *sensitive fingers.* 2 easily hurt or offended, *She is very sensitive about her age.*
3 affected by something, *Photographic paper is sensitive to light.*
sensitively *adverb*, **sensitivity** *noun*

sensitize *verb* (sensitizes, sensitizing, sensitized)
make a thing sensitive to something.

sensor *noun* (*plural* sensors)
a device or instrument for detecting a physical property such as light, heat, or sound.

sensory *adjective*
1 to do with the senses. 2 receiving sensations, *sensory nerves.*

sensual *adjective*
1 to do with physical pleasure. 2 liking or suggesting physical or sexual pleasures.

sensuous *adjective*
giving pleasure to the senses, especially by being beautiful or delicate.

sentence *noun* (*plural* sentences)
1 a group of words that express a complete thought and form a statement, question, exclamation, or command. 2 the punishment announced to a convicted person in a lawcourt.

sentence *verb* (sentences, sentencing, sentenced)
give someone a sentence in a lawcourt, *The judge sentenced him to a year in prison.*
[from Latin *sententia* = opinion]

sententious *adjective*
giving moral advice in a pompous way.
[same origin as *sentence*]

sentient *adjective*
capable of feeling and perceiving things, *sentient beings.*
[from Latin *sentiens* = feeling]

sentiment *noun* (*plural* sentiments)
1 an opinion. 2 sentimentality.
[from Latin *sentire* = feel]

sentimental *adjective*
showing or arousing tenderness or romantic feeling or foolish emotion.
sentimentally *adverb*, **sentimentality** *noun*

sentinel *noun* (*plural* sentinels)
a sentry. [via French from Italian]

sentry *noun* (*plural* sentries)
a soldier guarding something.
[origin unknown]

sepal *noun* (*plural* **sepals**)
each of the leaves forming the calyx of a
bud. [from French]

separable *adjective*
able to be separated.

separate *adjective*
1 not joined to anything. 2 not shared.
separately *adverb*

separate *verb* (**separates, separating,
separated**)
1 make or keep separate; divide. 2 become
separate. 3 stop living together as a
married couple. **separation** *noun*, **separator**
noun [from se- + Latin *parare* = prepare]

sepia *noun*
reddish-brown. [Greek, = cuttlefish (from
which the dye was originally obtained)]

sepsis *noun*
a septic condition.

septet *noun* (*plural* **septets**)
1 a group of seven musicians. 2 a piece of
music for seven musicians.
[from Latin *septem* = seven]

septic *adjective*
infected with harmful bacteria that cause
pus to form.
[from Greek *septikos* = made rotten]

sepulchral (*say* sep-**ul**-kral) *adjective*
1 to do with a sepulchre. 2 (of a voice)
sounding deep and hollow.

sepulchre (*say* sep-**ul**-ker) *noun* (*plural*
sepulchres)
a tomb. [from Latin *sepultum* = buried]

sequel *noun* (*plural* **sequels**)
1 a book or film etc. that continues the
story of an earlier one. 2 something that
follows or results from an earlier event.
[from Latin *sequi* = follow]

sequence *noun* (*plural* **sequences**)
1 the following of one thing after another;
the order in which things happen. 2 a
series of things.
[from Latin *sequens* = following]

sequestrate *verb* (**sequestrates,
sequestrating, sequestrated**)
confiscate property until the owner pays a
debt or obeys a court order. **sequestration**
noun [from Latin]

sequin *noun* (*plural* **sequins**)
a tiny bright disc sewn on clothes etc. to
decorate them. **sequinned** *adjective*
[via French and Italian from Arabic *sikka*
= a coin]

seraph *noun* (*plural* **seraphim** or **seraphs**)
a kind of angel. [from Hebrew]

seraphic (*say* ser-**af**-ik) *adjective*
angelic, *a seraphic smile.*
seraphically *adverb*

serenade *noun* (*plural* **serenades**)
a song or tune played by a lover to his lady.
serenade *verb* (**serenades, serenading,
serenaded**)
sing or play a serenade to someone.
[via French from Italian *sereno* = serene]

serendipity *noun*
the ability to make pleasant or interesting
discoveries by accident. **serendipitous**
adjective. [made up by an 18th-century
writer, Horace Walpole, from the title of a
story *The Three Princes of Serendip* (who
had this ability)]

serene *adjective*
calm and cheerful.
serenely *adverb*, **serenity** *noun*
[from Latin]

serf *noun* (*plural* **serfs**)
a farm labourer who worked for a
landowner in the Middle Ages, and who
was not allowed to leave. **serfdom** *noun*
[same origin as *servant*]

serge *noun*
a kind of strong woven fabric.
[from old French]

sergeant (*say* sar-**jent**) *noun* (*plural*
sergeants)
a soldier or policeman who is in charge of
others. [from old French; related to *serve*]

sergeant major *noun* (*plural* **sergeant
majors**)
a soldier who is one rank higher than a
sergeant. [from *sergeant* + *major* = greater]

serial *noun* (*plural* serials)
a story or film etc. that is presented in separate parts. [from *series*]

USAGE: Do not confuse with *cereal*.

serialize *verb* (serializes, serializing, serialized)
produce a story or film etc. as a serial.
serialization *noun*

serial killer *noun* (*plural* serial killers)
a person who commits a series of murders for no apparent reason.

serial number *noun* (*plural* serial numbers)
a number put onto an object, usually by the manufacturers, to distinguish it from other identical objects.

series *noun* (*plural* series)
1 a number of things following or connected with each other. 2 a number of games or matches between the same competitors. 3 a number of separate radio or television programmes with the same characters or on the same subject.
[Latin, = row or chain]

serious *adjective*
1 solemn and thoughtful; not smiling.
2 sincere; not casual; not light-hearted, *a serious attempt.* 3 causing anxiety, not trivial, *a serious accident.* seriously *adverb*, seriousness *noun* [from Latin]

sermon *noun* (*plural* sermons)
a talk given by a preacher, especially as part of a religious service.
[from Latin *sermo* = talk, conversation]

serpent *noun* (*plural* serpents)
a snake. [from Latin *serpens* = creeping]

serpentine *adjective*
twisting and curving like a snake, *a serpentine road.*

serrated *adjective*
having a notched edge.
[from Latin *serratum* = sawn]

serried *adjective*
arranged in rows close together, *serried ranks of troops.*
[from Latin *serere* = join together]

serum (*say* seer-um) *noun* (*plural* sera or serums)
1 the thin pale-yellow liquid that remains from blood when the rest has clotted. 2 this fluid used medically, usually for the antibodies it contains. [Latin, = whey]

servant *noun* (*plural* servants)
a person whose job is to work or serve in someone else's house.
[from Latin *servus* = slave]

serve *verb* (serves, serving, served)
1 work for a person or organization or country etc. 2 sell things to people in a shop. 3 give out food to people at a meal.
4 spend time in something; undergo, *He served a prison sentence.* 5 be suitable for something, *This will serve our purpose.*
6 start play in tennis etc. by hitting the ball. server *noun*
it serves you right you deserve it.

serve *noun* (*plural* serves)
a service in tennis etc.
[same origin as *servant*]

service *noun* (*plural* services)
1 working for a person or organization or country etc. 2 something that helps people or supplies what they want, *a bus service.*
3 the army, navy, or air force, *the armed services.* 4 a religious ceremony.
5 providing people with goods, food, etc., *quick service.* 6 a set of dishes and plates etc. for a meal, *a dinner service.* 7 the servicing of a vehicle or machine etc. 8 the action of serving in tennis etc.

service *verb* (services, servicing, serviced)
1 repair or keep a vehicle or machine etc. in working order. 2 supply with services.
[from Latin *servitium* = slavery]

serviceable *adjective*
usable; suitable for ordinary use or wear.

service charge *noun* (*plural* service charges)
1 an amount added to a restaurant or hotel bill to reward the waiters and waitresses for their service. 2 money paid to the landlord of a block of flats for services used by all the flats, e.g. central heating or cleaning the stairs.

service industry *noun* (*plural* service industries)
an industry which sells service, not goods.

serviceman *noun* (*plural* **servicemen**)
a man serving in the armed forces.

service road *noun* (*plural* **service roads**)
a road beside a main road, for use by
vehicles going to the houses or shops etc.

services *plural noun*
an area beside a main road with a garage,
shop, restaurant, lavatories, etc. for
travellers to use.

servicewoman *noun* (*plural*
servicewomen)
a woman serving in the armed forces.

serviette *noun* (*plural* **serviettes**)
a piece of cloth or paper used to keep your
clothes or hands clean at a meal.
[French, from *servir* = to serve]

servile *adjective*
to do with slaves or like a slave; slavish.
servility *noun* [same origin as *servant*]

serving *noun* (*plural* **servings**)
a helping of food.

servitude *noun*
the condition of being obliged to work for
someone else and having no independence;
slavery. [same origin as *servant*]

sesame *noun*
an African plant whose seeds can be eaten
or used to make an edible oil. [from Greek]

session *noun* (*plural* **sessions**)
1 a meeting or series of meetings, *The
Queen will open the next session of
Parliament.* 2 a time spent doing one thing,
a recording session.
[from Latin *sessio* = sitting]

set *verb* (**sets, setting, set**)
This word has many uses, including 1 put
or fix (*Set the vase on the table. Set a date for
the wedding*), 2 make or become firm or
hard (*Leave the jelly to set*), 3 give someone
a task (*This sets us a problem*), 4 put into a
condition (*Set them free*), 5 go down below
the horizon (*The sun was setting*).
set about 1 start doing something.
2 (*informal*) attack somebody.
set off 1 begin a journey. 2 start something
happening. 3 cause something to explode.
set out 1 begin a journey. 2 display or
make known.

set sail begin a voyage.
set to 1 begin doing something vigorously.
2 begin fighting or arguing.
set up 1 place in position. 2 establish, *set
up house.* 3 cause or start, *set up a din.*

set *noun* (*plural* **sets**)
1 a group of people or things that belong
together. 2 a radio or television receiver.
3 the way something is placed, *the set of his
jaw.* 4 a badger's burrow. 5 the scenery or
stage for a play or film. 6 a group of games
in a tennis match. [from Old English]

set-aside *noun*
the policy of paying farmers not to use
some of their land because too much food is
being produced.

setback *noun* (*plural* **setbacks**)
something that stops progress or slows it
down.

set book *noun* (*plural* **set books**)
a book that must be studied for a literature
examination.

set square (*plural* **set squares**)
a device shaped like a right-angled
triangle, used in drawing lines parallel to
each other etc.

settee *noun* (*plural* **settees**)
a long soft seat with a back and arms.
[probably from *settle*²]

setter *noun* (*plural* **setters**)
a dog of a long-haired breed that can be
trained to stand rigid when it scents game.

set theory *noun*
the branch of mathematics that deals with
sets and the relations between them.

setting *noun* (*plural* **settings**)
1 the way or place in which something is
set. 2 music for the words of a song etc.

settle¹ *verb* (**settles, settling, settled**)
1 arrange; decide or solve something, *That
settles the problem.* 2 make or become calm
or comfortable or orderly; stop being
restless, *Stop chattering and settle down!*
3 go and live somewhere, *They settled in
Canada.* 4 sink; come to rest on something,
Dust had settled on his books. 5 pay a bill or
debt.
[from Old English *setlan*; related to *settle*²]

settle² *noun* (*plural* settles)
a long wooden seat with a high back and arms.
[from Old English *setl* = a place to sit]

settlement *noun* (*plural* settlements)
1 settling something. 2 the way something is settled. 3 a small number of people or houses established in a new area.

settler *noun* (*plural* settlers)
one of the first people to settle in a new country; a pioneer or colonist.

set-up *noun* (*informal*)
the way something is organized or arranged.

seven *noun* (*plural* sevens) & *adjective*
the number 7. **seventh** *adjective* & *noun*
[from Old English]

seventeen *noun* & *adjective*
the number 17. **seventeenth** *adjective* & *noun* [from Old English]

seventy *noun* (*plural* seventies) & *adjective*
the number 70. **seventieth** *adjective* & *noun* [from Old English]

sever *verb* (severs, severing, severed)
cut or break off. **severance** *noun*
[from old French; related to *separate*]

several *adjective* & *noun*
more than two but not many. [from *sever*]

severally *adverb*
separately. [from *several*]

severance pay *noun*
money paid to a worker who is no longer needed by his or her employer. [from *sever*]

severe *adjective*
1 strict; not gentle or kind. 2 intense or forceful, *severe gales*. 3 very plain, *a severe style of dress*. **severely** *adverb*, **severity** *noun*
[from Latin]

sew *verb* (sews, sewing, sewed, sewn or sewed)
1 join things together by using a needle and thread. 2 work with a needle and

thread or with a sewing machine.
[from Old English]

USAGE: Do not confuse with *sow*.

---

sewage (*say* soo-ij) *noun*
liquid waste matter carried away in drains.

sewer (*say* soo-er) *noun* (*plural* sewers)
a large underground drain for carrying away sewage. [from old French]

sewing machine *noun* (*plural* sewing machines)
a machine for sewing things.

sex *noun* (*plural* sexes)
1 each of the two groups (*male* and *female*) into which living things are placed according to their functions in the process of reproduction. 2 the instinct that causes members of the two sexes to be attracted to one another. 3 sexual intercourse.
[from Latin]

sexism *noun*
discrimination against people of a particular sex, especially women.
sexist *adjective* & *noun*

sextant *noun* (*plural* sextants)
an instrument for measuring the angle of the sun and stars, used for finding your position when navigating. [from Latin *sextus* = sixth (because early sextants consisted of an arc of one-sixth of a circle)]

sextet *noun* (*plural* sextets)
1 a group of six musicians. 2 a piece of music for six musicians.
[from Latin *sextus* = sixth]

sexton *noun* (*plural* sextons)
a person whose job is to take care of a church and churchyard. [from old French]

sextuplet *noun* (*plural* sextuplets)
each of six children born to the same mother at one time. [same origin as *sextet*]

sexual *adjective*
1 to do with sex or the sexes. 2 (of reproduction) happening by the fusion of male and female cells.
sexually *adverb*, **sexuality** *noun*

sexual harassment *noun*
annoying or upsetting someone, especially
a woman, by touching her or making
obscene remarks or gestures.

sexual intercourse *noun*
an intimate act between two people, in
which the man puts his penis into the
woman's vagina, to express love, for
pleasure, or to conceive a child.

sexy *adjective* (**sexier, sexiest**) (*informal*)
1 sexually attractive. **2** concerned with
sex.

SF *abbreviation*
science fiction.

shabby *adjective* (**shabbier, shabbiest**)
1 in a poor or worn-out condition;
dilapidated. **2** poorly dressed. **3** unfair or
dishonourable, *a shabby trick.*
shabbily *adverb*, **shabbiness** *noun*
[from Old English *sceabb* = scab]

shack *noun* (*plural* **shacks**)
a roughly-built hut.
[probably from a Mexican word]

shackle *noun* (*plural* **shackles**)
an iron ring for fastening a prisoner's
wrist or ankle to something.
shackle *verb* (**shackles, shackling, shackled**)
put shackles on a prisoner.
[from Old English]

shade *noun* (*plural* **shades**)
1 slight darkness produced where
something blocks the sun's light. **2** a device
that reduces or shuts out bright light. **3** a
colour; how light or dark a colour is. **4** a
slight difference, *The word had several
shades of meaning.* **5** (*poetical*) a ghost.
shade *verb* (**shades, shading, shaded**)
1 shelter something from bright light.
2 make part of a drawing darker than the
rest. **3** move gradually from one state or
quality to another, *evening shading into
night.* [from Old English *sceadu*]

shadow *noun* (*plural* **shadows**)
1 the dark shape that falls on a surface
when something is between the surface
and a light. **2** an area of shade.
shadowy *adjective*

shadow *verb* (**shadows, shadowing,
shadowed**)
1 cast a shadow on something. **2** follow a
person secretly. [same origin as *shade*]

Shadow Cabinet *noun*
members of the Opposition in Parliament
who act as spokesmen on important
matters.

shady *adjective* (**shadier, shadiest**)
1 giving shade, *a shady tree.* **2** in the shade,
a shady place. **3** not completely honest;
disreputable, *a shady deal.*

shaft *noun* (*plural* **shafts**)
1 a long slender rod or straight part, *the
shaft of an arrow.* **2** a ray of light. **3** a deep
narrow hole, *a mine shaft.*
[from Old English]

shaggy *adjective* (**shaggier, shaggiest**)
1 having long rough hair or fibre. **2** rough,
thick, and untidy, *shaggy hair.*
[from Old English]

shah *noun* (*plural* **shahs**)
the title of the former ruler of Iran.
[from Persian *shah* = king]

shake *verb* (**shakes, shaking, shook, shaken**)
1 move quickly up and down or from side
to side. **2** disturb; shock; upset, *The news
shook us.* **3** tremble; be unsteady, *His voice
was shaking.* **shaker** *noun*
shake hands clasp a person's right hand
with yours in greeting or parting or as a
sign of agreement.
shake *noun* (*plural* **shakes**)
1 shaking; a shaking movement.
2 (*informal*) a moment, *I'll be there in two
shakes.* **shaky** *adjective*, **shakily** *adverb*
[from Old English]

shale *noun*
a kind of stone that splits easily into layers.
[probably from German]

shall *auxiliary verb*
1 used with *I* and *we* to express the
ordinary future tense, e.g. *I shall arrive
tomorrow*, and in questions, e.g. *Shall I
shut the door?* (but *will* is used with other
words, e.g. *they will arrive; will you shut the
door?*). **2** used with words other than *I* and

we in promises, e.g. *Cinderella, you shall go to the ball!* (but *I will go* = I promise or intend to go). [from Old English]

USAGE: If you want to be strictly correct, keep to the rules given here, but nowadays many people use *will* after *I* and *we* and it is not usually regarded as wrong.

shallot *noun* (*plural* **shallots**)
a kind of small onion. [from French]

shallow *adjective* (**shallower, shallowest**)
1 not deep, *shallow water*. 2 not capable of deep feelings, *a shallow character*.
shallowness *noun* [origin unknown]

shallows *plural noun*
a shallow part of a stretch of water.

sham *noun* (*plural* **shams**)
something that is not genuine; a pretence.
sham *adjective*
sham *verb* (**shams, shamming, shammed**)
pretend. [probably from *shame*]

shamble *verb* (**shambles, shambling, shambled**)
walk or run in a lazy or awkward way.
[origin unknown]

shambles *noun*
a scene of great disorder or bloodshed.
[from an old word *shamble* = a slaughter-house or meat-market]

shame *noun*
1 a feeling of great sorrow or guilt because you have done wrong. 2 dishonour or disgrace. 3 something you regret, *It's a shame that it rained.*
shameful *adjective*, **shamefully** *adverb*
shame *verb* (**shames, shaming, shamed**)
make a person feel ashamed.
[from Old English]

shamefaced *adjective*
looking ashamed.

shameless *adjective*
not feeling or looking ashamed.
shamelessly *adverb*

shampoo *noun* (*plural* **shampoos**)
1 a liquid substance for washing the hair.
2 a substance for cleaning a carpet etc. or washing a car. 3 a wash with shampoo, *a shampoo and set.*

shampoo *verb* (**shampoos, shampooing, shampooed**)
wash or clean with a shampoo. [originally = to massage: from Hindi *champo* = press!]

shamrock *noun* (*plural* **shamrocks**)
a plant rather like clover, the national emblem of Ireland. [Irish]

shandy *noun* (*plural* **shandies**)
a mixture of beer and lemonade or some other soft drink. [origin unknown]

shank *noun* (*plural* **shanks**)
1 the leg, especially the part from knee to ankle. 2 a long narrow part, *the shank of a pin.* [from Old English]

shan't (*mainly spoken*)
shall not.

shantung *noun*
soft Chinese silk. [named after Shandong, a province of China, where it was made]

shanty¹ *noun* (*plural* **shanties**)
a shack. [from Canadian French]

shanty² *noun* (*plural* **shanties**)
a sailors' song with a chorus.
[probably from French *chanter* = sing]

shanty town *noun* (*plural* **shanty towns**)
a settlement consisting of shanties.

shape *noun* (*plural* **shapes**)
1 a thing's outline; the appearance an outline produces. 2 proper form or condition, *Get it into shape.* 3 the general form or condition of something, *the shape of British industry.*
shape *verb* (**shapes, shaping, shaped**)
1 make into a particular shape. 2 develop, *It's shaping up nicely.* [from Old English]

shapeless *adjective*
having no definite shape.

shapely *adjective* (**shapelier, shapeliest**)
having an attractive shape.

share *noun* (*plural* **shares**)
1 a part given to one person or thing out of something that is being divided. 2 each of the equal parts forming a business company's capital, giving the person who holds it the right to receive a portion (a *dividend*) of the company's profits.

share *verb* (shares, sharing, shared)
1 give portions of something to two or more people. 2 have or use or experience something that others have too, *share a room*; *share the responsibility*.
[from Old English]

shareholder *noun* (*plural* shareholders)
a person who owns shares in a company.

shareware *noun*
computer software which is given away or which you can use free of charge.

shark¹ *noun* (*plural* sharks)
a large sea fish with sharp teeth.
[origin unknown]

shark² *noun* (*plural* sharks)
a person who exploits or cheats people.
[same origin as *shirk*]

sharp *adjective*
1 with an edge or point that can cut or make holes. 2 quick at noticing or learning things, *sharp eyes*. 3 steep or pointed; not gradual, *a sharp bend*. 4 forceful or severe, *a sharp frost*. 5 distinct; loud and shrill, *a sharp cry*. 6 slightly sour. 7 (in music) one semitone higher than the natural note, *C sharp*. **sharply** *adverb*, **sharpness** *noun*

sharp *adverb*
1 sharply, *turn sharp right*. 2 punctually, *at six o'clock sharp*. 3 (in music) above the correct pitch, *You were singing sharp*.

sharp *noun* (*plural* sharps)
(in music) a note one semitone higher than the natural note; the sign (#) that indicates this. [from Old English]

sharpen *verb* (sharpens, sharpening, sharpened)
make or become sharp. **sharpener** *noun*

sharp practice *noun*
dishonest or barely honest dealings in business.

sharpshooter *noun* (*plural* sharpshooters)
a skilled marksman.

shatter *verb* (shatters, shattering, shattered)
1 break violently into small pieces.
2 destroy, *It shattered our hopes*. 3 upset greatly, *We were shattered by the news*.
[origin unknown]

shave *verb* (shaves, shaving, shaved)
1 scrape growing hair off the skin. 2 cut or scrape a thin slice off something.
shaver *noun*

shave *noun* (*plural* shaves)
the act of shaving the face.
close shave (*informal*) a narrow escape.
[from Old English]

shavings *plural noun*
thin strips shaved off a piece of wood or metal.

shawl *noun* (*plural* shawls)
a large piece of material worn round the shoulders or head or wrapped round a baby. [from Persian or Urdu]

she *pronoun*
the female person or animal being talked about. [Middle English; related to *he*]

sheaf *noun* (*plural* sheaves)
1 a bundle of cornstalks tied together. 2 a bundle of arrows, papers, etc. held together. [from Old English]

shear *verb* (shears, shearing, sheared, sheared or, in sense 1, shorn)
1 cut or trim; cut the wool off a sheep.
2 break because of a sideways or twisting force, *the bolts sheared off*. **shearer** *noun*
[from Old English]

USAGE: Do not confuse with *sheer*.

shears *plural noun*
a cutting tool shaped like a very large pair of scissors and worked with both hands.
[from Old English]

sheath *noun* (*plural* sheaths)
1 a close-fitting cover. 2 a cover for the blade of a knife or sword etc. 3 a condom.
[from Old English]

sheathe *verb* (sheathes, sheathing, sheathed)
1 put into a sheath, *He sheathed his sword*.
2 put a close covering on something.
[from *sheath*]

shed¹ *noun* (*plural* sheds)
a simply-made building used for storing things or sheltering animals, or as a workshop. [from *shade*]

shed² *verb* (sheds, shedding, shed)
1 let something fall or flow, *The tree shed its leaves. We shed tears.* 2 give off, *A heater sheds warmth.* 3 get rid of, *The company has shed 200 workers.* [from Old English]

sheen *noun*
a shine or gloss.
[from Old English *sciene* = beautiful]

sheep *noun* (*plural* sheep)
an animal that eats grass and has a thick fleecy coat, kept in flocks for its wool and its meat. [from Old English]

sheepdog *noun* (*plural* sheepdogs)
a dog trained to guard and herd sheep.

sheepish *adjective*
1 bashful. 2 embarrassed or shamefaced.
sheepishly *adverb*, **sheepishness** *noun*
[originally = innocent or silly: from *sheep* + *-ish*]

sheepshank *noun* (*plural* sheepshanks)
a knot used to shorten a rope.

sheer¹ *adjective*
1 complete or thorough, *sheer stupidity.*
2 vertical, with almost no slope, *a sheer drop.* 3 (of material) very thin;
transparent. [from Old English *scir*
= shining, noble, or pure]

sheer² *verb* (sheers, sheering, sheered)
swerve; move sharply away.
[probably from old German]

USAGE: Do not confuse with *shear*.

sheet¹ *noun* (*plural* sheets)
1 a large piece of lightweight material used on a bed in pairs for a person to sleep between. 2 a whole flat piece of paper, glass, or metal. 3 a wide area of water, ice, flame, etc. [from Old English *scete*]

sheet² *noun* (*plural* sheets)
a rope or chain fastening a sail.
[from Old English *sceata*]

sheikh (*say* shayk *or* sheek) *noun* (*plural* sheikhs)
the leader of an Arab tribe or village.
[from Arabic *shaykh* = elder, old man]

shelf *noun* (*plural* shelves)
1 a flat piece of wood, metal, or glass etc. fixed to a wall or in a piece of furniture so that things can be placed on it. 2 a flat level surface that sticks out; a ledge.
[from old German]

shelf-life *noun* (*plural* shelf-lives)
the length of time something can be kept in a shop before it becomes too old to sell, *newspapers have a shelf-life of only a day.*

shell *noun* (*plural* shells)
1 the hard outer covering of a nut, egg, snail, tortoise, etc. 2 the walls or framework of a building, ship, etc. 3 a metal case filled with explosive, fired from a large gun.

shell *verb* (shells, shelling, shelled)
1 take something out of its shell. 2 fire explosive shells at something.
shell out (*informal*) pay out money.
[from Old English]

shellfish *noun* (*plural* shellfish)
a sea animal that has a shell.

shelter *noun* (*plural* shelters)
1 something that protects people from rain, wind, danger, etc. 2 protection, *Seek shelter from the rain.*
shelter *verb* (shelters, sheltering, sheltered)
1 provide with shelter. 2 protect. 3 find a shelter, *They sheltered under the trees.*
[origin unknown]

shelve *verb* (shelves, shelving, shelved)
1 put things on a shelf or shelves. 2 fit a wall or cupboard etc. with shelves.
3 postpone or reject a plan etc. 4 slope, *The bed of the river shelves steeply.* [from *shelf*]

shepherd *noun* (*plural* shepherds)
a person whose job is to look after sheep.
shepherd *verb* (shepherds, shepherding, shepherded)
guide or direct people. [from *sheep* + *herd*]

shepherdess *noun* (*plural* shepherdesses)
(*now usually poetical*) a woman whose job is to look after sheep.

shepherd's pie *noun*
a dish of minced beef or lamb under a layer of mashed potato.

sherbet *noun*
a fizzy sweet powder or drink.
[from Arabic *sharbat* = a drink]

sheriff *noun* (*plural* **sheriffs**)
the chief law officer of a county, whose
duties vary in different countries. [from
Old English *scir* = shire + *refa* = officer]

sherry *noun* (*plural* **sherries**)
a kind of strong wine.
[named after Jerez de la Frontera, a town
in Spain, where it was first made]

Shetland pony *noun* (*plural* **Shetland
ponies**)
a kind of small, strong, shaggy pony,
originally from the Shetland Isles.

shield *noun* (*plural* **shields**)
1 a large piece of metal, wood, etc. carried
to protect the body. **2** a model of a
triangular shield used as a trophy. **3** a
protection.
shield *verb* (**shields**, **shielding**, **shielded**)
protect from harm or from being
discovered.
[from Old English]

shift *verb* (**shifts**, **shifting**, **shifted**)
1 move or cause to move. **2** (of an opinion
or situation) change slightly.
shift for yourself manage without help; rely
on your own efforts.
shift *noun* (*plural* **shifts**)
1 a change of position or condition etc. **2** a
group of workers who start work as
another group finishes; the time when they
work, *the night shift*. **3** a straight dress
with no waist. [from Old English]

shifty *adjective*
evasive, not straightforward;
untrustworthy.
shiftily *adverb*, **shiftiness** *noun*

Shi'ite (*say* shee-eyt) *noun* (*plural* **Shi'ites**)
a member of one of the two main branches
of Islam, based on the teachings of
Muhammad and his son-in-law, Ali.
[from Arabic *shia* = the party of Ali]

shilling *noun* (*plural* **shillings**)
a former British coin, = 5p.
[from Old English]

shilly-shally *verb* (**shilly-shallies**, **shilly-
shallying**, **shilly-shallied**)
be unable to make up your mind.
[from *shall I? shall I?*]

shimmer *verb* (**shimmers**, **shimmering**,
shimmered)
shine with a quivering light, *The sea
shimmered in the moonlight.* **shimmer** *noun*
[from Old English]

shin *noun* (*plural* **shins**)
the front of the leg between the knee and
the ankle.
shin *verb* (**shins**, **shinning**, **shinned**)
climb by using the arms and legs, not on a
ladder. [from Old English]

shindig *noun* (*plural* **shindigs**) (*informal*)
1 a noisy party. **2** a shindy.
[origin unknown]

shindy *noun* (*plural* **shindies**) (*informal*)
1 a din. **2** a noisy argument; a brawl.
[origin unknown]

shine *verb* (**shines**, **shining**, **shone**, in sense 4
shined)
1 give out or reflect light; be bright. **2** be
excellent, *He doesn't shine in maths.* **3** aim a
light, *Shine your torch on it.* **4** polish, *Have
you shined your shoes?*
shine *noun*
1 brightness. **2** a polish. [from Old English]

shingle *noun*
pebbles on a beach. [origin unknown]

Shinto *noun*
a Japanese religion which includes
worship of ancestors and nature.

shiny *adjective* (**shinier**, **shiniest**)
shining or glossy.

ship *noun* (*plural* **ships**)
a large boat, especially one that goes to sea.
ship *verb* (**ships**, **shipping**, **shipped**)
transport goods etc., especially by ship.
[from Old English]

-ship *suffix*
forms nouns meaning 'condition' (e.g.
friendship, hardship), position (e.g.
chairmanship), or skill (e.g. *seamanship*).
[from Old English]

shipment noun (plural shipments)
1 the process of shipping goods. 2 the amount shipped.

shipping noun
1 ships, Britain's shipping. 2 transporting goods by ship.

shipshape adjective
in good order; tidy.

shipwreck noun (plural shipwrecks)
1 the wrecking of a ship by storm or accident. 2 a wrecked ship.
shipwrecked adjective

shipyard noun (plural shipyards)
a place where ships are built or repaired.

shire noun (plural shires)
a county.
the Shires the country areas of (especially central) England, away from the cities.
[from Old English]

shire horse noun (plural shire horses)
a kind of large, strong horse used for ploughing or pulling carts.

shirk verb (shirks, shirking, shirked)
avoid a duty or work etc. selfishly or unfairly. shirker noun [probably from German Schurke = scoundrel]

shirr verb (shirrs, shirring, shirred)
gather cloth into folds by rows of threads run through it. [origin unknown]

shirt noun (plural shirts)
a piece of clothing for the top half of the body, made of light material and with a collar and sleeves.
in your shirtsleeves not wearing a jacket over your shirt.
[from Old English]

shirty adjective (informal)
annoyed. [perhaps from Keep your shirt on! = calm down, don't be angry]

shiver verb (shivers, shivering, shivered)
tremble with cold or fear. shiver noun, shivery adjective [origin unknown]

shoal¹ noun (plural shoals)
a large number of fish swimming together. [same origin as school²]

shoal² noun (plural shoals)
1 a shallow place. 2 an underwater sandbank. [from Old English]

shock¹ noun (plural shocks)
1 a sudden unpleasant surprise. 2 great weakness caused by pain or injury etc. 3 the effect of a violent shake or knock. 4 an effect caused by electric current passing through the body.
shock verb (shocks, shocking, shocked)
1 give someone a shock; surprise or upset a person greatly. 2 seem very improper or scandalous to a person. [from French]

shock² noun (plural shocks)
a bushy mass of hair. [origin unknown]

shocking adjective
1 causing indignation or disgust.
2 (informal) very bad, shocking weather.

shock wave noun (plural shock waves)
a sharp change in pressure in the air around an explosion or an object moving very quickly.

shod past tense of shoe.

shoddy adjective (shoddier, shoddiest)
of poor quality; badly made or done, shoddy work. shoddily adverb, shoddiness noun [origin unknown]

shoe noun (plural shoes)
1 a strong covering for the foot. 2 a horseshoe. 3 something shaped or used like a shoe.
be in somebody's shoes be in his or her situation.
shoe verb (shoes, shoeing, shod)
fit with a shoe or shoes. [from Old English]

shoehorn noun (plural shoehorns)
a curved piece of stiff material for easing your heel into the back of a shoe.
[originally made from a cow's horn]

shoelace noun (plural shoelaces)
a cord for lacing up and fastening a shoe.

shoestring noun
on a shoestring using only a small amount of money, travel the world on a shoestring.

shoo interjection
a word used to frighten animals away.
shoo verb

shoot *verb* (shoots, shooting, shot)
1 fire a gun or missile etc. 2 hurt or kill by shooting. 3 move or send very quickly, *The car shot past us.* 4 kick or hit a ball at a goal. 5 (of a plant) put out buds or shoots. 6 slide the bolt of a door into or out of its fastening. 7 film or photograph something, *They shot the film in Africa.*
shoot *noun* (*plural* shoots)
1 a young branch or new growth of a plant. 2 an expedition for shooting animals.
[from Old English]

shooting star *noun* (*plural* shooting stars)
a meteor.

shop *noun* (*plural* shops)
1 a building or room where goods or services are on sale to the public. 2 a workshop. 3 talk that is about your own work or job, *She is always talking shop.*
shop *verb* (shops, shopping, shopped)
go and buy things at shops. **shopper** *noun*
shop around compare goods and prices in several shops before buying.
[from old French]

shopfitter *noun* (*plural* shopfitters)
a person whose job is to make or fit counters, shelves, display stands, etc. in shops.

shop floor *noun*
1 the workers in a factory, not the managers. 2 the place where they work.

shopkeeper *noun* (*plural* shopkeepers)
a person who owns or manages a shop.

shoplifter *noun* (*plural* shoplifters)
a person who steals goods from a shop after entering as a customer.
shoplifting *noun*

shopping *noun*
1 buying goods in shops. 2 the goods bought.

shop-soiled *adjective*
dirty, faded, or slightly damaged through being displayed in a shop.

shop steward *noun* (*plural* shop stewards)
a trade-union official who represents his or her fellow workers.

shop window *noun* (*plural* shop windows)
1 a window in a shop where goods are displayed. 2 an opportunity to show off your abilities, *The exhibition will be a shop window for British industry.*

shore¹ *noun* (*plural* shores)
the land along the edge of a sea or of a lake.
[from old German or old Dutch *schore*]

shore² *verb* (shores, shoring, shored)
prop something up with a piece of wood etc.
[from old German or old Dutch *schoren*]

shorn *past participle* of **shear**.

short *adjective*
1 not long; occupying a small distance or time, *a short walk.* 2 not tall, *a short person.* 3 not enough; not having enough of something, *We are short of water.* 4 curt. 5 (of pastry) rich and crumbly because it contains a lot of fat. **shortness** *noun*
for short as an abbreviation, *Raymond is called Ray for short.*
short for an abbreviation of, *'Ray' is short for Raymond.*
short *adverb*
suddenly, *She stopped short.*
[from Old English]

shortage *noun* (*plural* shortages)
lack or scarcity of something; insufficiency.

shortbread *noun*
a rich sweet biscuit, made with butter.

shortcake *noun*
shortbread.

short circuit *noun* (*plural* short circuits)
a fault in an electrical circuit in which current flows along a shorter route than the normal one.

short-circuit *verb* (short-circuits, short-circuiting, short-circuited)
cause a short circuit.

shortcoming *noun* (*plural* shortcomings)
a fault or failure to reach a good standard.

short cut *noun* (*plural* short cuts)
a route or method that is quicker than the usual one.

shorten *verb* (shortens, shortening, shortened)
make or become shorter.

shortfall *noun* (*plural* shortfalls)
a shortage; an amount lower than needed or expected.

shorthand *noun*
a set of special signs for writing words down as quickly as people say them.

short-handed *adjective*
short-staffed.

shortlist *noun* (*plural* shortlists)
a list of the most suitable people or things, from which a final choice will be made.

shortlist *verb* (shortlists, shortlisting, shortlisted)
put on a shortlist.

shortly *adverb*
1 in a short time; soon, *They will arrive shortly.* 2 in a few words. 3 curtly.

shorts *plural noun*
trousers with legs that do not reach to the knee.

short-sighted *adjective*
1 unable to see things clearly. 2 lacking imagination or foresight.

short-staffed *adjective*
not having enough workers or staff.

short-tempered *adjective*
easily becoming angry.

shot¹ *past tense* of shoot.

shot² *noun* (*plural* shots)
1 the firing of a gun or missile etc.; the sound of this. 2 something fired from a gun; lead pellets for firing from small guns. 3 a person judged by skill in shooting, *He's a good shot.* 4 a heavy metal ball thrown as a sport. 5 a stroke in tennis, cricket, billiards, etc. 6 a photograph; a filmed scene. 7 an attempt, *Have a shot at the crossword.* 8 an injection of a drug or vaccine.

shot *adjective*
(of fabric) woven so that different colours show at different angles, *shot silk.*
[from Old English]

shotgun *noun* (*plural* shotguns)
a gun for firing small shot at close range.

should *auxiliary verb*
used to express 1 obligation or duty, = ought to (*You should have told me*), 2 something expected (*They should be here by ten o'clock*), 3 a possible event (*if you should happen to see him*), 4 with *I* and *we* to make a polite statement (*I should like to come*) or in a conditional clause (*If they had supported us we should have won*).
[past tense of *shall*]

USAGE: In sense 4, although *should* is strictly correct, many people nowadays use *would* and this is not regarded as wrong.

shoulder *noun* (*plural* shoulders)
1 the part of the body between the neck and the arm, foreleg, or wing. 2 a side that juts out, *the shoulder of the bottle.*

shoulder *verb* (shoulders, shouldering, shouldered)
1 take something on your shoulder or shoulders. 2 push with your shoulder. 3 accept responsibility or blame.
[from Old English]

shoulder blade *noun* (*plural* shoulder blades)
either of the two large flat bones at the top of your back.

shouldn't (*mainly spoken*)
should not.

shout *noun* (*plural* shouts)
a loud cry or call. [origin unknown]

shout *verb* (shouts, shouting, shouted)
give a shout; speak or call loudly.
[origin unknown]

shove *verb* (shoves, shoving, shoved)
push roughly. **shove** *noun*
shove off (*informal*) go away.
[from Old English]

shovel *noun* (*plural* shovels)
a tool like a spade with the sides turned up, used for lifting coal, earth, snow, etc.

shovel *verb* (shovels, shovelling, shovelled)
1 move or clear with a shovel. 2 scoop or push roughly, *He was shovelling food into his mouth.* [from Old English]

show verb (shows, showing, showed, shown)
1 allow or cause something to be seen, *Show me your new bike.* 2 make a person understand; demonstrate, *Show me how to use it.* 3 guide, *Show him in.* 4 treat in a certain way, *She showed us much kindness.* 5 be visible, *That scratch won't show.* 6 prove your ability to someone, *We'll show them!*
show off 1 show something proudly. 2 try to impress people.
show up 1 make or be clearly visible; reveal a fault etc. 2 (*informal*) arrive.
show noun (*plural* shows)
1 a display or exhibition, *a flower show.* 2 an entertainment. 3 (*slang*) something that happens or is done, *He runs the whole show.* [from Old English]

show business noun
the entertainment industry; the theatre, films, radio, and television.

showcase noun (*plural* showcases)
1 a glass case for displaying something in a shop, museum, etc. 2 a situation or setting in which something can be presented attractively, *The programme is a showcase for new acts.*

showdown noun (*plural* showdowns)
a final test or confrontation.

shower noun (*plural* showers)
1 a brief fall of rain or snow. 2 a lot of small things coming or falling like rain, *a shower of stones.* 3 a device or cabinet for spraying water to wash a person's body; a wash in this.
shower verb (showers, showering, showered)
1 fall or send things in a shower. 2 wash under a shower. [from Old English]

showery adjective
(of weather) with many showers.

show house noun (*plural* show houses)
a furnished and decorated house on a new estate that can be shown to people who are thinking of buying a house there.

showjumping noun
a competition in which riders make their horses jump over fences and other obstacles, with penalty points for errors. **showjumper** noun

showman noun (*plural* showmen)
1 a person who presents entertainments. 2 someone who is good at attracting attention. **showmanship** noun

showpiece noun (*plural* showpieces)
a fine example of something for people to see and admire.

showroom noun (*plural* showrooms)
a large room where goods are displayed for people to look at.

showy adjective (showier, showiest)
likely to attract attention; brightly or highly decorated.
showily adverb, **showiness** noun

shrapnel noun
pieces of metal scattered from an exploding shell. [named after H. Shrapnel, a British officer who invented it in about 1806]

shred noun (*plural* shreds)
1 a tiny piece torn or cut off something. 2 a small amount, *There is not a shred of evidence.*
shred verb (shreds, shredding, shredded)
cut into shreds. **shredder** noun
[from Old English]

shrew noun (*plural* shrews)
1 a small mouse-like animal. 2 (*old use*) a bad-tempered woman who is constantly scolding people. **shrewish** adjective
[from Old English]

shrewd adjective
having common sense and good judgement; clever. **shrewdly** adverb, **shrewdness** noun
[from old sense of *shrew* = spiteful or cunning person]

shriek noun (*plural* shrieks)
a shrill cry or scream.
shriek verb (shrieks, shrieking, shrieked)
give a shriek. [imitating the sound]

shrift noun
short shrift curt treatment.
[originally = a short time allowed for someone to confess to a priest before being executed: from *shrive*]

shrill *adjective*
sounding very high and piercing.
shrilly *adverb*, **shrillness** *noun*
[probably from Old English]

shrimp *noun* (*plural* **shrimps**)
a small shellfish, pink when boiled.
[origin unknown]

shrimping *noun*
fishing for shrimps.

shrine *noun* (*plural* **shrines**)
an altar, chapel, or other sacred place.
[originally = a container for holy relics: via
Old English from Latin *scrinium* = a case
or chest]

shrink *verb* (**shrinks, shrinking, shrank,
shrunk**)
1 make or become smaller. 2 move back to
avoid something. 3 avoid doing something
because of fear, conscience,
embarrassment, etc. **shrinkage** *noun*
[from Old English]

shrive *verb* (**shrives, shriving, shrove,
shriven**) (*old use*)
(of a priest) hear a person's confession and
give absolution. [from Old English]

shrivel *verb* (**shrivels, shrivelling, shrivelled**)
make or become dry and wrinkled.
[probably from Old Norse]

shroud *noun* (*plural* **shrouds**)
1 a cloth in which a dead body is wrapped.
2 each of a set of ropes supporting a ship's
mast.
shroud *verb* (**shrouds, shrouding, shrouded**)
1 wrap in a shroud. 2 cover or conceal, *The
town was shrouded in mist.*
[from Old English]

shrove *past tense* of **shrive**.
Shrove Tuesday the day before Lent, when
pancakes are eaten, originally to use up fat
before the fast.
[from the past tense of *shrive*, because it
was the custom to be shriven on this day]

shrub *noun* (*plural* **shrubs**)
a woody plant smaller than a tree; a bush.
shrubby *adjective* [from Old English]

shrubbery *noun* (*plural* **shrubberies**)
an area planted with shrubs.

shrug *verb* (**shrugs, shrugging, shrugged**)
raise your shoulders as a sign that you do
not care, do not know, etc. **shrug** *noun*
shrug something off treat it as
unimportant.
[origin unknown]

shrunken *adjective*
having shrunk.

shudder *verb* (**shudders, shuddering,
shuddered**)
1 shiver violently with horror, fear, or
cold. 2 make a strong shaking movement.
shudder *noun*
[from old German or old Dutch]

shuffle *verb* (**shuffles, shuffling, shuffled**)
1 walk without lifting the feet from the
ground. 2 slide playing cards over each
other to get them into random order.
3 shift or rearrange. **shuffle** *noun*
[probably from old German]

shun *verb* (**shuns, shunning, shunned**)
avoid; deliberately keep away from
something. [from Old English]

shunt *verb* (**shunts, shunting, shunted**)
move a train or wagons on to another
track; divert. **shunt** *noun*, **shunter** *noun*
[origin unknown]

shut *verb* (**shuts, shutting, shut**)
1 move a door, lid, or cover etc. so that it
blocks an opening; make or become closed.
2 bring or fold parts together, *Shut the
book.*
shut down 1 stop something working.
2 stop business.
shut up 1 shut securely. 2 (*informal*) stop
talking or making a noise.
[from Old English]

shutter *noun* (*plural* **shutters**)
1 a panel or screen that can be closed over
a window. 2 the device in a camera that
opens and closes to let light fall on the film.
shuttered *adjective* [from *shut*]

shuttle *noun* (*plural* **shuttles**)
1 a holder carrying the weft-thread across
a loom in weaving. 2 a train, bus, or
aircraft that makes frequent short
journeys between two points. 3 a space
shuttle.

shuttle *verb* (shuttles, shuttling, shuttled)
move, travel, or send backwards and
forwards. [from Old English]

shuttlecock *noun* (*plural* shuttlecocks)
a small rounded piece of cork or plastic
with a crown of feathers, struck to and fro
by players in badminton etc.
[from *shuttle* and *cock*]

shy[1] *adjective* (shyer, shyest)
afraid to meet or talk to other people;
timid. **shyly** *adverb*, **shyness** *noun*
shy *verb* (shies, shying, shied)
move suddenly in alarm (of a horse).
[from Old English]

shy[2] *verb* (shies, shying, shied)
throw a stone etc.
shy *noun* (*plural* shies)
a throw. [origin unknown]

SI *noun*
an internationally recognized system of
metric units of measurement, including
the metre and kilogram.
[short for French *Système International
d'Unités* = International System of Units]

Siamese *adjective*
to do with or belonging to Siam (now called
Thailand) or its people. **Siamese** *noun*

Siamese cat *noun* (*plural* Siamese cats)
a cat with short pale fur with darker face,
ears, tail, and feet.

Siamese twins *plural noun*
twins who are born with their bodies
joined together. [after two famous twins
born in Siam (now called Thailand), who
were joined near the waist]

sibilant *adjective*
having a hissing sound, *a sibilant
whisper.*
sibilant *noun* (*plural* sibilants)
a speech-sound that sounds like hissing,
e.g. *s*, *sh*. [from Latin *sibilans* = hissing]

sibling *noun* (*plural* siblings)
a brother or sister. [from Old English *sib*
= related by birth, a blood relative, + -*ling*]

sibyl *noun* (*plural* sibyls)
a prophetess in ancient Greece or Rome.

sick *adjective*
1 ill; physically or mentally unwell.
2 vomiting or likely to vomit, *I feel sick.*
3 distressed or disgusted. 4 making fun of
death, disability, or misfortune in an
unpleasant way.
sick of tired of.
[from Old English]

sicken *verb* (sickens, sickening, sickened)
1 begin to be ill. 2 make or become
distressed or disgusted, *Vandalism sickens
us all.* **sickening** *adjective*

sickle *noun* (*plural* sickles)
1 a tool with a narrow curved blade, used
for cutting corn etc. 2 something shaped
like this blade, e.g. the crescent moon.
[from Old English]

sickle-cell anaemia *noun*
a severe form of anaemia which is passed
on in the genes, and which causes pain in
the joints, fever, jaundice, and sometimes
death. [so called because the red blood cells
become sickle-shaped]

sickly *adjective*
1 often ill; unhealthy. 2 making people
feel sick, *a sickly smell.* 3 weak, *a sickly
smile.*

sickness *noun* (*plural* sicknesses)
1 illness. 2 a disease. 3 vomiting.

side *noun* (*plural* sides)
1 a surface, especially one joining the top
and bottom of something. 2 a line that
forms part of the boundary of a triangle,
square, etc. 3 either of the two halves into
which something can be divided by a line
down its centre. 4 the part near the edge
and away from the centre. 5 the place or
region next to a person or thing, *He stood at
my side.* 6 one aspect or view of something,
Study all sides of the problem. 7 one of two
groups or teams etc. who oppose each
other.
on the side as a sideline.
side by side next to each other.
side *adjective*
at or on a side, *the side door.*
side *verb* (sides, siding, sided)
side with take a person's side in an
argument.
[from Old English]

sideboard *noun* (*plural* sideboards)
a long piece of furniture with drawers and cupboards for china etc. and a flat top.

sidecar *noun* (*plural* sidecars)
a small compartment for a passenger, fixed to the side of a motorcycle.

side effect *noun* (*plural* side effects)
an effect, especially an unpleasant one, that a medicine has on you as well as the effect intended.

sidelight *noun* (*plural* sidelights)
1 a light at the side of a vehicle or ship. 2 light from one side.

sideline *noun* (*plural* sidelines)
1 something done in addition to the main work or activity. 2 a line at the side of a football pitch etc.; the area just outside this.

sidelong *adjective*
towards one side; sideways, *a sidelong glance*. [from *side* + Old English *-ling* = extending in a certain direction]

sidereal (*say* sid-**eer**-ee-al) *adjective*
of or measured by the stars.
[from Latin *sideris* = of a star]

sideshow *noun* (*plural* sideshows)
a small entertainment forming part of a large one, e.g. at a fair.

sidetrack *verb* (sidetracks, sidetracking, sidetracked)
take someone's attention away from the main subject or problem.

sidewalk *noun* (*plural* sidewalks)
(*American*) pavement.

sideways *adverb* & *adjective*
1 to or from one side, *Move it sideways*. 2 with one side facing forwards, *We sat sideways in the bus*.

siding *noun* (*plural* sidings)
a short railway line by the side of a main line.

sidle *verb* (sidles, sidling, sidled)
walk in a shy or nervous manner.
[from *sidelong*]

siege *noun* (*plural* sieges)
the besieging of a place.
lay siege to begin besieging.
[from old French]

sienna *noun*
a kind of clay used in making brownish paints. [from *Siena*, a town in Italy]

sierra *noun* (*plural* sierras)
a range of mountains with sharp peaks, in Spain or parts of America.
[Spanish, from Latin *serra* = a saw]

siesta (*say* see-**est**-a) *noun* (*plural* siestas)
an afternoon rest. [from Latin *sexta hora* = sixth hour, midday]

sieve (*say* siv) *noun* (*plural* sieves)
a device made of mesh or perforated metal or plastic, used to separate the smaller or soft parts of something from the larger or hard parts.
sieve *verb* (sieves, sieving, sieved)
put something through a sieve.
[from Old English]

sift *verb* (sifts, sifting, sifted)
1 sieve. 2 examine and analyse facts or evidence etc. carefully. **sifter** *noun*
[from Old English]

sigh *noun* (*plural* sighs)
a sound made by breathing out heavily when you are sad, tired, relieved, etc.
sigh *verb* (sighs, sighing, sighed)
make a sigh. [probably from Old English]

sight *noun* (*plural* sights)
1 the ability to see. 2 a thing that can be seen or is worth seeing, *Our roses are a wonderful sight*. 3 an unsightly thing, *You do look a sight in those clothes!* 4 a device looked through to help aim a gun or telescope etc.
at sight or **on sight** as soon as a person or thing has been seen.
in sight 1 visible. 2 clearly near, *Victory was in sight*.

USAGE: Do not confuse with **site**.

sight *verb* (sights, sighting, sighted)
1 see or observe something. 2 aim a gun or telescope etc.
[from Old English]

sightless *adjective*
blind.

sight-reading *noun*
playing or singing music at sight, without preparation.

sightseeing *noun*
visiting interesting places in a town etc.
sightseer *noun*

sign *noun* (*plural* **signs**)
1 something that shows that a thing exists, *There are signs of decay.* **2** a mark, device, or notice etc. that gives a special meaning, *a road sign.* **3** an action or movement giving information or a command etc. **4** any of the twelve divisions of the zodiac, represented by a symbol.

sign *verb* (**signs**, **signing**, **signed**)
1 make a sign or signal. **2** write your signature on something; accept a contract etc. by doing this. **3** use signing.
sign on 1 accept a job etc. by signing a contract. **2** sign a form to say that you are unemployed and want to claim benefit.
[same origin as *signify*]

signal *noun* (*plural* **signals**)
1 a device, gesture, or sound etc. that gives information or a command. **2** a message made up of such things. **3** a sequence of electrical impulses or radio waves.

signal *verb* (**signals**, **signalling**, **signalled**)
make a signal to somebody. **signaller** *noun*

USAGE: Do not use this word in mistake for *single* in the phrase *to single out.*

signal *adjective*
remarkable, *a signal success.* **signally** *adverb* [same origin as *signify*]

signal box *noun* (*plural* **signal boxes**)
a building from which railway signals, points, etc. are controlled.

signalman *noun* (*plural* **signalmen**)
a person who controls railway signals.

signatory *noun* (*plural* **signatories**)
a person who signs an agreement etc.

signature *noun* (*plural* **signatures**)
a person's name written by himself or herself.
[from Latin *signare* = make a mark]

signature tune (*plural* **signature tunes**)
a special tune always used to announce a particular programme, performer, etc.

signet ring *noun* (*plural* **signet rings**)
a ring with a person's initials or a design engraved on it. [same origin as *signify*]

significant *adjective*
1 having a meaning; full of meaning. **2** important, *a significant event.*
significantly *adverb*, **significance** *noun*

signification *noun*
meaning.

signify *verb* (**signifies**, **signifying**, **signified**)
1 be a sign or symbol of; mean. **2** indicate, *She signified her approval.* **3** be important; matter. [from Latin *signum* = sign]

signing or **sign language** *noun*
a way of communicating by using gestures etc. instead of sounds, used mainly by deaf people.

signpost *noun* (*plural* **signposts**)
a sign at a road junction etc. showing the names and distances of places down each road.

Sikh (*say* seek) *noun* (*plural* **Sikhs**)
a member of a religion founded in northern India, believing in one God and accepting some Hindu and some Islamic beliefs. **Sikhism** *noun*
[from Sanskrit *sisya* = disciple]

silage *noun*
fodder made from green crops stored in a silo.

silence *noun* (*plural* **silences**)
absence of sound or talk.

silence *verb* (**silences**, **silencing**, **silenced**)
make a person or thing silent.

silencer *noun* (*plural* **silencers**)
a device for reducing the sound made by a gun or a vehicle's exhaust system etc.

silent *adjective*
1 without any sound. **2** not speaking.
silently *adverb*
[from Latin *silere* = to be silent]

silhouette (*say* sil-oo-et) *noun* (*plural* silhouettes)
a dark shadow seen against a light background. **silhouette** *verb*
[named after a French author, É. de Silhouette, who made paper cut-outs of people's profiles from their shadows]

silica *noun*
a hard white mineral that is a compound of silicon, used to make glass.

silicon *noun*
a substance found in many rocks, used in making transistors, chips for microprocessors, etc.
[from Latin *silex* = flint or quartz]

silicone *noun*
a compound of silicon used in paints, varnish, and lubricants.

silk *noun* (*plural* silks)
1 a fine soft thread or cloth made from the fibre produced by silkworms for making their cocoons. 2 a length of silk thread used for embroidery.
silken *adjective*, **silky** *adjective*
[from Old English, probably from Latin]

silkworm *noun* (*plural* silkworms)
the caterpillar of a kind of moth, which feeds on mulberry leaves and spins itself a cocoon.

sill *noun* (*plural* sills)
a strip of stone, wood, or metal underneath a window or door. [from Old English]

silly *adjective* (sillier, silliest)
foolish or unwise. **silliness** *noun*
[from Old English *saelig* = happy, blessed by God, later = innocent, helpless]

silo (*say* sy-loh) *noun* (*plural* silos)
1 a pit or tower for storing green crops (see *silage*) or corn or cement etc. 2 an underground place for storing a missile ready for firing. [Spanish]

silt *noun*
sediment laid down by a river or sea etc.
silt *verb* (silts, silting, silted)
silt up block or clog or become blocked with silt.
[origin unknown]

silver *noun*
1 a shiny white precious metal. 2 the colour of silver. 3 coins or objects made of silver or silver-coloured metal. 4 a silver medal, usually given as second prize.
silvery *adjective*

silver *adjective*
1 made of silver. 2 coloured like silver.
silver *verb* (silvers, silvering, silvered)
make or become silvery.
[from Old English]

silver wedding *noun* (*plural* silver weddings)
a couple's 25th wedding anniversary.

simian *adjective*
like a monkey.
[from Latin *simia* = monkey]

similar *adjective*
nearly the same as another person or thing; of the same kind. **similarly** *adverb*, **similarity** *noun* [from Latin *similis* = like]

simile (*say* sim-il-ee) *noun* (*plural* similes)
a comparison of one thing with another, e.g. *He is as strong as a horse. We ran like the wind.* [same origin as *similar*]

simmer *verb* (simmers, simmering, simmered)
boil very gently.
simmer down calm down.
[origin unknown]

simper *verb* (simpers, simpering, simpered)
smile in a silly affected way. **simper** *noun*
[origin unknown]

simple *adjective* (simpler, simplest)
1 easy, *a simple question.* 2 not complicated or elaborate. 3 plain, not showy, *a simple cottage.* 4 without much sense or intelligence. 5 not of high rank; ordinary, *a simple countryman.* **simplicity** *noun*
[from Latin]

simple-minded *adjective*
naive or foolish.

simpleton *noun* (*plural* simpletons) (*old use*)
a foolish person.

simplify *verb* (simplifies, simplifying, simplified)
make a thing simple or easy to understand.
simplification *noun*

simply *adverb*
1 in a simple way, *Explain it simply.*
2 without doubt; completely, *It's simply marvellous.* 3 only or merely, *It's simply a question of time.*

simulate *verb* (simulates, simulating, simulated)
1 reproduce the appearance or conditions of something; imitate, *This device simulates a space flight.* 2 pretend, *They simulated fear.* **simulation** *noun*
[same origin as *similar*]

simulator *noun* (*plural* simulators)
a machine or device for simulating actual conditions or events, often used for training, *a flight simulator.*

simultaneous (*say* sim-ul-**tay**-nee-us)
adjective
happening at the same time. **simultaneously**
adverb [from Latin]

sin *noun* (*plural* sins)
1 the breaking of a religious or moral law.
2 a very bad action.

sin *verb* (sins, sinning, sinned)
commit a sin. **sinner** *noun*
[from Old English]

since *conjunction*
1 from the time when, *Where have you been since I last saw you?* 2 because, *Since we have missed the bus we must walk home.*

since *preposition*
from a certain time, *She has been here since Christmas.*

since *adverb*
between then and now, *He ran away and hasn't been seen since.*
[from Old English *sithon* = then]

sincere *adjective*
without pretence; truly felt or meant, *my sincere thanks.*
sincerely *adverb*, **sincerity** *noun*
Yours sincerely see *yours.*
[from Latin *sincerus* = clean or pure]

sine *noun* (*plural* sines)
(in a right-angled triangle) the ratio of the length of a side opposite one of the acute angles to the length of the hypotenuse.
(Compare *cosine.*) [same origin as *sinus*]

sinecure (*say* sy-nik-yoor) *noun* (*plural* sinecures)
a paid job that requires no work.
[from Latin *sine cura* = without care]

sinew *noun* (*plural* sinews)
a tendon. [from Old English]

sinewy *adjective*
slim, muscular, and strong.

sinful *adjective*
1 guilty of sin. 2 wicked.
sinfully *adverb*, **sinfulness** *noun*

sing *verb* (sings, singing, sang, sung)
1 make musical sounds with the voice.
2 perform a song. **singer** *noun*
[from Old English]

singe (*say* sinj) *verb* (singes, singeing, singed)
burn something slightly.
[from Old English]

single *adjective*
1 one only; not double or multiple.
2 suitable for one person, *single beds.*
3 separate, *We sold every single thing.* 4 not married. 5 for the journey to a place but not back again, *a single ticket.* **singly** *adverb*

single *noun* (*plural* singles)
1 a single person or thing. 2 a single ticket.
3 a record with one short piece of music on each side.

single *verb* (singles, singling, singled)
single out pick out or distinguish from other people or things.
[from Latin]

single file *nouns*
in single file in a line, one behind the other.

single-handed *adjective*
without help.

single-minded *adjective*
with your mind set on one purpose only.

single parent *noun* (*plural* single parents)
a person bringing up a child or children without a partner.

singles bar *noun* (*plural* singles bars)
a bar where unmarried people go to drink and meet each other.

singlet *noun* (*plural* singlets)
a man's garment worn under or instead of a shirt; a vest. [originally = a jacket something like a doublet: from *single* with a pun on *double* and *doublet*]

singsong *adjective*
having a monotonous tone or rhythm, *a singsong voice.*

singsong *noun* (*plural* singsongs)
1 informal singing by a gathering of people. 2 a singsong tone.

singular *noun* (*plural* singulars)
the form of a noun or verb used when it stands for only one person or thing, *The singular is 'man', the plural is 'men'.*

singular *adjective*
1 to do with the singular. 2 uncommon or extraordinary, *a woman of singular courage.* **singularly** *adverb*, **singularity** *noun*
[from Latin *singulus* = single]

sinister *adjective*
1 looking evil or harmful. 2 wicked, *a sinister motive.* [from Latin, = on the left (which was thought to be unlucky)]

sink *verb* (sinks, sinking, sank, sunk)
1 go or cause to go under the surface or to the bottom of the sea etc., *The ship sank. They sank the ship.* 2 go or fall slowly downwards, *He sank to his knees.* 3 dig or drill, *They sank a well.* 4 invest money in something.
sink in become understood.

sink *noun* (*plural* sinks)
a fixed basin with a drainpipe and usually a tap or taps to supply water.
[from Old English]

sinuous *adjective*
with many bends or curves.
[same origin as *sinus*]

sinus (*say* sy-nus) *noun* (*plural* sinuses)
a hollow part in the bones of the skull, connected with the nose, *My sinuses are blocked.* [Latin, = curve]

-sion *suffix* see -ion.

sip *verb* (sips, sipping, sipped)
drink in small mouthfuls. **sip** *noun*
[probably from *sup*]

siphon *noun* (*plural* siphons)
1 a pipe or tube in the form of an upside-down U, arranged so that liquid is forced up it and down to a lower level. 2 a bottle containing soda water which is released through a tube.

siphon *verb* (siphons, siphoning, siphoned)
flow or draw out through a siphon.
[Greek, = pipe]

sir *noun*
1 a word used when speaking politely to a man, *Please sir, may I go?* 2 **Sir** the title given to a knight or baronet, *Sir John Moore.* [from *sire*]

sire *noun* (*plural* sires)
1 the male parent of a horse or dog etc. (Compare *dam²*.) 2 a word formerly used when speaking to a king.

sire *verb* (sires, siring, sired)
be the sire of, *This stallion has sired several winners.*
[from French; related to *senior*]

siren *noun* (*plural* sirens)
1 a device that makes a long loud sound as a signal. 2 a dangerously attractive woman. [named after the Sirens in Greek legend, women who by their sweet singing lured seafarers to shipwreck on the rocks]

sirloin *noun*
beef from the upper part of the loin.
[from *sur-²* + old French *loigne* = loin]

sirocco *noun* (*plural* siroccos)
a hot dry wind that reaches Italy from Africa.
[from Arabic *sharuk* = east wind]

sisal (*say* sy-sal) *noun*
fibre from a tropical plant, used for making ropes. [named after Sisal, a port in Mexico from which it was exported]

sissy *noun* (*plural* sissies)
a timid or cowardly person.
[from *sis* = sister]

sister *noun* (*plural* sisters)
1 a daughter of the same parents as another person. 2 a woman who is a fellow

member of an association etc. **3** a nun. **4** a female hospital nurse in charge of others.
sisterly *adjective* [from Old English]

sisterhood *noun* (*plural* **sisterhoods**)
1 being sisters. **2** companionship and mutual support between women. **3** a society or association of women.

sister-in-law *noun* (*plural* **sisters-in-law**)
1 the sister of a married person's husband or wife. **2** the wife of a person's brother.

sit *verb* (**sits, sitting, sat**)
1 rest with your body supported on the buttocks; occupy a seat, *We were sitting in the front row.* **2** seat; cause someone to sit. **3** (of birds) perch; stay on the nest to hatch eggs. **4** be a candidate for an examination. **5** be situated; stay. **6** (of Parliament or a lawcourt etc.) be assembled for business. [from Old English]

sitar *noun* (*plural* **sitars**)
an Indian musical instrument that is like a guitar. [Hindi, from Persian and Urdu *sih* = three + *tar* = string]

sitcom *noun* (*plural* **sitcoms**)
a situation comedy.

site *noun* (*plural* **sites**)
the place where something happens or happened or is built etc., *a camping site.*

USAGE: Do not confuse with *sight.*

site *verb* (**sites, siting, sited**)
provide with a site; locate. [from Latin *situs* = position]

sit-in *noun* (*plural* **sit-ins**)
a protest in which people sit down or occupy a public place and refuse to move.

sitting room *noun* (*plural* **sitting rooms**)
a room with comfortable chairs for sitting in.

sitting tenant *noun* (*plural* **sitting tenants**)
a tenant who is entitled to stay if the place he or she rents is bought by someone else.

situated *adjective*
in a particular place or situation.

situation *noun*
1 a position, with its surroundings. **2** a state of affairs at a certain time, *The police faced a difficult situation.* **3** a job. [same origin as *site*]

situation comedy *noun* (*plural* **situation comedies**)
a comedy series on radio or television, based on how characters react to unusual or comic situations.

six *noun* (*plural* **sixes**) & *adjective*
the number 6. **sixth** *adjective* & *noun*
at sixes and sevens in disorder or disagreement.
[from Old English]

sixteen *noun* & *adjective*
the number 16. **sixteenth** *adjective* & *noun*
[from Old English]

sixty *noun* (*plural* **sixties**) & *adjective*
the number 60. **sixtieth** *adjective* & *noun*
[from Old English]

size¹ *noun* (*plural* **sizes**)
1 the measurements or extent of something. **2** any of the series of standard measurements in which certain things are made, *a size eight shoe.*
size *verb* (**sizes, sizing, sized**)
arrange things according to their size.
size up 1 estimate the size of something. **2** form an opinion or judgement about a person or thing.
[originally, a law fixing the amount of a tax: from old French *assise* = law, court session]

size² *noun*
a gluey substance used to glaze paper or stiffen cloth etc.
size *verb* (**sizes, sizing, sized**)
treat with size. [origin unknown]

sizeable *adjective*
large or fairly large.

sizzle *verb* (**sizzles, sizzling, sizzled**)
make a crackling or hissing sound.
[imitating the sound]

skate¹ *noun* (*plural* **skates**)
1 a boot with a steel blade attached to the sole, used for sliding smoothly over ice. **2** a roller-skate.

skate *verb* (skates, skating, skated)
move on skates. **skater** *noun* [from Dutch]

skate² *noun* (*plural* skate)
a large flat edible sea fish. [from Old Norse]

skateboard *noun* (*plural* skateboards)
a small board with wheels, used for riding
on (as a sport) while standing.
skateboarder, skateboarding *nouns*

skein *noun* (*plural* skeins)
a coil of yarn or thread. [from old French]

skeleton *noun* (*plural* skeletons)
1 the framework of bones of the body. 2 the
shell or other hard part of a crab etc. 3 a
framework, e.g. of a building. **skeletal**
adjective [from Greek *skeletos* = dried-up]

sketch *noun* (*plural* sketches)
1 a rough drawing or painting. 2 a short
account of something. 3 a short amusing
play.
sketch *verb* (sketches, sketching, sketched)
make a sketch. [from Greek *schedios* = done
without practice or preparation]

sketchy *adjective*
rough and not detailed or careful.

skew *adjective*
askew or slanting.
skew *verb* (skews, skewing, skewed)
make a thing askew. [from old French]

skewer *noun* (*plural* skewers)
a long pin pushed through meat to hold it
together while it is being cooked. **skewer**
verb [origin unknown]

ski (*say* skee) *noun* (*plural* skis)
each of a pair of long narrow strips of
wood, metal, or plastic fixed under the feet
for moving quickly over snow.
ski *verb* (skies, skiing, skied)
travel on skis. **skier** *noun* [Norwegian]

skid *verb* (skids, skidding, skidded)
slide accidentally.
skid *noun* (*plural* skids)
1 a skidding movement. 2 a runner on a
helicopter, for use in landing.
[probably from Old Norse *skith* = ski]

skilful *adjective*
having or showing great skill.
skilfully *adverb*

skill *noun* (*plural* skills)
the ability to do something well. **skilled**
adjective [from Old Norse]

skilled *adjective*
1 skilful; highly trained or experienced.
2 (of work) needing skill or special
training.

skim *verb* (skims, skimming, skimmed)
1 remove something from the surface of a
liquid; take the cream off milk. 2 move
quickly over a surface or through the air.
3 read something quickly.
[from old French *escume* = scum]

skimp *verb* (skimps, skimping, skimped)
supply or use less than is needed, *Don't
skimp on the food.* [origin unknown]

skimpy *adjective* (skimpier, skimpiest)
scanty or too small.

skin *noun* (*plural* skins)
1 the flexible outer covering of a person's
or animal's body. 2 an outer layer or
covering, e.g. of a fruit. 3 a skin-like film
formed on the surface of a liquid.
skin *verb* (skins, skinning, skinned)
take the skin off something.
[from Old Norse]

skin diving *noun*
swimming under water with flippers and
breathing apparatus but without a diving
suit. **skin diver** *noun*

skinflint *noun* (*plural* skinflints)
a miserly person.

skinhead *noun* (*plural* skinheads)
a youth with very closely cropped hair.

skinny *adjective* (skinnier, skinniest)
very thin.

skip¹ (skips, skipping, skipped)
1 move along lightly, especially by hopping
on each foot in turn. 2 jump with a
skipping rope. 3 go quickly from one
subject to another. 4 miss something out,
You can skip chapter six.
skip *noun* (*plural* skips)
a skipping movement.
[probably from a Scandinavian language]

skip² *noun* (*plural* **skips**)
a large metal container for taking away builders' rubbish etc.
[from Old Norse *skeppa* = basket]

skipper *noun* (*plural* **skippers**) (*informal*)
a captain. [from old German or old Dutch *schip* = ship]

skipping rope *noun* (*plural* **skipping ropes**)
a rope, usually with a handle at each end, that is swung over your head and under your feet as you jump.

skirmish *noun* (*plural* **skirmishes**) (*informal*)
a small fight or conflict. **skirmish** *verb*
[from old French]

skirt *noun* (*plural* **skirts**)
1 a piece of clothing for a woman or girl that hangs down from the waist. 2 the part of a dress below the waist.
skirt *verb* (**skirts, skirting, skirted**)
go round the edge of something.
[from Old Norse]

skirting or **skirting board** *noun* (*plural* **skirtings, skirting boards**)
a narrow board round the wall of a room, close to the floor.

skit *noun* (*plural* **skits**)
a satirical sketch or parody, *He wrote a skit on 'Hamlet'.* [origin unknown]

skittish *adjective*
frisky; lively and excitable.
[origin unknown]

skittle *noun* (*plural* **skittles**)
a wooden bottle-shaped object that people try to knock down by bowling a ball in the game of **skittles**. [origin unknown]

skive *verb* (**skives, skiving, skived**) (*informal*)
dodge work. **skiver** *noun*
[probably from French *esquiver* = dodge]

skulk *verb* (**skulks, skulking, skulked**)
loiter stealthily.
[probably from a Scandinavian language]

skull *noun* (*plural* **skulls**)
the framework of bones of the head.
[probably from a Scandinavian language]

skullcap *noun* (*plural* **skullcaps**)
a small close-fitting cap worn on the top of the head.

skunk *noun* (*plural* **skunks**)
a North American animal with black and white fur that can spray a bad-smelling fluid. [a Native American word]

sky *noun* (*plural* **skies**)
the space above the earth, appearing blue in daylight on fine days. [from Old Norse]

skydiving *noun*
the sport of jumping from an aeroplane and performing manoeuvres before opening your parachute. **skydiver** *noun*

skylark *noun* (*plural* **skylarks**)
a lark that sings while it hovers high in the air.

skylight *noun* (*plural* **skylights**)
a window in a roof.

skyline *noun* (*plural* **skylines**)
1 the horizon, where earth and sky appear to meet. 2 the outline of buildings etc. against the sky.

skyscraper *noun* (*plural* **skyscrapers**)
a very tall building.

slab *noun* (*plural* **slabs**)
a thick flat piece. [origin unknown]

slack *adjective*
1 not pulled tight. 2 not busy; not working hard. **slackly** *adverb*, **slackness** *noun*
slack *verb* (**slacks, slacking, slacked**)
avoid work; be lazy. **slacker** *noun*
[from Old English]

slacken *verb* (**slackens, slackening, slackened**)
make or become slack.

slacks *plural noun*
trousers for informal occasions.

slag *noun*
waste material separated from metal in smelting. [from old German]

slag heap *noun* (*plural* **slag heaps**)
a mound of waste matter from a mine etc.

slain *past participle* of **slay**.

slake *verb* (slakes, slaking, slaked)
quench, *slake your thirst.*
[from Old English]

slalom *noun* (*plural* slaloms)
a ski race down a zigzag course.
[Norwegian *sla* = sloping + *låm* = track]

slam *verb* (slams, slamming, slammed)
1 shut loudly. **2** hit violently. **slam** *noun*
[probably from a Scandinavian language]

slander *noun* (*plural* slanders)
a spoken statement that damages a
person's reputation and is untrue.
(Compare *libel.*) **slanderous** *adjective*
slander *verb* (slanders, slandering,
slandered)
make a slander against someone.
slanderer *noun*
[from old French; related to *scandal*]

slang *noun*
words that are used very informally to add
vividness or humour to what is said,
especially those used only by a particular
group of people, *teenage slang.*
slangy *adjective* [origin unknown]

slanging match *noun* (*plural* slanging
matches)
a noisy quarrel, with people shouting
insults at each other.

slant *verb* (slants, slanting, slanted)
1 slope. **2** present news or information etc.
from a particular point of view.
[probably from a Scandinavian language]

slap *verb* (slaps, slapping, slapped)
1 hit with the palm of the hand or with
something flat. **2** put forcefully or
carelessly, *We slapped paint on the walls.*
slap *noun* [imitating the sound]

slapdash *adjective*
hasty and careless.

slapstick *noun*
comedy with people hitting each other,
falling over, etc. [from *slap* + *stick*[1]]

slash *verb* (slashes, slashing, slashed)
1 make large cuts in something. **2** cut or
strike with a long sweeping movement.
3 reduce greatly, *Prices were slashed.*
slash *noun* (*plural* slashes)
a slashing cut. [probably from old French]

slat *noun* (*plural* slats)
each of the thin strips of wood or metal or
plastic arranged so that they overlap and
form a screen, e.g. in a venetian blind.
[from old French *esclat* = piece, splinter]

slate *noun* (*plural* slates)
1 a kind of grey rock that is easily split into
flat plates. **2** a piece of this rock used in
covering a roof or (formerly) for writing
on. **slaty** *adjective*
slate *verb* (slates, slating, slated)
1 cover a roof with slates. **2** (*informal*)
criticize severely. [same origin as *slat*]

slattern *noun* (*plural* slatterns) (*old use*)
a slovenly woman. **slatternly** *adjective*
[origin unknown]

slaughter *verb* (slaughters, slaughtering,
slaughtered)
1 kill an animal for food. **2** kill people or
animals ruthlessly or in great numbers.
slaughter *noun* [from Old Norse]

slaughterhouse *noun* (*plural*
slaughterhouses)
a place where animals are killed for food.

slave *noun* (*plural* slaves)
a person who is owned by another and
obliged to work for him or her without
being paid. **slavery** *noun*
slave *verb* (slaves, slaving, slaved)
work very hard.
[from Latin *sclavus* = captive]

slave-driver *noun* (*plural* slave-drivers)
a person who makes others work very
hard.

slaver (*say* slav-er or slay-ver) *verb* (slavers,
slavering, slavered)
have saliva flowing from the mouth, *a
slavering dog.* [origin unknown]

slavish *adjective*
1 like a slave. **2** showing no independence
or originality.

slay *verb* (slays, slaying, slew, slain) (*poetical*)
kill. [from Old English]

sled *noun* (*plural* sleds) (*now mainly
American*)
a sledge.
[from old German; related to *sledge*]

sledge *noun* (*plural* **sledges**)
a vehicle for travelling over snow, with strips of metal or wood instead of wheels. **sledging** *noun*
[from old Dutch; related to *sled*]

sledgehammer *noun* (*plural* **sledgehammers**)
a very large heavy hammer.
[from Old English *slecg* = sledgehammer, + *hammer*]

sleek *adjective*
smooth and shiny.
[a different spelling of *slick*]

sleep *noun*
the condition or time of rest in which the eyes are closed, the body relaxed, and the mind unconscious. **sleepy** *adjective*, **sleepily** *adverb*, **sleepiness** *noun*
sleep *verb* (**sleeps, sleeping, slept**)
have a sleep.
[from Old English]

sleeper *noun* (*plural* **sleepers**)
1 someone who is asleep. 2 each of the wooden or concrete beams on which the rails of a railway rest. 3 a railway carriage with beds or berths for passengers to sleep in; a place in this.

sleeping bag (*plural* **sleeping bags**)
a padded bag to sleep in, especially when camping.

sleepless *adjective*
unable to sleep.

sleepwalker *noun* (*plural* **sleepwalkers**)
a person who walks about while asleep. **sleepwalking** *noun*

sleet *noun*
a mixture of rain and snow or hail.
[probably from Old English]

sleeve *noun* (*plural* **sleeves**)
1 the part of a garment that covers the arm. 2 the cover of a record.
up your sleeve hidden but ready for you to use.
[from Old English]

sleeveless *adjective*
without sleeves.

sleigh (*say as* slay) *noun* (*plural* **sleighs**)
a sledge, especially a large one pulled by horses. **sleighing** *noun* [originally American, from Dutch; related to *sled*]

sleight (*say as* slight) *noun*
sleight of hand skill in using the hands to do conjuring tricks etc.
[from Old Norse]

slender *adjective*
slim. **slenderness** *noun* [origin unknown]

sleuth (*say* slooth) *noun* (*plural* **sleuths**)
a detective.
[from Old Norse *sloth* = a track or trail]

slew *past tense* of **slay**.

slice *noun* (*plural* **slices**)
1 a thin piece cut off something. 2 a portion.
slice *verb* (**slices, slicing, sliced**)
1 cut into slices. 2 cut from a larger piece, *Slice the top off the egg.* 3 cut cleanly, *The knife sliced through the apple.*
[from old French]

slick *adjective*
1 quick and clever or cunning. 2 slippery.
slick *noun* (*plural* **slicks**)
1 a large patch of oil floating on water. 2 a slippery place. [from Old English]

slide *verb* (**slides, sliding, slid**)
1 move or cause to move smoothly on a surface. 2 move quietly or secretly, *The thief slid behind a bush.*
slide *noun* (*plural* **slides**)
1 a sliding movement. 2 a smooth surface or structure on which people or things can slide. 3 a photograph that can be projected on a screen. 4 a small glass plate on which things are placed to be examined under a microscope. 5 a fastener to keep hair tidy.
[from Old English]

slight *adjective*
very small; not serious or important. **slightly** *adverb*, **slightness** *noun*
slight *verb* (**slights, slighting, slighted**)
insult a person by treating him or her without respect. [from Old Norse]

slim *adjective* (**slimmer, slimmest**)
1 thin and graceful. 2 small, *a slim chance.* **slimness** *noun*

slim *verb* (slims, slimming, slimmed)
make yourself thinner. **slimmer** *noun*
[from old German or old Dutch]

slime *noun*
unpleasant wet slippery stuff. **slimy**
adjective, **sliminess** *noun* [from Old English]

sling *noun* (*plural* slings)
1 a loop or band placed round something to
support or lift it. **2** a looped strap used to
throw a stone etc.
sling *verb* (slings, slinging, slung)
1 support or lift with a sling. **2** (*informal*)
throw. [from old Dutch or Old Norse]

slink *verb* (slinks, slinking, slunk)
move in a stealthy or guilty way. **slinky**
adjective [from Old English]

slip *verb* (slips, slipping, slipped)
1 slide accidentally; lose your balance by
sliding. **2** move or put quickly and quietly,
*Slip it in your pocket. We slipped away from
the party.* **3** escape from, *The dog slipped its
leash. It slipped my memory.*
slip up make a mistake.
slip *noun* (*plural* slips)
1 an accidental slide or fall. **2** a mistake.
3 a small piece of paper. **4** a petticoat. **5** a
pillowcase.
give someone the slip escape or avoid him
or her skilfully.
[probably from old German or old Dutch]

slipper *noun* (*plural* slippers)
a soft comfortable shoe to wear indoors.

slippery *adjective*
smooth or wet so that it is difficult to stand
on or hold. **slipperiness** *noun*

slip road *noun* (*plural* slip roads)
a road by which you enter or leave a
motorway.

slipshod *adjective*
careless; not systematic.
[originally = wearing slippers or badly
fitting shoes; from *slip* + *shod*]

slit *noun* (*plural* slits)
a narrow straight cut or opening.
slit *verb* (slits, slitting, slit)
make a slit or slits in something.
[from Old English]

slither *verb* (slithers, slithering, slithered)
slip or slide unsteadily. [from Old English]

sliver (*say* sliv-er) *noun* (*plural* slivers)
a thin strip of wood or glass etc.
[from Middle English *slive* = to split or to
cut a piece off]

slob *noun* (*plural* slobs) (*informal*)
a careless, untidy, lazy person. [from an old
word *slab* = mud or slime, + *slobber*]

slobber *verb* (slobbers, slobbering,
slobbered)
slaver or dribble. [probably from old Dutch
slobberen = paddle in mud]

sloe *noun* (*plural* sloes)
the small dark plum-like fruit of
blackthorn. [from Old English]

slog *verb* (slogs, slogging, slogged)
1 hit hard. **2** work or walk hard and
steadily. **slog** *noun*, **slogger** *noun*
[origin unknown]

slogan *noun* (*plural* slogans)
a phrase used to advertise something or to
sum up the aims of a campaign etc., *Their
slogan was 'Ban the bomb!'* [from Scottish
Gaelic *sluagh-ghairm* = battle-cry]

sloop *noun* (*plural* sloops)
a small sailing ship with one mast.
[from Dutch]

slop *verb* (slops, slopping, slopped)
spill liquid over the edge of its container.
[probably from Old English]

slope *verb* (slopes, sloping, sloped)
lie or turn at an angle; slant.
slope off (*informal*) go away.
slope *noun* (*plural* slopes)
1 a sloping surface. **2** the amount by which
something slopes. [origin unknown]

sloppy *adjective* (sloppier, sloppiest)
1 liquid and splashing easily. **2** careless or
slipshod, *sloppy work.* **3** weakly
sentimental, *a sloppy story.* **sloppily** *adverb*
sloppiness *noun* [from *slop*]

slops *plural noun*
1 slopped liquid. **2** liquid waste matter.

slosh *verb* (*informal*) (sloshes, sloshing, sloshed)
1 splash or slop. 2 pour liquid carelessly. 3 hit. [a different spelling of *slush*]

slot *noun* (*plural* slots)
a narrow opening to put things in. **slotted** *adjective* [from old French]

sloth (rhymes with *both*) *noun* (*plural* sloths)
1 laziness. 2 a South American animal that lives in trees and moves very slowly. **slothful** *adjective* [from *slow*]

slot machine *noun* (*plural* slot machines)
a machine worked by putting a coin in the slot.

slouch *verb* (slouches, slouching, slouched)
stand, sit, or move in a lazy awkward way, not with an upright posture. **slouch** *noun*
[origin unknown]

slough[1] (rhymes with *cow*) *noun* (*plural* sloughs)
a swamp or marshy place.
[origin unknown]

slough[2] (*say* sluf) *verb* (sloughs, sloughing, sloughed)
shed, *A snake sloughs its skin periodically.*
[probably from old German]

slovenly (*say* sluv-en-lee) *adjective*
careless or untidy. **slovenliness** *noun*
[probably from Dutch]

slow *adjective*
1 not quick; taking more time than is usual. 2 showing a time earlier than the correct time, *Your watch is slow.* 3 not clever; not able to understand quickly or easily. **slowly** *adverb*, **slowness** *noun*
slow *adverb*
slowly, *Go slow.*
slow *verb* (slows, slowing, slowed)
go more slowly; cause to go more slowly, *The storm slowed us down.*
[from Old English]

slow motion *noun*
movement in a film or on television which has been slowed down.

slow-worm *noun* (*plural* slow-worms)
a small European legless lizard that looks like a snake, and gives birth to live young.

sludge *noun*
thick mud. [origin unknown]

slug *noun* (*plural* slugs)
1 a small slimy animal like a snail without a shell. 2 a pellet for firing from a gun.
[probably from a Scandinavian language]

sluggard *noun* (*plural* sluggards)
a slow or lazy person. [from *slug*]

sluggish *adjective*
slow-moving; not alert or lively. [from *slug*]

sluice (*say* slooss) *noun* (*plural* sluices)
1 a sluice-gate. 2 a channel carrying off water.
sluice *verb* (sluices, sluicing, sluiced)
wash with a flow of water.
[from old French]

sluice-gate *noun* (*plural* sluice-gates)
a sliding barrier for controlling a flow of water.

slum *noun* (*plural* slums)
an area of dirty overcrowded houses.
[origin unknown]

slumber *verb* (slumbers, slumbering, slumbered)
sleep. **slumber** *noun*, **slumberer** *noun*, **slumberous** or **slumbrous** *adjective*
[from Old English]

slump *verb* (slumps, slumping, slumped)
fall heavily or suddenly.
slump *noun* (*plural* slumps)
a sudden great fall in prices or trade.
[origin unknown]

slur *verb* (slurs, slurring, slurred)
1 pronounce words indistinctly by running the sounds together. 2 mark with a slur in music.
slur *noun* (*plural* slurs)
1 a slurred sound. 2 discredit, *It casts a slur on his reputation.* 3 a curved line placed over notes in music to show that they are to be sung or played smoothly without a break.
[probably from old German or old Dutch]

slurry *noun*
a semi-liquid mixture of water and cement, clay, or manure etc. [origin unknown]

slush *noun*
partly melted snow on the ground.
slushy *adjective*
[imitating the sound when you walk in it]

sly *adjective* (**slyer, slyest**)
1 unpleasantly cunning or secret.
2 mischievous, *a sly smile.* **slyly** *adverb,*
slyness *noun* [from Old Norse]

smack[1] *noun* (*plural* **smacks**)
1 a slap. 2 a loud sharp sound, *It hit the*
wall with a smack. 3 (*informal*) a hard hit
or blow.
smack *verb* (**smacks, smacking, smacked**)
1 slap. 2 hit hard.
smack your lips close and then part them
noisily in enjoyment.
smack *adverb* (*informal*)
forcefully or directly, *The ball went smack*
through the window.
[from old German or old Dutch]

smack[2] *noun* (*plural* **smacks**)
a slight flavour of something; a trace.
smack *verb* (**smacks, smacking, smacked**)
have a slight flavour or trace, *His manner*
smacks of conceit.
[from Old English]

smack[3] *noun* (*plural* **smacks**)
a small sailing boat used for fishing etc.
[from Dutch]

small *adjective*
not large; less than the usual size.
smallness *noun*
the small of the back the smallest part of the
back (at the waist).
[from Old English]

smallholding *noun* (*plural* **smallholdings**)
a small area of land used for farming.
smallholder *noun*

small hours *plural noun*
the early hours of the morning, after
midnight.

small-minded *adjective*
selfish; petty.

small print *noun*
the details of a contract, especially if in
very small letters or difficult to
understand.

small talk *noun*
conversation about unimportant things.

smart *adjective*
1 neat and elegant; dressed well. 2 clever.
3 forceful; brisk, *She ran at a smart pace.*
smartly *adverb,* **smartness** *noun*
smart *verb* (**smarts, smarting, smarted**)
feel a stinging pain. **smart** *noun*
[from Old English]

smart card *noun* (*plural* **smart cards**)
a card like a credit card with a
microprocessor built in, which stores
information or enables you to draw or
spend money from your bank account.

smarten *verb* (**smartens, smartening,**
smartened)
make or become smarter.

smash *verb* (**smashes, smashing, smashed**)
1 break noisily into pieces. 2 hit or move
with great force. 3 destroy or defeat
completely.
smash *noun* (*plural* **smashes**)
1 the action or sound of smashing. 2 a
collision. 3 a disaster.
[imitating the sound]

smash hit *noun* (*plural* **smash hits**)
something very successful.

smashing *adjective* (*informal*)
excellent or beautiful. **smasher** *noun*
[from *smash*]

smattering *noun*
a slight knowledge of a subject or a foreign
language. [origin unknown]

smear *verb* (**smears, smearing, smeared**)
1 rub something greasy or sticky or dirty
on a surface. 2 try to damage someone's
reputation. **smeary** *adjective*
smear *noun* (*plural* **smears**)
1 smearing; something smeared.
2 material smeared on a slide to be
examined under a microscope. 3 a smear
test. [from Old English]

smear campaign *noun* (*plural* **smear**
campaigns)
an organized attempt to ruin someone's
reputation by spreading rumours about
him or her.

smear test *noun* (*plural* smear tests)
the taking and examination of a sample of
the cervix lining, to check for faulty cells
which may cause cancer.

smell *verb* (smells, smelling, smelt or
smelled)
1 be aware of something by means of the
sense organs of the nose, *I can smell smoke.*
2 give out a smell.
smell *noun* (*plural* smells)
1 something you can smell; a quality in
something that makes people able to smell
it. 2 an unpleasant quality of this kind.
3 the ability to smell things. **smelly**
adjective [origin unknown]

smelt *verb* (smelts, smelting, smelted)
melt ore to get the metal it contains.
[from old German or old Dutch]

smile *noun* (*plural* smiles)
an expression on the face that shows
pleasure or amusement, with the lips
stretched and turning upwards at the ends.
smile *verb* (smiles, smiling, smiled)
give a smile.
[probably from a Scandinavian language]

smirch *verb* (smirches, smirching, smirched)
1 soil. 2 disgrace or dishonour a
reputation. **smirch** *noun* [origin unknown]

smirk *noun* (*plural* smirks)
a self-satisfied smile.
smirk *verb* (smirks, smirking, smirked)
give a smirk. [from Old English]

smite *verb* (smites, smiting, smote, smitten)
hit hard. [from Old English]

smith *noun* (*plural* smiths)
1 a person who makes things out of metal.
2 a blacksmith. [from Old English]

smithereens *plural noun*
small fragments. [from Irish]

smithy *noun* (*plural* smithies)
a blacksmith's workshop.

smitten *past participle* of smite.
be smitten with be suddenly affected by a
disease or desire or fascination etc.

smock *noun* (*plural* smocks)
1 an overall shaped like a very long shirt.
2 a loose top worn by a pregnant woman.

smock *verb* (smocks, smocking, smocked)
stitch into close gathers with embroidery.
smocking *noun* [from Old English]

smog *noun*
a mixture of smoke and fog.
[from *smoke* + *fog*]

smoke *noun*
1 the mixture of gas and solid particles
given off by a burning substance. 2 a
period of smoking tobacco, *He wanted a
smoke.* **smoky** *adjective*
smoke *verb* (smokes, smoking, smoked)
1 give out smoke. 2 have a lighted
cigarette, cigar, or pipe between your lips
and draw its smoke into your mouth; do
this as a habit. 3 preserve meat or fish by
treating it with smoke, *smoked haddock.*
smoker *noun* [from Old English]

smokeless *adjective*
without producing smoke.

smokescreen *noun* (*plural* smokescreens)
1 a mass of smoke used to hide the
movement of troops. 2 something that
conceals what is happening.

smooth *adjective*
1 having a surface without any lumps,
wrinkles, roughness, etc. 2 moving without
bumps or jolts etc. 3 not harsh, *a smooth
flavour.* **smoothly** *adverb*, **smoothness** *noun*
smooth *verb* (smooths, smoothing,
smoothed)
make a thing smooth.
[from Old English]

smote *past tense* of smite.

smother *verb* (smothers, smothering,
smothered)
1 suffocate. 2 cover thickly, *The buns were
smothered in sugar.* 3 restrain or conceal,
She smothered a smile. [from Old English]

smoulder *verb* (smoulders, smouldering,
smouldered)
1 burn slowly without a flame. 2 continue
to exist inwardly, *Their anger smouldered.*
[origin unknown]

smudge *noun* (*plural* smudges)
a dirty mark made by rubbing something.
smudgy *adjective*

smudge *verb* (smudges, smudging, smudged)
make a smudge on something; become smudged. [origin unknown]

smug *adjective*
self-satisfied; too pleased with your own good fortune or abilities.
smugly *adverb*, **smugness** *noun*
[from old German *smuk* = pretty]

smuggle *verb* (smuggles, smuggling, smuggled)
bring something into a country etc. secretly or illegally. **smuggler** *noun*
[from old German or old Dutch]

smut *noun* (*plural* smuts)
1 a small piece of soot or dirt. 2 indecent talk or pictures etc. **smutty** *adjective*
[origin unknown]

snack *noun* (*plural* snacks)
1 a small meal. 2 food eaten between meals. [from old Dutch]

snack bar *noun* (*plural* snack bars)
a small café where snacks are sold.

snack food *noun* (*plural* snack foods)
food such as peanuts, crisps, popcorn, etc. sold to be eaten between meals.

snag *noun* (*plural* snags)
1 a difficulty. 2 a sharp projection. 3 a tear in material that has been caught on something sharp.
[probably from a Scandinavian language]

snail *noun* (*plural* snails)
a small animal with a soft body and a shell. [from Old English]

snail's pace *noun*
a very slow pace.

snake *noun* (*plural* snakes)
a reptile with a long narrow body and no legs. **snaky** *adjective* [from Old English]

snap *verb* (snaps, snapping, snapped)
1 break suddenly or with a sharp sound. 2 bite suddenly or quickly. 3 say something quickly and angrily. 4 take something or move quickly. 5 take a snapshot of something.

snap *noun* (*plural* snaps)
1 the action or sound of snapping. 2 a snapshot. 3 **Snap** *noun* a card game in which players shout 'Snap!' when they see two similar cards.

snap *adjective*
sudden, *a snap decision.*
[probably from old German or old Dutch]

snapdragon *noun* (*plural* snapdragons)
a plant with flowers that have a mouth-like opening.

snappy *adjective*
1 snapping at people. 2 quick and lively. **snappily** *adverb*

snapshot *noun* (*plural* snapshots)
an informal photograph.

snare *noun* (*plural* snares)
a trap for catching birds or animals.
snare *verb* (snares, snaring, snared)
catch in a snare. [from Old English]

snarl[1] *verb* (snarls, snarling, snarled)
1 growl angrily. 2 speak in a bad-tempered way. **snarl** *noun* [imitating the sound]

snarl[2] *verb* (snarls, snarling, snarled)
make or become tangled or jammed, *Traffic was snarled up.* [from *snare*]

snatch *verb* (snatches, snatching, snatched)
seize; take quickly, eagerly, or by force.
snatch *noun* (*plural* snatches)
1 snatching. 2 a short and incomplete part of a song, conversation, etc.
[origin unknown]

sneak *verb* (sneaks, sneaking, sneaked)
1 move quietly and secretly. 2 (*informal*) take secretly, *He sneaked a biscuit from the tin.* 3 (*slang*) tell tales.
sneak *noun* (*plural* sneaks)
a tell-tale. **sneaky** *adjective*, **sneakily** *adverb*
[probably from Old English]

sneer *verb* (sneers, sneering, sneered)
speak or behave in a scornful way. **sneer** *noun* [probably from Old English]

sneeze *verb* (sneezes, sneezing, sneezed)
send out air suddenly and uncontrollably through the nose and mouth in order to get rid of something irritating the nostrils. **sneeze** *noun*

not to be sneezed at (*informal*) worth having.
[from Old English *fneosan*, imitating the sound]

sniff *verb* (sniffs, sniffing, sniffed)
1 make a sound by drawing in air through the nose. 2 smell something. **sniff** *noun*, **sniffer** *noun* [imitating the sound]

sniffer dog *noun* (*plural* sniffer dogs)
a dog trained to find drugs, explosives, etc. by smell.

sniffle *verb* (sniffles, sniffling, sniffled)
1 sniff slightly. 2 keep on sniffing. **sniffle** *noun* [imitating the sound]

snigger *verb* (sniggers, sniggering, sniggered)
giggle slyly. **snigger** *noun* [imitating the sound]

snip *verb* (snips, snipping, snipped)
cut with scissors or shears in small quick cuts. **snip** *noun*
[from old German or old Dutch]

snipe *noun* (*plural* snipe)
a marsh bird with a long beak.
snipe *verb* (snipes, sniping, sniped)
shoot at people from a hiding place. **sniper** *noun*
[probably from a Scandinavian language; the verb because the birds are shot from a hiding place]

snippet *noun* (*plural* snippets)
a small piece of news, information, etc. [from *snip*]

snivel *verb* (snivels, snivelling, snivelled)
cry or complain in a whining way. [from Old English]

snob *noun* (*plural* snobs)
a person who despises those who have not got wealth, power, or particular tastes or interests. **snobbery** *noun*, **snobbish** *adjective* [origin unknown]

snooker *noun*
a game played with cues and 21 balls on a special cloth-covered table. [origin unknown]

snoop *verb* (snoops, snooping, snooped)
pry; ask or look around secretly. **snooper** *noun* [from Dutch]

snooze *noun* (*plural* snoozes)
a nap. **snooze** *verb* [origin unknown]

snore *verb* (snores, snoring, snored)
breathe very noisily while sleeping. **snore** *noun* [imitating the sound]

snorkel *noun* (*plural* snorkels)
a tube through which a person swimming under water can take in air. **snorkelling** *noun* [from German]

snort *verb* (snorts, snorting, snorted)
make a rough sound by breathing forcefully through the nose. **snort** *noun* [imitating the sound]

snout *noun* (*plural* snouts)
an animal's projecting nose, or nose and jaws. [from old German or old Dutch]

snow *noun*
frozen drops of water that fall from the sky in small white flakes.
snow *verb* (snows, snowing, snowed)
send down snow.
be snowed under be overwhelmed with a mass of letters or work etc.
[from Old English]

snowball *noun* (*plural* snowballs)
snow pressed into a ball for throwing. **snowballing** *noun*

snow-blindness *noun*
temporary blindness caused by the glare of light reflected by snow.

snowdrop *noun* (*plural* snowdrops)
a small white flower that blooms in early spring.

snowdrift *noun* (*plural* snowdrifts)
a large heap or bank of snow piled up by the wind.

snowflake *noun* (*plural* snowflakes)
a flake of snow.

snowline *noun*
the level above which snow never melts.

snowman *noun* (*plural* snowmen)
a figure made of snow.

snowplough *noun* (*plural* **snowploughs**)
a vehicle or device for clearing a road or railway tract etc. by pushing snow aside.

snowshoe *noun* (*plural* **snowshoes**)
a frame rather like a tennis racket for walking on soft snow.

snowstorm *noun* (*plural* **snowstorms**)
a storm in which snow falls.

snow white *adjective*
pure white.

snowy *adjective*
1 with snow falling, *snowy weather*.
2 covered with snow, *snowy roofs*. 3 pure white.

snub *verb* (**snubs, snubbing, snubbed**)
treat in a scornful or unfriendly way.
snub *noun* (*plural* **snubs**)
scornful or unfriendly treatment.
[from Old Norse]

snub-nosed *adjective*
having a short turned-up nose.

snuff¹ *noun*
powdered tobacco for taking into the nose by sniffing.
[from old Dutch *snuffen* = snuffle]

snuff² *verb* (**snuffs, snuffing, snuffed**)
put out a candle by covering or pinching the flame. **snuffer** *noun* [origin unknown]

snuffle *verb* (**snuffles, snuffling, snuffled**)
sniff in a noisy way. **snuffle** *noun*
[same origin as *snuff¹*]

snug *adjective* (**snugger, snuggest**)
1 cosy. 2 fitting closely. **snugly** *adverb*,
snugness *noun* [probably from Dutch]

snuggle *verb* (**snuggles, snuggling, snuggled**)
press closely and comfortably; nestle.
[from *snug*]

so *adverb*
1 in this way; to such an extent, *Why are you so cross?* 2 very, *Cricket is so boring*.
3 also, *I was wrong but so were you*.
or so or about that number.
so far up to now.
so long! (*informal*) goodbye.
so what? (*informal*) that is not important.

so *conjunction*
for that reason, *They threw me out, so I came here*. [from Old English]

soak *verb* (**soaks, soaking, soaked**)
make a person or thing very wet. **soak** *noun*
soak up take in a liquid in the way that a sponge does.
[from Old English]

so-and-so *noun* (*plural* **so-and-sos**)
a person or thing that need not be named.

soap *noun* (*plural* **soaps**)
1 a substance used with water for washing and cleaning things. 2 a soap opera.
soapy *adjective*
soap *verb* (**soaps, soaping, soaped**)
put soap on something.
[from Old English]

soap opera *noun* (*plural* **soap operas**)
a television serial about the everyday lives of a group of people.
[originally American, where they were sponsored by soap manufacturers]

soar *verb* (**soars, soaring, soared**)
1 rise high in the air. 2 rise very high,
Prices were soaring.
[from old French; related to *aura*]

sob *verb* (**sobs, sobbing, sobbed**)
make a gasping sound when crying.
sob *noun* [probably from old Dutch]

sober *adjective*
1 not drunk. 2 serious and calm. 3 (of colour) not bright. **soberly** *adverb*, **sobriety**
(*say* so-**bry**-it-ee) *noun*
sober *verb* (**sobers, sobering, sobered**)
make or become sober. [from Latin]

sob story *noun* (*plural* **sob stories**)
an account of someone's experiences, told to get your help or sympathy, *she gave me some sob story about having her purse stolen*.

so-called *adjective*
named in what may be the wrong way,
This so-called gentleman slammed the door.

soccer *noun*
Association football. [short for *Association*]

sociable *adjective*
liking to be with other people, friendly.
sociably *adverb*, **sociability** *noun*
[same origin as *social*]

social *adjective*
1 living in a community, not alone, *Bees are social insects.* 2 of life in a community, *social science.* 3 concerned with people's welfare, *social worker.* 4 helping people to meet each other, *a social club.* 5 sociable.
socially *adverb*
[from Latin *sociare* = unite, associate]

socialism *noun*
a political system where wealth is shared equally between people, and the main industries and trade etc. are controlled by the government. (Compare *capitalism.*)
[from French; related to *social*]

socialist *noun* (*plural* **socialists**)
a person who believes in socialism.

social security *noun*
money and other assistance provided by the government for those in need through being ill, disabled, unemployed, etc.

social services *plural noun*
welfare services provided by the government, including schools, hospitals, and pensions.

society *noun* (*plural* **societies**)
1 a community; people living together in a group or nation. 2 a group of people organized for a particular purpose, *the school dramatic society.* 3 company; companionship, *We enjoy the society of our friends.* [same origin as *social*]

sociology (*say* soh-see-ol-o-jee) *noun*
the study of human society and social behaviour.
sociological *adjective*, **sociologist** *noun*
[from Latin *socius* = companion, ally, + *-logy*]

sock[1] *noun* (*plural* **socks**)
a short stocking reaching only to the ankle or below the knee. [from Old English]

sock[2] *verb* (**socks, socking, socked**) (*slang*)
hit hard; punch, *He socked me on the jaw.*
sock *noun* [origin unknown]

socket *noun* (*plural* **sockets**)
1 a hollow into which something fits, *a tooth-socket.* 2 a device into which an electric plug or bulb is put to make a connection. [from old French]

sod *noun* (*plural* **sods**)
a piece of turf.
[from old German or old Dutch]

soda *noun*
1 sodium bicarbonate. 2 soda water.
[probably from Persian]

soda water *noun*
water made fizzy with carbon dioxide, used in drinks.
[because originally it was made with *soda*]

sodden *adjective*
made very wet.
[the old past participle of *seethe*]

sodium *noun*
a soft white metal.
[from *soda*, to which it is related]

sodium bicarbonate *noun*
a soluble white powder used in fire extinguishers and fizzy drinks, and to make cakes rise; baking soda.

sodium carbonate *noun*
white powder or crystals used to clean things; washing soda.

sofa *noun* (*plural* **sofas**)
a kind of settee.
[from Arabic *suffa* = long stone bench]

soft *adjective*
1 not hard or firm; easily pressed. 2 smooth, not rough or stiff. 3 gentle; not loud. **softly** *adverb*, **softness** *noun*
[from Old English]

soft drink *noun* (*plural* **soft drinks**)
a cold drink that is not alcoholic.

soften *verb* (**softens, softening, softened**)
make or become soft or softer.
softener *noun*

soft furnishings *plural noun*
cushions, curtains, rugs, loose covers for chairs, etc.

soft-hearted *adjective*
sympathetic and easily moved.

software *noun*
computer programs, disks, etc. (Compare *hardware*.)

softwood *noun* (*plural* softwoods)
wood from pine trees or other conifers, which is easy to saw.

soggy *adjective* (soggier, soggiest)
very wet and heavy, *soggy ground*.
[from dialect *sog* = swamp]

soil¹ *noun* (*plural* soils)
1 the loose earth in which plants grow.
2 territory, *on British soil*. [old French *soil*]

soil² *verb* (soils, soiling, soiled)
make a thing dirty.
[from old French *suillier*]

sojourn (*say* soj-ern) *verb* (sojourns, sojourning, sojourned)
stay at a place temporarily.
sojourn *noun* (*plural* sojourns)
a temporary stay. [from old French]

solace (*say* sol-as) *verb* (solaces, solacing, solaced)
comfort someone who is unhappy or disappointed. **solace** *noun*
[from Latin *solari* = to console]

solar *adjective*
from or to do with the sun.
[from Latin *sol* = sun]

solar panel *noun* (*plural* solar panels)
a panel designed to catch the sun's rays and use their energy for heating or to make electricity.

solar power *noun*
electricity or other forms of power derived from the sun's rays.

solar system *noun*
the sun and the planets that revolve round it.

solder *noun*
a soft alloy that is melted to join pieces of metal together. **solder** *verb*
[from Latin *solidare* = make firm or solid]

soldier *noun* (*plural* soldiers)
a member of an army. [from old French]

sole¹ *noun* (*plural* soles)
1 the bottom surface of a foot or shoe. 2 a flat edible sea fish.
sole *verb* (soles, soling, soled)
put a sole on a shoe. [from Latin *solum*]

sole² *adjective*
single; only, *She was the sole survivor*.
solely *adverb* [from Latin *solus*]

solemn *adjective*
1 not smiling or cheerful. 2 dignified or formal. **solemnly** *adverb*, **solemnity** *noun*
[from Latin]

solemnize *verb* (solemnizes, solemnizing, solemnized)
1 celebrate a festival. 2 perform a marriage ceremony. **solemnization** *noun*

solenoid *noun* (*plural* solenoids)
a coil of wire that becomes magnetic when an electric current is passed through it.
[from Greek *solen* = channel]

sol-fa *noun*
a system of syllables (*doh, ray, me, fah, soh, la, te*) used to represent the notes of the musical scale. [*sol* was an earlier spelling of *soh*; the names of the notes came from syllables of a Latin hymn]

solicit *verb* (solicits, soliciting, solicited)
ask for or try to obtain, *solicit votes* or *solicit for votes*. **solicitation** *noun*
[same origin as *solicitous*]

solicitor *noun* (*plural* solicitors)
a lawyer who advises clients, prepares legal documents, etc.
[old French; related to *solicit*]

solicitous *adjective*
anxious and concerned about a person's comfort, welfare, etc.
solicitously *adverb*, **solicitude** *noun*
[from Latin *sollicitus* = worrying]

solid *adjective*
1 not hollow; with no space inside.
2 keeping its shape; not liquid or gas.
3 continuous, *for two solid hours*. 4 firm or strongly made; not flimsy, *a solid foundation*. 5 showing solidarity; unanimous. **solidly** *adverb*, **solidity** *noun*

solid *noun* (*plural* solids)
1 a solid thing. 2 a shape that has three dimensions (length, width, and height or depth). [from Latin]

solidarity *noun*
1 being solid. 2 unity and support for each other because of agreement in opinions, interests, etc.

solidify *verb* (solidifies, solidifying, solidified)
make or become solid.

solids *plural noun*
solid food; food that is not liquid, *Is your baby eating solids yet?*

soliloquy (*say* sol-il-ok-wee) *noun* (*plural* soliloquies)
a speech in which a person speaks his or her thoughts aloud without addressing anyone. **soliloquize** *verb*
[from Latin *solus* = alone + *loqui* = speak]

solitaire *noun* (*plural* solitaires)
1 a game for one person, in which marbles are moved on a special board until only one is left. 2 a diamond or other precious stone set by itself.
[French; related to *solitary*]

solitary *adjective*
1 alone, without companions. 2 single, *a solitary example*. 3 lonely, *a solitary valley*.
[from Latin *solus* = alone]

solitary confinement *noun*
a form of punishment in which a prisoner is kept alone in a cell and not allowed to talk to others.

solitude *noun*
being solitary.

solo *noun* (*plural* solos)
something sung, played, danced, or done by one person. **solo** *adjective* & *adverb*, **soloist** *noun* [Italian, – alone]

solstice (*say* sol-stiss) *noun* (*plural* solstices)
either of the two times in each year when the sun is at its furthest point north or south of the equator.
summer solstice about 21 June.
winter solstice about 22 December.
[from Latin *sol* = sun + *sistere* = stand still]

soluble *adjective*
1 able to be dissolved. 2 able to be solved. **solubility** *noun* [same origin as *solve*]

solution *noun* (*plural* solutions)
1 a liquid in which something is dissolved. 2 the answer to a problem or puzzle. [same origin as *solve*]

solve *verb* (solves, solving, solved)
find the answer to a problem or puzzle. [from Latin *solvere* = unfasten]

solvent *adjective*
1 having enough money to pay all your debts. 2 able to dissolve another substance. **solvency** *noun*

solvent *noun* (*plural* solvents)
a liquid used for dissolving something.

sombre *adjective*
dark and gloomy.
[from *sub-* + Latin *umbra* = shade]

sombrero (*say* som-**brair**-oh) *noun* (*plural* sombreros)
a hat with a very wide brim.
[Spanish; related to *sombre*]

some *adjective*
1 a few; a little, *some apples*; *some sugar*. 2 an unknown person or thing, *Some fool left the door open*. 3 about, *We waited some 20 minutes*.
some time at some point in time, *Come and see me some time* (not 'sometime'). *They left some time ago.*

some *pronoun*
a certain number or amount that is less than the whole, *Some of them were late*. [from Old English]

-some *suffix*
forms 1 adjectives meaning 'quality or manner' (e.g. *handsome, quarrelsome*), 2 nouns from numbers, meaning 'a group of this many' (e.g. *foursome*).
[from Old English]

somebody *pronoun*
1 some person. 2 an important or impressive person.

somehow *adverb*
in some way.

someone *pronoun*
somebody.

somersault *noun* (*plural* somersaults)
a movement in which you turn head over
heels before landing on your feet.
somersault *verb* [from Latin *supra* = above
+ *saltus* = a leap]

something *noun*
some thing; a thing which you cannot or do
not want to name.
something like rather like, *It's something
like a rabbit*; approximately, *It cost
something like £10.*

sometime *adjective*
former, *her sometime friend.* (Compare
some time in the entry for *some*).

sometimes *adverb*
at some times but not always, *We sometimes
walk to school.*

somewhat *adverb*
to some extent, *He was somewhat annoyed.*

somewhere *adverb*
in or to some place.

somnambulist *noun* (*plural*
somnambulists)
a sleepwalker. [from Latin *somnus* = sleep
+ *ambulare* = to walk]

somnolent *adjective*
sleepy or drowsy. **somnolence** *noun*
[from Latin *somnus* = sleep]

son *noun* (*plural* sons)
a boy or man who is someone's child.
[from Old English]

sonar *noun*
a device for finding objects under water by
the reflection of sound waves.
[from *son*ar navigation and *r*anging]

sonata *noun* (*plural* sonatas)
a piece of music for one instrument or two,
in several movements.
[from Italian *sonare* = to sound]

song *noun* (*plural* songs)
1 a tune for singing. **2** singing, *He burst
into song.*
a song and dance (*informal*) a great fuss.
for a song bought or sold very cheaply.
[from Old English]

songbird *noun* (*plural* songbirds)
a bird that sings sweetly.

songster *noun* (*plural* songsters)
1 a singer. **2** a songbird.

sonic *adjective*
to do with sound or sound waves.
[from Latin *sonus* = sound]

sonic boom *noun* (*plural* sonic booms)
a loud noise caused by the shock wave of
an aircraft travelling faster than the speed
of sound.

son-in-law *noun* (*plural* sons-in-law)
a daughter's husband.

sonnet *noun* (*plural* sonnets)
a kind of poem with 14 lines.
[from Italian *sonetto* = a little sound]

sonny *noun* (*informal*)
boy or young man, *Come on, sonny!*

sonorous (*say* sonn-er-us) *adjective*
giving a loud deep sound; resonant.
[from Latin *sonor* = sound]

soon *adverb*
1 in a short time from now. **2** not long after
something.
as soon as willingly, *I'd just as soon stay
here.*
as soon as at the moment that.
sooner or later at some time in the future.
[from Old English]

soot *noun*
the black powder left by smoke in a
chimney or on a building etc. **sooty**
adjective [from Old English]

soothe *verb* (soothes, soothing, soothed)
1 calm. **2** ease pain or distress. **soothingly**
adverb [from Old English]

soothsayer *noun* (*plural* soothsayers)
a prophet.
[from an old word *sooth* = truth, + *say*]

sop *noun* (*plural* sops)
1 a piece of bread dipped in liquid before
being eaten or cooked. **2** something
unimportant given to pacify or bribe a
troublesome person.

sop *verb* (sops, sopping, sopped)
sop up soak up liquid like a sponge.
[from Old English]

sophisticated *adjective*
1 of or accustomed to fashionable life and
its ways. 2 complicated, *a sophisticated
machine*. **sophistication** *noun*
[from Latin *sophisticare* = tamper with,
mix with something]

sophistry (*say* sof-ist-ree) *noun* (*plural*
sophistries)
a piece of reasoning that is clever but false
or misleading. [from Greek *sophos* = wise]

soporific *adjective*
causing sleep or drowsiness.
[from Latin *sopor* = sleep + *facere* = make]

sopping *adjective*
very wet; drenched. [from *sop*]

soppy *adjective*
1 very wet. 2 (*informal*) sentimental in a
silly way. [from *sop*]

soprano *noun* (*plural* sopranos)
a woman, girl, or boy with a high singing
voice. [Italian, from *sopra* = above]

sorcerer *noun* (*plural* sorcerers)
a wizard. **sorceress** *noun*, **sorcery** *noun*
[from old French]

sordid *adjective*
1 dirty and nasty. 2 dishonourable; selfish
and mercenary, *sordid motives*. **sordidly**
adverb, **sordidness** *noun*
[from Latin]

sore *adjective*
1 painful or smarting. 2 (*informal*)
annoyed or offended. 3 serious or
distressing, *in sore need*. **soreness** *noun*
sore *noun* (*plural* sores)
a sore place. [from Old English]

sorely *adverb*
seriously; very, *I was sorely tempted to run
away*.

sorrel[1] *noun*
a herb with sharp-tasting leaves.
[from old French *sur* = sour]

sorrel[2] *noun* (*plural* sorrels)
a reddish-brown horse.
[from old French *sor* = yellowish]

sorrow *noun* (*plural* sorrows)
unhappiness or regret caused by loss or
disappointment.
sorrowful *adjective*, **sorrowfully** *adverb*
sorrow *verb* (sorrows, sorrowing, sorrowed)
feel sorrow; grieve. [from Old English]

sorry *adjective* (sorrier, sorriest)
1 feeling pity, regret, or sympathy.
2 wretched, *His clothes were in a sorry state*.
[from Old English]

sort *noun* (*plural* sorts)
a group of things or people that are similar;
a kind or variety.
out of sorts slightly unwell or depressed.
sort of (*informal*) rather; to some extent, *I
sort of expected it*.

USAGE: Correct use is *this sort of thing* or
these sorts of things (not 'these sort of
things').

sort *verb* (sorts, sorting, sorted)
arrange things in groups according to their
size, kind, etc. **sorter** *noun*
sort out disentangle; select; (*slang*) deal
with and punish someone.
[from Latin]

sortie *noun* (*plural* sorties)
1 an attack by troops coming out of a
besieged place. 2 an attacking expedition
by a military aircraft.
[from French *sortir* = go out]

SOS *noun* (*plural* SOSs)
an urgent appeal for help.
[the international Morse code signal of
extreme distress, chosen because it is easy
to recognize, but often said to stand for
Save Our Souls]

sotto voce (*say* sot-oh **voh** chee) *adverb*
in a very quiet voice.
[Italian, = under the voice]

sought *past tense* of seek.

soul *noun* (*plural* souls)
1 the invisible part of a person that is
believed to go on living after the body has

died. **2** a person's mind and emotions etc.
3 a person, *There isn't a soul about.*
[from Old English]

soulful *adjective*
having or showing deep feeling.
soulfully *adverb*

sound[1] *noun* (*plural* **sounds**)
1 vibrations that travel through the air
and can be detected by the ear; the
sensation they produce. **2** sound
reproduced in a film etc. **3** a mental
impression, *We don't like the sound of his
plans.*
sound *verb* (**sounds, sounding, sounded**)
1 produce or cause to produce a sound.
2 give an impression when heard, *He
sounds angry.* **3** test by noting the sounds
heard, *A doctor sounds a patient's lungs
with a stethoscope.* [from Latin]

sound[2] *verb* (**sounds, sounding, sounded**)
test the depth of water beneath a ship.
sound out try to find out what a person
thinks or feels about something.
[from *sub-* + Latin *unda* = a wave]

sound[3] *adjective*
1 in good condition; not damaged.
2 healthy; not diseased. **3** reasonable;
correct, *His ideas are sound.* **4** reliable;
secure, *a sound investment.* **5** thorough;
deep, *a sound sleep.*
soundly *adverb*, **soundness** *noun*
[from Old English *gesund* = healthy]

sound[4] *noun* (*plural* **sounds**)
a strait, *Plymouth Sound.* [from Old
English *sund* = swimming or sea]

sound barrier *noun*
the resistance of the air to objects moving
at nearly supersonic speed.

sound bite *noun* (*plural* **sound bites**)
a very short part of a speech or statement
broadcast on radio or television because it
seems to sum up the person's opinion in a
few words.

sound effects *plural noun*
sounds produced artificially to make a
play, film, etc. seem more realistic.

soundtrack *noun* (*plural* **soundtracks**)
the sound that goes with a cinema film.

soup *noun* (*plural* **soups**)
liquid food made from stewed bones, meat,
fish, vegetables, etc.
in the soup (*informal*) in trouble.
[from old French]

sour *adjective*
1 tasting sharp like unripe fruit. **2** stale
and unpleasant, not fresh, *sour milk.* **3** bad-
tempered. **sourly** *adverb*, **sourness** *noun*
sour *verb* (**sours, souring, soured**)
make or become sour. [from Old English]

source *noun* (*plural* **sources**)
the place from which something comes.
[from old French; related to *surge*]

sour grapes *plural noun*
pretending that something you want is no
good because you know you cannot have it.
[from a fable in which a fox says that the
grapes he cannot reach are probably sour]

souse *verb* (**souses, sousing, soused**)
1 soak or drench. **2** soak fish in pickle.
[from old French]

south *noun*
1 the direction to the right of a person who
faces east. **2** the southern part of a country,
city, etc.
south *adjective & adverb*
towards or in the south. **southerly** (*say* suth-
er-lee) *adjective*, **southern** *adjective*,
southerner *noun*, **southernmost** *adjective*
[from Old English]

south-east *noun, adjective, & adverb*
midway between south and east. **south-
easterly** *adjective*, **south-eastern** *adjective*

southward *adjective & adverb*
towards the south. **southwards** *adverb*

south-west *noun, adjective, & adverb*
midway between south and west. **south-
westerly** *adjective*, **south-western** *adjective*

souvenir (*say* soo-ven-eer) *noun* (*plural*
souvenirs)
something that you keep to remind you of a
person, place, or event.
[from French *se souvenir* = remember]

sou'wester *noun* (*plural* **sou'westers**)
a waterproof hat with a wide flap at the
back. [from *south-wester*, a wind from the
south-west, often bringing rain]

sovereign *noun* (*plural* sovereigns)
1 a king or queen who is the ruler of a country; a monarch. 2 an old British gold coin, originally worth £1.

sovereign *adjective*
1 supreme, *sovereign power*. 2 having sovereignty; independent, *sovereign states*. [from old French; related to *super-*]

sovereignty *noun*
the power a country has to govern itself and make its own laws.

sow¹ (rhymes with *go*) *verb* (sows, sowing, sowed, sown or sowed)
put seeds into the ground so that they will grow into plants. **sower** *noun*
[from Old English *sawan*]

USAGE: Do not confuse with *sew*.

sow² (rhymes with *cow*) *noun* (*plural* sows)
a female pig. [from Old English *sugu*]

soya bean (*plural* soya beans)
a kind of bean from which edible oil and flour are made. [via Dutch from Japanese]

soy sauce *noun*
a Chinese or Japanese sauce made from fermented soya beans.

spa *noun* (*plural* spas)
a health resort where there is a spring of water containing mineral salts. [from *Spa*, a town in Belgium with a mineral spring]

space *noun* (*plural* spaces)
1 the whole area outside the earth, where the stars and planets are. 2 an area or volume, *This table takes too much space.* 3 an empty area; a gap. 4 an interval of time, *within the space of an hour*.

space *verb* (spaces, spacing, spaced)
arrange things with spaces between, *Space them out.* [from Latin *spatium* = a space]

spacecraft *noun* (*plural* spacecraft)
a vehicle for travelling in outer space.

spaceman *noun* (*plural* spacemen)
an astronaut.

spaceship *noun* (*plural* spaceships)
a spacecraft.

space shuttle *noun* (*plural* space shuttles)
a spacecraft for repeated use to and from outer space.

space station *noun* (*plural* space stations)
a satellite which orbits the earth and is used as a base by scientists and astronauts.

space suit *noun* (*plural* space suits)
a protective suit which enables an astronaut to survive in space.

space walk *noun* (*plural* space walks)
moving about or walking by an astronaut outside the spacecraft.

spacewoman *noun* (*plural* spacewomen)
a female astronaut.

spacious *adjective*
providing a lot of space; roomy.
spaciousness *noun*

spade¹ *noun* (*plural* spades)
a tool with a long handle and a wide blade for digging. [from Old English *spadu*]

spade² *noun* (*plural* spades)
a playing card with black shapes like upside-down hearts on it, each with a short stem. [from Italian *spada* = sword]

spadework *noun*
hard or uninteresting work done to prepare for an activity or project.

spaghetti *noun*
pasta made in long thin sticks.
[Italian, = little strings]

span *noun* (*plural* spans)
1 the length from end to end or across something. 2 the distance from the tip of the thumb to the tip of the little finger when the hand is spread out. 3 the part between two uprights of an arch or bridge. 4 the length of a period of time.

span *verb* (spans, spanning, spanned)
reach across, *A bridge spans the river.*
[from Old English]

spangle *noun* (*plural* spangles)
a small piece of glittering material.
spangled *adjective* [from old Dutch]

spaniel *noun* (*plural* spaniels)
a kind of dog with long ears and silky fur.
[from old French *espaigneul* = Spanish
(because it originated in Spain)]

spank *verb* (spanks, spanking, spanked)
smack a person on the bottom as a
punishment. [imitating the sound]

spanking *adjective*
brisk and lively, *at a spanking pace.*
[from *spank*]

spanner *noun* (*plural* spanners)
a tool for gripping and turning the nut on a
bolt etc. [German, from *spannen* = tighten]

spar¹ *noun* (*plural* spars)
a strong pole used for a mast or boom etc.
on a ship. [from Old Norse]

spar² *verb* (spars, sparring, sparred)
1 practise boxing. 2 quarrel or argue.
[from Old English]

spare *verb* (spares, sparing, spared)
1 afford to give something, *Can you spare a
moment?* 2 be merciful towards someone;
not hurt or harm a person or thing. 3 use
or treat economically, *No expense will be
spared. Spare the rod and spoil the child!*
spare *adjective*
1 not used but kept ready in case it is
needed; extra, *a spare wheel.* 2 thin; lean.
sparely *adverb*, **spareness** *noun*
go spare (*slang*) become very annoyed.
[from Old English]

spare time *noun*
time not needed for work.

sparing (*say* spair-ing) *adjective*
economical; grudging. **sparingly** *adverb*
[from *spare*]

spark *noun* (*plural* sparks)
1 a tiny glowing particle. 2 a flash
produced electrically.
spark *verb* (sparks, sparking, sparked)
give off a spark or sparks.
[from Old English]

sparking plug *noun* (*plural* sparking
plugs)
a spark plug.

sparkle *verb* (sparkles, sparkling, sparkled)
1 shine with tiny flashes of light. 2 show
brilliant wit or liveliness. **sparkle** *noun*
[from *spark*]

sparkler *noun* (*plural* sparklers)
a sparking firework.

spark plug *noun* (*plural* spark plugs)
a device that makes a spark to ignite the
fuel in an engine.

sparrow *noun* (*plural* sparrows)
a small brown bird. [from Old English]

sparse *adjective*
thinly scattered; not numerous, *a sparse
population.* **sparsely** *adverb*, **sparseness**
noun [from Latin *sparsum* = scattered]

spartan *adjective*
simple and without comfort or luxuries.
[named after the people of Sparta in
ancient Greece, famous for their
hardiness]

spasm *noun* (*plural* spasms)
1 a sudden involuntary movement of a
muscle. 2 a sudden brief spell of activity
etc. [from Greek]

spasmodic *adjective*
1 to do with or caused by a spasm.
2 happening or done at irregular intervals.
spasmodically *adverb*

spastic *noun* (*plural* spastics)
a person suffering from spasms of the
muscles and jerky movements, especially
caused by cerebral palsy.

USAGE: Do not use this word to mean a
clumsy or stupid person.

spat¹ *past tense* of **spit¹**.

spat² *noun* (*plural* spats)
a short gaiter. [from *spatter*]

spate *noun* (*plural* spates)
a sudden flood or rush. [origin unknown]

spathe (rhymes with *bathe*) *noun* (*plural*
spathes)
a large petal-like part of a flower, round a
central spike. [from Greek]

spatial *adjective*
to do with space. [same origin as *space*]

spatter *verb* (spatters, spattering, spattered)
1 scatter in small drops. **2** splash, *spattered with mud*. **spatter** *noun* [origin unknown]

spatula *noun* (*plural* spatulas)
a tool like a knife with a broad blunt flexible blade, used for spreading or mixing things. [from Latin *spathula* = small spear]

spawn *noun*
1 the eggs of fish, frogs, toads, or shellfish. **2** the thread-like matter from which fungi grow.
spawn *verb* (spawns, spawning, spawned)
1 produce spawn. **2** be produced from spawn. **3** produce something in great quantities. [from old French]

spay *verb* (spays, spaying, spayed)
sterilize a female animal by removing the ovaries. [from old French]

speak *verb* (speaks, speaking, spoke, spoken)
1 say something; talk. **2** talk or be able to talk in a foreign language, *Do you speak French?*
speak up 1 speak more loudly. **2** give your opinion.
[from Old English]

speaker *noun* (*plural* speakers)
1 a person who is speaking. **2** someone who makes a speech. **3** a loudspeaker.
the Speaker the person who controls the debates in the House of Commons or a similar assembly.

spear *noun* (*plural* spears)
a weapon for throwing or stabbing, with a long shaft and a pointed tip.
spear *verb* (spears, spearing, speared)
pierce with a spear or with something pointed. [from Old English]

spearmint *noun*
mint used in cookery and for flavouring chewing gum.
[from *spear* + *mint*¹ (probably because the leaves are shaped like spearheads)]

special *adjective*
1 of a particular kind; for some purpose, not general, *special training*. **2** exceptional, *Take special care of it*.
[same origin as *species*]

special effects *plural noun*
illusions created for films or television by using props, trick photography, or computer images.

specialist *noun* (*plural* specialists)
an expert in one subject, *a skin specialist*.

speciality *noun* (*plural* specialities)
1 a special quality or product. **2** something in which a person specializes.

specialize *verb* (specializes, specializing, specialized)
give particular attention or study to one subject or thing, *She specialized in biology*.
specialization *noun*

specially *adverb*
1 in a special way. **2** for a special purpose.

species (*say* spee-shiz) *noun* (*plural* species)
1 a group of animals or plants that are very similar. **2** a kind or sort, *a species of sledge*. [Latin, = appearance, form, or kind]

specific *adjective*
definite or precise; of or for a particular thing, *The money was given for a specific purpose*. **specifically** *adverb*
[same origin as *species*]

specific gravity *noun*
the weight of something as compared with the same volume of water or air.

specify *verb* (specifies, specifying, specified)
name or list things precisely, *The recipe specified cream, not milk*. **specification** *noun*
[same origin as *species*]

specimen *noun* (*plural* specimens)
1 a sample. **2** an example, *a fine specimen of an oak tree*. [Latin, from *specere* = to look]

specious (*say* spee-shus) *adjective*
seeming good but lacking real merit, *specious reasoning*. [same origin as *species*]

speck *noun* (*plural* specks)
a small spot or particle. [from Old English]

speckle *noun* (*plural* speckles)
a small spot or mark. **speckled** *adjective*
[from old Dutch]

specs *plural noun* (*informal*)
spectacles.

spectacle *noun* (*plural* **spectacles**)
1 an impressive sight or display. 2 a
ridiculous sight.
[from Latin *spectaculum* = a public show]

spectacles *plural noun*
a pair of lenses set in a frame, worn in
front of the eyes to help the wearer to see
clearly. **spectacled** *adjective*

spectacular *adjective*
impressive. [same origin as *spectacle*]

spectator *noun* (*plural* **spectators**)
a person who watches a game, show,
incident, etc.
[from Latin *spectare* = to look at]

spectre *noun* (*plural* **spectres**)
a ghost. **spectral** *adjective*
[same origin as *spectrum*]

spectrum *noun* (*plural* **spectra**)
1 the bands of colours seen in a rainbow.
2 a wide range of things, ideas, etc.
[Latin, = image]

speculate *verb* (**speculates, speculating,
speculated**)
1 form opinions without having any
definite evidence. 2 make investments in
the hope of making a profit but risking a
loss. **speculation** *noun*, **speculator** *noun*,
speculative *adjective*
[from Latin *speculari* = spy out]

sped *past tense* of **speed**.

speech *noun* (*plural* **speeches**)
1 the action or power of speaking. 2 words
spoken. 3 a talk to an audience.
[from Old English]

speechless *adjective*
unable to speak because of great emotion.

speed *noun* (*plural* **speeds**)
1 a measure of the time in which
something moves or happens. 2 quickness
or swiftness.
at speed quickly.
speed *verb* (**speeds, speeding, sped** (in
senses 3 and 4 **speeded**))
1 go quickly, *The train sped by*. 2 send

quickly, *to speed you on your way*. 3 travel
too fast. 4 make or become quicker, *This
will speed things up*. [from Old English]

speedboat *noun* (*plural* **speedboats**)
a fast motor boat.

speed camera *noun* (*plural* **speed
cameras**)
a camera by the side of a road which
automatically photographs any vehicle
which is going too fast.

speed hump *noun* (*plural* **speed humps**)
a ridge built across a road to make vehicles
slow down.

speed limit *noun* (*plural* **speed limits**)
the maximum speed at which vehicles may
legally travel on a particular road.

speedometer *noun* (*plural* **speedometers**)
a device in a vehicle, showing its speed.
[from *speed* + *meter*]

speedway *noun* (*plural* **speedways**)
a track for motorcycle racing.

speedwell *noun* (*plural* **speedwells**)
a wild plant with small blue flowers.
[from *speed* + *well²* (perhaps because the
plant often grows by the roadside)]

speedy *adjective* (**speedier, speediest**)
quick or swift. **speedily** *adverb*

speleology (*say* spel-ee-ol-o-jee) *noun*
the exploration and study of caves.
[from Greek *spelaion* = cave, + *-logy*]

spell¹ *noun* (*plural* **spells**)
a saying or action etc. supposed to have
magical power.
[from Old English *spel* = speech, story]

spell² *noun* (*plural* **spells**)
1 a period of time. 2 a period of a certain
work or activity etc.
[from Old English *spelian* = take someone's
place, take over a task]

spell³ *verb* (**spells, spelling, spelled** or **spelt**)
1 put letters in the right order to make a
word or words. 2 have as a result, *Wet
weather spells ruin for crops*. **speller** *noun*
[via old French from Germanic]

spellbound *adjective*
entranced as if by a magic spell.

spend *verb* (spends, spending, spent)
1 use money to pay for things. 2 use up,
Don't spend too much time on it. 3 pass time,
We spent a holiday in Spain.
[from Old English]

spendthrift *noun* (*plural* spendthrifts)
a person who spends money extravagantly
and wastefully. [from *spend* + an old sense
of *thrift* = prosperity, earnings]

sperm *noun* (*plural* sperms or sperm)
the male cell that fuses with an ovum.
[from Greek *sperma* = seed]

spermatozoon (*say* sper-ma-toe-zoe-on)
noun (*plural* spermatozoa)
a sperm.
[from *sperm* + Greek *zoion* = animal]

spew *verb* (spews, spewing, spewed)
1 vomit. 2 cast out in a stream, *The volcano
spewed out lava.* [from Old English]

sphere *noun* (*plural* spheres)
1 a perfectly round solid shape; the shape
of a ball. 2 a field of action or interest etc.,
*That country is in Russia's sphere of
influence.* **spherical** *adjective*
[from Greek *sphaira* = ball]

spheroid *noun* (*plural* spheroids)
a solid which is sphere-like but not
perfectly spherical.

sphinx *noun* (*plural* sphinxes)
a stone statue with the body of a lion and a
human head, especially the huge one
(almost 5,000 years old) in Egypt.
[from Greek]

spice *noun* (*plural* spices)
a substance used to flavour food, often
made from dried parts of plants. **spicy**
adjective [from old French]

spick and span *adjective*
neat and clean. [*span* is from Old Norse;
spick is probably from old Dutch]

spider *noun* (*plural* spiders)
a small animal with eight legs that spins
webs to catch insects on which it feeds.
[from Old English *spithra* = spinner]

spike *noun* (*plural* spikes)
1 a pointed piece of metal; a sharp point.
2 a long narrow projecting part.
spiky *adjective*

spike *verb* (spikes, spiking, spiked)
1 put spikes on something. 2 pierce with a
spike.
spike a person's guns spoil his or her plans.
[origin unknown]

spill *verb* (spills, spilling, spilt or spilled)
1 let something fall out of a container.
2 become spilt, *The coins came spilling out.*
spillage *noun*

spill *noun* (*plural* spills)
1 spilling. 2 something spilt. 3 a fall.
[from Old English]

spin *verb* (spins, spinning, spun)
1 turn round and round quickly. 2 make
raw wool or cotton into threads by pulling
and twisting its fibres. 3 (of a spider or
silkworm) make a web or cocoon out of
threads from its body.
spin a yarn tell a story.
spin out cause to last a long time.

spin *noun* (*plural* spins)
1 a spinning movement. 2 a short
excursion in a vehicle. [from Old English]

spinach *noun*
a vegetable with dark green leaves.
[via Spanish and Arabic from Persian]

spinal *adjective*
to do with the spine.

spinal cord *noun* (*plural* spinal cords)
the thick cord of nerves enclosed in the
spine, that carries impulses to and from
the brain.

spindle *noun* (*plural* spindles)
1 a thin rod on which thread is wound. 2 a
pin or bar that turns round or on which
something turns. [from Old English]

spindly *adjective*
thin and long or tall. [from *spindle*]

spin doctor *noun* (*plural* spin doctors)
a person whose job is to make information
or events seem favourable to his or her
employer, usually a politician or political
party.

spin-drier *noun* (*plural* spin-driers)
a machine in which washed clothes are
spun round and round to dry them.

spindrift *noun*
spray blown along the surface of the sea.
[from an old word *spoon* = be blown by the
wind, + *drift*]

spine *noun* (*plural* spines)
1 the line of bones down the middle of the
back. 2 a thorn or prickle. 3 the back part
of a book where the pages are joined
together. [from Latin]

spine-chilling *adjective*
very frightening, but in a way you enjoy, *a
spine-chilling horror film.*

spineless *adjective*
1 without a backbone. 2 lacking in
determination or strength of character.

spinet *noun* (*plural* spinets)
a small harpsichord. [from old French]

spinney *noun* (*plural* spinneys)
a small wood or thicket. [from old French]

spinning wheel *noun* (*plural* spinning
wheels)
a household device for spinning fibre into
thread.

spin-off *noun* (*plural* spin-offs)
a by-product.

spinster *noun* (*plural* spinsters)
a woman who has not married.
[the original meaning was 'one who spins'
(because many unmarried women used to
earn their living by spinning, which could
be done at home)]

spiny *adjective*
covered with spines; prickly.

spiral *adjective*
going round and round a central point and
becoming gradually closer to it or further
from it; twisting continually round a
central line or cylinder etc. **spirally** *adverb*
spiral *noun* (*plural* spirals)
a spiral line or course.
spiral *verb* (spirals, spiralling, spiralled)
move in a spiral.
[from Greek *speira* = winding]

spire *noun* (*plural* spires)
a tall pointed part on top of a church tower.
[from Old English]

spirit *noun* (*plural* spirits)
1 the soul. 2 a person's mood or mind and
feelings, *He was in good spirits.* 3 a ghost or
a supernatural being. 4 courage or
liveliness, *She answered with spirit.* 5 a
kind of quality in something, *the romantic
spirit of the book.* 6 a strong distilled
alcoholic drink.
spirit *verb* (spirits, spiriting, spirited)
carry off quickly and secretly, *They
spirited her away.*
[from Latin *spiritus* = breath]

spirited *adjective*
brave; self-confident and lively.

spirit level *noun* (*plural* spirit levels)
a device consisting of a tube of liquid with
an air bubble in it, used to find out whether
something is level.

spiritual *adjective*
1 to do with the human soul; not physical.
2 to do with the Church or religion.
spiritually *adverb*, **spirituality** *noun*
spiritual *noun* (*plural* spirituals)
a religious folk song, especially of Black
people in America.

spiritualism *noun*
the belief that the spirits of dead people
communicate with living people.
spiritualist *noun*

spirituous *adjective*
containing a lot of alcohol; distilled,
spirituous liquors.

spit¹ *verb* (spits, spitting, spat or spit)
1 send out drops of liquid etc. forcibly from
the mouth, *He spat at me.* 2 fall lightly, *It's
spitting with rain.*
spit *noun*
saliva or spittle. [from Old English *spittan*]

spit² *noun* (*plural* spits)
1 a long thin metal spike put through meat
to hold it while it is being roasted. 2 a
narrow strip of land sticking out into the
sea. [from Old English *spitu*]

spite *noun*
a desire to hurt or annoy somebody.
spiteful *adjective*, **spitefully** *adverb*,

spitefulness *noun*
in spite of not being prevented by, *We went out in spite of the rain.*
[same origin as *despite*]

spitfire *noun* (*plural* spitfires)
a fiery-tempered person.

spitting image *noun*
an exact likeness.

spittle *noun*
saliva, especially when it is spat out.
[from Old English]

spittoon *noun* (*plural* spittoons)
a receptacle for people to spit into.

splash *verb* (splashes, splashing, splashed)
1 make liquid fly about in drops. 2 (of liquid) be splashed. 3 wet by splashing, *The bus splashed us.*
splash *noun* (*plural* splashes)
1 the action or sound or mark of splashing. 2 a striking display or effect.
[imitating the sound]

splatter *verb* (splatters, splattering, splattered)
splash noisily. [imitating the sound]

splay *verb* (splays, splaying, splayed)
spread or slope apart. [from *display*]

spleen *noun* (*plural* spleens)
1 an organ of the body, close to the stomach, that helps to keep the blood in good condition. 2 bad temper or spite, *He vented his spleen on us.* [from Latin]

splendid *adjective*
1 magnificent; full of splendour.
2 excellent. **splendidly** *adverb*
[from Latin *splendidus* = shining]

splendour *noun*
a brilliant display or appearance.
[from Latin *splendere* = shine brightly]

splice *verb* (splices, splicing, spliced)
1 join pieces of rope etc. by twisting their strands together. 2 join pieces of film or wood etc. by overlapping the ends.
[probably from old Dutch]

splint *noun* (*plural* splints)
a straight piece of wood or metal etc. tied to a broken arm or leg to hold it firm.

splint *verb* (splints, splinting, splinted)
hold with a splint.
[from old German or old Dutch]

splinter *noun* (*plural* splinters)
a thin sharp piece of wood, glass, stone, etc. broken off a larger piece.
splinter *verb* (splinters, splintering, splintered)
break into splinters.
[from old German or old Dutch]

splinter group *noun* (*plural* splinter groups)
a group of people that has broken away from a larger group or movement.

split *verb* (splits, splitting, split)
1 break into parts; divide. 2 (*slang*) reveal a secret.
split *noun* (*plural* splits)
1 the splitting or dividing of something. 2 a place where something has split.
the splits an acrobatic position in which the legs are stretched widely in opposite directions.
[from Dutch]

split second *noun* a very brief moment of time; an instant.

split-second *adjective*
1 very quick. 2 (of timing) very precise.

splodge *noun* (*plural* splodges)
a dirty mark or stain. [origin unknown]

splurge *verb* (splurges, splurging, splurged) (*informal*)
to spend a lot of money on something, especially a luxury, *she splurged her first week's wages on a make-over.*
[originally American; origin unknown]

splutter *verb* (splutters, spluttering, spluttered)
1 make a quick series of spitting sounds.
2 speak quickly but not clearly. **splutter** *noun* [imitating the sound]

spoil *verb* (spoils, spoiling, spoilt or spoiled)
1 damage something and make it useless or unsatisfactory. 2 make someone selfish by always letting them have what they want.
spoil *noun* (*plural* spoils)
plunder or other things gained by a victor, *the spoils of war.* [from Latin]

spoilsport *noun* (*plural* spoilsports)
a person who spoils other people's enjoyment of things.

spoke¹ (*plural* spokes)
each of the bars or rods that go from the centre of a wheel to its rim.
[from Old English]

spoke² *past tense* of speak.

spokesman *noun* (*plural* spokesmen)
a spokesperson, especially a man.
[from *spoke²*]

spokesperson *noun* (*plural* spokespersons)
a person who speaks on behalf of a group of people.

spokeswoman *noun* (*plural* spokeswomen)
a female spokesperson.

spoliation *noun*
pillaging. [from Latin]

sponge *noun* (*plural* sponges)
1 a sea creature with a soft porous body.
2 the skeleton of this creature, or a piece of a similar substance, used for washing or padding things. 3 a soft lightweight cake or pudding. **spongy** *adjective*
sponge *verb* (sponges, sponging, sponged)
1 wipe or wash something with a sponge.
2 live by cadging from people, *He sponged on his friends*. **sponger** *noun*
[via Old English from Greek]

sponsor *noun* (*plural* sponsors)
someone who provides money or help etc. for a person or thing, or who gives money to a charity in return for something achieved by another person.
sponsorship *noun*
sponsor *verb* (sponsors, sponsoring, sponsored)
be a sponsor for a person or thing.
[from Latin *sponsum* = promised]

spontaneous (*say* spon-tay-nee-us) *adjective*
happening or done naturally; not forced or suggested by someone else.
spontaneously *adverb*, **spontaneity** *noun*
[from Latin *sponte* = of your own accord]

spoof *noun* (*plural* spoofs)
1 a hoax. 2 a parody. [originally = a card game invented and named by an English comedian, Arthur Roberts (1852–1933)]

spook *noun* (*plural* spooks) (*informal*)
a ghost. **spooky** *adjective*, **spookiness** *noun*
[Dutch]

spool *noun* (*plural* spools)
a rod or cylinder on which something is wound. [via old French from Germanic]

spoon *noun* (*plural* spoons)
a small device with a rounded bowl on a handle, used for lifting things to the mouth or for stirring or measuring things.
spoonful *noun* (*plural* spoonfuls)
spoon *verb* (spoons, spooning, spooned)
take or lift something with a spoon.
[from Old English]

spoonerism *noun* (*plural* spoonerisms)
an accidental exchange of the initial letters of two words, e.g. by saying *a boiled sprat* instead of *a spoiled brat*.
[named after Canon Spooner (1844–1930), who made mistakes of this kind]

spoon-feed *verb* (spoon-feeds, spoon-feeding, spoon-fed)
1 feed a baby or invalid with a spoon.
2 provide someone with so much help or information that he or she does not have to make any effort.

spoor *noun*
the track left by an animal. [Afrikaans]

sporadic *adjective*
happening or found at irregular intervals; scattered. **sporadically** *adverb*
[from Greek *sporas* = sown, scattered]

spore *noun* (*plural* spores)
a tiny reproductive cell of a plant such as a fungus or fern. [from Greek *spora* = seed]

sporran *noun* (*plural* sporrans)
a pouch worn in front of a kilt. [via Scottish Gaelic from Latin *bursa* = purse]

sport *noun* (*plural* sports)
1 an athletic activity; a game or pastime, especially outdoors. 2 games of this kind, *Are you keen on sport?* 3 (*informal*) a person who behaves fairly and generously, *Come on, be a sport!*

sport *verb* (sports, sporting, sported)
1 play; amuse yourself. 2 wear, *He sported a gold tiepin.* [from old French]

sporting *adjective*
1 connected with sport; interested in sport.
2 behaving fairly and generously.

sporting chance *noun*
a reasonable chance of success.

sportive *adjective*
playful.

sports car *noun* (*plural* sports cars)
an open low-built fast car.

sports jacket *noun* (*plural* sports jackets)
a man's jacket for informal wear (not part of a suit).

sportsman *noun* (*plural* sportsmen)
1 a man who takes part in sport. 2 a person who shows sportsmanship.

sportsmanship *noun*
sporting behaviour; behaving fairly and generously to rivals.

sportswoman *noun* (*plural* sportswomen)
1 a woman who takes part in sport. 2 a woman who shows sportsmanship.

spot *noun* (*plural* spots)
1 a small round mark. 2 a pimple. 3 a small amount, *We had a spot of trouble.* 4 a place. 5 a drop, *a few spots of rain.*
on the spot without delay or change of place; under pressure to take action, *This really puts him on the spot!*
spot *verb* (spots, spotting, spotted)
1 mark with spots. 2 (*informal*) notice, *We spotted her in the crowd.* 3 watch for and take note of, *train-spotting.* **spotter** *noun*
[probably from old German or old Dutch]

spot check *noun* (*plural* spot checks)
a check, usually without warning, on one of a group of people or things.

spotless *adjective*
perfectly clean.

spotlight *noun* (*plural* spotlights)
1 a strong light that can shine on one small area. 2 public attention, *The Royal Family are used to being in the spotlight.*

spotty *adjective*
marked with spots.

spouse *noun* (*plural* spouses)
a person's husband or wife.
[from old French; related to *sponsor*]

spout *noun* (*plural* spouts)
1 a pipe or similar opening from which liquid can pour. 2 a jet of liquid.
spout *verb* (spouts, spouting, spouted)
1 come or send out as a jet of liquid.
2 (*informal*) speak for a long time.
[from old Dutch]

sprain *verb* (sprains, spraining, sprained)
injure a joint by twisting it. **sprain** *noun*
[origin unknown]

sprat *noun* (*plural* sprats)
a small edible fish. [from Old English]

sprawl *verb* (sprawls, sprawling, sprawled)
1 sit or lie with the arms and legs spread out loosely. 2 spread out loosely or untidily. **sprawl** *noun* [from Old English]

spray[1] *verb* (sprays, spraying, sprayed)
scatter tiny drops of liquid over something.
spray *noun* (*plural* sprays)
1 tiny drops of liquid sprayed. 2 a device for spraying liquid. [origin unknown]

spray[2] *noun* (*plural* sprays)
1 a single shoot with its leaves and flowers.
2 a small bunch of flowers.
[from Old English]

spread *verb* (spreads, spreading, spread)
1 open or stretch something out to its full size, *The bird spread its wings.* 2 make something cover a surface, *We spread jam on the bread.* 3 become longer or wider, *The stain was spreading.* 4 make or become more widely known or felt or distributed etc., *We spread the news. Panic spread.*
spread *noun* (*plural* spreads)
1 the action or result of spreading. 2 a thing's breadth or extent. 3 a paste for spreading on bread. 4 (*informal*) a large or grand meal. [from Old English]

spreadeagled *adjective*
with arms and legs stretched out, *He lay spreadeagled on the bed.*
[originally = a picture of an eagle with legs and wings stretched out, used as an emblem on a knight's shield, inn sign, etc.]

spreadsheet *noun* (*plural* spreadsheets)
a computer program for handling
information, especially figures, displayed
in a table.

spree *noun* (*plural* sprees)
a lively outing. [origin unknown]

sprig *noun* (*plural* sprigs)
a small branch; a shoot. [from old German]

sprightly *adjective* (sprightlier, sprightliest)
lively and full of energy. [from *sprite*]

spring *verb* (springs, springing, sprang,
sprung)
1 jump; move quickly or suddenly, *He
sprang to his feet.* 2 originate or arise, *The
trouble has sprung from carelessness.*
3 present or produce suddenly, *They
sprang a surprise on us.*
spring *noun* (*plural* springs)
1 a springy coil or bent piece of metal. 2 a
springing movement. 3 a place where
water comes up naturally from the ground.
4 the season when most plants begin to
grow. [from Old English]

springboard *noun* (*plural* springboards)
a springy board from which people jump in
diving and gymnastics.

springbok *noun* (*plural* springboks or
springbok)
a South African gazelle.
[Afrikaans, from Dutch *springen* = to
spring + *bok* = buck, antelope]

spring-clean *verb* (spring-cleans, spring-
cleaning, spring-cleaned)
clean a house thoroughly in springtime.

spring onion *noun* (*plural* spring onions)
a small onion with a long green stem, eaten
raw in salads.

spring roll *noun* (*plural* spring rolls)
a Chinese pancake filled with vegetables
and (sometimes) meat, and fried until
crisp.

springtime *noun*
the season of spring.

springy *adjective* (springier, springiest)
able to spring back easily after being bent
or squeezed. **springiness** *noun*

sprinkle *verb* (sprinkles, sprinkling,
sprinkled)
make tiny drops or pieces fall on
something. **sprinkler** *noun*
[probably from old Dutch]

sprinkling *noun* (*plural* sprinklings)
a few here and there.

sprint *verb* (sprints, sprinting, sprinted)
run very fast for a short distance. **sprint**
noun, **sprinter** *noun* [from Old Norse]

sprite *noun* (*plural* sprites)
an elf, fairy, or goblin. [from *spirit*]

sprocket *noun* (*plural* sprockets)
each of the row of teeth round a wheel,
fitting into links on a chain.
[origin unknown]

sprout *verb* (sprouts, sprouting, sprouted)
start to grow; put out shoots.
sprout *noun* (*plural* sprouts)
1 a shoot of a plant. 2 a Brussels sprout.
[probably from Old English]

spruce¹ *noun* (*plural* spruces)
a kind of fir tree. [from *Pruce*, the old name
of Prussia, an area in central Europe,
where it was grown]

spruce² *adjective*
neat and trim; smart.
spruce *verb* (spruces, sprucing, spruced)
smarten, *Spruce yourself up.*
[probably from *spruce jerkin*, made of
leather from Prussia (see *spruce¹*)]

spry *adjective* (spryer, spryest)
active, nimble, and lively.
[origin unknown]

spud *noun* (*plural* spuds) (*informal*)
a potato. [origin unknown]

spume *noun*
froth or foam. [from Latin]

spur *noun* (*plural* spurs)
1 a sharp device worn on the heel of a
rider's boot to urge a horse to go faster. 2 a
stimulus or incentive. 3 a projecting part.
on the spur of the moment on an impulse;
without planning.
spur *verb* (spurs, spurring, spurred)
urge on; encourage. [from Old English]

spurious *adjective*
not genuine. [from Latin]

spurn *verb* (spurns, spurning, spurned)
reject scornfully. [from Old English]

spurt *verb* (spurts, spurting, spurted)
1 gush out. 2 increase your speed
suddenly.
spurt *noun* (*plural* spurts)
1 a sudden gush. 2 a sudden increase in
speed or effort. [origin unknown]

sputter *verb* (sputters, sputtering,
sputtered)
splutter. **sputter** *noun* [from Dutch]

sputum *noun*
saliva or phlegm. [Latin]

spy *noun* (*plural* spies)
someone who works secretly for one
country, person, etc. to find out things
about another.
spy *verb* (spies, spying, spied)
1 be a spy. 2 keep watch secretly. 3 see or
notice, *She spied a house.* 4 pry.
[from old French *espier* = espy]

squabble *verb* (squabbles, squabbling,
squabbled)
quarrel or bicker. **squabble** *noun*
[origin unknown]

squad *noun* (*plural* squads)
a small group of people working or being
trained together.
[from old French; related to *squadron*]

squadron *noun* (*plural* squadrons)
part of an army, navy, or air force.
[from Italian; related to *squad*]

squalid *adjective*
dirty and unpleasant.
squalidly *adverb*, **squalor** *noun*
[from Latin *squalidus* – rough, dirty]

squall *noun* (*plural* squalls)
1 a sudden storm or gust of wind. 2 a
baby's loud cry.
squall *verb* (squalls, squalling, squalled)
(of a baby) cry loudly.
[probably from *squeal* and *bawl*]

squander *verb* (squanders, squandering,
squandered)
spend money or time etc. wastefully.
[origin unknown]

square *noun* (*plural* squares)
1 a flat shape with four equal sides and
four right angles. 2 an area surrounded by
buildings, *Leicester Square.* 3 the number
produced by multiplying something by
itself, *9 is the square of 3* $(9 = 3 \times 3)$.
square *adjective*
1 having the shape of a square. 2 forming a
right angle, *The desk has square corners.*
3 equal or even, *The teams are all square
with six points each.*
squarely *adverb*, **squareness** *noun*
square foot, square metre, etc., the area of a
surface with sides that are one foot or one
metre etc. long.
square *verb* (squares, squaring, squared)
1 make a thing square. 2 multiply a
number by itself, *5 squared is 25.* 3 match;
make or be consistent, *His story doesn't
square with yours.* 4 (*informal*) bribe.
[from old French; related to *quadrant*]

square deal *noun*
one that is honest and fair.

square meal *noun* (*plural* square meals)
a good satisfying meal.

square-rigged *adjective*
with the sails set across the ship, not
lengthways.

square root *noun* (*plural* square roots)
the number that gives a particular number
if it is multiplied by itself, *3 is the square
root of 9* $(3 \times 3 = 9)$.

squash¹ *verb* (squashes, squashing,
squashed)
1 press something so that it loses its shape;
crush. 2 pack tightly. 3 suppress or quash.
squash *noun* (*plural* squashes)
1 a crowded condition. 2 a fruit-flavoured
soft drink. 3 a game played with rackets
and a soft ball in a special indoor court.
[a different spelling of *quash*]

squash² *noun* (*plural* squashes)
a kind of gourd used as a vegetable.
[from a Native American word]

squat *verb* (**squats, squatting, squatted**)
1 sit on your heels; crouch. **2** use an unoccupied building for living in without permission. **squat** *noun*, **squatter** *noun*
squat *adjective*
short and fat. [from *ex-* + old French *quatir* = press down, crouch]

squaw *noun* (*plural* **squaws**)
a North American Indian woman or wife. [a Native American word]

USAGE: This word is now considered to be offensive.

squawk *verb* (**squawks, squawking, squawked**)
make a loud harsh cry. **squawk** *noun* [imitating the sound]

squeak *verb* (**squeaks, squeaking, squeaked**)
make a short high-pitched cry or sound. **squeak** *noun*, **squeaky** *adjective*, **squeakily** *adverb* [imitating the sound]

squeal *verb* (**squeals, squealing, squealed**)
make a long shrill cry or sound. **squeal** *noun* [imitating the sound]

squeamish *adjective*
easily disgusted or shocked. **squeamishness** *noun* [from old French]

squeeze *verb* (**squeezes, squeezing, squeezed**)
1 press something from opposite sides, especially to get liquid out of it. **2** force into or through a place, *We squeezed through a gap in the hedge.* **squeezer** *noun*
squeeze *noun* (*plural* **squeezes**)
1 the action of squeezing. **2** a drop of liquid squeezed out, *Add a squeeze of lemon.* **3** a time when money is difficult to get or borrow. [origin unknown]

squelch *verb* (**squelches, squelching, squelched**)
make a sound like someone treading in thick mud. **squelch** *noun* [imitating the sound]

squib *noun* (*plural* **squibs**)
a small firework that hisses and then explodes. [origin unknown]

squid *noun* (*plural* **squids**)
a sea animal with eight short tentacles and two long ones. [origin unknown]

squiggle *noun* (*plural* **squiggles**)
a short curly line. [probably from *squirm* + *wriggle*]

squint *verb* (**squints, squinting, squinted**)
1 be cross-eyed. **2** peer; look with half-shut eyes at something. **squint** *noun* [origin unknown]

squire *noun* (*plural* **squires**)
1 the man who owns most of the land in a country parish or district. **2** a young nobleman in the Middle Ages who served a knight. [from *esquire*]

squirm *verb* (**squirms, squirming, squirmed**)
wriggle. [origin unknown]

squirrel *noun* (*plural* **squirrels**)
a small animal with a bushy tail and red or grey fur, living in trees. [from Greek]

squirt *verb* (**squirts, squirting, squirted**)
send or come out in a jet of liquid. **squirt** *noun* [imitating the sound]

St. or **St** *abbreviation*
1 Saint. **2** Street.

stab *verb* (**stabs, stabbing, stabbed**)
pierce or wound with something sharp.
stab *noun* (*plural* **stabs**)
1 the action of stabbing. **2** a sudden sharp pain, *She felt a stab of fear.* **3** (*informal*) an attempt, *I'll have a stab at it.* [origin unknown]

stability *noun*
being stable.

stabilize *verb* (**stabilizes, stabilizing, stabilized**)
make or become stable. **stabilization** *noun*, **stabilizer** *noun*

stable¹ *adjective*
1 steady or firmly fixed; not likely to move or change. **2** sensible and dependable. **stably** *adverb* [from Latin *stare* = to stand]

stable² *noun* (*plural* **stables**)
a building where horses are kept.
stable *verb* (**stables, stabling, stabled**)
put or keep in a stable. [from old French; related to *stable*¹]

staccato *adverb* & *adjective*
(in music) played with each note short and separate. [Italian, from *distaccare* = detach]

stack *noun* (*plural* stacks)
1 a neat pile. 2 a haystack. 3 (*informal*) a large amount, *a stack of work.* 4 a single tall chimney; a group of small chimneys.
stack *verb* (stacks, stacking, stacked)
pile things up. [from Old Norse]

stadium *noun* (*plural* stadiums)
a sports ground surrounded by seats for spectators. [Latin]

staff *noun* (*plural* staffs or, in sense 4, staves)
1 the people who work in an office, shop, etc. 2 the teachers in a school or college. 3 a stick or pole used as a weapon or support or as a symbol of authority. 4 a set of five horizontal lines on which music is written.
staff *verb* (staffs, staffing, staffed)
provide with a staff of people, *The centre is staffed by volunteers.* [from Old English]

stag *noun* (*plural* stags)
a male deer. [probably from Old English]

stage *noun* (*plural* stages)
1 a platform for performances in a theatre or hall. 2 a point or part of a process, journey, etc., *the final stage.*
stage *verb* (stages, staging, staged)
1 present a performance on a stage.
2 organize, *We decided to stage a protest.*
[from old French]

stagecoach *noun* (*plural* stagecoaches)
a horse-drawn coach that formerly ran regularly from one point to another along the same route.
[so called because it ran in stages, picking up passengers at points along the route]

stage fright *noun*
fear or nervousness before or while performing to an audience.

stage left *adverb*
on the left side of the stage when facing the audience.

stage-manage *verb* (stage-manages, stage-managing, stage-managed)
1 be stage manager. 2 organize and control an event so that it has a particular effect.

stage manager *noun* (*plural* stage managers)
the person in charge of the scenery, lighting, sound, etc. during a performance.

stage right *adverb*
on the right side of the stage when facing the audience.

stage-struck *adjective*
fascinated by the theatre and longing to be an actor.

stagger *verb* (staggers, staggering, staggered)
1 walk unsteadily. 2 shock deeply; amaze, *We were staggered at the price.* 3 arrange things so that they do not coincide, *Please stagger your holidays so that there is always someone here.* **stagger** *noun*
[from Old Norse]

stagnant *adjective*
1 not flowing. 2 not active or developing, *business is stagnant.*
[from Latin *stagnum* = a pool]

stagnate *verb* (stagnates, stagnating, stagnated)
1 be stagnant. 2 be dull through lack of activity or variety. **stagnation** *noun*

staid *adjective*
steady and serious in manner; sedate.
[old past participle of *stay*]

stain *noun* (*plural* stains)
1 a dirty mark on something. 2 a blemish on someone's character or past record. 3 a liquid used for staining things.
stain *verb* (stains, staining, stained)
1 make a stain on something. 2 colour with a liquid that sinks into the surface.
[from an old word *distain* = dye]

stained glass *noun*
pieces of coloured glass held together in a lead framework to make a picture or pattern.

stainless *adjective*
without a stain.

stainless steel *noun*
steel that does not rust easily.

stair *noun* (*plural* stairs)
each of the fixed steps in a series that lead from one level or floor to another in a building. [from Old English]

staircase *noun* (*plural* staircases)
a flight of stairs.

stairway *noun* (*plural* stairways)
a staircase.

stairwell *noun* (*plural* stairwells)
the space going up through a building, which contains the stairs.

stake *noun* (*plural* stakes)
1 a thick pointed stick to be driven into the ground. 2 the post to which people used to be tied for execution by being burnt alive. 3 an amount of money bet on something. 4 an investment that gives a person a share or interest in an enterprise.
at **stake** being risked.
stake *verb* (stakes, staking, staked)
1 fasten, support, or mark out with stakes. 2 bet or risk money etc. on an event.
stake a claim claim or obtain a right to something.
[from Old English]

stalactite *noun* (*plural* stalactites)
a stony spike hanging like an icicle from the roof of a cave.
[from Greek *stalaktos* = dripping]

USAGE: See note at *stalagmite*.

stalagmite *noun* (*plural* stalagmites)
a stony spike standing like a pillar on the floor of a cave.
[from Greek *stalagma* = a drop]

USAGE: Remember that a *stalagmite* stands up from the ground, while a *stalactite* hangs down from the ceiling.

stale *adjective*
not fresh. **staleness** *noun*
[old French, = at a standstill]

stalemate *noun*
1 a drawn position in chess when a player cannot make a move without putting his or her king in check. 2 a deadlock; a situation in which neither side in an argument will give way. [from old French *stale* = at a standstill, + *mate*²]

stalk¹ *noun* (*plural* stalks)
a stem of a plant etc.
[from Old English *stalu*]

stalk² *verb* (stalks, stalking, stalked)
1 track or hunt stealthily. 2 walk in a stiff or dignified way.
[from Old English *stealcian*]

stall¹ *noun* (*plural* stalls)
1 a table or counter from which things are sold. 2 a place for one animal in a stable or shed.
stall *verb* (stalls, stalling, stalled)
1 stop suddenly, *The car engine stalled.* 2 put an animal into a stall.
[from Old English]

stall² *verb* (stalls, stalling, stalled)
delay things deliberately so as to avoid having to take action. [from an old word *stall* = a decoy or a pickpocket's helper]

stallion *noun* (*plural* stallions)
a male horse. [from old French]

stalls *plural noun*
the seats in the lowest level of a theatre.

stalwart *adjective*
sturdy; strong and faithful, *my stalwart supporters*. [from Old English]

stamen *noun* (*plural* stamens)
the part of a flower bearing pollen.
[Latin, = thread]

stamina *noun*
strength and ability to endure things for a long time.
[Latin, plural of *stamen* (referring to the threads of life spun by the fates)]

stammer *verb* (stammers, stammering, stammered)
keep repeating the same syllables when you speak. **stammer** *noun*
[from Old English]

stamp *noun* (*plural* stamps)
1 a small piece of gummed paper with a special design on it; a postage stamp. 2 a small device for pressing words or marks on something; the words or marks made by this. 3 a distinctive characteristic, *His story bears the stamp of truth.*

stamp *verb* (stamps, stamping, stamped)
1 bang a foot heavily on the ground. 2 walk with loud heavy steps. 3 stick a stamp on something. 4 press a mark or design etc. on something.
stamp out put out a fire etc. by stamping; stop something, *stamp out cruelty*.
[probably from Old English]

stampede *noun* (*plural* stampedes)
a sudden rush by animals or people.
stampede *verb*
[from Spanish *estampida* = crash, uproar]

stance *noun* (*plural* stances)
1 the way a person or animal stands. 2 a person's attitude to something.
[French, related to *stable*[1]]

stanchion *noun* (*plural* stanchions)
an upright bar or post forming a support.
[from old French]

stand *verb* (stands, standing, stood)
1 be on your feet without moving, *We were standing at the back of the hall*. 2 set or be upright; place, *We stood the vase on the table*. 3 stay the same, *My offer still stands*. 4 be a candidate for election, *She stood for Parliament*. 5 tolerate or endure, *I can't stand that noise*. 6 provide and pay for, *I'll stand you a drink*.
it stands to reason it is reasonable or obvious.
stand by be ready for action.
stand for 1 represent. 2 tolerate.
stand up for support or defend.
stand up to 1 resist bravely. 2 stay in good condition in hard use.

stand *noun* (*plural* stands)
1 something made for putting things on, *a music stand*. 2 a stall where things are sold or displayed. 3 a grandstand. 4 a stationary condition or position, *He took his stand near the door*. 5 resistance to attack, *We made a stand*.
[from Old English]

standard *noun* (*plural* standards)
1 how good something is, *a high standard of work*. 2 a thing used to measure or judge something else. 3 a special flag, *the royal standard*. 4 an upright support.
standard *adjective*
1 of the usual or average quality or kind. 2 regarded as the best and widely used, *the standard book on spiders*. [from old French]

standardize *verb* (standardizes, standardizing, standardized)
make things be of a standard size, quality, etc. **standardization** *noun*

standard lamp *noun* (*plural* standard lamps)
a lamp on an upright pole that stands on the floor.

standard of living *noun*
the level of comfort and wealth that a country or a person has.

standby *noun* (*plural* standbys)
1 something or someone kept to be used when needed. 2 readiness, *Troops were on standby during the crisis*.

stand-in *noun* (*plural* stand-ins)
a deputy or substitute.

standing *noun*
1 a person's status or reputation. 2 the period for which something has existed, *a contract of five years' standing*.

standing order *noun* (*plural* standing orders)
an instruction to a bank to make regular payments, or to a trader to supply something regularly.

stand-offish *adjective*
cold and formal; not friendly.

standpipe *noun* (*plural* standpipes)
a pipe connected directly to a water supply, especially one set up in the street to provide water in an emergency.

standpoint *noun* (*plural* standpoints)
a point of view.

standstill *noun*
a stop; an end to movement or activity.

stanza *noun* (*plural* stanzas)
a verse of poetry. [Italian]

staple[1] *noun* (*plural* staples)
1 a small piece of metal pushed through papers and clenched to fasten them together. 2 a U-shaped nail. **staple** *verb*, **stapler** *noun* [from Old English]

staple² *adjective*
main or usual, *Rice is their staple food.*
staple *noun* [from old French]

star *noun* (*plural* **stars**)
1 a large mass of burning gas that is seen
as a speck of light in the sky at night. 2 a
shape with rays from it; an asterisk. 3 an
object or mark of this shape showing rank
or quality, *a five-star hotel.* 4 a famous
performer; one of the chief performers in a
play or show etc.
star *verb* (**stars, starring, starred**)
1 perform or present as a star in a show
etc. 2 mark with an asterisk or star
symbol. [from Old English]

starboard *noun*
the right-hand side of a ship or aircraft
when you are facing forward. (Compare
port¹.) [from Old English *steor* = paddle for
steering (usually mounted on the right-
hand side), + *board*]

starch *noun* (*plural* **starches**)
1 a white carbohydrate in bread, potatoes,
etc. 2 this or a similar substance used to
stiffen clothes. **starchy** *adjective*
starch *verb* (**starches, starching, starched**)
stiffen with starch. [from Old English]

stardom *noun*
being a star performer.

stare *verb* (**stares, staring, stared**)
look at something intensely. **stare** *noun*
[from Old English]

starfish *noun* (*plural* **starfish** or **starfishes**)
a sea animal shaped like a star with five
points.

stark *adjective*
1 complete or unmistakable, *stark
nonsense.* 2 desolate and bare; without
cheerfulness, *the stark lunar landscape.*
starkly *adverb*, **starkness** *noun*
stark *adverb*
completely, *stark naked.*
[from Old English]

starlight *noun*
light from the stars.

starling *noun* (*plural* **starlings**)
a noisy black bird with speckled feathers.
[from Old English]

starry *adjective*
full of stars.

starry-eyed *adjective*
made happy by foolish dreams or
unrealistic hopes.

start *verb* (**starts, starting, started**)
1 begin or cause to begin. 2 begin a
journey. 3 make a sudden movement
because of pain or surprise. **starter** *noun*
start *noun* (*plural* **starts**)
1 the beginning; the place where a race
starts. 2 an advantage that someone starts
with, *We gave the young ones ten minutes'
start.* 3 a sudden movement.
[from Old English]

startle *verb* (**startles, startling, startled**)
surprise or alarm someone.
[from Old English]

starve *verb* (**starves, starving, starved**)
1 suffer or die from lack of food; cause to do
this. 2 (*informal*) be very hungry.
starvation *noun* [from Old English]

state *noun* (*plural* **states**)
1 the quality of a person's or thing's
characteristics or circumstances;
condition. 2 a grand style, *She arrived in
state.* 3 an organized community under one
government (*the State of Israel*) or forming
part of a republic (*the 50 States of the USA*).
4 a country's government, *Help for the
earthquake victims was provided by the
state.* 5 (*informal*) an excited or upset
condition, *Don't get into a state about the
robbery.*
state *verb* (**states, stating, stated**)
express something in spoken or written
words. [same origin as *stable¹*]

stately *adjective* (**statelier, stateliest**)
dignified, imposing, or grand. **stateliness**
noun [from *state*]

stately home *noun* (*plural* **stately homes**)
a large and magnificent house belonging to
an aristocratic family.

statement *noun* (*plural* **statements**)
1 words stating something. 2 a formal
account of facts, *The witness made a
statement to the police.* 3 a written report of
a financial account, *a bank statement.*

state school noun (plural state schools)
a school which is funded by the
government and which does not charge
fees to pupils.

statesman noun (plural statesmen)
a person, especially a man, who is
important or skilled in governing a
country. **statesmanship** noun

stateswoman noun (plural stateswomen)
a woman who is important or skilled in
governing a country.

static adjective
not moving or changing. [from Greek]

static electricity noun
electricity that is present in something, not
flowing as current.

station noun (plural stations)
1 a place where a person or thing stands or
is stationed; a position. 2 a stopping place
on a railway with buildings for passengers
and goods. 3 a building equipped for people
who serve the public or for certain
activities, the police station. 4 a
broadcasting establishment with its own
frequency.
station verb (stations, stationing, stationed)
put someone in a certain place for a
purpose, He was stationed at the door to take
the tickets.
[from Latin statio = a stand, standing]

stationary adjective
not moving, The car was stationary when
the van hit it.

USAGE: Do not confuse with stationery.

stationer noun (plural stationers)
a shopkeeper who sells stationery.
[from Latin stationarius = a tradesman
(usually a bookseller) who had a shop or
stand (as opposed to one who sold goods
wherever he could)]

stationery noun
paper, envelopes, and other articles used in
writing or typing.

USAGE: Do not confuse with stationary.

statistic noun (plural statistics)
a piece of information expressed as a
number, These statistics show that the
population has doubled.
statistical adjective, **statistically** adverb
[from German]

statistician (say stat-is-tish-an) noun
(plural statisticians)
an expert in statistics.

statistics noun
the study of information based on the
numbers of things.

statuary noun
statues.

statue noun (plural statues)
a model made of stone or metal etc. to look
like a person or animal.
[same origin as stable¹]

statuesque (say stat-yoo-esk) adjective
like a statue in stillness or dignity.

statuette noun (plural statuettes)
a small statue.

stature noun
1 the natural height of the body.
2 greatness because of ability or
achievement. [same origin as stable¹]

status (say stay-tus) noun (plural statuses)
1 a person's or thing's position or rank in
relation to others. 2 high rank or prestige.
[same origin as stable¹]

status quo (say stay-tus kwoh) noun
the state of affairs as it was before a
change. [Latin, = the state in which]

status symbol noun (plural status
symbols)
something that you own because it shows
off your wealth or position in society,
rather than because you like it or need it.

statute noun (plural statutes)
a law passed by a parliament. **statutory**
adjective [from Latin statuere = set up,
decree; related to stable¹]

staunch adjective
firm and loyal, our staunch supporters.
staunchly adverb [from old French]

stave noun (plural **staves**)
1 each of the curved strips of wood forming the side of a cask or tub. 2 a staff in music (see staff 4).

stave verb (**staves, staving, staved** or **stove**)
dent or break a hole in something, The collision stove in the front of the ship.
stave off keep something away, We staved off the disaster.
[from staves (see staff)]

stay¹ verb (**stays, staying, stayed**)
1 continue to be in the same place or condition; remain. 2 spend time in a place as a visitor. 3 satisfy temporarily, We stayed our hunger with a sandwich.
4 pause. 5 show endurance in a race or task.
stay put (informal) remain in place.

stay noun (plural **stays**)
1 a time spent somewhere, We made a short stay in Rome. 2 a postponement, a stay of execution. [same origin as stable¹]

stay² noun (plural **stays**)
a support, especially a rope or wire holding up a mast etc.
[via old French from Germanic]

stead noun
in a person's or **thing's stead** instead of this person or thing.
stand a person in good stead be very useful to him or her.
[from Old English]

steadfast adjective
firm and not changing, a steadfast refusal.

steady adjective (**steadier, steadiest**)
1 not shaking or moving; firm. 2 regular; continuing the same, a steady pace. **steadily** adverb, **steadiness** noun [from stead]

steak noun (plural **steaks**)
a thick slice of meat (especially beef) or fish. [from Old Norse]

steal verb (**steals, stealing, stole, stolen**)
1 take and keep something that does not belong to you; take secretly or dishonestly.
2 move secretly or without being noticed, He stole out of the room. [from Old English]

stealthy (say stelth-ee) adjective (**stealthier, stealthiest**)
quiet and secret, so as not to be noticed.

stealth noun, **stealthily** adverb, **stealthiness** noun [probably from Old English and related to steal]

steam noun
1 the gas or vapour that comes from boiling water; this used to drive machinery. 2 energy, He ran out of steam.
steamy adjective

steam verb (**steams, steaming, steamed**)
1 give out steam. 2 cook or treat by steam, a steamed pudding. 3 move by the power of steam, The ship steamed down the river.
[from Old English]

steam engine noun (plural **steam engines**)
an engine driven by steam.

steamer noun (plural **steamers**)
1 a steamship. 2 a container in which things are steamed.

steamroller noun (plural **steamrollers**)
a heavy vehicle with a large roller used to flatten surfaces when making roads.
[because the first ones were powered by steam]

steamship noun (plural **steamships**)
a ship driven by steam.

steed noun (plural **steeds**) (poetical)
a horse. [from Old English]

steel noun (plural **steels**)
1 a strong metal made from iron and carbon. 2 a steel rod for sharpening knives.
[from Old English]

steel band noun (plural **steel bands**)
a West Indian band of musicians with instruments usually made from oil drums.

steel wool noun
a mass of fine, sharp steel threads used for cleaning a surface or rubbing it smooth.

steely adjective
1 like or to do with steel. 2 cold, hard, and severe, a steely glare.

steep¹ adjective
1 sloping very sharply, not gradually.
2 (informal) unreasonably high, a steep price. **steeply** adverb, **steepness** noun
[from Old English]

steep² *verb* (steeps, steeping, steeped)
soak thoroughly, saturate.
[probably from a Scandinavian language]

steepen *verb* (steepens, steepening,
steepened)
make or become steeper.

steeple *noun* (*plural* steeples)
a church tower with a spire on top.
[from Old English]

steeplechase *noun* (*plural* steeplechases)
a race across country or over hedges or
fences. [so called because the race
originally had a distant church steeple in
view as its goal]

steeplejack *noun* (*plural* steeplejacks)
a person who climbs tall chimneys or
steeples to do repairs.

steer¹ *verb* (steers, steering, steered)
make a car, ship, or bicycle etc. go in the
direction you want; guide. **steersman** *noun*
[from Old English *stieran*]

steer² *noun* (*plural* steers)
a young castrated bull kept for its beef.
[from Old English *steor*]

steering wheel *noun* (*plural* steering
wheels)
a wheel for steering a car, boat, etc.

stellar *adjective*
to do with a star or stars.
[from Latin *stella* = star]

stem¹ *noun* (*plural* stems)
1 the main central part of a tree, shrub, or
plant. 2 a thin part on which a leaf, flower,
or fruit is supported. 3 a thin upright part,
e.g. the thin part of a wineglass between
the bowl and the foot. 4 the main part of a
verb or other word, to which endings are
attached. 5 the front part of a ship, *from
stem to stern*.
stem *verb* (stems, stemming, stemmed)
stem from arise from; have as its source.
[from Old English]

stem² *verb* (stems, stemming, stemmed)
stop the flow of something.
[from Old Norse]

stench *noun* (*plural* stenches)
a very unpleasant smell.
[from Old English]

stencil *noun* (*plural* stencils)
a piece of card, metal, or plastic with pieces
cut out of it, used to produce a picture,
design, etc.
stencil *verb* (stencils, stencilling, stencilled)
produce or decorate with a stencil.
[from old French]

stentorian *adjective*
very loud, *a stentorian voice*.
[from the name of Stentor, a herald in
ancient Greek legend]

step *noun* (*plural* steps)
1 a movement made by lifting the foot and
setting it down. 2 the sound or rhythm of
stepping. 3 a level surface for placing the
foot on in climbing up or down. 4 each of a
series of things done in some process or
action, *The first step is to find somewhere to
practise*.
in step 1 stepping in time with others in
marching or dancing. 2 in agreement.
watch your step be careful.
step *verb* (steps, stepping, stepped)
tread or walk.
step in intervene.
step on it (*informal*) hurry.
step up increase something.
[from Old English *steppan*]

step- *prefix*
related through remarriage of one parent.
[from Old English *steop-*]

stepbrother *noun* (*plural* stepbrothers)
the son of one of your parents from an
earlier or later marriage.

stepchild *noun* (*plural* stepchildren)
a child that a person's husband or wife has
from an earlier marriage.
stepdaughter, stepson *nouns*

stepfather *noun* (*plural* stepfathers)
a man who is married to your mother but
was not your natural father.

stepladder *noun* (*plural* stepladders)
a folding ladder with flat treads.

stepmother *noun* (*plural* stepmothers)
a woman who is married to your father but
was not your natural mother.

steppe *noun* (*plural* **steppes**)
a grassy plain with few trees, especially in Russia. [from Russian]

stepping stone *noun* (*plural* **stepping stones**)
1 each of a line of stones put into a shallow stream so that people can walk across. 2 a way of achieving something, or a stage in achieving it, *good exam results can be a stepping stone to a career.*

steps *plural noun*
a stepladder.

stepsister *noun* (*plural* **stepsisters**)
the daughter of one of your parents from an earlier or later marriage.

stereo *adjective*
stereophonic.

stereo *noun* (*plural* **stereos**)
1 stereophonic sound or recording. 2 a stereophonic record player or radio. [from *stereophonic*]

stereophonic *adjective*
using sound that comes from two different directions so as to give a natural effect. [from Greek *stereos* = solid, three-dimensional + *phone* = sound]

stereoscopic *adjective*
giving the effect of being three-dimensional, e.g. in photographs. [from Greek *stereos* = solid, three-dimensional + *skopein* = look at]

stereotype *noun* (*plural* **stereotypes**)
a standardized character; a fixed idea etc., *The stereotype of a hero is one who is tall, strong, brave, and good-looking.* [originally = a kind of printing which appeared three-dimensional: from Greek *stereos* = solid, three-dimensional, + *type*]

sterile *adjective*
1 not fertile; barren. 2 free from germs.
sterility *noun* [from Latin]

sterilize *verb* (**sterilizes, sterilizing, sterilized**)
1 make a thing free from germs, e.g. by heating it. 2 make a person or animal unable to reproduce.
sterilization *noun*, **sterilizer** *noun*

sterling *noun*
British money.

sterling *adjective*
1 genuine, *sterling silver.* 2 excellent; of great worth, *her sterling qualities.* [probably from Old English *steorra* = star + *-ling* (because some early coins had a star on them)]

stern¹ *adjective*
strict and severe, not lenient or kindly.
sternly *adverb*, **sternness** *noun*
[from Old English]

stern² *noun* (*plural* **sterns**)
the back part of a ship. [from Old Norse]

steroid *noun* (*plural* **steroids**)
a substance of a kind that includes certain hormones and other natural secretions. [from Greek]

stethoscope *noun* (*plural* **stethoscopes**)
a device used for listening to sounds in a person's body, e.g. heartbeats and breathing. [from Greek *stethos* = breast + *skopein* = look at]

stew *verb* (**stews, stewing, stewed**)
cook slowly in liquid.

stew *noun* (*plural* **stews**)
a dish of stewed food, especially meat and vegetables.
in a stew (*informal*) very worried or agitated.
[from old French]

steward *noun* (*plural* **stewards**)
1 a man whose job is to look after the passengers on a ship or aircraft. 2 an official who keeps order or supervises the arrangements at an event. [from Old English *stig* = house or hall, + *ward*]

stewardess *noun* (*plural* **stewardesses**)
a woman whose job is to look after the passengers on a ship or aircraft.

stick¹ *noun* (*plural* **sticks**)
1 a long thin piece of wood. 2 a walking stick. 3 the implement used to hit the ball in hockey, polo, etc. 4 a long thin piece of something, *a stick of rock.* [from Old English *sticca*]

stick² *verb* (**sticks, sticking, stuck**)
1 push a thing into something, *Stick a pin in it.* 2 fix or be fixed by glue or as if by

this, *Stick stamps on the parcel.* **3** become
fixed and unable to move, *The boat stuck on
a sandbank.* **4** (*informal*) endure or
tolerate, *I can't stick that noise!*
5 (*informal*) impose a task on someone, *We
were stuck with the clearing up.*
stick out 1 come or push out from a surface;
stand out from the surrounding area. **2** be
very noticeable.
stick to 1 remain faithful to a friend or
promise etc. **2** keep to and not alter, *He
stuck to his story.*
stick together 1 stay together. **2** support
each other.
stick up for (*informal*) stand up for.
[from Old English *stician*]

sticker *noun* (*plural* **stickers**)
an adhesive label or sign for sticking to
something.

sticking plaster *noun* (*plural* **sticking
plasters**)
a strip of adhesive material for covering
cuts.

stick insect *noun* (*plural* **stick insects**)
an insect with a long thin body and legs,
which looks like a twig.

stickleback *noun* (*plural* **sticklebacks**)
a small fish with sharp spines on its back.
[from Old English *sticel* = thorn]

stickler *noun* (*plural* **sticklers**)
a person who insists on something, *a
stickler for punctuality.*
[from Old English *stihtan* = put in order]

sticky *adjective* (**stickier, stickiest**)
1 able or likely to stick to things. **2** (of
weather) hot and humid, causing
perspiration. **3** (*informal*) uncooperative,
She was very sticky about letting me come.
stickily *adverb*, **stickiness** *noun*
come to a sticky end die or end in a painful
or unpleasant way.

stiff *adjective*
1 not bending or moving or changing its
shape easily. **2** not fluid; hard to stir, *a stiff
dough.* **3** difficult, *a stiff examination.*
4 formal in manner; not friendly. **5** severe
or strong, *a stiff breeze.* **stiffly** *adverb*,
stiffness *noun* [from Old English]

stiffen *verb* (**stiffens, stiffening, stiffened**)
make or become stiff. **stiffener** *noun*

stifle *verb* (**stifles, stifling, stifled**)
1 suffocate. **2** suppress, *She stifled a yawn.*
[from old French]

stigma *noun* (*plural* **stigmas**)
1 a mark of disgrace; a stain on a
reputation. **2** the part of a pistil that
receives the pollen in pollination.
[from Greek]

stigmatize *verb* (**stigmatizes, stigmatizing,
stigmatized**)
brand as something disgraceful, *He was
stigmatized as a coward.*

stile *noun* (*plural* **stiles**)
an arrangement of steps or bars for people
to climb over a fence. [from Old English]

stiletto *noun* (*plural* **stilettos**)
a dagger with a narrow blade.
[Italian, = little dagger]

stiletto heel *noun* (*plural* **stiletto heels**)
a high pointed shoe-heel.

still[1] *adjective*
1 not moving, *still water.* **2** silent. **3** not
fizzy. **stillness** *noun*
still *adverb*
1 without moving, *Stand still.* **2** up to this
or that time, *He was still there.* **3** in a
greater amount or degree, *You can do still
better.* **4** nevertheless, *They've lost. Still,
they tried, and that was good.*
still *verb* (**stills, stilling, stilled**)
make or become still. [from Old English]

still[2] *noun* (*plural* **stills**)
an apparatus for distilling alcohol or other
liquid. [from *distil*]

stillborn *adjective*
born dead. [from *still*[1] + *born*]

still life *noun* (*plural* **still lifes**)
a painting of lifeless things such as
ornaments and fruit.

stilted *adjective*
stiffly formal. [originally = raised on stilts]

stilts *plural noun*
1 a pair of poles with supports for the feet
so that the user can walk high above the
ground. **2** posts for supporting a house etc.
above marshy ground. [Middle English,
from a Germanic language]

stimulant *noun* (*plural* stimulants)
something that stimulates.

stimulate *verb* (stimulates, stimulating, stimulated)
1 make more lively or active. 2 excite or interest. **stimulation** *noun*

stimulus *noun* (*plural* stimuli)
something that stimulates or produces a reaction. [Latin, = goad]

sting *noun* (*plural* stings)
1 a sharp-pointed part of an animal or plant, often containing a poison, that can cause a wound. 2 a painful wound caused by this part.

sting *verb* (stings, stinging, stung)
1 wound or hurt with a sting. 2 feel a sharp pain. 3 stimulate sharply, *I was stung into answering rudely.* 4 (*slang*) cheat a person by overcharging; extort money from someone. [from Old English]

stingray *noun* (*plural* stingrays)
a fish with a flat body, fins like wings, and a poisonous spine in its tail.

stingy (*say* stin-jee) *adjective* (stingier, stingiest)
mean, not generous; giving or given in small amounts. **stingily** *adverb*, **stinginess** *noun* [from *sting*]

stink *noun* (*plural* stinks)
1 an unpleasant smell. 2 (*informal*) an unpleasant fuss or protest.

stink *verb* (stinks, stinking, stank or stunk, stunk)
have an unpleasant smell.
[from Old English]

stint *noun* (*plural* stints)
1 a fixed amount of work to be done. 2 limitation of a supply or effort, *They gave help without stint.*

stint *verb* (stints, stinting, stinted)
limit; be niggardly, *Don't stint them of food.* [from Old English]

stipend (*say* sty-pend) *noun* (*plural* stipends)
a salary, especially one paid to a clergyman. [from Latin *stips* = wages + *pendere* = to pay]

stipple *verb* (stipples, stippling, stippled)
paint, draw, or engrave in small dots.
[from Dutch]

stipulate *verb* (stipulates, stipulating, stipulated)
insist on something as part of an agreement. **stipulation** *noun* [from Latin]

stir *verb* (stirs, stirring, stirred)
1 mix a liquid or soft mixture by moving a spoon etc. round and round in it. 2 move slightly; start to move. 3 excite or stimulate, *They stirred up trouble.*

stir *noun*
1 the action of stirring. 2 a disturbance; excitement, *The news caused a stir.*
[from Old English]

stir-fry *verb* (stir-fries, stir-frying, stir-fried)
to cook by frying quickly over a high heat while stirring and tossing.

stirrup *noun* (*plural* stirrups)
a metal part that hangs from each side of a horse's saddle, for a rider to put his or her foot in. [from Old English]

stitch *noun* (*plural* stitches)
1 a loop of thread made in sewing or knitting. 2 a method of arranging the threads, *cross stitch.* 3 a sudden sharp pain in the side of the body, caused by running.

stitch *verb* (stitches, stitching, stitched)
sew or fasten with stitches.
[from Old English]

stoat *noun* (*plural* stoats)
a kind of weasel also called an ermine.
[origin unknown]

stock *noun* (*plural* stocks)
1 a number of things kept ready to be sold or used. 2 livestock. 3 a line of ancestors, *a man of Irish stock.* 4 liquid made by stewing meat, fish, or vegetables, used for making soup etc. 5 a garden flower with a sweet smell. 6 shares in a business company's capital (see *share* 2). 7 the main stem of a tree or plant. 8 the base, holder, or handle of an implement etc. 9 a kind of cravat.

stock *verb* (stocks, stocking, stocked)
1 keep goods in stock. 2 provide a place with a stock of something.
[from Old English]

stockade noun (plural stockades)
a fence made of stakes. [from Spanish]

stockbroker noun (plural stockbrokers)
a broker who deals in stocks and shares.

stock car noun (plural stock cars)
an ordinary car strengthened for use in
races where deliberate bumping is allowed.

stock exchange noun (plural stock
exchanges)
a place where stocks and shares are bought
and sold.

stocking noun (plural stockings)
a garment covering the foot and part or all
of the leg. [from stock]

stockist noun (plural stockists)
a shopkeeper who stocks a certain kind of
goods.

stock market noun (plural stock markets)
1 a stock exchange. 2 the buying and
selling of stocks and shares.

stockpile noun (plural stockpiles)
a large stock of things kept in reserve.
stockpile verb

stocks plural noun
a wooden framework with holes for a
seated person's legs, used like the pillory.
[from stock]

stock-still adjective
quite still.

stocktaking noun
the counting, listing, and checking of a
shop's stock or a company's goods and
resources.

stocky adjective (stockier, stockiest)
short and solidly built, a stocky man.
[from stock]

stodge noun
stodgy food.
[probably from stuff and podgy]

stodgy adjective (stodgier, stodgiest)
1 (of food) heavy and filling. 2 dull and
boring, a stodgy book. **stodginess** noun

stoical (say stoh-ik-al) adjective
bearing pain or difficulties etc. calmly
without complaining. **stoically** adverb,
stoicism noun [named after ancient Greek
philosophers called Stoics]

stoke verb (stokes, stoking, stoked)
put fuel in a furnace or on a fire. **stoker**
noun [from Dutch]

stole[1] noun (plural stoles)
a wide piece of material worn round the
shoulders by women. [from Old English]

stole[2] past tense of steal.

stolid adjective
not excitable; not feeling or showing
emotion. **stolidly** adverb, **stolidity** noun
[from Latin]

stomach noun (plural stomachs)
1 the part of the body where food starts to
be digested. 2 the abdomen.
stomach verb (stomachs, stomaching,
stomached)
endure or tolerate. [from Greek]

stone noun (plural stones)
1 a piece of rock. 2 stones or rock as
material, e.g. for building. 3 a jewel. 4 the
hard case round the kernel of plums,
cherries, etc. 5 a unit of weight equal to
14 pounds, She weighs 6 stone.
stone verb (stones, stoning, stoned)
1 throw stones at somebody. 2 remove the
stones from fruit. [from Old English]

stone- prefix
completely, stone-cold.

Stone Age noun
the earliest period of human history, when
tools and weapons were made of stone.

stone circle noun (plural stone circles)
a circle of large stones or boulders, put up
in prehistoric times.

stone-cold adjective
extremely cold; completely without
warmth.

stone-deaf adjective
completely deaf.

stoneware noun
a kind of pottery with a hard shiny surface.

stony *adjective*
1 full of stones. 2 like stone; hard. 3 not answering, *a stony silence.*

stooge *noun* (*plural* stooges) (*informal*)
1 a comedian's assistant, used as a target for jokes. 2 an assistant who does dull or routine work.
[originally American; origin unknown]

stool *noun* (*plural* stools)
1 a movable seat without arms or a back. 2 a footstool. 3 a lump of faeces.
[from Old English]

stoop *verb* (stoops, stooping, stooped)
1 bend your body forwards and down. 2 lower yourself, *He would not stoop to cheating.* stoop *noun* [from Old English]

stop *verb* (stops, stopping, stopped)
1 bring or come to an end; not continue working or moving. 2 stay. 3 prevent or obstruct something. 4 fill a hole, especially in a tooth.

stop *noun* (*plural* stops)
1 stopping; a pause or end. 2 a place where a bus or train etc. regularly stops. 3 a punctuation mark, especially a full stop. 4 a lever or knob that controls pitch in a wind instrument or allows organ pipes to sound. [from Old English]

stopcock *noun* (*plural* stopcocks)
a valve controlling the flow of liquid or gas in a pipe.

stopgap *noun* (*plural* stopgaps)
a temporary substitute.

stoppage *noun* (*plural* stoppages)
1 an interruption in the work of a factory etc. 2 an amount taken off someone's wages. 3 a blockage.

stopper *noun* (*plural* stoppers)
a plug for closing a bottle etc.

stop press *noun*
late news put into a newspaper after printing has started.
[because the printing presses are stopped to allow the late news to be added]

stopwatch *noun* (*plural* stopwatches)
a watch that can be started and stopped when you wish, used for timing races etc.

storage *noun*
the storing of things.

storage heater *noun* (*plural* storage heaters)
an electric heater that gives out heat that it has stored.

store *noun* (*plural* stores)
1 a stock of things kept for future use; place where these are kept. 2 a shop, especially a large one.
in store 1 being stored. 2 going to happen, *There's a surprise in store for you.*
set store by something value it greatly.

store *verb* (stores, storing, stored)
keep things until they are needed.
[from old French]

storey *noun* (*plural* storeys)
one whole floor of a building. [from Latin]

USAGE: Do not confuse with *story*.

stork *noun* (*plural* storks)
a large bird with long legs and a long beak. [from Old English]

storm *noun* (*plural* storms)
1 a very strong wind usually with rain, snow, etc. 2 a violent attack or outburst, *a storm of protest.* stormy *adjective*
storm in a teacup a great fuss over something unimportant.

storm *verb* (storms, storming, stormed)
1 move or behave violently or angrily, *He stormed out of the room.* 2 attack or capture by a sudden assault, *They stormed the castle.*
[from Old English]

story *noun* (*plural* stories)
1 an account of a real or imaginary event. 2 the plot of a play or novel etc. 3 (*informal*) a lie, *Don't tell stories!*
[from Latin *historia* = history]

USAGE: Do not confuse with *storey*.

stout *adjective*
1 rather fat. 2 thick and strong. 3 brave and determined, *a stout defender of human rights.* stoutly *adverb*, stoutness *noun*
stout *noun*
a kind of dark beer.
[from old French]

stove¹ *noun* (*plural* **stoves**)
1 a device containing an oven or ovens. **2** a device for heating a room.
[from old German or old Dutch]

stove² *past tense* of **stave**.

stow *verb* (**stows, stowing, stowed**)
pack or store something away.
stowage *noun*
stow away hide on a ship or aircraft so as to travel without paying. **stowaway** *noun*
[from *bestow*]

straddle *verb* (**straddles, straddling, straddled**)
be astride; sit or stand across something, *A long bridge straddles the river.*
[from Old English]

straggle *verb* (**straggles, straggling, straggled**)
1 grow or spread in an untidy way. **2** lag behind; wander on your own. **straggler** *noun*, **straggly** *adjective* [origin unknown]

straight *adjective*
1 going continuously in one direction; not curving or bending. **2** tidy; in proper order. **3** honest and frank, *a straight answer.*
straightness *noun*
straight *adverb*
1 in a straight line or manner. **2** directly; without delay, *Go straight home.*
straight away immediately.
[old past participle of *stretch*]

USAGE: Do not confuse with *strait*.

straight away *adverb*
immediately.

straighten *verb* (**straightens, straightening, straightened**)
make or become straight.

straightforward *adjective*
1 easy, not complicated. **2** honest and frank.

strain¹ *verb* (**strains, straining, strained**)
1 stretch tightly. **2** injure or weaken something by stretching or working it too hard. **3** make a great effort. **4** put something through a sieve or filter to separate liquid from solid matter.

strain *noun* (*plural* **strains**)
1 straining; the force of straining. **2** an injury caused by straining. **3** something that uses up strength, patience, resources, etc. **4** exhaustion. **5** a part of a tune.
[from old French]

strain² *noun* (*plural* **strains**)
1 a breed or variety of animals, plants, etc.; a line of descent. **2** an inherited characteristic, *There's an artistic strain in the family.* [from Old English]

strainer *noun* (*plural* **strainers**)
a device for straining liquids, *a tea-strainer.*

strait *adjective* (*old use*)
narrow or restricted.

strait *noun* (*plural* **straits**)
a narrow stretch of water connecting two seas. [from Latin *strictus* = tightened]

USAGE: Do not confuse with *straight*.

straitened *adjective*
in straitened circumstances short of money. [from *strait*]

straitjacket *noun* (*plural* **straitjackets**)
a strong jacket-like garment put round a violent person to restrain his or her arms.

strait-laced *adjective*
very prim and proper.

straits *plural noun*
1 a strait, *the Straits of Dover.* **2** a difficult condition, *We were in dire straits when we lost our money.*

strand¹ *noun* (*plural* **strands**)
1 each of the threads or wires etc. twisted together to form a rope, yarn, or cable. **2** a single thread. **3** a lock of hair.
[origin unknown]

strand² *noun* (*plural* **strands**)
a shore.

strand *verb* (**strands, stranding, stranded**)
1 run or cause to run onto sand or rocks in shallow water. **2** leave in a difficult or helpless position, *We were stranded when our car broke down.* [from Old English]

strange *adjective*
1 unusual or surprising. 2 not known or seen or experienced before.
strangely *adverb*, **strangeness** *noun*
[from Latin *extraneus* = extraneous]

stranger *noun* (*plural* **strangers**)
1 a person you do not know. 2 a person who is in a place or company that he or she does not know.

strangle *verb* (**strangles, strangling, strangled**)
1 kill by squeezing the throat to prevent breathing. 2 restrict something so that it does not develop. **strangler** *noun*
[from Greek]

strangulate *verb* (**strangulates, strangulating, strangulated**)
squeeze so that nothing can pass through.
strangulation *noun*
[from Latin *strangulare* = strangle]

strap *noun* (*plural* **straps**)
a flat strip of leather or cloth etc. for fastening things or holding them in place.
strap *verb* (**straps, strapping, strapped**)
fasten with a strap or straps; bind.
[via old German or old Dutch from Latin]

strapping *adjective*
tall and healthy-looking, *a strapping lad.*

strata *plural* of **stratum**.

stratagem *noun* (*plural* **stratagems**)
a cunning method of achieving something; a plan or trick. [same origin as *strategy*]

strategic *adjective*
1 to do with strategy. 2 giving an advantage, *a strategic move.*
strategical *adjective*, **strategically** *adverb*

strategist *noun* (*plural* **strategists**)
an expert in strategy.

strategy *noun* (*plural* **strategies**)
1 a plan or policy to achieve something, *our economic strategy.* 2 the planning of a war or campaign. (Compare *tactics*.)
[from Greek *strategos* = a general]

stratified *adjective*
arranged in strata. **stratification** *noun*

stratosphere *noun*
a layer of the atmosphere between about 10 and 60 kilometres above the earth's surface. [from *stratum* + *sphere*]

stratum (*say* strah-tum or stray-tum) *noun*
(*plural* **strata**)
a layer. [Latin, = something spread]

USAGE: The word *strata* is a plural. It is incorrect to say 'a strata' or 'this strata'; correct use is *this stratum* or *these strata*.

straw *noun* (*plural* **straws**)
1 dry cut stalks of corn. 2 a narrow tube for drinking through. [from Old English]

strawberry *noun* (*plural* **strawberries**)
a small red juicy fruit, with its seeds on the outside. [probably because straw is put around the plants to keep slugs away]

stray *verb* (**strays, straying, strayed**)
leave a group or proper place and wander; get lost.
stray *adjective*
that has strayed; wandering around lost, *a stray cat.* **stray** *noun* [from old French]

streak *noun* (*plural* **streaks**)
1 a long thin line or mark. 2 a trace, *a streak of cruelty.* **streaky** *adjective*
streak *verb* (**streaks, streaking, streaked**)
1 mark with streaks. 2 move very quickly. 3 run naked in a public place for fun or to get attention. [from Old English]

streaky bacon *noun*
bacon with alternate strips of lean and fat.
[from *streak*]

stream *noun* (*plural* **streams**)
1 water flowing in a channel; a brook or small river. 2 a flow of liquid or of things or people. 3 a group in which children of similar ability are placed in a school.
stream *verb* (**streams, streaming, streamed**)
1 move in or like a stream. 2 produce a stream of liquid. 3 arrange schoolchildren in streams according to their ability.
[from Old English]

streamer *noun* (*plural* **streamers**)
a long narrow ribbon or strip of paper etc.

streamline verb (streamlines, streamlining, streamlined)
1 give something a smooth shape that helps it to move easily through air or water. 2 organize something so that it works more efficiently.
streamlined adjective

street noun (plural streets)
a road with houses beside it in a city or village.
[via Old English from Latin strata via = paved way]

strength noun (plural strengths)
1 how strong a person or thing is; being strong. 2 an ability or good quality, Patience is your great strength.
[from Old English]

strengthen verb (strengthens, strengthening, strengthened)
make or become stronger.

strenuous adjective
needing or using great effort.
strenuously adverb
[from Latin strenuus = brave, energetic]

stress noun (plural stresses)
1 a force that acts on something, e.g. by pressing, pulling, or twisting it; strain.
2 emphasis, especially the extra force with which you pronounce part of a word or phrase. 3 distress caused by having too many problems or too much to do.

stress verb (stresses, stressing, stressed)
put a stress on something; emphasize.
[from distress]

stretch verb (stretches, stretching, stretched)
1 pull something or be pulled so that it becomes longer or wider or larger. 2 be continuous, The wall stretches right round the estate. 3 push out your arms and legs etc.

stretch noun (plural stretches)
1 the action of stretching. 2 a continuous period of time or area of land or water.
[from Old English]

stretcher noun (plural stretchers)
a framework for carrying a sick or injured person.

strew verb (strews, strewing, strewed, strewn or strewed)
scatter things over a surface.
[from Old English]

striated (say stry-ay-tid) adjective
marked with lines or ridges. **striation** noun
[from Latin stria = a groove or furrow]

stricken adjective
overcome or strongly affected by an illness, grief, fear, etc. [past participle of strike]

strict adjective
1 demanding obedience and good behaviour, a strict teacher. 2 complete or exact, the strict truth. **strictly** adverb, **strictness** noun [same origin as strait]

stricture noun (plural strictures)
1 criticism. 2 constriction. [from Latin]

stride verb (strides, striding, strode, stridden)
walk with long steps.

stride noun (plural strides)
1 a long step when walking or running.
2 progress.
get into your stride settle into a fast and steady pace of working.
take something in your stride manage or deal with something without difficulty.
[from Old English]

strident (say stry-dent) adjective
loud and harsh. **stridently** adverb, **stridency** noun [from Latin]

strife noun
conflict; fighting or quarrelling.
[from old French]

strike verb (strikes, striking, struck)
1 hit. 2 attack suddenly. 3 produce by pressing or stamping something, They are striking some special coins. 4 light a match by rubbing it against a rough surface.
5 sound, The clock struck ten. 6 make an impression on someone's mind, She strikes me as truthful. 7 find gold or oil etc. by digging or drilling. 8 stop work until the people in charge agree to improve wages or conditions etc. 9 go in a certain direction, We struck north through the forest.
strike off or **out** cross out.
strike up begin playing or singing; start a friendship etc.

strike *noun* (*plural* **strikes**)
1 a hit. **2** an attack. **3** a stoppage of work, as a way of making a protest (see sense 8 of the verb). **4** a sudden discovery of gold or oil etc.
on strike (of workers) striking.
[from Old English]

striker *noun* (*plural* **strikers**)
1 a person or thing that strikes something. **2** a worker who is on strike. **3** a football player whose function is to try to score goals.

striking *adjective*
1 that strikes. **2** noticeable.
strikingly *adverb*

string *noun* (*plural* **strings**)
1 cord used to fasten or tie things; a piece of this or similar material. **2** a piece of wire or cord etc. stretched and vibrated to produce sounds in a musical instrument. **3** a line or series of things, *a string of buses*.
string *verb* (**strings, stringing, strung**)
1 fit or fasten with string. **2** thread on a string. **3** remove the tough fibre from beans.
string out 1 spread out in a line. **2** cause something to last a long time.
[from Old English]

stringed *adjective*
(of musical instruments) having strings.

stringent (*say* **strin**-jent) *adjective*
strict, *There are stringent rules.*
stringently *adverb*, **stringency** *noun*
[from Latin *stringere* = to bind]

strings *plural noun*
stringed instruments.

stringy *adjective*
1 like string. **2** containing tough fibres.

strip[1] *verb* (**strips, stripping, stripped**)
1 take a covering or layer off something. **2** undress. **3** deprive a person of something.
strip *noun*
the distinctive clothes worn by a sports team while playing.
[probably from Old English]

strip[2] *noun* (*plural* **strips**)
a long narrow piece or area.
[from old German]

strip cartoon *noun* (*plural* **strip cartoons**)
a comic strip (see *comic*).

stripe *noun* (*plural* **stripes**)
1 a long narrow band of colour. **2** a strip of cloth worn on the sleeve of a uniform to show the wearer's rank. **striped** *adjective*, **stripy** *adjective* [probably from old German and related to *strip*[2]]

strip light *noun* (*plural* **strip lights**)
a fluorescent lamp in the form of a tube.

stripling *noun* (*plural* **striplings**)
a youth. [from *strip*[2] + *-ling*]

stripper *noun* (*plural* **strippers**)
1 something that strips, *paint stripper*. **2** a person who performs striptease.

striptease *noun* (*plural* **stripteases**)
an entertainment in which a person slowly undresses.

strive *verb* (**strives, striving, strove, striven**)
1 try hard to do something. **2** carry on a conflict. [from old French]

strobe *noun* (*plural* **strobes**) (short for **stroboscope**)
a light that flashes on and off continuously.
[from Greek *strobos* = whirling]

stroke[1] *noun* (*plural* **strokes**)
1 a hit. **2** a movement or action. **3** the sound made by a clock striking. **4** a sudden illness that often causes paralysis.
[from *strike*]

stroke[2] *verb* (**strokes, stroking, stroked**)
move your hand gently along something.
stroke *noun* [from Old English]

stroll *verb* (**strolls, strolling, strolled**)
walk in a leisurely way. **stroll** *noun*, **stroller** *noun* [from German]

strong *adjective*
1 having great power, energy, effect, flavour, etc. **2** not easy to break, damage, or defeat. **3** having a certain number of members, *an army 5,000 strong.*
strongly *adverb*
strong *adverb*
strongly, *going strong.* [from Old English]

stronghold *noun* (*plural* strongholds)
1 a fortified place. 2 an area where many people live or think in a particular way, *a Tory stronghold*.

strong point *noun* (*plural* strong points)
a strength; something that you are very good at, *Maths is her strong point*.

strongroom *noun* (*plural* strongrooms)
a room designed to protect valuable things from fire and theft.

strontium *noun*
a soft silvery metal.
[named after Strontia in the Scottish highlands, where it was discovered]

strove *past tense* of **strive**.

structure *noun* (*plural* structures)
1 something that has been constructed or built. 2 the way something is constructed or organized.
structural *adjective*, **structurally** *adverb*
[from Latin *struere* = build]

struggle *verb* (struggles, struggling, struggled)
1 move your arms, legs, etc. in trying to get free. 2 make strong efforts to do something. 3 try to overcome an opponent or a problem etc.
struggle *noun* (*plural* struggles)
the action of struggling; a hard fight or great effort. [origin unknown]

strum *verb* (strums, strumming, strummed)
1 sound a guitar by running your fingers across its strings. 2 play badly or casually on a musical instrument.
[imitating the sound]

strut *verb* (struts, strutting, strutted)
walk proudly or stiffly.
strut *noun* (*plural* struts)
1 a bar of wood or metal strengthening a framework. 2 a strutting walk.
[probably from old German]

strychnine (*say* strik-neen) *noun*
a bitter poisonous substance. [from Greek]

stub *noun* (*plural* stubs)
1 a short stump left when the rest has been used or worn down. 2 a counterfoil.

stub *verb* (stubs, stubbing, stubbed)
bump your toe painfully.
stub out put out a cigarette by pressing it against something hard.
[from Old English]

stubble *noun*
1 the short stalks of corn left in the ground after the harvest is cut. 2 short hairs growing after shaving. [from old French]

stubborn *adjective*
obstinate. **stubbornly** *adverb*, **stubbornness** *noun* [origin unknown]

stubby *adjective*
short and thick.

stucco *noun*
plaster or cement used for coating walls and ceilings, often moulded into decorations. **stuccoed** *adjective*
[Italian]

stuck-up *adjective* (*informal*)
conceited or snobbish.

stud¹ *noun* (*plural* studs)
1 a small curved lump or knob. 2 a device like a button on a stalk, used to fasten a detachable collar to a shirt.
stud *verb* (studs, studding, studded)
set or decorate with studs etc., *The necklace was studded with jewels*.
[from Old English *studu*]

stud² *noun* (*plural* studs)
1 a number of horses kept for breeding; the place where they are kept. 2 a stallion.
[from Old English *stod*]

student *noun* (*plural* students)
a person who studies a subject, especially at a college or university.
[from Latin *studere* = to study]

studio *noun* (*plural* studios)
1 the room where a painter or photographer etc. works. 2 a place where cinema films are made. 3 a room from which radio or television broadcasts are made or recorded. [Italian; related to *study*]

studious *adjective*
1 keen on studying. 2 deliberate, *with studious politeness*.
studiously *adverb*, **studiousness** *noun*

study *verb* (studies, studying, studied)
1 spend time learning about something.
2 look at something carefully.
study *noun* (*plural* studies)
1 the process of studying. 2 a subject
studied; a piece of research. 3 a room
where someone studies. 4 a piece of music
for playing as an exercise.
[from Latin *studium* = zeal]

stuff *noun*
1 a substance or material. 2 things, *Leave
your stuff outside.* 3 valueless matter, *stuff
and nonsense!*
stuff *verb* (stuffs, stuffing, stuffed)
1 fill tightly. 2 fill with stuffing. 3 push a
thing into something, *He stuffed the
notebook into his pocket.* 4 (*informal*) eat
greedily. [from old French]

stuffing *noun*
1 material used to fill the inside of
something; padding. 2 a savoury mixture
put into meat or poultry etc. before
cooking.

stuffy *adjective* (stuffier, stuffiest)
1 badly ventilated; without fresh air.
2 with blocked breathing passages, *a stuffy
nose.* 3 formal and boring. **stuffily** *adverb*,
stuffiness *noun*

stultify *verb* (stultifies, stultifying, stultified)
prevent from being effective, *Their
stubbornness stultified the discussions.*
stultification *noun*
[from Latin *stultus* = foolish]

stumble *verb* (stumbles, stumbling,
stumbled)
1 trip and lose your balance. 2 speak or do
something hesitantly or uncertainly.
stumble *noun*
stumble across or **on** find accidentally.
[from Old Norse]

stumbling block *noun* (*plural* stumbling
blocks)
an obstacle; something that causes
difficulty.

stump *noun* (*plural* stumps)
1 the bottom of a tree trunk left in the
ground when the rest has fallen or been cut
down. 2 something left when the main part
is cut off or worn down. 3 each of the three
upright sticks of a wicket in cricket.

stump *verb* (stumps, stumping, stumped)
1 walk stiffly or noisily. 2 put a batsman
out by knocking the bails off the stumps
while he or she is out of the crease. 3 (of a
question or problem) be too difficult for
somebody.
stump up (*informal*) produce the money to
pay for something.
[from old German or old Dutch]

stumpy *adjective*
short and thick. **stumpiness** *noun*

stun *verb* (stuns, stunning, stunned)
1 knock a person unconscious. 2 daze or
shock, *She was stunned by the news.*
[from old French]

stunt[1] *verb*
prevent a thing from growing or
developing normally, *a stunted tree.*
[probably from Old English]

stunt[2] *noun* (*plural* stunts)
something unusual or difficult done as a
performance or to attract attention.
[originally American: origin unknown]

stupefy *verb* (stupefies, stupefying,
stupefied)
make a person dazed. **stupefaction** *noun*
[from Latin *stupere* = be amazed]

stupendous *adjective*
amazing or tremendous. **stupendously**
adverb [same origin as *stupefy*]

stupid *adjective*
1 not clever or thoughtful. 2 without
reason or common sense.
stupidly *adverb*, **stupidity** *noun*
[from Latin *stupidus* = dazed]

stupor (*say* stew-per) *noun* (*plural* stupors)
a dazed condition. [same origin as *stupefy*]

sturdy *adjective* (sturdier, sturdiest)
strong and vigorous or solid. **sturdily**
adverb, **sturdiness** *noun* [from old French]

sturgeon *noun* (*plural* sturgeon)
a large edible fish.
[via old French from Germanic]

stutter *verb* (stutters, stuttering, stuttered)
stammer. **stutter** *noun*
[imitating the sound]

sty¹ *noun* (*plural* **sties**)
a pigsty. [from Old English *sti*]

sty² or **stye** *noun* (*plural* **sties** or **styes**)
a sore swelling on an eyelid. [from Old English *stigend* = rising, swelling]

style *noun* (*plural* **styles**)
1 the way something is done, made, said, or written etc. **2** elegance. **3** the part of a pistil that supports the stigma in a plant. **stylistic** *adjective*

style *verb* (**styles, styling, styled**)
design or arrange something, especially in a fashionable style. **stylist** *noun*
[from old French; related to *stylus*]

stylish *adjective*
in a fashionable style.

stylus *noun* (*plural* **styluses** or **styli**)
the device like a needle that travels in the grooves of a record to produce the sound.
[from Latin *stilus* = pointed writing instrument]

suave (*say* swahv) *adjective*
smoothly polite. **suavely** *adverb*, **suavity** *noun* [from Latin *suavis* = sweet, pleasant]

sub *noun* (*plural* **subs**) (*informal*)
1 a submarine. **2** a subscription. **3** a substitute.

sub- *prefix* (often changing to **suc-, suf-, sum-, sup-, sur-, sus-** before certain consonants)
1 under (as in *submarine*). **2** subordinate, secondary (as in *subsection*).
[from Latin *sub* = under]

subaltern *noun* (*plural* **subalterns**)
an army officer ranking below a captain.
[from Latin *subalternus* = inferior, lower in rank]

subaqua *adjective*
to do with underwater sports, such as diving. [from *sub-* + Latin *aqua* = water]

subatomic *adjective*
1 smaller than an atom. **2** forming part of an atom.

subconscious *adjective*
to do with our own mental activities of which we are not fully aware.
subconscious *noun*

subcontinent *noun* (*plural* **subcontinents**)
a large mass of land not large enough to be called a continent, *the Indian subcontinent*.

subcontractor *noun* (*plural* **subcontractors**)
a person or company hired by another company to do a particular part of their work. **subcontract** *verb*

subdivide *verb* (**subdivides, subdividing, subdivided**)
divide again or into smaller parts. **subdivision** *noun*

subdue *verb* (**subdues, subduing, subdued**)
1 overcome; bring under control. **2** make quieter or gentler. [from old French]

subject *noun* (*plural* **subjects**)
1 the person or thing being talked about or written about etc. **2** something that is studied. **3** (in grammar) the word or words naming who or what does the action of a verb, e.g. '*the book*' in *the book fell off the table*. **4** someone who is ruled by a particular king, government, etc.

subject *adjective*
ruled by a king or government etc.; not independent.
subject to 1 having to obey. **2** liable to, *Trains are subject to delays during fog.* **3** depending upon, *Our decision is subject to your approval.*

subject (*say* sub-jekt) *verb* (**subjects, subjecting, subjected**)
1 make a person or thing undergo something, *They subjected him to torture.* **2** bring a country under your control.
subjection *noun*
[from *sub-* + Latin *-jectum* = thrown]

subjective *adjective*
1 existing in a person's mind and not produced by things outside it. **2** depending on a person's own taste or opinions etc. (Compare *objective*.)

sub judice (*say* joo-dis-ee) *adjective*
being decided by a judge or lawcourt.
[Latin, = under a judge]

subjugate *verb* (**subjugates, subjugating, subjugated**)
bring under your control; conquer.
subjugation *noun*
[from *sub-* + Latin *jugum* = a yoke]

subjunctive *noun* (*plural* subjunctives)
the form of a verb used to indicate what is
imagined or wished or possible. There are
only a few cases where it is commonly used
in English, e.g. *'were'* in *if I were you* and
'save' in *God save the Queen.*
[from *sub-* + Latin *junctum* = joined]

sublet *verb* (sublets, subletting, sublet)
let to another person a house etc. that is let
to you by a landlord.

sublime *adjective*
1 noble or impressive. **2** extreme; not
caring about the consequences, *with
sublime carelessness.* [from Latin]

submarine *adjective*
under the sea, *We laid a submarine cable.*
submarine *noun* (*plural* submarines)
a ship that can travel under water.

submerge *verb* (submerges, submerging,
submerged)
go under or put under water or other
liquid. **submergence** *noun*, **submersion**
noun [from *sub-* + Latin *mergere* = dip]

submissive *adjective*
willing to obey. [from *submission*]

submit *verb* (submits, submitting,
submitted)
1 let someone have authority over you;
surrender. **2** put forward for
consideration, testing, etc., *Submit your
plans to the committee.* **submission** *noun*
[from *sub-* + Latin *mittere* = send]

subnormal *adjective*
below normal.

subordinate *adjective*
1 less important. **2** lower in rank.
subordinate *noun* (*plural* subordinates)
a person working under someone's
authority or control.
subordinate *verb* (subordinates,
subordinating, subordinated)
treat as being less important than another
person or thing. **subordination** *noun*
[from *sub-* + Latin *ordinare* = arrange]

subordinate clause *noun* (*plural*
subordinate clauses)
a clause which adds details to the main
clause of the sentence, but cannot be used
as a sentence by itself.

suborn *verb* (suborns, suborning, suborned)
bribe or incite someone secretly.
[from *sub-* + Latin *ornare* = equip]

sub-plot *noun* (*plural* sub-plots)
a secondary plot in a play etc.

subpoena (*say* sub-peen-a) *noun* (*plural*
subpoenas)
an official document ordering a person to
appear in a lawcourt.
subpoena *verb* (subpoenas, subpoenaing,
subpoenaed)
summon by a subpoena. [from Latin *sub
poena* = under a penalty (because there is a
punishment for not obeying)]

sub-post office *noun* (*plural* sub-post
offices)
a small local post office, often in a shop,
which offers fewer services than a main
post office.

subscribe *verb* (subscribes, subscribing,
subscribed)
1 contribute money to a project or charity
etc. **2** pay regularly so as to be a member of
a society, get a periodical, have the use of a
telephone, etc. **3** sign, *subscribe your name.*
4 say that you agree, *We cannot subscribe to
this theory.* **subscriber** *noun*, **subscription**
noun [from *sub-* + Latin *scribere* = write]

subsequent *adjective*
coming after in time or order; later.
subsequently *adverb*
[from *sub-* + Latin *sequens* = following]

subservient *adjective*
under someone's power; submissive.
subservience *noun*
[from *sub-* + Latin *serviens* = serving]

subset *noun* (*plural* subsets)
a group or set forming part of a larger
group or set.

subside *verb* (subsides, subsiding, subsided)
1 sink. **2** become less intense, *Her fear
subsided.* **subsidence** *noun*
[from *sub-* + Latin *sidere* = settle]

subsidiary *adjective*
1 less important; secondary. **2** (of a
business) controlled by another, *a
subsidiary company.*
[same origin as *subsidy*]

subsidize *verb* (subsidizes, subsidizing, subsidized)
pay a subsidy to a person or firm etc.

subsidy *noun* (*plural* subsidies)
money paid to an industry etc. that needs help, or to keep down the price at which its goods etc. are sold to the public.
[from Latin *subsidium* = assistance]

subsist *verb* (subsists, subsisting, subsisted)
exist; keep yourself alive, *We subsisted on nuts*. subsistence *noun*
[from Latin *subsistere* = stand firm]

subsoil *noun*
soil lying just below the surface layer.

subsonic *adjective*
not as fast as the speed of sound. (Compare *supersonic*.)

substance *noun* (*plural* substances)
1 matter of a particular kind. 2 the main or essential part of something, *We agree with the substance of your report but not with its details*. [from Latin *substantia* = essence]

sub-standard *adjective*
not up to the normal or required standard; inferior or unsatisfactory.

substantial *adjective*
1 of great size, value, or importance, *a substantial fee*. 2 solidly built, *substantial houses*. 3 actually existing. substantially *adverb* [same origin as *substance*]

substantiate *verb* (substantiates, substantiating, substantiated)
produce evidence to prove something. substantiation *noun*
[same origin as *substance*]

substation *noun* (*plural* substations)
a subsidiary station for distributing electric current.

substitute *noun* (*plural* substitutes)
a person or thing that acts or is used instead of another.
substitute *verb* (substitutes, substituting, substituted)
put or use a person or thing as a substitute. substitution *noun*
[from *sub-* + Latin *statuere* = to set up]

subterfuge *noun* (*plural* subterfuges)
a deception.
[from Latin *subterfugere* = escape secretly]

subterranean *adjective*
underground.
[from *sub-* + Latin *terra* = ground]

subtitle *noun* (*plural* subtitles)
1 a secondary or additional title. 2 words shown on the screen during a film, e.g. to translate a foreign language.

subtle (*say* sut-el) *adjective*
1 slight and delicate, *a subtle perfume*. 2 ingenious; not immediately obvious, *a subtle joke*. subtly *adverb*, subtlety *noun*
[from Latin]

subtotal *noun* (*plural* subtotals)
the total of part of a group of figures.

subtract *verb* (subtracts, subtracting, subtracted)
deduct; take away a part, quantity, or number from a greater one. subtraction *noun* [from *sub-* + Latin *tractum* = pulled]

subtropical *adjective*
of regions that border on the tropics.

suburb *noun* (*plural* suburbs)
a district with houses that is outside the central part of a city. suburban *adjective*
[from *sub-* + Latin *urbs* = city]

suburbia *noun*
1 suburbs. 2 the way people in the suburbs live and think.

subvert *verb* (subverts, subverting, subverted)
1 get someone to be disloyal to their government, religion, standards of behaviour, etc. 2 overthrow a government etc. in this way. subversion *noun*, subversive *adjective*
[from *sub-* + Latin *vertere* = to turn]

subway *noun* (*plural* subways)
an underground passage.

suc- *prefix*
1 under. 2 subordinate, secondary. see **sub-**.

succeed *verb* (succeeds, succeeding, succeeded)
1 be successful. 2 come after another

person or thing; become the next king or
queen, *She succeeded to the throne; Edward
VII succeeded Queen Victoria.*
[from *suc-* + Latin *cedere* = go]

success *noun* (*plural* **successes**)
1 doing or getting what you wanted or
intended. 2 a person or thing that does
well, *The show was a great success.*
[same origin as *succeed*]

successful *adjective*
having success; being a success.
successfully *adverb*

succession *noun* (*plural* **successions**)
1 a series of people or things. 2 the process
of following in order. 3 succeeding to the
throne; the right of doing this.
[same origin as *succeed*]

successive *adjective*
following one after another, *on five
successive days.* **successively** *adverb*

successor *noun* (*plural* **successors**)
a person or thing that succeeds another.

succinct (*say* suk-**sinkt**) *adjective*
concise; expressed briefly. **succinctly** *adverb*
[originally = encircled: from *suc-* + Latin
cingere = gird]

succour (*say* suk-er) *noun & verb* (**succours**,
succouring, **succoured**)
help. [from old French]

succulent *adjective*
juicy. [from Latin *succus* = juice]

succumb (*say* suk-**um**) *verb* (**succumbs**,
succumbing, **succumbed**)
give way to something overpowering.
[from *suc-* + Latin *cumbere* = to lie]

such *adjective*
1 of the same kind; similar, *Cakes, biscuits,
and all such foods are fattening.* 2 of the
kind described, *There's no such person.* 3 so
great or intense, *It gave me such a fright!*
[from Old English]

such-and-such *adjective*
particular but not now named, *He promises
to come at such-and-such a time but is
always late.*

suchlike *adjective*
of that kind.

suck *verb* (**sucks**, **sucking**, **sucked**)
1 take in liquid or air through almost-
closed lips. 2 squeeze something in your
mouth by using your tongue, *sucking a
toffee.* 3 draw in, *The canoe was sucked into
the whirlpool.* **suck** *noun*
suck up to (*informal*) flatter someone in the
hope of winning their favour.
[from Old English]

sucker *noun* (*plural* **suckers**)
1 a thing that sucks something.
2 something that can stick to a surface by
suction. 3 a shoot coming up from a root or
underground stem. 4 (*informal*) a person
who is easily deceived.

suckle *verb* (**suckles**, **suckling**, **suckled**)
feed on milk at the mother's breast or
udder.

suction *noun*
1 sucking. 2 producing a vacuum so that
things are sucked into the empty space,
Vacuum cleaners work by suction.
[from Latin]

sudden *adjective*
happening or done quickly or without
warning. **suddenly** *adverb*, **suddenness** *noun*
[from old French]

suds *plural noun*
froth on soapy water.
[probably from old German or old Dutch]

sue *verb* (**sues**, **suing**, **sued**)
start a lawsuit to claim money from
somebody. [from old French]

suede (*say* swayd) *noun*
leather with one side rubbed to make it
velvety. [from French *gants de Suède*
= gloves from Sweden]

suet *noun*
hard fat from cattle and sheep, used in
cooking.
[from old French; related to *sebum*]

suf- *prefix*
1 under. 2 subordinate, secondary. see **sub-**.

suffer *verb* (**suffers**, **suffering**, **suffered**)
1 feel pain or sadness. 2 experience

something bad, *suffer damage*. **3** (*old use*) allow or tolerate. **sufferer** *noun*, **suffering** *noun* [from *suf-* + Latin *ferre* = to bear]

sufferance *noun*
on sufferance allowed but only reluctantly. [from Latin *sufferentia* = suffering]

suffice *verb* (**suffices, sufficing, sufficed**)
be enough for someone's needs. [from *suf-* + Latin *facere* = make or do]

sufficient *adjective*
enough. **sufficiently** *adverb*, **sufficiency** *noun* [same origin as *suffice*]

suffix *noun* (*plural* **suffixes**)
a letter or set of letters joined to the end of a word to make another word (e.g. in forget*ful*, lion*ess*, rust*y*) or a form of a verb (e.g. sing*ing*, wait*ed*). [from *suf-* + Latin *figere* = fix]

suffocate *verb* (**suffocates, suffocating, suffocated**)
1 make it difficult or impossible for someone to breathe. **2** suffer or die because breathing is prevented. **suffocation** *noun* [from *suf-* + Latin *fauces* = throat]

suffrage *noun*
the right to vote in political elections. [from Latin]

suffragette *noun* (*plural* **suffragettes**)
a woman who campaigned in the early 20th century for women to have the right to vote.

suffuse *verb* (**suffuses, suffusing, suffused**)
spread through or over something, *A blush suffused her cheeks*. [from *suf-* + Latin *fusum* = poured]

sugar *noun*
a sweet food obtained from the juices of various plants (e.g. sugar cane, sugar beet). **sugar** *verb*, **sugary** *adjective* [via old French, Italian, Latin, Arabic, and Persian from Sanskrit]

suggest *verb* (**suggests, suggesting, suggested**)
1 give somebody an idea that you think is useful. **2** cause an idea or possibility to come into the mind. **suggestion** *noun*, **suggestive** *adjective* [from Latin]

suggestible *adjective*
easily influenced by people's suggestions.

suicide *noun* (*plural* **suicides**)
1 killing yourself deliberately, *commit suicide*. **2** a person who deliberately kills himself or herself. **suicidal** *adjective* [from Latin *sui* = of yourself, + *-cide*]

suit *noun* (*plural* **suits**)
1 a matching jacket and trousers, or a jacket and skirt, that are meant to be worn together. **2** clothing for a particular activity, *a diving suit*. **3** any of the four sets of cards (clubs, hearts, diamonds, spades) in a pack of playing cards. **4** a lawsuit.

USAGE: Do not confuse with *suite*.

suit *verb* (**suits, suiting, suited**)
1 be suitable or convenient for a person or thing. **2** make a person look attractive. [from Latin *sequi* = to go together or follow]

suitable *adjective*
satisfactory or right for a particular person, purpose, or occasion etc. **suitably** *adverb*, **suitability** *noun*

suitcase *noun* (*plural* **suitcases**)
a rectangular container for carrying clothes, usually with a hinged lid and a handle.

suite (*say as* sweet) *noun* (*plural* **suites**)
1 a set of furniture. **2** a set of rooms. **3** a set of attendants. **4** a set of short pieces of music. [French; related to *suit*]

USAGE: Do not confuse with *suit*.

suitor *noun* (*plural* **suitors**)
a man who is courting a woman. [from Latin *secutor* = follower]

sulk *verb* (**sulks, sulking, sulked**)
be silent and bad-tempered because you are not pleased. **sulks** *plural noun*, **sulky** *adjective*, **sulkily** *adverb*, **sulkiness** *noun* [origin unknown]

sullen *adjective*
sulking and gloomy. **sullenly** *adverb*, **sullenness** *noun* [from old French; related to *sole*²]

sully *verb* (**sullies, sullying, sullied**)
soil or stain something; blemish,

The scandal sullied his reputation.
[same origin as *soil*²]

sulphur *noun*
a yellow chemical used in industry and in medicine. **sulphurous** *adjective* [from Latin]

sulphuric acid *noun*
a strong colourless acid containing sulphur.

sultan *noun* (*plural* **sultans**)
the ruler of certain Muslim countries.
[Arabic, = ruler]

sultana *noun* (*plural* **sultanas**)
a raisin without seeds.
[Italian, literally = sultan's wife]

sultry *adjective*
1 hot and humid, *sultry weather.*
2 suggesting passion or sexual desire, *her sultry smile.* **sultriness** *noun*
[origin unknown]

sum *noun* (*plural* **sums**)
1 a total. 2 a problem in arithmetic. 3 an amount of money.
sum *verb* (**sums, summing, summed**)
sum up 1 summarize, especially at the end of a talk etc. 2 form an opinion of a person, *sum him up.*
[from Latin *summa* = main thing]

sum- *prefix*
1 under. 2 subordinate, secondary. see **sub-**.

summarize *verb* (**summarizes, summarizing, summarized**)
make or give a summary of something.

summary *noun* (*plural* **summaries**)
a statement of the main points of something said or written.
summary *adjective*
1 brief. 2 done or given hastily, without delay, *summary punishment.* **summarily** *adverb* [same origin as *sum*]

summer *noun* (*plural* **summers**)
the warm season between spring and autumn. **summery** *adjective*
[from Old English]

summer house *noun* (*plural* **summer houses**)
a small building providing shade in a garden or park.

summit *noun* (*plural* **summits**)
1 the top of a mountain or hill. 2 a meeting between the leaders of powerful countries, *a summit conference.*
[from Latin *summus* = highest]

summon *verb* (**summons, summoning, summoned**)
1 order someone to come or appear.
2 request firmly, *He summoned the rebels to surrender.*
summon up gather or prepare, *Can you summon up the energy to get out of bed?*
[from *sum-* + Latin *monere* = warn]

summons *noun* (*plural* **summonses**)
a command to appear in a lawcourt.

sump *noun* (*plural* **sumps**)
a metal case that holds oil round an engine.
[from old German or old Dutch]

sumptuous *adjective*
splendid and expensive-looking.
sumptuously *adverb*
[from Latin *sumptus* = cost, expense]

sun *noun* (*plural* **suns**)
1 the star round which the earth travels.
2 light and warmth from the sun, *Go and sit in the sun.* 3 any star in the universe round which planets travel.
sun *verb* (**suns, sunning, sunned**)
warm something in the sun, *sunning ourselves on the beach.* [from Old English]

sunbathe *verb* (**sunbathes, sunbathing, sunbathed**)
expose your body to the sun, especially to get a tan.

sunbeam *noun* (*plural* **sunbeams**)
a ray of sun.

sunbed *noun* (*plural* **sunbeds**)
a bench that you lie on under a sunlamp.

sunblock *noun*
sunscreen.

sunburn *noun*
redness of the skin caused by the sun.
sunburnt *adjective*

sundae (*say* sun-day) *noun* (*plural* **sundaes**)
a mixture of ice cream and fruit, nuts,

cream, etc. [from *Sunday* (because sundaes were originally sold then, possibly to use up ice cream not sold during the week)]

sunder *verb* (sunders, sundering, sundered) (*poetical*)
break apart; cut off. [from Old English]

sundial *noun* (*plural* sundials)
a device that shows the time by a shadow on a dial.

sundown *noun*
sunset.

sundries *plural noun*
various small things. [from *sundry*]

sundry *adjective*
various or several.
all and sundry everyone.
[from Old English]

sunflower *noun* (*plural* sunflowers)
a very tall flower with golden petals round a dark centre. [so called because the flower head turns to follow the sun]

sunglasses *plural noun*
dark glasses to protect your eyes from strong sunlight.

sunken *adjective*
sunk deeply into a surface, *Their cheeks were pale and sunken.*

sunlamp *noun* (*plural* sunlamps)
a lamp which uses ultraviolet light to give people an artificial tan.

sunlight *noun*
light from the sun. **sunlit** *adjective*

Sunni *noun* (*plural* Sunnis)
a member of one of the two main branches of Islam; about 80% of Muslims are Sunnis. [from Arabic *sunna* = law or custom]

sunny *adjective* (sunnier, sunniest)
1 full of sunshine. 2 cheerful, *She was in a sunny mood.* **sunnily** *adverb*

sunrise *noun* (*plural* sunrises)
the rising of the sun; dawn.

sunscreen *noun*
an oil or lotion that you put on your skin to protect it from the sun's harmful rays.

sunset *noun* (*plural* sunsets)
the setting of the sun.

sunshade *noun* (*plural* sunshades)
a parasol or other device to protect people from the sun.

sunshine *noun*
sunlight with no cloud between the sun and the earth.

sunspot *noun* (*plural* sunspots)
1 a dark place on the sun's surface. 2 a sunny place.

sunstroke *noun*
illness caused by being in the sun too long.

sun visor *noun* (*plural* sun visors)
a flap at the top of a vehicle's windscreen that shields your eyes from the sun.

sup *verb* (sups, supping, supped)
drink liquid in sips or spoonfuls.
[from Old English]

sup- *prefix*
1 under. 2 subordinate, secondary. see **sub-**.

super *adjective* (*slang*)
excellent or superb. [from *super-*]

super- *prefix*
1 over or on top (as in *superstructure*). 2 of greater size or quality etc. (as in *supermarket*). 3 extremely (as in *superabundant*). 4 beyond (as in *supernatural*). [from Latin *super* = over]

superannuation *noun*
regular payments made by an employee towards his or her pension.
[from *super-* + Latin *annus* = a year]

superb *adjective*
magnificent or excellent. **superbly** *adverb*
[from Latin *superbus* = proud]

supercilious *adjective*
haughty and scornful. **superciliously** *adverb*
[from Latin *supercilium* = eyebrow]

superficial *adjective*
on the surface; not deep or thorough.
superficially *adverb*, **superficiality** *noun*
[from *super-* + Latin *facies* = face]

superfluous *adjective*
more than is needed. **superfluity** *noun*
[from *super-* + Latin *fluere* = flow]

superglue *noun*
a kind of strong glue that sticks very
quickly.

superhuman *adjective*
1 beyond ordinary human ability,
superhuman strength. 2 higher than
human; divine.

superimpose *verb* (**superimposes,
superimposing, superimposed**)
place a thing on top of something else.
superimposition *noun*

superintend *verb* (**superintends,
superintending, superintended**)
supervise. [from *super-* + Latin *intendere*
= direct, intend]

superintendent *noun* (*plural*
superintendents)
1 a supervisor. 2 a police officer above the
rank of inspector.

superior *adjective*
1 higher in position or rank, *She is your
superior officer.* 2 better than another
person or thing. 3 conceited.
superiority *noun*
superior *noun* (*plural* **superiors**)
a person or thing that is superior to
another. [Latin, = higher]

superlative *adjective*
of the highest degree or quality, *superlative
skill.* **superlatively** *adverb*
superlative *noun* (*plural* **superlatives**)
the form of an adjective or adverb that
expresses 'most', *The superlative of 'great'
is 'greatest'.* (Compare *positive* and
comparative.)
[from Latin *superlatum* = carried above]

superman *noun* (*plural* **supermen**)
a man with superhuman powers.

supermarket *noun* (*plural* **supermarkets**)
a large self-service shop that sells food and
other goods.

supernatural *adjective*
not belonging to the natural world,
supernatural beings such as ghosts.

supersede *verb* (**supersedes, superseding,
superseded**)
take the place of something, *Cars
superseded horse-drawn carriages.*
[from *super-* + Latin *sedere* = sit]

USAGE: This word is often spelt
incorrectly. Note that it ends '-sede' and
not '-cede'.

supersonic *adjective*
faster than the speed of sound. (Compare
subsonic.)

superstition *noun* (*plural* **superstitions**)
a belief or action that is not based on
reason or evidence, e.g. the belief that it is
unlucky to walk under a ladder.
superstitious *adjective*
[from Latin *superstare* = stand over]

superstore *noun* (*plural* **superstores**)
a very large supermarket selling a wide
range of goods.

superstructure *noun* (*plural*
superstructures)
1 a structure that rests on something else.
2 a building as distinct from its
foundations.

supertanker *noun* (*plural* **supertankers**)
a very large tanker.

supervene *verb* (**supervenes, supervening,
supervened**)
happen and interrupt or change
something, *The country was prosperous
until an earthquake supervened.*
[from *super-* + Latin *venire* = come]

supervise *verb* (**supervises, supervising,
supervised**)
be in charge of a person or thing and
inspect what is done. **supervision** *noun,*
supervisor *noun,* **supervisory** *adjective*
[from *super-* + Latin *visum* = seen]

superwoman *noun* (*plural* **superwomen**)
a woman with superhuman powers.

supine (*say* soop-I'n) *adjective*
1 lying face upwards. (The opposite is
prone.) 2 not taking action. [from Latin]

supper *noun* (*plural* **suppers**)
a meal eaten in the evening.
[from old French *soper* = sup]

supplant *verb* (supplants, supplanting, supplanted)
take the place of a person or thing that has been ousted. [from Latin *supplantare* = to trip someone up]

supple *adjective*
bending easily; flexible.
supplely *adverb*, **suppleness** *noun*
[from *sup-* + Latin *plicare* = to fold, bend]

supplement *noun* (*plural* supplements)
1 something added as an extra. 2 an extra section added to a book or newspaper, *the colour supplement*. **supplementary** *adjective*
supplement *verb* (supplements, supplementing, supplemented)
add to something, *She supplements her pocket money by working on Saturdays*. [same origin as *supply*]

suppliant (*say* sup-lee-ant) or **supplicant**
noun (*plural* suppliants, supplicants)
a person who asks humbly for something. [from old French; related to *supplicate*]

supplicate *verb* (supplicates, supplicating, supplicated)
beg humbly; beseech. **supplication** *noun*
[from Latin *supplicare* = kneel]

supply *verb* (supplies, supplying, supplied)
give or sell or provide what is needed or wanted. **supplier** *noun*
supply *noun* (*plural* supplies)
1 an amount of something that is available for use when needed. 2 the action of supplying something.
[from *sup-* + Latin *-plere* = fill]

supply teacher *noun* (*plural* supply teachers)
a teacher who takes the place of a regular teacher when he or she is away.

support *verb* (supports, supporting, supported)
1 keep a person or thing from falling or sinking. 2 give strength, help, or encouragement to someone, *Support your local team*. 3 provide with the necessities of life, *She has two children to support*. **supporter** *noun*, **supportive** *adjective*
support *noun* (*plural* supports)
1 the action of supporting. 2 a person or thing that supports.
[from *sup-* + Latin *portare* = carry]

suppose *verb* (supposes, supposing, supposed)
think that something is likely to happen or be true.
supposedly *adverb*, **supposition** *noun*
be supposed to be expected to do something; have as a duty.
[from old French]

suppress *verb* (suppresses, suppressing, suppressed)
1 put an end to something forcibly or by authority, *Troops suppressed the rebellion*. 2 keep something from being known or seen, *They suppressed the truth*.
suppression *noun*, **suppressor** *noun*
[from *sup-* + Latin *pressus* = pressed]

supreme *adjective*
1 most important or highest in rank. 2 greatest, *supreme courage*.
supremely *adverb*, **supremacy** *noun*
[from Latin *supremus* = highest]

sur-¹ *prefix*
1 under. 2 subordinate, secondary. see **sub-**.

sur-² *prefix*
= super- (as in *surcharge, surface*).
[from old French]

surcharge *noun* (*plural* surcharges)
an extra charge.

sure *adjective*
1 convinced; feeling no doubt. 2 certain to happen or do something, *Our team is sure to win*. 3 reliable; undoubtedly true.
sureness *noun*
for sure definitely.
make sure 1 find out exactly. 2 make something happen or be true, *Make sure the door is locked*.
sure *adverb* (*informal*)
surely.
sure enough certainly; in fact.
[from old French; related to *secure*]

surely *adverb*
1 in a sure way; certainly or securely. 2 it must be true; I feel sure, *Surely we met last year?*

surety *noun* (*plural* sureties)
1 a guarantee. 2 a person who promises to pay a debt or fulfil a contract etc. if another person fails to do so.
[from old French; related to *security*]

surf *noun*
the white foam of waves breaking on a rock or shore. [origin unknown]

surface *noun* (*plural* surfaces)
1 the outside of something. 2 any of the sides of an object, especially the top part. 3 an outward appearance, *On the surface he was a kindly man.*
surface *verb* (surfaces, surfacing, surfaced)
1 put a surface on a road, path, etc. 2 come up to the surface from under water. [French]

surface mail *noun*
letters and parcels etc. carried by sea or over land, not by air.

surfboard *noun* (*plural* surfboards)
a board used in surfing.

surfeit (*say* ser-fit) *noun*
too much of something. **surfeited** *adjective* [from *sur-*² + Latin *facere* = do]

surfing *noun*
balancing yourself on a board that is carried to the shore on the waves. **surfer** *noun*

surf-riding *noun*
surfing. **surf-rider** *noun*

surge *verb* (surges, surging, surged)
move forwards or upwards like waves. **surge** *noun* [from Latin *surgere* = rise]

surgeon *noun* (*plural* surgeons)
a doctor who treats disease or injury by cutting or repairing the affected parts of the body.

surgery *noun* (*plural* surgeries)
1 the place where a doctor or dentist etc. regularly gives advice and treatment to patients. 2 the time when patients can visit the doctor etc. 3 the work of a surgeon. **surgical** *adjective*, **surgically** *adverb* [from Greek *cheirourgia* = handiwork]

surly *adjective* (surlier, surliest)
bad-tempered and unfriendly. **surliness** *noun* [originally = majestic, haughty: from *sir* + *-ly*]

surmise *verb* (surmises, surmising, surmised)
guess or suspect. **surmise** *noun* [from old French *surmettre* = accuse]

surmount *verb* (surmounts, surmounting, surmounted)
1 overcome a difficulty. 2 get over an obstacle. 3 be on top of something, *The church tower is surmounted by a steeple.* [from French]

surname *noun* (*plural* surnames)
the name held by all members of a family. [from French]

surpass *verb* (surpasses, surpassing, surpassed)
do or be better than all others; excel. [from French]

surplus *noun* (*plural* surpluses)
an amount left over after spending or using all that was needed. [from *sur-*² + Latin *plus* = more]

surprise *noun* (*plural* surprises)
1 something unexpected. 2 the feeling caused by something that was not expected.
surprise *verb* (surprises, surprising, surprised)
1 be a surprise to somebody. 2 come upon or attack somebody unexpectedly. **surprisingly** *adverb* [from old French]

surrealism *noun*
a style of painting etc. that shows strange shapes like those seen in dreams and fantasies.
surrealist *noun*, **surrealistic** *adjective* [from *sur-*² + French *réalisme* = realism]

surrender *verb* (surrenders, surrendering, surrendered)
1 give yourself up to an enemy. 2 hand something over to another person, especially when compelled to do so.
surrender *noun* [from *sur-*² + French *rendre* = give, deliver]

surreptitious (*say* su-rep-tish-us) *adjective*
stealthy. **surreptitiously** *adverb* [from Latin *surrepticius* = stolen, taken secretly]

surrogate (*say* su-rog-at) *noun* (*plural* surrogates)
a deputy. [from Latin]

surrogate mother noun (plural
surrogate mothers)
a woman who agrees to conceive and give
birth to a baby for a woman who cannot do
so herself, using a fertilized egg of the other
woman or sperm from the other woman's
partner.

surround verb (surrounds, surrounding,
surrounded)
come or be all round a person or thing;
encircle.
[from sur-² + Latin undare = rise in waves]

surroundings plural noun
the things or conditions round a person or
thing.

surveillance (say ser-vay-lans) noun
a close watch kept on a person or thing,
Police kept him under surveillance.
[from sur-² + French veiller = to watch]

survey (say ser-vay) noun (plural surveys)
1 a general look at something. 2 an
inspection of an area, building, etc.

survey (say ser-vay) verb (surveys,
surveying, surveyed)
make a survey of something; inspect.
surveyor noun
[from sur-² + Latin videre = see]

survival noun (plural survivals)
1 surviving; the likelihood of surviving.
2 something that has survived from an
earlier time; a relic.

survive verb (survives, surviving, survived)
stay alive; go on living or existing after
someone has died or after a disaster.
survivor noun
[from sur-² + Latin vivere = to live]

sus- prefix
1 under. 2 subordinate, secondary. see sub-.

susceptible (say sus-ept-ib-ul) adjective
likely to be affected by something, She is
susceptible to colds. susceptibility noun
[from Latin susceptum = caught up]

suspect (say sus-pekt) verb (suspects,
suspecting, suspected)
1 think that a person is not to be trusted or
has committed a crime; distrust. 2 have a
feeling that something is likely or possible.

suspect (say sus-pekt) noun (plural
suspects)
a person who is suspected of a crime etc.
suspect adjective
[from sus- + Latin specere = to look]

suspend verb (suspends, suspending,
suspended)
1 hang something up. 2 postpone; stop
something temporarily. 3 deprive a person
of a job or position etc. for a time.
[from sus- + Latin pendere = hang]

suspender noun (plural suspenders)
a fastener to hold up a sock or stocking by
its top.

suspense noun
an anxious or uncertain feeling while
waiting for something to happen or become
known. [same origin as suspend]

suspension noun
1 suspending. 2 the springs etc. in a
vehicle that lessen the effect of rough road
surfaces. 3 a liquid containing small pieces
of solid material which do not dissolve.

suspension bridge noun (plural
suspension bridges)
a bridge supported by cables.

suspicion noun (plural suspicions)
1 suspecting or being suspected; distrust.
2 a slight belief. [same origin as suspect]

suspicious adjective
feeling or causing suspicion.
suspiciously adverb

sustain verb (sustains, sustaining, sustained)
1 support. 2 keep someone alive. 3 keep
something happening. 4 undergo; suffer,
We sustained a defeat.
[from sus- + Latin tenere = hold, keep]

sustenance noun
food and drink; nourishment.
[same origin as sustain]

suture (say soo-cher) noun (plural sutures)
surgical stitching of a cut.
[from Latin suere = sew]

suzerainty (say soo-zer-en-tee) noun
1 the partial control of a weaker country
by a stronger one. 2 the power of an
overlord in feudal times. [from old French]

svelte *adjective*
slim and graceful. [via French from Italian]

SW *abbreviation*
1 south-west. 2 south-western.

swab (*say* swob) *noun* (*plural* swabs)
1 a mop or pad for cleaning or wiping something; a small pad for cleaning a wound. 2 a specimen of fluid from the body taken on a swab for testing.
swab *verb* (swabs, swabbing, swabbed)
clean or wipe with a swab. [from Dutch]

swagger *verb* (swaggers, swaggering, swaggered)
walk or behave in a conceited way; strut.
swagger *noun*
[probably from a Scandinavian language]

swain *noun* (*plural* swains) (*old use*)
1 a country lad. 2 a suitor.
[from Old Norse]

swallow¹ *verb* (swallows, swallowing, swallowed)
1 make something go down your throat.
2 believe something that ought not to be believed. **swallow** *noun*
swallow up take in and cover; engulf, *She was swallowed up in the crowd.*
[from Old English *swelgan*]

swallow² *noun* (*plural* swallows)
a small bird with a forked tail and pointed wings. [from Old English *swealwe*]

swamp *noun* (*plural* swamps)
a marsh. **swampy** *adjective*
swamp *verb* (swamps, swamping, swamped)
1 flood. 2 overwhelm with a great mass or number of things. [origin unknown]

swan *noun* (*plural* swans)
a large usually white swimming bird with a long neck. [from Old English]

swank *verb* (swanks, swanking, swanked) (*informal*)
boast or swagger; show off.
swank *noun* (*informal*)
showing yourself or your possessions off in a conceited way. [origin unknown]

swansong *noun* (*plural* swansongs)
a person's last performance or work. [from the old belief that a swan sang sweetly when about to die]

swap *verb* (swaps, swapping, swapped) (*informal*)
exchange. **swap** *noun*
[formerly = seal a bargain by slapping each other's hands; imitating the sound]

swarm¹ *noun* (*plural* swarms)
a large number of insects or birds etc. flying or moving about together.
swarm *verb* (swarms, swarming, swarmed)
1 gather or move in a swarm. 2 be crowded or overrun with insects, people, etc. [from Old English]

swarm² *verb* (swarms, swarming, swarmed)
climb by gripping with the hands or arms and legs. [origin unknown]

swarthy *adjective*
having a dark complexion. **swarthiness** *noun* [from Old English]

swashbuckling *adjective*
1 daring; loving adventure and fighting.
2 (of a film etc.) showing daring adventures set in the past.
[from an old word *swash* = hit, + *buckler*]

swastika *noun* (*plural* swastikas)
an ancient symbol formed by a cross with its ends bent at right angles, adopted by the Nazis as their sign.
[from Sanskrit *svasti* = well-being, luck]

swat *verb* (swats, swatting, swatted)
hit or crush a fly etc. **swatter** *noun*
[originally American, a different spelling of *squat*]

swathe *verb* (swathes, swathing, swathed)
wrap in layers of bandages, paper, or clothes etc. [from Old English]

sway *verb* (sways, swaying, swayed)
1 swing gently; move from side to side.
2 influence, *His speech swayed the crowd.*
sway *noun* [origin unknown]

swear *verb* (swears, swearing, swore, sworn)
1 make a solemn promise, *She swore to tell the truth.* 2 make a person take an oath, *We swore him to secrecy.* 3 use curses or coarse words in anger or surprise etc.

swear by have great confidence in
something.
[from Old English]

swear word noun (plural swear words)
a word considered rude or shocking, often
used by someone who is angry.

sweat (say swet) noun
moisture given off by the body through the
pores of the skin; perspiration.
sweaty adjective
sweat verb (sweats, sweating, sweated)
give off sweat; perspire. [from Old English]

sweater noun (plural sweaters)
a jersey or pullover.

sweatshirt noun (plural sweatshirts)
a thick cotton jersey worn for sports or
casual wear.

swede noun (plural swedes)
a large kind of turnip with purple skin and
yellow flesh. [short for Swedish turnip
(because it originally came from Sweden)]

sweep verb (sweeps, sweeping, swept)
1 clean or clear with a broom or brush etc.
2 move or remove quickly, The floods
swept away the bridge. 3 go smoothly,
quickly, or proudly, She swept out of the
room. **sweeper** noun
sweep noun (plural sweeps)
1 the process of sweeping, Give this room a
good sweep. 2 a chimney sweep. 3 a
sweepstake. [from Old English]

sweeping adjective
general or wide-ranging, He made sweeping
changes.

sweepstake noun (plural sweepstakes)
a kind of lottery used in gambling on the
result of a horse race etc.
[so called because the winner 'sweeps up'
all the other players' stakes]

sweet adjective
1 tasting as if it contains sugar; not bitter.
2 very pleasant, a sweet smell. 3 charming
or delightful.
sweetly adverb, **sweetness** noun
sweet noun (plural sweets)
1 a small shaped piece of sweet food made
with sugar, chocolate, etc. 2 a pudding; the
sweet course in a meal. 3 a beloved person.
[from Old English]

sweetbread noun (plural sweetbreads)
an animal's pancreas used as food.

sweetcorn noun
the juicy yellow seeds of maize.

sweeten verb (sweetens, sweetening,
sweetened)
make or become sweet. **sweetener** noun

sweetheart noun (plural sweethearts)
a person you love very much.

sweetmeat noun (plural sweetmeats) (old
use)
a sweet. [from an old sense of meat = food]

sweet pea noun (plural sweet peas)
a climbing plant with fragrant flowers.

sweet potato noun (plural sweet
potatoes)
a root vegetable with reddish skin and
sweet yellow flesh.

swell verb (swells, swelling, swelled, swollen
or swelled)
make or become larger in size or amount
or force.
swell noun (plural swells)
1 the process of swelling. 2 the rise and fall
of the sea's surface.
swell adjective (American informal)
very good. [from Old English]

swelled head noun (informal)
conceit.

swelling noun (plural swellings)
a swollen place.

swelter verb (swelters, sweltering,
sweltered)
feel uncomfortably hot. [from Old English]

swerve verb (swerves, swerving, swerved)
turn to one side suddenly. **swerve** noun
[from Old English]

swift adjective
quick or rapid.
swiftly adverb, **swiftness** noun
swift noun (plural swifts)
a small bird rather like a swallow.
[from Old English]

swig verb (swigs, swigging, swigged) (informal)
drink quickly, taking large mouthfuls. **swig** noun [origin unknown]

swill verb (swills, swilling, swilled)
pour water over or through something; wash or rinse.
swill noun
1 the process of swilling, Give it a swill. 2 a sloppy mixture of waste food given to pigs. [from Old English]

swim verb (swims, swimming, swam, swum)
1 move the body through the water; be in the water for pleasure. 2 cross by swimming, She swam the Channel. 3 float. 4 be covered with or full of liquid, Our eyes were swimming in tears. 5 feel dizzy, His head swam. **swimmer** noun
swim noun (plural swims)
the action of swimming, We went for a swim. **swimsuit** noun [from Old English]

swimming bath noun (plural swimming baths)
a public swimming pool.

swimming costume noun (plural swimming costumes)
the clothing a woman wears to go swimming; a bikini or swimsuit.

swimming pool noun (plural swimming pools)
an artificial pool for swimming in.

swimming trunks plural noun
shorts which a man wears to go swimming.

swimsuit noun (plural swimsuits)
a one-piece swimming costume.

swindle verb (swindles, swindling, swindled)
cheat a person in business etc.
swindle noun, **swindler** noun
[from German Schwindler = a fool, a cheat]

swine noun (plural swine)
1 a pig. 2 a very unpleasant person. 3 (informal) a difficult thing, This crossword's a real swine!
[from Old English]

swing verb (swings, swinging, swung)
1 move to and fro while hanging; move or turn in a curve, The door swung open. 2 change from one opinion or mood etc. to another.
swing noun (plural swings)
1 a swinging movement. 2 a seat hung on chains or ropes etc. so that it can be moved backwards and forwards. 3 the amount by which votes or opinions etc. change from one side to another. 4 a kind of jazz music.
in full swing full of activity; working fully. [from Old English]

swingeing (say swin-jing) adjective
1 (of a blow) very powerful. 2 huge in amount, a swingeing increase in taxes. [from Old English]

swipe verb (swipes, swiping, swiped)
1 hit hard. 2 (informal) steal something.
swipe noun [a different spelling of sweep]

swirl verb (swirls, swirling, swirled)
move round quickly in circles; whirl. **swirl** noun [probably from old Dutch]

swish verb (swishes, swishing, swished)
move with a hissing sound. **swish** noun
swish adjective (informal)
smart and fashionable. [imitating the sound]

Swiss roll noun (plural Swiss rolls)
a thin sponge cake spread with jam or cream and rolled up.

switch noun (plural switches)
1 a device that is pressed or turned to start or stop something working, especially by electricity. 2 a change of opinion, policy, or methods. 3 mechanism for moving the points on a railway track. 4 a flexible rod or whip.
switch verb (switches, switching, switched)
1 turn something on or off by means of a switch. 2 change or transfer or divert something. [probably from old German]

switchback noun (plural switchbacks)
a railway at a fair, with steep slopes up and down alternately.

switchboard noun (plural switchboards)
a panel with switches etc. for making telephone connections or operating electric circuits.

swivel verb (swivels, swivelling, swivelled)
turn round.

swivel *noun* (*plural* swivels)
a device joining two things so that one can revolve without turning the other.
[from Old English]

swollen *past participle* of swell.

swoon *verb* (swoons, swooning, swooned) (*old use* or *poetical*)
faint. **swoon** *noun* [from Old English]

swoop *verb* (swoops, swooping, swooped)
come down with a rushing movement; make a sudden attack. **swoop** *noun*
[probably from *sweep*]

swop *verb* (swops, swopping, swopped)
swap.

sword (*say* sord) *noun* (*plural* swords)
a weapon with a long pointed blade fixed in a handle or hilt. **swordsman** *noun*
[from Old English]

swot *verb* (swots, swotting, swotted) (*slang*)
study hard. **swot** *noun*
[a dialect word for *sweat*]

sycamore *noun* (*plural* sycamores)
a tall tree with winged seeds, often grown for its timber. [from Greek]

sycophant (*say* sik-o-fant) *noun* (*plural* sycophants)
a person who tries to win people's favour by flattering them. **sycophantic** *adjective*, **sycophantically** *adverb*, **sycophancy** *noun*
[from Greek]

syl- *prefix*
1 with, together. 2 alike. see syn-.

syllable *noun* (*plural* syllables)
a word or part of a word that has one vowel sound when you say it, '*Cat*' *has one syllable,* '*el-e-phant*' *has three syllables*. **syllabic** *adjective*
[from *syl-* + Greek *lambanein* = take]

syllabus *noun* (*plural* syllabuses)
a summary of the things to be studied by a class or for an examination etc.
[from Greek]

sylph *noun* (*plural* sylphs)
a slender girl or woman.
[probably from Latin *sylvestris nympha* = nymph of the woods]

sym- *prefix*
1 with, together. 2 alike. see syn-.

symbol *noun* (*plural* symbols)
1 a thing used as a sign, *The cross is a symbol of Christianity*. 2 a mark or sign with a special meaning (e.g. +, −, and ÷ in mathematics). **symbolic** *adjective*, **symbolical** *adjective*, **symbolically** *adverb*
[from Greek *symbolon* = token]

USAGE: Do not confuse with *cymbal*.

symbolism *noun*
the use of symbols to represent things.

symbolize *verb* (symbolizes, symbolizing, symbolized)
make or be a symbol of something.

symmetrical *adjective*
able to be divided into two halves which are exactly the same but the opposite way round, *Wheels and butterflies are symmetrical*.
symmetrically *adverb*, **symmetry** *noun*
[from *sym-* + Greek *metron* = a measure]

sympathize *verb* (sympathizes, sympathizing, sympathized)
show or feel sympathy. **sympathizer** *noun*

sympathy *noun* (*plural* sympathies)
1 the sharing or understanding of other people's feelings, opinions, etc. 2 a feeling of pity or tenderness towards someone who is hurt, sad, or in trouble. **sympathetic** *adjective*, **sympathetically** *adverb*
[from *sym-* + Greek *pathos* = feeling]

symphony *noun* (*plural* symphonies)
a long piece of music for an orchestra.
symphonic *adjective*
[from *sym-* + Greek *phone* = sound]

symptom *noun* (*plural* symptoms)
a sign that a disease or condition exists, *Red spots are a symptom of measles*.
symptomatic *adjective*
[from Greek *symptoma* = chance, accident]

syn- *prefix* (changing to syl- or sym- before certain consonants)
1 with, together (as in *synchronize*). 2 alike (as in *synonym*). [from Greek]

synagogue (*say* sin-a-gog) *noun* (*plural* synagogues)
a place where Jews meet for worship.
[from Greek *synagoge* = assembly]

synchronize (*say* sink-ron-I'z) *verb*
(synchronizes, synchronizing, synchronized)
1 make things happen at the same time.
2 make watches or clocks show the same time. **3** happen at the same time.
synchronization *noun*
[from *syn-* + Greek *chronos* = time]

syncopate (*say* sink-o-payt) *verb*
(syncopates, syncopating, syncopated)
change the strength of beats in a piece of music. syncopation *noun* [from Latin]

syndicate *noun* (*plural* syndicates)
1 a group of people or firms who work together in business. **2** a group of people who buy something together, or who gamble together, sharing the cost and any gains.
[from *syn-* + Greek *dike* = judgement]

syndrome *noun* (*plural* syndromes)
a set of symptoms. [from *syn-* + Greek *dramein* = to run]

synod (*say* sin-od) *noun* (*plural* synods)
a council of senior members of the clergy.
[from Greek *synodos* = meeting]

synonym (*say* sin-o-nim) *noun* (*plural* synonyms)
a word that means the same or almost the same as another word, *'Large' and 'great' are synonyms of 'big'*.
synonymous (*say* sin-on-im-us) *adjective*
[from *syn-* + Greek *onyma* = name]

synopsis (*say* sin-op-sis) *noun* (*plural* synopses)
a summary.
[from *syn-* + Greek *opsis* = view, seeing]

syntax (*say* sin-taks) *noun*
the way words are arranged to make phrases or sentences.
syntactic *adjective*, syntactically *adverb*
[from *syn-* + Greek *taxis* = arrangement]

synthesis (*say* sin-thi-sis) *noun* (*plural* syntheses)
combining different things to make something. synthesize *verb*
[from *syn-* + Greek *thesis* = placing]

synthesizer *noun* (*plural* synthesizers)
an electronic musical instrument that can make a large variety of sounds.

synthetic *adjective*
artificially made; not natural. synthetically *adverb* [same origin as *synthesis*]

syringe *noun* (*plural* syringes)
a device for sucking in a liquid and squirting it out.
[from Greek *syrinx* = pipe, tube]

syrup *noun*
a thick sweet liquid. syrupy *adjective*
[from Arabic *sharab* = a drink]

system *noun* (*plural* systems)
1 a set of parts, things, or ideas that are organized to work together. **2** a way of doing something, *a new system of training motorcyclists*. [from Greek]

systematic *adjective*
methodical; carefully planned.
systematically *adverb*

Tt

tab *noun* (*plural* tabs)
a small flap or strip that sticks out.
[origin unknown]

tabard *noun* (*plural* tabards)
a kind of tunic decorated with a coat of arms. [from old French]

tabby *noun* (*plural* tabbies)
a grey or brown cat with dark stripes.
[originally = a kind of striped silk material: named after al-Attabiyya, a district of Baghdad where it was made]

tabernacle *noun* (*plural* tabernacles)
(in the Bible) the portable shrine used by the ancient Jews during their wanderings in the desert.
[from Latin *tabernaculum* = tent or shed]

table *noun* (*plural* tables)
1 a piece of furniture with a flat top supported on legs. **2** a list of facts or figures

table 725 tact

arranged in order. **3** a list of the results of multiplying a number by other numbers, *multiplication tables*.

table *verb* (**tables, tabling, tabled**)
put forward a proposal etc. for discussion at a meeting.
[from Latin *tabula* = plank, tablet, or list]

tableau (*say* tab-loh) *noun* (*plural* **tableaux,** *say* tab-lohz)
a dramatic or attractive scene, especially one posed on a stage by a group of people who do not speak or move.
[French; related to *table*]

tablecloth *noun* (*plural* **tablecloths**)
a cloth for covering a table, especially at meals.

table d'hôte (*say* tahbl **doht**) *noun*
a restaurant meal served at a fixed price. (Compare *à la carte*).
[French, = host's table]

tablespoon *noun* (*plural* **tablespoons**)
a large spoon for serving food.
tablespoonful *noun*

tablet *noun* (*plural* **tablets**)
1 a pill. **2** a solid piece of soap. **3** a flat piece of stone or wood etc. with words carved or written on it. [from old French *tablete* = small table or slab]

table tennis *noun*
a game played on a table divided by a net, over which you hit a small ball with bats.

tabloid *noun* (*plural* **tabloids**)
a newspaper with pages that are half the size of larger newspapers. [originally, the trade mark of a kind of pill, later = something in a smaller form than usual]

taboo *adjective*
not to be done or used or talked about.
taboo *noun* [from Tongan *tabu* = sacred]

tabor (*say* tay-ber) *noun* (*plural* **tabors**)
a small drum. [from old French]

tabular *adjective*
arranged in a table or in columns.

tabulate *verb* (**tabulates, tabulating, tabulated**)
arrange information or figures in a table or list. **tabulation** *noun*

tabulator *noun* (*plural* **tabulators**)
a device on a typewriter or computer that automatically sets the positions for columns.

tachograph (*say* tak-o-grahf) *noun* (*plural* **tachographs**)
a device that automatically records the speed and travelling time of a motor vehicle in which it is fitted.
[from Greek *tachos* = speed, + *-graph*]

tacit (*say* tas-it) *adjective*
implied or understood without being put into words; silent, *tacit approval*.
[from Latin *tacitus* = not speaking]

taciturn (*say* tas-i-tern) *adjective*
saying very little. **taciturnity** *noun*
[same origin as *tacit*]

tack¹ *noun* (*plural* **tacks**)
1 a short nail with a flat top. **2** a tacking stitch. **3** (in sailing) the direction taken when tacking.
tack *verb* (**tacks, tacking, tacked**)
1 nail something down with tacks. **2** fasten material together with long stitches. **3** sail a zigzag course to take advantage of what wind there is.
tack on (*informal*) add an extra thing.
[from old French]

tack² *noun*
harness, saddles, etc.
[from *tackle* = equipment]

tackle *verb* (**tackles, tackling, tackled**)
1 try to do something that needs doing.
2 try to get the ball from someone else in a game of football or hockey.
tackle *noun* (*plural* **tackles**)
1 equipment, especially for fishing. **2** a set of ropes and pulleys. **3** tackling someone in football or hockey.
[probably from old German]

tacky¹ *adjective*
sticky, not quite dry, *The paint is still tacky.* **tackiness** *noun*
[from *tack¹* = a fastening]

tacky² *adjective*
(*informal*) showing poor taste or style.
[origin unknown]

tact *noun*
skill in not offending people.

tactful *adjective*, **tactfully** *adverb*, **tactless** *adjective*, **tactlessly** *adverb*
[from Latin *tactus* = sense of touch]

tactics *noun*
1 the method of arranging troops etc. skilfully for a battle. 2 the methods you use to achieve something or gain an advantage.
tactical *adjective*, **tactically** *adverb*, **tactician** *noun*
[from Greek *taktika* = things arranged]

USAGE: *Strategy* is a general plan for a whole campaign, *tactics* is for one part of this.

tactile *adjective*
to do with the sense of touch.
[same origin as *tact*]

tadpole *noun* (*plural* **tadpoles**)
a young frog or toad that has developed from the egg and lives entirely in water.
[from *toad* + *poll* = head]

taffeta *noun*
a stiff silky material.
[from Persian *taftan* = to shine]

tag¹ *noun* (*plural* **tags**)
1 a label tied on or stuck into something. 2 a metal or plastic point at the end of a shoelace.
tag *verb* (**tags, tagging, tagged**)
1 label something with a tag. 2 add as an extra thing, *A postscript was tagged on to her letter.* 3 (*informal*) go with other people, *Her sister tagged along.*
[origin unknown]

tag² *noun*
a game in which one person chases the others. [origin unknown]

tail *noun* (*plural* **tails**)
1 the part that sticks out from the rear end of the body of a bird, fish, or animal. 2 the part at the end or rear of something. 3 the side of a coin opposite the head, *Heads or tails?*
tail *verb* (**tails, tailing, tailed**)
1 remove stalks etc. from fruit, *top and tail gooseberries.* 2 (*informal*) follow a person or thing.
tail off become fewer, smaller, or slighter etc.; cease gradually.
[from Old English]

tailback *noun* (*plural* **tailbacks**)
a long line of traffic stretching back from an obstruction.

tailless *adjective*
without a tail.

tailor *noun* (*plural* **tailors**)
a person who makes men's clothes.
tailor *verb* (**tailors, tailoring, tailored**)
1 make or fit clothes. 2 adapt or make something for a special purpose.
[from old French]

taint *noun* (*plural* **taints**)
a small amount of decay, pollution, or a bad quality that spoils something.
taint *verb* (**taints, tainting, tainted**)
give something a taint.
[from old French; related to *tint*]

take *verb* (**takes, taking, took, taken**)
This word has many uses, including 1 get something into your hands or possession or control etc. (*take this cup*; *we took many prisoners*), 2 make use of (*take a taxi*) or indulge in (*take a holiday*), 3 carry or convey (*Take this parcel to the post*), 4 perform or deal with (*When do you take your music exam?*), 5 study or teach a subject (*Who takes you for maths?*), 6 make an effort (*take trouble*) or experience a feeling (*Don't take offence*), 7 accept; endure (*I'll take a risk*), 8 require (*It takes a strong man to lift this*), 9 write down (*take notes*), 10 make a photograph, 11 subtract (*take 4 from 10*), 12 assume (*I take it that you agree*). **taker** *noun*
take after be like a parent etc.
take in deceive somebody.
take leave of say goodbye to.
take off (of an aircraft) leave the ground and become airborne. **take-off** *noun*
take on 1 begin to employ someone. 2 play or fight against someone. 3 (*informal*) show that you are upset.
take over take control. **takeover** *noun*
take place happen or occur.
take up 1 start something. 2 occupy space or time etc. 3 accept an offer.
[from Old Norse]

takeaway *noun* (*plural* **takeaways**)
1 a place that sells cooked meals for customers to take away. 2 a meal from this.

takings *plural noun*
money received.

talcum powder
a scented powder put on the skin to make it
feel smooth and dry. [from *talc*, the
substance from which it is made]

tale *noun* (*plural* **tales**)
a story. [from Old English]

talent *noun* (*plural* **talents**)
a special or very great ability.
talented *adjective*
[from Greek *talanton* = sum of money]

talisman *noun* (*plural* **talismans**)
an object that is supposed to bring good
luck.
[from Greek *telesma* = consecrated object]

talk *verb* (**talks, talking, talked**)
speak; have a conversation. **talker** *noun*
talk *noun* (*plural* **talks**)
1 talking; a conversation. 2 an informal
lecture.
[from Middle English; related to *tale*]

talkative *adjective*
talking a lot.

tall *adjective*
1 higher than the average, *a tall tree.*
2 measured from the bottom to the top, *It is
10 metres tall.* **tallness** *noun*
[from Old English]

tallow *noun*
animal fat used to make candles, soap,
lubricants, etc. [from old German]

tall story *noun* (*plural* **tall stories**)
(*informal*) a story that is hard to believe.

tally *noun* (*plural* **tallies**)
the total amount of a debt or score.
tally *verb* (**tallies, tallying, tallied**)
correspond or agree with something else,
Does your list tally with mine?
[from Latin]

Talmud *noun*
the collection of writings that contain
Jewish religious law.
[Hebrew, = instruction]

talon *noun* (*plural* **talons**)
a strong claw. [from Latin]

tambourine *noun* (*plural* **tambourines**)
a circular musical instrument with metal
discs round it, tapped or shaken to make it
jingle. [from French]

tame *adjective*
1 (of animals) gentle and not afraid of
people; not wild or dangerous. 2 not
exciting; dull.
tamely *adverb*, **tameness** *noun*
tame *verb* (**tames, taming, tamed**)
make an animal become tame. **tamer** *noun*
[from Old English]

Tamil *noun* (*plural* **Tamils**)
1 a member of a people of southern India
and Sri Lanka. 2 their language.

tam-o'-shanter *noun* (*plural* **tam-o'-
shanters**)
a beret with a wide top.
[named after Tam o' Shanter, hero of a
poem by the Scottish poet Robert Burns]

tamp *verb* (**tamps, tamping, tamped**)
pack or ram down tightly. [from French]

tamper *verb* (**tampers, tampering,
tampered**)
meddle or interfere with something.
[from *temper*]

tampon *noun* (*plural* **tampons**)
a plug of soft material that a woman puts
into her vagina to absorb the blood during
her period. [French]

tan *noun* (*plural* **tans**)
1 light brown colour. 2 brown colour in
skin that has been exposed to sun.
tan *verb* (**tans, tanning, tanned**)
1 make or become brown by exposing skin
to the sun. 2 make an animal's skin into
leather by treating it with chemicals.
[probably from Latin]

tandem *noun* (*plural* **tandems**)
a bicycle for two riders, one behind the
other. [Latin, = at length]

tandoori *noun*
a style of Indian cooking in which food is
cooked in a clay oven (a **tandoor**).
[from Persian or Urdu]

tang *noun* (*plural* **tangs**)
a strong flavour or smell. [from Old Norse]

tangent *noun* (*plural* **tangents**)
a straight line that touches the outside of a
curve or circle.
[from Latin *tangens* = touching]

tangerine *noun* (*plural* **tangerines**)
a kind of small orange from Tangier in
Morocco. [named after Tangier]

tangible *adjective*
1 able to be touched. 2 real or definite,
tangible benefits. **tangibly** *adverb*, **tangibility**
noun [from Latin *tangere* = to touch]

tangle *verb* (**tangles, tangling, tangled**)
make or become twisted into a confused
mass. **tangle** *noun*
[probably from a Scandinavian language]

tango *noun* (*plural* **tangos**)
a ballroom dance with gliding steps.
[American Spanish, perhaps from an
African language]

tank *noun* (*plural* **tanks**)
1 a large container for a liquid or gas. 2 a
heavy armoured vehicle used in war.
[from Gujarati or Marathi, languages
spoken in India]

tankard *noun* (*plural* **tankards**)
a large mug for drinking beer from, usually
made of silver or pewter. [origin unknown]

tanker *noun* (*plural* **tankers**)
1 a large ship for carrying oil. 2 a large
lorry for carrying a liquid. [from *tank*]

tanner *noun* (*plural* **tanners**)
a person who tans animal skins into
leather. **tannery** *noun*

tannin *noun*
a substance obtained from the bark or fruit
of various trees (also found in tea), used in
tanning and dyeing things.
[from French; related to *tan*]

tantalize *verb* (**tantalizes, tantalizing,
tantalized**)
tease or torment a person by showing him
or her something good but keeping it out of
reach. [from the name of Tantalus in Greek
mythology, who was punished by being
made to stand near water and fruit which
moved away when he tried to reach them]

tantamount *adjective*
equivalent, *The Queen's request was
tantamount to a command*. [from Italian
tanto montare = amount to so much]

tantrum *noun* (*plural* **tantrums**)
an outburst of bad temper.
[origin unknown]

tap[1] *noun* (*plural* **taps**)
a device for letting out liquid or gas in a
controlled flow.
tap *verb* (**taps, tapping, tapped**)
1 take liquid out of something, especially
through a tap. 2 obtain supplies or
information etc. from a source. 3 fix a
device to a telephone line so that you can
overhear conversations on it.
[from Old English]

tap[2] *noun* (*plural* **taps**)
1 a quick light hit; the sound of this. 2 tap-
dancing.
tap *verb* (**taps, tapping, tapped**)
hit a person or thing quickly and lightly.
[from French]

tap-dancing *noun*
dancing with shoes that make elaborate
tapping sounds on the floor.
tap-dance *noun*, **tap-dancer** *noun*

tape *noun* (*plural* **tapes**)
1 a narrow strip of cloth, paper, plastic, etc.
2 a narrow plastic strip coated with a
magnetic substance and used for making
recordings. 3 a tape recording. 4 a tape-
measure.
tape *verb* (**tapes, taping, taped**)
1 fix, cover, or surround something with
tape. 2 record something on magnetic tape.
get or **have something taped** (*slang*) know
or understand it; be able to deal with it.
[from Old English]

tape deck *noun* (*plural* **tape decks**)
the part of a stereo system on which you
can play cassette tapes.

tape-measure *noun* (*plural* **tape-
measures**)
a long strip marked in centimetres or
inches for measuring things.

taper *verb* (**tapers, tapering, tapered**)
1 make or become thinner towards one
end. 2 make or become gradually less.

taper *noun* (*plural* tapers)
a very thin candle.
[via Old English from Latin]

tape recorder *noun* (*plural* tape recorders)
a machine for recording sounds or computer data on magnetic tape and reproducing them. **tape recording** *noun*

tapestry *noun* (*plural* tapestries)
a piece of strong cloth with pictures or patterns woven or embroidered on it.
[from French *tapis* = carpet]

tapeworm *noun* (*plural* tapeworms)
a long flat worm that can live as a parasite in the intestines of people and animals.

tapioca *noun*
a starchy substance in hard white grains obtained from cassava, used for making puddings.
[from Tupi (a South American language)]

tapir (*say* tay-per) *noun* (*plural* tapirs)
a pig-like animal with a long flexible snout.
[via Spanish or Portuguese from Tupi (a South American language)]

tar *noun*
a thick black liquid made from coal or wood etc. and used in making roads.
tar *verb* (tars, tarring, tarred)
coat something with tar.
[from Old English]

tarantula *noun* (*plural* tarantulas)
a large kind of spider found in southern Europe and in tropical countries.
[from Italian]

tardy *adjective* (tardier, tardiest)
slow or late. **tardily** *adverb*, **tardiness** *noun*
[from Latin *tardus* = slow]

target *noun* (*plural* targets)
something aimed at; a thing that someone tries to hit or reach.
target *verb* (targets, targeting, targeted)
aim at or have as a target.
[from Old English]

tariff *noun* (*plural* tariffs)
a list of prices or charges.
[via French and Italian from Arabic]

tarmac *noun*
an area surfaced with tarmacadam, especially on an airfield.
[*Tarmac* is a trade mark]

tarmacadam *noun*
a mixture of tar and broken stone, used for making a hard surface on roads, paths, playgrounds, etc.

tarnish *verb* (tarnishes, tarnishing, tarnished)
1 make or become less shiny, *The silver had tarnished.* **2** spoil or blemish, *The scandal tarnished his reputation.* **tarnish** *noun* [from French *terne* = dark, dull]

tarot cards (rhymes with *barrow*) *plural noun*
a special pack of cards used for fortune-telling. [via French from Italian]

tarpaulin *noun* (*plural* tarpaulins)
a large sheet of waterproof canvas.
[from *tar* + *pall*[1]]

tarragon *noun*
a plant with leaves that are used to flavour salads etc. [from Latin]

tarry[1] (*say* tar-ee) *adjective*
covered with or like tar.

tarry[2] (*say* ta-ree) *verb* (tarries, tarrying, tarried) (*old use*)
stay for a while longer; linger.
[origin unknown]

tart[1] *noun* (*plural* tarts)
1 a pie containing fruit or sweet filling. **2** a piece of pastry with jam etc. on top.
[from Latin]

tart[2] *adjective*
1 sour. **2** sharp in manner, *a tart reply.*
tartly *adverb*, **tartness** *noun*
[origin unknown]

tartan *noun*
a pattern with coloured stripes crossing each other, especially one that is used by a Scottish clan. [probably from old French *tiretaine*, a kind of material]

tartar[1] *noun* (*plural* tartars)
a person who is fierce or difficult to deal with. [named after the Tartars, warriors from central Asia in the 13th century]

tartar² *noun* (*plural* tartars)
a hard chalky deposit that forms on teeth.
[from Latin]

tartlet *noun* (*plural* tartlets)
a small pastry tart.

task *noun* (*plural* tasks)
a piece of work to be done.
take a person to task rebuke him or her.
[from old French; related to *tax*]

task force *noun* (*plural* task forces)
a group specially organized for a particular
task.

taskmaster *noun* (*plural* taskmasters)
a person who sets a lot of difficult tasks for
other people to do, *a hard taskmaster*.

tassel *noun* (*plural* tassels)
a bundle of threads tied together at the top
and used to decorate something. **tasselled**
adjective [from old French]

taste *verb* (tastes, tasting, tasted)
1 take a small amount of food or drink to
try its flavour. 2 be able to perceive
flavours. 3 have a certain flavour.
taste *noun* (*plural* tastes)
1 the feeling caused in the tongue by
something placed on it. 2 the ability to
taste things. 3 the ability to enjoy beautiful
things or to choose what is suitable, *Her
choice of clothes shows her good taste.* 4 a
liking, *I've developed quite a taste for skiing.*
5 a very small amount of food or drink.
[from old French]

tasteful *adjective*
showing good taste.
tastefully *adverb*, **tastefulness** *noun*

tasteless *adjective*
1 having no flavour. 2 showing poor taste.
tastelessly *adverb*, **tastelessness** *noun*

tasty *adjective* (tastier, tastiest)
having a strong pleasant taste.

tattered *adjective*
badly torn; ragged. [from *tatters*]

tatters *plural noun*
rags; badly torn pieces.
in tatters torn to pieces, *My coat was in
tatters.*
[from Old Norse]

tatting *noun*
a kind of handmade lace. [origin unknown]

tattle *verb* (tattles, tattling, tattled)
gossip. **tattle** *noun* [from old Flemish]

tattoo¹ *verb* (tattoos, tattooing, tattooed)
mark a person's skin with a picture or
pattern by using a needle and some dye.
tattoo *noun* (*plural* tattoos)
a tattooed picture or pattern.
[from a Polynesian language]

tattoo² *noun* (*plural* tattoos)
1 a drumming or tapping sound. 2 an
entertainment consisting of military
music, marching, etc. [from Dutch]

tatty *adjective*
1 ragged; shabby and untidy. 2 cheap and
gaudy. **tattily** *adverb*, **tattiness** *noun*
[from Old English *taettec* = rag]

taunt *verb* (taunts, taunting, taunted)
jeer at or insult someone. **taunt** *noun*
[from French *tant pour tant* = tit for tat]

taut *adjective*
stretched tightly. **tautly** *adverb*, **tautness**
noun [probably from *tough*]

tauten *verb* (tautens, tautening, tautened)
make or become taut.

tautology *noun* (*plural* tautologies)
saying the same thing again in different
words, e.g. *You can get the book free for
nothing* (where *free* and *for nothing* mean
the same). [from Greek *tauto* = the same
+ *logos* = word]

tavern *noun* (*plural* taverns) (*old use*)
an inn or public house. [from Latin]

tawdry *adjective*
cheap and gaudy. **tawdriness** *noun*
[from *St Audrey's lace* (cheap finery
formerly sold at St Audrey's fair at Ely)]

tawny *adjective*
brownish-yellow.
[from old French; related to *tan*]

tax *noun* (*plural* taxes)
1 money that people or business firms
have to pay to the government, to be used
for public purposes. 2 a strain or burden,
The long walk was a tax on his strength.

tax *verb* (taxes, taxing, taxed)
1 put a tax on something. **2** charge someone a tax. **3** pay the tax on something, *I have taxed the car up to June.* **4** put a strain or burden on a person or thing, *Will it tax your strength?* **5** accuse, *I taxed him with leaving the door open.*
taxable *adjective*, **taxation** *noun*
[from Latin *taxare* = calculate]

taxi *noun* (*plural* taxis)
a car that carries passengers for payment, usually with a meter to record the fare to be paid. **taxicab** *noun*

taxi *verb* (taxies, taxiing, taxied)
(of an aircraft) move along the ground or water, especially before or after flying.
[short for *taximeter cab*, from French *taxe* = tariff, charge + *mètre* = meter]

taxidermist *noun* (*plural* taxidermists)
a person who prepares and stuffs the skins of animals in a lifelike form. **taxidermy** *noun* [from Greek *taxis* = arrangement + *derma* = skin]

taxpayer *noun* (*plural* taxpayers)
a person who pays tax.

TB *abbreviation*
tuberculosis.

tea *noun* (*plural* teas)
1 a drink made by pouring hot water on the dried leaves of an evergreen shrub (the *tea-plant*). **2** these dried leaves. **3** a meal in the afternoon or early evening. **teacup** *noun*, **tea leaf** *noun*, **tea table** *noun*, **teatime** *noun* [via Dutch from Chinese]

tea bag *noun* (*plural* tea bags)
a small bag holding about a teaspoonful of tea.

teacake *noun* (*plural* teacakes)
a kind of bun usually served toasted and buttered.

teach *verb* (teaches, teaching, taught)
1 give a person knowledge or skill; train. **2** give lessons, especially in a particular subject. **3** show someone what to do or avoid, *That will teach you not to meddle!*
[from Old English]

teachable *adjective*
able to be taught.

teacher *noun* (*plural* teachers)
a person who teaches others, especially in a school.

tea cloth *noun* (*plural* tea cloths)
a tea towel.

teak *noun*
the hard strong wood of an evergreen Asian tree. [via Portuguese from a south Indian language]

teal *noun* (*plural* teal)
a kind of duck. [origin unknown]

team *noun* (*plural* teams)
1 a set of players forming one side in certain games and sports. **2** a set of people working together. **3** two or more animals harnessed to pull a vehicle or a plough etc.
team *verb* (teams, teaming, teamed)
put or join together in a team.
[from Old English]

teamwork *noun*
the ability of a team or group to work well together.

teapot *noun* (*plural* teapots)
a pot with a lid and a handle, for making and pouring tea.

tear[1] (*say* teer) *noun* (*plural* tears)
a drop of the water that comes from the eyes when a person cries. **teardrop** *noun*
in tears crying.
[from Old English *taeher*]

tear[2] (*say* tair) *verb* (tears, tearing, tore, torn)
1 pull something apart, away, or into pieces. **2** become torn, *Newspaper tears easily.* **3** run or travel hurriedly.
tear *noun* (*plural* tears)
a split made by tearing.
[from Old English *teran*]

tearful *adjective*
in tears; crying easily. **tearfully** *adverb*

tear gas *noun*
a gas that makes people's eyes water painfully.

tease *verb* (teases, teasing, teased)
1 amuse yourself by deliberately annoying or making fun of someone. **2** pick threads apart into separate strands.

tease *noun* (*plural* **teases**)
a person who often teases others.
[from Old English]

teasel *noun* (*plural* **teasels**)
a plant with bristly heads formerly used to
brush up the surface of cloth. [from *tease* 2]

teaser *noun* (*plural* **teasers**)
a difficult problem.

teaspoon *noun* (*plural* **teaspoons**)
a small spoon for stirring tea etc.
teaspoonful *noun*

teat *noun* (*plural* **teats**)
1 a nipple through which a baby sucks
milk. 2 the cap of a baby's feeding bottle.
[from old French]

tea towel *noun* (*plural* **tea towels**)
a cloth for drying washed dishes, cutlery,
etc.

tech (*say* tek) *noun* (*plural* **techs**) (*informal*)
a technical college.

technical *adjective*
1 to do with technology. 2 to do with a
particular subject and its methods, *the
technical terms of chemistry.* **technically**
adverb [from Greek *technikos* = skilled in
an art or craft]

technical college *noun* (*plural* **technical
colleges**)
a college where technical subjects are
taught.

technicality *noun* (*plural* **technicalities**)
1 being technical. 2 a technical word or
phrase; a special detail.

technician *noun* (*plural* **technicians**)
a person whose job is to look after
scientific equipment and do practical work
in a laboratory.

technique *noun* (*plural* **techniques**)
the method of doing something skilfully.
[French, related to *technical*]

technology *noun* (*plural* **technologies**)
the study of machinery, engineering, and
how things work.
technological *adjective*, **technologist** *noun*
[from Greek *techne* = craft, skill, + *-ology*]

teddy bear *noun* (*plural* **teddy bears**)
a soft furry toy bear. [named after US
President Theodore ('Teddy') Roosevelt,
who liked hunting bears]

tedious *adjective*
annoyingly slow or long; boring. **tediously**
adverb, **tediousness** *noun*, **tedium** *noun*
[from Latin *taedium* = tiredness]

tee *noun* (*plural* **tees**)
1 the flat area from which golfers strike
the ball at the start of play for each hole.
2 a small piece of wood or plastic on which
a golf ball is placed for being struck.
[origin unknown]

teem[1] *verb* (**teems, teeming, teemed**)
be full of something, *The river was teeming
with fish.* [from Old English]

teem[2] *verb* (**teems, teeming, teemed**)
rain very hard; pour. [from Old Norse]

-teen *suffix*
a form of 'ten' added to numbers from *three*
to *nine* to form *thirteen* to *nineteen*.

teenage *adjective*
to do with teenagers.

teenaged *adjective*
in your teens.

teenager *noun* (*plural* **teenagers**)
a person in his or her teens.

teens *plural noun*
the time of life between 13 and 19 years of
age.

teeny *adjective* (**teenier, teeniest**) (*informal*)
tiny. [a different spelling of *tiny*]

teeter *verb* (**teeters, teetering, teetered**)
stand or move unsteadily. [from Old Norse]

teething *noun*
(of a baby) having its first teeth beginning
to grow through the gums.

teetotal *adjective*
never drinking alcohol. **teetotaller** *noun*
[from *total* with *tee* added for emphasis]

Teflon *noun* (*trade mark*)
a type of plastic used as a non-stick coating

for pans. [from poly*tetrafl*uoroethylene, its scientific name]

tele- *prefix*
far; at a distance (as in *telescope*).
[from Greek]

telecommunications *plural noun*
communications over a long distance, e.g. by telephone, telegraph, radio, or television.

telegram *noun* (*plural* **telegrams**)
a message sent by telegraph.

telegraph *noun*
a way of sending messages by using electric current along wires or by radio.
telegraphic *adjective*, **telegraphy** *noun*

telepathy (*say* til-**ep**-ath-ee) *noun*
communication of thoughts from one person's mind to another without speaking, writing, or gestures.
telepathic *adjective*
[from *tele-* + Greek *pathos* = feeling]

telephone *noun* (*plural* **telephones**)
a device or system using electric wires or radio etc. to enable one person to speak to another who is some distance away.
telephone *verb* (**telephones**, **telephoning**, **telephoned**)
speak to a person on the telephone.
[from *tele-* + Greek *phone* = sound, voice]

telephonist (*say* til-**ef** on-ist) *noun* (*plural* **telephonists**)
a person who operates a telephone switchboard.

telescope *noun* (*plural* **telescopes**)
an instrument using lenses to magnify distant objects. **telescopic** *adjective*
telescope *verb* (**telescopes**, **telescoping**, **telescoped**)
1 make or become shorter by sliding overlapping sections into each other.
2 compress or condense something so that it takes less space or time.
[from *tele-* + Greek *skopein* = look at]

teletext *noun*
a system for displaying news and information on a television screen.

televise *verb* (**televises**, **televising**, **televised**)
broadcast something by television.
[from *television*]

television *noun* (*plural* **televisions**)
1 a system using radio waves to reproduce a view of scenes, events, or plays etc. on a screen. 2 an apparatus for receiving these pictures. 3 televised programmes.

telex *noun* (*plural* **telexes**)
a system for sending printed messages by telegraphy; a message sent by this system.
telex *verb* [from *teleprinter* (the machine used) + *exchange*]

tell *verb* (**tells**, **telling**, **told**)
1 make a thing known to someone, especially by words. 2 speak, *Tell the truth.*
3 order, *Tell them to wait.* 4 reveal a secret, *Promise you won't tell.* 5 decide or distinguish, *Can you tell the difference between butter and margarine?* 6 produce an effect, *The strain began to tell on him.*
7 count, *There are ten of them, all told.*
tell off (*informal*) reprimand.
tell tales report something naughty or bad that someone has done.
[from Old English]

telling *adjective*
having a strong effect, *a very telling reply.*

tell-tale *noun* (*plural* **tell-tales**)
a person who tells tales.
tell-tale *adjective*
revealing or indicating something, *There was a tell-tale spot of jam on his chin.*

telly *noun* (*plural* **tellies**) (*informal*)
1 television. 2 a television set.

temerity (*say* tim-**erri**-tee) *noun*
rashness or boldness. [from Latin]

temp *noun* (*plural* **temps**)
a secretary or other worker who works for short periods of time in different companies. [from *temporary*]

temper *noun* (*plural* **tempers**)
1 a person's mood, *He is in a good temper.*
2 an angry mood, *She was in a temper.*
lose your temper lose your calmness and become angry.
temper *verb* (**tempers**, **tempering**, **tempered**)
1 harden or strengthen metal etc. by

heating and cooling it. **2** moderate or soften the effects of something, *tempering justice with mercy.* [via Old English from Latin *temperare* = mix]

temperament *noun* (*plural* **temperaments**)
a person's nature as shown in the way he or she usually behaves, *a nervous temperament.* [same origin as *temper*]

temperamental *adjective*
1 likely to become excitable or moody suddenly. **2** to do with a person's temperament. **temperamentally** *adverb*

temperance *noun*
1 moderation or self-restraint. **2** drinking little or no alcohol.
[from Latin *temperantia* = moderation]

temperate *adjective*
neither extremely hot nor extremely cold, *Britain has a temperate climate.*
[originally = not affected by strong emotions: same origin as *temper*]

temperature *noun* (*plural* **temperatures**)
1 how hot or cold a person or thing is. **2** an abnormally high temperature of the body. [from Latin *temperatus* = tempered]

tempest *noun* (*plural* **tempests**)
a violent storm.
[from Latin *tempestas* = weather]

tempestuous *adjective*
stormy; full of commotion.

temple[1] *noun* (*plural* **temples**)
a building where a god is worshipped.
[from Latin *templum* = consecrated place]

temple[2] *noun* (*plural* **temples**)
the part of the head between the forehead and the ear.
[from Latin *tempora* = sides of the head]

tempo *noun* (*plural* **tempos** or **tempi**)
the speed or rhythm of something, especially of a piece of music.
[Italian, from Latin *tempus* = time]

temporary *adjective*
lasting for a limited time only; not permanent.
temporarily (*say* tem-per-er-il-ee) *adverb*
[from Latin *temporis* = of a time]

temporize *verb* (**temporizes, temporizing, temporized**)
avoid giving a definite answer, in order to postpone something.
[from Latin *tempus* = time]

tempt *verb* (**tempts, tempting, tempted**)
try to persuade or attract someone, especially into doing something wrong or unwise. **temptation** *noun*, **tempter** *noun*, **temptress** *noun* [from Latin *temptare* = test]

ten *noun* (*plural* **tens**) & *adjective*
the number 10. [from Old English]

tenable *adjective*
able to be held or defended, *a tenable theory; the job is tenable for one year only.*
[French, from *tenir* = to hold]

tenacious (*say* ten-ay-shus) *adjective*
1 holding or clinging firmly to something. **2** obstinate and persistent.
tenaciously *adverb*, **tenacity** *noun*
[from Latin *tenere* = to hold]

tenant *noun* (*plural* **tenants**)
a person who rents a house, building, or land etc. from a landlord. **tenancy** *noun*
[French, = holding]

tend[1] *verb* (**tends, tending, tended**)
have a certain tendency, *Prices tend to rise.*
[same origin as *tender*[2]]

tend[2] *verb* (**tends, tending, tended**)
look after, *Shepherds were tending their sheep.* [from *attend*]

tendency *noun* (*plural* **tendencies**)
the way a person or thing is likely to behave, *She has a tendency to be lazy.*

tender[1] *adjective*
1 easy to chew; not tough or hard. **2** easily hurt or damaged; sensitive or delicate, *tender plants.* **3** gentle and loving, *a tender smile.* **tenderly** *adverb*, **tenderness** *noun*
[from Latin *tener* = soft]

tender[2] *verb* (**tenders, tendering, tendered**)
offer something formally, *He tendered his resignation.*
tender *noun* (*plural* **tenders**)
a formal offer to supply goods or carry out work at a stated price, *The council asked for tenders to build a school.*
legal tender kinds of money that are legal

for making payments, *Are pound notes still legal tender?*
[from Latin *tendere* – stretch, hold out]

tender³ *noun* (*plural* **tenders**)
1 a truck attached to a steam locomotive to carry its coal and water. 2 a small boat carrying stores or passengers to and from a larger one. [from *tend²*]

tendon *noun* (*plural* **tendons**)
a strong strip of tissue that joins muscle to bone. [same origin as *tender²*]

tendril *noun* (*plural* **tendrils**)
1 a thread-like part by which a climbing plant clings to a support. 2 a thin curl of hair etc. [from French; related to *tender¹*]

tenement *noun* (*plural* **tenements**)
a large house or building divided into flats or rooms that are let to separate tenants. [from Latin *tenementum* = holding]

tenet (*say* ten-it) *noun* (*plural* **tenets**)
a firm belief held by a person or group. [Latin, = he or she holds]

tenner *noun* (*plural* **tenners**) (*informal*)
a ten-pound note; £10.

tennis *noun*
a game played with rackets and a ball on a court with a net across the middle. [from old French]

tenon *noun* (*plural* **tenons**)
a piece of wood etc. shaped to fit into a mortise. [French, from *tenir* = to hold]

tenor *noun* (*plural* **tenors**)
a male singer with a high voice. [from Latin]

tense¹ *noun* (*plural* **tenses**)
the form of a verb that shows when something happens, e.g. he *came* (**past tense**), he *comes* or *is coming* (**present tense**), he *will come* (**future tense**). [from Latin *tempus* = time]

tense² *adjective*
1 tightly stretched. 2 nervous or worried and unable to relax.
tensely *adverb*, **tenseness** *noun*
tense *verb* (**tenses**, **tensing**, **tensed**)
make or become tense.
[from Latin *tensum* = stretched]

tensile *adjective*
1 to do with tension. 2 able to be stretched.

tension *noun* (*plural* **tensions**)
1 how tightly stretched a rope or wire is. 2 a feeling of anxiety or nervousness about something that is just about to happen. 3 voltage, *high-tension cables*.
[from Latin *tensio* = stretching]

tent *noun* (*plural* **tents**)
a shelter made of canvas or other material. [from French; related to *tense²*]

tentacle *noun* (*plural* **tentacles**)
a long flexible part of the body of certain animals (e.g. snails, octopuses), used for feeling or grasping things or for moving. [from Latin]

tentative *adjective*
cautious; trying something out, *a tentative suggestion*. **tentatively** *adverb*
[same origin as *tempt*]

tenterhooks *plural noun*
on tenterhooks tense and anxious.
[from *tenter* = a machine with hooks for stretching cloth to dry]

tenth *adjective* & *noun*
next after the ninth. [from Old English]

tenuous *adjective*
very slight or thin, *tenuous threads*; *a tenuous connection*.
[from Latin *tenuis* = thin]

tenure (*say* ten-yoor) *noun* (*plural* **tenures**)
the holding of a position of employment, or of land, accommodation, etc.
[old French, from *tenir* = to hold]

tepee (*say* tee-pee) *noun* (*plural* **tepees**)
a tent formerly used by Native Americans, made by fastening skins or mats over poles. [a Native American word]

tepid *adjective*
only slightly warm; lukewarm, *tepid water*. [from Latin *tepere* = to be warm]

term *noun* (*plural* **terms**)
1 the period of weeks when a school or college is open. 2 a definite period, *a term of imprisonment*. 3 a word or expression, *technical terms*.

term *verb* (**terms, terming, termed**)
name; call something by a certain term,
This music is termed jazz.
[from French; related to *terminus*]

termagant *noun* (*plural* **termagants**)
a bad-tempered bullying woman.
[named after Tervagant, a fierce god in
medieval plays]

terminable *adjective*
able to be terminated.

terminal *noun* (*plural* **terminals**)
1 the place where something ends; a
terminus. **2** a building where air
passengers arrive or depart. **3** a place
where a wire is connected in an electric
circuit or battery etc. **4** a device for
sending information to a computer, or for
receiving it.
terminal *adjective*
1 to do with or at the end or boundary of
something. **2** in the last stage of a fatal
disease, *terminal cancer*. **terminally** *adverb*
[same origin as *terminus*]

terminate *verb* (**terminates, terminating,
terminated**)
end; stop finally. **termination** *noun*
[same origin as *terminus*]

terminology *noun* (*plural* **terminologies**)
the technical terms of a subject.
terminological *adjective*
[via German from Latin]

terminus *noun* (*plural* **termini**)
the end of something; the last station on a
railway or bus route.
[Latin, = end, limit, or boundary]

termite *noun* (*plural* **termites**)
a small insect that is very destructive to
timber. [from Latin]

terms *plural noun*
1 a relationship between people, *They are
on friendly terms.* **2** conditions offered or
accepted, *peace terms.*

tern *noun* (*plural* **terns**)
a seabird with long wings.
[probably from a Scandinavian language]

terrace *noun* (*plural* **terraces**)
1 a level area on a slope or hillside. **2** a

paved area beside a house. **3** a row of
houses joined together. **terraced** *adjective*
[from French; related to *terrain*]

terracotta *noun*
1 a kind of pottery. **2** the brownish-red
colour of flowerpots.
[Italian, = baked earth]

terra firma *noun*
dry land; the ground. [Latin, = firm land]

terrain *noun* (*plural* **terrains**)
a stretch of land, *hilly terrain.*
[from Latin *terra* = earth]

terrapin *noun* (*plural* **terrapins**)
an edible freshwater turtle of North
America. [a Native American word]

terrestrial *adjective*
to do with the earth or land.
[same origin as *terrain*]

terrible *adjective*
very bad; distressing. **terribly** *adverb*
[same origin as *terror*]

terrier *noun* (*plural* **terriers**)
a kind of small lively dog.
[from old French *chien terrier* = earth-dog
(because they were used to dig out foxes
from their earths)]

terrific *adjective* (*informal*)
1 very great, *a terrific storm.* **2** excellent.
terrifically *adverb*
[from Latin *terrificus* = frightening]

terrify *verb* (**terrifies, terrifying, terrified**)
fill someone with terror.
[same origin as *terrific*]

territory *noun* (*plural* **territories**)
an area of land, especially one that belongs
to a country or person. **territorial** *adjective*
[same origin as *terrain*]

terror *noun* (*plural* **terrors**)
1 very great fear. **2** a terrifying person or
thing. [from Latin *terrere* = frighten]

terrorist *noun* (*plural* **terrorists**)
a person who uses violence for political
purposes.
terrorism *noun*

terrorize *verb* (terrorizes, terrorizing, terrorized)
fill someone with terror; frighten someone by threatening them. **terrorization** *noun*

terse *adjective*
using few words; concise or curt.
tersely *adverb*, **terseness** *noun*
[from Latin *tersum* = polished]

tertiary (*say* ter-sher-ee) *adjective*
to do with the third stage of something; coming after secondary.
[from Latin *tertius* = third]

tessellate *verb* (tessellates, tessellating, tessellated)
fit shapes into a pattern without overlapping or leaving gaps. **tessellated** *adjective*, **tessellation** *noun* [from Latin *tessella* = a small piece of wood, bone, or glass, used as a token or in a mosaic]

test *noun* (*plural* tests)
1 a short examination. 2 a way of discovering the qualities, abilities, or presence of a person or thing, *a test for radioactivity.* 3 (*informal*) a test match.
test *verb* (tests, testing, tested)
carry out a test on a person or thing. **tester** *noun* [from Latin]

testament *noun* (*plural* testaments)
1 a written statement. 2 either of the two main parts of the Bible, the Old Testament or the New Testament. [from Latin *testari* = act as a witness, make a will]

testator *noun* (*plural* testators)
a person who has made a will.
[same origin as *testament*]

testicle *noun* (*plural* testicles)
either of the two glands in the scrotum where semen is produced. [from Latin]

testify *verb* (testifies, testifying, testified)
give evidence; swear that something is true. [from Latin *testis* = witness]

testimonial *noun* (*plural* testimonials)
1 a letter describing someone's abilities, character, etc. 2 a gift presented to someone as a mark of respect.
[same origin as *testify*]

testimony *noun* (*plural* testimonies)
evidence; what someone testifies.

test match *noun* (*plural* test matches)
a cricket or Rugby match between teams from different countries.

test tube *noun* (*plural* test tubes)
a tube of thin glass with one end closed, used for experiments in chemistry etc.

test-tube baby *noun* (*plural* test-tube babies)
a baby that develops from an egg that has been fertilized outside the mother's body and then placed back in the womb.

testy *adjective*
easily annoyed; irritable.
[from old French *testif* = headstrong]

tetanus *noun*
a disease that makes the muscles become stiff, caused by bacteria.
[from Greek *tetanos* = a spasm]

tête-à-tête (*say* tayt-ah-tayt) *noun* (*plural* tête-à-têtes)
a private conversation, especially between two people. [French, = head to head]

tether *verb* (tethers, tethering, tethered)
tie an animal so that it cannot move far.
tether *noun* (*plural* tethers)
a rope for tethering an animal.
at the end of your tether unable to endure something any more.
[from Old Norse]

tetra- *prefix*
four. [from Greek]

tetrahedron *noun* (*plural* tetrahedrons)
a solid with four sides (i.e. a pyramid with a triangular base).
[from *tetra-* + Greek *hedra* = base]

text *noun* (*plural* texts)
1 the words of something written or printed. 2 a sentence from the Bible used as the subject of a sermon etc.
[from Latin *textus* = literary style]

textbook *noun* (*plural* textbooks)
a book that teaches you about a subject.

textiles *plural noun*
kinds of cloth; fabrics.
[from Latin *textum* = woven]

texture *noun* (*plural* **textures**)
the way that the surface of something feels.
[from Latin *textura* = weaving]

thalidomide *noun*
a medicinal drug that was found (in 1961)
to cause babies to be born with deformed
arms and legs.
[from its chemical name]

than *conjunction*
compared with another person or thing,
His brother is taller than he is or *taller than
him.* [from Old English]

thank *verb* (**thanks, thanking, thanked**)
tell someone that you are grateful to him or
her.
thank you I thank you.
[from Old English]

thankful *adjective*
grateful.

thankfully *adverb*
1 in a grateful way. 2 I am grateful that;
fortunately, *Thankfully, John remembered
to lock the door.*

USAGE: Some people say it is incorrect to
use *thankfully* to mean 'I am grateful that'
or 'fortunately', and say that it should only
be used to mean 'in a grateful way'. This
first use is very common in informal
language but you should probably avoid it
when you are writing or speaking
formally.

thankless *adjective*
not likely to win thanks from people, *a
thankless task.*

thanks *plural noun*
1 statements of gratitude. 2 (*informal*)
thank you.
thanks to as a result of; because of, *Thanks
to your help, we succeeded.*

thanksgiving *noun*
an expression of gratitude, especially to
God.

that *adjective* & *pronoun* (*plural* **those**)
the one there, *That book is mine. Whose is
that?*
that *adverb*
to such an extent, *I'll come that far but no
further.*

that *relative pronoun*
which, who, or whom, *This is the record
that I wanted. We liked the people that we
met on holiday.*

that *conjunction*
used to introduce a wish, reason, result,
etc., *I hope that you are well. The puzzle was
so hard that no one could solve it.*
[from Old English]

thatch *noun*
straw or reeds used to make a roof.

thatch *verb* (**thatches, thatching, thatched**)
make a roof with thatch. **thatcher** *noun*
[from Old English]

thaw *verb* (**thaws, thawing, thawed**)
melt; stop being frozen.

thaw *noun* (*plural* **thaws**)
a period of warm weather that thaws ice
and snow. [from Old English]

the *adjective* (called the *definite article*)
a particular one; that or those.
[from Old English]

theatre *noun* (*plural* **theatres**)
1 a building where plays etc. are
performed to an audience. 2 a special room
where surgical operations are done, *the
operating theatre.* [from Greek *theatron*
= place for seeing things]

theatrical *adjective*
to do with plays or acting.
theatrically *adverb*

theatricals *plural noun*
performances of plays etc.

thee *pronoun* (*old use*)
the form of *thou* used as the object of a verb
or after a preposition. [from Old English]

theft *noun* (*plural* **thefts**)
stealing. [from Old English]

their *adjective*
1 belonging to them, *Their coats are over
there.* 2 (*informal*) belonging to a person,
Somebody has left their coat on the bus.
[from Old Norse]

USAGE: Do not confuse with *there.*

theirs *possessive pronoun*
belonging to them, *These coats are theirs.*

USAGE: It is incorrect to write *their's.*

them *pronoun*
the form of *they* used as the object of a verb
or after a preposition, *We saw them.*
[from Old Norse]

theme *noun* (*plural* **themes**)
1 the subject about which a person speaks,
writes, or thinks. **2** a melody. [from Greek]

theme park *noun* (*plural* **theme parks**)
an amusement park where the rides and
attractions are based on a particular
subject.

theme tune *noun* (*plural* **theme tunes**)
a special tune always used to announce a
particular programme, performer, etc.

themselves *pronoun*
they or them and nobody else. (Compare
herself.)

then *adverb*
1 at that time, *We were younger then.*
2 after that; next, *Make the tea, then pour it
out.* **3** in that case, *If this is yours, then this
must be mine.* [from Old English]

thence *adverb*
from that place. [from Old English]

theology *noun*
the study of religion.
theological *adjective*, **theologian** *noun*
[from Greek *theos* = a god, + *-logy*]

theorem *noun* (*plural* **theorems**)
a mathematical statement that can be
proved by reasoning.
[from Greek *theorema* = theory]

theoretical *adjective*
based on theory not on experience.
theoretically *adverb*

theorize *verb* (**theorizes, theorizing,
theorized**)
form a theory or theories.

theory *noun* (*plural* **theories**)
1 an idea or set of ideas put forward to
explain something. **2** the principles of a
subject rather than its practice.

in theory according to what should happen
rather than what may in fact happen.
[from Greek *theoria* = thinking about,
considering]

therapeutic (*say* therra-pew-tik) *adjective*
treating or curing a disease etc., *Sunshine
can have a therapeutic effect.*

therapy *noun* (*plural* **therapies**)
treatment to cure a disease etc.
[from Greek *therapeia* = healing]

there *adverb*
1 in or to that place etc. **2** used to call
attention to something (*There's a good
boy!*) or to introduce a sentence where the
verb comes before its subject (*There was
plenty to eat*). [from Old English]

USAGE: Do not confuse with *their.*

thereabouts *adverb*
near there.

thereafter *adverb*
from then or there onwards.

thereby *adverb*
by that means; because of that.

therefore *adverb*
for that reason. [from *there* + *fore*]

therm *noun* (*plural* **therms**)
a unit for measuring heat, especially from
gas. [from Greek *therme* = heat]

thermal *adjective*
1 to do with heat; worked by heat. **2** hot,
thermal springs. [same origin as *therm*]

thermo- *prefix*
heat. [same origin as *therm*]

thermodynamics *noun*
the science dealing with the relation
between heat and other forms of energy.

thermometer *noun* (*plural*
thermometers)
a device for measuring temperature.

Thermos *noun* (*plural* **Thermoses**) (*trade
mark*)
a kind of vacuum flask.
[from Greek *thermos* = hot]

thermostat *noun* (*plural* **thermostats**)
a piece of equipment that automatically keeps the temperature of a room or piece of equipment steady. **thermostatic** *adjective*, **thermostatically** *adverb*
[from *thermo-* + Greek *statos* = standing]

thesaurus (*say* thi-**sor**-us) *noun* (*plural* **thesauruses** or **thesauri**)
a kind of dictionary containing sets of words grouped according to their meaning. [from Greek *thesauros* = storehouse, treasury]

these *plural* of **this**.

thesis *noun* (*plural* **theses**)
a theory put forward, especially a long essay written by a candidate for a university degree. [Greek, = placing]

thews *plural noun* (*literary*)
muscles; muscular strength.
[from Old English]

they *pronoun*
1 the people or things being talked about. **2** people in general, *They say the show is a great success.* **3** (*informal*) he or she; a person, *I am never angry with anyone unless they deserve it.* [from Old Norse]

they're (*mainly spoken*)
they are.

USAGE: Do not confuse with *their* and *there*.

thick *adjective*
1 measuring a lot or a certain amount between opposite surfaces. **2** (of a line) broad, not fine. **3** crowded with things; dense, *a thick forest; thick fog.* **4** fairly stiff, *thick cream.* **5** (*informal*) stupid. **thickly** *adverb*, **thickness** *noun* [from Old English]

thicken *verb* (**thickens, thickening, thickened**)
make or become thicker.

thicket *noun* (*plural* **thickets**)
a number of shrubs and small trees etc. growing close together. [from Old English]

thickset *adjective*
1 having a stocky or burly body. **2** with parts placed or growing close together.

thief *noun* (*plural* **thieves**)
a person who steals things. **thievish** *adjective*, **thievery** *noun*, **thieving** *noun* [from Old English]

thigh *noun* (*plural* **thighs**)
the part of the leg between the hip and the knee. [from Old English]

thimble *noun* (*plural* **thimbles**)
a small metal or plastic cap worn on the end of the finger to push the needle in sewing. [from Old English]

thin *adjective* (**thinner, thinnest**)
1 not thick; not fat. **2** feeble, *a thin excuse.* **thinly** *adverb*, **thinness** *noun*
thin *verb* (**thins, thinning, thinned**)
make or become less thick. **thinner** *noun* [from Old English]

thine *adjective* & *possessive pronoun* (*old use*)
belonging to thee. [from Old English]

thing *noun* (*plural* **things**)
an object; something which can be seen, touched, thought about, etc.
[from Old English]

things *plural noun*
1 personal belongings, *Can I leave my things here?* **2** circumstances, *Things are looking good.*

think *verb* (**thinks, thinking, thought**)
1 use your mind; form connected ideas. **2** have as an idea or opinion, *We think we shall win.* **thinker** *noun* [from Old English]

third *adjective*
next after the second. **thirdly** *adverb*
third *noun* (*plural* **thirds**)
1 the third person or thing. **2** one of three equal parts of something.
[from Old English]

Third World *noun*
the poorest and underdeveloped countries of Asia, Africa, and South America. [originally called 'third' because they were not considered to be politically connected with the USA and its allies (the *First World*) or with the Communist countries led by Russia (the *Second World*)]

thirst *noun*
1 a feeling of dryness in the mouth and

throat, causing a desire to drink. **2** a strong desire, *a thirst for adventure.*
thirsty *adjective*, **thirstily** *adverb*
thirst *verb* (**thirsts, thirsting, thirsted**)
have a strong desire for something.
[from Old English]

thirteen *noun & adjective*
the number 13. **thirteenth** *adjective & noun*
[from Old English]

thirty *noun* (*plural* **thirties**) & *adjective*
the number 30. **thirtieth** *adjective & noun*
[from Old English]

this *adjective & pronoun* (*plural* **these**)
the one here, *This house is ours. Whose is this?*
this *adverb*
to such an extent, *I'm surprised he got this far.* [from Old English]

thistle *noun* (*plural* **thistles**)
a prickly wild plant with purple, white, or yellow flowers. [from Old English]

thistledown *noun*
the very light fluff on thistle seeds.

thither *adverb* (*old use*)
to that place. [from Old English]

thong *noun* (*plural* **thongs**)
a narrow strip of leather etc. used for fastening things. [from Old English]

thorax *noun* (*plural* **thoraxes**)
the part of the body between the head or neck and the abdomen. **thoracic** *adjective*
[Greek, = breastplate]

thorn *noun* (*plural* **thorns**)
1 a small pointed growth on the stem of a plant. **2** a thorny tree or shrub.
[from Old English]

thorny *adjective* (**thornier, thorniest**)
1 having many thorns. **2** like a thorn.
3 difficult, *a thorny problem.*

thorough *adjective*
1 done or doing things carefully and in detail. **2** complete in every way, *a thorough mess.* **thoroughly** *adverb*, **thoroughness** *noun* [a different spelling of *through*]

thoroughbred *adjective*
bred of pure or pedigree stock.
thoroughbred *noun*

thoroughfare *noun* (*plural* **thoroughfares**)
a public road or path that is open at both ends. [from an old sense of *thorough* = through, + *fare* = to progress]

those *plural* of **that**.

thou *pronoun* (*old use*, in speaking to one person)
you. [from Old English]

though *conjunction*
in spite of the fact that; even if, *We must look for it, though we probably shan't find it.*
though *adverb*
however, *She's right, though.*
[from Old English]

thought[1] *noun* (*plural* **thoughts**)
1 something that you think; an idea or opinion. **2** the process of thinking, *She was deep in thought.*
[from Old English; related to *think*]

thought[2] *past tense* of **think**.

thoughtful *adjective*
1 thinking a lot. **2** showing thought for other people's needs; considerate.
thoughtfully *adverb*, **thoughtfulness** *noun*

thoughtless *adjective*
1 careless; not thinking of what may happen. **2** inconsiderate.
thoughtlessly *adverb*, **thoughtlessness** *noun*

thousand *noun* (*plural* **thousands**) & *adjective*
the number 1,000. **thousandth** *adjective & noun* [from Old English]

USAGE: Say *a few thousand* (not 'a few thousands').

thrall *noun*
in thrall to somebody in his or her power; in a state of slavery. [from Old Norse]

thrash *verb* (**thrashes, thrashing, thrashed**)
1 beat someone with a stick or whip; keep hitting very hard. **2** defeat someone

thoroughly. **3** move violently, *The crocodile thrashed its tail.*
[a different spelling of *thresh*]

thread *noun* (*plural* threads)
1 a thin length of any substance. **2** a length of spun cotton, wool, or nylon etc. used for making cloth or in sewing or knitting. **3** the spiral ridge round a screw.
thread *verb* (threads, threading, threaded)
1 put a thread through the eye of a needle. **2** pass a strip of film etc. through or round something. **3** put beads on a thread.
[from Old English]

threadbare *adjective*
(of cloth) with the surface worn away so that the threads show.

threat *noun* (*plural* threats)
1 a warning that you will punish, hurt, or harm a person or thing. **2** a sign of something undesirable. **3** a person or thing causing danger. [from Old English]

threaten *verb* (threatens, threatening, threatened)
1 make threats against someone. **2** be a threat or danger to a person or thing.

three *noun* (*plural* threes) & *adjective*
the number 3. [from Old English]

three-dimensional *adjective*
having three dimensions (length, width, and height or depth).

thresh *verb* (threshes, threshing, threshed)
beat corn in order to separate the grain from the husks. [from Old English]

threshold *noun* (*plural* thresholds)
1 a slab of stone or board etc. forming the bottom of a doorway; the entrance. **2** the beginning, *We are on the threshold of a great discovery.* [from Old English]

thrice *adverb* (*old use*)
three times. [from Old English]

thrift *noun*
1 careful spending or management of money or resources. **2** a plant with pink flowers. **thrifty** *adjective*, **thriftily** *adverb*
[Old Norse, = thriving]

thrill *noun* (*plural* thrills)
a feeling of excitement.

thrill *verb* (thrills, thrilling, thrilled)
have or give a feeling of excitement.
thrilling *adjective* [from Old English]

thriller *noun* (*plural* thrillers)
an exciting story, play, or film, usually about crime.

thrive *verb* (thrives, thriving, throve, thrived or thriven)
grow strongly; prosper or be successful.
[from Old Norse]

throat *noun* (*plural* throats)
1 the tube in the neck that takes food and drink down into the body. **2** the front of the neck. [from Old English]

throaty *adjective*
1 produced deep in the throat, *a throaty chuckle.* **2** hoarse. **throatily** *adverb*

throb *verb* (throbs, throbbing, throbbed)
beat or vibrate with a strong rhythm, *My heart throbbed.* **throb** *noun*
[imitating the sound]

throes *plural noun*
severe pangs of pain.
in the throes of struggling with, *We are in the throes of exams.*
[origin unknown]

thrombosis *noun*
the formation of a clot of blood in the body.
[from Greek *thrombos* = lump]

throne *noun* (*plural* thrones)
a special chair for a king, queen, or bishop at ceremonies.
[from Greek *thronos* = high seat]

throng *noun* (*plural* throngs)
a crowd of people.
throng *verb* (throngs, thronging, thronged)
crowd, *People thronged the streets.*
[from Old English]

throstle *noun* (*plural* throstles) (*poetical*)
a thrush. [from Old English]

throttle *noun* (*plural* throttles)
a device that controls the flow of fuel to an engine; an accelerator.

throttle *verb* (throttles, throttling, throttled)
strangle.
throttle back or **down** reduce the speed of
an engine by partially closing the throttle.
[from *throat*]

through *preposition*
1 from one end or side to the other end or
side of, *Climb through the window.* **2** by
means of; because of, *We lost it through
carelessness.* **3** at the end of; having
finished successfully, *He is through his
exam.*
through *adverb*
1 through something, *We squeezed through.*
2 with a telephone connection made, *I'll
put you through to the president.* **3** finished,
Wait till I'm through with these papers.
through *adjective*
1 going through something, *No through
road.* **2** going all the way to a destination, *a
through train.* [from Old English]

throughout *preposition* & *adverb*
all the way through.

throve *past tense* of **thrive.**

throw *verb* (throws, throwing, threw,
thrown)
1 send a person or thing through the air.
2 put something in a place carelessly or
hastily. **3** move part of your body quickly,
He threw his head back. **4** put someone in a
certain condition etc., *It threw us into
confusion.* **5** move a switch or lever in
order to operate it. **6** shape a pot on a
potter's wheel. **throw** *noun,* **thrower** *noun*
throw away 1 get rid of something because
it is useless or unwanted. **2** waste, *You
threw away an opportunity.*
[from Old English]

thrum *verb* (thrums, thrumming, thrummed)
sound monotonously; strum. **thrum** *noun*
[imitating the sound]

thrush[1] *noun* (*plural* thrushes)
a songbird with a speckled breast.
[from Old English]

thrush[2] *noun*
a disease causing tiny white patches in the
mouth and throat. [origin unknown]

thrust *verb* (thrusts, thrusting, thrust)
push hard. **thrust** *noun* [from Old Norse]

thud *verb* (thuds, thudding, thudded)
make the dull sound of a heavy knock or
fall. **thud** *noun* [originally Scots; probably
from Old English]

thug *noun* (*plural* thugs)
a rough and violent person. **thuggery** *noun*
[from Hindi: the Thugs were robbers and
murderers in India in the 17th–19th
centuries]

thumb *noun* (*plural* thumbs)
the short thick finger set apart from the
other four.
be under a person's thumb be completely
under his or her influence.
thumb *verb* (thumbs, thumbing, thumbed)
turn the pages of a book etc. quickly with
your thumb.
thumb a lift hitch-hike.
[from Old English]

thumbnail *adjective*
a thumbnail account or description is a
short one that gives only the main facts.

thumbscrew *noun* (*plural* thumbscrews)
a former instrument of torture for
squeezing the thumb.

thump *verb* (thumps, thumping, thumped)
1 hit or knock something heavily. **2** punch.
3 thud. **4** throb or beat strongly, *My heart
was thumping.* **thump** *noun*
[imitating the sound]

thunder *noun*
1 the loud noise that is heard with
lightning. **2** a similar noise, *a thunder of
applause.* **thunderous** *adjective,*
thunderstorm *noun,* **thundery** *adjective*
thunder *verb* (thunders, thundering,
thundered)
1 sound with thunder. **2** make a noise like
thunder; speak loudly. [from Old English]

thunderbolt *noun* (*plural* thunderbolts)
a lightning flash thought of as a destructive
missile.

thunderstruck *adjective*
amazed.

thus *adverb*
1 in this way, *Hold the wheel thus.*
2 therefore. [from Old English]

thwart *verb* (**thwarts, thwarting, thwarted**)
frustrate; prevent someone from achieving
something. [from Old Norse]

thy *adjective* (*old use*)
belonging to thee. [from *thine*]

thyme (*say as* time) *noun*
a herb with fragrant leaves. [from Greek]

thyroid gland *noun* (*plural* **thyroid
glands**)
a large gland at the front of the neck.
[from Greek *thyreos* = a shield (because of
the shape of the gland)]

thyself *pronoun* (*old use*)
thou or thee and nobody else. (Compare
herself.)

tiara (*say* tee-**ar**-a) *noun* (*plural* **tiaras**)
a woman's jewelled crescent-shaped
ornament worn like a crown. [from Greek]

tic *noun* (*plural* **tics**)
an unintentional twitch of a muscle,
especially of the face.
[via French from Italian]

tick[1] *noun* (*plural* **ticks**)
1 a small mark (usually ✓) put by
something to show that it is correct or has
been checked. **2** a regular clicking sound,
especially that made by a clock or watch.
3 (*informal*) a moment, *Back in a tick*.
tick *verb* (**ticks, ticking, ticked**)
1 put a tick by something. **2** make the
sound of a tick.
tick off (*informal*) reprimand someone.
[probably from old German or old Dutch]

tick[2] *noun* (*plural* **ticks**)
a bloodsucking insect. [from Old English]

ticket *noun* (*plural* **tickets**)
1 a printed piece of paper or card that
allows a person to travel on a bus or train,
see a show, etc. **2** a label showing a thing's
price. [via French from old Dutch]

tickle *verb* (**tickles, tickling, tickled**)
1 touch a person's skin lightly in order to
produce a slight tingling feeling and
laughter. **2** (of a part of the body) have a
slight tingling or itching feeling. **3** amuse
or please somebody. [origin unknown]

ticklish *adjective*
1 likely to laugh or wriggle when tickled.
2 awkward or difficult, *a ticklish situation*.

tidal *adjective*
to do with or affected by tides.

tidal wave *noun* (*plural* **tidal waves**)
a huge sea wave.

tiddler *noun* (*plural* **tiddlers**) (*informal*)
a very small fish. [origin unknown]

tiddlywink *noun* (*plural* **tiddlywinks**)
a small counter flicked into a cup by
pressing with another counter in the game
of **tiddlywinks**. [origin unknown]

tide *noun* (*plural* **tides**)
1 the regular rise and fall in the level of the
sea which usually happens twice a day.
2 (*old use*) a time or season, *Christmas-tide*.
tide *verb* (**tides, tiding, tided**)
tide a person over provide him or her with
what is needed, for a short time.
[from Old English]

tidings *plural noun* (*formal*)
news. [probably from Old Norse]

tidy *adjective* (**tidier, tidiest**)
1 with everything in its right place; neat
and orderly. **2** (*informal*) fairly large, *It
costs a tidy amount*.
tidily *adverb*, **tidiness** *noun*
tidy *verb* (**tidies, tidying, tidied**)
make a place tidy. [originally = at the right
time or season: from *tide*]

tie *verb* (**ties, tying, tied**)
1 fasten something with string, ribbon, etc.
2 arrange something into a knot or bow.
3 make the same score as another
competitor.
tie *noun* (*plural* **ties**)
1 a strip of material worn passing under
the collar of a shirt and knotted in front.
2 a result when two or more competitors
have equal scores. [from Old English]

tie-break or **tie-breaker** *noun* (*plural* **tie-
breaks, tie-breakers**)
a way to decide the winner when
competitors have tied, especially an
additional question in a quiz or an
additional game at the end of a set in
tennis.

tier (*say* teer) *noun* (*plural* tiers)
each of a series of rows or levels etc. placed one above the other. **tiered** *adjective*
[from French *tire* = rank[1]]

tiff *noun* (*plural* tiffs)
a slight quarrel. [origin unknown]

tiger *noun* (*plural* tigers)
a large wild animal of the cat family, with yellow and black stripes. [from Greek]

tight *adjective*
1 fitting very closely. 2 firmly fastened.
3 fully stretched; tense. 4 in short supply, *Money is tight at the moment.* 5 stingy, *He is very tight with his money.* 6 (*slang*) drunk.
tightly *adverb*, **tightness** *noun*
[probably from Old English]

tighten *verb* (tightens, tightening, tightened)
make or become tighter.

tightrope *noun* (*plural* tightropes)
a tightly stretched rope high above the ground, on which acrobats perform.

tights *plural noun*
a garment that fits tightly over the feet, legs, and lower part of the body.

tigress *noun* (*plural* tigresses)
a female tiger.

tile *noun* (*plural* tiles)
a thin square piece of baked clay or other hard material, used in rows for covering roofs, walls, or floors. **tiled** *adjective*
[via Old English from Latin]

till[1] *preposition & conjunction*
until. [from Old English *til* = to]

USAGE: It is better to use *until* rather than *till* when the word stands first in a sentence (e.g. *Until last year we had never been abroad*) or when you are speaking or writing formally.

---

till[2] *noun* (*plural* tills)
a drawer or box for money in a shop; a cash register. [origin unknown]

till[3] *verb* (tills, tilling, tilled)
plough land to prepare it for cultivating.
[from Old English *tilian* = try]

tiller *noun* (*plural* tillers)
a handle used to turn a boat's rudder.
[from old French]

tilt *verb* (tilts, tilting, tilted)
move into a sloping position.
tilt *noun*
a sloping position.
at full tilt at full speed or force.
[origin unknown]

timber *noun* (*plural* timbers)
1 wood for building or making things. 2 a wooden beam. [from Old English]

timbered *adjective*
made of wood or with a wooden framework, *timbered houses.*

timbre (*say* tambr) *noun* (*plural* timbres)
the quality of a voice or musical sound.
[French; related to *timpani*]

time *noun* (*plural* times)
1 all the years of the past, present, and future; the continuous existence of the universe. 2 a particular point or portion of time. 3 an occasion, *the first time I saw him.*
4 a period suitable or available for something, *Is there time for a cup of tea?* 5 a system of measuring time, *Greenwich Mean Time.* 6 (in music) rhythm depending on the number and stress of beats in the bar. 7 (in mathematics) **times** multiplied by, *Five times three is 15* ($5 \times 3 = 15$).
in time 1 not late. 2 eventually.
on time punctual.
time *verb* (times, timing, timed)
1 measure how long something takes.
2 arrange when something is to happen.
timer *noun* [from Old English]

timeless *adjective*
not affected by the passage of time; eternal.

time limit *noun* (*plural* time limits)
a fixed amount of time within which something must be done.

timely *adjective*
happening at a suitable or useful time, *a timely warning.*

timetable *noun* (*plural* timetables)
a list showing the times when things will happen, e.g. when buses or trains will arrive and depart, or when school lessons will take place.

timid *adjective*
easily frightened. **timidly** *adverb*, **timidity** *noun* [from Latin *timidus* = nervous]

timing *noun*
the way something is timed.

timorous *adjective*
timid. [from Latin *timor* = fear]

timpani *plural noun*
kettledrums. [Italian]

tin *noun* (*plural* **tins**)
1 a silvery-white metal. 2 a metal container for food.
tin *verb* (**tins, tinning, tinned**)
seal food in a tin to preserve it. [from Old English]

tincture *noun* (*plural* **tinctures**)
1 a solution of medicine in alcohol. 2 a slight trace of something. [from Latin *tinctura* = dyeing]

tinder *noun*
any dry substance that catches fire easily. [from Old English]

tine *noun* (*plural* **tines**)
a point or prong of a fork, comb, or antler. [from Old English]

tinge *verb* (**tinges, tingeing, tinged**)
colour something slightly; tint. **tinge** *noun* [same origin as *tint*]

tingle *verb* (**tingles, tingling, tingled**)
have a slight pricking or stinging feeling. **tingle** *noun* [probably from *tinkle*]

tinker *noun* (*plural* **tinkers**) (*old use*)
a person travelling about to mend pots and pans etc.
tinker *verb* (**tinkers, tinkering, tinkered**)
work at something casually, trying to improve or mend it. [origin unknown]

tinkle *verb* (**tinkles, tinkling, tinkled**)
make a gentle ringing sound. **tinkle** *noun* [imitating the sound]

tinny *adjective*
1 like tin. 2 (of a sound) unpleasantly thin and high-pitched.

tinsel *noun*
strips of glittering material used for decoration.
[from old French; related to *scintillate*]

tint *noun* (*plural* **tints**)
a shade of colour, especially a pale one.
tint *verb* (**tints, tinting, tinted**)
colour something slightly. [from Latin *tingere* = to dye or stain]

tiny *adjective* (**tinier, tiniest**)
very small. [origin unknown]

-tion *suffix* see **-ion**.

tip[1] *noun* (*plural* **tips**)
the part right at the top or end of something.
tip *verb* (**tips, tipping, tipped**)
put a tip on something. [from Old Norse]

tip[2] *noun* (*plural* **tips**)
1 a small present of money given to someone who has helped you. 2 a small but useful piece of advice; a hint. 3 a slight push.
tip *verb* (**tips, tipping, tipped**)
1 give a person a tip. 2 name someone as a likely winner, *Which team would you tip to win the championship?* **tipper** *noun* [probably from *tip*[1]]

tip[3] *verb* (**tips, tipping, tipped**)
1 tilt or topple. 2 empty rubbish somewhere.
tip *noun* (*plural* **tips**)
1 the action of tipping something. 2 a place where rubbish etc. is tipped. [probably from a Scandinavian language]

tipple *verb* (**tipples, tippling, tippled**)
drink alcohol. **tipple** *noun*, **tippler** *noun* [origin unknown]

tipsy *adjective*
slightly drunk. [from *tip*[3]]

tiptoe *verb* (**tiptoes, tiptoeing, tiptoed**)
walk on your toes very quietly or carefully. **on tiptoe** walking or standing on your toes.

tiptop *adjective* (*informal*)
excellent; very best, *in tiptop condition.* [from *tip*[1] + *top*[1]]

tirade (*say* ty-rayd) *noun* (*plural* tirades)
a long angry or violent speech.
[via French from Italian]

tire *verb* (tires, tiring, tired)
make or become tired. [from Old English]

tired *adjective*
feeling that you need to sleep or rest.
tired of having had enough of something
and impatient or bored with it.

tiresome *adjective*
annoying.

tiro *noun* (*plural* tiros)
a beginner. [Latin, = recruit]

tissue *noun* (*plural* tissues)
1 tissue paper. 2 a paper handkerchief.
3 the substance forming any part of the
body of an animal or plant, *bone tissue*.
[from old French; related to *textiles*]

tissue paper *noun*
very thin soft paper used for wrapping and
packing things.

tit[1] *noun* (*plural* tits)
a kind of small bird. [probably from a
Scandinavian language]

tit[2] *noun*
tit for tat something equal given in return;
retaliation.
[originally 'tip for tap': from *tip*[2] + *tap*[2]]

titanic (*say* ty-tan-ik) *adjective*
huge. [from the *Titans*, gigantic gods and
goddesses in Greek legend]

titanium *noun*
a strong silver-grey metal used to make
light alloys that do not corrode easily.

titbit *noun* (*plural* titbits)
a nice little piece of something, e.g. of food,
gossip, or information.
[from a dialect word *tid* = tender, + *bit*[1]]

tithe *noun* (*plural* tithes)
one-tenth of a year's output from a farm
etc., formerly paid as tax to support the
clergy and church.
[from Old English *teotha* = tenth]

titillate *verb* (titillates, titillating, titillated)
stimulate or excite you pleasantly.
titillation *noun*
[from Latin *titillare* = to tickle]

titivate *verb* (titivates, titivating, titivated)
put the finishing touches to something;
smarten up. **titivation** *noun*
[origin unknown]

title *noun* (*plural* titles)
1 the name of a book, film, song, etc. 2 a
word used to show a person's rank or
position, e.g. *Dr, Lord, Mrs.* 3 a
championship in sport, *the world
heavyweight title.* 4 a legal right to
something. [from Latin]

titled *adjective*
having a title as a noble.

titter *verb* (titters, tittering, tittered)
giggle. **titter** *noun* [imitating the sound]

TNT *abbreviation*
trinitrotoluene; a powerful explosive.

to *preposition*
This word is used to show 1 direction or
arrival at a position (*We walked to school.
He rose to power*), 2 limit (*from noon to two
o'clock*), 3 comparison (*We won by six goals
to three*), 4 receiving or being affected by
something (*Give it to me. Be kind to
animals*).
Also used before a verb to form an
infinitive (*I want to see him*) or to show
purpose etc. (*He does that to annoy us*), or
alone when the verb is understood (*We
meant to go but forgot to*).

to *adverb*
1 to or in the proper or closed position or
condition, *Push the door to.* 2 into a state of
activity, *We set to and cleaned the kitchen.*
to and fro backwards and forwards.
[from Old English]

toad *noun* (*plural* toads)
a frog-like animal that lives mainly on
land. [from Old English]

toad-in-the-hole *noun*
sausages baked in batter.

toadstool *noun* (*plural* toadstools)
a fungus (usually poisonous) with a round
top on a stalk.

toady *verb* (**toadies, toadying, toadied**)
flatter someone to make them want to help you. **toady** *noun* [short for *toad-eater*]

toast *verb* (**toasts, toasting, toasted**)
1 heat bread etc. to make it brown and crisp. 2 warm something in front of a fire etc. 3 drink in honour of someone.
toast *noun* (*plural* **toasts**)
1 toasted bread. 2 the call to drink in honour of someone; the person honoured in this way. [from Latin *tostum* = dried up]

toaster *noun* (*plural* **toasters**)
an electrical device for toasting bread.

tobacco *noun*
the dried leaves of certain plants prepared for smoking in cigarettes, cigars, or pipes or for making snuff. [via Spanish from a Central American language]

tobacconist *noun* (*plural* **tobacconists**)
a shopkeeper who sells cigarettes, cigars, etc.

toboggan *noun* (*plural* **toboggans**)
a small sledge used for sliding downhill. **tobogganing** *noun* [via Canadian French from a Native American language]

tocsin *noun* (*plural* **tocsins**)
a bell rung as an alarm signal. [from old French]

today *noun*
this present day, *Today is Monday.*
today *adverb*
on this day, *Have you seen him today?* [from *to* (preposition) + *day*]

toddler *noun* (*plural* **toddlers**)
a young child who has only recently learnt to walk. **toddle** *verb* [origin unknown]

toddy *noun* (*plural* **toddies**)
a sweetened drink made with spirits and hot water.
[from Sanskrit *tadi*, a tree whose sugary sap was made into an alcoholic drink]

to-do *noun* (*plural* **to-dos**)
a fuss or commotion.

toe *noun* (*plural* **toes**)
1 any of the separate parts (five in humans) at the end of each foot. 2 the part of a shoe or sock etc. that covers the toes. [from Old English]

toffee *noun* (*plural* **toffees**)
a sticky sweet made from heated butter and sugar. [origin unknown]

toga (*say* **toh-ga**) *noun* (*plural* **togas**)
a long loose garment worn by men in ancient Rome.
[Latin, from *tegere* = to cover]

together *adverb*
with another person or thing; with each other, *They went to the party together.* [from Old English]

toggle *noun* (*plural* **toggles**)
a short piece of wood or metal etc. used like a button. [originally a sailors' word; origin unknown]

toil *verb* (**toils, toiling, toiled**)
1 work hard. 2 move slowly and with difficulty. **toiler** *noun*
toil *noun*
hard work. [from old French]

toilet *noun* (*plural* **toilets**)
1 a bowl-like object, connected by pipes to a drain, which you use to get rid of urine and faeces. 2 a room containing a toilet. 3 the process of washing, dressing, and tidying yourself.
[from French]

toilet paper *noun*
paper for use in a toilet.

token *noun* (*plural* **tokens**)
1 a piece of metal or plastic that can be used instead of money. 2 a voucher or coupon that can be exchanged for goods. 3 a sign or signal of something, *a token of our friendship.*
[from Old English]

tolerable *adjective*
able to be tolerated. **tolerably** *adverb*

tolerant *adjective*
tolerating things, especially other people's behaviour, beliefs, etc.
tolerantly *adverb*, **tolerance** *noun*

tolerate *verb* (tolerates, tolerating, tolerated)
allow something without protesting or interfering. **toleration** *noun*
[from Latin *tolerare* = endure]

toll[1] (rhymes with *hole*) *noun* (*plural* tolls)
1 a charge made for using a road, bridge, etc. 2 loss or damage caused, *The death toll in the earthquake is rising.* [via Old English and Latin from Greek *telos* = a tax]

toll[2] (rhymes with *hole*) *verb* (tolls, tolling, tolled)
ring a bell slowly. **toll** *noun*
[probably from Old English]

tom *noun* (*plural* toms)
a male cat. **tomcat** *noun* [short for *Thomas*]

tomahawk *noun* (*plural* tomahawks)
a small axe used by Native Americans.
[from Algonquin, a Native American language]

tomato *noun* (*plural* tomatoes)
a soft round red or yellow fruit eaten as a vegetable. [via French, Spanish, or Portuguese from Nahuatl (a Central American language)]

tomb (*say* toom) *noun* (*plural* tombs)
a place where someone is buried; a monument built over this. [from Greek]

tombola *noun*
a kind of lottery. [from Italian *tombolare* = tumble (because often the tickets are drawn from a revolving drum)]

tomboy *noun* (*plural* tomboys)
a girl who enjoys rough noisy games etc.
[from *tom* (short for *Thomas*) + *boy*]

tombstone *noun* (*plural* tombstones)
a memorial stone set up over a grave.

tome *noun* (*plural* tomes)
a large heavy book.
[from Greek *tomos* = roll of papyrus]

tommy-gun *noun* (*plural* tommy-guns)
a small machine-gun.
[from the name of its American inventor, J. T. Thompson (died 1940)]

tomorrow *noun* & *adverb*
the day after today.
[from *to* (preposition) + *morrow*]

tom-tom *noun* (*plural* tom-toms)
a drum beaten with the hands.
[from Hindi *tam tam*, imitating the sound]

ton *noun* (*plural* tons)
1 a unit of weight equal to 2,240 pounds or about 1,016 kilograms. 2 a large amount, *There's tons of room.* 3 (*slang*) a speed of 100 miles per hour. [a different spelling of *tun*]

tone *noun* (*plural* tones)
1 a sound in music or of the voice. 2 each of the five larger intervals between notes in a musical scale (the smaller intervals are *semitones*). 3 a shade of a colour. 4 the quality or character of something, *a cheerful tone.* **tonal** *adjective*, **tonally** *adverb*

tone *verb* (tones, toning, toned)
1 give a particular tone or quality to something. 2 be harmonious in colour.
tone down make a thing quieter or less bright or less harsh.
tone up make a thing brighter or stronger.
[from Greek *tonos* = tension]

tone-deaf *adjective*
not able to tell the difference between different musical notes.

tongs *plural noun*
a tool with two arms joined at one end, used to pick up or hold things.
[from Old English]

tongue *noun* (*plural* tongues)
1 the long soft muscular part that moves about inside the mouth. 2 a language. 3 the leather flap on a shoe or boot underneath the laces. 4 a pointed flame.
[from Old English]

tongue-tied *adjective*
too shy to speak.

tongue-twister *noun* (*plural* tongue-twisters)
something that is difficult to say quickly and correctly, e.g. 'She sells seashells'.

tonic *noun* (*plural* tonics)
1 a medicine etc. that makes a person healthier or stronger. 2 a keynote in music. **tonic** *adjective* [same origin as *tone*]

tonight *noun & adverb*
this evening or night.
[from *to* (preposition) + *night*]

tonnage *noun*
the amount a ship or ships can carry,
expressed in tons.

tonne *noun* (*plural* **tonnes**)
a metric ton (1,000 kilograms). [French]

tonsil *noun* (*plural* **tonsils**)
either of two small masses of soft tissue at
the sides of the throat. [from Latin]

tonsillitis *noun*
inflammation of the tonsils.

too *adverb*
1 also, *Take the others too.* 2 more than is
wanted or allowed etc., *That's too much
sugar for me.* [from Old English]

tool *noun* (*plural* **tools**)
an object that helps you to do a particular
job, *A saw is a tool for cutting wood or
metal.* [from Old English]

toot *noun* (*plural* **toots**)
a short sound produced by a horn. **toot**
verb [imitating the sound]

tooth *noun* (*plural* **teeth**)
1 one of the hard white bony parts that are
rooted in the gums, used for biting and
chewing things. 2 one of a row of sharp
parts, *the teeth of a saw.* **toothache** *noun*,
toothbrush *noun*, **toothed** *adjective*
fight tooth and nail fight very fiercely.
[from Old English]

toothpaste *noun* (*plural* **toothpastes**)
a paste for cleaning your teeth.

toothpick *noun* (*plural* **toothpicks**)
a small pointed piece of wood etc. for
removing bits of food from between your
teeth.

toothy *adjective*
having large teeth.

top¹ *noun* (*plural* **tops**)
1 the highest part of something. 2 the
upper surface. 3 the covering or stopper of
a bottle, jar, etc. 4 a piece of clothing for
the upper part of the body.
on top of in addition to something.

top *adjective*
highest, *at top speed.*

top *verb* (**tops, topping, topped**)
1 put a top on something. 2 be at the top of
something, *She tops the list.* 3 remove the
top of something.
top up fill up something that is half empty.
[from Old English]

top² *noun* (*plural* **tops**)
a toy that can be made to spin on its point.
[origin unknown]

topaz *noun* (*plural* **topazes**)
a kind of gem, often yellow. [from Greek]

top hat *noun* (*plural* **top hats**)
a man's tall stiff black or grey hat worn
with formal clothes.

top-heavy *adjective*
too heavy at the top and likely to
overbalance.

topic *noun* (*plural* **topics**)
a subject to write, learn, or talk about.
[from Greek *topos* = place]

topical *adjective*
connected with things that are happening
now, *a topical film.* **topically** *adverb*,
topicality *noun* [originally = covering a
particular place or topic]

topless *adjective*
not wearing any clothes on the top half of
the body.

topmost *adjective*
highest.

topography (*say* top-**og**-ra-fee) *noun*
(*plural* **topographies**)
the position of the rivers, mountains,
roads, buildings, etc. in a place.
topographical *adjective*
[from Greek *topos* = place, + -*graphy*]

topping *noun* (*plural* **toppings**)
food that is put on the top of a cake,
dessert, pizza, etc.

topple *verb* (**topples, toppling, toppled**)
1 fall over; totter and fall. 2 make
something fall; overthrow. [from *top¹*]

top secret *adjective*
extremely secret, *top secret information.*

topsy-turvy *adverb & adjective*
upside down; muddled. [probably from *top*¹
+ Middle English *terve* = turn upside down]

torch *noun* (*plural* **torches**)
1 a small electric lamp that you can carry
in your hand. **2** a stick with burning
material on the end, used as a light.
[from old French]

toreador (*say* torree-a-dor) *noun* (*plural*
toreadors)
a bullfighter. [from Spanish *toro* = bull]

torment *verb* (**torments, tormenting,
tormented**)
1 make someone suffer greatly. **2** tease;
keep annoying someone. **tormentor** *noun*
torment *noun* (*plural* **torments**)
great suffering.
[from old French; related to *torture*]

tornado (*say* tor-**nay**-doh) *noun* (*plural*
tornadoes)
a violent storm or whirlwind.
[from Spanish *tronada* = thunderstorm]

torpedo *noun* (*plural* **torpedoes**)
a long tube-shaped missile that can be fired
under water to destroy ships.
torpedo *verb* (**torpedoes, torpedoing,
torpedoed**)
attack or destroy a ship with a torpedo.
[Latin, = a large sea fish that can give an
electric shock which causes numbness]

torpid *adjective*
slow-moving, not lively. **torpidly** *adverb*,
torpidity *noun*, **torpor** *noun*
[from Latin *torpidus* = numb]

torrent *noun* (*plural* **torrents**)
1 a rushing stream; a great flow. **2** a heavy
downpour of rain. [from Latin]

torrential *adjective*
(of rain) pouring down violently.

torrid *adjective*
1 very hot and dry. **2** passionate, *a torrid
love affair*. [from Latin *torridus* = parched]

torsion *noun*
twisting, especially of one end of a thing
while the other is held in a fixed position.
[French; related to *torture*]

torso *noun* (*plural* **torsos**)
the trunk of the human body.
[Italian, = stump]

tortoise *noun* (*plural* **tortoises**)
a slow-moving animal with a shell over its
body. [from Latin]

tortoiseshell (*say* **tort**-a-shell) *noun*
(*plural* **tortoiseshells**)
1 the mottled brown and yellow shell of
certain turtles, used for making combs etc.
2 a cat or butterfly with mottled brown
colouring.

tortuous *adjective*
1 full of twists and turns, *a tortuous path*.
2 complicated and not easy to follow,
tortuous logic. **tortuosity** *noun*
[from Latin *tortum* = twisted]

USAGE: Do not confuse with *torturous*.

torture *verb* (**tortures, torturing, tortured**)
make a person feel great pain or worry.
torture *noun*, **torturer** *noun*
[same origin as *tortuous*]

torturous *adjective*
like torture, *a torturous wait for news of
survivors*.

USAGE: Do not confuse with *tortuous*.

Tory *noun* (*plural* **Tories**)
a Conservative. **Tory** *adjective*
[from Irish *toraidhe* = an outlaw]

toss *verb* (**tosses, tossing, tossed**)
1 throw something, especially up into the
air. **2** spin a coin to decide something
according to which side of it is upwards
after it falls. **3** move restlessly or unevenly
from side to side. **toss** *noun*
[origin unknown]

toss-up *noun* (*plural* **toss-ups**)
1 the tossing of a coin. **2** an even chance.

tot¹ *noun* (*plural* **tots**)
1 a small child. **2** (*informal*) a small
amount of spirits, *a tot of rum*.
[originally a dialect word]

tot² *verb* (**tots, totting, totted**)
tot up (*informal*) add up.
[from *total*]

total *adjective*
1 including everything, *the total amount.*
2 complete, *total darkness.* **totally** *adverb*

total *noun* (*plural* **totals**)
the amount you get by adding everything
together.

total *verb* (**totals, totalling, totalled**)
1 add up the total. 2 amount to something,
The cost of the damage totalled £500.
[from Latin *totum* = the whole]

totalitarian *adjective*
using a form of government where people
are not allowed to form rival political
parties. [from *totality*]

totality *noun*
the whole of something.

totem pole *noun* (*plural* **totem poles**)
a pole carved or painted by Native
Americans with the symbols (*totems*) of
their tribes or families. [from Ojibwa, a
Native American language]

totter *verb* (**totters, tottering, tottered**)
walk unsteadily; wobble. **tottery** *adjective*
[from old Dutch]

toucan (*say* **too**-kan) *noun* (*plural* **toucans**)
a tropical American bird with a huge beak.
[via French and Portuguese from Tupi (a
South American language)]

touch *verb* (**touches, touching, touched**)
1 put your hand or fingers etc. on
something lightly. 2 be or come together so
that there is no space between. 3 hit
something gently. 4 move or meddle with
something. 5 reach, *The thermometer
touched 30° Celsius.* 6 affect someone's
feelings, e.g. by making them feel
sympathy, *The sad story touched our hearts.*
7 (*slang*) persuade someone to give or lend
you money.
touch and go an uncertain situation.
touch down 1 (of an aircraft) land. **2** (in
Rugby football) touch the ball on the
ground behind the goal line.
touch up improve something by making
small additions or changes.

touch *noun* (*plural* **touches**)
1 the action of touching. 2 the ability to
feel things by touching them. 3 a small
amount; a small thing done, *the finishing
touches.* 4 a special skill or style of
workmanship, *She hasn't lost her touch.*

5 communication with someone, *We lost
touch with him.* 6 the part of a football field
outside the playing area. [from old French]

touchable *adjective*
able to be touched.

touchdown *noun* (*plural* **touchdowns**)
the action of touching down.

touching *adjective*
causing you to have kindly feelings such as
pity or sympathy.

touchline *noun* (*plural* **touchlines**)
one of the lines that mark the side of a
sports pitch.

touchstone *noun* (*plural* **touchstones**)
a test by which the quality of something is
judged. [formerly, a kind of stone against
which gold and silver were rubbed to test
their purity]

touchy *adjective* (**touchier, touchiest**)
easily offended. **touchily** *adverb*, **touchiness**
noun [origin unknown]

tough *adjective*
1 strong; difficult to break or damage.
2 difficult to chew. 3 firm or stubborn; able
to stand hardship. 4 difficult, *a tough
decision.* **toughly** *adverb*, **toughness** *noun*
[from Old English]

toughen *verb* (**toughens, toughening,
toughened**)
make or become tough.

tour *noun* (*plural* **tours**)
a journey visiting several places.

tour *verb* (**tours, touring, toured**)
make a tour.
[from old French; related to *turn*]

tourism *noun*
the industry of providing services for
people on holiday in a place.

tourist *noun* (*plural* **tourists**)
a person who makes a tour or visits a place
for pleasure.

tournament *noun* (*plural* **tournaments**)
a series of contests.
[from old French; related to *turn*]

tourniquet (*say* **toor**-nik-ay) *noun* (*plural* **tourniquets**)
a strip of material etc. pulled tightly round an arm or leg to stop bleeding from an artery. [from French]

tousle (*say* **towz**-el) *verb* (**tousles, tousling, tousled**)
ruffle someone's hair.
[probably from an Old English word meaning 'to pull or shake']

tout (rhymes with *scout*) *verb* (**touts, touting, touted**)
try to sell something or get business.

tout *noun* (*plural* **touts**)
a person who sells tickets for a sports match, concert, etc. at more than the original price.
[from Old English]

tow[1] (rhymes with *go*) *verb* (**tows, towing, towed**)
pull something along behind you. **tow** *noun*
[from Old English *togian*]

tow[2] (rhymes with *go*) *noun*
short light-coloured fibres of flax or hemp.
[from Old English *tow*]

toward *preposition*
towards.

towards *preposition*
1 in the direction of, *She walked towards the sea.* 2 in relation to; regarding, *He behaved kindly towards his children.* 3 as a contribution to, *Put the money towards a new bicycle.* 4 near, *towards four o'clock.*
[from Old English]

towel *noun* (*plural* **towels**)
a piece of absorbent cloth for drying things. **towelling** *noun*
[via old French from Germanic]

tower *noun* (*plural* **towers**)
a tall narrow building.

tower *verb* (**towers, towering, towered**)
be very high; be taller than others, *Skyscrapers towered over the city.*
[from Greek]

town *noun* (*plural* **towns**)
a place with many houses, shops, offices, and other buildings.
[from Old English *tun* = enclosure]

town hall *noun* (*plural* **town halls**)
a building with offices for the local council and usually a hall for public events.

township *noun* (*plural* **townships**)
a town in South Africa where Black people live.

towpath *noun* (*plural* **towpaths**)
a path beside a canal or river, originally for use when a horse was towing a barge etc.

toxic *adjective*
poisonous; caused by poison. **toxicity** *noun*
[from Greek]

toxicology *noun*
the study of poisons. **toxicologist** *noun*
[from *toxic* + *-ology*]

toxin *noun* (*plural* **toxins**)
a poisonous substance, especially one formed in the body by germs. [from *toxic*]

toy *noun* (*plural* **toys**)
a thing to play with.

toy *adjective*
1 made as a toy. 2 (of a dog) of a very small breed kept as a pet, *a toy poodle.*

toy *verb* (**toys, toying, toyed**)
toy with handle a thing or consider an idea casually.
[origin unknown]

toyshop *noun* (*plural* **toyshops**)
a shop that sells toys.

trace[1] *noun* (*plural* **traces**)
1 a mark left by a person or thing; a sign, *There was no trace of the thief.* 2 a very small amount.

trace *verb* (**traces, tracing, traced**)
1 copy a picture or map etc. by drawing over it on transparent paper. 2 follow the traces of a person or thing; find, *The police have been trying to trace her.* **tracer** *noun*
[from old French; related to *tract*[1]]

trace[2] *noun* (*plural* **traces**)
each of the two straps or ropes etc. by which a horse pulls a cart.
kick over the traces become disobedient or reckless.
[from old French; related to *traction*]

traceable *adjective*
able to be traced.

tracery *noun*
a decorative pattern of holes in stone, e.g. in a church window. [from *trace*[1]]

track *noun* (*plural* **tracks**)
1 a mark or marks left by a moving person or thing. 2 a rough path made by being used. 3 a road or area of ground specially prepared for something (e.g. racing). 4 a set of rails for trains or trams etc. 5 one of the songs or pieces of music on a CD, tape, etc. 6 a continuous band round the wheels of a tank or tractor etc.
keep track of keep yourself informed about where something is or what someone is doing.
track *verb* (**tracks, tracking, tracked**)
1 follow the tracks left by a person or animal. 2 follow or observe something as it moves. **tracker** *noun*
track down find a person or thing by searching.
[from old French]

track record *noun* (*plural* **track records**)
a person's past achievements.

track suit *noun* (*plural* **track suits**)
a warm loose suit of the kind worn by athletes etc. before and after contests or for jogging.

tract[1] *noun* (*plural* **tracts**)
1 an area of land. 2 a series of connected parts along which something passes, *the digestive tract*.
[from Latin *tractus* = drawing, draught]

tract[2] *noun* (*plural* **tracts**)
a pamphlet containing a short essay, especially about religion.
[via Old English from Latin]

traction *noun*
1 pulling a load. 2 the ability of a vehicle to grip the ground, *The wheels were losing traction in the snow*. 3 a medical treatment in which an injured arm, leg, etc. is pulled gently for a long time by means of weights and pulleys. [from Latin *tractum* = pulled]

traction engine *noun* (*plural* **traction engines**)
a steam or diesel engine for pulling a heavy load along a road or across a field etc.

tractor *noun* (*plural* **tractors**)
a motor vehicle for pulling farm machinery or other heavy loads.
[same origin as *traction*]

trade *noun* (*plural* **trades**)
1 buying, selling, or exchanging goods. 2 business of a particular kind; the people working in this. 3 an occupation, especially a skilled craft.
trade *verb* (**trades, trading, traded**)
buy, sell, or exchange things. **trader** *noun*
trade in give a thing as part of the payment for something new, *He traded in his motorcycle for a car*.
[from old German]

trade mark *noun* (*plural* **trade marks**)
a firm's registered symbol or name used to distinguish its goods etc. from those of other firms.

tradesman *noun* (*plural* **tradesmen**)
a person employed in trade, especially one who sells or delivers goods.

trade union *noun* (*plural* **trade unions**)
a group of workers organized to help and protect workers in their own trade or industry.

tradition *noun* (*plural* **traditions**)
1 the passing down of beliefs or customs etc. from one generation to another. 2 something passed on in this way.
traditional *adjective*, **traditionally** *adverb*
[from Latin *tradere* = to hand on, deliver, or betray]

traffic *noun*
1 vehicles, ships, or aircraft moving along a route. 2 trading, especially when it is illegal or wrong, *drug traffic*.
traffic *verb* (**traffics, trafficking, trafficked**)
deal in something, especially illegally. **trafficker** *noun* [from French]

traffic lights *plural noun*
coloured lights used as a signal to traffic at road junctions etc.

traffic warden *noun* (*plural* **traffic wardens**)
an official who assists police to control the movement and parking of vehicles.

tragedian (*say* tra-jee-dee-an) *noun* (*plural* tragedians)
1 a person who writes tragedies. 2 an actor in tragedies.

tragedy *noun* (*plural* tragedies)
1 a play with unhappy events or a sad ending. 2 a very sad or distressing event. [from Greek]

tragic *adjective*
1 very sad or distressing. 2 to do with tragedies, *a great tragic actor*.
tragically *adverb*

trail *noun* (*plural* trails)
1 a track, scent, or other sign left where something has passed. 2 a path or track made through a wild region.
trail *verb* (trails, trailing, trailed)
1 follow the trail of something; track. 2 drag or be dragged along behind; lag behind. 3 hang down or float loosely. [from Latin *tragula* = net for dragging a river]

trailer *noun* (*plural* trailers)
1 a truck or other container pulled along by a vehicle. 2 a short piece from a film or television programme, shown in advance to advertise it. [from *trail*]

train *noun* (*plural* trains)
1 a railway engine pulling a line of carriages or trucks that are linked together. 2 a number of people or animals moving in a line, *a camel train*. 3 a series of things, *a train of events*. 4 part of a long dress or robe that trails on the ground at the back.
train *verb* (trains, training, trained)
1 give a person instruction or practice so that he or she becomes skilled. 2 practise, *She was training for the race*. 3 make something grow in a particular direction. 4 aim a gun etc., *Train that gun on the bridge*. [from French; related to *traction*]

trainee *noun* (*plural* trainees)
a person who is being trained.

trainer *noun* (*plural* trainers)
1 a person who trains people or animals. 2 a soft rubber-soled shoe of the kind worn for running or by athletes etc. while exercising.

traipse *verb* (traipses, traipsing, traipsed)
walk wearily; trudge. [origin unknown]

trait (*say as* tray *or* trayt) *noun* (*plural* traits)
one of a person's characteristics. [from French; related to *tract*]

traitor *noun* (*plural* traitors)
a person who betrays his or her country or friends. **traitorous** *adjective*
[from old French; related to *tradition*]

trajectory *noun* (*plural* trajectories)
the path taken by a moving object such as a bullet or rocket.
[from *trans-* + Latin *jactum* = thrown]

tram *noun* (*plural* trams)
a public passenger vehicle running on rails in the road. [from old German or old Dutch *trame* = plank, shaft of a cart]

tramlines *plural noun*
1 rails for a tram. 2 the pair of parallel lines at the side of a tennis court.

tramp *noun* (*plural* tramps)
1 a person without a home or job who walks from place to place. 2 a long walk. 3 the sound of heavy footsteps.
tramp *verb* (tramps, tramping, tramped)
1 walk with heavy footsteps. 2 walk for a long distance. [probably from old Dutch]

trample *verb* (tramples, trampling, trampled)
tread heavily on something; crush something by treading on it. [from *tramp*]

trampoline *noun* (*plural* trampolines)
a large piece of canvas joined to a frame by springs, used by gymnasts for jumping on. [from Italian]

trance *noun* (*plural* trances)
a dreamy or unconscious state rather like sleep.
[from old French; related to *transient*]

tranquil *adjective*
calm and quiet. **tranquilly** *adverb*,
tranquillity *noun* [from Latin]

tranquillizer *noun* (*plural* tranquillizers)
a medicine used to make a person feel calm.

trans- *prefix*
1 across; through. 2 beyond.
[from Latin *trans* = across]

transact *verb* (transacts, transacting, transacted)
carry out business. **transaction** *noun*
[from *trans-* + Latin *agere* = do]

transatlantic *adjective*
across or on the other side of the Atlantic Ocean.

transcend *verb* (transcends, transcending, transcended)
go beyond something; surpass.
[from *trans-* + Latin *scandere* = climb]

transcribe *verb* (transcribes, transcribing, transcribed)
copy or write something out. **transcription** *noun* [from *trans-* + Latin *scribere* = write]

transcript *noun* (*plural* transcripts)
a written copy.
[from Latin *transcriptum* = written out]

transept *noun* (*plural* transepts)
the part that is at right angles to the nave in a cross-shaped church.
[from *trans-* + Latin *septum* = partition]

transfer *verb* (transfers, transferring, transferred)
1 move a person or thing to another place. 2 hand over.
transferable *adjective*, **transference** *noun*
transfer *noun* (*plural* transfers)
1 the transferring of a person or thing. 2 a picture or design that can be transferred onto another surface.
[from *trans-* + Latin *ferre* = carry]

transfigure *verb* (transfigures, transfiguring, transfigured)
change the appearance of something greatly. **transfiguration** *noun*
[from *trans-* + Latin *figura* = figure]

transfix *verb* (transfixes, transfixing, transfixed)
1 make a person or animal unable to move because of fear or surprise etc. 2 pierce and fix with something pointed.
[from *trans-* + Latin *fixum* = fixed]

transform *verb* (transforms, transforming, transformed)
change the form or appearance or character of a person or thing.
transformation *noun*
[from *trans-* + Latin *formare* = to form]

transformer *noun* (*plural* transformers)
a device used to change the voltage of an electric current.

transfusion *noun* (*plural* transfusions)
putting blood taken from one person into another person's body. **transfuse** *verb*
[from *trans-* + Latin *fusum* = poured]

transgress *verb* (transgresses, transgressing, transgressed)
break a rule or law etc. **transgression** *noun*
[from *trans-* + Latin *gressus* = gone]

transient *adjective*
passing away quickly; not lasting.
transience *noun*
[from *trans-* + Latin *iens* = going]

transistor *noun* (*plural* transistors)
1 a tiny semiconductor device that controls a flow of electricity. 2 (also **transistor radio**) a portable radio that uses transistors. **transistorized** *adjective*
[from *transfer* + resi*stor*]

transit *noun*
the process of travelling from one place to another. [from *trans-* + Latin *itum* = gone]

transition *noun* (*plural* transitions)
the process of changing from one condition or form etc. to another. **transitional** *adjective* [same origin as *transit*]

transitive *adjective*
(of a verb) used with a direct object after it, e.g. *change* in *change your shoes* (but not in *change into dry shoes*). (Compare *intransitive*.) **transitively** *adverb*
[from Latin *transitivus* = passing over]

transitory *adjective*
existing for a time but not lasting.
[same origin as *transit*]

translate *verb* (translates, translating, translated)
put something into another language.

translatable *adjective*, **translation** *noun*, **translator** *noun*
[from *trans-* + Latin *latum* = carried]

transliterate *verb* (**transliterates, transliterating, transliterated**)
write a word in the letters of a different alphabet or language. **transliteration** *noun*
[from *trans-* + Latin *littera* = letter]

translucent (*say* tranz-**loo**-sent) *adjective*
allowing light to shine through but not transparent.
[from *trans-* + Latin *lucens* = shining]

transmigration *noun*
1 migration. 2 the passing of a person's soul into another body after his or her death.
[from *trans-* + Latin *migratio* = migration]

transmission *noun* (*plural* **transmissions**)
1 transmitting something. 2 a broadcast. 3 the gears by which power is transmitted from the engine to the wheels of a vehicle.

transmit *verb* (**transmits, transmitting, transmitted**)
1 send or pass on from one person or place to another. 2 send out a signal or broadcast etc. **transmitter** *noun*
[from *trans-* + Latin *mittere* = send]

transmute *verb* (**transmutes, transmuting, transmuted**)
change something from one form or substance into another.
transmutation *noun*
[from *trans-* + Latin *mutare* = to change]

transom *noun* (*plural* **transoms**)
1 a horizontal bar of wood or stone dividing a window or separating a door from a window above it. 2 a small window above a door.
[from French; related to *transverse*]

transparency *noun* (*plural* **transparencies**)
1 being transparent. 2 a transparent photograph that can be projected onto a screen.

transparent *adjective*
able to be seen through.
[from *trans-* + Latin *parens* = appearing]

transpire *verb* (**transpires, transpiring, transpired**)
1 (of information) become known; turn out, *It transpired that she had known nothing at all about it.* 2 happen, *The police need to know what transpired on the yacht.* 3 (of plants) give off watery vapour from leaves etc. **transpiration** *noun*
[from *trans-* + Latin *spirare* = breathe]

transplant *verb* (**transplants, transplanting, transplanted**)
1 remove a plant and put it to grow somewhere else. 2 transfer a part of the body to another person or animal.
transplantation *noun*

transplant *noun* (*plural* **transplants**)
1 the process of transplanting. 2 something transplanted.
[from *trans-* + Latin *plantare* = to plant]

transport *verb* (**transports, transporting, transported**)
take a person, animal, or thing from one place to another.
transportation *noun*, **transporter** *noun*

transport *noun*
the action or means of transporting people, animals, or things, *The city has a good system of public transport.*
[from *trans-* + Latin *portare* = carry]

transpose *verb* (**transposes, transposing, transposed**)
1 change the position or order of something. 2 put a piece of music into a different key. **transposition** *noun*
[from *trans-* + Latin *positum* = placed]

transverse *adjective*
lying across something. **transversely** *adverb*
[from *trans-* + Latin *versum* = turned]

transvestite *noun* (*plural* **transvestites**)
a person who likes wearing clothes intended for someone of the opposite sex.
[from *trans-* + Latin *vestire* = to dress]

trap *noun* (*plural* **traps**)
1 a device for catching and holding animals. 2 a plan or trick for capturing, detecting, or cheating someone. 3 a device for collecting water etc. or preventing it from passing. 4 a two-wheeled carriage pulled by a horse.

trap verb (traps, trapping, trapped)
catch or hold a person or animal in a trap.
trapper noun [from Old English]

trapdoor noun (plural trapdoors)
a door in a floor, ceiling, or roof.

trapeze noun (plural trapezes)
a bar hanging from two ropes as a swing
for acrobats. [French; related to trapezium]

trapezium noun (plural trapeziums or
trapezia)
a quadrilateral in which two opposite sides
are parallel and the other two are not.
[from Greek trapeza = table]

trapezoid noun (plural trapezoids)
a quadrilateral in which no sides are
parallel. [same origin as trapezium]

trappings plural noun
1 the clothes or possessions that show your
rank or position. 2 an ornamental harness
for a horse. [from French drap = cloth]

trash noun
rubbish or nonsense. **trashy** adjective
[origin unknown]

trauma (say traw-ma) noun (plural
traumas)
a shock that produces a lasting effect on a
person's mind. **traumatic** adjective,
traumatize verb [Greek, = a wound]

travail noun (old use)
hard or laborious work. **travail** verb
[French]

travel verb (travels, travelling, travelled)
move from place to place. **travel** noun,
traveller noun [from travail]

travel agent noun (plural travel agents)
a person whose job is to arrange travel and
holidays for people.

traveller's cheque noun (plural traveller's
cheques)
a cheque for a fixed amount of money that
is sold by banks and that can be exchanged
for money in foreign countries.

traverse verb (traverses, traversing,
traversed)
go across something. **traversal** noun
[same origin as transverse]

travesty noun (plural travesties)
a bad or ridiculous form of something, His
story is a travesty of the truth.
[from trans- + Italian vestire = to clothe]

trawl verb (trawls, trawling, trawled)
fish by dragging a large net along the
seabed. [from old Dutch; related to trail]

trawler noun (plural trawlers)
a boat used in trawling.

tray noun (plural trays)
1 a flat piece of wood, metal, or plastic,
usually with raised edges, for carrying
cups, plates, food, etc. 2 an open container
for holding letters etc. in an office.
[from Old English]

treacherous adjective
1 betraying someone; disloyal. 2 not to be
relied on; dangerous, It's snowing and the
roads are treacherous. **treacherously** adverb,
treachery noun [from old French trechier
= to trick or deceive]

treacle noun
a thick sticky liquid produced when sugar
is purified. **treacly** adjective [originally
= ointment for an animal bite; from Greek
therion = wild or poisonous animal]

tread verb (treads, treading, trod, trodden)
walk or put your foot on something.
tread noun (plural treads)
1 a sound or way of walking. 2 the top
surface of a stair; the part you put your
foot on. 3 the part of a tyre that touches
the ground.
[from Old English]

treadle noun (plural treadles)
a lever that you press with your foot to
turn a wheel that works a machine.
[from tread]

treadmill noun (plural treadmills)
1 a wide mill-wheel turned by the weight of
people or animals treading on steps fixed
round its edge. 2 monotonous routine
work.

treason noun
betraying your country.
treasonable adjective, **treasonous** adjective
[from old French; related to tradition]

treasure *noun* (*plural* treasures)
1 a store of precious metals or jewels. 2 a precious thing or person.

treasure *verb* (treasures, treasuring, treasured)
value greatly something that you have. [same origin as *thesaurus*]

treasure hunt *noun* (*plural* treasure hunts)
a game in which people try to find a hidden object.

treasurer *noun* (*plural* treasurers)
a person in charge of the money of a club, society, etc.

treasure trove *noun*
gold or silver etc. found hidden and with no known owner.

treasury *noun* (*plural* treasuries)
a place where money and valuables are kept.
the Treasury the government department in charge of a country's income.

treat *verb* (treats, treating, treated)
1 behave in a certain way towards a person or thing. 2 deal with a subject etc. 3 give medical care in order to cure a person or animal. 4 put something through a chemical or other process, *The fabric has been treated to make it waterproof.* 5 pay for someone else's food, drink, or entertainment, *I'll treat you to an ice cream.*

treat *noun* (*plural* treats)
1 something special that gives pleasure. 2 the process of treating someone to food, drink, or entertainment. [from Latin *tractare* = to handle or manage]

treatise *noun* (*plural* treatises)
a book or long essay on a subject. [from old French; related to *treat*]

treatment *noun* (*plural* treatments)
the process or manner of dealing with a person, animal, or thing.

treaty *noun* (*plural* treaties)
a formal agreement between two or more countries. [from French; related to *treat*]

treble *adjective*
three times as much or as many.

treble *noun* (*plural* trebles)
1 a treble amount. 2 a person with a high-pitched or soprano voice.

treble *verb* (trebles, trebling, trebled)
make or become three times as much or as many. [from old French; related to *triple*]

tree *noun* (*plural* trees)
a tall plant with a single very thick hard stem or trunk that is usually without branches for some distance above the ground. [from Old English]

trefoil *noun*
a plant with three small leaves (e.g. clover). [from Latin *tres* = three + *folium* = leaf]

trek *noun* (*plural* treks)
a long walk or journey.

trek *verb* (treks, trekking, trekked)
go on a long walk or journey. [from Dutch *trekken* = pull]

trellis *noun* (*plural* trellises)
a framework with crossing bars of wood or metal etc. to support climbing plants. [from old French]

tremble *verb* (trembles, trembling, trembled)
shake gently, especially with fear. **tremble** *noun* [from French; related to *tremulous*]

tremendous *adjective*
1 very large; huge. 2 excellent.
tremendously *adverb* [from Latin *tremendus* = making someone tremble]

tremor *noun* (*plural* tremors)
a shaking or trembling movement. [Latin]

tremulous *adjective*
trembling from nervousness or weakness.
tremulously *adverb*
[from Latin *tremere* = tremble]

trench *noun* (*plural* trenches)
a long narrow hole cut in the ground.

trench *verb* (trenches, trenching, trenched)
dig a trench or trenches. [from old French; related to *truncate*]

trenchant *adjective*
strong and effective, *trenchant criticism.* [old French, = cutting]

trend *noun* (*plural* **trends**)
the general direction in which something is going. [from Old English]

trendy *adjective* (*informal*)
fashionable; following the latest trends.
trendily *adverb*, **trendiness** *noun*

trepidation *noun*
fear and anxiety; nervousness.
[from Latin *trepidare* = be afraid]

trespass *verb* (**trespasses, trespassing, trespassed**)
1 go on someone's land or property unlawfully. 2 (*old use*) do wrong; sin.
trespasser *noun*
trespass *noun* (*plural* **trespasses**) (*old use*)
wrongdoing; sin.
[from old French *trespasser* = go beyond]

tress *noun* (*plural* **tresses**)
a lock of hair. [from French]

trestle *noun* (*plural* **trestles**)
each of a set of supports on which a board is rested to form a table. **trestle-table** *noun*
[from old French, = small beam]

tri- *prefix*
three (as in *triangle*). [from Latin or Greek]

trial *noun* (*plural* **trials**)
1 the trying of a person in a lawcourt.
2 testing a thing to see how good it is. 3 a test of qualities or ability. 4 an annoying person or thing; a hardship.
on trial 1 being tried in a lawcourt. 2 being tested.
trial and error trying out different methods of doing something until you find one that works.
[from old French; related to *try*]

triangle *noun* (*plural* **triangles**)
1 a flat shape with three sides and three angles. 2 a percussion instrument made from a metal rod bent into a triangle.
triangular *adjective*
[from *tri-* + Latin *angulus* = angle]

tribe *noun* (*plural* **tribes**)
1 a group of families living in one area as a community, ruled by a chief. 2 a set of people. **tribal** *adjective*, **tribally** *adverb*, **tribesman** *noun* [from Latin]

tribulation *noun* (*plural* **tribulations**)
great trouble or hardship.
[from Latin *tribulare* = to press or oppress]

tribunal (*say* try-**bew**-nal) *noun* (*plural* **tribunals**)
a committee appointed to hear evidence and give judgements when there is a dispute.
[from Latin *tribunale* = tribune's seat]

tribune *noun* (*plural* **tribunes**)
an official chosen by the people in ancient Rome. [from Latin]

tributary *noun* (*plural* **tributaries**)
a river or stream that flows into a larger one or into a lake. [same origin as *tribute*]

tribute *noun* (*plural* **tributes**)
1 something said, done, or given to show respect or admiration. 2 payment that one country or ruler was formerly obliged to pay to a more powerful one.
[from Latin *tribuere* = assign, grant, share]

trice *noun* (*old use*)
in a trice in a moment.
[from old Dutch *trisen* = pull quickly, tug]

triceps (*say* **try**-seps) *noun* (*plural* **triceps**)
the large muscle at the back of the upper arm. [Latin, = three-headed (because the muscle is attached at three points)]

trick *noun* (*plural* **tricks**)
1 a crafty or deceitful action; a practical joke, *Let's play a trick on Jo.* 2 a skilful action, especially one done for entertainment, *magic tricks.* 3 the cards picked up by the winner after one round of a card game such as whist.
trick *verb* (**tricks, tricking, tricked**)
1 deceive or cheat someone by a trick.
2 decorate, *The building was tricked out with little flags.* [from old French]

trickery *noun*
the use of tricks; deception.

trickle *verb* (**trickles, trickling, trickled**)
flow or move slowly. **trickle** *noun*
[imitating the sound]

trickster *noun* (*plural* **tricksters**)
a person who tricks or cheats people.

tricky *adjective* (trickier, trickiest)
1 difficult; needing skill, *a tricky job.*
2 cunning or deceitful. **trickiness** *noun*

tricolour (*say* trik-ol-er) *noun* (*plural* tricolours)
a flag with three coloured stripes, e.g. the national flag of France or Ireland.

tricycle *noun* (*plural* tricycles)
a vehicle like a bicycle but with three wheels.

trident *noun* (*plural* tridents)
a three-pronged spear, carried by Neptune and Britannia as a symbol of their power over the sea.
[from *tri-* + Latin *dens* = tooth]

triennial (*say* try-en-ee-al) *adjective*
happening every third year.
[from *tri-* + Latin *annus* = year]

trier *noun* (*plural* triers)
a person who tries hard.

trifle *noun* (*plural* trifles)
1 a pudding made of sponge cake covered in custard, fruit, cream, etc. 2 a very small amount. 3 something that has very little importance or value.
trifle *verb* (trifles, trifling, trifled)
treat a person or thing without seriousness or respect, *She is not a woman to be trifled with.* [from old French]

trifling *adjective*
small in value or importance.

trigger *noun* (*plural* triggers)
a lever that is pulled to fire a gun.
trigger *verb* (triggers, triggering, triggered)
trigger off start something happening.
[from Dutch *trekker* = puller]

trigonometry (*say* trig-on-om-it-ree) *noun*
the calculation of distances and angles by using triangles. [from Greek *trigonon* = triangle + *metria* = measurement]

trilateral *adjective*
having three sides. [from *tri-* + *lateral*]

trilby *noun* (*plural* trilbies)
a man's soft felt hat. [named after Trilby O'Ferrall, the heroine of a popular book and play, who wore a similar hat]

trill *verb* (trills, trilling, trilled)
make a quivering musical sound. **trill** *noun*
[from Italian]

trillion *noun* (*plural* trillions)
1 a million million million. 2 (*American*) a million million. [from *tri-* + *million*]

trilogy *noun* (*plural* trilogies)
a group of three stories, poems, or plays etc. about the same people or things.
[from *tri-* + Greek *-logia* = writings]

trim *adjective*
neat and orderly.
trimly *adverb*, **trimness** *noun*
trim *verb* (trims, trimming, trimmed)
1 cut the edges or unwanted parts off something. 2 decorate a hat or piece of clothing by adding lace, ribbons, etc.
3 arrange sails to suit the wind.
trim *noun* (*plural* trims)
1 condition, *in good trim.* 2 cutting or trimming, *Your beard needs a trim.* 3 lace, ribbons, etc. used to decorate something.
[from Old English]

Trinity *noun*
God regarded as three persons (Father, Son, and Holy Spirit). [from Latin]

trinket *noun* (*plural* trinkets)
a small ornament or piece of jewellery.
[origin unknown]

trio *noun* (*plural* trios)
1 a group of three people or things.
2 a group of three musicians or singers.
3 a piece of music for three musicians.
[Italian, from Latin *tres* = three]

trip *verb* (trips, tripping, tripped)
1 catch your foot on something and fall; make someone do this. 2 move with quick light steps. 3 operate a switch.
trip up 1 stumble. 2 make a slip or blunder.
3 cause a person to do either of these.
trip *noun* (*plural* trips)
1 a journey or outing. 2 the action of tripping; a stumble. 3 (*informal*) hallucinations caused by taking a drug.
[from old French]

tripartite *adjective*
having three parts; involving three groups, *tripartite talks.*
[from *tri-* + Latin *partitus* = divided]

tripe *noun*
1 part of an ox's stomach used as food.
2 (*slang*) nonsense. [French]

triple *adjective*
1 consisting of three parts. 2 involving three people or groups, *a triple alliance.*
3 three times as much or as many.
triply *adverb*
triple *verb* (**triples, tripling, tripled**)
treble.
[from Latin *triplus* = three times as much]

triple jump *noun*
an athletic contest in which competitors try to jump as far as possible by doing a hop, step, and jump.

triplet *noun* (*plural* **triplets**)
each of three children or animals born to the same mother at one time. [from *triple*]

triplicate *noun*
in triplicate as three identical copies.
[from *tri-* + Latin *plicare* = to fold]

tripod (*say* **try**-pod) *noun* (*plural* **tripods**)
a stand with three legs, e.g. to support a camera.
[from *tri-* + Greek *podes* = feet]

tripper *noun* (*plural* **trippers**)
a person who is making a pleasure trip.

trireme (*say* **try**-reem) *noun* (*plural* **triremes**)
an ancient warship with three banks of oars. [from *tri-* + Latin *remus* = oar]

trisect *verb* (**trisects, trisecting, trisected**)
divide something into three equal parts.
trisection *noun*
[from *tri-* + Latin *sectum* = cut]

trite (rhymes with *kite*) *adjective*
worn out by constant repetition; hackneyed, *a few trite remarks.*
[from Latin *tritum* = worn by use]

triumph *noun* (*plural* **triumphs**)
1 a great success or victory; a feeling of joy at this. 2 a celebration of a victory.
triumphal *adjective*, **triumphant** *adjective*, **triumphantly** *adverb*
triumph *verb* (**triumphs, triumphing, triumphed**)
1 be successful or victorious. 2 rejoice in success or victory. [from Latin]

triumvirate *noun* (*plural* **triumvirates**)
a ruling group of three people.
[from Latin *trium virorum* = of three men]

trivet *noun* (*plural* **trivets**)
an iron stand for a pot or kettle etc., placed over a fire.
[from *tri-* + Latin *pedes* = feet]

trivia *plural noun*
unimportant details or pieces of information. [same origin as *trivial*]

trivial *adjective*
small in value or importance.
trivially *adverb*, **triviality** *noun*
[from Latin *trivialis* = commonplace]

troglodyte *noun* (*plural* **troglodytes**)
a person living in a cave in ancient times.
[from Greek *trogle* = hole]

troll (rhymes with *hole*) *noun* (*plural* **trolls**)
(in Scandinavian mythology) a supernatural being, either a giant or a friendly but mischievous dwarf.
[from Old Norse]

trolley *noun* (*plural* **trolleys**)
1 a small table on wheels or castors. 2 a small cart or truck. [probably from dialect *troll* = to roll or flow]

trolleybus *noun* (*plural* **trolleybuses**)
a bus powered by electricity from an overhead wire to which it is connected.
[from an old sense of *trolley* = a pulley that runs along a track or wire]

trombone *noun* (*plural* **trombones**)
a large brass musical instrument with a sliding tube.
[from Italian *tromba* = trumpet]

troop *noun* (*plural* **troops**)
1 an organized group of soldiers, Scouts, etc. 2 a number of people moving along together.

USAGE: Do not confuse with *troupe.*

troop *verb* (**troops, trooping, trooped**)
move along as a group or in large numbers, *They all trooped in.*
[from Latin *troppus* = herd]

trooper *noun* (*plural* **troopers**)
a soldier in the cavalry or in an armoured unit. [from *troop*]

troops *plural noun*
armed forces.

trophy *noun* (*plural* **trophies**)
a prize or souvenir for a victory or other success. [from Greek]

tropic *noun* (*plural* **tropics**)
a line of latitude about 23½° north of the equator (**tropic of Cancer**) or 23½° south of the equator (**tropic of Capricorn**).
the tropics the hot regions between these two latitudes.
[from Greek *trope* = turning (because the sun seems to turn back when it reaches these points)]

tropical *adjective*
to do with the tropics, *tropical fish*.

troposphere *noun*
the layer of the atmosphere extending about 10 kilometres upwards from the earth's surface.
[from Greek *tropos* = turning, + *sphere*]

trot *verb* (**trots, trotting, trotted**)
1 (of a horse) run, going faster than when walking but more slowly than when cantering. **2** (*informal*) go, *Trot round to the chemist.*
trot out (*informal*) produce or repeat, *He trotted out the usual excuses.*

trot *noun*
a trotting run.
on the trot (*informal*) one after the other without a break, *She worked for ten days on the trot.*
[via old French from Germanic]

troth (rhymes with *both*) *noun* (*old use*)
loyalty; a solemn promise.
[a different spelling of *truth*]

trotter *noun* (*plural* **trotters**)
an animal's foot as food, *pigs' trotters.*
[from *trot*]

troubadour (*say* troo-bad-oor) *noun*
(*plural* **troubadours**)
a poet and singer in southern France in the 11th–13th centuries.
[from old French *trover* = write in verse]

trouble *noun* (*plural* **troubles**)
1 difficulty, inconvenience, or distress.
2 a cause of any of these.

take trouble take great care in doing something.
trouble *verb* (**troubles, troubling, troubled**)
1 cause trouble to someone. **2** give yourself trouble or inconvenience etc., *Don't trouble to reply.* [from old French]

troublesome *adjective*
causing trouble or annoyance.

trough (*say* trof) *noun* (*plural* **troughs**)
1 a long narrow open container, especially one holding water or food for animals. **2** a channel for liquid. **3** the low part between two waves or ridges. **4** a long region of low air pressure. [from Old English]

trounce *verb* (**trounces, trouncing, trounced**)
defeat someone heavily. [origin unknown]

troupe (*say as* troop) *noun* (*plural* **troupes**)
a company of actors or other performers. [French, = troop]

USAGE: Do not confuse with *troop.*

trousers *plural noun*
a piece of clothing worn over the lower half of the body, with a separate part for each leg. [from Irish or Scottish Gaelic]

trousseau (*say* troo-soh) *noun* (*plural* **trousseaus** or **trousseaux**)
a bride's collection of clothing etc. to begin married life. [from French, = bundle]

trout *noun* (*plural* **trout**)
a freshwater fish that is caught as a sport and for food. [from Greek]

trowel *noun* (*plural* **trowels**)
1 a small garden tool with a curved blade for lifting plants or scooping things. **2** a small tool with a flat blade for spreading mortar etc. [from Latin *trulla* = scoop]

troy weight *noun*
a system of weights used for precious metals and gems, in which 1 pound = 12 ounces. [said to be from a weight used at Troyes in France]

truant *noun* (*plural* **truants**)
a child who stays away from school without permission. **truancy** *noun*

play truant be a truant.
[old French, = criminal, probably of Celtic origin]

truce *noun* (*plural* **truces**)
an agreement to stop fighting for a while.
[from Old English]

truck[1] *noun* (*plural* **trucks**)
1 a lorry. **2** an open container on wheels for transporting loads; an open railway wagon. **3** an axle with wheels attached, fitted under a skateboard.
[probably from *truckle* = a pulley or castor]

truck[2] *noun*
have no truck with refuse to have dealings with, *I'll have no truck with fortune-tellers!*
[origin unknown]

truculent (*say* truk-yoo-lent) *adjective*
defiant and aggressive.
truculently *adverb*, **truculence** *noun*
[from Latin *truculentus* = wild, fierce]

trudge *verb* (**trudges, trudging, trudged**)
walk slowly and heavily. [origin unknown]

true *adjective* (**truer, truest**)
1 representing what has really happened or exists, *a true story*. **2** genuine or proper; not false, *He was the true heir*. **3** accurate. **4** loyal or faithful, *Be true to your friends*.
trueness *noun* [from Old English]

truffle *noun* (*plural* **truffles**)
1 a soft sweet made with chocolate. **2** a fungus that grows underground and is valued as food because of its rich flavour.
[probably from Dutch]

truism *noun* (*plural* **truisms**)
a statement that is obviously true, especially one that is hackneyed, e.g. 'Nothing lasts for ever'.

truly *adverb*
1 truthfully. **2** sincerely or genuinely, *We are truly grateful*. **3** accurately. **4** loyally or faithfully.
Yours truly see *yours*.

trump[1] *noun* (*plural* **trumps**)
a playing card of a suit that ranks above the others for one game.

trump *verb* (**trumps, trumping, trumped**)
beat a card by playing a trump.
trump up invent an excuse or an accusation etc.
[from *triumph*]

trump[2] *noun* (*plural* **trumps**) (*old use*)
a blast of a trumpet.
[from old French *trompe* = trumpet]

trumpet *noun* (*plural* **trumpets**)
1 a metal wind instrument with a narrow tube that widens near the end. **2** something shaped like this.
trumpet *verb* (**trumpets, trumpeting, trumpeted**)
1 blow a trumpet. **2** (of an elephant) make a loud sound with its trunk. **3** shout or announce something loudly. **trumpeter** *noun* [same origin as *trump*[2]]

truncate *verb* (**truncates, truncating, truncated**)
shorten something by cutting off its top or end. **truncation** *noun*
[from Latin *truncare* = maim]

truncheon *noun* (*plural* **truncheons**)
a short thick stick carried as a weapon, especially by police.
[from old French; related to *trunk*]

trundle *verb* (**trundles, trundling, trundled**)
roll along heavily, *He was trundling a wheelbarrow. A bus trundled up.*
[related to Old English *trendel* = ball]

trunk *noun* (*plural* **trunks**)
1 the main stem of a tree. **2** an elephant's long flexible nose. **3** a large box with a hinged lid for transporting or storing clothes etc. **4** the human body except for the head, arms, and legs. [from Latin]

trunk road *noun* (*plural* **trunk roads**)
an important main road.
[regarded as a 'trunk' from which smaller roads branch off]

trunks *plural noun*
shorts worn by men and boys for swimming, boxing, etc.

truss *noun* (*plural* **trusses**)
1 a framework of beams or bars supporting a roof or bridge etc. **2** a bundle of hay etc. **3** a type of padded belt worn to support a hernia.

truss *verb* (trusses, trussing, trussed)
1 tie up a person or thing securely
2 support a roof or bridge etc. with trusses.
[from old French]

trust *verb* (trusts, trusting, trusted)
1 believe that a person or thing is good, truthful, or strong. 2 let a person have or use something in the belief that he or she will behave responsibly, *Don't trust him with your CD player!* 3 hope, *I trust that you are well.*
trust to rely on, *trusting to luck.*

trust *noun* (*plural* trusts)
1 the belief that a person or thing can be trusted. 2 responsibility; being trusted, *Being a prefect is a position of trust.*
3 money legally entrusted to a person with instructions about how to use it.
trustful *adjective*, **trustfully** *adverb*, **trustworthy** *adjective*
[from Old Norse]

trustee *noun* (*plural* trustees)
a person who looks after money entrusted to him or her.

trusty *adjective* (*old use*)
trustworthy or reliable, *my trusty sword.*

truth *noun* (*plural* truths)
1 something that is true. 2 the quality of being true.
[from Old English]

truthful *adjective*
1 telling the truth, *a truthful boy.* 2 true, *a truthful account of what happened.*
truthfully *adverb*, **truthfulness** *noun*

try *verb* (tries, trying, tried)
1 attempt. 2 test something by using or doing it, *Try sleeping on your back.*
3 examine the accusations against someone in a lawcourt. 4 be a strain on, *Very small print tries your eyes.*
try on put on clothes etc. to see if they fit.

try *noun* (*plural* tries)
1 an attempt. 2 (in Rugby football) putting the ball down behind the opponents' goal line in order to score points.
[from old French]

trying *adjective*
putting a strain on someone's patience; annoying.

tsar (*say* zar) *noun* (*plural* tsars)
the title of the former ruler of Russia.
[Russian, from Latin *Caesar*]

tsetse fly (*say* tet-see) *noun* (*plural* tsetse flies)
a tropical African fly that can cause sleeping sickness in people whom it bites.
[from Setswana (a language spoken in southern Africa)]

T-shirt *noun* (*plural* T-shirts)
a short-sleeved shirt shaped like a T.

tsunami *noun* (*plural* tsunamis)
a huge sea wave caused by an underwater earthquake. [Japanese, from *tsu* = harbour + *nami* = a wave]

tub *noun* (*plural* tubs)
a round open container holding liquid, ice cream, soil for plants, etc.
[probably from old Dutch]

tuba (*say* tew-ba) *noun* (*plural* tubas)
a large brass wind instrument with a deep tone. [Italian from Latin, = war trumpet]

tubby *adjective* (tubbier, tubbiest)
short and fat. **tubbiness** *noun* [from *tub*]

tube *noun* (*plural* tubes)
1 a long hollow piece of metal, plastic, rubber, glass, etc., especially for liquids or air etc. to pass along. 2 a container made of flexible material with a screw cap, *a tube of toothpaste.* 3 the underground railway in London. [from Latin]

tuber *noun* (*plural* tubers)
a short thick rounded root (e.g. of a dahlia) or underground stem (e.g. of a potato) that produces buds from which new plants will grow. [Latin, = a swelling]

tuberculosis *noun*
a disease of people and animals, producing small swellings in the parts affected by it, especially in the lungs. **tubercular** *adjective*
[from Latin *tuberculum* = little swelling]

tubing *noun*
tubes; a length of tube.

tubular *adjective*
shaped like a tube.

TUC *abbreviation*
Trades Union Congress.

tuck *verb* (**tucks, tucking, tucked**)
1 push a loose edge into something so that it is hidden or held in place. **2** put something away in a small space, *Tuck this in your pocket.*
tuck in (*informal*) eat heartily.
tuck *noun* (*plural* **tucks**)
1 a flat fold stitched in a garment. **2** (*slang*) food, especially sweets and cakes etc. that children enjoy. **tuck shop** *noun*
[from Old English]

-tude *suffix*
forms nouns meaning 'quality or condition' (e.g. *altitude, solitude*).
[from French]

tuft *noun* (*plural* **tufts**)
a bunch of threads, grass, hair, or feathers etc. growing close together. **tufted** *adjective*
[from old French]

tug *verb* (**tugs, tugging, tugged**)
1 pull something hard or suddenly. **2** tow a ship.
tug *noun* (*plural* **tugs**)
1 a hard or sudden pull. **2** a small powerful boat used for towing others.
[Middle English; related to *tow*[1]]

tug of war *noun*
a contest between two teams pulling a rope from opposite ends.

tuition *noun*
teaching. [from Latin *tuitio* = looking after something]

tulip *noun* (*plural* **tulips**)
a large cup-shaped flower on a tall stem growing from a bulb.
[from Persian *dulband* = turban (because the flowers are this shape)]

tulle (*say* tewl) *noun*
a very fine silky net material used for veils, wedding dresses, etc. [named after Tulle, a town in France, where it was first made]

tumble *verb* (**tumbles, tumbling, tumbled**)
1 fall or roll over suddenly or clumsily.
2 move or push quickly and carelessly.
tumble *noun*

tumble to (*informal*) realize what something means.
[from old German]

tumbledown *adjective*
falling into ruins.

tumble-drier *noun* (*plural* **tumble-driers**)
a machine that dries washing by turning it over many times in heated air.

tumbler *noun* (*plural* **tumblers**)
1 a drinking glass with no stem or handle.
2 a part of a lock that is lifted when a key is turned to open it. **3** an acrobat.

tumbrel or **tumbril** *noun* (*plural* **tumbrels, tumbrils**) (*old use*)
an open cart of the kind used to carry condemned people to the guillotine during the French Revolution. [from old French]

tummy *noun* (*plural* **tummies**) (*informal*)
the stomach. [imitating a small child trying to say 'stomach']

tumour (*say* tew-mer) *noun* (*plural* **tumours**)
an abnormal lump growing on or in the body. [from Latin *tumere* = to swell]

tumult (*say* tew-mult) *noun*
an uproar; a state of noisy confusion and agitation. [from Latin]

tumultuous (*say* tew-**mul**-tew-us) *adjective*
making a tumult; noisy, *a tumultuous welcome.*

tun *noun* (*plural* **tuns**)
a large cask or barrel. [from Old English]

tuna (*say* tew-na) *noun* (*plural* **tuna**)
a large edible sea fish with pink flesh.
[American Spanish; related to *tunny*]

tundra *noun*
the vast level Arctic regions of Europe, Asia, and America where there are no trees and the subsoil is always frozen.
[from Lappish (the language spoken in Lapland)]

tune *noun* (*plural* **tunes**)
a short piece of music; a pleasant series of musical notes.
tuneful *adjective*, **tunefully** *adverb*
in tune at the correct musical pitch.

tune *verb* (tunes, tuning, tuned)
1 put a musical instrument in tune.
2 adjust a radio or television set to receive a certain channel. 3 adjust an engine so that it runs smoothly. **tuner** *noun*
[a different spelling of *tone*]

tungsten *noun*
a grey metal used to make a kind of steel.
[from Swedish *tung* = heavy + *sten* = stone]

tunic *noun* (*plural* tunics)
1 a jacket worn as part of a uniform. 2 a garment reaching from the shoulders to the hips or knees. [from Latin]

tunnel *noun* (*plural* tunnels)
an underground passage.
tunnel *verb* (tunnels, tunnelling, tunnelled)
make a tunnel.
[from old French *tonel* = barrel]

tunny *noun* (*plural* tunnies)
a tuna. [from Latin]

turban *noun* (*plural* turbans)
a covering for the head made by wrapping a strip of cloth round a cap. [from Persian]

turbid *adjective*
(of water) muddy, not clear.
turbidly *adverb*, **turbidity** *noun*
[from Latin *turba* = crowd, disturbance]

turbine *noun* (*plural* turbines)
a machine or motor driven by a flow of water, steam, or gas. [from Latin *turbo* = whirlwind, spinning top]

turbojet *noun* (*plural* turbojets)
a jet engine or aircraft with turbines.
[from *turbine* + *jet*[1]]

turbot *noun* (*plural* turbot)
a large flat edible sea fish.
[via old French from old Swedish]

turbulent *adjective*
1 moving violently and unevenly, *turbulent seas*. 2 unruly.
turbulently *adverb*, **turbulence** *noun*
[same origin as *turbid*]

tureen *noun* (*plural* tureens)
a deep dish with a lid, from which soup is served at the table.
[from French *terrine* = earthenware pot]

turf *noun* (*plural* turfs or turves)
1 short grass and the earth round its roots.
2 a piece of this cut from the ground.
the turf horse racing.
turf *verb* (turfs, turfing, turfed)
cover ground with turf.
turf out (*slang*) throw out.
[from Old English]

turgid (*say* ter-jid) *adjective*
1 swollen and thick. 2 pompous and boring, *a turgid speech*.
[from Latin *turgere* = to swell]

turkey *noun* (*plural* turkeys)
a large bird kept for its meat.
[originally the name of a different bird which was imported from Turkey]

turmoil *noun*
wild confusion or agitation, *Her mind was in turmoil*. [origin unknown]

turn *verb* (turns, turning, turned)
1 move round; move to a new direction.
2 change in appearance etc.; become, *He turned pale*. 3 make something change, *You can turn milk into butter*. 4 move a switch or tap etc. to control something, *Turn that radio off*. 5 pass a certain time, *It has turned midnight*. 6 shape something on a lathe.
turn down 1 fold down. 2 reduce the flow or sound of something. 3 reject, *We offered her a job but she turned it down*.
turn out 1 send out. 2 empty something, especially to search or clean it. 3 happen.
4 prove to be, *The visitor turned out to be my uncle*.
turn up 1 appear or arrive. 2 increase the flow or sound of something.
turn *noun* (*plural* turns)
1 the action of turning; a turning movement. 2 a change; the point where something turns. 3 an opportunity or duty etc. that comes to each person in succession, *It's your turn to wash up*. 4 a short performance in an entertainment.
5 (*informal*) an attack of illness; a nervous shock, *It gave me a nasty turn*.
good turn a helpful action.
in turn in succession; one after another.
[from Greek *tornos* = lathe]

turncoat *noun* (*plural* turncoats)
a person who changes his or her principles or beliefs.

turner *noun* (*plural* **turners**)
a person who makes things on a lathe.
turnery *noun*

turning *noun* (*plural* **turnings**)
a place where one road meets another,
forming a corner.

turning point *noun* (*plural* **turning points**)
a point where an important change takes
place.

turnip *noun* (*plural* **turnips**)
a plant with a large round white root used
as a vegetable. [from Latin]

turnout *noun* (*plural* **turnouts**)
the number of people who attend a
meeting, vote at an election, etc., *Despite
the rain, there was a pretty good turnout.*

turnover *noun* (*plural* **turnovers**)
1 the amount of money received by a firm
selling things. **2** the rate at which goods
are sold or workers leave and are replaced.
3 a small pie made by folding pastry over
fruit, jam, etc.

turnpike *noun* (*plural* **turnpikes**) (*old use*)
a toll gate; a road with toll gates.
[originally = a barricade: from *turn* + *pike*]

turnstile *noun* (*plural* **turnstiles**)
a revolving gate that lets one person in at a
time.

turntable *noun* (*plural* **turntables**)
a circular revolving platform or support,
e.g. for the record in a record player.

turpentine *noun*
a kind of oil used for thinning paint,
cleaning paintbrushes, etc. [from Latin]

turpitude *noun*
wickedness. [from Latin *turpis* = shameful]

turps *noun* (*informal*)
turpentine.

turquoise *noun* (*plural* **turquoises**)
1 a sky-blue or greenish-blue colour. **2** a
blue jewel. [from French *pierre turquoise*
= Turkish stone]

turret *noun* (*plural* **turrets**)
1 a small tower on a castle or other

building. **2** a revolving structure
containing a gun. **turreted** *adjective*
[from old French *tourete* = small tower]

turtle *noun* (*plural* **turtles**)
a sea animal that looks like a tortoise.
turn turtle capsize.
[probably from French *tortue* = tortoise]

turtle-dove *noun* (*plural* **turtle-doves**)
a wild dove. [from Old English]

tusk *noun* (*plural* **tusks**)
a long pointed tooth that sticks out from
the mouth of an elephant, walrus, etc.
[from Old English]

tussle *noun* (*plural* **tussles**)
a struggle or conflict over something.
tussle *verb* (**tussles, tussling, tussled**)
take part in a tussle.
[originally Scots; origin unknown]

tussock *noun* (*plural* **tussocks**)
a tuft or clump of grass. [origin unknown]

tutor *noun* (*plural* **tutors**)
1 a teacher who teaches one person or
small group, not in a school. **2** a teacher of
students in a college or university.
[Latin, = guardian]

tutorial *noun* (*plural* **tutorials**)
a meeting in which students discuss a
subject with their tutor.

tutu (*say* too-too) *noun* (*plural* **tutus**)
a ballet dancer's short stiff frilled skirt.
[French]

TV *abbreviation*
television.

TVEI *abbreviation*
Technical and Vocational Education
Initiative.

twaddle *noun*
nonsense. [possibly from *tattle*]

twain *noun* & *adjective* (*old use*)
two. [from Old English *twegen* = two]

twang *verb* (**twangs, twanging, twanged**)
1 play a guitar etc. by plucking its strings.
2 make a sharp sound like that of a wire
when plucked. **twang** *noun*
[imitating the sound]

tweak *verb* (tweaks, tweaking, tweaked)
pinch and twist or pull something sharply.
tweak *noun*
[from Old English]

tweed *noun*
thick woollen twill, often woven of mixed colours.
[originally a mistake; the Scottish word *tweel* (= twill) was wrongly read as *tweed* by being confused with the River Tweed]

tweeds *plural noun*
clothes made of tweed.

tweet *noun* (*plural* tweets)
the chirping sound made by a small bird.
[imitating the sound]

tweezers *plural noun*
small pincers for picking up or pulling very small things. [from French *étui*
= prison, in English = a case of surgical instruments, including tweezers]

twelve *noun* & *adjective*
the number 12. **twelfth** *adjective* & *noun*
[from Old English]

twenty *noun* (*plural* twenties) & *adjective*
the number 20. **twentieth** *adjective* & *noun*
[from Old English]

twice *adverb*
1 two times; on two occasions. 2 double the amount. [from Old English]

twiddle *verb* (twiddles, twiddling, twiddled)
twirl or finger something in an idle way; twist something quickly to and fro. **twiddle**
noun, **twiddly** *adjective* [origin unknown]

twig[1] *noun* (*plural* twigs)
a small shoot on a branch or stem of a tree or shrub. [from Old English]

twig[2] *verb* (twigs, twigging, twigged)
(*informal*)
realize what something means.
[origin unknown]

twilight *noun*
dim light from the sky just after sunset or just before sunrise. [from Old English *twi-*
= twice, double, + *light*]

twill *noun*
material woven so that there is a pattern of diagonal lines. [from Old English *twi*
= double, + Latin *licium* = thread]

twin *noun* (*plural* twins)
1 either of two children or animals born to the same mother at one time. 2 either of two things that are exactly alike.

twin *verb* (twins, twinning, twinned)
1 put things together as a pair. 2 if a town is twinned with a town in a different country, the two towns exchange visits and organize cultural events together.
[from Old English]

twine *noun*
strong thin string.

twine *verb* (twines, twining, twined)
twist or wind together or round something.
[from Old English]

twinge *noun* (*plural* twinges)
a sudden pain; a pang. [from Old English]

twinkle *verb* (twinkles, twinkling, twinkled)
shine with tiny flashes of light; sparkle.
twinkle *noun* [from Old English]

twirl *verb* (twirls, twirling, twirled)
twist quickly. **twirl** *noun* [origin unknown]

twist *verb* (twists, twisting, twisted)
1 pass threads or strands round something or round each other. 2 turn the ends of something in opposite directions. 3 turn round or from side to side, *The road twisted through the hills.* 4 bend something out of its proper shape. 5 (*informal*) swindle somebody. **twister** *noun*

twist *noun* (*plural* twists)
a twisting movement or action. **twisty**
adjective [from Old English]

twit *noun* (*plural* twits) (*slang*)
a silly or foolish person.
[from *at* + Old English *witan* = to blame]

twitch *verb* (twitches, twitching, twitched)
move or pull with a slight jerk. **twitch** *noun*
[probably from old German]

twitter *verb* (twitters, twittering, twittered)
make quick chirping sounds. **twitter** *noun*
[imitating the sound]

two *noun* (*plural* **twos**) & *adjective*
the number 2.
be in two minds be undecided about
something.
[from Old English]

two-faced *adjective*
insincere or deceitful.

tycoon *noun* (*plural* **tycoons**)
a rich and influential business person.
[from Japanese *taikun* = great prince]

tying *present participle* of **tie**.

type *noun* (*plural* **types**)
1 a kind or sort. **2** letters or figures etc.
designed for use in printing.
type *verb* (**types, typing, typed**)
write something by using a typewriter.
[from Greek *typos* = impression]

typescript *noun* (*plural* **typescripts**)
a typewritten document.

typewriter *noun* (*plural* **typewriters**)
a machine with keys that are pressed to
print letters or figures etc. on a piece of
paper. **typewritten** *adjective* [the word
typewriter at first meant the person using
the machine, as well as the machine itself]

typhoid fever *noun*
a serious infectious disease with fever,
caused by harmful bacteria in food or
water etc. [from *typhus*]

typhoon *noun* (*plural* **typhoons**)
a violent hurricane in the western Pacific
or East Asian seas.
[from Chinese *tai fung* = great wind]

typhus *noun*
an infectious disease causing fever,
weakness, and a rash.
[from Greek *typhos* = vapour]

typical *adjective*
1 having the usual characteristics or
qualities of a particular type of person or
thing, *a typical school playground*. **2** usual
in a particular person or thing, *He worked
with typical carefulness*. **typically** *adverb*
[same origin as *type*]

typify (*say* tip-if-I) *verb* (**typifies, typifying,
typified**)
be a typical example of something, *He*
*typifies the popular image of a football
manager*.

typist *noun* (*plural* **typists**)
a person who types.

typography (*say* ty-**pog**-ra-fee) *noun*
the style or appearance of the letters and
figures etc. in printed material.
[from *type* + -*graphy*]

tyrannize (*say* tirran-I'z) *verb* (**tyrannizes,
tyrannizing, tyrannized**)
rule or behave like a tyrant.

tyrannosaurus *noun* (*plural*
tyrannosauruses)
a huge flesh-eating dinosaur that walked
upright on its large hind legs. [from Greek
tyrannos = ruler + *sauros* = lizard]

tyranny (*say* tirran-ee) *noun* (*plural*
tyrannies)
1 government by a tyrant. **2** the way a
tyrant behaves towards people.
tyrannical *adjective*, **tyrannous** *adjective*

tyrant (*say* ty-rant) *noun* (*plural* **tyrants**)
a person who rules cruelly and unjustly;
someone who insists on being obeyed.
[from Greek *tyrannos* = ruler with full
power]

tyre *noun* (*plural* **tyres**)
a covering of rubber fitted round a wheel to
make it grip the road and run more
smoothly. [from *attire*]

Uu

ubiquitous (*say* yoo-**bik**-wit-us) *adjective*
found everywhere, *The ubiquitous
television aerials spoil the view*. **ubiquity**
noun [from Latin *ubique* = everywhere]

-uble *prefix* see **-able**.

U-boat *noun* (*plural* **U-boats**)
a German submarine of the kind used in
the Second World War. [short for German
Unterseeboot = undersea boat]

udder *noun* (*plural* **udders**)
the bag-like part of a cow, ewe, female goat,
etc. from which milk is taken.
[from Old English]

UFO *abbreviation*
unidentified flying object.

ugly *adjective* (**uglier, ugliest**)
1 unpleasant to look at; not beautiful.
2 hostile and threatening, *The crowd was
in an ugly mood.* **ugliness** *noun*
[from Old Norse *uggligr* – frightening]

UHF *abbreviation*
ultra-high frequency (between 300 and 3000
megahertz).

UHT *abbreviation*
ultra heat-treated; used to describe milk
that has been treated at a very high
temperature so that it will keep for a long
time.

UK *abbreviation*
United Kingdom.

ukulele (*say* yoo-kul-**ay**-lee) *noun* (*plural*
ukeleles)
a small guitar with four strings.
[Hawaiian, literally = jumping flea]

ulcer *noun* (*plural* **ulcers**)
a sore on the inside or outside of the body.
ulcerated *adjective*, **ulceration** *noun*
[from Latin]

ulterior *adjective*
beyond what is obvious or stated, *an
ulterior motive.* [Latin, = further]

ultimate *adjective*
furthest in a series of things; final, *Our
ultimate destination is London.* **ultimately**
adverb [from Latin *ultimus* = last]

ultimatum (*say* ul-tim-**ay**-tum) *noun*
(*plural* **ultimatums**)
a final demand or statement that unless
something is done by a certain time action
will be taken or war will be declared.
[same origin as *ultimate*]

ultra- *prefix*
1 beyond (as in *ultraviolet*). **2** extremely;
excessively (as in *ultramodern*).
[from Latin *ultra* = beyond]

ultramarine *noun*
deep bright blue. [from *ultra-* + Latin *mare*
= sea (because it was originally imported
'across the sea' from the East)]

ultrasonic *adjective*
(of sound) beyond the range of human
hearing.

ultraviolet *adjective*
(of light-rays) beyond the violet end of the
spectrum and so not visible to the human
eye.

umber *noun*
a kind of brown pigment.
[from Italian *terra di Ombra* = earth of
Umbria (a region in central Italy)]

umbilical (*say* um-**bil**-ik-al) *adjective*
to do with the navel.
[from Latin]

umbilical cord *noun* (*plural* **umbilical
cords**)
the tube through which a baby receives
nourishment before it is born, connecting
its body with the mother's womb.

umbrage *noun*
take umbrage take offence.
[originally = shadow or shade: from Latin
umbra = shadow]

umbrella *noun* (*plural* **umbrellas**)
1 a circular piece of material stretched
over a folding frame with a central stick
used as a handle, or a central pole, which
you open to protect yourself from rain or
sun. **2** a general protection.
[from Italian *ombrella* = a little shade]

umlaut *noun* (*plural* **umlauts**)
a mark (¨) placed over a vowel in German
to indicate a change in its pronunciation.
[German, from *um* = about + *Laut* = a
sound]

umpire *noun* (*plural* **umpires**)
a referee in cricket, tennis, and some other
games.
umpire *verb* (**umpires, umpiring, umpired**)
act as an umpire. [from French *non* = not
+ *per* = an equal, peer²]

UN *abbreviation*
United Nations.

un- *prefix*
1 not (as in *uncertain*). 2 (before a verb) reversing the action (as in *unlock* = release from being locked). [from Old English]

NOTE: Many words beginning with this prefix are not listed here if their meaning is obvious.

unable *adjective*
not able to do something.

unaccountable *adjective*
1 unable to be explained, *For some unaccountable reason I completely forgot your birthday*. 2 not accountable for what you do. **unaccountably** *adverb*

unadulterated *adjective*
pure; not mixed with things that are less good. [from *un-* + *adulterate*]

unaided *adjective*
without help.

unanimous (*say* yoo-**nan**-im-us) *adjective*
with everyone agreeing, *a unanimous decision*. **unanimously** *adverb*, **unanimity** (*say* yoo-nan-**im**-it-ee) *noun*
[from Latin *unus* = one + *animus* = mind]

unassuming *adjective*
modest; not arrogant or pretentious. [from *un-* + *assume*]

unavoidable *adjective*
not able to be avoided.

unaware *adjective*
not aware.

unawares *adverb*
unexpectedly; without warning, *His question caught me unawares*.

unbearable *adjective*
not able to be endured. **unbearably** *adverb*

unbeatable *adjective*
unable to be defeated or surpassed.

unbeaten *adjective*
not defeated; not surpassed.

unbecoming *adjective*
1 not making a person look attractive. 2 not suitable or fitting. [from *un-* + *become* (sense 2)]

unbeknown *adjective*
without someone knowing about it, *Unbeknown to us, they were working for our enemies*. [from *un-* + *be-* + *know*]

unbelievable *adjective*
not able to be believed; incredible. **unbelievably** *adverb*

unbend *verb* (**unbends, unbending, unbent**)
1 change from a bent position; straighten up. 2 relax and become friendly.

unbiased *adjective*
not biased.

unbidden *adjective*
not commanded or invited. [from *un-* + *bid*²]

unblock *verb* (**unblocks, unblocking, unblocked**)
remove an obstruction from something.

unborn *adjective*
not yet born.

unbridled *adjective*
not controlled or restrained, *unbridled rage*.

unbroken *adjective*
not broken or interrupted.

unburden *verb* (**unburdens, unburdening, unburdened**)
remove a burden from the person carrying it.
unburden yourself tell someone your secrets or problems so that you feel better.

uncalled for *adjective*
not justified; impertinent.

uncanny *adjective* (**uncannier, uncanniest**)
strange or mysterious, *an uncanny coincidence*. **uncannily** *adverb*, **uncanniness** *noun* [from *un-* + an old sense of *canny* = knowing, able to be known]

unceremonious *adjective*
1 without formality or ceremony. 2 offhand or abrupt.

uncertain *adjective*
1 not certain. 2 not reliable, *His aim is*

rather uncertain. **uncertainly** *adverb*, **uncertainty** *noun*
In no uncertain terms clearly and forcefully.

uncharitable *adjective*
making unkind judgements of people or actions. **uncharitably** *adverb*

uncle *noun* (*plural* **uncles**)
the brother of your father or mother; your aunt's husband.
[from Latin *avunculus* = uncle]

unclothed *adjective*
naked.

uncomfortable *adjective*
not comfortable. **uncomfortably** *adverb*

uncommon *adjective*
not common; unusual.

uncompromising (*say* un-**komp**-rom-I-zing) *adjective*
not allowing a compromise; inflexible.

unconcerned *adjective*
not caring about something; not worried.

unconditional *adjective*
without any conditions; absolute, *unconditional surrender*.
unconditionally *adverb*

unconscious *adjective*
not conscious; not aware of things.
unconsciously *adverb*, **unconsciousness** *noun*

uncontrollable *adjective*
unable to be controlled or stopped.
uncontrollably *adverb*

uncooperative *adjective*
not cooperative.

uncouple *verb* (**uncouples, uncoupling, uncoupled**)
disconnect.

uncouth (*say* un-**kooth**) *adjective*
rude and rough in manner; boorish.
[from *un-* + Old English *cuth* = known]

uncover *verb* (**uncovers, uncovering, uncovered**)
1 remove the covering from something.
2 reveal or expose, *They uncovered a plot to kill the king*.

unction *noun*
1 anointing with oil, especially in a religious ceremony. **2** unctuousness.
[from Latin *unguere* = to oil or smear]

unctuous (*say* unk-**tew**-us) *adjective*
having an oily manner; polite in an exaggerated way. **unctuously** *adverb*, **unctuousness** *noun* [same origin as *unction*]

undecided *adjective*
1 not yet settled; not certain. **2** not having made up your mind yet.

undeniable *adjective*
impossible to deny; undoubtedly true.
undeniably *adverb*

under *preposition*
1 below or beneath, *Hide it under the desk*.
2 less than, *under 5 years old*. **3** governed or controlled by, *The country prospered under his rule*. **4** in the process of; undergoing, *The road is under repair*.
5 using, *He writes under the name of 'Lewis Carroll'*. **6** according to the rules of, *This is permitted under our agreement*.
under way in motion or in progress.
under *adverb*
in or to a lower place or level or condition, *Slowly the diver went under*.
under *adjective*
lower, *the under layers*. [from Old English]

under- *prefix*
1 below or beneath (as in *underwear*).
2 lower; subordinate (as in *under-manager*). **3** not enough; incompletely (as in *undercooked*).

underarm *adjective & adverb*
1 moving the hand and arm forward and upwards. **2** in or for the armpit.

undercarriage *noun* (*plural* **undercarriages**)
an aircraft's landing wheels and their supports.

underclothes *plural noun*
underwear. **underclothing** *noun*

undercover *adjective*
done or doing things secretly, *an undercover agent*.

undercurrent *noun* (*plural* **undercurrents**)
1 a current that is below the surface or

below another current. **2** an underlying feeling or influence, *an undercurrent of fear*.

undercut *verb* (**undercuts, undercutting, undercut**)
sell something for a lower price than someone else sells it.

underdeveloped *adjective*
1 not fully developed or grown. **2** (of a country) poor and lacking modern industrial development.

underdog *noun* (*plural* **underdogs**)
a person or team that is expected to lose a contest or struggle.

underdone *adjective*
not thoroughly done; undercooked.

underestimate *verb* (**underestimates, underestimating, underestimated**)
make too low an estimate of a person or thing.

underfoot *adverb*
on the ground; under your feet.

undergarment *noun* (*plural* **undergarments**)
a piece of underwear.

undergo *verb* (**undergoes, undergoing, underwent, undergone**)
experience or endure something; be subjected to, *The new aircraft underwent intensive tests*.

undergraduate *noun* (*plural* **undergraduates**)
a student at a university who has not yet taken a degree.

underground *adjective* & *adverb*
1 under the ground. **2** done or working in secret.
underground *noun*
a railway that runs through tunnels under the ground.

undergrowth *noun*
bushes and other plants growing closely, especially under trees.

...erhand *adjective*
...e or doing things in a sly or secret way.

underlie *verb* (**underlies, underlying, underlay, underlain**)
1 be the basis or explanation of something. **2** be or lie under something.

underline *verb* (**underlines, underlining, underlined**)
1 draw a line under a word etc. **2** emphasize something.

underling *noun* (*plural* **underlings**)
a person working under someone's authority or control; a subordinate.

underlying *adjective*
1 forming the basis or explanation of something, *the underlying causes of the trouble*. **2** lying under something, *the underlying rocks*.

undermine *verb* (**undermines, undermining, undermined**)
weaken something gradually.

underneath *preposition* & *adverb*
below or beneath. [from *under-* + Old English *neothan* = beneath]

underpants *plural noun*
a piece of men's underwear covering the lower part of the body, worn under trousers.

underpass *noun* (*plural* **underpasses**)
a road that goes underneath another.

underpay *verb* (**underpays, underpaying, underpaid**)
pay someone too little.

underprivileged *adjective*
having less than the normal standard of living or rights in a community.

underrate *verb* (**underrates, underrating, underrated**)
have too low an opinion of a person or thing.

undersell *verb* (**undersells, underselling, undersold**)
sell something at a lower price than another person.

undersigned *adjective*
who has or have signed at the bottom of this document, *We, the undersigned, wish to protest*.

undersized *adjective*
of less than the normal size.

understand *verb* (understands, understanding, understood)
1 know what something means or how it works or why it exists. **2** know and tolerate a person's ways. **3** have been told, *I understand that you would like to speak to me.* **4** take something for granted, *Your expenses will be paid, that's understood.*
understandable *adjective*, **understandably** *adverb* [from Old English]

understanding *noun*
1 the power to understand or think; intelligence. **2** sympathy or tolerance. **3** agreement in opinion or feeling, *a better understanding between nations.*

understatement *noun* (*plural* understatements)
an incomplete or very restrained statement of facts or truth, *To say they disagreed is an understatement; they had a violent quarrel.*

understudy *noun* (*plural* understudies)
an actor who learns a part in order to be able to play it if the usual performer is ill or absent.
understudy *verb* (understudies, understudying, understudied)
be an understudy for an actor or part.

undertake *verb* (undertakes, undertaking, undertook, undertaken)
agree or promise to do something.

undertaker *noun* (*plural* undertakers)
a person whose job is to arrange funerals and burials or cremations.

undertaking *noun* (*plural* undertakings)
1 a job or task that is being undertaken. **2** a promise or guarantee. **3** the business of an undertaker.

undertone *noun* (*plural* undertones)
1 a low or quiet tone, *They spoke in undertones.* **2** an underlying quality or feeling etc., *His letter has a threatening undertone.*

undertow *noun*
a current below that of the surface of the sea and moving in the opposite direction.

underwater *adjective* & *adverb*
placed, used, or done beneath the surface of water.

underwear *noun*
clothes worn next to the skin, under indoor clothing.

underweight *adjective*
not heavy enough.

underwent *past tense* of **undergo**.

underworld *noun*
1 the people who are regularly involved in crime. **2** (in myths and legends) the place for the spirits of the dead, under the earth.

underwrite *verb* (underwrites, underwriting, underwrote, underwritten)
guarantee to finance something, or to pay for any loss or damage etc.
underwriter *noun*
[because the underwriter used to sign his or her name underneath the names of the other people in the agreement]

undesirable *adjective*
not desirable; objectionable.
undesirably *adverb*

undeveloped *adjective*
not yet developed.

undignified *adjective*
not dignified.

undo *verb* (undoes, undoing, undid, undone)
1 unfasten or unwrap. **2** cancel the effect of something, *He has undone all our careful work.*

undoing *noun*
be someone's undoing be the cause of their ruin or failure.

undoubted *adjective*
certain; not regarded as doubtful, *She has undoubted talent.* **undoubtedly** *adverb*

undress *verb* (undresses, undressing, undressed)
take your clothes off.

undue *adjective*
excessive; too great. **unduly** *adverb*

undulate *verb* (undulates, undulating, undulated)
move like a wave or waves; have a wavy appearance. **undulation** *noun*
[from Latin *unda* = a wave]

undying *adjective*
everlasting.

unearth *verb* (unearths, unearthing, unearthed)
1 dig something up; uncover something by digging. 2 find something by searching.

unearthly *adjective*
1 unnatural; strange and frightening.
2 (*informal*) very early or inconvenient, *We had to get up at an unearthly hour.*

uneasy *adjective*
1 worried or anxious. 2 uncomfortable.
uneasily *adverb*, **uneasiness** *noun*

uneatable *adjective*
not fit to be eaten.

uneconomic *adjective*
not profitable.

unemployed *adjective*
without a job. **unemployment** *noun*

unending *adjective*
not coming to an end.

unequal *adjective*
not equal.
unequalled *adjective*, **unequally** *adverb*

unequivocal *adjective*
not at all ambiguous; completely clear, *an unequivocal reply.*

unerring (*say* un-er-ing) *adjective*
making no mistake, *unerring accuracy.*
[from *un-* + *err*]

uneven *adjective*
1 not level or regular. 2 unequal.
unevenly *adverb*, **unevenness** *noun*

unexceptionable *adjective*
not in any way objectionable.
[from *un-* + *exception* as in 'take exception']

USAGE: Do not confuse with *unexceptional.*

unexceptional *adjective*
not exceptional; quite ordinary.

USAGE: Do not confuse with *unexceptionable.*

unexpected *adjective*
not expected.
unexpectedly *adverb*, **unexpectedness** *noun*

unfair *adjective*
not fair; unjust.
unfairly *adverb*, **unfairness** *noun*

unfaithful *adjective*
not faithful; disloyal.

unfamiliar *adjective*
not familiar. **unfamiliarity** *noun*

unfasten *verb* (unfastens, unfastening, unfastened)
open the fastenings of something.

unfavourable *adjective*
not favourable. **unfavourably** *adverb*

unfeeling *adjective*
not caring about other people's feelings; unsympathetic.

unfit *adjective*
1 unsuitable. 2 not in perfect health because you do not take enough exercise.
unfit *verb* (unfits, unfitting, unfitted)
make a person or thing unsuitable.

unfold *verb* (unfolds, unfolding, unfolded)
1 open; spread out. 2 make or become known slowly, *as the story unfolds.*

unforeseen *adjective*
not foreseen; unexpected.

unforgettable *adjective*
not able to be forgotten.

unforgivable *adjective*
not able to be forgiven.

unfortunate *adjective*
1 unlucky. 2 unsuitable or regrettable, *an unfortunate remark.* **unfortunately** *adverb*

unfounded *adjective*
not based on facts. [from *un-* + *found*^{2}]

unfreeze *verb* (unfreezes, unfreezing, unfroze, unfrozen)
thaw; cause something to thaw.

unfriendly *adjective*
not friendly. **unfriendliness** *noun*

unfrock *verb* (unfrocks, unfrocking, unfrocked)
dismiss a person from being a priest. [from *un-* + an old sense of *frock* = a priest's robe]

unfurl *verb* (unfurls, unfurling, unfurled)
unroll; spread out, *They unfurled a large flag.*

unfurnished *adjective*
without furniture, *an unfurnished flat.*

ungainly *adjective*
awkward-looking or clumsy; ungraceful. **ungainliness** *noun* [from *un-* + Middle English *gainly* = graceful]

ungodly *adjective*
1 not giving reverence to God; not religious. 2 (*informal*) outrageous; very inconvenient, *She woke me at an ungodly hour.* **ungodliness** *noun*

ungovernable *adjective*
uncontrollable.

ungracious *adjective*
not kindly or courteous. **ungraciously** *adverb*

ungrateful *adjective*
not grateful. **ungratefully** *adverb*

unguarded *adjective*
1 not guarded. 2 without thought or caution; indiscreet, *He said this in an unguarded moment.*

unguent (*say* ung-went) *noun* (*plural* unguents)
an ointment or lubricant. [same origin as *unction*]

unhappy *adjective*
1 not happy; sad. 2 unfortunate or unsuitable, *an unhappy coincidence.* **unhappily** *adverb*, **unhappiness** *noun*

unhealthy *adjective*
not healthy. **unhealthiness** *noun*

unheard-of *adjective*
never known or done before; extraordinary.

unhinge *verb* (unhinges, unhinging, unhinged)
cause a person's mind to become unbalanced.

uni- *prefix*
one; single (as in *unicorn*). [from Latin *unus* = one]

unicorn *noun* (*plural* unicorns)
(in legends) an animal that is like a horse with one long straight horn growing from its forehead. [from *uni-* + Latin *cornu* = horn]

uniform *noun* (*plural* uniforms)
special clothes showing that the wearer is a member of a certain organization, school, etc.
uniform *adjective*
always the same; not varying, *The desks are of uniform size.* **uniformly** *adverb*, **uniformity** *noun* [from *uni-* + Latin *forma* = form]

uniformed *adjective*
wearing a uniform.

unify *verb* (unifies, unifying, unified)
make a number of things into one thing; unite. **unification** *noun* [same origin as *unit*]

unilateral *adjective*
done by one person or group or country etc., *a unilateral decision.* [from *uni-* + *lateral*]

unilateral disarmament *noun*
getting rid of nuclear weapons without waiting for other countries to agree to do the same.

unimpeachable *adjective*
completely trustworthy, *unimpeachable honesty.* [from *un-* + *impeach* + *-able*]

uninhabitable *adjective*
unfit to live in.

uninhabited *adjective*
with nobody living there.

uninhibited *adjective*
having no inhibitions.

uninterested *adjective*
not interested; showing or feeling no
concern.

USAGE: See the note at *disinterested*.

union *noun* (*plural* **unions**)
1 the joining of things together; uniting.
2 a trade union. [from Latin *unio* = unity]

unionist *noun* (*plural* **unionists**)
1 a member of a trade union. 2 a person
who wishes to unite one country with
another.

Union Jack *noun* (*plural* **Union Jacks**)
the British flag.

unique (*say* yoo-**neek**) *adjective*
being the only one of its kind, *This jewel is
unique*. **uniquely** *adverb*
[French, from Latin *unicus* = one and only]

USAGE: *Unique* does not mean 'unusual' or
'remarkable', so avoid saying things like
very unique or *most unique*.

unisex *adjective*
designed to be suitable for both sexes, *a
unisex hairdresser's*.

unison *noun*
in unison 1 with all sounding or singing the
same tune etc. together, or speaking in
chorus. **2** in agreement.
[from *uni-* + Latin *sonus* = sound]

unit *noun* (*plural* **units**)
1 an amount used as a standard in
measuring or counting things, *Centimetres
are units of length; pence are units of money.*
2 a group, device, piece of furniture, etc.
regarded as a single thing but forming part
of a larger group or whole, *an army unit*;
a sink unit. [from Latin *unus* = one]

unite *verb* (**unites, uniting, united**)
join together; make or become one thing.
[same origin as *unit*]

United Kingdom *noun*
Great Britain and Northern Ireland.

USAGE: See note at *Britain*.

unity *noun*
1 being united; being in agreement.

2 something whole that is made up of
parts. 3 (in mathematics) the number one.

universal *adjective*
to do with or including or done by
everyone or everything. **universally** *adverb*

universe *noun*
everything that exists, including the earth
and living things and all the heavenly
bodies. [from Latin *universus* = combined
into one]

university *noun* (*plural* **universities**)
a place where people go to study at an
advanced level after leaving school.
[from Latin *universitas*, literally = the
universe, later = a community or group of
people (i.e. the teachers and students)]

unjust *adjective*
not fair or just.

unkempt *adjective*
looking untidy or neglected.
[from *un-* + an old word *kempt* = combed]

unkind *adjective*
not kind. **unkindly** *adverb*, **unkindness** *noun*

unknown *adjective*
not known.

unlawful *adjective*
not legal.

unleaded *adjective*
(of petrol) without added lead.

unleash *verb* (**unleashes, unleashing,
unleashed**)
1 set a dog free from a leash. 2 let a strong
feeling or force be released.

unleavened (*say* un-**lev**-end) *adjective*
(of bread) made without yeast or other
substances that would make it rise.

unless *conjunction*
except when; if ... not, *We cannot go unless
we are invited.*

unlike *preposition*
not like, *Unlike me, she enjoys cricket.*
unlike *adjective*
not alike; different, *The two children are
very unlike.*

unlikely *adjective* (unlikelier, unlikeliest)
not likely to happen or be true.

unlimited *adjective*
not limited; very great or very many.

unload *verb* (unloads, unloading, unloaded)
remove the load of things carried by a ship,
aircraft, vehicle, etc.

unlock *verb* (unlocks, unlocking, unlocked)
open something by undoing a lock.

unlucky *adjective*
not lucky; having or bringing bad luck.
unluckily *adverb*

unmanageable *adjective*
unable to be managed.

unmarried *adjective*
not married.

unmask *verb* (unmasks, unmasking,
unmasked)
1 remove a person's mask. 2 reveal what a
person or thing really is.

unmentionable *adjective*
too bad or embarrassing to be spoken of.

unmistakable *adjective*
not able to be mistaken for another person
or thing. **unmistakably** *adverb*

unmitigated *adjective*
absolute, *an unmitigated disaster*.
[from *un-* + *mitigate*]

unnatural *adjective*
not natural or normal. **unnaturally** *adverb*

unnecessary *adjective*
not necessary; more than is necessary.

unnerve *verb* (unnerves, unnerving,
unnerved)
make someone lose courage or
determination.

unoccupied *adjective*
not occupied.

unofficial *adjective*
not official. **unofficially** *adverb*

unorthodox *adjective*
not generally accepted, *an unorthodox
method*.

unpack *verb* (unpacks, unpacking,
unpacked)
take things out of a suitcase, bag, box, etc.

unparalleled *adjective*
having no parallel or equal.

unparliamentary *adjective*
impolite or abusive.

USAGE: It is a rule of debates in
Parliament that speakers must be polite to
each other. Impolite language is
'unparliamentary'.

unpick *verb* (unpicks, unpicking, unpicked)
undo the stitching of something.

unpleasant *adjective*
not pleasant.
unpleasantly *adverb*, **unpleasantness** *noun*

unpopular *adjective*
not popular.

unprecedented (*say* un-press-id-en-tid)
adjective
that has never happened before.
[from *un-* + *precedent*]

unprejudiced *adjective*
impartial.

unprepared *adjective*
not prepared beforehand; not ready or
equipped.

unprepossessing *adjective*
not attractive.

unprincipled *adjective*
without good moral principles;
unscrupulous.

unprintable *adjective*
too rude or indecent to be printed.

unprofessional *adjective*
not professional; not worthy of a member
of a profession.

unprofitable *adjective*
not producing a profit or advantage.
unprofitably *adverb*

unqualified *adjective*
1 not officially qualified to do something.
2 not limited, *We gave it our unqualified
approval.*

unravel *verb* (unravels, unravelling,
unravelled)
1 disentangle. 2 undo something that is
knitted. 3 investigate and solve a mystery
etc. [from *un-* + an old word *ravel* = tangle]

unready *adjective*
not ready; hesitating.

USAGE: In the title of the English king
Ethelred the Unready the word means
'lacking good advice or wisdom'.

unreal *adjective*
not real; existing in the imagination only.
unreality *noun*

unreasonable *adjective*
1 not reasonable. 2 excessive or unjust.
unreasonably *adverb*

unreel *verb* (unreels, unreeling, unreeled)
unwind from a reel.

unrelieved *adjective*
without anything to vary it, *unrelieved
gloom.*

unremitting *adjective*
never stopping or relaxing; persistent.
[from *un-* + *remit*]

unrequited (*say* un-ri-**kwy**-tid) *adjective*
(of love) not returned or rewarded.
[from *un-* + *requite* = reward or pay back]

unreserved *adjective*
1 not reserved. 2 without restriction;
complete, *unreserved loyalty.*
unreservedly *adverb*

unrest *noun*
restlessness; trouble caused because people
are dissatisfied.

unripe *adjective*
not yet ripe.

unrivalled *adjective*
having no equal; better than all others.

unroll *verb* (unrolls, unrolling, unrolled)
open something that has been rolled up.

unruly *adjective*
difficult to control; disorderly.
unruliness *noun*
[from *un-* + *rule*]

unsavoury *adjective*
unpleasant or disgusting.

unscathed *adjective*
uninjured. [from *un-* + Middle English
scathe = harm or injure]

unscrew *verb* (unscrews, unscrewing,
unscrewed)
undo something that has been screwed up.

unscrupulous *adjective*
having no scruples about wrongdoing.

unseat *verb* (unseats, unseating, unseated)
throw a person from horseback or from a
seat on a bicycle etc.

unseemly *adjective*
not proper or suitable; indecent.

unseen *adjective*
not seen; invisible.
unseen *noun* (*plural* unseens)
a passage for translation without previous
preparation.

unselfish *adjective*
not selfish.

unsettled *adjective*
1 not settled or calm. 2 (of weather) likely
to change.

unshakeable *adjective*
not able to be shaken; firm.

unshaven *adjective*
(of a man) not recently shaved.

unsightly *adjective*
not pleasant to look at; ugly.
unsightliness *noun*

unskilled *adjective*
not having or not needing special skill or
training.

unsociable *adjective*
not sociable.

unsocial *adjective*
not social.

unsocial hours time spent working when most people are free.

unsolicited *adjective*
not asked for, *unsolicited advice*.
[from *un-* + *solicit*]

unsound *adjective*
not sound; damaged, unhealthy, unreasonable, or unreliable.
[from *un-+ sound³*]

unspeakable *adjective*
too bad to be described; very objectionable.

unstable *adjective*
not stable; likely to change or become unbalanced.

unsteady *adjective*
not steady.

unstinted *adjective*
given generously. [from *un-* + *stint*]

unstuck *adjective*
come unstuck 1 cease to stick. **2** (*informal*) fail or go wrong.

unsuccessful *adjective*
not successful.

unsuitable *adjective*
not suitable.

untenable *adjective*
not able to be justified or defended.

unthinkable *adjective*
too bad or too unlikely to be worth considering.

unthinking *adjective*
thoughtless.

untidy *adjective* (untidier, untidiest)
not tidy. **untidily** *adverb*, **untidiness** *noun*

untie *verb* (unties, untying, untied)
undo something that has been tied.

until *preposition* & *conjunction*
up to a particular time or event.
[from Old Norse]

USAGE: See the note on *till¹*.

untimely *adjective*
happening too soon or at an unsuitable time.

unto *preposition* (*old use*)
to. [from *until* + *to* (preposition)]

untold *adjective*
1 not told. **2** too much or too many to be counted, *untold wealth* or *wealth untold*.

untoward *adjective*
inconvenient or unfortunate, *if nothing untoward happens.*
[from *un-* + *toward* = fortunate, promising]

untraceable *adjective*
unable to be traced.

untrue *adjective*
not true.

untruth *noun* (*plural* untruths)
an untrue statement; a lie.
untruthful *adjective*, **untruthfully** *adverb*

unused *adjective*
1 (*say* un-**yoozd**) not yet used, *an unused stamp*. **2** (*say* un-**yoost**) not accustomed, *He is unused to eating meat.*

unusual *adjective*
not usual; strange or exceptional.
unusually *adverb*

unutterable *adjective*
too great to be described, *unutterable joy*.
[from *un-* + *utter* + *-able*]

unvarnished *adjective*
1 not varnished. **2** plain and straightforward, *the unvarnished truth*.

unveil *verb* (unveils, unveiling, unveiled)
1 remove a veil or covering from something. **2** reveal.

unwanted *adjective*
not wanted.

unwarrantable *adjective*
not justifiable.
unwarrantably *adverb*
[from *un-* + *warrant* + *-able*]

unwarranted *adjective*
not justified; uncalled for.

unwary *adjective*
not cautious or careful about danger.
unwarily *adverb*, **unwariness** *noun*

unwell *adjective*
not in good health.

unwholesome *adjective*
not wholesome.

unwieldy *adjective*
awkward to move or control because of its
size, shape, or weight. **unwieldiness** *noun*
[from *un-* + *wield*]

unwilling *adjective*
not willing. **unwillingly** *adverb*

unwind *verb* (unwinds, unwinding,
unwound)
1 unroll. 2 (*informal*) relax after a time of
work or strain.

unwise *adjective*
not wise; foolish. **unwisely** *adverb*

unwitting *adjective*
1 unintentional. 2 unaware.
unwittingly *adverb*

unwonted (*say* un-wohn-tid) *adjective*
not customary or usual, *She spoke with
unwonted rudeness.* **unwontedly** *adverb*
[from *un-* + *wont*]

unworn *adjective*
not yet worn.

unworthy *adjective*
not worthy.

unwrap *verb* (unwraps, unwrapping,
unwrapped)
open something that is wrapped.

up *adverb*
1 to or in a higher place or position or
level, *Prices went up.* 2 so as to be upright,
Stand up. 3 out of bed, *It's time to get up.*
4 completely, *Eat up your carrots.*
5 finished, *Your time is up.* 6 (*informal*)
happening, *Something is up.*
up against 1 close to. 2 (*informal*) faced
with difficulties, dangers, etc.
ups and downs 1 ascents and descents.
2 alternate good and bad luck.
up to 1 until. 2 busy with or doing
something, *What are you up to?* 3 capable

of, *I don't think I'm up to it.* 4 needed from,
It's up to us to help her.
up to date 1 modern or fashionable.
2 giving recent information etc.

USAGE: Use hyphens when this is used as
an adjective before a noun, e.g. *up-to-date
information* (but *The information is up to
date*).

up *preposition*
upwards through or along or into, *Water
came up the pipes.* [from Old English]

upbraid *verb* (upbraids, upbraiding,
upbraided) (*formal*)
scold or reproach someone.
[from Old English]

upbringing *noun*
the way someone is trained during
childhood.

update *verb* (updates, updating, updated)
bring a thing up to date.

upheaval *noun* (*plural* upheavals)
a sudden violent change or disturbance.
[from *up-* + *heave*]

uphill *adverb*
up a slope.
uphill *adjective*
1 going up a slope. 2 difficult, *It was an
uphill struggle.*

uphold *verb* (upholds, upholding, upheld)
support or maintain a decision or belief
etc.

upholster *verb* (upholsters, upholstering,
upholstered)
put covers, padding, and springs etc. on
furniture. **upholstery** *noun*
[from *uphold* = maintain and repair]

upkeep *noun*
keeping something in good condition; the
cost of this.

uplands *plural noun*
the higher parts of a country or region.
upland *adjective*

uplifting *adjective*
making you feel more cheerful.

upon *preposition*
on. [from *up* (adverb) + *on* (preposition)]

upper *adjective*
higher in place or rank etc.

upper class *noun* (*plural* **upper classes**)
the highest class in society, especially the
aristocracy. **upper-class** *adjective*

uppermost *adjective*
highest.
uppermost *adverb*
on or to the top or the highest place, *Keep
the painted side uppermost.*
[from *upper* + *most*]

upright *adjective*
1 vertical or erect. 2 strictly honest or
honourable.
upright *noun* (*plural* **uprights**)
a post or rod etc. placed upright, especially
as a support.

uprising *noun* (*plural* **uprisings**)
a rebellion or revolt.

uproar *noun*
an outburst of noise or excitement or
anger.

uproarious *adjective*
very noisy.

uproot *verb* (**uproots, uprooting, uprooted**)
1 remove a plant and its roots from the
ground. 2 make someone leave the place
where he or she has lived for a long time.

upset *verb* (**upsets, upsetting, upset**)
1 overturn; knock something over. 2 make
a person unhappy or distressed. 3 disturb
the normal working of something; disrupt,
This has really upset my plans.
upset *adjective*
1 unhappy or distressed. 2 slightly ill, *an
upset stomach.*
upset *noun* (*plural* **upsets**)
1 a slight illness, *a stomach upset.* 2 an
unexpected result or setback, *There has
been a major upset in the quarter-finals.*

upshot *noun* (*plural* **upshots**)
an outcome. [originally = the final shot in
an archery contest]

upside down *adverb* & *adjective*
1 with the upper part underneath instead
of on top. 2 in great disorder; very untidy,
Everything had been turned upside down.

upstairs *adverb* & *adjective*
to or on a higher floor.

upstart *noun* (*plural* **upstarts**)
a person who has risen suddenly to a high
position, especially one who then behaves
arrogantly. [from an old verb *upstart* = to
spring up suddenly]

upstream *adjective* & *adverb*
in the direction from which a stream flows.

uptake *noun*
quick on the uptake quick to understand.
slow on the uptake slow to understand.

uptight *adjective* (*informal*)
tense and nervous or annoyed.

upward *adjective* & *adverb*
going towards what is higher. **upwards**
adverb [from *up* + *-ward*]

uranium *noun*
a heavy radioactive grey metal used as a
source of nuclear energy.
[named after the planet Uranus]

urban *adjective*
to do with a town or city.
[from Latin *urbis* = of a city]

urbane *adjective*
having smoothly polite manners.
urbanely *adverb*, **urbanity** *noun*
[same origin as *urban*]

urbanize *verb* (**urbanizes, urbanizing,
urbanized**)
change a place into a town-like area.
urbanization *noun*

urchin *noun* (*plural* **urchins**)
1 a poorly dressed or mischievous boy. 2 a
sea urchin. [from Latin *ericius* = hedgehog]

Urdu (*say* **oor**-doo) *noun*
a language related to Hindi, spoken in
northern India and Pakistan.

urge *verb* (**urges, urging, urged**)
1 try to persuade a person to do something.
2 drive people or animals onward.
urge *noun* (*plural* **urges**)
a strong desire. [from Latin]

urgent *adjective*
needing to be done or dealt with
immediately. **urgently** *adverb*, **urgency**
noun [from Latin *urgens* = urging]

urinal (*say* yoor-**rye**-nal) *noun* (*plural*
urinals)
a bowl or trough fixed to the wall in a
men's public toilet, for men to urinate into.
[from Latin *urinalis* = urinary]

urinate (*say* yoor-in-ayt) *verb* (**urinates**,
urinating, **urinated**)
pass urine out of your body. **urination** *noun*

urine (*say* **yoor**-in) *noun*
waste liquid that collects in the bladder
and is passed out of the body. **urinary**
adjective [from Latin]

urn *noun* (*plural* **urns**)
1 a large metal container with a tap, in
which water is heated. 2 a container
shaped like a vase, usually with a foot,
especially a container for holding the ashes
of a cremated person. [from Latin]

US *abbreviation*
United States (of America).

us *pronoun*
the form of *we* used when it is the object of
a verb or after a preposition.
[from Old English]

USA *abbreviation*
United States of America.

usable *adjective*
able to be used.

usage *noun* (*plural* **usages**)
1 use; the way something is used. 2 the
way words are used in a language, *English
usage often differs from American usage.*

use (*say* yooz) *verb* (**uses**, **using**, **used**)
perform an action or job with something,
Use soap for washing. **user** *noun*
used to 1 was or were in the habit of doing,
We used to go by train. 2 accustomed to or
familiar with, *I'm used to his strange
behaviour.*
use up use all of something.

use (*say* yooss) *noun* (*plural* **uses**)
1 the action of using something; being
used, *the use of computers in schools.* 2 the
purpose for which something is used, *Can

you find a use for this crate?* 3 the quality of
being useful, *These scissors are no use at
all.* [from Latin]

used *adjective*
not new; second-hand, *used cars.*

useful *adjective*
able to be used a lot or to do something that
needs doing.
usefully *adverb*, **usefulness** *noun*

useless *adjective*
not useful; producing no effect, *Their
efforts were useless.*
uselessly *adverb*, **uselessness** *noun*

usher *noun* (*plural* **ushers**)
a person who shows people to their seats in
a public hall or church etc.

usher *verb* (**ushers**, **ushering**, **ushered**)
lead someone in or out; escort someone as
an usher.
[from Latin *ostiarius* = doorkeeper]

usherette *noun* (*plural* **usherettes**)
a woman who shows people to their seats
in a cinema or theatre.

USSR *abbreviation*
(*old use*) Union of Soviet Socialist
Republics.

usual *adjective*
such as happens or is done or used etc.
always or most of the time. **usually** *adverb*
[from Latin *usum* = used]

usurp (*say* yoo-**zerp**) *verb* (**usurps**, **usurping**,
usurped)
take power or a position or right etc. from
someone wrongfully or by force.
usurpation *noun*, **usurper** *noun*
[from Latin *usurpare* = seize in order
to use]

usury (*say* **yoo**-zher-ee) *noun*
the lending of money at an excessively
high rate of interest. **usurer** *noun*
[from Latin]

utensil (*say* yoo-**ten**-sil) *noun* (*plural*
utensils)
a tool, device, or container, especially one
for use in the house, *cooking utensils.*
[from Latin *utensilis* = fit for use]

uterus (*say* yoo-ter-us) *noun* (*plural* uteruses)
the womb. [Latin]

utilitarian *adjective*
designed to be useful rather than decorative or luxurious; practical. [from *utility*]

utility *noun* (*plural* utilities)
1 usefulness. 2 an organization that supplies water, gas, electricity, etc. to the community. [from Latin *utilis* = useful]

utilize *verb* (utilizes, utilizing, utilized)
use; find a use for something. **utilization** *noun* [from French]

utmost *adjective*
extreme or greatest, *Look after it with the utmost care.* **utmost** *noun* [from Old English *utemest* = furthest out]

Utopia (*say* yoo-toh-pee-a) *noun* (*plural* Utopias)
an imaginary place or state of things where everything is perfect. **Utopian** *adjective* [Latin, = nowhere; used in 1516 as the title of a book by Sir Thomas More, in which he describes an ideal society]

utter[1] *verb* (utters, uttering, uttered)
say or speak; make a sound with your mouth. **utterance** *noun* [from old Dutch]

utter[2] *adjective*
complete or absolute, *utter misery.* **utterly** *adverb* [from Old English *uttra* = outer]

uttermost *adjective* & *noun*
utmost.

U-turn *noun* (*plural* U-turns)
1 a U-shaped turn made in a vehicle so that it then travels in the opposite direction. 2 a complete change of policy.

Vv

vacant *adjective*
1 empty; not filled or occupied. 2 without expression; blank, *a vacant stare.*
vacantly *adverb*, **vacancy** *noun* [from Latin *vacans* = being empty]

vacate *verb* (vacates, vacating, vacated)
leave or give up a place or position. [from Latin *vacare* = be empty or free from work]

vacation (*say* vak-ay-shon) *noun* (*plural* vacations)
1 a holiday, especially between the terms at a university. 2 vacating a place etc. [same origin as *vacate*]

vaccinate (*say* vak-sin-ayt) *verb* (vaccinates, vaccinating, vaccinated)
inoculate someone with a vaccine. **vaccination** *noun*

vaccine (*say* vak-seen) *noun* (*plural* vaccines)
a substance used to immunize a person against a disease. [from Latin *vacca* = cow (because serum from cows was used to protect people from the disease smallpox)]

vacillate (*say* vass-il-ayt) *verb* (vacillates, vacillating, vacillated)
keep changing your mind; waver. **vacillation** *noun* [from Latin *vacillare* = sway]

vacuous (*say* vak-yoo-us) *adjective*
1 empty-headed; unintelligent. 2 without expression, *a vacuous stare.* **vacuously** *adverb*, **vacuousness** *noun*, **vacuity** *noun* [same origin as *vacuum*]

vacuum *noun* (*plural* vacuums)
1 a completely empty space; a space without any air in it. 2 (*informal*) a vacuum cleaner. **vacuum** *verb* [from Latin *vacuus* = empty]

vacuum cleaner *noun* (*plural* vacuum cleaners)
an electrical device that sucks up dust and dirt etc.

vacuum flask *noun* (*plural* vacuum flasks)
a container with double walls that have a vacuum between them, used for keeping liquids hot or cold.

vagabond *noun* (*plural* vagabonds)
a person with no settled home or regular work; a vagrant. [same origin as *vagary*]

vagary (*say* vay-ger-ee) *noun* (*plural* vagaries)
an impulsive change or whim, *the vagaries of fashion*. [from Latin *vagari* = wander]

vagina (*say* va-jy-na) *noun* (*plural* vaginas)
the passage that leads from the vulva to the womb. [Latin, = sheath]

vagrant (*say* vay-grant) *noun* (*plural* vagrants)
a person with no settled home or regular work; a tramp. **vagrancy** *noun*
[from old French; related to *vagary*]

vague *adjective*
not definite or clear.
vaguely *adverb*, **vagueness** *noun*
[from Latin *vagus* = wandering]

vain *adjective*
1 conceited, especially about your appearance. 2 useless, *They made vain attempts to save her*. **vainly** *adverb*
in vain with no result; uselessly.
[from Latin *vanus* = empty]

USAGE: Do not confuse with *vane* or *vein*.

valance *noun* (*plural* valances)
a short curtain round the frame of a bed or above a window.
[from old French *avaler* = to hang down]

vale *noun* (*plural* vales)
a valley.
[from old French; related to *valley*]

valediction (*say* val-id-ik-shon) *noun* (*plural* valedictions)
saying farewell. **valedictory** *adjective* [from Latin *vale* = farewell + *dicere* = to say]

valency *noun* (*plural* valencies)
the power of an atom to combine with other atoms, measured by the number of hydrogen atoms it is capable of combining with. [from Latin *valentia* = power]

valentine *noun* (*plural* valentines)
1 a card sent on St Valentine's day (14 February) to the person you love. 2 the person to whom you send this card.

valet (*say* val-ay or val-it) *noun* (*plural* valets)
a man's servant who looks after his clothes etc. [French; related to *vassal*]

valetudinarian *noun* (*plural* valetudinarians)
a person who is excessively concerned about keeping healthy.
[from Latin *valetudo* = health]

valiant *adjective*
brave or courageous. **valiantly** *adverb*
[from old French; related to *value*]

valid *adjective*
1 legally able to be used or accepted, *This passport is out of date and not valid*. 2 (of reasoning) sound and logical. **validity** *noun*
[from Latin *validus* = strong]

valley *noun* (*plural* valleys)
1 a long low area between hills. 2 an area through which a river flows, *the Nile valley*. [from Latin]

valour *noun*
bravery. **valorous** *adjective*
[from Latin *valor* = strength]

valuable *adjective*
worth a lot of money; of great value.
valuably *adverb*

valuables *plural noun*
valuable things.

value *noun* (*plural* values)
1 the amount of money etc. that is considered to be the equivalent of something, or for which it can be exchanged. 2 how useful or important something is, *They learnt the value of regular exercise*.
value *verb* (values, valuing, valued)
1 think that something is valuable.
2 estimate the value of a thing.
valuation *noun*, **valuer** *noun*
[from Latin *valere* = be strong]

valueless *adjective*
having no value.

valve *noun* (*plural* **valves**)
1 a device for controlling the flow of gas or liquid through a pipe or tube. 2 a device that controls the flow of electricity in old televisions, radios, etc. 3 each piece of the shell of oysters etc. **valvular** *adjective* [from Latin *valva* = a panel of a folding door]

vamp *noun* (*plural* **vamps**) (*informal*)
an attractive woman who deliberately sets out to lead men astray. [from *vampire*]

vampire *noun* (*plural* **vampires**)
a ghost or revived corpse supposed to leave a grave at night and suck blood from living people. [from Serbo-Croat (a Slavonic language spoken in the Balkan countries)]

van[1] *noun* (*plural* **vans**)
1 a covered vehicle for carrying goods.
2 a railway carriage for luggage or goods, or for the use of the guard.
[short for *caravan*]

van[2] *noun*
the vanguard or forefront.

vandal *noun* (*plural* **vandals**)
a person who deliberately breaks or damages things, especially public property. **vandalism** *noun* [named after the Vandals, a Germanic tribe who invaded the Roman Empire in the 5th century, destroying many books and works of art]

vandalize *verb* (**vandalizes, vandalizing, vandalized**)
damage things as a vandal.

vane *noun* (*plural* **vanes**)
1 a weathervane. 2 the blade of a propeller, sail of a windmill, or other device that acts on or is moved by wind or water. [from Old English]

USAGE: Do not confuse with *vain* or *vein*.

vanguard *noun*
1 the leading part of an army or fleet. 2 the first people to adopt a fashion or idea etc. [from French *avant* = before + *garde* = guard]

vanilla *noun*
a flavouring obtained from the pods of a tropical plant.
[from Spanish *vainilla* = little pod]

vanish *verb* (**vanishes, vanishing, vanished**)
disappear completely. [from Latin]

vanity *noun*
conceit; being vain.

vanquish *verb* (**vanquishes, vanquishing, vanquished**)
conquer. [from Latin *vincere* = conquer]

vantage point *noun* (*plural* **vantage points**)
a place from which you have a good view of something.
[from Middle English *vantage* = advantage]

vapid *adjective*
not lively or interesting; dull. [from Latin *vapidus* = without flavour, insipid]

vaporize *verb* (**vaporizes, vaporizing, vaporized**)
change or be changed into vapour.
vaporization *noun*, **vaporizer** *noun*

vapour *noun* (*plural* **vapours**)
a visible gas to which some substances can be converted by heat; steam or mist.
[from Latin *vapor* = steam]

variable *adjective*
likely to vary; changeable.
variably *adverb*, **variability** *noun*
variable *noun* (*plural* **variables**)
something that varies or can vary;
a variable quantity.

variance *noun*
the amount by which things differ.
at variance differing or conflicting.
[from Latin *variare* = vary]

variant *adjective*
differing from something, *'Gipsy' is a variant spelling of 'gypsy'*. **variant** *noun*
[same origin as *variance*]

variation *noun* (*plural* **variations**)
1 varying; the amount by which something varies. 2 a different form of something.

varicose *adjective*
(of veins) permanently swollen.
[from Latin]

varied *adjective*
of different sorts; full of variety.

variegated (*say* vair-ig-ay-tid) *adjective*
with patches of different colours.
variegation *noun* [same origin as *various*]

variety *adjective* (*plural* **varieties**)
1 a quantity of different kinds of things.
2 the quality of not always being the same;
variation. 3 a particular kind of
something, *There are several varieties of
spaniel.* 4 an entertainment that includes
short performances of various kinds.
[same origin as *various*]

various *adjective*
1 of several kinds; unlike one another, *for
various reasons.* 2 several, *We met various
people.* **variously** *adverb*
[from Latin *varius* = changing]

varnish *noun* (*plural* **varnishes**)
a liquid that dries to form a hard shiny
usually transparent coating.
varnish *verb* (**varnishes, varnishing,
varnished**)
coat something with varnish.
[from French]

vary *verb* (**varies, varying, varied**)
1 make or become different; change. 2 be
different. [same origin as *various*]

vascular *adjective*
consisting of tubes or similar vessels for
circulating blood, sap, or water in animals
or plants, *the vascular system.*
[from Latin *vasculum* = little vessel]

vase *noun* (*plural* **vases**)
an open usually tall container used for
holding cut flowers or as an ornament.
[from Latin *vas* = vessel]

Vaseline *noun* (*trade mark*)
petroleum jelly for use as an ointment.
[from German *Wasser* = water, + Greek
elaion = oil]

vassal *noun* (*plural* **vassals**)
a humble servant or subordinate.
[from Latin *vassallus* = manservant]

vast *adjective*
very great, especially in area, *a vast
expanse of water.*
vastly *adverb*, **vastness** *noun*
[from Latin *vastus* = unoccupied, desert]

VAT *abbreviation*
value added tax; a tax on goods and
services.

vat *noun* (*plural* **vats**)
a very large container for holding liquid.
[from Old English]

vaudeville (*say* vawd-vil) *noun*
a kind of variety entertainment. [French]

vault *verb* (**vaults, vaulting, vaulted**)
jump over something, especially while
supporting yourself on your hands or with
the help of a pole.
vault *noun* (*plural* **vaults**)
1 a vaulting jump. 2 an arched roof. 3 an
underground room used to store things.
4 a room for storing money or valuables.
5 a burial chamber.
[from Latin *volvere* = to roll]

vaulted *adjective*
having an arched roof.

vaulting horse *noun* (*plural* **vaulting
horses**)
a padded wooden block for vaulting over in
gymnastics.

vaunt *verb* (**vaunts, vaunting, vaunted**) (*old
use* or *poetical*)
boast. **vaunt** *noun*
[from Latin *vanus* = vain]

VCR *abbreviation*
video cassette recorder.

VDU *abbreviation*
visual display unit.

veal *noun*
calf's flesh used as food.
[from Latin *vitulus* = calf]

vector *noun* (*plural* **vectors**)
(in mathematics) a quantity that has size
and direction (e.g. velocity, = speed in a
certain direction). **vectorial** *adjective*
[Latin, = carrier, traveller]

Veda (*say* vay-da or vee-da) *noun*
the most ancient and sacred literature of
the Hindus. **Vedic** *adjective*
[Sanskrit, = sacred knowledge]

veer *verb* (veers, veering, veered)
change direction; swerve.
[from old French]

vegan *noun* (*plural* vegans)
a person who does not eat or use any
animal products. [from *veg* (short for
vegetable) + *-an* = belonging to]

vegetable *noun* (*plural* vegetables)
a plant that can be used as food.
[from Latin *vegetare* = enliven, animate]

vegetarian *noun* (*plural* vegetarians)
a person who does not eat meat.
vegetarianism *noun*
[from *vegetable* + *-arian*]

vegetate *verb* (vegetates, vegetating,
vegetated)
live a dull or inactive life.
[originally = grow like a vegetable: same
origin as *vegetable*]

vegetation *noun*
1 plants that are growing. 2 vegetating.
[from Latin *vegetatio* = the power to grow]

vehement (*say* vee-im-ent) *adjective*
showing strong feeling, *a vehement refusal.*
vehemently *adverb*, **vehemence** *noun*
[from Latin]

vehicle *noun* (*plural* vehicles)
a means of transporting people or goods,
especially on land.
[from Latin *vehere* = carry]

veil *noun* (*plural* veils)
a piece of thin material worn to cover the
face or head.
take the veil become a nun.

veil *verb* (veils, veiling, veiled)
1 cover something with a veil. 2 partially
conceal something, *veiled threats.*
[from Latin]

vein *noun* (*plural* veins)
1 any of the tubes that carry blood from all
parts of the body to the heart. (Compare
artery.) 2 a line or streak on a leaf, rock,
insect's wing, etc. 3 a long deposit of
mineral or ore in the middle of a rock.
4 a mood or manner, *She spoke in a serious
vein.* [from Latin]

USAGE: Do not confuse with *vain* or *vane.*

veld (*say* velt) *noun*
an area of open grassland in South Africa.
[Afrikaans, from Dutch *veld* = field]

vellum *noun*
smooth parchment or writing paper.
[from old French *veel* = veal (because
parchment was made from animals' skins)]

velocity *noun* (*plural* velocities)
speed in a given direction.
[from Latin *velox* = swift]

velour (*say* vil-oor) *noun*
a thick velvety material.
[from French *velours* = velvet]

velvet *noun*
a woven material with very short soft furry
fibres on one side. **velvety** *adjective*
[from Latin *villus* = soft fur]

venal (*say* veen-al) *adjective*
able to be bribed. **venality** *noun*
[from Latin *venalis* = for sale]

vend *verb* (vends, vending, vended)
offer something for sale.
[from Latin *vendere* = sell]

vendetta *noun* (*plural* vendettas)
a long-lasting bitter quarrel; a feud.
[Italian, from Latin *vindicta* = vengeance]

vending machine *noun* (*plural* vending
machines)
a slot machine from which you can obtain
drinks, chocolate, cigarettes, etc.

vendor *noun* (*plural* vendors)
a seller. [from *vend*]

veneer *noun* (*plural* veneers)
1 a thin layer of good wood covering the
surface of a cheaper wood in furniture etc.
2 an outward show of some good quality, *a
veneer of politeness.* [via German from
French *fournir* = furnish]

venerable *adjective*
worthy of being venerated, especially
because of great age.

venerate *verb* (venerates, venerating,
venerated)
honour with great respect or reverence.
veneration *noun*
[from Latin *venerari* = revere]

venereal (*say* vin-**eer**-ee-al) *adjective*
to do with sexual intercourse.
[from *Venus*, the Roman goddess of love]

venereal disease *noun* (*plural* **venereal diseases**)
a disease passed on by sexual intercourse.

venetian blind *noun* (*plural* **venetian blinds**)
a window blind consisting of horizontal strips that can be adjusted to let light in or shut it out. [from Latin *Venetia* = Venice]

vengeance *noun*
revenge.
with a vengeance very strongly or effectively.
[from old French; related to *vindictive*]

vengeful *adjective*
seeking vengeance.
vengefully *adverb*, **vengefulness** *noun*

venial (*say* veen-ee-al) *adjective*
(of sins or faults) pardonable, not serious.
[from Latin *venia* = forgiveness]

venison *noun*
deer's flesh as food.
[old French, from Latin *venatio* = hunting]

Venn diagram *noun* (*plural* **Venn diagrams**)
(*in mathematics*) a diagram in which circles are used to show the relationships between different sets of things.
[named after an English mathematician, John Venn]

venom *noun*
1 the poisonous fluid produced by snakes, scorpions, etc. **2** very bitter feeling towards somebody; hatred. **venomous** *adjective*
[from Latin *venenum* = poison]

vent *noun* (*plural* **vents**)
an opening in something, especially to let out smoke or gas etc.
give vent to express your feelings openly.
vent *verb* (**vents, venting, vented**)
1 make a vent in something. **2** give vent to feelings. [from Latin *ventus* = wind]

ventilate *verb* (**ventilates, ventilating, ventilated**)
let air move freely in and out of a room etc.

ventilation *noun*, **ventilator** *noun*
[same origin as *vent*]

ventral *adjective*
on or to do with the abdomen, *This fish has a ventral fin.*
[from Latin *venter* = abdomen]

ventriloquist *noun* (*plural* **ventriloquists**)
an entertainer who makes his or her voice sound as if it comes from another source.
ventriloquism *noun* [from Latin *venter* = abdomen + *loqui* = speak]

venture *noun* (*plural* **ventures**)
something you decide to do that is risky.
venture *verb* (**ventures, venturing, ventured**)
risk; dare to do or say something or to go somewhere, *We ventured out into the snow.*
[from *adventure*]

venturesome *adjective*
ready to take risks; daring.

venue (*say* **ven**-yoo) *noun* (*plural* **venues**)
the place where a meeting, sports match, etc. is held. [from French *venir* = come]

veracity (*say* ver-**as**-it-ee) *noun*
truth. **veracious** (*say* ver-**ay**-shus) *adjective*
[from Latin *verus* = true]

veranda *noun* (*plural* **verandas**)
a terrace with a roof along the side of a house. [via Hindi from Portuguese *varanda* = railing, balcony]

verb *noun* (*plural* **verbs**)
a word that shows what a person or thing is doing, e.g. *bring, came, sing, were.*
[from Latin *verbum* = word]

verbal *adjective*
1 to do with or in words; spoken, not written, *a verbal statement.* **2** to do with verbs. **verbally** *adverb* [same origin as *verb*]

verbatim (*say* ver-**bay**-tim) *adverb* & *adjective*
in exactly the same words, *He copied his friend's essay verbatim.*
[same origin as *verb*]

verbose *adjective*
using more words than are needed.
verbosely *adverb*, **verbosity** (*say* ver-**boss**-it-ee) *noun* [same origin as *verb*]

verdant *adjective*
(of grass or fields) green. [from old French]

verdict *noun* (*plural* **verdicts**)
a judgement or decision made after considering something, especially that made by a jury.
[from Latin *verus* = true + *dictum* = said]

verdigris (*say* **verd**-i-grees) *noun*
green rust on copper or brass.
[from French *vert-de-gris*, literally = green of Greece]

verdure *noun*
green vegetation; its greenness.
[from old French *verd* = green]

verge *noun* (*plural* **verges**)
1 the extreme edge or brink of something, *on the verge of madness*. **2** a strip of grass along the edge of a road or path etc.
verge *verb* (**verges, verging, verged**)
verge on border on something; be close to something, *This puzzle verges on the impossible*.
[from old French; related to *verger*]

verger *noun* (*plural* **vergers**)
a person who is caretaker and attendant in a church. [originally = someone who carried a bishop's staff of office: from Latin *virga* = rod]

verify *verb* (**verifies, verifying, verified**)
check or show that something is true or correct. **verifiable** *adjective*, **verification** *noun* [same origin as *veracity*]

verisimilitude *noun*
an appearance of being true or lifelike.
[from Latin *verus* = true + *similis* = like]

veritable *adjective*
real; rightly named, *a veritable villain*. **veritably** *adverb* [French; related to *verity*]

verity *noun* (*plural* **verities**)
truth. [from Latin *veritas* = truth]

vermicelli (*say* verm-i-**sel**-ee) *noun*
pasta made in long thin threads.
[Italian, = little worms]

vermilion *noun* & *adjective*
bright red.
[from Latin *vermiculus* = little worm]

vermin *plural noun*
1 pests (e.g. foxes, rats, mice) regarded as harmful to domestic animals, crops, or food. **2** unpleasant or parasitic insects, e.g. lice. **verminous** *adjective*
[from Latin *vermis* = worm]

vernacular (*say* ver-**nak**-yoo-ler) *noun* (*plural* **vernaculars**)
the language of a country or district, as distinct from an official or formal language.
[from Latin *vernaculus* = domestic]

vernal *adjective*
to do with the season of spring.
[from Latin *ver* = spring]

verruca (*say* ver-**oo**-ka) *noun* (*plural* **verrucas**)
a kind of wart on the sole of the foot.
[Latin, = wart]

versatile *adjective*
able to do or be used for many different things. **versatility** *noun*
[from Latin *versare* = to turn]

verse *noun* (*plural* **verses**)
1 writing arranged in short lines, usually with a particular rhythm and often with rhymes; poetry. **2** a group of lines forming a unit in a poem or song. **3** each of the short numbered sections of a chapter in the Bible. [via Old English from Latin *versus* = a line of writing]

versed *adjective*
versed in experienced or skilled in something.
[from Latin *versatus* = engaged in something]

version *noun* (*plural* **versions**)
1 a particular person's account of something that happened. **2** a translation, *modern versions of the Bible*. **3** a special or different form of something, *the latest version of this car*.
[from Latin *versum* = turned, transformed]

versus *preposition*
against; competing with, *Arsenal versus Liverpool*. [Latin, = against]

vertebra *noun* (*plural* **vertebrae**)
each of the bones that form the backbone.
[Latin]

vertebrate *noun* (*plural* **vertebrates**)
an animal that has a backbone. (The opposite is *invertebrate*.) [from *vertebra*]

vertex *noun* (*plural* **vertices**, *say* ver-tis-eez)
the highest point of a cone or triangle, or of a hill etc. [Latin, = top of the head]

vertical *adjective*
at right angles to something horizontal; upright. **vertically** *adverb*
[same origin as *vertex*]

vertigo *noun*
a feeling of dizziness and loss of balance, especially when you are very high up. [Latin, = whirling around]

verve (*say* verv) *noun*
enthusiasm and liveliness. [French, = vigour]

very *adverb*
1 to a great amount or intensity; extremely, *It was very cold.* 2 (used to emphasize something), *on the very next day; the very last drop.*
very *adjective*
1 exact or actual, *It's the very thing we need.* 2 extreme, *at the very end.*
[from old French *verai* = true]

vespers *plural noun*
a church service held in the evening. [from Latin *vesper* = evening]

vessel *noun* (*plural* **vessels**)
1 a ship or boat. 2 a container, especially for liquid. 3 a tube carrying blood or other liquid in the body of an animal or plant. [from old French; related to *vase*]

vest *noun* (*plural* **vests**)
a piece of underwear covering the trunk of the body.
vest *verb* (**vests, vesting, vested**)
1 give something as a right, *The power to make laws is vested in Parliament.* 2 (*old use*) clothe.
[from Latin *vestis* = a piece of clothing]

vested interest *noun* (*plural* **vested interests**)
a strong reason for wanting something to happen, usually because you will benefit from it.

vestibule *noun* (*plural* **vestibules**)
1 an entrance hall or lobby. 2 a church porch. [from Latin]

vestige *noun* (*plural* **vestiges**)
a trace; a very small amount, especially of something that formerly existed. **vestigial** *adjective* [from Latin *vestigium* = footprint]

vestment *noun* (*plural* **vestments**)
a ceremonial garment, especially one worn by clergy or choir at a service. [same origin as *vest*]

vestry *noun* (*plural* **vestries**)
a room in a church where vestments are kept and where clergy and choir put these on. [from Latin *vestiarium* = wardrobe]

vet *noun* (*plural* **vets**)
a person trained to give medical and surgical treatment to animals.
vet *verb* (**vets, vetting, vetted**)
check a thing to see if it has any mistakes or faults. [short for *veterinary surgeon*]

vetch *noun*
a plant of the pea family. [from Latin]

veteran *noun* (*plural* **veterans**)
a person who has had long service or experience in something, *a war veteran.* [from Latin *vetus* = old]

veteran car *noun* (*plural* **veteran cars**)
a car that is at least 80 years old.

veterinary (*say* vet-rin-ree) *adjective*
to do with the medical and surgical treatment of animals, *a veterinary surgeon.* [from Latin *veterinae* = cattle]

veto (*say* vee-toh) *noun* (*plural* **vetoes**)
1 a refusal to let something happen. 2 the right to prohibit something.
veto *verb* (**vetoes, vetoing, vetoed**)
refuse or prohibit something. [Latin, = I forbid]

vex *verb* (**vexes, vexing, vexed**)
annoy; cause somebody worry. **vexation** *noun*, **vexatious** *adjective* [from Latin *vexare* = to shake]

vexed question *noun* (*plural* **vexed questions**)
a problem that is difficult or much discussed.

VHF *abbreviation*
very high frequency.

via (*say* vy-a) *preposition*
through; by way of, *The train goes from London to Exeter via Bristol.*
[Latin, = by way of]

viable *adjective*
able to work or exist successfully; practicable, *a viable plan.* **viability** *noun*
[French, from *vie* = life]

viaduct *noun* (*plural* **viaducts**)
a long bridge, usually with many arches, carrying a road or railway over a valley or low ground.
[from Latin *via* = road + *ducere* = to lead]

vial *noun* (*plural* **vials**)
a small glass bottle.
[a different spelling of *phial*]

viands (*say* vy-andz) *plural noun*
food. [from French]

vibrant *adjective*
full of energy; lively.
[same origin as *vibrate*]

vibraphone *noun* (*plural* **vibraphones**)
a musical instrument like a xylophone with metal bars under which there are tiny electric fans making a vibrating effect.
[from *vibrate* + Greek *phone* = voice]

vibrate *verb* (**vibrates, vibrating, vibrated**)
1 shake very quickly to and fro. **2** make a throbbing sound. **vibration** *noun*
[from Latin *vibrare* = shake]

vicar *noun* (*plural* **vicars**)
a member of the clergy who is in charge of a parish. [same origin as *vicarious* (because originally a vicar looked after a parish for another clergyman, or for a monastery)]

vicarage *noun* (*plural* **vicarages**)
the house of a vicar.

vicarious (*say* vik-air-ee-us) *adjective*
not experienced yourself but felt by imagining you share someone else's experience, *We felt a vicarious thrill by watching people skiing.*
[from Latin *vicarius* = substitute]

vice[1] *noun* (*plural* **vices**)
1 evil or wickedness. **2** an evil or bad habit; a bad fault. [from Latin *vitium* = fault]

vice[2] *noun* (*plural* **vices**)
a device for gripping something and holding it firmly while you work on it.
[from Latin *vitis* = vine]

vice- *prefix*
1 authorized to act as a deputy or substitute (as in *vice-captain, vice-president*). **2** next in rank to someone (as in *vice-admiral*).
[Latin, = in place of, by a change]

vice versa *adverb*
the other way round, *which do you prefer—blue spots on a yellow background or vice versa?*
[Latin, = the position being reversed]

vicinity *noun*
the area near or round something. [from Latin *vicinus* = neighbouring, a neighbour]

vicious *adjective*
1 cruel and aggressive. **2** severe or violent. **viciously** *adverb*, **viciousness** *noun*
[same origin as *vice*[1]]

vicious circle *noun* (*plural* **vicious circles**)
a situation where a problem produces an effect which itself produces the original problem or makes it worse.

vicissitude (*say* viss-iss-i-tewd) *noun*
(*plural* **vicissitudes**)
a change of circumstances or fortune.
[from Latin *vicissim* = in turn]

victim *noun* (*plural* **victims**)
someone who is injured, killed, robbed, etc.
[from Latin *victima* = a person or animal sacrificed to a god]

victimize *verb* (**victimizes, victimizing, victimized**)
make a victim of someone; punish a person unfairly. **victimization** *noun*

victor *noun* (*plural* **victors**)
the winner. [same origin as *victory*]

Victorian *adjective*
belong to the time of Queen Victoria (1837–1901). **Victorian** *noun*

victory *noun* (*plural* **victories**)
success won against an opponent in a
battle, contest, or game. **victorious** *adjective*
[from Latin *victum* = conquered]

victualler (*say* vit-ler) *noun* (*plural*
victuallers)
a person who supplies victuals.
licensed victualler a person who holds the
license of a public house.

victuals (*say* vit-alz) *plural noun* (*old use*)
food and drink. [from Latin *victus* = food]

video *noun* (*plural* **videos**)
1 recorded or broadcast pictures. **2** a video
recorder or recording. **3** a visual display
unit. [Latin, = I see]

video game *noun* (*plural* **video games**)
a game in which you press electronic
controls to move images on a screen.

video recorder *noun* (*plural* **video
recorders**)
a machine for recording a television
programme etc. on magnetic tape for
playing back later.

videotape *noun* (*plural* **videotapes**)
magnetic tape suitable for recording
television programmes.

vie *verb* (**vies**, **vying**, **vied**)
compete; carry on a rivalry, *vying with
each other*. [probably from *envy*]

view *noun* (*plural* **views**)
1 what can be seen from one place, e.g.
beautiful scenery. **2** sight; range of vision,
The ship sailed into view. **3** an opinion, *She
has strong views about politics*.
in view of because of.
on view displayed for inspection.
with a view to with the hope or intention of.
view *verb* (**views**, **viewing**, **viewed**)
1 look at something. **2** consider.
viewer *noun*
[from Latin *videre* = to see]

viewpoint *noun* (*plural* **viewpoints**)
a point of view.

vigil (*say* vij-il) *noun* (*plural* **vigils**)
staying awake to keep watch or to pray, *a
long vigil*. [from Latin]

vigilant (*say* vij-il-ant) *adjective*
watchful. **vigilantly** *adverb*, **vigilance** *noun*
[from Latin *vigilans* = keeping watch]

vigilante (*say* vij-il-an-tee) *noun* (*plural*
vigilantes)
a member of a group who organize
themselves, without authority, to try to
prevent crime and disorder in a small area.
[Spanish, = vigilant]

vigorous *adjective*
full of strength and energy.
vigorously *adverb*

vigour *noun*
strength and energy. [from Latin]

Viking *noun* (*plural* **Vikings**)
a Scandinavian trader and pirate in the
8th–10th centuries. [from Old Norse]

vile *adjective*
1 extremely disgusting. **2** very bad or
wicked. **vilely** *adverb*, **vileness** *noun*
[from Latin *vilis* = cheap, unworthy]

vilify (*say* vil-if-I) *verb* (**vilifies**, **vilifying**,
vilified)
say unpleasant things about a person or
thing. **vilification** *noun* [same origin as *vile*]

villa *noun* (*plural* **villas**)
a house, especially a holiday home abroad.
[Latin, = country house]

village *noun* (*plural* **villages**)
a group of houses and other buildings in a
country district, smaller than a town and
usually having a church. **villager** *noun*
[old French; related to *villa*]

villain *noun* (*plural* **villains**)
a wicked person or a criminal.
villainous *adjective*, **villainy** *noun*
[from Latin *villanus* = villager]

villein (*say* vil-an or vil-ayn) *noun* (*plural*
villeins)
a tenant in feudal times.
[a different spelling of *villain*]

vim *noun* (*informal*)
vigour. [originally American; probably
from Latin]

vindicate *verb* (vindicates, vindicating, vindicated)
1 clear a person of blame or suspicion.
2 prove something to be true or worth while. **vindication** *noun*
[from Latin *vindicare* = set free]

vindictive *adjective*
showing a desire for revenge; spiteful.
vindictively *adverb*, **vindictiveness** *noun*
[from Latin *vindicta* = vengeance]

vine *noun* (*plural* vines)
a climbing or trailing plant whose fruit is the grape. [from Latin *vinum* = wine]

vinegar *noun*
a sour liquid used to flavour food or in pickling.
[from Latin *vinum* = wine + *acer* = sour]

vineyard (*say* vin-yard) *noun* (*plural* vineyards)
a plantation of vines producing grapes for making wine.

vintage *noun* (*plural* vintages)
1 the harvest of a season's grapes; the wine made from this. 2 the period from which something comes.
[from French; related to *vine*]

vintage car *noun* (*plural* vintage cars)
a car made between 1917 and 1930.

vinyl *noun*
a kind of plastic. [from Latin]

viola[1] (*say* vee-oh-la) *noun* (*plural* violas)
a musical instrument like a violin but slightly larger and with a lower pitch.
[Spanish or Italian]

viola[2] (*say* vy-ol-a) *noun* (*plural* violas)
a plant of the kind that includes violets and pansies. [Latin, = violet]

violate *verb* (violates, violating, violated)
1 break a promise, law, or treaty etc.
2 break into somewhere; treat a person or place without respect.
violation *noun*, **violator** *noun*
[from Latin *violare* = treat violently]

violence *noun*
force that does harm or damage. **violent** *adjective*, **violently** *adverb* [from Latin]

violet *noun* (*plural* violets)
1 a small plant that often has purple flowers. 2 purple. [related to *viola*[2]]

violin *noun* (*plural* violins)
a musical instrument with four strings, played with a bow. **violinist** *noun*
[from Italian *violino* = small viola[1]]

VIP *abbreviation*
very important person.

viper *noun* (*plural* vipers)
a small poisonous snake.
[from Latin *vipera* = snake]

virago (*say* vir-ah-goh) *noun* (*plural* viragos)
a fierce or bullying woman.
[Latin, = female soldier]

virgin *noun* (*plural* virgins)
a person, especially a girl or woman, who has never had sexual intercourse.
virginal *adjective*, **virginity** *noun*
virgin *adjective*
not yet touched or used, *virgin snow*.
[from Latin]

virginals *plural noun*
an instrument rather like a harpsichord, used in the 16th–17th centuries.
[from Latin *virginalis* = to do with virgins (because it was often played by young women)]

virile (*say* vir-I'l) *adjective*
having masculine strength or vigour, especially sexually. **virility** *noun*
[from Latin *vir* = man]

virology *noun*
the study of viruses. **virological** *adjective*, **virologist** *noun* [from *virus* + *-ology*]

virtual *adjective*
being something in effect though not strictly in fact, *His silence was a virtual admission of guilt.* [same origin as *virtue*]

virtually *adverb*
nearly or almost.

virtual reality *noun*
an image or environment produced by a computer that is so realistic that it seems to be part of the real world.

virtue *noun* (*plural* **virtues**)
1 moral goodness; a particular form of this, *Honesty is a virtue.* 2 a good quality or advantage, *Jamie's plan has the virtue of simplicity.*
virtuous *adjective*, **virtuously** *adverb*
in virtue of because of.
[from Latin *virtus* = worth]

virtuoso (*say* ver-tew-**oh**-soh) *noun* (*plural* **virtuosos** or **virtuosi**)
a person with outstanding skill, especially in singing or playing music. **virtuosity** *noun*
[Italian, = skilful]

virulent (*say* **vir**-oo-lent) *adjective*
1 strongly poisonous or harmful, *a virulent disease.* 2 bitterly hostile, *virulent criticism.*
virulence *noun* [same origin as *virus*]

virus *noun* (*plural* **viruses**)
1 a very tiny living thing, smaller than a bacterium, that can cause disease. 2 a disease caused by a virus. 3 a hidden set of instructions in a computer program that is designed to destroy data. [Latin, = poison]

visa (*say* **vee**-za) *noun* (*plural* **visas**)
an official mark put on someone's passport by officials of a foreign country to show that the holder has permission to enter that country. [Latin, = things seen]

visage (*say* **viz**-ij) *noun* (*plural* **visages**)
a person's face.
[from Latin *visus* = sight, appearance]

vis-à-vis (*say* veez-ah-**vee**) *adverb* & *preposition*
1 in a position facing one another; opposite to. 2 as compared with.
[French, = face to face]

viscera (*say* **vis**-er-a) *plural noun*
the intestines and other internal organs of the body. [Latin, = soft parts]

viscid (*say* **vis**-id) *adjective*
thick and gluey. **viscidity** *noun*
[same origin as *viscous*]

viscose (*say* **vis**-kohs) *noun*
fabric made from viscous cellulose.

viscount (*say* **vy**-kownt) *noun* (*plural* **viscounts**)
a nobleman ranking below an earl and

above a baron. **viscountess** *noun*
[from old French *visconte* = vice-count]

viscous (*say* **visk**-us) *adjective*
thick and gluey, not pouring easily.
viscosity *noun*
[from Latin *viscus* = a sticky substance spread on branches to catch birds]

visible *adjective*
able to be seen or noticed, *The ship was visible on the horizon.* **visibly** *adverb*,
visibility *noun* [from Latin]

USAGE: Do not confuse with *visual.*

vision *noun* (*plural* **visions**)
1 the ability to see; sight. 2 something seen in a person's imagination or in a dream. 3 foresight and wisdom in planning things. 4 a person or thing that is beautiful to see. [from old French; related to *visible* and *visual*]

visionary *adjective*
extremely imaginative or fanciful.

visionary *noun* (*plural* **visionaries**)
a person with extremely imaginative ideas and plans.

visit *verb* (**visits**, **visiting**, **visited**)
1 go to see a person or place. 2 stay somewhere for a while. **visitor** *noun*

visit *noun* (*plural* **visits**)
1 going to see a person or place. 2 a short stay somewhere.
[from Latin *visitare* = go to see]

visitant *noun* (*plural* **visitants**)
1 a visitor, especially a supernatural one. 2 a bird that is a visitor to an area while migrating.

visitation *noun* (*plural* **visitations**)
an official visit, especially to inspect something.

visor (*say* **vy**-zer) *noun* (*plural* **visors**)
1 the part of a helmet that covers the face. 2 a shield to protect the eyes from bright light or sunshine.
[from old French; related to *visage*]

vista *noun* (*plural* **vistas**)
a long view. [Italian, = view]

visual *adjective*
to do with or used in seeing; to do with sight. **visually** *adverb*
[from Latin *visus* = sight]

USAGE: Do not confuse with *visible*.

visual aid *noun* (*plural* **visual aids**)
a picture, slide, film, etc. used as an aid in teaching.

visual display unit *noun* (*plural* **visual display units**)
a device that looks like a television screen and displays data being received from a computer or fed into it.

visualize *verb* (**visualizes, visualizing, visualized**)
form a mental picture of something. **visualization** *noun*

vital *adjective*
1 connected with life; necessary for life to continue, *vital functions such as breathing.* 2 essential; very important. **vitally** *adverb*
[from Latin *vita* = life]

vitality *noun*
liveliness or energy.

vitamin (*say* vit-a-min or vy-ta-min) *noun* (*plural* **vitamins**)
any of a number of substances that are present in various foods and are essential to keep people and animals healthy. [from Latin *vita* = life + *amine*, a kind of chemical related to amino acids, which vitamins were once thought to contain]

vitiate (*say* vish-ee-ayt) *verb* (**vitiates, vitiating, vitiated**)
spoil or damage something and make it less effective. **vitiation** *noun*
[same origin as *vice*[1]]

vitreous (*say* vit-ree-us) *adjective*
like glass in being hard, transparent, or brittle, *vitreous enamel.*
[from Latin *vitrum* = glass]

vitriol (*say* vit-ree-ol) *noun*
1 sulphuric acid or one of its compounds. 2 savage criticism. **vitriolic** *adjective*
[from Latin]

vituperation *noun*
abusive words. [from Latin *vituperare* = to blame or find fault]

vivacious (*say* viv-ay-shus) *adjective*
happy and lively. **vivaciously** *adverb*, **vivacity** *noun* [from Latin *vivus* = alive]

viva voce (*say* vy-va voh-chee) *adjective* & *adverb*
in a spoken test or examination.
[Latin, = with the living voice]

vivid *adjective*
1 bright and strong or clear, *vivid colours; a vivid description.* 2 active and lively, *a vivid imagination.* **vividly** *adverb*, **vividness** *noun* [from Latin *vividus* = full of life]

vivisection *noun*
doing surgical experiments on live animals.
[from Latin *vivus* = alive + *sectio* = cutting]

vixen *noun* (*plural* **vixens**)
a female fox. [from Old English]

vizier (*say* viz-eer) *noun* (*plural* **viziers**)
(in former times) an important Muslim official.
[from Arabic *wazir* = chief counsellor]

vocabulary *noun* (*plural* **vocabularies**)
1 a list of words with their meanings. 2 the words known to a person or used in a particular book or subject etc.
[from Latin *vocabulum* = name]

vocal *adjective*
to do with or using the voice. **vocally** *adverb*
[from Latin *vocis* = of the voice]

vocal cords *plural noun*
two strap-like membranes in the throat that can be made to vibrate and produce sounds.

vocalist *noun* (*plural* **vocalists**)
a singer, especially in a pop group.

vocation *noun* (*plural* **vocations**)
1 a person's job or occupation. 2 a strong desire to do a particular kind of work, or a feeling of being called by God to do something.
[from Latin *vocare* = to call]

vocational *adjective*
teaching you the skills you need for a particular job or profession, *vocational training*.

vociferate (*say* vo-**sif**-er-ayt) *verb*
(**vociferates, vociferating, vociferated**)
say something loudly or noisily.
vociferation *noun* [from Latin *vocis* = of the voice + *ferre* = carry]

vociferous (*say* vo-**sif**-er-us) *adjective*
noisily and forcefully expressing your views. [same origin as *vociferate*]

vodka *noun* (*plural* **vodkas**)
a strong alcoholic drink very popular in Russia. [from Russian *voda* = water]

vogue *noun* (*plural* **vogues**)
the current fashion, *Very short hair for women seems to be the vogue*.
in vogue in fashion, *Stripy dresses are definitely in vogue*.
[via French from Italian]

voice *noun* (*plural* **voices**)
1 sounds formed by the vocal cords and uttered by the mouth, especially in speaking, singing, etc. 2 the ability to speak or sing, *She has lost her voice*. 3 someone expressing a particular opinion about something, *Emma's the only dissenting voice*. 4 the right to express an opinion or desire, *I have no voice in this matter*.
voice *verb* (**voices, voicing, voiced**)
say something, *We voiced our opinions*. [from Latin]

void *adjective*
1 empty. 2 having no legal validity.
void *noun* (*plural* **voids**)
an empty space or hole.
[from old French; related to *vacant*]

voile (*say* voil) *noun*
a very thin almost transparent material. [French, = veil]

volatile (*say* **vol**-a-tyl) *adjective*
1 evaporating quickly, *a volatile liquid*.
2 changing quickly from one mood or interest to another. **volatility** *noun*
[from Latin *volatilis* = flying]

volcano *noun* (*plural* **volcanoes**)
a mountain with an opening at the top from which lava and hot gases etc. flow.
volcanic *adjective* [Italian, from *Vulcan*, the ancient Roman god of fire]

vole *noun* (*plural* **voles**)
a small animal rather like a rat.
[from Old Norse]

volition *noun*
using your own will in choosing to do something, *She left of her own volition*.
[from Latin *volo* = I wish]

volley *noun* (*plural* **volleys**)
1 a number of bullets or shells etc. fired at the same time. 2 hitting back the ball in tennis etc. before it touches the ground.
volley *verb* (**volleys, volleying, volleyed**)
send or hit something in a volley or volleys. [from Latin *volare* = to fly]

volleyball *noun*
a game in which two teams hit a large ball to and fro over a net with their hands.

volt *noun* (*plural* **volts**)
a unit for measuring electric force.
[named after an Italian scientist, A. Volta, who discovered how to produce electricity by a chemical reaction]

voltage *noun* (*plural* **voltages**)
electric force measured in volts.

volte-face (*say* volt-**fahs**) *noun*
a complete change in your attitude towards something.
[French]

voluble *adjective*
talking very much.
volubly *adverb*, **volubility** *noun*
[from Latin *volubilis* = rolling]

volume *noun* (*plural* **volumes**)
1 the amount of space filled by something.
2 an amount or quantity, *The volume of work has increased*. 3 the strength or power of sound. 4 a book, especially one of a set. [from Latin *volumen* = a roll (because ancient books were made in a rolled form)]

voluminous (*say* vol-**yoo**-min-us) *adjective*
1 bulky; large and full, *a voluminous skirt*.

2 able to hold a lot, *a voluminous bag.*
[from Latin *voluminosus* – having many
turns or coils]

voluntary *adjective*
1 done or doing something willingly, not
because you are forced to do it. 2 unpaid,
voluntary work. **voluntarily** *adverb*
voluntary *noun* (*plural* **voluntaries**)
an organ solo, often improvised, played
before or after a church service.
[from Latin *voluntas* = the will]

volunteer *verb* (**volunteers, volunteering,
volunteered**)
give or offer something of your own accord,
without being forced to.
volunteer *noun* (*plural* **volunteers**)
a person who volunteers to do something,
e.g. to serve in the armed forces.
[from French; related to *voluntary*]

voluptuous *adjective*
giving a luxurious feeling, *voluptuous
furnishings.*
[from Latin *voluptas* – pleasure]

vomit *verb* (**vomits, vomiting, vomited**)
bring up food etc. from the stomach and
out through the mouth; be sick. **vomit** *noun*
[from Latin]

voodoo *noun*
a form of witchcraft and magical rites,
especially in the West Indies.
[via American French from a West African
language]

-vore *suffix*
forms nouns meaning 'eating or feeding on
something' (e.g. *carnivore*).
[same origin as *voracious*]

voracious (*say* vor-ay-shus) *adjective*
greedy; devouring things eagerly.
voraciously *adverb*, **voracity** *noun*
[from Latin *vorare* = devour]

-vorous *suffix*
forms adjectives correspoding to nouns in
-vore (e.g. *carnivorous*).

vortex *noun* (*plural* **vortices**)
a whirlpool or whirlwind. [Latin]

vote *verb* (**votes, voting, voted**)
show which person or thing you prefer by

putting up your hand, making a mark on a
paper, etc. **voter** *noun*
vote *noun* (*plural* **votes**)
1 the action of voting. 2 the right to vote.
[from Latin *votum* = a wish or vow]

votive *adjective*
given in fulfilment of a vow, *votive offerings
at the shrine.* [same origin as *vote*]

vouch *verb* (**vouches, vouching, vouched**)
vouch for guarantee that something is true
or certain, *I will vouch for his honesty.*
[from old French; related to *vocation*]

voucher *noun* (*plural* **vouchers**)
a piece of paper that can be exchanged for
certain goods or services; a receipt.
[from *vouch*]

vouchsafe *verb* (**vouchsafes, vouchsafing,
vouchsafed**)
grant something in a gracious or
condescending way, *She did not vouchsafe a
reply.* [from *vouch* + *safe*]

vow *noun* (*plural* **vows**)
a solemn promise, especially to God or a
saint.
vow *verb* (**vows, vowing, vowed**)
make a vow.
[from old French; related to *vote*]

vowel *noun* (*plural* **vowels**)
any of the letters a, e, i, o, u, and sometimes
y, which represent sounds in which breath
comes out freely. (Compare *consonant.*)
[from Latin *vocalis littera* = vocal letter]

voyage *noun* (*plural* **voyages**)
a long journey on water or in space.
voyage *verb* (**voyages, voyaging, voyaged**)
make a voyage. **voyager** *noun*
[from old French]

vulcanize *verb* (**vulcanizes, vulcanizing,
vulcanized**)
treat rubber with sulphur to strengthen it
vulcanization *noun*
[from *Vulcan,* the ancient Roman god of
fire (because the rubber has to be made
very hot)]

vulgar *adjective*
rude; without good manners. **vulgarly**
adverb, **vulgarity** *noun* [from Latin *vulgus*
= the common or ordinary people]

vulgar fraction noun (plural vulgar fractions)
a fraction shown by numbers above and below a line (e.g. $\frac{2}{3}$, $\frac{5}{8}$), not a decimal fraction.

vulnerable adjective
able to be hurt or harmed or attacked. **vulnerability** noun
[from Latin vulnus = wound]

vulture noun (plural vultures)
a large bird that feeds on dead animals. [from Latin]

vulva noun (plural vulvas)
the outer parts of the female genitals. [Latin]

vying present participle of vie.

Ww

W. abbreviation
1 west. 2 western.

wacky adjective (wackier, wackiest)
crazy or silly. [from whack + -y]

wad (say wod) noun (plural wads)
a pad or bundle of soft material or banknotes, papers, etc.
wad verb (wads, wadding, wadded)
pad something with soft material. [from Dutch]

waddle verb (waddles, waddling, waddled)
walk with short steps, swaying from side to side. **waddle** noun [probably from wade]

wade verb (wades, wading, waded)
walk through water or mud etc. **wader** noun [from Old English]

wafer noun (plural wafers)
a kind of thin biscuit.
[from old French; related to waffle¹]

wafer-thin adjective
very thin.

waffle¹ (say wof-el) noun (plural waffles)
a small cake made of batter and eaten hot. [from Dutch]

waffle² (say wof-el) noun (informal)
vague wordy talk or writing. **waffle** verb
[from an old word waff = to bark or yelp]

waft (say woft) verb (wafts, wafting, wafted)
carry or float gently through the air or over water. [from old German or Dutch]

wag¹ verb (wags, wagging, wagged)
move quickly to and fro, a dog wagging its tail. **wag** noun [from Old English]

wag² noun (plural wags)
a person who makes jokes.
[from an old word waghalter = someone likely to be hanged]

wage noun or **wages** plural noun
a regular payment to someone in return for his or her work.
wage verb (wages, waging, waged)
carry on a war or campaign.
[via old French from Germanic]

wager (say way-jer) noun (plural wagers)
a bet. **wager** verb
[from old French; related to wage]

waggle verb (waggles, waggling, waggled)
move quickly to and fro; wag. **waggle** noun
[from wag]

wagon noun (plural wagons)
1 a cart with four wheels, pulled by a horse or an ox. 2 an open railway truck, e.g. for coal. [from Dutch]

wagoner noun (plural wagoners)
the driver of a horse-drawn wagon.

wagtail noun (plural wagtails)
a small bird with a long tail that it moves up and down.

waif noun (plural waifs)
a homeless and helpless person, especially a child. [from old French]

wail verb (wails, wailing, wailed)
make a long sad cry. **wail** noun
[from Old Norse]

wain noun (plural wains) (old use)
a farm wagon. [from Old English]

wainscoting *noun*
wooden panelling on the wall of a room.
[from old German]

waist *noun* (*plural* waists)
the narrow part in the middle of your body.
[probably from Old English]

USAGE: Do not confuse with *waste*.

waistcoat *noun* (*plural* waistcoats)
a short close-fitting jacket without sleeves,
worn over a shirt and under a jacket.

waistline *noun* (*plural* waistlines)
the amount you measure around your
waist, which indicates how fat or thin you
are.

wait *verb* (waits, waiting, waited)
1 stay somewhere or postpone an action
until something happens; pause. 2 be
postponed, *This question must wait until
our next meeting.* 3 wait on people.
wait on 1 hand food and drink to people at
a meal. 2 be an attendant to someone.
wait *noun*
an act or time of waiting, *We had a long
wait for the train.*
[from old French; related to *wake*[1]]

waiter *noun* (*plural* waiters)
a man who serves people with food and
drink in a restaurant.

waiting list *noun* (*plural* waiting lists)
a list of people waiting for something to
become available.

waiting room *noun* (*plural* waiting
rooms)
a room provided for people who are
waiting for something.

waitress *noun* (*plural* waitresses)
a woman who serves people with food and
drink in a restaurant.

waive *verb* (waives, waiving, waived)
not insist on having something, *She waived
her right to travel first class.*
[from Old French]

USAGE: Do not confuse with *wave*.

wake[1] *verb* (wakes, waking, woke, woken)
1 stop sleeping, *Wake up! I woke when I
heard the bell.* 2 stop someone sleeping, *You
have woken the baby.*
wake *noun* (*plural* wakes)
(in Ireland) a party held after a funeral.
[from Old English]

wake[2] *noun* (*plural* wakes)
1 the track left on the water by a moving
ship. 2 currents of air left behind a moving
aircraft.
in the wake of following.
[probably from Old Norse]

wakeful *adjective*
unable to sleep.

waken *verb* (wakens, wakening, wakened)
wake.

walk *verb* (walks, walking, walked)
move along on your feet at an ordinary
speed. **walker** *noun*
walk *noun* (*plural* walks)
1 a journey on foot. 2 the manner of
walking. 3 a path or route for walking.
[from Old English]

walkabout *noun* (*plural* walkabouts)
an informal stroll among a crowd by an
important visitor.

walkie-talkie *noun* (*plural* walkie-talkies)
(*informal*)
a small portable radio transmitter and
receiver.

walking stick *noun* (*plural* walking sticks)
a stick used as a support while walking.

Walkman *noun* (*plural* Walkmans) (*trade
mark*)
a personal stereo.

walk of life *noun* (*plural* walks of life)
a person's occupation or social position.

walkover *noun* (*plural* walkovers)
an easy victory.

wall *noun* (*plural* walls)
1 a continuous upright structure, usually
made of brick or stone, forming one of the
sides of a building or room or supporting
something or enclosing an area. 2 the
outside part of something, *the stomach
wall.*

wall *verb* (**walls, walling, walled**)
enclose or block something with a wall, *a walled garden*.
[from Old English]

wallaby *noun* (*plural* **wallabies**)
a kind of small kangaroo.
[from an Australian Aboriginal language]

wallet *noun* (*plural* **wallets**)
a small flat folding case for holding banknotes, documents, etc.
[via old French from Germanic]

wallflower *noun* (*plural* **wallflowers**)
a garden plant with fragrant flowers, blooming in spring. [because it is often found growing on old walls]

wallop *verb* (**wallops, walloping, walloped**) (*slang*)
thrash. **wallop** *noun*
[from old French; related to *gallop*]

wallow *verb* (**wallows, wallowing, wallowed**)
1 roll about in water, mud, etc. 2 get great pleasure by being surrounded by something, *wallowing in luxury*.
wallow *noun* [from Old English]

wallpaper *noun* (*plural* **wallpapers**)
paper used to cover the inside walls of rooms.

walnut *noun* (*plural* **walnuts**)
an edible nut with a wrinkled surface.
[from Old English]

walrus *noun* (*plural* **walruses**)
a large Arctic sea animal with two long tusks. [probably from Dutch]

waltz *noun* (*plural* **waltzes**)
a dance with three beats to a bar.
waltz *verb* (**waltzes, waltzing, waltzed**)
dance a waltz.
[from German *walzen* = revolve]

wan (*say* wonn) *adjective*
pale from being ill or tired.
wanly *adverb*, **wanness** *noun*
[from Old English]

wand *noun* (*plural* **wands**)
a thin rod, especially one used by a magician. [from Old Norse]

wander *verb* (**wanders, wandering, wandered**)
1 go about without trying to reach a particular place. 2 leave the right path or direction; stray. **wanderer** *noun*
wander *noun*
a wandering journey. [from Old English]

wanderlust *noun*
a strong desire to travel.

wane *verb* (**wanes, waning, waned**)
1 (of the moon) show a bright area that becomes gradually smaller after being full. (The opposite is *wax*.) 2 become less, smaller, or weaker, *His popularity waned*.
wane *noun*
on the wane becoming less or weaker.
[from Old English]

wangle *verb* (**wangles, wangling, wangled**) (*slang*)
get or arrange something by using trickery, clever planning, etc., *He's managed to wangle himself a trip to Paris*.
wangle *noun* [origin unknown]

want *verb* (**wants, wanting, wanted**)
1 wish to have something. 2 need, *Your hair wants cutting*. 3 be without something; lack.
want *noun* (*plural* **wants**)
1 a wish to have something. 2 lack or need of something. [from Old Norse]

wanted *adjective*
(of a suspected criminal) that the police wish to find or arrest.

wanton (*say* wonn-ton) *adjective*
irresponsible; without a motive, *wanton damage*. [from Old English]

war *noun* (*plural* **wars**)
1 fighting between nations or groups, especially using armed forces. 2 a serious struggle or effort against crime, disease, poverty, etc.
at war taking part in a war.
[via old French from Germanic]

warble *verb* (**warbles, warbling, warbled**)
sing with a trilling sound, as some birds do.
warble *noun*
[via old French from Germanic]

warbler *noun* (*plural* **warblers**)
a kind of small bird.

ward *noun* (*plural* **wards**)
1 a room with beds for patients in a hospital. **2** a child looked after by a guardian. **3** an area electing a councillor to represent it.
ward *verb* (**wards, warding, warded**)
ward off keep something away.
[from Old English]

-ward *suffix*
forms adjectives and adverbs showing direction (e.g. *backward, forward, homeward*). [from Old English]

warden *noun* (*plural* **wardens**)
an official who is in charge of a hostel, college, etc., or who supervises something. [from old French; related to *guardian*]

warder *noun* (*plural* **warders**) (*old use*)
an official in charge of prisoners in a prison. [from old French; related to *guard*]

wardrobe *noun* (*plural* **wardrobes**)
1 a cupboard to hang clothes in. **2** a stock of clothes or costumes. [from old French *warder* = to guard, + *robe*]

-wards *suffix*
forms adverbs showing direction (e.g. *backwards, forwards*).
[from Old English *-weardes* = -ward]

ware *noun* (*plural* **wares**)
manufactured goods of a certain kind, *hardware; silverware*.
wares *plural noun* goods offered for sale. [from Old English]

warehouse *noun* (*plural* **warehouses**)
a large building where goods are stored.

warfare *noun*
fighting a war.

warhead *noun* (*plural* **warheads**)
the head of a missile or torpedo etc., containing explosives.

warlike *adjective*
1 fond of making war. **2** threatening war.

warm *adjective*
1 fairly hot; not cold or cool. **2** friendly or enthusiastic, *a warm welcome*. **warmly** *adverb*, **warmness** *noun*, **warmth** *noun*
warm *verb* (**warms, warming, warmed**)
make or become warm. [from Old English]

warm-blooded *adjective*
having blood that remains warm permanently.

warn *verb* (**warns, warning, warned**)
tell someone about a danger etc. that may affect them, or about what they should do, *I warned you to take your wellingtons*.
warning *noun* [from Old English]

warp (*say* worp) *verb* (**warps, warping, warped**)
1 bend or twist out of shape, e.g. by dampness. **2** distort a person's ideas, judgement, etc., *Jealousy warped his mind*.
warp *noun*
1 a warped condition. **2** the lengthwise threads in weaving, crossed by the weft. [from Old English]

warpath *noun*
on the warpath angry and getting ready for a fight or argument.

warrant *noun* (*plural* **warrants**)
a document that authorizes a person to do something (e.g. to search a place) or to receive something.
warrant *verb* (**warrants, warranting, warranted**)
1 justify, *Nothing can warrant such rudeness*. **2** guarantee.
[from old French; related to *guarantee*]

warranty *noun* (*plural* **warranties**)
a guarantee.
[from old French; related to *guarantee*]

warren *noun* (*plural* **warrens**)
1 a piece of ground where there are many burrows in which rabbits live and breed. **2** a building or place with many winding passages. [from old French]

warring *adjective*
occupied in war.

warrior *noun* (*plural* **warriors**)
a person who fights in battle; a soldier. [from old French]

warship *noun* (*plural* **warships**)
a ship used in war.

wart *noun* (*plural* **warts**)
a small hard lump on the skin, caused by a virus. [from Old English]

wartime *noun*
a time of war.

wary (*say* **wair**-ee) *adjective*
cautious; looking carefully for possible
danger or difficulty. **warily** *adverb*, **wariness**
noun [from Old English]

wash *verb* (**washes**, **washing**, **washed**)
1 clean something with water or other
liquid. 2 be washable, *Cotton washes easily*.
3 flow against or over something, *Waves
washed over the deck*. 4 carry along by a
moving liquid, *A wave washed him
overboard*. 5 (*informal*) be accepted or
believed, *That excuse won't wash*.
wash out (*informal*) if an event is washed
out, it is abandoned because of rain.
wash up wash dishes and cutlery etc. after
use. **washing-up** *noun*
wash *noun* (*plural* **washes**)
1 the action of washing. 2 clothes etc. being
washed. 3 the disturbed water behind a
moving ship. 4 a thin coating of colour.
[from Old English]

washable *adjective*
able to be washed without becoming
damaged.

washbasin *noun* (*plural* **washbasins**)
a small sink for washing your hands etc.

washer *noun* (*plural* **washers**)
1 a small ring of rubber or metal etc.
placed between two surfaces (e.g. under a
bolt or screw) to fit them tightly together.
2 a washing machine.

washing *noun*
clothes etc. being washed.

washing machine *noun* (*plural* **washing
machines**)
a machine for washing clothes etc.

washing soda *noun*
sodium carbonate.

wash-out *noun* (*plural* **wash-outs**) (*slang*)
a complete failure.

wasn't (*mainly spoken*)
was not.

wasp *noun* (*plural* **wasps**)
a stinging insect with black and yellow
stripes round its body. [from Old English]

wassail (*say* **woss**-al) *noun* (*old use*)
spiced ale drunk especially at Christmas.
wassailing *noun*
[from Norse *ves heill* = be in good health]

wastage *noun*
loss of something by waste.

waste *verb* (**wastes**, **wasting**, **wasted**)
1 use something in an extravagant way or
without getting enough results. 2 fail to
use something, *You wasted an opportunity*.
3 make or become gradually weaker or
useless.
waste *adjective*
1 left over or thrown away because it is not
wanted. 2 not used; not usable, *waste land*.
lay waste destroy the crops and buildings
etc. of an area.
waste *noun* (*plural* **wastes**)
1 wasting a thing, not using it well, *a waste
of time*. 2 things that are not wanted or not
used. 3 an area of waste land, *the wastes of
the Sahara Desert*.
wasteful *adjective*, **wastefully** *noun*,
wastefulness *noun*
[from Latin *vastus* = empty]

USAGE: Do not confuse with *waist*.

wastrel (*say* **way**-strel) *noun* (*plural*
wastrels)
a person who wastes his or her life and
does nothing useful. [from *waste*]

watch *verb* (**watches**, **watching**, **watched**)
1 look at a person or thing for some time.
2 be on guard or ready for something to
happen, *Watch for the traffic lights to turn
green*. 3 take care of something.
watcher *noun*
watch *noun* (*plural* **watches**)
1 the action of watching. 2 a turn of being
on duty in a ship. 3 a device like a small
clock, usually worn on the wrist.
[from Old English]

watchdog *noun* (*plural* **watchdogs**)
1 a dog kept to guard property. 2 a person
or committee whose job is to make sure
that companies do not do anything harmful
or illegal.

watchful *adjective*
watching closely; alert.
watchfully *adverb*, **watchfulness** *noun*

watchman *noun* (*plural* watchmen)
a person employed to look after an empty
building etc., especially at night.

watchword *noun* (*plural* watchwords)
a word or phrase that sums up a group's
policy; a slogan, *Our watchword is 'safety
first'.*

water *noun* (*plural* waters)
1 a colourless odourless tasteless liquid
that is a compound of hydrogen and
oxygen. 2 a lake or sea etc. 3 the tide, *at
high water.*
pass water urinate.

water *verb* (waters, watering, watered)
1 sprinkle or supply something with water.
2 produce tears or saliva, *It makes my
mouth water.*
water down dilute.
[from Old English]

water closet *noun* (*plural* water closets)
a toilet with a pan that is flushed by water.

watercolour *noun* (*plural* watercolours)
1 paint made with pigment and water (not
oil). 2 a painting done with this kind of
paint.

watercress *noun*
a kind of cress that grows in water.

waterfall *noun* (*plural* waterfalls)
a stream flowing over the edge of a cliff or
large rock.

watering can *noun* (*plural* watering cans)
a container with a long spout, for watering
plants.

water lily *noun* (*plural* water lilies)
a plant that grows in water, with broad
floating leaves and large flowers.

waterlogged *adjective*
completely soaked or swamped in water.
[from *water* + *log*¹ (because water was said
to 'lie like a log' in the hold of a
waterlogged ship]

watermark *noun* (*plural* watermarks)
1 a mark showing how high a river or tide
rises or how low it falls. 2 a design that can
be seen in some kinds of paper when they
are held up to the light.

waterproof *adjective*
that keeps out water, *a waterproof jacket.*
waterproof *verb*

watershed *noun* (*plural* watersheds)
1 a turning point in the course of events.
2 a line of high land from which streams
flow down on each side. [from *water* + Old
English *scead* = division, a parting]

water-skiing *noun*
the sport of skimming over the surface of
water on a pair of flat boards (**water-skis**)
while being towed by a motor boat.

waterspout *noun* (*plural* waterspouts)
a column of water formed when a
whirlwind draws up a whirling mass of
water from the sea.

water-table *noun* (*plural* water-tables)
the level below which the ground is
saturated with water.

watertight *adjective*
1 made or fastened so that water cannot get
in or out. 2 that cannot be changed or set
aside or proved to be untrue, *a watertight
excuse.*

waterway *noun* (*plural* waterways)
a river or canal that ships can travel on.

waterworks *noun*
a place with pumping machinery etc. for
supplying water to a district.

watery *adjective*
1 like water. 2 full of water. 3 containing
too much water.

watt *noun* (*plural* watts)
a unit of electric power.
[named after James Watt, a Scottish
engineer, who studied energy]

wattage *noun* (*plural* wattages)
electric power measured in watts.

wattle¹ *noun* (*plural* wattles)
1 sticks and twigs woven together to make
fences, walls, etc. 2 an Australian tree with
golden flowers. [from Old English]

wattle² *noun* (*plural* wattles)
a red fold of skin hanging from the throat
of turkeys and some other birds.
[origin unknown]

wave *noun* (*plural* **waves**)
1 a ridge moving along the surface of the sea etc. or breaking on the shore. 2 a wave-like curve, e.g. in hair. 3 the wave-like movement by which heat, light, sound, or electricity etc. travels. 4 the action of waving.
wave *verb* (**waves, waving, waved**)
1 move loosely to and fro or up and down. 2 move your hand to and fro as a signal or greeting etc. 3 make a thing wavy. 4 be wavy. [from Old English]

USAGE: Do not confuse with *waive*.

waveband *noun* (*plural* **wavebands**)
the wavelengths between certain limits.

wavelength *noun* (*plural* **wavelengths**)
the size of a sound wave or electromagnetic wave.

wavelet *noun* (*plural* **wavelets**)
a small wave.

waver *verb* (**wavers, wavering, wavered**)
1 be unsteady; move unsteadily. 2 hesitate; be uncertain. [from Old Norse]

wavy *adjective*
full of waves or curves.
wavily *adverb*, **waviness** *noun*

wax¹ *noun* (*plural* **waxes**)
1 a soft substance that melts easily, used to make candles, crayons, and polish. 2 beeswax. **waxy** *adjective*
wax *verb* (**waxes, waxing, waxed**)
coat or polish something with wax. [from Old English *waex*]

wax² *verb* (**waxes, waxing, waxed**)
1 (of the moon) show a bright area that becomes gradually larger. (The opposite is *wane*.) 2 become stronger or more important. [from Old English *weaxan*]

waxen *adjective*
1 made of wax. 2 like wax.

waxwork *noun* (*plural* **waxworks**)
a model of a person etc. made in wax.

way *noun* (*plural* **ways**)
1 a line of communication between places, e.g. a path or road. 2 a route or direction. 3 a distance to be travelled. 4 how something is done; a method or style.

5 a respect, *It's a good idea in some ways.* 6 a condition or state, *Things were in a bad way.*
get or **have your own way** make people let you do what you want.
give way 1 collapse. 2 let somebody else move first. 3 yield.
in the way forming an obstacle or hindrance.
no way (*informal*) that is impossible!
under way see *under*.
way *adverb* (*informal*)
far, *That is way beyond what we can afford.* [from Old English]

wayfarer *noun* (*plural* **wayfarers**)
a traveller, especially someone who is walking.

waylay *verb* (**waylays, waylaying, waylaid**)
lie in wait for a person or people, especially in order to talk to them or rob them.

-ways *suffix*
forms adverbs showing direction or manner (e.g. *sideways*). [from *way*]

wayside *noun*
fall by the wayside fail to continue doing something.

wayward *adjective*
disobedient; wilfully doing what you want. [from *away* + *-ward*]

WC *abbreviation*
water closet.

we *pronoun*
a word used by a person to refer to himself or herself and another or others. [from Old English]

weak *adjective*
not strong; easy to break, bend, defeat, etc. **weakness** *noun* [from Old English]

weaken *verb* (**weakens, weakening, weakened**)
make or become weaker.

weakling *noun* (*plural* **weaklings**)
a weak person or animal.

weakly *adverb*
in a weak manner.

weakly *adjective*
sickly; not strong.

weal *noun* (*plural* **weals**)
a ridge raised on the flesh by a cane or whip etc. [from Old English *walu* = ridge]

wealth *noun*
1 a lot of money or property; riches. 2 a large quantity, *The book has a wealth of illustrations.* [from Old English]

wealthy *adjective* (**wealthier, wealthiest**)
having wealth; rich. **wealthiness** *noun*

wean *verb* (**weans, weaning, weaned**)
make a baby take food other than its mother's milk. [from Old English]

weapon *noun* (*plural* **weapons**)
something used to harm or kill people in a battle or fight. **weaponry** *noun*
[from Old English]

wear *verb* (**wears, wearing, wore, worn**)
1 have clothes, jewellery, etc. on your body. 2 damage something by rubbing or using it often; become damaged in this way, *The carpet has worn thin.* 3 last while in use, *It has worn well.*
wearable *adjective*, **wearer** *noun*
wear off 1 be removed by wear or use. 2 become less intense.
wear on pass gradually, *The night wore on.*
wear out 1 use or be used until it becomes weak or useless. 2 exhaust.
[from Old English]

wearisome *adjective*
causing weariness.

weary *adjective* (**wearier, weariest**)
1 tired. 2 tiring, *It's weary work.*
wearily *adverb*, **weariness** *noun*
weary *verb* (**wearies, wearying, wearied**)
tire. [from Old English]

weasel *noun* (*plural* **weasels**)
a small fierce animal with a slender body and reddish-brown fur. [from Old English]

weather *noun*
the rain, snow, wind, sunshine etc. at a particular time or place.
under the weather feeling ill or depressed.
weather *verb* (**weathers, weathering, weathered**)
1 expose something to the effects of the weather. 2 come through something successfully, *The ship weathered the storm.*
[from Old English]

weathercock or **weathervane** *noun*
(*plural* **weathercocks, weathervanes**)
a pointer, often shaped like a cockerel, that turns in the wind and shows from which direction it is blowing.

weave *verb* (**weaves, weaving, wove, woven**)
1 make material or baskets etc. by crossing threads or strips under and over each other. 2 put a story together, *She wove a thrilling tale.* 3 (*past tense & past participle* **weaved**) twist and turn, *He weaved through the traffic.* **weaver** *noun*
weave *noun* (*plural* **weaves**)
a style of weaving, *a loose weave.*
[from Old English]

web *noun* (*plural* **webs**)
1 a cobweb. 2 a network. [from Old English *webb* = a piece of woven cloth]

webbed or **web-footed** *adjective*
having toes joined by pieces of skin, *Ducks have webbed feet; they are web-footed.*
[from *web*]

wed *verb* (**weds, wedding, wedded**)
1 marry. 2 unite two different things.
[from Old English]

wedding *noun* (*plural* **weddings**)
the ceremony when a man and woman get married.

wedge *noun* (*plural* **wedges**)
1 a piece of wood or metal etc. that is thick at one end and thin at the other. It is pushed between things to force them apart or prevent something from moving. 2 a wedge-shaped thing.
wedge *verb* (**wedges, wedging, wedged**)
1 keep something in place with a wedge. 2 pack tightly together, *Ten of us were wedged in the lift.*
[from Old English]

wedlock *noun*
being married; matrimony. [from Old English *wedlac* = marriage vow]

wee *adjective* (*Scottish*)
little. [from Old English]

weed noun (plural **weeds**)
a wild plant that grows where it is not wanted.
weed verb (**weeds, weeding, weeded**)
remove weeds from the ground.
[from Old English *weod*]

weedy adjective (**weedier, weediest**)
1 full of weeds. 2 thin and weak.

week noun (plural **weeks**)
a period of seven days, especially from Sunday to the following Saturday.
[from Old English]

weekday noun (plural **weekdays**)
a day other than Saturday or Sunday.

weekend noun (plural **weekends**)
Saturday and Sunday.

weekly adjective & adverb
happening or done once a week.

weeny adjective (informal)
tiny. [from *wee* + *tiny*]

weep verb (**weeps, weeping, wept**)
1 shed tears; cry. 2 ooze moisture in drops.
weep noun, **weepy** adjective
[from Old English]

weeping adjective
(of a tree) having drooping branches, *a weeping willow*.

weevil noun (plural **weevils**)
a kind of small beetle. [from Old English]

weft noun
the threads on a loom that are woven across the warp. [from Old English]

weigh verb (**weighs, weighing, weighed**)
1 measure the weight of something. 2 have a certain weight, *What do you weigh?* 3 be important; have influence, *Her evidence weighed with the jury*.
weigh anchor raise the anchor and start a voyage.
weigh down 1 keep something down by its weight. 2 depress or trouble somebody.
weigh up estimate or assess something.
[from Old English]

weight noun (plural **weights**)
1 how heavy something is; an object's mass expressed as a number according to a scale of units. (Compare *mass* 3.) 2 a piece of metal of known weight, especially one used on scales to weigh things. 3 a heavy object. 4 importance or influence.
weighty adjective, **weightless** adjective

weight verb (**weights, weighting, weighted**)
put a weight on something.
[from Old English]

weightlifting noun
the sport of lifting a heavy weight.
weightlifter noun

weir (say weer) noun (plural **weirs**)
a small dam across a river or canal to control the flow of water.
[from Old English]

weird adjective
very strange; uncanny. **weirdly** adverb, **weirdness** noun [from Old English]

USAGE: When spelling this word, note that the 'e' comes before the 'i', not the other way round.

welcome noun (plural **welcomes**)
a greeting or reception, especially a kindly one.
welcome adjective
1 that you are glad to receive or see, *a welcome gift*. 2 gladly allowed, *You are welcome to come*.
welcome verb (**welcomes, welcoming, welcomed**)
show that you are pleased when a person or thing arrives. [from *well²* + *come*]

weld verb (**welds, welding, welded**)
1 join pieces of metal or plastic by heating and pressing or hammering them together. 2 unite people or things into a whole.
[from Old English]

welfare noun
people's health, happiness, and comfort.
[from *well²* + *fare*]

welfare state noun
a system in which a country's government provides money to pay for health care, social services, benefits, etc.

well¹ noun (plural **wells**)
1 a deep hole dug to bring up water or oil from underground. 2 a deep space, e.g. containing a staircase.

well *verb* (**wells, welling, welled**)
rise or flow up, *Tears welled up in our eyes.*
[from Old English *wella* = spring of water]

well² *adverb* (**better, best**)
1 in a good or suitable way, *She swims well.*
2 thoroughly, *Polish it well.* 3 probably or
reasonably, *This may well be our last
chance.*
well off 1 fairly rich. 2 in a good situation.
well *adjective*
1 in good health, *He is not well.*
2 satisfactory, *All is well.*
[from Old English *wel* = prosperously]

well-being *noun*
good health, happiness, and comfort.

wellingtons *plural noun*
rubber or plastic waterproof boots.
wellies *plural noun* (*informal*)
[named after the first Duke of Wellington,
who wore long leather boots]

well-known *adjective*
1 known to many people. 2 known
thoroughly.

well-mannered *adjective*
having good manners.

well-meaning *adjective*
having good intentions.

wellnigh *adverb*
almost.

well-read *adjective*
having read a lot of good books.

well-to-do *adjective*
fairly rich.

welsh *verb* (**welshes, welshing, welshed**)
cheat someone by avoiding paying what
you owe them or by breaking an
agreement. **welsher** *noun* [origin unknown]

welt *noun* (*plural* **welts**)
1 a strip or border. 2 a weal
[origin unknown]

welter *verb* (**welters, weltering, weltered**)
(of a ship) be tossed to and fro by waves.
welter *noun*
a confused mixture; a jumble, *a welter of
information.*
[from old German or old Dutch]

wen *noun* (*plural* **wens**)
a large but harmless tumour on the head or
neck. [from Old English]

wench *noun* (*plural* **wenches**) (*old use*)
a girl or young woman. [from Old English]

wend *verb* (**wends, wending, wended**)
wend your way go.
[from Old English]

weren't (*mainly spoken*)
were not.

werewolf *noun* (*plural* **werewolves**)
(in legends) a person who sometimes
changes into a wolf.
[from Old English *wer* = man, + *wolf*]

west *noun*
1 the direction where the sun sets, opposite
east. 2 the western part of a country,
city, etc.
west *adjective*
1 situated in the west, *the west coast.*
2 coming from the west, *a west wind.*
west *adverb*
towards the west, *We sailed west.*
[from Old English]

westerly *adjective*
to or from the west.

western *adjective*
of or in the west.
western *noun* (*plural* **westerns**)
a film or story about cowboys or American
Indians in western North America during
the 19th and early 20th centuries.

westward *adjective & adverb*
towards the west. **westwards** *adverb*

wet *adjective* (**wetter, wettest**)
1 soaked or covered in water or other
liquid. 2 not yet dry, *wet paint.* 3 rainy, *wet
weather.* **wetly** *adverb*, **wetness** *noun*
wet *verb* (**wets, wetting, wet** or **wetted**)
make a thing wet. [from Old English]

whack *verb* (**whacks, whacking, whacked**)
(*informal*)
hit someone or something hard. **whack**
noun [imitating the sound]

whale *noun* (*plural* **whales**)
a very large sea animal.

a whale of a (*informal*) very good or great, *We had a whale of a time.* [from Old English]

whaler *noun* (*plural* whalers)
a person or ship that hunts whales.

whaling *noun*
hunting whales.

wharf (*say* worf) *noun* (*plural* wharves or wharfs)
a quay where ships are loaded and unloaded. [from Old English]

what *adjective*
used to ask the amount or kind of something (*What kind of bike have you got?*) or to say how strange or great a person or thing is (*What a fool you are!*).
what *pronoun*
1 what thing or things, *What did you say?* **2** the thing that, *This is what you must do.*
what's what (*informal*) which things are important or useful.
[from Old English]

whatever *pronoun*
1 anything or everything, *Do whatever you like.* **2** no matter what, *Keep calm, whatever happens.*
whatever *adjective*
of any kind or amount, *Take whatever books you need. There is no doubt whatever.*

wheat *noun*
a cereal plant from which flour is made.
wheaten *adjective* [from Old English]

wheedle *verb* (wheedles, wheedling, wheedled)
coax. [probably from German]

wheel *noun* (*plural* wheels)
1 a round device that turns on a shaft that passes through its centre. **2** a horizontal revolving disc on which clay is made into a pot.
wheel *verb* (wheels, wheeling, wheeled)
1 push a bicycle or trolley etc. along on its wheels. **2** move in a curve or circle; change direction and face another way, *He wheeled round in astonishment.* [from Old English]

wheelbarrow *noun* (*plural* wheelbarrows)
a small cart with one wheel at the front and legs at the back, pushed by handles.

wheelchair *noun* (*plural* wheelchairs)
a chair on wheels for a person who cannot walk.

wheel clamp *noun* (*plural* wheel clamps)
a device that can be locked around a vehicle's wheel to stop it from moving, used especially on cars that have been parked illegally.

wheelie bin *noun* (*plural* wheelie bins)
a large dustbin on wheels.

wheeze *verb* (wheezes, wheezing, wheezed)
make a hoarse whistling sound as you breathe. **wheeze** *noun*, **wheezy** *adjective* [probably from Old Norse]

whelk *noun* (*plural* whelks)
a shellfish that looks like a snail. [from Old English]

whelp *noun* (*plural* whelps)
a young dog; a pup. [from Old English]

when *adverb*
at what time; at which time, *When can you come to tea?*
when *conjunction*
1 at the time that, *The bird flew away when I moved.* **2** although; considering that, *Why do you smoke when you know it's dangerous?* [from Old English]

whence *adverb* & *conjunction*
from where; from which.
[from Old English]

whenever *conjunction*
at whatever time; every time, *Whenever I see it, I smile.*

where *adverb* & *conjunction*
in or to what place or that place, *Where did you put it? Leave it where it is.*
where *pronoun*
what place, *Where does she come from?* [from Old English]

whereabouts *adverb*
in or near what place, *Whereabouts are you going?*
whereabouts *plural noun*
the place where something is, *Do you know the whereabouts of my radio?*

whereas *conjunction*
but in contrast, *Some people enjoy sport, whereas others hate it.*

whereby *adverb*
by which.

wherefore *adverb* (*old use*)
why. [from *where* + *for* (preposition)]

whereupon *conjunction*
after which; and then.

wherever *adverb*
in or to whatever place.

whet *verb* (whets, whetting, whetted)
whet your appetite stimulate it.
[from Old English *hwettan* = sharpen]

USAGE: Do not confuse with *wet.*

whether *conjunction*
as one possibility; if, *I don't know whether to believe her or not.* [from Old English]

whetstone *noun* (*plural* whetstones)
a shaped stone for sharpening tools.
[from *whet* = sharpen, + *stone*]

whey (*say as* way) *noun*
the watery liquid left when milk forms curds. [from Old English]

which *adjective*
what particular, *Which way did he go?*
which *pronoun*
1 what person or thing, *Which is your desk?*
2 the person or thing referred to, *The film, which is a western, will be shown on Saturday.* [from Old English]

whichever *pronoun & adjective*
no matter which; any which, *Take whichever you like.*

whiff *noun* (*plural* whiffs)
a puff or slight smell of smoke, gas, etc.
[imitating the sound of a puff]

Whig *noun* (*plural* Whigs)
a member of a political party in the 17th–19th centuries, opposed to the Tories.
[from *whiggamer*, a Scottish Presbyterian rebel in 1648]

while *conjunction*
1 during the time that; as long as, *Whistle while you work.* 2 although; but, *She is dark, while her sister is fair.*
while *noun*
a period of time, *a long while.*
while *verb* (whiles, whiling, whiled)
while away pass time, *We whiled away the afternoon on the river.* [from Old English]

whilst *conjunction*
while.

whim *noun* (*plural* whims)
a sudden wish to do or have something.
[origin unknown]

whimper *verb* (whimpers, whimpering, whimpered)
cry or whine softly. **whimper** *noun*
[imitating the sound]

whimsical *adjective*
impulsive and playful. **whimsically** *adverb*, **whimsicality** *noun* [from *whim*]

whine *verb* (whines, whining, whined)
1 make a long high miserable cry or a shrill sound. 2 complain in a petty or feeble way. **whine** *noun* [from Old English]

whinny *verb* (whinnies, whinnying, whinnied)
neigh gently or happily. **whinny** *noun*
[imitating the sound]

whip *noun* (*plural* whips)
1 a cord or strip of leather fixed to a handle and used for hitting people or animals.
2 an official of a political party in Parliament. 3 a pudding made of whipped cream and fruit or flavouring.
whip *verb* (whips, whipping, whipped)
1 hit a person or animal with a whip.
2 beat cream until it becomes thick.
3 move or take something suddenly, *He whipped out a gun.* 4 (*informal*) steal something.
whip up stir up people's feelings etc., *She whipped up support for her plans.*
[from old German or old Dutch]

whippet *noun* (*plural* whippets)
a small dog rather like a greyhound, used for racing. [from *whip*]

whirl *verb* (whirls, whirling, whirled)
turn or spin very quickly. **whirl** *noun*
[from Old Norse]

whirlpool *noun* (*plural* whirlpools)
a whirling current of water.

whirlwind *noun* (*plural* whirlwinds)
a strong wind that whirls round a central point.

whirr *verb* (whirrs, whirring, whirred)
make a continuous buzzing sound. **whirr** *noun* [imitating the sound]

whisk *verb* (whisks, whisking, whisked)
1 move or brush something away quickly and lightly. 2 beat eggs etc. until they are frothy.
whisk *noun* (*plural* whisks)
1 a kitchen tool used for whisking things. 2 a whisking movement. [from Old Norse]

whisker *noun* (*plural* whiskers)
1 a hair of those growing on a man's face, forming a beard or moustache if not shaved off. 2 a long bristle growing near the mouth of a cat etc. **whiskery** *adjective* [from *whisk*]

whisky *noun* (*plural* whiskies)
a strong alcoholic drink. [from Scottish Gaelic *uisge beatha* = water of life]

whisper *verb* (whispers, whispering, whispered)
1 speak very softly. 2 talk secretly. **whisper** *noun* [from Old English]

whist *noun*
a card game usually for four people. [origin unknown]

whistle *verb* (whistles, whistling, whistled)
make a shrill or musical sound, especially by blowing through your lips.
whistler *noun*
whistle *noun* (*plural* whistles)
1 a whistling sound. 2 a device that makes a shrill sound when air or steam is blown through it. [from Old English]

Whit *adjective*
to do with Whitsun.

whit *noun*
the least possible amount, *not a whit better*. [from Old English]

White *noun* (*plural* Whites)
a person with a light-coloured skin.
White *adjective*

white *noun* (*plural* whites)
1 the very lightest colour, like snow or salt. 2 the transparent substance (*albumen*) round the yolk of an egg, which turns white when it is cooked.
white *adjective*
1 of the colour white. 2 very pale from the effects of illness or fear etc. 3 (of coffee) with milk.
whiteness *noun*
[from Old English]

whitebait *noun* (*plural* whitebait)
a small silvery-white fish.
[from *white* + *bait* (because it was used as bait to catch larger fish)]

white elephant *noun* (*plural* white elephants)
a useless possession.

white-hot *adjective*
extremely hot; so hot that heated metal looks white.

white lie *noun* (*plural* white lies)
a harmless or trivial lie that you tell in order to avoid hurting someone's feelings.

white meat *noun*
poultry, veal, rabbit, and pork.

whiten *verb* (whitens, whitening, whitened)
make or become whiter.

whitewash *noun*
1 a white liquid containing lime or powdered chalk, used for painting walls and ceilings etc. 2 concealing mistakes or other unpleasant facts so that someone will not be punished.
whitewash *verb*

whither *adverb* & *conjunction* (*old use*)
to what place. [from Old English]

USAGE: Do not confuse with *wither*.

whiting *noun* (*plural* whiting)
a small edible sea fish with white flesh. [from Dutch *wijt* = white]

Whitsun *noun*
Whit Sunday and the days close to it. [from *Whit Sunday*]

Whit Sunday
the seventh Sunday after Easter.
[from Old English *hwit* = white, because people used to be baptized on that day and wore white clothes]

whittle *verb* (whittles, whittling, whittled)
1 shape wood by trimming thin slices off the surface. **2** reduce something by removing various things from it, *whittle down the cost.* [from Old English]

whiz *verb* (whizzes, whizzing, whizzed)
1 move very quickly. **2** sound like something rushing through the air. [imitating the sound]

who *pronoun*
which person or people; the particular person or people, *This is the boy who stole the apples.* [from Old English]

whoa *interjection*
a command to a horse to stop or stand still. [origin unknown]

whoever *pronoun*
1 any or every person who. **2** no matter who.

whole *adjective*
1 complete. **2** not injured or broken.
whole *noun*
1 the full amount. **2** a complete thing.
on the whole considering everything; mainly.
[from Old English]

wholefood *noun* (*plural* wholefoods)
food that has been processed as little as possible.

wholemeal *adjective*
made from the whole grain of wheat etc. [from *whole* + *meal²*]

whole number *noun* (*plural* whole numbers)
a number without fractions.

wholesale *noun*
selling goods in large quantities to be resold by others. (Compare *retail*.)
wholesaler *noun*
wholesale *adjective & adverb*
1 on a large scale; including everybody or everything, *wholesale destruction.* **2** in the wholesale trade.

wholesome *adjective*
good for health; healthy, *wholesome food.*
wholesomeness *noun* [from an old sense of *whole* = healthy, + *-some*]

wholly *adverb*
completely or entirely.

whom *pronoun*
the form of *who* used when it is the object of a verb or comes after a preposition, as in *the boy whom I saw* or *to whom we spoke.*

whoop (*say* woop) *noun* (*plural* whoops)
a loud cry of excitement. **whoop** *verb*
[imitating the sound]

whoopee *interjection*
a cry of joy.

whooping cough (*say* hoop-ing) *noun*
an infectious disease that causes spasms of coughing and gasping for breath. [because of the sound the person makes gasping for breath]

whopper *noun* (*plural* whoppers) (*slang*)
something very large. [from Middle English *whop* = to strike or beat]

whopping *adjective* (*slang*)
very large or remarkable, *a whopping lie.* [from *whopper*]

whorl *noun* (*plural* whorls)
1 a coil or curved shape. **2** a ring of leaves or petals. [a different spelling of *whirl*]

who's (*mainly spoken*)
who is; who has.

USAGE: Do not confuse with *whose*.

whose *pronoun*
belonging to what person or persons; of whom; of which, *Whose house is that?* [from Old English]

USAGE: Do not confuse with *who's*.

why *adverb*
for what reason or purpose; the particular reason on account of which, *This is why I came.* [from Old English]

wick *noun* (*plural* wicks)
1 the string that goes through the middle of a candle and is lit. **2** the strip of material

that you light in a lamp or heater etc. that uses oil. [from Old English]

wicked *adjective*
1 morally bad or cruel. 2 very bad; severe, *a wicked blow*. 3 mischievous, *a wicked smile*. **wickedly** *adverb*, **wickedness** *noun* [from Old English *wicca* = witch]

wicker *noun*
thin canes or osiers woven together to make baskets or furniture etc. **wickerwork** *noun* [from a Scandinavian language]

wicket *noun* (*plural* **wickets**)
1 a set of three stumps and two bails used in cricket. 2 the part of a cricket ground between the wickets.
[via old French from Germanic]

wicket-gate *noun* (*plural* **wicket-gates**)
a small gate used to save opening a much larger one.
[from an old sense of *wicket* = small gate]

wicketkeeper *noun* (*plural* **wicketkeepers**)
the fielder in cricket who stands behind the batsman's wicket.

wide *adjective*
1 measuring a lot from side to side; not narrow. 2 measuring from side to side, *The cloth is one metre wide*. 3 covering a great range, *a wide knowledge of birds*. 4 fully open, *staring with wide eyes*. 5 far from the target, *The shot was wide of the mark*. **widely** *adverb*, **wideness** *noun*
wide *adverb*
1 widely. 2 completely or fully, *wide awake*. 3 far from the target, *The shot went wide*. [from Old English]

widen *verb* (**widens, widening, widened**)
make or become wider.

widespread *adjective*
existing in many places or over a wide area, *a widespread belief*.

widow *noun* (*plural* **widows**)
a woman whose husband has died.
widowed *adjective* [from Old English]

widower *noun* (*plural* **widowers**)
a man whose wife has died. [from *widow*]

width *noun* (*plural* **widths**)
how wide something is; wideness.
[from *wide*]

wield *verb* (**wields, wielding, wielded**)
hold something and use it, *wielding a sword*. [from Old English]

wife *noun* (*plural* **wives**)
the woman to whom a man is married.
[from Old English *wif* = woman]

wig *noun* (*plural* **wigs**)
a covering made of real or artificial hair, worn on the head. [short for *periwig*, from old French *perruque*]

wigeon *noun* (*plural* **wigeon**)
a kind of wild duck. [origin unknown]

wiggle *verb* (**wiggles, wiggling, wiggled**)
move from side to side; wriggle. **wiggle** *noun* [from old German or old Dutch]

wigwam *noun* (*plural* **wigwams**)
a tent formerly used by Native Americans, made by fastening skins or mats over poles. [a Native American word]

wild *adjective*
1 living or growing in its natural state, not looked after by people. 2 not cultivated, *a wild landscape*. 3 not civilized, *the Wild West*. 4 not controlled; very violent or excited. 5 very foolish or unreasonable, *these wild ideas*. **wildly** *adverb*, **wildness** *noun* [from Old English]

wildebeest *noun* (*plural* **wildebeest**)
a gnu. [Afrikaans, = wild beast]

wilderness *noun* (*plural* **wildernesses**)
a wild uncultivated area; a desert. [from Old English *wild deor* = wild deer, + *-ness*]

wildlife *noun*
wild animals.

wile *noun* (*plural* **wiles**)
a piece of trickery. [origin unknown]

wilful *adjective*
1 obstinately determined to do what you want, *a wilful child*. 2 deliberate, *wilful murder*. **wilfully** *adverb*, **wilfulness** *noun* [from *will²* + *-ful*]

will¹ *auxiliary verb*
used to express the future tense, questions, or promises. [from Old English *wyllan*]

USAGE: See the entry for *shall*.

will² *noun* (*plural* **wills**)
1 the mental power to decide and control what you do. **2** a desire; a chosen decision, *I went to the party against my will.*
3 determination to do something, *They set to work with a will.* **4** a written statement of how a person's possessions are to be disposed of after his or her death.
at will whenever you like, *You can come and go at will.*
will *verb* (**wills, willing, willed**)
use your will-power; influence something by doing this, *I was willing you to win!* [from Old English *willa*]

willing *adjective*
ready and happy to do what is wanted.
willingly *adverb*, **willingness** *noun*
[from *will²*]

will-o'-the-wisp *noun* (*plural* **will-o'-the-wisps**)
1 a flickering spot of light seen on marshy ground. **2** an elusive person or hope. [from *William* + *of* + *the* + an old sense of *wisp* = small bundle of straw burned as a torch]

willow *noun* (*plural* **willows**)
a tree or shrub with flexible branches, usually growing near water.
[from Old English]

will-power *noun*
strength of mind to control what you do.

willy-nilly *adverb*
whether you want to or not.
[from *will I, nill I* (= will I, will I not)]

wilt *verb* (**wilts, wilting, wilted**)
lose freshness or strength; droop.
[originally dialect; probably from old Dutch]

wily (*say* wy-lee) *adjective*
cunning or crafty. **wiliness** *noun* [from *wile*]

wimp *noun* (*plural* **wimps**)
(*informal*) a weak or timid person.
[perhaps from *whimper*]

wimple *noun* (*plural* **wimples**)
a piece of cloth folded round the head and neck, worn by women in the Middle Ages.
[from Old English]

win *verb* (**wins, winning, won**)
1 defeat your opponents in a battle, game, or contest. **2** get or achieve something by a victory or by using effort or skill etc., *She won the prize.*
win *noun* (*plural* **wins**)
a victory. [from Old English]

wince *verb* (**winces, wincing, winced**)
make a slight movement because of pain or embarrassment etc. [from old French]

winch *noun* (*plural* **winches**)
a device for lifting or pulling things, using a rope or cable etc. that winds on to a revolving drum or wheel.
winch *verb* (**winches, winching, winched**)
lift or pull something with a winch.
[from Old English]

wind¹ (rhymes with *tinned*) *noun* (*plural* **winds**)
1 a current of air. **2** gas in the stomach or intestines that makes you feel uncomfortable. **3** breath used for a purpose, e.g. for running or speaking. **4** the wind instruments of an orchestra.
get or **have the wind up** (*slang*) feel frightened.
wind *verb* (**winds, winding, winded**)
put a person out of breath, *The climb had winded us.* [from Old English *wind*]

wind² (rhymes with *find*) *verb* (**winds, winding, wound**)
1 go or turn something in twists, curves, or circles. **2** wind up a watch or clock etc.
winder *noun*
wind up 1 make a clock or watch work by tightening its spring. **2** close a business.
3 (*informal*) end up in a place or condition, *He wound up in jail.*
[from Old English *windan*]

windbag *noun* (*plural* **windbags**)
(*informal*)
a person who talks too much.

windfall *noun* (*plural* **windfalls**)
1 a piece of unexpected good luck, especially a sum of money. **2** a fruit blown off a tree by the wind.

wind instrument *noun* (*plural* **wind instruments**)
a musical instrument played by blowing, e.g. a trumpet.

windlass *noun* (*plural* **windlasses**)
a machine for pulling or lifting things (e.g. a bucket from a well), with a rope or cable that is wound round an axle by turning a handle. [via old French from Old Norse *vindass* = winding-pole]

windmill *noun* (*plural* **windmills**)
a mill worked by the wind turning its sails.

window *noun* (*plural* **windows**)
1 an opening in a wall or roof etc. to let in light and often air, usually filled with glass. 2 the glass in this opening. 3 an area on a VDU screen used for a particular purpose. [from Old Norse *vind* = wind, air + *auga* = eye]

window-shopping *noun*
looking at things in shop windows but not buying anything.

windpipe *noun* (*plural* **windpipes**)
the tube by which air passes from the throat to the lungs.

windscreen *noun* (*plural* **windscreens**)
the window at the front of a motor vehicle.

windsurfing *noun*
surfing on a board that has a sail fixed to it.

windward *adjective*
facing the wind, *the windward side of the ship*.

windy *adjective*
with much wind, *It's windy outside*.

wine *noun* (*plural* **wines**)
1 an alcoholic drink made from grapes or other plants. 2 dark red colour. [same origin as *vine*]

wing *noun* (*plural* **wings**)
1 one of the pair of parts of a bird, bat, or insect, that it uses for flying. 2 one of the pair of long flat parts that stick out from the side of an aircraft and support it while it flies. 3 a part that sticks out at one end or side of something; **the wings** the sides of a theatre stage out of sight of the audience. 4 the part of a motor vehicle's body above a

wheel. 5 a player at either end of the forward line in football or hockey etc. 6 a section of a political party, with more extreme opinions than the others.
on the wing flying.
take wing fly away.

wing *verb* (**wings, winging, winged**)
1 fly; travel by means of wings, *The bird winged its way home*. 2 wound a bird in the wing or a person in the arm. [from Old Norse]

winged *adjective*
having wings.

wingless *adjective*
without wings.

wink *verb* (**winks, winking, winked**)
1 close and open your eye quickly, especially as a signal to someone. 2 (of a light) flicker or twinkle.

wink *noun* (*plural* **winks**)
1 the action of winking. 2 a very short period of sleep, *I didn't sleep a wink*. [from Old English]

winkle *noun* (*plural* **winkles**)
a kind of edible shellfish.
winkle *verb* (**winkles, winkling, winkled**)
winkle out extract; prise a thing out, *I managed to winkle out some information*. [short for *periwinkle*[2]]

winner *noun* (*plural* **winners**)
1 a person or animal etc. that wins. 2 something very successful, *Her latest book is a winner*.

winnings *plural noun*
money won.

winnow *verb* (**winnows, winnowing, winnowed**)
toss or fan grain etc. so that the loose dry outer part is blown away. [from Old English]

winsome *adjective*
charming and attractive. [from Old English *wynn* = a pleasure, + *-some*]

winter *noun* (*plural* **winters**)
the coldest season of the year, between autumn and spring.
wintry *adjective*

winter *verb* (winters, wintering, wintered)
spend the winter somewhere.
[from Old English]

wipe *verb* (wipes, wiping, wiped)
dry or clean something by rubbing it.
wiper *noun*
wipe out 1 cancel, *wipe out the debt.*
2 destroy something completely.
[from Old English]

wire *noun* (*plural* wires)
1 a strand or thin flexible rod of metal. **2** a
piece of wire used to carry electric current.
3 a fence etc. made from wire. **4** a telegram.
wire *verb* (wires, wiring, wired)
1 fasten or strengthen something with
wire. **2** fit or connect something with wires
to carry electric current.
[from Old English]

wireless *noun* (*plural* wirelesses) (*old use*)
a radio. [because it does not need wires to
conduct sound]

wiry *adjective*
1 like wire. **2** lean and strong.

wisdom *noun*
1 being wise. **2** wise sayings. [from Old
English *wis* = wise, + *-dom*]

wisdom tooth *noun* (*plural* wisdom
teeth)
a molar tooth that may grow at the back of
the jaw of a person aged about 20 or more.

wise *adjective*
knowing or understanding many things;
judging well. **wisely** *adverb*
[from Old English *wis*]

-wise *suffix*
forms adverbs meaning 'in this manner or
direction' (e.g. *otherwise, clockwise*).
[from Old English *wise* = way or manner]

wish *verb* (wishes, wishing, wished)
1 feel or say that you would like to have or
do something or would like something to
happen. **2** say that you hope someone will
get something, *Wish me luck!*
wish *noun* (*plural* wishes)
1 something you wish for; a desire. **2** the
action of wishing, *Make a wish when you
blow out the candles.* [from Old English]

wishbone *noun* (*plural* wishbones)
a forked bone between the neck and breast
of a bird (sometimes pulled apart by two
people; the person who gets the bigger part
can make a wish).

wishful *adjective*
desiring something.

wishful thinking *noun*
believing something because you wish it
were true rather than on the facts.

wisp *noun* (*plural* wisps)
1 a few strands of hair or bits of straw etc.
2 a small streak of smoke or cloud etc.
wispy *adjective* [origin unknown]

wistaria (*say* wist-air-ee-a) *noun*
a climbing plant with hanging blue, purple,
or white flowers. [named after an
American professor, C. Wistar]

wistful *adjective*
sadly longing for something. **wistfully**
adverb, **wistfulness** *noun* [from Middle
English *whist* = quiet, + *-ful*]

wit *noun* (*plural* wits)
1 intelligence or cleverness, *Use your wits.*
2 a clever kind of humour. **3** a witty
person.
at your wits' end not knowing what to do.
[from Old English]

witch *noun* (*plural* witches)
a person, especially a woman, who uses
magic to do things. [from Old English]

witchcraft *noun*
the use of magic, especially for evil
purposes.

witch doctor *noun* (*plural* witch doctors)
a magician in a primitive tribe whose job
is to use magic, cure people, etc.

witch-hunt *noun* (*plural* witch-hunts)
a campaign to find and punish people who
hold views that are considered to be
unacceptable or dangerous.

with *preposition*
used to indicate **1** being in the company or
care etc. of (*Come with me*), **2** having (*a
man with a beard*), **3** using (*Hit it with a
hammer*), **4** because of (*shaking with
laughter*), **5** feeling or showing (*We heard it*

with pleasure), **6** towards or concerning (*I was angry with him*), **7** in opposition to; against (*Don't argue with your father*), **8** being separated from (*We had to part with it*). [from Old English]

withdraw *verb* (**withdraws, withdrawing, withdrew, withdrawn**)
1 take back or away; remove, *She withdrew money from the bank.* **2** go away from a place or people, *The troops withdrew from the frontier.* **withdrawal** *noun* [from Old English *with-* = away, back, + *draw*]

wither *verb* (**withers, withering, withered**)
1 shrivel or wilt. **2** make something shrivel or wilt. [a different spelling of *weather*]

USAGE: Do not confuse with *whither*.

withering *adjective*
scornful or sarcastic, *a withering remark.*

withers *plural noun*
the ridge between a horse's shoulder blades. [origin unknown]

withhold *verb* (**withholds, withholding, withheld**)
refuse to give or allow something (e.g. information or permission). [from Old English *with-* = away, back, + *hold*]

within *preposition* & *adverb*
inside; not beyond something.
[from Old English]

without *preposition*
1 not having, *without food.* **2** free from, *without fear.* **3** (*old use*) outside, *without the city wall.*
without *adverb* (*old use*)
outside, *We looked at the house from within and without.* [from Old English]

withstand *verb* (**withstands, withstanding, withstood**)
endure something successfully; resist.
[from Old English *with-* = against, + *stand*]

withy *noun* (*plural* **withies**)
a thin flexible branch for tying bundles etc.
[from Old English]

witness *noun* (*plural* **witnesses**)
1 a person who sees or hears something

happen, *There were no witnesses to the accident.* **2** a person who gives evidence in a lawcourt.
witness *verb* (**witnesses, witnessing, witnessed**)
1 be a witness of something, *Did anyone witness the accident?* **2** sign a document to confirm that it is genuine. [from *wit*]

witted *adjective*
having wits of a certain kind, *quick-witted.*

witticism *noun* (*plural* **witticisms**)
a witty remark.

wittingly *adverb*
intentionally. [from *wit*]

witty *adjective* (**wittier, wittiest**)
clever and amusing; full of wit.
wittily *adverb*, **wittiness** *noun*

wizard *noun* (*plural* **wizards**)
1 a male witch; a magician. **2** a person with amazing abilities. **wizardry** *noun*
[from an old sense of *wise* = a wise person]

wizened (*say* wiz-end) *adjective*
full of wrinkles, *a wizened face.*
[from Old English]

woad *noun*
a kind of blue dye formerly made from a plant. [from Old English]

wobble *verb* (**wobbles, wobbling, wobbled**)
stand or move unsteadily; shake slightly.
wobble *noun*, **wobbly** *adjective*
[origin unknown]

woe *noun* (*plural* **woes**)
1 sorrow. **2** misfortune. **woeful** *adjective*,
woefully *adverb* [from Old English]

woebegone *adjective*
looking unhappy. [from *woe* + an old word *bego* = attack, surround]

wok *noun* (*plural* **woks**)
a Chinese cooking pan shaped like a large bowl. [from Chinese]

wold *noun* (*plural* **wolds**)
an area of low hills. [from Old English]

wolf *noun* (*plural* **wolves**)
a fierce wild animal of the dog family.

wolf *verb* (wolfs, wolfing, wolfed)
eat something greedily. [from Old English]

woman *noun* (*plural* women)
a grown-up female human being.
womanhood *noun* [from Old English]

womanizer *noun* (*plural* womanizers)
a man who has sexual affairs with many
women.

womanly *adjective*
having qualities that are thought to be
typical of women.

womb (*say* woom) *noun* (*plural* wombs)
the hollow organ in a female's body where
babies develop before they are born; the
uterus. [from Old English]

wombat *noun* (*plural* wombats)
an Australian animal rather like a small
bear. [an Aboriginal word]

women's lib or **women's liberation**
noun
the freedom of women to have the same
rights, opportunities, and status as men.

wonder *noun* (*plural* wonders)
1 a feeling of surprise and admiration or
curiosity. 2 something that causes this
feeling; a marvel.
no wonder it is not surprising.
wonder *verb* (wonders, wondering,
wondered)
1 feel that you want to know; try to form an
opinion, *We are still wondering what to do
next.* 2 feel wonder. [from Old English]

wonderful *adjective*
marvellous or excellent.
wonderfully *adverb*

wonderment *noun*
a feeling of wonder.

wondrous *adjective* (*old use*)
wonderful.

wont (*say* wohnt) *adjective* (*old use*)
accustomed, *He was wont to dress in rags.*
wont *noun*
a habit or custom, *He was dressed in rags,
as was his wont.* [from Old English]

won't (*mainly spoken*)
will not.

woo *verb* (woos, wooing, wooed) (*old use*)
1 court a woman. 2 seek someone's favour.
wooer *noun* [from Old English]

wood *noun* (*plural* woods)
1 the substance of which trees are made.
2 many trees growing close together.
[from Old English]

woodcock *noun* (*plural* woodcock)
a bird with a long bill, often shot for sport.

woodcut *noun* (*plural* woodcuts)
an engraving made on wood; a print made
from this.

wooded *adjective*
covered with growing trees.

wooden *adjective*
1 made of wood. 2 stiff and showing no
expression or liveliness. **woodenly** *adverb*

woodland *noun* (*plural* woodlands)
wooded country.

woodlouse *noun* (*plural* woodlice)
a small crawling creature with seven pairs
of legs, living in rotten wood or damp soil
etc.

woodpecker *noun* (*plural* woodpeckers)
a bird that taps tree trunks with its beak to
find insects.

woodwind *noun*
wind instruments that are usually made of
wood, e.g. the clarinet and oboe.

woodwork *noun*
1 making things out of wood. 2 things
made out of wood.

woodworm *noun* (*plural* woodworms)
the larva of a kind of beetle that bores into
wooden furniture etc.

woody *adjective*
1 like wood; consisting of wood. 2 full of
trees.

woof *noun* (*plural* woofs)
the gruff bark of a dog.
[imitating the sound]

wool *noun* (*plural* wools)
1 the thick soft hair of sheep and goats etc.

2 thread or cloth made from this.
[from Old English]

woollen *adjective*
made of wool.

woollens *plural noun*
woollen clothes.

woolly *adjective*
1 covered with wool or wool-like hair.
2 like wool; woollen. 3 not thinking
clearly; vague or confused, *woolly ideas.*
woolliness *noun*

word *noun* (*plural* **words**)
1 a set of sounds or letters that has a
meaning, and when written or printed has
no spaces between the letters. 2 a promise,
He kept his word. 3 a command or spoken
signal, *Run when I give the word.* 4 a
message; information, *We sent word of our
safe arrival.*
word for word in exactly the same words.
word *verb* (**words, wording, worded**)
express something in words, *Word the
question carefully.*
[from Old English]

wording *noun*
the way something is worded.

word of honour *noun*
a solemn promise.

word-perfect *adjective*
having memorized every word perfectly,
He was word-perfect at the rehearsal.

word processor *noun* (*plural* **word
processors**)
a kind of computer used for editing and
printing words typed into it.

wordy *adjective*
using too many words; not concise.

wore *past tense* of wear.

work *noun* (*plural* **works**)
1 something you have to do that needs
effort or energy, *Digging is hard work.*
2 the use of effort or energy to do
something (contrasted with *play* or
recreation). 3 a job; employment.
4 something produced by work, *The
teacher marked our work.* 5 a piece of
writing, painting, music, etc., *the works of

William Shakespeare.*
at work working.
out of work having no work; unable to find
paid employment.
work *verb* (**works, working, worked**)
1 do work. 2 have a job; be employed, *She
works in a bank.* 3 act or operate correctly
or successfully, *Is the lift working?* 4 make
something act; operate, *Can you work the
lift?* 5 shape or press etc., *Work the mixture
into a paste.* 6 make a way; pass, *The grub
works its way into timber.*
work out 1 find an answer by thinking or
calculating. 2 have a particular result.
work up make people become excited;
arouse.
[from Old English]

workable *adjective*
that can be used or will work.

worker *noun* (*plural* **workers**)
1 a person who works. 2 a member of the
working class. 3 a bee or ant etc. that does
the work in a hive or colony but does not
produce eggs.

workforce *noun* (*plural* **workforces**)
the number of people who work in a
particular industry, country, etc.

working class *noun* (*plural* **working
classes**)
people who work for wages, especially in
manual or industrial work.

workman *noun* (*plural* **workmen**)
a man employed to do manual labour; a
worker.

workmanship *noun*
a person's skill in working; the result of
this.

work of art *noun* (*plural* **works of art**)
a fine picture, building, etc.

worksheet *noun* (*plural* **worksheets**)
a sheet of paper with a set of questions
about a subject for students, often used
with a textbook.

workshop *noun* (*plural* **workshops**)
a place where things are made or mended.

work-shy *adjective*
avoiding work; lazy.

world *noun* (*plural* **worlds**)
1 the earth with all its countries and peoples. 2 a planet, *creatures from another world*. 3 the people or things belonging to a certain activity, *the world of sport*. 4 a very great amount, *It will do him a world of good. She is worlds better today.* [from Old English]

worldly *adjective*
1 to do with life on earth, not spiritual. 2 interested only in money, pleasure, etc. 3 experienced about people and life. **worldliness** *noun*

worm *noun* (*plural* **worms**)
1 an animal with a long small soft rounded or flat body and no backbone or limbs. 2 an unimportant or unpleasant person. **wormy** *adjective*

worm *verb* (**worms, worming, wormed**)
move along by wriggling or crawling. **worm out** gradually get someone to tell you something by constantly and cleverly questioning them, *We eventually managed to worm the truth out of them.* [from Old English]

wormwood *noun*
a woody plant with a bitter taste. [from Old English]

worn *past participle* of **wear**.

worn-out *adjective*
1 exhausted. 2 damaged by too much use.

worried *adjective*
feeling or showing worry.

worry *verb* (**worries, worrying, worried**)
1 be troublesome to someone; make a person feel slightly afraid. 2 feel anxious. 3 hold something in the teeth and shake it, *The dog was worrying a rat.* **worrier** *noun*

worry *noun* (*plural* **worries**)
1 the condition of worrying; being uneasy. 2 something that makes a person worry. [from Old English]

worse *adjective* & *adverb*
more bad or more badly; less good or less well. [from Old English; related to *war*]

worsen *verb* (**worsens, worsening, worsened**)
make or become worse.

worship *verb* (**worships, worshipping, worshipped**)
1 give praise or respect to God or a god. 2 love or respect a person or thing greatly. **worshipper** *noun*

worship *noun* (*plural* **worships**)
1 worshipping; religious ceremonies. 2 a title of respect for a mayor or certain magistrates, *his worship the mayor*. [from Old English *weorth* = worth, + -*ship*]

worshipful *adjective*
(in titles) respected, *the Worshipful Company of Goldsmiths*.

worst *adjective* & *adverb*
most bad or most badly; least good or least well. [from Old English]

worsted *noun*
a kind of woollen material. [named after Worstead, a place in Norfolk, where it was made]

worth *adjective*
1 having a certain value, *This stamp is worth £100*. 2 deserving something; good or important enough for something, *That book is worth reading*.

worth *noun*
value or usefulness. [from Old English]

worthless *adjective*
having no value; useless. **worthlessness** *noun*

worthwhile *adjective*
important or good enough to deserve the time or effort needed, *a worthwhile job*. [from *worth the while* = worth the time]

worthy *adjective*
having great merit; deserving respect or support, *a worthy cause*. **worthiness** *noun*
worthy of deserving, *This charity is worthy of your support*. [from *worth*]

would *auxiliary verb*
used 1 as the past tense of *will*[1] (*We said we would do it*), in questions (*Would you like to come?*), and in polite requests (*Would you come in, please?*), 2 with *I* and *we* and the verbs *like, prefer, be glad*, etc. (e.g. *I would like to come, we would be glad to help*),

where the strictly correct use is *should*, **3** of something to be expected (*That's just what he would do!*).

USAGE: For sense 2, see the note on *should* 4.

would-be *adjective*
wanting or pretending to be, *a would-be comedian.*

wouldn't (*mainly spoken*)
would not.

wound[1] (*say* woond) *noun* (*plural* **wounds**)
1 an injury done by a cut, stab, or hit. **2** a hurt to a person's feelings.
wound *verb* (**wounds, wounding, wounded**)
1 cause a wound to a person or animal. **2** hurt a person's feelings, *She was wounded by these remarks.*
[from Old English]

wound[2] (*say* wownd) *past tense* of **wind**[2].

wraith *noun* (*plural* **wraiths**)
a ghost. [originally Scots: origin unknown]

wrangle *verb* (**wrangles, wrangling, wrangled**)
have a noisy argument or quarrel.
wrangle *noun*, **wrangler** *noun*
[probably from old Dutch]

wrap *verb* (**wraps, wrapping, wrapped**)
put paper or cloth etc. round something as a covering.
wrap *noun* (*plural* **wraps**)
a shawl, coat, or cloak etc. worn for warmth. [origin unknown]

wrapper *noun* (*plural* **wrappers**)
a piece of paper etc. wrapped round something.

wrath (rhymes with *cloth*) *noun*
anger. **wrathful** *adjective*, **wrathfully** *adverb*
[from Old English]

wreak (*say as* reek) *verb* (**wreaks, wreaking, wreaked**)
inflict or cause, *Fog wreaked havoc with the flow of traffic.* [from Old English]

USAGE: Note that the past form of *wreak* is *wreaked* not *wrought.* The adjective *wrought* is used to describe metal that has been shaped by hammering or rolling.

wreath (*say* reeth) *noun* (*plural* **wreaths**)
1 flowers or leaves etc. fastened into a circle, *wreaths of holly.* **2** a curving line of mist or smoke.
[from Old English *writhan* = writhe]

wreathe (*say* reeth) *verb* (**wreathes, wreathing, wreathed**)
1 surround or decorate something with a wreath. **2** cover, *Their faces were wreathed in smiles.* **3** move in a curve, *Smoke wreathed upwards.*
[from *wreath* and *writhe*]

wreck *verb* (**wrecks, wrecking, wrecked**)
damage or ruin something so badly that it cannot be used again.
wreck *noun* (*plural* **wrecks**)
1 a wrecked ship or building or car etc. **2** a person who is left very weak, *a nervous wreck.* **3** the wrecking of something.
[via old French from Old Norse]

wreckage *noun*
the pieces of a wreck.

wren *noun* (*plural* **wrens**)
a very small brown bird.
[from Old English]

wrench *verb* (**wrenches, wrenching, wrenched**)
twist or pull something violently.
wrench *noun* (*plural* **wrenches**)
1 a wrenching movement. **2** pain caused by parting, *Leaving home was a great wrench.* **3** an adjustable tool rather like a spanner, used for gripping and turning bolts, nuts, etc. [from Old English]

wrest *verb* (**wrests, wresting, wrested**)
take something away using force or effort, *We wrested his sword from him.*
[from Old English]

wrestle *verb* (**wrestles, wrestling, wrestled**)
1 fight by grasping your opponent and trying to throw him or her to the ground. **2** struggle with a problem etc. **wrestle** *noun*, **wrestler** *noun* [from Old English]

wretch *noun* (*plural* **wretches**)
1 a person who is very unhappy or who you pity. **2** a person who is disliked; a rascal. [from Old English]

USAGE: Do not confuse with *retch.*

wretched *adjective*
1 miserable or unhappy. 2 of bad quality.
3 not satisfactory; causing a nuisance, *This wretched car won't start.* **wretchedly** *adverb*,
wretchedness *noun* [from *wretch*]

wriggle *verb* (wriggles, wriggling, wriggled)
move with short twisting movements.
wriggle *noun*, **wriggly** *adjective*
wriggle out of avoid work or blame etc.
cunningly.
[from old German]

wring *verb* (wrings, wringing, wrung)
1 twist and squeeze a wet thing to get water
etc. out of it. 2 squeeze something firmly or
forcibly. 3 get something by a great effort,
We wrung a promise out of him. **wring** *noun*
wringing wet so wet that water can be
squeezed out of it.
[from Old English]

wringer *noun* (*plural* wringers)
a device with a pair of rollers for squeezing
water out of washed clothes etc.

wrinkle *noun* (*plural* wrinkles)
1 a small furrow or ridge in the skin. 2 a
small crease in something.
wrinkle *verb* (wrinkles, wrinkling, wrinkled)
make wrinkles in something; form
wrinkles. [origin unknown]

wrist *noun* (*plural* wrists)
the joint that connects the hand and arm.
[from Old English]

wristwatch *noun* (*plural* wristwatches)
a watch for wearing on the wrist.

writ (*say* rit) *noun* (*plural* writs)
a formal written command issued by a
lawcourt etc.
Holy Writ the Bible.
[from Old English]

write *verb* (writes, writing, wrote, written)
1 put letters or words etc. on paper or
another surface. 2 be the author or
composer of something, *write books* or
music. 3 send a letter to somebody. **writer**
noun, **writing** *noun* [from Old English]

writhe *verb* (writhes, writhing, writhed)
1 twist your body because of pain.
2 wriggle. 3 suffer because of great shame.
[from Old English]

wrong *adjective*
1 incorrect; not true, *the wrong answer.*
2 morally bad; unfair; unjust, *It is wrong to
cheat.* 3 not working properly, *There's
something wrong with the engine.*
wrongly *adverb*, **wrongness** *noun*

wrong *adverb*
wrongly, *You guessed wrong.*

wrong *noun* (*plural* wrongs)
something morally wrong; an injustice.
in the wrong having done or said
something wrong.

wrong *verb* (wrongs, wronging, wronged)
do wrong to someone; treat a person
unfairly. [probably from Old Norse]

wrongdoer *noun* (*plural* wrongdoers)
a person who does wrong.
wrongdoing *noun*

wrongful *adjective*
unfair or unjust; illegal, *wrongful arrest.*
wrongfully *adverb*

wrought *adjective*
(of metal) worked by being beaten out or
shaped by hammering or rolling etc.,
wrought iron.
[the old past participle of *work*]

USAGE: See note at *wreak.*

wry *adjective* (wryer, wryest)
1 slightly mocking or ironic, *a wry smile.*
2 twisted or bent out of shape. (Compare
awry.) **wryly** *adverb*, **wryness** *noun*
[from Old English]

Xx

xenophobia (*say* zen-o-foh-bee-a) *noun*
strong dislike of foreigners. [from Greek
xenos = foreigner, + *phobia*]

Xerox (*say* zeer-oks) *noun* (*plural* Xeroxes)
(*trade mark*)
a photocopy made by a special process.
xerox *verb* [from Greek *xeros* = dry

(because the process does not use liquid chemicals, as earlier photocopiers did)]

-xion *suffix* see -ion.

Xmas *noun*
Christmas.
[the X represents the Greek letter called chi, the first letter of *Christos* = Christ]

X-ray *noun* (*plural* X-rays)
a photograph or examination of the inside of something, especially a part of the body, made by a kind of radiation (called X-rays) that can penetrate solid things.
X-ray *verb* (X-rays, X-raying, X-rayed)
make an X-ray of something.

xylophone (*say* zy-lo-fohn) *noun* (*plural* xylophones)
a musical instrument made of wooden bars that you hit with small hammers. [from Greek *xylon* = wood + *phone* = sound]

Yy

-y[1] and **-ie** *suffixes*
form names showing fondness, or diminutives (e.g. *daddy*, *pussy*).
[origin unknown]

-y[2] *suffix*
forms adjectives meaning 'to do with' or 'like' (e.g. *angry*, *horsy*, *messy*, *sticky*).
[from Old English]

yacht (*say* yot) *noun* (*plural* yachts)
1 a sailing boat used for racing or cruising. **2** a private ship. **yachting** *noun*, **yachtsman** *noun*, **yachtswoman** *noun*
[from Dutch *jaghtschip* = fast pirate ship]

yak *noun* (*plural* yaks)
an ox with long hair, found in central Asia.
[from Tibetan]

yam *noun* (*plural* yams)
the edible starchy tuber of a tropical plant, also known as a sweet potato.
[from Portuguese or Spanish, probably from a West Indian word]

Yank *noun* (*plural* Yanks) (*informal*)
a Yankee.

yank *verb* (yanks, yanking, yanked)
(*informal*)
pull something strongly and suddenly. **yank** *noun* [origin unknown]

Yankee *noun* (*plural* Yankees)
an American, especially of the northern USA.
[probably from Dutch *Janke* = Johnny]

yap *verb* (yaps, yapping, yapped)
bark shrilly. **yap** *noun*
[imitating the sound]

yard[1] *noun* (*plural* yards)
1 a measure of length, 36 inches or about 91 centimetres. **2** a long pole stretched out from a mast to support a sail.
[from Old English *gerd*]

yard[2] *noun* (*plural* yards)
an enclosed area beside a building or used for a certain kind of work, *a timber yard.*
[from Old English *geard*]

yardstick *noun* (*plural* yardsticks)
a standard by which something is measured. [from *yard*[1]]

yarn *noun* (*plural* yarns)
1 thread spun by twisting fibres together, used in knitting etc. **2** (*informal*) a tale or story. [from Old English]

yarrow *noun*
a wild plant with strong-smelling flowers.
[from Old English]

yashmak *noun* (*plural* yashmaks)
a veil worn in public by Muslim women in some countries.
[from Turkish *yaşmak* = hide yourself]

yawl *noun* (*plural* yawls)
a kind of sailing boat or fishing boat.
[from old German or Dutch]

yawn *verb* (yawns, yawning, yawned)
1 open the mouth wide and breathe in deeply when feeling sleepy or bored.
2 form a wide opening, *A pit yawned in front of us.* **yawn** *noun* [from Old English]

ye *pronoun* (*old use*, in speaking to two or more people)
you. [from Old English]

yea (*say* yay) *adverb* (*old use*)
yes. [from Old English]

year *noun* (*plural* **years**)
1 the time the earth takes to go right round the sun, about 365¼ days. **2** the time from 1 January to 31 December; any period of twelve months. **yearly** *adjective & adverb* [from Old English]

yearling *noun* (*plural* **yearlings**)
an animal between one and two years old.

yearn *verb* (**yearns, yearning, yearned**)
long for something. [from Old English]

yeast *noun*
a substance that causes alcohol and carbon dioxide to form as it develops, used in making beer and wine and in baking bread etc. [from Old English]

yell *verb* (**yells, yelling, yelled**)
give a loud cry; shout. **yell** *noun* [from Old English]

yellow *noun* (*plural* **yellows**)
the colour of buttercups and ripe lemons.
yellow *adjective*
1 of yellow colour. **2** (*informal*) cowardly. **yellowness** *noun* [from Old English]

yellow pages *plural noun*
a special telephone directory giving addresses and telephone numbers of businesses, arranged according to what services they provide.

yelp *verb* (**yelps, yelping, yelped**)
give a shrill bark or cry. **yelp** *noun* [from Old English *gielpan* = to boast]

yen¹ *noun* (*plural* **yen**)
a unit of money in Japan.
[from Japanese *en* = round]

yen² *noun* (*plural* **yens**)
a longing for something. [from Chinese]

yeoman (*say* yoh-man) *noun* (*plural* **yeomen**) (*old use*)
a man who owns and runs a small farm. **yeomanry** *noun* [probably from *young man*]

Yeoman of the Guard *noun* (*plural* **Yeomen of the Guard**)
a member of the British sovereign's bodyguard, wearing Tudor dress as uniform.

yes *adverb*
used to agree to something (= the statement is correct) or as an answer (= I am here). [from Old English]

yesterday *noun & adverb*
the day before today. [from Old English]

yet *adverb*
1 up to this time; by this time, *The post hasn't come yet.* **2** eventually, *I'll get even with him yet!* **3** in addition; even, *She became yet more excited.*
yet *conjunction*
nevertheless, *It is strange, yet it is true.* [from Old English]

yeti *noun* (*plural* **yetis**)
a very large animal thought to live in the Himalayas, sometimes called the 'Abominable Snowman'. [from Tibetan]

yew *noun* (*plural* **yews**)
an evergreen tree with dark green needle-like leaves and red berries.
[from Old English]

yield *verb* (**yields, yielding, yielded**)
1 give in or surrender. **2** agree to do what is asked or ordered; give way, *He yielded to persuasion.* **3** produce as a crop or as profit etc.
yield *noun* (*plural* **yields**)
the amount yielded or produced, *What is the yield of wheat per acre?* [from Old English]

yodel *verb* (**yodels, yodelling, yodelled**)
sing or shout with the voice continually going from a low note to a high note and back again. **yodeller** *noun* [from German]

yoga (*say* yoh-ga) *noun*
a Hindu system of meditation and self-control. [Sanskrit, literally = union]

yoghurt (*say* yog-ert) *noun*
milk thickened by the action of certain bacteria, giving it a sharp taste.
[from Turkish]

yoke *noun* (*plural* yokes)
1 a curved piece of wood put across the necks of animals pulling a cart or plough etc. **2** a shaped piece of wood fitted across a person's shoulders, with a pail or load hung at each end. **3** a close-fitting upper part of a piece of clothing, from which the rest hangs.
yoke *verb* (yokes, yoking, yoked)
harness or join things by means of a yoke. [from Old English]

USAGE: Do not confuse with *yolk*.

yokel (*say* yoh-kel) *noun* (*plural* yokels)
a simple country fellow. [origin unknown]

yolk (rhymes with *coke*) *noun* (*plural* yolks)
the round yellow part inside an egg. [from Old English *geolu* = yellow]

USAGE: Do not confuse with *yoke*.

Yom Kippur (*say* yom kip-oor) *noun*
the Day of Atonement, a solemn Jewish religious festival, a day of fasting and repentance. [Hebrew]

yon *adjective* & *adverb* (*dialect*)
yonder. [from Old English]

yonder *adjective* & *adverb*
over there. [Middle English; related to *yon*]

yore *noun*
of yore of long ago, *in days of yore*. [from Old English]

Yorkshire pudding *noun* (*plural* Yorkshire puddings)
baked batter, usually eaten with roast beef. [from *Yorkshire*, a former county in northern England, where it was first made]

you *pronoun*
1 the person or people being spoken to, *Who are you?* **2** anyone or everyone; one, *You can't tell what will happen next.* [from Old English]

young *adjective*
having lived or existed for only a short time; not old.

young *plural noun*
children or young animals or birds, *The robin was feeding its young.* [from Old English]

youngster *noun* (*plural* youngsters)
a young person; a child.

your *adjective*
belonging to you. [from Old English]

USAGE: Do not confuse with *you're*.

you're (*mainly spoken*)
you are.

USAGE: Do not confuse with *your*.

yours *possessive pronoun*
belonging to you.
Yours faithfully, Yours sincerely, Yours truly ways of ending a letter before you sign it. (*Yours faithfully* and *Yours truly* are more formal than *Yours sincerely*.)

USAGE: It is incorrect to write *your's*.

yourself *pronoun* (*plural* yourselves)
you and nobody else. (Compare *herself*.)

youth *noun* (*plural* youths)
1 being young; the time when you are young. **2** a young man. **3** young people.
youthful *adjective*, **youthfulness** *noun*
[from Old English]

youth club *noun* (*plural* youth clubs)
a club providing leisure activities for young people.

youth hostel *noun* (*plural* youth hostels)
a place, often in the countryside, where young people can stay cheaply when they are on holiday.

yowl *verb* (yowls, yowling, yowled)
wail or howl. **yowl** *noun*
[imitating the sound]

yo-yo *noun* (*plural* yo-yos)
a round wooden or plastic toy that moves up and down on a string that you hold. [probably from a language spoken in the Philippines]

Yule *noun* (*old use*)
the Christmas festival, also called **Yuletide**. [from Old English]

yuppie *noun* (*plural* **yuppies**)
(*informal*) a young middle class person with a professional job, who earns a lot of money and spends it on expensive things. [from the initial letters of *young urban professional*, + *-ie*]

Zz

zap *verb* (**zaps, zapping, zapped**) (*slang*)
1 attack or destroy something forcefully.
2 change quickly from one section of a videotape etc. to another.
[imitating the sound of a blow or shot]

zeal *noun*
enthusiasm or keenness. **zealous** (*say* zel-us) *adjective*, **zealously** *adverb* [from Greek]

zealot (*say* zel-ot) *noun* (*plural* **zealots**)
a zealous person; a fanatic.

zebra (*say* zeb-ra) *noun* (*plural* **zebras**)
an African animal of the horse family, with black and white stripes all over its body. [Italian, Spanish, or Portuguese]

zebra crossing *noun* (*plural* **zebra crossings**)
a place for pedestrians to cross a road safely, marked with broad white stripes.

zebu (*say* zee-bew) *noun* (*plural* **zebus**)
an ox with a humped back, found in India, East Asia, and Africa. [from French]

zenith *noun*
1 the part of the sky directly above you.
2 the highest point, *His power was at its zenith.* [from Arabic]

zephyr (*say* zef-er) *noun* (*plural* **zephyrs**)
a soft gentle wind. [from Greek *Zephyros* = god of the west wind]

zero *noun* (*plural* **zeros**)
1 nought; the figure 0. 2 the point marked 0 on a thermometer etc.
[from Arabic *sifr* = cipher]

zero hour *noun*
the time when something is planned to start.

zest *noun*
great enjoyment or interest.
zestful *adjective*, **zestfully** *adverb*
[from French]

zigzag *noun* (*plural* **zigzags**)
a line or route that turns sharply from side to side.
zigzag *verb* (**zigzags, zigzagging, zigzagged**)
move in a zigzag.
[via French from German]

zinc *noun*
a white metal. [from German]

zip *noun* (*plural* **zips**)
1 a zip fastener. 2 a sharp sound like a bullet going through the air. 3 liveliness or vigour. **zippy** *adjective*
zip *verb* (**zips, zipping, zipped**)
1 fasten something with a zip fastener.
2 move quickly with a sharp sound.
[imitating the sound]

zip fastener or **zipper** *noun* (*plural* **zip fasteners, zippers**)
a fastener consisting of two strips of material, each with rows of small teeth that interlock when a sliding tab brings them together.

zither *noun* (*plural* **zithers**)
a musical instrument with many strings stretched over a shallow box-like body. [from Greek]

zodiac (*say* zoh-dee-ak) *noun*
a strip of sky where the sun, moon, and main planets are found, divided into twelve equal parts (called **signs of the zodiac**), each named after a constellation. [from Greek *zoidion* = image of an animal]

zombie *noun* (*plural* **zombies**)
1 (*informal*) a person who seems to be doing things without thinking, usually because he or she is very tired. 2 (in voodoo) a corpse that has been brought back to life by witchcraft.
[from a Bantu language]

zone *noun* (*plural* **zones**)
an area of a special kind or for a particular purpose, *a war zone*; *a no-parking zone*. [Greek, = girdle]

zoo *noun* (*plural* zoos)
a place where wild animals are kept so that people can look at them or study them. [short for *zoological gardens*]

zoology (*say* zoh-ol-o-jee) *noun*
the study of animals. **zoological** *adjective*, **zoologist** *noun*
[from Greek *zoion* = animal, + *-logy*]

zoom *verb* (zooms, zooming, zoomed)
1 move very quickly, especially with a buzzing sound. **2** rise quickly, *Prices had zoomed.* **zoom** *noun* [imitating the sound]

zoom lens *noun* (*plural* zoom lenses)
a camera lens that can be adjusted continuously to focus on things that are close up or far away.

Zulu *noun* (*plural* Zulus)
a member of a Black people in South Africa.

Appendices

APPENDIX 1

Prefixes and suffixes

Prefixes

A prefix is placed at the beginning of a word to change its meaning or to form a new word. The following prefixes have entries at their alphabetical places in the dictionary.

a-	auto-	dys-	in-	ortho-	semi-
ab-	be-	e-	infra-	out-	step-
abs-	bene-	ef-	inter-	over-	sub-
ac-	bi-	electro-	intra-	pan-	suc-
ad-	bio-	em-	intro-	para-	suf-
aero-	cata-	en-	ir-	penta-	sum-
af-	cath-	epi-	iso-	per-	sup-
Afro-	centi-	equi-	kilo-	peri-	super-
ag-	circum-	eu-	mal-	phil-	sur-
al-	co-	ex-	mega-	philo-	sus-
ambi-	col-	extra-	micro-	photo-	syl-
amphi-	com-	for-	milli-	poly-	sym-
an-	con-	fore-	mini-	post-	syn-
ana-	contra-	geo-	mis-	pre-	tele-
Anglo-	cor-	hecto-	mono-	pro-	tetra-
ant-	counter-	hepta-	multi-	proto-	thermo-
ante-	cross-	hetero-	neo-	pseudo-	trans-
anti-	de-	hexa-	non-	psycho-	tri-
ap-	deca-	homo-	ob-	quadri-	ultra-
apo-	deci-	hydr-	oc-	quasi-	un-
ar-	demi-	hydro-	octa-	radio-	under-
arch-	di-	hyper-	octo-	re-	uni-
as-	dia-	hypo-	of-	retro-	vice-
at-	dif-	il-	omni-	se-	
aut-	dis-	im-	op-	self-	

Suffixes

A suffix is placed at the end of a word to form another word or to form a plural, past tense, comparative, superlative, etc. The following suffixes have entries at their alphabetical places in the dictionary.

-able	-cy	-gen	-iest	-less	-sion
-arch	-dom	-gon	-iferous	-ling	-some
-archy	-ed	-gram	-ification	-logical	-teen
-arian	-ee	-graph	-ing	-logist	-tion
-ary	-er	-graphy	-ion	-logy	-tude
-ate	-esque	-hood	-ise	-ly	-uble
-ation	-ess	-ible	-ish	-most	-vore
-bility	-est	-ic	-ism	-ness	-vorous
-ble	-ette	-ical	-ist	-oid	-ward
-cide	-faction	-ician	-ite	-ology	-wards
-cle	-ferous	-icity	-itis	-or	-ways
-cracy	-fold	-ics	-ive	-pathy	-wise
-crat	-ful	-ie	-ize	-phobia	-xion
-cule	-fy	-ier	-kin	-ship	-y

APPENDIX 2

Some foreign words and phrases used in English

ad hoc done or arranged only when necessary and not planned in advance. [Latin, = for this]

ad infinitum (*say* in-fin-I-tum) without limit; for ever. [Latin, = to infinity]

ad nauseam (*say* naw-see-am) until people are sick of it. [Latin, = to sickness]

aide-de-camp (*say* ayd-der-**kahm**) a military officer who is the assistant to a senior officer. [French, = camp-helper]

à la carte ordered and paid for as separate items from a menu. (Compare *table d'hôte*.) [French, = from the menu]

alfresco *adjective & adverb* in the open air, *an alfresco meal*. [from Italian *al fresco* = in the fresh air]

alter ego another, very different, side of someone's personality. [Latin, = other self]

au fait (*say* oh **fay**) knowing a subject or procedure etc. well. [French, = to the point]

au gratin (*say* oh **grat**-an) cooked with a crisp topping of breadcrumbs or grated cheese. [French]

au revoir (*say* oh rev-**wahr**) goodbye for the moment. [French, = to be seeing again]

avant-garde (*say* av-ahn-**gard**) *noun* people who use a very modern style in art or literature etc. [French, = vanguard]

bête noire (*say* bayt **nwahr**) a person or thing you greatly dislike. [French, = black beast]

bona fide (*say* boh-na fy-**dee**) genuine; without fraud, *Are they bona fide tourists or spies?* [Latin, = in good faith]

bona fides (*say* boh-na fy-**deez**) honest intention; sincerity, *We do not doubt his bona fides*. [Latin, = good faith]

bon voyage (*say* bawn vwah-**yah***zh*) pleasant journey! [French]

carte blanche (*say* kart **blahnsh**) freedom to act as you think best. [French, = blank paper]

c'est la vie (*say* sel la **vee**) life is like that. [French, = that is life]

chef-d'oeuvre (*say* shay **dervr**) a masterpiece. [French, = chief work]

compos mentis in your right mind; sane. (The opposite is **non compos mentis**.) [Latin, = having control of the mind]

cordon bleu (*say* kor-dawn **bler**) (of cooks and cookery) first-class. [French, = blue ribbon]

corps de ballet (*say* kor der **bal**-ay) the whole group of dancers (not the soloists) in a ballet. [French]

corps diplomatique (*say* kor dip-lom-at-**eek**) the diplomatic service. [French]

coup de grâce (*say* koo der **grahs**) a stroke or blow that puts an end to something. [French, = mercy-blow]

coup d'état (*say* koo day-**tah**) the sudden overthrow of a government. [French, = blow of State]

crème de la crème (*say* krem der la krem) the very best of something. [French, = cream of the cream]

curriculum vitae (*say* veet-I) a brief account of a person's education, career, etc. [Latin, = course of life]

déjà vu (*say* day-*zh*a **vew**)
a fooling that you have already
experienced what is happening now.
[French, = already seen]

de rigueur (*say* der rig-**er**)
proper; required by custom or etiquette.
[French, = of strictness]

de trop (*say* der **troh**)
not wanted; unwelcome.
[French, = too much]

doppelgänger (*say* **dop**-el-geng-er)
noun
the ghost of a living person.
[German, = double-goer]

dramatis personae (*say* **dram**-a-tis per-
sohn-I)
the characters in a play.
[Latin, = persons of the drama]

en bloc (*say* ahn **blok**)
all at the same time; in a block. [French]

en masse (*say* ahn **mass**)
all together. [French, = in a mass]

en passant (*say* ahn pas-ahn)
by the way. [French, = in passing]

en route (*say* ahn **root**)
on the way. [French]

entente (*say* ahn-**tahnt** *or* on-**tont**)
noun
a friendly understanding between nations.
[French]

esprit de corps (*say* es-pree der **kor**)
loyalty to your group.
[French, = spirit of the body]

eureka (*say* yoor-**eek**-a)
interjection
I have found it! [Greek]

exeunt (*say* **eks**-ee-unt)
verb
they leave the stage. [Latin, = they go out]

ex gratia (*say* eks **gray**-sha)
given without being legally obliged to be
given, *an ex gratia payment.*
[Latin, = from favour]

faux pas (*say* foh **pah**)
an embarrassing blunder.
[French, = false step]

hara-kiri *noun*
a form of suicide formerly used by
Japanese officers when in disgrace.
[from Japanese *hara* = belly, *kiri* = cutting]

hoi polloi the ordinary people; the masses.
[Greek, = the many]

Homo sapiens human beings regarded as
a species of animal. [Latin, = wise man]

hors-d'oeuvre (*say* or-**dervr**)
noun
food served as an appetizer at the start of a
meal. [French, = outside the work]

in camera in a judge's private room, not in
public. [Latin, = in the room]

in extremis (*say* eks-**treem**-iss)
at the point of death; in very great
difficulties.
[Latin, = in the greatest danger]

in memoriam in memory (of). [Latin]

in situ (*say* **sit**-yoo)
in its original place. [Latin]

joie de vivre (*say* *zh*wah der **veevr**)
a feeling of great enjoyment of life.
[French, = joy of life]

laissez-faire (*say* lay-say-**fair**) *noun*
a government's policy of not interfering.
[French, = let (them) act]

maître d'hôtel (*say* metr doh-**tel**)
a head waiter. [French, = master of house]

milieu (*say* **meel**-yer) *noun*
environment; surroundings.
[French, from *mi* = mid + *lieu* = place]

modus operandi (*say* moh-dus op-er-and-
ee)
1 a person's way of working. **2** the way a
thing works. [Latin, = way of working]

nem. con. *abbreviation*
unanimously. [short for Latin *nemine
contradicente* = with nobody disagreeing]

nom de plume a writer's pseudonym.
[French, = pen-name (this phrase is not
used in France)]

non sequitur (*say* non sek-wit-er)
a conclusion that does not follow from the
evidence given. [Latin, = it does not follow]

nota bene (*say* noh-ta ben-ee)
(usually shortened to NB) note carefully.
[Latin, = note well]

nouveau riche (*say* noo-voh reesh)
a person who has only recently become
rich. [French, = new rich]

objet d'art (*say* ob-zhay dar)
a small artistic object.
[French, = object of art]

par excellence (*say* par eks-el-ahns)
more than all the others; to the greatest
degree.
[French, = because of special excellence]

pas de deux (*say* pah der der)
a dance (e.g. in a ballet) for two persons.
[French, = step of two]

pâté de foie gras (*say* pat-ay der fwah
grah)
a paste or pie of goose-liver.
[French, = paste of fat liver]

per annum for each year; yearly. [Latin]

per capita (*say* kap-it-a)
for each person. [Latin, = for heads]

persona grata (*say* per-soh-na grah-ta)
a person who is acceptable to someone,
especially a diplomat acceptable to a
foreign government. (The opposite is
persona non grata.)
[Latin, = pleasing person]

pièce de résistance (*say* pee-ess der ray-
zees-tahns)
the most important item. [French]

placebo (*say* plas-ee-boh)
noun (*plural* **placebos**) a harmless
substance given as if it were medicine,
usually to reassure a patient.
[Latin, = I shall be pleasing]

poste restante (*say* rest-ahnt)
a part of a post office where letters etc. are
kept until called for.
[French, = letters remaining]

prima facie (*say* pry-ma fay-shee)
at first sight; judging by the first
impression.
[Latin, = on first appearance]

quid pro quo (*say* kwoh)
something given or done in return for
something.
[Latin, = something for something]

raison d'être (*say* ray-zawn detr)
the purpose of a thing's existence.
[French, = reason for being]

rigor mortis (*say* ry-ger mor-tis)
stiffening of the body after death.
[Latin, = stiffness of death]

RIP *abbreviation*
may he or she (or they) rest in peace.
[short for Latin *requiescat* (or *requiescant*)
in pace]

sang-froid (*say* sahn-frwah)
noun
calmness in danger or difficulty.
[French, = cold blood]

savoir faire (*say* sav-wahr fair)
noun
knowledge of how to behave socially.
[French, = knowing how to do]

sotto voce (*say* sot-oh voh-chee)
in a very quiet voice.
[Italian, = under the voice]

status quo (*say* stay-tus kwoh)
the state of affairs as it was before a
change. [Latin, = the state in which]

sub judice (*say* joo-dis-ee)
being decided by a judge or lawcourt.
[Latin, = under a judge]

table d'hôte (*say* tahbl doht)
a restaurant meal served at a fixed
inclusive price. (Compare **à la carte**.)
[French, = host's table]

terra firma dry land; the ground.
[Latin, = firm land]

tête-à-tête (*say* tayt-ah-**tayt**)
noun
a private conversation, especially between two people. [French, = head to head]

vis-à-vis (*say* veez-ah-**vee**) *adverb* &
preposition
1 in a position facing one another; opposite to. 2 as compared with.
[French, = face to face]

viva voce (*say* vy-va **voh**-chee)
in a spoken test or examination.
[Latin, = with the living voice]

volte-face (*say* volt-**fahs**) *noun*
a complete change in your attitude towards something. [French]

APPENDIX 3

Days of the week

The days of the week were named more than a thousand years ago, in Anglo-Saxon times, and the English names are based on those given by the ancient Romans. They are named after the planets, taking the order of these from ancient astronomy.

Sunday   from Old English *sunnandaeg* = day of the sun; the Latin name was *solis dies*.

Monday   from Old English *monandaeg* = day of the moon; the Latin name was *lunae dies*. Compare French *lundi*.

Tuesday   from Old English *Tiwesdaeg* = day of Tiw, the Old English name of the Norse god of war, whose name was substituted for that of Mars, the Roman god of war; the Latin name was *Martis dies* = day of Mars. Compare French *mardi*.

Wednesday from Old English *Wodnesdaeg* = day of Woden or Odin, the chief Norse god, whose name was substituted for that of Mercury, the Roman messenger-god; the Latin name was *Mercurii dies*. Compare French *mercredi*.

Thursday   from Old English *thuresdaeg* = day of thunder, named after Thor, the Norse god of thunder, whose name was substituted for that of Jove or Jupiter, the Roman god who controlled thunder and lightning; the Latin name was *Jovis dies* = day of Jupiter. Compare French *jeudi*.

Friday   from Old English *Frigedaeg* = day of Frigg, wife of the god Odin (see *Wednesday*); the Latin name was *Veneris dies* = day of Venus. Compare French *vendredi*.

Saturday   from the Old English *Saeternesdaeg* = day of Saturn, a Roman god; the Latin name was *Saturni dies*. Compare French *samedi*.

Months of the year

The names of the months go back to ancient Roman times, and some are named after Roman gods and goddesses.

January   is named after Janus, god of gates and beginnings, who faced two ways (past and future), whose festival was held on 9 January.

February   is named after *februa*, an ancient Roman feast of purification held in this month.

March   is named after Mars, god of war, several of whose festivals were held in this month. It was originally the first month of the year and the months September–December were counted from here.

April   is from its Latin name *Aprilis*. The Romans considered this month to be sacred to Venus, goddess of love, and its name may be taken from that of her Greek equivalent Aphrodite.

May   is named after the goddess Maia, who was worshipped in this month.

June   is named after Juno, queen of the gods.

July   is named after Julius Caesar, who was born in this month.

August   is named after Augustus Caesar, the first Roman emperor, who was given the name Augustus (Latin, = majestic) in 27 BC.

September   is from Latin *septem* = seven, because it was the seventh month in the ancient Roman calendar (see the note on *March*).

October   is from Latin *octo* = eight (eighth month).

November   is from Latin *novem* = nine (ninth month).

December   is from Latin *decem* = ten (tenth month).

Signs of the zodiac

The strip of sky called the *zodiac* is divided into twelve equal sections, each named after a group of stars (its *sign*) that was formerly situated in it. When seen from the Earth, the sun appears to move through each section in turn during one year. The dates given below are the approximate times when it enters and leaves each sign.

In ancient times, people believed that stars and planets influenced the entire world and all that happened in it, including crops, medicine, and people's lives. The key to a person's whole life was thought to lie in the way the planets were arranged (called a *horoscope*) at his or her birth. Many newspapers and magazines print forecasts of what is about to happen to those born under each sign, but only a few people treat them seriously.

The names of the signs are derived from the Latin word with the same meaning.

Aries	the Ram	21 March–20 April
Taurus	the Bull	21 April–20 May
Gemini	the Twins	21 May–20 June
Cancer	the Crab	21 June–21 July
Leo	the Lion	22 July–22 August
Virgo	the Virgin	23 August–21 September
Libra	the Scales	22 September–22 October
Scorpio	the Scorpion	23 October–21 November
Sagittarius	the Archer	22 November–21 December
Capricorn	the Goat	22 December–20 January
Aquarius	the Water-carrier	21 January–19 February
Pisces	the Fishes	20 February–20 March

APPENDIX 4

Countries of the world

Country	People	Adjective
Afghanistan	Afghans	Afghan
Albania	Albanians	Albanian
Algeria	Algerians	Algerian
America (*see* United States of America)		
Andorra	Andorrans	Andorran
Angola	Angolans	Angolan
Anguilla	Anguillans	Anguillan
Antigua and Barbuda	Antiguans, Barbudans	Antiguan, Barbudan
Argentina	Argentinians	Argentinian or Argentine
Armenia	Armenians	Armenian
Australia	Australians	Australian
Austria	Austrians	Austrian
Azerbaijan	Azerbaijanis or Azeris	Azerbaijani
Bahamas	Bahamians	Bahamian
Bahrain	Bahrainis	Bahraini
Bangladesh	Bangladeshis	Bangladeshi
Barbados	Barbadians	Barbadian
Belarus	Belorussians	Belorussian
Belgium	Belgians	Belgian
Belize	Belizians	Belizian
Benin	Beninese	Beninese
Bermuda	Bermudans	Bermudan
Bhutan	Bhutanese	Bhutanese
Bolivia	Bolivians	Bolivian
Bosnia-Herzegovina	Bosnians	Bosnian
Botswana	Batswana or Citizens of Botswana	Botswanan
Brazil	Brazilians	Brazilian
Britain (part of the United Kingdom)	British or Britons	British
Brunei Darussalam	People of Brunei	Bruneian or Brunei
Bulgaria	Bulgarians	Bulgarian
Burkina Faso	Burkinans	Burkinan or Burkina
Burma (now called *Myanmar*)	Burmese	Burmese
Burundi	People of Burundi	Burundi
Cambodia	Cambodians	Cambodian

Country	People	Adjective
Cameroon	Cameroonians	Cameroonian
Canada	Canadians	Canadian
Cape Verde Islands	Cape Verdeans	Cape Verdean
Cayman Islands	Cayman Islanders	Cayman Islands
Central African Republic	People of the Central African Republic	Central African Republic
Chad	Chadians	Chadian
Chile	Chileans	Chilean
China, People's Republic of	Chinese	Chinese
China, Republic of (Taiwan)	Taiwanese	Taiwanese
Colombia	Colombians	Colombian
Comoros	Comorans	Comoran
Congo	Congolese	Congolese
Costa Rica	Costa Ricans	Costa Rican
Croatia	Croats	Croatian
Cuba	Cubans	Cuban
Cyprus	Cypriots	Cypriot
Czech Republic	Czechs	Czech
Denmark	Danes	Danish
Djibouti	Djiboutians	Djiboutian
Dominica	Dominicans	Dominican
Dominican Republic	Dominicans	Dominican
Ecuador	Ecuadoreans	Ecuadorean
Egypt	Egyptians	Egyptian
El Salvador	Salvadoreans	Salvadorean
England (part of the United Kingdom)	English	English
Equatorial Guinea	Equatorial Guineans	of Equatorial Guinea
Eritrea	Eritreans	Eritrean
Estonia	Estonians	Estonian
Ethiopia	Ethiopians	Ethiopian
Falkland Islands	Falkland Islanders	Falkland Islands
Fiji	Fijians	Fijian
Finland	Finns	Finnish
France	French	French
Gabon	Gabonese	Gabonese
Gambia	Gambians	Gambian
Georgia	Georgians	Georgian
Germany	Germans	German
Ghana	Ghanaians	Ghanaian
Gibraltar	Gibraltarians	Gibraltarian

Country	People	Adjective
Great Britain (*see* United Kingdom)		
Greece	Greeks	Greek
Grenada	Grenadians	Grenadian
Guatemala	Guatemalans	Guatemalan
Guinea	Guineans	Guinean
Guinea-Bissau	People of Guinea-Bissau	Guinea-Bissau
Guyana	Guyanese	Guyanese
Haiti	Haitians	Haitian
Honduras	Hondurans	Honduran
Hong Kong	Inhabitants of Hong Kong	Hong Kong
Hungary	Hungarians	Hungarian
Iceland	Icelanders	Icelandic
India	Indians	Indian
Indonesia	Indonesians	Indonesian
Iran	Iranians	Iranian
Iraq	Iraqis	Iraqi
Ireland, Republic of	Irish	Irish
Israel	Israelis	Israeli
Italy	Italians	Italian
Ivory Coast	People of the Ivory Coast	Ivory Coast or Ivorian
Jamaica	Jamaicans	Jamaican
Japan	Japanese	Japanese
Jordan	Jordanians	Jordanian
Kazakhstan	Kazakhs	Kazakh
Kenya	Kenyans	Kenyan
Kiribati	Kiribatians	Kiribatian
Korea (*see* North, South Korea)		
Kuwait	Kuwaitis	Kuwaiti
Kyrgyzstan	Kyrgyz	Kyrgyz
Laos	Laotians	Laotian
Latvia	Latvians	Latvians
Lebanon	Lebanese	Lebanese
Lesotho	Basotho	Lesotho
Liberia	Liberians	Liberian
Libya	Libyans	Libyan
Liechtenstein	Liechtensteiners	Liechtenstein
Lithuania	Lithuanians	Lithuanian
Luxembourg	Luxembourgers	Luxembourgian

Country	People	Adjective
Macedonia	Macedonians	Macedonian
Madagascar	Malagasies	Malagasy
Malawi	Malawians	Malawian
Malaysia	Malaysians	Malaysian
Maldives	Maldivians	Maldivian
Mali	Malians	Malian
Malta	Maltese	Maltese
Marshall Islands	Marshall Islanders	Marshall Islands
Mauritania	Mauritanians	Mauritanian
Mauritius	Mauritians	Mauritian
Mexico	Mexicans	Mexican
Micronesia	Micronesians	Micronesian
Moldavia	Moldavians	Moldavian
Monaco	Monégasques	Monégasque
Mongolia	Mongolians	Mongolian
Montenegro	Montenegrins	Montenegrin
Montserrat	Montserratians	Montserrat
Morocco	Moroccans	Moroccan
Mozambique	Mozambicans	Mozambican
Myanmar (until 1989 called *Burma*)		
Namibia	Namibians	Namibian
Nauru	Nauruans	Nauruan
Nepal	Nepalese	Nepalese
Netherlands	Dutch	Dutch
New Zealand	New Zealanders	New Zealand
Nicaragua	Nicaraguans	Nicaraguan
Niger	Nigeriens	Nigerien
Nigeria	Nigerians	Nigerian
Northern Ireland (part of the United Kingdom)	Northern Irish	of Northern Ireland
North Korea	North Koreans	North Korean
Norway	Norwegians	Norwegian
Oman	Omanis	Omani
Pakistan	Pakistanis	Pakistani
Panama	Panamanians	Panamanian
Papua New Guinea	Papua New Guineans	Papua New Guinean
Paraguay	Paraguayans	Paraguayan
Peru	Peruvians	Peruvian
Philippines	Filipinos	Philippine
Pitcairn Islands	Pitcairn Islanders	Pitcairn
Poland	Poles	Polish

Country	People	Adjective
Portugal	Portuguese	Portuguese
Puerto Rico	Puerto Ricans	Puerto Ricans
Qatar	Qataris	Qatari
Romania	Romanians	Romanian
Russia (Russian Federation)	Russians	Russian
Rwanda	Rwandans	Rwandan
St Helena	St Helenians	St Helenian
St Kitts-Nevis	People of St Kitts-Nevis	Kittsian, Nevisian
St Lucia	St Lucians	St Lucian
St Vincent and the Grenadines	St Vincentians	St Vincent
San Marino	People of San Marino	San Marino
São Tomé and Principe	People of São Tomé and Principe	of São Tomé and Principe
Saudi Arabia	Saudi Arabians	Saudi Arabian
Scotland (part of the United Kingdom)	Scots	Scottish, Scots, or Scotch
Senegal	Senegalese	Senegalese
Seychelles	Seychellois	Seychellois
Sierra Leone	Sierra Leoneans	Sierra Leonean
Singapore	Singaporeans	Singaporean
Slovakia	Slovaks	Slovak
Slovenia	Slovenes	Slovenian
Solomon Islands	Solomon Islanders	Solomon Islands
Somalia	Somalis	Somali
South Africa	South Africans	South African
South Korea	South Koreans	South Korean
Spain	Spaniards	Spanish
Sri Lanka	Sri Lankans	Sri Lankan
Sudan	Sudanese	Sudanese
Suriname	Surinamers	Surinamese
Swaziland	Swazis	Swazi
Sweden	Swedes	Swedish
Switzerland	Swiss	Swiss
Syria	Syrians	Syrian
Taiwan	Taiwanese	Taiwanese
Tajikistan	Tajiks	Tajik
Tanzania	Tanzanians	Tanzanian
Thailand	Thais	Thai
Togo	Togolese	Togolese
Tonga	Tongans	Tongan

Country	People	Adjective
Trinidad and Tobago	Trinidadians and Tobagans or Tobagonians	Trinidadian, Tobagan or Tobagonian
Tunisia	Tunisians	Tunisian
Turkey	Turks	Turkish
Turkmenistan	Turkmens	Turkmen
Turks and Caicos Islands	Turks and Caicos Islanders	Turks and Caicos Islands
Tuvalu	Tuvaluans	Tuvaluan
Uganda	Ugandans	Ugandan
Ukraine	Ukrainians	Ukrainian
United Arab Emirates	People of the United Arab Emirates	of the United Arab Emirates
United Kingdom	British	British
United States of America	Americans	American
Uruguay	Uruguayans	Uruguayan
Uzbekistan	Uzbeks	Uzbek
Vanuatu	People of Vanuatu	Vanuatu
Vatican City	Vatican citizens	Vatican
Venezuela	Venezuelans	Venezuelan
Vietnam	Vietnamese	Vietnamese
Virgin Islands	Virgin Islanders	Virgin Islands
Wales (part of the United Kingdom)	Welsh	Welsh
Western Samoa	Western Samoans	Western Samoan
Yemen, Republic of	Yemenis	Yemeni
Yugoslavia (**Montenegro** and **Serbia**)	Yugoslavs (Montenegrins and Serbians)	Yugoslav (Montenegrin and Serbian)
Zaïre	Zaïreans	Zaïrean
Zambia	Zambians	Zambian
Zimbabwe	Zimbabweans	Zimbabwean

APPENDIX 5

Weights and Measures

Note The conversion factors are not exact unless so marked. They are given only to the accuracy likely to be needed in everyday calculations.

1. METRIC, WITH BRITISH EQUIVALENTS

Linear Measure

1 millimetre	= 0.039 inch
1 centimetre = 10 mm	= 0.394 inch
decimetre = 10 cm	= 3.94 inches
metre = 10 dm	= 1.094 yards
decametre = 10 m	= 10.94 yards
1 hectometre = 100 m	= 109.4 yards
1 kilometre = 1,000 m	= 0.6214 mile

Square Measure

1 square centimetre	= 0.155 sq. inch
square metre = 10,000 sq. cm	= 1.196 sq. yards
1 are = 100 sq. metres	= 119.6 sq. yards
1 hectare = 100 ares	= 2.471 acres
square kilometre = 100 hectares	= 0.386 sq. mile

Cubic Measure

1 cubic centimetre	= 0.061 cu. inch
1 cubic metre = 1,000,000 cu. cm	= 1.308 cu. yards

Capacity Measure

1 millilitre	= 0.002 pint (British)
1 centilitre = 10 ml	= 0.018 pint
1 decilitre = 10 cl	= 0.176 pint
1 litre = 10 dl	= 1.76 pints
1 decalitre = 10 l	= 2.20 gallons
1 hectolitre = 100 l	= 2.75 bushels
1 kilolitre = 1,000 l	= 3.44 quarters

Weight

1 milligram	= 0.015 grain
1 centigram = 10 mg	= 0.154 grain
1 decigram = 10 cg	= 1.543 grains
1 gram = 10 dg	= 15.43 grains
1 decagram = 10 g	= 5.63 drams
1 hectogram = 100 g	= 3.527 ounces
1 kilogram = 1,000 g	= 2.205 pounds
1 tonne (metric ton) = 1,000 kg	= 0.984 (long) ton

2. BRITISH AND AMERICAN, WITH METRIC EQUIVALENTS

Linear Measure

1 inch	= 25.4 mm exactly
1 foot = 12 inches	= 0.3048 metre
1 yard = 3 feet	= 0.9144 metre exactly
1 (statute) mile = 1,760 yards	= 1.609 km

Square Measure

1 square inch	= 6.45 sq. cm
1 square foot = 144 sq. in.	= 9.29 sq. dm
1 square yard = 9 sq. ft.	= 0.836 sq. metre
1 acre = 4,840 sq. yd.	= 0.405 hectare
1 square mile = 640 acres	= 259 hectares

Cubic Measure

1 cubic inch	= 16.4 cu. cm
1 cubic foot = 1,728 cu. in.	= 0.0283 cu. metre
1 cubic yard = 27 cu. ft.	= 0.765 cu. metre

Avoirdupois Weight

1 grain	= 0.065 gram
1 dram	= 1.772 grams
1 ounce = 16 drams	= 28.35 grams
1 pound = 16 ounces = 7,000 grains	= 0.4536 kilogram (0.45359237 exactly)
1 stone = 14 pounds	= 6.35 kilograms
1 quarter = 2 stones	= 12.70 kilograms

Capacity Measure

British

1 pint = 34.68 cu. in.	= 20 fluid oz. = 0.568 litre
1 quart = 2 pints	= 1.136 litres
1 gallon = 4 quarts	= 4.546 litres
1 peck = 2 gallons	= 9.092 litres
1 bushel = 4 pecks	= 36.4 litres
1 quarter = 8 bushels	= 2.91 hectolitres

American dry

1 pint = 33.60 cu. in.	= 0.550 litre
1 quart = 2 pints	= 1.101 litres
1 peck = 8 quarts	= 8.81 litres
1 bushel = 4 pecks	= 35.3 litres

American liquid

1 pint = 16 fluid oz. = 28.88 cu. in.	= 0.473 litre
1 quart = 2 pints	= 0.946 litre
1 gallon = 4 quarts	= 3.785 litres

1 hundredweight = 4 quarters	= 50.80 kilograms
1 (long) ton = 20 hundredweight	= 1.016 tonnes
1 short ton = 2,000 pounds	= 0.907 tonne

3. POWER NOTATION

This expresses concisely any power of ten (any number that is composed of factors 10), and is sometimes used in the dictionary. 10^2 or ten squared $= 10 \times 10 = 100$; 10^3 or ten cubed $= 10 \times 10 \times 10 = 1,000$. Similarly, $10^4 = 10,000$ and $10^{10} = 1$ followed by ten noughts $= 10,000,000,000$. Proceeding in the opposite direction, dividing by ten and subtracting one from the index, we have $10^2 = 100$, $10^1 = 10$, $10^0 = 1$, $10^{-1} = \frac{1}{10}$, $10^{-2} = \frac{1}{100}$, and so on; $10^{-10} = 1/10^{10}$ $= 1/10,000,000,000$.

TEMPERATURE

ahrenheit: Water boils (under standard conditions) at 212° and freezes at 32°.
Celsius or Centigrade: Water boils at 100° and freezes at 0°.
elvin: Water boils at 373.15 K and freezes at 273.15 K.

Celsius	Fahrenheit	Celsius	Fahrenheit
−17.8°	0°	50°	122°
−10°	14°	60°	140°
0°	32°	70°	158°
10°	50°	80°	176°
20°	68°	90°	194°
30°	86°	100°	212°
40°	104°		

 convert Celsius into Fahrenheit: multiply by 9, divide by 5, and add 32.
 convert Fahrenheit into Celsius: subtract 32, multiply by 5, and divide
 y 9.

5. METRIC PREFIXES

	Abbreviation or symbol	Factor		Abbreviation or symbol	Factor
deca-	da	10	deci-	d	10^{-1}
hecto-	h	10^2	centi-	c	10^{-2}
kilo-	k	10^3	milli-	m	10^{-3}
mega-	M	10^6	micro-	μ	10^{-6}
giga-	G	10^9	nano-	n	10^{-9}
tera-	T	10^{12}	pico-	p	10^{-12}
peta-	P	10^{15}	femto-	f	10^{-15}
exa-	E	10^{18}	atto-	a	10^{-18}

These prefixes may be applied to any units of the metric system: hectogram (abbreviated hg) = 100 grams; kilowatt (abbreviated kW) = 1,000 watts.

6. SI UNITS

Basic SI units

Quantity	Unit	Symbol
Length	Metre	m
Mass	Kilogram	kg
Time	Second	s
Electric current	Ampere	A
Temperature	Kelvin	K
Light intensity	Candela	cd
Amount of substance	Mole	mol

Derived SI units

Quantity	Unit	Symbol
Area	Square metre	m^2
Volume	Cubic metre	m^3
Frequency	Hertz	Hz
Force	Newton	N
Pressure	Pascal	Pa
Energy	Joule	J
Power	Watt	W
Electric potential	Volt	V
Electrical resistance	Ohm	Ω
Electric charge	Coulomb	C
Radioactivity	Becquerel	Bq

Basic SI units and derived SI units

The seven basic SI units have scientific standards that define the size of the units with great precision. All derived units are related to the basic SI units. Each unit has its own entry in the dictionary.

Note: SI stands for Système International, the international system of units of measurement.